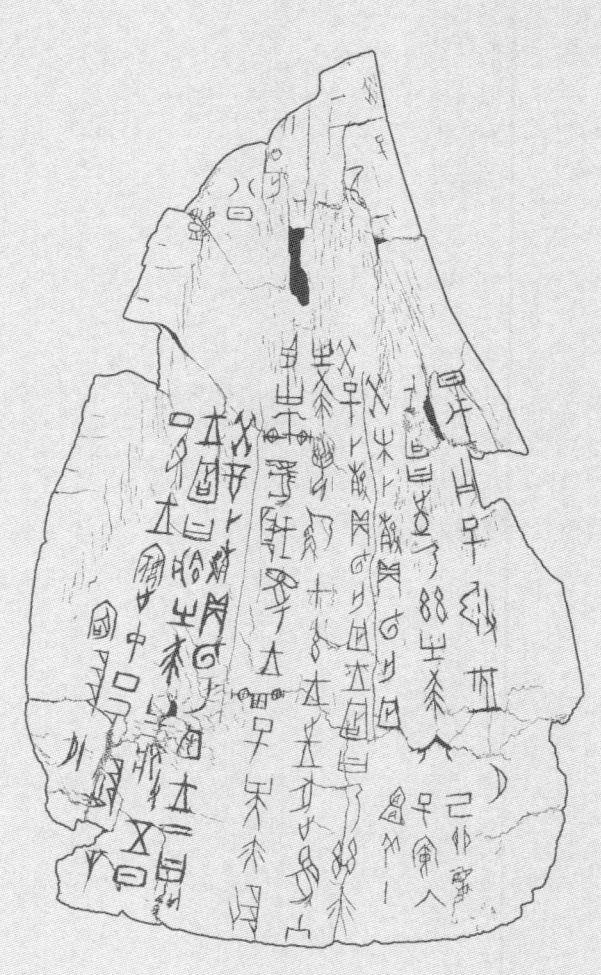

本書爲"古文字與中華文明傳承發展工程"項目成果（YWZ-J012），得到教育部語信司和中國文字學會的支持和指導，謹此致謝！

主編 劉釗

副主編 陳劍

傳承中華基因

甲骨文發現一百二十年來甲骨學論文精選及提要

(二)

商務印書館
The Commercial Press

許進雄

鑽鑿對卜辭斷代的重要性

殷代的卜占通常是在牛肩胛骨及龜腹、背甲上施燒灼以徵驗的。他們總是在甲骨的反面鑿鑽窪洞,以使燒灼時甲骨表面裂成一直一斜如卜字的卜兆。在不同的時代這些窪洞鑿成各異的形狀,有裨益於區分卜辭的時期。本文特別著重於討論某些學者命名的王族卜辭和多子族卜辭的卜骨,想借重牛肩胛骨上鑿鑽的各種形狀的窪洞的事實,來證明這一類的卜辭應分屬於第一和第四期,而不應歸屬與武丁同時的特別的一類。

分期是甲骨文研究的一個非常重要的問題。董彥堂先生發現了卜辭中的貞人名後,擴充成十項標準以斷定卜辭的時代。他分卜辭時代爲五期:第一期爲武丁及其前世,第二期爲祖庚和祖甲,第三期爲廩辛和康丁,第四期爲武乙和文武丁,第五期爲帝乙和帝辛①。他的分法大部分是被接受的,但第四期文武丁的卜辭却引起不少的爭論②。爭論是起於第一期與第四期有不少的相似點,所以董先

---

① 董作賓《甲骨文斷代研究例》,《史語所集刊》外編第一種上册,1933。
② 主張王族卜辭爲第一期的有:
 (a)貝塚茂樹、伊藤道治《甲骨文斷代研究法の再檢討——董氏文武丁時代を中心として》,《東方學報》第 23 期,京都:1953。
 (b)貝塚茂樹《京都大學人文科學研究所藏甲骨文字》,京都:1969,頁 101—122。
 (c)陳夢家《殷虛卜辭綜述》,1956,頁 135—172。
 (d)胡厚宣《甲骨續存自序》,1955。
 (e)屈萬里《殷虛文字甲編考釋》,臺北:1961,頁 315。
主張王族卜辭應爲第四期文武丁的有:
 (a)董作賓《殷虛文字乙編自序》,1949。
 (b)島邦男《殷墟卜辭研究》,弘前:1958,頁 1—34。
 (c)李學勤《評陳夢家〈殷虛卜辭綜述〉》,《考古學報》1957 年第 3 期。
 (d)嚴一萍《甲骨文斷代研究新例》,《史語所集刊》外編第四種,1961,頁 488—503。

生聲稱第四期的文武丁是第一期武丁的復古期①。而持反對意見的人，以爲董先生的第四期文武丁卜辭應是與武丁約略同時代的一羣卜辭。陳夢家稱這一羣爭論的卜辭爲自組卜辭，貝塚茂樹教授則分爲王族卜辭與多子族兩組，爲方便起見，以後都稱此類卜辭爲王族卜辭。在討論此類卜辭前，先讓筆者説明何以鑿鑽能作爲斷代的標準。

由於鑿鑽的窟洞只是用來幫助兆紋的裂開容易些，並不意在鑿成一定的形狀，所以很難單由鑿鑽來判定卜骨的正確時期，但對長鑿形狀的檢驗，有幾點是對卜辭時代的判別很有價值的。長鑿的形狀在第一期總是兩肩筆直兩頭尖如 ◐ 形的（圖1a、1b、2、3和4）。第一期以後，除少數仍契刻第一期的形狀外，已鑿成頭尖兩肩彎曲如 ◐ 形（圖5和6），或兩頭平如 ◐ 形（圖7、8和9），兩頭斜如 ◐ 形的（圖10a）。鑿的長度比普通的長得多的只發現於第一期以後。第一期以後鑿的兩肩經常被挖寬，由於這第二次的挖刻，使得鑿的長度與寬度的比例，第一期比後期大得多，換句話説，第一期的鑿看起來是瘦些。另外還有一種長鑿，其長度比平常的短些，只發現於第四期（尤其是文武丁的）與陳夢家所稱的自組的卜骨。

再檢驗長鑿與圓鑿的挖刻形態也是有助於分期的。普通鑿鑽的窟洞可分爲兩種主要形式：形式一 a 是長鑿的長度約等於其旁邊的圓鑿的兩倍大，此圓鑿經常是作半圓形，或高或低地挖刻在長鑿旁邊（圖1a），火就燒灼在圓洞上。形式一 b 是没有圓鑿而只有長鑿存在的（圖1b）。形式二 a 是圓鑿的，其直徑約等於或大於長鑿的長度並包攝長鑿（圖26—36）。形式二 b 是没有長鑿而只有圓鑽的（圖34—39）。

長鑿與圓鑿相聯的一 a 形式是被認爲在小屯發掘的甲骨中最普通的形式。雖然貝塚氏也指出火直接燒灼於没有圓鑿相聯的長鑿的例子（圖1b 形式），似乎認爲這種例子在所有五期中都是不常見的②。這種見解與皇家安大略博物館的明義士與懷特氏所藏的甲骨現象是有點出入的。仔細檢驗此博物館所藏的甲骨，發現在第二、三和四期的卜骨上，被認爲是挖刻的圓鑿，大都只是燒灼後剥落的窟洞而已。顯然的，没人注意到這些窟洞是燒灼後骨的表面剥落了所造成的。如果沿著長鑿旁的燒灼面剥落，其剥落處是很容易被誤認爲圓鑿的（圖10）。由没有被

---

① 董作賓《殷虛文字乙編自序》。
② 陳夢家《殷虛卜辭綜述》，頁11 説："鑽鑿並施，鑿者較多，鑽者較少。"鑽鑿的含意不太清楚。

燒灼或雖燒灼而不剝落的圓鑿實例，知圓鑿的直徑大於長鑿長度之半而其契刻面的坡度是很緩的，如果燒灼的剝落面很小，不平且不成形狀，則很容易可推知此剝落面不是原有的挖刻窪洞（圖5b、11a和c）。

此博物館的藏骨，沒有晚於第一期的未燒灼或雖燒灼而保存完好狀態的圓鑿實例①。由於此博物館所藏第二期的卜骨不很多，很難肯定地說第二期沒有這種例子，但是，第三和第四期沒有於長鑿之旁挖刻圓鑿的習慣是應該不成問題的。否則，最少也可發現一例如第一期那麼常見的，未燒灼或雖燒灼而仍保持完好狀態的圓鑿。雖然很難說第五期也是直接把火燒灼在長鑿之旁的，但此博物館唯一合適之例也是這樣的（圖6）②。

圓鑿有個很重要的功能，它能造成更大更薄的表面使兆紋容易裂開。兆紋的剝裂總是由燒灼處和最薄處開端的，如果火燒灼在圓鑿的上部，裂開處也比較容易朝上，反之，兆紋則比較容易朝下。如果沒有圓鑿，兆紋就比較不容易裂開，兆紋分歧的也大都是直接於長鑿旁燒灼的結果。骨的厚薄對兆紋裂開是否容易是很有關係的，這由沒有圓鑿的燒灼，因而需要更多的火和熱度，所以其燒灼面比較大的事實推出來的③。雖然圓鑿有使兆紋容易裂開的作用，但也可能導致貞人利用其職權來控制兆坼的弊端，而不能不取消圓鑿的使用。如果這假設是對的，那就足以說明何以後期常挖寬長鑿的兩肩，使骨頭有較大的薄弱面。

基於此事實，可以區別出卜骨是早期或晚期的。大概地說，前期（第一期）的卜骨有個窄而尖頭的長鑿和與之相聯的圓鑿。後期的只有一個長鑿，此長鑿如不是非常的長，就是看起來肥些。對於皇家安大略博物館所藏的這一大批卜骨，這區別是個很重要的事實。第二、三和五期的卜辭是比較容易與他期區別的，如果有一版卜辭不屬於這幾期，那麼它就屬於第一或第四期。貝塚茂樹教授所稱的王族卜辭不屬於第二、三、五期或第四期的武乙，如果它不自成爲一個集

---

① 貝塚茂樹《京都大學所藏甲骨文字》，頁119—123指出第二期有未灼的圓鑿，但拓本B1641顯示有分歧的兆坼，可能該穴也是剝落面。
② 甲上的鑿洞常與骨上的不同，通常是於長鑿旁刻一平行線條，然後挖個指甲形的穴與長鑿相聯如圖12，與骨上的半圓形頗爲不同。甲上也有一些直接於長鑿旁燒灼而不刻圓鑿的，圖13是背甲上的例子，腹甲上的可見《殷虛文字丙編》頁16的解說。由於甲質脆弱，難以判明長鑿旁的圓穴是挖成的或燒灼剝落面。雖然第三、四期骨上無挖圓鑿的習慣，看起來大部分的甲都有長鑿與圓鑿的，這可能是由於甲骨體質上的不同。
③ 張秉權《殷虛文字丙編》上輯二，頁174說："平常在龜甲較薄之處，我們可以發現僅作棗核狀的凹穴（其左或右側無指甲狀凹穴），但是這裏的那個未灼過的棗核狀凹穴，却在甚厚的腹甲上，這是不常見的例子。"可見骨的薄厚與兆紋裂開的易否很有關係。

團，那麼就一定屬於第一期或是第四期的文武丁了。雖然這兩期的相似點使得很難區別它們，但自鑿鑽形態的觀點，這並不是複雜的問題。

由於此博物館沒有刻著貞人名的王族卜辭卜骨，無法確定舉出的例子會被接受爲王族卜辭，故現在利用貝塚教授所舉的例子，來看看王族卜辭的鑿洞是近於第一期或後期。圖 14 有幾種樣子的鑿鑽，洞 a 是個第一期常見的長鑿圓鑿相連的形式，雖然該圓鑿不知是否剝落面，而長鑿的兩肩又是與後期的彎曲相似。洞 b 沒有圓鑿而長鑿又是平頭的。介於 a 和 b 而有點破損的洞，也可看出是直接於長鑿上燒灼的。洞 c 是個複式的長鑿（長鑿的兩肩被挖寬了），很明顯沒有相聯的長鑿和圓鑿，長鑿的最深線不在中央而在右邊第二道弧的中央，可見忘了畫出左邊第一道肩，如 ◐，所謂的圓鑿也可看出是剝落面。洞 d 是個圓鑽，其旁邊的半圓窪洞當然是剝落面。可見這些窪洞大都是後期的形式。圖 15 雖然例子不很明顯，亦可看出長鑿的頭不如第一期的尖，而兩肩也彎曲，短肥的長鑿也是後期的形態。圖 16 的長鑿也是短肥形的，圖上顯示長鑿兩肩都有燒灼的痕跡。由此博物館藏骨的實例，這種情形都是以火直接燒灼於長鑿的內壁而灼到另一肩的，因此半圓的窪洞也是剝落而成的。圖 17 是此館的藏骨，字體很像貝塚教授所說的王族卜辭，上面多種樣態的窪洞都是後期的形式。由於圖 14 到 17 所顯示的鑿形都是後期形式，所以它們都應屬於第四期，因此王族卜辭的卜骨不必都劃入第一期。

由於鑿鑽的問題是沒有目驗過大批甲骨的人所不能研究的，所以只有貝塚教授寫過鑿鑽與斷代的關係文章[1]。他贊成王族卜辭是第一期的，但因爲王族卜辭不與第一期貞人同現於一版，所以他主張這些卜辭是有別於殷王朝的另一個機關占卜的[2]。他用鑿鑽的施用情形來加強其論調。貝塚教授分鑿鑽爲標準與多種形式兩類，形式一 a 是標準型，二 a 與 二 b 則爲不正常型。除了一例[3]，他將不正常型的都歸入王族卜辭。他認爲最原始的鑽鑿技術是直接於甲骨上燒灼的方法，然後再由不正常型進展到長鑿與圓鑿相聯的標準型。根據貝塚教授的看法，就成了

---

[1] 貝塚茂樹《京都大學所藏甲骨文字》，頁 117—122，陳夢家於《殷虛卜辭綜述》頁 11 也討論到鑿穴，但沒說到與斷代的關係。明義士於其編輯的《殷虛卜辭後編》的（A 三）3076 號拓本下注云："First offered to me Feb.16, 1926. The hole found somewhat earlier." 該版著錄於《戰後南北所見甲骨錄》的明義士舊藏甲骨文字 478。該版刻辭可疑，可見明義士已注意到鑿穴與時代的關係而懷疑其刻辭了。

[2] 貝塚茂樹、伊藤道治《斷代研究法的再檢討》，頁 173。

[3] 見圖 13 及本文討論。

王族卜辭的卜骨含有一些比較原始的鑽鑿技法。因爲他認爲比較簡陋的技巧一定是早期的，所以他把王族卜辭歸類於第一期而不是第四期①。

由發掘的報告，知鑽鑿的技巧雖然是由最原始的直接於甲骨上燒灼的方法，進展到容易控制兆紋的長鑿圓鑿相聯的技法，但實例顯示較簡陋的方法不一定是屬於早期的。此博物館有一片直接於骨上燒灼的例子，但却是第四期的東西。圖18顯示没有一條如長鑿所應有的深的長溝。那個窪洞很淺、不平，又不成任何長鑿的形狀，只是由直接於骨上燒灼所成的剥落面，並不是鑿或鑽成的②。由這一骨及第三、四期的卜骨没有挖刻圓鑿於長鑿旁的習慣，知卜骨上技巧較簡陋的鑿鑽不一定屬於早期的，所以王族卜辭卜骨上所顯示較簡陋的窪洞也不必非與第一期武丁同時代的東西不可。

貝塚教授把形式二較簡陋的窪洞都歸入王族卜辭，在討論刻有這種簡陋窪洞的卜辭時，是應該來自王族卜辭的集團，還是應該歸屬於第一期前，有一點是先得澄清的。"上吉"是出現於第一期很頻繁而不在他期出現的"兆側刻辭"，貝塚教授指出兩例王族卜辭而有自組貞人名的甲骨，上面刻有"上吉"的兆側刻辭，證明王族卜辭與第一期同時而使用這個術語③。但是他舉出的例子都是值得懷疑的。他説圖19上的術語"不若"、"見"和"上吉"都是兆側刻辭。"不若"、"見"和"上吉"這幾個字看起來都比其他刻辭刻得淺些，兩段刻辭用線劃開，這幾個兆側刻辭都屬於下一句，難道一個貞辭用上三個判斷吉凶的術語？ 尤其"不若"與"上吉"是相反的意思，而"不若"與"見"也不曾被用作兆側刻辭。圖20的"上吉"不刻在習慣的兆坼所向的一邊，而與月名刻在一起的也是僅見的。總之，"上吉"是第一期僅見的兆側刻辭，如果王族卜辭也使用此種術語，何以僅此兩見，而且也不用"不牾黽"等第一期所常見的兆側刻辭。

貝塚教授指出京都大學人文科學研究所藏甲骨，刻有形式二 a 的圓鑿大於並包含長鑿的例子有四版（圖21—24）。除圖21外，他把其他三骨都歸屬於王族卜辭。後來他覺得它們都有相同形態的鑿洞，不如也把它改屬爲王族卜辭的好④。筆者同意他把第一骨歸入第一期，但把四骨都歸入王族卜辭是值得討

---

① 貝塚茂樹《京都大學所藏甲骨文字》，頁122。
② 該骨可與《京津》4505、《佚存》58、59和《萃編》959綴合，可能那幾版也有於骨上直接燒灼的情形。
③ 貝塚茂樹《京都大學所藏甲骨文字》，頁116—117。他也指出《拾遺》448有"不牾黽"的兆側刻辭。但該版只有一"牾"字於命辭之中，並不作爲兆側刻辭。
④ 《京都大學所藏甲骨文字》，頁122。

論的。圖 22 的卜辭全文應是"干支卜，今條方其大出"，或"干支卜，今條方不大出"①。某些地方這些刻辭雖與常見的第一期刻辭有些不同，如不記貞人名，𠂤（條）和𰀁（方）刻作𰀁、𰀂，但是這種形式在第一期是不乏其例的。如圖 25、26 和圖 22 的文辭和字體都是一樣的，而其上刻有兆側刻辭的"上吉"，"上吉"是只出現於第一期的術語。唯一的例外，見於《甲編》2742 片爲第三期刻辭。因此圖 21、22、25 和 26 的卜辭只是第一期的，並不是特別集團的王族的卜辭。圖 23 是卜問有關雀的，雀作𰀂是第一期的字體，雖然也沒有貞人名，亦無悖於把他看作第一期。圖 24 的字體與有第一期貞人名的《殷虛書契續編②》4・29・1 和《殷虛文字乙編》5317 是相似的。貝塚氏所舉的這幾個圓鑿大於並包攝長鑿的王族卜辭的例子，有許多特徵是第一期共有的，但不足以動搖第一期不必再分出特別的小集團的論調。

此博物館和他處的收藏也有圓鑿大於並包攝長鑿的例子。圖 27 與圖 22、25、26 等是同類的貞問。圖 28 之"之夕雨"與"五月"作"𰀁𰀂"和"𰀃𰀄"都是第一期的形式。圖 29 的干支形式是很早的，雖然缺貞人名與卜貞字，也是第一期所有的現象③。圖 30 的其菫（𰀁𰀂）卜問是第一期所特有的。圖 31 的卜旬夕，其夕（𰀁）與禍（𰀂）的字體近於第二期，但其反面有刻辭，是比較少行於第二期而盛行於第一期的，所以是第一期到第二期的過渡期卜骨。

看起來圓鑿大於並包攝長鑿的鑿法是第一期所特有的，但不必是王族卜辭的特性。如果這種鑿法的卜骨上，發現有王族貞人名的卜辭，則王族卜辭與第一期同時或稍前的説法是相當有理由的，但可惜沒有這種例子。

貝塚教授也把無鑿而只有圓鑽（形式二 b）的卜骨全部歸屬王族卜辭（圖 32、33）。有些只有圓鑽的卜骨是可屬於第一期的。如圖 34、35 都有"上吉"的兆側刻辭，所以是第一期的。圖 36 是於己亥日卜問庚日之雨，以干名日是第三期最爲盛行，但他期也有。由於字體像是比較早期的，故就算它是第一期的（骨上的長鑿是晚期的）。

其他這種圓鑽的例子就不容易歸屬於第一期了。圖 32 的辛寫作𰀁是第四期所常見的，也不見於貝塚教授的王族和多子族卜辭干支對照表④。第一期的寮祭

---

① 參考島邦男《殷虛卜辭綜類》，東京：1979，頁 187—188 的"今條"和頁 459 的"方出"項下。
② 編者按："編"，原文誤作"論"，今徑改。
③ 參考《京都》B0830。
④ 《斷代研究法的再檢討》，頁 78 後的附表。

作 ，而圖 33 的 是第四期的形式，所以他所舉的兩例都是近於第四期的。如果所有圓鑽的例子，都像圓鑿大於長鑿的例子，顯示出近於第一期的，則説明貝塚教授所舉的兩例是第四期的自是靠不住。但是圓鑽的例子不全是第一期的，第四期的例子也不少的。圖 37—39 的卜辭其序辭都是干支貞的形式。這種形式是第四期所特有的，雖也可在第一期找出數例來，但説這三骨都是第一期的就太巧合了。而且其干支字的庚（ ）卯（ ）子（ ）也是後期的形式，而不在貝塚教授的王族、多子族卜辭干支表上的。因此這三骨一定是第四期的，而很多有圓鑽的卜骨歸屬於第四期是比第一期妥當的。由以上所論，知所有圓鑽和圓鑿大於並包含長鑿的卜骨是與第一期同時的王族卜辭的説法是不成立的。

貝塚教授把𠂤組卜辭包括在其王族卜辭内，陳夢家也主張𠂤組貞人是第一期，他説：

> 以上的敘述，可得到一個結論，即𠂤組①卜辭屬於武丁的晚期。由於稱謂，可知𠂤組和賓組很多相同的，在下節中將要詳論賓組之所以必屬於武丁時代。由於字體，可知𠂤組一方面遵守賓組的舊法，一方面已產生了新形式。𠂤組的紀時法和賓組也是大同而小異。𠂤組某種卜辭形式，或同於賓組，或爲𠂤組所特有，或下接祖甲卜辭，與字體的情形一樣，足以表示𠂤組當武丁之晚葉，開下代的新式。𠂤組祭法見於賓組，而"出""又"通用亦顯示交替之跡。至其稱號中，或守武丁舊制，或開新例如大乙、上甲諸例。凡此可見𠂤組大部分和賓組發生重疊的關係，小部分與下一代重疊，它正是武丁和祖庚卜辭的過渡。

陳夢家在此所説的紀時法、字體、卜辭形式等的大同小異，舊制新例等，看起來並無客觀的標準，如殷人祭祀先人恒以干支名之，父與伯叔的稱呼並無分別，故每一期都可能有父戊的稱謂。雖然𠂤②組卜辭在某些方面與第一期很相似，但由鑿鑽形態的事實，把𠂤組卜辭歸入第一期是很難的③。

理論上王族卜辭的貞人是不與第一期的貞人同出現於一版的。從第一期的卜辭裏分出一部分而使成一特別集團也是論爭焦點之一。貝塚教授舉出幾個第一期貞人與王族卜辭貞人同現於一版的例子，來支持他的王族卜辭與第一期同

---

① 包括無貞人名而字體與有𠂤組貞人名卜辭相似的卜辭。
② 編者按："𠂤"，原文誤作"出"，今徑改。
③ 《殷虛卜辭綜述》，頁 153。

時的主張①。可以《殷虛文字甲編》2361（圖 40）爲他舉出的典型例子。他説第一期貞人（賓）與王族卜辭貞人（扶）同在該版上，可是該版的賓作，字體與第一期的貞人賓是很不同的，該字在文中的意義根本不曉得，除非他們涉及相同的事類，是很難逕指出現於不同時期的卜辭的相似字體爲同一人的。如果王族卜辭與第一期是同時的，則彼此間的關係當不只表現於其曖昧的幾版的。由鑿鑽的觀點，能證明王族卜辭有貞人名的是第四期，而不是與第一期同時的王族卜辭的一部分②。

　　有兩種形態的鑿鑽只出現於自組貞人的卜辭和後期的卜骨。圖 41—46③ 是自組貞人卜辭而在骨的表面有長鑿的，長鑿旁的圓鑿也可能和背面一樣是燒灼的剝落面。第三期（圖 47—50）和第四期（圖 51、52）也有這種於卜骨下方的表面上鑿洞的習慣。此博物館還有不少這種例子，因爲都順著長鑿的深溝破裂，所以拓本很難表現出來，如圖 18 就有這樣的兩個長鑿。第一期與第二期貞人的卜骨上從來沒有這種於骨上鑿洞的例子，因此可推定第一期是沒有這種習慣的。大量的第三期和第四期的卜骨上，於表面挖刻長鑿並燒灼之，可見是那一段時期的一種特性，卜骨有自組貞人名的也有這種特別習慣，可見也應屬於這一時期。

　　從第二種鑿洞看來，自組貞人的卜骨更明確地屬於第四期的文武丁。簡言之，第一期的鑿洞都挖得很小心，個個都有差不多的形狀和大小，第一期以後則挖成各種各樣的形態而且也大些。但是文武丁的卜骨（圖 53—61）有些是很小的，形狀也不像第一期那樣的整潔。其他卜骨上有這種長鑿的，也只在自組貞人名的卜骨。《殷虛文字甲編》的 387、2335、2383、2387、2908、2930，《乙編》的 9067、9088 和 9104 都是有自組貞人名的刻辭，上面都有這種特別小的鑿洞，所以王族卜辭中的自組貞人卜辭可確定是第四期的，也可能是文武丁朝的。

　　嚴一萍先生也指出一些事實來反對王族卜辭，他指出三例：一例有自組貞人

---

① 參考貝塚茂樹《京都大學所藏甲骨文字》頁 50—52 和頁 111。他指出《甲編》234 的自組貞人扶與第一期貞人内同現於一版，但屈翼鵬先於《甲編》考釋，已指出那是卜丙之誤。其他的例證也像此不能確切地肯定爲貞人名的。
② 《殷虛文字甲編》和《乙編》還有很多有自組貞人名的卜辭。雖然由拓本很難看出真正的鑿穴形狀，仍可看出《乙編》的 8659、9067、9071、9074、9080、9085、9086、9088 和 9091 等都沒有第一期的長鑿形。
③ 圖 40 到 45 取自《甲編》，《乙編》的 8670、8672、8674、9066、9077、9084、9093 等也是於表面鑿洞的。與此批材料同時被發掘的第一期卜辭也無此種現象。

名，一例的字體是𠂤組的，一例是普通的王族卜辭，不可能屬於武丁或其前世的①。他的意見符合本文所陳述的，即王族卜辭屬於不與第一期同時的另外一個集團。

本文可歸納成下列幾點：

一、雖然鑿鑽的技巧有精粗之別，但並不能作爲年代的序列標準。

二、圓鑿大於並包攝長鑿出現於第一期，只有圓鑽的也常現於第四期，並不只是出現於王族卜辭。

三、一般地説，王族卜辭的鑿洞更近於第三、第四期。

四、圓鑿包攝長鑿和未灼或灼而保留完好的狀態的圓鑿，常常出現在第一期的卜骨。如果王族卜辭是與第一期約略同時的，則有𠂤組貞人名的卜骨上也應有此等鑿洞。既然無此例子，把𠂤組貞人名的卜辭歸屬於第一期就不能不成問題了。

五、於骨下方的表面挖刻鑿洞只出現於𠂤組貞人及第三、四期的卜骨上。又除了幾例可能是武乙的卜辭外，有特別小的長鑿的卜骨只出現於𠂤組貞人與文武丁的卜辭。所以𠂤組貞人集團應該是與第四期文武丁同時的。

六、貝塚教授的所謂王族卜辭可析爲：（一）無貞人名而屬於第一期武丁的。（二）無貞人名但屬於第四期的。（三）有貞人名而屬於第四期的文武丁。

圖版出處：

1. ROM960・237・620 + 622。　　　　　　　　　　　（《安明》1134）
2. 《京都》B0802。頁 300。　　　　　　　　　　　　（《合》14145）
3. 《京都》B0836。頁 308。
4. 《京都》B1067。頁 337。　　　　　　　　　　　　（《合》17687）
5. ROM960・237・150。　　　　　　　　　　　　　　（《合》33986）
6. ROM960・237・84。　　　　　　　　　　　　　　（《合》39080）
7. 《京都》B1597。頁 424。　　　　　　　　　　　　（《合》24719）
8. 《京都》B1547。頁 119。　　　　　　　　　　　　（《合》23225）

---

① 嚴一萍《甲骨文斷代研究新例》，頁 488、495—503。他指出：1.《佚存》884，祭自上甲廿示。自上甲數起，第二十示是武乙，所以此骨是屬於文武丁以後的（李學勤於《評陳夢家〈殷虛卜辭綜述〉》已指出）。2.《乙編》8660"出般庚"，直書先祖名必屬遠祖，般庚爲武丁父輩，武丁時應稱父庚，故此骨必晚於武丁時期。3.《京都》3099，於二月置一閏月，與武丁置於年尾稱十三月之習慣相違。

9. 《京都》B2381。頁120。　　　　　　　　　　（《合》33809）
10. ROM960・237・130。　　　　　　　　　　（《合》30213）
11. ROM960・237・1960。　　　　　　　　　 （《合》34230）
12. ROM960・237・3694。　　　　　　　　　 （《合》36328）
13. ROM960・237・3622＋3667＋3690。　　 （《合》35957）
14. 《京都》B3221。頁120。　　　　　　　　　　（《合》21078）
15. 《京都》B3222。頁118。　　　　　　　　　　（《合》32941）
16. 《京都》B3242。頁119。　　　　　　　　　　（《合》21664）
17. ROM931・52・867。　　　　　　　　　　　（《懷特》1629）
18. ROM960・237・298。　　　　　　　　　　（《合》32940）
19. 《京都》B3220。　　　　　　　　　　　　　　（《合》20611）
20. 《續存》1122。　　　　　　　　　　　　　　（《合》20185）
21. 《京都》B707。
22. 《京都》B3228。　　　　　　　　　　　　　　（《合》6714）
23. 《京都》B3230。　　　　　　　　　　　　　　（《合》20172）
24. 《京都》B3227。　　　　　　　　　　　　　　（《合》7731）
25. 《明》857。　　　　　　　　　　　　　　　　（《合》6693）
26. 《庫方》1739。　　　　　　　　　　　　　　（《合》39906）
27. ROM931・52・39。　　　　　　　　　　　　（《懷特》0943）
28. 《庫方》1737。　　　　　　　　　　　　　　（《合》40287）
29. ROM931・52・572。　　　　　　　　　　　（《懷特》0925）
30. ROM931・52・730。　　　　　　　　　　　（《懷特》0921）
31. ROM960・237・38。　　　　　　　　　　　（《合》8410）
32. 《京都》B3226。　　　　　　　　　　　　　　（《合》20509）
33. 《京都》B3221。　　　　　　　　　　　　　　（《合》21078）
34. 《續存》723。　　　　　　　　　　　　　　　（《合》10982）
35. ROM931・52・1031。　　　　　　　　　　（《懷特》0982）
36. ROM960・237・960。　　　　　　　　　　（《合》32146）
37. ROM960・237・99。　　　　　　　　　　　（《安明》2796）
38. ROM960・237・802。　　　　　　　　　　（《合》34153）
39. ROM960・237・790。　　　　　　　　　　（《合》34154）

40. 《甲編》2361。
41. 《甲編》2352。　　　　　　　　　　　　　　　（《合》21204）
42. 《甲編》2851。　　　　　　　　　　　　　　　（《合》31526）
43. 《甲編》2930。　　　　　　　　　　　　　　　（《合》21217）
44. 《甲編》2380＋2385＋2387＋3・2・0189。　　（《合》20464）
45. 《甲編》2278＋2335。　　　　　　　　　　　　（《合》19773）
46. 《甲編》2378＋2356。　　　　　　　　　　　　（《合》20440）
47. ROM960・237・240。　　　　　　　　　　　　（《合》28507）
48. 《京津》4581。　　　　　　　　　　　　　　　（《合》29378）
49. 《甲編》2862＋2873。　　　　　　　　　　　　（《合》31338）
50. ROM960・237・576。　　　　　　　　　　　　（《安明》2146）
51. ROM960・237・4584＋5021。　　　　　　　　（《安明》2704）
52. 《甲編》737＋808＋2・2・2440。　　　　　　（《合》32001）
53. ROM960・237・812＋1982＋3548。　　　　　（《合》33357）
54. ROM960・237・105。　　　　　　　　　　　　（《安明》2772）
55. ROM960・237・318。　　　　　　　　　　　　（《安明》2693）
56. ROM960・237・793。　　　　　　　　　　　　（《合》20027）
57. ROM960・237・321。　　　　　　　　　　　　（《合》32151）
58. ROM960・237・1958。　　　　　　　　　　　 （《合》32778）
59. ROM960・237・296＋772＋1046＋5108。　　　（《合》32257）
60. ROM960・237・135＋878。　　　　　　　　　 （《安明》2387）
61. ROM960・237・40＋5062。　　　　　　　　　 （《安明》2597）

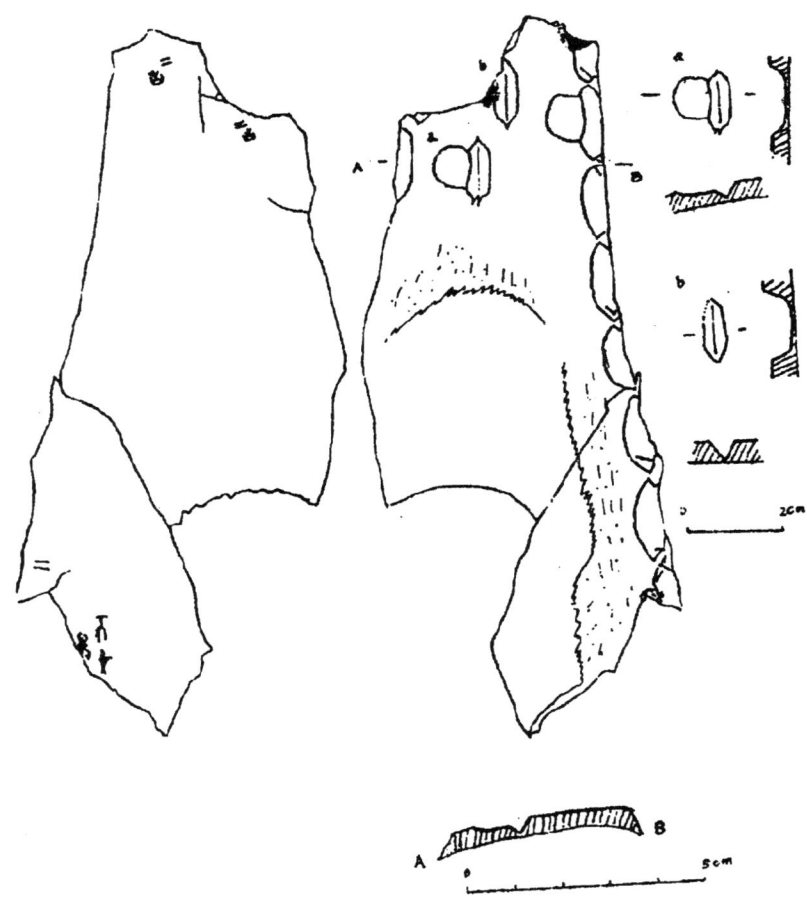

图 1　《安明》1134

圖 2　《人》B0802b P.300

圖 3　《人》B0836b P.308

圖 4　《人》B1067 P.337

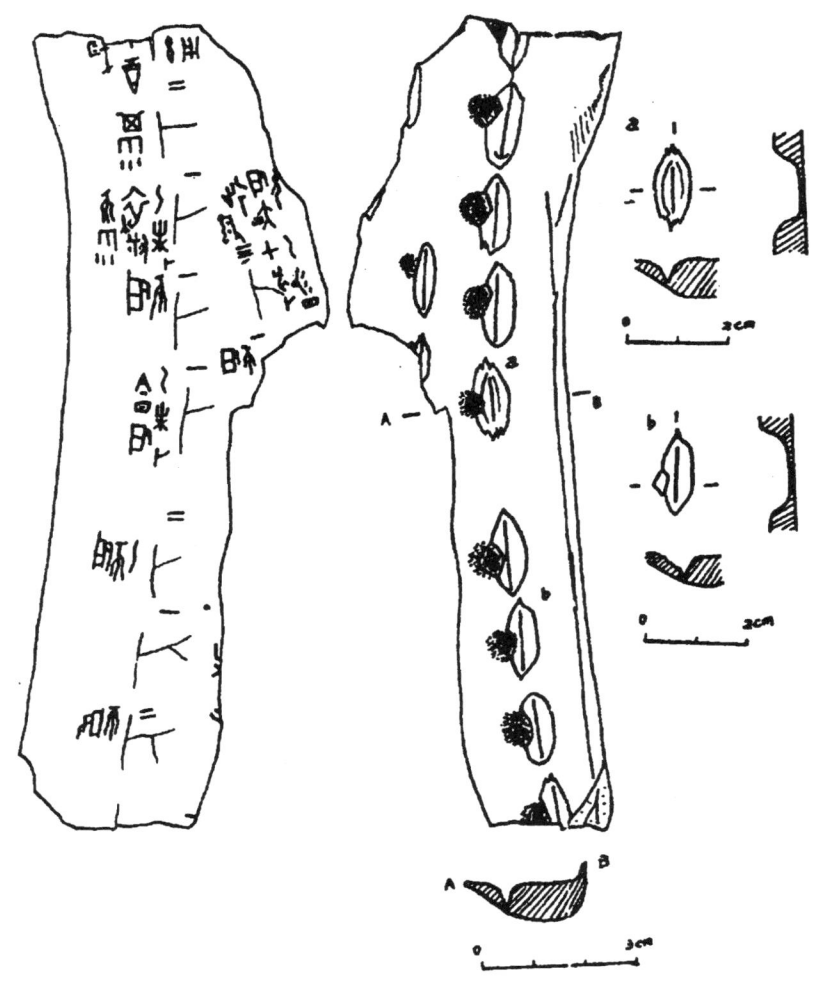

图 5 《合》33986

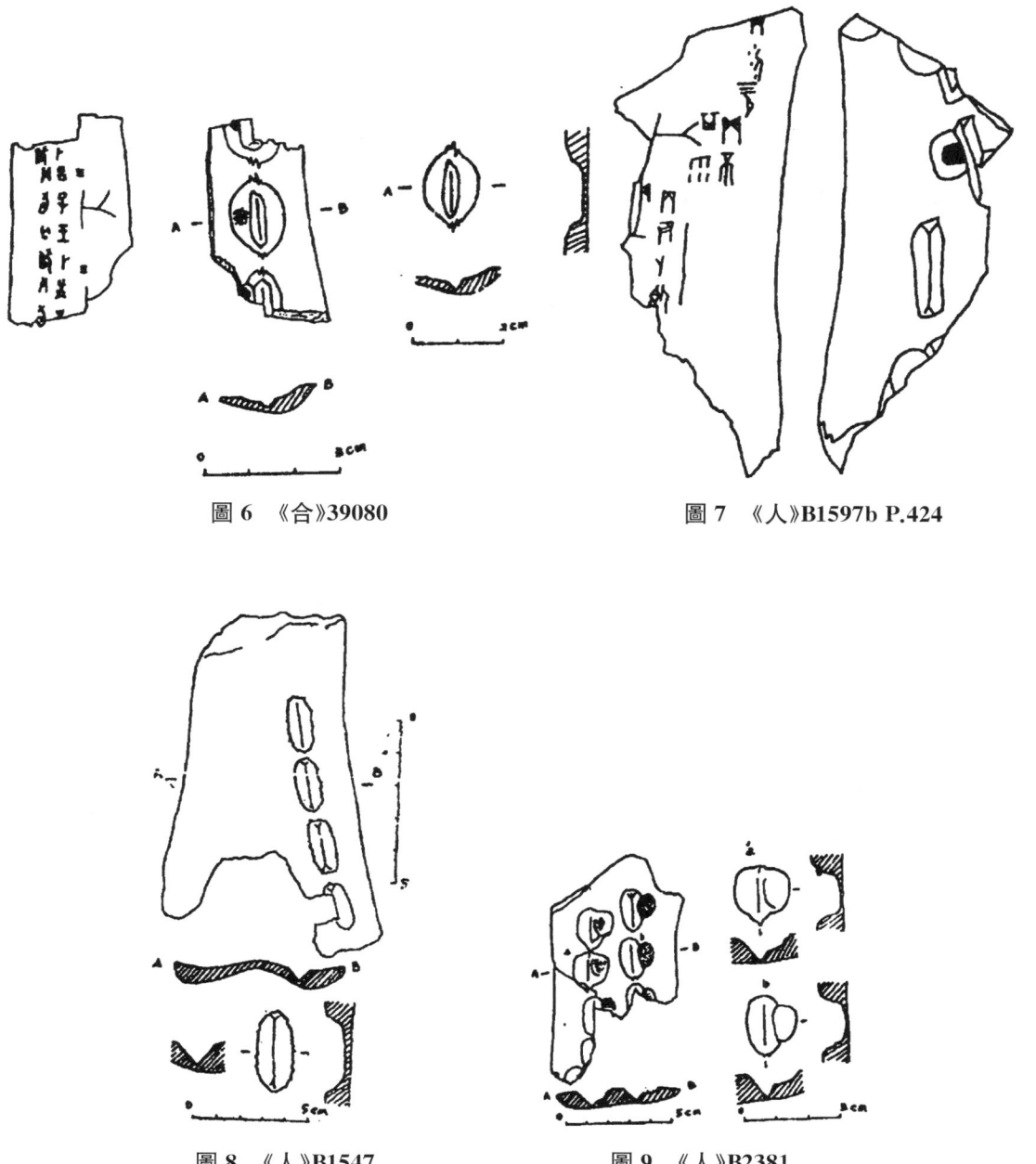

圖 6 《合》39080　　　　圖 7 《人》B1597b P.424

圖 8 《人》B1547　　　　圖 9 《人》B2381

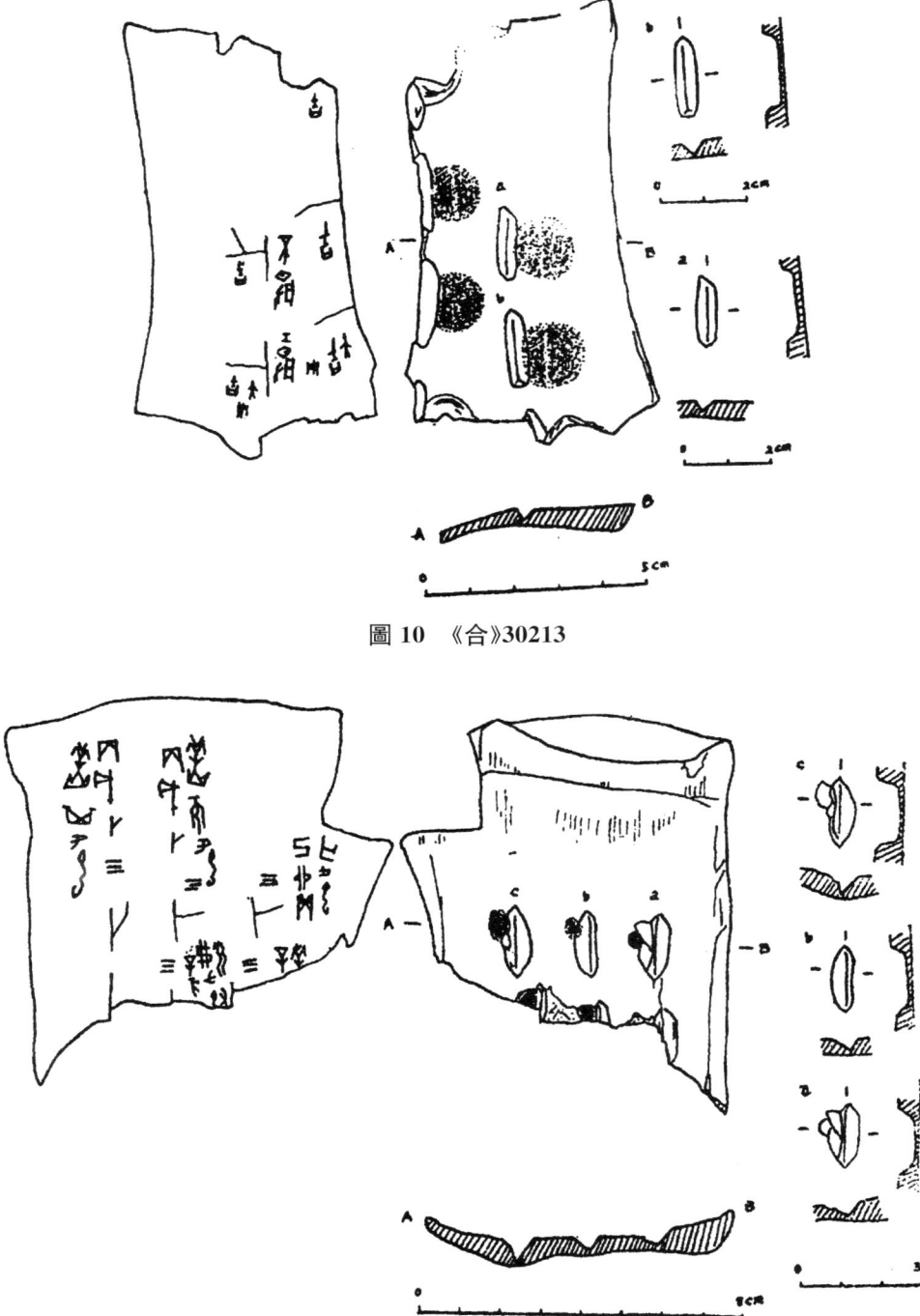

圖 10 《合》30213

圖 11 《合》34230

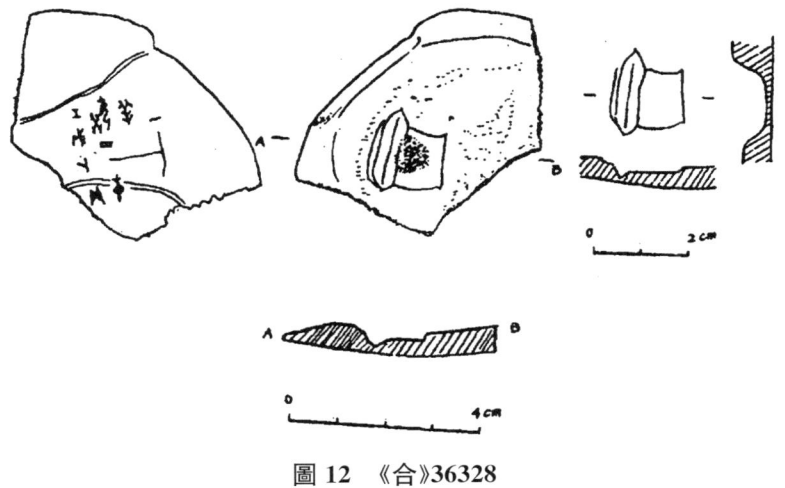

圖 12　《合》36328

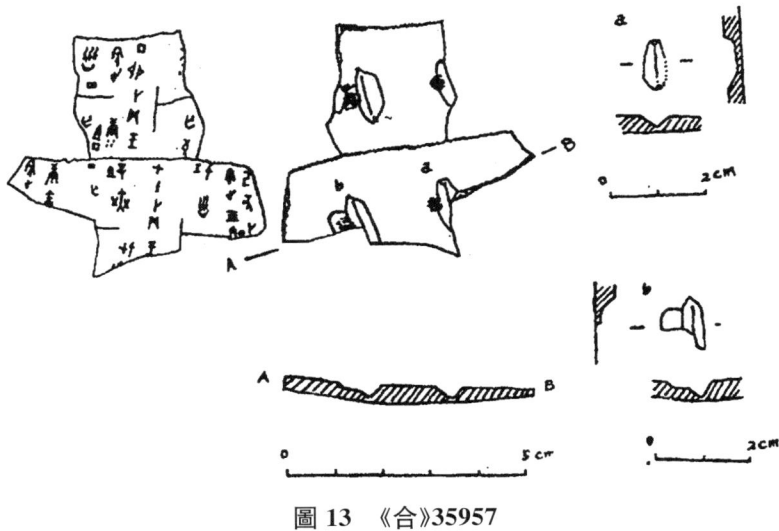

圖 13　《合》35957

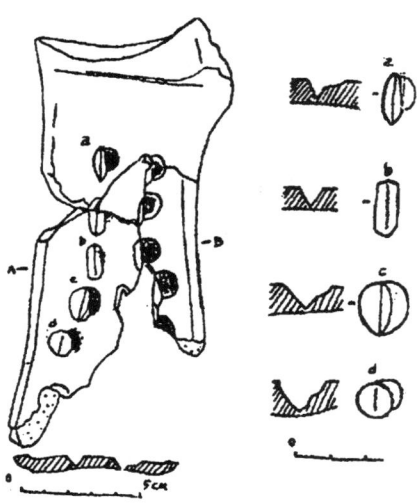

图 14 《人》B3221

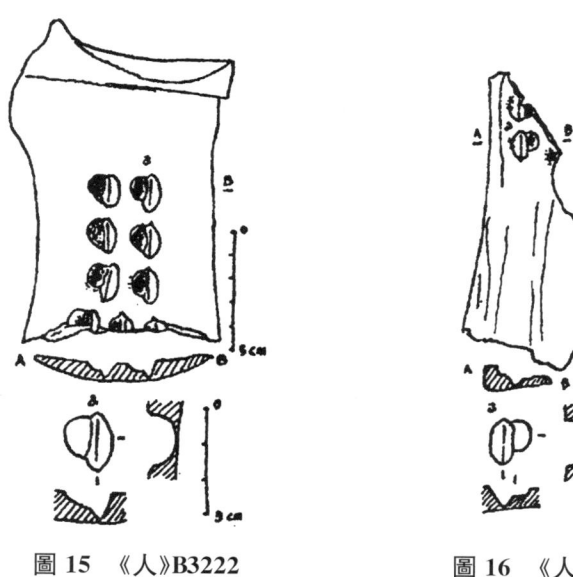

图 15 《人》B3222　　　图 16 《人》B3242

圖 17 《懷特》1629

圖 18 《合》32940×與《存》58、59・414
《甲》882＞同爲一版×參考《萃》959 考釋

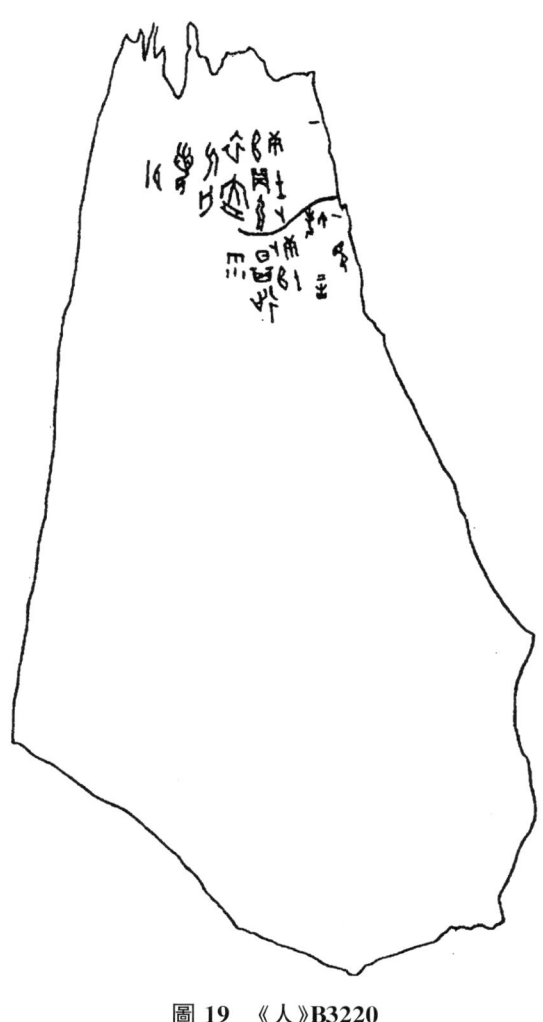

圖 19　《人》B3220

圖 20　《續存》1122
　　　　《合》20185

圖 21　《人》B707　　　圖 22　《人》B3228　　　圖 23　《人》B3230

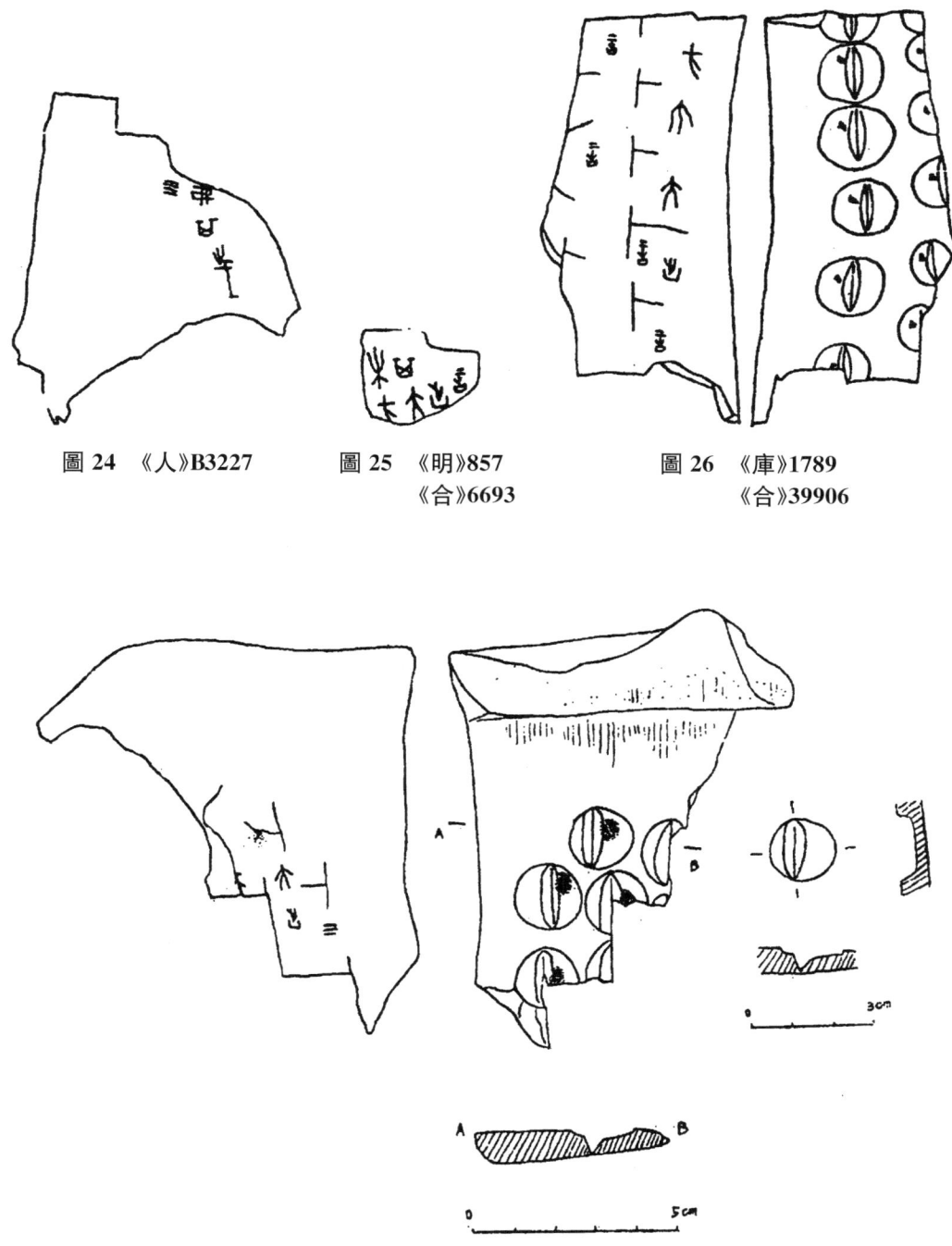

圖 24　《人》B3227　　圖 25　《明》857
　　　　　　　　　　　　　　《合》6693　　圖 26　《庫》1789
　　　　　　　　　　　　　　　　　　　　　　　《合》39906

圖 27　《懷特》0943

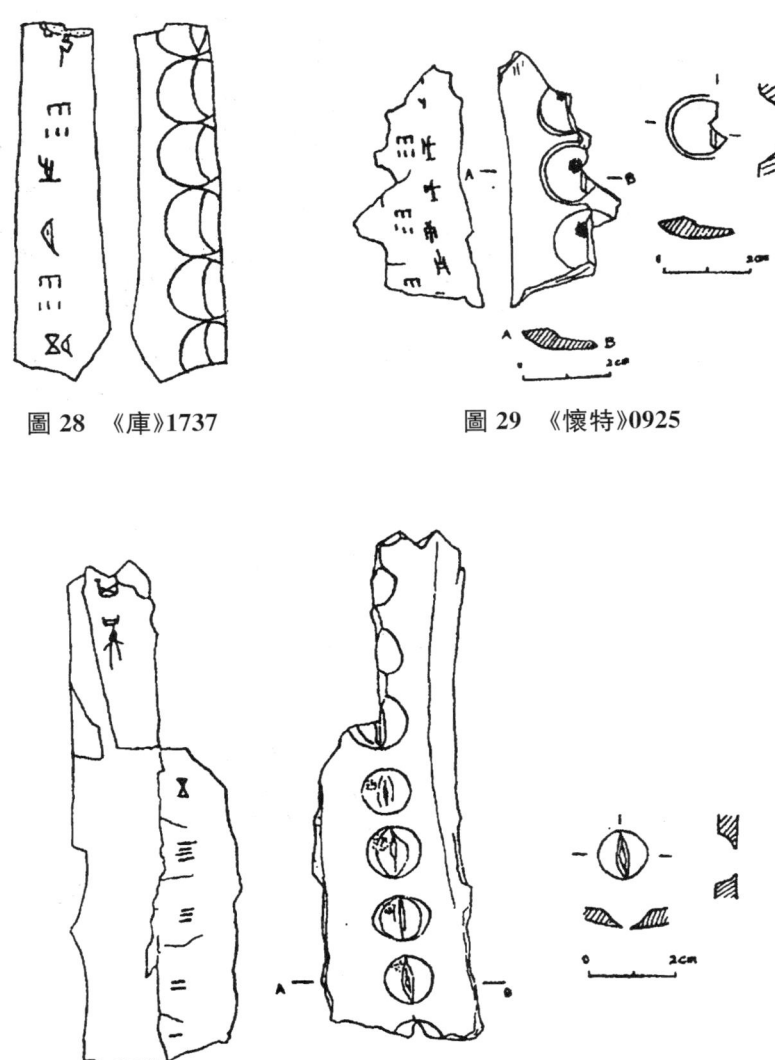

圖 28　《庫》1737　　圖 29　《懷特》0925

圖 30　《懷特》0921

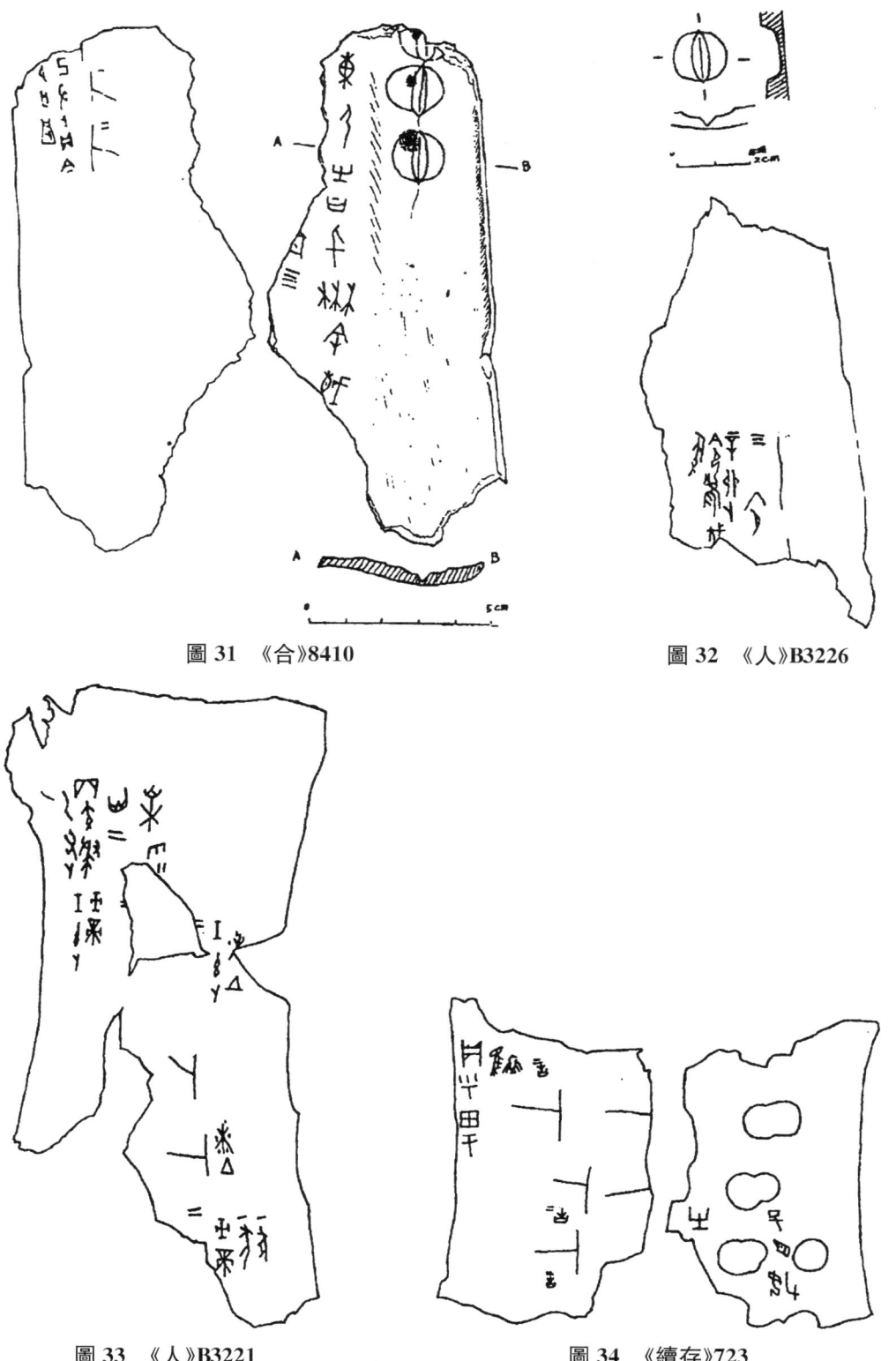

圖 31 《合》8410　　　　　圖 32 《人》B3226

圖 33 《人》B3221　　　　圖 34 《續存》723

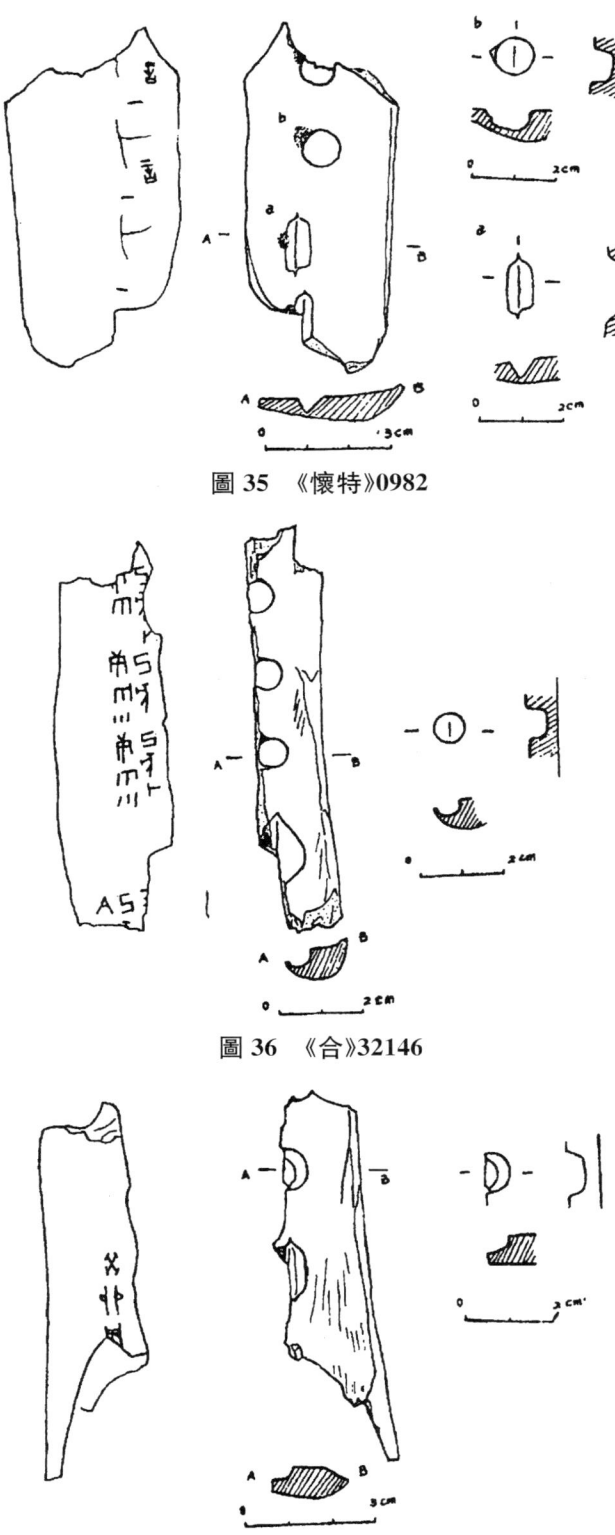

圖 35 《懷特》0982

圖 36 《合》32146

圖 37 《安明》2796

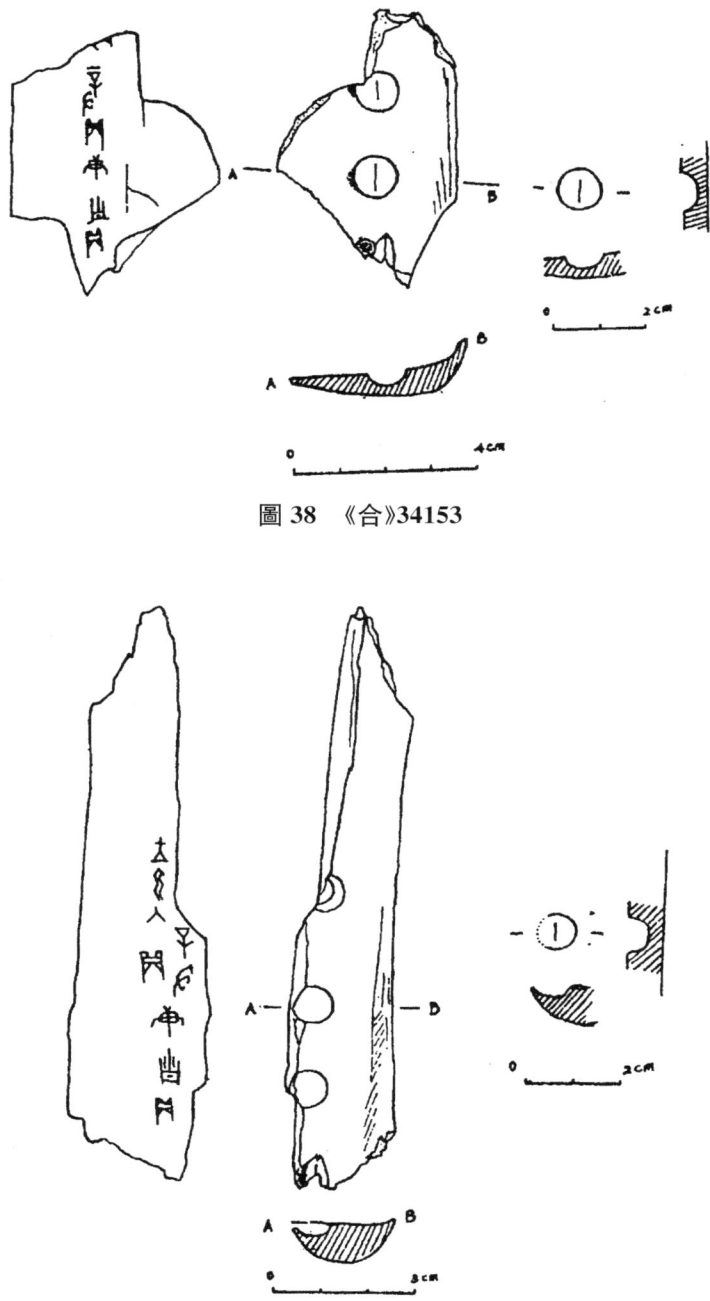

圖 38 《合》34153

圖 39 《合》34154

圖 40　《甲》2361　　　　圖 41　《甲》2352

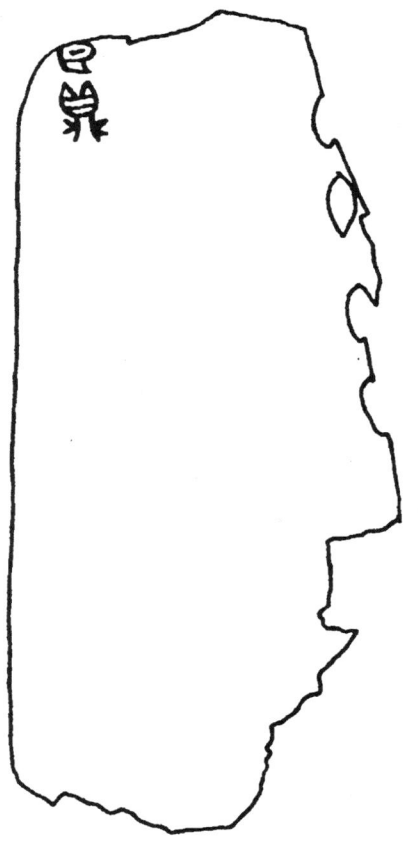 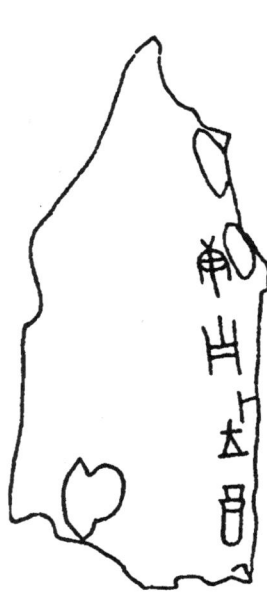

圖 42　《甲》2851　　　　圖 43　《甲》2930

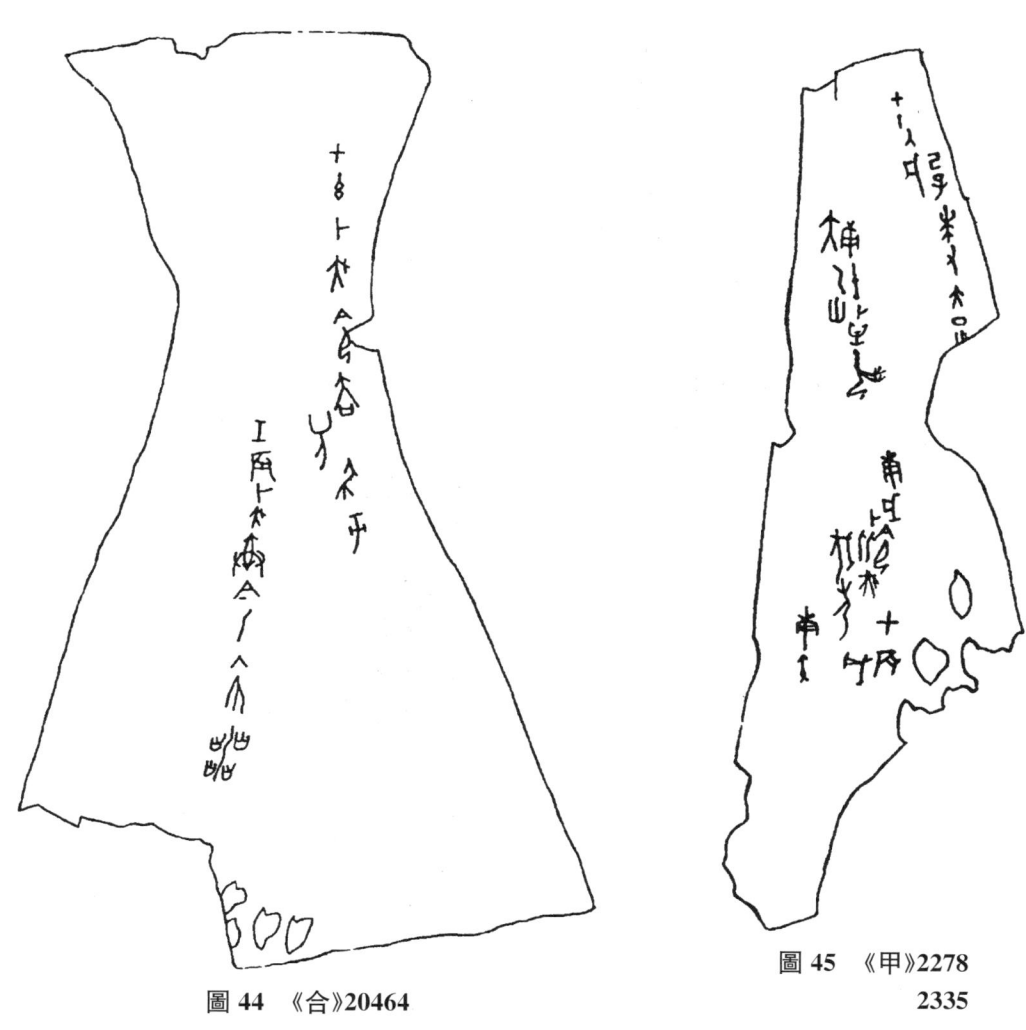

圖 44 《合》20464

圖 45 《甲》2278
　　　　　　2335

圖 46　《甲》2378
　　　　　　2356

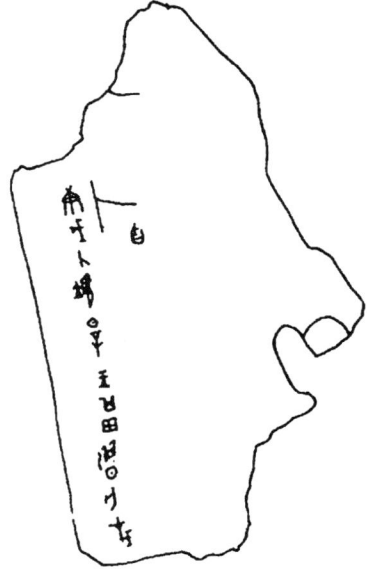

圖 47　《合》28507

圖 48　《京》4581

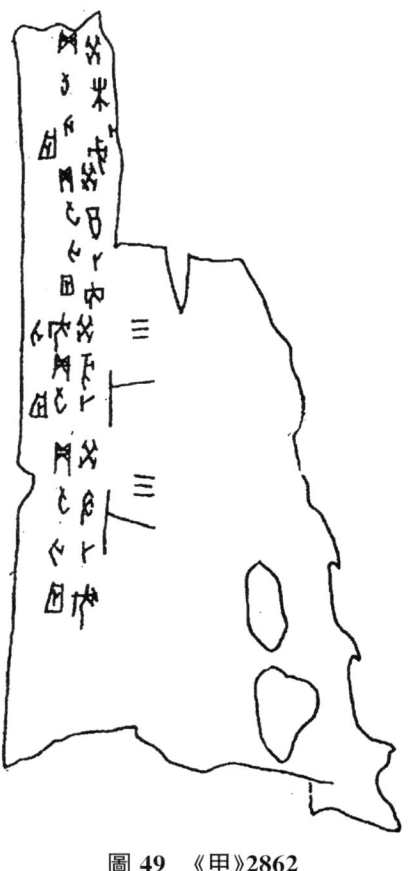

圖 49　《甲》2862
　　　　　　2873

圖 50　《安明》2146

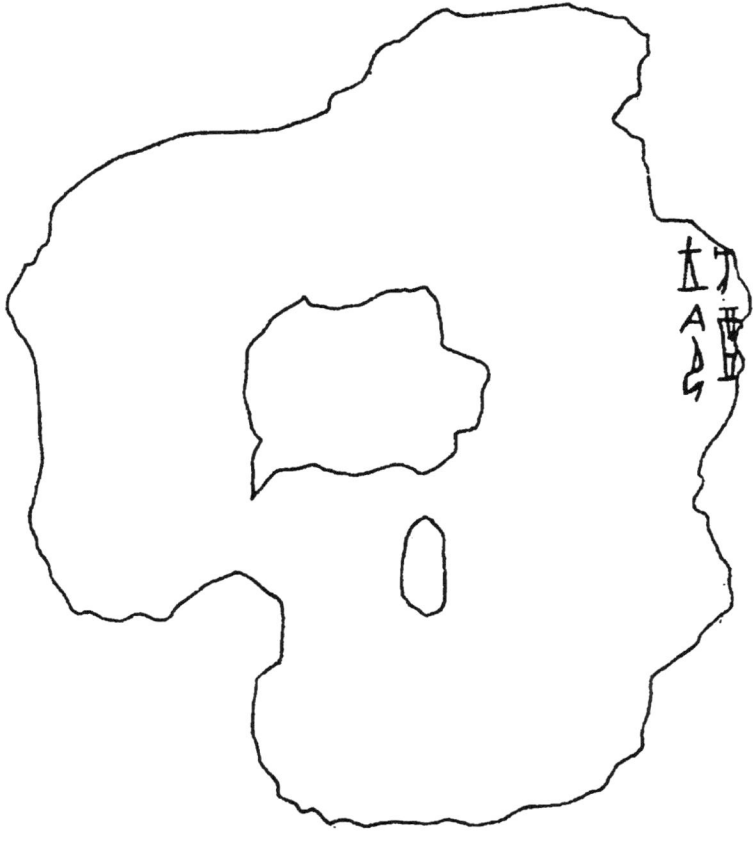

圖 51　《安明》2704

圖 52 《甲》737
808
2・2・0440

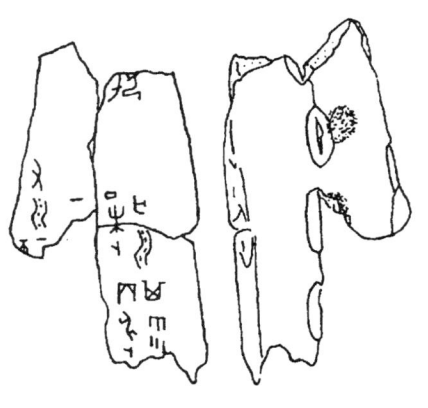

圖 53 《合》33357

圖 54 《安明》2772

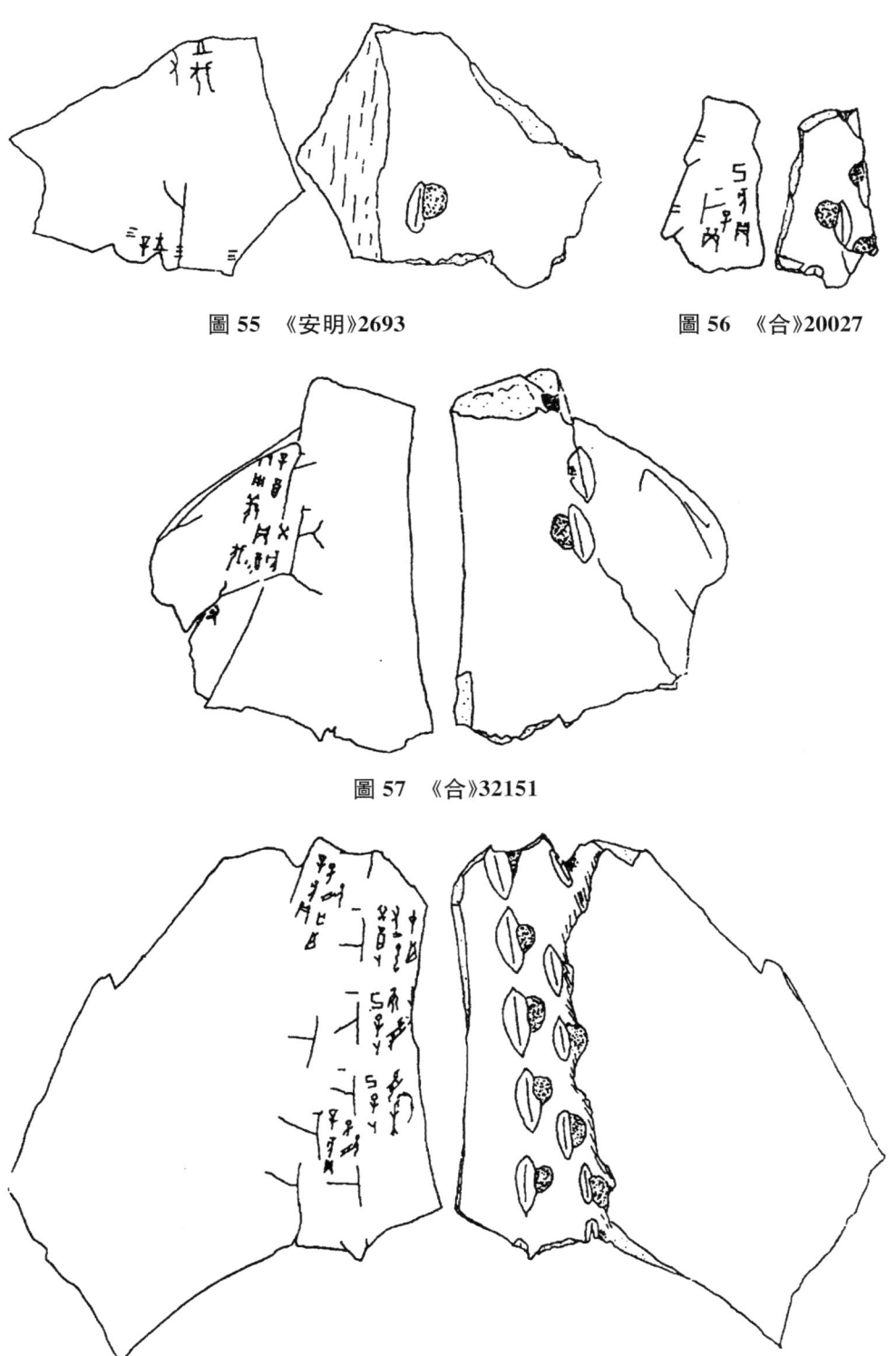

圖 55　《安明》2693　　　　　　　　圖 56　《合》20027

圖 57　《合》32151

圖 58　《合》32778

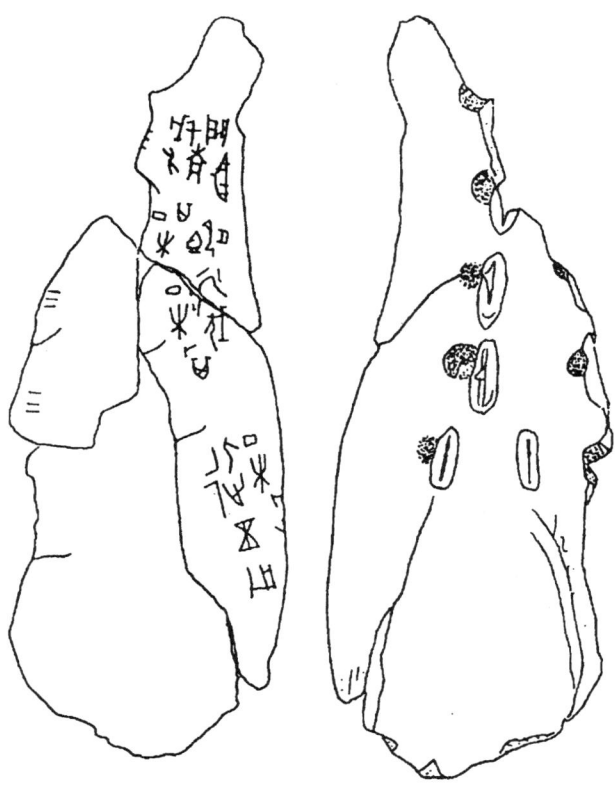

圖 59 《合》32257

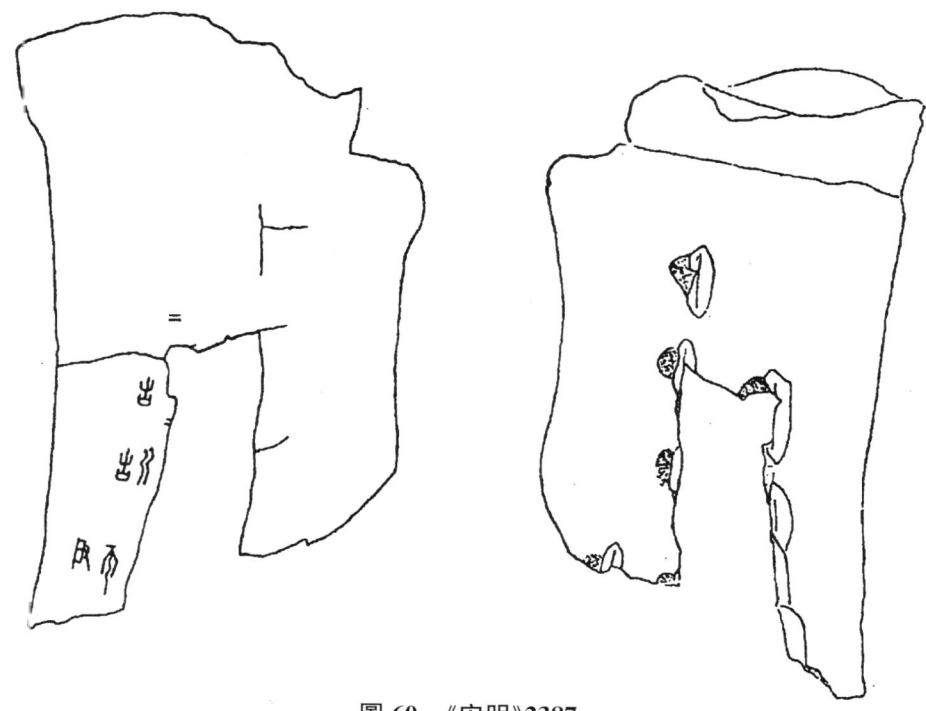

圖 60 《安明》2387

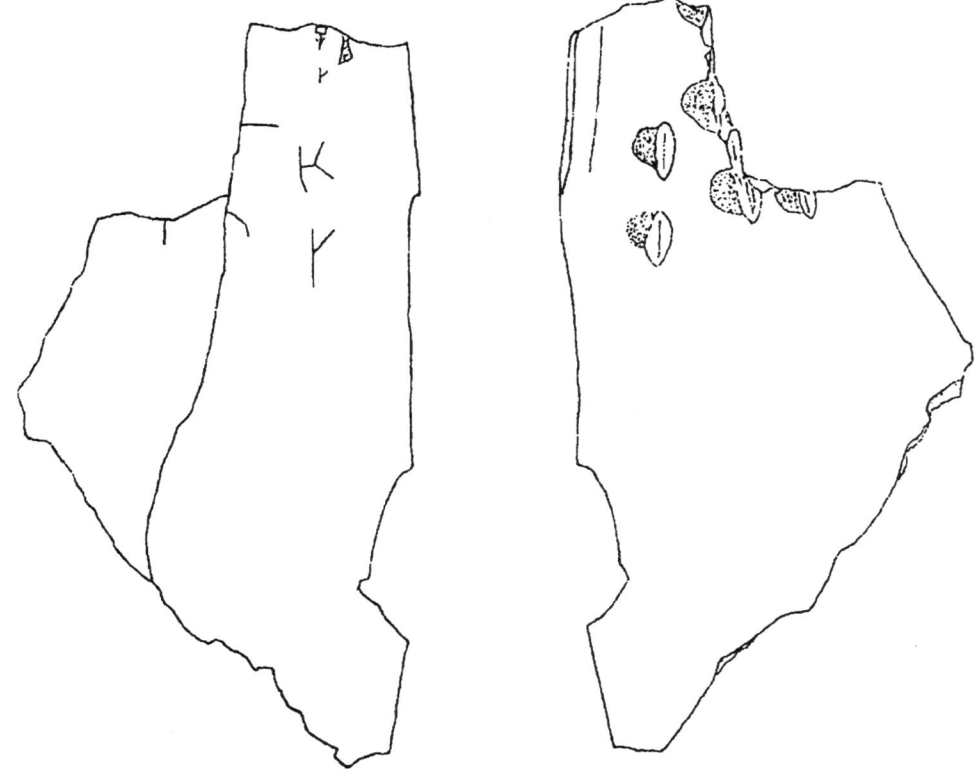

图 61 《安明》2597

原载《中国文字》第 37 期，1970 年；收入《许进雄古文字论集》，中华书局，2010 年。今据后者收入。

David N. Keightley(吉德煒)

SHIH CHENG 釋貞: A NEW HYPOTHESIS ABOUT THE NATURE OF SHANG DIVINATION(釋貞:商代占卜本質的新假設)(節選)

Chinese, Japanese, and Western scholars have generally regarded the oracle bone inscriptions of Shang as questions: "Is the spirit of Grandfather Hsin inuring me?"; "Will the Garrison-Governor get as far as the Cha-region?"; "Should the altar be sprinkled with the blood of the Ch'iang who were brought in?"① Two assumptions have guided this choice of the interrogative: 1) that the oracle-bone form 鼎, which appears in the prefatory formula of most of the oracle inscriptions, is equivalent to the modern Cheng 貞 (irregular chen); and 2) that cheng 貞, following the Shuo-wen 說文 definition, Cheng pu wen yeh 貞卜問也, means "to question by crack-making." It is the thesis of this essay that the second of these generally accepted assumptions (which has made me uneasy for several years) is wrong, and that the oracle inscriptions of Shang were not questions but predictions. What they recorded were not queries, but tentative statements of intent proclaimed to the spirits for their approval or disapproval.②

---

① Herrlee Glessner Creel, The Birth of China (New York, 1937), p.196; Noel Barnard, Monumenta Serica, 22(1963), 219; DKDS, p.90. For a standard view of the oracle bone inscriptions as questions, see CSPT, pp.184-185.

② To the best of my knowledge, only Jao Tsung-yi has suggested that 貞 in certain contexts may be affirmative(i.e. declarative) and that it is often incorrect to add question marks at the end of the inscriptions(YTCP, pp.70-71). But his evidence is minimal. (Cf. the critique at Ping-pien, p.445.)

The argument of this essay may be likened to a jigsaw; it is composed of many pieces of evidence, some stronger than others, but all, it is hoped, interlocking to produce a convincing picture. The reader is asked to reserve judgment until the picture is clear before him. For convenience, a summary of the major points is given on pp. 67-69.

I. THE FORM OF THE GRAPH

The standard divination formula consisted of the kan-chih 干支 day-date, followed by the verb pu 卜, "crack-making," followed by the name of the diviner, followed by 鼎, followed by the divination sentence. The purpose of this essay is to discover the meaning of 鼎. The first question to answer, therefore, is: may the oracle-bone character 鼎 be taken as equivalent to the modern 貞? Or, put more exactly, can we demonstrate graphic, phonetic, and semantic ties between the two characters that persuade us that no philological violence is being done by taking 貞 as the direct descendant of 鼎?

At first sight, the graphs seem to share no common features. Modern 貞 is composed of a cowrie element, pei 貝 (oracle-bone form 貝) and a divination crack, pu 卜 (oracle-bone form 卜). The oracle character 鼎,① by contrast, is assumed to be a simplified picture of a ting-cauldron 鼎 (oracle-bone forms 鼎, 鼎). That assumption must first be checked, and we must then explain, if we are to demonstrate a filiation between 鼎 and 貞, the substitution of the "cowrie" and "crack" elements in the later form of the graph.

A. The Interchangeability of 鼎 and 鼎.

There is little doubt that 鼎 or 鼎 was used in certain divinations in place of the standard 鼎. This is indicated by the following attested inscriptions:

---

① Minor variations appear in the shape of this graph (e.g. YHPT, p. 150); and the variations seem to be related to the date of the inscriptions and to different groups of diviners involved (e.g. Kaizuka Shigeki 貝塚茂樹 and Itō Michiharu 伊藤道治, "Kōkotsubun dantai kenkyūhō no saikentō 甲骨文斷代研究法の再檢討," Tōhōgakuhō 東方學報, 23 (March, 1953), esp. pp. 36-40). Such considerations, however, do not affect the thesis of this essay.

[1] 己巳❲卜❳婦X允亡田   (Yi-pien, 8695)

On the day chi-ssu [the diviner] ❲卜❳-ing: "Fu-X really not calamitied."

[2] 己巳❲卜❳婦X允亡田   (Yi-pien, 8888)

On the day chi-ssu [the diviner] ❲卜❳-ing: "Fu-X really not calamitied."

These and other examples (see IKBS, pp. 396.1-396.2; cf. Ping-pien, pp. 445-446) suggest that ❲卜❳ and ❲卜❳ could be used interchangeably. Phonology also supports the view that ❲卜❳ (*tieng) was interchangeable with ❲卜❳ (*tieng), for in three cases ❲卜❳ was replaced by ❲口❳ (*tieng; modern form ting 丁) in the prefatory formula of the oracle-bone inscriptions (IKBS, p. 577.1). Probably, the ❲卜❳ form was more common than ❲卜❳ in the divination formulas because it was easier to incise, the lines being straight rather than curved.① The substition of the homophone ❲口❳ represented perhaps a desire for still more graphic simplicity.

B. The Interchangeability of the 鼎 and 貝 Elements.

Extant Chou inscriptions provide no certain epigraphic filiation between ❲卜❳ and 貞. Some scholars identify 貞,② a graph which does appear on Western Chou bronzes and which does combine 卜 and 鼎, as 貞 (e.g., ST, p.11b). The graph in question, however, usually has to be taken as a vessel name, and has been read as the modern tzu 鼒;③ occasionally it is a person's name.④ It is never, so far as I have been able to discover, a verbal or divinatory, 貞.

A link between ❲卜❳ and 貞 is provided, however, by the comment of Hsü Shen 許慎 in the Shuo-wen that ku wen yi pei (cheng?) wei ting, chou wen yi ting wei pei

---

① Cf. CKWT, p.1107. Ch'en Meng-chia believes that the more elaborate, most tripod-like forms of the graph were, in fact, the earliest (YHPT, pp.150-151).

② The belief (e.g., ST, p.13a) that a prototype of this character, written ❲卜❳ or ❲卜❳, appears in the oracle bones (GSR, No.834g) is mistaken. I can find only two characters (T'ieh-yün 鐵雲, 45.2; Shih-yi 拾遺, 8.9) which scholars have attempted to interpret in this way, and in both cases the supposed ㇏ or ∣ element is probably a chip in the bone. Two dubious cases, compared with thousands of instances of ❲卜❳ without the ㇏ element, cannot be accepted as evidence of a 鼎 prototype in the oracle bones.

③ CWP, 7.16a. Jung Keng suggests that the appearance of 鼒 rather than 鼎 in the Shuo-wen may result from an error in transmission.

④ On the San-shih-p'an 散氏盤. See Na Chih-liang 那志良, Liang-chien chu-ming-te kuo-pao 兩件著名的國寶 (Taipei, 1964), p.60; SMSG, p.659.

(cheng?)古文㠯貝(貞?)爲鼎,籀文㠯鼎爲貝(貞?), "the ku-wen script used the pei (cheng?) element in place of the ting element, and the chou-wen script used the ting element in place of the pei(cheng?) element."① That this substitution of 貝 for 鼎 was common in ancient times is shown by Hsü Shen's statement that the chou-wen forms of 則, 員, and 霣, were written 䣋, 鼎, and 霛 respectively(SWCT, 7 上, p. 35b).

The idea that the lower element in modern 貞 was not originally 貝 but 鼎, receives support from the statement of the later Han scholar Ching Fang 京房 that 貞 was a phonetic abbreviation(sheng-sheng 省聲)of 鼎(SWCT, 3 下, p. 42a). We may suppose that Ching Fang had observed, in the ancient divination texts in which he was well-versed (SMSG, p.660; cf. n.72 below), a divinatory 貞 written 鼎.

---

① SWCT, 7 上, pp. 35b-36a. Tuan Yü-ts'ai 段玉裁 believes that the text should read 古文㠯貝... etc. Most scholars, however, have agreed with the Shuo-wen text of Hsü Ch'ien 徐鍇:古文㠯貞爲鼎,籀文㠯鼎爲貞(e.g., CKWT, pp.1104, 1106, 1107; YTCP, p.71; ST, p.12b). I see no way to resolve the dilemma with certainty, and indeed my own conclusion is that little graphic distinction was made between 貝 and 貞 in ku-wen or chou-wen script. There is no doubt that the interchangeability of 貞(＊tieng) and 鼎(＊tieng) elements in Chou times may be explained on phonetic grounds, whereas the interchangeability of 貞 and 貝(＊pwad) is phonetically impermissible. However, Chou inscriptions certainly confirm the interchangeability of the 貝 and 鼎 elements(e.g. modern pin 賓 might be written either as 賓 or 賓 (CWP, 6.19a; KJKG, No.411)). Whether Chou inscriptions also confirm the interchangeability of 貞 and 鼎 depends upon whether or not the 貞 of the Chou inscriptions is taken to be an alternate form of 鼎(with CKWT, pp. 1107, 1108; SWKL, p.1383a, 下; DKW, No.48319), or as the antecedent of 肅(with CWP, 7.16a). These two alternatires may not be mutually exclusive. One inscription, on the 瘵鼎(Fu K'ai-sen 福開森, Li-tai chu-lu chi-chin mu 歷代著錄吉金目(Changsha, 1939), p.852 上), contains the phrase 乍其□鼎鼎,which would indicate, at least in this one case, that the two words are not the same(cf. the commentary of Wu K'ai-sheng 吳闓生, Chi-chin-wen lu 吉金文錄 1.35b). But it seems entirely possible that most of the time there was no clear semantic or graphic distinction between 貝 and 貞 when used as elements in other bronse-inscription characters; at least, a preliminary survey of the vessels called 鼎 by their inscriptions reveals no characteristics of form or size that would distinguish them from vessels described as 鼎. My own conclusion, therefore, is that both the 貝 and 貞 elements were used interchangeably with 鼎 in Chou graphs. The interchange was originally permitted on grounds of the phonetic identity of 貞 and 鼎, but 貝 came to participate in the interchange because of its graphic similarity to 貞. Probably, it was necessary, for reasons of space, to lop the top 卜 off 貞 when fitting it in as the bottom element of another character. When 貞 was fitted in as the top element, as in 鼎, there was sufficient space, and the lopping did not have to take place. Lo Chen-yü 羅振玉 has proposed that the interchangeability of the 鼎 and 貝 elements was probably due to the graphic similarity of 鼎 and 貝 in oracle-bone script(CKWT, p.1104), but the graphs do not seem sufficiently alike.

C. Summary of the Graphic Evidence (See. Fig. 1).

The oracle-bone form 𝌀 was an alternate, simpler form of 𝌀 or 𝌀, a picture of a <u>ting</u>-cauldron. A graph combining 卜 and 鼎 elements appears on Western Chou bronze inscriptions, but as the name of a vessel (or person), not as a divinatory 貞. Nevertheless, Chou inscriptions, together with Han accounts of the Chou scripts and phonology, indicate: 1) that 鼎, 貞, and 貝 could be used interchangeably in antiquity as elements in other characters, and 2) that in particular, 貞 was thought to be a phonetic abbreviation of 鼎. This suggests a reasonably certain graphic and phonological filiation between oracle-bone 𝌀 (<u>ting</u>-cauldron and divinatory verb), Chou bronze 𝌀 (vessel name and person's name, and, if Ching Fang is right, divinatory verb); descending by a substitution (which was common) of 貝 for 鼎, to the small-seal 貞 (divinatory verb) and the modern 貞. We may, in short, accept as a reasonably well-supported convention, that oracular 𝌀 may be transcribed as 貞 in modern script.

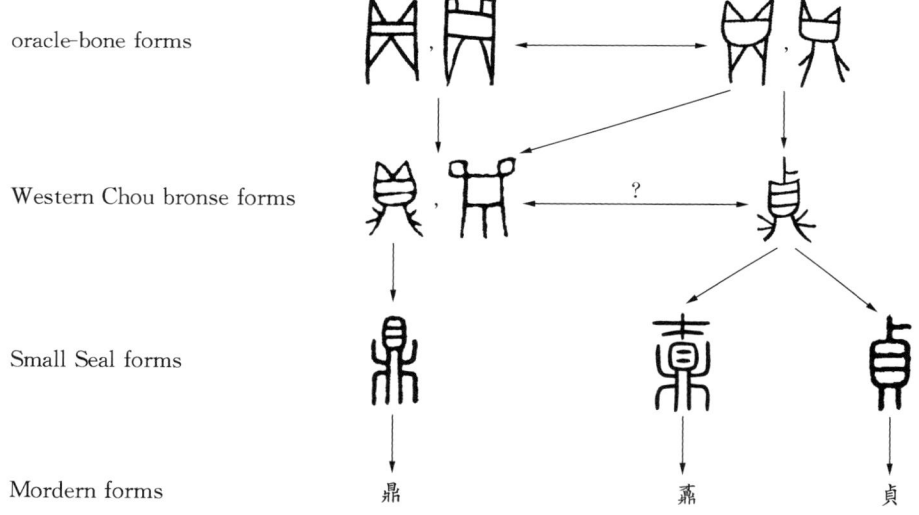

Fig. 1. The evolution of the graphs 鼎, 鼏, and 貞.

II. THE APPARENT SOURCE OF THE <u>SHUO-WEN</u> DEFINITION

As we shall see below (section III), the <u>Shuo-wen</u> definition (A. D. 121), cheng pu wen yeh 貞卜問也, is supported by virtually no classical usage. It seems probable, in fact, that Hsü Shen's definition was not derived from his reading of pre-Han texts, but from the commentary of Cheng Ssu-nung 鄭司農 (fl. AD 89, d. 114) to the Chou-li,① which says, cheng wen yeh 貞問也, "cheng is to question." Why did Cheng Ssu-nung offer this definition?

The passage in question is found in his commentary to a sentence in the Chou-li (Ch'un-kuan 春官, "T'ien-fu 天府"): chi tung ch'en yü yi cheng lai sui chih mei o 季冬陳玉以貞來歲之媺惡 which we may translate, temporarily following Biot (I, 482), "A la fin de l'hiver, il dispose les objects en jade qui servent à determiner si l'année suivante sera bonne ou mauvaise." Cheng Ssu-nung comments: 貞問也易曰師貞丈人吉問於丈人國語曰貞於陽卜 "Cheng is to question. The Yi-ching says: 'Shih cheng chang jen chi 師貞丈人吉'; [this means] 'Ask the chang-jen.' The Kuo-yü says: 'cheng yü yang pu 貞於陽卜' (CLCY, 38.27 b.6). Do these two passages cited by Cheng Ssu-nung support his contention that cheng wen yeh 貞問也?

His interpretation of the Yi-ching passage is markedly at variance with traditional views. Far from taking cheng 貞 in the sense of "question", the commentators Wang Pi 王弼 (226-249) and K'ung Ying-ta 孔穎達 (574-648) take it as cheng 正; so does the t'uan 彖 itself (SSCC, 2, p.8a). According to Legge, the hexagram Shih 師 indicates how "with firmness and correctness, and (a leader of) age and experience, there will be good fortune...." (The I Ching (New York, 1963), pp. 71-72). According to Wilhelm, "The army needs perseverance/And a strong man./Good fortune...." (Cary F. Baynes, Tr., The I Ching or Book of Changes (Princeton, 1969), p. 32; my italics in both cases). As Juan Yüan 阮元 (1764-1849) noted, cheng 貞 occurs frequently in the Yi-ching; this would be the only case in which it means "question"; Cheng Ssu-nung's proof is probably wrong (CLCY, 38. 28a. 13-28b. 2). Cheng 貞 does not mean "question" in this

---

① This is the view of Tuan Yü-ts'ai (SWCT, 3 下, 42a) and Ch'en Pang-huai 陳邦懷 (CKWT, p.1106). Such an interpretation is supported by a peculiarity of Hsü Shen's definition which should be noted as possible evidence of the carelessness or unease with which he defined cheng 貞. He correctly defined the next character in the Shuo-wen, hui 卟, as yi kua chih shang t'i yeh 易卦之上體也, "the upper part (i.e. the top trigram) of an Yi-ching hexagram." It is curious, therefore, that he did not provide the complimentary technical definition of cheng 貞 as "the lower trigram," a meaning of which he must have been equally aware. (Cf. n. 16 below.)

passage. And it certainly does not mean "question by crack-making," for how could one "question the old man by crack-making"?

The Kuo-yü phrase cited by Cheng Ssu-nung comes from a passage in the "Wu-yü 吳語"in which Chin and Wu contest for supremacy at Huang-ch'ih 黃池 in 482 B.C. "The house of Chou has been humbled, the feudal lords no longer pay their ritual dues to the Son of Heaven. We request to cheng yü yang pu 貞於陽卜 and gather in the feudal lords[descended from] Kings Wen and Wu." It is possible, as Cheng proposes, that cheng meant "question": "We request to question by crack-making with fire(i. e. by tortoise-shell divination)." But Wei Chao 韋昭(204-273) comments, cheng cheng yeh 貞正也,(SPTK, 19. 10b. 4) thus: "We request to rectify[the matter of the hegemony] by tortoise-shell divination." He was, in fact, apparently following the earlier Kuo-yü commentaries of Chia K'uei 賈逵(A. D. 30-101) and K'ung Chao 孔晁(whom I have not identified)(CLCY, 38. 28b. 5). Wei Chao was presumably aware of Cheng Ssu-nung's interpretation—he cites Cheng's opinions elsewhere in his commentary—but he chose not to follow it. Neither the Yi-ching nor the Kuo-yü passage, therefore, conclusively support Cheng Ssu-nung's opinion that cheng 貞 means "to question," and the standard commentaries refute it.

The Chou-li uses the term cheng 貞 elsewhere: fan kuo ta cheng pu li chün pu ta feng.... 凡國大貞卜立君卜大封....(CLCY, 47. 10 b. 3), "Whenever the state performs the Grand Cheng(Biot, II, 73, 'la grande consultation des sorts'), and divines about the enthroning of a prince and the establishment of a great principality...." Once again, Ssu-nung comments: cheng wen yeh, kuo yu ta yi wen yü shih kuei 貞問也國有大疑問於蓍龜(CLCY, 47. 10 b. 5), "Cheng is to question. When the state has a great problem[the ta-pu 大卜, "Grand Augurer"] asks the milfoil and tortoise." But here again the context does not require the sense of "question." Ta cheng 大貞 is simply the name of the ceremony. And it should be noted that the phrase ta cheng 大貞 occurs in the Yi-ching several times, where cheng 貞 merely has the sense of cheng 正. Thus hsiao cheng chi ta cheng hsiung 小貞吉大貞凶(Hexagram 3, line 5), "small correctness brings good fortune, great correctness brings misfortune"(cf. Legge, p.63; Baynes, p.19). The Chou-li's Ta-cheng 大貞 ceremony may simply have been a "Great Rectification."

How did the commentator Cheng Hsüan 鄭玄(127-200) explicate cheng 貞 in these Chou-li passages? He was apparently in a quandary. On the one hand, he wished to include the sense of "question" indicated by his predecessor, Ssu-nung; but on the other hand, he wished to introduce the second—and apparently, to him, more fundamental—meaning of cheng 正. He labored mightily to combine the two. His commentary to the "T'ien-fu 天府" passage reads: wen shih chih cheng yüeh cheng 問事之正曰貞 (CLCY, 38.27b.4) "to ask about the correctness of an enterprise is called cheng." And, to the second, "Ta-pu 大卜", passage he comments: cheng chih wei wen, wen yü cheng che pi hsien cheng chih, nai ts'ung wen yen 貞之爲問問於正者必先正之乃從問焉 (CLCY, 47.10b.6), "As to cheng's being a question, one who questions about what is correct (cheng 正), must first rectify (cheng 正) it (the matter to be questioned? the method of questioning?), and only then proceed to question the matter." What Cheng Hsüan is doing in this passage, I think, is trying to indicate that Cheng Ssu-nung may include the sense of "question" if he wishes, but that the primary sense—what you have to do before you proceed to question—is cheng 正, "rectify or regulate."

Cheng Hsüan makes this quite clear in his commentary to yet a third Chou-li passage. The main text reads: kuo ta ch'ien ta shih tse cheng kuei 國大遷大師則貞龜 (CLCY, 47.12b-13a), which Biot (II, 74), here following Ssu-nung, translates, "Quand on fait, au nom de l'Etat, un grand changement de capitale, une grande reunion d'armée, il [the ta-pu] interroge la tortue." But Cheng Hsüan disagrees. He comments: cheng kuei yü pu wei yeh 正龜於卜位也 (CLCY, 47.13a.1), "[cheng kuei 貞龜 means] he regulates the tortoise at the place of divination."

The "Ta-pu" section of the Chou-li, in fact, weakens Ssu-nung's position. The Grand Augurer performs various kinds of operations, singly or in combination, on the tortoise, depending on the occasion. He may ch'en kuei 陳龜 "display the tortoise"①; cheng kuei 貞龜 "regulate (or question?) the tortoise;" tso kuei 作龜 "prepare the tortoise"; or ming kuei 命龜 "give the charge to the tortoise" (CLCY, 47.10b-13b). It is this last phrase which interests us, for, ac-

---

① Since this is the only occurrence of the phrase in the Classics, its exact meaning is uncertain. Sun Yi-jang suggests that it corresponds to cheng kuei 貞龜, and that ch'en kuei 陳龜 probably had no particular connection with the divination itself, but referred perhaps to displaying the shells as a ritual courtesy to the spirits (CLCY, 47.13b.1-6).

cording to Cheng Hsüan, it means: kao kuei yi so pu chih shih 告龜以所卜之事 (CLCY, 47.12a.8), "to inform the tortoise about the subject matter to be divined"; and in his commentary to the Li-chi 禮記, he stresses the questioning aspect of ming kuei defining it as: kao yi so wen shih yeh 告以所問事也 (SSCC, 40.13a), "to inform the tortoise about the subject matter it will be asked about," or, as Couvreur renders it, "propose à la tortue les questions" (Li ki: mémoires sur les bienséances et les cérémonies (Paris, 1950), II, 123). We will return to this phrase later (pp. 15-17), but it seems possible that if ming kuei meant to "question the tortoise," cheng kuei, which was an alternative procedure practised by the ta-pu, did not.

Finally, it should be noted that elsewhere in the Chou-li, Cheng Hsüan omits the "question" dimension of cheng 貞 altogether, as indeed the context demands. Thus, the main text informs us that the ta-chu 大祝 (Grand Invocator) is to, in Biot's translation, "demander une longe rectitude" (II, 85). Commenting on this phrase, ch'iu yung cheng 求永貞, Cheng Hsüan notes, once again, cheng cheng yeh 貞正也 (CLCY, 49.1a.4), and it is hard to see how it could mean anything else. The Grand Invocator would hardly seek a long "questioning."

In short, Cheng Hsüan, throughout his commentary to the Chou-li is consistent in his emphasis on cheng 正 as the core meaning of cheng 貞. It is permissible to consider, therefore, the idea that cheng pu wen yeh 貞卜問也 was not a meaning innate to 閂 in archaic times, but was artificially inseminated into the word by the academic notations of the Han scholars Cheng Ssu-nung and Hsü Shen.① To verify that supposition it will

---

① There is ample precedent for such lèse-majesté. "It is now common knowledge that many of the definitions given by Hsü Shen have been proved to be wrong in the light of the recent studies on bronze and bone inscriptions" (Wu Shih-ch'ang, "On the Marginal Notes Found in Oracle Bone Insdriptions," T'oung Pao, 43 (1955), 66). Cheng Hsüan misunderstood the meaning of 契 in its oracular context (Edouard Chavannes "La divination par l'écaille de tortue dans la haute antiquité chinoise," Journal asiatique, serie 10, vol. 17 (1911), 131-132). And Karlgren, in fact, has remarked that the commentaries of all the great Han scholiasts "are so full of discrepancies and contradictions that they simply cannot be considered as 'sources' for the knowledge of pre-Han China" ("Some Sacrifices in Chou China," Bulletin of the Museum of Far Eastern Antiquities, 40 (1968), 2). Such strictures apply with great force in the present essay when we consider that the commentators had never seen a Shang oracle inscription.

next be necessary to explore the usages of cheng 貞 in the post-Shang texts to see if divination contexts there demand that cheng mean "to question by crack-making."

III. DIVINATION TERMS(cheng 貞, pu 卜, ming 命) IN CHOU AND OTHER EARLY TEXTS

A. Cheng in the Early Dictionaries

The Shuo-wen(A.D. 121) definition, cheng pu wen yeh 貞卜問也, "cheng means to question by crack-making," is not supported by other early dictionaries. The Shih-ming 釋名(ca. A.D. 200), "Shih yen yü 釋言語"section, says: cheng ting yeh, ching wan pu tung kan yeh 貞定也精完不動惑也(DKW, No. 36658, definition 2), "cheng means settle, fix; the feeling that the essence is complete and unmoving." And the Kuang-ya 廣雅(A.D. 230), "Shih-ku 釋詁" section, says: cheng cheng yeh 貞正也(DKW, No. 36658, definition 1), "cheng is regulate, rectify."

The value of such dictionary definitions is uncertain. Nevertheless, we can note that Liu Hsi 劉熙, the author of the Shih-ming, frequently followed Hsü Shen's Shuo-wen definitions(Bodman, p.7); his failure to do so in this case was presumably the result of conscious disagreement. The Kuang-ya, like the Erh-ya 爾雅, was primarily a collection of earlier definitions found in commentaries to the classics(Bodman, p.8), and in this instance its compiler, Chang Yi 張揖, was presumably following the earlier definition of Cheng Hsüan, cheng cheng yeh 貞正也(p.8 above)①. But it is suggestive that neither of the two dictionaries immedi-

---

① The Kuang-ya, "Shih-ku 釋詁," in fact, offers an alternate definition, cheng tang yeh 貞當也 (DKW, no. 36658, meaning 3), presumably taken from the commentary of Ma Jung 馬融 (A.D. 79-166) to the "Lo kao." But the meaning, as Karlgren remarks, is "obscure and ambiguous" them(Glosses on the Book of Documents, no.1752); the phonology(* tâng as a loan for * tiĕng) offers no strong support; and I know of no other passages where cheng 貞 may be read as tang 當. Ma Jung's gloss, and thus the resultant Kuang-ya definition, is probably anomalous. But for another view see YTCP, p.27; Ping-pien, p.445.

ately following the Shuo-wen in time, accepted, or even noted, Hsü Shen's cheng pu wen yeh. Indeed, I suspect—though I have not checked this thoroughly—that the "question" definition of cheng did not reappear in a Chinese dictionary until the K'ang-hsi tz'u-tien of 1716.

B. Cheng 貞 in Pre-Han Texts

Another early "definition" of cheng 貞 appears in the Chia-tzu hsin-shu 賈子新書. Whatever the exact date of this text,① it offers another early explidation which is again not in the Shuo-wen tradition: yen hsing pao yi, wei chih cheng, fan cheng wei wei 言行抱一謂之貞反貞爲僞 (Wang Yün-wu 王雲五, ed., Hsin-shu 新書 (Shanghai, 1937), p. 82): "to embrace unity in speech and action is called cheng 貞; to be the opposite of cheng is to be false." In this passage, cheng 貞 has the sense of "genuineness, correctness, and sincerity," a meaning (i. e. cheng 正) well attested in the pre-Han texts (see below).

The pre-Han texts, in fact, offer no support to the view of Cheng Ssu-nung and Hsü Shen that cheng pu wen yeh.

1) The Tso-chuan

In the Tso-chuan, cheng 貞 is sometimes used in connection with milfoil divination, either as a technical term for the inner trigram, or in its common, Yi-ching, sense of "firmly correct" (p. 5 above) in the interpretation of a hexagram; cheng 貞 (with the sense of 正) is also used to describe human characteristics: "sincere devotion," "incorrupt," "solidity", using Legge's translations (pp. 154, 577, 640) in each case.

Only one instance may support the Shuo-wen definition. The Tso, for Ai 哀 17, records how the ruler of Wei himself divined about a dream by milfoil (kung ch'in shih chih 公親筮之); the diviner gave a reading (chan 占), Which was falsely

---

① The supposed author, Chia Yi 賈誼, was a man of the 2nd century B.C. Creel concludes that "Although the authenticity of parts of this work has been attacked, it seems probable that what we have now is essentially the work as it existed at an early date, with such losses and alterations as are normal" (Herrlee G. Creel, What is Taoism? And Other Studies in Chinese Cultural History (Chicago and London, 1970), p. 107, n. 74).

auspicious, and then absconded. Thereupon wei hou cheng pu 衛侯貞卜 (Legge, p. 850: "The marquis again consulted the tortoise shell"), and obtained a new interpretation. Tu Yü 杜預 (A.D. 222-284) glosses cheng pu 貞卜 as cheng pu meng chih chi hsiung yeh 正卜夢之吉兇也 "he correctly divined the good or bad fortune of the dream." The Meiji commentator, Takezoe Shin'ichiro, first cites the Shuo-wen definition, cheng pu wen yeh, but then, citing the "Wu-yü 吳語" passage discussed above (pp. 5-6), says: cheng yen chi ting chih yeh 貞言稽定之也 (TSHC, Ai 17, pp. 37-38), "cheng means to examine and settle it." He also cites some of the commentaries to the Chou-li already discussed (pp. 4-8 above). Takezoe, in fact, like Cheng Hsüan, is still attempting to combine differing, almost contradictory, meanings: on the one hand, "to ask," but on the other hand, "to settle." Once again, neither commentator, Tu Yü or Takezoe, is willing to follow without qualifications, Hsü Shen's cheng pu wen yeh.

If we substitute Hsü Shen's definition, pu wen yeh 卜問也 for cheng 貞 in the Tso phrase, we obtain wei hou pu wen pu 衛侯卜問卜, "the marquis of Wei questioned the cracks by crack-making," which is redundant. This seems an unfair procedure, perhaps, but it assumes some significance when we consider that cheng 貞 is not used to preface any of the other numerous divinations which appear in the Tso-chuan. The divinatory verb, as it is in this case too, is always pu 卜.① If pu alone meant "to consult the tortoise-shell" (pp. 13-15 below), why would it have been necessary, in this single instance in the Tso, to add the prefatory cheng 貞? The context of the Ai 17 passage suggests a possible reason. The ruler was dissatisfied with the previous milfoil divination and presumably wanted to "correct" (both to ensure it was done correctly, and thus, perhaps, to correct the results that the absconding diviner had falsified) this second divination by tortoise-shell, as Tu Yü proposed. Hence the addition of the verb cheng 貞 in the sense of cheng 正.②

---

① See Ch'un-ch'iu ching-chuan yin-te 春秋經傳引得 (Peiping, 1937), pp. 185-187. Typical are the cases of divination in the paragraphs immediately preceding the one under consideration. They simply use pu 卜 as the verb: wo pu fa wei 我卜伐衛, "I consulted the tortoise-shell about attacking Wei," and wang pu chih 王卜之, "The king consulted the tortoise-shell" (Legge, p. 850).

② The Wei 衛 state supposedly maintained the laws and political system of Shang (Li Ya-nung 李亞農, Li Ya-nung shih-lun-chi 李亞農史論集 (Shanghai, 1964), pp. 686 ff. This may explain why the cheng 貞 (as descendant of oracular 鼎) appears in this one instance in the Tso-chuan.)

2) The Shang-shu

The Shang-shu 尚書 contains one passage which links cheng 貞 to divination in a way which might support Hsü Shen's definition.① The "Lo kao 洛誥," which is generally acknowledged to be a text of Western Chou, if not early Western Chou, date, records how the Duke of Chou chose the site of the new city at Lo by a series of divinations, whose results he then presented by messenger to the king in the Western capital. The king said: "When he [the Duke of Chou] had fixed the site, he sent a messenger to come; and he has come to show me the grace and constant auspiciousness of the oracles. We two men have both verified (sc. the reading of the oracles)" (Karlgren, Documents, pp. 51-52). The phrase that has puzzled the commentators is the last one: Wo erh jen kung cheng 我二人共貞. Karlgren discusses the matter (cf. n. 12 above) and concludes that when cheng 貞 "has its sense of 'divination inquiry' it really means 'to verify, to determine what is correct'." Here he is following the commentators like Cheng Hsüan and Takezoe, who have tried to combine the senses of "inquire" and "settle" in one word. This is possible, but the context is so vague here, that it would also be possible to take cheng 貞 in the Shuo-wen sense, to indicate that the king had also enquired about the site (or about the Duke of Chou's divinations), so that the last part might read, "We two men have both questioned by crack-making."② As in the Tso-chuan, however, the divinatory verb in the rest of the "Lo kao," is always pu 卜, never cheng 貞. Whatever this passage means, it offers no unequivocal support for Hsü Shen's definition. I note it here as a matter for later resolution.

3) Conclusion

There is, so far as I have been able to determine, no other pre-Han usage which supports the Shuo-wen definition. This point is worth stressing. In the Lun-yü, Tso-chuan, Kuo-yü, Shang-shu (both spurious and genuine), Han-fei-tzu, Lao-tzu, Chan-kuo-ts'e, and Huai-nan-tzu, cheng 貞 (when it is not a ersonal name, or the technical name for the interior, lower, trigram) must al-

---

① There is no need to discuss here the use of cheng 貞 in the "Hung fan 洪範," in the sense of the "lower trigram" (Karlgren, Documents, pp. 32-33, per. 22).

② This is evidently the way Chang Ping-ch'üan takes it (LCTP, p. 401).

ways be treated as cheng 正.① The verb for tortoise-shell divination in all pre-Han texts is always pu 卜. Even the Yi-ching and the T'ai-hsüan-ching 太玄經 make no use of cheng 貞 in the sense that the Shuo-wen proposes. These are, of course, milfoil divination texts, not texts for tortoise-shell divination; but when we consider that pu 卜, rather than cheng 貞, continues to be the verb in the two Shih-chi chapters (127 and 128) that deal with divination,② in the Ch'un-ch'iu fan-lu 春秋繁露, and in the Po-hu-t'ung 白虎通, chapter 22, "Shih kuei 蓍龜," "Divination with the Milfoil and the Tortoise-Shell," we realize that Cheng Ssu-nung and Hsü Shen, in taking cheng 貞 as "to question by crack-making" were conferring a meaning upon the word for which there is no firm support in the classical Chou texts as we now have them, and no support whatever in Han divination texts. It is interesting to remark that in the early 4th-century work, Pao-p'u-tzu 抱朴子 by Ko Hung 葛洪 compound cheng-jen 貞人, which any modern student of oracle-bones would now translate as "diviner," meant, in fact, a cheng-jen 正人, "a man

---

① SWKL, p.1383a 下, cites several appearances of cheng 貞 in the classics, which generally have the meaning of cheng 正, e.g. from the Lun-yü (15.36): chün tsu cheng erh pu liang 君子貞而不諒, which Legge (p.305) translates as, "The superior man is correctly firm, and not firm merely." See too, KJGK, p.468, no.121-4. Cheng 貞 is sometimes glossed as hsin 信 or ch'eng 誠, "sincerity" (DKW, no.36658, meaning 4); these are probably extended meanings of cheng 正; in any event, they contain no sense of "question."

② As a noun, cheng 貞 occurs in the compound liang-cheng 良貞 twice in Shih-chi, chapt.128, but the precise meaning of cheng 貞 is obscure in both cases: 1) chin jih liang jih hsing ji liang cheng 今日良日行一良貞 (SKK, 128.34.9). Herbert Pohl translates: "Today is now an auspicious day, and will bring about a fortunate sign" (Shi Ki Kapitel 128: Ein Beitrag zur altchinesischen Divination, (Ph.D. dissertation, Universität Hamburg, 1948), p.61); but there is no reason to translate cheng 貞 as sign (Zeichen). Noguchi Sadao 野口定男 takes cheng 貞 to mean pu 卜, and translates: "Today is a good day, truly suitable for performing a crack-making (Shiki, 史記, vol.12 in the series Chūgoku koten bungaku zenshū 中國古典文學全集 (Tokyo, 1971), p.324). 2) chih jen ssu chih jen sheng mou shen liang cheng mou yü ch'iu mou wu... 知人死知人生某身良貞某欲求某物 (SKK, 128.35.4-5). Pohl (p.62) omits the phrase entirely; Noguchi (p.325) merely repeats the kanji 良貞 with a furigana reading of ta da). The passage can be translated: "[You, divine tortoise] know about the dying of men, know about the living of men. When a certain person carries out a liang cheng, when a certain person desires to seek a certain thing... [the cracks assume the following forms]." In both these passages liang cheng 良貞 presumably has the general sense of "a good divining," but there is no reason to take it, as the Shuo-wen definition would require us to do, as "a good questioning. The compound liang-cheng appears nowhere else in Chinese literature.

who preserves his rectitude"(DKW, No. 36658-113). None of the Chou and Han terms applied to diviners, in fact—pu-jen 卜人, tsung-jen 宗人, chan-jen 占人, shih-kuan 史官①—contain the character cheng 貞.

All this is not to deny that there was some connection between cheng 貞 and tortoise-shell divination. This is indicated by the cracle-bone inscriptions themselves(section I above), by the Chou-li and Kuo-yü passages(section II), and by the Tso-chuan(Ai 17) and Shang-shu passages(section III, B). Our goal must be to find out what that connection was.

C. The Meaning of the Verb Pu 卜

Even if we grant that cheng 貞 contains no necessary sense of "question," it may still be objected that the divination sentences should be treated as questions because of the verb pu 卜 which usually prefaces them, in both the oracle-bone and Chou texts. In fact, there are no grounds for such a view. The Shuo-wen: merely gives pu cho po kuei yeh 卜灼剝龜也, "pu means to burn and crack the tortoise-shell"(SWCT, 3 下, 41b). And Legge, in his translation of the Tso-chuan, customarily renders pu 卜 as "divine about," "consult the tortoise shell about," "divine by tortoise shell about"; Couvreur, likewise, employs the verb "consulter." In none of the Chou classics, in fact, have I found a passage in which pu 卜 should be taken as governing an interrogative sentence.

In several passages, pu 卜 has the opposite sense, meaning not "question" but "predict." Thus, in the Shih-ching(Mao no. 166, par. 4), chün yüeh pu erh wan shou wu chiang 君曰卜爾萬壽無疆, "the(dead) lords say: 'We predict for you a myriad years of life, without limit'"(Karlgren, The Book of Odes, p. 110; Legge has, "We give to thee/Myriads of years…", She, p. 257). A similar usage appears in Mao no. 209: shen shih yin shih pu erh po fu 神嗜飲食卜爾百福 "the spirits enjoy the wine and food; they predict for you a hundred blessings"(Karlgren, Odes, p. 163, par. 4; Legge: "They confer upon you…", She, p. 371; italics added in each case).

---

① The first three terms appear in the Yi-li, "Shih sang li 士喪禮"; the last in the Chou-li(SASA, p. 129).

The predictive nature of pu-divination is indicated by a passage in the Tso-chuan that is most important for the thesis of this essay:

> In the spring [of 609 B.C.] the Marquis of Ch'i was preparing for the time when he should take the field [to attack Lu], when he fell ill, and his physician said that he would die before autumn. The duke [of Lu] heard of it, and consulted the tortoise-shell, saying, "May his death take place before the time [of his taking the field]!" Hui-pei communicated the subject enquired about to the shell. Ch'u-ch'iu, the diviner, read the divination, and said, "The marquis of Ch'i will die before that time..."
>
> (Wen 18, Legge, Tso, p. 281, modified)

The last part of the text reads kung wen chih pu yüeh shang wu chi ch'I hui pei ling kuei pu ch'u ch'iu chan chih yüeh ch'I hou pu chi ch'i 公聞之卜曰尚無及期惠伯令龜卜楚丘占之曰齊侯不及期 Every commentator, and every Japanese and Western translation I have consulted, supports the predictive, wishful, optative, interpretation of the shang 尚, and thus of the pu 卜 in this passage.① (For a similar use of shang 尚, in pu 卜 divination, see TSHC, Chao 5, p. 40; also, p. 16 below.)

Pu 卜 also has the sense of "forecast" in at least one other passage in the Tso (Hsüan 宣 12, 3 Tso): yi wo pu yeh cheng pu k'o ts'ung 以我卜也鄭不可從, "According as I should divine, the counsel of Cheng is not to be followed" (Legge, p. 318); Couvreur gives "predict" (vol. I, p. 623). "Divine" here is used in the loose sense of "estimate" or "guess," for the context makes it clear that no actual divination was involved.②

In conclusion, the divinatory verb pu 卜 has no innate sens of "question" in

---

① TSHC, Wen 18, p. 42; Kojima Kenkichirō 兒島獻吉郎, tr., Shun jū sashiden 春秋左氏傳, vol. 5 in the series Kokushi kambun taisei 國譯漢文大成 (Tokyo, 1934), p. 255; Takeuchi Teruo 竹内照夫, tr., Shunjū sashiden 春秋左氏傳 vol. 2 in the series Chūgoku koten bungaku taikei 中國古典文學大系 (Tokyo, 1968), p. 141; Couvreur, vol. 1, p. 545.

② Another instance in which pu 卜 may have this predictive sense appears in the Tso, Chao 昭 26. Legge, following Tu Yü, translates yi pu yen 以卜焉 as "and form an opinion in the case" (p. 716). Takezoe, however, apparently feels that an actual divination may have been intended (TSHC, Chao 26, p. 44).

Chou texts, and, on the contrary, in certain cases has the sense of "predict." Three passages (Tso, Wen 18, Chao 5; and Chao 17 on p. 16 below) suggest that divinations might be couched in the form of a wish or intent, rather than as questions, a point to which we shall return.

D. The Meaning of the Phrase ming-kuei 命龜 or ling-kuei 令龜

As we have already seen (p. 7 above), ming-kuei 命龜 was a technical term used in the Chou-li and Li-chi for informing the tortoise about the subject-matter of the divination. A variant also occurred in the Tso-chuan passage (Wen 18) just cited: hui pei ling kuei 惠伯令龜, "Hui-pei communicated the subject inquired about to the shell." The phrase may also be found in the Shang-shu, "Chin-t'eng 金滕," par. 8, where the Duke of Chou, addressing the departed spirits of the Chou kings, says: chin wo chi ming yü yüan kuei 今我即命于元龜, which I propose to translate as "Now I will forthwith give the charge to the great tortoise." Commentators and translators have resisted this straightforward translation① because, I think, they have been reluctant to admit that divination involved giving an order or charge rather than asking a question. But the fact that the text appears to say just that cannot be easily dismissed, especially when the "ordering" of the tortoise is congruent both with the optative nature of pu-divining (see p. 14 above) and with the general thesis of this essay that the divination sentences

---

① There are two problems involved in translating this passage. First, were the orders to the tortoise, as I believe (cf. Karlgren, Documents, p. 35), or were they to be received from the tortoise, as Legge translates? Legge's view depends upon taking chi ming 即命 as equivalent to chiu shou ming 就受命, "go and receive the order" (Shoo, p. 355, n.; cf. SSSY, p. 68, no. 15). Not only is this unnecessary, but it is contradicted by Lagge's own translation of a similar passage in the "Lo kao," par. 7: chin wang chi ming yüeh.... 今王即命曰, where Legge takes chi 即 in the sense of "immediately," thus, "Let the king instantly give orders, saying..." (Shoo, p. 439). The second problem involves the precise meaning of chi 即. There are three possibilities: a) chi 即 means "to go to" (cf. Karlgren, Documents, p. 52, par. 7), thus, "Now I will go to give the charge to the great tortoise"; b) chi 即 means "forthwith, thereupon" (GSR, No. 399), thus, "I will forthwith give the charge to the great tortoise"; c) chi 即 indicates the perfective aspect, thus, "Now I have given the charge to the great tortoise" (cf. EAC, p. 49). Rather arbitrarily, I take chi 即 in the sense of meaning b), but whichever meaning is adopted, the force of ming 命 remains the same: the "charge" was given to the tortoise-shell.

were indicative and not interrogative.

Yet another passage in the Shang-shu may lend some support to this interpretation. In the "Ta kao 大誥," king Ch'eng says: ning wang yi wo ta pao kuei shao t'ien ming, chi ming yüeh yu ta chien yü his t'u, his t'u jen yi pu ching jüeh tzu ch'un 寧王遺我大寶龜紹天命即命曰有大艱于西土西土人亦不靜越茲蠢, which I would translate as: "I have used the precious tortoise handed down to me by the serene(dead) kings, to transmit(to me) Heaven's bright(will). I gave the charge to the tortoise saying: 'There will be great difficulties in the Western lands, and the people of the Western lands will be likewise not peaceful.' Now they are crawling about"(Karlgren, Documents, p.36, par.3, modified). In short, I suggest that the passage refers to a predictive charge or prognostication given to the tortoise, together with a verification about what actually happened.① The similarity of the content of this "charge" to that found in some oracle-bone divinations has been noted(Chia-pien k'ao-shih, No.2094(1); KTZ, p.495).

That the divination sentence was conceived of as a charge or order is confirmed by a passage in the Tso-chuan(Chao 昭 17, 6 Tso): ch'ieh ch'u ku ssu ma ling kuei, wo ch'ing kai pu, ling yüeh fang yeh yi ch'i shu ssu chih, ch'u shih chi chih, shang ta k'o chih, chi 且楚故司馬令龜我請改卜令曰魴也以其屬死之楚師繼之尚大克之吉(TSHC, Chao 17, p.64), "'Moreover, it is the old custom of Ch'u for the marshal to give the charge to the shell; allow me to divine again.' [Accordingly], he charged it, saying: 'I, Fang, and my followers will die in the conflict, but the army of Ch'u will continue it. May we greatly defeat the enemy.' The divination was auspicious." It is clear from this passage that the ling 令 "charge," was given to the tortoise-shell(rather than vice-versa as Legge believed in translating the Shang-shu, "Chin-t'eng," passage above; see n.23); furthermore, the first part of the charge was declarative, not interrogative; and the presence of shang 尚, (as in the Tso, Wen 18 passage above, p.14) indicates that the

---

① The passage has occasioned much dispute. For views which give some support to my interpretation see KTZ, pp.491, 495. The alternative view, that the ming 命 refers to the instructions given by the tortoise(Legge, Shoo, p.365; SSSY, p.71, n.8) seems refuted by the occurrence of the compound ming-kuei 命龜 in later texts(see pp.15-17 above).

last part was optative.①

On the basis of the divination passages analyzed in this and the preceding section, it seems that the divination was conceived of as a three-fold process: 1) the diviner gave the verbal charge to the tortoise shell in the form of a prediction or wish(this was the ming-kuei 命龜 stage); 2) the crack-making(pu 卜)was carried out for that particular charge; 3) the cracks were read(chan 占). The concept of a "charge" also appears in classical accounts of Yi-ching divination. The Yi-ching, "His-tz'u chuan 繫辭傳, says: shih yi chün tzu chiang yu wei yeh, chiang yu hsing yeh, wen yen erh yi yen, ch'I shou ming yeh ju hsiang 是以君子將有爲也將有行也問焉而以言其受命也如響, "Therefore, when a superior men is about to take action of a more private or of a public character, he asks(the Yi-ching), using words. It receives his charge like an echo"(Legge, The I-ching, vol. 16 of The Sacred Books of the East(Oxford, 1899), p. 369, modified; SSCC, 7. 24a). Likewise, the account of milfoil divination in the Yi-li, "Shao lao k'uei shih li 少牢饋食禮," shows that the subject to be divined was conceived of as a ming 命, "charge," couched in the indicative, not the interrogative(SSCC, 47. 2a-3b; cf. John Steele, The I-Li or Book of Etiquette and Ceremonial(London, 1917), vol. 2, p. 158, par. e, p. 159, par. g).

Finally, it should be noted that the technical term used by modern scholars for the putative divination "question" is still ming 命(e.g. YHPT, p. 86). This term derives from the usage of the Chou texts, and it is my hypothesis that it should be taken literally, that the divination sentences of Chou were indeed "charges" and not queries. As I shall hope to show in the next section, the oracle-bone inscriptions of Shang were similarly not interrogative, but were "charges" too—indicative and predictive—recorded on the shell and bone.

IV. THE ORACLE-BONE FORMULA

It is not only dissatisfaction with the usage of cheng 貞 in traditional texts that

---

① Legge(Tso, p. 668) and Couvreur(III, p. 282) both ignore the shang 尚; Kojims(vol. 6, p. 297) and Takeuchi(vol. 2, p. 393) both translate shang 尚 as expressing a wish.

leads me to question the Shuo-wen definition. The translation of 貞 as "ask" in the oracle-bone inscriptions themselves also leads to certain difficulties. The rejection of the Shuo-wen definition resolves these difficulties in some cases, and in others provides solutions that are, at least, equally valid. This section cannot prove conclusively that the divination sentences could not have been questions; but it will try to show that such a proposal is feasible. It relies for part of its persuasiveness upon the use of "Ockham's razor" (entities should not be multiplied needlessly), for it can be shown that treating the cracle-bone inscriptions as statements simplifies the interpreting of the divination process. The oracular examples given below are translated, in most cases, in both the traditional way, and in the new manner I am proposing (given in capitals).

A. Declarative Statements After 貞.

Though most scholars accept cheng 貞 as pu wen 卜問, we frequently find inscriptions in which they treat the first characters after the 貞, not as a question, but as a statement of fact.① For example:

[3] 戊辰卜壴貞又來𡆥自獸今日
　　其征于且丁　　　　　　　　　　(Chia-pien, No. 2772)

Crack-making on the day wu-ch'en, (the diviner) Shu asking: "There have come disasters from hunting. Today should we continue (yesterday's) sacrifice to Tsu Ting?"②

It is true that we can subordinate the first part of the divination: "Since disasters have come from hunting, should we continue yesterday's sacrifice to Tsu Ting today?" But there are no grammatical indicators of the need for such subordination. And it is at least possible that if the first part of the divination is not a question, the last part may not be either. Thus, I would propose: [3] CRACK-MAKING ON THE DAY WU-CH'EN, (THE DIVINER) SHU 貞-

---

① Chang Ping-ch'üan agrees that some oracle-bone inscriptions do contain, in part, statements of fact(CSPT, p.184).
② Following the k'ao-shih of Ch'ü Wan-li. For another interpretation, which does not affect the argument here, see YTCP, p.896.

ING: "THERE HAVE COME DISASTERS FROM HUNTING AND (THUS) TODAT WE CONTINUE (YESTERDAY'S) SACRIFICE TO TSU TING." In other words, the recorded divination may be regarded as a "charge" to the shell, a statement of fact and intent.

Another example of the same problem:

[4] 戊午卜𣪯貞我狩歔举 (Ping-pien, No. 284(4))

Crack-making on the day wu-wu, (the diviner) K'o asking: "We are going to chase at Ch'iu; any capture?"①

Again, either the first three characters after the 貞 are not part of a question, which is anomalous if cheng 貞 is "to ask"; or, they must be subordinated ("If we chase at Ch'iu, any capture?"), for which there is no grammatical indicator. I would propose instead a simple forecast: [4] "WE ARE GOING TO CHASE AT CH'IU AND CAPTURE."

Chou Hung-hsiang, in fact, has proposed a "Cause-and-Result" category of oracle-bone inscriptions in which he eliminates the interrogative sense of cheng 貞. Thus he translates:

[5] 貞疾齒卯于父乙 (Ch'ien-pien, 1.25.1)

as a statement: "Because (an ancestor?) is making (the king's?) teeth sick, we will therefore offer a (propitiatory)② Yü-sacrifice to Fu Yi." And again, he translates:

[6] 貞王夢白牛隹田 (Fu-shih, 人名6)

as "Because the king dreamed of a white ox, there will as a result be disaster" (PTTC, p. 125). While I fully agree with the declarative form of Chou's translations (e.g. I would translate [6] as "THE KING HAS DREAMED OF A WHITE OX AND THERE WILL BE DISASTER"), I do not know how he translates (or in fact omits translating) cheng 貞 in these two cases, or how he justifies ignoring the Shuo-wen definition in these cases and not in others. Chou, in fact, proceeds

---

① Translation taken from Li Chi, The Beginnings of Chinese Civilization (Seattle and London, 1957, p. 23).

② On the nature of this sacrifice see DKDS, p. 51, n. 1.

to postulate the existence of "Cause-and-Result" pairs:

[7] 貞羽甲午用多〻

貞亡壱 　　　　　　　　　　　　　　(Yi-pien, No. 7128)

Asking: "On the next chia-wu day should we sacrifice the To-〻 (perhaps a group of captives)?"

Asking: "There will be no curse?"

He argues that <u>because</u> one was to "sacrifice the to-〻" <u>therefore</u> there would be "no curse" (<u>PTTC</u>, p. 126). If such a construction is put on these two sentences, it is hard to see why question-marks are needed at the end of them. I believe that two separate yet related "charges" would be a simpler explanation: [7]: 𠁣-ING: "ON THE NEXT CHIA-WU DAY WE WILL SACRIFICE THE TO-〻"; 𠁣-ING: "THERE WILL BE NO CURSE." The sentences are declarative, not interrogative.

B. <u>The Problem of Multiple Questions</u>

When a divination appears too long, many commentators insert question-marks according to taste to break it up into several shorter questions:

[8] 乙丑卜狄貞今日乙王其田湄

日亡𢦏不冓大雨大吉 　　　　　　　(Chia-pien, No. 1604)

Crack-making on the day yi-ch'ou, (the diviner) 狄 asking: "On this yi-day the king will hunt, will the whole day be without disaster? Will he not encounter a great rain?"

(The prognostication:) Greatly aupicious.

This translation and punctuation are taken from <u>Chia-pien k'ao-shih</u>. It is true that the <u>wang tsai</u> 亡𢦏 appears frequently at the end of inscriptions, so that there is some justification for breaking the sentence at that point. But why only two questions? Why not three? "On this yi-day should the king hunt? Will the whole day... etc?" Or, if there were two (or three) separate questions, how were they answered? Was there only one crack, or two, or three? Since these supposedly separate questions within the single divination have no separate crack-numbers associated with them individually, it seems unlikely that two (or three) separate questions were in the diviner's mind. I am reluctant, in fact, to believe that one 㢑 could preface two (or three) separate questions. It seems simpler (with Ockham) to assume that 㢑 precedes one homogenous inscription unit. I would propose as translation [8]: "ON THIS YI-DAY THE KING WILL HUNT, THE WHOLE DAY WILL BE WITHOUT DISASTER, AND HE WILL NOT ENCOUNTER A GREAT RAIN." The spirits' response to this forecast was "Greatly auspicious."

A similar instance is:

[9] 庚申貞今來甲子酒王大钊
于大甲煑六小窜卯九牛不冓雨 (Nan-pei, 明 432)

On the day keng-shen, asking: "On the coming chia-tzu day shall wine-libation be offered to Ta Chia in the Great Purification of the king? Shall we make burnt-offering of six small lao and ritually dismember nine cattle? Will we not encounter rain?"

This translation and punctuation are taken from DKDS, no. 5.26b. But how can we decide with certainty which are the separate questions? It would be in better accord with the absence of any grammatical-break indicators to take the divination as a single statement of intents: [9] ON THE DAY KENG-SHEN, 㢑-ING: "ON THE COMING CHIA-IZU DAY WE WILL OFFER WINE LIBATION TO TA CHIA IN THE GREAT PURIFICATION OF THE KING, WE WILL MAKE BURNT OFFERING OF SIX SMALL LAO, AND RITUALLY DISMEMBER NINE CATTLE, AND WE WILL NOT ENCOUNTER RAIN." I would regard such divinations, in fact, as a "package-deal," to which the answer would not be a series of yeses and nos, but a general "auspicious," meaning that the series of actions forecast, summed together, would have a favorable outcome. The charge to the shell may be conceived of in these cases as a chain of linked human acts, as when a child says, "I'll do this and then I'll do this and then I'll do that and then it won't rain on my birthday." In such chain-predictions the last link is generally impersonal or natural, beyond human control (cf. divination [8]), but now involved by the chain of contingent events that humans have established by the divinatory charge.

C. Two Diviners "Questioning" Together

A few inscriptions indicate that the divination "question" was posed jointly by two diviners. Thus, in the traditional view:

[10] 癸未卜爭☒貞旬亡囧　　　　　　　　　　(Ts'ui-pien, No. 1424)

　　Crack-making on the day kuei-wei, (the diviners) Cheng and ☒ asking: "Will the next ten days be without disaster?"①

It is hard to understand how or why two men could have asked the same question simultaneously. It is possible, therefore, that ☒ had some other meaning which would more readily admit of joint participation by two diviners.

D. The Problem of the Double Negative.

Oracle-bone inscriptions are generally paired, with the positive sentence placed on the right side of the shell, the negative divination on the left(PTTC, introd., p. 4). Thus, in the traditional translations:

[11] 丙辰卜㱿貞我受黍年
　　　丙辰卜㱿貞我弗受黍年四月　　　　　　(Ping-pien, No. 8)

　　Crack-making on the day ping-ch'en, (the diviner) K'o asking: "Will we receive millet harvest?"

　　Crack-making on the day ping-ch'en, (the diviner) K'o asking: "Will we not receive millet harvest?"(Divination made) in the fourth month.

This is straightforward: on the right-hand, the oracle is asked if something will happen, on the left hand if it will not. The use of the negative, however, raises problems in more complex divinations. Again, following the traditional formula:

[12] 貞羽丁卯求舞㞢雨
　　　羽丁卯勿亡其雨　　　　　　　　　　　(Ping-pien, No. 442(6)(7))

---

① Other examples are given and discussed at LCTP, p. 400.

Asking: "On the next ting-mao day if we perform a (rain-) seeking dance, will there be rain?"

"On the next ting-mao day if we do not [perform a rain seeking dance]①, will there be no rain?"

The meaning of this second query is not unfathomable, but it does seem unnecessarily convoluted to ask a question containing a double negative. It would seem simpler to regard both divinations as declarative statements: [12] 関-ING: "ON THE NEXT TING MAO DAY WE WILL PERFORM A (RAIN-) SEEKING DANCE AND THERE WILL BE RAIN"; "ON THE NEXT TING-MAO DAY WE WILL NOT [PERFORM A RAIN-SEEKING DANCE] AND THERE WILL BE NO RAIN." Here the statement of negative intent, followed by the negative forecast, is simply the mirror alternative to the positive divination: i. e. "dance plus rain" is opposed to "no dance and no rain."

The use of double negatives in the oracle bone inscriptions has been discussed in detail by Chou Hung-hsiang (PTTC, pp. 75-82). On the basis of double-negatives in the Shih-ching (Mao No. 194, par. 7; 258, par. 1), he argues that the oracular double-negative is positive in effect (cf. EAC, pp. 46-47) and violates the general (though not mandatory) principle that the paired inscriptions should be in positive-negative opposition. Thus, if we continue to use Ping-pien No. 442 above as an example, [12]: "If we do not perform a rain-seeking dance, will there be no rain?", is, in Chou's view, equivalent to, and thus not in proper opposition to, "If we perform a rain-seeking dance, will there be rain?" But this absence of opposition between the two divinations disappears if we translate them as declarative sentences: "dance plus rain" is the opposite of "no dance and no rain." That is, the double negatives do not cancel each other, as they would do in a question; they simply negate two separate events, as in a declarative statement.

---

① The principle of pairing requires us to supply the missing characters. There is a danger of error if pairs are not considered together since the abbreviation of the full statement may not be remarked. (See Ping-pien k'ao-shih, p. 513; PTTC, pp. 60, ff.).

E. Failure of the Response to Match the Supposed Question

1) The Intensifier yün 允

Yün, meaning "really," appears in the verification sentences which may follow a divination. A good example of this is the typical, complete divination inscription given by Ch'en Meng-chia(YHPT, p.86):

[13] 庚子卜争貞羽辛丑啓

貞羽辛丑不其啓

王固曰今夕其雨羽辛丑啓

之夕允雨辛丑啓　　　　　　　　　　　(Ching-hua, No. 7 and 8)

[Positive Question] Crack-making on the day keng-tzu, (the diviner) Cheng asking: "On the next hsin-ch'ou day will it be clear?"

[Negative Question] Asking: "On the next hsin-ch'ou day will it be not clear?"

[Prognostication] The king interpreted the cracks and said: "This evening it will rain. The next hsin-ch'ou day will be clear."

[Verification] That evening it really rained. On hsin-ch'ou it was clear.

Notice that in this case, the yün 允 is used to confirm not the "question" itself, but the prognostication, which was declarative, not interrogative: Prognostication: "This evening it will rain..." Verifications: "That evening it really did rain." In the traditional view, however, this prognostication-verification link is not always present. Thus:

[14] 癸巳卜殼貞今日不雨

允不　　　　　　　　　　　　　　　　(Ping-pien, No.263(10))

Crack-making on the day kuei-ssu, (the diviner) K'o asking: "Today will there be no rain?"

It really did not [rain].

For the verification to "match" the "question," it is necessary to supply an answer (prognostication: "it will not rain today"). Yet such an answer is not inscribed. Its absence, which is common in cases of this sort, may be explained if we take the divination as declarative: [14] CRACK-MAKING ON THE DAY

KUEI-SSU, (THE DIVINER) K'O 門-ING: "TODAY IT WILL NOT RAIN," followed by the verification: "IT REALLY DID NOT [RAIN]." In this way, the verification matches the forecast exactly.

I am suggesting, in short, that in most divinations it is simpler to take the "question" as a tentative prognostication ([14] "TODAY IT WILL NOT RAIN"), and the verification with yün 允 as a verification of that prognostication (IT REALLY DID NOT RAIN), rather than as verification of a frequently missing response to a "question." This conclusion is supported by the fact that yün 允 does appear in the divination charge itself on occasion. Thus, following the traditional view:

[15] 貞咸允左王
貞咸弗左王   (Ping-pien, No. 41(16)(17))

Asking: "Will Hsien really assist the king?"
Asking: "Will Hsien not assist the king?"

But the use of "really" in a "question" raises problems. Did it mean that the Shang distrusted the spirits to whom the oracles were addressed? On the other hand, if we reject the question form in favor of the forecast form: [15] 門-ING: "HSIEN WILL REALLY ASSIST THE KING"; 門-ING: "HSIEN WILL NOT ASSIST THE KING," then we simply have an intensification of the positive forecast which presumably served to strengthen its efficacy. (On the magical aspect of the divinations see pp. 49-61 below.)

2) The Terms of the Response

The divinations were not answered in terms of "yes" or "no," but in grades of auspiciousness: shang chi 上吉, chi 吉, hsiao chi 小吉, etc. For example:

[16] 庚申卜王貞余伐不三月(一)
庚[申](卜)王貞余勿伐不(一上吉)

(Ping-pien, No. 1(5)(6))

CRACK-MAKING ON THE DAY KENG-SHEN, THE KING 門-ING: "I WILL ATTACK PU." [Divination made] in the third month. (crack one). [CRACK-MAKING] ON THE DAY KENG [-SHEN], THE KING

㢅-ING: "I WILL NOT ATTACK PU." (crack one: Extremely auspicious).

The answer, "extremely auspicious," given to a "question" is less well matched than when given to a forecast (cf. divination [8] above). "Extremely auspicious" is not a direct answer to "Should I attack Pu?" It can, of course, be argued that the full "question" was understood to be, "If I attack Pu, will it be auspicious?", hence the answer, "It will be extremely auspicious." But no divination has been found phrased that way. Once again (to wield Ockham's razor) it is simpler to take the divination as a forecast, rather than multiply our entities needlessly (by elaborating the "question," or by supplying the missing answer), as the question-form requires us to do.

3) Tzu yung 茲用

This notation appears after certain divinations, meaning "Use this," or "We used this," the "this," according to Ch'ü Wan-li, Chia-pien k'ao-shih, no. 2, citing Hu Hou-hsüan) referring to the results of a particular divination. Ch'ü has to supply "results" because "use this question" would make little sense. Yet, if we could dispense with the "question" and "results" we would have a simpler solution: "use this divination," i.e. "use this charge." Consider the traditional view:①

[17] 癸丑貞甲寅酒大卯自上甲袞六小宰
茲用上甲不遘雨大乙不遘雨大丁遘雨

(Nan-pei, Ming 明, No. 432)

On the day kuei-ch'ou, asking: "On the day chia-yin, shall we perform a wine libation and a Great Purification, beginning with Shang Chia? Shall we thus make burnt offering of six small lao?"

This was used. On [the day of] Shang Chia we did not encounter rain. On [the day of] Ta Yi we did not encounter rain. On [the day of] Ta Ting we encountered rain.

What was used? Certainly not the "questions." The results? But none are indicated on the bone. It is simpler to treat the divination as a forecast: [17]: ON

---

① Cf. the previous discussion of this inscription, at divination [9].

THE DAY KUEI-CH'OU, 鼎-ING: "ON THE DAY CHIA-YIN WE SHALL OFFER A WINE LIBATION AND A GREAT PURIFICATION, BEGINNING WITH SHANG CHIA, AND WE SHALL MAKE BURNT OFFERING OF SIX SMALL LAO." THIS WAS USED... etc. In other words, this forecast or statement of intent was used, was put into effect, with the results described.

F. The Absence of a Response

The majority of the inscriptions apparently record neither prognostications, such as wang chan yüeh 王固曰, "The king interpreted the cracks and said," nor crack notations such as "Extremely auspicious." We do not know what most of the divination responses were.① This absence is puzzling if the divinations were indeed questions. What would have been the value of recording questions, and storing them like archives, if the answers were missing? What would have been the value of incising the questions, frequently in quintuplicate, when it was presumably the answers that were of more concern? It seems clear that the prognostication—or, more exactly, the recording of the prognostication—was not important to the Shang diviners. For some reason they did not need to record it with great frequency.

As I have already suggested(p. 25 above), one explanation is that the "question" was indeed the prognostication, and thus the "answer" too. Once the confirmation had been made by reading the cracks, the charge itself was the indicator of the result. Thus, the oracle-bone archives of Shang may be regarded not as a series of generally answerless questions, but as a series of royal charges or instructions to the shell, some of which were accepted favorably by the spirits, others of which were rejected, but all of which were a record of a charge and thus of a potential result. The fact that we may not know the nature(auspicious or inauspi-

---

① This may be an erroneous view, fostered by decades of scholarship that worked only with inscription fragments. My preliminary studies suggest the possibility that a complete "set" of questions, such as those that have been reconstituted on the Ping-pien plastra, will always, at some stage in the questioning, record a crack notation, such as chi 吉, shang chi 上吉, etc. (See pp. 51-52 below.) Even if this be proven, there would still seem to be a striking imbalance between the energy and emphasis involved in incising thousands of "questions" into the bones, and the tiny, and easily overlooked, notations like chi 吉.

cious) of this result① is immaterial; the point is that the Shang, by incising the charges, were also recording the results.

G. The Grammar of the Divinations

If we discount the Shuo-wen definition of cheng 貞, there are no other indications, particles, or grammatical constructions in the divinations which would make them interrogative. Chang Tsung regards 隹 (modern transcription 隹) and 㞢 (variant 㞢)(modern transcriptions 㞢 and 叀) as interrogative particles (DKDS, pp. 35, 88, 324). But the classical particle wei 唯 (or hui 叀, in the sense of wei 唯) with which he identifies these two forms has no question function. It is highly unlikely that it served this function in the oracle bones. In my opinion, 隹 and 㞢 (or its variant 㞢) should rather be taken as modal copula to indicative positive, subjunctive mood, with restriction or intensification, this last usage often resulting in a transposition of the expected word order.②

To give one type of divination record where 㞢 or 隹 clearly cannot have had an interrogative sense:

[18] 王固曰㞢艱　　　　　　　　　　　　　　　(Yi-pien, No. 3423)

The king read the cracks and said: "There will be troubles."

[19] [王]固不隹艱　　　　　　　　　　　　　　(Hsü-pien, 4.29.1)

[The king] read the cracks: "There will not be troubles."

Similarly, the non-interrogative nature of wei 隹 is clearly indicated by its use in the dating formula found in both the oracle inscriptions and bronze inscriptions of Shang. Thus:

---

① This may be an erroneous view, fostered by decades of scholarship that worked only with inscription fragments. My preliminary studies suggest the possibility that a complete "set" of questions, such as those that have been reconstituted on the Ping-pien plastra, will always, at some stage in the questioning, record a crack notation, such as chi 吉, shang chi 上吉, etc. (See pp. 51-52 below.) Even if this be proven, there would still seem to be a striking imbalance between the energy and emphasis involved in incising thousands of "questions" into the bones, and the tiny, and easily overlooked, notations like chi 吉.

② For a fuller discussion, see my working paper, "Hui 叀 in Oracle Bone Inscriptions," typescript, August, 1970.

[20] …在二月隹王十祀彡日…　　　　　　　　　(Chia-pien, No. 3939)

… in the second month, it was (the king's) tenth (sacrificial-cycle =) year, the days for the yung-ceremony…

Or, on bronze:

[21] 乙亥…才六月隹王六祀羽日①

On the day yi-hai… in the sixth month, it was the king's sixth (sacrificial-cycle =) year, the days of the yü-ceremony…

Further, wei 隹 (=維) occurs in Chou texts in non-interrogative contexts that resemble those of the Shang oracle-bone inscriptions. Consider, for example, Shih-ching, Mao no. 189:

nai chan wo meng　乃占我夢
chi meng wei ho　吉夢維何
wei hsiung wei pi　維熊維羆
wei hui wei she　維虺維蛇
t'ai jen chan chih　大人占之
wei hsiung wei pi　維熊維羆
nan tzu chih hsiang　男子之祥
wei hui wei she　維虺維蛇
nü tzu chih hsiang　女子之祥

"'Divine my dreams!' Which are the auspicious dreams? There are black bears and brown-and-white bears, there are snake-brood and snakes. The Great Man (chief diviner) divines them: 'There are black bears and brown-and-white bears, they are good omens of sons; there are snake-brood and snakes, they are good omens of daughters'" (Karlgren, Odes, p. 131, modified). Compare this with

[22] 貞王夢隹大甲
　　　貞王夢不隹大甲　　　　　　　　　　　(Ping-pien, No. 212(5)(6))

which (if we allow for the moment that cheng 貞 does not mean "question") may

---

① cited at YHPT, p. 233, which cites many other bronze inscriptions with this formula.

be translated, in accordance with the usage of the Shih-ching as: [22] (THE DIVINER) K'O 貞-ING: "THE KING'S DREAM WAS (OF) TA CHIA"; 貞-ING: "THE KING'S DREAM WAS NOT (OF) TA CHIA." A shang-chi 上吉 written by the first crack of the affirmative charge suggests that the dream was indeed about Ta Chia (but cf. the problems of interpretation raised at pp. 51-52 below).

Again, another Shih-ching usage reminiscent of the oracle-bone formula appears in Mao no. 272:

wo chiang wo hsiang　我將我享
wei yang wei niu　維羊維牛
wei t'ien ch'i yu chih　維天其右之

"We present our offerings. /There are sheep, there are oxen; /May Heaven esteem them" (following the translation of Creel, Origins, p. 505). This may be compared with:

[23] 辛未卜㝢貞曰䧹羊六月　　　　　(Ping-pien, No. 116(1))
CRACK-MAKING ON THE DAY HSIN-WEI, (THE DIVINER) NET 貞-ING: "WE SAY①: 'IT WILL BE A SHEEP.'" (DIVINATION MADE) IN THE SIXTH MONTH.

[24] 壬戌卜貞母癸祊叀羊　　　　　(Hsü-pien, 1.25.7)
CRACK-MAKING ON THE DAY JEN-HSU, 貞-ING: "IN THE PENG-SACRIFICE TO MU-KUEI, IT WILL BE A SHEEP."

In the absence of any indications to the contrary, a phrase like wei yang 隹羊 may be taken as indicative in both the Shih-ching and oracle-bone inscriptions.

Kuo Mo-jo has argued that hu 乎 (oracle-bone form 𠂎) does appear as an interrogative particle at the end of an oracle-bone sentence (Ts'ui-pien, no. 425, k'ao-ahih; cf. DKDS, no. 9. 24). But in the single instance he cites, the character is probably not hu 乎 (CKWT, 5.1634). I can find no other instance in which hu 乎 ends a divination (see the abbreviated listing at IKBS, p. 504.2 ff.).

Ocassionally, a negative pu 不 is placed at the end of the divination sentence,

---

① See p. 37 below.

instead of occurring before the verb. Thus, following the traditional translation:

[25] 庚辰卜辛巳雨

　　庚辰卜辛巳雨不　　　　　　　　　　　　(Nan-pei, 輔仁, No. 52)

Crack-making on the day keng-ch'en: "On the day hsin-ssu, will it rain?"

Crack-making on the day keng-ch'en: "On the day hsin-ssu, will it rain or not?"

But as Chou Hung-hsiang has demonstrated (PTTC, p. 80, cf. p. 89), this is simply a transposition of normal word order; it implies no interrogative sense and may be translated as [25]: CRACK-MAKING ON THE DAY KENG-CH'EN: "ON THE DAY HSIN-SSU IT WILL NOT RAIN."

The hypothesis that the individual sentences were indeed not questions is supported by the "sample divinations" provided by Ch'u Shao-sun 褚少孫 in Shih-chi, chapt. 128, Kuei-ts'e lieh-chuan, 龜策列傳, "On Divination by Tortoise Shell and Divining Straw." Ch'u does present the divinations as questions, but in precisely the "A-not-A" form we would expect if my hypothesis is correct. Thus: pu sui chung ho chia shu pu shu. Shu shou yang tsu k'ai… pu shu tsu han… 卜歲中禾稼孰不孰。孰,首仰足開…不孰足肣…(SKK, 128, 38.2), "Crack-making as to whether in the year the crops will ripen or not ripen? If they will ripen, the (cracks at the) head (of the shell) will rise up(?), and the (cracks at the) foot (of the shell) will open up(?)… If they will not ripen, the (cracks at the) foot will contract…" Similarly, pu t'ien yü pu yü. yü shou yang yu wai, wai kao nei hsia. pu yü shou yang tsu k'ai… 卜天雨不雨,雨首仰有外,外高內下,不雨首仰足開…(SKK, 128, 39.8), "Crack-making as to whether Heaven will make rain or not make rain. If it will make rain, the cracks at the head of the shell will rise up and be exposed(?), the outside (of the cracks?) being higher than the inside(?). If it will not make rain, the cracks at the head will rise up, and the cracks at the feet will open up…" Ch'u offers other "sample divinations" in the chi pu chi 吉不吉 form (e.g. SKK, 128, 37.8, 10).

Two points are worth noticing. First, the divining verb is pu 卜, not cheng 貞. Second, the interrogative form with a particle such as hu 乎 at the end of the sentence is never used. It seems reasonable to conclude, therefore, that the tradition of tortoise-shell divination recorded in Shih-chi 128 (which may not, of course, have resembled Shang practice, cf. SKK, 128, 56.6) frames the "question" as two indicative statements, one positive, the other negative. It was the juxtaposition of the two contrasting forecasts, that characteristic Chinese apposition of opposites, that generated the "question" by confronting the spirits with alternatives from which to choose.

H. The Context of the Divinations

It is the thesis of this section that divinations concerning sacrifice and ritual-request were performed at the same time as the sacrifice or ritual to which they refer. The "charge" to the shell may thus be regarded not as a question, "Should we seek harvest?", but as a description (or prayer), "We are seeking harvest," intended both to inform the spirits about, and to win their approval for, the sacrifice being offered, or the request being made. The presentation to the spirits of tablets, with prayers written on them, is well documented in the Chou texts (Yü Hsing-wu 于省吾, Yin-ch'i p'in-chih hsü-pien 殷契駢枝續編 (1941), pp. 12a-b; CLCY, 49.1a-b). Perhaps some of the inscribed oracle bones served a similar function.

If we treat such divinations as questions, problems of interpretation arise. For example, the traditional translations:

[26] 貞于王亥求年　　　　　　　　　　　　　　(Hou-pien, 1.1.1)

Asking: "Shall we seek a good harvest from Wang Hai?"

[27] 貞求方于丁　　　　　　　　　　　　　　　(T'ieh-yün, 51.4)

Asking: "Shall we seek [assistance against] the Fang from (ancestor) Ting?"

are curious because they are questions that ask about asking. In this view, the Shang first divined if they should ask a certain spirit about something, and once that divination had been answered, they then proceeded to perform the actual asking ceremony, having obtained a guarantee of success in advance. This seems cautious and time-consuming. Presumably, the strategic problem in "seeking" divinations of this sort was, "If we ask Wang Hai, will we get a good harvest?", "If we seek assistance from Ting, will we get it?" Not, should we ask so-and-so, but will we get what we want? Taking the divinations as statements economizes, with Ockham, the "seeking" process: [26]: 鬥-ING "WE ARE SEEKING A GOOD HARVEST FROM WANG HAI"; [27] : 鬥-ING: "WE ARE SEEKING [ASSISTANCE AGAINST] THE FANG FROM TING." To which the response "auspicious" would inform the celebrants that they were indeed performing the right ceremony and would receive the harvest or assistance sought.

What evidence supports the view that the divinations and sacrifices occurred simultaneously? In the first place, it can be shown that the divinations and sacrifices were performed in the same place. Sacrifices to the ancestors took place in the ancestral temple(Chao Lin, Marriage, Inheritance, and Lineage Organization in Shang-Chou China (Taipei, 1970), pp. 50-51; cf. the inscriptions at IKBS, pp. 270. 2-271. 4). Similarly, the oracle-bone inscriptions do on occasion record that the questioning of the oracle took place in the temples of the dead kings (DKDS, p. 263, citing Jimbun, no. 2142, Ts'ui-pien, no. 12, Chih-hsü, no. 64). That divinations, at least in Chou times, did take place in the ancestral temple, the site of the ancestral sacrifices, is confirmed by a passage in the Tso-chuan: pu chih yi shou kuei yü tsung t'iao 卜之以守龜於宗祧, "Our ruler consulted the tortoise-shell of the State about it in the ancestral temple"(Legge, Tso, p. 854, Ai 23). If sacrifices took place in the temple, and if divinations also took place in the temple, there is at least the possibility that they may, on occasion, have taken place in conjunction with one another.

Several pieces of evidence, much of it admittedly negative, support this interpretation. In the first place, so far as I can tell, none of the divinations about offering sacrifice have prognostications attached to them(cf. KTZ, pp. 474-475; IKBS, pp. 307. 3-311. 1). If the divinations were queries of the form, "Should we offer sacrifice A to ancestor X?" we would expect to find some prognostications of the form, "The king interpreted the cracks and said: 'Auspicious. We will offer sacrifice A to ancestor X.'" Similarly, we would expect to find some verifications of the form, "We really did offer sacrifice A to ancestor X." But no divination about sacrifice has this kind of prognostication or verification attached to it.

One possible explanation for this feature of the oracular record would be that the sacrifice divinations did not require prognostication or verification because they were carried out simultaneously, or almost simultaneously, with the sacrifice itself. The auspicious or inauspicious response of the divination indicated at once the success of the associated sacrifice or ritual. I would suggest that, as a general rule, prognostications or verifications were attached only to divinations about future events, when there was a significant interval between the divination and the result (the Ching-hua inscriptions are a classic case of this; see IKBS, 307.3). Conversely, the absence of prognostications or verifications suggests that the divination was of immediate applicability, and was therefore not a direct question about doing something in the future, but a description of something being done.

Such an interpretation is supported by the fact that not a single ch'iu nien 求年 divination, and only two ch'iu yü 求雨 divinations (Pu-tz'u, no. 244; Hsü-ts'un, 2.216; recorded at IKBS, p. 206.2) divine about a ceremony to be offered on a future day, which suggests that they were generally carried out on the same day as the ch'iu nien or ch'iu yü ceremony itself. Furthermore, nearly all the "seek harvest" and "seek rain" divinations (IKBS, pp. 194.2-195.1; 206.2-206.3) are couched in positive terms. If the divinations were simply a query about the advisability of seeking harvest or rain, we would then expect pairs of the form : "Should we seek harvest from X"; "Should we not seek harvest from X?" But such negative sentences are rare.① This suggests that the ch'iu nien 求年 and ch'iu yü 求雨 divinations referred to a ritual request that was actually being carried out at the time of divination. To divine that "We are not seeking rain" or "We are not seeking harvest" at a time when the actual ceremony for seeking rain or seeking

---

① There are three negative divinations of the form wu ch'iu yü ho 勿求于河 (Hsü-pien, 1.35.4; Yi-ts'un, no. 145; Yi-pien, no. 2969; listed at IKBS, p. 206.3) and two of the form wu ch'iu nien yü pang 勿求年于邦 (Fu-shih, 歲, 18; Ch'ien-pien, 4.17.3; listed at IKBS, p. 194.4). I believe that in these cases a prayer request was being offered, and the divination was simply to define the details; hence these negative pair sentences, "We are not seeking from the Yellow River," or "We are not seeking harvest at Pang." The performance of the seeking ritual itself was not in question.

harvest was taking place would have been at odds with the truth. Therefore, few such positive-negative divinations were made. The "pairing" was instead effected by changing the recipient of the sacrifice ritual (cf. PTTC, p. 97; Jimbun, no. 2361). Thus:

[28] 癸未貞求年于河
癸未貞求年于夒　　　　　　　　　　　　　　　(Yi-ts'un, No. 376)

ON THE DAY KUEI-WEI 囚-ING: "WE ARE SEEKING HARVEST FROM THE YELLOW RIVER."

ON THE DAY KUEI-WEI 囚-ING: "WE ARE SEEKING HARVEST FROM (ANCESTOR) KUEI."

Presumably the divination indicated which of these two spirits would receive favorably the sacrifice that was under way or about to take place.

Similar considerations apply to the ch'iu sheng 求生, "seek offspring," divinations (IKBS, pp. 163.2-163.3).① Thus, rather than the traditional translation:

[29] 癸未貞其求生于高妣丙　　　　　　　　　　(Ch'ien-pien, 1.33.3)

On the day kuei-wei, asking: "Should we seek offspring from the high ancestress Ping?"

I would offer: ON THE DAY KUEI-WEI, 囚-ING: "WE ARE SEEKING OFFSPRING FROM THE HIGH ANCESTRESS PING." For in these prayer-divinations too, we never find a pu ch'iu sheng 不求生 form. The question "pairing" is effected by varying the recipient of the prayer-request. Thus, in the case of this divination the pair sentence reads: [29] 貞其求生于高□庚 囚-ING: "WE ARE SEEKING OFFSPRING FROM HIGH [ANCESTRESS] KENG."② The consistent absence of the negative formula again suggests that the divination accompanied the ceremony or

---

① IKBS, pp. 163.2-163.3. For the meaning of the phrase see Ikeda Suetoshi 池田末利, Inkyo shokei kōhen shakubun kō 殷虛書契後編釋文稿 (Hiroshima, 1964), I, 26.6; Itō Michiharu 伊藤道治, "Indai ni okeru sosen saishi to tiejin shūdan 殷代における祖先祭祀と貞人集團," Kenkyū shigaku 研究史學, 28 (March, 1962), p. 32, n. 19.

② The rubbing I have seen is illegible; here I follow the transcription at IKBS, p. 163.3. Yeh Yü-sen 葉玉森, Yin-hsü shu-ch'i ch'ien-pien chi-shih 殷虛書契前編集釋 (1934), I, p. 108a, gives Pi Yin 妣寅, but this must be in error; the ancestresses were not named by earthly branches.

prayer, which could, not therefore, be referred to as not occurring.

In short, I am suggesting that these oracle-bone inscriptions may be taken as an integral part of a sacrifice, ritual-request, or prayer—specifying its content or recipient, and giving indications as to the success of the undertaking. These divinations were not questions about future actions to be taken (unless, of course, the divination refers to time future); they were statements which were to both define, and permit the evaluation of, current actions.

I. The wang yüeh 王曰 divinations

If the oracle-bone inscriptions do represent charges to the shell, we should expect to find some indication of this in the content of the divinations. I believe, in fact, that the inscriptions record oral statements, spoken (yüeh 曰) or cried out (hu 乎) by the king, or the diviner, in order to catch the attention of the spirits and assert the charge. Some inscriptions, in fact, lacking the cheng 貞, permit a translation that supports this viewpoint. Thus:

[30] 甲子王卜曰翌乙丑其酒𤞗于①唐不雨　　　　（Hsü-ts'un, 1.148）
ON THE DAY CHIA-TZU THE KING MADE CRACKS, SAYING: "ON THE NEXT YI-CH'OU WE WILL OFFER WINE LIBATION AND A FEATHERDANCE TO T'ANG AND IT WILL NOT RAIN."②

There is no evident reason to take divinations of this wang pu yüeh 王卜曰 form (e.g. Hou-pien, II. 27. 13; Hsü-ts'un, 1.1594) as questions. Divinations of the form, cheng[wang] yüeh 貞[王]曰 also appear:

[31] 貞王曰亡其疾　　　　（Hsü-pen, 4.29.1）
冏-ING: "THE KING SAYS: 'THERE WILL BE NO SICKNESS.'"

[32] 己亥卜殻貞曰戈氏齒[于]王
　　　貞勿曰戈氏齒[于]王　　　　（Chui-ho, No.144）
CRACK-MAKING ON THE DAY CHI-HAI, THE DIVINER K'O 冏-

---

① 編者按："于"，原文誤脫，今徑補。
② Following the translation of DKDS, no. 10. 19; Chang, however, translates the yüeh 曰 as "question," but I know of no reason to do so.

ING: "[THE KING?] SAYS THAT KE WILL (TAKE =) BRING IVORY TO THE KING."

卣-ING: [THE KING?] DOES NOT SAY THAT KE WILL BRING IVORY [TO THE] KING."

Such translations seem preferrable to the traditional views [31] "Asking: 'Should the king say, "There will be no sickness"?'"; [32] "Asking: 'Should [the king?] not say that Ke will bring ivory [to the] king'?"

J. The Use of the Verb hu 乎

Without wishing to make a detailed study of the matter here, I would also suggest that the verb hu 乎 confirms the oral, even exclamatory, nature of the divination charge. Thus,

[33] 貞乎子汰祝一牛于(?)父甲　　　　　　　(Ping-pien, No. 117(33))①

卣-ING: "CRY OUT: 'TZU TA IS OFFERING ONE OX IN THE CHU CEREMONY TO FU CHIA'."

Or, another translation, more controversial in nature:

[34] 貞宙王往伐呂

貞叀呂乎伐呂

貞叀自般乎伐

貞叀子盡乎伐　　　　　　　(Shih-to, 2.185)

卣-ING: "IT IS THE KING WHO GOES TO ATTACK THE HU."

卣-ING: "IT IS KUNG (ABOUT WHOM THE KING) CRIES OUT: 'ATTACK'."

卣-ING: "IT IS SHIH P'AN (ABOUT WHOM THE KING) CRIES OUT: 'ATTACK'."

卣-ING: "IT IS TZU CHIN (ABOUT WHOM THE KING) CRIES OUT: 'ATTACK'."②

---

① I follow the transcription at SASA, p. 63, in taking the second 乎 not as hu 乎 but as yü 于.
② Following the translation at DKDS, no. 6.29 for the personal names.

The oral nature of secular charges is well documented in the Western Chou bronze inscriptions where the formula wang hu A ts'e ming Y 王乎A冊命Y is common,① "The king cried out: let (officer) A command Y by means of a document," and the content of the command then follows. It may not be too far-fetched to suggest that the oracular charge to the spirits of Shang became the documentary charge to the officers of Western Chou, cried out and written down in both cases to render them efficacious.

In conclusion, the use of the verb yüeh 曰, "say," and hu 乎 "cry out," suggests that the divinations were statements proclaimed to the spirits and to the shell. Questions could certainly have been proclaimed too, but yüeh 曰 is not an interrogative verb, and hu 乎 (judging from its use in Western Chou bronze inscriptions) was used in affirmatory, rather than interrogative, contexts.

V. THE MEANING OF 鼎

I am not sure what 鼎 really meant in the oracle-bone formula. And we never will be sure unless a Shang dictionary or divination manual is excavated. What follows is extrapolation based on the evidence available.

As we have seen, there was a strong tradition running from Cheng Hsüan to Change Yi, Wei Chao, and Tu Yü, that cheng 貞 (*tiěng/ťiäng) meant cheng 正 (*ťiěng/tśiäng-). Such a tradition was self-reinforcing; Chang Yi's Kuang-ya derived from classical commentaries, such as Cheng Hsüan's; Wei Chao and Tu Yü were presumably influenced by both Cheng Hsüan and the Kuang-ya. But the very reiteration of the tradition suggests the general validity attributed to it. Though these traditional glosses were partly paranomastic, the identity between cheng 貞 and cheng 正 was not simply phonological; it was clearly semantic as well, since

---

① Kuo Mo-jo 郭沫若, Liang-chou chin-wen-tz'u ta-hsi t'u-lu k'ao-shih 兩周金文辭大系圖錄考釋 (Peking, 1957), pp. 72a, 74b, 75b, 77a, 78b, 79a, 79b, 80a, 85b, 88b, 100a, 102b, 115a, 116b, 117a, etc. On the use of this phrase in the bronze inscriptions, cf. H. G. Creel, Studies in Early Chinese Culture (Baltimore, 1937), p. 44; Origins, p. 126.

the meaning of cheng 正 serves admirably in almost all classical occurrences of cheng 貞.

The Shih-ming, by contrast, gives cheng 貞 as equivalent to ting 定(*d'ieng/d'ieng-)①. Bodman notes that there is good reason to believe that Liu Hsi 劉熙, the compiler of the Shih-ming, "chose his glosses for sound similarity at the expense of close resemblance in meaning"(p.2). But it is far from certain that Liu was matching sounds at the expense of meaning in this case. In the first place, cheng 正(*t̂ieng/tśiäng) rather than ting 定 would seem to have been equally acceptable as a sound gloss for cheng 貞; and in the second place, as we have already noted(p.9), the Shih-ming definitions frequently follow either those of Hsü Shen or Cheng Hsüan. The fact that in this case Liu chose to follow neither of his famous predecessors, nor follow the sound gloss that was found acceptable by Chang Yi, suggests that he had reasons for thinking that ting 定, rather than cheng 正, was a better gloss for cheng 貞.

The difference is perhaps minimal, for it is clear that cheng 正 and ting 定 were also related semantically, as well as phonetically, in antiquity(e.g. CLCY, 6.10b.10; 11b.5), and that there was certainly a pre-Han word group that linked 鼎(*tieng), 貞(*tieng), 正(*tieng), and 定(*d'ieng).② The etymon from which 貞 derived, therefore, presumably contained the sense of "correct, regulate, proper"(正), on the one hand, and "settle, establish, fix"(定), on the other. In the oracle-bone context, what could 貞 have been regulating or establishing?

Karlgren's suggestion that when cheng 貞 "has its sense of 'divination inquiry' it really means 'to verify, to determine what is correct'"(Glosses, no. 1752) is plausible at first glance, and indeed I believe, generally correct. But I think it is clear that the verifying, the determining what is correct, did not involve the actual interpretation of the oracle, which, so far as we can tell from the oracle

---

① Nicholas Cleaveland Bodman, A Linguistic Study of the Shih Ming(Cambridge, Mass., 1954), no.684, p.96.
② GSR, nos.833, 834. Cf. KJGK, nos.120-122. Tōdō extends the scope of the word family to include, among other words, t'ing 聽(*t'ieng), so that cheng 貞 has the sense of "hearing the will of the spirits by means of divination."

record, was rarely, if ever, performed by the diviner. In inscription [13] above, the diviner Cheng was 冏-ing, but it was the king who actually interpreted the cracks and prognosticated (cf. divinations [18], [19]). Thus, following Karlgren, we would arrive at a tentative translation: [13]: Crack-making on the day keng-tzu, Cheng determining/verifying what was correct: "On the next hsin-ch'ou day it will be clear..." The king interpreted the cracks and said... etc.

The question then becomes, what aspects of the divination process would require verifying, rectifying, or determining, in this way? There are several possible answers, and they do not exclude one another:

1) As we now understand the process, the divination involved the following sequence of events: a depression (hereafter referred to as a "pit") was bored in the back of the shell or bone, making it sufficiently thin for cracking at that point; heat was then applied by some device such as a hot ember or poker to the pit, and as it was applied (causing a crack to form in the shell or bone), a statement (either mental, or if I am right about the function of yüeh 曰 and hu 乎 (see pp. 37-39 above), oral) was addressed as a charge to the shell; once the crack was formed, a sequence numeral (usually from 1 to 10) was written beside the crack to identify its place in the sequence (e.g. Ping-pien no. 49) and presumably to relate the particular crack to the particular question; the divination statement was then written on the shell or bone with a brush; and at a later date the brush-written characters were incised into the shell or bone.

It would seem that the chance of error would be greatest in linking the original (oral or mental?) charges to the cracks, and in linking the cracks to the written charges later. Several practices were apparently designed to prevent error.① First, as we have seen, the cracks were numbered. Second, the ⼘-shaped cracks were on occasion cut more deeply into the shell themselves (YTKT, p. 27), presumably to identify and preserve them more clearly. Third, dividing boundaries were at times inscribed on crowded shell surfaces, to separate the divination sentences, forming as it were a series of compartments or "spheres of influ-

---

① Chang Ping-ch'üan has suggested that the "sets" themselves were instituted mainly to avoid the confusion that would have resulted without such orderly record-keeping (LCTP, p. 393).

ence" for each divination (CKPW, pp. 49, 57, n. 1; PTTC, pp. 29 ff.). It is possible, therefore, that the diviner's function as he 閖-ed was "to keep things straight," to ensure the correctness of these technical, bureaucratic procedures, to ensure that the right crack was numbered in accord with the right statement, that the right written characters were recorded for the right statement, that the divination statement for one crack did not invade the domain of another.

The boring of the pits themselves was another technical matter which required regulation. Chang Ping-ch'üan notes that four pits on one plastron were unburned, apparently because they had been bored in shell that was too thick for the heat to crack easily; hence the diviner rejected them (Ping-pien k'ao-shih, p. 321). I doubt that the diviner was actually involved in the routine task of boring the pits, but it may have been part of his function to make sure, prior to the divination, that the pits had been made correctly.

Some support for the view that 閖 meant cheng 正 may be found in Shih-chi 128. Describing the preparation of the shell, Ch'u Shao-sun says: pu hsien yi tsao cho tsuan. tsuan chung yi yu cho. kuei shou ke san. yu fu cho so tsuan chung yüeh cheng shen, cho shou yüeh cheng tsu. ke san. 卜先以造灼鑽。鑽中已又灼。龜首各三，又復灼所鑽中曰正身，灼首曰正足各三, "Prior to making the crack, one burns out a depression with (a burning stick from) the stove. When the center of the depression has been completed, one applies heat again. Three times in all at the head of the tortoise shell. The repeated burning of what has been bored out (?) is, in the middle (of the plastron) called cheng shen 正身, 'regulating the body'; burning the head (of the shell) [is called cheng shou] 正首, 'regulating the head'; burning the foot (of the shell)] is called cheng tsu 正足, 'regulating the foot.' In each case, one does it three time."① As Takigawa notes, the method of divination which this chapter presents differs from that found in classical texts; he

---

① SKK, 128.34.3-5; reading 造 as 竈. The characters in square brackets were added following the suggestion of Chang Wen-hu 張文虎. The passage is corrupt and my translation tentative. For a different translation see Pohl, Schi Ki Kapital 128, p. 61; Noguchi Sadao, Shiki, vol. 12, p. 324; Shiki retsuden kōgi 史記列傳講義, in Kambun gaku kōgi 漢文學講義 (Tokyo, 1913), vol. 10, p. 1614.

therefore proposes that Ch'u was basing himself on the practices found in Ch'in-Han divination texts, rather than on the procedures of the Three Dynasties (SKK, 128.56). Nevertheless, it is interesting to find "rectification," or "regulation," associated with the burning of the pits. Conceivably, 閑 referred to a similar procedure in Shang times.

2) In addition to these technical aspects, there were undoubtedly features of ritual correctness of which we know little. These are suggested by the presence of both unburned, unscorched pits and, more especially, the presence of unnumbered cracks. Ping-pien, no. 184, is an example of the first; 174 pits were bored in the back of this large plastron, but only 43 of them were actually used; 131 were not. Why, after arduous preparation, a plastron should have been largely unused in this way, is not clear; perhaps a ritual error was discovered, causing the plastron to be

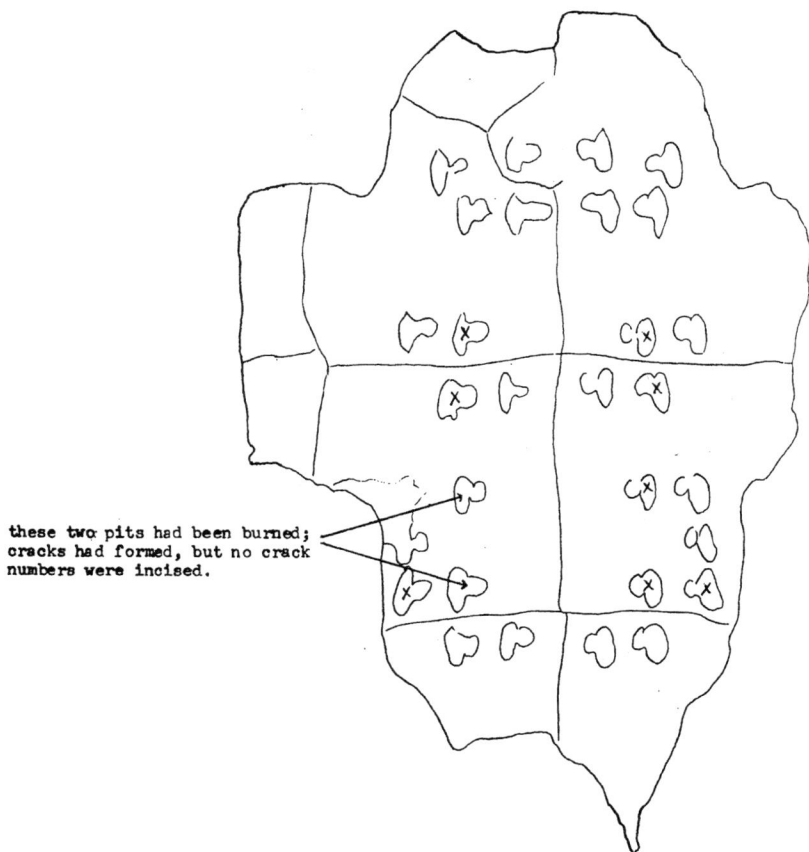

these two pits had been burned; cracks had formed, but no crack numbers were incised.

Figure 2　Ping-pien, No. 58
X marks the pits which had not been burned.

rejected for further divination. Ping-pien, no. 58, provides a still more interesting example; 30 pits were bored, and 8 of these were not scorched; of these 8 unused pits, 6 were arranged symmetrically, 3 on the right and 3 on the left. What is significant is that in 2 out of the remaining 22 pits that were scorched and produced cracks, the cracks so produced were not numbered; and it is precisely the 2 unused pits on the other side of the median line which correspond to those 2 pits whose cracks were numberless. Figure 2 will make this clear. As Chang Ping-ch'üan suggests, it seems that after the crack-making had taken place in these two pits on the left side, some irregularity was discovered, the divinations were rejected, and the two corresponding pits on the right were not used at all. This suggests that Shang divination had its rules and regulations (Ping-pien k'ao-shih, pp. 93-94). If such strict observance of rules, either technical or ritual, did take place while the crack-making was actually under way (as the example of Ping-pien, no. 58, suggests), it is reasonable to suppose that it was the diviner who was responsible for such matters. 閂 in the sense of cheng 正 would fit such an interpretation. And it would also accord with the sense of "pure," "chaste," "proper," which cheng 貞 has in the Chou texts. Indeed, the Pao-p'u-tzu use of cheng-jen 貞人, noted above (p. 13), as "one who preserves his rectitude," suggests that the oracle-bone diviner was a man who preserved the rectitude of the entire operation.①

3) A further type of regulation might have involved the actual wording of the charge. Chang Ping-ch'üan has noted that it commonly happens in oracle-bone inscriptions that the scope of the prognostication exceeds the scope of the original charge (Ping-pien k'ao-shih, p. 460). For instance, the charge in Ping-pien, no. 394, lists the names of two ancestors who are thought to be cursing the

---

① Shih-chi, chapt. 127, "Jih che lieh chuan 日者列傳," "The Diviners of Lucky Days," may contain an echo of such ideas about rectification (cheng 正). Ssu-ma Ch'ien noted that "When the former kings managed the affairs of state, they invariably consulted the tenteise on the milfoil stalks and coserved the sun and moon before undertaking the charge of Heaven. Only after determining the correct hour and day did they come and go" (cheng shih jih nai hou ju 正時日乃後入) (SKK, 127.8.2; tr. Watson, Records, II, 472). "When the diviner sets to work, he first sweeps a place and spreads his mat, straightens his hat and arranges his sash (cheng ch'i kuan tai 正其冠帶), and only then does he begin to discuss business" (Burton Watson, Records of the Grand Historian of China (New York and London, 1961), Vol. II, p. 472; SKK, 127.8.7-8).

Shang. The prognostication on the other side of the shell (Ping-pien, no. 395) lists five ancestors who it had been determined were actually doing the cursing. We will encounter a similar instance in divination [39] below, in which the king's prognostication ("If it is a ting-day... If it is a keng-day...") far exceeds the scope of the charge. Such instances suggest, according to Chang, that the initial charge was frequently more detailed than the inscribed charge which was eventually written down. Thus he suggests that, in Ping-pien, no. 394, cracks actually were made about each of the five ancestors who appear in the prognostication, but that the names of only two appear in the abbreviated, recorded charge. If this is so, it may well have been part of the diviner's function both to frame the full but unrecorded charge, and also to decide on the abbreviated form that the recorded charge should take. This, too, would require "regulation."

4) The use of the ting-cauldron graph in the oracle-bone inscriptions to depict cheng 貞 may have had semantic as well as phonological significance. It is a hypothesis at least worth exploring that 鼎 actually meant "cauldron" in the divination formula. Thus 争貞 would not mean "Cheng asking" or "Cheng regulating," but "Cheng cauldroning," thus "Cheng presiding at the cauldron." Ma Wei-ch'ing 馬薇廎 states that the Western Chou bronze character for ting 鼎 sometimes included a pu 卜 element on top (cf. p. 3 above) because the cauldron was frequently used in divination questioning.① This is a plausible suggestion, for we know that Shang inscriptions frequently recorded a ritual offering by depicting the implement involved (Lefeuvre, "Serie 臼", p. 8; cf. pp. 23-24). It might therefore be possible to treat the character 鼎, which does appear in the bronze inscriptions (see p. 3 above) as meaning "a ting for 卜-ing," that is, a cauldron to be used in crack-making. How such a cauldron might have been used in divining, however, is uncertain. If, as Shirakawa has suggested (SMSG, p. 657), water was sprinkled on the heated bone to assist the cracking (presumably the steam generated increased the stress), then it is possible that a cauldron containing water was at hand, and that the diviner sprinkled water at the crucial moment to cause the cracks to

---

① "Ts'ung yi-ming so-chien yi-ch'i-chih ming-ch'eng 從彝銘所見彝器之名稱," Chung-kuo wen-tzu 中國文字, 42 (December, 1971), p. 8a.

form. But I know of no textual evidence to support such a hypothesis.

Professor Chou Hung-hsiang has determined that it is necessary to soften scapula by boiling them, before inscriptions can be incised, even with surgical steel(conversation, September 10, 1970). Thus, it is not beyond the realm of possibility that the divination process, at some point, involved the actual boiling of shells in a tripod.① No classical text links cauldrons to divination in this way either. Thus, although cauldrons may have been involved in the divination process—hence the temptation to use the picture of the cauldron as a loan word—I doubt that 鼎 itself had the meaning of "cauldron" in the divination formula.

There may, indeed, be another explanation for the use of this particular graph. Just as tien 奠 meaning "to place, fix, settle," was a picture of a vessel, perhaps on a support(GSR, no. 363; CKWT, 5. 1585-1587), so 鼎 may have functioned in the same way, to mean "to rectify, to make stable, to make firm, like the putting down of a tripod."② Such a meaning may have been in Cheng Hsüan's mind when he glossed cheng kuei 貞龜 as cheng kuei yü pu wei yeh 正龜於卜位也(CLCY, 47. 13a; cf. p. 7 above), "he regulates(=correctly places?) the tortoise at the place of divination."

How then should we translate 鼎? If we start with 貞 = 正 as "regulate" we are led to the Indo-European root, reg-, "To move in a straight line," with derivatives meaning "to direct in a straight line, lead, rule." Among the words in the group are "correct, direct, rectify, regulate, reckon," and, interestingly, "interrogate".③ If we start with 貞 = 定 as "fix," Karlgren's "determine what is correct," we are led to the Indo-European root, dhīgw, "to stick, fix," with deriva-

---

① Such an interpretation would be supported by the claim of the Sung dynasty Chi-yün 集韻 that an old form of cheng 貞 was 鼒(DKW, no. 2826). This might well be taken as a picture of a shell(here simplified to an eye) being cracked, in a vessel, over flames. But no bronze graph supports this claim.
② Cf. the Yi-li, "Shih sang li 士喪禮": pu jen pao kuei chiao hsien tien kuei hsi shou chiao tsai pei 卜人抱龜燋先奠龜西首燋在北(SSCC, 37, p. 19b), "The diviner lifts up the shell in his arms, the tinder being carried in front, and lays it in the doorway, with its head to the west, the tinder being to the north of it"(John Steele, The I-Li or Book of Etiquette and Ceremonial(London, 1917), Vol. 2, p. 75).
③ William Morris, editor, The American Heritage Dictionary of the English Language(Boston, New York, etc., 1969), p. 1536.

tives such as "dig, ditch, dike, affix, orucify, prefix." The idea of "dig" would accord well with the incision of the oracle bone inscriptions into the shell or bone (cf. Waley's comments on the need to "fix" an oracle, pp. 49-50 below), but Chinese permits no such link between cheng 貞 and ting 定 and "dig."

Of all the possibilities, I would suggest that "regulate" be used, as the most inclusive English term available. That 鼎 did not merely equal cheng 正 in the oracle-bone inscriptions is suggested by the fact that the two graphs do appear in the same inscription. Cheng 正 is frequently used in the sense of to "regulate, straighten out," hence "attack" (i. e. as a loan for cheng 征) an enemy tribe (IKBS, pp. 70. 4-71. 3; 73. 2-73. 4); on other occasions cheng 正 seems to have the sense of "favorable,"① which is not incompatible with the sense of "regulated." All these inscriptions containing cheng 正 are usually prefaced with 鼎. I suspect that it was precisely the meanings of "verify" and "determine," even of "affirm" or "affix," which distinguished 鼎 from cheng 正, "regulate." This seems all the more likely when we consider that although the oracle-bone form for ting 定 (*d'ieng) was 𓎹, which is related both graphically and semantically to cheng 正 (*ţieng; oracle-bone form 𓎺), ting 定 in the oracle bones was apparently used only as a place-name (CKWT, 7. 2447; IKBS, p. 70. 4). This suggests that the sense of "determine" or "fix"—as in settling a tripod (see p. 46 above)-had to be carried by a related graph, such as 鼎.

Thus, I propose that we translate the standard pattern 辛亥卜爭貞 as "Crack-making on the day hsin-hai, with Cheng regulating." And that what was "regulated" be thought to include the correct form of the pits, the correct placing of the shell, the correct phrasing of the charge, the correct identification of the cracks, and the correct observation of other technical rules and ritual observances. The purpose of the formula was presumably bureaucratic—to identify the diviner responsible for the correct execution of the divining.②

---

① Lefeuvre, "Serie 卩," p. 59, n. 108, citing the work of Chin Hsiang-heng.
② It is possible that Ma Jung had a sense of this meaning when he glossed the "Lo Kao's" wo erh jen kung cheng 我二人共貞 (cf. n. 12 above) as cheng tang yeh 貞當也, "We two men have jointly undertaken/been jointly responsible for (the divination)."

Father Paul L-M. Serruys has suggested (in conversation) that the core meaning of cheng 貞 in Chou texts, where (glossed as cheng 正) it is thought to have the sense of virtuous constancy, is "attested," hence "tested," referring to someone who is a "tested," reliable person. Thus, he has suggested that 鼎 in the oracle bones might mean "test," and the prefatory formula would read "Crack-making on the day XY, the diviner A testing (the following hypothesis)."① I should be delighted to accept this interpretation—for it confirms my view that the inscriptions were not interrogative but declarative—but I am not certain that it can be supported. In the first place, there is a difference in meaning between something that has been "attested" (and thus, with Karlgren, "verified") and something that is about to be "tested" (and is as yet "unverified"). "Test" would be quite at variance with the sense of "determine" (ting 定; see CLCY, 6.10b.10; 11b.5) or "decide" (chüeh 決, see p. below) that cheng 正 clearly possessed. Cheng 正 in classical usage has the sense of something certain and determined, not of something hypothetical; I have found no cases in which it may precede a hypothesis.② In the second place, if one looks in Giles dictionary (no. 607), for example, at the compounds containing cheng 貞—such as cheng-lieh 貞烈, "chaste, even to death," cheng-chieh 貞潔, cheng-shu 貞淑 "pure, undefiled, as a virgin," cheng-nü 貞女, "a virtuous woman; a virgin," shou-cheng 守貞, "to keep one's purity" (said of a girl whose fiancé has died, and who elects to remain unmarried ever afterwards, ping-cheng yü-chieh 冰貞玉潔, "ice chastity and jade purity, i.e. pure, unsullied"—it seems clear that "purity" (i.e. correctness) rather than "testing" was the core meaning of cheng 貞. One could, of course, argue that true purity must have been tested, but this is speculative. On the whole, and with reluc-

---

① Professor Peter A. Boodberg also pointed out (in conversation) that if Serruys is correct, cheng 貞 as a technical name for the inner trigram (cf. n.9 above) might refer to a two-stage process of hexagram enquiry in which the first, bottom trigram represented a "test probe."

② It is true that cheng 偵 (*tiěng) means to "test" as well as to "observe, examine, verify" (GSR, 834k), but I can find no instance in which cheng 偵 was used as a divination term. It is only the Sung dynasty Chi-yün which notes that 偵 was sometimes written for 貞 (DKW, no.36658, definition 11). I am reluctant, therefore, to believe that oracular 貞 was merely an abbreviated form of 偵.

tance, I believe that the sense of "correct" rather than "test" is closer to the core meaning of both cheng 貞 and cheng 正.① And therefore, for want of a better word, I offer "regulate" as the best translation of 貞.

VI. THE MAGICAL ASPECT: A HYPOTHESIS

We do not fully understand the metaphysics of Shang divination. We do not even know with certainty the actual sequence of the record-making; that is, we do not know at what point in time (before or after the event?) the divinations were written on the bone or shell, and at what point they were incised. What follows, therefore, is a tentative, exploratory, attempt to answer the basic question: What did the Shang diviner think he was doing? It attempts to show, from yet another point of view, that it is unsatisfactory to treat the divinations simply as enquiries. And it attempts to show that "regulate," as a translation for 貞, may be appropriate for reasons concerned with the nature of the divination process itself.

A. The Engraving of the Inscriptions

We have not yet taken account of the fact that the divination charges, prognostications, and verifications, were not simply written on the bone or shell with a brush; they were incised, cut into the shell or bone with bronze knives (YTKT, passim.); these incisions required considerable skill and energy, and were carved on an assembly-line basis. The impulse to carts was not simply that of the bureaucrat-record keeper, or historian, though these impulses were undoubtedly present. We have already noted that, on occasion, the cracks were themselves incised (see p. 42 above). The motive here may be related to Waley's observation

---

① It is true that cheng 偵 (*tiěng) means to "test" as well as to "observe, examine, verify" (GSR, 834k), but I can find no instance in which cheng 偵 was used as a divination term. It is only the Sung dynasty Chi-yün which notes that 偵 was sometimes written for 貞 (DKW, no. 36658, definition 11). I am reluctant, therefore, to believe that oracular 貞 was merely an abbreviated form of 偵.

that "an omen is regarded as in itself a momentary, evanescent thing. Like silverprints, it requires 'fixing.' Otherwise it will refer only to the moment at which it was secured."① The carving of the inscriptions too, presumably involved the same desire to "fix" the charge. But more than that, I would suggest that the impulse to carve was that of the magician. I believe that the divinations were not simply forecasting devices, but that they existed on the narrow borderland between prophecy and magic, between hypothesis, fore-knowledge, and knowledge.②

In this view, the charges represent spells applied to future events. The act of divination not only forecast the future, it also helped, in some magical way, to induce it. If this is a true hypothesis—and the traditional Chinese attitude towards the Yi-ching, which has regarded the hexagrams not just as symbols, but as "causative factors behind natural phenomena" (SACC, vol. 2, p. 336, note b) is congruent with such a view—then the oracle-bone inscriptions may have been incised in order to "congeal" the future they had forecast, in order to ensure that it did indeed happen. The very form of the crack itself, suggesting a divergence and definition of two alternate roads into the future, implies not only that the two "roads" were established by the paired sentences of the charge, but also that, by analogical magic, the formation of the crack somehow defined and induced the future course of events. The crack was a symbolic representation of the future, which had to be read. But it was, at the same time, the future itself. And if this were true of the crack, it would also have been true of the charge. The logographic script, with its tendency to reify at least certain concepts, would presumably have encouraged the development of this magical tendency; to incise the word for "man," for instance, was indeed to incise, symbolically, the man himself.

It is harder to explain the engraving of the inscriptions if they were interroga-

---

① "The Book of Changes," Bulletin of the Museum of Far Eastern Antiquities, 5(1933), 136.
② "It may very well be that not only did the seeking of oracles help to incorporate the supernatural into the everyday, but that the writing itself was imbued with magical properties" (Judith M. Treistman, The Prehistory of China (Garden City, N.Y., 1972), p.108).

tive.① A question is not a spell. Engraving a question gives no power to influence the future. Nobody carves "Was Kilroy here?" Carving implies assertion: "Kilroy was here!" And the affirmation continues to mark, to scar, the future, telling later generations not only that Kilroy was indeed here, but, in a sense, that he still is. The engracing of the oracle inscriptions had the same intent: to impress the forecast events upon the future by scarring it, and doing so, in the case of the sets, not once but many times. The full divination process then, from the mental "charge" to the eventual engraving of the written "charge"(which was, as we have seen(p. 28) no longer simply a "charge" but also an "answer") was not simply quizzical. It was an affirmative, incisive, attempt to establish magical guarantees, or at least magical links, in an attempt to regulate the future.②

B. The Negating Forecasts

The hypothesis that incising the inscriptions gave magical power to the divination forecasts faces the obvious difficulty that approximately half the divinations, expressed as they were in terms of positive and negative alternatives, were undesirable, or at least negative and thus negating, forecasts. Thus:

[35] 戊午卜㞢貞般往來亡囚

貞般往來其出囚　　　　　　　　(Ping-pien, No. 130(1)(2))

CRACK-MAKING ON THE DAY WU-WU, (THE DIVINER) 㞢 REGULATING:

"PAN, GOING AND COMING, WILL HAVE NO DISASTERS."

---

① "Why [the Shang] wrote down any of the questions, and how they selected those which were to be written, is a mystery... One can hardly conceive of a less momentous question than 'Will it rain tonight?' yet we find this question, carved with the expenditure of no little labour, time and again"(H. G. Creel, The Birth of China (New York, 1937), p.193). If this is a charge, "IT WILL RAIN TONIGHT," and If the charge has magical efficacy to actually make it rain, then Creel's question would seem to be answered. The oracle-bone inscriptions were not simply requests for information about the future. They affected it.

② The occasional smearing of the inscriptions with colored pigments—sometimes with red, the auspicious color, the color of life(?)—may have been a further magical attempt to render the charges more potent.

REGULATING: "PAN, GOING AND COMING, WILL HAVE DISASTERS."

Sentence number 2, by the very fact that it is incised into the bone, would, according to my hypothesis, help make the undesirable(a disaster befalling Pan) occur. My tentative answer to this objection is that in every case where an undesirable outcome is one part of the charge-pair, that undesirability is countered by the notation of "auspicious" written by one or more of the related cracks. Thus, in the case of divination, [35] shang chi 上吉, "extremely auspicious," is noted after crack number five of sentence 1, and after crack number two of sentence 2. According to this explanation, the shang-chi 上吉 need not necessarily be attached to the inauspicious forecast; it may instead be attached to the auspicious forecast, the other sentence of the pair(e.g. attached to Ping-pien, no.5(5), rather than to 5(6)), but it will occur within the full set. There are many instances in which this hypothesis cannot be verified, precisely because in these cases we do not have the complete set of cracks. ① When the complete set is available, ② and even in many cases when it is not, ③ any undesirable magic generated by the negative half of the inscription pair is countered by the "auspicious" notation, also incised, that, as it were, renders the net effect of the divination auspicious. (I have so far found only one exception to this theory—Ping-pien, no.496(3)(4)—and it is possible that an "auspicious" notation might have been incised on the missing fragment of shell at the lower right corner.) According to this theory, only divinations resulting in auspicious prognostications would have been incised.

C. The Inauspicious Forecasts

But there is a further objection to the supposed magical power of the divination forecasts. A small number of the incised inscriptions do indeed register unfa-

---

① E.g. Ping-pien nos. 165(17); 104(3); 110(5); 358; 209; 88; 452; 407(11); 124; 269, etc.
② E.g. Ping-pien, nos. 345(2)(4); 293(5); 5; 8(2); 10(2); 326(4)(6); 332(1)(2)(7)(8); 172(7); 338, etc.
③ Ping-pien, nos. 1(19); 3(11); 51(8); 502(11); 454(3); 332(3),(4); 332(17); 269; 442(1)(2); 76(8); 291; 370; 411(1)(3).

vorable prognostications. These are all variants of the general form, wang chan yüeh pu chi 王固曰不吉 (IKBS, pp. 308.1-308.2), "The king read the cracks and said, 'Inauspicious'." A few examples will illustrate the problem.

1. Inauspicious Forecasts (non-specific).

First, there are inauspicious forecasts of a non-specific nature. For example:

[36] 癸巳卜㱿貞旬亡㕚.王固曰㞢希,其㞢來艱.

三至五日.丁酉允.㞢來㛷自西.沚𢦏告土方正(＝征)

于我東鄙戋二邑.呂方亦侵我西鄙田   (Ching-hua, No.2)

CRACK-MAKING ON THE DAY KUEI-SSU, (THE DIVINER) K'O REGULATING: "IN THE NEXT TEN DAYS THERE WILL BE DISASTERS." THE KING READ THE CRACKS AND SAID: "THERE WILL BE HARM. THERE WILL COME MIS-FORTUNES IN 3 TO 5 DAYS." ON THE DAY TING-YU, [FOUR DAYS LATER], THERE REALLY DID COME TROUBLES FROM THE WEST. 沚𢦏 REPORTED THAT THE T'U-FANG ATTACKED IN OUR EASTERN BORDER AND (CUT-DOWN =) DESTROYED TWO SETTLEMENTS. THE KUNG-FANG ALSO PASTURED THEIR CATTLE IN THE FIELDS OF OUR WESTERN BORDER.

In such cases, the verification (The T'u-fang attacked... the Kung-fang pastured...) serves to define the non-specific prognostication (there will be harm).

2. Inauspicious Forecasts (specific, but qualified)

In other cases, however, the inauspicious prognostication is specific, but in need of qualification:

[37] [己]丑卜𡧊貞羽乙[未]酒黍于祖乙□(王)固曰

㞢希□(不)其雨六日[甲]午夕月㞢食乙未酒

多古率條遣(?)   (Ping-pien, No.57(1))

CRACK MAKING ON THE DAY CHI-CH'OU, (THE DIVINER) PIN REGULATING: "ON THE NEXT YI-WEI DAY WE WILL OFFER WINE AND MILLET TO ANCESTOR YI..." THE KING READ THE CRACKS AND SAID: "THERE WILL BE HARM... IT WILL NOT RAIN." ON THE SIXTH DAY, CHIA-WU, IN THE EVENING, THE

MOON WAS ECLIPSED. ON THE DAY YI-WEI WE OFFERED WINE. THE TO-KUNG...①

[38] 丙申卜殼貞來乙巳酒下乙．王固曰酒隹出希．

其出酸乙巳酒明雨伐既雨咸伐亦雨．

改卯鳥星 (Ping-pien, No. 207(3))

CRACK MAKING ON THE DAY PING-SHEN, (THE DIVINER) K'O REGULATING: "ON THE COMING YI-SSU DAY WE WILL OFFER WINE TO HSIA-YI." THE KING READ THE CRACKS AND SAID: "WE WILL OFFER WINE. THERE WILL BE HARM. THERE WILL BE THE BREAKING OF THE WINE VESSEL(?)." ON THE DAY YI SSU WE OFFERED WINE. AT DAYBREAK IT RAINED. AT THE DECAPITATION SACRIFICE IT HAD RAINED. AT THE DECAPITATION SACRIFICE TO HSIEN IT ALSO RAINED. WE CLUBBED TO DEATH AND DISMEMBERED A SNAKE IN OFFERING TO THE BIRD STAR.②

It should be noticed that in these two cases the prognostication was inauspicious (it will not rain... breaking of the wine vessel...) but the misfortune that actually did follow (an eclipse... rain...) was not the precise misfortune that had been forecast. A similar discrepancy between the prognostication and inauspicious result also appears in a typical child-bearing divination:

[39] 甲申卜殼貞（婦）好娩㚰王固曰其隹丁娩㚰

其隹庚娩弘吉三旬出一日甲寅娩

不㚰隹女 (Ping-pien, No. 247(1))

CRACK MAKING ON THE DAY CHIA-SHEN, (THE DIVINER) K'O REGULATING: "FU HAO'S CHILD-BEARING WILL BE GOOD." THE KING READ THE CRACKS AND SAID: "IF IT IS A TING-DAY CHILD-BEARING, IT WILL BE GOOD. IF IT IS A KENG-DAY CHILD-BEARING IT WILL BE EXTREMELY AUSPICIOUS." ON THE 31ST DAY, CHIA-YIN, SHE GAVE BIRTH. IT WAS NOT GOOD. IT WAS A GIRL.

---

① I can offer no certain translation for the last three characters.
② Following the translation of DKDS, no. 14.28.

And a divination about the same event:

[40] 王固曰其隹丁娩妿,其庚弘吉

其隹壬戌不吉 (Ping-pien, No. 248(7))

THE KIND READ THE CRACKS AND SAID: "IF IT IS A TING-DAY CHILD BEARING IT WILL BE GOOD. IF IT IS A KENG-DAY IT WILL BE EXTREMELY AUSPICIOUS. IF IT IS A JEN-HSÜ DAY, IT WILL BE INAUSPICIOUS."

In these cases, we have a series of specific forecasts, which were not fulfilled by the event (the baby came on one of the days not specified by the king), but in which the "non-good" event (the birth of a girl) did not contradict the auspicious prognostications; rather, it failed to satisfy the specific contingencies established by the prognostication.

By contrast with these cases in which a forecast (either inauspicious, or qualifiedly auspicious) is proven at least partly right by the event, I know of no forecasts (auspicious or inauspicious) of which it is recorded that they were proven wrong by the event. That is, forecasts of the form, (prognostication:) "Auspicious. It will not rain on XY day", (verification:) "It did rain on XY day", or of the form, (prognostication:) "Inauspicious. It will rain on XY day", (verification:) "It did not rain on XY day," do not appear. It seems that auspicions prognostications were recorded only when confirmed (or at least not invalidated, as in divinations [39] and [40]) by the event; and inauspicious prognostications were recorded only when an inauspicious, validating, verification could also be recorded.

This hypothesis thus suggests that inauspicious forecasts which, to a greater or lesser degree, were proven correct, were engraved; inauspicious forecasts which proved in error, were rejected, not simply because they had been inauspicious, but because they had been both inauspicious and inefficacious. Such an explanation might explain why some 90% of the oracle-bone fragments found at Hsiao-t'un had been cracked but had no writing on them; these were perhaps the givers of inauspicious and inefficacious forecasts of which no further record needed to be made.

There may be a middle group of divinations consisting of inauspicious prognostications, but with no verification or crack notation given, and whose rationale cannot be interpreted with certainty.① If this is the case, I would suggest that these prognostication were engraved because they had indeed proved correct; and the very fact that they were correct is indicated by the fact that they were engraved. No further notation or verification was needed(just as no further prognostication was needed for the bulk of the divinations themselves in which the "question," i.e. charge, was the "answer").

D. Avoidance of the Undesirable

It should also be noted that the oracle-bone inscriptions generally prefer to view and record the world in auspicious terms. References to disaster are usually couched in the negative, "defusing," way. Thus, all phrases containing the word tsai 災 are in the negative form wang tsai 亡災, "no disaster"(IKBS, pp. 184.3-185.4).② The phrase, wang chan pu chi 王固不吉 does not appear as frequently as wang chen chi(IKBS, pp.308.1-308.2). Shang chi 上吉 appears more frequently than hsiao chi 小吉.③ Cracks are marked shang-chi, chi, hsiao-chi, but never, so far as I know, pu chi 不吉. In a similar vein, it has been remarked that "there are more oracle characters standing for pleasures than those standing for pains."④ It is usually the negative sentence of a pair that is abbreviated, or has its prefatory formula omitted(PTTC, pp.127, 60), suggesting perhaps that, despite the balance of the pair, there was some intent to render the negative charge shorter and thus weaker than the full, positive charge. There is nothing surprising about this. We all, like the Shang, wish to hear good fortune foretold; we all, like the Shang, dislike to hear the bad. And there was undoubtedly a reluctance(which we still

---

① As indicated above(pp.51-52) this may be an erroneous view. All full sets of inscriptions may indeed have been classified "auspicious," etc.
② Cf. I-hsiung Ju, "The Ancient Chinese Metaphysical Characters Through the Oracle Writing," Unitas(Manila), 42.1(March, 1969), pp.94-96.
③ Wu Shih-ch'ang, "On the Marginal Notes Found in Oracle Bone Inscriptions," T'oung Pao, 43(1955), 45.
④ Ju, "Metaphysical," p.98.

share; witness such sayings as "Don't say that, or you'll make it happen," or shuo ts'ao ts'ao ts'ao ts'ao chiu tao 説曹操曹操就到) to introduce unpleasant events into the spectrum of the future.

E. The Metaphysical Balance

This indeed suggests a further solution to the presence of inauspicious alternatives in all the oracle-bone divinations. Each inauspicious charge was "balanced" by its opposite, auspicious, counterpart on the other side of the shell, thus weakening, as it were, its potentiality for harm(and vice versa). The very system of balance suggests the typical Chinese interest in homeostatic stability, in maintaining the status quo, rather than in risk-taking and vigorous change by executive decision. The oracular process of Shang—witness the large number of cracks that might be made for one set of divinations—was nothing if it were not cautious. And indeed, we may be making an error in labelling the pair sentences as auspicious and inauspicious. That is, a forecast of disaster or enemy attack, if valid, might have been distasteful, but by giving warning it served as auspiciously as could be expected under the circumstances. That is, forecasts with inauspicious content were nevertheless, if verified, "auspicious," because valid and useful, indications of the future and of the efficacy of the divination process, and thus worthy of record.

The fact that both sides of a "question"—the good and the bad—were engraved illustrates the balanced dualism of the Chinese world-view even in Shang times. Lucky and unlucky, good and bad, were seen as inextricably entwined, not as contradictory.① Both alternatives were presented for choice because that was the way the world was viewed. There was a fundamental, organic tension, be-

---

① Liu Pai-min 劉百閔 has suggested that a "law of duality" rather than a "law of contradiction" underlay the system of Yi-ching divination. (See Revue bibliographique de sinologie, 6(1960), no. 559.) Similarly, Ch'u Chai and Winberg Chai have found in the Yi-ching the suggestion of "the theory that everything involves its own negation... The universe is composed of pairs of opposites, such as good and evil, right and wrong, subjective and objective, positive and negative... The phenomenon and its negation are necessary parts making up the whole. We cannot have, for instance, a positive without a negative, or vice versa. They are correlatives which involve each other..." (I Ching: Book of Changes, Translated by James Legge, edited with Introduction and Study Guide by Ch'u Chai with Winberg Chai(New Hyde Park, N.Y., 1964), pp. lxxvi, lxxvii.)

tween the possible choices facing man. Only by facing both possibilities, by giving each possibility, as it were, a fair chance to make its mark on the future, could the divination itself be fair, in accord with reality, and thus valid. The engraving of both alternatives documented the reality and fairness of the divination and thus validated the king's decision-making. For there is a strong documentary impulse here; that is, the inauspicious or negative alternative is still engraved, even though, once the cracks have been read (or once the outcome of the event is known?), it is known to be inapplicable. And that documentary impulse can best be explained, I think, in terms of the need to validate the entire divination process, by making it an accurate, correct, reflection of reality.

The realism of this cautious approach becomes apparent when we consider that the king's magic can hardly have been infallible. It cannot have rained every time that he said it world. The balanced divinations, therefore, provide an explanation for possible failure. The king's magic was not felt to be sufficiently strong, nor was the universe felt to be sufficiently obedient or unambiguous, for unequivocal attempts at regulation to be made. In addition to its magical, regulatory nature, therefore, I would suggest that the divination process also served a ritual function, representing not simply an attempt to regulate the world, but also an attempt to identify with it, which-ever course of action resulted.

If so, the Shang divination process was not simply one of assertion; it was also one of rectification, both of the world and of the self.① The character 閃 may have had the sense of regulating, correcting, the difference between the right, auspicious, forecasts, and the wrong, inauspicious, ones. At the same time, the Shang kings, as they divined, were concerned with correctness, with performing the right sacrifices, to the right ancestors, at the right time, so that the right consequences would result. The emphasis was not so much on diverting the future as it was on establishing and confirming the correct relationships between auspicious and inauspicious possibilities, between men and the spirits, so that properly regulated blessings would ensue. The divinations were a record of what was

---

① For an indication that divination could not be engaged in for selfish or improper ends, see Couvreur, Li ki, vol. 2, p. 6, par. 13. Cf. CLCY, 38.27b.8.

correct. The magic was one of harmonious integration rather than mere causation. Such a hypothesis would certainly be consonant with, for example, the later beliefs of the Yin-yang or Wu-hsing theorists, who sought to control the world by correctly identifying and allying themselves with its metaphysical forces.

F. The Power of Divination

Some evidence can be cited to support the attribution of magical powers to the divinations.① We have already seen(pp.33-37) that the divinations associated with sacrifice may be regarded as prayers, in other words, as statements addressed to the spirits which were expected to have material or spiritual(the distinction was not a sharp one to the Shang) effect. If magic is "essentially an art of doing things"② then prayers are a form of magic.③

A magical interpretation accords particularly well with the "harvest" divinations. For example:

[41] 貞西土受年
　　　貞西土不其受年　　　　　　　　(Ping-pien, No.332(1)(2))

Asking: "Will the western lands receive harvest?"
Asking: "Will the western lands not receive harvest?"

Two shang-chi 上吉 notations by cracks 4 and 5 of the negative question suggest that the response read in the cracks was favorable, and that the answer was presumably: "the western lands will receive harvest." But, what had been accomplished by this? The anxieties of the Shang king might have been assuaged; the inhabitants of the western lands could be told that the king had enquired and that

---

① For a late example in which the power to forecast rain was associated with the power to make it, see Arthur Waley, tr., Monkey(New York, 1958), pp.96-98. Cf. too the fate of Ching Fang (p.3 above) who was executed after correctly forecasting a great flood(Herbert A. Giles, A Chinese Biographical Dictionary(Taipei, 1962), no.398).

② H. Hubert and M. Mauss, "Esquisse d'une Théorie Générale de la Magie," Année Sociologique, 7(1904), 56; cited by SACC, vol.2, p.280.

③ "Primitive forms of Prayer certainly appear often to have form or intent of incantation or spell" (S.G.F. Brandon, Dictionary of Comparative Religion(New York, 1970, p.507).

the answer had been auspicious. But the entire process is remarkably passive when we consider the energy and attention that the Shang elite invested in the divination process.① I would suggest instead, a different translation: [41] REGULATING: "THE WESTERN LANDS WILL RECEIVE HARVEST"; REGULATING: "THE WESTERN LANDS WILL NOT RECEIVE HARVEST," as two magical charges, two statements about the future. The "extremely auspicious" result indicated that the king had, by divining, actually done something magical to make the harvest happen. The fact that the Shang king apparently conducted such "harvest" divinations for all the quarters of his domains, and also for the various tribal-nations who happened to be allies of the Shang (cf. YHPT, pp.313-316, 639), indicates that the king's divining was thought to have more value, more charisma, than a mere enquiry would be likely to possess.

Certain Chou texts suggest that the tortoise-shell was thought to possess decisive (magical) powers. The Shih-ching, Mao no.244, describes how the Chou founders established the capital of Hao:

k'ao pu wei wang 考卜維王
chai shih hao ching 宅是鎬京
wei kuei cheng chin 維龜正之
wu wang ch'eng chih 武王成之

"The one who examined the oracle-cracks was the king; /He took his residence in the Hao capital; /It was the tortoise-shell that regulated it, /King Wu completed it" (Karlgren, Odes, p.199, modified). This suggests that the tortoise oracle was thought to have some regulating (cheng 正) power. Similarly, the Shang-shu, "P'an keng 盤庚," contains the sentences, tiao yu ling ko fei kan wei pu 弔由靈各非敢違卜, "I graciously follow the intelligent and discerning ones, but I dare not disobey the oracle-cracks" (Karlgren, Documents, p.26, par.41, modified). Similarly, in the Tso-chuan, Yen-tzŭ 晏子 is credited with saying wei pu pu hsiang 違卜不祥 "to go against the oracle-cracks is inauspicious" (Legge, p.589, modified;

---

① Consider, for example, Chia-pien, no.3917, which records 26 evening divinations on 26 successive days, with two diviners involved.

Chao 3). The cracks (pu 卜) were apparently thought to have a power that had to be respected. Similarly, the Shang-shu "Shao kao 召誥," records that t'ai pao chao chih yü lo pu chai, chüeh chi te pu tse ching ying 太保朝至于洛卜宅厥既得卜則經營, "the grand guardian in the morning arrived at Lo and made cracks about the site. When he had obtained the cracks, he planned and laid out (the city)" (Karlgren, Documents, p. 48, per. 2, modified). The cracks undoubtedly indicated that a certain site was auspicious; but there is at least the possibility here that the grand guardian could not proceed with the planning until the cracks had been made and obtained.

In conclusion, a study of the form and content of the Shang divinations and the responses to them, together with an appreciation of the attention paid to the crack-making and inscribing process, suggests that they were more than mere requests for information. Shang divination was part of an early Chinese attempt to comprehend, identify, identify with, and thus influence, the spiritual forces that shaped the world.

VII. CONCLUSIONS

A. The New Translation Applied to the Chou Texts

Is "regulate" (with its related senses of "define" and "correct") an appropriate translation for cheng 貞 in the Chou texts considered previously (pp. 10-12)? I will consider here only the most puzzling passages.

a) Chou li, "T'ien fu": chi tung ch'en yü yi cheng lai sui chih mei o 季冬陳玉以貞來歲之媺惡 (see pp. 4-5). "At the end of winter, [the t'ien-fu] arranges the jade objects in order to regulate the good or bad of the coming year." This makes sense if one accepts the magical, spell-casting, yüeh-ling 月令-like nature of the ceremony. What the text is saying, I believe, is that the correct disposition of the jade objects will in fact affect, correctly regulate (cf. Biot's "déterminer"), future events. Cheng Hsüan's commentary, wen shih chih cheng yüeh cheng 問事之正曰

貞 should perhaps be translated, "to ask about correctly regulating affairs is called cheng 貞," but he is mistaken in introducing the idea of "ask." In particular, it should be stressed that the t'ien-fu 天府 was not an officer of divination, and that this Chou-li passage makes no mention of tortoise-shell divination. (For Sun Yi-jang's attempt to explain this, see CLCY, 38.27b.12-13.)

b) Tso-chuan, Ai 17: wei hou cheng pu 衛侯貞卜 (see pp. 10-11 above). "The ruler of Wei regulated the crack-making...." This accords well with the context; having been deceived by the milfoil diviner, the ruler wished to ensure that all was correct in the divination by tortoise; therefore he acted as the presiding official responsible for the correctness of the procedures.

c) Kuo-yü, "Wu-yü": ch'ing cheng yü yang pu 請貞於陽卜 (see p. 5 above). "We request to regulate (the matter) by fire-divination...." This too accords with the context; the stress is not on asking questions, but on settling and correcting the issue of who should properly be hegemon.

d) Shang-shu, "Lo kao": wo erh jen kung cheng 我二人共貞 (see pp. 11-12 above). "We two men have both regulated [the divination? the future?]." As already indicated, the context here is ambiguous. It is not possible to establish the correct meaning of cheng 貞 with certainty, though the full passage does appear to stress future time: "When he had fixed the site, he sent a messenger to come; and he has come to show me the grace and constant auspiciousness of the oracles. We two men have both regulated [the future]. May the prince with me for myriads and ten myriads of years reverence Heaven's grace." (Karlgren, Documents, pp. 51-52, modified).

It would seem, in short, that "regulate" is an appropriate translation for cheng 貞 in the Chou texts about divination; as in the oracle-bone inscriptions of Shang,① its use

---

① If cheng 貞 has no interrogative sense, we may also retranslate, with no inappropriateness, the oracle-bone inscriptions given in the first paragraph of this paper: "The spirit of Grandfather Hsin is injuring me" (if the inscription cited by Creel is Ch'ien-pien, 1.11.5, 貞祖辛𡆥我, "cuase" is probably a better translation than 'injure' for 𡆥); "The Governor General will not get as far as the Cha-region" (Chia-pien, no. 807(1); SASA, p. 315, gives a somewhat different translation); "We are sprinkling the altar with the blood of the Ch'iang who were brought in" (Chia-pien, no. 59). In each case, the auspiciousness of the charge was to be read in the cracks.

raises no insurmountable problems. And it should be remembered, that in at least one case, Cheng Hsüan believed that cheng kuei 貞龜 indeed meant cheng kuei 正龜 (see p. 7 above) and that Tu Yü thought cheng pu 貞卜 meant cheng pu 正卜 (p. 10 above).

B. The Disappearance of Oracular Cheng 貞

Why did oracular pu 卜 survive as the verb in Chou divination contexts? Why did cheng 貞, which is as ubiquitous as pu in the oracle-bone inscriptions, virtually disappear? Presumably, the cheng involved some aspect of Shang divination practice that the Chou did not use. Perhaps the Chou stress on ethical correctness, rather than mere ritual correctness, meant that divination was no longer hedged around with so many regulations and restrictions. Chou plastromancy, as we can discern it in the Tso-chuan and Chou-li seems not to have involved the frequent repetion of crack-making, or the use of sets of charges, that was integral to Shang plastromancy, and which, we have suggested, was one of the features which needed regulation (see p. 42 above). Similarly, Chou plastromancy did not involve the writing or incising of a record into the shell, a shang practice that had apparently been forgotten; as a result, the need for careful regulation between charge, crack, and written record, would have been absent. It my be suggested as a hypothesis then, that the simpler plastromancy of Chou was concerned only with making and reading the crack—hence the use of pu 卜 as the verb. The need for complex bureaucratic, ritual, or magical correctness, that was integral to Shang plastromancy, had disappeared; hence the verb cheng 貞 was no longer used. It is significant that the only appearance of oracular cheng 貞 in the Tso-chuan (Ai 17) concerns a case where the ruler had reason to be concerned about the correctness of the procedure, about the proper relationship between charge, crack, and prognostication (see pp. 10-11, 61, above). And it is significant too, perhaps, that the ta cheng 大貞 ceremony, which involved crack-making (see p. 6 above) appeared only in the Chou-li, a text concerned primarily with correct ritual procedures.

C. The Hypothesis Reconsidered

The error of the Shuo-wen definition, cheng pu wen yeh 貞卜問也, may lie not simply in Hsü Shen's definition, but also in the literalness with which scholars have taken it. Hsü Shen knew that <u>cheng</u> 貞 was in some way linked to divination, and he associated divination with the asking of questions. In a loose sense, he was correct; divination, to the extent that it implies a quest for certainty about future events, does involve a questioning, an enquiry. My main concern in this paper has been to show, not that Shang divination did not involve a querying of the future (the sentence pairs of the A-not-A form did generate questions), but that Shang divination charges, considered singly, were not couched in interrogative terms. Thus, if there was an initial question in the king's mind, such as "Should I attack the T'u-fang?," it was presented to the shell, not as a question, but broken down into two discrete alternatives: "I will attack the T'u-fang" and "I will not attack the T'u-fang."

We must be wary about imposing our own grammatical categories upon the Shang language. It may well be that in making affirmative statements about the future, the Shang diviners saw no distinction between the indicative and the interrogative.① To raise what is to us a "question," was to them perhaps an act of "prediction." Whatever may be will be, and whatever will be should be. The very fact that the shell and the spirits were being charged to consider the matter at all may have served to combine "Will it rain tomorrow?", "It will rain tomorrow?", and "It <u>will</u> rain tomorrow!" into one pregnant impulse, querying and asserting at the same time. If we must think in terms of "question" and "answer," the written divination should be regarded as an answer, rather than as a question, delineating the course of action to be followed according to whether the response to the divination was auspicious or not. The divination was not so much an enquiry but a consultation, in which symptoms (the charges) were stated, and reactions elicited. But there are mysteries here which we shall possibly never grasp. We cannot say with certainty that the divination charges were not questions. All we can say is that the grammar and content of the oracle-bone inscriptions, considered

---

① Indeed, if we ignore the traditional interpretation of <u>cheng</u> 貞, I can think of no oracle-bone sentence which contains a grammatical question. It may be that the written language had not yet evolved ways for recording questions; hence the A-not-A form of the inscriptions.

with the later uses of cheng 貞 in the classics, gives no reason for thinking that they had to be questions. If by some accident the definitions of Cheng Ssu-nung and Hsü Shen had been lost to us, a completely different interpretation of 貞 might long ago have been provided.

D. Scapulimancy in Other Cultures

It is of some value to test the hypothesis that the divination sentences were not questions, by studying the methods of scapulimancy used in other cultures. For two reasons, however, the evidence is by no means conclusive. First, the Chinese were, so far as I know, the only people who employed writing in conjunction with scapulimancy or plastromancy. There are no divination texts of other cultures which are strictly comparable to the oracle-bone inscriptions, and we are reduced, therefore, to guessing what was in the mind of these scapulimancers of other cultures. Second, reports about scapulimancy elsewhere (like those about scapulimancy in China) have not paid attention to the point at issue; the reports are frequently vague or silent about whether a query or a forecast was involved.

An early Chinese account (ea. A. D. 297) of scapulimancy in Japan records that the Japanese ch'e cho ku erh pu, yi chan chi hsiung, hsien kao so pu, ch'i tz'u ling kuei fa, shih huo ch'e chan ch'ao 輒灼骨而卜以占吉凶先告所卜其辭如令龜法視火坼占兆 "abruptly apply heat to bones and make cracks, in order to read in the cracks good or bad fortune. First they announce the object of divination, using the same manner of speech as in (our) method of charging the tortoise-shell; then they examine the cracks made by the fire and read the crack-omens."[①] This indicates that the subject-matter of the divination was "announced," as in the Chinese method of "charging" the shell (offering further support for the hypothesis that the "charge" was oral; see pp. 37-39 above); no mention is made of questions being asked.

Accounts of scapulimancy in North America are not conclusive. Thus, a

---

① Based on Ryūsaku Tsunoda and L. Carrington Goodrich, Japan in the Chinese Dynastic Histories (South Pasadena, 1951, mimeo.), p. 12, modified. For the Chinese text see San-kuo chih 三國志, Wei-shu 魏書 (K'ai-ming, ed., 1936), Ch. 30, p. 1006.1.

1634 account of scapulimancy among the Algonquian-speaking natives near Quebec reported: "Ils mettent au feu vn certain os plat de Porc épic, puis ils regardent à sa couleur s'ils feront bonne chasses de ces animaux."①② In such a case, no particular "charge" or "question" appears to have been involved; the choice of the purcupine bone itself apparently determined the subject-matter of the divination. Equally inconclusive is a modern account: "I knew a Saluteaux who could foretell the future by heating an animal shoulder blade and reading the cracks." The actual format of the "foretelling" is not detailed.

That the cracking of the bone may have had a magical efficacy for the Shang is supported by the fact that, among certain Indian tribes, the practice of scapulimancy was restricted to persons of certain status:

> The bones used are the rabbit shoulder blade and the grouse breastbone. What burns on the bone, will come; if the shape of an animal burns, luck in hunting it will follow; if the shape of a mādjímanidu (evil spirit) appears, a mādjímanidu will come. Only old folks and fathers of families are allowed to indulge in the practice, children being prohibited from doing so. Once, it is related, some children were burning a shoulder blade while their parents were away, and the figure of a mādjímanidu burned upon the blade, whereupon the mādjímanidu himself put in an appearance; so the children were stopped.③

The magic of scapulimancy, in short, was not to be trifled with. This may perhaps be related to the Li-chi's injunction that the subject of divination by either tortoise-shell or milfoil must be a morally appropriate (yi 義) rather than a selfish one.④

An 11th-century Byzantine account of "barbarian" scapulimancy reports:

---

① cited by John M. Cooper, "Scapulimancy," in Essays in Anthropology, Presented to A. L. Kroeber(1936), p.29.
② Cooper, "Scapulimancy," p.30.
③ Cooper, "Northern Algonkian Scrying and Scapulimancy," in W. Koppers, ed., Festschrift Publication d'hommage offerte au P.W.Schmidt(Vienna, 1928), pp.214-215; cf. his "Scapulimancy," p.32.
④ Couvreur, Li-ki, vol.2, p.6; cf. CLCY, 38.27b.8.

Now those who intend to obtain an oracle, having selected a sheep or lamb of the flock, <u>first put in their minds or even declare with the tongue that which they wish to learn about</u>. Then having sacrificed [not just "killed"] (the animal) they separate the shoulder blade from the whole body as (being) the instrument of oracular response, and having roasted this with charcoal and having stripped off the flesh they then have <u>visible signs of the issue of their questions</u>. But they <u>foretell the future</u> with other members also. Accordingly they put <u>judgment</u> of life and death in the excellence of the sharp projection in the middle of the shoulder blade. And if this is white and pure on either side, then they accept this as <u>a symbol of life</u>; but if it is burned up, they take this as <u>a token of death</u>. In the middle part of the shoulder blade they put <u>judgments</u> of calamities from the air. For if in the middle of the shoulder blade the two thin plates on both parts of the sharp projection should appear white and pure, they <u>foretell</u> a peaceful condition for the air; but if they are spotted, they <u>prophesy</u> the opposite. <u>If anyone asks about war</u>, if in the right part of the shoulder blade a red cloud-like spot should appear or in the other part a long and dark line, give response that there will be a great war. But if you should see both parts white according to nature, declare as the oracle that there is to be peace. And in brief <u>in all questions</u>, what is rather red and dark and burned up is connected with the more unfavorable issue of events, while the opposite of this is connected with the more favorable issue.①

That they "declare with the tongue that which they wish to learn about," and that they "foretell the future" suggests that the mode of divination was not necessarily interrogative; but on the other hand, there is reference to "questions," though how precisely any of these terms are to be taken is not clear. The subject-matter seems to have been established partly by the declaration (ie. the charge), and partly by the area of bone being scrutinized. "If anyone asks about war..." suggests that questions may have been asked. But the phrase is ambiguous; it may

---

① Michael Psellus, cited by Cooper, "Scapulimancy," p. 34; italics added.

indeed refer simply to a "declaration" in which the diviner said, "We are divining about war."

The extent to which such examples from other cultures may bear upon Shang divination is uncertain. The "barbarian" divination referred to in the Byzantine account did involve pyro-scapulimancy, but no cracks were formed by the heat. And among the North American Indians who practiced scapulimancy, interpretation was "by the location or shape more of burned spots than of cracks or fissures, thus contrasting with the uniform Asiatic method of interpretation by cracks."① In these cases, the method of divination was by no means identical with that of Shang. At most, these examples suggest that the hypothesis presented in this paper is possibly correct.

It may do no harm to close with a commonplace Western version of "scapulimancy"—wish-bone pulling. One makes a wish. One does not ask a question. The bone cracks, and one knows whether or not the wish will be granted. Such wishing may be in the tradition of the optative charges (containing shang 尚, see pp. 14, 16 above) of early China.

E. Summary

It may be helpful at this point to summarize the evidence presented in this essay:

1) The Shuo-wen definition is firmly supported by no classical usage; it rests upon interpretations, sometimes forced, of passages, frequently ambiguous, in the Chou texts (pp. 4-8).

2) Han and Chin commentators either ignored, or seriously modified, the Shuo-wen definition, preferring instead of "question," the sense of "regulate/rectify" (cheng 正) or "fix" (ting 定) (pp. 9-11).

3) The operative verb for tortoise-shell divination in Chou texts is always pu 卜, not cheng 貞; pu itself has no interrogative sense and on occasion clearly has a predictive sense (pp. 13-15).

4) Chou texts indicate that the divination involved an order or charge (ming

---

① Cooper, "Scapulimancy," p. 32.

命) to the shell; an order is not a question(pp. 15-17).

5) Some divinations in the Tso-chuan were optative, expressing wishes about the future; they were not questions(pp. 14, 16).

6) To read the oracle-bone inscriptions as questions raises certain difficulties of interpretation; these difficulties are solved if we regard the oracle-bone inscriptions as declarative charges of intent and forecast(pp. 18-39).

7) The grammar of the oracle-bone inscriptions contains no indications that these were interrogative sentences(pp. 28-33). The phrasing of the sample divinations in Shih-chi, chapt. 128, is likewise not interrogative(pp. 32-33).

8) Certain "prayer" divinations are better regarded as declarative descriptions of actual sacrifices, not as questions about the future desirability of performing the sacrifices(pp. 33-37).

9) The graphic, semantic, and phonological evidence suggests that 貞 belonged to a word-family whose basic meaning was "regulate, correct, stabilize," a word-family which contains no idea of interrogation(pp. 1-4, 40-41).

10) It is suggested that 貞 in the oracle-bone formula referred to "regulating" the technical and ritual aspects of the divination, and possibly to "regulating," or getting in correct relationship with, the future(pp. 41-47).

11) An analysis of scapulimancy in other cultures offers some support, but not decisively, for this new view(pp. 64-67).

Much of the argument, as noted earlier, depends upon the application of Ockham's razor. The assumption has been that the simpler, more "rational" explanations offered by this hypothesis are to be preferred. There is no reason to believe that Shang divination was "simple" or that its "rationality" was ours. Nevertheless, the consistency of the indications, which either suggest, or permit the suggestion, that the inscription sentences were not questions, together with the fact that this conclusion accords well with what appears to have been the rationale of Shang and Chou sacrifice and divination, suggests that the method and the hypothesis are valid.

In conclusion, it should be remarked that the hypothesis accords well with the limitations of scapulimantic enquiry itself. Faced with a direct question, such as

"What should I do?" or "Whom should I ally with?" the cracks, by their very nature, would have been dumb. They had no voice of their own, could formulate no answers of their own. They could offer responses only when the possible "answers" had already been proposed to them: "I will do this," "I will ally with so-and-so"(e.g. the set of questions starting with Ping-pien, no. 12). No seer or medium gave the king fresh insights into the situation. Even at this early date, Chinese divination was relatively impersonal(there being no human, ecstatic, intermediary) and also relatively humanistic(in that the charges offered were always the king's, never the spirits').

The hypothesis also accords well with the character of Chinese civilisation in general, which has been noted less for its interest in asking question, more for its qualities of self-confidence and conviction. Questions, when they appear in early documents such as the Shang-shu, for instance, are almost always rhetorical; the answer is known before the question is asked. Similarly, in art, the "supreme confidence" of the Shang bronze-masters has been remarked upon.① It is hard to believe that the Shang kings—the ancestors of the confident Chinese culture of later times, and the sponsors of this assertive, declarative bronze style—were querelous men, continually asking if they would receive assistance from the spirits or not, if they should go hunting or not, etc. The Shang kings sought to bring their own plans into accord with the wishes of the spirits, but they did so by informing the spirits, by "charges," what it was they proposed to do. They were not, as a true questioner does, simply seeking information. They were, as one who gives orders does, seeking approval and response.

I believe that the hypothesis presented in this essay, which says in essence that oracular cheng 貞 should be read as cheng 正, would have been acceptable to Chia Yi, Chia K'uei, Cheng Hsüan, Wang Pi, Liu Hsi, Chang Yi, Wei Chao, Tu Yü, Ko Hung, and K'ung Ying-ta(see. pp. 4-13 above). It is worth stressing that there is nothing particularly heterodox about the hypothesis here advanced. Its originality lies primarily in suggesting that oracle-bone scholars, rather than fol-

---

① Peter C. Swann, Chinese Monumental Art(New York, 1963), p.37.

low, as they have for the last sixty-odd years, the erroneous indications given by Cheng Ssu-nung and Hsü Shen, return to the fold of orthodox commentary and dictionary tradition. In which tradition, if I may end with a pun, cheng pu wen yeh 貞卜問也.

美國加利福尼亞蒙特雷太平洋沿岸亞洲研究學會會議論文（Asian Studies on the Pacific Coast Conference, Monterey, Colifornia, June），1972 年。

曾毅公

論甲骨綴合

一　甲骨的性質

在中國古代的奴隸社會商王朝的後期，從盤庚時，自奄——現在的山東省曲阜縣一帶——遷到殷，就是現在的河南省安陽市西北五華里的洹河南岸小屯村北一帶，建立了都邑，商人在這裡統治着各個部族的統治者侯伯和人民，以及奴隸。因爲這裡是商王朝的統治中心，朝廷、宗廟、政治、經濟等等，都掌握在商王朝手裡，他們自稱這裡是"大邑商"或"天邑商"。他們在這裡統治了273年，被周王朝毀滅了。因爲部族之間的敵愾關係，所以周部族的統治者，稱商部族爲"殷"，爲"戎殷"（"殷"和"衣"、"夷"的聲音相近，古書上叙述商人爲"衣"爲"殷"爲"戎衣"），商人的後裔宋，自己稱他們先人或自稱還是商。這商人的故都，被周部族毀滅後，已成爲廢墟，所以在秦漢之際，洹河、小屯一帶，稱爲"殷墟"。這和商的先人曾建都在河南商丘，中國歷代稱那裡叫"商丘"，是一個意思。

在中國歷史上，從宋代一直到清代末年，殷墟就是出古器物的一個有名的地方。尤其在清代同治中，在農田裡，常有半化石的龜甲、獸骨出現，這些半化石，被農民們當作止血的"刀創藥"和中草藥的"龍骨"和"敗龜版"。數十年間，農民在農閒時間，挖掘"龍骨"等作爲副業，大部分成批的論斤發賣給藥材商，零星的磨粉爲"刀尖藥"。到1899年，才爲古器物學家王懿榮在北京藥店所發現，經過研究，認爲是與青銅器上的銘文文字有同等價值，經過古董商人大力收購，逐漸爲學者所注意。可惜在1900年秋，帝國主義者八國聯軍侵陷北京時，王殉了國難。1903年，另一位古文字學、古器物學的學者、《老殘游記》的作者

劉鶚，受羅振玉的鼓舞，出版了第一部龜甲獸骨文字拓本《鐵雲藏龜》，興起了甲骨文字的研究。龜甲獸骨文字經過七十多年的研究和新的發現發掘；甲骨學從"金石學"的附庸，已成爲專門的科學，是探索古代史奴隸社會商王朝歷史、政治、經濟、文化、藝術等等學術上的第一手寶貴資料。

說到龜甲獸骨文字，是把文字刻（少數是用毛筆寫的）在那時占卜所用的龜甲和牛肩胛骨上，因爲那時的人很迷信，尤其是統治者的王朝，凡是有所行動，都要用占卜來決定他的趨向。占卜有專門的人才，大概就是"巫"吧，後來在周王朝叫作"太卜"。把占卜時所要詢問的事，記錄在占卜所出現的"兆"紋旁邊，就是卜辭。

我們從這些"卜辭"中，探索那時的社會上的政治經濟、意識、文化等面貌。因爲卜辭經過"巫"者的占卜，和記錄者的記錄，我們想這記錄者，也就是王朝的"史"官，周王朝叫作"太史"。

從現存的青銅器銘文、陶器、玉器、石器、文字和甲骨卜辭等等看，知道商王朝那時文字的應用，已很普遍。甲骨、青銅、陶、玉、石等的文字，雖然爲數很多，統計單字約在四千六百字左右，但是記事文辭却很簡短，周王朝的歷史書現在還保存著的《尚書》上說，祇有殷代的先人是有文書典册的（《尚書·多士》："惟殷先人，有典有册。"），所以我們想，在商王朝，記載朝廷史事的鴻篇鉅作的長文典册是會有的，祇不過現在還沒有發現罷了。再從甲骨卜辭上的"再册"、"祝册"、"工典"等文，也不難推想這種長文典册是會存在的。我們再看殷墟出土的遺物，如陶、石、玉等器物和甲骨上，也有用毛筆書寫的文字，這也可以證明用毛筆書寫在竹木上的簡册在商王朝也曾經使用了。1945年4月，前中央研究院在洹河北岸侯家莊南地發掘，獲得一整叠大龜（著錄在《殷虛文字甲編》3913—3919號），前六版是龜腹甲，後一版是背甲大半，我們看出土時叠壓情狀的照片，縱觀就呈現出 ⊞ 形樣子。1971年12月，考古研究所的安陽工作隊在小屯村西約160多米，此去洹河約600多米的一處殷代南北向的大溝內，發現一堆完整牛胛骨，計21枚卜骨，重叠著堆放在一起，井然有序。郭老在他的《安陽新出土的牛胛骨及其刻辭》（《考古》1972年第2期及1972年8月人民出版社版《出土文物二三事》）說："……卜骨或卜龜甲是以三枚爲一組，一次卜用三龜或三骨，卜畢后儲存，在當初想必有帛以裹之，有繩以纏之，有篋以藏之，年代既久，帛朽、繩爛，化爲灰土，便僅剩下了甲與骨。"侯家莊的腹甲六版也是三的倍數，加上一枚背甲，似乎可與骨臼

刻辭的"三屯又一"的數字相合①。

二 甲骨的形態

商代用作貞卜的原料，在安陽小屯出土的貞卜文字，絕大多數是龜的腹甲和少數背甲，肩胛骨絕大多數是牛胛骨。龜的種屬，大概都是中國膠龜 Ocadia sinensis 和地龜（？）Geoclenys（秉志定名爲安陽田龜 Testudo Anyangensis），都是現在尚存的種類（見《中國地質學會會誌》1937年十七卷第一號下美年《河南安陽遺龜》）②。前者僅產於南方，後者很廣泛地產於中國並常有人工培養。前者產生在福建、廣東、廣西、海南和臺灣，商人的足跡，是否能達到這樣遠的南方，是否能輾轉運到現在河南北部？很成疑問。根據竺可楨《中國近五千年來氣候變遷的初步研究》推斷，亞熱帶的膠龜，也可能產於商代人勢力活動的地區，貢獻到商代都城天邑商來，就如商王田獵，也可以在他們的田獵區狩獲到象和虎一樣，雖然在現在黃河流域下游已不生產了象和虎。牛的肩胛骨，用在占卜上的大概都是水牛，因爲水牛的胛骨，要比黃牛大得多。至於商王室作占卜用的，據說也有鹿、馬、猪、羊的，但最多的還是牛胛骨。我們爲給卜用甲骨文字作綴合復原工作，應當熟悉它們的部位和形態。

甲　龜甲

龜殼的解剖，是構成龜殼的上下甲，也就是上面凸起的背甲，和下面較爲平

---

① 卜骨一左一右爲一屯，與腹甲一枚可視爲從中縫分爲左右甲相同，則卜用三龜，骨則需有六。勹字郭老釋包，"知勹爲勹，則刻辭中之若干勹，即言卜骨之包裹，（如爲竹木簡當爲若干册，如爲帛當爲若干卷，以爲骨故言包耳"（見《古代銘刻彙考續編》十頁，七頁引佚 586勹字謂身之繁文）。勹于省吾先生釋屯（《雙劍誃殷契駢枝》）。按《墨子·節用上》："若純三年而字子，生可以二三年（人）矣。"《周易》屯卦："六二，屯如邅如，乘馬班如，匪寇，婚媾。女子貞，不字，十年，乃字。"又《象》曰："屯，剛柔始交而難生。"疑屯與身勹、勹、勹同象身孕姙之形。家鄉謂婦人有孕，俗言"重身"；《毛詩·大明》："大任有身。"傳："身重也。"箋："謂懷孕也。"《廣雅》云："有娠也。"《爾疋》："純'壬'大也。"重即屯。勹作尸，正與勹同，作勹，正與勹同，蓋即勹勹之譌變。郭老謂勹即身之繁文，知勹亦爲"身"字。

② 在《殷虛文字乙編》4330一版大龜甲，伍獻文參考葛萊氏 Gray《大英博物館龜類誌》，證明這大龜和現在產生馬來半島的龜類是同種（《乙編序》）。

正的腹甲。背甲、腹甲之間，即左右的前後足出口處的中間，每一個甲牆相連接，即"甲橋"。鋸解之後，這個"甲橋"聯屬於腹甲，成爲腹甲的雙珥，仰置起來，成爲腹甲的支柱。有的雙珥再加工，把靠近背甲鋸口的邊緣，錯治成較爲整齊的弧形。背甲則從脊甲的正中，平均對鋸爲二，然後把近脊處的凸凹不平的部分，加以錯刮，成爲較平整的半月形。有的較小的背甲，則在近脊處凸凹不平部分，和首尾及邊緣較薄的部分，一并鋸去，成爲一個不很規則的長橢圓的鞋底形，并在中間穿一個圓孔。這是就安陽出土已見到的龜背甲和龜腹甲的原料。再經一段錯平、刮光的工序，然後在背甲和腹甲的反面，加工鑿、鑽，以備貞卜時應用。所謂正面，即表面，爲較爲平滑、細緻，密度較大，接近瓷面的部分；反面則大半多爲粗糙、疏松的海綿狀的組織。

Ⅰ. 背甲

背殼隆凸，周緣較爲光滑。全部背甲可分爲五個部分：一脊甲，二肋甲，三甗甲，四背鱗紋，五背盾紋。

一、脊甲

脊甲又分爲三部分：

子：頸甲　在龜首出口處，在脊甲中是一塊最大的甲，前緣最長，成六角形。

丑：脊甲　在頸甲之次，連續向後排列，一共有八塊。第一脊甲四角形，長大於寬。第二至第八，皆六角形。

寅：尻甲　在第八脊甲之次，也連續向後排列，一共三塊。第一上尻甲，四角形，長大於寬，上窄下寬。第二上尻甲，六角形，寬大於長。尻甲四角形，後緣中向少有凹入，寬大於長。

二、肋甲

左右各八塊，第一肋甲七角形，第二至第八，皆五角形，第八最短。

三、甗甲

左右各十一塊。第一甗甲前緣較薄，厚度向後逐漸增加。第二大致相同，第三的腹面，是"甲橋"的前端。第四、五、六的甗甲，皆四角形，腹面隆起，是"甲橋"的本部。第七甗，是四角形，腹面向後漸薄，它的前部是"甲橋"的後端。第八、九、十皆四角形。第十一爲五角形。第八至十一各甲的邊緣，皆較薄於中部。

四、背鱗紋

脊、肋和甗各甲之間，有齒形紋相互連接，構成各甲的分界綫，我們叫它爲

背鱗紋。

五、背盾紋

在背甲全面各脊、肋、䚡甲之中，分佈着大小不同的淺溝，淺溝構成不同形狀的盾板，總計有 38 個盾紋板：

子：頸板　在頸甲前部邊緣正中，成"U"字形，最小，四角形，長大於寬。

丑：脊板　皆較大，六角形，第二、三、四形體相似，第五似七角形（左右尻甲的盾板，移作䚡盾板計）。

寅：肋板　計左右各四板，形體相似，皆五角形，第二較大於第一、第三，第四最小，每肋板發長，溝紋皆清晰而長。

卯：䚡板　左右各十二板（包括尻甲），皆四角形，大小比較相同，但較脊板、肋板爲小。

Ⅱ. 腹甲

腹甲的中間稍凹，兩旁稍凸。"甲橋"部分（四足出口之中間）仰立，經鋸解錯治後，尚存自背甲延展盾紋四綫的殘存（較小的腹甲則將殘存盾紋與甲橋鱗紋，全部鋸削錯治成半月形的"甲珥"）。全腹甲可分爲八個部分：（1）舌腹甲（首甲）；（2）內腹甲（中甲）；（3）上腹甲（前甲）；（4）下腹甲（後甲）；（5）劍腹甲（尾甲）；（6）甲橋（珥甲）；（7）腹鱗紋；（8）腹盾紋。腹甲在貞卜時，皆不像背甲從中間鋸開，而存原狀。自首甲至尾甲的正中，有一條自生的鱗紋和盾紋所謂"千里路"，把腹甲分爲左右，我們稱這左邊一半爲左首甲、左前甲、左後甲和左尾甲，右邊的也如此。用各部分甲間的鱗紋，來定它們的名稱。

（一）舌腹甲（一般稱首甲）　舌腹甲的前側較厚，後側向上延展，爲"甲橋"的前下端。

（二）內腹甲（一般稱中甲）　近於三角的菱形，寬大於長，在舌腹甲與上腹甲之間中部。

（三）上腹甲（一般稱前甲）　在內腹甲與舌腹甲的下方，以"甲橋"中間的橫縫（鱗紋）爲界，與下腹甲相鄰，其左右爲珥甲的上部。

（四）下腹甲（一般稱後甲）　前側向上延展，爲"甲橋"的下端。

（五）劍腹甲（一般稱尾甲）　居於腹甲的最後，尻部中間突出的分爲兩岐，它前部邊緣的寬度，二倍於後緣。

（六）甲橋　在上下腹甲的兩側，居於前後足出甲口的中間，原與背甲相

連，斜向上延展，成爲腹甲的雙珥。大的腹甲，經鋸解後，祇少加錯治，即留作貞卜備用品；較小的腹甲，祇從向背甲延展的根部，加以錯治，留下小的珥形，使成爲半月弧形的珥甲。

（七）腹鱗紋　在左右首甲、中甲、前後甲、尾甲之間，有齒形紋相連接，我們稱它們爲腹鱗紋。

（八）腹盾板

子、喉盾板　左右喉板最小，楔形，它的尖端，與內腹甲的尖端相接。

丑、腕板　它的淺溝橫行通過中甲及"千里路"，成一直綫，在前足出口處的上端。

寅、胸板　在"甲橋"中間與前後甲鱗紋之上，通過"千里路"，向上微屈的直綫。

卯、腹板　腹板下盾紋在後足出口處的上端，成一微屈綫通過"千里路"的直綫。腹板較大於胸板。

辰、脛板　居於腹板的下盾紋之下，脛板較小於胸板。

巳、臀板　居於腹甲最後端，兩岐形，大於喉板而小於肢板及脛板，下緣突凹，爲尾的出口處。

午、腋板與胅板　在"甲橋"之上下端。大龜腹甲，在貞卜用甲，尚有存留，即"甲橋"上端之窄而長的四板。較小的腹甲，在貞卜用甲則已被鋸去。

乙　牛肩胛骨

肩胛骨有左右之分，左右肩胛骨合起來稱爲一夕①，單獨一個稱爲一骨②或一丿③，它的作用，和背甲從中間鋸爲左右兩半，稱左右背甲，大概是相同。在殷墟出土的肩胛骨，絕大多數是牛的肩胛骨。當然鹿、羊、豬的肩胛骨也間或有之，但我們既不是古生物學家，實在不能分析它們的骨頭確屬何獸，祇能就大體上知道是牛的。

肩胛骨的頂端，有一半月形凹入，即納入"肱骨頭"的盂形部分，我們稱它

---

① 見第916頁注①。
② 林2·30·12"￤示四￤一骨"，即四副零一骨，共計九骨。
③ 林1·18·14"利示三￤又一丿"，丿疑即子禾子釜"關鋘節于廬琲"的琲，秦公簋蓋刻欵的"西一斗七升大半升"的半升，器口刻欵的"西元器一斗七升拳"的拳。今山東曲阜人稱半斗爲"一撇子"，琲是會意字，拳是形聲字，丿是象骨臼的半圓形。今山東曲阜的"撇"正是"八"字一半的撇。

爲"骨臼"。在"骨臼"的一端略下有一個突出的"喙突",我們稱它爲"臼角"(在左肩胛骨的左方,右肩胛骨則在右方)。在背面沿此"喙突",側向下方有隆起,再突起一道壁立的"骨峰",延展至"骨扇"一邊的下端:"喙突"側向下方隆起部分的另一側,即"骨峰"的對面,亦有小隆起,沿着骨背的邊緣向下延展至"骨扇"的另一方的下端,兩個隆起形成一個八字形,"骨峰"我們稱爲"胛岡",其上部下部的分歧處我們稱它爲"胛岡上窩"與"胛岡下窩",骨扇上的"骨峰"與隆起部分,我們統稱爲"骨扇"。"骨峰"一側的邊緣轉薄,隆起一側的邊緣較厚而圓,我們稱這隆起厚而圓的部分爲"邊條"或"骨條"。這個"骨條"至骨肩下部逐漸轉薄,不論面部或背面,它的磁面,質地比較疏松,所以往往從這裡斷折。殷墟商人對卜骨的整治:他們把"喙突"部分,連用"骨臼"的一角,鋸去一部分,成一正角缺口;把"骨峰"連根鋸去削平。並削平"骨臼"下部隆起的部分。

三　甲骨的坑位與綴合

甲　甲骨的坑位

董作賓在他的《甲骨斷代研究例》裡①,把坑位作爲甲骨斷代的十標準之一,但是坑位作爲斷代標準是有其限度的②。李濟在《殷虛文字甲編》裡寫的《跋彥堂自序》裡,談前中央研究院在河南省安陽縣小屯村北地第四次發掘"E"區第十六坑的文物出土情況,對董氏提出他對以坑位來作斷代的意見;之後,陳夢家在《殷虛卜辭綜述》裡也闡述了坑位對斷代的局限性。這些是對甲骨斷代研究進一步的貢獻。但是坑位對甲骨斷代是有其局限性,而對甲骨殘片的綴合和復原,則有其密切性和重要性。人所周知,古文物在地下的埋藏,不論是古人的有意埋藏,或無意的堆積,這些古文物絕大多數是聚集在一起的。經過長久

---

① 見《歷史語言研究所集刊》外集《蔡元培先生六十五歲紀念論文集》,1933年。
② 四十年前殷墟發掘,有"大連坑"、"橫溝"、"縱溝"、"斜溝"及"甲乙丙丁"、"ABCD",又有"北支"、"南斜"等等,這些"坑位"是發掘時人爲的"坑位",而決不是古人建築時所作的所謂圓井、窟窖、"陶復"等等原坑位,並且也不說出坑位限界,所以一個"大連坑"同是在"B"出的文物,可能不是一個坑,我們又如何區別甲骨是一個時期的呢?

時間的埋藏，受到地下濕潮氣和土壤酸化作用而朽敗，受到地層的傾壓，發掘時受到鍬鏟的敲擊，或出土後輾轉運輸的震蕩，都容易使古文物損傷和破碎，尤其是質地脆弱的東西，如龜甲和獸骨。除去古文物當在埋藏或堆積時，無意中遺失在其他地方外，大多是留在原坑中。在古陵墓裡的殉葬品，都是如此。當然甲骨文字，是奴隸社會商王朝的貞卜時的記錄的卜辭，大多是埋藏在圓井或窟窖中，也是這樣。

我們從 1899 年到 1928 年秋季，前中央研究院在殷墟發掘止，安陽小屯村南，迄小屯村東北洹河南岸一帶，盜掘甲骨，村人所謂"挖字骨頭"，成為小屯農民農閑時的副業。我們再從羅振玉訪知甲骨出自安陽小屯村的記載，和逐漸訪知甲骨出土地在村東北"劉家廿畝地"、"朱坤十四畝"、"何家七畝"，以及"村中張學獻家菜園"和"村南大道"等等，再證以《安陽發掘報告》的記載和地圖，大概得到一個比較明確的概念。1930 年的暑假，筆者曾因友人的約請，參加一個暑期講習班，在安陽小住月餘，那時正遇上軍閥內戰，交通斷絕，雖在兵荒馬亂，土匪亂擾的時候，因為處在這動亂的環境裡，也曾請當地友人，携帶著略聆這"洹水南、殷墟上"的遺址，也曾向村人打聽些發掘甲骨的"佚聞佳話"，又從古董販子口中，知道些前中央研究院發掘的情況。並且附帶著在安陽南關龍王廟訪查元代的白話碑，首先發現了碑側的石工題記，使我進一步注意到"和尚"、"也里可溫"、"先生"、"荅失蠻"等宗教傳教士，為什麼能受到統治者那樣的保護和優待。

1928—1937 年，前中央研究院歷史語言研究所，在河南省安陽縣洹河兩岸，作了 15 次科學發掘，雖然出了幾期報告，但都是些零星的、片段的。從發掘開始，二三十年以後，才勉強出版了考古特刊報告之二《小屯》《殷墟文字》甲、乙兩編四册，共輯錄了甲骨拓本一萬三千多片。遺憾的是作為斷代憑證的伴出器物，還沒有有系統的發表出來。至於發掘的坑位、層次等記錄和圖表，也還沒有一個比較詳細的報告。祇有在《甲編》的序言中，簡略地舉出五個區中各一坑，作為董氏甲骨斷代的例證，而語焉不詳，《乙編》序言，附錄了坑位和拓本編號對照表。當我們在做綴合工作時，發現不少"跳坑"以及坑位的重號和缺號，拓本與寫本的不符，甚至有拓本掉換等等現象，便使人疑惑在整理、著錄和編輯時，是否不大認真？一則曰："片甲隻字，涓滴歸公"，再則曰："為了節約篇幅，一些不重要的單辭隻字，不與收錄。""涓滴歸公"，固然表現出董氏的廉介，但是摒棄不少不重要的單辭雙字（甚至無字的碎甲骨），也不是對學術研究上的科學態

度。凡是搞甲骨文字的人，都有這樣的感覺，單辭隻字，更可能是在綴合工作上，有重要的關鍵性。舉一明顯的例子，《殷契拾掇》第二集的作者郭若愚在它的序言中説：“上海市文物管理委員會所藏甲骨……由李亞農先生編輯了《殷契摭佚續編》。……在小孩子的手裡，看到一片甲骨上還有一個半字（本編399C片），忽然覺得這骨版和《摭佚續編》125片是可以拼合的，結果是的確不錯。”

至於無字甲骨，在綴合中也是有意義的，如張秉權在他那《殷虛文字丙編》中用"無號碎甲"及"有登記號"的帶字甲來綴合，因爲他有便利的工作條件。我們祇根據拓本來作綴合，當然有一定的困難了。胡厚宣在滬得自洋莊古董商葉叔重的一批牛骨，當轉手讓與郭若愚時，經郭手綴合的無字牛骨，現藏清華大學，也可以見到黏合的痕跡。

乙　發掘出土甲骨與過去著録材料的綴合

殷墟發掘出土的甲骨，有的可與過去著録中的材料相綴合，例如，第一次安陽試掘，在村北"朱坤十四畝地"內所掘之E9坑所出的牛骨，與已出版的著録甲骨能綴合的，如：

甲 297（寫本 1）＋庫 1661＋金 382

董氏已談到E9坑是個已翻掘多次的熟坑，甲297一片是在翻過的填土內所得，那麼，在1904年以後，經庫方之手，而轉賣到英國博物院和金璋的二片，當然也是出"E9坑"的窖藏之中。

甲 346（寫本 108）＋庫 1569＋前 2·17·7

甲346出于E9坑的擾土中，庫方和羅振玉所得二片，當亦出於E9坑的窖藏之中。

或與不同次發掘出土的材料綴合，如：

甲 310（寫本 10）＋2242

甲310也是出土於E9坑的翻掘的填土中，但第二次村北祇開掘了"T、U、V……"幾個坑，都是在"朱坤的十四畝地"內，那麼這幾片牛骨，都是在挖土中獲得的，可能是一個肩胛骨一版所折。

1929年春第二次在村中發掘所獲肩胛骨，大多在村中張學獻家東牆外場院和南邊田中，如：

甲 712（2·2·296）＋明後 3104（攈 828）—甲 724

我們知道明義士在 1923 年所得一批肩胛骨，都是在張學獻家菜地左右一坑所出，筆者曾在北京與明義士整理修復綴合過。我們再看甲 712 和 724 二殘片，和明後 3104 字體是一樣，文例也相同，並且可以相互綴合。那麼甲編雖沒發表他的坑位，我們從明氏舊藏甲骨和出土地址相對證，可以確定它們是同坑所藏。甲 724 雖不能相接合，也可以知道它們是同時所卜。再從 712 卜次"三"看，可能是一套卜辭，但非同版。

現在我們再試以《甲編》所著錄的拓本，根據已知坑位和已見著錄的試舉幾例於後：

合 331 = 甲 346 + 庫 1569 + 前 2·17·7

合 332 = 甲 387 + 甲 709 + 寫本（甲失錄）195 反

合 333 = 甲 433 + 庫 1134—庫 1009—1121 + 庫 1153

合 5 + 6 = 甲 248 + 甲 254 + 甲 264 + 粹 425

綴 328（佚 986）= 甲 2282 + 佚 256

合 38 = 甲 2442 + 佚 278

甲 2477—錄 174

甲 2738 + 明後（攟 500、胡 408）

合 51（綴 62）= 甲 2799 + 佚 257 + 佚 266

合 52（綴 61）= 甲 2803 + 佚 255

合 354 = 甲 2900 + 錄 180

合 37 = 甲 3004 + 吉 282

合 58 = 甲 3020 + 甲 3014 + 吉 283

丙　發掘出土甲骨與晚近流散材料的綴合

第十三次到第十五次的坑位，算是公開出來了，我們也知道十三、十五次（十四次祇出了二片甲骨），大多是"生坑"，沒經過盜掘，地層多數是沒經過擾亂（如 YH127 坑的甲骨是整個一個幾噸重的甲骨塊），但也有一部分材料流出，這當然是少數，如董氏在《殷契佚存》序言中所說，當第三次殷墟發掘時，前中央研究院和河南民族博物館，因爭掘甲骨發生糾紛時，在"B"區"大連坑"和"E"區附近，河南博物館有一批甲骨被盜（是裝在一隻綠布小箱裡），流落到北京琉璃廠古玩店，被美國人施密士購得，即著錄在《殷契佚存》裡的部分拓本。這一部分拓本中，有的可以和"B"區"大連坑"的"橫十三溝"丙北支一坑所出

綴合，證明它們原是一體：

綴 328 = 合 29 = 甲 2282 + 佚 256（重見佚 986）
綴 61 = 合 52 = 甲 2803 + 佚 255
綴 62 = 合 51 = 甲 2799 + 佚 257 + 佚 256
合 38 = 甲 2442 + 佚存 278
綴 356 = 合 50 = 甲 2775 + 2776

再證以綴 356（合 50）與甲 2442 + 佚存 278，雖不知它們是一坑所出，但皆是出於大連坑是無疑問的。

前中央研究院所流失的甲骨、拓本、照片的情況，恐怕不僅是上述一小箱甲骨。當北京淪陷前後，和北京解放前，也見到了一些甲骨、拓本和照片，有可能是前中央研究院流出來的。如：

（1）在淪陷時期，雙劍誃于省吾先生，用高昂的價格，購到第三次殷墟發掘一大批甲骨拓本，裝成數大册。北京解放後，經陳夢家介紹，把全部雙劍誃藏甲骨拓本，讓與前燕京大學，現藏北大圖書館。

（2）于省吾先生，在華北淪陷時期，也從古玩店中購到三片比較完整的大半龜版和一片牛骨刻辭，三片龜甲收在他的著作《雙劍誃古器物圖錄》卷下 32、33 兩頁上，第一片是腹甲，存在右首甲、中甲和左右腹甲和左右珥甲的上端，第二片是腹甲的後甲、尾甲和珥甲下端一部分，也是刻兆，同於 YH127 所出。1954 年在考古研究所校補《殷虛文字綴合》稿時，發現郭若愚把乙編 4473 一片右珥甲下端，和右後甲及右珥甲下部，4630 一片右珥甲下部和這二半龜綴合，左右珥甲卜辭，正是對貞。北京解放後雙劍誃所藏甲骨，經陳夢家介紹，全部讓與清華大學。

（3）第 3 次殷墟發掘的甲骨照片大部分，在北京解放後，爲歷史博物館資料室所收購，照片原甲骨上有出土時編號。

（4）前師大歷史系教授李泰棻，著有《癡厂藏金》、《癡厂藏契》，《藏金》兩集已出版，大多出於殷墟，《藏契》未出版。勝利後，胡厚宣先生自川飛京，收購甲骨。《癡厂藏契》大部分爲胡所得，時筆者蒙胡先生不棄，以癡厂所藏二整龜見示[①]（即

[①] 這兩塊整龜，大約在北京淪陷前短時期歸癡厂所得，已用漿糊紙條在背面黏上。再經過兩次長途運輸，受到飛機、輪船、大車等轉運時的顛簸震動，整理時已破碎成數十小片。現仍按原形放在匣內，以棉花等物保護，等待修復。

《戰後京津新獲甲骨集》1、2及899，2是反面，因用漿糊紙條黏着，不能施拓，故為摹本），兆紋也經重刻，同於13次YH127坑所出。聞胡先生携回重慶後，將平津戰後新獲甲骨和青銅器，在渝售票展覽一月，所得甲骨歸北京圖書館駐渝辦事處。此批甲骨1900多片，於勝利復員時，回到北京。解放後，筆者曾加以整理（時《殷虛文字甲編》及《乙編》上中二輯，及《戰後平津新獲甲骨集》摹寫本均已出版），發現所謂"四方風名"龜腹甲的首甲①、中甲和上腹甲的一部分（北圖5396）可與乙編4548，4876，5459，4883，4794，5161等片相綴合（《乙編》下輯出版後，又補綴上乙6533），兆紋也是經過重刻的。

（5）北京解放前夕，筆者在工作之暇，訪唐蘭同志於米糧庫寓所，適書賈白某來，持整龜二版求售，索價甚低。時在圍城中，唐頗猶豫，余勸勉收之。白去後，余謂此二版兆經複刻，頗似《乙編》所錄。後唐以此二版，貢獻於國家，並蒙以拓本見惠（《殷虛卜辭綜述》圖版十九，即喆厂藏拓），現藏歷史博物館。

（6）當北京圖書館采訪部移交胡售甲骨於金石組時，又發現一大半龜，珥甲上部，已缺其一，因破碎待修復。1954年《戰後京津新獲甲骨集》（群聯版）收此全拓於1266（又見上海《文物周刊》《大龜七版》）。我以乙5340，5343，5383三殘片和京津1266綴合成一整龜（《殷虛文字丙編》上輯，在62年左右，北京圖書館從香港購到此書，知張秉權亦已綴合）。

（7）1958年北京圖書館，承文化部文物局撥來大批甲骨保管，其中包括善齋（劉體智晦之）、沐園（羅伯昭）、智厂（郭若愚）、天津孟氏（孟廣慧）、南陽徐氏（炳昶）……等家舊藏。其中有布匣三函，為"獻字13738—13740"，計73小殘片，北圖編號為5200—5272。其中5252一殘片，存"曰風"二字，是右上腹甲的一部分，並且尚有一小段盾紋，再從字體比較，似與"四方風名"相同，試以北圖5396一片相較，正可補充"辛亥卜，内貞：禘于北方〔曰〕夷〔風〕曰卻，秦年"兩個殘文，它的盾文也正好銜接，反面的鑿、鑽、灼痕跡，也若合符節，證明它們確係同版。

（8）因受"曰風"殘片的啟示，再詳細審視這三匣73片甲面的紋理、色澤，都是玉黃色，疑它們可能是一批一坑所出，也可能與YH127坑有關。把5237，5251，5232三殘片綴合，從字體和龜甲的部位比較，正可補足乙編4810所缺殘的右上腹甲和右珥甲的一部分，可綴成為一個比較完整的龜腹甲。

---

① 四方風名首甲，因背面無文字，又無修復經驗，當時用石膏在背面作了一個床，但很覺得不理想。

（9）北圖 5238 是左下腹甲接近左珥甲的一殘片，文曰："壬午卜，殻貞：亘弗戈殼？"適與《殷虛文字綴合》272（乙 6848＋6111①）B 片右下腹甲近珥甲一辭"壬午卜，殻貞：亘允其戈殼"爲左右對貞，它上部的鱗紋，也可與 A 片的鱗紋相密接。故知 3238 殘片，也是 YH127 坑遺甲中流出來的。

（10）北圖 5244，5228，5220 和 5230 四片殘甲，綴合爲"甲午卜，亘貞：南土②受年？""甲午囗"，附兆次："一、〔二〕、三、四、五"，與乙編 7970＋8327＋8322 三殘片，再可綴成一個不很完整的龜腹甲。在北圖 5244 的中甲左方的"甲午囗"下所缺殘的卜辭下，又可用乙編中甲中縫（"千里路"）下補足左方對貞的"甲午〔卜，亘〕貞：南土不其受年？"和兆次"四、五"，適成爲左右對貞、兆次相對稱卜年的一組完整卜辭。不過乙編 8322 左邊上的"勿告于父囗"一片殘文，恐怕是乙編編者的誤綴，因爲從龜版本身的尺寸看，是不適合的。這片小龜版可參閱乙編 3287（東土受年）、3409（西土受年）、3952（北土受年）和 8176＋8776 的亞受年。

（11）北圖 5248、5215、5245、5221、5214、5239、5213、5225、5227 共十個小殘片③，可綴成一個比較少有殘缺的完整的腹甲的尾甲。其卜辭爲：

一、囗〔甾〕正〔化戈叙〕？兆辭："上吉"，兆次：一、二、三、四、五、〔六〕、七。

二、"甲辰卜，殻貞：我牵丝玉黄尹，若？"兆辭："上吉"，兆次：〔一、二、三〕、四、〔五〕、六、〔七〕。

三、"貞：我牵丝玉黄尹，弗若？"

這一的卜辭與乙編 7799 的中甲卜辭左右對，可以對照參證，而二、三兩卜辭，可與乙編 7799＋2327 左右上腹甲的二卜辭互相對照，一則是卜人殻於甲午日卜問，王用丝（絲）玉祭禮於咸，一則是卜人殻在甲辰日卜問，我用丝（絲）玉祭祀於黄（衡）尹。這尾甲破碎成十小片後，流落到北京，解放後原藏者捐獻國家，歸到北京圖書館，首甲、中甲和上下腹甲一部分與這十碎片的尾甲，從甾化和絲玉特殊聯繫，可能原是一個整甲。

（12）乙編 2678＋2071＋2591＋6344＋5839 五殘片，綴合起來，是下腹甲、

---

① 編者按："6111"，原文誤作"61111"，今據實際出處徑改。
② 編者按："土"，原文誤作"士"，今徑改。
③ 編者按：原稿如此，僅有九個編號。

珥甲和尾甲的一大部分，祇是下腹甲中縫左右部分殘缺了，這片卜辭，主要是卜問"疾身"的（身體有病）。北圖 5219＋5240＋5247 三殘片，是下腹甲中縫左右的一部分，也是卜"疾身"的卜辭，並且右下腹甲的盾紋，與左珥甲下部殘存的盾紋，遙遙可相銜接，殘存的"兆次"數字，也可左右互補，也當是一甲所折開，使一部分存在北京，一部分流浪臺北。

（13）第十五次 YH251 坑出土的乙 8710，與《思泊藏契》拓本中的一片，可以綴合，李學勤同志曾發表於《帝乙時代的非王卜辭》一文①。因爲第十五次發掘是在 1937 年 3 月 16 日到 6 月 19 日止，這時距離"七七"蘆溝橋日本侵入華北，祇相差半月，殷墟發掘事業，從此停止，中國即轉入抗戰時期。思泊所藏拓本的原甲，聽説原藏已故章草書家羅復堪先生家，此後不知其下落。

跋

李學勤

1950 年至 1951 年，我常去北京圖書館讀甲骨等方面書籍，得以見到當時在館中管理金石圖書的曾毅公先生。

曾毅公先生（1903—1991 年），北京香山人，係滿族。二十年代起，協助加拿大漢學家明義士（James Mellon Menses）整理研究甲骨。三十年代，著有《甲骨叕存》、《甲骨地名通檢》、《殷虚書契續編校記》等書，蜚聲學界。1941 年，太平洋戰爭爆發，他自齊魯大學返京，備歷艱苦。抗戰勝利，1947 年經于省吾先生介紹，任職於北京圖書館。建國後的 1950 年，將《甲骨叕存》增訂爲《甲骨綴合編》，使他成爲早期對甲骨綴合貢獻最多的學者。

1952、1953 兩年，曾先生和我都參加了《殷虚文字綴合》的工作，該書於 1955 年由科學出版社出版。我們還一起編纂過拓本《甲骨文攟》。不過在五十年代中期以後，他的研究重點已轉移到石刻，對於甲骨便不措意了。這幾十年，他在甲骨學領域没有發表過新作。因此，當我聽到他晚年尚有研究甲骨的遺稿時，實在感覺十分驚奇。

原來，曾毅公先生在"文革"期間遭受了大家不難想見的苦難，被送往湖北

---

① 《考古學報》，第 44 頁，1958 年第 1 期。

"五七"干校，1972年因年老體衰，幸得回京。他剛剛鬆下一口氣，竟能不忘學術，重拾故業，在那樣沉重的氛圍中寫出長篇甲骨論文。這種骨氣和精神，難道不是我們應該敬佩和學習的麼？

曾毅公先生在1973年前後撰著的這篇文稿，由國家圖書館善本部保存，我看到的是他的哲嗣曾龍先生給我的複印件。原稿並未完成，已有的幾部份都反覆寫了多次，其間結構、內容均有不小改變。全文沒有篇題，也沒有提綱。承曾龍先生囑加整理，深覺並非易事。

經過再三通讀，我大膽揣測曾毅公先生是要在他一生研究的基礎上，對甲骨綴合作出理論與方法的總結。他在文中先爲一般讀者着想，概述什麼是甲骨，接着作爲綴合工作的準備，又詳細描寫了甲骨的構造及整治過程。文章的後半，專門討論了甲骨出土坑位在綴合中的作用，並舉出許多實例來說明。值得注意的是，他在甲骨形態的敘述上，充分引用了動物解剖的知識；在甲骨綴合的例證裏，特別重視發掘材料同過去著錄及一些晚近流散甲骨的關係，這些皆爲前人所未及，不少綴合也是前未公佈的成果，堪稱對甲骨學的新貢獻。

我所做的，祇是在全篇各段落選取文字最完整、內涵最多的一稿，盡可能把它們連綴起來。對於原有的觀點和語句，除個別必要的地方外，一律不作改動。篇題和幾處小標題是我試加的，後者用斜體字表明。這項工作不知能否不違背曾毅公先生的本意，但我的心願是以此作爲對曾先生的紀念。

2000年4月14日

原載《華學》第4輯，紫禁城出版社，2000年。

Paul L-M. Serruys(司禮義)

STUDIES IN THE LANGUAGE OF THE SHANG ORACLE INSCRIPTIONS

（商代甲骨文中的语言研究）

This collection of notes on some general problems related to the writing and the language(mostly in its grammatical aspects) of the Shang bone and shell inscriptions was begun as a review of the recent work of Chang Tsung-tung, *Der Kult der Shang-Dynastie im Spiegel der Orakelin-schriften* (*Eine paläographische Studie zur Religion im archaischen China*).[1] This is an important work, not only or mostly for its own special topic of research, the Shang religion, but for the study of the Shang bone texts itself. It was felt that the usual kind of review would not suffice to discuss in full the intricate problems involved in this field of research. Therefore these notes are intended as comments regarding any study of Shang oracle inscriptions in general rather than direct criticisms of Chang's book, which merely provided the occasion.

With the growing number of new publications, comprising special topical studies, editions of various bone collections with transcription and discussion of texts, indexes, dictionaries and an increasing number of mono-graphies or studies on individual characters, the factual information contained in or to be derived from these materials has become more and more widely available to historians as well as philologists and linguists. To quote D.V. Keightley(Review of Shima Kunio 島邦男, *Inkyo bokuji sōrui* 殷墟卜辭綜類, Tokyo 1967. Hereafter: Shima, *Index*): "Shang oracle writings need no longer remain the exclusive realm of philologists. I hope that this review by introducing a major new reference work to Western scholars will assist all those, especially the historians interested in earliest Chinese records." (*Monumenta Serica*, xxviii, p. 467) One can only agree with this aim. However, the problems of decipherment, the comparative analysis of the graphs, and the study of the language of these texts still loom as the biggest, the most important, and, in spite of all efforts, still insufficiently solved elements; they are preliminary, even *conditio sine qua non*, for any kind of reliable and sound historical or cultural (including religious) interpretations. Because of this, it still remains a fact that the historians will have to wait for reliable, accurate and justified translations and also the necessary comments from the philologists and linguists to qualify the degrees of certainty or doubtfulness at various levels of translation and interpretation, or they must themselves go through the efforts of doing the spade work, and double as philologists and linguists. While evaluating here Chang's success and contributions toward the solution of these problems connected with textual collation, transcription and translation of the texts, before even dealing with the exposition and interpretation of the facts contained in them, we want merely to clarify and stress some basic methodological requirements in any work of this type. We should mention at least the following separate steps: (1) dating of the bone fragments; (2) transcription of the graphs in original shape and sequence; (3) identification of graphs and their analysis, their possible equation or ancestral connection with later and better known graphic forms in successive periods of Chinese writing; (4) determination of meaning and usage of the graphs in the texts or within certain idiomatic expressions; (5) function of certain graphs in the grammatical system; and, last not least, (6) specific problems of syntax in the language of the Shang texts. Thus, we can see that at each step the student of Shang bone texts has to make decisions and opt for solutions that may seriously affect his translations and, then also, his historical and cultural interpretations. Some of these problems are dealt with by the author in his introductory remarks, but unfortunately in a too general outline.

I. DATING AND PERIODICIZATION

The *dating* and *periodicization* of the oracular bones (discussed pp. 19-29) will necessarily have significance in relation to the selection of the passages used in the discussion of the Shang religion. The author follows the basic, widely accepted division, first established and later refined by Tung Tso-pin. When he differs from Tung's periods, the author proposes some subdivisions in which he mainly follows the theory of Ikeda Suetoshi 池田末利 in his book *Inkyo shokei kōhen shakubun kō* 殷虛書契後編釋文稿 (Hiroshima 1964) (Chang, *op. cit.*, p. 20); yet, he remains at least within Tung's general framework and simply reassigns some inscriptions to different periods; he does not go as far as proposing a new hypothesis such as Kaizuka's, which assumes besides the Royal Court other sources of divination texts, for instance, the Princely Houses and Clan organizations. (cf. Kaizuka Shigeki 貝塚茂樹, *Kyōto daigaku Jimbun kagaku kenkyūjo zō kōkotsu monji* 京都大學人文科學研究所藏甲骨文字, Kyoto 1960.) Tung Tso-pin's theory of two successive schools of divination (conservative-innovative) following each other over the periods is rejected by Chang as a mere *ad hoc* explanation without clarifying whether the explanation is unsatisfactory or whether the fact itself, if admitted, needs no explanation at all.[2] The method of dating and dividing fragments of inscribed bones to certain periods, from Wu Ting 武丁 till Ti Hsin 帝辛 (ca. 210 or 220 years), is presented as a generally accepted procedure, the criteria being: the signatures of the diviners, the names of kings and Shang ancestors, and the complex system of sacrifices. Not mentioned by Chang is a criterion used first by Kaizuka, based on the forms of the chiselled hollows in oracle bones, discussed also by Hsü Chin-hsiung 許進雄 in *The Menzies Collection of Shang Dynasty Oracle Bones*, Vol. I: *A Catalogue*. Toronto 1970. Preface, pp. 3-8. Cf. also Hstü's article 鑽鑿對卜辭斷代的重要性 *Tsuantsao tui pu-ts'u tuan-tai ti chung-yao-hsing* in *Chung-kuo wen-tzu* 中國文字 (abbr. *CKWT*) Vol. 37, 1970. (Taiwan "National" University) and his forthcoming English version, The Importance of Chiselled Hollows in the Periodic Classification of Oracle Bones(*Monumenta Serica*); note also the comments made by Ching Hsiang-heng 金祥恒 and Yen Yi-p'ing 嚴一萍 in *CKWT*, Vol. 44, 1972.

Yet doubts soon must creep in when one observes how many actual pieces can thus be dated with certainty. Two thirds of the pieces have no signatures or diviner's names; then other criteria(kings' names, clan names, language idiomatisms, graphic peculiarities) are applied. But the problems of transcription of names, language, and script features are not that simply settled. Impressed by the complexity and variety in the system of sacrifices, one is also struck by the lack of basic agreement and solid arguments as to what they were and how they were distinguished and starts to wonder about their use as criteria for dating. Most of all, these criteria even taken together afford little solidity for attributing a *small* and *isolated* fragment of sometimes unknown origin to a given period with such offhand certitude and confidence.

II. TRANSCRIPTION OF THE TEXTS

Chang writes the graphs in their original shape, but his transcription is linear, from left to right, so as to fit into the German text, consisting of (1) a word-to-word identification of the meaning of each graph, (2) a translation of the text with commentary. Graphs are analyzed and interpreted in footnotes, in the order in which they appear(a full index of graphs is given at the end). This feature will be welcome to the reader who wishes to be acquainted with this kind of script. Yet a lot is left unsaid, which ought to be said, in order not to leave the tiro with misconceptions about the bone texts. The ideal Shang materials are those bones or shells that have come to us unbroken and with their full context of other shells and pieces. Such conditions are rare and only present to some extent in the materials published by the *Academia Sinica* (Taiwan). If the pieces have come to us as broken fragments, then depending on the knowledge of the origin of the piece and the conditions of the actual finding, the content of the inscriptions, etc., the full set of pieces might be restored with relative certainty. But it is important to realize that only such complete or restored pieces offer us sufficient context to interpret the texts with confidence. Only from the study of a complete set does it become clear in what direction a text is to be read, which sentences are related or parallel to each other, and in what sequence they must be read. As to the direction of reading: some lines go downward all the way till the end of the sentence, sometimes to be resumed again after a number of graphs at the top; some go from left to right or from right to left until the end. Or, in other cases, we have to read in one line horizontally, left to right or right to left. To illustrate this:

```
    I         II          III           IV              V                VI
    1       1   6        5   1       ↓1  4  6        1  3    (1)       7  5    (2)
    2       2   7        6   2        2  5  7        2  4     →        8  6     ←
    3       3   8        7   3        3                                          ↑
    4       4   9        8   4         →             5  7    (2)       3  1    (1)
  ↓ 5       5            9             5  3  1       6  8     →        4  2     ←
                         ←             6  4  2
                                       7             ↓9 11   (3)
                                            ←         10 12   →

         VII                                        VIII
     1  3         1                  1  2  3  4  5  6     6  5  4  3  2  1
     2  4  5  6 . 5  4  3  2            ─────────→           ←─────────
         →         ←
```

Arrows ↳ ↵ ↓ → ← indicate direction of reading the sentences. Each number stands for a graph and at the same time indicates the place it obtains in the sentence.

II and III are supposed to be opposite statements; IV, VII and VIII contain their opposite statements in negative and affirmative form. V and VI show the possibilities of upward and downward sequences in the levels of reading the various portions.

In complete sets, affirmative statements are mostly paralleled by negative ones at the other side or another spot on the same bone or shell. This will indicate the context needed to determine the meaning of the whole message and each sentence that is part of it. By comparing these parallel lines it can be determined in what sequence the different sentences shall be read. This sequence may follow different figurations: downward from *level* to *level* (V), or upward (VI) from left side to right or *vice versa*. In the sequence of related sentences, certain statements are repeated with slight changes, sometimes shortening previously mentioned parts but adding others of a different nature referring to time, place, persons or objects involved, quantity, etc. When no such sufficient context exists, i.e., for pieces so fragmentary as to consist only of three to four actually visible graphs, the reading may become quite problematic, and all solutions are often mere subjective guesswork. Chang does not even mention all these factors in his introduction. Yet, for instance, his text 16.5 is completely different from Kaizuka's (Kyoto Collection No. 3035) from which it is taken.

Chang 16.5　壬午卜帝豕〔犬〕
Kaizuka 1)　壬午卜豕犬.…
　　　　2)　☐乍邑帝☐
　☐ means indefinite number of graphs missing

Scholars with some experience in dealing with Shang bone texts may well know that a certain idiom or formula appears elsewhere; they even may have made a subjective estimate of how frequently it appears in certain contexts, and on this basis they may propose a certain reading and interpretation. As to these reconstructed "mental" contexts and interpretations, we say that indeed such a reading is possible, among maybe other possible combinations depending on other contexts; but what if some day this fragment happens to find its wider context by being fitted into a set with other pieces, as has been done in many cases? Even then, we must point out that this reassembling and fitting of fragmentary pieces into a "successful" puzzle is in itself an adventurous thing. See, for instance, Chang Ping-ch'üan 張秉權 On the Oracle Bone Transcriptions in Sets. 論成套卜辭 *Bulletin of the Institute of History and Philology* (abbrev. *BIHP*) (*Wai-pien* 外編 No. 4, 1960. *Academia Sinica* Studies Presented to Tung Tsopin on his sixty-fifth Birthday, Pt. I, pp. 398-401.) Chang's transcriptions, being always linear from left to right, regardless of the original bone, result in some anomalies and even mistakes. In the original bone certain graphs will appear in mirror-like shapes (e.g., 亡 *wang*: 𠔿 or 𠄐, 亥 *hai*: 𠂌 or 𠂉, etc.) depending on whether they appear on the right or left side of the opposite sentences. In this case we cannot exactly speak of variant graphs. At the same time, it appears that *only* a certain type and a limited number of graphs are *regularly* written in mirror form. In Chang we find *fu-ting* "Father Ting" sometimes written 父丁 sometimes 丁父 in his linear transcription without comment. But worse, where he transcribes in linear fashion what in the original is a *downward* reading text, he has separated the elements of a graph into two different graphs, thus making 洹 into 亘水, understood as "Huan river" for what in reality is 洹 "the Huan(river)". Also 今水 for 汵 or as Ch'ü Wan-li (*Chia pien* 1110) writes 㝬, and 有水 for what is really 㝬 or 洧 (*Yi pien* 1577). All these remarks may seem rather specious, but the detailed discussion of some oracular statements and their translations will show the importance of the interpretation in the light of a full context, either with immediate opposites or with a wider context of other statements in the same bone or shell.

To transcribe the individual graphs is not so simple as what may be described as copying the graphs as they seem to appear on the bones; for any kind of copy is already an interpretation. In each case, Chang had in reality to decide on how to isolate and trace what is essential in the picto-graph and what are mere variables, accidents of particular execution, effects of chipping, and pits or cracks of the bone. It is important to realize in what sequence the strokes are carved and in what direction, because this may show what simplifications or variations are most probable; it may also show the true distinction between mere variants and really different characters.[3] When certain variants have been established, then the work might be started in assigning the variants to different periods or different kinds of texts. Some of these points have been clarified for a few cases, but an immense number of problematic forms remain unsolved.

III. IDENTIFICATION OF CHARACTERS

"Identification" of characters is at best a wide notion: vague, protean, multifaceted, elastic, and elusive. It involves many aspects and levels; the ideal "identification" might be the one that will provide information concerning at least four different aspects at the same time: (1) What does the graphic *concrete* unit of lines or drawing actually represent? For instance, Chang's example (p. 16, note 1): [a man holding an axe *behind* his back]; this element "behind," which is an interpretation, will influence the answer to the next level of questions. (2) What does this graphic representation stand for in terms of language, i.e., the word, which by syntactic position in the sentence may function as noun, verb, adjective, or adverb: [a surprise attack; make a surprise attack; sneaking, surprising; by surprise, etc.][4] (3) What does this graph correspond to in successive periods of the Chinese writing; does it continue to appear in later texts, in basically *unchanged* form, leaving aside details of execution and graphic style, or is this graph replaced by a partially or completely new form (obtained by addition, transformation, combination of different elements, etc.)?[5] (4) Finally, how was it pronounced or, at least, can we pronounce or read it according to its modern equivalent, once we have decided upon the various levels of identification mentioned before? If we cannot propose any reading, then possibly, by approximation, we can find some sort of phonetic hint in the script, or some possible cognates in later characters of which the pronunciation is known. It may seem fanciful or illusory to bring considerations of "sound" into the identification of the Shang graphs. Yet, like it or not, the problem of sound does emerge every time the identification of the bone graphs is discussed. In oblique, hidden ways, sound is resorted to for the identification of meaning and function of certain graphs; it is important that these

implications be made clear. For, in fact, it is basic to the nature of the writing that every graph stands for a *word* and that it does so by either a pictographic or by a phonographic function, or both combined. By facing this problem, we should at least know what solutions cannot be admitted in light of the little we know about the oldest Chinese phonological reconstructions. This could be illustrated with many examples.[6]

These and other related problems involving writing and language are indeed very complex. Chang has dealt with them too cavalierly and in a simplistic fashion (pp. 4-18). True, this is not his main point of focus and research; but it led him to erroneous simplifications, wrong identifications, and unsupported solutions.

After these general observations, we now enter into some problems in more detail, using the selections of bone texts made by Chang and his translations and comments. The remarks that follow will deal with (1) questions of grammar and syntax and (2) explanations and analyses of individual graphs, proposed by Chang in his footnotes.

IV. GRAMMAR AND SYNTAX OF THE BONE INSCRIPTIONS

Well aware of the importance of grammar and syntax, Chang has commendably made a list of grammatical auxiliaries (pp. 324-25); other grammatical notes are scattered throughout the work. In matters of syntax, a serious attempt has been made toward a consistent system in the word order, so as to have a measure of accuracy in reading, parsing, and punctuating the sentences, and hence also in translating. These efforts are clearly seen in the word-for-word account of each separate quote followed by a more readable finished translation. Yet, these principles are gravely (and also silently) contradicted by many specific modes of translation. To demonstrate this, we have chosen to test Chang's grammatical notes on (1) the function of the interrogative particles supposedly found in *wei* 隹 and (?) 叀, *ch'i* 其, *hu* 乎 and *pu* 不; (2) the various negatives *pu* 不, *fu* 弗, (?) 弜, *wu* 勿 and 母, *fei* 非 and *wei* 未.

1. *Interrogative Sentences*

Probably the idea that 隹 and 叀, 其, 乎 and 不 have interrogative functions is the result of the fact that almost all sentences in the whole corpus of Chang's quotes are thought to be interrogative sentences: "Shall we do this? Shall we not do this?" "Shall it rain?" or "Shall there be no rain?" In this, Chang has followed a generally accepted and widespread opinion, never positively proved. But he has made it worse by introducing in each supposed oracular query *two* verbs, "to ask" (fragen), e. g., 壬寅卜殻貞⋯ "Am Tage Jen-yin fragte K'o das Orakel . . . ," which he puts in literal sequence as "Jen-yin/*fragen*/K'o/*fragen*/. . ." without distinction between 卜 and 貞. He cites as proof for his translations the *Shuo Wen* 説文 definitions 卜, 灼剝龜也 and 貞, 卜問也. Yet, neither of the terms in the Bone texts does necessarily mean "to ask, to question". In fact, 卜 means "to apply a firing process to cause cracks in the shell or bone".

This, of course, was done to observe the reactions, "approval or disapproval," of the other world on certain possible courses of action and events; but it does not therefore imply a *grammatical interrogative* sentence, introduced by 卜 "to ask". As to the graph 貞, written in various ways, it is a pictograph of a *ting* vessel, but is seldom used with such a sense in the bones; aside from the introductory formula of divination, it is used as a place-name and as a verb "to sacrifice". Cf. Li Chi 李濟 *et al.*, *Study of the Bronze Ting Cauldron* 殷虛出土銅鼎形器之研究 (*Archaeologica Sinica*, New Series, No. 4, Nankang, Taiwan, 1970, pp. 63-81); also Shima, *Index*, pp. 396-67; Li Hsiao-ting, *op. cit.*, pp. 1103-1108 and 2333; T'ien Ch'ien-chün 田倩君, *CKWT*, Vol. 11, 1963, 釋鼎 and Yen Yi-p'ing 嚴一萍 *CKWT*, ibid., 證鼎; and in particular, Yim Lee(Li Yen 李棪) in his review of Shima's *Index* (*The Journal of the Institute of Chinese Studies of the Chinese University of Hong Kong*, Vol. II No. 1, 1969, p. 197), where several instances are given of the graph 口 (i.e., 丁) serving as loan graph for 鼎 or 貞, even of cases of such variations within the *same* text. Though 貞 is usually defined in accordance with *Shuo wen* as "to ask, query," this meaning is almost unique to the *Shuo wen* and *Chou Li* 周禮 (i.e., a rather late development and rare in occurrence) as against the more frequent and regular meaning 貞：正也定也善也,信也; there is a majority of usages of *chen* 貞 (adjective + noun): "reliable, good, fine, correct". If we try to explain 貞 of the introductory formula of divination, not in the light of *Shuo Wen* and later, rare usages, but of a majority of usages, we can only think of a verbal sense "to test, to try out, to make *true*, correct" in the sense of "find out the *right* (course of action)" parallel with "tried, tested, reliable, correct, good". In this hypothesis, X X 卜, Y 貞 would simply mean: "In the bone divination of day X X, diviner Y *tested* the proposition, or *proposed* for test(i.e., rectification) the following course of action or alternative courses of action. ..."

a) *Hu* 乎: *final interrogative?*

Once this is accepted, it will be clear why Chang has only *one* case where the solution "*hu* 乎: final interrogative" can be applied (p. 140, text 9.24): 丁未卜夫(=扶) 㞢咸戊學戊乎, "At the divination of day Ting-wei(diviner) Fu[7] [tests the proposition]: we shall make a sacrifice to Hsien Wu; Hsüeh Wu(i.e., Teacher Wu) will call out(the order) (or: will be called out to)". To translate this as an interrogative sentence: "Should a sacrifice be made to Hsien Wu *and* Hsüeh Wu?", when viewed in the light of the later classical language, would seem perfectly correct and ordinary. Yet, why is there in this enormous number of supposed interrogative sentences only *one* case of *hu*? Furthermore, there is no probable reason why here *hu* should be interrogative and everywhere else a verb: "to call out". The *Ping-pien* (see note 9) has among the 200 first sets of reassembled complete oracular shells *two* cases of *hu* in final position: set 66(2) and set 97(12-13) 王固曰吉其乎 "The king prognosticated saying: consider lucky that we. . . ." A prognostication is never a question but a statement interpreting the divinatory answer. 其隹甲娩吉乎見庚其隹丁弘吉, "If it is a Chia day that she will deliver(the baby), it will be lucky to call upon (X, someone previously mentioned or implied). Seeing the Keng day(i.e., letting pass by the day Keng), if it be a Ting day, (it will) increase the luck".

b) *Final pu* 不

In a similar way the use of final *pu* 不, supposedly "interrogative particle" is illustrated by only *one* case in the entire collection of Chang's oracular texts (p. 140, 9.24): 丁未夫出咸戊牛不, "(At the divination of) day Ting-wei, diviner Fu [tests the proposition]: 'We shall sacrifice oxen to Hsien-wu. It shall not [be so]'". Already Yang Lien-sheng somewhere pointed out that interpreting *pu* as a final interrogative particle is nothing but reading Shang texts in the light of modern spoken Chinese.

c) *Particles Wei* 隹 *and* 叀

These "interrogative" particles 隹 and 叀 are explained as particles "die vor dem Wort stehten, auf das sich die Frage bezieht"; by "Wort" is meant probably a noun or a nominal structure, although elsewhere Chang speaks more clearly of nouns and verbs or verbal phrases. Among the two forms, 隹 is distinguished from 叀 by another special function, a so-called "Füllwort" used before indications of a year; but no further indication is given for distinguishing them in other sentences. What is striking is that 隹 and 叀 are perhaps the most frequent, ever-returning words in the oracle bone sentences, almost like the ever-present final particle *yeh* 也 in classical Chinese. In fact they appear as much in interpretive prognostications (statements) as in supposed "questions". 隹 is a verbal (copulative) term which from Shang texts on has persisted down to the Classical times of Chou (Bronze inscriptions, *Shu ching* and *Shih ching*) and it is even occasionally found as late as *Meng-tzu, Hsün-tzu*, etc. Thus, it is clear that 隹 "(to be) + noun" (e.g., 隹王 "it is the king" or "he is king") and the formula 隹 + verbal phrase (as a unit) (e.g., 隹來 "It is that he will come") and 隹 + date of year, month, etc., in inscriptions on bone or bronze (e.g., 隹王三祀, "It was the third cult year of the king") are all regular applications of the same function and rule of 隹 (Classical 惟, 維) "to be". The word 叀 is explained by Chang (p. 88) as having the same function as 隹; thus 叀牛三百 is translated as: "*or perhaps* oxen 300". This solution is unwarranted and has a serious weakness: it does not explain why two signs should be created and then used at the same time, even within the same line, without any difference. They are not "interrogative" for they appear in plain interpretive statements (introduced by 王固曰). The task is really to explain in what conditions 叀 is used as against the predominant and later solely surviving 隹 and why. (cf. note 63)

d) *The particle ch'i* 其

In like manner, the presence of *ch'i* 其 in plain interpretive statements speaks against the hypothesis of *ch'i* 其 functioning as an interrogative particle. Another explanation, viz., that this particle is an adverbial or even a more abstract grammatical word, seems quite preferable:[8] yet, in this latter interpretation, it is not shown why in certain contexts *ch'i* is present and in others not, often in perfect parallel, opposite alternatives: *ch'i* + verbal phrase opposed to negated verbal phrase without *ch'i* and *vice versa*. Leaving aside the function of *ch'i* as a particle introducing or marking subordinated clauses (a valuable suggestion made by Chang, but without attempt to specify in more detail), we find that the presence or absence of *ch'i* is a sign of very clear contrasts between two different kinds of oracular propositions: presence of *ch'i* marks the proposition or the alternative among possible courses of action, which is considered less desirable, less preferred, often positively feared and resorted to only if really unavoidable. This rule applies regardless of whether the proposition is expressed in negative or affirmative sentences. An exhaustive list of such cases from Chang's material will follow. But, since we need examples where the *full* context of opposites can be ascertained, we take first the cases as they appear in the first 200 sets of the *Academia Sinica* collection.[9]

PP1(1, 3)我弋冑 and (2, 3)我弗其弋冑: "We shall destroy Chou"; "We shall not destroy Chou" (*ch'i*: less desirable outcome). Compare 134(5) X X X (name of person) 弋弋魚隹 and (6) X X X 弗其弋: "X X X (name of person) shall destroy the tribes Tsai, Chüeh and Wei," "(he) shall not destroy (them)". 171(3)子閈弋基方缶 and (4)子閈弗其弋基方缶: "Tzu-shang shall destroy Chi Fang and Fou (supposedly a hostile group)"; "Tzu-shang shall not destroy Chi Fang and Fou". 177(1)亘允其弋鼓 and (2)亘弗弋鼓: "Huan truly will destroy (the tribe) Ku '(not desired alternative)'; Huan will not destroy Ku". Compare also 83(5) and (6).

PP1(9, 15)隻缶 and (10, 11, 16, 17) X 弗其隻缶: "(He) will catch the Fou"; "X will not catch the Fou". Compare 32(24)在北史出隻羌 and (25)在北史

亡其隻羌: "The envoy who is in the North will have (opportunity) to catch a Ch'iang (tribesman)"; "The envoy who is in the North will not have (opportunity) to catch a Ch'iang". 86(4)王隻鷹、允隻 and (5)不其隻: "The king will catch a *ch'ai* animal"; (post factum added statement:) "Indeed he caught (it)"; "It will not be caught". (9)王弗其隻兕 and (10)王隻兕: "The king will not catch a rhinoceros"; "The king will catch a rhinoceros".

PP2(11)我其出囚 and (12)我亡囚: "We shall have disastrous (evil) influence"; "We shall not have evil influence". 5(1, 3, 5, 7, 9) X 亡囚古; and (2, 4, 6, 8, 10) X 其出囚: "X will not have evil influence on Ku(?)"; "X will have evil influence (on him)". Compare p. 78: X 其出囚 and X 亡囚 "X will have evil influence" and "X will not have evil influence". The same sentence is frequently found with different subjects. P. 108 (*Yi pien* 3422) X X X 亡囚 and X X 其出囚. 117(1)貯其出囚 and (2)貯亡囚: "Chu will have evil influence..." "Chu will not have evil influence". 128(6) X 往來亡囚, and (8) X 其出囚: "By his going and coming, X will not have evil influence"; "X will have evil influence". (130. 1-2 has the same with another name as subject.) 165(16)王入于商亡乍囚 and (17)王入于商其出乍囚: "The king when entering into the Shang (city) will not have (opportunity) to cause evil influence"; "King when entering into Shang, will have risk to cause evil influence".

Other examples with 出 *or* 亡

29(2)鳳其出疾弗其殷: "Feng will have sickness; he might not ... (recover?)" [or: "by wind (because of cold) have sickness ..."]. 61(5)雩丁亡貝 and (6)雩丁其出貝: "Performing rain dance on Ting day we will not have loss". "Performing rain dance on Ting day, we will have loss". P. 132 (*Yi pien* 5451) ᛋ其出疾 and ᛋ亡疾: "Tun will have sickness"; "Tun will not have sickness". P. 166 (*Hsü* 3.45.5) 子阱其出災: "Tzu-ching will have disaster". 117(16)其出來婞 and (17)亡來婞: "We will have imminent (lit. coming) difficulty"; "We will not have imminent difficulty". 139(3)其出再帚好禍 and (5)亡再帚好禍: "(He) will have (cause, chance, risk) to build up (i. e., because of) Lady Hao's bad luck"; "He will not have (risk) of causing Lady Hao's bad luck". 157(1)今丙戌焱姙出从雨 and (2)姙亡其从雨: "On present day Ping-hsü, burning (at the stake) woman

Tsai, we will have ensuing rain"; "As to woman Tsai, we will not have ensuing rain". *Ch'ien* 5.33.2 勿尞亡其从雨 and 尞㞢从雨: "Do not burn (any victim at the stake), then we will not have ensuing rain. Burn (victims at the stake), then we will have ensuing rain". The prohibitive "don't" and its counterpart "do burn" are often used in the function of conditional: "If we do not burn ..." and "if we burn ..." This is comparable to similar structures in other languages, e. g., Classical Greek usage of negative *me* (Cf. Hansjakob Seiler, Abstract Structures for Moods in Greek. *Language*, *Journal of the Linguistic Society of America*, Vol. 47, 1. 1971, p. 81): "If one looks at a number of conditional sentences ... it seems odd that the protasis should invariably be negated by means of the prohibitive negation". *Yi Pien* 1228 叀姓尞㞢雨 against 6319 勿尞姓亡其雨: "If we consider woman Tsai (whom we) burn at the stake, then we will have rain"; "Do not burn (i. e., *if* we do not burn) at the stake woman Tsai, we will not have rain". 160(1)其㞢令般 and (2)勿令: "We have (cause) to command Pan"; "Do not command (him)" (般 may also be a verb: command to + verb.) 175(1)屯其㞢疾 and (2) 屯亡疾: "Tun will have sickness. Tun will not have sickness". 190(1, 3)帚好不征㞢疾 and (2, 4)帚好其征㞢疾: "Lady Hao will not for long time have sickness; Lady Hao will for protracted time have sickness". 199(9)舞岳㞢雨 and (10)岳亡其雨: "If we perform a dance on the Yüeh (mountain) (or: to Yüeh mountain god), we will have rain"; "As to Yüeh (rites) (or: Yüeh mountain god), there will not be any rain (lit. not have rain)".

Verb 雨 "to rain"

PP2(15)今夕雨 and (16)今夕不其: "(Present time) today, in the evening, it will rain"; "Today in the evening it will not [understood: 雨 rain]". 66(1)□帝不其令雨: "God will not command rain". 87(6)今日其雨 and (7)今日不雨: "Today it will rain"; "Today it will not rain". (Rain is usually mentioned in circumstances where it is expected and needed, except in cases, as this, where rain is mentioned in context with hunting, etc.) 93(1)其雨 and (2)不雨: "It will rain"; "It will not rain". 116(8)羽丁丑王步于壴, (10)羽丁丑勿步, (11)羽丁丑其雨, (12)羽丁丑不雨: "Next Ting ch'ou day the king will make a walk to (at?) Shu. Next Ting-ch'ou day, he (the king) should not take a walk. Next Ting-ch'ou day it will rain. Next Ting-ch'ou day it will not rain". 149(11)帝令雨, (12)帝不其令雨: "God will command rain. God will not command rain" (opposite case to the prior one). 149(21)征雨, (22)不其征雨: "For protracted time it will rain. It will not rain for protracted time". 151(1)自今至于庚申其雨, (2)自今于丁巳至于庚申不雨: "Starting from present (Ting-ssu day) reaching till Keng-shen day, it will rain. Starting from present Ting-ssu day reaching till Keng-shen day, it will not rain". (This sequence taken from PP is probably to be reversed, because Ting-ssu is omitted in the affirmative sentence.) 152(7)其雨, (8)不雨: "It will rain. It will not rain". (13)羽癸丑其雨, (14)羽甲寅其雨: "Next Kuei-ch'ou day it will rain. Next Chia-yin day it will rain" (*ch'i*: less desirable event; obviously a special day is sought for some outside activity wherefore rain is not desired). 154(1)王固曰其夕雨熱明, (3)王固曰癸丑其雨、三日癸丑允雨; "The king prognosticating says: it will rain at evening time. (But, next) morning, it will clear up; The king prognosticating says: on a Kuei day it will rain. The third day, a Kuei-ch'ou day, indeed it rained". (First *ch'i*: predictive testing statement; last clause, no *ch'i*: post factum statement.) 155(5)自今至于丙午雨, (6)自今至于丙午不其雨: "Starting at present (time) reaching till Ping-wu day, it will rain; Starting at present time reaching to Ping-wu day, it will not rain".

Verb 死 "*to die*"

P. 20(*Yi pien* 5347)雀其死 and 雀不死: "Ch'üeh will die" (not desirable alternative); "Ch'üeh will not die".

Verb 受 "*to receive*" "*to reap*"

PP8(1)我受黍年, (2)我弗其受黍年: "The Wo(we?) will receive millet harvest; The Wo(we?) will not obtain (good) millet harvest". [10](1)X受年, (2)不其受年: "X will receive good harvest"; "(They) will not be receiving..." 12(1)...受出又, (2)弗其受出又: "... will receive abundant assistance; They will not receive abundant assistance". 55(5)我受年, (6)我不其受年: "We (the Wo?) will obtain (good) harvest"; "The Wo (we?) will not be receiving a (good) harvest". Compare also 76(1) X X 受年, and (2) X X X 弗其受年. 81(1)王立黍受年, and (2)王勿立黍弗其受年: "The king presiding over the millet planting will receive (good) harvest; The king ought not to preside (i.e., If the king does not preside) over millet planting, we will not obtain(good) harvest". Compare P.182(*Yi pien* 7009)...受年 and...不其受年.176(7, 9, 11)冓不其受年 and(8, 10, 12)冓受年: "Kou will not be receiving good harvest; Kou will obtain good harvest".

Verb 疾 "*to be sick, have as sickness*"

PP12(9)疾齒龍 and(10)不其龍: "Having a toothache, it will get better. It will not get better".[10] 83(7)王骨龍,(8)王骨不其龍:"The king's bones will get better; the king's bones will not get better". 96(20)㞢疾身不其龍 and 㞢疾身…龍(Compare p. 209, *Yi pien* 960): "Having sick body, he will not get better; Having sick body, he will get better". 96(5)王其疾㞢 "The king might have as sickness baleful influences"[11]. P.133(*Ping pien* 106)王其疾目 and ... 王弗疾目: "The king will have pain in the eyes. The king will not have pain in the eyes". 106 same.

Verb 來 "*to come, cause to come*"

PP94(1)㞢來自西,(2)亡其來自西: "(He) will have(opportunity) to come from the West; He will not have(opportunity) to come from the West". 25(3)今□不其來,(5)☒歸春母來余其从: "At present, X will not come ...; ... will return; in Spring, Mother comes, I may (*de rigueur*) have to follow ..."[12] 32(20) X 來,(21)不其來: "X will come. He will not come". 33(2, 3) same. 81(5, 7)畫來牛,(6, 8)畫弗其來牛: "Hua will cause to come(bring) oxen; Hua will not bring oxen".

Verb 挈 "*to lead, to bring along*"

PP201(3.6)辜□挈大,(4, 6)辜弗其挈大: "Pi will lead on Ta; Pi will not lead Ta". 199(7)旨挈,(8)弗其挈: "Chih will lead(bring someone?); He will not lead". 185(1, 3)戋挈虭夗,(2, 4)戋弗其挈虭夗: "ch'ien will lead Ch'en(?) to cut grass; ch'ien will not lead Ch'en to cut grass". 178(1)旃眔殸挈羌,(2)旃眔①殸不挈羌: "Jan and K'o will lead on ch'iang(prisoners?); Jan and K'o will not be leading any ch'iang". 144(7)王挈之,(8)王固曰其勿挈: "The king will lead(someone) [make?] to go; The king prognosticating says: One ought not to lead".[13]

---

① 編者按:"眔",原文誤作"罪",今徑改。

Various Verbs

PP41(12, 14)且乙肯王,(13, 15)且乙弗其肯王: "Tsu-yi will afflict the king; Tsu-yi will not afflict the king". 71 and 73(1, 3)帝隹其冬兹邑,(2, 4)帝弗冬兹邑: "God will(lit. As to God, it is that he will) bring to end this city; God will not bring to end this city". 67(7)帝其降我莫,(8)帝不我降莫: "God will send down on us drought; God will not send down on us drought". P. 123(*Yi pien* 3069)子目娩㚸 and 子目娩不其㚸: "Tzumu in giving birth will be lucky(i. e., have a son); Tzu-mu in giving birth will not be lucky". 96(16)帚嫊娩㚸,(17)帚嫊娩不其㚸: "Lady Hua in giving birth will be lucky; Lady Hua in giving birth will not be lucky". P. 136(*Yi pien* 743 + 1724)帚好㚸 and 不其㚸: "Lady Hao will be lucky; She will not be lucky". 90(9)小臣㚸,(10)小臣不其㚸: "The Small Servant will be lucky; The Small servant will not be lucky".

FP86(6)罕麋,(7)弗其罕麋: "He will catch by net a deer; He will not catch a deer(in the net)". 96(13)羽乙亥啓,(14)羽乙亥不其啓: "Next Yi-hai day it will be clear(weather); Next Yi-hai day it will not be clearing up".

P. 158(*Lu* 705)辛卯卜貞方不出于唐 and *Chia pien* 2924 方其出于唐: "The Fang will not come out at T'ang; The Fang will come out at T'ang(ch'i: less desirable, because 'come out' equals 'to invade')". 117(20)羽癸卯帝不令鳳夕窖,(21)羽癸卯帝其令鳳: "Next Kuei-mao day God will not command it to be windy; at night it will be overcast; Next Kuei-mao day God will order it to be windy". 119(4)雀弗其敗亘我,(3)雀敗亘我: "The Ch'üeh will not defeat the Huan and the Wo(Ch'üeh are considered allies against the others, enemies of Shang), The Ch'üeh will defeat the Huan and Wo". P. 178(*Shou* 2.27.12)帚婏年蒦 and ...年不其蒦: "Lady Ching, her harvest will be reaped; (Her) harvest will not be reaped". 126(5)乎見湔匆弗其羅,(6)乎見湔匆羅: "Call upon the Ch'ien, ch'ien and X to cut grass, they will not catch any(game) in their nets; Calling upon the Ch'ien, ch'ien and X to cut grass, they will catch(game) in their nets". 155(3)弖召王史,(4)弖弗其召王史: "Kung will fittingly perform the King's service; Kung will not fittingly perform the king's service".[14] 165(8)不🜚,(9)其🜚,(12)羽乙卯王入不🜚,(13)其🜚.[15] P. 248(*Hsü ts'un* 550)今䆉方其征于䢼: "This Autumn the X and Fang will make a military attack upon Hui".[16]

174(3)禱田元祉, (4)禱弗其田元祉: "Li(?) will harm(by his influence) Yüan-hsi; Li will not harm Yüan-hsi". 193(1, 3, 5)不曰之, (2, 4, 6)其曰之: "He will not declare to go; He will declare to go".

These examples with regular statements in opposition show in their obvious context that *ch'i* is always attached to the least desirable alternative, clearly seen in "have luck, good harvest, catch game"; opposed to "have sickness, have bad influence". Some of these verbs(e.g., to rain) may, according to context and circumstances, take *ch'i*. Others are unclear because of our lack of exact knowledge of what is really implied or of the context in which the event is put("to attack, to defeat, to destroy"); but the mutual exclusiveness of *ch'i* in the opposition of negative and affirmative sentences shows the consistence of its usage. There are, however, a number of cases that still deserve closer investigation.

Incomplete opposition of the sentences

128(9)羽乙未其尞, (10)羽乙未勿衣尞: "On next Yi-wei day we might make a burning sacrifice. (*ch'i*: but would rather not); Next Yi-wei day we ought not at the Yi-sacrifice make a *liao*(burning) sacrifice".[17] 141(1)王其戉奚, (2)勿戉奚: "The king might (*ch'i*: but would rather not) make human sacrifice (of a shaman)" (cf. Shima, *Kenkyū*, p.339); "Do not ..."[18] 80(1)壬其阱罕, (2)弗其罕: "The king rather than use the pitfall method shall use a net(to catch game); He will not use a net(to catch game)" (*ch'i* in the first clause affects 阱 not 罕, in the second it affects 罕). P.22(*Yi pien* 5253) X 弗其伐 X X X and X 戈 X X X: "X will not attack X X X. X will destroy X X X". 7(1, 3, 5)丙辰卜㱿貞其改羌, (2, 4, 6)于庚申伐羌: "At divination on Ping-ch'en day, Chung tests [the proposition]: we might(*ch'i*: but rather not) beat the ch'iang. Coming to Keng-shen day we shall sacrifice(i.e., behead) a ch'iang."

Prognostications

PP1 王固曰丁巳我毋其戈于來甲子戈: "The king prognosticating says: on Ting-ssū day the Wo ought not be attacked, but by next coming Chia-tzū day [seven days later] we will destroy(them)". 42(2)我允其來, (5)王固曰吉戈隹甲不更丁, (6)我來卅: "The Wo really might come(*ch'i*: less desirable); The king prognosticating says: it is auspicious; (when) destroying, it will be a Chia day;

(we) will not assume(it be) a Ting day. The Wo came, they were thirty". 77 王固曰吉隹其亡工言叀其徝: "The king prognosticating says: it is auspicious; being(the case that) we do not have(cause) to 工言(?), assume that we inspect...."[19] 66(5)王固曰帝隹今二月令霝其隹丙不(令)雨、隹庚其吉,(6)王固曰吉其霝: "The king prognosticating says: as to God, it is the present second month that He will command there be hail(or sleet?); if it is on a Ping day that it will not(by his) command rain, then it means the Keng day will be auspicious. The king prognosticating says: it is auspicious that there be sleet(hail?)"[20]. 99 王固曰吉陮至其隹辛: "The king prognosticating says: it is auspicious that when Yin arrives, it will be a Hsin day". 149(1)妥㸚舞,(2)妥不其㸚舞,(5)王固曰不吉其㸚齒: "T'o being lead on will perform dance. T'o will not be lead on to dance... The king prognosticating says: it is not considered auspicious that he bring ivory(teeth)".[21] 157(11)奚來白馬王固曰吉其來,(12)奚不其來白馬五: "The Hsi will bring white horses. The Hsi will not be bringing white horses, amounting to five. The king prognosticating says: it will be auspicious that they come". 170(1)矢象,(2)王固曰吉其□象: "Promise ivory. The king prognosticating says: it is auspicious that they(promise) ivory". This translation of *shih* 矢 as equal to 誓 "to swear, make a promise" is doubtful indeed, and the meaning may simply be that of "shoot arrows at elephants...." The context is insufficient to decide.[22] From these examples it appears that the *ch'i* used in prognosticating statements is really the same as *ch'i* marking subordination: it is auspicious that, consider (it) auspicious that...." (Cf. infra, p. 37 sq.)

ch'i present in both the opposite sentences

P.178(*Hou* 40.15)帚黍其雈 and 帚井黍不其雈: "Lady Ching(her) millet will be harvested. Lady Ching's millet will not be harvested". 47(7)其屮來齒,(8)其亡來齒: "(One) might have occasion that they will bring(ivory) teeth. (One) might not have occasion that they will bring ivory". 76(3)方其戈我史,(4)方弗其戈我史,(5)我史弗其戈方,(6)我史其戈方: "The Fang(tribe) might destroy our envoy. The Fang might not destroy our envoy. Our envoy might not destroy the Fang. Our envoy might destroy the Fang". 63(3)今日其雨,(4)今日不其雨,(5)羽乙巳其雨,(6)羽乙巳不其雨,(7)羽丁未其雨,(8)羽丁未不其雨:

"Today it might rain. Today it might not rain. Next Yi-ssu day it might rain. Next Yi-ssu day it might not rain. Next Ting-wei day it might rain. Next Ting-wei day it might not rain". P.161(*Yi pien* 3381)□挈卅馬允其夲羌 and 虞卅馬弗其夲羌: "X(probably Chü) leading 30 men from the Ma(tribe) really might shackle(take prisoners) the ch'iang. Chü's 30 Ma(tribesmen) might not shackle the ch'iang". 124(15)缶其來見王,(16)缶不其來見王: "Fou might come to visit the king. The Fou might not come to visit the king". 141(11)旨其伐出蠱羅,(12)旨弗其伐出蠱羅: "As to Chih, he might attack You-ku-lo. As to Chih he might not attack You-ku-lo". 202(4)今日王出,(9)雨,(10)不其雨,(11)其雨,(12)不其雨: "The king today will go out. It will rain. It might not rain. It might rain and it might not rain". 4(1)羽辛酉其出,(2)其戍: "Next Hsin-yu day (we) might make a sacrifice. It might become open(clear weather)". This double use of *ch'i* seems to contradict the solution we presented above, unless we can consider this usage as special cases of *ch'i* as a mark of subordinative clauses, where the main verb is understood Yet main verbs are usually expressed, for instance, 貞 "test a statement," 令 "to command," 吉 "to be auspicious, find auspicious". Since the majority of divinations are couched in terms of what the diviner already considers desirable, it might be proposed that this exceptional pattern here could be used when such a decision or opinion concerning preference or desirability was not expressed or could not be formed. The underlying main clause might then have been: "we shall prepare for the eventuality that ... we shall expect that. ..."

Mixing of stative-passive sentences and active-transitive sentences

P.9(*T'ieh* 181.3)雀往正犬不其毕: "The Ch'üeh will proceed to punish the Ch'üan tribe. But they will not be caught". 120(12)𝄞隻羌,(3)𝄞不其隻羌,(15)王其逐咒隻弗亞咒隻豕二,(16)弗其隻咒,(17)其逐咒隻弗亞咒: "The Tsu (Shu?足~疋) will capture the ch'iang. But the Tsu(Shu?) will not be capturing the ch'iang. The king, if he chases the rhinoceros, will capture it; he will not drive the rhinoceros into the enclosure, yet the captured swine will be two(in number). He will not capture rhinos. If he chases rhinos, not capturing, he will drive the rhinos into the enclosure".[23] 124(7)降曾千牛,(8)不其降曾千牛千人:

"(we) will send down and offer with written record 1000 oxen; we will not send down and offer with written record 1000 oxen and 1000 men". [24] P. 193 (*Yi pien* 781+2341) 乎□豕隻 and X 不其隻豕: "Call upon X (i. e., commit order to X) that the swine will be captured. X will not be capturing the swine". 132 (1-6) 不羍羌, (7-8) 其羍羌: "(They) will not be shackled by the ch'iang. They will be shackled by the ch'iang".

ch'i sometimes can be understood in opposition to the parallel line, and translated as "rather than". 156 (3) 王其从取, (4) 勿从取: "The king, rather than follow (someone) to take (prisoners?), he ought not follow to take (prisoners?)". 142 (1) 目其希疾, (2) 目不希疾: "Mu rather than that he suffer bad effect from sickness, Mu will not suffer ominous effects from sickness". 124 (3) 缶其醬我旅, (14) 缶不我醬旅: "The Fou rather than to bring for us together troops, they will not for us gather troops". [25] 122 (1) 其沚于姶, (2) 勿于姶: "Rather than ... (?) to Lady Tzu, one ought not to go to Tzu".

Though a number of difficult passages remain and certainly more could be found in other text collections, we think we have given a general theory that can consistently explain most of the cases. When comparing these examples taken from *Ping Pien* volumes (down to set 202) with the selections of Chang's material, we see that the cases of *ch'i* used for marking the subordinate clauses are by far more numerous than those of *ch'i* affecting a main clause to indicate a less desirable alternative.

P. 47 (2.6) 貞王夢隹囚貞王其疾目: "Test [the proposition]: the king had a dream. It is (> it means, it spells) disaster. Test [the proposition]: the king might have eye sickness". P. 61 (3.31) 其御匕辛于多母御、弜: "Rather than make exorcist rites to the Ancestral Mother Hsin, and make exorcist rites to the many (ancestral) mothers. Do not (弜 equals 勿)(make any such rites)". [26] P. 64 (4.1) 乙子(=巳)卜酨子漁卯不其易□(=日): "Yi-ssu day divination: when making wine libations, Prince Yü will perform an exorcist rite; it might not (*ch'i*: less desirable) bring sunshine (lit. change to sun; cf. note on 易, p. 69). P. 83 (5.8) 貞卜丙弗壱王、其出囚(=禍): "Test [the proposition]: (Ancestor) Pu Ping does not endanger (exert harmful influence upon) the king. But it (he?) might have bad influence". [27]

P.97(6.8)(a)癸辛貞王令多尹🐚(=培、封、鋤)田于西受禾、癸亥貞其求禾自上甲.(b)乙丑貞王令封田于京戊辰貞求自上甲其燎. This piece taken from the Kyoto Collection No. 2363 is not cited in its entire and full context. Kaizuka (*op. cit.*, Fig. 92 and Plate 38) reproduces the piece itself and others which he thinks belong together. See Fig. next page.

The text runs as follows: (1)癸亥貞于𡇎🐚(=鋤)田, (2)癸亥貞王令多尹🐚田于西受禾, (3)癸亥貞多尹弜🐚受禾, (4)戊辰貞䆫禾自上甲其燎, (5)癸亥貞其䆫禾自上甲, (6)乙丑貞王令🐚田于京. If we examine the bone (original rubbing and Kaizuka's hand copy), we see that Kaizuka follows a regular sequence of reading, level by level, starting from below: "(1) At Kuei-hai day (divination), test [the proposition]: at 𡇎 (place name) we shall 🐚 hoe the fields.²⁸ (2) At Kuei-hai day (divination), test [the proposition]: the king shall command the many managers (officials) to hoe the fields in the West; (thus) we will obtain (a good) harvest. (3) At Kuei-hai day (divination, test [the proposition]: the many officials ought not to (do so, as suggested in (2)), thus we will obtain a (good) harvest. (4) At Wu-ch'en day (divination) [five days later], in praying for harvest start from Shang-chia (ancestor), we might (but preferably not) make a burning sacrifice (and, from there, move down to other ancestors). (5) At Kuei-hai day (divination), test [the proposition]: when praying for harvest, we shall start with Shang-chia.²⁹ (6) At Yi-ch'ou day (divination) [two days after Kuei-hai], the king shall order to hoe the field at Ching."

From this full context, it appears that 2-3 and 4-5 are meant as mutually exclusive alternatives of action. This opposition is ignored in the sequence adopted by Chang. Especially in (4) "prayer for harvest" is mentioned only as an option with possible but less preferred addition of burning sacrifices. That this is so, is implied by (5), where "burning sacrifice" is now silently eliminated and further determination is sought concerning the sort of prayers to be made.

Kaizuka has tried to further supply a more full context to this set of divinatory statements by adding the bone fragments from *Ts'ui pien* 1223, 1554, 1221. This reads: (7) 1223 lower part: 甲子貞于下𡰥刖🐚田: "Chia-tzu day (divination) (one day after Kuei-hai): at Lower Yi-X (place), we shall hoe the fields". (8) 1223 top half: 甲子貞于□方卣田: "[Chia-]tzu day(divination), at X-region, we shall hoe the fields". (9)于龍卣田: "At Lung(place) we shall hoe the fields". (10) 1544 王令卣田嚨: "The king commands to hoe the fields at Lung". (11)1221 己巳王☒刖卣田: "On Chi-ssu day(six days after Kuei-hai) the king ... [commands? ... at Lower] Yi to hoe the fields". (12)壬辰貞辛卯☒: "At Jen-ch'en day divination(ninth day), test [the proposition]: on Hsin-mao day (sixteen days after Kuei-hai). ..."

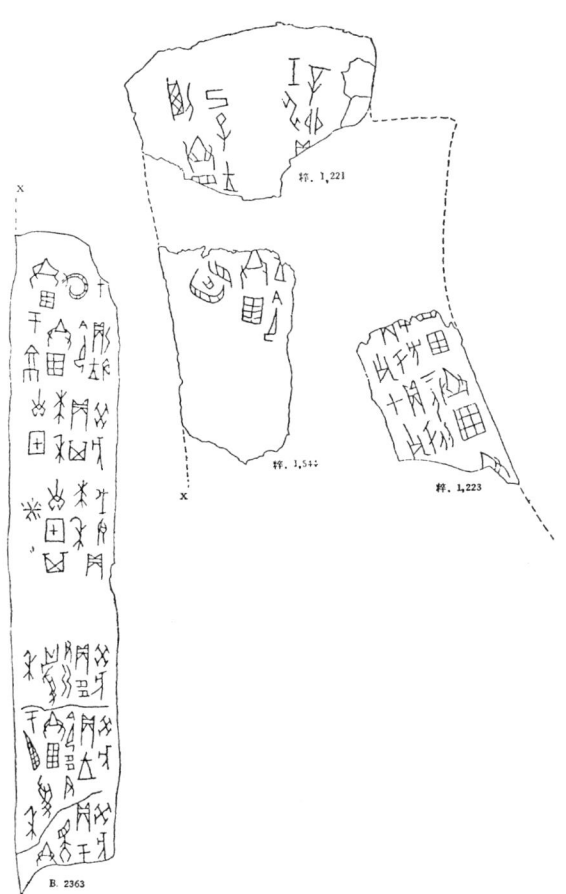

B 2363 is supposed to be joined to bone 1,544 at the point x.

From the figure of the Kaizuka arrangement it is hardly convincing that these pieces should be added to the Kyoto unit; moveover, the writing 龍 and 嚨 in the same bone poses a problem, and the graph 刖 in sentence(11) is not similar to that in(7). (☒indicates that more than one graph is supposed to be missing in the original, □ stands for *one* missing graph.)

P. 103(6.24)叀戊田、弜往田不畢、既求王其田杏 Ch'ü Wan-li(*Chia pien* 2608) puts these under three separate statements, followed by a fourth: X 子卜☒ 雨. Then we have: (1) "Consider it a Wu day(on which) we shall hunt. (2) Do not go forward to hunt; (for) nothing will be caught(in the nets) [lit. something will not be netted]. (3) After having made prayers, the king might(*ch'i: de rigueur*) hunt at Yung". (4) "At X-ssu day(divination) ... it will rain". P. 104(6.25)癸酉卜其父甲一牛: "Kuei-hai day divination: there might, on the other hand(*ch'i*) be brought as sacrifice to Father Chia one ox". (The role of the verb is really found in the *numeral*; literally: "to Father Chia it shall *be* one ox".) P. 105(6.27)貞求于上甲受我又、勿求于上甲不我其(受又): "Test [the proposition]: do pray to Shang-chia(and he) will hand over to us(his) assistance; do not pray to Shang-chia(and he) will not give us assistance", ("do pray" and "do not pray" are instances of imperative, prohibitive functioning as conditional: "if we pray ... , if we do not pray ... ".) Chang has translated this text by telescoping the two sentences into one and splitting it up again in two: "Should a ritual prayer be addressed to Shang-chia? Will he then grant us assistance?"

P. 107(6.32) (a)乙丑卜方出其求: "At Yi-ch'ou day divination: the Fang go out, one might(*ch'i*: as well, *de rigueur*) pray ... [context doubtful, original bone very unclear]. P. 117(7.19) (b)庚申貞王其告于大示、庚申貞王于父丁告: "Kengshen day(divination), test [the proposition]: the king might(as less preferable alternative) make an announcement to Ta-shih. At Keng-shen day(divination), test [the proposition]: as to the king, to Father Ting [stress position, i.e., to Ting and not to Ta-shih], shall he make an announcement". P. 122 (7.28)其告䖵上甲二牛三牛四牛: "Rather than make an announcement(rite) to Shang-chia about the locusts, we have two oxen, three oxen(or even) four oxen (brought as sacrifice)". P. 123(7.31)庚辰貞日又戠非冎隹若、庚辰貞日又戠其告于父丁用牛九在𦦲: Chang reads this as *one* sentence, though this is impossible because of the repeated "dated introductory formula," and he translates: "On day Keng-ch'en, ask at 𦦲(place): there is a solar eclipse; is it inauspicious [lit. is it not disaster?] or is all fine? Should a ritual announcement be made(about that) to Father Ting with sacrifice of nine oxen?" More accurately: "At Keng-ch'en day (divination), test [the proposition]: the sun has chopped off(aspect);³⁰ to remove the baneful influence will be agreeable. At Keng-ch'en day(divination), test [the proposition]: the sun has chopped off(aspect); one might(*ch'i: de rigueur*), while making announcement to Father Ting, sacrifice oxen; sacrificed oxen will be nine. It will be at 𡎚(place) (or: it was done at...?)".

P.134(9.8)父丁鼐三咒其五咒不雨 Ch'ü Wan-li(*Chia pien* 840) puts this in a longer context with different parsing and sequence: (1)于旦,(2)于南門,(3)父丁鼐三咒,(4)其五咒,(5)☒不雨. On the basis of the bone fragment itself, it is clear that one cannot take them as *one* sentence as Chang does: "To Father Ting offer boiled(in a *ting* vessel) three or four rhinos; will it(at this offering) rain?" Ch'ü reads it: "(1) At dawn; (2) At the Southern Gate; (3) The sacrificial offering to Father Ting will amount to three rhinos(鼐 equals 鼎, used as term for 'sacrifice,' cf. supra, p.11); (4) (or) on the other hand(*ch'i*: if need be, but not preferably so) five rhinos. (5) ... it will not rain". P.148(10.9)甲子貞且乙日壱其雨:Chang translates: "On day Chia-tzu the oracle was asked: will the sun of Tsu-yi(which should appear on the next day Yi-ch'ou) bring a curse? or will it rain (i.e., will the sun not appear)?" This should be read as *one* sentence: "On day Chia-tzu, we test [the proposition]: the sun(i.e., day) of Tsu-yi having ominous influence(壱), it will(*ch'i*: less desired) rain. [or: the day of Tsu-yi will have as harmful(effect) (*ch'i*:) that it will rain.]" P.167(12.1)貞羽甲戌河其令雨、貞羽甲戌河不令雨: "Test [the proposition]: next Chia-hsü day, the Ho(river god) will command it to rain(*ch'i*: less desired event). Next Chia-hsü day, as to the Ho(river god) it will, by his command, not rain". (On cases of "rain" implying less desirable outcome, c.f., supra, p.17. The use of the negative 不 with verbs like 令, instead of what might be expected, *viz*. 弗, is explained below, under the discussion on the negatives.) P.174(12.20)丙戌卜即貞其告執于河: "At Ping-hsü day(divination), (diviner) Chi tests [the proposition]: one might [*ch'i*: if need be] announce an offering of prisoners to the Ho(river god). (Set incomplete; the alternative is missing)". P.171(12.13)貞勿舞河亡其雨:"Test [the proposition]: one ought not perform a ritual dance to the Ho(river god); there is no occasion(chance) that it will rain". (i.e., "if we do not perform ... there will be no chance …") (cf. supra, p. 16). P.175(12.22)庚辰貞日又戈㞢凹隹若、庚辰貞日又戈其告于河: (almost identical with 7.31 mentioned before, except for last part): "… we might on the other hand(*ch'i*) make a ritual announcement to the Ho(river god). P.177(12.31)丁子(=巳)卜其袞于河牢(件)(=沈)㚔: "Ting-ssu day divination: one might(*ch'i: de rigueur*) burn in sacrifice to Ho(river god) a pen raised ox and drown a slave girl".[31] P.180(12.42)殻貞洹其乍兹邑凹: "(Diviner) K'o tests [the proposition]: 'Huan(river god) might on the other hand (*ch'i*) cause this city disaster'." P.186(13.3)乙丑卜岳弗壱禾丙戌岳其壱. This is taken from Kyoto bone 2370, which Kaizuka reads in a different sequence: (1)丙戌卜岳其壱 then separated by several items(2-9) comes(10)乙酉卜岳弗壱禾. Kaizuka's reading of this bone from left to right and downward in successive levels seems preferable, yet Chang's sequence is not excluded though he gives no reason for his choice of reading. For our purpose here, suffice it to note that it is clear that *ch'i* marks a less desirable alternative: "Yi-you day divination: the Yüeh (mountain god) will not bring harm to the rice plants. On Ping-hsü day (divination) [here Kaizuka reads 卜, but rubbing is unclear]: the Yüeh(mountain god) may on the other hand cause disaster".

P.209(14.44) … 未卜其求雨于兒: "At divination of X-wei day: one might [*ch'i*: if need be] pray for rain to Erh". P.211(15.1)乙亥卜殻羽丙子帝其令雨: "At divination of day Yi-hai, K'o [tests the proposition]: next Ping-tzu day [i.e., one day later] God might on the other hand(*ch'i*) command rain". P.212(15.4)貞帝其及今十三月令雷(~霰). 帝其于生一月令雷(~霰): "Test [the proposition]: God might, by the time we reach the present thirteenth month command a hailstorm. God might at the(newly) born first moon command a hailstorm". Cf. note 20: 𦊆 equals 霰 or 雷 or 電. This divination line shows two propositions both introduced by *ch'i*; the choice is not about the event of the hail(or thunder) storm itself, but the date on which it is expected to happen. (On double *ch'i*, cf. supra, p.24.) We can compare this with the quote 15.3; cf. p.52.

P.213(15.7)貞羽癸卯帝其令䨖(=風): "Test [the proposition]: next Kueimao day, God might command it to be windy". Chang translates the latter part: "dem Wind(gott) einem Befehl verteilen". The mythology of the wind being conceived as messenger of God (first proposed by Tung Tso-pin) may be underlying here, but the construction is exactly the same as in "command rain, etc." and it is not clear what the "Befehl" given to the wind is. P. 213 (15.8) Chang cites a passage which has one alternative only: 庚戌卜貞帝其降堇: "At divination of Keng-hsü day, test [the proposition]: God might send down drought". A similar text in *Ping pien* 63 has both opposites: 戊申卜爭貞帝其降我堇、一月、戊申卜爭貞帝不降堇: "At divination of day Wu-shen, (diviner) Cheng tests [the proposition]: God might make fall upon us a drought; first month. At Wu-shen day divination, Cheng tests [the proposition]: God will not send down on us a drought". P. 216 (15.16) 貞勿伐🀆(=胡)方帝不我其受又: "Test [the proposition]: we ought not attack the Hu (country) (cf. note 16) (for) God might not give us (lit. make receive) his assistance". (i.e., "If we do not ... God will not ...") P. 219 (15.24) 丙辰卜㱿貞帝隹其冬(=終)茲邑. In *Ping pien* 73 (71) this sentence is repeated twice in its full context with its negative counterpart (without *ch'i*), 貞帝弗冬茲邑 and in addition two more lines 羽庚申煉于黃奭 and 貞我舞雨, which allows for a better understanding: "At divination of day Ping-*ch'en*, (diviner) K'o tests [the proposition]: as to God, it is that he might bring to end this city. Test [the proposition]: God will not bring to end this city. On next Keng-shen day [four days later] we will perform an axe-dance for Huang's wife. Test: we will have a ritual dance for rain". Chang translates 終茲邑 "den *Bau* dieser Stadt beenden lassen". But without supplying the element "building (of a city,)" 終 can be understood as "to bring to end, make something end" in the sense of "destroy": the context indicates a situation of drought where the survival of a city is in danger. In this context the use of *ch'i* with the affirmative sentence 其終 as against 不終 (no *ch'i*) is clearly fitting. On 黃奭: according to Kuo Mo-jo and T'ang Lan, the term refers to Huang *Yin's* wife, but Shima (*Kenkyū*, p. 249) considers it equivalent to Huang Pao 保 (by taking 奭: modern 婦 as a loan for 保). Kuo and T'ang seem more convincing and simple. Cf. note infra, p. 95. On 煉 "axe dance," i.e., modern 戣, cf. Shima, *Index* 349, *Kenkyū*, p. 209 and Chang, p. 191, note 1.

P. 220 (15.28) 貞帝其作我孽: "Test [the proposition]: God might make for us suffering". P. 221(15.30) 帝其乍王占 (This should be part of a set, though the fragment lacks its contrastive alternative statement): "God might(*ch'i*: on the other hand) make(cause) the king a disaster". P. 229(16.24) 貞生八月帝不其令多雨勿乎雀帝于西: "Test [the proposition]: at the(newly) born 8th moon, God might command to have abundant rain; do not call upon the Ch'üeh tribes to make a Ti sacrifice at the West". Chang translates: "Will God in the coming 8th month of the year *perhaps* give command for abundant rain? Should the Ch'üeh not be ordered to make a sacrifice to Ti(God) *and* to the God of the West?" Observe here the use of 令 and 乎 in the same context: one is "God's command" and the second is "*we* call upon the Ch'üeh" to 帝 i. e. 禘 "to bring a Ti-sacrifice" at a certain place. This latter structure is parallel to other sentences such as: 帝于瀧, 帝于南, 帝于岳, 帝于北, 帝于東 etc. Shima, *Kenkyū*, p. 301 understands 帝于河 as "to associate Ho(river god) in the Ti sacrifice".

P. 224(16.6) 其乎戍禦羌方于義且乙戈羌方不桑(=喪)眾、其淔帝乎禦羌方于止(=之)戈 Chang translates: "Should one in the Yi-Tsu-yi(temple) command the frontier guard to ward against the ch'iang country? Will we destroy(defeat) the ch'iang country and not lose citizens? Should we make Ti-sacrifice at the river Ning? Should we command to ward against ch'iang country? 于之戈 Will we in *this* (enterprise) destroy them?" This excerpt taken from the Kyoto Collection, bone 2142 is not complete. The whole is preceded by two lines: 戍其徲每歸于止若、戈羌方 and 戍其歸乎媽王弗每 The lines quoted by Chang are further followed by 方其大出. Kaizuka takes 止 as a placename(not as Chang who reads this as 之 pronoun "it"), and this is supported by 止 in the first line. "The frontier guards, if they were to tarry(Kaizuka erroneously takes 徲 as identical with 歸), it will be inauspicious; but to return at Chih will be agreeable. If the frontier guard, when returning, call upon the 雝(Yung tribe), the king will not cause disaster. If calling upon the frontier guard to ward against the ch'iang and Fang at the(temple city) Tsu-yi, (then) in destroying the ch'iang and Fang, there will not be lost any multitudes(of troops). If at the river Ning we make a Ti-sacrifice, and call out to ward against the ch'iang and Fang at Chih, we will destroy(them). The Fang might on the other hand(*ch'i*) in great(number) come out(to invade)." (Compare

Wu ch'i-ch'ang, *T'oung Pao*, Vol. 43, 1955, p. 55) In this set of divinatory sentences, all the functions of *ch'i* are to introduce the subordinate clauses "if . . . ," except the last one: *ch'i . . . ch'u*(出). The phrase 義且乙 is explained by Chang (p. 224, note 3) in the sense of "Beiname von Tsu-yi," yet he translates "in I-Tsu-i" as "im Tempel von I-Tsu-i". Kaizuka refers to Chin Hsiang-heng's article in *Ta-lu tsa-chih* 大陸雜誌(Vol. 19.3) where 義 is explained as a posthumous temple name, but adds that 義 often stands for 宗 "shrine, sacrificial tablets of ancestors". This would provide a simpler translation: 于義且乙 "going to (or: at) Ancestral Shrine, Tsu-yi". Same structure as 示壬, cf. note 37.

P. 244(18.2) 壬申卜多🀆舞不其从雨: "Divination of day Jen-ch'en: if the many Shih perform a dance, it still might not, as a result (lit. ensuingly) rain". P. 245(18.8) 其雩于㫺于楚又雨(于)盂(又)雨 [bracketed characters are filled in by Kuo Mo-jo in *Ts'ui pien* 547]: "Rather than have a rain dance at X (place name), if in Ch'u(we have it), there will be rain; (or if) in Yü(have it), there will be rain". P. 246(18.9) 王其乎戍雩盂又雨叀亥雩盂田又雨: "The king, rather than call upon Shu to perform rain dance at Yü to have rain, we shall assume(consider that) Hai perform the rain dance at the Yü fields to have rain". P. 252(18.23) . . . 卜其焚玨: "(On X X day) divination: we might(less desired course of action) burn on the stake Hsü. . . ." P. 249(18.15) 其用燎牛…: "(One) might use for burning(on a stake) oxen. . . ."³² P. 117(7.19) (a) 己未貞王其告其从亞侯: "On(divination of) day Chi-wei, test [the proposition]: the king might [*ch'i*: if need be] make announcement that he will follow Lord of Ya". (b) 庚申貞王其告于大示、庚申貞王于父丁告: "(On divination of) day Keng-shen, test [the proposition]: the king might make an announcement to Ta-shih. (On divination of) day Keng-shen, test [the proposition]: the king(rather than previous alternative) to Father Ting (stress), he will make an announcement".³³ P. 256(19.1) 婦𡥜不其妨、貞御婦𡥜: "Lady Hsieh might not (less desired event, *ch'i*) be lucky(in child birth); we test [the proposition]: perform an exorcist rite over Lady Hsieh". P. 257(19.4) (b) 貞王其疾🀆貞王出夢不隹乎余钟🀆: "Test [the proposition]: the king might after all have as sickness a fault(i.e., be sick, be afflicted because of a committed fault). Test [the proposition]: the king had a dream; it is not that one shall call upon (someone), but I shall exorcize the evil". The phrase 疾囗 is unusual compared with the frequent usages such as 疾齒、疾目, and the translation is only tentative; another solution would be: "... as to the king, after all (less desired alternative) the sickness is ominous ..." (still *ch'i* should immediately precede the verb). P.39(1.13) 婓其 壱王貞婓弗其壱王: "E will cause harm to the king. E will not cause harm to the king". P.44(1.25) 貞𠂤弗其凸(=禍)風屮疾: "Test [the proposition]: Shu will not cause evil effect that by wind (cold) one have sickness". Chang translates 𠂤 as "to have pain over the whole body".[34]

ch'i 其 *used as mark of subordination*

In the following examples (from Chang's selections) we will discuss some of the cases of *ch'i* used as a mark of subordination. P.77(4.24) 丁丑卜宕貞子 雋(=雖)其钾王于丁妻二匕己堂垾三十三羌十: "At divination of day Ting-ch'ou, (diviner) Pin tests [the proposition]: Prince Yung, when making an exorcist rite for King Ting's wife, second ancestral Mother Chi, then he will bring as offering (in cooking vessel), rams numbering 33 and Ch'iang (prisoners) numbering 10".[35] P.85(5.13) 其䏇坰又大雨弜(=勿)䏇亡大雨: "When making a recorded written exorcist ritual, we will have big rain. Do not make record written sacrifices, (and then) we will not have big rain". ("If we do not ... we will not. ...") P.89(5.23) 丁未貞其大钾王自上甲血用白豕九下示卝(=蠱)牛在父丁宗: "At (divination of) day Ting-wei, test [the proposition]: if having great exorcist rites, the king starting with Shang-chia (down to the other ancestors) shall bring as sacrifice (in blood-filled vessels) white swine, numbering nine, and (in) Hsia-shih (lower ancestral shrines) he shall bring as sacrifice with blood sprinkling ritual an ox. Being at Fu-ting's temple (one made this divination)". The last sentence of this divinatory text is independent from the previous ones. Chang as in many other instances combines this with the date given at the beginning of the first sentence. This results in a complete misrepresentation of the actual text. P.91(5.26) 丁卯貞㚔厶(=以)羌其用自上甲卝(=蠱)至于父丁: "On (divination of) day Ting-mao, test [the proposition]: Chia will lead the ch'iang (prisoners); when sacrificing them, starting from Shang-chia, we will perform the ritual of sprinkling blood on the altar and reach down (in this rite) to Father Ting". P. 93 (5.27) 丁未卜何貞卯于小乙舞匕庚其寇₍₌宕₎₍賓₎鄉 This fragment is mentioned in *Chia-pien* with a context of several more lines, not given by Chang yet related to the date of the banquet and other possible ritual actions: (1) 壬子卜何貞翌癸丑其又匕癸鄉, (2) 癸巳卜何貞翌甲午鳳于父甲鄉: "At divination of Jen-tzu day, (diviner) Ho tests [the proposition]: next Kuei-ch'ou [one day later] when making sacrifices to the ancestral Mother Kuei, we shall have a banquet. At divination of day Kuei-ssu, (diviner) Ho tests [the proposition]: next day Chia-wu, when presenting offerings to Father Chia, we shall have a banquet. At Ting-wei day divination, Ho tests [the proposition]: in making exorcism for Hsiao-yi, performing ritual dances for ancestral mother Keng, one might on the other hand (*ch'i*: but rather not) treat as guest and offer a banquet".[36] P. 93 (5.28) 貞其征卯于大戊鄉: "Test [the proposition]: when continuing to make exorcist rites for Ta-wu (then) we will have a banquet". Ch'ü Wan-li (*Chia-pien* 2689) has a parallel line, 貞其征鄉于又河鄉: "When continuing to make exorcist rites to Ho (river god), we will have a banquet". P. 95 (6.4) 壬寅卜其求禾于示壬舞眾酒茲用: "At divination of day Jen-yin: when praying for harvest to Shih-jen[37] we will have ritual dancing and a wine libation. This was applied". P. 98 (6.9) 其求₍~案₎于襲₍~穀₎尞九羊: "When praying for rain to X-ancestor, burn as offering 9 sheep". P. 99 (6.13) 其求₍~案₎雨于伊舞: "When praying for rain to Yi (not Yi-yin) we will have a ritual dance".[38]

P. 102 (6.20) 癸未貞其求生于高匕丙: "At divination of day Kuei-wei, test [the proposition]: in praying for life (?) to the High ancestral Mother Ping. ..." Incomplete text? Compare P. 102 (6.22) 辛子₍₌巳₎貞其求于匕庚匕丙牡白豕: "At Hsinssu day (divination), test [the proposition]: in making prayers, we shall bring as offering to Ancestresses Keng and Ping a bull, a ram and a white swine". Chang understands 求生 as "praying for life" i.e., for progeny: this seems superior to Kaizuka's translation as "to pray for *long* life". P. 106 (6.31) 其求在父甲王受又求在且丁〔王受又〕: "When prayer is directed to (lit. is at) Father Chia, the king will receive assistance. When praying is directed to Ancestor Ting. ..." P. 111 (7.8) ... 殷貞🔲方衛₍₌還₎率伐不王其正告于且乙勾又: "[On X day divination] K'o tests [the proposition]: Hu(?) and Fang spied on Shuai and attacked Pi; as to the king, if he goes on a punitive expedition, (then) he shall make an announcement to Tsu-yi, and pray for assistance". P. 113 (7.12) 丁子(=巳)卜宕貞叀于王亥🐚卯十牛三🐚告其从戉乘(=望乘)正下𦤞(~危):"At Ting-ssu day divination, Pin tests [the proposition]: we shall offer as burning sacrifice to Wang-hai a deer(a goat?), slaughter ten oxen, three deer(goats?), announce that we will follow Wang-ch'eng to punish the Lower Hsi(Wei?)".[39]

P.118(7.22) □未貞王其令望乘帚(=歸)其告且[乙]一牛父丁一[牛]:"At divination of day X-wei, test [the proposition]: the king, if he commands Wang-ch'eng to return, and when making an announcement to Tsu-yi(about it), there be one ox, and to Fu-ting also there be one ox(offered in sacrifice)". P. 120 (7.23)貞王其往出省从西告于且丁:"Test [the proposition]: the king, when he proceeds and leaves to inspect and follows the Western(direction), then he will make an announcement to Tsu-ting". P. 120(7.24)貞王其去癸告于且乙:"The king, when leaving the Kuei region, shall make an announcement to Tsu-yi". P.121(7.26)丁卯貞其告于父丁其𠦪一牛:"At divination of Ting-mao day, test [the proposition]: one might on the other hand(ch'i) make an announcement to Father Ting, that when going on a hunt there be one ox(offered in sacrifice)". On this special graph for "hunt" 𠦪, cf. supra note 3. It would seem more natural to the general structure of the text and the grammar, if this graph was not "to hunt" but a term for "sacrificing or offering," then there would be a parallel structure with double ch'i:其告父丁 and 其…一牛. The text would then simply read: "One might make an announcement to Father Ting; one might … (verb: sacrifice?) one ox". P.122(7.29) … 卜其告火自後且丁:"… (day) divination: when announcing fire, start with later generation's Tsu-ting". P.125(7.32)辛亥卜出貞鼓🐚告于唐九牛、一月:"At divination of day Hsin-hai, Ch'u tests [the proposition]: when beating drums at continuing sacrifice, we make announcement to T'ang, there will be nine oxen(offered in sacrifice). First month".[40] P. 128 (8.8)辛丑卜王其又彳(=升)伐大乙叀舊𤕌用人十五:"At Hsin-ch'ou day divination, the king, when offering and making ascend decapitated victims(humans) to Ta-yi, shall assume(consider) that with old written statement the used victims will amount to fifteen". Chang mistakenly considers 蒜 as a *ho-wen* for 大子冊 and translates the line: etwa/alt/Versprechen des Kronprinzen/gebrauchen/Menschen/15/, i.e., "Should the king offer 15 men in cultic decapitation to Ta-yi, *in order to fulfill the old promise* of the Heir Apparent 太子". Cf. supra note 24.

P.135(9.9)乙丑其又ᵢ(=升)戋于且乙白坰三王在...卜: "Yi-ch'ou day(divination): when offering and sacrificing(by killing) oxen to Tsu-yi, the white bulls will be three. The king being at ... made the divination". 坰 is the 牛 "ox" with the special mark 土(for male animals). Chang translates the last sentence 王在...卜 as if it made one with the date 乙丑 of the beginning of the first sentence. P.138(9.19)己子(=巳)貞其𩡠南囧米叀乙亥、己子(=巳)貞王米囧其𩡠又且乙 This quote, taken from *Chiapien* 903 is copied incorrectly and in a sequence different from that of Ch'ü Wan-li's, which has: (1)己巳貞王米囧其登于且乙,(2)己巳貞王其登南囧米叀乙亥: "At Chi-ssu day(divination), test [the proposition]: as to the king's grain stores, when bringing offerings, then offer to Tsu-yi. At Chi-ssu day(divination), test [the proposition]: the king when offering to the South the stored grain, consider it to be on day Yi-hai". Chang translates these two sentences, which both explicitly start with the formula x x 貞 as one: "On Chi-ssu day the oracle was asked whether the king on Yi-hai day should offer grain from South Chiung to Ancestor Tsu-yi". The two lines differ by the additional use of the words 南, 其, and 叀 in one sentence, and the different position of the word 米 in each of them. P.138(9.21)甲申卜何貞羽乙酉其𩡠(=登)且乙鄉: "At divination of day Chiashen, Ho tests [the proposition]: next Yi-yu day, if we make offering (of wine?) to Tsu-yi, then we shall give a banquet". (Chang translates this as two different sentences connected by "and".) P.139(9.22) (a)庚戌卜何貞羽辛亥其又𩡠(=後)比辛鄉, (b)癸酉卜何貞羽甲午𩡠(=登)于父甲鄉: "At Keng-hsü day divination, Ho tests [the proposition]: next Hsin-hai day, when making a sacrifice to (後) later generation's Ancestral Mother Hsin, we shall present a banquet. At Kuei-yu day divination, Ho tests [the proposition]: next Chia-wu day when offering to Father Chia, give a banquet". P.141(9.29)壬申卜其桼子癸叀豕牛牢: "At Jen-shen day divination: if we perform branch-tree(ritual)[41] to prince Tzu-kuei, we consider(i.e., plan for) a pig(or) make it an ox or a pen raised ox(as sacrificial victim)".

P. 142(9.32) 己未卜其又于子東小宰 This is a parallel text, obviously incomplete: "At Chi-wei day divination: we might(*ch'i*: if need be) bring as offering to Prince Tzu-kao(Ching? 東) a small penned sheep". P. 148(10.11) 癸酉卜王貞羽甲戌王其𡩜大甲𩰤亡𡆥: "At Kuei-yu day divination, the king tests [the proposition]: next Chia-hsü day(one day later), if the king treats as guest Ta-chia and makes food sacrifice, then he will have no disaster". Chang translates 𡩜大甲 as "den *Darsteller* von Ta Chia empfangen". Whether in Shang sacrifices the ancestors were made present at the rituals of sacrifice in the person of the "representative" 尸 (as in Chou texts) is not sure. Literally 𡩜, 宾 is "to treat X as guest". Shima, *Kenkyū*, p. 311, explains the expression 王宾… in certain contexts as "to go *in person* (to the ancestral temple) to worship".

P. 151(10.15) [癸]丑卜即貞羽乙[卯]酚于且乙其兄(=羞) 又伐羌十卯五宰: "At divination of day Kuei-ch'ou, diviner Chi tests [the proposition]: next Yi-mao day(two days later) we will make a harmonizing ritual sacrifice to Tsu-yi. When offering sacrifice(又), the decapitated ch'iang(victims) will amount to ten, and we will slaughter five penned sheep".[42] P. 153(10.19) 甲子王卜曰羽乙丑其酒朋唐不雨: "On Chia-tzu day the king made divination and said: next Yi-ch'ou day(one day later) if we make wine libation and feather dance to T'ang, (still) it will not rain". P. 154(20.21) 卜其召大乙五牛王受[又]: "On divination of day X X, if we offer as victims in harmonizing sacrifice to Ta-yi five oxen, then the king will receive(assistance)". P. 170(12.12) 其求年于河、叀今年亥酚受年、卅牛受年、其用舊𦎫廿年受年: "If we pray for harvest to Ho(river god), we shall consider(it that) on present day Hsin-hai we make wine libation, then we will receive a (good) harvest. If there be 30 oxen, we shall receive a good harvest. If we sacrifive with old written document of announcement 30 oxen, then we receive a (good) harvest". (Cf. note 24.)

P. 177(12.29) … 卜□其件于河叀羊: "… divination(of day X X) K'ou [tests the proposition]: if we shall drown an ox as victim to Ho(river god), consider(it to be) a reddish-brown one".[43] P. 178(12.33) 癸亥卜爭羽辛未王其酒河不雨: "At divination of day Kuei-hai, Cheng tests [the proposition]: next day Hsin-wei(eight days later) the king, if he will make wine libation to the Ho(river god), it will not rain". P.179(12.36)貞其求我于河又雨:"Test [the proposition]: if, praying the Wo go to the Ho(river god), we will have rain".⁴⁴ P.181(12.41)戊子貞其尞于洹泉大三牢宜牢:"At Wu-tzu day(divination), test [the proposition]: if we make burning sacrifice to the Huan sources, then at the most, we shall make offerings(on slanted offering table) of three penned oxen". *Ibid*. (12.45)王其又于滴在又厂尞又雨:"The king when bringing offerings to the Shang(river god), if situated at the right rock shores, he makes a burning sacrifice, then we will have rain".

P.186(13.7)癸酉卜其取岳雨:"Divination of day Kuei-yu: if we take ears (i.e., make ear offerings) to the Yüeh(mountain god), it will rain". P.187(3.8)丁酉卜王朁岳尞叀犬十眔豚十又大雨叀羊十豚十:"At divination of day Ting-yu: as to the king, if we announce by written record sacrifices to the Yüeh(mountain god) by burning and consider(plan it to be) dogs numbering ten, and young piglets numbering ten, then we will have big rains; or we consider(it) sheep numbering ten and young piglets numbering ten". P.190(13.22)癸子(=己)貞其㶣丰山雨 This line, taken from *Chia-pien* 3642, is transcribed by Ch'ü Wan-li as 其㶣玉山雨(*Chia-pien* 788 writes 㶣, 636 has 㶣, explained as 㶣"hand holding torch" used for 炬 "to burn a sacrifice"): "At Kuei-tzu day(divination) test [the proposition]: if we make a burning sacrifice on the Yüeh(mountain; to Yüeh mountain god?) it will rain."⁴⁵ P.196(14.10)其又尞亳土又雨:"If making offerings, we burn(victims) to the earth god of P'o, then we have rain".⁴⁶ *Ibid*. (14.12)戊子卜其又戋于亳土三小牢十小牢:"At Wu-tzu day divination: if we make offerings, then we shall kill with axe for the earth god of P'o three or even ten small penned sheep". P.197(14.13)癸丑卜其又亳土叀袼 Ch'ü Wan-li has a more complete text(*Chia-pien* 1640): (1)其方…疾足,(2)癸丑卜其又亳土叀袼:"At divination of Kuei-ch'ou day, if we make an offering to the earth god of P'o then we shall consider it should be a harmonizing(propitiatory) rite".⁴⁷

P.199(14.15)甲子卜其求雨于東方:"At divination of day Chia-tzu, if we seek rain from the Eastern direction …"[sentence incomplete. Other possibility: "We might [*ch'i*: if need be] seek rain from. …"] P.200(14.21) …卜其簪求雨于南…:"At (X X day) divination: if we …, then pray for rain at the

South".⁴⁸ P.203(14.28)丙申卜㱿貞來乙子(=巳)酒下乙王固曰酒隹㞢希(=求?)其㞢 設、乙子(=巳)酒胆(=明)雨伐既雨咸伐亦雨㝬卯鳥星: "At divination day Ping-shen, K'o tests [the proposition]: next coming day Yi-ssu(nine days later) we shall make wine offering to Hsia-yi. The king prognosticating says: to pour wine is(> means) to have a calamity. One might on the other hand have a 設 sacrifice (?). On day Yi-ssu, a wine libation was made, next dawn(of the day) it rained. When making a beheading sacrifice, it was fully(既) raining; when to Hsien(i.e., 湯?) a beheading sacrifice was made, it rained increasingly more(or: continuously). We shall make an exorcist ritual and slaughter sacrificial victims to the Bird star".⁴⁹

P.209(14.43) 其求(~㱿)禾于咒賣罕卯: "When praying for harvest to ..., we shall burn (in sacrifice) a penned sheep and slaughter animals (such like oxen)". P.219(15.25)壬子卜爭我其乍邑帝弗ナ(=左)若吉三月: "At divination of day Jen-tzu, diviner Cheng tests [the proposition]: if we make the city, God will not assist and agree to(it). But consider lucky the third month". P.243(18.1)王 固曰其㞢雨甲辰丙午亦雨多: "The king prognosticating says: though we will have rain on day Chia-ch'en, on Ping-wu day the rain will be increasingly (亦) abundant". It is doubt-ful that 亦 should mean "also" in the bone texts: rather as an adverb with a fuller sense, it may mean "additionally, increasingly". P.248 (18.13)癸丑卜其尞于河尞雨: "At divination of day Kuei-ch'ou: if making a burning(of a sacrificial victim) at the stake, we make(this) burning at the river Ho, it will rain".⁵⁰ P.254(18.27)庚子卜貞王其觀耤叀往,于月: "At divination of day Keng-tzu, test [the proposition]: if the king watches the ploughing, then we consider that he shall go out. Twelfth month".

These examples of the use of *ch'i* require some additional comments. In particular those cases illustrating the function of *ch'i*, subordination mark, may indeed leave some doubts in our minds. For one thing, it would be rather unusual if one and the same particle would be used for functions so strongly diverging, at least when viewed in the respective translations by which this particle has been expressed. Moreover, a good number of these texts illustrating *ch'i* (subordination mark) are certainly open for other types of solutions. Already in cases like 7.26 and

14.15 other possibilities of analyzing and translating were mentioned. Strictly speaking, wherever the *ch'i* clause precedes another clause and the latter was taken as a main clause, one could equally consider both clauses as separate and independent, or at least apply the analysis where the *ch'i* clause is translated according to the formula: "Rather than doing this ... (*ch'i*: less desirable alternative), we shall do that". This solution might even seem preferable, since it will have been observed how some of Chang's texts have unusually long and complex types of sentences, which compared with other edited texts (for instance, Chang Ping-ch'üan) admit several break-ups into shorter sentences.

Yet in spite of that, a number of sentences will remain where *ch'i* (subordination mark) is still left as the only probable grammatical analysis. Among these must be counted the cases where the *ch'i* clause *follows* the main verb, for instance, "consider lucky that ... , assume that ... ," etc. The most striking case of this *ch'i* function is the (at first sight) quite exceptional pattern *wang ch'i* 亡其 as for instance in 亡其雨: "there will be no rain" (*ch'i*, less desirable alternative) and 亡其受又: not have (cause, chance) to receive assistance". As Takashima observed the pattern *wang ch'i* 亡其 is used throughout with few instances of 其亡 as would be expected when compared with all other cases where *ch'i precedes* the verb as in 其出囚: "there will be baneful influence," etc. The hypothesis presented to explain this exception is simply that *wang* 亡 is treated as a main verb "not have" followed by what is really an object clause, and that 亡其雨 literally means: "not have [chance] that it might rain". The few instances of 其亡 are: *Ping pien*⁷⁷ 王固曰吉隹其亡工言叀其徝 translated above, p. 23. Here 其亡 is a case of *ch'i* used as mark of subordinate clause, dependent from the verb 隹. Another case is *Ping pien* 47 (7, 8) 其出來齒 opposed to 其亡來齒 (double *ch'i*, also subordinative): "Whether they will have occasion to bring ivory," "or they will not have occasion to bring ivory".

To assume a function of *ch'i* (subordination mark) even already among the Shang texts would have the advantage of affording a possible bridge with the later classical *modal ch'i*. In order to understand the connection as well as the contrast between *ch'i* (subordination mark) and *ch'i* (less desirable alternative) a clearer analysis is needed for the latter. As pointed out before, the translation "perhaps, may be" is not only inadequate, but misleading. Yet, the translations suggested, such as "if need be, if unavoidable, *de rigueur*, one might after all ..." though more accurate, still being periphrastic, do not indicate the basic sense of *ch'i*.

Since the "less desirable alternatives" are mentioned in the divinatory texts, they were quite definite and factual, though undesirable, possibilities, and obviously they were so by the will of the gods or the ancestral spirits. If so, *ch'i* would simply stand for an *adverbial* term: "if(the gods) do wish so," i.e., "by divine *fiat*". This interpretation would permit(1) the shift to subordination function in clauses of the type: "rather than doing *a*, do *b*," where the original *ch'i* "less desirable" is still clearly preserved. (2) the function of double *ch'i* (as described above). (3) The function of *ch'i* in subordination before and after the main verb. (4) The development into the *modal ch'i* of later classical Chinese, which basically functions as an optative, exhortative and "probability" particle, a broadening of the original *ch'i*: "if(they) wish so". In the case of the *modal ch'i* development, it must be stressed that this is still in no way related to *ch'i* pronoun. The latter is in fact late, and not appearing in the Chou bronze texts until the later periods, while the *modal ch'i* is attested already in the earliest pieces.

2. *The Negatives*

Chang mentions the negative patterns: 弜 + negated clause; 不 and 弗 before verb or adjective predicate, 非 and 亡 before noun, but also 亡 as a mark of negative perfective(p. 40), probably as a parallel function to the use of *you* 出 which on one occasion he explains as indicating "perfective" (p. 114), 未"negative perfective" and 勿"prohibitive". On p. 61(3.31) he identifies 弜 as an equivalent of 弗. Here he is probably following Chang Tsung-ch'ien 張宗騫(On Similar Use of *Pi* 弜 and *Fu* 弗 in Oracle Inscriptions 卜辭弜弗通用考 *Yen-ching Journal*, No. 28, 1940.) If we examine the variants of 弜 shown in Sun Hai-po's and Chin Hsiang-heng's dictionaries of bone graphs, we see that though 弜 may be graphically related to 弓 nothing of the kind can be said of 弗. On the other hand 弜 shows graphic similarities with 勿. Chang explains the graph *wu* 勿 exclusively in the light of *Shuo wen* (p. 55, note 2). Yet, as is often the case, Hsü Shen in his *Shuo wen* may propose a new interpretation of graphs, basing himself either on the fact that a graph may have changed in shape or merged with another, or because the sound and etymology of the word (represented by the graph) as understood in his time suggested differently. The real argument for 弜 as a variant of 勿 (and not 弗) is the fact observed by Ch'ü Wan-li, that 弜 is almost exclusively found in period III of the bone inscriptions. In these pieces we can see that the negatives 弗, 不, 亡 are in no way lacking, but that it is exactly 勿 which is glaringly absent. When 勿 is found the form 弜 is lacking and *vice versa*. This (with a possible low proportion of exceptions or overlaps) seems decisive. In a paper read at the Annual Meeting of the American Oriental Society (New York, March 15, 1969), *Negatives in the Language of the Bone Inscriptions of Shang*, this interpretation, 弜 equals 勿 (against 弜 equals 弗 of Chang Tsung-ch'ien) was argued by me, together with a general outline of the differences of the negatives 不 versus 弗 and 毋 versus 勿, to correct the all too vague identifications of 勿, 不, 弗 as *t'ung yung* 同用, given, in *some* cases at least, by Kuan Hsieh-ch'u 管燮初 (*Yin-hsü chia-ku k'o-ts'u ti yü-fa yen-chiu* 殷虛甲骨刻辭的語法研究, 1953, p. 41) and Ch'en Meng-chia 陳夢家 (*Yin-hsü pu-ts'u tsung-shu* 殷虛卜辭綜述, 1956, pp. 127-129).

a) *Fei* 非, *a negative?*

The explanation of 𫞦 (equals 非) "negative + noun" is applied to the line 7.31 (p. 123) 庚辰貞日又戠 𫞦 日隹若庚辰貞日又戠其告于父丁用牛在黎 There are no further cases mentioned. A negative "not be + noun" found only *once* in such an extensive material becomes suspicious; furthermore, the regular negative of "to be" is not 非 (a much later occurrence in classical texts) but 不隹. If one still insists on 非 "negative," then it must be explained why it is so rare and in what way it differs from the regular 不隹. In translating 𫞦 as a basic form of 排 "to remove, push away, brush aside" we obtain a better and simpler translation. (Cf. supra, p. 30)

b) *Wei* 未, *a negative?*

Parallel to 非 we find also 未 to which Chang attributes the function of "negative with perfective aspect": "not yet" (pp. 256-257), again supported by one solitary example(19.3): [辛]酉卜旻未(未)出生辛酉卜其钔旻. First we ought to observe the ordinary graphic shape of 未, when used as a cyclical character (未, 未) and the way it appears here 未. We suggest that we probably have here a graphic variant of 求 (changed to 未: 求) and we translate: "Hsin-yu day divination: Lady Mu will *pray* to have successful delivery; Hsin-yu day divination: we might on the other hand(*ch'i*: less desirable course of action) have an exorcist rite over Lady Mu". For this kind of confusion between 求 and 未 compare also the cases already mentioned above, note 3. The expression 出生 "successful delivery" literally "have life" could also mean "have(male) progeny" (Li Hsiao-ting, *op.cit.*, 2099).

That *wei* 未, negative perfective particle, is highly improbable is because we find at least one case of the positive perfective particle 既 negated by *pu* 不 in Jao Tsung-yi, *op. cit.*, p. 703 (and more examples are given in Shima, *Index*, p.51). 辛亥卜湋貞龍不既骍其亦求更丁巳酻 "On Hsin-hai day divination, diviner Yang tests [the proposition]: the dragon(constellation) has not yet acted(risen, appeared); if, continuingly we(want to) pray, then consider(it be) a Ting-ssu day(for) wine libation". It is interesting to note in this context that in many *Shih ching* passages we find a contrast of the same kind between *wei* and *chi*: 君子未來, 君子既來 which suggests that 未 may very well take a later function and represent a fusion or contraction of 不既. "not yet" On the true negatives and their distinctive functions, I will here take the examples from Chang for discussion and when necessary refer to parallel or more complete lines from *Ping-pien*.

c) *Pu* 不 and *fu* 弗

1.1 疾齒不隹出壱、不隹父乙貞不隹止: "Having a toothache(lit. having as sickness the teeth) is not that(i.e., does not mean that) there is harmful influence; it is not(due) to Father Yi. Test [the proposition]: it is not...."[51] 1.12 不隹多介壱王父辛不壱: "It does not mean that 'many buffcoats' will harm the king. Father Hsin is not harmful(to any one)". Concerning 多介 "*to chieh*," Chang follows the explanation of Yang Shu-ta(*Chia wen shuo* 甲文説, p. 38) *viz.* as a name of a Shang king. 1.24 不隹婁壱子宀: "It is not E who harms Prince Mien". 2.1-2 不隹囚 "It is not(> it does not spell) disaster". 2.4 辛未

〔卜〕殷貞王夢兄戍何从、不隹囚: "At Hsin-wei day divination, K'o tests [the proposition]: the king dreamt of older brother Wu; Ho followed (i.e., Ho accompanying Wu?) It is not (> it does not spell) disaster". 2.9 貞王囚(=尤?)隹蠱貞帚好夢、不隹父乙. 貞隹父乙囚王: "Test [the proposition]: the king is suffering bad effects; it is (because of) magic. Test [the proposition]: Lady Hao dreamt; it is not Father Yi. Test [the proposition]: it is Father Yi who causes pain to the king". 蠱 is translated as "parasites" by Chang. Cf. Shirakawa Shizuka 白川静 in *Kōkotsu kimbun gaku ronsō* 甲骨金文學論叢 Vol. 7, 1958, pp. 73-133 with a discussion on the wide implications of 蠱, not only as physical body parasites, but as also "magic noxious influences". Also, Shima, *Index* 386, Li Hsiao-ting, *op. cit.*, 3929. 2.10 貞王夢帚好不隹哥: "The king dreamt Lady Hao is not (who) will bring suffering". 2.11 貞王夢不隹兄戍: "Test [the proposition]: the king dreamt; it is not older Brother Wu". 2.13 乙丑卜殷貞甲子㘝乙丑王夢牧石麋(?)不隹囚隹又: "At Yi-ch'ou day divination, K'o tests [the proposition]: on Chia-tzu day down to Yi-ch'ou day (60 and 61 days before), the king dreamt he herded a stone elk(?). It is not (a sign of) disaster. It is a blessing".

5.17 乙未貞隹卡壱㘝弖卯㘝 This line is differently arranged and transcribed by Ch'ü Wan-li as part of a much longer context (*Chia-pien* 562): (1)伊雨?(2)不伊雨?(3)不往冓雨?(4)乙未貞隹上下壱㘝?(5)不隹上下壱㘝?(6)丁酉貞…?(7)戊戌卜出雨?(8)己亥貞酒夔于戠?(9)弖御㘝: "It is rain. It is not rain (i.e., it forebodes or does not forebode rain). We shall not proceed, (for) we will encounter rain. On Yi-wu day (divination), test [the proposition]: it is (i.e., refers to) the upper and lower (divinities) which will harm Pi(?). It is not that upper and lower (divinities) will harm Pi(?). On Ting-yu day (divination), test [the proposition]: … on Mou-hsü day (divination) … rain. At Chi-hai day (divination), test [the proposition]: we shall bring wine libation, make holocaust sacrifice to. … We ought not to make exorcist rites for (or: on) Pi". Ch'ü Wan-li according to the traditional way, puts a question mark after each sentence. Chang explains 卡 as a combination of 上甲 and 下乙 which he compares to the *ho-wen* 仒 equal to 下乙, yet both cases are not the same. Ch'ü (*Chia-pien* 2416, 3629) on the contrary, reads 上下 "upper and lower deities". 㘝 is transcribed by Ch'ü as 伃. Chang calls this graph "nicht identifizierbar," but recognizes 匕 is probably *phonetic* (which stands over the lower part that is simply 皀); though used as a name, the whole graph must mean "ladle" or "ritual vessel and ladle". 15.5 ... 宁貞霰(雷?)不隹囚: "Diviner Pin test [the proposition]: the hail(sleet? thunder?) is not a sign of disaster". 15.29 王囚隹咎、貞不隹帝咎王: "The king's bad omen is(〉 means) an evil influence. Test [the proposition]: it does not mean that God will be harmful to the king". 1.14 女娥弗壱王: "Girl (woman?) Ko will not harm to the king". 1.16 貞牅隹壱盡戍弗求(希): (On X X day divination) test [the proposition]: having bellyache is(〉 means) a baleful influence; Chin Wu does not cause evil effects(to the king)". This text 1.16 is the same as that of 1.10 only more complete. The graph 牅 (compare Chang p. 52 牅 for 牅) is not found in Shima, *Index*, but the passage is quoted, p.6, *s.v.*, 牅, in the expression 牅牅 "to be sick in the body...(身)". 12.2 庚申卜永貞河壱雨貞河弗壱雨: "On Keng-shen day divination, diviner Yung tests [the proposition]: Ho(river god) will not harm the rain". 84. The phrase, literally translated as "to harm the rain," is open to two different interpretations: harm i.e., prevent, stop the rain(which we desire) (so understood by Chang) or it could also be "to bring as harm rain" opposed to "not bring as harm rain". The expression is found elsewhere and regularly, e.g., *Ts'ui pien* 75:隹王亥壱雨 but transcribed by Kuo with different punctuation, separating 雨 "it will rain" as an independent sentence from the rest. 壱雨 can be considered a verb+object, for "bring as harm something" a pattern comparable to 疾 + object: "have as sickness/the teeth, etc." Shima, *Index* 85 has a sentence 隹卬壱雨: "It is 卬 who will cause as harm the rain".

13.3   乙酉卜岳弗壱禾其壱禾丙戌其壱:"At Yi-you day divination, test [the proposition]: Yüeh(mountain god) will not harm the plants. On the other hand, he might (*ch'i*) still harm the plants. At Ping-hsü day (divination): Yüeh (mountain god) will harm(the plants)". 1.2 貞王疾隹匕己壱貞隹匕庚貞不死: "Test [the proposition]: the king's sickness is a harm(caused by) ancestral Mother Chi. Test [the proposition]: it is ancestral Keng(not Chi, who does the harm). Test [the proposition]: he will not die". On 死 "to die" cf. supra, note 5. 1.25 貞乎弗其囚凡(=風)出疾:"... will not cause evil effect..." (This line has been translated in full on p. 37) 2.5 庚辰卜貞多鬼夢不至囧: "At Keng-Shen day divination, test [the proposition]: the many spirits of the dead causing dreams, it will not reach to the point that it be harmful". Chang translates the phrase 不至囧: "Kommt ein Unheil nicht zu?", literally: /nicht/ ankommen/ Unheil/. Yet in this sequence 囧 cannot be subject. The translation offered: "not reach to (the point that it) be harmful" assumes that 囧 is not even object of 至 in causative sense "make arrive," because the negative used is 不. Yet the negative 不 could be present in such patterns, if they are understood as "stative" predicates, with an "eventive aspect," comparable to the type of negations in weather predictions "(God will) not send down rain," etc. Then, it would mean: "will not be causing harm".

15.25 帝弗又若: "God will not assist(or) find(it) agreeable". 12.3 河弗壱我禾: "Ho(river god) will not harm(prevent) our harvest". 5.26(a)癸丑貞甲寅酒大御自上甲衆六十小羍兹用上甲不冓雨大乙不冓雨大丁冓雨,(b)庚申貞今來甲子酒王大御于大甲衆六十小羍卯九牛不冓雨: "At Kuei-ch'ou day divination, test [the proposition]: on day Chia-yin(next day) making wine libation, we greatly perform exorcist rites, starting from Shang-chia(down to other ancestors); offer as holocaust 60 small penned sheep. This was used (i. e., applied); but (with) Shang-chia, we were not encountering rain; with Ta-yi there was no encountering rain; with Ta-ting, we encountered rain. At Keng-shen day(divination), test [the proposition]: when at the present, the next Chia-tzu day(four days later), we make wine libation and greatly perform exorcist rites for Ta-chia, burn in holocaust 60 small sheep and slaughter 9 oxen, then we will not encounter rain." 6.24 叀戊田弜(勿)往田不擒既求王其田杏: "Considering it a Wu day(on which) to hunt, we ought not proceed to hunt, (for it) will not be caught(i.e., nothing will be caught); having made prayers, the king might (*de rigueur: ch'i*) hunt at Yung". ("ought not ... for nothing will be caught" is equivalent to "if we do not proceed ... it will not be caught"). From the context it appears that it has already been found out that it is not advisable to go hunting, yet it does not say any harm will necessarily follow, simply that nothing will be caught. Hence, the *ch'i* clause leaves open a possibility of hunting at another place. This is why the whole oracular statement should probably be taken as one, not as four separate consecutive questions.

10.24 乙亥卜何貞宎唐不冓雨十月: "At Yi-hai day divination, diviner Ho tests [the proposition]: in treating T'ang as guest, if we offer food as sacrificial gifts, there will not be encountering rain. Tenth month". Chang translates 冓雨 in a sort of passive, "vom Regen überrascht werden". 冓 does not necessarily imply "surprise" or "unforeseen rain". 14.30 尞云不雨: "Though we bring holocaust as sacrifice to the cloud(god), it will not rain". 15.3 戊子卜殻貞帝及三月令雨貞帝弗及今三月令雨王固曰丁雨不叀辛旬丁酉允雨: "At Wu-tzu day divination, K'o tests [the proposition]: God will make it reach the fourth month to have rain. Test: God will not make it reach the fourth month to have rain(*ch'i*: less desirable alternative). The king prognosticating says: on a Ting day it will rain; we do not expect(consider, plan for) a Hsin day. On the decade's day Ting-yu, in fact it rained". Chang translates: "On day Wu-tzu, K'o asked the oracle whether God until this month, the fourth of the year, will give a command that it will rain. The king prognosticated saying: it will rain on day Ting or *perhaps* on day Hsin. On day Ting-yu of the following decade it did indeed rain." The two first sentences which clearly have a separate introductory formula 貞... are translated as one; this allows Chang to avoid the problem of 及 and 弗.

15.6 云自北申隹厶雨不咎隹好: "The clouds starting from the North extend (roll out, unfold); it is(> means) they will make rain. They are not harming, but are a good thing"[52]. 15.22 壬寅卜宾貞若茲不雨帝隹茲邑龍不若: "At Jenyin day divination, diviner Pin tests [the proposition]: that it does not rain like this (i.e., it fails to rain for such a long time), as to God, it is this city Lung(?) which is not compliant, pleasing".[53] 15.32 帝弗吉于王: "God does not give good luck to the king". 16.6 不喪眾: "not be losing its masses". (cf. supra, p.35) 16.36 辛未卜帝鳳不用雨: "Hsin-wei day divination: we shall perforin the Ti-sacrifice to(the god of the) Wind. It was not applied, for it rained".[54] 17.1 庚辰王弗疾朕𢎥①: "On day Keng-ch'en(divination)... king [tests the proposition]: they will not cause suffering on my grandee X... (?)"[55] 18.20 (a)于癸烄凡于甲烄凡

---

① 編者按: "𢎥", 原文誤作 "𢎥", 下文不誤。今據甲骨原拓及下文徑改。

弜烄凡不雨: "... either on a Kuei day we shall burn(a sacrifice) at the stake to the Wind(god), or on a Chia day we shall make a burning sacrifice at the stake to the Wind(god). We ought not burn at the stake(a victim) to the Wind(god), for it will not rain". ("... ought not ..." i.e., "if we do not ... it will not rain".)⁵⁶

From these examples and those already given to illustrate the use of *ch'i*, it will be clear that we have consistently tried to tie the negative *pu* with stative, intransitive or passive verbs, and *fu* with active-transitive verbs. Some of the verbs are always treated as intransitive, stative(e.g., to rain, etc.), others can be both(e.g., to harm, to be harmful); others though intransitive(e.g., to reach a point) can be turned into transitive, causative: "to make reach"; others can be transitive or passive: "to catch by net in hunt" and "to be caught," depending on the negative used. There is a striking exception to this rule: when the transitive verb has a personal *pronoun* object, *pu* is used with inversion of the regular sequence. 6.27 貞求于上甲受我又勿求于上甲不我其〔受又〕: "Test [the proposition]: making a prayer to Shang-chia, he will extend to us (hand us) assistance. Do not make prayers to Shang-chia(i.e., if we do not...) he will not *on us* extend his assistance". 14.36 庚戌卜殻貞蛊不我壱: "At Keng-hsü day divination, K'o tests [the proposition]: (their) black magic will not harm us". 15.11 貞帝不我莫: "Test [the proposition]: God will not(lit. drought us) inflict on us a drought". 15.16 貞勿伐⎕帝不我其受又: "Test [the proposition]: we ought not attack the Hu(?) (i.e., if we do not..), God might not(*ch'i*) extend to us his help". Chang translates this last text in two separate questions: "Should war not be made against the Hu? Will God not grant us help?"

Another exception is that verb phrases, referring to weather, even if consisting of transitive verb + object(令雨 "command rain," 冓雨 "encounter rain," 降莫 "send down drought," 易日 "change to sun > sunny weather") are still treated as stative intransitive verbs. 15.24 帝不其令多雨: " As to God, we might not by his command have abundant rain". 15.9 貞帝不降大莫、九月: "Test [the proposition]: God will not send down great drought. Ninth month". 12.1 貞羽甲戌河不令雨: "Test [the proposition]: next Chiahsü day Ho(river god) will not command rain". 4.1 乙子(=巳)卜酒子漁钔不其易日: "At Yi-ssu day divination: making wine libation, if

Prince Yü performs exorcist rites, it still may not change to sunny weather".

The same usage of the negative *pu* 不 with transitive verbs + object is not only found in sentences relating to events connected with "weather," but also with other transitive verbs + object, which may even appear elsewhere negated by the "normally expected" negative *fu* 弗. The difference can be explained in *analogy* with the cases of predictions connected with weather, in the sense that for instance in the sentence 不受年 as distinguished from 弗受年("not receive" or "not grant good harvest"), a specific aspect(*"eventive"*) is being stressed where the predication 受年"to receive" or "grant harvest" is considered a mere *event* happening to the interested party for whom the divination is performed.

d) *Negative* 亡(*opposed to* 出)

1.8 貞疾止隹出壱: "Test [the proposition]: having sickness in the foot, it is(> means) there is evil influence". Compare 1.15 … 爿臣亡壱我: "The sick servant(?) does not have(occasion, cause) to harm us".[57] 5.13 其酚坯又大雨弜酚亡大雨: "If with written record we perforin exorcist rites, we will have a big rain. We ought not have any written record(rite), (for) there will not be big rains". (i.e., if we do not have …) 10.16 丙辰卜旅貞羽丁子(=巳)酚于中丁衣亡壱在八月: "At Ping-ch'en day divination, diviner Lü tests [the proposition]: on next Ting-ssu day, in performing harmonizing sacrifice to Chung-ting, we bring Yi-sacrifice, there will be no disaster. It is in the eighth monthn". 10.17 甲戌卜尹貞窆夕禍亡囚在六月、貞亡丈(?)乙亥卜尹貞大乙祭亡囚: "At Chia-hsü day divination, diviner Yin tests [the proposition]: the king shall, treating as guests (the gods), on the eve before present a wine libation; there will be no disaster. It was at the sixth moon. Test: there will be no harm. At Yi-hai day divination, diviner Yin tests [the proposition]: the king will treat as guest ancestor Ta-yi, and bring meat sacrifice; there will be no evil influencen."[58] (Compare 10.18; 10.20.) 10.27 癸卯王卜貞肜羽日自上甲至多後衣亡壱自馘在九月隹王五〔祀〕: "At Kuei-mao day, king's(own) divination, test: when offering wine libation, making sun dance, we start from Shang-chia to reach down to the many later generations (of king ancestors) to offer Yi-sacrifice, we will have no harm or any originating (> resulting) evil effects. It is in the ninth month; it is the king's fifth cultic year". Chang explains 自 in the expression 自㞢 as "selbst, sogar". This implies that 自 would have developed from "selbst" into some vague adverbial function "sogar," but it is not explained how. 自 as a verb "to start from, originate" makes good sense "originating > arising evil effects". In this text, again 壱 and 㞢 occur together and must mean two different kinds of "bad, ominous" things.

e) *Prohibitive* 勿 (*or* 弜)

3.12 〔于〕母庚卸帚好齒勿于母庚卸:"To Mother Keng, we shall make exorcist rite over Lady Hao's teeth(toothache?); do not to Mother Keng make any ritual exorcism". In this idiomatic usage of 卸 "to make an exorcist rite," the direct object is the person or the suffering, the feared harm over which the exorcism is made; the indirect object with 于 refers to the deity or ancestral spirit to whom the ritual is addressed. 3.23 勿卸雀于母庚:"Do not make ritual exorcism on Ch'üeh to Mother Keng". (cf. 4.18.) 3.24 丙午卜勿卸雀于兄丁:"Ping-wu day divination: do not ritually exorcize Ch'üeh to Older Brother Ting". 4.17 己卯卜殻貞卸帚好于父乙㝬羊㞢豕酻十窂貞勿酻: "At Chi-mao day divination, K'o tests [the proposition]: ritually exorcize Lady Hao to Father Yi, and offer(ready cooked in vessel) a sheep, bring as offering swine and sacrifice with written record ten penned sheep. Test: do no offer with record(any such sacrifice)". 4.18 丙子卜殻貞勿卸帚媟于庚酻庚窂酻庚三窂:"At Ping-tzu day divination, K'o tests [the proposition]: do not make exorcist rites over Lady Hsieh for Keng; bring as record-documented offerings to Keng a penned sheep(or) bring as recorded offering to Keng three penned sheep". 6.26 貞勿乎伐⿰方貞勿昇人羊貞昇人千:"Test [the proposition]: do not call out(the order) to attack the Hu(?) and Fang. Test: do not make ascend and present as sacrificial victims 3000 men. Test: make ascend in sacrifice(only) 1000 men".[59] 6.29 貞求于黃尹貞勿求于黃尹:"Test [the proposition]: do pray to Huang Yin. Test: do not pray to Huang Yin". On Huang Yin, cf. supra note 6. Chang here again mistakenly transcribes Yi-yin. 7.6 貞勿于父乙告疾身:"Test [the proposition]: do not announce to Father Yi that(someone) has pain in the body". Chang(p.110) explains the graph 𠂆 as "kniegelenk". He gives no sources for this identification and adds that this graph "hat in späteren Zeiten kein Equivalent". The classical language equivalent of "knee, knee joint" is 郤, 膝 and probably corresponds to the bone graph 从. Shima, *Index* 447 transcribes the same phrase(7.6) as 疾身. 12.17 辛未卜㱿貞王勿徣伐[ ]方:"At Hsinwei day divination, K'o tests [the proposition]: the king ought not to go against and attack the Hu(?) and the Fang". 7.25 貞王勿出田丁未卜争貞王告于且乙:"Test [the proposition]: the king ought not to go out to hunt. Divination of Ting-wei day, Cheng tests [the proposition]: the king shall make announcement to Tsu-yi". 14.14 貞勿求年于邦土:"Test [the proposition]: we ought not to pray for harvest to the Earth god of Pang". On p. 127 Chang explains 邦土 as a place name 邦社. Shima, *Kenkyū*, p. 229 thinks it does not refer to a particular place name but to a general common term "earth spirit of vegetation (邦 not 邦)". 15.20 王勿从蔑帝若:"Test [the proposition]: as to the king, he ought not to follow X, and God will find it agreeable".⁶⁰ 15.23 王勿乍邑:"As to the king, he ought not to make the city". 16.2 勿帝犬勿帝虎…:"Do not offer a dog in Ti-sacrifice; do not offer a tiger in Ti-sacrifice".⁶¹ 16.20 豹勿帝于瀤:"As to Pao, do not make a Ti-sacrifice to Kuei(river god)". Chang explains 豹 as a name of a king. But when we compare 14.31 己丑卜争貞亦乎雀爇于云豹貞勿乎雀爇于云豹:"At divination of day Chi-ch'ou, diviner Cheng tests [the proposition]: continuing call upon the Ch'üeh to burn in sacrifice to the Cloud(god) a leopard; Test: do not call upon the Ch'üeh to burn in sacrifice to the Cloud(god) a leopard," it seems quite possible that here in 16.20 豹 is really an emphatically exposed object of the verb 帝:"as to a leopard, do not offer(it) as victim in Ti-sacrifice at the Kuei river". Shima, *Index* 225 moreover quotes this text as having 虎(not 豹); *ibid*., 246 the same text is quoted but with an additional character (雨)added at the end.

16.24 勿乎雀帝于西:"Do not call upon the Ch'üeh to make a Ti-sacrifice at the West". 16.28 貞勿方旁:"Do not make Ti-sacrifice in(to?) the four directions". This quote from 16.28 is preceded by 貞方帝一羌二犬卯一牛:"We shall in all directions offer in Ti-sacrifice one ch'iang(prisoner), two dogs and slaughter one ox". This and the following negative opposite are translated by Chang as if they were one sentence. Furthermore, though we follow Chang in his translation of 方, there is some doubt, for 方 may have been another "sacrificial term"(祊)used in combination with 帝. 18.28 弜耤…: "Do not plough ..." (period Ⅲ, use of 弜 for 勿). 12.13 貞勿舞河亡其雨: "Test [the proposition]: do not (i.e., if we do not) perform dance for the Ho (river god), we will not have rain". 18.17 勿焚姓亡其雨: "Do not burn (i.e., if we do not ...) at the stake (woman) Tsai, we might not have any rain".

f. *Prohibitive* 毋

Besides the prohibitive negative particles 勿 and 弜, we find a small number of cases with 毋 (taken from the *Ping pien* collection): 331(6) 毋其隹衣: "It ought not be a Yi-sacrifice". 332(2) 王固曰勿雨隹其風既雨毋其既雨: "The king prognosticating says: it ought not, when raining, be (so) that it is windy. It will be finished raining; it ought not be finished raining". P.5(*Yi-pien* 3219) 百牛至百牛毋其至: "Hundred oxen will be arriving. Hundred oxen ought not be arriving".[62] Compare 76(10-11) 至于庚寅夋遒既若毋至于庚寅夋不若: "Until Keng-yin day, when making exorcist rites, we will get to the point that it will be fully agreeable. It ought not be reaching till Keng-yin day, for the exorcist rites will not be agreeable". P.136(*Ping-pien* 90) 小臣又其妨癸酉卜甲戌毋妨: "Small Servant has (chance) that it be lucky; (but) from Kuei-yu day passing to Chia-hsü day, it ought not be considered lucky". 178(5-6) 帚妌其㞢子 negated as 帚妌毋其㞢子: "Lady Ching might have a son; Lady Ching ought not be expected (?) to have a son".[63] 197(2-3) 㞢㡀 opposed to 毋其徙㞢㡀: "It will have ominous effect. It ought not be that it continues to have ominous effect". Compare for instance 40(14-15) 㞢于父甲 negated as 勿㞢于父甲 "Perform a sacrifice to Father Chia; do not perform a sacrifice to Father Chia".

Though this survey, hopefully, brings some clarity and system into the grammar of the negatives of the Shang texts, it must be admitted that some baffling cases still wait a final solution. In this respect, however, the Shang materials are not different from many other passages in later Chinese texts. The problem of the uses and forms of negatives in Chinese in general has been the object of some interesting observations and comments on all sorts of unusual, exceptional, and at first sight highly irregular or illogical usages, by Yang Lien-sheng 楊聯陞 in *Miscellaneous Notes on Negatives in Classical and Modern Chinese*, 漢

語否定詞雜談 (*Tsing Hua Journal of Chinese Studies*, New Series, IX, No. 1-2, Studies in Linguistics, Presented to Dr. Yuen Ren Chao on His Eightieth Birthday, September 1971, pp. 160-191.)

In the Shang texts, one such problem is the fact that when comparing the prohibitive forms used with about 75 different verbs in the *Ping-pien* collection, the occurrences of 毋 are in a very slender minority, and those of 勿 are used with *all kinds* of verbs both in stative-passive and active-transitive function. Though it seems that, parallel to the contrastive use of 不 and 弗, we can assign a stative-intransitive aspect to the function of 毋 and a transitive-active or causative function in connection with 勿, the exceptions in respect to 勿 are quite numerous and striking. To attempt a solution through an historical development whereby 勿 would gradually assume all the functions of 毋 seems to promise little success, since the 毋 and 勿 opposition is quite well preserved in the Chou bronze inscriptions. To resort to solutions by "deletion" or "supplementing" of certain words, is dangerous; such solutions require a clear and well established *context* based on a solid and reliable *reading* of the Shang texts.

Another difficulty is the relation between 隹 and 叀. Usually both are considered the same. Yet the regular negation of 隹 is 不隹, the negation of 叀 is overwhelmingly expressed by 勿隹 with only rare cases of 不叀. For instance: 39(5) 王固曰吉戋隹甲不叀丁: "The king prognosticating says: it is lucky. To destroy (the enemy) shall be (> shall happen on) a Chia day. It shall not be considered a Ting day". 264(1) 隹丁不叀…: "It shall be a Ting day, it will not be considered … (X-day)". *Chia-pien* 2670 叀 and … 不其叀…: "It shall be considered …, … it might after all not be considered. …"[64] A full scale examination of the usages of the negatives in declarative sentences shows that many verbs can be negated by 不 as well as by 弗, depending on the actual function of the verb in the particular context. But some verbs, because of their natural semantic content, are exclusively or to a great extent limited to either the negative particle 不 or 弗. The case of 叀 and 隹, however, seems to be a flagrant exception by this regular opposition of 叀 and 勿隹.

To conclude these remarks on grammar and Chang's views of the grammar of

Shang inscription texts, and the translations based on his views, it is clear that a rigorous search for consistent and logical grammatical rules will help us to refine and improve our understanding of the oracular statements. It is precisely this part of the language analysis that will provide a minimum of certitude about what is said rather than a mere vague indication as to what sort of topic the oracle is talking about.

V. GRAPHIC ANALYSIS

In the remaining part of this review some special cases will be discussed relating to the identification and explanation of separate bone graphs. These are examples, taken from Chang's work, that are not directly connected with grammatical or syntactic functions, but only with the graphic analysis, the meaning and usage in the texts, and problems regarding sound or pronunciation. A number of such instances have already been mentioned with the texts or in footnotes, as they occurred in oracular sentences quoted above.

In the transcription and identification of graphs, often solutions and analyses were offered which are new but lack sufficient evidence to carry conviction. Often the source or basis for presenting such a solution is not given.

P. 104　新 having 辛 as phonetic is explained as "Frische Wunde". No grounds are given for this interpretation. Maybe 辛 "pictograph of an awl-like puncturing tool" is understood as "etymonic" for "to stab, to punish"? From Li Hsiao-ting, *op.cit*., p.407, we see that two variants exist, one with 辛 and 斤, and another with 辛 + 木 and 斤. Hence, there is equal ground that 辛 on top of 木 + 斤 may refer to a word "to chop wood with an axe" with phonetic 辛. The variant 新 could be a simplification. Then 新 is simply the original form of 薪 "firewood, brush wood, chop firewood".

P.89　白 is explained as the pictograph of 貌 "Gesicht". Again no source given. Probably he has in mind the *Shuo wen* analysis of 皃(*SWKL* 3832)从人从白、白象人面形. 皃 is a variant of 貌(with 豹 as reduced phonetic). The analysis that 白 in 皃 represents acc. to *Shuo wen* "a human face" does not mean that 白 alone "white" is the pictograph of "face," not even in Hsü Shen's opinion. The graph 白 alone and in various other combinations may very well be the result of different graphic representations that have converged into one. We can think of 白 "acorn" (in 樂: 櫟 and 皂), "thumb" (in 百, Kuo Mo-jo), "target" (的 cf. Serruys, *Monumenta Serica*, XIX, 1960, pp.138-143).

P.203 It is stated that 毃 in bone form 🅐 "stellt die Zerschlagung eines Weinkruges mit dem Knüppel dar"; no modern corresponding graph is given. Chang Ping-ch'üan (PP 207) transcribes 毃, Shima, *Index* 94 writes 殳; in *Kenkyū*, pp.323-324 a number of variants are given. The interpretation "beating (a vessel)" or "punishing, killing" (a human victim) proposed by Wu Ch'i-ch'ang, is rejected by Shima in favor of "to dance," a reading still less probable. Li Hsiao-ting, *op. cit.*, 1099, identifies the graph as 殳, but gives no meaning that will fit in the bone text usages. He quotes, however, Ch'ü Wan-li, who transcribes 殳* *d'ug*, with *ku-wen* 殺* *t'wad*; "baton" > "to beat"; in the bone texts it is used in the sense of 用牲之名, e.g., 出殳, "have a sacrifice by beating to death the victim," 殳六人 "beat to death six men"; these lines are found in parallel with other sacrificial terms: 殳二人, 卯二牢. This action 殳 can both be auspicious or inauspicious: 出殳吉; 其出殳不吉.

P.106 Chang explains 🅑 as a variant of 🅒 (盡) used as a place name or personal name. The distinction between 皿 or 🅓 is very clear however. This has been interpreted in various ways (Shima, *Index* 452), and Li Hsiao-ting, *op. cit.*, 981 proposes 妻 as the corresponding modern form, identical with 嬖* *ngiad* "to govern, regulate" (妻: signifying, 乂 phonetic part), e.g., *Yi pien* 1054: 旨正不其妻 "Chih attacking, it will not be put under control". Yet the explanation 妻 is not so simple and probable from a graphic point of view because of the identification 🅓 = 乂; on the contrary, 🅒 is more probably *hua* 畫. Cf. Cheng Te-k'un, "The T'u-lu colour-container of the Shang-chou period," *Bulletin of the Museum of Far Eastern Antiquities*, Vol.37, Stockholm 1965, p.246.

P.215 🅔 (variant p.219 🅕) Chang sees in this form a pictograph of an "arbeitende Hand". It is without exception accepted by all as corresponding to modern 乍 and 作 "to do, to make". Li Hsiao-ting (*op. cit.*, 2637 and 3807) prefers to leave the interpretation of the graph unsolved. Against the opinion of Chang there is the explanation of Kuo Mo-jo that it is basically a variant graph of 孔, bone form 孑 and this still seems the most probable solution, ∀ or ∀ cannot readily be taken as "a hand," but it can be seen as a simplified form of 孑, the "kneeling" part of the figure being left out. In the variants of ∀, the different additions ∨ or ↓, ⋈, ⋈ etc. are variations of ⊞ (玉), implying "to work (on jade, and other objects)". Yeh Yü-sen's objection that 孔 *always* shows a "man kneeling" and that 乍 does not, does not seem to be an obstacle in view of the kind of simplifications that can be observed among certain variants of the graph. Chin Hsiang-heng in *CKWT*, Vol. 19 gives more variants of the bone graph for 乍 and attributes three basic meanings to it: 爲, 祚, and 治.

P. 109 告 is explained as the pictograph for the derived character 梏 "Maulkorb" (gag, muzzle). Yet 梏 means "manacles" and written 牿, it means "beam attached to horns (to prevent oxen to harm in butting)". This interpretation does not explain 告 "to announce" except by simply applying the principle of loan graph, and in that case it does not matter what 告 originally was. The *Shuo wen* interpretation, called "umständig und unklar" is not based on the original pictographic sense of 告 but on a mythological motive of "ox, accuser and punisher in ordeals". Other solutions proposed, however, are for instance that of Chang Yi-jen 張以仁 (*Ta-lu tsa-chih*), Vol. 33.4, 1966, pp. 109-111, and Shirakawa Shizuka 白川静 (*Kōkotsu kimbungaku ronsō*), 甲骨金文學論叢, Vol. 4 (1961), p. 154: 載書關係 説 where the top part is interpreted as 木 "tree, pole" and 凵 is "document, record *attached* to a pole" > to announce, announcement.

P. 56 韋 is explained by Chang as "klaffen, auseinandergehen" (p. 56); this repeats a late *Shuo wen* interpretation 相背 because 舛 seems to indicate that the "feet" go in "opposite" directions. But this cannot be applied to the Shang bone graph (Shima, *Index* 74). Li Hsiao-ting (*op. cit.*, 1929) follows the majority of authors in taking it as "feet going around": 圍 "to surround, defend" etc.

P. 35 㞢 is explained as 祟 "Fluch, verfluchen". This rather specific meaning does not derive so naturally from the fact that in texts it represents a *verb*, the agent or subject of which is usually a dead ancestor or a deity and the result is "sickness or disaster" among the living. Moreover, 㞢 with pronunciation *t'o* (Shima, *Index* 82; Li Hsiao-ting, *op. cit.*, 597.3933) cannot be taken as a word, identical with 祟 *sui*, even if the meanings were supposedly similar. The explanation of 㞢＞祟 by graphic substitutions 止 into 出 and 它, 虫 into 示 strikes us as farfetched and a mere *ad hoc* solution. On 祟 cf. Shima, *Index*, 209; Li Hsiao-ting, *op. cit.*, 97, and Pai Yü-cheng 白玉崢 in *CKWT*, Vol. 34, 1964 (pp. 10-11) and Vol. 39, 1971 (pp. 10-11).

P. 56 [graph] with several variants, is explained by Chang as a pictograph for "das Messen einer Matte [graph] bzw. einer 'Stange' mit ausgebreiteten Armen …" With Ch'ü Wan-li he considers this graph as corresponding to the modern 度. It is true that 度 is a measure and may even belong to the same phonetic series as 席, but the *graphic* analysis given by T'ang Lan (followed by Li Hsiao-ting, *op. cit.*, 1031, 4437) shows how almost every part of the graph leads to 尋 *$dzi\partial m$* "to measure" (cf. *Erh Ya* 尋：舒兩肱也 "to stretch both arms"). Among the bone texts, *Chia-pien* 1159 has the expression [graph] 舟于河 which, of course, would fit perfectly with the identification 度＞渡 "to cross the river in a boat". But 舟 is here direct object of 度, and "cross the river *in* a boat" would presumably be something different than 度舟于… (but 舟度于…?). It would be grammatically much more acceptable if [graph] were read 尋＝彤 *$t'i\partial m$* "to float, make float (a boat) on the river" (Cf. Serruys, *Monumenta Serica*, XXI, 1962, pp. 227-228). Finally, in the variant [graph] we need not explain | as "eine Stange", for it is probably a mere simplification of the drawing [graph] "mat".

The two last examples bring us to some cases where the author has completely ignored the lights that can be had from Chinese historical phonology: in some cases we find statements involving phonology that are erroneous and in others where phonology is not even considered.

P. 168 先, bone form [graph] and variant [graph], is analyzed with *Shuo wen* as 从儿从之. It is quite probable that the lower part 人 (bone graphs do not distinguish 几 and 人) is phonetic, in the same way it is phonetic in 年 (bone form [graph]) and 千 ([graph] marked with 一二三 as additional signifiers). In this way there is no need to explain 先: "Es stellt einen *Fuss* dar, der *vor einem anderen Mensch steht*"; this is only a subjective play on supposed semantic associations. Furthermore, it is not true that 炎 became *uniformly* 秂 in Chou time bronze inscriptions (cf. Jung Keng, *Chin Wen pien* No. 0941), but only by late Chou and *Shuo wen* time. Therefore, it is not sure at all that once 炎 became 秂, 秃 (originally 炎) now can be used for 禿 *t'u* "bald". Rather, 秃 the original form of which we do not know consisted of 禾 or a *similar element* that played a phonetic role (as *Shuo wen* suggest), probably a corruption or reduction of 秀 * *siuk*.

P. 60 㞢 is identified with 仙 (following Yang Shu-ta). Phonologically this needs some explanation because of the difference of initials * *g-*/* *d-*.

P. 64 易, bone form ⧆, "to give" is explained by Chang as a pictograph of "tin" because a (Chou) bronze vessel, the Te-ting 德鼎 (cf. *CKWT*, Vol. 37, 1970, pp. 48-49 and Vol. 40, 1971, pp. 1-4) has a graph ⧆, used in the sense of "to give, to grant". But it does not prove that either 益 or 易 is pictographically the same, and should mean "tin". Both are found in the bone texts (Shima, *Index* 384, 494), but are phonologically not identical (cf. Karlgren, *Grammata Serica*, 849-50 益 * ·*iək*/易 * *diěk*.) According to Li Hsiao-ting (*op. cit.*, 3823, 4055) the word is indeed used for "grant, give," but not as frequently as the occurrences of 易 for "change." If 益 and 易 have no relations, then Yang Shu-ta's explanation that 易 is "the sun breaking through the clouds," hence "to change into sunny weather," gains new probability; the usage of 易 for "to give" should be explained as a phonetic loan. Cf. also *CKWT*, Vol. 30, 1968, pp. 18-19, Lee Yim's review of Shima's *Index*, pp. 194-195.

P. 111 徬: a graph, presumably without modern equivalent, explained by Chang as "to spy"; he rightly doubts the explanation of T'ang Lan that this be the same graph as 還, bone form ⧆. But on what basis can Chang consider the element 方 as "phonetic" in 徬, if we cannot propose any solution as to graph or pronunciation?

VI. CONCLUSION

The conclusion from all the preceding observations for the readers of this review to draw should *not* be that the author has produced anything less than an amazing piece of work. In spite of the restrictive comments, and in spite of the corrections suggested and many other points that could be made (and were not made), one can only admire how much information has been condensed and presented in this book.[65] The fact is that the problems encountered in this field of research, even for the ordinary tasks of straightforward transcription of a text, translation and interpretation of its meaning are extremely involved, intricate and practically overwhelming. When a substantial number of texts have to be brought together into a *consistent* picture, where the problems of graphics, meaning, grammar, punctuation, etc., are facing the scholar at the same time, one wonders whether there is hardly a line of some length that does not provide a number of points of wide ranging controversy. The readers will realize that even before the main task, *viz.*, to present a survey of the cultic religious facts of Shang times, the author has had to struggle at each step with a considerable number of preliminary yet crucially important questions. No matter how enticing the task of *reconstructing* a general body of texts from fragmented, scattered pieces of bones and interpreting these collected texts within the framework of a general theory of social-religious philosophical concepts, it will seem to many a task still, to a great extent, premature and nigh impossible. But first attempts, regardless how imperfect or incomplete, have to be made, for they lay the ground on which much can be cleared and gained. The errors and inaccuracies in the preliminary philological and linguistic clearing work do not, in my opinion, substantially alter or undermine the description of the Shang religious factual elements. Undoubtedly it presents a great effort toward the study of Shang religion. The amount of material collected, classified and compared will be extremely helpful to all.

The author has divided his material from the point of view of the *object* of the religious and cultic acts: the spirits of the dead, the ancestors, the Supreme God, the powers of Nature, connected with rain, wind, seasons, agriculture, and daily life. The exposition of facts is made in close connection with numerous texts, amounting to no less than about 500 extracts of a length of 4 to 50 characters. It describes the things that were done in relation to those living in the mysterious, numinous sphere of religion: sacrifices and offerings of all kinds, conciliatory, propitiatory, imprecatory, eucha-ristic; exorcisms, interpretation of dreams, down to crass magic and sorcery, etc. Yet, in spite of the neat chapter divisions, the readers nevertheless may find the picture confusing, blurred, imbalanced. But this may be just because of the nature of the sources.

This is the first work of this kind and this scope in a Western language, but not in Chinese and Japanese. In spite of the syntheses found in Shima, Kaizuka, Hu Hou-hsüan, Ch'en Meng-chia, etc., we still need clarification on many things, such as the excessively rich nomenclature concerning sacrificial, ritual activities (sacrifices by burning, holocaust, drowning, strangling of victims, beating, dismembering, cooking in vessels, blood sprinkling), all often simply mentioned as 祭名; such also as the variety and degrees of ominous, dangerous, harmful, disastrous, evil "influences" or events, things and persons that are feared, foreseen and must be avoided; problems related to religion and the calendar: the festivals, seasons, months and weeks and special days for doing certain things; religion and nature: rivers and mountains, but also the role played by buildings, mausoleums, shrines and temples. Those are the aspects that need monographic treatment to bring much needed clarity. Some of these problems are probably mostly linguistic in nature; some have been treated already but in a scattered and fragmentary way, here and there in the available literature on the broad subject of "bone inscriptions". This book would, probably, have gained in value if the studies of other scholars had been summarized and unified to serve as a background and basis for the studies of its own topics of research.

When perusing this work, any reader will want to know, for instance, how *comprehensive* is the material collected and presented? Is it merely a selection of some of the best known and understood parts? A selection it is, for it is obvious that we have only a part of the available material; but on the other hand, much of this material in the bone inscriptions is repetitious and redundant. Next comes the question to what extent the selected material can be considered *representative*. In view of the variety of sources quoted and the fact that each separate text example given is often referred to various sources and different kinds of parallel texts, we may feel sure that the major basic categories have been quite intensively researched.

On the level of interpretation: to let the texts speak for themselves demands more than mere translation and immediate comments on meaning and context. We will need complete and detailed study on how, for instance, each kind of sacrifice, or type of divinations, celebrations, etc., fits in the general overall picture of the religious activity, the general framework of culture and social organization. It is obvious that, at this stage, no one would expect the author to do all this at once. In this regard, H. Köster's harshly worded criticisms (*Sinologica*, *Zeitschrift für Chinesische Kultur und Wissenschaft*, Vol. 12, 3/4, 1972, pp. 209-210) are perhaps exaggerated and only partly true. But on the other hand, we notice that much of the interpretation, occasionally provided, is based on information, facts and comparisons derived from written historical texts like *Tso Chuan*, *Kuo Yü*, etc.; these sources, though relatively late, may, of course, contain much ancient lore and stories that will help us understand the times of Shang; but the reliability and authenticity of such information decreases still more when taken from late Chou works like *Li Chi* and *Chou li*. Yet the whole literature buried in the bronze inscriptions of Chou has been left untouched; true, much of the bronze texts is extremely narrow in scope, to a certain degree repetitive and often unrelated, but the little that could be gleaned from those sources would by its very nature provide a much more solid basis for comparison and interpretation.

A look at the author's bibliography is interesting; we find in the first place the "Fachliteraturn" in a narrow sense related to the field of Shang oracular texts. If we compare with the bibliographies given in Shima (*Kenkyū* and *Index*), Kaizuka, Ch'en Meng-chia, etc., we will see that the major basic collections and studies have been mentioned and utilized. It is not a full bibliography, for such a list would be immense; cf. for instance P'eng Shu-ch'i 彭樹杞 (Madge P'eng), An Annotated Bibliography of the Publications on the Inscribed Oracle Bones Excavated from the Yin Ruins, *Chinese Culture. A Quarterly Review*, 1965, pp. 97-149, which perhaps gives the most complete list of books and articles up to 1964; the flow of publications has not stopped since. In the second place, we find some relevant bibliography on archeology, anthropology, comparative religion. To this reviewer, it is not clear to what extent or in what way these works have guided or influenced the author's method or judgment in regard to the facts of the Shang religion. In the third place, there are some titles referring to linguistics and philology, such as Chomsky(*Aspects of Grammar*), Leisi(*Wortinhalt*), Ullmann(*Semantics*), P'ei Hsüeh-hai(Chinese Grammatical Particles), etc., which seem to have had little to do with the methods and results obtained by the author. On the other hand, studies like those of Hu Kuang-huei 胡光煒, *Chia-ku wen-li* 甲骨文例 (1928) or Kuan Hsieh-ch'u 管燮初, *Yin-hsü chia-ku k'o-tz'u yü-fa yen-chiu* 殷虛甲骨刻辭語法研究 (1953) are missing. Perhaps the author merely wished to claim company with the major deities of the modern linguistic pantheon, like Chomsky. It would have been better if the *principles* of sound grammatical analysis displayed, for instance, by von der Gabelentz(*vetus atque probus*), to name only one, had been observed; then one would not have felt free to suggest solutions such as in 3.25 庚戌死收 (really 歺廾): "Am Tage Keng-hsü starb Shou," where an analysis like [sterben / Shou] is suggested with a *subject* following the verb.

The author has written an important book. Many times he has hacked his way through the thicket of problems to push boldly forward, maybe here and there too boldly. Careful reading of his work will stimulate and inspire many scholars to reconsider certain points. Students interested in the field will be fascinated and find in it a useful introduction and a great help, if duly warned about the pitfalls and the complexity of the problems.

University of Washington, Seattle.

NOTES

1. The book reviewed in this article appears in the series *Veröffent-lichungen des Ostasiatischen Seminars der Johann-Wolfgang-Goethe-Universität*. Frankfurt/Main, Reihe B, Band 1. Wiesbaden, Otto Harras-sowitz, 1971, vi-p.331.

2. Still, Tung Tso-pin has reasserted his theory as late as 1964, when he published his *Fifty Years of Studies in Oracle Inscriptions*, Tokyo, Chap. IV,

pp. 66-106. This theory is given new significance in a wider scope of studies by Chang Kuang-chih, Some Dualistic Phenomena in Shang Society, *Journal of Asian Studies*, Vol. 24, 1964.

3. The study of the variants is important: in many cases they give us hints as to the analysis and explanation and the reason for changes or substitutions of certain parts in the graphs. Thus, f.i. 争 of which Shima, *Index* 100, gives only one form 〾. One may wonder how the scholars came to identify this with the modern form 争. Yet upon close examination of the rubbings we find neatly distinguished variants showing 〾, i.e., two 〾 "hand with stick" hitting each other: "to struggle, to fight". Chang indicates the variants of 卯 (pp. 51-52, 69, 76, 78) as, 〾, 〾, 〾, 〾, 〾. Among them, the *type* 卯, viz. 〾, 〾 (and probably, by further reduction of strokes |〾) is the form that we find in the Chou bronze inscriptions. We therefore suggest that 〾 is the more original form, representing a person kneeling before 土 (earth mound, altar?); later this was further expanded by addition of signifiers 卯, 御. Subsequently, the element 土 was replaced by 午 (in archaic shapes 〾, |, |) which played the role of *phonetic*. On p. 118, Chang explains 〾 as a variant of 〾, 伐. It is basically the same form but more reduced in lines. But by the same token, Chang contradicts himself when he interprets this same graph (p. 85, item 5.12) differently, namely now as a simplification of 秂 (modern 年). The expression 卯伐 (in Chang's reading 卯年) 大乙, which is translated "reinigen" (Ernte)/Ta-yi (i.e., das Orakel wurde befragt: ob die Ernte vom Fluch des Ta-yi gereinigt werden sollte). Much simpler would be: "In making exorcist ritual we shall make beheading (of human victims) to Ta-yi". This is clear also from the difference in the sentence structure with 于 or without 于; cf. 5.11: 卯年于上甲五月 "Make exorcist ritual (over) the harvest *to* Shangchia. Fifth month".

The negative 不 has variants 〾, 〾, 〾, 〾 (according to Chang pp. 35, 49, 92). Yet it looks suspicious that the *same* bone text should have two variants of the same graphs 不 as strongly different as these. For instance 5.26 has (a) 上甲〾 冓雨大乙〾冓雨 but also (b) 卯九年〾冓雨. Similarly, for 用 we find p. 76 the variants 〾, 〾 and 〾. Shima, *Index* p. 50 has a quote from *Ts'ui* 322: 己未卜其〾父

庚⋯丁宗𢆶𠬪 where we find both forms on the *same* bone piece. However, cases where variants of the same graph appear in the *same* context are not excluded; this is shown in the occurrences of graphs 貞, 鼎 and 丁 (cf. infra); sometimes they seem to be bound with specific contexts, such as f. i. 亡它 as against 㞢㞢 (presence or absence of the element 止) (See Lee Yim 李棪, Review of Shima's *Index*, in *Journal of the Institute of Chinese Studies*, Chinese University of Hong Kong, Vol. 2, No. 1, 1969, p. 196). Again, p. 141 Chang takes 𡧊 as a variant of the *ho-wen* (合文) graph 𡨄 i.e. 小军. Yet, Shima, *Index* p. 213, does not have this particular variant. Furthermore, Chang has understood the graphs 𡧊 and 军 as the Han commentators explained the meaning of 牢 "a pair of oxen". Against this, we may refer to the study of K'ung Te-ch'eng 孔德成 (*Bulletin of the College of Arts*. "National" Taiwan University, Vol. 15, 1966) which on the basis of many quotes from classical texts and following the analysis of *Shuo wen*, explains the word as "sheep or ox specially *raised in a pen* for sacrifices". See also Yen Yi-p'ing 嚴一萍, *Lao yi hsin-shih* 牢義新釋 in *Chung-kuo wen-tzu* 中國文字 (abbrev. *CKWT*), Vol. 39. "National" Taiwan University, 1970.

P. 113, the graph 𡴂 is explained as a pictograph of "antlers (of a deer)". But it could as well be a mere variant of 𢉩 (Shima, *Index* p. 229), identified as 鷹 by Li Hsiao-ting 李孝定 (*Chia-ku wen-tzu chi-shih* 甲骨文字集釋 Taipei, 1965, p. 3051). On the other hand, T'ang Chien-yüan 唐健垣 in *CKWT*, Vol. 28, p. 3 (1968) mentions Kao Hung-chin's idea that 𡴂 is a variant of 南, a kind of a bell, but in this instance read as 令 and applied as a loangraph for 羚 "goat, ram". This solution involves a number of steps and assumptions, all in need of more substantiation.

P. 121, Chang mentions 𤣤 as a variant for 獸. This graph is not found in Shima, *Index* p. 445, where we find however three variants: 𤣥, 𤣦 and 𠂎.

P. 145: as variants of 魯 are given 𠚎, 𠚏, 𠚐, 𧆞 and on p. 154 𠙹. This agrees with Shima, *Index* p. 127 sq. where we have also 𠙹 and 𠚎. But Shima, *Inkyo bokuji kenkyū* 殷墟卜辭研究, Tokyo, 1958 (hereafter Shima, *Kenkyū*, p. 169) rejects the explanation of 𠚎 as a variant of 魯 (on rather weak arguments) and tries to identify this form 𠚎 (defined in *Shuo wen* and *Erh ya* 爾

雅 as 祜, 福也). Kaizuka, *op. cit.*, *Index*, p.33) mentions a rather unusual variant of 咎 viz. ⌐⌐. Cf. Pai Yü-cheng 白玉崢, *Ch'i-wen chü-li chiao-tu* 契文舉例校讀 in *CKWT*, Vol.43, 1972, pp.4-5.

P. 145, Chang also distinguishes as variants forms 衣 and 衣 for modern 衣. In Chou bronze texts and *Shuo wen* forms, the direction of the lower line is always downward and to the *right*: 衣. Chang concludes from this that the Shang garment could be *closed* (buttoned?) sometimes on the right, sometimes on the left side, but that by Confucius' time the right side style of closing it had become specifically "Chinese". This seems mere speculation, for this right or left turning line below may simply represent the hanging *flap of a poncho-like garment*, and not the left or right side closing or buttoning of a robe. This difference is more probably due to the *direction* in writing the graphs, depending whether they are written on the left or right side of opposite sentences in a set; the two forms are merely mirrorlike distinctions of the same graph.

P. 122, Chang gives three variants for the graph corresponding to 蝗 "locust": 蝗, 蝗, 蝗, but at the same time also admits the meaning of "autumn" (秋). His explanation that "locusts were being scared away at harvest times (秋) by burning grass" (hence the addition of the element 火) needs further proof. Moreover, it does not explain the different readings *huang* and *ch'iu* (Cf. Shima, *Index*, p.426).

From these examples, it can be seen that the problem of the variants is a very complex one. It involves different factors of sound as well as factors of graphic nature, such as substitutions and transformations of certain parts in the structure of the graph. One may assume that the greater the variety of such variants, ordered according to the periods of the bone inscriptions in which they appear, the better also will be the chances to explain the structure, meaning and development of the graph. But even then, there are unsolved cases. As an example, one might mention the graph 夒, which even after the elimination of some doubtful forms, presents no less than 43 variants collected from a total of 202 different bone fragments. (Cf. Chang Ping-ch'üan, Some Examples of the Comparative Study of the Oracle Bone Inscriptions. Discussion of the theories on the graph 夒, in *Bulle-*

tin of the Institute of History and Philology (abbr. *BIHP*) Vol. 20, pt. 2, 1949, pp. 175-221 and also Akatsuka Kiyoshi 亦塚忠, On the Origin of the Worship of the Mount 山 in Yin Dynasty, *The Oracle Bone Journal*, No. 6 Tokyo 1958). Yet it remains doubtful what is the correct transcription, as several readings are proposeed: 岳, 羔, 奈, 荅 etc. with different corresponding meanings. Besides the *true* variants, there are also cases of graphs that are in fact different in origin and representative, pictographic intent, i. e., they stand for originally entirely different graphs, words and meanings, but they have become so closely similar in graphic form as to merge into one; at least, for us they are hard to distinguish. One example is the frequent confusion between the graphs for 求 "to pray, beg, ask" and 希 "evil, ominous, bad effect or influence". Thus, pp. 203-204 (14.28) Chang has the expression 出希 "to have evil effect" which he transcribes as if it were 出求 (Shima, *Index*, pp. 206 and 209). In this instance, however, Chang translates 求 as "Tadel," referring us to a passage in *Lun yü* (incorrectly understood). It is simply a case of confusion of graphs 求 for 希. Perhaps a similar convergence of graphs may explain the curious case of the pictograph "locust" being used for "autumn": a convergence may be [in sense of "perhaps"] between a pictograph "tortoise+fire" (i. e., "to scorch, burn" > "autumn") and the pictograph "locust".

4. This example refers to Chang's explanation of the graph 羲: "Der Mann hält eine Streitaxt hinter dem Rücken verborgen, um bei nächster Gelegenheit anzugreifen". He calls it an example of graphic forms "so originall illustrativ, dass man ihre Bedeutungen leicht ablesen kann". The danger in "reading" such meanings in the pictographs that look so "illustratively transparent" is obvious. As there is no text adduced to support the meaning "attack by surprise," it remains a mere subjective interpretation of the pictograph. On p. 98 (6.9 and note 1), we find it written slightly differently 羲 in a text 其求雨于羲 (Hsi) 燎九羊 which is translated in *two* separate parts: "Should a ritual prayer for rain be addressed to Hsi? Should (at this point) nine pairs of sheep be offered in cultic burning?" (Compare our translation p. 39). Chang admits that the graph here stands for the name of an Ancestor, and transcribes it *Hsi*, on the basis of his pictographic in-

terpretation and his identification of the *meaning* with the *word* 襲 "to invade"; but is 襲 the only word for "invade, make a surprise attack" and therefore the only *word* that could be meant? The underlying reasoning implies several levels and assumptions, without giving the proof to support each of these assumptions. Yet this name of Ancestor, the graph and others similar to it have been discussed at length by scholars in the past, summarized in Li Hsiao-ting, *op. cit.*, p. 2839, s. v. 戠. Cf. also Shima, *Index*, pp. 211-212 and Kaizuka, *op. cit.*, p. 140(bone 0001). The graph could be related to 蔑(Shima, *Kenkyū*, p. 240 sq., Li Hsiao-ting, *op. cit.* 1307). Cf. also T'ien Ch'ien-chün 田倩君, *CKWT*, Vol. 18, 釋夒 pp. 8-9.

5. On p. 17, Chang gives an example of a development of a graph from Shang, *viz.* 𤕫 to Chou(seal graph 𤵸, but also bronze inscriptions 疒) to *Shuo wen* and later 疾. He notes that a Shang variant 𥎦 exists with 矢 as phonetic. Yet the situation is more complex, for the examples in Shima(*Index*, 447-448) show that the most frequently occurring form 𤕫 is usually construed with a direct object(name of body or body-part) in the sense of "have(as) sickness the feet, the teeth, the eyes, etc." as against 𥎦 (Shima, *Index*, 40) in sentences like 又疾 "have sickness," 𠂆疾 and 㠯疾 "remove, transpose(?), repress sickness," and also 疾 with a noun(for a person or a thing) as direct object, in the sense of "to inflict pain, cause suffering to(someone)". In Chou time inscriptions and Classics, the form 疾 is used for both usages and the once more frequent Shang graph, i. e., 𤕫, seems to have disappeared. But 疾 is in fact a combination of the element 疒 (taken from 𤕫) and the element 矢, extracted from 𥎦. This is a case of originally *two* different graphs for *two* different usages, merging into one graph for both (probably related) words: "to have sickness, be sick," and "to inflict pain". This must have happened by the end of Shang. Cf. Pai Yü-cheng 白玉崢 *Ch'i-wen chü-li chiao-tu* 契文舉例校讀(*CKWT*, Vol. 35, 1970, pp. 16-17 and Vol. 37, 1970, p. 2; Chou Ch'ing-hai 周清海 *Tu-ch'i hsiao-chi* 讀契小記, *CKWT*, Vol. 41, 1971, pp. 3-4). There are also other cases of double graphs for similar or closely related meanings and words, e. g., "to die" written 死 and 𠚫, 𡖉 (Shima, *Index* 12, 40, 414; Li Hsiao-ting, *op. cit.*, p. 3401). The latter two forms probably used in a

more specialized meaning, disappeared while the form 死 continued through later periods. (Cf. Li Hsiao-ting, Notes on the Oracle Bone Inscriptions I, *BIHP*, Vol. 36, pt. 1, 1965, p. 285).

Finally, we have a number of graphs for which a *modern form* may be proposed as an adequate translation, but by no means as a true *graphic* descendant. Such is e. g. 㛰 "to deliver, to give birth" which is generally transcribed 娩. Yet this character is a late word and certainly has no graphic connection with the Shang graph and most probably is not even related with the *word* now read 娩.

6. Though the problem of the pronunciation of Shang graphs is a nigh unsurmountable one, it should be recognized; at least some solutions can be accepted as possible, such as 卯(analyzed as having a phonetic 午), 矦 (with phonetic element 矢). The graph 卯 read *mao* when used as a cyclical character, probably stands for the later more fully developed compound 劉 "to slaughter, kill, cut up". Chang's identification of 卯 with modern 剖 is phonetically less convincing than 劉, and the fact that 卯 *may be* a pictograph of a "shafted" jade-knife used to "dismember, dissect" animals does not lead necessarily to a meaning "to dismember".

In certain cases 立 is used for 涖 ("to supervise, to preside over"); Cf. Yen Yi-p'ing 嚴一萍 *CKWT*, Vol. 5, 釋立. Chang p. 253 tries to take it as a causative verb: "stehen > hinstellen," implying that the king himself would be doing the "(rice) planting" (立禾).

This is not the place to suggest phonological reconstructions; yet certain proposed loan usages must be removed as impossible; thus 于 and 與 cannot be used for each other (Chang, p. 182, note 2), nor 以 for 與. Also Chang (p. 99, text 6.13) copies a name I-yin from the graphs 㕊 and 阝 written as one, but elsewhere (p. 82, 5.4) we find 伊 simply as one graph for 伊 "Yin". On the other hand we find also (p. 82, 5.5) 㕊 阝 transcribed as I-yin (though p. 201 has 㕊, now interpreted as a scribe's mistake for 㕊 "yellow" 黃). This I-yin 㕊 尹 is identified with 寅 尹, because 㕊 is considered equivalent with 寅 and, according to Karlgren (*Grammata Serica*, No. 450), 寅 has two readings *i* and *yin*. But 伊 is not *yin* but *yi* (Karlgren *·iər*) and this cannot be identical with 寅 *yi(n)*, *dien* and *diər*. Against Karlgren's bone graph examples for 寅, Shima(*Index* p.363) has 寅: 寅 clearly distinguished from 黃 (*Index*, p.364) and its variant 黃 for 黃. Hence we must read 伊尹 I-yin and 黃尹 Huang-yin. Though 人尹 for 尸尹 or 夷尹 may be phonetically acceptable, there seems to be no such combinations (cf. Shima, *Index*, p.5).

It is clear from the examples quoted above that phonetic reconstruction in fact may be very much needed and to a certain extent possible, within limits. Basic to it is the assumption that a solid continuity in language usage and script can be observed from the last periods of Shang down to the Early Chou times in bone and bronze forms. If a number of graphs in both levels can be correctly identified and analyzed, with variants and substitutions which allow us to conclude that certain parts may function as phonetic elements in the graphs, then a systematic comparison could be attempted as a start. Li Hsiao-ting's study, *Ts'ung liu-shu ti kuan-tien k'an chia-ku wen-tzu* 從六書的觀點看甲骨文字, *Journal of Nan Yang University* 南洋大學學報 Vol. 2, Singapore, 1968, pp.84-106, is such an attempt in this direction; yet, though he successfully shows the emergence of phonetic compounds, and the use of different phonetic elements, he does not tackle any of the problems such phonetic elements create in terms of actual pronunciation and reconstructions, as f. i. the appearance of the *same* phonetic element both in 鳳 (final-*m*) and in 槃 (final-*n*), etc.

7. For 夫 or 扶, name of a diviner, cf. the list of diviners in Jao Tsung-yi 饒宗頤, *Oracle Bone Diviners of the Yin Dynasty* 殷代貞人物通考, Hong Kong, 1959, p.657: 夫 and variant 夫 = 扶.

8. Takashima Ken-ichi in a study on *ch'i* 其 (part of his preliminary research for a Ph. D. dissertation at the University of Washington, and to be published as a separate article in Japanese) has suggested that *ch'i* is a word or a particle with morphological and syntactic functions, "expressing the modality of uncertain feeling and subject deletion"; he proposes that the best English rendering of this "morpho-syntactic" particle is still "perhaps". At the time, I myself expressed full agreement with the proposed English rendering, yet I have since come to the opinion that it does not really explain any of the cases and important aspects of

ch'i. Even after certain modifications (f. i. omitting the "subject deletion" theory), *ch'i does not express primarily "uncertain feelings" but a definitely certain* judgment and opinion, *viz*. that the proposition carrying the particle *ch'i* represents the "less desired alternative," and the English "perhaps, may be" does not seem to account for the real meaning implied by absence and presence of *ch'i* in certain opposite sentences.

9. Examples are taken from Chang Ping-ch'üan 張秉權, *Yin-hsü wen-tzu ping-pien* 殷虛文字丙編 (abbr. *Ping-pien* and PP), Vols. 1-3, Taiwan 1957-67. In the reference system, PP 1(1, 3) stands for *Ping-pien*, set No. 1, lines 1 and 3; P. 108, however, refers to the *page* in Chang's current discussion on certain points of interpretation of the text, whenever a quote is made from other extant bone collections. In all my quotes I have followed mostly Chang Ping-ch'üan's mode of transcribing the bone graphs in modern type characters. The same has been done for all quotes made from Chang Tsung-tung whenever possible. In this mode of transcribing, a certain convention is observed by which the modern graph is always kept as similar as possible in *structure* and form to the original, thus 隻 (for 獲), but also new graphs are used, e. g. 㞢, as distinguished from 又 (though both are equivalent in the meaning "to sacrifice" and are used for 有, 右, etc.)

10. *Lung* 龍 written 𠂇 with other variants, is explained by Chang Ping-ch'üan(*Ping-pien* p. 32) as a loan graph for 凶 "bad, ominous," and as a verb "to get worse, to have bad effect, etc." This seems improbable. Though the phonetic considerations in a hypothesis of 凶 * *xiung* being written by 龍 * *liung* (suggesting an Archaic Chinese * * xl-?) can be argued, there is no positive reason given from the context or the graph analysis for this theory. It seems curious that "dragon" would be used as a loan for "bad, ominous". Yet, this idea is followed by Kaizuka (*op. cit*. bone 93, p. 167) without questioning. Shima, *Index* 242 gives several examples of 疾 and other similar words followed by 龍 and the *negated* phrase usually carrying the particle *ch'i*. There is also the phrase 婦 + name, followed by 龍 or 婦龍(without specific name): here too I am inclined to understand it as: "Lady X will get better". Li Hsiao-ting(*op. cit*. 1474) cites Yeh Yü-shen 葉玉森 as the

only author to have identified a Shang graph corresponding to the modern 凶, namely 囟, which is read by the majority of scholars as equivalent with 禍. Shima, *Kenkyū*, p. 277 explains 囟 as strictly different from 龍, and standing for 虯 "hornless dragon" (following T'ang Lan), and also occurring in the name of the Shang king 囟甲, written in the *Shih chi*(史記) as 沃甲. Shima finds in the *Shih chi* name enough grounds to identify 囟 with 沃 and to consider it as a loan graph for 祅 "disastrous," f. i. 告囟 "to announce disaster" and 疾囟 "sickness becoming dangerous, worse". Yen Yi-p'ing and also Ting Su 丁驌 (*CKWT*, Vol. 32, 1969) and Li Hsiao-ting(*op. cit.* 3477) isolate from 囟 the graphic element 勺, explained as 旬 = 眴 "dazed, confused" and by extension "dangerous, uncertain". The latter part of the explanation is farfetched and unconvincing. The final solution of 囟 is still awaiting further study as can be concluded from Lee Yim in his review of Shima's *Index*, pp. 193-194.

11. On 卣, Chang(p. 38) follows T'ang Lan and Shima in explaining it as a pictograph of 卣, used as a loan graph for 尤 "extraordinary, ominous," and as a verb "be under bad influence, feel bad"; on p. 199, again with Shima and T'ang Lan, he takes it as a loan for 幽 "dark, black". Jao Tsung-yi takes it as verb 囿 = 衈 "to sacrifice, to smear with victim's blood," and Kuo Mo-jo as 幽 but in the sense of "to bury" (*Erh Ya*). In the expression 卣 雨, T'ang Lan and Shima (against Yang Shu-ta) see in it a loan character for 脩: "long(lasting) rain". The hypothesis of T'ang and Shima seems to explain the occurrences of the graph well enough as far as it gives a reasonably acceptable *meaning* in certain contexts. Yet the fact that 卣 is *only* used in a series of loan applications and never for itself as 卣 "pitcher, flask" inspires some doubt. This use as loan graph is not to be compared with f. i. 叀 used exclusively as a *particle*. Furthermore, Li Hsiao-ting (*op. cit*, 1615, 4227) shows cases of simultaneous occurrences of the graphs 卣 and 尤 in the bone texts. Pai Yü-cheng(*CKWT*, Vol. 44, 1972, pp. 12-13) reads it as 辜 "to rip open(sacrificial victims, such as dogs)" and further applies it to a reading 咎 "fault, calamity". All this shows the need for further research on this point before anything can be stated with some degree of certitude.

12. In this series of sentences we need to distinguish 出來 and other phrases

with 㞢 + verb from the structure 其从, as in 25(3 and 5), in spite of superficially similar translations. + verb in Shang texts and in Chou inscriptions and Classics (有 + verb) is a regular pattern to be understood according to context as "to have [cause, opportunity, chance, reason, risk] to(+ verb do something)". It is opposed to the negative 亡 or 無 + verb "to have no cause at all [no opportunity, etc.]," which contrasts with the unemphatic plain 不 + verb. On the other hand, when 其从 is translated "have to follow" it is to render the idea that *ch'i* implies a less desired course of action, which one may have to follow. On p. 114(7.13) Chang suggests that 㞢 following a verb and preceding that verb's object is used in a special function to give a perfective aspect to an "aspectually neutral" verb. The line in question is 貞告土方于上甲受㞢擎, which is translated: "Shall a ritual announcement be made concerning the T'u country to Shang-chia? Will we obtain/ have/assistance?" The last graph is explained as equivalent to 又 = 祐. Chang indeed considers the element 又 in 擎 as the essential part, meaning "help, assistance," while 隹 is more a decorative elaboration and excessive addition, comparable to the Bird Script of later Chou times, where all characters were either transformed into a birdlike shape or given additional parts in the form of a bird. All this is highly improbable: (1) why only this sole example? (2) the Bird Script, a late Chou development, has no direct connection with the Shang script. Obviously, 叙 must go together "to hold a bird in the hand"; 隹 and 擎 are really variants of the same graph "to catch birds with a net". Shima, *Index* 407 gives also 敊, 叢 and 夒. We translate the line: "Test [the proposition]: announcing(the matter of) the T'u country(?) to Shang-chia, we will receive assistance(㞢 = 又) to catch(them" (or: "He will grant(us that we) have(occasion) to catch them"). Shima, *Index*, p. 407 quotes a parallel line from *Ning* 3.70 貞弗其受㞢隹 "We might not receive assistance to catch(them)" (or: "... grant assistance to ..."). Pai Yü-cheng (*CKWT*, Vol. 33, 1969, p. 21 and Vol. 39, 1971, pp. 4-5) shows clearly that 舀, 皋 and 隹 with variants, though *graphically* related to 羅, 離, 禽 is really identical as *a word* with 畢 "to catch(birds) with net". (The "net" having a *handle* clearly distinguishes it from 羅, etc.) Cf. also Chang Che 張哲 *CKWT*, Vol. 10, 釋畢.

13. 挈 is Chang Ping-ch'üan's modern transcription of the bone graph 㕣 or

⌐. The theories mentioned in Li Hsiao-ting(*op. cit*. 3737) can be summarized as follows: when not used as a place name or a personal name, this graph functions as a verb, the meaning of which is expressed by a pictograph representing "a man holding something before himself, dangling like a thread" > "to hold hanging(before oneself)" > "bring along, lead(armies, men), bring(sacrificial victims, etc.), present(as offering, gift), to hold, use(something)". The opinions differ quite seriously when they try to identify the *word* this graph is supposed to represent: 挈, 提, 包, 持, 氐(make arrive, lead). Some, f. i. Chin Hsiang-heng 金祥恒 (*CKWT*, Vol. 8, 1962 釋⌐), Shima(*Kenkyū*, p. 250) and T'ien Ch'ien-chün 田倩君(*CKWT*, Vol. 21, 釋以) identify it with ㇗ = 以. Kaizuka thinks that at least from Period IV on the form ⌐ was simply confused with or taken over by ㇗ (以). Li Hsiao-ting rejects this because ⌐ and ㇗ after all are clearly distinguishable and distinguished.

14. On this expression 召王事, cf. Chin Hsiang-heng 金祥恒 (*CKWT*, No. 8) with reference to Yang Shu-ta's opinion.

15. This graph, to my knowledge, has not been identified. Kaizuka(*op. cit*. bone 3029) and Kuo Mo-jo(*Ts'ui pien* 1074) both have it once in different sentences, but give no comment, no translation. From Shima(*Index* 419) we can only say that the *affirmative* phrase with ⊗ *only* and almost always is marked by the presence of *ch'i* 其; presumably, it must imply something less desirable. (12): "Next Yi-mao day the king when entering will not ..." (13) "He might (but would rather not) ..."

16. ⌐ is transcribed in *Ping pien* 71(3) as 基. Chang reads it *Hu*(i. e. 胡)and explains it(p. 83) as a pictograph of the chin. However, 胡 is "dewlap," the part under the chin, and the chin usually is 臣, read *yi*(Karlgren, *Grammata Serica*, No. 960 *giəg). 胡方 is understood by Chang as referring to *one* specific neighboring tribe of Shang and in this he follows Shima(*Kenkyū*, p. 384) who bases himself on Yeh Yü-sen and many others. But since 方 Fang also occurs as a tribe's name, it is difficult to decide whether 胡方 stands for one or two. In view of the fact that the bone texts are extremely terse and that from the point of view of the bone language there is no need for a supplemental addition of 方 in the sense of

"country," it seems possible to take 方 as a name also. Li Hsiao-ting (*op. cit*. 409, 410, 422) follows T'ang Lan who offers a solution which is quite different from that of Chang. He explains the graph 𠯑 as composed of 𠮷 (i.e. 工) and the element 日 (mouth) (often used to mark "names"), i.e. 吾. Tung Tso-pin has argued that this 𠯑方 stands for Kuei-fang 鬼方 in the later bone inscriptions and the Classics. Whether 𠯑 is to be read 胡 is doubtful. That 𠯑 became later to be written 鬼 is generally accepted (Cf. Li Chi 李濟, The Excavations at Anyang and the Study of Ancient History of China, *BIHP*, Vol. 40, pt 2, 1969, pp. 921-922) but the explanation of the graphic and phonetic aspects of 𠯑 (吾 *$kung$*?, 基*$-i\partial g$*, 臣*$-i\partial g$*) and the later (鬼*$-i\partial r \sim -i\partial d$*) remains a problem. In the same text, 征于總 is the transcription of Chang Ping-ch'üan, yet the presence of 于 seems to indicate that instead of 征 one might better read 偉, 衛. Cf. Huang Jan-wei 黃然偉 (*CKWT*, 14, p. 20), Yen Yi-p'ing (*CKWT*, 15), T'ang Chien-yüan 唐健垣 (*CKWT*, 28, 1968) and Pai Yü-cherg (*CKWT*, 31, 1969, pp. 11-12) where it is shown that 正, 征 never has the proposition *yü* 于.

17. The graph 衣 has been explained by the majority of scholars as a term for "sacrifice" and, more specifically, "a universal, grand sacrifice intended for the entire series of ancestors and gods" (Li Hsiao-ting, *op. cit*. 2721). Only Shima (*Kenkyū*, p. 279) rejects this explanation first proposed by Wang Kuo-wei, and instead takes 衣 as a loan graph for 殷 "grand, solemn". He adduces texts such as f.i. 貞王田羌衣逐亡𢦏 where 衣 "sacrifice" seems to make little sense, but rather "The king hunting (in, for?) Ch'iang, *greatly* shall pursue them and have no disaster". Yet, the texts where 衣 has indeed a "religious" implication connected with sacrifices are the great majority of occurrences in the bone material. Chang p. 145 simply explains 衣 as "ein Kleid opfern," without any comments or discussion.

18. As to the character 㩜, Li Hsiao-ting (*op. cit*. 4587) transcribes it as 繫 "to tie up prisoners or criminals". Shima (*Kenkyū*, p. 338) follows this general idea but argues it should be read like 毌, 母 or 十. This is based on doubtful variants and parallel lines that are maybe too easily assumed to be the same.

19. The character 徝 in the original form 𢓊 is explained by some as 省 "to inspect, investigate," by others as 循 "to make an inspection *tour*". In the first hy-

pothesis it is taken as a mere graphic variant of 省. Safest reading is probably 循. (Li Hsiao-ting, *op. cit*. 563.)

20. The reading 霰 is that of Chang Ping-ch'üan. On p. 212 Chang has a similar text, where with Shima, Yü Hsing-wu and others, he transcribes it as 雷 "thunder". According to *Shuo wen* (cf. *Shuo-wen chieh-tzu ku-lin* 説文解字詁林 5184), 霰 means 稷雪也 "snow flakes as (hard) as grain kernels". The graph 雹 suggests "hail":雹.

21. The first sentence being parallel to the second, its opposite, which has the negative 不, both have been translated in the passive. The meaning 齒 "teeth > ivory" can be supported from parallels in the Classics.

22. In the passage of text 157(11) and (12), the last sentence of the translation corresponds to the six last characters at the end of (11). In reality the first and the last sentences of the original text must go together and should logically follow each other as corresponding positive and negative propositions; only after these two divinatory propositions have been examined in the oracle, can the interpretation be given. This interpretation was added to the first sentence because this proposed alternative was found to be the right one. The lines of the passage 170 (1) and (2) are discussed by Ch'en P'an in the article, Relations between Hunting and Sacrifices in Ancient China. A Revised Version (*BIHP*, Vol. 36, Pt 1, 1965, p. 326). Ch'en understands 矢 as "to shoot at," identical with 射. However, 射 in the bone texts is found to have its own proper forms 矢 and 射, which seem to be mostly used as nouns: "archery, archer, etc." (Cf. Shima, *Index* 373 and 378-379).

23. This character 亞, as transcribed by Chang Ping-ch'üan, is clearly different from 㐫; yet, Li Hsiao-ting, *op. cit*. 577 and Shima, *Index* p. 70 take it as 㐫, i.e., 彶 a *ku-wen* variant given in *Shuo wen* for 復, 退 "to withdraw". Among other meanings suggested, we find "to stop," "to be late, to delay". Kaizuka (bone 2089) follows Chin Hsiang-heng (in *Hsü Chia-ku-wen pien* 續甲骨文編 2.26, 1959) and writes 卻: "to expel". Chin Hsiang-heng (*CKWT*, Vol. 17, 釋 ⌾) shows on what meager and fragmentary material this is built. "To stop" is the suggested explanation of ⌾ 雨, explained as inversion of 雨止! The most frequent

expressions are 㲋麋, 㲋兕, 㲋豕 which are explained as "to trap". But the graph analysis does not show how this could be "a trap" or "to trap". Whether the top part of 㲋 is the same as 內 or not, if one starts from the clear and certain element "foot" it might be explained as a pictographic unit 㲋 "to drive into *an enclosure*, to make enter into a corral, a fence". If 冂 is considered, or has become later to be identical with 內, as a *phonetic*, the basic sense would still be preserved, and 㲋雨 might be explained as "delayed, slow down, protracted(?) rain".

24. 冊 "make announcements by written document" is a ritual performance that accompanies all sorts of sacrifices and offerings. Cf. Pai Yü-cheng 白玉峥, *Ch'i-wen chü-li chiao-tu* 契文舉例校讀 in *CKWT*, Vol. 33, 1969 (p. 13). Chang (p. 70) quotes Shirakawa as the source for his translation "to promise, make a vow". The graph has a number of variants (Shima, *Index*, p. 423 sq.) and among them the complex form 䇂, which Chang (p. 128) has completely misunderstood.

25. Li Hsiao-ting, *op. cit*. 1883, mentions Ch'en Meng-chia as a source for some examples of 舊 in verbal function "to store, to gather together". However, the exact meaning when used together with 旅 is still uncertain.

26. On 弜 = 勿, cf. infra the discussion on the various negatives. The structure of a verb, e. g. 卯 followed by its indirect object (without 于), but also with 于 noun, and 于 + noun + verb, allows for different patterns applied for un-emphatic and emphatic position of the noun, the latter showing 于 with its noun *before* the verb. This difference of uses of the proposition 于 can be observed regularly in the bone texts.

27. So far it has not been made clear what the terms for different kinds of ominous and evil effects mentioned in the bone texts really mean when used in contradistinction with each other. Here, 壱 clearly is not the same as 冎.

28. The graph 坄 is explained by Chang as "häufeln," i. e. "to earth up (a plant)". (Shima, *Kenkyū*, pp. 494-495). He considers it as the equivalent of the later *Shuo wen* graph 培: but why not as well, or even better 封 (Karlgren, *Grammata Serica*, 1197, i) which has more graphic similarity with 坄? Kuo Mo-jo, according to Kaizuka, proposes a meaning "to build a vegetable garden on the sides of a field"; Yang Shu-ta reads it as 礦 "to mine a mountain side," and Ch'en Meng-

chia explains it as 糞田 "to fertilize the fields". Kaizuka and also Hu Hou-hsüan 胡厚宣(*Li-shih yen-chiu* 歷史研究, No. 7, 1957) follow Hsü Chungshu's solution: 鋤 "to hoe, to earth up with a hoe". Graphically speaking, 封 seems the most probable reading.

29. In this line the graph 求 is understood as "to pray" by both Chang and Kaizuka (though the latter transcribes it 桼, a script variant also preferred by Kuo Mo-jo). Shima(*Kenkyū*, p. 315) seems to accept both 求 and 桼, because they have more or less the same meaning in the general context. Yet, this is clearly another case of confusion or convergence of graphs that are originally different and stand for different words and meanings: 求 = 求 "to beg, pray" and 桼 = 祓 "a sacrifice" or 貴 "abundant, flourishing, beautiful". (Cf. Li Hsiao-ting, op. cit. pp. 3237 and 2733; Pai Yü-cheng, *CKWT*, Vol. 34, 1969, pp. 11-12). Lung Yü-ch'un 龍宇純 devoted a detailed study to this graph 桼 in *BIHP* (Vol. 34, pt 2, 1963, pp. 405-433) entitled: On the Archaic Character 桼 and Related Problems in the Oracle Bone and Bronze inscriptions. In this study, the possible convergence of two graphs 求 and 桼 is excluded and all the cases are explained as graphic variants standing for 桼. Though he finds evidence for this hypothesis in the fact that 求 and 桼 are always clearly distinguished in the Chou bronze inscriptions, he does not show this to be the case for the bone forms. But he further argues that expressions like 桼囗方 make no sense if the graph in case were read 求: "to *beg* the Kuei-fang(people)". The meaning is obviously to be sought in 桼囗方. The graph 桼 is explained with plenty of evidence from the bone texts and later classical passages to be the pictograph of "a plant with hanging *roots*," and is used as a verb (read 拔) "to uproot, to eradicate" and by extension "to eliminate, to expel *by means of ritual, sacrificial* actions (all kinds of evils)" and then written 祓 in later texts. The line 桼囗方 then would mean "to *avert* (by sacrificial rites) the Kuei-fang(dangers, menace)". Since Lung considers this to be the basic and general meaning, it is only by further extension that this graph is used in the sense of "to pray," a sense derived from "to seek (by *sacrificial, ritual* actions) to *obtain*" things like good harvest, rain, etc.

30. On the meaning of 妝, taken here as "to remove" and not as negative,

cf. infra, the discussion on the negatives. The graph 戠 originally written 𢦍 with variants 𢦏 and 𢦒 (Shima, *Index* 334-335, *Kenkyū*, p. 270) is usually explained in the phrase 日出戠 or 月出戠 as equivalent to the later classical expression 有飤. Only Shima disagrees with the accepted translation "eclipse of sun or moon". The graph is explained as standing for 臘 or 截 "to chop meat, offer chopped meat". Thus the line, used by Shima as reason to reject the interpretation "eclipse" (as it would seem to make no acceptable sense): 甲子卜貞日戠于甲寅 may simply mean: "On Chia-tzu day, test [the proposition]: to the sun make chopped-meat offerings on Chia-yin day". The eclipse of sun or moon, being expressed by 戠 was then understood as the sun or moon being chopped and diminished in size. It is not certain that each time this expression was used, a true "astronomical" eclipse must have occurred. Chang (p. 183) also takes 戠 as a loan graph for 垎 "brown," for instance in 12. 47 燎瀧戠三牢 analyzed as: "verbrennen/ Schildkröten Fluss/braun/3/paar Rinder/". This is not necessary: "Burn in sacrifice to the Kuei (river god) chopped meat (amounting to) three oxen".

31. The graph 𠂂 representing an ox being drowned (in 巛 water) is identified by Chang with the modern character 沈 (p. 170, note 1). It is shown how probably *Shuo wen* originally did not understand the "corrupt" graphic element 巿 of the bone graph to represent the ox being sunk head first. Yet, this explanation is insufficient without at the same time showing that the confusion or convergence of 牛 (turned head downward) with 尢 was also conditioned by the fact that 尢 was reinterpreted as a phonetic element. On the other hand, there is the graph 𤞞 (Chang p. 176; Shima, *Kenkyū*, p. 348) usually transcribed as 貍, which could equally be considered a variant of 𠂂. Cf. Pai Yü-cheng 白玉崢, *Ch'i-wen chü-li chiao-tu* 契文舉例校讀 in *CKWT*, Vol. 44, 1972, pp. 8-9.

The graph 陵 (bone form 𨽸) is interpreted by Chang as two separate characters: "ein Mann und eine Jungfrau als Konkubine". This is not probable since 卩 alone is not used as 人, and there are on the other hand enough examples to show that 陵 is equivalent to 嬖 "slave girl". (Shima, *Index* 136; *Kenkyū*, p. 337 and Li Hsiao-ting, *op. cit.* 3671).

32. 𦬊 in modern transcription 芙, 堇 is explained by Chang as the pictograph

of a "hunchback"; he quotes a *Tso chuan* text to show that in general misformed persons were used in such occasions of natural disaster, and probably more could be quoted. (Cf. Katō Jōken 加藤常賢 *Religion and Thought in Ancient China*, I. The Dwarfs and Hunchbacks of Antiquity. 中國古代の宗教と思想 Kyōto 1954.) On pp. 213-214 Chang explains the upper part of the graph as "mouth" (die Schil-derung eines buckligen Mens chen, der in der Regel einen rückwärts geneigten Kopf hat ...) Yet, there are variants that have no such top element (e.g. 𡕥, Shima, *Index* 38, *Kenkyū*, pp. 193-193) and this would take away the essential characteristic of the pictograph. It is perhaps better to explain it with Karlgren(*Grammata Serica*, 480 b) as "a man (prisoner?) with back-bound hands". The element on top 口 may simply be added for 嘆 "to sigh, exclaim"; since 𡕥 is frequently used for 嘆 "drought," 莫 is further distinguished by adding 火 (𡕥) to mean 煤, 難 "to burn". Chang translates: "Should a hunchback *and* an ox be sacrificed at the stake?" This is impossible; literally we might say: "use (as victim) a hunchback (at the stake) and an ox"; then, the sacrifice of the ox is not specified in its form as against the burning at the stake of the human victim. This is why we translated 薰 as noun "burnifig," indirect object of 用.

33. For Ya hou 亞侯 cf. Shima, *Kenkyū*, p. 428. This text b) has a clear example of the use of 于 in 1) 告于…(regular, unemphatic) as against 于…告 (于+ noun, put before the verb, for emphasis).

34. In footnote (p. 44) Chang explains the graph 𢎘 as presumably a pictograph of "a man having pain over the whole body" (shivers?). Shima, *Index*, pp. 1-8 lists this graph among the many derivations of the graph 人, and lists the same text under 𢎘, (= 弔, 尗, i.e., a name "Shu," cf. *Index* 474); the meaning should then be: "*Shu* will not be cause. …"

35. Chang explains (p. 50) the graph 卣, with variant 卣 (p. 72), the latter not in Shima (*Index* 402), as the pictograph of 卣 "drinking cup" (Li Hsiao-ting, *op. cit.* 4061), but translates it, when used as a verb "gesotten in Schüsseln darbringen" (pp. 71 and 77). But it seems much simpler to take 卣 (once this is accepted as the modern equivalent of the bone graph) as a loan for 斷 "to cut in pieces, dismember (victims)". When used between two cyclical dates, Chang ex-

plains it as a loan graph for 到 "until". Yet 到* tog for 亞* tŭk, though defendable, is less probable than 闗 (same phonetic series as 亞), which *Shuo wen* defines as 過也 "to meet, to reach". Pai Yü-cheng (*CKWT*, Vol. 36, 1970, p. 5) follows Yü Hsing-wu in reading it in the sense of "darkness, overcast," "evening," Chin Hsiang-heng (*CKWT*, Vol. 25), 釋咠 reviews the major opinions and distinguishes it carefully from 咠 finally to settle for 亞, i.e., the later graph 禋 (or 煙) "sacrifice".

36. Chang considers 舞 a variant of 舞 = 舞 "to dance" and a loan for a word "wife". Shima, *Kenkyū*, p. 93 and p. 326 gives a long list of variants, but only Li Hsiao-ting (*op. cit.* 1161) after reviewing the many different opinions on the meaning of the graph, points out that 舞 and 舞 are graphically not the same, and not even the same in meaning, usage or sound. With Chang Cheng-lang 張政烺 he identifies it with the later 爽 * kiug used as a loan word for 仇 * g'iug (same as 逑 "mate, companion" in *Shih ching*). In the latter theory, 爽匕庚 would mean: "associating with ancestral Mother Keng".

37. *Shih-jen* 示壬 like *Shih-kuei* 示癸 are names of Shang ancestors. They probably mean literally: "The Altar Jen, the Altar Kuei," where the altar or tablet is taken as the personification of the ancestor himself; this would parallel the constructions *Tsu-chia* 且甲 "Ancestor Chia," originally "Ancestral Tablet Chia" and *Hsiung Yi* 兄乙 "Older brother Yi". Chang (p. 89, note 2) interprets 示, originally 丅, as a pictograph of an "altar, shrine tablet" and rejects Kuo Mo-jo's explanation of 丅 as a phallic symbol. Yet, when explaining 冂, modern 礬, he, on the contrary, holds that the element 冂 is not merely a "stone altar" but a "phallic stone". The same lack of proof is found in both cases.

38. Compare note 5, last paragraph where the transcription of 伊 as 尸尹 is discussed. Chang translates 6.13 with two separate sentences, and thus seems to leave the presence of *ch'i* unaccounted for.

39. On the graph 𩵋, explained by Chang as "antlers," cf. note 3. Wang Ch'eng (with first graph transcribed in various ways 㫃, 𦕠, 望) is a frequently mentioned personality in the bone inscriptions (Shima, *Index* p. 110). Lower Hsi, name of a neighboring tribe, (下𦥑) is mostly transcribed as 下危 (f. i. Chang

Ping-ch'üan *et al*.) This graph 㕣 is explained by Chang according to Kao Hung-chin 高鴻縉 (*Chung-kuo tzu-li* 中國字例, Taipei, 1964) as a pictograph of a horn used as a wedge or pin to loosen knots. Shima (*Kenkyū*, pp. 389-390) discusses at length the various transcriptions, but never attempts to give a graphic analysis or reading. Yü Hsing-wu 于省吾 on the basis of seal forms like 㠯, argues for the identity with the modern graph 危, in the sense of "dangerously tottering, toppling". Since the bone graph seems only to be used as a name of a country or a tribe, it is difficult to further prove or disprove these theories.

40. Chang translates 鼓彡 as a binom: "to drum + to beat the drum". This use of binomial constructs is improbable in such a terse and extremely economical style as that of the bone texts. Though in the graph 彭 f.i. the element 彡 (in its various forms) may well indicate the repeated drum beats, alone 彡 (variants 彡, cf. Shima, *Kenkyū*, p. 296; Li Hsiao-ting, *op. cit*. 2759) stands for the character 肜: 繹祭也 "continuous sacrifices": 彡夕 → 彡日 → 彡龠 "evening sacrifice," followed by the "next day sacrifice" and finally third day, concluding with the "龠 sacrifice". This 彡 = 肜 is also written 融 and by some commentaries (phonetically) equated with 尋. Cf. Chin Hsiang-heng 金祥恒, *CKWT*, Vol. 29, 釋肜. Chang p. 155 (10.25) quotes the line 彡日父甲: "... der Sonne des Vaters Chia ein Trommelspiel vorführen" which is really: "make the continuing sacrifices on the (following second day) for Father Chia"; furthermore, p. 144 (10.1) 彡酒于... is not "Trommelspiel vorülhren und Wein vergiessen..." but: "at the continuous sacrifices make wine libations to..."; p. 150 (10.13) 彡夕亡囚 is not: "... am Abend trommeln..., wird es kein Unheil geben?", but: "The previous evening of the continuing sacrifices will have no evil (ominous influences)". In the text (7.32) we must fill in: "We will have continuous sacrifices...".

41. 祡 is explained by Chang as having the variant 叔 "offensichtlich die Darstellung eines Zweiges auf dem Altar," but is not further identified with any modern character or reading. Yet Shima (*Index* 154-155, *Kenkyū*, p. 263) and Li Hsiao-ting (*op. cit*. 927) explain it as 叔. Kaizuka (*op. cit Index* 44) explains it as "burning twigs, e.g. aromatic Artemisium, etc., brought as sacrifice or offering on the ancestral altar," and transcribes 叔; Tung Tso-pin reads this 祡 "burn in

sacrifice". The readings 叙 *sui* and 柴 *ts'ai* cancel each other out.

42. 冓 is taken by Chang as a short form of 冓. But in addition he supplies the word 雨: "Shall we be surprised (überrascht) by sudden rain?" Kuo Mo-jo's transcription (*Ts'ui-pien* 239) leaves a blank for 冓 without explanation. Shima, *Index* 455 has no such simplified form of 冓. No matter what the reading of this graph is, there is no basis whatsoever to expand it into 冓雨. In our analysis, this should be some sort of an adverb preceding the verb 又 "to sacrifice, to offer," but since it is not identified, it is omitted in the translation.

43. 羊 is explained by Chang (p. 135) as 骍 on the basis of the *Shuo wen* definition of 埩 "red brown (earth)," here applied to the color of the animals. This is generally accepted (Shima, *Index* 214; Li Hsiao-ting, *op. cit.* p. 3047 s. v. 骍) but it is not entirely certain. (Li Hsiao-ting, *op. cit.* 3299 and Kaizuka, bone 2732-33).

44. Chang translates: "Should I (singular!) go to the Ho river?" According to Ch'en Meng-chia 陳夢家 (*Yin-hsü pu-tz'u ts'ung-shu* 殷虛卜辭綜述, 1956, p. 94 sq.), 我 is mostly used in a plural sense "we, our". Chang explains 我 (bone form 扌) as a pictograph of a saw or a trident-like weapon. This is an incomplete analysis, for (Li Hsiao-ting, *op. cit.* 3797) this only accounts for the graphic part 丯, the other part 厂 = 戈, may well be a phonetic.

45. This explanation of 㶷 "torch, burn a torch" is not sure. The graph is supposed to have a number of variants (Shima, *Kenkyū*, p. 284), which are all closely similar but not always identical and may occasionally have been confused. (Cf. Ii Hsiao-ting *op. cit.* 869 and 2283.) The transcription of 㶷 as modern 熱 "to burn" has been argued with equal plausibility.

46. Chang translates this as two independent sentences, which leaves the presence of *ch'i* unexplained.

47. In Chang's translation the function of 叀 (cf. infra note 64) is entirely ignored. His literal word-for-word explanation has: /etwa/; this insertion of "etwa" is irrelevant, for it implies nothing real in the content, and is omitted in Chang's own translation.

48. Ch'ü Wan-li (*Chia-pien* 753) quotes this line differently than Chang. Ch'ü puts a stop after the character 南 and instead of 方, he writes 甲, beginning a

new sentence too fragmentary to translate: 甲☒眔☒. Chang takes 簪, written in bone form 妾, as "Frauenname," but Ch'ü considers it a *verb* with the general sense of "sacrifice". If the sequence of the transcription is indeed that given by Ch'ü, then the position of 其 would suggest that 妾 is a verb. Shima, *Index* 137 lists two other examples of this word in presumably verbal function: (1)于大乙且乙妾求年王受又: "To Ancestors Ta-yi and Tsu-yi make a 'X'-sacrifice to pray for a good harvest; the king will receive assistance," and (2)弜卬又其妾于舞工王受又 This text is taken from *Ts'ui-pien* 538 and transcribed by Kuo Mo-jo as 弜卬又其簪于燕壬… The meaning of 妾, apart from the *graphic* representation (簪 and 旡, cf. Li Hsiao-ting, *op. cit*. 2807), as a *verb* remains unsolved, and the identification or definition 祭名 "name of sacrifice" is another example of the tendency to solve all problems of *nouns* as being "personal names" and *verbs* as being "types of sacrifice".

49. 求 is mistaken for 希; cf. supra note 3. The interpretation of 求 as "Tadel" cannot be supported by referring to *Lun Yü* 15.21 求諸己: "to seek it in one self"; "it" refers to one's faults; if the commentary to *Lun Yü* explained the line by replacing 求 by 責 "exact, demand," he did not thereby in any way imply that 求 = 責 "Tadel".

50. Except for the different reading (suggested by the phonetic 交), the term 窔 seems to have hardly any difference from the word 薰.

51. This is the very first quote of Chang's work, taken from *Yi-pien*, but also found in *Ping-pien* 239, which Chang Ping-ch'üan read in an entirely different way: (1)貞隹之.(2)貞不隹之.(3)貞帚曰.(4)帚勿曰.(5)疾齒隹㞢 㞢.(6)疾齒不隹㞢㞢.(7)隹☐乙.(8)不隹父乙. The difference as far as our translation is concerned is with (1) and (2). The original text certainly has the graph 㞢 = 之 and not 止 which is 止(Li Hsiao-ting, *op. cit*. 2061). This makes the interpretation quite difficult, not because of grammar or wording but simply because of lack of context and indications as to what the situation really was and to what the oracular statement really refers. Tentatively we suggest: "Test [the proposition]: it is (> means) that (he?) will go. It does not mean that (he) will go. The lady shall 曰 yüeh ... (declare? speak?). The lady ought not to declare(?), etc."

52. 𓏼 is explained by Chang as "thunder," therefore he understands the sentence as: "The clouds come from the North *and* it thunders". 𓏼 originally is 申 without the element 雨 and could also simply mean 申 "to extend, develop, unroll". The use of 厶 (= 以) in the sense of "make(rain), bring along(rain)" seems to indicate a different usage and meaning of 以 than that observed for the graph 𓏼 (usually transcribed as 㧑), sometimes considered equivalent with 以. Cf. supra note 13.

53. The place name 龍 is written in a different way than 𠂤, to which the meaning "bad, ominous" is sometimes ascribed(cf. note 10). But it is also different from the place names proposed by Kaizuka(bone 2365), cf. p. 27. This shows that these different graphs may not be variants at all, and if so, they may not refer to the same places.

54. Chang translates: "... whether a sacrifice will be made to the wind together with(*ge meinsam mit*) Ti". This is probably the same idea as Shima's (cf. supra, p. 42). However, where the formula shows an opposition between 帝于河 and simply 帝河, a difference may be implied. 不用雨 could also be translated: "(This course of action) not being used, it(still) will rain(?)".

55. Chang's analysis that 𠂤 is a mere variant of 𠂤 = 天"top, head" is not proved nor probable. Shima, *Index* 29 keeps them quite clearly distinguished. Furthermore, *Index* p. 31, he seems to follow Li Hsiao-ting(*op. cit.* p. 195) who reads this graph as 㫃 *liu*, possibly a pictograph of a lizard-like animal(a reading first suggested by T'ang Lan). Aside from the *graphic* problem, it is quite unusual to have the expression 疾 + body part separated by the unnecessary word 朕"my" or any other pronoun, since the subject of the verb 疾 is always the owner of the body part that suffers. It is against the regular usage of terse and compact statements found in the bone texts. Pai Yü-cheng(*CKWT*, Vol. 33, 1969, p. 32) explains 𠂤 simply as a personal name. In that sense the use of the pronoun "my"朕 still seems strange. (Cf. Han Yao-lung 韓耀隆 on the use of the first personal pronouns in the bone inscriptions, *CKWT*, Vol. 18). It seems from a comparison of the examples in Shima, *Index* 29-30, that 𠂤 is more similar to 𠂤(= 夫)than to 𠂤 (proposed by Chang); the translation proposed is tentative at the most, assuming that 𠂤 may

stand for 夫.

56. Chang takes 凡 as a personal name. The tendency to explain everything unclear or unidentifiable as a "personal name," or a "place name" is one of the weaknesses and temptations in the studies on the oracle bones in general; it is an easy and last resort solution. Yet here we can simply read(as was done before in other cases): 炙風 "to make a burning sacrifice(of a victim at the stake) to the Wind(god)". (凡＝風).

57. Chang's full transcription is 我家舊老疒臣: "mein/Familie/ehemalig/blind und krank/Untertan..." The graph 疒, however, is not "blind" as suggested by Chang in this passage and again on p. 243, in the quote 18.1 多疒舞: "Many blind men will dance," instead of: "The many old men will dance," but simply "old". (Shima, *Index* 11 and 108, Li Hsiao-ting, *op. cit.* 2739, Serruys, *Ac. Sinica BIHP* Vol. 29, 1957, pp. 152-154). The graph 舺 is interpreted by Chang as a *ho-wen*(合文) of which the second part is 卜, a shortened variant of 疒 ＝疾. Yet a binom 舊老 is also excluded. Though the graph 舺 seems to be nonexistent, Shima(*Index* 447) has many examples of a phrase 疾臣 and Li Hsiao-ting has one variant of 疾 written 舺. The actual graph as given in Lo Chen-yü 羅振玉 (*Yin-hsü shu-ch'i ch'ien-pien* 殷虛書契前編(4:5.4) is 舺 and quite different from 疒. We suggest then: "My family's old and sick(舺＝疾) servant..."

58. This text has the expressions 亡尤 and 亡囚 within the same oracular statement; it is clear that 尤 and 囚 are not exactly the same. Shima, *Kenkyū*, pp. 264-267 understands the phrase 夕禍 as perform evening sacrifice and 禍 itself as being identical with 祼 "to make a libation". (Shima, *Index* 155). Li Hsiao-ting(*op. cit.* 1869 and 57) reads it as 福. Chang p. 137 explains it as a *Chüeh* vessel 爵 with "drops" added, but he does not conclude to a reading 灒＝禍 "pour out a cup," though this would seem much simpler than to identify it with 祼. Pai Yü-cheng(*CKWT*, Vol. 35, 1970, p. 12) lists the various opinions of the authors and the variants according to the successive periods. He reads it 福, but with the specific meaning of "ritual of presentation of a *vessel* with *wine*" (based on *Chou Li* and *Kuo Yü* texts).

59. Chang following Yang Shu-ta, identifies 登 with 登 "to ascend" and in

the causative sense "to make ascend > to offer". On the other hand, Shima(*Index* 95 and 1) and Ii Hsiao-ting(*op. cit.* 1763) read it as equivalent to modern 升 and 饗. The bone graph 豋 which is clearly corresponding to 登 should indeed be distinguished from 豋 (consisting of 豆 on top of 升). The latter form 升 is then considered as a basic graph which is further elaborated by adding 豆, with the sense "to present" and possibly related to 饗 in the sense of "to present(food)".

60. Chang p. 217 reads 㦻 as *fa*, i. e., modern 瞂 "shield". He quotes the *Kuang yün*(廣韻) form 戜, given there as a variant of the *Shuo wen* form 瞂, to substantiate the identification. But it is probably pure coincidence that such a variant cropped up in the *Kuang yün* and it may have nothing to do with the bone graph 㦻. Both Shima(*Index* 338) and Li Hsiao-ting(*op. cit.* 3539) instead read it as 馘. Li after reviewing the different opinions on 㦻, points out that: 瞂 玬 "shield" in bone script is really 玬 (Cf. Kaizuka, *op. cit. Index*, p.55), and explains the lower part 冃 as "head hanging down" from the 戈 "ax," i. e., "a scalp". This would explain how 冃 could be shortened to 冂 in the bronze graph of Chou time 馘 or 馘 (Jung Keng 容庚, *Chin-wen pien* 金文編, No. 1511). Yet, 冃 appears also in the phrase 多冃 (name of a place or a tribe in Shang). Jao Tsung-yi, *op. cit.*, p. 168 and 561 reads it as 首 "head, leader, to lead". Chang reads 盾 as *Shun*, but Li Hsiao-ting(*op. cit.* 2853) interprets the top part as 下 and takes the whole as 視. As long as the graphs are used only as "names" there is great difficulty in establishing the real analysis of the graph.

61. 帝犬 etc. is translated as "to sacrifice to Ti a dog, etc." by Chang. Shima, *Index* p. 216, has examples of sacrifices made to Ti of dogs, swine, sheep, oxen, but rarely a tiger. (Shima, *Index* 225 has two cases.)

62. The expected regular negation of 至 would be either 不至: "X will not arrive" or 弗至: "X will not make arrive". In all the cases quoted here with 毋其, we consider *ch'i* as marking an object clause of an implicit verb after 毋: "ought not (be thought the case) that they will arrive".

63. The negative of 出 is 亡, and it is only when 出 is used in its sense of "sacrifice, to offer" that its negative is mostly 勿出 "do not sacrifice ..." Again as observed in note above(110) 毋其 is understood as having a verb understood: "ought

not be expected..."

64. 不叀丁 in the first example could also be analyzed as: "if not(so), then assume(it to be) a Ting day". In my paper(AOS meeting, New York, March 15, 1969), *Negatives in the Language of the Bone Inscriptions of Shang*, I proposed that 隹 being the regular, normal copulative verb "to be," 叀 is the causative counterpart of 隹, i.e., "to cause to be > consider, assume, make". This rule I have tried to connect with the usage of the negatives 不 or 弗, 毋 or 勿. But the negative of 叀, if any is 不叀, and 弗叀 or 勿叀 seem to be nonexistent. In a privately circulated notice, Hui 叀 *in Oracle Bone Inscriptions*, Professor David N. Keightley pointed out the weaknesses of this solution and suggested instead that 叀 would seem to require a positive subjunctive sense "should". This idea is probably inspired by Dobson's *Early Archaic Chinese* and *Late Archaic Chinese* grammatical studies where it is asserted that classical and pre-classical Chinese has special verbs to mark subjunctive or conditional mood, e.g. 無, 維. In the case of conditionals, I have shown that such is not so: conditionals are expressed by context, sentence parallelism or special particles (Review article, *Monumenta Serica XXII*, 1, 1963, p. 268 sq.). In the case of subjunctive mood, the same can be assumed for no such verbs functioning as "subjunctives" have been shown. After further investigation and study of 叀, it seems now that it is simply a verb meaning "to consider, estimate, assume," which can be used with attributive complements: "consider X as Y," frequently reduced to phrases where one object is omitted "to consider(something as) Y". In that sense it is not treated as a true active transitive verb, requiring the negative 弗, but is used in analogy with copulative verbs that have the negative 不. Thus 隹 could appear in contrast with 叀: (1)隹王… "It is the king(who) …" and (2)叀王饗"Consider(it) the king, who will offer the banquet," and again (1)隹丁"It is day Ting, when …" contrasted with (2)叀丁… "Consider(it) a Ting day(for a certain contemplated action.)" In this sense 隹 and 叀 are not truly cognates as in the hypothesis of 叀 causative of 隹, but by nature of the semantic content and usage, they are close and subject to analogical treatment. Compare *Ch'ien* 7.3.2 令多子族…召王事 and *Hou* 下, 38.1 叀多尹令…召王事:"Command the many princely clans … harmoniously to cooperate

for the king's service," and "Consider(it) the many officials(?)(whom) to command to. ..." If this is so, it might be more understandable how 叀 was later used to constitute the graph 惠 "to be kind, considerate, thoughtful". In *Shuo wen* (*SWKL* 1673) 叀 is defined as 專小謹也 "Specially(even) in small(things), be diligent, attentive" and was read *chuan*. A *hui* reading seems to be unknown to Hsü Shen and we have no documentary source to prove the reading *hui* except the unanimous opinion of the scholars that (1) 叀 in the bone texts is somehow similar to 隹, (2) that some *Shih ching* occurrences of 惠 really must have been used instead of 維 or a word related to 維. (Chou Fa-kao 周法高 Notes on Ancient Chinese Grammar, *BIHP*, Vol. 22, 1950). To date the most detailed study of 叀 and 隹 in Shang bone texts is that of Han Yao-lung 韓耀隆, *Chia-ku pu-ts'u chung Hui, Wei. yung-fa t'an chiu* 甲骨卜辭中叀隹用法探究 (*CKWT*, Vol. 43, 1972, pp. 1-33). The author, after discussing the graphic analysis of 叀 and 隹, first lists the various usages of both particles separately; then he comes to what is really the core of the problem: the *distinct* and *similar* (though certainly not identical) usages and meanings of the two words. As to the graphic aspect, Han shows that ฿ (early period variant) and 叀 (later period variant) are pictographs of a "whorl," used as a loan graph for a grammatical word, and that the original graphic meaning is nowhere found in the bone inscriptions. Chang (p. 88) also explains 叀 as a pictograph for "whorl," basing himself on Kao Hung-chin 高鴻縉, *Chung-kuo tzu-li* 中國字例 (Taipei 1964). As to the grammatical aspect of the usage of 隹 and 叀, aside from the extensive collection of representative sentences and contexts in which these words are found, the results of Han are rather disappointing. He finds that 叀 and 隹 are in the majority of cases identical in meaning, function and in *all* cases identical in *pronunciation*. The differences are merely found to be complementary distributional in nature; in the end the true nature of 叀 and 隹 is left unexplained and the problem itself of *how* they complement each other and how they are distinguished remains untouched. The reason for Han's failure in explaining the usage of 叀 and 隹 is undoubtedly because of the tendency to list *supposedly* parallel, mutually explanatory sentences, that are in reality not parallel or similar at all, and that have often been extracted from entirely different contexts;

and secondly because of the frequent mistake by which texts are compared on the basis of mere *superficial substitution* of one particle or word by another. Thus f.i. the sentence 叀王从沚馘 is explained as identical with 王从沚馘: "The king shall follow Chih-x," because the sentence is otherwise the same and 由此可證叀純係一發語詞 "it can be proved from this that 叀 is merely an 'introductory' particle"; but we find also 王叀沚馘从… (where 叀 obtains different position in the sentence), yet again it is assumed that it is the same as 王从沚馘, except that 叀 in this instance causes the object of 从 "to follow" to be placed *before* the verb. But what is the nature of 叀, which allows it to reverse the regular verb-object sequence? We suggest instead that the pattern 叀王… means "Consider, assume the king to follow Chih-x," and the pattern 王叀…: "As to the king, consider, assume Chih-x [as whom] he (the king) shall follow". In this analysis, the first pattern simply proposes that the king shall follow someone, and its opposite alternative that the king shall not follow, while the second pattern opposes the alternative "whether to follow a certain person" against the alternative of following someone *else* or nobody at all.

In the sentences: "叀 + date + verb," Han explains f.i. 王叀今六月出 or 王叀今辛未步 as *mere* equivalent phrases for 王于今六月出 or 王于辛未步 and he simply says that 叀 has the same meaning as 于 (叀義同于當無疑也). Yet, he mentions a case like 叀于甲子酒㸂 which, if it is correctly transcribed (Ch'ü Wan-li, *Chia pien* 795 transcribes differently: 叀甲子酒于殷), should have inspired some doubt. In the same way, 兹旬叀雨: "This decade-week, it … rain" is explained by Han as if it were the same as: 兹旬其雨: "This decade-week it will rain (less desired)," and 王固曰叀出 is parallelled with a similar phrase 王固曰其出疾: "… if go out, he will suffer sickness," and 叀兹卜用: "Assume, consider this divination (as what) we shall use (apply again)" is equalled with the *imaginary* line (no source given) 其用兹卜 where *ch'i* 其 is a mystery.

When treating the uses of 隹, Han finds again that 隹父乙降囗 is identical with 父乙降囗 (because 隹 is 發語詞無義); yet, he does not explain why this very same sentence is negated as 不隹父乙降囗 (and not, if 隹 were merely 發語詞, something like *隹父乙不降囗). Again, as for 叀, in 子漁隹出它 Han explains it as equivalent with 子漁其出它 which is completely missing the role of *ch'i* 其, and leads him to explain 子央隹其疾 and 隹其不雨 as cases where 隹 *and* 于 are identical function words *used in combination!* Furthermore, parallel to 叀, 隹 in 隹今八月又事 is explained as 于今八月又事. In the end, there is no difference attributed to these various patterns and no explanation is given why these various phrases would have been used at random within the same divinatory contexts. Han observes however (1) the regular phenomenon that 叀 is negated by 勿隹 in the great majority of occurrences, that (2) with verbs of command (令, 乎) we have mostly the patterns with 叀, seldom with 隹 e. g. 叀罕乎伐吾方 "Assume, consider Pi (whom) we call upon to attack ..." and 叀多子族令...: "Assume the many princely clans (whom we) command to ...," that (3) 隹 + personal name, e. g. 隹父乙: "It is Father Yi," finds no counterpart with 叀. So much for the theory of Han Yao-lung.

Though in *Shuo wen* the reading 叀 *chuan* had for Hsü Shen no relation with *hui* 惠, still 叀 *chuan* was used as the *pu shou* (部首, radical) under which *Shuo wen* classified 惠, defined as 仁也 and analyzed as 从心从叀. This analysis implies that Hsü Shen could not accept 叀 as the phonetic element in a character read by him as *hui*, at least not in the opinion of his time and in the regular pronunciation of 叀 in his time, but the element 叀 still was in some way "etymonic". The *Ku wen* form of 惠, written 蕙 is so similar to the Chou bronze form 𤉙 (Karlgren, *Grammata Serica* 533 d), that (in spite of *Shuo wen's* analysis, where the top element 艸 is taken as a tripled 中 of the Small Seal variant form) 叀 may have developed from a pictograph of an insect (蠭) instead of the pictograph of "whorl". This would indicate the possibility of a graphic convergence of 甫, 叀 (Shang graph for "whorl") with the graph 虫 (in 蠭) for "insect," but also that another reading for "whorl," *viz. chuan* was applied to the graph 叀. Li Hsiao-ting (article in *Journal of Nan Yang University*, Vol. 2, 1968, p. 102) suggests that 艸 of the *Ku wen* graph 蕙 was simply 艸 added as "phonetic," but concludes also that there was a graphic convergence of *chuan* and *hui*. Though 叀 *hui* was unknown to Hsü Shen, a vague connection was still recognized between 惠 and 叀 (*chuan*). 叀 (of Shang bones) had become obsolete and lost, yet the derivate 惠 "to be kind, considerate" survived and was still used in certain passages of *Shih ching*, in a function and meaning similar to that of 維.

65. The publishers of Chang's work (in their *Neuerscheinungen*, February 1972) present his work with a statement in which one may recognize some of the features I mentioned in a short review (*Journal of Asian Studies*, Vol. 31, 1972, p. 388) as required and expected in any study of this nature:

In dieser Arbeit werden die für die shangzeitliche Religion relevanten Orakelknocheninschriften aus dem 14. bis 11. Jahrhundert v. Chr. zum ersten Male in der Geschichte dieser Disziplin mit verbindlichen Übersetzungen und Interpretationen präsentiert. Anhand der 495 Beispielsätze wird versucht, verschiedene Kultriten und das Gesamtbild der Glaubensvorstellungen jener Zeit darzustellen und die archaische Phase der chinesischen Geistesgeschichte durch Vergleiche mit der Zeit der Philosophen aufzuhellen. Ausgestattet mit einer Abhandlung über die Entzifferungs- und Auswertungsmethodik, ausführlichen Glossen zu einzelen Schriftzeichen sowie einem umfassenden Zeichenlexikon und Erläuterungen zu grammatischen Hilfswörtern, kann dieses Buch ausserdem als Einführung in die chinesische Paläographie dienen, die bislang von den europäisch-amerikanischen Fachkreisen unberücksichtigt gelassen wurde.

Mutatis mutandis . . . seu cum grano . . . concedo.

原載《通報》第 60 卷第 1—3 期(*T'oung Pao*, LX, 1-3)，1974 年。

嚴一萍

殷虛書契前編的三種不同版本

羅振玉氏所輯殷虛書契前編八卷，用玻璃版影印於民國元年壬子（一九一二）；民國二十年（一九三一）曾再版過一次。以前北平、上海一帶的舊書商，根據一個字以辨別初版或再版；倘若初印者，一定將售價提高。所謂一字，就是序文第二頁第三行"婦弟范恒齋"句中之"范"字，初版本誤作"茫"，再版本則已經改正。其實初版再版的分別，不僅序中一字之差而已，它的內容也實在有許多不同處。最顯而易見的，為再版本修整拓本，完全失去原物的邊緣，使綴合更加不容易。而拓本移易，也使編號有許多不同的地方，此點最使研究者困惑。我在重印殷虛書契前編時，將初版本與再版本仔細對照，發現初版本的編號，在再版本中有所改變的，共達三十九處。這三十九處的不同，我在重印殷虛書契前編的時候，已經揭出加以對照，此處不再重複了。這許多不同，即使在研究甲骨的人，也很少知道。但是還有一種殷虛書契前編石印本，更沒有人知道了，那是宣統三年辛亥（一九一一），發表在國學叢刊上的，原定每月出版一冊，國學叢刊一共出了兩冊就停刊了。因此殷虛書契前編也只印了二卷。羅振玉在這個石印本的前面，也寫了一篇序，序文也與後來的不同：

宣統庚戌（二年）夏，予既考安陽所出龜甲、獸骨刻辭，為殷商王室之遺蹟，大卜之所掌，竊以為：此殷代國史之一斑，其可貴重等於《尚書》、《春秋》，乃亟為殷商貞卜文字考以章顯之，並手拓其遺文。顧是時，所見甲與骨才數千，巾笥所儲才七八百枚耳。好之既篤，不能自已，復遣廠友視繼先、秋良臣，大索於洹水之陽，先後所見乃達二萬枚，汰其贗作，得尤異者三千餘。於是范君恒齋兆昌，家弟子敬振常，助予拓墨，几案充斥，積塵在襟。殘臘歲朝，氈墨不離左右，匝歲始畢。因略加類次為《殷虛書契前編》二十卷，其先後之次，則首人名、次地

名、歲名、數名，又次則文之可讀者，字之可識者，而以字之未可釋及書體之特殊者殿焉。其說解則別寫爲後編。噫！予之致力於此蓋逾年，由選別而考證，而拓墨，而編次，昕夕孜孜，至忘寢食，儕輩每笑其癡絕，予亦未嘗不自哈也。然於斯學第闢其途徑，至於闡明，未逮十一。斯編既出，所冀當世鴻達，有以啓予，此則予所日望者矣。辛亥正月，上虞羅振玉書於京邸之龜堂。

他說分二十卷，但是經我核對一遍，他所發表的二卷，還抵不上後來八卷本的第一卷，而且，二十卷本一的百二十二個編號之中，有五個編號根本不見於八卷本中。如：

一・三一・三①
一・十四・二
一・二十三・二
一・三十一・二
一・三十一・四

二十卷本卷二的九十九編號之中，也有二個編號不見於八卷本中。如：

二・六・二
二・十三・二

最使人驚異的，羅氏在編二十卷本的時候，頗能存甲骨之真，到了編印八卷本的時候，就任意剪削，把甲骨的原形改變了。例如：

二十卷本卷一	八卷初印本卷一	
一・六・四	一・五・四	已刪去一半（見附圖）那刪去的不知下落。
一・十一・二	一・八・五	已剪去左邊
一・十二・四	一・九・五	已剪去右邊
一・十五・三	一・十一・一	已剪去下邊
一・十六・四	一・十二・一	已剪去右邊
一・十八・二	一・十二・五	已剪去右邊
一・十八・二	一・十二・七	已剪去上邊及右邊
一・十八・四	一・十二・八	已剪去右邊及下邊
一・十九・二	一・十三・二	已剪去右邊
一・十九・四	一・十三・七	已剪去上邊及右邊
一・二十二・三	一・十四・七	

---

① 編者按："一・三一・三"，原文誤作"一・一三・三"，今據實際出處徑改。

	一・十六・三	已分成兩塊（見附圖）
一・二十三・四	一・十六・八	已剪去上邊
一・二十五・四	一・十九・一	已剪去右邊及下邊
一・二十六・一	一・十九・二	已剪去右邊
一・二十六・二	一・十九・四	已剪去左邊及下邊
一・二十六・三	一・十九・三	已剪去下邊

二十卷本卷二

二・一・一	一・二十二・六	已剪去左邊及右邊
二・三・一	一・二十四・三	已剪去上邊及下邊
二・二十二・二	一・三十六・二	已剪去上邊
二・二十八・二	一・三十八・五	已剪去下邊

卷二有一版是二・二十六・三編號，我在前編中遍查無着，結果，在殷虛書契後編中查到了，號碼是後上二・九。

現在把二十卷本《殷虛書契前編》所載的一・六・四與一・二十三・三兩塊完整的背甲摹在下邊，再對照八卷本的分割情形，便可以一目了然。

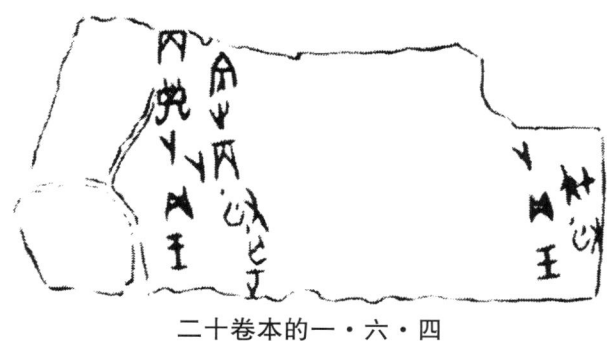

二十卷本的一・六・四

八卷本的一・五・四已刪去右邊的一半已不知下落

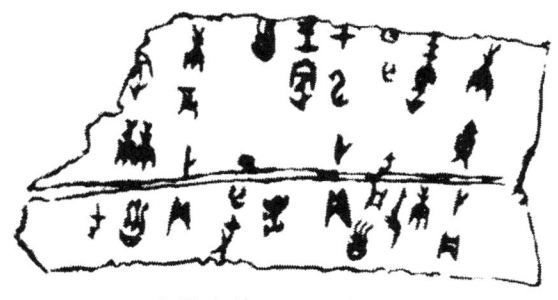

二十卷本的一·二十二·三

八卷本的一·十四·七　一·十六·三已分成兩塊

這兩片是左甗背甲刻辭，屬於第五期的祭祀卜辭。"祭"祭、"叠"祭是五種祀典裏的兩種。五種祭祀是極有規律的祭祀方式，創始於祖甲，一直到帝辛，從沒有間斷過，雖然先師董彥堂先生的《殷曆譜》裏，只有發現祖辛、帝乙、帝辛三王的祀譜，但是我已經譜出一個文武丁祀譜（見《"中央研究院"歷史語言研究所集刊》第四十六本第二分《文武丁祀譜》一文），廩辛、康丁、武乙的祀譜，目前祇因材料的缺乏還不能譜出，但是絕對不會沒有。這兩片卜辭，第一片（一·六·四）釋文是：

（甲戌）卜貞：王（室）大甲祭，（亡尤）。

丙子卜貞：王室外丙祭，亡尤。

八卷本的《殷虛書契前編》，把大甲的一條割掉了。第二片（一·二十二·三）的釋文是：

庚辰卜貞：王室南庚叠，亡尤。

甲申卜貞：王室虎（陽）甲叠，亡尤。

庚寅卜貞：王室般庚叠，亡尤。

太子太丁未立而卒，於是迺立太丁之弟外丙，是爲帝外丙。外丙即位二年崩，立外丙之弟中壬，是爲帝中壬。帝中壬即位四年崩，伊尹乃立太丁之子太

甲，太甲、成湯適長孫也。

《史記・殷本紀》説："帝祖丁崩，立弟沃甲之子南庚，是爲帝南庚。南庚崩，立弟祖丁之子陽甲，是爲帝陽甲。……帝陽甲崩，弟盤庚立，是爲帝盤庚。"卜辭所祭的就是這五世。"祭"祭是五種祀典的第三種祭祀。"㚔"祭是五種祀典的第五種祭祀。第四種是壹祭。第三種祭祀，是複疊舉行的。因爲是複疊舉行，所以我們可以看出這兩片甲骨是屬於同一時期所卜的。請看祀譜：

癸丑	甲寅	祭上甲		
癸亥	甲子		壹上甲	
癸酉	甲戌	祭大甲		㚔上甲

（甲戌）卜貞：王（宜）大甲祭。亡尤。

| | 丙子 | 祭外丙 | | |

丙子卜貞：王宜外丙祭。亡尤。　　　　　　　　　（二十卷本前編一・六・四）

癸未	甲申	祭小甲	壹大甲	
癸巳	甲午		壹小甲	㚔大甲
癸卯	甲辰	祭戔甲		㚔小甲
癸丑	甲寅	祭羌甲	壹戔甲	
	庚申	祭南庚		
癸亥	甲子	祭虎（陽）甲	壹羌甲	㚔戔甲
	庚午	祭般庚	壹南庚	
癸酉	甲戌		壹虎（陽）甲	
	庚辰		壹般庚	㚔南庚

庚辰卜貞：王宜南庚㚔，亡尤。

| 癸未 | 甲申 | 祭祖甲 | | 㚔虎（陽）甲 |

甲申卜貞：王宜般庚㚔，亡尤。

| | 庚寅 | | | 㚔般庚 |

庚寅卜貞：王宜般庚㚔，亡尤。　　　　　　　　　（二十卷本前編一・二二・三）

由這個祀譜看，正好是銜接一週，所以是同一時期卜的，或者，甚至於是同一背甲，也未可知。羅振玉把第一片卜辭割掉了大甲的祭祀，把第二片卜辭又分成兩塊，完全失去了聯繫。如果這兩片卜辭刻上一個月份，我們還可以根據帝乙、帝辛祀譜查出它的年代，是帝乙的，還是帝辛的，可惜現在沒有辦法，那祇有等待將來綴合以後了。

至於失去的七片，一片是一期的。二片是二期的，四片是五期的。我現在逐一把它考釋在下面：

（1）二十卷本前編一·十四·二

丁亥卜貞：翌庚寅出于且庚。十月。

這是第一期卜辭，不記貞人。是在十月丁亥卜"出"祭祖庚，"翌庚寅"、是在四天之後，這"翌"字不一定指"明天"。"出"祭卜辭在第一期中最多，絕無規律可尋，只有文武丁時代是循着五種祀典的次序卜祭，我曾經根據一塊綴合後的文武丁時代腹甲，譜出一個"出"祭的祀譜，原文刊在"中央研究院"歷史語言研究所的紀念董作賓先生六十五歲論文集，茲不贅。

（2）二十卷本前一·十三·三

己酉卜，即貞：告于母辛，宙農。十月。

"即"是第二期貞人，"母辛"是合文，卜告于母辛"宙農"的事。宙讀唯，農指農事言。

（3）二十卷本前編二·六·二

□　　□
　　□□卜大（貞）：□父丁歲□障□

"大"也是第二期貞人，是卜歲祭父丁的事，父丁即是武丁。是另一條卜辭，辭殘無法猜測。

（4）二十卷本前編一·二三·二

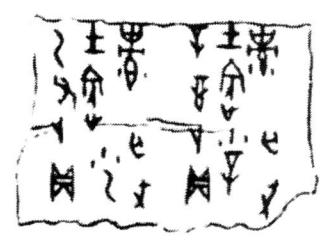

　　辛酉卜貞：王窑小辛壹，亡尤。
　　乙丑卜貞：王窑小乙壹，亡尤。

這是五期卜辭，是記五種祀典裏的壹祭。《史記·殷本紀》說："帝盤庚崩，弟小辛立，是爲帝小辛。帝小辛崩，弟小乙立，是爲帝小乙。"祭的就是這二世。與前述一·六·四和一·二三·三兩片卜辭雖然同樣是五種祭祀，但是不能容納在同一個譜裏，它應當是較後的一個祀典的祭祀，大約要在五年以後，方纔可以再輪到。

（5）二十卷本前編一·三一·四

　　丙□（卜貞）：□　大丁其□
　　甲寅（卜貞）：□　　□用□其牢□
　　□于□用□
　　□□（卜貞）：□升□

這也是第五期卜辭，甲寅以牢祭的可能是武乙，拓片不清楚，不能辨認。如果是武乙，與丙申祭大丁的時間相隔太近，有些不可能。總是無法猜測的。

（6）二十卷本前編二・一三・二

丙申（卜貞）：□文丁其□羊□

這是祭文武丁卜辭，與前面的一片，應屬於五期帝辛時代。

（7）二十卷本前編一・三一・二

羊用，亡尤。

茲用。

這是泛祭的卜辭，沒有指定先祖妣的名字，當是第三期的卜辭。

一九七五年十一月十七日修改於美國

原載《新加坡南洋大學文物彙刊》第 2 號，1976 年；收入《萍廬文集》第 1 輯，《嚴一萍先生全集・甲編》之十七，藝文印書館，1989 年。今據《萍廬文集》收入。

于豪亮

説引字

雲夢睡虎地秦簡辛 81 簡："輕車、趜張、引强"，引字寫作 ✐。長沙馬王堆帛書《周易·萃》："引吉"，引字寫作 ✐；帛書《經法》"法者，引得失以繩"的引字和《導引圖》中的引字，則與《周易》中的引字寫法完全相同。把秦簡同帛書的引字相比較，不難看出兩者寫法大體相同，不同的是帛書引字所從的弓字末一筆向上延伸，字形稍有變化而已。

這個引字，常見於金文和甲骨文之中。秦簡的寫法同甲骨文、金文的寫法相同，帛書的寫法也同甲骨文、金文的寫法極相近。在甲骨文和金文中，以前都將這個字釋爲弘，根據秦簡和帛書，可以肯定這個字是引字，不是弘字。因爲"引强"不可釋爲"弘强"；《周易·萃》的"引吉"，又有今本對照；《導引圖》中引字多次出現，更不可釋爲弘字。

我們知道這個字不是弘字而是引字以後，就可以對與這個字有關的甲骨文、金文的詞句作進一步的考察。

甲骨文常見"引吉"一詞，以前釋爲"弘吉"。釋爲"弘吉"，對於這樣一種情況無法作出合理的解釋：《爾雅·釋詁》："弘，大也。""弘吉"就是"大吉"，兩者的含義完全相同。但是，在甲骨文中，在同一時期、同一字體的卜辭中，我們既看到了使用"引吉"這個詞，又看到了使用"大吉"這個詞。例如：

乙巳卜，貞王田狳，往來亡（無）巛（災）？王㞢曰引吉。在三月。

（《前》二·三六·七）

戊戌王卜，貞田弋，往來亡（無）巛（災）？王㞢曰大吉。丝御，獲狼十又三。

（《前》二·二七·五）

這兩條是帝乙時的卜辭；筆迹相同，是同一人的手筆，所卜也同是田獵的事。然而在卜辭中却既有"⼻吉"又有"大吉"。如果象前人那樣，釋"⼻吉"爲"弘吉"，而"弘吉"又是"大吉"，爲什麽不乾脆統統寫成"大吉"，而要有的寫成"⼻吉"，有的寫成"大吉"？

把"⼻吉"釋爲"引吉"，問題就可以迎刃而解了。《爾雅·釋詁》："引，長也。"《釋訓》："子子孫孫，引無極也。""引吉"就是"長吉"，和"大吉"的含義並不相同。因此，對於同一時期，同一卜人所卜的事也相同，而用詞有"引吉"和"大吉"之分，也就容易理解了。

卜辭有"引吉"，又有"大吉"，同《周易》頗爲一致。《周易·萃》之六二："引吉，無咎"；《萃》之九四："大吉，無咎。"也是既有"引吉"，又有"大吉"。這樣看來，《周易》實在是殷代占卜的繼承和發展。如果釋爲"弘吉"就與《周易》不合，因爲《周易》並没有"弘吉"一詞。所以，從《周易》我們也可以推知，此字必然是"引"，不是"弘"。

釋此字爲"引"，也有助於對金文字句的理解。

毛公鼎："丕顯文武，皇天引厭厥德。"叔夷鎛："余引厭乃心。"這兩句話同《書·洛誥》"萬年厭乃德"的句子相同。"萬年"是長久之意，"引"也是長久之意。如果釋爲"弘"，就與《洛誥》的"萬年"含義不合。這也可以證明此字當釋爲"引"。

毛公鼎："令女（汝）辪（乂）我邦我家内外……死（尸）母（毋）童余一人在立（位），引唯乃智（智）。"童讀爲動，《左傳·宣公十一年》："冬，楚子爲陳夏氏亂故，伐陳，謂陳人無動，當討於少西氏。"動，義爲動摇。毛公鼎的"母（毋）童"同《左傳》的"無動"含義相同。"引唯乃智"的引也是長久之意。銘文記述周宣王任命毛公主持内外一切事務，希望他鞏固王位，並表示自己永遠依靠毛公的才智。釋此字爲引，文義就比較通順易懂，釋爲弘就不可通。

毛公鼎："無唯正虡（昏），引其唯王智（智），廼爲是喪我國。"文義是：無論王正確與否，老是認爲王有才智，這樣就會亡國，釋此字爲引就可以通讀，釋爲弘就不可通。

秦公殷和秦公鐘都有"高引有慶"一語。《廣雅·釋詁一》："高，遠也。"《國語·周語三》："有慶未賞不怡"，注："慶，福也。"因此"高引有慶"即"長久有福"的意思，舊釋引爲弘，也不可通。

毛公肇鼎："其用畜，亦引唯考。"畜讀爲侑，《爾雅·釋詁》："侑，報也。"

字亦作右,《詩·雝》:"既右烈考,又右文母。"考,《國語·周語三》:"所以脩潔百物,考神納賓也。"注:"考,合也。……用之宗廟,合致神人。"唯讀作爲。意思是,鑄作此鼎,既用之於侑祭,又永爲合祭之用。

這裡需要指出的是,金文中有引字。吴彝的"秦引、朱虢、鈒、虎冟",牧敦的"朱虢、引、斬、虎冟",正好與《詩·韓奕》的"鞹鞃淺幭"相當。虢與鞹通,冟與幭通,虎皮即淺毛,因此引就是鞃字。引既是鞃,當然可以讀爲弘。毛公鼎:"引我邦我家",录伯戜敦:"惠引天令(命)",這個引正讀爲弘,作弘大解。毛公鼎中引字凡三見,引(弘)字一見,前人將引字釋爲弘字,不但不能正確解釋此字的含義,也不能説明爲什麽在同一篇銘文中,同一個字會有兩種截然不同的寫法。

因此,甲骨文和金文中的 引 字,應釋爲"引"。

原題《説"引"字》,載《考古》1977 年第 5 期;收入《于豪亮學術文存》(篇題略去引號),中華書局,1985 年;又收入《于豪亮學術論集》,上海古籍出版社,2015 年。今據後者收入。

David S. Nivison（倪德衛）

THE PRONOMINAL USE OF THE VERB YU (GIǓG: 㞢, 㞢, 㞢, 有)* IN EARLY ARCHAIC CHINESE（動詞"㞢、㞢、㞢、有"在早期古漢語中的代詞性用法）

* (I have resolved Shang graphs into modern forms wherever this is possible without prejudice to the argument.)

1. The word yu 有 in Classical Chinese usually has the apparent meaning of the existential quantifier in logic, and the grammatical functin of a transitive verb. (That is, e.g., in Nan jen yu yen … 南人有言… "Among the southern people there is a saying …," the word yen 言 "saying" is the grammatical object of yu 有, and if we substitute a pronoun the substitute has to be the object pronoun chih 之.) Yu 有 also is used in a noun phrase before a group name or general term, and the analysis of its syntax and meaning in this use is the problem that motivates this paper. The use is rare except before dynasty names, where it has continued to the present, e.g., yu Yin 有殷, yu Ming 有明, etc. The analysis of this latter use has been disputed by Chinese grammarians for the past three centuries. Two interpretations have emerged. At present, one interpretation appears to be accepted by prominent Chinese linguists and philologists, while the other is generally followed by the leading Western translators of early texts.

The two interpretations are these:

1.1 In all such expressions, yu 有 has its related verbal meaning, "have" ("[for] ... there is ..." becoming "... has ..."), and the whole phrase, e.g., yu Yin 有殷, means "the possessors of the Yin," i.e., "The rulers of the Yin." So also yu pang 有邦, "the ruler of a state," i.e., a feudal lord. This is the view of the Ch'ing grammarian Liu Ch'i 劉淇, whose book on grammatical words, Chu-tzu pien-lueh 助字辨略 was published in 1711. In chapter 3, in a section on the word yu, he aruges for his view, citing the Sung Dynasty commentator to the Analects of Confucius, Hsing Ping 邢昺. Hsing writes (commenting on Analects 8.20) that the early emperors took the names of the states they came from as their dynasty-names (kuo-hao 國號), so that, e.g., "when Shun possessed the world, he was called yu Yü shih 有虞氏" (he of the lineage of the possessors of Yü) — Yü 虞 being, presumably, the name of Shun's state.

In this view Liu has been followed by James Legge. I do not know that this is where Legge got his interpretation of yu 有 in such phrases (probably he got it directly from Hsing Ping), but he consistently translates them as Liu would have him. The first occurrence of the idiom in the (ku-wen) Shang Shu, for example, is yu Miao 有苗 in the "Counsels of the Great Yü 禹)," where Yü is bidden by Shun to lead the vassal lords against the Miao and persuade them to accept the blessings of civilization. Here (The Chinese Classics, III, p.64, section 3) Legge notes that "we might render the characters literally — 'the possessor of Meaou,'" and he says "such is generally the force of 有 before the name of a country throughout the Shoo." Karlgren and Dobson both handle such uses of yu 有 in Shang Shu texts the same way Legge does. Karlgren elsewhere has seen that there is a problem to be explained (see his "Glosses on the Siao Ya Odes," BMFEA 16(1944): 118-19; and see also section 2.1 below). But Dobson does not see this to be a sepcial use in his Early Archaic Chinese (Toronto, 1959).

1.2 The second interpretation to be noted is that of Wang Yin-chih 王引之 in his well-known book on grammatical words, Ching-chuan shih-tz'u 經傳釋詞 (author's preface 1798). In chapter 3 of that work we find a section on yu 有. Here Wang says, "When one character doesn't make a complete phrase 成詞, one adds the character yu 有 to match it. Thus Yü, Hsia, Yin and Chou are all names of dynasties, and one calls them respectively yu Yü 有虞, yu Hsia 有夏, yu

Yin 有殷, and yu Chou 有周." And he adds that this is the account that should be given whenever yu 有 occurs before a state-name. But it is not limited to use before names of states, and Wang claims a multitude of other examples, most of them from the Shang Shu, e. g., yu pang 有邦 (presumably "the states"), yu chia 有家 ("the families"), yu fang 有方 ("the regions"), yu Hsia 有夏 ("the Chinese states"), yu chung 有衆 ("the multitudes"); and from the Shih, yu pei 有北 ("the regions of the north"). Wang concludes, "interpreters of the Classics have not understood that yu is here a particle, and always explain it as yu meaning 'have.' This is a mistake."

Dictionaries in Chinese and Japanese usually follow Wang, as do the grammarians P'ei Hsüeh-hai 裴學海 and Yang Shu-ta 楊樹達, who both take yu here as a meaningless particle. Furthermore, it is easy to discover early Classical commentary that gives some support to Wang and that offers interpretation inconsistent with Liu's view. We need look no farther than K'ung Ying-ta 孔穎達, in the T'ang Dynasty, commenting on the account of the Miao campaign already mentioned. In this Shang Shu passage the phrase yu Miao 有苗 occurs twice in near succession. The first occurrence is glossed by K'ung as yu Miao kuo 有苗國, and again yu Miao chih kuo 有苗之國. The second occurrence is glossed as yu Miao chih chün 有苗之君. I assume that the two glosses are parallel, the second being "the ruler of the Miao," and the first therefore "the state of the Miao." In the second case K'ung must be understanding the phrase yu Miao to mean just "the Miao," but to refer in this context to the ruler of those people — quite a possible interpretation. If we go back even farther to the third century commentary of the man who probably forged the chapter, we find the first occurrence glossed san Miao chih min 三苗之民 "the people of the three Miao [tribes]." Neither K'ung Ying-ta nor the third century forger can possibly be understanding yu as "have."

2. So here we have a disagreement with quite deep roots, about the interpretation of a usage that occurs quite frequently in historical texts that are certainly important enough so that one would like to translate them correctly. And on either side of this difference of view we have distinguished scholars who deserve respect. Can we straighten the matter out for them?

2.1   I must turn now away from forged material, which has served well enough to elicit the difference, to some genuine Shang Shu chapters of the ninth or tenth century B.C. In the To-fang 多方 chapter ("Numerous Regions" #38) I count twelve cases of my usage, and in the Chün Shih 君奭 chapter ("Prince Shih" #36) perhaps eight. There is no lack of material, but it is hard to find something that cuts. Just as in ecclesiastical usage "Rome" can refer to the Pope, and "California" to the bishop of California, so it could perfectly well have been (Chinese being at least as flexible as English) that a phrase that may have meant, e.g., "the Hsia," could be used quite regularly to refer to the ruler of Hsia, and so on. But in the Chün Shih chapter Wang has found a case of yu Hsia in which "Hsia" is not the dynasty, but just "Chinese states." Section 12 in Karlgren goes "But that Wen Wang was still able to make concordant the Hsia (i.e., Chinese states) in our possession was because he had such men as Shu of Kuo ···"; and Legge's translation substantially agrees. They may be right in making yu "in our possession," i.e., "possessed"; but this is an interpretation quite different from the one they always give to, e.g., wo yu Chou 我有周 "we the rulers of Chou," and one would think it should be the same. Karlgren tries to resolve this dilemma by arguing that "yu Yü shih" originally was "the lord who possesses Yü," i.e., "the yu-Yü lord." The word shih could now be deleted, giving "(he who) possesses Yü." But also the component yu-Yü could be detached as an apparent fief name, and understood with different syntax as "the possessed Yü." Finally, he thinks, both usages persisted. But if usage before the Shang Shu is to decide the matter, we must turn to the evidence. This is found in the Shang oracle bone inscriptions, as early as 1200 B.C.

2.2   In Shang material the graph 有（ ） is not found, but there is no doubt that the graphs 㞢 and (in later Shang periods) 㞢 represent the same word, i.e., Karlgren's *gi̭ŭg. The evidence in this earliest material is, I believe, decisive. There, noun-phrases of the form "yu NP" occur fairly often, and in great variety. And it is quite clear in most of them, and probably true of all, that they cannot be verb-object structures of the supposed "possessor of" sort. Yu in these noun-phrases is a modifying word of some kind, and that seems to me to be in effect what Wang Yin-chih is asserting of their syntax. But if we take post-Shang usage to be a continuation of Shang idiom, then Wang Yin-chih and Yang Shu-ta are wrong in thinking yu here to be meaningless, and wrong again, I believe, in thinking it has nothing to do with yu meaning "there is" or "has."

My thesis is that we should see a noun-phrase of the form "yu X" as deriving from a sentence meaning "… has X," or "in(or for) … there is(was, will be) X," where X is a general term of some kind. I would want to develop the argument as follows: the sentence "… yu pang," if it means "… has a state," would yield the term "yu pang," with the meaning "the state that … has," or simply "his(our, your) state." If this hypothetical sentence means "in … there are states," then the derived term yu pang would mean "the states there"; and(to generalize) when a hypothetical sentence is simply "yu X," "there is(an) X," or "there are X's," the derived term "yu X" will mean simply "the X" or "the(various) X's."(This preliminary analysis will require further refinement.) In early literary materials this construction is already rare; but in Shang inscriptions it occurs frequently, and may play many different roles.

2.3 While most scholars have managed not to notice the problem at all, there are some exceptions. Besides Wang Yin-chih, P'ei Hsüeh-hai and Yang Shu-ta, I must mention James Legge again. Usually he translates this usage incorrectly, but sometimes he gets it right, and sometimes sees what it must be. In the character index to his translation of the Shang Shu(p.685), Legge observes of the word yu that "the term must often be construed as if it were preceded by a 所," and he notes in particular the expression 有眾. This is exactly right, and if the import of Legge's observation had been fully appreciated there would be no need for this paper. Wu Ch'i-ch'ang(1971: 1960 Taipei ed., pp.10-11), writing in 1934, argued that one of the meanings of 㞢 is 此"this," and some of his examples are good ones. Kaizuka Shigeki(人, 1960: 146/12) and Ch'en Meng-chia(1956: 96-7) both argue that 㞢(or 才) in 受㞢(or 才)才 has the sense of a demonstrative pronoun. They are right, but neither gives any analysis to show why this should be so, and Ch'en's reasoning from his evidence as to just what pronominal functions 㞢 can have in this phrase is faulty, as Takashima(p.336) argues. Takashima is mistaken, I think, in rejecting Ch'en's basic claim that 㞢 functions as a pronoun; but Ch'en himself does not extend his own idea, often interpreting 㞢 as a name (pp. 323, 503) and 㞢 as "right" (p. 517) where his pronoun theory would have worked at least as well. Shima Kunio in his concordance treats the middle 㞢 or 㞢 in 受㞢(㞢)㞢, 受㞢(㞢)年 as meaning 尤 "much," the meaning ("abundant") accepted also by Takashima and Serruys. But Shima (S 506.4) does recognize that 㞢 following 于 is a special problem, and gives twenty-two examples, though he does not suggest a meaning. And since Shima does not index common words like 㞢 and 㞢 but only gives a sampling of their use, I have had to collect most of the 250-plus examples in my list (at the end of this paper) as I happened on them.

Finally one of the most useful discussions, specifically of the graph 㞢, is Yen I-p'ing's short article 說「㞢」, in 中國文字 47 (1973). Quoting Wang Yin-chih, he recognizes that 㞢 sometimes functions as a "particle" 語助, concluding that the matter needs more research, and (p. 6b) offering thirteen examples (of which I would accept all but the first two). But — a demonstration that the matter does need more research — we find Yen (p. 3a) classing 㞢 in 受㞢㞢, 受㞢年 simply under the meaning "have," 非無.

3. I shall begin by translating three inscriptions on one plastron (丙 182-3), using the order-numbers assigned by Chang Ping-ch'uan in this Academica Sinica collection. (I would reject a few of Chang's graph-identifications.)

182(1)   壬   辰   卜   殼   貞: 呼   子
          Jen   ch'en   pu   Ch'üeh   chen   Hu   Tzu
          窒   卯   㞢   母   于   父   乙;
          pin   yü   yu   mu   yü   Fu   I
          㞢   宰,   㞢   及,   三   豛,   五
          t'ou   lao   ts'e   fu   san   hua   wu
          宰.
          lao

Jen-chen (day 29) crack, Ch'üeh divining: "We should have (Princess) Tzu-pin yü-supplicate for her mother to Fu Yi; she will t'ouflagon sacrifice a sacrificial sheep, (and) make ts'e-inscribed prayer promise of a fu-captive human victim, three floral sets and five sacrificial sheep."

(This inscription, on the left center of the face of the plastron, is repeated on the right center(2), with a few words added or omitted.)

182(7)	乙	巳	卜，	㱿	貞：	呼	子
	I	ssu	pu	Ch'üeh	chen	Hu	Tzu
	窜	㞢	于	出	祖	牢．	
	pin	yu	yü	yu	tsu	lao	

I-ssu(day 42) crack, Ch'üeh divining: "We should have(Princess) Tzu-pin make offering to her grandfather, (using) sacrificial sheep."

(This inscription, below and to the right of(1), is repeated in negative form(8) on the left side, and again in positive form(9) on the right side farther down. There is a final abbreviated negative on the left, "(She) should not make offering.")

183(4)	王	其	㞢	用	入	羋
	Wang	ch'i	yu	yung	ju	pi

The king should perhaps also use the incoming catch.

(This inscription on the lower left of the back of the plastron, has an abbreviated negative(5) on the lower right.)

3.1　The situation, briefly, appears to be this: one of the royal wives is sick. It is suspected that King Wu Ting's father, Fu Yi, is responsible and must be appeased with sacrifices. It is proposed that these sacrifices to father-in-law Fu Yi be made by the sick lady's daughter(probably; perhaps a son), Tzu-pin. In 182(1),(2), therefore, we have "Tzu-pin yü-supplicates for her(㞢) mother to Fu Yi …," while in 182(7),(8),(9) we have "Tzu-pin makes offering to her(㞢) grandfather …"(on a later day: the proposed offering here is more modest). The entire context of family relationships shows that 㞢(yu) has to mean "her" in these inscriptions.

183(4) is probably related to an inscription(182(3)) on the face of the plastron(perhaps also(5),(6)), proposing sacrifices by the king to his high ancestor Shang Chia, probably intended as an independent appeal for his wife's recovery. I assume 183(4) to be an offer to increase the stakes.

4. Inscription 4 on 丙 183 in my translation reads "The King should perhaps also use the incoming catch." By this I intended, use(i. e., offer to Shang Chia) the game caught(recently or imminently) in a royal hunt conducted by the King himself or a subordinate, and sent in or brought in to the capital. (Game, probably; but war-captives could have been meant.)

In this interpretation the three transitive verbs 用 "use," 入 "send in," and 犁 "catch" are related in exactly one of dozens of mathematically possible ways, without the availability of any of the Classical pronouns and particles —所,之,者, 其,也,而, etc. — that a Classical Chinese writer could use to reduce or eliminate syntatic ambiguity. I suggest that the Shang language simply would not have worked unless this ambiguity were restricted by certain strict conventions. A full description of those conventions is a task for much more research. For now, let us try out the assumption that the needed conventions include at the top of the list the ones that would yield the meaning I have gotten from the phrase 用入犁. They would then be as follows(for simplicity I consider the problem only for transitive verbs):

4.1 C(1) "Verb(b) Verb(a)": If Verb(b) is the main verb of its sentence or clause. read this "Verb(b)(其)所 Verb(a)." Here "(其)所 Verb(a) functions as Noun object of Verb(b)." Examples:

> 入犁 "He sends in what he(or someone) catches."
> 用犁 "He uses what he(or someone) catches."

C(2) "Verb Noun": If "Verb" is not the main verb in its sentence or clause, read this "(其)所 Verb 之 Noun." Example:

> 入犁 "(What someone catches =) the catch that he(or someone) sends in."
> (Taking 犁, i. e., 所犁, as a noun.)

C(3) In the sequences

> "Verb(c)   Verb(b)   Verb(a)"
> "Verb(c)   Verb(b)   Noun"

consider Verb(c) related to Verb(a) by C(1); then consider Verb(b) related to what follows by C(2). These conventions together indicate for 用入单 the syntax that was assumed in the translation:

用(其)所入之所单

4.2 These are proposed as conventions not rules: think of them as one thinks of the speech class of a word — e.g., we try 人 as a noun before trying something else, 入 as a verb before trying something else, etc. It will be possible to do other things with words when context and sense make it sufficiently obvious. In the above case in effect we think of(a) the sentence 用单 as formed first and construed by C(1); then(b) the term 入单, construed by C(2), and substituted for 单 in(a). But following some other convention than C(3), we might have thought of the constituent 入单 as interpreted first by C(1), getting

用(其)所[入(其)所单]

with the possible meaning "…(use=) sacrifice the one who had his catch(sent in=) confiscated." And this structure, though quite mad here, might sometimes have a use, filled in with other words, and in the right context.

4.3 One can readily find evidence for holding that C(1-3) are in fact the dominant convention set for interpreting EAC (Early Archaic Chinese) syntax. Consider an example from Shang Shu 38 多方:

(1) 38.3 我惟大降尔命

(Karlgren: "I grandly(send down orders to you=) give you my commands.")

(2) 38.23 乃有不用我降尔命,
  我乃其大罚殛之.

(Karlgren: "If there are those who do not(use=) obey the orders which I have sent down to you, I will greatly punish and kill them.")

Abstracting out the verbs, notice that 降…命 in(1) obeys C(1); but in(2) 降…命 obeys C(2), and 用…降…命 obeys C(3). (But here there is something more complicated, for C(1-3) do not explain the relation of 有 to what follows: The structure 乃…乃…forces a comarison of '有 + noun-phrase' with 'verb-phrase + 之'; this shows that 'noun-phrase' must be the reference of 之; and this rules out the possibility of interpreting 有不用… as 有所不用…, perhaps "if there are occasions when(people) do not obey …" and requires 有不用…者 "If there are those who do not obey …")

4.4 Or, consider the constantly encountered use of 有(㞢, 㞢) before a (single) verb. Serruys(1974, pp.96-98) argues for interpreting "yu + Verb" as "have [cause, opportunity, chance, reason, risk] to(+verb) do something," and says that in this sense it is often found in oracle and bronze inscriptions and in the early Classics. (In fact it occurs occasionally throughout Classical Chinese.) Serruys here gives a good list of senses when 㞢/㞢 precedes an intransitive verb(since such a verb must be in "oblique" relation to any "object"). When the verb is transitive, A.C. Graham's remark("The Grammar of the Mohist Dialectical Chapters," p.91, in A Symposium on Chinese Grammar, Aug. 1970) is the right one: here, "the reference is forward, to an implicit object"; and he gives examples: 有求"seek something,"有指"point something out," etc. In other words, what the sentence "yu Verb" amounts to is "有所 Verb," quite in accord with C(1).

5. Keeping C(1-3) in mind, look again at the phrase 钔㞢母 in 丙 182(1). C(1) does not apply, but C(2-3) do. The result is

钔(其)所㞢之母

i.e., "… supplicate for the mother whom she has," or "supplicate for her mother." It seems that the mysterious pronominal "meaning" of 㞢 is just what we should expect from regular features of EAC syntax. This is, it is not a special meaning of 㞢, but a quite ordinary use of the word, and surely the Shang speaker in employing this use continued to think of the word as the ordinary 㞢 and not something else. This use is assisted, of course, by the fact that 㞢 easily means "have."

5.1 This "possessive pronoun" use of 㞢/㞢 is illustrated, probably, by the following in the list: 1-45; 66-80; 86-87; 93-95; 130-131; 134, 136-138; 204-254—i.e., about half of the total list. This use is unproblematic, but other uses do need comment.

5.2 As I have argued (2.2), to see what is referred to by 㞢/㞢 in a phrase "Verb yu Noun" we must imagine a sentence "... yu Noun," and see what could fill in the blank, when yu is understood verbally, either as "has/have" or as "there is/are." When the appropriate English for sentential yu is "has/have," then "pronominal" yu is "possessive." When the English ought to be "there is/are (were, will be)," there is a variety of possibilities. Examples:

(1) No reference, or indefinite reference: appropriate translation "the." E.g., 48, 92; probably 85, 135; probably others. (In syntax "yu Noun.")

(2) Location: appropriate translation "there." E.g., hunting: 49-64, 140-142; agriculture: 96-123 (年, some cases only, the reference being to the place where the crop is planted), 124-128, 129. (The last is unique, in that the place-name is not deleted, and so perhaps this is a "possessive" case.)

(3) Specification of kind: appropriate translations "of it" (i.e., planted crop; most cases of 年 96-123); "of them" (i.e., captives or game, 178-180); "about it" (kind of trouble, 192-196).

(4) Problem or project: appropriate translation "in this (matter)." This is the use in the most frequently occurring yu-phrase, 受㞢㞢, 受㞢㞢. 155-177 in the list are only a sample. But what exactly can yu refer to here? Ch'en Meng chia (1956, pp.96-97) thinks it can refer here to an enemy tribe or state ("We will be granted aid against them"), and this is acceptable; but of course what is meant is "... aid in our defense against them" or "... aid in our attack against them": the reference will be to the project or problem at hand. Ch'en also thinks yu can refer to Ti, the principal Shang deity. I believe this unlikely, because I have never seen the phrase 受帝㞢 "receive Ti's aid"; but the sequence "受 + tribe name + 㞢" often occurs (e.g., S 131.4). One might argue that the final 㞢 in this phrase means "divine aid," so one should not expect to see 帝 before 㞢. But not all divine aid is necessarily aid from Ti. Some would entertain the possibility that this sequence could mean "receive aid from the X's"; and again I think this unlikely, for two reasons: whenever a tribe or state name appears in this sequence, it is the name of a people that from every other indication (and there is sometimes much other evidence) is hostile to the Shang; and I believe that the scholarship that

identifies 㞢 in 受㞢/㞢 as 祐 "divine aid" is almost certainly right. Furthermore, although the sequence 受我㞢 "grant us aid" is common (e. g., S 463.2-3), 㞢 in 受㞢㞢 does not, I think, mean "to us"; for the negation of 受我㞢 is 不我其受㞢, showing that 我 is indirect object of 受, and not a modifier of 㞢. Obviously, I also think that the meaning "abundant" for 㞢/㞢, both in 受㞢/㞢㞢 and 受㞢/㞢年, must now be relegated to the history of scholarship in the field. It was at least useful in making provisional sense of these phrases, without giving them meanings that would lead to misinterpretation of surrounding contexts.

5.3　Two more types of use have not been covered, and applying the foregoing analysis to them requires a more technical treatment: (5) unspecified quantity: appropriate translation "some" or "the (understood amount of)"; (6) No reference, or indefinite or not prominent reference, in syntax "Verb yu Verb": translate as if "Verb 所 Verb."

(5) Unspecified quantity: examples, list 143-154.

That these inscriptions containing the phrase 㞢鬯 (or 㞢鬯) exhibit the "pronominal" use of yu is shown by list 143 and 144.

143，—叀㞢鬯用福 "… it should be some" (or "the") "fragrant wine that we use in the fu-offering," shows 㞢 in the structure "hui yu object verb." Compare with this the list examples 20, 137-142, and see my argument in 6.2(g).

144，—父己𢀛㞢鬯 "… to Fu Chi we make sui-offering of some fragrant wine," can be compared with 明 757 cited in my comment to 144, which has the same syntax with a number (一, i. e., 一卣) in place of 㞢: "To Tsu Hsin we make sui-offering of one yu (卣) of fragrant wine." On this, see my argument in 6.2(e).

The problem is that I have explained the pronominal reference of yu in "yu Noun" as deriving from the component "…" in a hypothetical sentence "… yu Noun," where yu (㞢 or 㞢) is the verb and "Noun" is its object. But in this case the hypothetical sentence would have to be "… yu 鬯 + Number + 卣": see the example (摭續 60) cited in the comment on list 146; and the reference that I suppose yu in the term "yu 鬯" to acquire is not "…" but "Number + 卣," which follows yu 鬯 in this hypothetical sentence.

Obviously, if this is right, the previously given informal explanation of the acquisition of reference for yu in a "yu Noun" term requires refinement. Perhaps better would be a semi-formal account along these lines: We can say that we suppose a sentence "… yu Noun …," which is progressively shortened by deleting elements that thereafter are "understood in context." Penultimately, we have the sentence "yu Noun," which then is used as a term by C(2). In this term "yu Noun," yu implicitly has the reference of everything that was deleted from the original sentence, and explicitly has the reference of the element in that sentence that we think of as the last element to be deleted.

Thus:

Original sentence 彡祖辛彳鬯五卣

"In sui-offering to Tsu Hsin there will be five yu of fragrant wine."

Deletion(1) 彳鬯五卣

"There will be five yu of fragrant wine (sc. in sui-offering to Tsu Hsin)."

Deletion(2) 彳鬯

"There will be some fragrant wine (sc. five yu of it (sc. in sui-offering to Tsu Hsin))."

Conversion to term (by C(2)) 彳鬯

"The (or some) fragrant wine (parenthetically, five yu of it (which, double parenthetically, was set aside for the sui-offering to Tsu Hsin))."

This term, with its referential shadow and penumbra, may now be used in any way a noun may be used in a Chinese sentence. Yu (彳) retains its reference, of course, only within the context that generates it; but that is true of any pronoun.

(5a) List 132-33, from 丙 302, illustrate another interesting usage analyzable in this way. Consider the (logically) possible sentence 隹甲辰迄至四日屮丁未 "Four days (inclusive) following chia-ch'en (day) there will be a (day designated) ting-wei." From this we can derive the term 屮丁, which (if today is chia-ch'en) will mean "this ting day," i.e., "ting-(wei" (the one following today)), i.e., the next ting day." That is just what 屮丁 means in these two examples, as we can establish from examining the entire plastron. 丙 302 contains thirteen inscriptions, all on the same subject, each either dated or containing an internal date. These two are (11) and (12), with the phrase 至于㞢丁, and (13) in a similar context has 至于丁未, obviously used in the same sense.

(6) No reference, or indefinite or not prominent reference, in syntax "Verb yu Verb." Examples: 181-191; 199-201(?); 202-203.

I am led to posit this category of use because I believe that what 203 (e. g.) means is, 事以所告啟; 在二月 "The business will begin according to what we announced; in the second month."

That is, at some earlier time there was an "announcement" to the Ancestors via oracle-cracking of some contemplated action; here the king double-checks and then goes ahead with it. So, also, 以㞢取 (181-191) seems to me to mean 以所取. Unfortunately, there are not many inscriptions that, like this one, force me to interpret this way, and there is very little context to work with. But "yu Verb" as a term here does seem to be "所 Verb."

If I interpret 203 correctly, how could 㞢 have this function? Do we, perhaps, face a different grammatical construction altogether? For a long time I thought so. But I now believe the matter can be explained quite within the framework of the present analysis.

First, reflect that this analysis has been unblushingly anachronistic. 用入㞢 does not really equal 用其所入之所㞢, because the function-words 其, 所, 之 as used here did not appear in the language until several centuries later. It is now time to set aside the fish-trap, and look just at what is really there.

The fish, to begin with, is a sentence "A yu B," "For A there is B." In this sentence yu "points" two ways, calling attention to A as "having" B, and to B as what there is in connection with A. When B is a noun and A is unexpressed and we are uninterested in it (perhaps it is just "everything") then the corresponding term "yu B" will mean "extant B," "B which there is," "some B," "the B," without our thinking of (or yu pointing toward) any further description of it.

Now, suppose B in the sentence "A yu B" is a verb. The import of C(1) was that in this case, since yu (㞢, 㞢) also is a verb, and is the main verb in the sentence, the meaning will be "A has something it B's"; or (per A. C. Graham) "A B's something." If now again we suppose "A" not only deleted but unthought of, the resulting sentence "yu B" will mean "something is B'd." And the term-conversion "yu B" of this sentence will then mean simply "the B'd thing," or "what is B'd," or "what (someone or something) B's." Place this carefully back in the fish-trap. Voila! 所 B.

We may now loosen this up a bit, and reflect that if "yu B" can mean 所 B at all, there is no reason to insist that A be completely invisible. Yu will have, potentially, its characteristic double-pointing wherever it is used. And so, whenever B is a verb, yu in a term "yu B" has to some extent a double "pronominal" function. Thus, 受屮擘 (178-180) will mean "we will be granted (something caught =) a catch of them," but also "we will be granted (something caught =) a catch (sc. of them)." Which way we read it will depend on what we are interested in. Perhaps the same option is available for interpreting the controversial 受屮ㄓ. For, ㄓ(祐) is reasonably taken as a "completable" verb, "(do something helpfully =) aid." The term 屮ㄓ could then mean either "(something (Ti, e.g.) does helpfully =) (divine) aid in this," or just (something (Ti or some spirit) does helpfully =) (divine) aid (sc. in some situation or other). And the last meaning proposed here is just 所ㄓ. When context encourages this interpretation, 受屮ㄓ would have exactly the same sense as simple 受ㄓ.

(5.4 The meaning "abundant" for 屮/ㄓ in this and similar contexts, e.g., 受屮年, 受屮擘, seemed to have a sound basis. 有 apparently means "abundant" in Shih Ching 170.1. But in such phrases one would expect a quantifying adverb (rather than a quantifying adjective before the object); e.g., Ch'un Ch'iu (207 Hsüan 16/4) 大有年; and S 29.3 遺 760 丁卯卜王大隻魚.)

6. If the pronominal hypothesis for Shang Chinese 屮/ㄓ is true, what else should we find? Finding expectations borne out does not prove a theory, but does progressively confirm it.

6.1 History being the process of gradual change that it usually is — especially in language — we could expect that there are, for a time, some survivals of the 屮/ㄓ idiom — with 有(㝢) the graph used — in free use in early literary material(and not just the stereotyped use before dynasty names, which continues into normal Classical usage.) A second supplementary list is attached of examples or possible examples found in the Shang Shu, Shih Ching and I Chou Shu. (The many examples of 有 before a dynasty or state name are not included.) Here I will examine several from the Shang Shu in addition to those already cited(1.2, 2.1 above):

書 4 皋陶謨 3:皋陶曰,都亦行有九德,亦言其人有德,乃言曰,載采采.

Legge(p.70) and Karlgren(p.8) both take 有九德, to mean "there are nine virtues," and so are forced to construe 行 as a noun. But, as Legge admits in a long note, this causes difficulty with 亦, which he obviously senses ought to be followed by a verb; so he(and the commentators he reviews) have to hunt for another meaning for it. Surely the sequence 亦…亦…ought to be in some way parallel(compare Shu 30.3 亦罔非酒惟行…亦罔非酒惟辜); and the antithesis 行…言 that would result seems to confirm this. These difficulties disappear if we take 有九德 as "the Nine Virtues." I am not sure of the translation, but perhaps it goes thus: "Kao Yao said, 'Oh, you should both practice the Nine Virtues, and also speak of others having virtues, saying "you serve me(well) in this and in that."'" Or, perhaps 采采 has the sense "(varicolored =) beautiful," giving "…saying 'your service is very fine.'"(For the "modal" 其 in 亦言其…, compare Tso Chuan 31-32, Huan 6/1…謂其上下皆有嘉德…, "…they meant that superiors and inferiors were all of admirable virtue …"(Legge, Classics, 5.49).)

書 5 益稷 4:予欲左右有民.

Legge(p.79): "I wish to help and support my people." Legge's commentary shows clearly that he is construing 有 correctly: he expands 有民 to 我所有之民 (as, in fact, does(pseudo) K'ung An-kuo). Karlgren(p.11) interprets similarly.

書 38 多方 15:天降時喪,有邦間之.

This should be, I think, "Heaven sent down ruin on this(one), and your state supplanted him."(One may argue here that 有邦 should refer to the Shang ruler. Perhaps so; but it can refer to the ruler even though it means "your state."

Similarly 有夏 in what immediately precedes <u>refers</u> to the Hsia ruler but <u>means</u> "The Hsia." Compare the use of fief names to refer to feudal lords in Shakespeare.)

書 38 多方 24：猷告爾有多方士暨殷多士

Legge(p. 504): "Oh! ho! I tell you, ye many officers of the various regions, and you, ye many officers of Yin." In his commentary, Legge expands 有方 to 所有之方, in exact accord with my C(2). Pseudo-K'ung had glossed 告爾有方 as 告汝眾方.

These examples and others seem to show that the <u>yu</u> idiom under study was used easily by Chou writers of EAC.

6.2 The pronoun thesis would lead one to expect still other things in Shang Chinese itself, and here the confirmation is equally good. We should predict that with enough material to sift we would find language like the following:

(a) Other possessive pronouns used where 㞢 or ㇱ might have been used. Examples are found in the list, under "comments," at 1, 68, 130.

(b) There should be similar structures with 㞢(ㇱ) omitted (just as 厥, 其, 此 etc., functionally similar in later Chinese, can be omitted). Examples are plentiful for most types of use. Number 85 is particularly significant. The list notes other examples at 53, 54, 202, 247; as for 受㞢ㇱ, note that 受ㇱ is common; so also 受年. The view that 㞢 or ㇱ is an adjective or a name is not ruled out by this, but the pronoun theory explains it more easily, because a possessive or demonstrative pronoun in Chinese usually says something that would be understood in the context anyway.

(c) We should expect 㞢 or ㇱ in the syntax "Verb <u>yu</u> Noun(Verb)" in texts dealing with a very wide variety of problems. In fact, the observed variety includes curing disease, routine sacrifices, rain-seeking, hunting, administrative matters, military activities, agriculture. Notice the predicament in which this puts anyone who holds that this <u>yu</u> is a word with a fixed meaning or reference. For he must choose whether to deny any significance to the <u>syntactic similarity</u> of the material assembled here, and to posit one meaning after another in different contexts, or he must ignore the contextual variety, picking a meaning that will fit in some cases but will often be bizarre. One does not receive "right" aid(155), nor does one supplicate to one's "Yu"(proper name) grandmother(10), nor yet recover from "abundant" illness(204) nor visit "abundant" temples (24). But a pronoun is at home anywhere.

(d) Denying that 玐 in these contexts means "right"(and passing by the fact that 屮 does not mean "right" in any case), we would expect that the reverse form 玐, which can mean "left," will occur in the material very infrequently, usually only when other graphs too are being reversed. That is just what we do find. (See comment on 粹 950 under(e) below, list 55.)

(e) We should expect to find sentences similar in form to sentences represented in the list, with a term(name of crop, place name, name of border peoples, etc.) appearing where 屮 or 玐 might have been used, that plausibly could be what 屮 or 玐 would refer to if it had been used. Particularly significant are groups of inscriptions on the same bone or shell. The following(see S 131.4, 卜 77) is cited by Ch'en Meng-chia(1956, p.96):

(i) 貞我受吾方玐

"Divining: 'We will be granted aid against the Kung-fang.'"

(ii) 貞弗其受屮玐

"Divining: 'We will not be granted aid against them.'"

For another example involving crops, see the plastron at 丙 8-9(S 196.3):

(i) 丙辰卜彀貞我受粟年

"Crack on ping-ch'en(day 53), Ch'üeh divining: 'We will receive the millet harvest.'"

There is a matching negative, and on the reverse side, opposite the positive:

(ii) 王固曰吉受屮年

"The king, reading, the cracks, said 'Good fortune: (we) will receive this harvest.'"

Not on the same place, but in convincing detail, are the following concerning hunting: (i) list 55 粹 950, (ii) list 57 續 3.44.3, in full:

(i) …[王?]涉滳至戠躬⼻豕㞢

"…[the king(?)] will cross the Shang River and go as far as Ch'ing(?), and will shoot pigs there. There will be a catch."

(ii) 王涉滳躬⼻鹿㞢

"The king will cross the Shang River and will shoot lu-deer there. There will be a catch."

(In 粹 950, yu is reversed; but so also are the two graphs before and after.) These show that the place Ch'ing(?) is across the Shang, where one goes to shoot deer. This fact, in turn, is confirmed by the following(S 378.4 拾 6.3):

(iii) 王其躬戠鹿亾戈㞢

"If the king shoots lu-deer at Ch'ing(?), he will suffer no harm. There will be a catch."

Here we find, as expected, the place-name where yu would occur. Other examples of this syntax: compare S 449.1 合 237…[妣?]庚克瘳王疒, "Pi Keng will successfully cure the king's illness," and S 449.2 南南 2.121 壬子卜貞亞興㞢 疒, "Crack on day jen-tzu, divining: 'The ya-officer(N.) will successfully recover from his illness'"(List 240). And compare S 209.4 前 3.29.2 希雨匃, "(We should) make hsi-appeal about rain harm"(i.e., appeal for less rain) with List 192-196 希㞢(⼻) 匃 "make hsi-appeal about harm from it," "make hsi-appeal about this(possible) harm."

(f) We should find cases where(even without such comparisons) the context, or even the sentence itself, identifies an antecedent for 㞢 or ⼻. 丙 182, dealt with in 3, 3.1, is the best example, but there are many; e.g., list 6, 12-13, 15, 27-28, 32, 87, 132-33, 137, 204, 242.

(g) We would find examples of both 㞢 and ⼻ in the same kind of material, occurring with the same words. Examples: before 宗(24-33); before 示(34-45); before names of game animals(49-64); before 行(93-95); in the structure "叀/吏 㞢/⼻ Noun Verb"(20, 137-143); before ⼻(155-177); before 年(96-123); before 尹(81-83); before 匃(192-196); after 𠔼(i.e., 𦥑, 興) and before 疒 of 疾(204-

240, 243-247). This increases the likelihood that 㞢/㞢 in this syntax is neither an adjective nor a name, but a special use of the ordinary word yu.

(h) Any new discovery, if it really is a discovery, is likely to resolve old problems. This is especially to be expected here, where what is discovered is a basic structural usage. I will give one striking example of how this discovery clears up a hopeless muddle. Consider list 204(丙 334) in full:

貞婦好㞢 且 㞢 疒

(The list directs attention to over forty similar examples.) Here are some of the ways in which scholars have previously attempted to translate this kind of inscription:

(i) N.(above, Lady Hao) will(have misfortune(凡, i.e., 禍) through wind(且, i.e., 風) catch a bad cold; she will be sick.

(ii) If N. bones(a victim)(凡) and p'an-sacrifices(it)(且, i.e., 盤), there will be sickness.

(iii) N.'s bones(凡, i.e., 骨) ache(且, i.e., 同, loan for 痛); there will be sickness.(Takashima, pp. 142-44, reviews scholarship on the problem in detail, without seeing any solution that he likes. Supporters of some of these interpretations would prefer to understand the inscriptions as questions.)

In each case, the translator takes for granted that 㞢 is verbal 有 "there will be," with 疒 "sickness" or "illness" as its object. This insures that he will look in wrong directions for the solutions to the two difficult problems, 㞢 and 且. But if we try the idea that 㞢 means "his" or "her" here, we see that the immediately preceding word 且 will then have to be the main verb in what must be a single simple sentence. Since other contexts(e.g., 丙 335) show that 㞢 且 or 㞢 且 㞢 疒 is something "fortunate"(吉), a fair guess for 且 is "recover(from)"(as Serruys noticed in a slightly different context: T'oung Pao 60[1974], p. 27); and graphic analysis confirms that it must here be 興. The adverbial 㞢 is more difficult. For some time I thought it must have something to do with "bone," or perhaps with "body"(體), and I let my imagination play on these possibilities. But no: the syntactic similarity of list 204(to 239, as above) with list 240 亞克興㞢疒 shows that

岂 (perhaps read 骩, * k'ôig, k'u here) must be a cognate used for (or else a phonetic loan for) 克 (克, * k'ək; k'o), "overcome," "succeed." There are other parallels for the two graphs (compare, e. g., S 307.2 佚 106 with S 132.2 甲 427); and it seems possible, even, that the second is an abbreviated modification of the first (岂, 岂, * 岂, 岂, then 克, later 克, becoming 克). (Since 克 is, like 岂, 岂, etc., a Period I graph, the abbreviating would have taken place very early, and it is not surprising that the Han lexicographers and philologists never guessed it.)

I conclude that the problem sentence means, simply, "Lady Hao will successfully recover from her illness." What was unintelligible becomes perfectly clear. This solution seems to work wherever there is context in which to test it.

So expectations the hypothesis warrants are borne out. Of course, a hypothesis is not proved with certainty in this way (no hypothesis is ever proved with certainty); but it is progressively confirmed by its successful predictions. Any single piece of evidence of the sorts described here could fairly be dismissed as "not proving anything." But anyone who would say this after seeing the whole spread of evidence needs to be asked, "What would satisfy you?"

This question is not rhetorical. A reasonable response would be to produce counterexamples and ask me to explain them.

I leave the search for counterexamples to my friends.

(I want to thank one friend in particular: Professor David N. Keightley, for counsel, instruction, and the use of his manuscript Sources of Shang History (1977, forthcoming); I have had valuable comments, also, from members of his seminar on oracle inscriptions at the University of California, Berkeley. Throughout this research I have continually gotten very valuable insights and information from the work of Professor Paul L-M Serruys and Professor Kenichi Takashima (see below). Professor Edwin G. Pulleyblank has given me valuable criticisms. Finally, my work would have been impossible without constant-use of Shima Kunio's concordance, Inkyo Bokuji Sōrui.)

Bibliography and Abbreviations

Chang Ping-ch'üan 張秉權. Chung-kuo K'ao-ku Pao-kao Chi 中國考古報告集 (Archaeologica Sinica) II, Hsiao T'un 小屯, Vol. 2, Yin-hsü Wen-tzu 殷虛文字, Ping-pien 丙編 (Fascicule Three). 6 Volumes. Taipei: Institute of History and Philosophy, Academia Sinica, 1957-1972 (abbreviated 丙; see S 589).

Ch'en Meng-chia 陳夢家. Yin Hsü Pu-tz'u Tsung-shu 殷虛卜辭綜述. Peking, 1956. Taipei reprint, 1971, published under name Ch'en Ting-ho 陳丁合. Pu-tz'u Tsung-shu.

Graham, Angus C. "The Grammar of the Mohist Dialectical Chapters." A Symposium on Chinese Grammar. Scandinavian Institute of Asian Studies Monograph Series No. 6 (Lund, Sweden, 1971), pp. 55-141.

GSR: Bernard Karlgren. "Grammata Serica Recensa." Bulletin of the Museum of Far Eastern Antiquities 29:1-332.

Karlgren: Bernard Karlgren. The Book of Documents, 1950; reprinted from BMFEA 22.

Legge: James Legge. The Chinese Classics. Vol. III The Shoo King, Vol. IV The She King (reprinted in China, 1939).

Li: Li Hsiao-ting 李孝定. Chia-ku Wen-tzu Chi-shih 甲骨文字集釋. 14 vols. Nankang, Taiwan, 1965.

Malmquist, N. G. D. "Some Observations on a Grammar of Late Archaic Chinese." T'oung Pao 48 (1960): 252-286.

Serruys 1974: Paul L-M Serruys. "Studies in the Language of the Shang Oracle Inscriptions." T'oung Pao 60 (1974): 12-120.

S: Shima Kunio 島邦男. Inkyo Bokuji Sōrui 殷墟卜辭綜類. 2d ed. Tokyo, Kyuko Shoin 汲古書院, 1971.

Takashima: Takashima, K. Negatives in the King Wu Ting Bone Inscriptions. Ann Arbor: University Microfilms, 1973.

Wang Yin-chih 王引之. Ching Chuan Shih Tz'u 經傳釋詞. 1799.

Wu Ch'i-ch'ang 吳其昌. Yin-hsü Shu-ch'I Chieh-ku 殷虛書契解詁. Taipei, 1960 and 1971 (originally a series of articles in Wen-che Chi-k'an 文哲季刊 3-6

[1934-37]).

Yen I-p'ing 嚴一萍. "Shuo 'Yu'" 説「㞢」, 7 double pages, first article in Chung-kuo Wen-tzu 中國文字 47(1973).

丙, etc.: All such abbreviations of titles of published collections of rubbings and other reproductions follow the list in S 589.

References to the Ch'un Ch'iu and commentaries use Harvard-Yenching concordance text page numbers.

EAC: Early Archaic Chinese

LAC: Late Archaic Chinese

The following lists assemble evidence for the hypothesis that 㞢(㞢) functions as a pronominal or demonstrative adjective, regularly in Shang Chinese (List Ⅰ) and occasionally in early Chou Chinese (List Ⅱ). Inscriptions are not quoted in full. List Ⅰ is intended to supplement, and to be used with, the sections on these words in Shima Kunio, Inkyo Bokuji Sōrui; I do not pretend, any more than would Shima, to be able to translate everything here presented, nor do I pretend to be sure that all of this material belongs in the list. It is presented here as at least including the evidence for my argument, and as a convenience for research for others who may wish to continue work on this problem.

Some of the graph identifications used here (and in the foregoing paper) are controversial. I have arbitrarily distinguished 㱿 and 㱿 as 疒 and 疾, respectively. 㱿 is often thought to be 希 ti, "porcupine," hence "curse." I read it 希 hsi, (1) "rare;" "uncommon," a mishap, something bad; (2) "appeal for;" "appeal about." 㱿, 㱿, 㱿, sometimes thought to be 龍 (metaphor for "recovery from illness") or 寵, must actually be 翏, 瘳 liao, ch'ou (bronze form 㱿, i.e., 㱿 with additions), "fly up," hence "recover." 凡 in these examples cannot be 般, 風, 同 or 痌 (see Li 3931, 3977 and Takashima 142-44) as sometimes supposed (by scholars trying to make two sentences out of 㱿凡㞢㱿) but must be 凡, 凡 (pictograph of a sail being raised), hence 凡, 興 hsing, "arise," "recover." I have transcribed 㱿(㱿) as 冎; normally 骨 "bone," it is here undoubtedly an early form of 㱿, i.e., 克 "overcome," hence "succeed in," "successfully." And the whole phrase

吕日㞢帅 must read 克興有疒 (as argued above, section 6.2(h)). 彳 (List 197-98), long supposed to be 循, really is what it looks like, i.e., 德, as a later paper will prove. 㠯 is debatable; I follow Sun I-jang's identification as 侣, interpreted as 以 (reserving the variant 㠯 for 㠯); this at least gives the meaning (see Li 3737).

Note: Malmquist (T'oung Pao 48[1960]: 276) calls attention to the fact that in the sentence "A 有 B," "B" must have indefinite reference; so that, e.g., one cannot say … 只有你, "there is only you…," but must say … 只有一個你. He gives examples also for LAC, and one can readily find them for EAC, e.g., Shu 36 (君奭) 時則有若伊尹, etc. (若 "like" being required to form a general term when prefixed to the proper name 伊尹). In the noun-phrase 有 B formed from the sentence A 有 B (by C2), it must then also be required that B by itself can have indefinite reference—though, of course, the whole term 有 B will have definite reference. This implies that B in such expressions cannot be the proper name of an individual. Hence my observation that the occurrence of 彳望乘 shows that (against the received opinions) 望乘 is a general term, and not the name of one of Wu Ting's generals (though conceivably it could be used in context to refer to one person). One must also wonder what to make of the proper (dynasty) name "Yin" in the noun-phrase 有殷: apparently by itself it normally is a general term, capable of indefinite reference, its meaning not yet clear to us. (Compare: 有河 (sentence) "there is a river;" 有河 (term) "the river," "the River.") The same thing must be said of the dynasty name 周. Notice, however, that the expression 有商 does not occur in genuine Shu texts (though there were several "Shang" cities: 天邑商, 大邑商, 中商, 商丘; see Ch'en, map, p. 683). So perhaps "Shang" was a true name, and not a general term used as a name. It may be objected that I have disregarded this conception of the way attributive 有 works in admitting #7 (京714) 㞢于㞢祖丁; for is not 祖丁 a proper posthumous name of an individual? Yes, normally, but only contextually; for consider 粹303 其彳四祖丁 "we should perhaps make offering to fourth ancestor Ting" (i.e., our fourth ting ancestor; cf. Kuo Mo-jo in loco citing Wang Kuo-wei's explanation). 㞢祖丁 in #7 must be "his grandfather Ting" or "his ting ancestor." (Similarly #8 㞢祖戊.)

LIST I		
NUMBER	INSCRIPTIONS WITH 㞢 (with 彳, inset)	PAGE IN SHIMA KUNIO (S), COLLECTION (SEE S 589), AND COMMENTS ("4/…" indicates "four similar examples at S…")
L 1-5	呼子窒㞢于㞢祖窒	S 538.2, 丙 182.4/S 538.2. See section 3 for translation, and compare S 538.3, 粹 878, 其㞢于我祖 "We should make an offering to our grandfather," with personal pronoun instead of 㞢; see section 6.2(a).
L 6	隹㞢祖彳𢦏	S 538.2, 前 6.20.3 "It is his grandfather who is (stepping on, i.e.) afflicting N." (Compare L 15, "grandmother" for "grandfather.")
L 7	呼子其㞢于㞢祖丁	S 39.2, 京 714. See "Note" for 㞢 before apparent names: "We should have Prince Tzu-N make an offering to his grandfather Ting."
L 8	翌乙巳子漁㞢用賓㞢祖戊	S 240.3, 續 3.47.7. "Tomorrow, i-ssu (day 42), having successfully recovered, Prince Tzu-yü will make a thank offering to his grandfather Wu."
L 9	…酚㞢祖	S 538.2, 存 2.220.
L 10-11	卯于㞢妣	S 544.4, 前 6.20.3.1/S 544.3. This completes the group including L 6 and L 15: "(N) should yü-supplicate to his grandmother."
L 12-13	卯子安于㞢妣	S 544.3, 誠 271.1/S 544.3. "We should yü-supplicate for Tzu-an to his (or her) grandmother."
L 14	呼子安福于㞢妣	S 544.3, 合 170. "We should have Tzu-an make a fu-offering to his (her) grandmother."
L 15	隹㞢妣彳𢦏	S 544.3, 前 6.20.3. "It is his grandmother who is (stepping on, i.e.) afflicting N." Compare L 6, same inscription group; 㞢 refers forward here.
L 16	…于㞢妣	S 544.4, 乙 3902.
L 17-18	卯㞢母于父乙	S 423.4, 丙 182(1-2). See section 3 for translation and analysis.
L 19	呼从來取㞢兄以	S 554.4, 合 323. "We should have him come with us and bring his elder brother with him." See comments on L 181-191.
L 20	宙㞢弟令祠…父	S 313.1, 存 1.1080. "It should be his younger brother we order to tz'u-sacrifice to…[their?] father;" syntax as in L 137-43; see section 6.2(g).
L 21	…食于㞢…	S 274.4, 乙 3697. Compare L 12-13.

續表一

LIST I		
L 22	🦴(?)以 ⛰ 兄(?)	S 9.4, 外 389.
L 23	⛰于⛰…	S 148.2, 掇 1.494. Compare L 1-5, L 7.
L 24-25	即ㄗ宗	S 270.4, 甲 1318. 1/S 270.4.
L 26	其🦴嶽ㄗ宗雨	S 270.4, 人 1943. "We should X-sacrifice to (the god of) Yüeh (Mountain) (at) his temple; (there will be) rain." (Shima questions 宗.) 🦴: S 206.1.
L 27	弜🦴即ㄗ宗大雨	S 270.4, 人 1943. "We should not proceed to his temple to X-sacrifice; (there will be) a big rain."
L 28	王其酒夒于ㄗ宗ㄓ大雨	S 270.4, 甲 1259. "The King should make a wine-offering to K'uei at his temple; (if he does,) there will be a big rain." (Compare L 87.)
L 29-30	即于ㄗ宗	S 270.4, 粹 16. 1/S 270.4. Context shows ㄗ宗 is "K'uei's temple."
L 31	…掃于ㄗ宗其ㄓ雨	S 270.4, 後下 8.17. "… perform a sweeping rite at his temple, there may be rain."
L 32	…其酒日于祖丁秦ㄗ宗	S 270.4, 寧 1.192. "… should, on wine-offering day, to Tsu Ting make a ch'in-sacrifice (in) his temple." (秦: see 甲, 考, 571.)
L 33	其求家🦴子母(?)于⛰宗若	S 270.4, 零 89. Possible translation: "… we should appeal for the (royal) family's (care, i.e.) continuance (from) the mothers of the princes, at their temples; they will approve." (Taking 🦴 or 🦴 as 膚, i.e. 慮; the rite 求家 🦴 must have some connection with the common formula ⛰母 N 🦴豕 (S 300 passim), usually interpreted "sacrifice to ancestral mother N, offering the skin/flesh 膚 of a pig," as in 甲 2426.)
L 34-36	隹⛰示	S 152.4, 乙 3728. 2/S 152.4.
L 37-38	⛰于⛰示	S 152.4, 合 245. One similar, 丙 184(9).
L 39	…⛰示	S 152.4, 明 1772.
L 40-41	勿共⛰示鄉	S 450.1, 存 2.195. 1/S 450.1 (陳 31). "He should not present a food offering at his altar stands …" See comment, L 74-77.
L 42-43	朕其以⛰示敦	S 215.2, 續 5.1.4. (With a negative matching inscription.)
L 44	…ㄗ示	S 153.3, 前 8.4.2. Compare 乙 8829, …父ㄗ示 (without ㄗ).

續表二

LIST I		
L 45	…取㲋曰㞢示…廼㞢方	S 153.2, 前 6.61.7. Possible translation: "… seek support, taking with us their altar stands… and then attack the Fang." (Note also 鐵 35.2 …㞢示; but this is doubtful.) See comment, L 74-77.
L 46	火于㞢社	S 172.3, 丙 86. No reference suggested in context: "We should make fire sacrifices at the soil altars." (The inscription opposite, 丙 87, reads "Today it will rain." The problem presumably affected a wide area.)
L 47	火于㞢水由犬	S 180.2, 乙 1577. "In fire-sacrificing to the river we should use a dog." ("River" is shui 水, not ho 河, here.)
L 48	其祉钾于㞢河鄉	S 90.1, 甲 2689. "We should proceed to yü-supplicate to The River, making an offering of food." "The River," i.e., the god of the Ho. (Ch'ü Wanli in 甲, 考 2689 calls attention to the phrase 有河 in I Chou Shu, 度邑 chapter; see List II (s).)
L 49	翌癸卯王亦東㞢出㞢㲋	S 419.1, 後下 13.14. "Tomorrow, kuei-mao (day 40), the King will also set up a corral(?㞢) on the east, and we will make the rhinoceroses there come out (into it)." Compare 摭續 121, 王其焚㞢廼㞢王子東立豕出㞢: "The King should burn off 㞢, and in doing so set up a corral. If the King stations himself on the east, as the pigs come out he will make a catch." (The meaning of 㞢, 㲋, here "rhinoceros," is uncertain.)
L 50	毕㞢㲋	S 405.3, 前 6.24.7.
L 51	毕㞢㲋	S 406.1, 寧 1.387. Compare S 406.1, 佚 265 毕㲋 (without 㞢).
L 52	叀壬…躬㞢㲋	S 223.2, 寧 1.387. Note 摭 1.406 王其躬㲋匕戈 (without 㞢), and 京 4487 其躬在喪㲋牢 (location in place of 㞢).
L 53	隻㞢虎	S 225.2, 乙 2115. Compare S 225.2, 後下 5.12…隻虎 (without 㞢).
L 54	盡㞢虎	S 225.2, 摭 1.405. Compare S 225.2, 合 366…葦虎 (without 㞢).
L 55-56	躬㞢豕	S 218.2, 粹 950.1/S 218.2. See 6.2(e) for full text and analysis.
L 57	躬㞢鹿	S 228.2, 續 3.44.3. See 6.2(e) for full text and analysis.
L 58-60	躬㞢麋	S 227.2, 甲 1284.2/S 227.2.

續表三

LIST I		
L 61	𤴔丿鹿	S 406.1, 拾 6.8. Compare L 140 (with 麋 instead of 鹿).
L 62	逐丿麋	S 405.1, 京 4503. S 405.1-2, many examples of 逐麋 (without 丿).
L 63	其从(豕 i.e.)逐日𤴔丿狐茲用	S 220.3, 佚 81. Probable translation: "'We should (chase, i.e.) hunt (following along…, i.e.) in that area.' (The crack) says, 'We will catch foxes there.' (Then use (it), i.e.) This crack is valid." Compare L 141.
L 64	…𤴔丿…允𤴔	S 406.1, 甲 1189. "'… will catch … there.' We actually did catch some."
L 65	…◈丿𤴔于入乙	S 406.2, 乙 8670. ◈, perhaps 入, "send in," "contribute," when said of animals for sacrifice. (Compare 入𤴔, analyzed in section 4.1.) "… contribute his catch to Ju I."
L 66-67	…呼丿見屮丿	S 441.3, 粹 1132.1/S 441.3. Possibly (taking 丿, i.e., 師 in two senses) "… have commander (N) (go forth and) display his forces."
L 68-69	行以屮師眾屮邑	S 441.4, 乙 7385. "Hsing should bring his units and his town (forces)." Note S 43.4, 卜 173 曰以乃邑 "(The King) says, 'bring your town (forces).'" (With the pronoun 乃 where 屮 could occur; see 6.2(a).)
L 70-71	以屮師自屮邑	S 441.4, 乙 4539. (This and the next are variants of the above.)
L 72-73	以屮師眔邑	S 441.4, 丙 500-501. Repeated twice (inscription defective). Note omission of 屮 before 邑, deletable without change of meaning.
L 74-77	今日祈屮令圂我于屮師乃共屮[示鄉]	S 450.1, 陳 31.3/S 441.4. Possible translation: "Today we should command Lu to (圂 us, i.e. (?)) protect us from injury (by appropriate sacrifices) in his army; so, he should present [food offerings] at his [ancestral altar stands]." It must have been the practice to take ancestral altars on campaign for protection: compare L 45, and also campaign inscriptions of Period V such as 甲 3659 (S 151.1-2) with the formula 上下于◈示受余丿 "The higher and lower (ancestral spirits) in their (?) altarstands will grant us aid." ("their" for ◈; 𢆉 might be expected, if a Shang form of 厥 existed; if this is right, again a possessive pronoun is used where 丿 could occur.) Take 祈, 祈 as 引. See also L 40 and L 134.

續表四

LIST I		
L 78	勿呼取㞢邑	S 43.1, 林 2.8.1. Compare S 112.4, 寧 3.86 呼取邑(㞢 is deletable).
L 79	啓㞢邑	S 43.1, 乙 4539. "He should deploy his town(forces)." See L 70-71.
L 80	羽以王族从㞢	S 249.3, 菁 11.7. (Shima Kunio, Inkyo Bokuji Kenkyū, Tokyo, 1958, p.471, has 㞢族 instead of 王族 in this inscription.)
L 81-82	令僉以㞢族尹吏㞢友	L 328.4, 前 7.1.4. Possibly "We should order Yung to take the tsu(banner) yin-officers and stand in the center of the allies." Perhaps "the" for 㞢 before tsu and "allies" should be "his" or "our." The meaning for 吏 is a guess; it must be the same as 仌, S 86.3, where 㞢 is replaced by a name.
L 83	宙古㞢保自㞢尹	S 92.4, 後下 13.12. Perhaps "What we do should be to make sure of having support from our yin-officers." In any case, 㞢 before 尹 is pronominal.
L 84	…以㞢元臣…	S 109.4, 前 4.32.5. "… bring the ranking officials.…"
L 85	其卯㞢事王受㞢	L 55.2, 粹 544. 㞢 here shows that simple 卯事 (㞢㞢) in 17 other cases at S 55.2 must be "verb object"; but the phrase should be related in sense to the term or title 御事 in the Shang Shu(e.g., Karlgren, "managers of affairs," at p.43). Perhaps, "They should take care of(the) affairs; the King will receive aid." See section 6.2(b).
L 86	至于㞢日酒㞢大雨	(Not in Shima.) 人 1948. Compare L 32 and L 132-33: "When his(scheduled sacrifice-) day comes, let there be a wine offering; it will rain heavily."
L 87	王其㞢于滴在㞢厂燓㞢雨	S 90.1, 寧 1.25. "The King should sacrifice to the Shang River at its banks with a fire-offering;(if he does,) there will be rain." Compare 128.
L 88	勿㞢帝于㞢囧	S 158.2, 乙 4915.
L 89	往于㞢敵	S 70.3, 庫 1987 反.
L 90-91	卯㞢敵	S 70.3, 餘 10.1. Two inscriptions, different ancestors(female).
L 92	戍及校于㞢	S 90.1, 甲 807(5). Copied incorrectly in Shima. This is one of a group, context indicating the following: "The shu(? dagger-axe-man officer)(Chia 甲) will overtake Chiao(?校, chief of the 戠-Fang) at his 㞢." 㞢 may mean "stronghold"—compare 㞢(邑) "stockade." But Ch'ü Wan-li says that 㞢 here is a "particle," as in 有殷, and that 㞢 is a place name(as it sometimes is; see S 45.2, 前 2.27.7).

續表五

LIST I		
L 93	征复业…	S 87.2, 金 715.
L 94	勿呼征复业行从⊕	S 87.2, 金 569. "We should not have them go on and resume their march westward."(⊕, 迺 for 西.)
L 95	[勿才]涉[迄羌弗]其得复才行	S 253.1, 合 380. "[They should not also] cross (the river) [and go as far as the Ch'iang (territory); they will not] be able to (reach it); they should resume their march."
L 96-118	受业年	S 196.3, 丙 8 反.22/S 196.3-4. Either "receive a harvest there" or "receive a harvest of it." See sections 5.2(2-4) and 5.4.
L 119-23	受才年	S 196.4, 甲 1369.4/S 196.4.
L 124-5	令卨…屎业田	S 6.1, 存 1.177.1/S 6.1. Compare 存 2.166 屎西單田 with place designation in place of 业. See 6.2(e) and 5.2(2).
L 126	令後…业田…年	(Not in Shima.) 甲 1167(4).
L 127-8	屎业律	S 464.4, 庫 116.1/S 464.4
L 129	王弜省㵂才工其雨	S 443.3, 庫 1090. "The King should not inspect his 工 at 㵂; it might rain." See section 5.2(2). 工 is here possibly 貢田, "tribute-fields," the yield going directly to the king; see L 131.
L 130	令追呼业尹工	S 418.1, 續 5.4.6. Possibly, "We should order (pursuit-collection, i.e.) collection of overdue yields from our tribute-fields under yin-officers." Compare 前 4.46.1 余𩛥朕南工 "I shall collect the yield from my south tribute-fields," with pronoun in place of 业. (For 𩛥, 呼 i.e. 奇, compare Li 393 quoting 今甲盤:政䲨成周四方積 with S 300.3 後下 8.1 奇畯四方; the meaning "collect the yield" is tentative.)
L 131	…龏屎业父工	S 241.3, 前 4.28.7. "…[at] Kung, and (ritually?) fertilize the yin-officers' tribute-fields there." (Or, "Kung should… his… fields." See L 124-5, for evidence that 工 is some kind of 田, and read 又 for 乂.)
L 132-133	日子商至于业丁作火戋	S 287.3, 丙 302. Positive-negative pair, analyzed in section 5.3(5a). "We should say, 'Tzu-shang on next ting-day should make a fire-attack; (if he does so,) he will harm them.'" (Paired with "We should not say, …" etc.)

續表六

LIST I		
L 134	尖得㞢牛	S 31.2, 續 1.14.2. "Lu will get the cattle." On Lu, see L 74, also S 31, passim, and Shima, Kenkyū 468-70. His importance (only the king stood above him) tempts the suggestion that "Lu" is not a surname but a title, the graph 尖(尖) being a combination of 大(太) and 子(子), "crown prince."
L 135	㞢眔止十二月	S 25.3, 後下 33.8. Possibly, "The multitude should stop." 止, 止 "stop work"? —following Yen I-p'ing, p.6b. But verbal uses of 止 are rare, and the interpretation is doubtful. 止 could be "this," with the following date, and 㞢眔 "We should (have, i.e.) raise a work force." See List II, g-j.
L 136	…取㞢貝	S 252.1, 鐵 104.4.
L 137	其㞢兄辛叀㣇車用㣇正	S 554.4, 南明 641. "In the 㞢-ritual for Hsiung Hsin it should be his chariot that we use; all will go properly."
L 138	叀㣇妹品	S 90.1, 人 1884.
L 139	叀㣇朢乘从	S 110.4, 南南 1.152. "It should be the (? our) wang-ch'eng we accompany." This inscription shows that "wang-ch'eng" is not a person's name. See "Note."
L 140	叀㣇麋毕	S 406.1, 甲 2079. Compare L 61. "It should be the mi-deer there that we (try to) catch."
L 141	叀㣇狐射毕	S 405.1, 掇 1.402. Compare L 63. "It should be the foxes there that we shoot. We will make a catch."
L 142	叀㣇囟楚亾戈毕	S 90.1, 人 2052. "It should be our newly cultivated fields that we burn off. We will suffer no harm, and will make a catch." (Or, "It should be the area to the west of us that we burn off;"—taking 囟 as 西 rather than 甾.)
L 143	叀㣇鬯用福	S 408.1, 續 6.12.5. See section 5.3(5) for full analysis of this inscription (and of others through L 154). Notice the companion inscription 鬯其用于福 "As for the fragrant wine, we should use it in the fu offering."
L 144	…父己㞢㣇鬯	S 408.1, 寧 1.204. Compare S 408.2 明 757 祖辛㞢一鬯 and see 5.3(5).
L 145	㞢祖乙㞢鬯	S 408.1, 遺 350. Compare S 523.4 合 205 㞢祖乙五宰 "We should make an offering to Tsu I of five sacrificial sheep," indicating here "We should make an offering to Tsu I of some fragrant wine."

續表七

LIST Ⅰ		
L 146	祖丁𦣞[甲]彡[邑]	S 395.3, 寧 1.190. Compare S 187.2 摭續 60 祖丁[甲]彡[邑]三卣([𦣞] and [甲] are sacrifice-verbs, from names of things or locations within a temple, where these sacrifices are performed. See S 187.1-2 and S 395.3-4. [𦣞][甲] is to do [甲] at the [𦣞].)
L 147	祖丁𦣞彡[邑]	S 395.3, 金 29.
L 148-154	弜彡[邑]	S 408.1, 寧 1.190. Negative paired with L 146; and so "We should not([𦣞][甲]) some fragrant wine." 6/S 408.1.
L 155-169	受㞢又	S 88.3, 續 3.5.3. 4/S 320.1-2, 10/S 88.3-4 (sample only). See full discussion, sections 5.2(4), 5.3(6), 5.4, and 6.2(e).
L 170-7	受又,受又	S 88.4, 甲 3913. 7/S 88.4 (sample only).
L 178-180	受㞢𨐨	S 463.2, 天 60. 2/S 463.2. See section 5.3(6).
L 181-191	竝弗其以㞢取	S 112.2, 天 94. 10/S 112.2-3. Probably "N 以㞢取" derives from the idiom "N 取 X 以"(S 112-3 passim), "N should seek/take X and will bring(it/him)," where 取 is "controllable"(the attempt, negated by 勿)and 以 "uncontrollable" (the result, negated by 弗其). (For this essential distinction, see Takashima, especially pp. 186-87.) The sentence then must mean "Ping will not bring his/the sought/taken(thing/person)" i.e., "Ping will not bring it back" (or, "take him along," or "get what he sought," etc.). See L 19 and 5.3(6). Note that 㞢 is deletable here: S 113.2 外 272 以取.
L 192-4	𢀈㞢夢勿希㞢匄亾匄十月	S 209.4, 續 3.41.4. 2/S 209.3. See analysis, 6.2(e). (Charge:) "In regard to the dream that Pi had, we should not make a hsi-appeal concerning harm from it." (Verification:) "There was no harm; 10th month."
L 195-6	希彡匄	S 209.3-4, 粹 401. One of a pair, about appeals to different ancestors.
L 197-8	辟㞢外	S 320.4, 丙 360. A positive-negative pair. Possibly "We will(闢 open up, i.e.) make effective(㞢德 what we te for, i.e.) the te, 'virtue' that we are seeking through sacrifices, in this matter." But this needs more study. If 𠂆 is a variant of 𠂆(辟), then S 359.3 天 579 shows 㞢 deletable(𠂆祉) and replaceable(𠂆舞祉).
L 199-201	孫弗其以㞢正	S 71.3, 乙 8227. 2/S 71.3. Possibly "Sun will not bring his charges."

續表八

LIST I		
L 202	聞㞢㞢	S114.3, 續 5.10.7. 㞢 (Li 677 舌) must be a verb of appeal to spirits. (See S 124.1-2.) 聞 (negated by 弗, S114.2-3) is the spirit's response: "They will heed what we ask." 㞢 is deletable: 續 5.30.10① … 聞㞢.
L 203	ㄓ曰ㄓ告啓	S 285.1, 南上 14. See analysis, section 5.3(6).
L 204-239	丏日㞢疒	S 306.2, 丙 334.35/S 306.2-3. See analysis, 5.3(6) and 6.2(h).
L 240	亞克興㞢疒	S 411.3, 南南 2.121. Translated in 6.2(e); see also 6.2(h).
L 241	㞢疒瘳	S 449.1, 乙 6412. "His illness will get better." (If valid, 20/S 447.)
L 242	王弗疒㞢骨	S 302.3, 甲 3510. Possibly "The king will not have an attack of his arthritis." (骨 unclear, may be 骨 "bones.") See the study of 骨 by Stanley L. Mickel, in "A Semantic Analysis of the Disaster Graphs of Period One Shang Dynasty Oracle Bones" (Ph. D. thesis at Indiana University, 1976) pp. 126-139.
L 243	子㞢丏㞢疒	S 306.3, 京 1681. Apparently without 日; but see listing at S 448.3.
L 244-6	…弗其日㞢疒	S 410.4, 合 219.2/S 410.4: without 丏(骨).
L 247	卩丏日ㄓ疾	S 306.3, 乙 125. Compare S 40.2 後下 3.2 … 日疾 (without ㄓ).
L 248-251	帚好不征㞢疒	S 449.1, 合 275. 4 inscriptions: "… continue her illness." (But perhaps "… keep on having illness.")
L 252-4	子弗疒㞢疒	S 448.4, 庫 1542. Possibly "The child will not be seriously sick."

LIST II	EXAMPLES FROM EARLY CHOU LITERATURE (6.1: translation in 6.1; C: 有 correctly construed in Legge, Classics; K: 有 correctly construed in Karlgren)	
a	Shu 4.3 皋陶謨:亦行有九德 6.1	
b	Shu 4.4 …濬明有家/亮采有邦 C71-2	
c	Shu 4.5 無教逸欲有邦 "Let(the ruler) not teach his state(s) ease and indulgence."	

---

① 編者按:"5.30.10",原文誤作"5.30.9",今據實際出處徑改。

續表

LIST II	EXAMPLES FROM EARLY CHOU LITERATURE(6.1: translation in 6.1; C: 有 correctly construed in Legge, Classics; K: 有 correctly construed in Karlgren)
d	Shu 4.6 天叙有典/天秩有禮 K 9 6.1
e	Shu 5.4 益稷:予欲左右有民(C 79, K 11)
f	Shu 16.1 盤庚:盤庚遷于殷,民不適有居;C and K both construe as ⋯適而有所居; probably it should be as if ⋯適于有居.
g	Shu 16.18 其有眾咸造 C 233, K 23
h	Shu 16.35 綏爰有眾 C 242, K 24
i	Shu 10.2 湯誓:今爾有眾⋯ C 174, K 20
j	Shu 10.3 有眾率怠弗協 C 175, K 20
k	Shu 32.13 召誥:有王雖小,元子哉 C 427, K 49
l	Shu 33.10 洛誥:伻嚮即有僚 C 440, K 52
m	Shu 38.15 多方:天降時喪,有邦間之 6.1
n	Shu 38.24 ⋯告爾有方⋯ 6.1(C 504, K 65) C 178
o	Shih 116.3 揚之水:我聞有命 K BMFEA 16:208
p	Shih 200.6 巷伯:取彼譖人,投畀豺虎;豺虎不食,投畀有北;有北不受,投畀有昊. C 348. Karlgren, BMFEA 16:241, insists on "Lord of the North," etc., and argues the point in "Glosses" —see above, sections 1.1, 2.1.
q	Shih 236.4 大明:天監在下,有命既集. L 434, K BMFEA 17:66.
r	I Chou Shu 43 商誓:王曰,霱,予天命維既咸汝,克承天休于我有周,斯小國于有命不易. "The King said, 'Oh! I have now fully declared to you Heaven's Mandate; and now that we have gained Heaven's grace on our Chou our state will not be casual about this Mandate.'"
s	I Chou Shu 44 度邑:顧瞻過于有河,宛瞻延于伊雒. "As I look back, my eye passes by the River; my wandering gaze follows the winding of the I and the Lo." See List I, L 48.

原載《古代中國》第 3 期,1977 年。

李學勤

殷墟甲骨兩系説與歷組卜辭

歷組卜辭問題的提出，是在 1977 年①，至今已有十年。贊成或反對新説的論著，陸續發表多篇，對促進討論的深入都有很多貢獻。這一問題之所以得到國内外許多學者的注意，是由於它涉及殷墟甲骨分期研究的一些帶根本性質的觀點。

我們曾一再談到，歷組卜辭屬於武丁至祖庚時期這個意見，并不是 1977 年纔提出的。明義士 1928 年起草的《殷虛卜辭後編序》已有此説，該序稿近來已發表了②。最近讀到聯邦德國法蘭克福大學張聰東先生的《甲骨文所見商代祀典》一書，始知他已提到有歷的卜辭應列於祖庚至祖甲前期，并舉出若干論據，這部書是 1970 年問世的③。現在提出歷組卜辭問題所藴含的新觀點，可概括爲我們以前講過的一句話，就是"同一王世不見得只有一類卜辭，同一類卜辭也不見得屬于一個王世"④。

甲骨分期的兩系説的基礎，便是上述這句話。將殷墟甲骨看成一系，按王世來分期，出現了"復古"等現象。克服這類困難，必須徹底採取類型學的方法，并充分運用考古發掘提供坑位和層位的依據，其結果勢必放棄一系説。

所謂兩系，是説殷墟甲骨的發展可劃爲兩個系統。一個系統是由賓組發展到出組、何組、黄組，另一個系統是由𠂤組發展到歷組、無名組⑤。林澐、彭裕商

---

① 李學勤：《論婦好墓的年代及有關問題》，《文物》1977 年第 11 期。
② 李學勤：《小屯南地甲骨與甲骨分期》附，《文物》1981 年第 5 期。
③ 張聰東：《甲骨文所見商代祀典》（德文），第 22—23 頁，1970 年。
④ 李學勤：《評陳夢家〈殷虛卜辭綜述〉》，《考古學報》1957 年第 3 期。
⑤ 王宇信：《西周甲骨探論》李學勤序，第 4 頁，1984 年。

兩同志對這個看法給予補正①。根據他們的看法，自組可能是兩系的共同起源，黃組可能是兩系的共同歸宿，這無疑是極有啓發的。

實際董作賓先生在《甲骨文斷代研究例》中已意識到兩系的存在，指出小屯村北主要出他所分一、二、五期，村中（包括村南）主要出他所分三、四期，不過他把兩者作爲一系對待了。陳夢家先生的《殷虛卜辭綜述》進一步強調了坑位的區別，對董說作出很多重要修改，只是尚不能擺脫一系的觀點。他把自組、子組、"午"組等列入武丁晚期，便是一系說的表現之一。

近年小屯南地的發掘，再次證實了坑位區別的存在。通觀《小屯南地甲骨》全書，其內涵和解放前這一地帶的出土品，以及《庫方》、《明後》、《萃編》、《寧滬》、《京都》、《懷特》等書所錄的若干收藏一樣，以董氏所分三、四期爲主。具體說來，是有一定數量的自組及"午"組，大量的是歷組和無名組卜辭。換句話說，是兩系中第二系的卜辭。

林澐同志已指出，《南地》書中罕見賓組卜辭。該書釋文部分所說武丁卜辭，絕大多數是自組（或林澐同志所分自賓間組）、"午"組卜辭。真正的賓組卜辭，可舉出 H92 出土的《南地》2663 胛骨，有卜人則。此人和 H47 與 T54（3）出土的兩片合成的《南地》2113 胛骨卜人丩當爲一人。值得注意的是，則在歷組屢次出現，可能與這一系有某種關係②。

出組卜辭在《南地》只見於 H57 所出 2384 胛骨，與歷組卜辭同版（詳見下述）。

何組卜辭有 T44（3）所出《南地》4327、T53（2B）所出《南地》4447，爲數極少，且係小片。

典型的黃組卜辭也難找到。《南地》釋文的帝乙卜辭，林澐同志已詳加分析，認爲是無名組晚期卜辭。M15 所出《南地》3564 有"武乙宗"，字體確已向黃組趨近，但其兆辭"引吉"的位置，却是典型的黃組卜辭所沒有的。

總之，《南地》甲骨中屬於兩系第一系的只占極少數。這和村北也出過幾片歷組無名組卜辭一樣，不影響問題的實質。

上述兩系并未將子組、"午"組等非王卜辭包括在內。另外在小屯以外，還可能存在性質不同的甲骨，如侯家莊 HS57 的卜辭，字近何組而有許多不同；四盤

---

① 林澐：《小屯南地發掘與殷墟甲骨斷代》，《古文字研究》第 9 輯。彭裕商：《也論歷組卜辭的時代》，《四川大學學報》1983 年第 1 期。
② 李學勤：《海外訪古記（一）》，《文博》1986 年第 5 期。

磨還出現了屬周人型式的卜骨，更爲顯例。這樣的例子還有一些。

兩系不同卜辭的并存，有多種多樣的證據。其中最明顯的一種例子，是不同卜辭同見一版。有關歷組，恰好有這樣的例證。1981 年，我在《小屯南地甲骨與甲骨分期》文中①，曾論及《南地》2384 胛骨，以爲它"爲論證歷組的年代提供了最好的證據"。當時只見到《小屯南地甲骨》上册，僅有該胛骨正面拓本，所論不能完全。最近，《小屯南地甲骨》下册問世，公布了此骨反面拓本，補足了這一缺憾。

《南地》2384 出土編號爲 H57：179，係牛右胛骨，上部自骨臼以下約五分之二已斷去，殘存左邊偏下部分，依拓本量，殘長 26.7，寬 9.5 厘米。反面可見鑽鑿兩行，靠邊緣一行有鑽鑿十處，都已灼過成兆；靠内一行存鑽鑿兩處，上一處成兆，下一處只有梭形的鑿，没有成兆。胛骨的折斷即在兩行鑽鑿的最上一兆。從正面看，兆枝都是向内的。

胛骨正面最下一兆，是反面鑽鑿靠邊緣一行最底下一處經灼造成的。正面兆幹上端右側刻有兆序"一"字。兆幹左側起有卜辭三行，第一行首字與兆幹上端相平，第二、三行右轉在兆枝下，所以卜辭肯定屬於這個兆。三行文字是：

庚辰貞，其陟□
高祖、囟，兹□。
王固："兹□。"

是歷組父丁類的字體。比較特别的，是辭中"王"字上有一横。這種寫法接近無名組卜辭，在個别歷組卜辭中也出現過，如《英藏》573。

此兆的上面還有九個兆，對應於反面靠邊緣一行鑽鑿的另九處。在拓本上可見一部分兆序，參考《南地》釋文，有自下向上相連的"一"、"二"、"三"、"四"，字顯較上面提到的最下一兆的"一"小。各兆卜辭均二行，左轉，位於兆幹左側，行高與兆幹長度一致。文字都是"庚辰卜王"。從文例、文體看，均屬出組卜辭。

字體不同的刻辭共存於一版甲骨，并不多見，而且大多是細微的差别，仍可列於同組。不同組的兩種字體并存，非常罕見，五十年代我舉過三例：

（1）《甲編》2904 胛骨，自組卜辭，右下隅刻干支表一行，屬自組的一種特

---

① 《文物》1981 年第 5 期。

殊字體，有學者稱之爲"歷自間組"或"自歷間組"①。

（2）《庫方》972 胛骨，"自歷間組"卜辭，左下隅刻干支表一列，係歷組字體（原骨 1979 年我曾觀察）。

（3）《乙編》8818 腹甲，中、下部爲子組卜辭，均爲庚申卜，而上部及右下近甲橋處有另一字體卜辭，有辛巳卜。後者我們曾稱之爲"婦女卜辭"。

姚孝遂同志 1963 年刊布一例②：

（4）吉林大學藏胛骨，賓組卜辭，下部刻干支表，係子組字體。

《南地》除 2384 外還有一例，該書序言已經提及。林澐同志曾加討論③：

（5）《南地》910 胛骨，歷組卜辭，反面有署辭"壬子，殼……"，是賓組字體。

英國劍橋大學圖書館所藏有一例：

（6）《英藏》2415 胛骨，歷組卜辭，反面有祭祀刻辭"丁卯，申出于丁三宰，在……"，是賓組字體。

肖良瓊同志提示一例：

（7）《合集》21643 胛骨，自組卜辭、子組卜辭並存。

加上《南地》2384，共得八例。除與歷組有關者外，其他根據近年研究，刻辭雖不同組，仍是同時期的。

《南地》2384 卜辭分屬兩組，卜日都是庚辰。編者認爲是武乙時期利用了庚、甲時期卜骨的空隙再刻辭而形成的④。不過，版上的歷組卜辭有鑽鑿卜兆，必須結合起來考慮。

商朝祖庚、祖甲之後是傳爲孿生的廩辛、康丁，然後是武乙。武乙爲祖庚、祖甲孫輩，相距多年，使用過的枯骨能否再卜，是有待實驗的問題。同時卜日均爲庚辰，未免太巧。如說用舊骨占卜例用同日，又沒有他例。

武乙時占卜，應按當時方式開兆，鑽鑿宜爲武乙時流行型式。如歷組是武乙時的，武乙時又只有歷組，《南地》此骨鑿型應爲長而兩端呈三角形的狹槽。可是版上有關鑽鑿却是編者所分"一型二式"。此式據同書統計表，除 2384 外没有列

---

① 裘錫圭：《論"歷組卜辭"的時代》，《古文字研究》第 6 輯；林澐：《小屯南地發掘與殷墟甲骨斷代》，同上第 9 輯。
② 姚孝遂：《吉林大學所藏甲骨選釋》，《吉林大學社會科學學報》1963 年第 3 期。
③ 林澐：《小屯南地發掘與殷墟甲骨斷代》。
④ 《小屯南地甲骨》釋文第 1010 頁。

於武乙時的。細看此處鑽鑿和版上其他鑽鑿銜接成行，形態全同，絕非後加。

如說此處鑽鑿是祖庚、祖甲時留下未用，也不可能。因爲出組胛骨慣例，位於下角的這第一處鑽鑿首先灼用，可看《合集》所收"卜王"各版，大都在第一兆辭末附記月分。《南地》2384 有一未用的鑿，前已述及，沒有鑽，也不曾灼。由此可知，祖庚、祖甲時即使留下一鑿，應爲未鑽未灼。而歷組的鑿是不這樣加鑽的。

由此可見，這一版確是歷組卜辭應提早到武丁晚年至祖庚時的有力證據。這樣，上舉歷組與其他組刻辭同版各例也都得到解釋了。

關於殷墟甲骨分期的兩系說以及歷組卜辭問題，今後還會繼續討論下去。相信這一討論會使甲骨研究得到進一步的發展。

附記：1986 年，中國古文字研究會第六屆年會在山東長島召開，會議要求討論甲骨分期問題。我寫了《殷墟甲骨分期的兩系說》一文，以摘要提交會議，并附以當時已寫好的另一小文《論小屯南地出土的一版特殊胛骨》的摘要。現在這篇就是以上述摘要爲基礎，刪去過於專門的部分，合并改寫而成。《特殊胛骨》全文已在《上海博物館集刊》第 4 期發表，《兩系說》則將刊於《古文字研究》。

原收入《李學勤集》，黑龍江教育出版社，1989 年；又收入《當代學者自選文庫·李學勤卷》，安徽教育出版社，1999 年。今據前者收入。

白玉崢

殷墟第十五次發掘成組卜甲

殷虛第十五次發掘，始於民國二十六年三月十六日，至同年六月十九日止，共工作三月餘。發掘所得，除殷時之墓葬遺跡及其他遺存外，獲有字龜版五四九版，有字骨版五〇版；兩者共計得五九九版。其拓本、悉數納入《殷虛文字乙編》。其龜版中，有甚多較完整與完整之卜用腹甲與背甲。董而理之，得成組之卜用腹甲甚多；唯其間若干卜甲，雖知其爲成組者，但經綴合後，仍難窺其全貌。茲擇其較爲完整者十組，及較有意義之綴合五版，今譯其辭。設有前賢考述未周者，間以鄙意附於辭末，以爲續貂。唯坐井之說未必有當，聊助談資云爾。

第一組

本組卜甲，係以兩版腹甲構成。其第一甲，爲綴合《小屯乙編》之八七一一、八七三〇、八七六二、八七九一、八八〇二、八八一二、八八三五、八八三六、八八四四、八八六八等十片碎甲而成，且爲一較完整之腹甲如附圖一。第三甲則爲《小屯乙編》之八八九六版。就其所紀卜兆序數審之，綴合之殘甲爲第一甲，《乙編》之腹甲乃其第三甲。其間序數二之腹甲則不悉其何之矣？兩卜甲均出土於YH二五一坑，經綴合之腹甲，其登記號雖至二十一九號之多，然據同坑出土之關係察之，在殷紂亡國之前夕，似爲完整之腹甲。若敢大膽的假設，其第二甲可能尚未出土？

本組卜甲所紀之干支爲庚戌、癸丑、癸亥、辛未、己丑、辛丑等，若據其順序以察其卜用之法，其法則有二焉：一、辛未爲本組卜甲最前之干支，以此爲

始，至癸亥止，約略呈不規則之右旋；自卜甲之中央始，先上再下，而迄版中爲止。二、庚戌爲最下之干支，以此爲始，順次至辛丑止，其軌跡略呈自下而上，自右而左。至何者爲是，則難得其實矣。若其卜用之時期，以無貞人之具名，遂缺乏簡捷之斷代憑據，僅可從其稱謂及其他條件，作委婉之推求。今其稱謂有妣辛、妣庚、帚妤、帚多、妌、嫒、娥、䜴、姎等。據其書體，在同版中則有帚㚬、帚㗊、帚㓁、妣甹、甹戌、甹未、甹丑、勹㚣、勹㚣、㚣、㚣等之異。茲先從稱謂中推求之：按殷虛五期中，就卜辭所可考知者，自大乙以下十七世三十王之配，其稱妣庚者爲祖辛、祖丁、小乙三王；其稱妣辛者爲大甲、祖丁、武丁三王。就妣庚之稱審之：凡稱且辛、且丁二王之配，必冠以高字。此妣庚既未冠高字，則其必爲小乙之配無疑。妣辛，當爲武丁之配矣。據此，本組卜甲當爲第四期之物矣。若再以書體及現示於版面之情況等互勘之，爲文武丁時之遺物炯然如揭矣。

茲將第一甲之殘辭，略據自下而上之卜用順序，今譯於後；其殘缺者，並據同組之他辭予以填實，而以〔　〕號界之，以明所殘。

1. 庚〔戌卜〕，貞：〔亡𡆥〕？ 右行
   又𡆥？ 下行

2. 癸丑卜，貞：子亡𡆥？ 左行
   〔又〕𡆥？ 下行

3. 貞：帚多妁？ 左行

4. 妣庚、周、三竿？ 右行
   妣庚竿六？ 左行

5. 勹屰妌？ 右行
   勹何嫒？ 左行

6. 使人〔先曰屰〕娥？ 右行
   勹娥？ 右行

7. 勹逆〔女〕？ 右行

8. 力。

9. 癸亥卜、子夕往屰以？ 右行

10. 辛未〔卜〕，作宀？ 右行

11. 己丑卜，又妣庚牝？ 右行

12. 夕，刜卸事，爰？ 右行

13. 馬不歺？ 右行

14. 辛〔丑〕卜，乎爰帚妤乳？ 右行

15. 正受禾？右行
16. 〔受禾？下行
　　弜受？左行

△：以同組卜甲之他辭審之，似爲△之急就者；亦如△之作△△然。

△、△、△：疑並爲人鬼之名；亦或爲人格化之天神名。娥曾見於第一期武丁時之卜辭。

△：當即宀，今則淪爲偏旁矣。乍宀，未詳其義。或釋爲"作宅"，然甲文中已有宅字。

△：或謂與△同，然在卜辭中之辭例各異，遽難定其爲同字。姑仍从舊説作爰。

△：今釋正；於本辭爲地名，或方國名。唯卜辭中以正爲地名之義僅此一見。於他辭率爲動詞，征也。又或爲名詞，月序也。

△：地名，或方國名，唯亦僅見於本組卜甲。或謂：字與△、△等同。然否，以俟考定。

第二組

本組卜甲，乃由兩版殘甲及一版較爲完整之腹甲構成；同爲YH二五一坑所出土。就其所記序數審之，乙八八八〇爲第一甲，乙八六九一爲第二甲，乙八八五二乃其第三甲；而以第三甲較爲完整。察其情形，本組卜甲可能於紂亡國之前夕即已殘碎分裂，東零西散；而於出土之後，遂未由復合矣。

據第三甲審之，本組卜甲所紀之干支日名，計爲癸卯、□辰、丁巳、戊午、甲戌、□□等；辰上之□，據此序列推斷，可能爲甲、但亦可能爲丙。若其爲甲，則甲戌後之所缺可能爲乙亥；則其兩間分別爲十四及十七。若其爲丙，此殘缺之干則無由推斷矣。然無論其爲甲爲丙，可得知者，本組卜甲之卜用時間，頗爲集中。此一現象，在此十組卜甲中，頗與他異。至其卜用之時期，以無貞人之具名，頗難簡捷瞭然。唯以稱謂及同坑出土之他組卜甲比勘之，仍屬方便。茲比附前組卜甲之坑位、稱謂等，本組卜甲當亦爲第四期文武丁時之遺物。

茲就第三甲之殘辭今譯於後：

1. 癸卯貞：用戋宰妣庚？ 左行
2. 祝亞𠃡豕？ 右行

   亞朿？
3. 囗辰卜，……首……乙……豕？ 左行
4. 用……十……？ 右行
5. 于來己……？ 左行
6. 丁巳卜，戋十宰妣庚？ 左行
7. 戊午卜，用十……？ 右行
8. 妣庚𤋱羌？用。 右行　三甲並同
9. ……卜……？
10. 妣庚。
11. 𠂤。
12. 甲戌卜，又妣庚羌？ 右行
13. ……乙……？

亞：孫籀廎氏之《契文舉例》隸定爲亞見《卜事篇》。後世學者，自羅振玉氏《書契考釋》以下，曾無異議，是釋亞已爲定論，惟雖論述繽紛，然於其初義之推求，率多拘於許說，未能會通其理，是正其書。然則，亞之初義爲何？余疑其爲"宮中道"也。此說並見許書，惜許氏立說之當時，固未之察也。《說文》："䆠，宮中道，从囗，象宮垣道上之形。"許氏此說，蓋誤以亞之初義，當於壺之說解也。且所爲說解，窒礙晦澀，索解匪易，其說遂不彰。今以殷墟發掘之墓址作平面之觀察，並與亞之構形比勘，兩者完全相一；是亞之初義，與墓址必有相互之關聯。殷人尚鬼，事死如事生，由是察知生人之居室，自其平面視之，亦若亞形，用知亞之初義爲"宮中道"。所謂"宮中道"者，乃於通道之左右，各予設窗或戶限，其頂設覆蓋之義也，與居舍無甚軒輊。其所異者，此乃專供通行者也。若以今語說之，"走廊"之義近似。且觀今時大廈内部之甬道，亦與亞形相合，是亞與行之構形略通，且並象四達之形。若就其異者論，行之構形，乃爲平面之描述，而亞則兼立體，其四向之丨或一，乃其頂之覆蓋也；此可從甲文中𠃡戩四○、一四與𠂤新綴四三八版等之構形證知之。是亞之初義爲"宮中道"，象四達之形，當無疑也。

𠂤：金祥恒先生《續文編》釋首卷九頁一。

第三組

本組卜甲是由兩版較小之腹甲所構成。第一甲如附圖二乃以乙八七一四及八七八四綴合而成，第二甲在《乙編》中之編號爲八八〇八。全組卜甲皆出土於 YH 二五一坑。

本組卜甲，紀事簡括，且於卜用當日之干支亦未之紀，惶及貞人之具名，若似“無乃大簡乎”？至其稱謂，亦僅“母庚”與“小母”而已。按母庚之稱，在五期卜辭中，見於第一期之武丁，及第四期之二王；於此三母庚中之一，再勘以同坑出土之他甲屬時，則本組卜甲所稱之“母庚”，定爲文武丁之母，武乙之妻，當無疑義。而本組卜甲之卜用時期，自當屬文武丁之時矣。

茲將第一甲之原辭今譯於左：

1. 于門？下行

2. 力羊？下行

3. 牀母庚？下行

4. 貞。

5. 力豩小母？用。左行

6. 力小母？下行

7. 力豩小母？下行

ナ：字不識。或釋爲[illegible]之省。以之釋第五組卜甲見後辭尚可達；若以之釋本組之辭則窒礙不達。又或釋爲劦之省，亦頗可商；蓋以之釋本組之辭，或亦可通；若以之釋第五組之辭，則又扞格不適。究當爲今之何字何意，尚待論定。茲姑隸作力，藉便説解。

爿：从《甲骨文字集釋》之説二三三一釋牀。“牀母庚”，其義不詳。然就辭例審之，似爲祭祀之義。

第四組

本組卜甲，是以若干碎甲，經綴合後而構成者。第一甲如附圖三係以乙八七二

七、八八五五、八九七〇、八九九三等四片所綴合；第二甲 如附圖四 係以乙八七〇四、八八二〇、八八二六、八八五七等四片所綴合；第三甲爲《乙編》之八七一三。全組卜甲以第二甲較爲完整。第一甲出土於 YH 二五一及 YH 二三〇兩坑；第二與第三兩甲，均出土於 YH 二五一坑。是第一甲在帝辛亡國之前夕即已破裂，於三千年之後，竟有部份又重復合，是亦其大幸也。

本組卜甲所紀之干支有四：辛巳、癸未、己丑、癸巳，緣此干支順序，得推知其卜用之序，爲先右後左，自下而上。癸巳日共有三卜，二左一右；此後，即未再卜用。其於稱謂，則有妣庚、中母、帚多、帚嫘及子㞢、子丁等。妣庚作 𩰫，帚多作 𠂤，是其異也。

至其卜用之時期，據妣庚之稱，及出土坑位之標準，例當第四期文武丁時之遺物。唯子丁之稱，在第四期中僅見於武乙時之卜辭；若據此標準，則本組卜甲當爲武乙時之遺物。然就版面之風格，書體及其他情形審之，咸皆大異其趣。然則，文武丁時亦有"子丁"歟？或者本組卜甲之卜用，適當武乙與文武丁二王交替之時矣。

兹將三卜甲之原辭今譯於後，並相互參酌補實其所缺。

第一甲

1. 辛巳卜，㱿又升妣庚豕？右行
2. 㱿〔又升妣庚小宰〕？左行
3. 于子丁？右行
4. 中母？
5. 癸未貞：帚多？右行
6. 癸巳卜，貞：帚嫘亡至口？右行

第二甲

1. 〔辛巳卜〕，㱿又〔升妣庚〕宰？右行
2. 〔㱿又〕升妣〔庚〕小宰？左行
3. 㱿又升妣庚㘚？左行
4. 于子丁？右行
5. 中母 下行
6. 癸未貞：帚多？右行
7. 癸巳卜，貞：帚嫘亡至口？右行

第三甲

1. 辛巳卜，㱿又升妣庚豕？右行

2. 攸又〔升妣庚小宰〕？

3. 于子丁？ 右行

4. 癸未貞：帚多？ 右行

5. 癸巳卜：子壴亡凷？ 左行

6. 癸巳卜，貞：帚嫘亡至口？ 右行

崢按：本辭之"帚嫘"，其帚字顯爲事後之補契，故緊契於嫘之左上，癸之右下。

島邦男之《卜辭綜類》三七一頁竟予失錄，殊非。又"亡至口"之亡，亦緊契於至之右方。緣是：若干學者遂釋爲"至口亡"，亦有以"至亡"釋爲一文者。今以前二甲證之，知所釋皆非。然此又可證知當時史官之自由精神，致有補書漏契之事，亦一耐人玩索之事也。

7. 癸巳卜，貞：帚嫘亡疾？ 左行

嫘：金祥恒先生《續文編》入於女部之後，定爲《説文》所無之字卷十二頁十三。李孝定先生之《集釋》从之卷十二頁三七〇七，並隸定爲娞。丁驌先生謂："亦即嫘"《中國文字》三十八册字。崢按：字蓋从女从〇〇；〇〇即畾即雷。甲骨文字有𤲳前四、一一、七片字，今釋爲雷；字若省𤲳，則當爲〇〇，用知嫘即嫘字，亦即嫘字。嬬、嫘，《説文》皆未錄。《大戴禮記·帝繫篇》："黃帝娶于西陵氏之子，謂之嫘祖。"此嬬或嫘之名氏，既見於黃帝時代，至殷商時代不得謂無此名氏。若單就姓氏之延續與擴展之情形論之，後世之雷姓，或其後裔歟？至若其字，《史記·五帝本紀》與《大戴記》同，作嫘；《索隱》引《帝王世紀》作累，《正義》又作儽。《漢書·古今人表》作絫，《國語·晉語》韋昭註引《帝繫》作纍；而《山海經·海内經》則作雷。雷浚《説文外編》卷十二《〈玉篇〉俗字》上："嫘，嫘祖也。字本作絫，後世變絫爲累，又加女旁也。"《索隱》之累，爲《説文》緦之古文，非雷氏謂變絫爲累也。《正義》之儽，《説文》雖無其字，但有僵字，則於此嬬似相若也。《人表》之絫，《國語》之纍，雖均入錄於《説文》，但其構形却與此異。是許書雖錄絫、纍、累、僵等字，但與嫘之名氏無涉，與嬬更無涉。而各家所作之嫘、累等，亦僅止於擬聲，甚或沿習而已，從未見有尋求其真確之本字之者，寧非奇哉？然而，《山海經》之作雷，或亦爲擬聲，但證以甲文之構形，不得謂爲無據。

金文中齊嬬姬簠有𩰫字，容氏《金文編》錄于女部之後，定爲《説文》所無之字卷十二頁二二。若從偏旁分析，除其妝飾，恰正與甲文合。至其从二或三〇，在

古文字中非其病也。又穌甫人盤及匜，均有 ⟨字⟩ 字，前修皆以姪爲釋，遂致短短五字之銘文，辭義扞格窒礙，無由通讀；今以嬬〔嫘〕爲釋，其銘文之義豁然開朗，辭通義達。至如嬭妊壺之 ⟨字⟩ 三代十二、七，僰嬀壺之 ⟨字⟩ 三代十二、六，亦莫不如斯也。

要之，釋嬬〔嫘〕，不僅於字之構形有據，且於名氏之徵實有證；若以之通讀甲金二文，莫不辭通達意，抒暢無礙。又爲文字之本真，當以隸作嬬最爲適當，然嫘字沿習已久，未便干俗，故譯辭從俗作嫘。

⟨字⟩：獨孫海波《校正文編》入錄於止部之後，隸定爲歨，爲《說文》所無之字《校編》二、十六。崢按：本字僅只兩見，即本組卜甲與燕一三四版。《燕》爲殘骨之賸辭，無由推勘其義；字於本組卜甲，例當人名。其字之構形與初義爲何？有俟論定，茲姑从孫氏作歨，藉便說解。

⟨字⟩：義不詳。辭僅見於本組卜甲。

第五組

本組卜甲，係由三版不太大之卜甲構成。第一甲係以碎甲三版綴合而成 如附圖五，其在《乙編》之編號爲八七一二、八九四四、八九四六。其中僅八七一二出土於 YH 二五一坑，餘二版均出土於 YH 三三〇坑；是此一腹甲，於出土前即已殘碎。第二、第三兩甲均完整，其《乙編》之編號，依次爲八八九三與八八九八；但其出土之坑位則異。八八九三出土於 YH 二五一坑，八八九八出土於 YH 二五三坑。是本組卜甲於出土之坑位有三。此可說明：本組卜甲在商紂亡國時，即已零散碎裂。然而，也可證明：殷商於亡國之前，其秩序即已紊亂不堪；也可揣知：帝辛"倉皇辭廟"之情狀。於今，"笙歌已散尊罍在"，且讓後人憑弔罷。

本組卜甲所紀之干支，計有甲申、癸巳、戊午、辛酉、乙丑等，以經綴合之第一版言；其干支位置頗爲零亂，若欲推求其卜用順序，頗費周折。若據卜用之慣例，並循干支之序推求，當以甲申爲始，至乙丑而止，呈左旋之二重圓。若純據干支序求之，則有二焉：一、以左甲橋之乙丑始，則呈先右再左旋之二圓。二、以右沿之乙丑始，則呈左旋之重圓。然而，何者爲是，頗難尋其真矣。至其卜用之時期，據辭中之稱謂及出土坑位，更參以前四組之例，當爲第四期文武丁

時之遺物。

兹將第一甲之原辭今譯如左：

1. 甲申卜，令啄宅正？

按：本辭除"甲申卜"爲下行外，餘爲二字平列，右行之二列。若無餘二甲及對貞辭之比勘，勢必誤讀爲"令宅啄正"。

2. 由徣宅正？ 左行
3. 癸巳卜，妫力？ 下行
　　　　　不力？ 下行
　　　　　妫力？ 下行
4. 妫自毓？ 右行
5. 癸巳卜，妫囗出？ 左行
6. 歸老？ 下行
7. 又罒啄亡口？ 右行
8. 〔又〕禽？ 下行
9. 戊午卜，又妣庚牝？ 右行
10. 辛酉卜，妫囗出？ 左行
11. 乙丑卜，帚亡祟？ 左行
12. 乙丑卜，又矤丁？ 左行

🐾：金祥恒先生《續文編》列於女部之後，爲《説文》所無之字，與 🐾 爲一字卷十二頁十三。孫海波《校正文編》从之，並隸定爲妫卷十二頁十三。李孝定先生《集釋》失錄。丁驌先生釋爲妫之省"帚妫，或省女旁作多，或只寫多字之一半，成帚妫。妫，顯即妫之省；惟不與帚字連用。妫字寫爲妫，作合文形，決非口向上之吹〔🐾〕字，亦非多女、多母兩字。各辭細讀之，仍是妫之省"《中國文字》三十八册。崝按：🐾，僅見於本組卜甲及第一組之第三甲。該甲妫、多、妫同見一版，且於其上冠以"帚"字；如此姻緣，推論妫與妫爲同字，雖僅單辭之據，亦可謂有憑有證，所論不誣。然就本組卜甲諸辭審之，其上皆未冠"帚"字，且其辭例亦不盡相若；遽以妫爲釋，仍嫌突兀。然就第一組第三甲"帚妫在老"之辭及本組卜甲"妫囗出"、"帚亡祟"、"歸老"之辭比勘之，帚妫雖未連用，而以其定爲妫之省，似又可通。兹从丁氏説，姑釋爲妫省，以俟他證。又爲便於説解，姑從孫氏之隸定，而非以 Ð 爲 ）或 ♪ 也。

🐾：商承祚釋老。本辭曰"歸老"，第一組有辭曰"在老"；老，當爲地名。此兩組卜甲既爲同時物，則似有相當之關聯。若得"往老"之辭，或可考知其實

情歟？

⺿凵：其義不詳；亦未悉其與前組卜甲之"亡至口"有否關聯。

𠀠：義亦不詳。丁驌先生謂其出爲"或係貞人署名"，"出，或即是外行之意"《中國文字》三十八冊。崝按：所論非是。蓋緣未能句讀其辭也。

第六組

本組卜甲，亦係以較小之三腹甲所構成。其實，第一甲僅殘存左後甲之左半而已；其在《乙編》之序列爲八九五八，YH 三三〇坑所出土。第二甲比較完整，《乙編》之序列爲八七二二，乃 YH 二五一坑所出。第三甲乃以碎甲綴合而成者如附圖六，《乙編》之序列爲八七四二、八七七九、八七八九、八七九三、八八二八等五版，均爲 YH 二五一坑所出；然仍僅爲左右兩後甲之殘。以同坑出土之他甲勘之，仍當爲第四期文武丁時之遺物。

茲將第三甲之殘辭之譯如左：

1. 甲辰卜，貞：羌野不歹？右行

〔其〕歹？下行

2. 馬𢀛？下行

𢀛：李孝定先生《集釋》失錄。按：字从重臣从子，《說文》所無，究爲何字何義？尚待論定。

第七組

本組卜甲，係以三版較小之腹甲構成。各皆殘缺；惟第三甲較爲完整。其在《乙編》之編號，依次爲八七一〇、八八〇四、八七二三，均出土於 YH 二五一坑。其所紀之干支，僅丁酉而已。亦頗乏斷代之簡捷依據；惟仍可據其出土坑位推斷，故定爲第四期文武丁時之遺物。

茲將全組之卜辭，依序今譯如左：

第一甲

1. 貞：飲？下行

2. 〔祝亞〕🈁豖? 左行

3. 〔祝亞〕🈁豖? 右行

4. 丁酉卜，來庚午用戋宰? 右行

按：原版"庚午"二字左右平列，下第三甲亦同。午字不類《補契》。然則，其辭或作"庚午戋宰? 用?"義亦可通，惟無辭例以資佐證。又島邦男《綜類》作"來庚用十戋宰"五十七頁。非是。

第二甲

1. 祝亞🈁豖? 右行

2. 羊祝? 下行

第三甲

1. 貞：飲? 下行

2. 祝亞🈁豖? 右行

3. 丁酉卜，來庚午用戋〔宰〕? 右行

𩚨：金祥恒先生《續文編》入錄於飲之後八、二四。茲姑隸作飲，以俟考之。

第八組

本組卜甲係以YH二五一坑同時出土之三版小腹甲構成。其在《乙編》中之編號，依次爲八六九七、八六九六、八八六一：其間以第二甲較爲完整，餘均殘缺甚多。其所紀之干支，僅乙卯、丁巳、丁亥而已。以同坑出土之他版，及本組卜甲最突兀的，以鼎爲貞證之，當爲第四期文武丁時之遺物。茲將全組原辭今譯如左：

第一甲

1. 乙卯貞：子𩵋? 右行

2. 丁巳，㳄兄豕? 右行

3. 𠂤🈁祟? 下行

按：島邦男《綜類》以本辭及下第五辭併爲一辭，作"鼎水𠂤🈁祟"七五及二一一。今以本組卜甲自身證之，知島邦此錄非是。

4. 丁亥鼎：登? 下行

5. 鼎：水? 下行

第二甲

1. 乙卯貞：子𠂤？右行

2. 丁巳，兄𠂤？右行

3. 示丁𠂤不？左行

4. 丁亥鼎：登？下行

按：右二辭島邦男《綜類》併爲一辭，作"丁亥鼎登示丁𠂤不"八○及四○一。

第三甲

1. 〔乙卯〕貞：子𠂤？右行

2. 丁巳，兄𠂤？右行

3. 丁示𠂤不？左行

4. 丁亥鼎：登？下行

按：右二辭：島邦男之《綜類》併爲一辭，作"……鼎登丁示……𠂤不"八○及四○一。

5. 鼎：水？下行

𠂤：金祥恆先生《續文編》列爲待問之字附二、五。李孝定先生《集釋》从之，列爲待考之字四七四六。又子𠂤，當爲人名，其事不詳。或爲文武丁之子歟？

第九組

本組卜甲，係由兩版稍大之腹甲構成。兩甲皆已殘缺，第二甲且殘缺一辭。其在《乙編》之編號，第一甲爲八八五八、第二甲爲八八○九；均出土於 YH 二五一坑。其所紀之干支，僅癸酉與乙亥而已。辭亦較簡略，而以鼎爲貞，則正與前組卜甲同，當亦爲第四期文武丁時之遺物。茲將兩甲之原辭今譯如左：

第一甲

1. 癸酉鼎。下行

2. 〔乙〕亥卜，大叩𠂤？十一月。右行

3. 乙亥卜，自小白弘？十一月。左行

第二甲

1. 癸酉鼎。下行

2. 〔乙亥卜，大叩𠂤……〕？十一月。左行

3. 乙亥卜，自小白弘？十一月。左行

叩：李孝定先生《集釋》定爲待考之字四六二二及四六九三頁。

第十組

本組卜甲，係以較小之腹甲三版所構成。第一甲爲上腹甲之部份；在《乙編》之編號爲八九六五，餘二甲均較完整，《乙編》之編號依序爲八七二八、八八一四。第一甲，出土於 YH 三三〇坑，餘均出土於 YH 二五一坑。是本組卜甲，於紂亡國之前即已散亂；今於三千年之下而予重合，亦一幸事。至其卜用時期，據現示於版面之情況，及出土之坑位例之，當亦爲第四期文武丁時之遺物。

兹將第二甲〔八七二八〕之原辭今譯於左：

1. 乙卯卜，貞：子攸亡疾？左行
2. 乙卯卜，貞：聑？下行

按：島邦男《卜辭綜類》七六以本辭及下第五辭，併爲一辭，錄作"乙卯卜貞聑先妣牛"。

3. 乙卯卜，貞：〔子〕夋？左行

按：第三甲〔八八一四〕之本辭，夋上有"子"；據前第五組之辭亦當有之。然則，本甲之子其或爲漏契歟？

4. 甲子卜，先夋？右行
5. 先妣牛？左行
6. 母□。
7. 帚□。
8. 丁示。下行

：金祥恒先生《續文編》釋聑十二、五。孫海波《校正文編》釋卍曰："或從聑"十二、四。

：金祥恒先生《續文編》釋允八、十九。孫海波《校正文編》錄作，釋允八、十三，又錄作，隸作夋，從於夂部之末五、二五。島邦男《卜辭綜類》定爲與明二五三、前四、三三、二片、前六、一三、三片爲同文七十五頁。峥按：釋允可商，孫氏錄作，非是，島邦之認定亦非。兹姑從孫氏之又作，隸爲夋。至其究當今之何字？何義？以俟考定。

附録（一）

本附録爲夫子以《乙編》之八八〇七、九〇三一兩版所綴合，並著錄於《中國書譜》四十六頁。經綴合後，爲一完整之卜用腹甲如附圖七。分別出土於 YH 二五一及 YH 三七一兩坑；是本腹在紂亡國之前即已碎裂。據其"以鼎爲貞"，及出土之坑位例之，當亦爲第四期文武丁時之遺物。

茲將原辭今譯如左：

1. 甲子卜，束禽羊？ 一。右行
2. 甲子卜，束禽羊？ 二。左行
3. 囲。一。
4. 囲。二。
5. 丙寅鼎：子弗条囚？ 一。左行
6. 丙寅鼎：宀？ 一。下行

𠂤：金祥恒先生《續文編》从於夂部之末五、三二，爲《說文》所無之字。孫海波《校正文編》入附錄上六一。或釋条，然否，以俟考定。

附録（二）

本附録係以第十五次發掘之殘腹甲兩版綴合而成如附圖八；在《乙編》之編號爲八八五四、及八八八九，皆出土於 YH 二五一坑。其"以鼎爲貞"，正與前第八及九兩組卜甲相同，當亦爲第四期文武丁時之遺物。

本殘甲雖殘存七辭，而其所紀之干支，僅爲甲子、甲戌、囗寅而已。循干支序及契刻位置，推求此寅上之缺文，疑其爲戊。若然，則此一腹甲之卜用次序爲：自上而下，自右而左。設其卜序反是，則此寅上之缺文，疑其爲甲。果其爲甲，則此一腹甲，乃爲連續之三甲日所特予卜用者；而於甲戌日卜用者最多。茲沿此序，今譯其辭如左：

1. 〔甲〕寅鼎：〔帚〕周疾……征？ 左行

按：此疾字原文作 𣦼 。

2. 甲戌卜，亡囗？ 左行

3. 甲戌卜，亡囗？ 右行

4. ……不允？ 左行

5. 甲戌鼎：呂？ 下行

6. 甲戌鼎：亡疾？三月。右行

按：此疾字原文作𠭥。

7. 甲子卜，鼎：㞢周𠂤征？ 左行

𠂤：諸家失錄。玆以拓印不清，姑如上作。其或仍當爲𠦒。

附錄（三）

本附錄係以碎甲三版綴合而成 如附圖九；其在《乙編》之序數爲八七〇六、八七一九、八八〇五均出土於YH二五一坑。當亦爲第四期文武丁時之遺物。

玆將原辭今譯如左：

1. 甲申卜，貞。下行

按：本辭之"卜"字，顯屬事後之補契，故緊貼於"申"字之右側。

2. 甲申卜，貞。右行

3. 甲申卜，貞。下行

4. 甲申卜，貞：子。左行

附錄（四）

本附錄係以三版殘甲綴合而成 如附圖十；其在《乙編》之編號爲八六九九、八八二二、八八八五；同爲YH二五一坑所出。據此，當亦爲第四期文武丁時之遺物。

玆將綴合後之殘辭今譯如左：

1. 壬午貞：㞢多亡囗？ 右行

2. 壬午貞：㞢多亡囗？ 左行

附錄（五）

　　本附錄係以背甲二版綴合而成 附圖十一，且爲一完整之左背甲；若謂其殘，亦僅邊甲一片而已。其在《乙編》中之編號爲八八〇六及八八九九七；分別出土於 YH 二五一及 YH 三三八兩坑，是本背甲在紂亡國時即已破裂爲二矣。而於三千年下之今日，竟又重圓，亦一大幸也。

　　本背甲之面積雖大，然僅刻四辭；且書體纖秀，致全甲之空間頗大。其辭、共契干支二，亦無由推尋其卜用之法。至其卜用之時期，況以 YH 二五一坑出土之卜甲，當爲第四期文武丁時之遺物。茲將原辭今譯如左：

1. 乙丑卜，又隻目，今日？ 右行
2. 甲午卜，龍禽？ 左行
3. 貞：一月。
4. 貞：帚亡疾，其征？ 右行

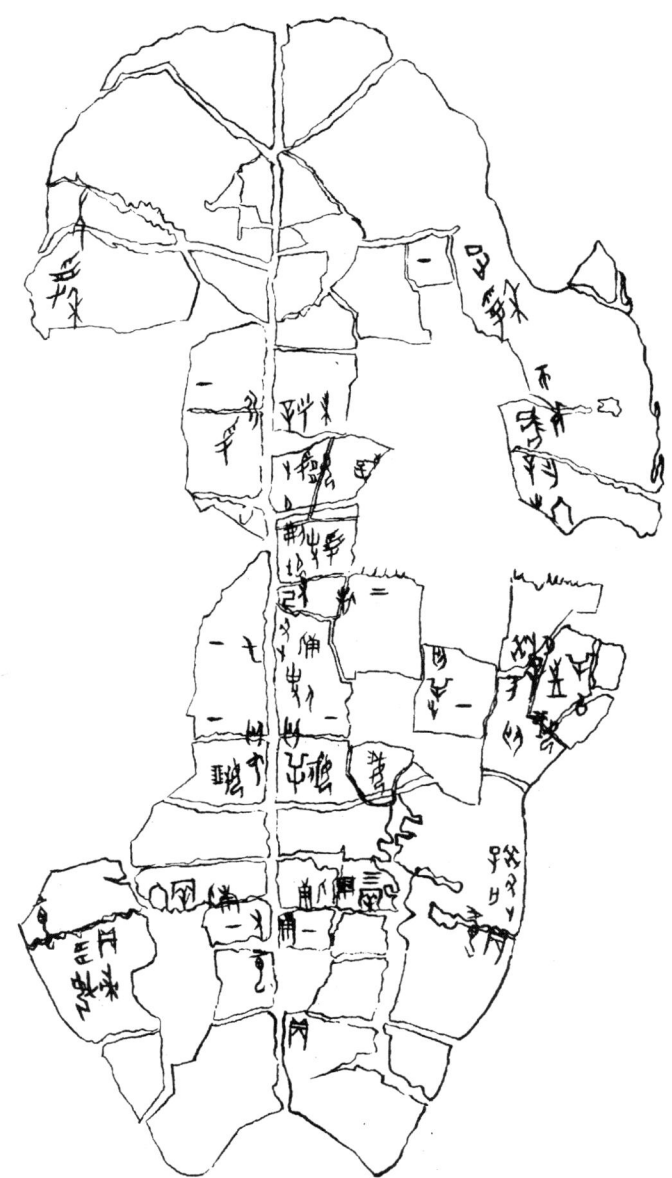

《乙》8711＋8730＋8762＋8791＋8802
＋8812＋8835＋8836＋8844＋8868

圖　一

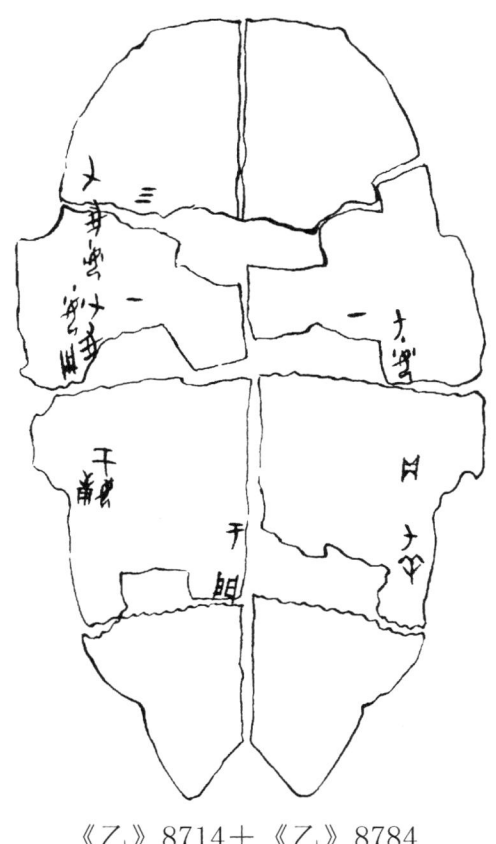

《乙》8714＋《乙》8784

《乙》8727＋《乙》8855
＋《乙》8970＋《乙》8993

圖 二　　　　　　　　　圖 三

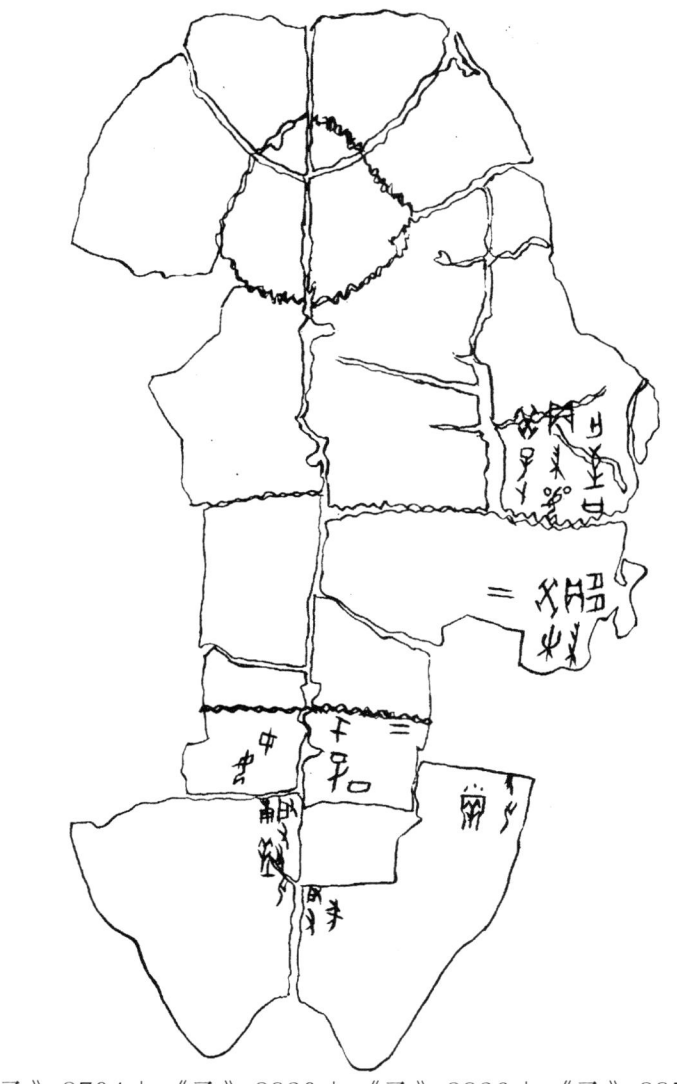

《乙》8704＋《乙》8820＋《乙》8826＋《乙》8857

圖 四

047 殷墟第十五次發掘成組卜甲　白玉崢

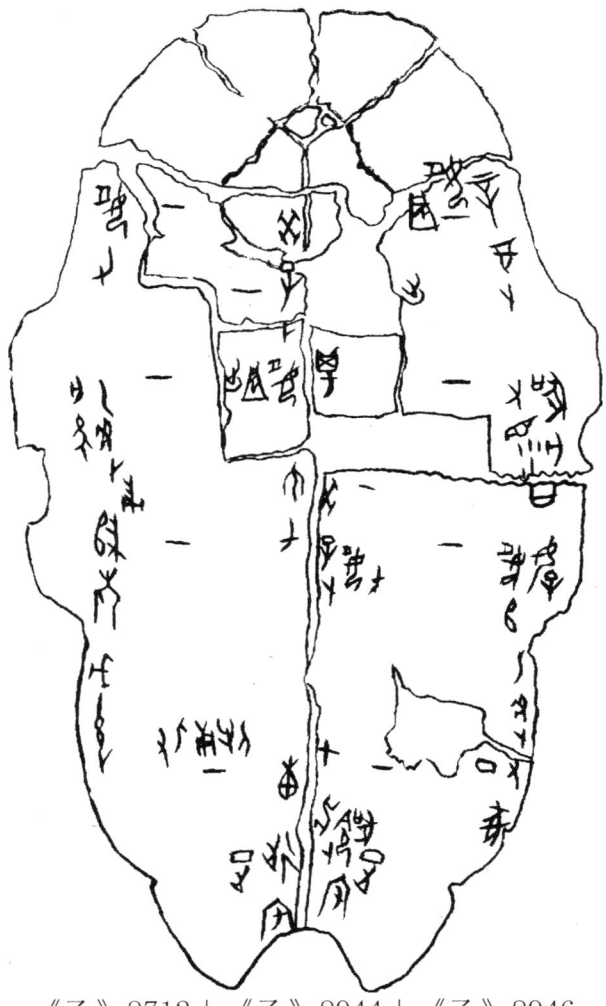

《乙》8712＋《乙》8944＋《乙》8946

圖　五

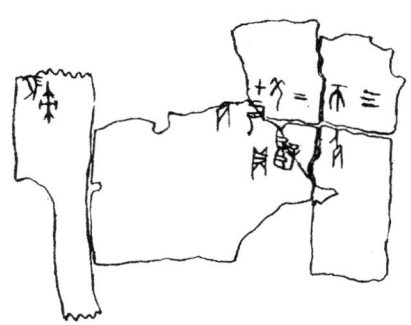

《乙》8742＋《乙》8779＋《乙》8789
＋《乙》8793＋《乙》8828

圖　六

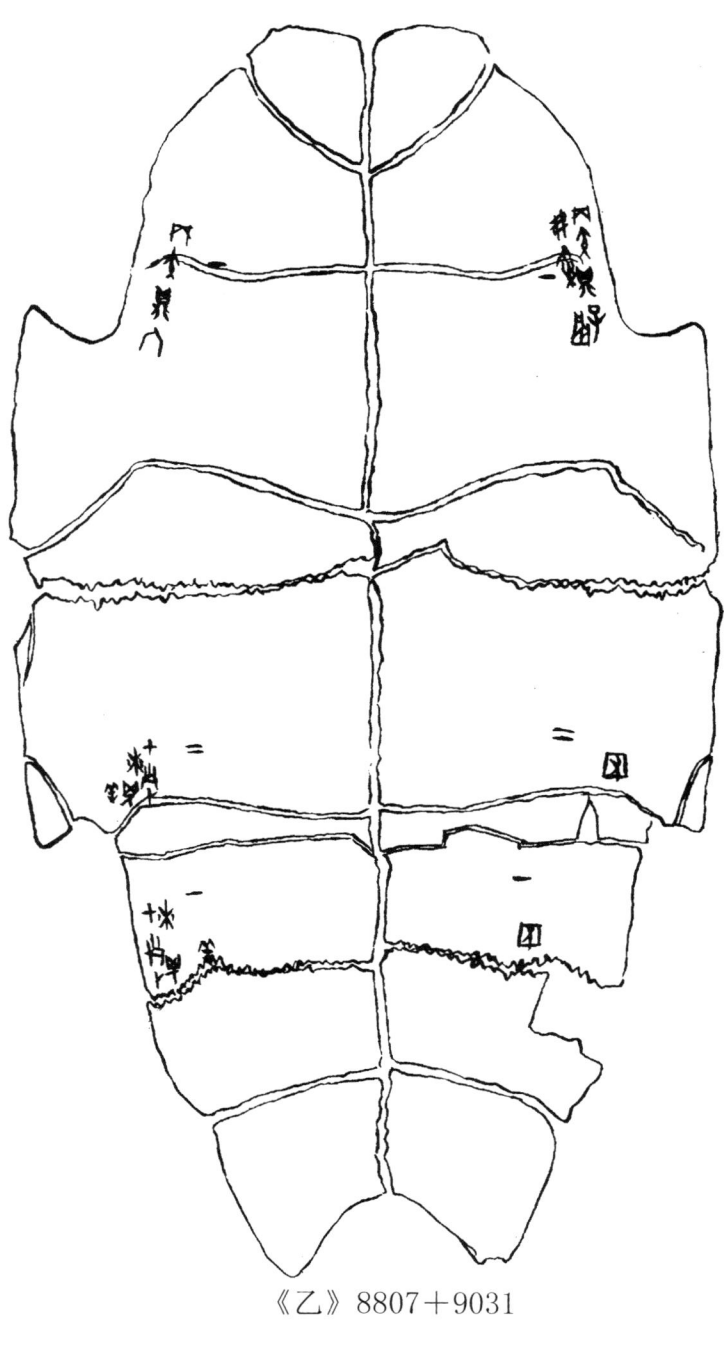

《乙》8807＋9031

圖 七

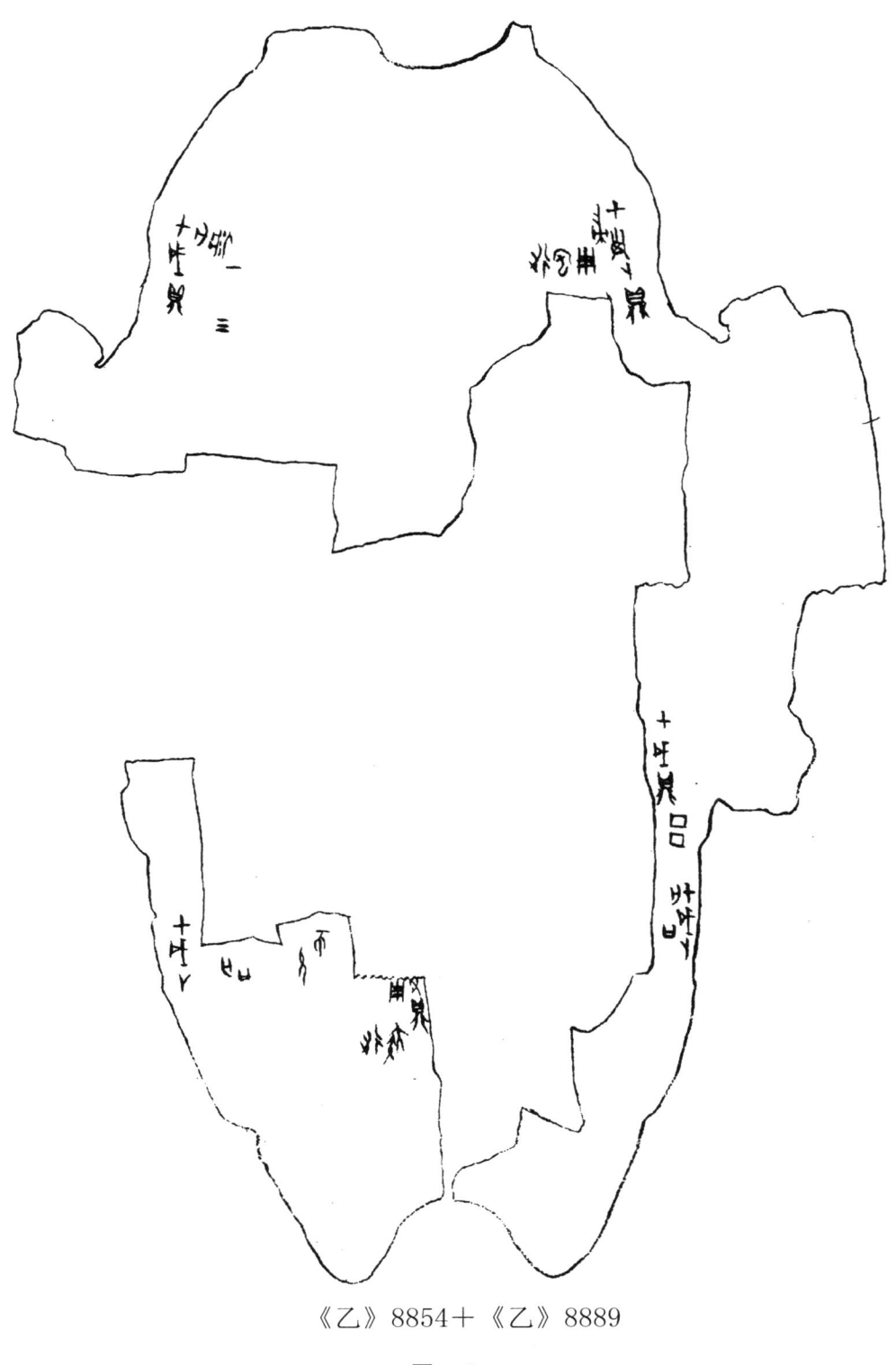

《乙》8854＋《乙》8889

圖 八

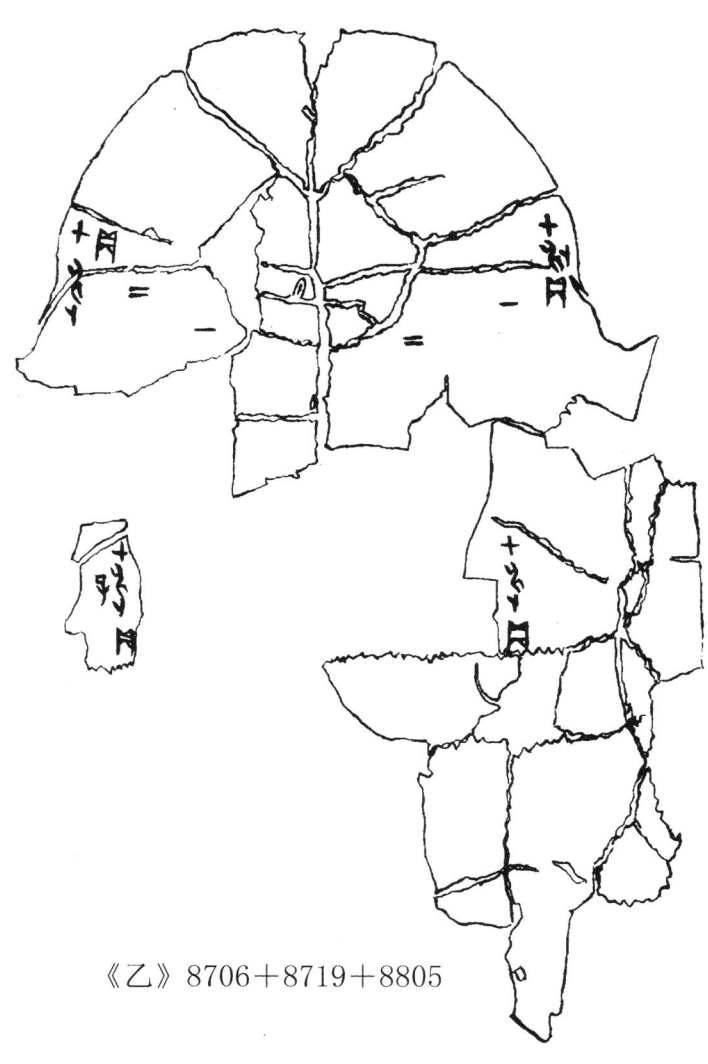

《乙》8706＋8719＋8805

圖 九

047 殷墟第十五次發掘成組卜甲　白玉崢

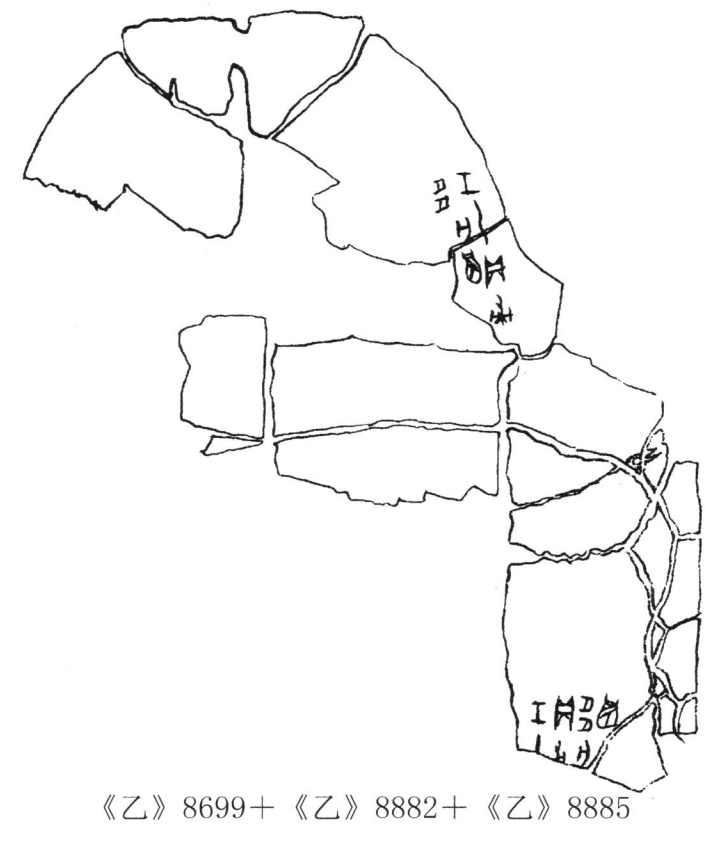

《乙》8699＋《乙》8882＋《乙》8885

圖　十

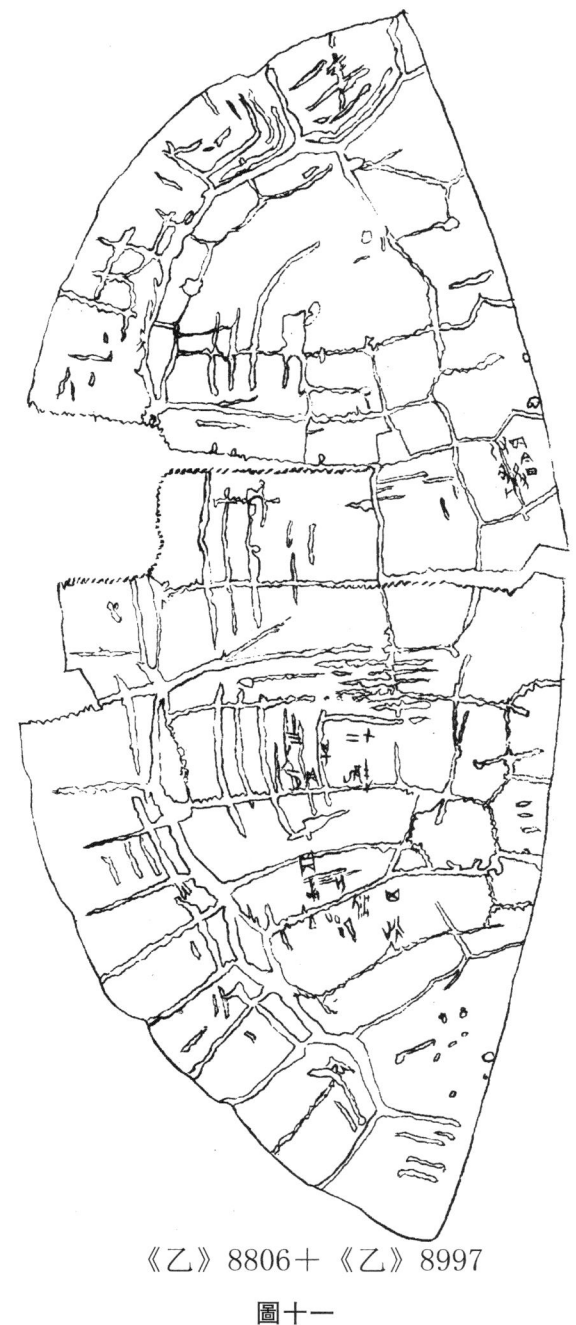

《乙》8806＋《乙》8997

圖十一

原載《董作賓先生逝世十四周年紀念刊》，藝文印書館，1978年；收入白玉崢:《楓林讀契集》，藝文印書館，1989年。今據前者收入。

于省吾

釋具有部分表音的獨體象形字
釋古文字中附劃因聲指事字的一例

釋具有部分表音的獨體象形字

　　《周禮》保氏教國子六藝，"五曰六書"，六書之名始見於此。《説文敘》段注："蓋有指事象形，而後有會意形聲。有是四者爲體，而後有轉注假借二者爲用。"按把所有文字劃分爲六個範疇的六書，段氏又把六書分析爲四體二用，都有着一定的邏輯性。但是，六書中尤其是指事的界劃和轉注的解釋，自來議論分歧，糾纏不清，在此撇開不談。《説文敘》於象形舉日月爲例，於形聲舉江河爲例，可見象形和形聲是不難辨別的。四體中的形聲字最後出現，以其便於應用，故《説文》一書九千餘字，形聲字約佔七千以上，後世則越發衍化繁殖。就造字來説，形聲字是以形符和聲符相配合而成，似乎容易創造。但是，它之所以最後出現，還是有着發生發展的過程。形聲字的如何起源，自來文字學家都没有作出適當的説明。我認爲，形聲字的起源，是從某些獨體象形字已發展到具有部分表音的獨體象形字，然後才逐漸分化爲形符和聲符相配合的形聲字。但在這一過渡期間之前，已經出現了兩個或幾個偏旁相配合的會意字，會意字的出現當然要先於形聲字。在會意字初步發展階段，即使出現了具有部分表音的獨體象形字，也不過是形聲字的萌芽而已。在會意字相當發展之後，形聲字才應運而出，會意字有時也附加聲符，則成爲會意兼聲的字，當然也屬於形聲的範疇。現在就甲骨文中具有部分表音的獨體象形字以及它如何演化爲形聲字，分條闡述之（周代金文也有兩個這一類型的字，因爲它與甲骨文有着連帶關係，故附列於後）。

　　一、《説文》羌作羗，並謂："羌，西戎牧羊人也，从人羊，羊亦聲。"按《説

文》據已譌的小篆，誤分羌字爲人與羊兩個偏旁。甲骨文前期羌字均作🕈，乃獨體象形字（第五期羌甲之羌，偶有作🕈者——前一·四一·七，周代金文因之），本象人戴羊角形，並非从羊。原始社會早期，人們爲了獵取野獸，往往披皮戴角，裝扮成野獸的樣子，以便接近於野獸而射擊之。後來戴角逐漸普及爲一般人的裝飾，以表示美觀。有的貴族婦女或部落酋長戴着雙角冠，以顯示尊榮。有的民族到奴隸社會甚至近現代，仍然保持着這種風尚（詳釋羌茍敬美）。至於《說文》謂羌从人羊，羊亦聲，已成爲會意兼形聲，與造字原意不符。總之，🕈爲獨體象形字，上部作𝀖形，既象人戴羊角形，同時也表示着以羊省聲爲音讀（甲骨文的宰字从羊省作𝀖者屢見）。但不能因此遂謂🕈字爲从人从羊省聲的形聲字。

二、《說文》："姜，神農居姜水，因以爲姓，从女羊聲。"按許説背於初文。甲骨文姜字作🕈，和🕈字的構形相仿，均爲獨體象形字。姜字上部从𝀖，既象女人戴羊角冠，同時也表示着姜字以羊省聲爲音符。

三、甲骨文秂字作🕈，研契諸家均誤釋爲往來之來。實則，秂字上部作禾省，下部爲來省聲，後世代以从禾來聲的秾字而秂字遂廢。《說文》："秾，齊謂麥秾也，从禾來聲。"甲骨文以麥爲大麥，以秂爲小麥（詳釋黍𥣬秂）。秂本爲獨體象形字，但其下部作來字的省體，也表示了秂字的音讀，然而不得謂爲从禾來省聲的形聲字。

四、甲骨文眉字有的作🕈形，象目上有眉形。又眉字也作🕈或🕈形，隸定作兜。兜字上部作𝀖，象人的眉形，這和🕈之上部作𝀖，象橫目以視，🕈之上部作🕈，象舉目以視，頗有相似之處。見兒兜三字都是獨體象形字，但是，見和兒的上部只是象目之橫與豎，而兜字的上部作𝀖，不僅象眉形，同時也表示着兜字的音讀。

五、《說文》："麋，鹿屬，从鹿米聲。麋冬至解其角。"《急就篇》的"貍兔飛鼯狼麋麛"，顏注："麋似鹿而大，冬至則角解。目上有眉，因以爲名也。"甲骨文麋字作🕈或🕈，其頭部作𝀖或𝀖，和人的眉目之眉同形。後世代之以从鹿米聲之麋，於是麋行而𪋮廢。總之，𪋮本爲獨體象形字，但其頭部作𝀖，也表示着𪋮字的音讀。

六、第一期早期自組甲骨文，有"弗疒朕天"（乙九〇六七）之貞，天字作🕈。此外，第一期甲骨文从天的字，如子𡕰世譜的𣦼字（影印拓本，也見庫一五〇六），右从天作🕈。又奀字（乙三八四三）下从天作🕈。第一期晚期的天字也有作🕈或🕈者。甲骨文晚期天字習見，均作🕈，爲了便於鍥刻，故上部化圓爲方。商

代金文天字，一般作🧍。天字構形的起源，是一個懸而未決的問題。《說文》："天，顛也，至高無上，从一大。"後世《說文》學家和近年來古文字學家對天字的說法，聚訟分歧，其至在六書歸屬問題上，也有指事會意象形之不同，令人困惑莫解。《說文》據已譌的小篆，而又割裂一與大爲二字，其荒謬自不待言。又《說文》既訓天爲顛，又訓顛爲頂。按顛頂雙聲，真耕通諧，但以聲爲訓，也解決不了它的造字本義。甲骨文早期的天字不多見，🧍形下部作夫，夫與大古通用，故甲骨文大甲也作夫甲。天字上部作〇或●，即古丁字，也即人之顛頂之頂字的初文。前文的"弗疒朕天"，是占卜人之顛頂之有無疾病。天本爲獨體象形字，由於天體高廣，無以爲象，故用人之顛頂以表示至上之義，但天字上部以丁爲頂，也表示着天字的音讀。

七、《說文》："須（俗作鬚），面毛也，从頁（首）从彡（所銜切）。"按甲骨文而字作𦓐或𦓑，即須字的初文（詳釋而）。周代金文始出現須字，作🗿或🗿（左右相連）。這是從獨體象形的而字，孳乳爲附加首形的須字。由於而字假作虛詞（《今文尚書》和《詩經》中的而字常見），久假不歸，遂別造須字以代之。《說文》依據小篆把須字分化爲"从頁从彡"，又誤以"毛飾畫文"之彡爲偏旁，遂成爲會意字。其實，即使後來分化爲二，也當作"从頁彡（讀須）聲"的形聲字。這和上一條的乘變爲秣同例。總之，須本爲獨體象形字，但其所連接的三邪劃，也表示着須字的音讀。

八、甲骨文和周代早期金文，均以🕺或🕺（隸變作無）爲舞。東周器余義鐘以訶遻爲歌舞。遻字从止，以表示行動，但遻字後世並未通行。甲骨文以亡爲有無之無，而周代金文則多借無爲有無之無。《說文》訓無爲豐，訓橆（後起字）爲亡，均與造字本義不符。《說文》舞字作𦐇，並謂"舞樂也，用足相背，从舛無聲"。《說文繫傳》："舛，兩足左右也，兩足左右蹈厲也。"按許氏不知缺疑，本諸小篆，割裂舞字形體以爲之解，乖謬之至。早期古文未見舞字。近年來房山縣琉璃河西周燕墓出土之圓盤形銅器上有"匽医舞易"四字，舞字作🕺，上部象人兩手執舞器，下部象兩足均有足止（趾），用以表示手舞足蹈之形。這是由無字孳乳爲舞，成爲舞字的初文。所謂"中流失船，一壺千金"。古文早期之人形，从止（趾，下同）與否本來無別，但後期則不盡然，比如周器穆公鼎的燊作🔥（甲骨文之炎字作🔥），是其例。然而《說文》也把燊字割裂爲"从炎舛"。古文無與舞均用作舞蹈字，只是有早晚期之別而已。周代多借無爲有無字，因而別制舞字以爲區別。總之，後起的舞爲獨體象形字，其上部既象左右執舞器，同時也

表示着舞字的音讀。

依據上述，前八條的羌、姜、乘、兔、甮、天和須、舞等字，除天字外，其它各字後世都分化爲形聲字。其中甮字，後世則代以從鹿米聲的麋。但它們在未分化爲形聲字以前，和天字相同，都是具有部分表音的獨體象形字。總之，具有部分表音的獨體象形字，是界乎象形和形聲兩者之間，可稱作"獨體形聲"，這類文字可能將來仍有發現。由此看來，本文對於六書的範疇，已經初次作出突破。

釋古文字中附劃因聲指事字的一例

説文解字敘："指事者，視而可識，察而見意，上下是也。"按上下二字以及一至九的紀數字，都屬於抽象指事。指事屬於六書之一。六書者，乃後人用歸納方法把所有文字劃分爲六個範疇。六書中的象形會意和形聲尚易辨認。而自來《説文》學家對於指事的説法，頗多分歧，在此不煩引述。象形和指事之別，物有形，故可象，事無形，故須有所指以見意。會意與指事之別，會意是由兩個或兩個以上的獨立偏旁所組成。而指事字的構成，有的連一個獨立偏旁也不具備，而由極簡的點劃所構成，這是原始的指事字；有的僅有一個獨立的偏旁，而附以並非正式偏旁的極簡單的點劃以發揮其作用，這是後起的指事字。本文所論證的是："古文字中附劃因聲指事字的一例。"這一類型的指事字，雖然也有音符，但和一般形聲字都爲一形一聲兩個正式偏旁所配合的迥然不同。本文所論列的指事字，和前人的説法雖然也有偶合之處，但不盡相同，而且，前人還未曾發現這一通例。這一類型指事字的特徵，是在某個獨體字上附加一種極簡單的點劃作爲標志，賦予它以新的含意，但仍因原來的獨體字以爲音符，而其音讀又略有轉變。這當然是陸續後起的指事字。現僅就一時所知，分條予以闡述。

史——吏。《説文》："史，記事者也，从又持中，中，正也。"又："吏，治人者也，从一从史，史亦聲。"又："事，職也，从史之省聲。"又："使，伶也，从人吏聲。"按古文字吏與事同字，有時與史通用。古文無使字，使乃後起的分化文。吳大澂《説文古籀補》謂史字象"手執簡形"。江永《周禮疑義舉要》："凡官府簿書謂之中，……其字从又从中，又者右手，以手持簿書也。"王國維《釋史》從江永説，而謂："是中者盛筭之器也。"按吳江王三氏之説都不可信。古文

字中與中迥別，中字卜辭屢見，乃㞢字的省文，與事字通用。其造字本義待考。依據《說文》則吏為會意兼形聲字，事為形聲字。甲骨文的吏與事均作㞢，既不從一，也不從之，則許說不攻自破。史與吏的初文，自應以甲骨文為準。㞢字的造字本義，係於㞢字豎劃的上端分作兩叉形，作為指事字的標誌，以別於史，而仍因史字以為聲。

束——東。甲骨文束字作㯮。東字並非從日，通常作㯮，中期有時作㯮或㯮。《說文》束作㯮，並謂："束，縛也，從口（音圍）木。"《說文》東作㯮，並謂："東，動也，從木。官溥說，從日在木中。"段注："木，榑木也，日在木中曰東。"朱駿聲《說文通訓定聲》："從日在木中，會意。木，叒木，榑桑也。《離騷》折若木以拂日。"按段朱二氏均傅會許說，毫不足據。林義光《文源》："古日作⊙不作㊀。"又引金文偏旁東束互作，並謂："東與束同字，東束雙聲對轉，束聲之涑亦轉入東部。四方之名，西南北皆借字，則東方亦不當獨制字也。"按林說甚是，但還不知東為指事字。甲骨文東與束每互作，例如：東方之東也作束（南北師二·五六，此例屢見），橐字或從束（乙三四七八，此例屢見），是其證。東字的造字本義，係於束字的中部附加一橫，作為指事字的標誌，以別於束，而仍因束字以為聲。

東——重。《說文》重字作㯮，並謂："重，厚也，從壬東聲。"按許氏據已譌的小篆為解，故誤為從壬。甲骨文無重字，而量字從重多作㯮，也有從㯮者（詳釋量）。周代金文的中甗和克鼎，量字也均從重作㯮，與甲骨文形同。又東周器陳侯因資錞"斢（紹）緟高祖黃啻（帝）"之緟，《說文》作緟。重字的造字本義，係於東字上部附加一個橫劃，作為指事字的標誌，以別於東，而仍因東字以為聲。

月——夕。《說文》月字作㠯，並謂："月，闕也，太陰之精，象形。"《說文》夕字作㠯，並謂："夕，莫也，從月半見。"段注："旦者日全見地上，莫者日在茻中，夕者月半見，皆會意象形也。"王筠《說文句讀》："黃昏之時，日光尚在，則月不大明，故曰半見。"林義光《文源》："夕月初本同字，暮時見月，因謂暮為月，猶晝謂之日，夜晴謂之星也。後分為二音，始於中加一畫為別，而加畫者乃用為本義之月，象月形者反用為引伸義之夕。"以上所引各說，林說有一定的道理，其餘都係望文生義，無一可取。月與夕之別雖然只爭一劃之有無，但也是文字學上的千古疑案。林氏已經看出這一疑案的是非，而不知其根本原由。甲骨文由第一期到第四期，月字作☽或☾，夕字作☽或☾，而第五期的月字作☽或☾，夕字作☽或☾。雖然前後期的月與夕也偶然有時相混，但畢竟是個別的現

象。至於西周金文的月字均作☽，夕字均作☾，兩者互作是極爲個別的，而在偏旁中則互見較多。西周金文月夕二字之所以顛倒，是由於沿襲了甲骨文的晚期作風，一直到小篆仍然如此。話又說回來，爲什麼甲骨文前四期的夕字在月字中間加一豎劃？夕字在六書中屬於哪個範疇？我認爲，月本有形可象，夕則無形可象，故夕字的造字本義，乃於月字的中間附加一個豎劃，作爲指事字的標志，以別於月，而仍因月字以爲聲。

　　白——百。《說文》："百，十十也，從一白。數，十百爲一貫，相章也。"按百字從一白，已與初文相背。戴侗《六書故》："百也當以白爲聲。"林義光《文源》："古作🜂，當爲白之或體，∧∧皆象薄膜虛起形。"戴說較舊解爲優，但誤認爲形聲，與造字本義不符。林說殊誤。甲骨文第一期早期的百字作🜂，稍後又孳乳作🜂，也省作🜂。此外，甲骨文還有借白以爲百者，如"三白羌"（燕二四五）即三百羌。百字的造字本義，係於白字中部附加一個折角形的曲劃，作爲指事字的標志，以別於白，而仍因白字以爲聲。

　　人——千。《說文》千字作𐅝，並謂："千，十百也，從十人聲。"按甲骨文千字作𐅝或𐅝，金文同。許氏不知古文十作丨，七作十，而割裂千字的下部，誤以爲從十百之十。孔廣居《說文疑疑》："千當訓從一人聲，十百千皆數之成，故皆從一。"孔氏謂千從人聲是對的，但以數之成爲言也誤。千字的造字本義，係在人字的中部附加一個橫劃，作爲指事字的標志，以別於人，而仍因人字以爲聲（人千疊韻）。

　　又——尤。《說文》尤字作𠃌，並謂："尤，異也，從乙又聲。"《說文繫傳》："乙者欲出而見閡，見閡則顯其尤異也。"徐灝《說文段注箋》："尤，過也，從乙，艸木出土也。物過盛則異於常，是曰尤。"林義光《文源》："又象手形，乙抽也，尤異之物自手中抽出之也。"許氏據已譌之小篆，誤認尤字從乙，又誤認爲形聲字。至於其他三家之說，也均紆回不通。甲骨文尤字習見，作𠃌或𠃌，金文作𠃌，上部皆從橫劃或邪劃，下部右側無從乙者。尤字的造字本義，係於又字上部附加一個橫劃或邪劃，作爲指事字的標志，以別於又，而仍因又字以爲聲。

　　弓——弘。《說文》弘字作𢎞，並謂："弘，弓聲也，從弓厶聲。厶古文肱字。"許氏誤以弘爲形聲字。甲骨文弘字作𢎞或𢎞，西周金文作𢎞。其弓背隆起處乃弓的高出部分，故典籍多訓弘爲高爲大，高與大義相因。金文弘字的右側已由邪劃變爲彎劃，而小篆的彎劃又與弓形分化爲二，故作弘。𢎞字的造字本義，係於弓背隆起處附一個邪劃，作爲指事字的標志，以別於弓，而仍因弓字以爲聲。

　　矢——寅。《說文》："寅，髕也，正月陽氣動，去黃泉，欲上出，陰尚彊，象

宀不達，髕寅於下也。"按許氏據訛的小篆妄爲之解，而自來《說文》學家仍拘泥許說，加以緣飾。近代文字學家多援引金文爲說，均無是處，無須列引。甲骨文早期干支的寅字均作🔺，即古矢字。後來一變爲🔺🔺🔺🔺，再變爲🔺🔺。金文早期作🔺🔺🔺🔺，晚期作🔺🔺🔺。總之，寅字的初文，係借用弓矢的矢字，所謂造字假借，這和借𠦪（鳳）爲風，借匚爲報同例。古音矢與寅雙聲，矢屬審紐三等，寅屬喻紐四等，並讀爲舌頭。本諸上述，則寅字的造字由來，假借弓矢之矢以爲寅。後來因爲矢與寅用各有當，故於矢字的中部加一方框，作爲指事字的標志，以別於矢，而仍因矢字以爲聲。當然，寅字後來訛化滋甚，與矢字大有出入，已脫離了指事字的範疇。

用——甬。《說文》用作🔺，並謂："用，可施行也，从卜中，衛宏說。"又甬作🔺，並謂："甬，艸木華甬甬然也，从𠃑用聲。"按許氏釋用和甬，根本不可靠。甲骨文用字的初文作🔺，即古桶字，後來又變爲🔺（詳釋用），西周金文車器"金甬"之甬屢見，均作🔺，後來又變爲🔺。江小仲鼎的"自作甬鼎"，曾姬無卹壺的"後嗣甬之"，均以甬爲用。甬字的造字本義，係於用字上部附加半圓形，作爲指事字的標志，以別於用，而仍因用字以爲聲。

口——甘。《說文》："甘，美也，从口含一，一道也。"按許說不足爲據，而自來解者又附和之，訓道爲味道。甘字《說文繫傳》以爲指事，這是對的。王筠《說文句讀》謂"以會意定指事字"，朱駿聲《說文通訓定聲》謂"會意兼指事"，俞樾《兒笘錄》以爲象形。以上各說，無一可通。甲骨文甘字作🔺，用作地名。甘之訓美見於周代典籍。古化文甘丹（邯鄲）之甘作🔺。甘字的造字本義，係於口字中附加一劃，作爲指事字的標志，以別於口，而仍因口字以爲聲（甘口雙聲）。

母——每。《說文》每作🔺，並謂："每，艸盛上出也，从屮母聲。"按許說不足爲據，而自來文字學家並無異議。甲骨文母與女互用無別。甲骨文每字作🔺或🔺，後來又變作🔺。甲骨文每字既不从屮也不作艸盛用，艸盛乃後起之義。甲骨文每字多用作悔吝之悔或晦冥之晦。每字的造字本義，係於母字的上部附加一個∨劃，作爲指事字的標志，以別於母，而仍因母字以爲聲。

母——毋。《說文》毋字作🔺，並謂："毋，止之也，从女有奸之者。"《禮記·曲禮》的"毋不敬"，陸氏《釋文》："《說文》云，止之詞。其字从女，內有一畫，象有奸之形，禁止之勿令奸。"按許說荒謬，而陸氏還予以附會，自來《說文》學家又隨聲附和，遂成定論。甲骨文和金文均借用母字以爲否定詞之

毋。《詛楚文》的"葉萬子孫毋相爲不利"，毋字作㑒。古鉩文作㑒，秦權和詔版毋字習見。毋字的造字本義，係把母字的兩點變爲一個橫劃，作爲指事字的標志，以別於母，而仍因母字以爲聲。

亼──今。《説文》："今，是時也，从亼ㄱ，ㄱ古文及。"段注："會意。ㄱ逮也，ㄱ亦聲。"王筠《説文句讀》："今與亼ㄱ皆平入疊韻，是亼ㄱ皆義又皆聲也。"徐灝《説文段注箋》："ㄱ即乙字，艸木冤曲難出之義。"林義光《文源》謂亼"即含之古文。亼爲口之倒文，亦口字。亼象口含物形"。按今字甲骨文早期作亼，後期作亼，金文作亼或亼。甲骨文作亼，爲今字的初文，然則《説文》以爲从ㄱ，以及諸家的解説，均失去了依據。我認爲，今字係从一亼聲（詳釋会），《説文》："亼，三合也，从入一，象三合之形，讀若集。"按《説文》从入一之説，殊誤。亼與集疊韻，均屬緝部。今字的造字本義，係於亼字的下部附加一個橫劃，作爲指事字的標志，以別於亼，而仍因亼字以爲聲。

小──少。《説文》："小，物之微也，从八丨，見而分之。"又："少，不多也，从小丿聲。"又："尐，少也，从小ㄱ聲，讀若輟。"按許氏釋小少尐三字並誤。甲骨文小與少同用，後世分化爲二字。甲骨文小字作小，既不从八也不从丨。小字作三小點以表示物之微小。甲骨文少字作少，無从丿者。果如許説，則小爲會意字，少與尐爲形聲字，均背於初文。少字，春秋時金文酃侯簋作少，弓鎛作少，蔡侯鐘作少，都是後起的變形。其中少字作少，本來反正無別。本諸上述，則少字的造字本義，係於小字下部附加一個小點，作爲指事字的標志，以別於小，而仍因小字以爲聲。

从──并。《説文》："并，相從也，从从幵聲。一曰，从持二爲并。"徐灝《説文段注箋》："并不得用幵爲聲。从持二干會意，於義爲長。"林義光《文源》："幵非聲，二人各持一干，亦非并聲。秦權量皇帝盡并兼天下，并皆作并，从二人並立，二并之象。"按許氏分爲兩種説法，徐氏以爲會意，均誤。林説較優，但也不夠明確。甲骨文并字作并、并或并。并字的造字本義，係於从字的下部附加一個或兩個橫劃，作爲二人相連的指事字的標志，以別於从，而仍因从字以爲聲（東耕通諧）。

高──喬。《説文》喬字作喬，並謂："喬，高而曲也，从夭从高省。"按許説殊誤。據古文字則喬字既不从夭，也不从高省。喬字東周金文邵鐘作喬。曾伯陭壺的鐈字从喬作鐈或鐈。喬字的造字本義，係於高字上部附加一個曲劃，作爲指事字的標志，以別於高，而仍因高字以爲聲。

大——太。《説文》："泰，滑也，从廾水，大聲。夳，古文泰如此。"段注："當作夳，从夰取滑之意也。"許説和段注均不可據。春秋時器䚄塙"太室"之太作夳。太字下从ヘ，依大字下部的空隙，因形隨勢而作曲劃。這和甲骨文百字作𤰃，也因白字上半三角形的空隙而加ヘ是相同的。太爲大的後起字。典籍中太與大每同用，又訓太爲大之極爲甚。由於用各有當，以致分化。太字的造字本義，係於大字下部附加一個折角形的曲劃，作爲指事字的標志，以別於大，而仍因大字以爲聲。

言——音。《説文》："言，直言曰言，論難曰語，从口辛聲。"又："音，聲也。……从言含一。"按甲骨文言字作𠱝，在偏旁中則作𠙵或𠱭（詳釋設）。許氏誤認爲形聲字。甲骨文有言無音。西周金文音字作𠱭，與言字作𠱝者互用無別，後來由於用各有當，因而分化。音字的造字本義，係於言字下部的口字中附加一個小橫劃，作爲指事字的標志，以別於言，而仍因言字以爲聲（言音古通用，詳鄂君啓節考釋）。

言——䇂。《説文》："䇂，快也，从言从中。"又："意，滿也，从心䇂聲。一曰，十萬曰意。"按許氏誤以䇂爲从中。䇂即十萬曰意之意的初文，俗字作億。甲骨文的劓字从䇂作𠱭（京都三〇一六），弔口鼎（西清二·二七）的"其萬䇂年"，䇂字作𠱭，命瓜（令狐）君壺的"至于萬䇂年"，䇂字作𠱭，从〇音聲。〇形中的點乃羨劃，古文字乘隙加點或劃者習見。甲骨文有言無音，往往以言爲音，讀爲歆饗之歆，周代金文的言與音以及偏旁中从言从音，每互作無別。漢魯峻碑的"永傳䇂年"，孔宙碑的"䇂載揚聲"，均以䇂爲億，猶存古文。䇂字的造字本義，係於言字中部附加一個圓圈，作爲指事字的標志，以別於言，而仍因言字以爲聲（言音古同用，音億雙聲）。

氏——氐。甲骨文氐字只一見，作𠄌（後下二一·六，辭已殘）。又甲骨文氏字習見，作𠄌或𠄍，余舊誤釋爲氐。甲骨文𥃳字常見，从氏作𠄌也作𠄍。由於鍥刻不便作實點，故氏字之點皆作〇形。周代金文氏字多作𠄌，其點皆在豎劃或邪劃的中部。後來變點爲橫則作𠄎，但無論點或橫，從没有在氏字下部者。石鼓文"其簍氏鮮"之氏作𠄌。周器害簋的氐字，从氏作𠄎。《説文》氐作𠄎，並謂："氐，至也，本也，从氏下箸一，一，地也。"按氏字下部本从點，後世變點爲橫，許氏遂誤以爲从一。典籍氏字多通氐，《爾雅·釋言》："氐，致也。"《説文》："致，送詣也。"《書·禹貢》的"覃懷氐績"，《史記·夏本紀》氐作致。按凡物由彼送至此爲致。甲骨文氏字訓爲致，於義均可通。氏字的造字本義，係於

氏字豎劃或邪劃的下部附加一點，作爲指事字的標志，以別於氏，而仍因氏字以爲聲（氐氏雙聲）。

止——世。甲骨文笹字只一見，作 形（續存上一二三七，辭已殘），舊不識。按笹字从竹世聲，世字作 ，需要加以說明。《說文》世字作 ，並謂："世，三十年爲一世，从卅而曳長之，亦取其聲也。"段注："曳長之謂末筆也。末筆曳長，即爲十二部之乁，从反厂，亦是抴引之義。世合卅乁會意，亦取乁聲爲聲，讀如曳也。"林義光《文源》：世"當爲葉之古文，象莖及葉之形。草木之葉重累百疊，故引伸爲世代之世"。按許說出諸杜撰，段氏還阿附其說，林氏又以草木莖葉爲解，這都無異後世的拆字和猜謎，毫無道理。其實，周代金文有的以止爲世（伯尊），有的以杫（从止聲，見楿簋）爲世，可見止與世有時通用。又世字師晨鼎和師遽簋作 ，寧簋作 ，在止字上部加一點或三點，以表示和止字的區別。石鼓文世字作 ，變三點爲三橫，爲《說文》所本。此外，最引人注意的是，周器祖日庚簋"用笹言孝"的笹字作 ，和甲骨文的 字完全相同，只是其三點有虛實之別而已。笹字雖然不見於後世字書，但簋文以笹爲世，也證明了笹从世聲，與世同用。因此可知，世字的造字本義，係於止字上部附加一點或三點，以別於止，而仍因止字以爲聲（止世雙聲）。

除上述外，還要加以說明的是，各個附劃因聲指事字，在沒有附加點或劃以前和既已附加點或劃以後，有的仍然同用，並非完全等齊劃一，判然分爲兩個字。例如文中所闡述的史與事，月與夕，朿與東，東與重，白與百，用與甬，小與少，言與音，止與世等，是其證。本文論證的結果，可以概括爲三項：一，附劃因聲指事字，是由於文字孳乳愈多而采取了因利乘便的方法，在獨體字上附加極爲簡單的點劃，作爲區別，既可以達到指其事的目的，而又因原字以爲聲符，一舉兩得。二，附劃因聲指事字所附加的各種點劃，只是起着記號的辨別作用，既不成爲偏旁，當然也不是個獨體字。自來《說文》學家把屬於這種類型的指事字，有的不知道它具有聲符，而誤作會意；有的知道它有聲符，而誤作形聲；有的也以爲指事字，而和會意或形聲字界劃不清。三，附劃因聲指事字的發現，不僅尋出了一個重要的通例，而更重要的是，可以徹底明瞭這些指事字的創造由來。

原收入《甲骨文字釋林》，中華書局，1979 年；又 2007 年（作爲《于省吾著作集》之一種）；又商務印書館，2010、2017 年。今據初版收入，並吸收了商務版書後林澐先生的兩條相關校勘意見。

郭若愚

049 | 釋䖵

我屢次見到甲骨文裏的䖵字，總覺得它應該是一個象形字，象一個什麼小動物。具體地說，象一隻蟲豸。

葉玉森以爲象蟬，他因此釋爲夏字；唐蘭以爲象龜，聯想到魏字，就釋爲秋字。

釋夏和秋似乎覺得很勉强，我覺得却象一隻蝗蟲，有觸角、身翼、肢足，一個蝗蟲的各部分都具備了。而且《鐵雲藏龜》153頁2片有此字，象蝗之外，還特别刻劃出蝗的口器。

《説文》："蝗，螽也，从虫皇聲。"

《説文》："螽，蝗也，从䖵冬聲。冬古文終字，螽或从虫眾聲。"

據此，蝗和螽在原來是同一意義的。段玉裁注："䖵部曰螽，蝗也。是爲轉注。……於春秋爲螽，今謂之蝗。按螽蝗古今語也。"《説文校義》："蝗、當作螽也。"殷人見到一群群飛蝗，就造䖵字，又因它是成群成隊的，就音爲衆。後來便發展爲形聲字螽，或𧓕（見《説文通訓定聲》），戰國及其以前是在䖵上加終爲螽，漢代以後又另用蝗字。《春秋》及《詩經》用螽。所以我認爲䖵字可釋爲螽。

螽字的引申意義是災禍。《春秋·桓五年》"秋，螽"，《榖梁》："蟲災也。"我國古代蟲害對於農業最有密切關係的便是蝗災，殷代的奴隸們對於這種成群結隊、到處吞噬農作物的飛蝗是十分恐懼的；殷王朝的奴隸主對它同樣是害怕的，占卜的史官也就把䖵字刻上了甲骨版。

……貞䖵其至。

庚申卜，出貞：今歲，䖵不至兹商？二月　　　《甲骨文録》687

這是祖庚祖甲時史官出貞卜的一片胛骨,在庚申那天正卜問蝗災的"其至"和"不至",卜問的地點在商,時間在二月。

庚午卜,貞:豕友亡蠱吕南。七月	《鄴二集》下 35・1
象蠱稱至商。六月	《甲骨文字》卷 2・15・8

（以上兩條郭沫若先生所增）

第一條卜辭是庚午那天卜問:"豕那地方沒有蠱災嗎?"吕南據意推測,可能是蝗災向南延展。這條卜辭卜問的時間是七月。第二條卜辭是卜問蠱至不至商,時間是六月。

戊申卜,貞:蠱……	《殷契卜辭》592
壬子卜,貞:□蠱□	《前編》6・51・3
□卜,蠱至。四月	《前編》4・5・5
庚戌卜,有蠱……	《甲骨文字》2・18・3
今蠱其有降歆。	《甲骨文字》2・26・13

這幾條都是卜問有關蠱的卜辭,因爲有殘,不能很清楚地知道蠱的意義,但如釋蠱爲蝗災,就都能讀通。如第五條説:"現在蝗災有沒有降到這裏的可能?"含義是很清楚的。

卜辭還有"告蠱"的記載。"告"是祭名,是祭祀祖先庇佑,免除蝗災:

□戊貞:其告蠱于高祖夒。六□	《粹編》2
其告蠱上甲。	《粹編》4
□□貞其告蠱于夒,□牛。	《粹編》14
其告蠱上甲,二牛、三牛、四牛。	《粹編》88
丁巳□,告蠱□由令。七月	《甲骨文字》2・18・2

告蠱的祖先有"高祖夒"及上甲,這是殷代的遠祖,亦就是威望較大的祖先。祭品用牛,有二、三、四頭。

蝗災一旦發生,又亟需灼龜卜問:

……賓貞:唯今蠱……	《後編》下 12・14
唯今夒。唯今蠱。于矛,迭申素	《粹編》1151
唯蠱令畢。唯□令田。	《粹編》946

蝗災發生,殷人也採用一些撲滅的方法。如燹字似乎告訴我們他們已採用燒

火滅蝗的辦法；"令畢"是採用網捕捉的方法。還有一些殘辭，含義也大致可以瞭解的：

今龘㗊黍□……　　　　　　　　　　　　　　　　　　　　《粹編》878

㗊字由四口組成，《說文》"㗊，眾口也"，正象蝗蟲成群結隊在吞噬農作物。黍是殷代常常種植的糧食，卜辭中屢見。

□□卜，□□龘□□至。四月　　　　　　　　　　　　　　《甲骨文字》2·18·4

郭沫若先生說：這辭該作"(干支)卜貞今龘方其至　四月"，龘方可以作爲方國名。但如釋龘爲蝗災，也可通。

庚午貞：龘大隻于帝五丯臣血□，在且(祖)乙宗卜。　　　　　　《粹編》12

隻字从隹冉聲，擬爲集字。那麼庚午這天貞卜的是說在"帝五丯"的地方(指五處地方)，都發生蝗災，因此在祖乙的宗廟裏卜問，還舉行祭典。

卜辭還有龜字：

己未宛龜夗往自□圍。　　　　　　　　　　　　　　　《後編》下41·1

……龜夗辛自□六人。八月　　　　　　　　　　　　　　《卜辭》124

辛字郭沫若先生說："辛字不識，他辭有'虎辛羊災'一例(《鐵雲》271·2)，虎羊當係虎方(南宮中鼎)、羊方(《前編》6·60·6)二國名。則辛當係攻伐之意。'辛□五人'要必爲人禍。"(見《甲骨文字研究·釋蝕》)則辛爲向蝗災攻伐，龜爲捕蝗之義。卜辭尚有魯、雀、象等文。商承祚說："魯字卜辭恆見。以文義釋之，亦是漁字，與魯同爲變體。从八口皆象取魚之具。"以此類推，雀爲捕鳥，象爲捕獸，龜爲捕蝗。

春秋時對於蝗災的記載，有文獻可徵了(并見《前漢書·五行志》)，今錄之以爲佐證：

釐公十五年八月，螽。

文公三年秋，雨螽于宋。

文公八年十月，螽。

宣公六年秋八月，螽。

宣公十三年秋，螽。

宣公十五年秋，螽。

襄公七年八月,螽。

哀公十二年冬十有二月,螽。

哀公十三年九月,螽。

哀公十三年十有二月,螽。

《前漢書》蝗災的記載是:

景帝中元三年秋,蝗。

武帝元光六年夏,蝗。

武帝元鼎五年秋,蝗。

武帝元封六年秋,蝗。

武帝太初元年夏,蝗從東方飛至敦煌。

武帝征和三年秋,蝗。四年夏,蝗。

平帝元始二年秋,蝗遍天下。

《後漢書》蝗災的記載是:

武帝建武四年,蝗。《古今注》:建武二十二年三月京師郡國十九蝗。二十三年京師郡國十八大蝗旱,草木盡。二十八年三月郡國八十蝗。二十九年四月武威、酒泉、清河、京兆、魏郡、弘農蝗。

武帝建武三十年六月,郡國十二大蝗。

武帝建和三十一年,郡國大蝗。

武帝中元元年三月,郡國六大蝗。

明帝永平四年十二月,酒泉大蝗,從塞外入。

明帝永平八年五月,河內、陳留蝗。九月,京都蝗。九年,蝗,從夏至秋。

安帝永初四年夏,蝗。

安帝永初五年夏,九州蝗。

安帝永初六年三月,去蝗處復蝗子生。七年夏,蝗。

安帝元初元年夏,郡國五蝗。

安帝元初二年夏,郡國二十蝗。

順帝延光元年六月,郡國蝗。

順帝永建五年,郡國十二蝗。

順帝永和元年秋七月,偃師蝗。

桓帝永興元年七月,郡國三十二蝗。二年六月,京都蝗。

桓帝永壽三年六月，京都蝗。

桓帝延熹元年五月，京都蝗。

靈帝熹平六年夏，七州蝗。

獻帝興平元年夏，大蝗。

獻帝建安二年五月，蝗。

以上所録各條，均經郭沫若先生校正。

〔作者附記〕 1947年夏季，我幸福地會見了郭沫若先生，向他學習殷契文字。郭先生誨人不倦，循循善誘，使我在短暫的時間裏，知道了一些甲骨文字的基本知識。我當時也學習了撰寫一些簡短的論文，請郭先生指正。郭先生除了爲我校對甲骨圖版、查考原書以及修改文字以外，諄諄教導我做學問要實事求是，不能信口開河。嚴師的教言，雖然事隔三十餘年，還是清音在耳，銘記於心。

這篇短文是比較像樣的一篇，當時郭先生認爲可備一説。今年（1979）夏季，我檢出原稿，見到了上面郭先生批改的字迹，使我感慨萬分。敬愛的郭沫若先生逝世已經一周年了。我寫了一篇紀念他的文章，此篇作爲附録，藉以表達懷念之情。今將此篇先予發表，請求讀者指正。

原載《上海師範學院學報》1979年第2期，有副題"向郭沫若先生學習殷契文字習作之一"；收入宋鎮豪、段志洪主編：《甲骨文獻集成》第13册，四川大學出版社，2001年；又省略副題收入郭若愚：《智龕金石書畫論集》，上海古籍出版社，2007年。今據後者收入。

林 澐

從武丁時代的幾種"子卜辭"試論商代的家族形態

長期以來，在多數甲骨研究者中有一種相當普遍的誤解，即以爲出於安陽小屯的全部甲骨刻辭都是王室之物。董作賓的"殷曆譜"體系，就是基於這種臆斷之上的。

在較深入地整理全部甲骨資料時，有個別研究者曾根據字體、祭祀對象、稱謂和卜人等特徵，認爲在小屯出土的卜辭中存在着"非王卜辭"①。但並未弄清這些"非王卜辭"的性質，却立了一些難以令人信服的假設。因此，這批數量雖少而有重要歷史價值的資料，至今還沒有引起史學界普遍的重視。

在研究我國階級社會産生和發展這一重大問題時，商代佔有特殊的地位。但當我們試圖恢復歷史的真面目時，又每苦於缺乏有關商代社會基本結構的直接史料。所謂的"非王卜辭"，恰恰在這方面提供了一些原始資料。

毛主席強調指出，在應用馬克思列寧主義的立場、觀點、方法認真研究中國歷史時，"要根據詳細的材料加以具體的分析，然後引出理論性的結論來"。本文只是一種初步嘗試，希望有更多的同志一起努力去做。

一　主要的三種"非王卜辭"的特徵和時代

在以前的研究者已經區別出來的"非王卜辭"中，數量最多而特別有研究價

---

① 貝塚茂樹、伊藤道治：《甲骨文斷代研究之再檢討》，《東方學報（京都）》第 23 期，1953 年。
李學勤：《帝乙時代的非王卜辭》，《考古學報》1958 年 1 期。

值的，有以下三種：

1. 甲種

集中出於小屯 YH251、YH253、YH330 三個灰坑中。其中 YH251 出土的乙 8712，同 YH330 出土的乙 8946、乙 8944 可以綴合（綴合後著錄爲合 22322），該版又和 YH253 的合 22324 爲同辭異刻的成套卜辭。這三坑出土的全爲卜甲，字體、稱謂和辭例相同，故可視爲一個整體。

這種卜辭不記卜人名。記干支的前辭形式有"干支卜貞"、"干支卜"、"干支貞"三種。字體的最大特色是同一字的寫法很不統一。如：合 22289 同一版上的貞字有 𠦝、𠁱 兩種寫法，合 22288 同一版上又有 𠦝、𠁱、𠁱 三種寫法，總計這種卜辭貞字的異體不下十種之多。

祭祀對象最主要是匕庚、匕丁、中母、小母、母庚、父丁、兄、子丁。其他還有匕己、匕辛、匕戊、中匕等。

這種卜辭在其他著錄中散見者，可舉合 22249、合 22269 等片爲例。

2. 乙種

集中出於小屯 YH127 這個灰坑。另外，YH448 出土的合 22467，也屬本羣。

這種卜辭也不記卜人名①。記干支的前辭形式有"干支卜貞"、"干支卜"、"干支貞"三種。字體最顯著特徵是筆劃轉折陡峭，基本沒有曲筆。例如：乙作 𠃌，申作 𠁙。貞字則多數作 𠁱。這種字體的干支表見於合 22093。

祭祀對象主要是內乙、下乙、祖庚、祖戊、父戊、父丁、子庚、匕乙、匕辛、匕癸、兄己。此外還有石甲、工乙、天戊、司戊、外戊、內己、祖己、祖辛、祖壬、祖丁、匕己（高匕己）、匕丁、匕壬、中匕、父己、父丙、父乙、母戊等。

合 22108、合 22305 是這種卜辭。此外，散見於《前》、《後》、《續》、《粹》、《鐵》、《京津》、《佚存》等著錄中。

---

① 過去有人認爲這種卜辭有卜人午和 𠁙，定名爲"午組卜辭"、"𠁙卜辭"。其實，午是祭名"卸（禦）"的省體，參看合 22047 及合 22092 兩版自明。𠁙 字見於合 22129 的那一條，辭殘不可通讀。見於合 22074 的兩條，凡冠 𠁙，均言"卸某至某"，似有合祭之義，不能確定爲卜人名。

3. 丙種

也集中出於 YH127 這個灰坑。YH090 僅出一片卜甲（合 21722），亦屬本群。甲編中發表的 1 區 9 坑和 2 區 26 坑出土的甲骨中，也有這種卜辭（合 21817、甲 158）。

卜人稱謂有子、余、我、𠂤、巡五種。記干支的前辭形式有"干支卜某貞"、"干支某卜貞"、"干支某卜"、"干支卜貞"、"干支卜"、"干支貞"六種。字體特色是細小而多曲筆，貞字一律作 ␣，其他各字也寫法劃一，幾乎沒有異構。干支表見合 21784、合 21783。

祭祀對象最主要是妣庚、妣丁、妣己、父庚、父戊、母庚、中母己、兄丁、子丁、␣甲及龍母。此外還有司妣甲、妣壬、二妣己、司妣、祖乙、南庚、司癸、小辛、司、␣、伊尹、小己、父甲、父辛等。

這種卜辭散見於其他甲骨著錄者甚多，不煩一一列舉。

另外，在 YH127 中還有兩類卜辭：（a）貞字作 ␣；（b）貞字作 ␣，刀法最劣。

在其他著錄中，如合 22227、合 21893、合 21954、合 21897、合 22231、合 22010、續 6·26·3、合 21872、京津 3156、合 21902、英 1915 等片均屬 a 類。合 22509、合 22469 屬 b 類。這兩類卜辭字體雖然和上述貞字作 ␣ 的很不相同，但主要祭祀對象也是妣庚、妣丁、妣己和子丁。其他辭例也和丙種有不少相同之處，又同出於 YH127 這一灰坑。而且，合 21872 這版，正面貞字作 a 式，反面貞字作 b 式。總之，以上三者之間關係密切。故將後兩類分別命名爲"丙種 a 屬"和"丙種 b 屬"，附入丙種之中。

關於這三種卜辭的斷代，過去分歧很大。如果拋棄"殷曆譜"一派種種主觀武斷的斷代標準，客觀地分析這一問題，有以下三種現象特別值得注意。

1. 同版現象

第一例：補 6829 這一完整龜甲上，"辛巳貞：啟弟"、"又羊，又豕，卒（邕）妣庚"，兩辭爲甲種字體，其餘各辭都是丙種字體。

第二例：合 21784 這一牛胛骨，下部是丙種字體的干支表，而上端是典型的武丁時代王室卜辭（即所謂"賓組卜辭"）字體的卜旬辭，卜人爲爭。羅氏輯錄

時無理地截去了拓本的上端。原骨現藏吉林大學文物室①。

第三例：合 22094 這一龜甲上，"壬寅卜，禦量于父戊。——壬寅卜，禦量于內乙"。是乙種字體。而"壬寅卜，禦石于□戊"、"乙巳，于天癸"、"其凶畀"等辭，都是典型的𠂤組大字字體。而所謂"𠂤組卜辭"，我在 1965 年已考定是武丁前期的王室卜辭，關於𠂤組卜辭之屬於武丁時代，則已由 1973 年安陽小屯南地的最新發掘成果所證實。

2. 同坑現象

甲編所錄甲骨，坑位記錄至今尚未全部發表。且因當時發掘水平低，地層坑位本不甚可靠。現僅就乙編坑位記錄列表說明如下：

發掘單位	出土非王卜辭種類	共存的其他甲骨
YH090	丙種（1 片，即合 21722）	無
YH127	乙種（100 片以上） 丙種（100 片以上） 丙種 a 屬（如合 21966、合 21983 等） 丙種 b 屬（如合 21891、合 21959 等）	武丁賓組（大量） 武丁𠂤組（合 20570、合 20476、合 20414 等十餘片）
YH251	甲種（大量）	無
YH253 YH330	甲種（大量） 甲種（大量）	無 武丁𠂤組（合 21220）
YH344	甲種（乙 8997，與 YH251 的乙 8806 可綴合，即合 22391） 丙種 a 屬（合 20240）	武丁𠂤組（大量）
YH371	甲種（合 22211、22293 等） 丙種（補 6860）	無
YH484	乙種（合 22467）	無

從表中可以清楚地看出，同坑現象跟同版現象一樣，說明這三種非王卜辭除了相互聯繫之外，只和武丁時代的王室卜辭有關係。

3. 地層現象

這方面已發表的資料很不完整。但舉幾個例子就足以說明問題。

第一例：從出土大量乙、丙兩種非王卜辭以及武丁時代王室卜辭的 YH127 來

---

① 姚孝遂：《吉林大學所藏甲骨選釋》，《吉林大學社會科學學報》1963 年 4 期。

看，它的上面是YH121，再往上是YH117，再往上是YM164。根據鄒衡同志系統的分期研究，YM164是屬於"殷墟文化第三期"（廩辛—文丁時代）的陶器墓，所以YH127出土物顯然應早於廩辛—文丁時代。

第二例：從出土兩片乙種非王卜辭的YH448來看，同出有225G式陶簋等物，屬於鄒衡分期系統的"殷墟文化第二期"，即不得晚於祖甲時代①。

由此可見，過去根據字體、前辭形式或辭例等方面的個別特徵，把這三種非王卜辭定在文丁或帝乙時代，是根本不能成立的。我們應當尊重客觀存在的同版關係、同坑關係和層位關係，把這三種非王卜辭的時代定在武丁之世。並從這個基礎上來修改舊有的對甲骨斷代標準的認識，使之進一步符合客觀實際。

二　非王卜辭的占卜主體——"子"

過去，對這三種非王卜辭的性質，有"子卜辭"、"婦女卜辭"、"多子族卜辭"等多種假說。要弄清非王卜辭的性質，必須首先判定這三種卜辭的占卜的主體究竟是何人。

在王室卜辭中，存在着多數卜人，但從卜辭的語氣來看，只有王自己卜問時，才用單數第一人稱代詞"余"和"朕"，而其他卜人則爲王而占卜，例如：

戊午卜，王，貞：勿禦子辥，余弗其子。　　　　　　　　　　（英1767，武丁𠂤組）

乙巳卜，𠂤，貞：王弗其子辥。　　　　　　　　　　　　　　（合20608，武丁𠂤組）

這說明王室卜辭雖是由多數卜人所卜，而主體是王。

在記卜人稱謂的丙種非王卜辭中，則可以看到另一種現象。只有當"子"卜問時，才用單數第一人稱代詞"余"和"朕"，例如：

乙丑子卜，貞：余有呼出墉。　（綴合編330＝前8·10·1＋京都B3241）

丙辰子卜，貞：朕……　　　　　　　　　　　　　　　　　　　（合21658）

□子子卜：朕在𠂤臣……　　　　　　　　　　　　　　　　　　（合21740）

而其他卜人則爲"子"而占卜，例如：

乙巳巡卜：方來巡，子自征。　　　　　　　　　　　　　　　　（補6828）

---

① 鄒衡：《試論殷墟文化分期》，《北京大學學報（人文科學）》1964年4—5期。

李學勤同志根據這一事實，判定丙種非王卜辭的占卜主體是"子"，並定名爲"子卜辭"，這是很對的。可是，他把"子"誤認爲丙種非王卜辭專有的私名，因而影響了他的結論的正確性。

實際上，在甲、乙兩種非王卜辭中，也有不少爲"子"占卜之辭，例如：

癸丑卜，貞：子亡蚩。——有蚩。　　　　　　　　　　（合 22246，甲種）

壬申卜，貞：子其曰亡事。——壬申卜，貞：有事。　　（合 22069，乙種）

子夕往旬逆娥。　　　　　　　　　　　　　　　　　　（合 22246，甲種）

而且，在甲種非王卜辭中，常見有"干支卜，貞：子"之語，與王室卜辭中習見的"干支卜，貞：王"辭例相同。

"子"這一稱謂，不僅見於這三種不同的非王卜辭中，而且見於綴有不同氏族徽號的青銅器銘文中。其中綴以 ![] 的有四器（卣，集成 5417；卣，集成 5394；觚，集成 9301；尊，集成 5965）。綴以 ![] 的有兩器（角，集成 9100；卣，集成 5355）。綴以 ![] 的一器（卣，集成 5353）。綴以 ![] 的一器（卣，集成 5375）。

就當今的青銅器斷代研究成果而言，文丁時代以前的青銅器還未出現成篇的銘文。因此，這些已經是成篇的銘文中所提到的"子"，和上述武丁時代三種非王卜辭中的"子"，顯然不可能是同一個人。

李學勤同志把這兩種時代不同的史料搞混了，而且還斷言：既然省卣（三代 13·38，即集成 5394）銘中小子省把子稱爲君，則子一定是私名。其實，西周銘文中，常在述受王賞賜後，稱"揚天子休"。難道可以因爲"王"又被稱爲"天子"，就斷言王也是私名嗎？而且，李學勤同志認爲，"君"在戰國以前是"夫人"的尊稱，所以"子"是女性。這種説法是缺乏根據的。試看師毀簋（集成 4311）銘中稱伯和父爲君，尸鎛（集成 285）銘中稱齊公爲君，伯和父、齊公當然不是什麽"夫人"，顯非女性。

實際上，在商周時代，"君"是一個對於長上通用的尊稱，並不限定性別。禹鼎（集成 2833）銘文中的"獲厥君噩侯馭方"，曶盨（集成 4469）銘文中的"俾復虐厥君厥師"，都是在這個意義上使用"君"字的。省卣銘中把子又稱爲君，恰恰説明子也是一種對長上的尊稱。既不足以證明子是私名，更不能證明子是女性。

至於"子"究竟是對什麽樣的人的尊稱，綴合編 330 這一骨版提供了重要綫索。該版有下列數辭並卜：

己丑子卜，貞：余有呼出墉。
　　己丑子卜，貞：子商呼出墉。
　　　　子𪓑呼出墉。
　　　　子□呼〔出墉〕。

既然"子"把自己和子商、子𪓑和子□等人並卜，説明"子"和這些人的身份相似。可是，第一個綴合了此版的貝塚茂樹，却恰恰又由此版而走入了歧途。他作了個不適當的推論："在同時再三卜問同一件事情，乃是卜辭的通例。如此則這個子商，正是子卜貞之子的自稱。"①

按照貝塚茂樹的邏輯，如果"父丁三牛"、"父丁三羊"、"父丁三殳"並卜，既然都是再三卜問祭父丁之事，則牛就是羊，人犧也和牛羊無別了。這顯然是荒謬的推論。何況，既然在再三卜問時，不僅提到子商，還提到子𪓑、子□。爲什麽不把子𪓑、子□也認爲是子的自稱呢？

而且，貝塚茂樹又斷言子商是武丁之子也同樣是缺乏根據的。卜辭中所見"子某"之稱，光是武丁時代就有好幾十個。到周代，男子稱"子某"仍然十分流行。因此，我們不能把卜辭中凡稱"子某"者，一概斷定是商王之子。就拿子商來説，他在武丁王室卜辭中佔有顯赫的地位，並且有令其祭祀商先公先王的記載，説明他和武丁有着血親關係。但我們現在還無法斷定他是商王的子輩，還是兄弟輩，抑或是父輩②。從丙種非王卜辭的祭祀對象來看，雖然有南庚、小辛、伊尹、⚓甲等和王室所祭相同，説明這種卜辭的"子"和商王有血親關係，但如果"子"是商王武丁之子，則祭祀對象中還可能出現的有祖甲（陽甲）、祖庚（盤庚）、祖辛（小辛）、祖乙（小乙）、父丁（武丁之兄丁）。可是，這幾種稱謂在丙種非王卜辭中一次也没遇到過。所以，子是武丁之子的説法是靠不住的。由此而再推論"多子族"是武丁之子構成的集團，這集團還有獨立的占卜機關，就更只是一連串的假想了。

我們認爲：第一，根據在武丁時代的非王卜辭和文丁以後的銅器銘文中都有"子"這一稱謂，這些屬於不同種類的卜辭當屬於不同徽號的氏族；第二，根據丙種非王卜辭中的"子"把自己和子商、子𪓑、子□並卜，以及第三，根據銅器

---

① 貝塚茂樹：《甲骨學概論》（鄭清茂譯），《大陸雜誌》17卷2期。
② 庫方1506（英2674）爲兒氏的世系表，拓本見考古研究所藏《孫壯所藏甲骨拓本》第138號。末一代爲"商"。該拓本上貞字作🦴，和武丁自組王室卜辭相同，所以有可能就是武丁卜辭中常見的"子商"的世系表。從這一世系表來看，"子商"當非武丁的親子。

銘文中"子"又被稱爲"君";可以推斷,"子"在商代是對子商那樣的男性貴族所通用的尊稱。《穀梁傳》宣公十年:"其曰子,尊之也。"注:"子者,人之貴稱。"《詩·大車》:"畏子不敢。"注:"子者,稱所尊敬之辭。"是後代訓詁中也保留了這方面的意義的證明。

子的本義應是指父母的後代,約當現代語中的"孩子"一詞。所以女兒古代也稱子(後來爲區別起見,又稱"女子子")。而它之轉化爲對男性顯貴人物的尊稱,並非中國特有的現象。例如,美洲的古代瑪雅人稱貴族爲"阿里默汗",本義爲"父母親的兒子"。歐洲的古羅馬人稱貴族爲 patricus,本義爲"父親的(後代)"。在新舊大陸上普遍存在的這一現象,說明在血緣紐帶還起相當大作用的階級社會初期,確切的父親血統對世襲貴族具有重大意義。《左傳》僖公九年:"凡在喪……公侯曰子。"注:"子,繼父之辭。"《禮記·曾子問》:"不俟子。"注:"嗣君也。"因爲必須是確切的"子",才有繼父嗣君的資格,所以"子"也就逐漸轉化爲一種對世襲貴族的尊稱了。

合27650:"叀多子〔饗〕。——叀多生〔饗〕。""多子"和"多生"並舉。我們傾向於把"多生"讀爲"多姓",則"多子"最有可能是指和商王同姓的貴族。所謂"多子族"應是對這種貴族家族的總稱,而"子"則是這些家族的首腦們通用的尊稱。在周代,琱生簋(集成4292、集成4293)銘中稱族長爲"宗君",而《禮記》中稱族長爲"宗子",正和前舉省卣銘中稱子爲君有着歷史淵源關係。

根據周代的文獻來看,顯貴的世族大家是有自己的祝宗卜史的,各自獨立進行占卜。在這種意義上,我們把上述三種非王卜辭分別命名爲甲種子卜辭、乙種子卜辭、丙種子卜辭。

三　子卜辭所反映的父權家族

進一步分析各種子卜辭的具體內容,不僅證明了我們對子卜辭性質的初步推斷是正確的,而且使我們得以瞭解商代各貴族家族的內部情況。

1. 構成家族的諸成員

在甲種子卜辭中,除了"子"以外,還爲以下諸人占卜咎休禍福、疾病、生

育等事，並爲這些人祭告先代亡靈。

第一類：子啟、啟弟、子𘀀、子𘀁。

第二類：婦多（或作姼、妠）、婦嫜、婦妥、婦周。

第三類：婦多子、婦嬃子。

可以設想，第一類是子的弟輩或子輩。第二類是他的妻妾、弟媳或兒媳。第三類則是他的子侄或孫輩。這樣正是構成了一個家族。

同樣，在乙種子卜辭中，除"子"之外，還有新、亳、㬎、虎等男性和婦石、婦夸（或作姱）、娘、姜、旻、𫝀等女性。在丙種子卜辭中，僅涉及卜生育之事的婦名就有十個以上。說明這些家族内部的親屬成員，人數是不少的。

特別值得注意的是，在某些卜辭中還指到了奴隸。

丙午，貞：多臣亡疾。　　　　　　　　　　　（合 22258，甲種）

甲辰，貞：羌馭不歺（烈）。——其歺。　　（合 22135，甲種）

甲寅卜，臣子來……　　　　　　　　　　　　（合 22374，甲種）

貞：臣子。　　　　　　　　　　　　　　　　（合 22394，甲種）

丁酉，貞：臣不又正。　　　　　　　　　　　（合 21789＋22042，丙種 b 屬）

丁亥，貞：我多臣不見。　　　　　　　　　　（合 21872 正，丙種 b 屬）

這些卜辭都說明家族内部存在着奴隸。在奴隸主心目中所關心的只是：第一，擔心奴隸"不馴"，起而反抗；第二，當奴隸被壓榨到瀕於死亡時，擔心作爲私有財產的一部分是否會有損失。

在武丁時代的王室卜辭中，也提到過"子效臣"（合 195）、"子商臣"（合 638），說明以子效、子商等人分别爲首領的各貴族家族都有自己的奴隸。考古發掘表明，商代中小型墓中也有殉葬奴隸的現象，所殉者有的是兒童。他們和墓主葬在同一墓穴中，顯然不是後來祭祀時所殺的人犧。而有些反縛雙手作掙扎狀的例子正表明是不自願的生殉。這些情況，都和子卜辭中提到各家族内部有奴隸是一致的。

2. 家族組織的經濟基礎

從甲種子卜辭簡略的記載中可以看出，家族是有自己的土地、牲畜和住宅的。

正受禾。——長受禾。　　　　　　　　　　　（合 22246）

這是占卜該家族在正、長兩地的農業收成。

  馬不步（烈）。   （合 22247）①

這是占卜該家族的馬匹是否利於役使。

  辛未卜，作宀。   （合 22246）

這是占卜是否蓋新房子。

  乙種子卜辭中有一條值得注意的卜辭：

  庚戌卜，朕耳鳴，屮禦于祖庚羊百，屮用五十八，屮女（毋）用。（合 22099）

證明該家族擁有頗大的畜羣。

  除了農牧業外，還經常進行田獵：

  丁未卜，田于西。——丁未卜，貞：其田于東。 （合 22043，乙種）
  甲辰卜，我，貞：累，獲。   （合 21761，丙種）

  因爲捕捉異族戰俘不僅可用作人犧，而且可以轉化爲奴隸，所以各家族都自己進行武裝活動：

  癸巳卜，獲妥。   （合 22147、合 22135，甲種）
  丙申余卜，巡牵𠦪。   （合 21709，丙種）
  癸巳余卜，印牵𠦪，弗獲。   （合 21708，丙種）

  當然，由於卜辭的簡略，如上述甲種子卜辭提到的正地和長地，是該家族世襲的私有土地，還是王所賜授而佔有的土地，抑或爲向該家族"納貢"之封邑，是無法肯定的。屬於家族的土地分佈情況也不清楚。但是，丙種子卜辭中有幾條記載，畢竟提供了一些線索：

  乙亥子卜，方征于我墉。   （合 40874）
  □丑卜，㱿貞：九月我入商。   （合 21718）

這似乎表明該家族在商王都城之外的地方，有自己的邑落。

3. 族長的權力

  從三種子卜辭可以看出，它們的占卜主體——"子"，都有呼令他人的權

---

① 乙 8812 和乙 8672、8990、8711、8730、8791、8802、8835、8884、8877 可以綴成一版（即合 22247），和乙 8896（合 22246）是成套卜辭。

力，例如：

  甲申卜，令豚宅正。   （合 22323，甲種）

  庚戌卜，貞：余令陕从羌田，亡囚。   （合 22043，乙種）

  庚戌，令㐰，惟來。㐰以龜二，若令。   （合 21562，丙種）

  根據現有材料，還不能斷定像豚、陕、㐰等是族長的子弟，抑或爲該族的"附庸"，是管事的僚屬，抑或爲奴隸中的首領。但是，可以看出，在家族中，有有權呼令他人的首腦，有受遣使的人物。綴有㐰這一氏號的薔卣（集成 5417）記載："子令小子薔先以人于莫。"直接指明了這個有權呼令他人的首腦就是"子"。

  在奴隸制產生以後，深刻地影響到社會上人與人之間的關係。在家族內部，不僅是奴隸、僚屬必須完全聽命於族長，即使在父子、兄弟、夫妻關係上，也無不染上奴隸制的色彩。

  商代晚期的省卣記載："子賞小子省貝五朋，省揚君賞。"西周的虞簋（集成 4167）記載："休朕甸君公伯賜厥臣弟虞"，均可證家族内部諸成員和族長的關係，是君臣關係。《左傳》哀公十一年記魯國三分公族之後，"孟氏使半爲臣，若子若弟"。《左傳》桓公二年"士有隸子弟"。可見，子弟對族長的關係，至少是半奴隸性的。族長操縱家族的全部財產權，家族成員所得的一份，至少在名義上必須受賜於族長。《商周金文錄遺》中有一卣，其銘爲："顯作母辛尊彝。顯賜婦㜏曰：用齍于乃姑宓。"（集成 5389）妻子的用器須受賜於夫，正是父權制的鮮明特徵。

  摩爾根在《古代社會》中，對父權家族作了如下概括："將相當數量的自由民和非自由民，以耕種土地和照料畜群爲目的而在父權之下組成家族。被淪爲奴隸的人和被用作僕役的人都處在婚姻關係中並和家長即他們的酋長一起組成一個父權家族。家長支配其成員和支配其財產的權力是這種家族的實質。"[1]馬克思在作該書摘要時，在這段話下面加了橫線予以強調[2]。恩格斯更明確地指出，父權家族（或譯作"家長制家庭"）的主要特點，不是多妻制，而其"主要標誌，一是把非自由人包括在家庭以内，一是父權"。[3]武丁時代的三種子卜辭，不正是活生

---

[1] 莫（摩）爾根：《古代社會》（楊東蓴、張栗原、馮漢驥譯），生活·讀書·新知三聯書店，1957年，541頁。譯文據人民出版社1965年版的《摩爾根古代社會一書摘要》作了修改。

[2] 馬克思：《摩爾根古代社會一書摘要》，人民出版社，1965年，36頁。

[3] 恩格斯：《家庭、私有制和國家的起源》，《馬克思恩格斯選集》，人民出版社，1972年，第4卷，52頁。

生地給我們描繪出一幅這種父權家族的圖景嗎？

恩格斯當初把羅馬的 Familia 作爲"這種家庭形式的完善的典型"。由於子卜辭的發現，可以斷定，在東方的黄河流域，至少在武丁時代，這種家庭形式業已存在。可證它在世界歷史範疇内具有普遍性，即使在東方，也並不缺乏"完善的典型"。

四　商王統治的支柱——"多子"和"多姓"

在初步探討了武丁時代父權家族的内部結構之後，進一步研究這些父權家族和商王室的關係，以及它們互相之間的關係，對弄清商代的社會結構是有益的。

在研究三種子卜辭的祭祀對象時，以前就已經有人注意到，在丙種子卜辭中，祭祀祖乙（合 21542）、南庚（合 21538 甲）、小辛（合 21538 乙）、𤰕甲（合 21805），是和武丁王室卜辭相同的。而乙種子卜辭的祭祀對象，除了一個"下乙"和武丁王室卜辭相同外，幾乎完全是另外一個系統。這種現象當然需要解釋。流傳的祭法有"同姓於宗廟，同祖於祖廟，同族於禰廟"之説，不同種類的子卜辭中祭祀對象的差別性，似乎表明着不同家族與商王在血緣親疏上的差別性。比如，可以推測，丙種子卜辭的子與王室血緣關係較近，乙種子卜辭的子與王室血緣關係較遠。至於像甲種子卜辭中三個主要祭祀對象匕庚、匕丁、子丁和丙種子卜辭相同，却未見祖乙、南庚、小辛之類王室祭祀對象，所以甲種子卜辭的子可能和丙種子卜辭的子是近親，但與王室血緣關係頗遠。基於這種想法，我們認爲"多子族"就是指這些和商王有血緣關係的父權家族，但是和王有最近血緣關係的親屬（可能是親兄弟、親子侄）則專稱"王族"。

在甲種子卜辭中還有一段很有趣的卜辭，在合 22246 這一完整龜版的下半段，有以下各辭：

(1) 使人先日逆。——先日何。
(2) 癸亥卜，子夕往勾逆娥。——勾逆女（毋）娥。
　　勾逆娥。
　　勾逆㛖。
　　勾逆姗。
(3) 勾何𤔲。——勾何女（毋）𤔲。

如果我們讀一下《儀禮·士婚禮》，很自然地會推想到這正是一組擇婚的占卜。其中逆和何是武丁王室卜辭中常見的族名，亦見於銅器銘文①。第（1）小段是遣使向逆、何兩族分別"納采"以前所卜。第（2）（3）兩段是在"問名"（參看《左傳》襄公十二年）之後，再進行選擇，以便決定娶哪個族的哪一名女子，好進而"納吉"。如果我們推測甲種子卜辭的子和商王是同姓沒有錯，那麼，按古代通行的"同姓不婚"的原則，逆、何兩族就應當與商王異姓。這樣，我們可以把逆、何兩族看成是"多姓"的代表。

在三種子卜辭中，片斷地可以看到各家族之間的往來關係。如合 21564 提到"逆多子，若"，合 21631 提到"多亞"。屬於丙種的合 21623 和屬於乙種的合 22092 都提到"亞雀"。他應當就是武丁王室卜辭中顯赫的"雀"。丙種子卜辭中常提到的"方"（原刻作囗，和丁作〇不同），則見於銅器銘文（集成 1064），也是一個族名。此外，如合 22065 提到"⿱宀六侯"，他也見於武丁王室卜辭。合 21546 提到"小王"，乙 8971、合 21901 都提到"王"，說明各家族和"諸侯"、王室也有往來關係。

如果超越純粹的血緣關係來看，武丁儼然是凌駕於諸同姓家族和異姓家族之上的"總族長"。他一方面直接統治王家的子弟、妻妾和大量奴隸；另一方面又通過多子和多姓，統治各家族的子弟和奴隸，成為當時最大的奴隸主。他一方面有獨立的王家經濟、官僚機關和軍隊，賴以維護其統治；另一方面則通過呼令各族"載王事"，並直接向各族徵取人力、物力，以鞏固和擴大自己的權勢。如果將武丁時代的王室卜辭和三種子卜辭的內容作綜合對照的研究，至少在下列三個重要問題上能加深我們的認識。

第一，王室的經濟來源，除王家的田地、畜群和手工業外，主要依賴各家族的貢納。在武丁時代王室卜辭中所見到的貢物，有牛、馬、卜用的龜和牛骨、象牙、貝、玉、石等，此外還有人犧、美女、舞伎、珍禽異獸。這在家族角度稱為"⿱入⿰丨丨"，在商王角度則稱為"取"。丙種子卜辭有貞問"有取"（合 21745）當指這類事。

特別要指出，王室的田地主要是靠徵調各家族的勞動力來耕作的。丙種子卜

---

① 見於武丁王室卜辭者，如"何不其⿱入⿰丨丨羌"（合 273 正）、"令逆比曲于⿱宀六"（合 4916）。見於銅器銘文者：何作⿱入⿰丨丨的有卣（集成 4910）、簋（集成 3065）；何作⿱入⿰丨丨的有爵（集成 8151）。逆則省作屰，見集成 8887、集成 8059 等（在武乙卜辭中逆也省作屰，如合 3521 正"貞：令旨比屰"）。

辭有貞問"我伇（及）藉于尸。——我尸藉今春"（合 21595）和王室卜辭的"呼雷藉于明"（合 14 正）、"呼藉于㞷北"（合 9509）正相呼應。可見，所謂"古者公田，藉而不稅"的制度，顯然不是周公首創的。在商代王室卜辭中可以看到，"協田"、"黍"（指播種）、"㞷田"等農事，都是調集"眾"（或泛稱"人"）來進行的。這種"眾"，根據西周金文，在身份上和"臣"有別，因而應該是指各父權家族的親屬成員。而且，由於在大量的武丁王室卜辭中，還沒有發現一條用奴隸耕作的記載，可見調集各家族勞動力來耕作名義上是"公田"的王室直屬領地，至少在商代武丁之世，對王室經濟仍有決定的意義。

第二，在武丁時代，根據王室卜辭的記載，商王已建立了和"武裝全民"不一致的常備武裝。其成員一方面來源於戰爭中俘獲的異族奴隸（"多臣、多馬羌"）①，另一方面是從各家族徵調的。在王室卜辭中，有"取馬"、"取射"和各家族"◊馬"、"◊射"的記載②。雖然有了這樣的常備軍，在大型戰爭中，商王仍須調集多數家族的成員。這在卜辭中稱為"❂人"（❂或省作❂）。通常是三千，多者達五千以上。丙種子卜辭有"在𠂤人歸"（合 21741），乙種子卜辭有"❂至𠂤，亡若"（合 22088），當均與這類徵調有關。這種調集還可能涉及家族奴隸。王室卜辭卜："州（族名）臣得。——州臣不〔其〕得。"（合 850）丙種子卜辭卜"朕在𠂤臣……"（合 21740）提供了這方面的材料。

由此可見，至少到武丁時代，商王在軍事上對各家族的武裝力量還有相當的依賴性，可能要到文丁時代"王作三師：右、中、左"（合 33006 右半）③之後，這種依賴性才得以降低。

第三，從武丁時代的王室卜辭可以看出，當時商王為了行使其統治權，已設置了一批專門的職官。但在農、祀、戎這三大事務中，還是常常臨時指派各家族的族長或主要成員去主持其事。今就子卜辭中提到過的"子商"和可能是異姓的"逆"，略舉數例如下：

---

① 恩格斯指出："雅典人在創立他們國家的同時，也創立了警察，即由步行的和騎馬的弓箭手組成的真正的憲兵隊，……不過，這種憲兵隊卻是由奴隸組成的。這種警察職務在自由的雅典人看來是非常卑賤的，以致他們寧願叫武裝的奴隸逮捕自己，而自己卻不肯去幹這種丟臉的事。"（《馬克思恩格斯選集》第 4 卷，114 頁）中國到周代還以罪隸和異族奴隸作警衛隊，見《周禮·司隸》。
② 卜辭中"馬"一詞，有時指馬匹，有時指騎士。如"貞：❂◊卅馬，允其𢦏羌"（合 500 正）當指騎士，而"貞：❂呼取白馬，◊？"（合 945 正）當指馬匹。
③ 關於該版的斷代，林澐《甲骨斷代中一個重要問題的再研究》一文中有專門討論。

叀子商令。——叀子效令西。——叀王自往西。　　　　　　（合 6928 正）

　　翌乙酉，呼子商酓伐于父乙。　　　　　　　　　　　　　　（合 969）

　　令子商先涉羌于河。　　　　　　　　　　　　　　　　　　（合 536）

　　呼子商从溝，屮鹿。　　　　　　　　　　　　　　　　　　（合 10948 正）

　　令逆比畫于🗆。　　　　　　　　　　　　　　　　　　　　（合 4916）

　　令逆……征牟……　　　　　　　　　　　　　　　　　　　（合 7054）

　　丙種子卜辭所卜的"我有呼出墉"（前引）、"自商令我"（合 21549）、"酓彡，我有事"（合 21586），顯然都是指這一類事而言。

　　正因爲各家族的力量在維持王權上有這樣重大而直接的關係，所以商王特別重視各家族族長的作用，不僅常常爲他們的咎休禍福進行占卜，而且通過封賞、宴射和祭祀來進行物質和精神上的籠絡。各期王室卜辭中的"賜多子女"（合 677）、"賜多女屮貝朋"（合 11438）、"叀多子〔饗〕——叀多姓饗"（合 27650）、"叀多姓射"（合 24142）以及丙種子卜辭中的"呼䍃逆有賞"（合 21626）、"呼㚔逆有賞"（合 21626）、"王用賞"（合 21908，丙種 b 屬），從不同角度説明了這個問題。

　　因此，在每一個家族中，除了奴隸之外，表面上是血緣親屬的人與人之間，族長和一般成員實應劃分成兩個不同的階級。前者是奴隸主階級，而後者實際是被統治的半奴隸階級。在族長中，可以參與或代商王主持祭祀先公先王，從而強調血緣紐帶而維持思想一致的同姓族長，地位又高於異姓族長。但不論是同姓或異姓的族長，都一同幫助商王統治各家族的普通成員，並動員各家族的力量來支持以商王爲頭子的奴隸主專政。所以，"多子"和"多姓"乃是商代王權的主要支柱。

　　馬克思説："現代家庭（按：即指羅馬人的 Familia）在萌芽時，不僅包含着奴隸制，而且也包含着農奴制，因爲它從一開始就是同田間耕作的勞役有關的。它以縮影的形式包含了一切後來在社會及其國家中廣泛發展起來的對立。"①從這個觀點來看武丁時代的父權家族，就更清楚它在我國古代史上的重要地位了。

餘　論

　　最後，對子卜辭的問題，再贅上幾句。

---

① 恩格斯：《家庭、私有制和國家的起源》，《馬克思恩格斯選集》，第 4 卷，53 頁。

在安陽發掘出來的大量甲骨刻辭中，非王卜辭並不止於本文所討論的三種。例如，甲編中發表的 E16 坑出土的所謂"刀卜辭"，辭中亦多見"子"這一稱謂。合 21703 正和合 21285 正兩片貞字作三足形的卜辭，也有"子不㞢"之辭。此外，以合 22301 爲代表的"亞卜辭"，合 22536 這一後岡出土的卜骨，擴續 274 這一字體拙劣的刻辭，甲編考釋中綴合的第三次發掘所得的大龜版，都不是王室卜辭。1971 年在小屯西地所出的二十一枚卜骨，裘錫圭同志認爲是"三、四期的非正統卜辭"①，很可能也是一種子卜辭。可見，今後隨着田野考古工作的進一步開展，不僅本文已討論過的三種子卜辭還會繼續出土，而且一定會發現更多種的商代以至周代的其他父權家族的卜辭。本文對商代父權家族的初步論證，必將進一步得到檢驗、補充和修正。這些工作肯定會有助於我們更深入地瞭解商代的社會結構，爲研究中國歷史和世界歷史的基本發展規律作出有益的貢獻。

1965 年 9 月初稿
1978 年 11 月第 7 稿

按語：

該文寫得很早，在判定字體類別上有不當之處。如認爲無想 240（即合 40857）是甲種子卜辭，黃天樹在 1999 年發表的《婦女卜辭》中已指出應該是師組小字類卜辭；認爲乙 6690（即合 22094）爲師組大字和乙種子卜辭同版，蔣玉斌在 2006 年的博士論文中已指出不是師組大字，而是乙種子卜辭 B 類字體；在就乙編坑位列表說明各類字體同坑現象時，把 YH371 坑中出的乙 9026—9031 都說成是甲種子卜辭，經周忠兵指出乙 9026—9028 都不是甲種子卜辭，而乙 9029 是丙種子卜辭；在結語部分又說綴 449（即合 20385 爲代表者）是子卜辭，周忠兵指出是歷組一類王卜辭。凡此類失誤，無關論文主旨，所以一並刪去。

又如在說明子卜辭的子之外其他卜人是爲子占卜，舉京津 3023（即合 21566）爲例：讀成"子有往來惟若"，實際是"中子又入，往來隹若"，與子無關，所以也刪去。

在丙種子卜辭中出現的作正方形或扁方形的人物，該文釋爲"方"，並引鼎銘（集成 1064）爲證。但 1991 年花東子卜辭出土後，這個作方形的人物是指武

---

① 裘錫圭：《讀〈安陽新出土的牛胛骨及其刻辭〉》，《考古》1972 年 5 期。

丁已無疑問。在《花東子卜辭所見人物研究》中我已改釋爲"辟",可參看。

該文中把有"王作三師右中左"的粹597（即合33006）定爲文丁時卜辭,是我在1965年做研究生畢業論文時的見解,即把有祭祀"父乙"的歷組一類卜辭,作爲是文丁時祭祀武乙的證據。實際上那是武丁時祭祀小乙。歷組一類卜辭既有武丁祭祀小乙的"父乙",又有祖甲祭祀武丁的"父丁",所以是武丁到祖甲時的卜辭。

原載《古文字研究》第1輯,中華書局,1979年;收入《林澐學術文集》,中國大百科全書出版社,1998年;又收入《林澐文集·古史卷》,上海古籍出版社,2019年。今據後者收入。

姚孝遂

商代的俘虜

目 錄

（一）緒言
（二）俘虜的名稱
    一、以方域爲名
      1. 羌　2. 大　3. 亘　4. 尸　5. 絴　6. 美　7. 㦰　8. 𠂤　9. 𠂤　10. 𠂤
11. 奚　12. 而　13. 印
    二、以俘獲或處理之方法爲名
      1. 㚔　2. 靰　3. 係　4. 俘　5. 伐　6. 戉
    三、敵方之首領
      1. 白　2. 囚
    四、女性的俘虜
      1. 姜　2. 妝　3. 奚　4. 嬉　5. 㚔
    五、通稱
      1. 人　2. 女
    六、其它
      1. 㚔　2. 㚔、卯　3. 屯
（三）俘虜的來源
    一、戰爭
    二、貢納
    三、田獵或牧芻

（四）俘虜的用途

    一、用作祭祀時的犧牲

      1. 俎　2. 伐　3. 馘　4. 尞　5. 沈　6. 饮　7. 葡　8. 见　9. 奈　10. 卯
11. 戋　12. 㫃　13. 彈　14. 用　15. 㞢

    二、用作奴隸

      1. 田獵　2. 征伐　3. 山田　4. 床上奴隸

（五）有關的比較和統計

（六）結語

（一）緒　言

    在古代社會，俘虜的命運是與當時的生産力發展水平密切聯繫着的。人類在最初的時候，"他們仍然是半畜牲的、野蠻的，在自然力量之前無能爲力的。……他們象動物一樣的貧乏，他們也難得比動物有較高的生産性"①。在這種情況下，他們就把捉到的俘虜當作食物拿來喫掉了，就象喫掉他們所捉到的野獸一樣。恩格斯曾經強調說："人若不食肉，就不會變成人。……有一個時期，肉食曾引起人喫人的現象。柏林人的祖先，範萊塔勃人或維爾茨人，在十世紀還喫過自己的父母呢。"②在澳洲的某些部落，"不祇食戰陣上所殺死的敵人，而且也食他們被殺死的伙伴。至於老死者，祇要還可供食用，他們也是喫掉的"③。當然，在盛行着以人爲食的時代，主要還是以俘虜爲對象，在我國古代的春秋、戰國之際，在某些地方，還有食人的殘餘迹象。《山海經·海內南經》："窫窳龍首……食人。""窫窳"是一個方國名。在《海內西經》亦稱之爲"窫窳之尸（夷）"。《列子·魯問》也說，楚之南有"啖人國"。及至東漢，交趾之西尚有"啖人國"，而《博物志》且載有"琅琊臨沂縣東界次睢有大叢社，民謂之食人社"。

    隨着人類社會的進步和發展，"食人現象已逐漸消滅，它祇當作宗教儀式或當作魔法纔保存着"④。但是，人們還是殘酷地把俘虜拿來殺掉了，盛行着以人

---

① 恩格斯《反杜林論》，一八四頁。
② 《馬克思恩格斯文選（兩卷集）》卷二，八六頁。
③ 莫爾根《古代社會》，四二一頁。
④ 《馬克思恩格斯文選（兩卷集）》卷二，一八八頁。

作祭品的風俗。①這種"以人作祭品的風俗",也就是早期的食人的遺風。人類在這一歷史階段,還沒有可能把大量的俘虜活着保留下來,供人役使,恩格斯曾詳細地説明這一點:"奴隸並不能使每個人得到好處,爲着要從奴隸身上得到好處,必須具備兩種東西:第一,奴隸所需的工具及對象;第二,維持奴隸困苦生活所需的資料。所以在奴隸制成爲可能以前,先應在生産的發展上達到一定的程度,並在分配的不平等上達到一定的程度。如果要使奴隸勞動成爲整個社會的支配生産方式,那麽,還需要更大得多的生産、商業和財富積蓄的增長。"②在這一時期,俘虜的命運也和前一時期一樣,也是被殘酷地殺掉了,但所不同的是:他們不是供活人食用,而是供死人"食用"。這就是殺人作爲祭祀時的犧牲,我們通稱之爲"人牲"的現象。

在原始社會的後期,當"生産已經發展到如此程度,使人的勞動力已能生産比簡簡單單維持勞動力所需要的數量更多的東西,維持大量勞動力所需的資料,已經具備了,運用這些勞動力的資料,也已經具備了。這樣,勞動力於是獲得了價值……所以俘虜開始被活着保留下來,而其勞動則開始被利用……奴隸制於是被發現了"③。

基於上述,在古代社會,人們對待俘虜的態度,是隨着社會生産力的發展水平之不同而有所變異的。換句話説,俘虜的命運是由社會的不同發展水平所決定的。在古代社會,俘虜的命運基本上有下列三種:最初是被殺喫掉;其次是被殺來用作祭祀的犧牲;最後是被活着保留下來强迫其從事勞動。

俘虜與奴隸之間有着密切的關係,古代奴隸多來源於戰爭中之俘虜,然而俘虜並不等於奴隸,這是大家都非常明確的事實。可是,有許多同志在引用具體資料以説明古代社會歷史問題的時候,却往往忽略了這一點,將一些俘虜誤認作奴隸。

不同的時代,不同的地區,對於奴隸有着不同的名稱。關於奴隸身份的確定,我們祇能通過他們在當時所處的社會地位及其實際活動來加以考察。在這一點上,採用"顧名思義"的辦法是非常危險的,事實上也是行不通的。

在甲骨刻辭中,有着大量的關於商代處置俘虜情況的記載。這一些記載是我們今天探討當時社會歷史的一項非常重要的資料,然而這一些資料在過去並没有

---

① 《馬克思恩格斯文選(兩卷集)》卷二,二九二頁。
② 恩格斯《反杜林論》,一六五頁。
③ 恩格斯《反杜林論》,一八五——一八六頁。

得到系統的、全面的整理和分析,因而也就沒有很好地得到利用。即令有一部分得到利用,可是也遭到了曲解,面目全非。我曾經在《人牲與人殉》一文中,詳細論證了殷墟發掘中"人牲"和"人殉"是兩種性質截然不同的考古迹象,應該嚴格加以區分。而且"人牲"的身份主要是俘虜,"人殉"的身份主要是奴隸。任何加以混同都是錯誤的(見《史學月刊》一九六〇年第九期)。這篇論文則是進一步對甲骨刻辭中有關俘虜的記載,系統地加以分析和整理,結合文獻資料加以說明,以便大家能夠更好地利用這一部份史料,從而更確切地瞭解當時的社會實際情況。這對於深入地探討我國古代社會歷史,當能提供一些幫助。

(二)俘虜的名稱

甲骨刻辭中關於俘虜的名稱極其繁雜,但大體上可以劃分成四個類別,即:

1. 以方域爲名:凡擄獲某"方"的戰俘,就直接用其所屬的"方"名稱呼之;

2. 以俘獲或處理的方法爲名:捕獲俘虜有各種不同的手段,處理俘虜也有各種不同的方法,在甲骨刻辭中就因此而形成了俘虜的各種不同名稱;

3. 敵方的首領;

4. 女性的俘虜。

以下就分別舉例加以說明。

一、以方域爲名

1. 羌

"羌"是甲骨刻辭中最爲常見的,數量最多的一種俘虜。同時,"羌"也是一個方國名。

"羌"字的變體很多,⇡、⇡、⇡、⇡、⇡、⇡都應當釋"羌",是不同時期的不同寫法。

　　叀甫乎令汕壱羌方　　　　　　　　　　　　　　　　前六・六〇・六
　　勿异人乎伐羌　　　　　　　　　　　　　　　　　　乙四五九八
　　往羌　　　　　　　　　　　　　　　　　　　　　　乙四三七四
　　往羌得　　　　　　　　　　　　　　　　　　　　　存一・六〇三

　　　　往羌不其得　　　　　　　　　　　　　　　　前四・五〇・八

以上是方域名的"羌"。有的同志解釋"往羌"爲羌人的逃亡，這是錯誤的。甲骨刻辭所有的"往"字祇有一個用法，都用作"前往"，沒有例外。我們試比較以下諸辭例：

　　　　乎婦往，其㞢得
　　　　乎婦往⩑得　　　　　　　　　　　　　　　　合三一五
　　　　令㪟往田　　　　　　　　　　　　　　　　　甲三四五九
　　　　㪟往田，不來歸　　　　　　　　　　　　　　甲三四七九
　　　　王叀往　　　　　　　　　　　　　　　　　　乙四五四二

這裏所列舉的，僅僅是"往"字的形體與"往羌"相同的例子，都作 𠂤 或 𠃊。顯而易見，即使是這種形體的"往"字，也不可能作逃亡解釋，"往田"是"前往田獵"，"田"是不可能"逃亡"的。"王"前往什麼地方，或前往做什麼事情，甲骨刻辭中此類的記載非常之多，不可能解釋成爲商王逃亡。

"往羌得"祇能是卜問前往羌地是否能有所虜獲。有如下的辭例：

　　　　𢦏得㞢牛　　　　　　　　　　　　　　　　　鐵三・三
　　　　㪟得舟；
　　　　㪟不其得舟　　　　　　　　　　　　　　　　合一二三

"乎婦往，其㞢得"，祇能解釋爲命令"婦"前往，是否有所得。不可能解釋爲命令"婦"逃亡，然後再把她抓回來。

在這裏由於牽涉到我們所要論證的問題，不得不占一點篇幅來加以申論。

　　　　在𩰚國羌⋯　　　　　　　　　　　　　　　　前七・一九・二
　　　　奉羌十人　　　　　　　　　　　　　　　　　林二・一三・二
　　　　追羌⋯隻⋯　　　　　　　　　　　　　　　　鐵九七・四
　　　　令戍光㞢隻羌芻五十　　　　　　　　　　　　乙四六九二
　　　　⋯隻四羌其至⋯　　　　　　　　　　　　　　合二八六

以上"羌"爲俘虜名。"羌芻"當爲羌人之牲畜。下文還將論及。

2. 大

　　　　大方　　　　　　　　　　　　　　　　　　　乙二二九
　　　　⋯來告大方出　　　　　　　　　　　　　　　粹一一五二

大方伐戛廿邑　　　　　　　　　　　　　　　　　　　　　　粹八〇一

有的同志認爲"大方"乃商人的自稱，這是錯誤的。甲骨刻辭中"××來告×方出"之例多見，乃是邊境守衛人員向商王報告敵方將要前來侵犯。上舉的"大方伐戛廿邑"，是指"大方"侵擾了商的廿個邊邑，這與《菁》一的"𡭊友角告曰，舌方出，𢦚我示𢦔田七十人五"和"沚戛告曰，土方征于我東邑，戈二邑，舌方亦𢦚我西啚田"，其内容是一致的。"大方"祇能是和"舌方"、"土方"一樣，都是商的敵方，不可能是商的自稱。

　　　　辛氏大
　　　　辛弗其氏大
　　　　乎取大
　　　　令❋取大氏　　　　　　　　　　　　　　　　　　　　合二一一
　　　　㗊大　　　　　　　　　　　　　　　　　　　　　　乙一七五二

以上"大"爲俘虜名。

　3. 亘

　　　　亘方　　　　　　　　　　　　　　　　　　　　　　粹一九三
　　　　亘戋其戈我　　　　　　　　　　　　　　　　　　　合二八二
　　　　雀𠦪亘，受又　　　　　　　　　　　　　　　　　　存一·六三八

以上"亘"爲方國名。

　　　　雀隻亘；雀弗其隻亘　　　　　　　　　　　　　　　乙四六九三
　　　　雀追亘㞢隻　　　　　　　　　　　　　　　　　　　乙五〇三

以上"亘"爲俘虜名。

　4. 尸

"尸"作⸝或⸜，與"人"字有別。亦即"夷"字。

　　　　㕚告伐尸方　　　　　　　　　　　　　　　　　　　粹一一八七
　　　　王叀㕚告从正尸　　　　　　　　　　　　　　　　　乙三八六〇
　　　　王叀帚好令正尸　　　　　　　　　　　　　　　　　續四·三〇·一

以上"尸"爲方域名。

　　　　翌乙未㳄澂尸　　　　　　　　　　　　　　　　　　乙一五一二

　　　　用十尸于丁，卯一牛　　　　　　　　　　　　　京津七三八

以上"尸"爲俘虜而用作祭牲。

　5. 絴

　　絴字從羊從糸，與羌字下從人者迥然有別，諸家多誤混入"羌"字，或混入"羊"字，均非是。

　　　　令衆人…入…絴方…望田　　　　　　　　　甲三五一〇
　　　　其氐絴方　　　　　　　　　　　　　　　　存一•三五一

以上"絴"爲方國名。

　　　　絴方其用，王受…　　　　　　　　　　　　京津四三八一
　　　　…王牽絴　　　　　　　　　　　　　　　　後下一二•一•六

以上"絴"爲俘虜名。

　6. 美

　　　　使人于美…　　　　　　　　　　　　　　　掇二•七八
　　　　…章…美…受又…　　　　　　　　　　　　林二•一三•九

以上"美"爲方域名。

　　　　其軏美　　　　　　　　　　　　　　　　　京津四一四一
　　　　叀且美用　　　　　　　　　　　　　　　　京津四一〇五

以上"美"爲俘虜名。

　7. 𣎵

　　此字形體多變異，作 𣎵、𣎵、𣎵、𣎵、𣎵 諸形。孫詒讓《契文舉例》釋"共"，以爲即《詩•皇矣》"侵阮徂共"之"共"（卷上，第三六頁）。葉玉森《殷墟書契前編集釋》卷一、第八八頁釋"垂"。均難以爲據。

　　　　祈于𣎵厎　　　　　　　　　　　　　　　　乙八四〇六
　　　　王…于𣎵　　　　　　　　　　　　　　　　珠六〇九

以上"𣎵"爲方域名。

　　　　酚匕庚𣎵
　　　　酚匕庚五𣎵　　　　　　　　　　　　　　　乙五二四七
　　　　㞢于匕庚十𣎵　　　　　　　　　　　　　　乙六七〇三

　　　　出匕己及【字】　　　　　　　　　　　　　　　　乙七四六五

以上"【字】"爲俘虜而用爲祭牲。

　8.【字】

　　【字】的或體作【字】，下從"尸"，王襄《類纂》釋"允"，鮑鼎《春秋國名考釋》釋"尢"，張秉權《丙編考釋》釋"老"，均不可據。葉玉森《前編集釋》、李孝定《集釋》則均誤入"先"字。【字】、與"先"之作【字】、【字】是有嚴格區分的。

　　　　王令弜伐【字】……　　　　　　　　　　　　　　佚三八三
　　　　令从……伐【字】　　　　　　　　　　　　　　　合二八
　　　　余乎弜章【字】……　　　　　　　　　　　　　　存二・三一九

以上"【字】"爲方國名。

　　　　王出匚于庚百【字】　　　　　　　　　　　　　　合一〇四
　　　　牽【字】　　　　　　　　　　　　　　　　　　　摭續一四二
　　　　氏【字】　　　　　　　　　　　　　　　　　　　金七八

以上"【字】"爲俘虜名。

　9.【字】

　　【字】字象虎頭而人身，自羅振玉以來，多誤混入"虎"字。實際上甲骨文的"虎"字皆象虎形，不從"人"，而【字】字則下從人，與"虎"字有嚴格的區分。"羌"爲羊頭人，【字】爲虎頭人，蓋以其頭飾之不同而命名。

　　　　【字】方其涉河東【字】，其……　　　　　　　　前六・六三・六

此爲方國名。

　　　　卯十【字】　　　　　　　　　　　　　　　　　　存二・七八七

此爲用【字】俘爲祭牲。此外尚有：

　　　　【字】其用　　　　　　　　　　　　　　　　　　掇一・三九一
　　　　又來【字】，其用于……　　　　　　　　　　　　明七一五
　　　　王其用【字】　　　　　　　　　　　　　　　　　甲七五七①

這乃是【字】而帶上刑具者，亦當爲俘獲之【字】方人員。可證【字】絶非虎字。

---

① 編者按："甲七五七"，原文誤作"甲七五一"，今據實際出處徑改。

10. 🅰

　　字象人張網形。金祥恒《續甲骨文編》入於"罟"字,蓋以《説文》"罟"字之或體作"罛",下從"孚",乃契文所從"🅱"之譌變,確否待考,高田忠周釋"舞",非是。契文"舞"作🅲或🅳,與🅱有別。

　　　　乎雀伐🅰　　　　　　　　　　　　　　　　　乙四三八〇
　　　　我戈🅰　　　　　　　　　　　　　　　　　　庫一七五〇

以上"🅰"爲國名。

　　　　我用🅰孚　　　　　　　　　　　　　　　　　乙六六九四

以上爲俘虜名。孚字作🅴,象以手持子,俘獲之義。引申爲俘獲之敵人亦謂之"孚"。

11. 奚

　　甲骨刻辭中的"奚"字,其形體變化多端,用法也很複雜。就其字形來説,基本上是象用手拘提俘虜辮髮之形。還有的則象用斧鉞以斫斷"奚"頭。"奚"在甲骨刻辭中用爲地名,爲人名,爲虜獲"奚"方的戰俘名,同時也爲一種斬首的用牲方法,詳見于省吾同志《殷代的奚奴》(《東北人民大學學報》一九五六年第一期)。

　　　　奚來白馬　　　　　　　　　　　　　　　　　乙三四四九
　　　　奚不其來牛　　　　　　　　　　　　　　　　合一四四
　　　　王从奚伐🅵　　　　　　　　　　　　　　　　乙七七四一

以上"奚"爲方域名。

　　　　钔小辛三牢,又🅶二　　　　　　　　　　　　前一·一六·五
　　　　皋其來屯🅷　　　　　　　　　　　　　　　　佚一五一

以上爲俘虜名。

12. 而

　　　　王重而白龜从伐…方;
　　　　王勿隹而白龜伐…　　　　　　　　　　　　　乙二九四八

"而"在此爲方國名。

　　　　牵羌…隻廿屮五,而二…　　　　　　　　　　後下三八·七

小臣牆从伐㠯危、美…人廿人四,而千五百七十…　　　綜圖一六·二

是俘獲"而方"之俘虜亦稱之爲"而"。

　　…而于且丁…羌甲一羌…　　　　　　　　　　　粹二六〇

此當是用"而"俘作爲祭牲。

13. 印

甲骨文"印"字作❦或❦，與"㚔"字之作❦者有別。至於陳夢家《卜辭綜述》二八四頁所謂之"印方"，字作❦，唐蘭《天釋》五四頁釋"巴"，李孝定《集釋》二七八三釋"儿"，均待考。"方❦自南，其昷❦"，當爲方國名。（乙一五一）

　　隻❦　　　　　　　　　　　　　　　　　　　　合三八〇
　　狩不其㠯❦　　　　　　　　　　　　　　　　　乙一四三
　　狩得❦　　　　　　　　　　　　　　　　　　　乙三九二
　　❦不執　　　　　　　　　　　　　　　　　　　乙一三五

以上"❦"均爲俘虜名。

二、以俘獲或處理之方法爲名

1. 㞢

《說文》："㞢，治也，从又，从卩。卩、事之節也。"這完全是依據小篆的形體來進行說解，與"㞢"字的本形、本義不符。甲骨文"㞢"字作❦，從手持人，抑之使跪之形。其用法主要有兩種：

一爲動詞，乃"虜獲"之義：

　　白旲允其㞢角　　　　　　　　　　　　　　　　佚九一
　　其㞢❦不…　　　　　　　　　　　　　　　　　京津一三三二

一爲名詞，乃俘虜名：

　　禱于匕己,㓨㞢卯宰　　　　　　　　　　　　　續一·三八·六
　　㓨匕庚十㞢,卯十宰　　　　　　　　　　　　　乙七五一
　　㓨㞢二人；㓨㞢一人　　　　　　　　　　　　　佚二一八
　　來庚用十㞢　　　　　　　　　　　　　　　　　乙八七二三

2. 執

"執"字象人帶上桎梏之形，主要也有兩種用法：

一爲動詞：

…隹執亘	乙四六九三
叀￼令執￼	南明九〇
執兕	粹九四一
執罷隻	京津一四七二
其執羌	京津四一四一

作動詞用的"執"字，既可指俘獲敵人，引申之，凡所俘獲，包括野獸亦可謂之"執"。"亘"、"￼"、"羌"指"人"，"兕"、"罷"則指野獸。

一爲名詞：

執其隻；不隻	乙四七六八
用執，用＆	存二·二六八
￼氏執	後下三一·八

3. 係

《說文》："係，結束也。"段玉裁《注》："絜束者，圍而束之也。俗通作繫。"

甲骨文"係"字作￼、￼、￼諸形，象以繩索縛人頸脖，或象以繒繳縛人全身。于省吾同志《釋係》一文，言之甚詳。

在甲骨刻辭中，縛束捆綁俘虜謂之"係"。由於行軍作戰並不一定都帶有繩索，所以有時就利用繒繳。《左傳》襄公十八年："乃弛弓而自後縛之"，也正是此意。

"係"用爲動詞：

| ￼其￼羌 | 存一·六〇〇 |
| 十羌￼ | 續二·一八·七 |

"係"用爲名詞：

| 夏￼ | 摭二·一五五 |
| 氏王￼ | 乙四六〇六 |

4. 俘

甲骨文"俘"字作￼、￼、￼諸形。《說文》以"俘"爲"軍所獲也"；以

"孚"爲"孵"之本字。實際上，"孚"從爪從子，象俘獲之形，金文即用爲"俘"字，與甲文同。"孚"與"俘"的區別，乃後世所分化。

甲骨刻辭捕獲謂之"俘"，爲動詞：

...克🈳二人　　　　　　　　　　　　　　　　　　　甲三九三三

...子🈳告曰，昔甲辰，方眔于虻，🈳人十出五人，五日戊申，方亦眔，🈳人十出六人。　　　　　　　　　　　　　　　　　　　　菁六

《菁》六所記載，乃商的邊邑遭到"方"國的侵犯，一次被擄去十五人，又一次被擄去十六人。

"俘"又用爲名詞，凡所捕獲之俘虜亦謂之"俘"：

我用🈳　　　　　　　　　　　　　　　　　　　　　乙六六九四
王役🈳　　　　　　　　　　　　　　　　　　　　　後下三二·八

5. 伐

甲骨刻辭的"伐"字除用作征伐之伐而外，尚有兩種用法：

一爲砍伐之伐，即"斬首"。這一點下文還要詳細加以說明。

一爲斬掉首級以供祭祀之用的一種"人牲"的名稱：

氐伐百　　　　　　　　　　　　　　　　　　　　　乙五〇〇一
五伐十宰；五伐五宰　　　　　　　　　　　　　　　後上二一·一二
曹且丁十伐十宰　　　　　　　　　　　　　　　　　乙四八三四

6. 㞢

"㞢"即今"歲"字。甲骨刻辭既用作"年歲"之意，也用作祭名，同時爲用牲的一種方法，相當於"劌"。其義爲"殺"。下文將進一步加以說明。

被用作"歲"祭時犧牲的俘虜，也稱之爲"歲"：

子美見，氐㞢于丁　　　　　　　　　　　　　　　　前七·二八·二
氐㞢　　　　　　　　　　　　　　　　　　　　　　契六二一
用子央㞢于丁　　　　　　　　　　　　　　　　　　林一·二〇·三

"氐"通作"致"，有"貢納"的意思。"氐歲"即進納供"歲"祭之犧牲。"用子央㞢于丁"即以"子央"所貢納之"㞢"以祭祀於祖丁，這是武丁時期的卜辭。

三、敵方之首領

1. 白

  方白用   京津五二八一

  白戠䩺，四月   天九〇

  羌二方白其用于…且丁、父甲   京津四〇三四

  其䩺白于父丁   南明六二一

甲骨刻辭的"白"字除用作白色之"白"及地名之"白"而外，如上所舉諸例，相當於後世的"伯"字，金文亦同。《說文》"伯，長也"。甲骨刻辭的這些"白"或"方白"，均指敵方之首領而言。實際上"白"就是"首"或"頭"。"首領"乃"白"字的引申義。"伯"是後起的孳乳字。商代的"與國"或"屬國"，其首領亦稱"白"。有人以爲即五等爵之"伯"，純屬牽強附會。

《京津》五二八一是一片人頭骨刻辭，把俘虜來的"方白"殺掉，用以祭祀，並在其頭骨上刻"方白用"三字，類似的例子還有：

  《京津》五二八二："…丑用于…義友…"

  《存》一·二三五八："…白…"

陳夢家《卜辭綜述》三二七尚列舉有《明氏》人頭骨刻辭，《甲室》人頭骨刻辭，《善齋》人頭骨刻辭及《掇二》人頭骨刻辭等等。胡厚宣《京津》、《續存》序言對此曾有所論及，認爲是"殺用戰俘酋長以祭祀祖先的記事刻辭"，極爲正確。

2. 囟

  羌方囟其用，王受又   甲五〇七

  用危方囟于匕庚   南明六六九

陳夢家《卜辭綜述》三二七謂："卜辭之⊕象頭殼之形，其義或爲首腦，或爲腦殼。"于省吾《從甲骨文看商代社會性質》謂："囟係指羌方與危方首領之頭顱言之。"（《東北人民大學學報》一九五七年二—三期合刊）

四、女性的俘虜

甲骨刻辭中女性的俘虜名大多是從相應的男性俘虜名孳化而來。

1. 姜

"姜"即女性的"羌"。

  帚于小乙三姜   錄二〇三
  王姜甾朕事   京津二二四五

2. 孜

"孜"即女性的"㚸"。

  邑人其見方𢎛，不其見方孜   外三四
  勿乎孜宅…   乙六四〇四
  孜用于且…   存一・一六一

3. 奚

"奚"即女性的"奚"。

  小母矢奚   前一・三・四
  且辛奚   續一・一九・三

4. 嬃

"嬃"即女性的"係"。孫海波《甲骨文編》六〇四頁以爲"母它"的合文；陳夢家《卜辭綜述》四九一頁讀作"它母"，以爲是"先妣之私名"，都是錯誤的。

"嬃"字僅見於《乙》四六七七，其辭爲"匕辛嬃"，同版卜辭尚有"母庚𤣥"，"母庚三牢"，均爲用牲以祭先妣之占卜。

同版又有"匕戊㚤"、"匕戊娅"、"匕戊𡝗"、"匕乙娅"、"匕辛婡"，是足以證明"先妣私名"之說不可據。"匕戊"不可能同時名"㚤"、名"娅"、名"𡝗"。而"娅"不可能同時爲"匕戊"及"匕乙"之私名。

所有這一些從女之字，都應當是女俘之名，與"𤣥"、"牢"一樣，是用作祭祀先妣的犧牲。

卜辭祭先妣多用牝牲，多用女俘。

"嬃"字所從之𠂤，乃象繒繳形，與 𢎛、𫝀 諸字所從之𠂤或𠃍 同，不是"它"字。男俘爲"係"，女俘爲"嬃"，均象用繒繳加以束縛。《左傳》襄公十八年"乃弛弓自後縛之"，就是戰爭中利用繒繳以縛系俘虜的明確記載。

5. 妾

陳夢家《卜辭綜述》（五九八頁）以爲"嬖"字，"指一種可爲犧牲的女奴"，

不確。其身份是"女奴"或是"女俘"在卜辭中都得不到證明。

不過,"奻"都是用作祭祀時的犧牲,沒有例外。她是擄掠自其它部族,這種可能性要大一些,現在暫且將之作為俘虜,列之於此。

  其燎于河牢,沈奻   後上二三・四
  王其又母戊一奻,此受又   粹三八〇

五、通稱

1. 人

在甲骨刻辭中,有的時候,俘虜泛稱為"人":

  羌三人   甲三三六一
  尸十人二   粹四一二
  伐十人   前一・一八・四
  囚二人   續五・一二・一
  克孚二人   甲三九三三
  用人牛;弜用人   南師一・一四九
  人于河其用   甲六九〇

2. 女

在甲骨刻辭中,"妾"、"女"、"母"三字往往可以通用。但女俘祇能稱之為"妾"或"女",不能稱之為"母"。"女"或"妾"在有的時候是一切女俘的通稱,正如"人"字有時是一切男俘的通稱一樣。

商代用動物為牲,有時對於其牝牡、毛色、大小,要求甚嚴,有時則要求不那麼嚴格,泛稱"牛"、"羊"、"犬"、"豕"而已。對於用人為牲也是如此,對於其性別、地區、來源,有時規定甚嚴,有時則祇用泛稱。

  出及女   合四三七
  帚妌來女   乙七七二六
  其氏角女   乙三五〇七
  燎女   外五〇

六、其它

1. 🅐

🅐字的變體很多,郭沫若釋"宰",葉玉森釋"寇"。究竟相當於現在的什麼

字，還很難確定。至於其爲一種俘虜的專名，則是可以肯定的。

畚☒	契六三九
叀夫令馭☒	南明九〇
亘奉☒	乙二五七二①
乎追☒及	鐵一一六·四
衍氏☒	乙五二八八
奉☒見	掇二·三〇九

從上述的例證中可以看出，☒都是俘獲來的，"奉☒見"，"見"讀爲"獻"，即將俘獲之☒獻納於商王。

☒可能爲方國名，但於卜辭中還得不到證明。

2. 𠬝、卬

"𠬝"當是"𠬝"的繁體；"卬"從辭例看來，也是俘虜之一種。

王出𠬝若	合二七三
勿乎取卬	珠二三
戕卬；勿戕卬	乙二五九四
又匕庚五卬，十牢不用	佚八九七

3. 屯

奉屯？王固曰，奉	乙二二七〇
𣪊來屯，戕	佚一五一
王戕多屯若于下乙	乙四一一九
翌甲午用多屯	乙七一二八
用侯（屯）自𠙻十示	合三三三

此外，甲骨刻辭中尚有"妥"字，象以手俘女形，但均用作人名，不用作俘虜名。又"灸"祭所用從女之字甚多，雖可推斷當爲女俘，但於卜辭中均得不到證明。凡此之類，皆摒而不錄。

平心《卜辭金文中所見社會經濟史實考釋》以爲"青"與"☒"均爲俘虜名（見《中華文史論叢》第一集），但於卜辭中難以確徵，不敢苟同。

---

① 編者按："乙二五七二"，原文誤作"乙二二七二"，今據實際出處徑改。

(三) 俘虜的來源

一、戰爭

俘虜的來源，祇可能是戰爭，商與其鄰近的"多方"之間，戰爭頻繁。商王經常派遣其臣僚去征伐"多方"。例如：

王叀婦好令正尸	續四·三〇·一
令五族伐羌	後下四二·六
登人伐下危，受屮又	續一·三七·一

有時商王與其它方國結成聯盟，共同征伐另一方國：

王叀沚馘从伐𢀛方，帝受我又	乙三七八七
王从壴乘伐下危，受屮又	乙二七〇〇

有時則商王親自出征：

呂方出，王自正，下上若，受我（又）	柏二五
王伐土方，受屮又	林二·七·九
王卄人五千正土方，受屮又	後上三一·六

至於與商鄰近的"多方"，也是在不斷地侵犯商的領域：

方其大出	福三
土方𢦔我田十人	菁六
土方征于我東啚，戈二邑。呂方亦𢦔我西啚田	菁二

甲骨刻辭中有關戰爭或邊境武裝衝突的記載，多至不可勝數。我們由此可以看出當時的戰爭或衝突是頻繁的。在這些頻繁的交戰過程中，商人曾經擄獲了大量的戰俘：

隻伇	乙三〇一
追隻羌	金五九六
…牵羌…隻廿屮五…	後下三八·七
…克俘二人…	甲三九三三

𢦏㝬	乙五二六五
㝬其係羌	存一·六〇〇
十羌係	續二·一八·七
拳羌十人	林二·一三·二

以上都是有關擄獲戰俘的辭例。"隻"就是現在的"獲"字。《公羊》昭廿四年傳："生得曰獲";《禮·檀弓》鄭《注》："獲謂係虜之";《周禮·朝士職》鄭《注》："俘而取之曰獲。"甲骨刻辭對於田獵取得禽獸叫做"隻",對於戰爭取得的俘虜也叫做"隻"。

乙、辛時期有一片牛骨刻辭曾有如下的記載:

小臣牆从伐,㠱危、美…人廿人四,而千五百七十,䤔百…,車二丙,厰百八十三,函五十,矢…又白麇于大乙,用雎白印…䤔于且乙,用美于且丁,俘日京易…

綜圖一六·二

這是有關商代晚期某一次大規模戰爭的記載。文辭雖然略有殘缺,但其大致内容還是清楚的。其大意是:

小臣牆參加了這次戰役,共擒獲危方、美方若干人,某方的廿四人,而方的一千五百七十人,䤔方的一百多人。同時還繳獲了二輛車,一百八十三個盾,五十付函甲,若干箭。把所俘獲的敵方首領殺掉以祭祀祖先。

從這一次戰爭中所俘獲人數之衆多,以及同時與好幾個敵方交戰的情況看來,商人一定是出動了不少的人員,並且還可能是聯合了不少的方國共同出征的。乙、辛時期的另一片刻辭記載着"余其从多田于多白正盂方白炎"(甲二四一六)可以互證。

在武丁時,曾記載有一次征伐某方,共出動了一萬三千人。這是甲骨刻辭中迄今所見的,有明確記載的最高出征人數。《粹》一一七一"…隻…其三萬,不…",此為甲骨刻辭中所有記數字之最高者,其所"獲"者是人是獸,則無法確知。

甲骨刻辭所記載的,一般的戰爭規模,其興師人數是"五千"、"三千",有時則祇有"五百"、"一千"。另外,我們從《菁華》的幾片大骨中,商人曾經加以大書特書的辭例,也可以看出某些迹象:

土方㞢于我東啚,戈二邑,吕方亦殷我西啚田	菁一
昔甲辰,方㞢于蚁,俘人十㞢五人。五日戊申,方亦㞢,俘人十㞢六人	菁五
土方殷我田十人	菁六

從上舉諸例中可以看出，土方和呂方從東西兩面夾攻，祇能使商的兩個邊邑受災。"方"在五天之內，兩次侵犯商境，共俘走了三十一人。"土方"一次俘走了商的十人。其規模都不會太大。象這樣的情況，與其說是戰爭，不如說是武裝衝突更來得恰當一些。這幾片都是武丁時期的刻辭。乙、辛時期征伐"人方"和"盂方"之役，則規模極大，且曠日持久，這和上述邊境上短暫的衝突是不可同日而語的。

二、貢納

商代的"俘虜"，除了直接來源於戰爭之外，值得加以注意的是，有些"俘虜"的很大一部份，是來自於"屬國"或"與國"的貢納。不可否認，這些"俘虜"究其根源仍然是在戰爭中所俘獲的。祇不過是把這些戰俘當作貢納物或禮品送給別人。因此，就商王朝來說，這就不是戰爭的"收入"，而是貢納物或禮品的"收入"了。

甲骨刻辭中常見有關於禮品或貢納物的記載：

妥氐羊	乙五三〇三
古來馬	乙五三〇五
氐牛五十	前一·二九·一
出來自南氐龜	乙六六七〇
省氐石	乙四六九三
癸來白馬	乙三三九四
…其來象三	後下五·一一
妻來牛	乙一二八三
雀氐猱	乙四七一八
氐牛四百	明一五一七
其氐車	京津一〇〇二
畢見百牛	前七·三二·四
氐魚	存一·三九〇

這些貢納物大多數是牲畜。也有"車"、"石"、"象"、"猱"、"魚"等等。"牛"、"羊"等貢物是作祭祀時的犧牲，這在卜辭中有明確的記載。"馬"有時是戰馬。《乙》三三八一有辭云："貞（龜）氐卅馬，允其牽羌"，"龜卅馬，弗其牽羌"。其

後一辭漏刻"氐"字。所"氐"之馬，乃供"牽羌"之用。其背面（《乙》三三八二）之"繇辭"云："王固曰，隹丁牽吉，隹甲不吉。"

甲骨刻辭中更爲常見的貢納物則是"俘虜"：

𡧒來一羌一牛	甲五二五
𡧒來戠	南師二·一一〇
妥來羌二人	存二·三四〇
倗眔殸氐羌	乙六三七三
犬隻羌其氐	乙六二一五
用望乘以羌自囗	佚八七五
用望乘來羌	粹五九六
用射䶂以羌自囗	粹二三五
䶂正化氐王係	乙四六〇六
子羑見，氐㚔于丁	前七·二八·二
氐伐百	乙五〇〇一
伐來屯	京津一三三三
衍氐卩	乙五二八八①
𡇒氐大	乙四〇八〇
邑人其見方𠂤	南師一·五九
帚姘來女	乙七四二六
其氐角女	乙三五〇七
…其來𠂤，不其來𩁹	乙四〇三〇
周氐𡚬	乙七三一二
媚子突入俎羌十	菁三

這些被當作貢納物的都是"俘虜"。貢納或餽遺的方法或者叫做"見（獻）"，或者叫做"氐（致）"，或者叫做"以"，或者叫做"來"，或者叫做"至"，或者叫做"入"。這可能是與貢納者的身份地位，以及和商王關係的親疏有關。

商王與這些貢納者的關係，有的是直接的臣屬，如"𡧒"、"倗"、"殸"、"婦姘"等等；有的是被征服的方國，如"奚"、"犬"；有的是時友時敵，如"周"。

以俘虜作貢納品或禮物，在周代銘刻及典籍中不乏記載。如：

---

① 編者按："乙五二八八"，原文誤作"乙五二八九"，今據實際出處徑改。

《虢季子白盤》："趄趄子白，獻馘于王"

《春秋》莊公六年："齊人來歸衛俘"

《春秋》僖公廿一年："楚人使宜申來獻捷"

《左傳》僖公廿八年："晉侯入曹，執曹伯，畀宋人"

又："晉人執魏侯，歸之于京師"

《左傳》宣公十五年："晉侯使趙同獻狄俘于周"

《史記·晉世家》：晉侯"獻楚俘于周（城濮之役所獲）"

三、田獵或牧芻

在邊境地區，商與鄰近的"多方"相互雜處，時常發生衝突，尤其是以放牧和打獵的時候爲甚，這種衝突當應屬於戰爭的範疇。但商人把這些在衝突中所獲得的俘虜，祇認爲是牧芻或田獵的"副業"收入。例如：

芻田其隻羌	京津一二七八
令彘田从戔至于瀧隻羌	前七·二·四
今日狩不其畢印	乙一四三

這些刻辭都是有關於在田獵中能否獲得俘虜的占卜。由於在田獵時經常擄獲敵方人員。積之既久，在出發田獵之前，就要占卜一番，貞問是否能和往常一樣，除了獵獲野獸之外，尚能得到額外的收穫——抓住俘虜。

從這裏我們可以連帶地看出另外兩個問題：一個是商代的疆域，在其邊境地區，是與多方雜處，閒有出入的；另一個是當時的田獵與戰爭有着密切的關係。郭沫若同志曾經指出："征伐與畋遊之事每多不可分，多於行師之次從事畋獵或盤遊"（《卜辭通纂攷釋》第一六二頁），這是對的。但不僅如此而已。在田獵的時候，還會因爲利害的關係，發生武裝衝突。也就是說，田獵這一行動本身，還會成爲戰爭的"導火綫"。

商人出發打獵，固然是全副武裝，準備必要時與遭遇的敵人進行戰鬥，而放牧也不例外。在當時放牧是一種很危險的事情。大批的牛羊，最容易引起敵人的覬覦。商人自己就曾經常搶掠敵方的牛羊牲畜。

甲骨刻辭有"告芻"（見《戩》三六·一四），這和"告鹿"、"告麥"的性質相同。胡厚宣同志認爲"告鹿"是"發現了野獸，就向殷王報告"（《甲骨續存序》），于省吾同志認爲"告麥的意義是商王在外邊的臣吏，窺伺鄰近部落所種或

收穫的麥子，對於商王作了一種情報。商王根據這種情報，纔進行掠奪"（見《商代的穀類作物》）。這些都是非常正確的。

"告芻"應該是商王的臣屬發現了鄰近方國在牧放中的牲畜，向商王報告，以便前往刼掠。

甲骨刻辭的"芻"字有兩種用法。一種是相當於《孟子·告子》"猶芻豢之悦我口"或《禮記·月令》"共寢廟之芻豢"之"芻"，指牛馬等食草的牲畜而言，乃名詞；一種是相當於《周禮·充人》"芻之三月"之"芻"，指牧放牲畜，乃動詞。

…氐芻其五百隹六	乙六八九六
允虫來自光,氐羌芻五十	珠六二〇
戉,光虫隻羌芻五十	乙四六九二
乎取㕚芻	乙五〇二六
乎取兆芻	合五九
洀氐牧芻	天三六

這些辭例説明商王的臣屬經常搶掠近鄰方國的牛羊，並貢納給商王。然則商人自己在放牧時，也得隨時準備戰鬥。至於遭到敵人的侵襲，也是意料中的事情。所以也有這樣的刻辭：

| 在易牧隻羌 | 珠七五八 |
| 牧隻羌 | 庫四二 |

放牧而獲得了"羌"，應該就是羌人來搶刼在放牧中的牲畜，結果被商的武裝放牧者所俘獲。由於這種情況在當時經常發生，所以就反映在貞問的卜辭中。無論是田獵也好，還是放牧也好，有時事先要貞卜一番，看看是否能有一點額外的牧獲——抓住俘虜。因此，商代"俘虜"的來源，除了戰爭和臣屬或盟國的貢納、餽遺以外，還別有門路，那就是田獵和放牧時的"副業"收入。

（四）俘虜的用途

一、用作祭祀時犧牲

商代對於俘虜的處置，根據甲骨刻辭的記載，主要是殺掉以祭祀神明或祖

先。商代經常地、大量地用俘虜作爲祭牲的現象，在世界古代史中，截至目前爲止，還找不出足以與之相比擬的例子。至於其手段之殘酷，名目之繁多，更是驚人。現在分別舉例説明於下：

1. 俎

《説文》："俎，禮俎也。从半肉在且上。"甲骨文"俎"字的形體雖然變化很多，但都象置肉於"且"之形。

"俎"字在卜辭中絶大多數用作動詞：

俎小牢	粹一八
俎大牢	粹六八
俎卅牛	後上二七·一〇
尞大牢，俎大牢	後上二二·七
三羊沈，五牛俎	南師一·五
俎牝	簠典九六

以上所"俎"者均爲牛羊。《儀禮·鄉飲酒》："賓辭以俎"，《注》："俎者，肴之貴者也。"卜辭用"俎"祭祀神靈祖先，犧牲都是以牛羊，或者是用"人"。祇有《乙》三〇九四"二羊二豕俎"，是唯一"俎"用"豕"的例子。

"俎"與"尞"、"沈"、"卯"等並舉，均爲用牲的方法。這種用牲方法，應該是"全牲"，不象"伐"或"戠"是砍掉了腦袋的。"俎"人時大多用的是"羌"：

癸酉俎于夒，羌三人，卯十牛，又	續一·五二·二
己未俎于夒，羌三，卯十牛，中	前六·二·三
己未俎…夒，羌…人，卯十牛，左	前六·二·二
…午俎…夒，尸十人二，卯十牛，中	粹四一二

其中祇有《粹》四一二是用"尸"於俎祭，比較特殊。郭沫若同志以爲"丂"字之異，並認爲此片可疑，蓋有未然。島邦男《卜辭綜類》四八四亦誤摹作"↑"。

《菁》三有辭云："媚子宷入俎羌十"，是指"媚子宷"貢納了準備用於"俎"祭的羌俘十名。董作賓以爲是"進納了伺候俎祭的羌人十名，意思是伺候俎祭時照料牛羊的羌人"，這和他把"伐羌"說成是會跳舞的羌人，同樣是出於臆測。

卜辭的"俎"這一種用牲方法，是行之於比較隆重的祀典。到了後世，把"俎"字的這一意義加以引申，於是乎便成爲：凡是隆重的祀典都叫做"俎"；

凡是"肴之貴者"也叫做"俎"。同時在形體上也發生了分化，成爲"俎"、"宜"二字。凡隆重的祀典均叫做"宜"。《爾雅·釋天》所謂"起大事，動大衆，必先有事乎社而後出謂之宜"。

卜辭還有一種用牲方法叫做"刞"，辭例很少，字不可識，與"俎"有別。其辭爲：

  刞羌百⋯   存一·三四七
  ⋯刞用百⋯   前六·三七·六

暫附於此以待考。

2. 伐

《廣雅·釋詁》："伐，殺也"；《管子·霸形》："伐鐘鼓之縣"，《注》"伐，斫斷也"。甲骨文的"伐"字作𢦏，就象斬首之形。其辭例爲：

  㞢于成卅伐   乙六〇四三
  㞢于囧一伐，卯十小宰   乙六六六五
  㞢于大甲，伐十㞢五   乙四九一六
  酚且乙，十伐㞢五，卯十宰   乙六四〇八
  王宔武丁伐十人，卯三牢，鬯⋯；
  王宔且庚伐二人，卯二牢，鬯⋯卣；
  王⋯庚且丁⋯人，卯二牢，鬯二卣；
  王宔文武丁伐十人，卯六牢，鬯六卣   前一·一八·四

"伐"就是砍掉頭顱，這是卜辭中最爲常見的用牲方法之一，引申之，凡被砍掉頭顱的"人牲"或是將被砍頭作爲祭牲的俘虜也叫做"伐"。早期金文的"伐"字作：

               參見《金文編》八〇四頁

正象以斧鉞斬首之形。《京津》三一〇二有"𢦏"字，辭殘，疑亦"伐"字之異構。據其字體，乃屬於"𠂤"組卜辭，屬於武丁早朝。此組貞人之字體多保留較原始之形態。

3. 䤾

"䤾"和"伐"一樣，都是斬首。但"䤾"字的形體較爲複雜，作𢦏、𢦏、𢦏、等形。象將俘虜的雙手反縛，抓住其髮辮，用斧鉞砍斷其頭顱。有的還帶

數小點，象血水淋漓之狀。

  王戠多屯　　　　　　　　　　　　　　　　　　　乙三四四二
  王戠多屯若干下乙　　　　　　　　　　　　　　　乙四一一九
  皋來屯，戠…十人　　　　　　　　　　　　　　　佚一五一

以上均用爲動詞。《佚》一五一商承祚《考釋》誤釋"人"作"月"，胡厚宣《南·師》二·一一〇及島邦男《卜辭綜類》四六九均誤摹作"月"。然島邦男對此曾表示懷疑。

  "戠"字含義的進一步引申，則凡用"戠"這一方法加以處置的俘虜，也稱之爲"戠"，用爲名詞，例如：

  卯小辛三宰，又戠二　　　　　　　　　　　　　　前一·一六·五
  …父庚…又戠二　　　　　　　　　　　　　　　　林二·五·九

在歷次殷陵和殷墟的發掘中，發現了不少無頭人尸骨，另外則有整坑的、失去了軀體的人頭，總數當以千計。這一些應當就是用"伐"或"戠"的方法處置俘虜的結果，是一種用人爲祭牲的現象，很多同志將這些斬首用作祭牲的現象解釋成爲屠殺奴隸，這是錯誤的。根據甲骨刻辭的記載，這些被斬首者，其身份是戰爭中的俘虜，並不是什麽奴隸。下文還將詳細論及。

  4. 炎

  甲骨刻辭的"炎"字從人在火上，這是處置俘虜的另一種方法——用火將之燒死，而其目的則是在於求雨，這是一種乞雨的祭祀。這種風俗一直流傳了很久。《左傳》僖公廿一年："夏大旱，公欲焚巫尪"；《禮記·檀弓》："歲旱，穆公召縣子而問焉，曰：天久不雨，吾欲暴尪而奚若？"

  如果向上推溯的話，則早在商代的初期，據傳說："湯時大旱七年，卜用人祀天。"（《文選·思玄賦》注引《淮南子》）至於說商湯自己"剪髮及爪自潔，居柴上，將自焚以祭天"，則未免故神其說了。

  其炎三㚻　　　　　　　　　　　　　　　　　　　　存二·七四四
  炎婞出雨　　　　　　　　　　　　　　　　　　　　佚一〇〇〇
  炎㚸出从雨　　　　　　　　　　　　　　　　　　　乙三四四九

卜辭用於"炎"祭最多者是"㚸"及"婞"，其身份在卜辭中無明確記載。"㚻"當爲女性之卩，則其身份乃女俘。陳夢家《卜辭綜述》六〇三頁以爲"婞"、

"妦""乃是女巫"。這是根據後世"焚巫"的記載,商代恐非如此。我們則認爲"嫭"與"妦"是女俘的可能性要大一些。根據卜辭所反映的情況,商代卜人、巫者的地位均甚尊崇,是不可能用作祭祀時犧牲的。

5. 沈

甲骨文的"沈"字,羅振玉謂:"象沈牛於水中,殆即貍沈之沈字。此爲本字,《周禮》作沈乃借字也。"(見《增訂殷虛書契考釋》卷中第六一頁)我們認爲,㳄或作㳄,所從之"牛"或正或倒,篆文㳄乃其形體之訛變,㳄與木形甚相近。

《周禮・大宗伯》:"以貍沈祭山林川澤",《注》:"川澤曰沈";《禮記・大傳》《注》:"祭水曰沈。"甲骨文的"沈"字形體,象投牛或羊入水。引申之,凡一切投入水中的用牲方法,均謂之"沈",並不限於牛、羊。而"沈"祭的主要對象則是"河":

使人于河,沈三羊,劋三牛	粹三六
尞于河三宰,沈三宰,俎一宰	合三三九
沈五牛,尞三牛,卯五牛	乙四五九五
桒禾于河,尞三宰,沈三牛,俎宰	掇一・五五〇

"沈"和"㶣"正好相對,"㶣"是用火燒,"沈"則是投諸水;"㶣"是求雨,"沈"則主要是防水。商人在自然災害面前,尤其是對於水災和旱災,還是無能爲力的。祇知屠殺俘虜或牲畜以祈求神祖的保祐。例如:

其出大水	後下三・四
今歲㐬大水;	
其出大水	金三七七
其告水入于上甲,祝大乙一牛,王受又	粹一四八
水其夓兹邑;	
⋯爲我家祖辛佐王;	
⋯家祖乙佐王	乙三一六二

商代的水災是頻繁的,人們認爲這是河神爲祟,就供奉犧牲以祭祀河神,認爲這樣就可以免去水災。

其尞于河宰,沈卯	後上二三・四

這是卜辭沈祭用人爲牲的唯一例子。與此有關的則有：

  郊玨酚河　　　　　　　　　　　　　　　　　　鐵一二七・二
  酚河卅牛，氏我女　　　　　　　　　　　　　　乙三〇九四
  乎帚奏于河宅　　　　　　　　　　　　　　　　乙五五二〇

"沈郊"或"郊玨酚河"，當爲後世"爲河伯娶婦"之所由來。商代之"河"，亦稱"高祖"（《摭續》二），爲其"先公"之一，祀典極爲隆重，當爲神祖之統一體。

 6. 攸（攴）

于省吾同志謂"攴字象以朴擊蛇之形…初義爲以朴擊蛇，引申爲割殺之義，攴即《說文》敀字，經傳假施爲之"（《殷契駢枝・釋攴》）。

"攴"在卜辭，是用牲方法之一種：

  攴牢　　　　　　　　　　　　　　　　　　　　存上二八・五
  攴羊　　　　　　　　　　　　　　　　　　　　存一・一四九四
  于兄己攴犬；
  攴二豭二牡于下乙；
  攴二豭二牡　　　　　　　　　　　　　　　　　乙四五四四
  攴卅牛　　　　　　　　　　　　　　　　　　　明一一六四

以上是"攴"牲畜。用人爲牲，也謂之"攴"：

  攴羌百…　　　　　　　　　　　　　　　　　　續二・二九・三
  勿攴羌百，十三月　　　　　　　　　　　　　　鐵一七六・一
  攴尸　　　　　　　　　　　　　　　　　　　　乙四四二三
  翌乙未，汎攴尸　　　　　　　　　　　　　　　乙一五一二
  亦攴人　　　　　　　　　　　　　　　　　　　前七・三一・三

 7. 苟

甲骨文苟字或又作苟，郭沫若《粹》三五五片《考釋》讀作"甒"；于省吾《駢續・釋苟》進而詳加論證，都是正確的。就其形體來說，小篆苟乃是形體的訛變。本來是象盛矢於器中之形，《說文》孳乳作"箙"。卜辭皆通假作"甒"，是一種用牲的方法。

《周禮・大宗伯》："以甒辜祭四方百物"，鄭《注》："甒，甒牲胷也。"《說

文》篆文作"副",訓爲"判"。錢大昕《養新錄》以爲"古讀副如劈",卜辭"萄"這種用牲方法,當是劈開牲胃,取出內臟,風乾以祭:

  翌辛亥出于司辛,萄出羌十   前五·九·六
  辛卯出三宰,萄羌…   前五·九·七
  出于母辛三宰,萄三牛,羌十   金六九四

《後上》二八·三和《佚》五四三同文,二者互相補充,其辭爲:

  丁亥卜殷貞,昔乙酉萄㫃卯大丁、大甲、且乙,百邑、百羌,卯三百宰。

8. 㲋

甲骨文的㲋字,即《説文》之"蠱",乃殺牲取血以祭,于省吾同志對此有詳盡之論證,見《駢枝·釋㲋》。這種祭禮,大致相當於後世之"釁":

  《左傳》僖公三十三年:"孟明稽首曰,君之惠,不以纍臣釁鼓,使歸就戮于秦…"杜《注》:"殺人以血塗鼓,謂之釁鼓。"

  《左傳》成公三年:"二國治戎,臣不才,不勝其任,以爲俘馘,執事不以釁鼓,使歸即戮,君之惠也。"

  《左傳》昭公五年:"吳子使其弟蹶由犒師。楚人執之,將以釁鼓。"

是在春秋時代,尚有屠殺戰爭中之俘虜,取血以塗鼓的風俗。此當即商代"㲋"人或牲畜,取血以祭的遺風。其辭例爲:

  出來羌,來甲戌㲋用   前六·六七·四
  …羌九㲋自…   甲三九二
  㲋用來羌   甲五九
  自囧㲋用人;其用人牛十又五   南明五二五
  㲋出伐;勿㲋出伐   合一三八
  于大示㲋出伐   存一·一八二四

9. 尞

甲骨文的"尞"字,"從木在火上,木旁諸點象火燄上騰之狀"(《增考》二六頁)。也是一種用牲之法。除牛、羊等牲畜之外,對於俘虜也是常常"尞"之,以作爲祭祀時的犧牲:

  尞于土羌,俎小宰   粹一八
  㞢年于夏,尞又羌   續一·五一·五

尞白人　　　　　　　　　　　　　　　　南誠一八
　　　尞白人　　　　　　　　　　　　　　　　鐵四三・一

《說文》："尞、柴祭天也"，卜辭"尞"多爲萎年祈雨之祭。此種祭祀多用牛羊，用人則比較少見。"白人"當指其膚色而言。或讀爲"百"，誤。卜辭"白"與"百"區分極爲嚴格。還有"白羌"（《契》二四五及《存》二・一九五），這和卜辭的"白牛"、"白馬"、"白羊"、"白豕"、"白兕"、"白鹿"、"白犾"當屬同一性質。《契》二四五《考釋》瞿潤緡謂"當如字讀"，所論甚是。

10．卯

王國維以爲"卯即劉之假借字"（《戩考》五頁）。《爾雅・釋詁》"劉，殺也"。實際上"劉"乃"卯"之孳乳字。卜辭的"卯"除用作干支以外，最常見的就是用牲方法。這種用牲方法多施之於牛、羊，但有時以人爲牲也用"卯"。

　　　其卯羌伊宀　　　　　　　　　　　　　　粹一五一
　　　卯五羌　　　　　　　　　　　　　　　　粹五九一
　　　卯⋯五人　　　　　　　　　　　　　　　存二・九〇四
　　　卯十𢦏　　　　　　　　　　　　　　　　存二・七八七

這種用牲之法，乃"因卯之字形取義，蓋言對剖也"（《卜通》第三九片考釋）。

11．歲（戉、戌）

甲骨文"歲"字作𢦏、𢦏等形，隸定作戉或戌。說者多謂"歲"與"戊"爲一字。實際上卜辭"歲"與"戊"已經分化，區分極嚴，從不相混。

卜辭"歲"亦爲用牲之法，其義爲"殺"。

　　　戉羌卅，卯三宀，萄一牛　　　　　　　　林二・三・一一
　　　戉羌卅，卯十牛　　　　　　　　　　　　前六・一六・一

《甲骨文錄》二六〇，孫海波《考釋》讀作：

　　　□旅□，□上甲歲□，□于唐五□，□羌十五歲亡尤

並謂"此辭既云歲□□于唐矣，復於羌十五下黏注歲字，文例甚奇"。孫氏誤讀"五十"爲"十五"，可以無論，但以爲所黏補之"歲"字列於"亡尤"之前，則恐未然。"歲"字當係補於"唐"字之下，島邦男《卜辭綜類》三四五讀作：

　　　⋯旅⋯上甲戉⋯于唐戉五⋯羌五十亡尤

這一釋讀較爲正確。

12. 卯

"卯"在卜辭中也是最常見的用牲方法之一。"卯"也是"殺"的意思：

卯㚔、三[木]、五宰	乙六七三二
钟帚好于父乙，卯㚔	庫一七〇一
勿卯匕庚㚔十[牢]、卅小宰	乙二四九一
卯匕庚十㚔，卯十宰	乙七五一
卯十㚔十青	乙二〇二三
卯匕庚五[木]	乙五二四七
钟于匕庚卯㚔，出十牛	存二·二七〇
卯匕己㚔[木]	乙三三八七
卯十㚔，卯小宰	乙二八〇二
卯羌五	庫一五五一
其卯卻	粹三八七
卯㚔一人；卯㚔二人	佚二一八

據《後上》二一·一〇"卯伐廿，鬯卅，牢卅，㚔卅……"，又《前》八·一二·六與此同文（爲第三卜），"卯"與"伐"似爲同義。《合》二五四亦有辭爲"卯且乙十伐出五，卯十宰出五"。

《合》三〇一"卯千牛、千人"是甲骨刻辭中用牲數字之最高者，屬於武丁時期。

胡厚宣同志《甲骨續存·序》説："人祭最多的'卯千人'，甚至'戈伐二千六百五十六人'。"①我們的意見則認爲，《後下》四三·九的"允戈伐二千六百五十六人"，乃"驗辭"，係指戰爭中斬伐敵人之數字，與"人祭"無關。用人爲牲，僅見"卜辭"，且其用牲之數，自二十以上，皆以十爲單位；自百以上，皆以百爲單位。即"廿"、"卅"……；"百"、"二百"、"三百"……等等。

尚有一值得注意之現象，即某種用牲方法，主要施之於某種特定之俘虜或牲畜。例如"卯"多施之於"㚔"、"[木]"；"俎"、"戉"則多施之於"羌"；"改"則多施之於"尸"；"沈"、"燎"則爲女俘等等。

---

① 胡厚宣同志《中國奴隸社會的人殉和人祭》一文已認爲《後下》四三·九"應該是戰爭斬伐的記録"（見《文物》一九七四年第八期第六三頁）。

13. 彈（弦）

甲骨文"彈"字作𢎨、𢎩、𢎪等形體。《太平御覽》引《字林》："彈，拼也，拼使戰動掉彈也。"甲骨文"彈"字從弓、從又，或從攴，正象"使戰動掉彈"之形。字亦作"䚡"，《玉篇》："青州謂彈曰䚡"；《廣雅·釋器》："䚡，彈也。"卜辭"彈"亦謂用牲之方法，"彈"有"擊"義，謂擊殺之。其辭例爲：

| 其彈廿人 | 掇一·三九二 |
| 其彈五十 | 後下六·七 |

引申之，凡是用此種祭法的祭祀也叫做"彈"，卜辭的祭名與用牲方法很多都是一致的。

| 彈，王受又；羌十人又五，王受又 | 粹五九三 |
| 其彈，三牢；五牢 | 粹一五四二 |

14. 用

卜辭的"用"字爲殺牲的通稱。《左傳》昭公十一年："楚子滅蔡，用隱太子于岡山"，杜《注》："用之，殺以祭山。"又僖公十九年："宋公使邾文公用鄫子于次睢之社"，杜《注》："蓋殺人而用祭。"

奚絆白鹽用于丁	後下三三·九
癸丑卜殼貞，五百𢦏用；旬壬戌，屮用𢦏百，三月	京津一二五五
其用人牛十又五	南明五二五
用羌	乙一九四一
用馭	乙八八七八
用五伐	乙八四六二
三百羌用于丁	續二·一六·三

15. 屮

"屮"字舊以爲"侑"之假借，認爲是祭名。實際上就是"有"字，和"用"一樣，都是用牲之通稱：

屮奚大乙卅	合二八
祐大甲，屮十羌	珠八六四
燎河一牛，屮三羌，卯三牛；	
屮于河三羌，卯三牛，燎…牛	合三〇一
屮艮母庚	鄴一·三七·三

二、用作奴隸

甲骨刻辭所記載的有關於俘虜的處置，除了極大一部份是作爲祭祀的犧牲而殺掉以外，也有一部份是被活着保留下來，驅使他們做一些勞役。這樣，這些俘虜就取得了奴隸的身份。這些勞役，可分爲下列諸種：

1. 田獵

乎多羌逐罡隻	續四・二九・二
乎羌逐…	庫一九七六
乎多羌…隻	京津一二八一
多羌隻鹿	前四・四八・一
…多羌…鹿	庫一九八

已著錄的數萬片甲骨中，僅此五條。而《庫》一九七六"乎羌逐…"尚殘缺，"逐"祇剩了一個"豕"字的殘體。

2. 征伐

令多馬羌御方	續五・二五・九
乎多㘝伐呂方	續三・二・三
乎㘝伐呂	前六・三〇・五

"㘝"和"羌"都是俘虜，都是經常被殺來用作祭祀時的犧牲。而其中有少數能够活着保留下來，充當軍士。雖然在出征作戰時生命還是沒有保障，但比起那些被殘酷殺掉充作"人牲"的俘虜，終究是要幸運得多。這些被活着保留下來而充當軍士的，其身份已不再是俘虜，而是屬於奴隸之列。

《林》二・一五・一九有"王…伐馬羌"，"馬羌"當是"羌"的一種，曾遭到商的侵伐。《粹》一五五四有"令多馬羌"，《錄》六二五有"…多馬羌臣"，說明"多馬羌"爲商的臣屬，受商的驅使。

這一類的刻辭，相對地說來，數量是很少的，總共不過十餘條。

3. ⛰田

關於"⛰田"的解釋，學術界意見分歧。我們比較傾向於"墾田"的説法。

《粹》一二二二"王令多絴⛰田"，這是數萬片甲骨中，唯一的記載其明確身份爲奴隸，而又從事農業生產的例子。《天》八一有"令衆絴"，令其從事什麼工作，則缺乏記載。"絴"字郭沫若同志隸作"兮"即"狗"，唐蘭同志隸作"羊"，

都是錯誤的。上文我們已經論及，"絴"是方國名，也是一種俘虜名。這兩片所記載的，則是"絴"這種俘虜，已取得了奴隸的身份。

4. 床上奴隸

在古代社會，女俘的命運大半是供統治階層的淫樂。根據甲骨刻辭，商代的女俘也逃脱不了這一悲慘的遭遇。

首先，當時的女俘有很多是被當作貢品或禮物進納給商王的：

婦妌來女	乙七四二六
其氏角女	乙三五〇七
夫(氏)角女	乙三〇〇五
入妾	前四・三五・五
周氏嬠	乙七三一二
不其見方㚻	南師一・五九

其次，甲骨刻辭中還有不少關於"取妾"的記載。"取"一般認為就是"娶"，我們認為這和後世"明媒正娶"的"娶"是不同的。甲骨刻辭常見"取牛"、"取羌"的辭例，"取女"、"取妾"實際上與此沒有什麽區別。

乎取女于林	乙三一八六
乎取莫女子	合二七六
允其取妾	乙七一六一
取⺁女	甲二二八七

此外，甲骨刻辭也有這樣的記載：

王余令角婦甾朕事	粹一二四四
王姜甾朕事	京津二二四五

"甾朕事"是侍候商王的意思。有許多女俘是冠以"婦"頭銜的：

婦妾	乙八八一五
婦媚	前六・二八・六
婦印	粹一二四一
婦㚻	甲三八

女俘既成了統治者洩欲的工具，則其身份已轉化成為奴隸。

（五）有關的比較和統計

　　上述的各種情況，我們是把甲骨刻辭所反映的整個時代作爲一個整體來加以論述的。但是，甲骨刻辭的早期（武丁）和晚期（帝乙、帝辛）之間，存在着很大的差異。我們從這一些差異中，可以看到商代在前後不同時期的發展變化，爲我們進一步地瞭解問題的實質，提供了一些寶貴的綫索。

　　殺戮俘虜作爲祭祀時的犧牲，以武丁時期最爲突出。上舉的各種繁雜的俘虜名稱、用牲方法，大多數都屬於武丁時期。

　　從用人爲牲的數量來看，早期和中期差不多每次祭祀都要殺人爲牲。尤其以早期爲甚，並且每次所用人牲的數量都相當大，最多有一次殺掉一千人的。到了晚期，祭祀仍然頻繁，但很少用人爲牲。即使用人的話，在一般的情況下，祇是"牢又一伐"而已。並且"用"俘虜中屬於敵方首領的現象比較突出。

　　從我們現在所收集到的六八八片甲骨，進行比較和分析，得到下列這些統計數字，可以看到商代早晚期明顯的變化：

　　一、早期——武丁時期，約六十年：

　　用人牲之記數者：五四一八人

　　用人牲之不記數者：二四七次

　　一次用人牲最高數：一〇〇〇人

　　總計用人牲片數：三七九片

　　二、中期——自祖庚至文丁，約九十年：

　　用人牲之記數者：一九五〇人

　　用人牲之不記數者：一八九次

　　一次用人牲最高數：三〇〇人

　　總計用人牲片數：二七七片

　　三、晚期——帝乙、帝辛時期，約四十年：

　　用人牲之記數者：七五人

　　用人牲之不記數者：二九次

　　一次用人牲最高數：三〇人

　　總計用人牲片數：三二片

從上述的比較和統計數字當中，我們可以看出，商代殺戮俘虜以作爲祭祀的犧

牲，是隨着時代的推移，而急劇地減少着的。到了帝乙、帝辛時期，這種殘酷的用人的制度雖仍然存在，並没有完全廢除，但近乎是一種殘餘的迹象。

總計各種俘虜的名稱，就目前我們所能掌握的來說，共有：羌、大、亘、尸、絴、美、㭒、㳄、㲋、覭、奚、而、印、及、軏、係、俘、伐、戉、白、囟、姜、㚔、妾、㚼、朋、服、从、屯等三十種。至於某些女俘的專名，尚未包括在内。所有這些俘虜，都曾當作祭祀的犧牲而加以殺戮過，無一例外。其殺戮的方法則有：俎、伐、歲、灸、沈、饮、菊、冗、袞、卯、戉、㬱、彈、用、㞢等十五種。其中祇有灸和沈兩種用牲方法專施之於女俘。

從甲骨刻辭的記載來看，相形之下，俘虜之能活着保留下來，能夠取得奴隸身份，其數量是很少的。我們現在祇發現有二十二片甲骨有這方面的記載。當然，女俘成爲統治階層淫樂的對象，也應算是奴隸，甲骨刻辭在這方面有所反映，但未作詳細的統計。可以肯定的一點是，女俘被殺來用作祭牲的數量比較少。

有一個非常明顯的事實，即在帝乙、帝辛時期，戰爭的規模和持續的時間都超過了早期和中期。戰爭中所得到的俘虜應該比過去增多。然而這些衆多的俘虜除了少數用作祭祀的犧牲以外，其下落如何，甲骨刻辭缺乏這方面的記載。我們可以推斷，這些俘虜的命運，祇能是淪爲奴隸。晚期的用人爲牲現象減少，應該是俘虜之多數淪爲奴隸的一種反映。社會向前發展了，生産力的提高，爲役使大批的奴隸提供了條件。處置俘虜的方法，由過去的以殺作祭牲爲主，轉變爲活着保留下來，成爲統治者會說話的工具，這是社會發展的必然結果。

（六）結　語

根據以上的論述，我們可以清楚地看出，在甲骨刻辭的早、中期，俘虜主要是被當作祭祀時的犧牲而殺戮掉了。其中祇有很少的一部份被活着保留下來成爲奴隸。其中僅僅祇有一條刻辭記載着"令多絴㞢田"，算是從事於當時主要生産部門——農業的勞動生産。其餘的如從事狩獵、充當軍士或擔當一些雜役，祇能是屬於家内奴隸的性質。及至晚期，殺人爲牲的現象急劇減少，雖然在晚期甲骨刻辭中没有關於驅使俘虜從事勞動生産，使之轉化成爲奴隸的記載，但我們完全有理由可以斷言，當時一定有較大量的俘虜被活着保留下來，轉

化成爲奴隸。

在西周初期,《書·多士》記載成王告殷之"多士",也就是周克殷所得的俘虜說:"今余惟不爾殺",而是強迫他們遷於洛邑,"攸服奔走臣我",成爲周人的奴隸。周初分封諸侯,有"殷民六族"、"殷民七族"、"懷姓九宗"(見《左傳》定公四年),也都是俘虜,均作爲奴隸而賞賜其臣屬。

《小盂鼎》記載着康王三十五年在一次征伐中就俘虜了一萬三千零八十一人,所殺掉的也僅僅是敵方的幾個首領,其它所有的俘虜均進獻於康王,並沒有殺掉。

《大盂鼎》記載着康王廿三年賞賜"盂""邦嗣四白,人鬲自馭至于庶人六百又五十又九夫,錫夷嗣王臣十又三白,人鬲千又五十夫",這些都當來自於戰爭中的俘虜,其結果都淪爲奴隸。

"周因于殷禮",從周初的情況,我們不難推想到商代晚期的情況。

或許有人會懷疑,是否卜辭早期的情況也是如此,祇是沒有記載下來而已。我們認爲,這種懷疑是不能成立的。大量屠殺俘虜作爲祭祀的犧牲,與大量地驅使俘虜爲奴隸,這兩種現象是不可能同時並存的。甲骨刻辭有這樣的記載:

丙午卜即貞,又氐羌翌丁未其用	京津三四二九
丙寅卜宁貞,出來羌來甲戌兇用	前六·六七·四
癸酉貞,射䑣以羌用自囧,于甲申	粹八一
癸酉卜萪貞,翌甲戌用…氐羌,易日…	存二·五三

一般地都是當天進納而來的準備用作祭牲的俘虜,第二天就"用"掉了,從"丙寅"到"甲戌",也不過是八天。很多進納的祭牲,還特別注明是供"伐"或"戓"等專門指定用途的。這些都不可能取得奴隸的身份。

俘虜並不等於奴隸。祇有把俘虜活着保留下來,強迫其從事某種勞役的時候,俘虜纔算是取得了奴隸的身份。從甲骨刻辭中所見到的情況是,俘虜在沒有能夠取得奴隸身份之前,就已經被當作祭祀的犧牲而殺掉了。有許多同志卻把他們的身份斷定爲奴隸,這是不恰當的,是不符合於實際情況的。

在古代社會,對於俘虜的如何處理,是受着當時社會生產方式所制約的。因此,研究當時人們如何去處理其所獲得的俘虜,這對於深入探討當時社會歷史,是一個值得注意的環節。本文對於甲骨刻辭中有關商代處理俘虜的情況,偏重於

資料的整理與分析。祇是希望能够通過這一些，爲研究商代歷史的同志提供某些可供參考的綫索。

一九六四年五月稿
一九七八年六月修訂

原載《古文字研究》第 1 輯，中華書局，1979 年；收入《姚孝遂古文字論集》，中華書局，2010 年。今據後者收入，同時參考前者校勘。

王宇信

商代的馬和養馬業

甲骨文中有一個用"金"——即銅的顏色表示馬色的"鎷"字。商代雖是青銅時代的高峰，但青銅主要用於鑄造華美、莊嚴的禮器、樂器、兵器等，極少用於鑄造生產工具。銅的顏色、性能雖在日常生活中已爲人們所熟悉，但這是一種非常寶貴的、爲廣大奴隸可望而不可及的金屬。因此，用銅的顏色——即"金"來表示馬色，說明馬在商代還是一種比較珍貴的役畜。

商代的馬是奴隸主貴族在戰爭和狩獵時用於騎、駕的主要畜力。因此，商奴隸主統治階級對養馬業特別重視，而且還設有專司養馬的"小臣"。養馬業較其它動物的馴養有了突出的發展。

我國古代的養馬業，自進入階級社會起，就處在國家政權的直接控制之①，其管理機構成爲國家機器的一個組成部分。有關古代"馬政"及養馬的技術成就，不少學者將《周禮》等古代文獻、各代史書《職官志》的有關記載，以及考古、文物等材料結合現代養馬科學進行研究，發表了不少寶貴意見，寫出了專門的養馬史著作。但關於商代養馬業的研究，由於"文獻不足徵"，很少有人全面涉及。我們擬據甲骨文中的材料，探索一下商代的馬和養馬業發展的情況。

（一）商代的馬和"相馬"

野生的馬被人類馴化爲役畜，在世界各民族歷史上，都較其它各種家畜爲

---

① 編者按："之"後似脫"中"字。

晚。我國仰韶文化遺址中雖有馬骨的發現①，但當時是母系氏族社會繁榮期，生產處在原始的鋤耕農業階段，男子主要從事的狩獵活動，祇不過是生活資料的一種補充。祇有到了畜牧業有了較大發展的父系氏族社會，男人們成爲"畜群的主人"，馬的馴養才有可能。我國馬的馴養，最早當始於龍山文化時代。山東省歷城縣城子崖的龍山文化層裏，發現了馬骨與牛骨，數量僅次於豬骨、狗骨，在各種動物骨骼中占第二位②。可能從公元前二千八百年前的原始社會末期，馬才開始被人們馴化爲役畜。

商族的祖先，以從事畜牧業而著稱。相傳"相土作乘馬"③。到了盤庚遷殷以後的商代晚期，養馬業更有了較大的發展。

甲骨文保存了不少關於商代的馬和養馬業的史料。商代的馬，不僅用途多樣，而且名目繁多。有的按毛色命名，有的按其特點命名，也有的命以專名。

按毛色區分的馬有如下幾種：如銅色的馬。

(1) 辛卯卜，在□貞，□王其步，叀鎷□。

（歷史研究所拓本七〇〇一號，山東博物館藏）

"鎷"即銅色的馬。形容馬色的"金"字即是商代的銅（對此我們將另撰專文，此不贅言）。步爲祭名，假爲酺④。此片爲第五期帝乙、帝辛時代的卜辭。意思是辛卯日卜問，王用銅色的馬爲祭牲麼？

白色的馬。郭沫若同志說："金文用白爲白色義者罕見，《作册大鼎》云：'公賞作册大白馬'，僅此而已。"⑤而甲骨文中的白馬却頗有幾例：

(2) 甲辰卜，㱿，〔貞〕奚來白馬。王占曰：吉，其來。　甲辰卜，㱿，貞奚不其來白馬五。

（乙3449，丙157）

(3) 貞叀乎取白馬氐。　　　　　　　　　　　　　　　　　（丙342）

(4) □白馬□。　　　　　　　　　　　　　　　　　　　　（龜2·15·14）

以上均爲第一期武丁時之卜辭。奚爲奴隸的一種身分⑥，在此也可能用爲管

---

① 山西省文管會：《晉南五縣古代人類文化遺址初步調查簡報》，《文物參考資料》，一九五六年，第九期。
② 《城子崖》，第九一頁，一九三四年版。
③ 《世本·作篇》。
④ 郭沫若：《殷契粹編考釋》，第二六頁。
⑤ 郭沫若：《金文餘釋》，《金文叢考》。
⑥ 于省吾：《殷代的奚奴》，《東北人民大學人文科學學報》，一九五六年，第四期。

理奚奴的人名；🐎爲人名。第二辭是甲辰那一天，貞人殼從正反兩方面問卜，首先問：是派奚貢入白馬五匹麼？又從反面問：不是派奚貢入白馬五匹吧？殷王看了正面一辭的卜兆後說：吉利，會將白馬貢來吧？第三辭是問，🐎這個人命令取白馬貢來麼？赤色的馬：

(5) 乙未卜，𡧊，貞在寧田，□□赤馬⊡。　　　　　（菁9·16① + 10·5，通732）

(6) 癸丑卜，𡧊，貞左赤馬其🐎，不𣪘。　　　　　　　　　　（鐵10·2）

(7) 乙未卜，𡧊，貞白貯入赤䭴，其🐎，不𣪘，吉。　（後下18·8，通733）

"左馬，右馬，蓋馬種之名也"，🐎字，"左旁從釆，釆字一作穗，從禾惠聲。疑均假爲㬅"②；于省吾先生謂此"㙁通惠"，又謂𣪘即束，"束有棱廉棘刺之意"，"其惠不吉，言其順不棘也。不棘謂馬之馴順，無棱廉棘刺，不驛突，利於服駕也"③。此說可從。此三辭均爲第三期廩辛、康丁時所卜。第六辭是說：癸丑日占卜，貞人𡧊問：左邊的赤馬很溫順不暴烈吧？第七辭是乙未日占卜，貞人𡧊問：自貯這個人貢來的赤䭴，很溫順，不暴烈，吉利麼？

(8) 叀䭴眔䮕子亡災。　　　　　　　　　　　　（前4·47·5，通730）

此爲第五期帝乙、帝辛時之卜辭。䭴，"從馬利聲，殆是許書之䮣字，《廣韻》䮣同䮕，《漢書·西域傳》'西與犁軒條支接'注'犁讀與驪同'，古利麗同音，故䭴字後亦從麗作"④。《說文解字》驪"馬深黑色，從馬麗聲"，䭴殆即深黑色的馬。這種深黑色的馬黃脊者爲䮕及小䮕。

(9) 叀䮕眔䮕亡災。　　　　　　　　　　　　　（前4·47·5，通730）

(10) 叀䮕眔小䮕亡災。　　　　　　　　　　　　（前4·47·5，通730）

(11) 戊午卜，在瀗貞，王其𤉢大兕，叀䭴眔䮕亡災，卒。

（前2·5·7下，通730）

此亦爲第五期卜辭。䮕字唐蘭先生謂："似以訓驪馬黃脊爲優。"⑤𤉢字于省吾先生說："應讀作窟……，窟作動詞用，即用窟穴以陷獸。"⑥最後一辭是戊午

---

① 編者按："9·16"，原文誤作"9·15"，今據實際出處徑改。
② 郭沫若：《卜辭通纂考釋》，第一五六頁。
③ 于省吾：《釋束》，《雙劍誃殷契駢枝》。
④ 羅振玉：《增訂殷墟書契考釋》(中)，第二九頁。
⑤ 唐蘭：《殷虛文字記》，第十頁。
⑥ 于省吾：《從甲骨文看商代的農田墾殖》，《考古》，一九七二年，第四期。

日卜，在潢地問，王要用窟穴陷大兕，用獵馬及深黑色黃脊的馬（䮄）去逐趕，没有災禍麽？這一卜應驗了，擒得了大兕。雜色的馬：

(12) 叀並駁。　　　　　　　　　　　　　　　　　　　　　　　（甲 298）

(13) 庚戌卜，貞，王□于慶駁䮄。　　　　　　　　（前 4·47·3，叕 71，綴 239）

並，二者相俱爲並。駁，《說文》云"馬色不純"。此駁馬，即雜色的馬。慶爲地名。第十二辭是問：用兩匹雜色的馬爲祭牲麽？

在甲骨文中，除了用騮、白、赤、深黑、黄、雜色來形容馬或爲馬名外，還有時用某種動物來表示馬的某些特點，並用此種動物爲馬命名。

有用鹿來表示馬的特點的。如上引第四辭之䮨即是。鹿類俊逸温順，伶俐機敏，奔跑迅速。此馬可能在性格或外形上具有鹿類的某些特點，故名之曰䮨。

有用豕來表示馬的特點的。如上引第十一辭之獵即是。豕馴化以後，軀體肥腯，行動遲滯；而野豕兇悍，善於奔突。此辭之馬爲田獵用，當具有野豕的某些特點，故名獵。

也有時用表示馬匹外形的專字。上引第十辭之䮷即是。"䮷字舊不識，毫即《說文》薹也，䮷从馬毫聲，字書所無，其義爲馬名，以聲類推之，疑即驕之或體，《說文》：'馬高六尺爲驕'"①，或因此馬軀體健壯雄偉，故名之曰驕。不僅如此，有時還給比較喜愛的馬直接命以專名。如瑪（上引第七辭）、䮦（上引第八辭）、䮄（上引第十三辭）。還有：

(14) □于馬□䮄逈。　　　　　　　　　　　　　　　　　（前 4·47·4，通 729）

馬在此辭做地名用。"'䮄逈'者，謂並駕二䮄"②；此外，還有犅、犕、瑪、犐、瑪、犕、焉等。如：

(15) 叀小犅用。　　　　　　　　　　　　　　　　　　　　　　（福 29）

(16) 戌其歸乎犕，王弗每。　　　　　　　　　　　　　　　　（京人 2142）

(17) 叀瑪眔犐用。　　　　　　　　　　　　　　　　　（簠典 62，續 2·25·11）

(18) 叀瑪用。　　　　　　　　　　　　　　　　　　　　　　　（福 29）

(19) 乙未卜，𡧊，貞舊乙，左犅其惠，不束。　　乙未卜，𡧊，貞□史入犅，王其惠，不束。　　乙未卜，𡧊，貞□子入犅，王乙惠。

　　　　　　　　　　　　　　　　　　　　（後下 18·8，龜 2·26·7，通 733，珠 318）

---

① 唐蘭：《殷虛文字記》，第一七頁。
② 郭沫若：《卜辭通纂考釋》，第一五五頁。

□史、舊乙等爲人名。此辭是乙未日卜，貞人貴問：舊乙這個人，左騳馴順，不暴烈吧？又問：□史貢入的騳，王覺得馴順，不暴烈難馭吧？最後問：□子進貢來的騳，王和乙都覺得馴順否？

(20) 叀左馬眔馬亡災。　　　　　　　　　　　　　　　　（前 4·47·5，通 730）

凡此種種，是躍然於甲骨之上的商代"名馬圖"。

商代的馬有上述各種命名，可能是這些不同的馬在祭祀、戎事或狩獵時有不同的用途與性能。有時商王反復卜問究竟是哪匹馬合適，原因也就在於此。有關這些卜辭，應是我國最早記載"相馬"的文字[①]。

我國古代的"相馬"，即今天所謂的"馬匹外形學"，對馬匹優劣的鑒定和優良品種的選擇是有着重要意義的。我國人民所熟知的相馬家伯樂、九方皋，在戰國時就廣爲流傳關於他們"相馬"的故事了。其記載見於《戰國策·楚策四》及《列子·說符》。此外，諸如《莊子》、《呂氏春秋·觀表篇》等也都提到了一些古代相馬的名家。但甲骨文的記載表明，"相馬"的開始，要比這些人早的多[②]。因此，作爲我國"相馬"的濫觴期，應從商代開始，至今最少已有三千年之久。

（二）商代的養馬業和"馬政"

在甲骨文中，我們發現：武丁期戰爭卜辭及與之交戰的方國，遠較其後各期爲多，而且就在第一期（武丁期）的全部卜辭中，戰爭卜辭也佔有相當大的比例。毋庸置疑，武丁及其後各朝所進行的歷次戰爭中，是需要不少馬匹爲之役用的。不僅如此，奴隸主統治階級還要用不少馬（或馬與車一起）去祭祀祖先或死後隨葬；而殷王經常的田遊，也是驅車逐馬，廝役相從，這在甲骨文中不乏記載。因此，我們可以想見商代的養馬業一定很發達。

商代馬匹的數量是不少的，見於甲骨文的數字有五十丙：

(21) ☐馬五十丙。　　　　　　　　　　　　　　　　　　（續 1·29·4）

此爲第一期卜辭。"丙"即爲匹[③]。有廿匹：

---

① 《福氏所藏甲骨文字考釋》，第九頁。
② 商代"相馬"的發明，謝承俠先生曾舉《通》730 爲證。見所著《中國養馬史》，第四八頁。
③ 于省吾：《殷代的交通工具和馴傳制度》，《東北人民大學人文科學學報》，一九五五年，第二期。

(22) □癸未□方于□𢀛□馬廿丙出□月，在臭卜。　　　　　（前2·19·1）

此亦爲第一期卜辭。此辭因殘，幾不能屬讀。有人根據殘痕補齊全辭，說："由此可知舌方人是馭馬的。"①所殘者是否爲舌方之舌字，我們姑且不論，但此辭所載馬數當爲二十匹以上。這麼多的馬匹，除了在商都附近繁殖以外，有相當一部分爲貢納而來：

(23) 甲申卜，𣪊，貞氏馬。　　　　　　　　　　　　　（乙7647）

(24) 貞氏馬。　　　　　　　　　　　　　　　　　　　（乙3943）

(25) □辰卜，𡆥，貞乎取馬于𪊭氏，三月。　　　（籃地44，續5·4·5）

(26) 𢎦氏馬自𠂤，十二月，允氏三丙。　　　　　　　　（乙4718）

(27) □𢎦□馬。　　　　　　　　　　　　　　　　　　（鐵30·4）

(28) □取弜馬，弗其氏在𠭯。　　　　　　　　　　　　（續5·8·3）

此外，還有前引第三辭之"取白馬氏"。以上皆爲第一期。"氏"應"讀底訓致"②，有致送之意。𪊭、𠂤、𠭯爲地名，𢎦、弜爲人名。其名爲弜者，即弜方國之首領，或爲弜方國之名。此人與武丁之妻婦好有着一定的關係③，著名的殷墟五號墓出土之大圓鼎及五個一組的銅鐃當爲其貢入④。

(29) 𡆥來馬。　不其來馬。　　　　　　　　　　　　　（丙342）

(30) □弜□來馬□丞。　　　　　　　　　　　　　　（後下30·12）

此外，還有前述第二辭之"𡩻來白馬"。"來"有貢來之意。除氏馬、來馬，還有"入"，前引第七辭之"自貯入赤瑪"，第十九辭之"入馮"即是。此自貯當爲廩辛、康丁時一名武將，其名還見於《摭續》41。我們可從該片得知，此人曾參與商王朝與危伯美及伐望的戰鬥。因此，自貯能給商王貢入赤色的名馬，倒是十分值得玩味的。還有：

(31) 乙未卜，𡧊，貞辰入馬，其惠。　　　（菁9·5＋菁10·16⑤，通732）

"入"字"有進貢之意"⑥。這是乙未日卜，貞人𡧊問：辰這個人貢入的馬，還

---

① 李學勤：《殷代地理簡論》，第六五頁。
② 于省吾：《釋氏》，《雙劍誃殷契駢枝》。
③ 《安陽殷墟五號墓座談紀要》，《考古》，一九七七年，第五期。
④ 《安陽殷墟五號墓的發掘》，《考古學報》，一九七七年，第二期。
⑤ 編者按："菁9·5＋菁10·16"，原文誤作"菁9·16＋菁10·5"，今據實際出處徑改。
⑥ 胡厚宣：《武丁時五種記事刻辭考》，《甲骨學商史論叢》，初集，第二冊。

馴順吧？這些氐、來、入的馬匹，與其它馬匹一起，飼養在商王專設的馬廄裏。

(32) ☐卜王其作墊棯于寫☐。　　　　　　　　　　　　（京4831）

(33) 王畜馬在絲寫☐母戊王受☐。　　　　　　　　　　（寧1·521）

(34) ☐絲寫☐。　　　　　　　　　　　　　　　　　　（寧1·522）

(35) ☐畜馬在絲寫☐。　　　　　　　　　　　　　　　（粹1551）

此均爲第三、四期卜辭。畜字"从幺从囿，明是養畜義，蓋謂系牛馬於囿也，字變爲畜"。寫字"爲廄之初文"①。"王畜馬在絲廄"，即把商王擁有的馬養畜在專設的馬廄裏。此廄和《周禮·夏官·司馬》"校人"中所談的"天子十有二閑"之"閑"，當爲同制。管理商王馬匹的官吏有"馬小臣"。

(36) ☐來告大方出，伐我自，叀馬小臣令。　　　　　　（粹1152）

(37) 丙寅卜，叀馬小臣☐。　　　　　　　　　　　　　（粹1156）

此"馬小臣"和《周禮·夏官·司馬》所設的校人、趣馬、巫馬、牧師、廋人、圉師、圉人等職掌管馬的教養、乘御、醫疾等事差不多。春秋時代的"校正"（《左》襄九年）及"馬正"（《左》襄廿五年）就是專司養馬的官吏。周代馬官所掌握的一些養馬技術，在甲骨文中就已開始了先河。

每年春季，當母馬受孕以後，便將頭一年所生的小駒使之"離之去母"（《大戴禮記·夏小正·四月》），以避免馬駒傷害孕馬。這在《周禮》校人、廋人職中，叫做"執駒"。有人認爲"執駒便是馴練小馬駕車"②。這不僅是爲了對小馬進行調教，使之利於服乘；而且對於保證馬匹的順利繁殖也有一定意義。

甲骨文中雖不見"駒"字，但有"䎽子"（上引第八辭）。這當與郿縣李村出土《駒尊》蓋銘之"雛子"、"駱子"相同。據考證，"雛、駱是小馬母親的名字，小馬尚未命名，所以稱雛子、駱子"③。雛子、駱子就是所賜之駒。因此，甲骨文中的"䎽子"當是䎽馬所生之駒。駒因才生下不久，尚不能服乘，甲骨文中又稱子馬。

(38) 甲辰卜，集子馬自大乙。　　　　　　　　　　　　（粹135）

這裏的"子馬"，應和"䎽子"一樣，當同指馬的小駒而言。甲骨文中有隻駒：

(39) ☐酉卜，角隻〔☐〕。　角不其隻〔☐〕。（龜2·12·5＋龜2·12·6）

---

① 郭沫若：《殷契粹編考釋》，第二〇七頁。
②③ 李學勤：《郿縣李村銅器考》，《文物參考資料》，一九五七年，第七期。

此爲第一期卜辭。角爲人名。隻字原爲以手抓鳥，假爲獲，有抓而獲得之意。🐎爲象意字，馬旁之子表示爲馬之子，此字當即駒之初文。此辭是先從正面問：某酉日卜，（殷王命令）角去隻駒麼？又從反面問：（殷王命令）角不去隻駒麼？這個名爲角的人，當爲商王朝的馬官。隻駒，就是將馬駒抓獲，很可能就是"執駒"。商王關心"執駒"，可見"執駒"已成爲"馬政"中一重要事項；到了周代，"執駒"成爲馬政中的重典。如《駒尊》銘載"王初執駒于啟"①，國王參加"執駒"典禮，說明了對馬政的重視。

隨着養馬業的發展，爲了提高馬的利用價值，即增强馬的任載力以及選擇優良品種，最早的馬匹去勢術也發明出來了。《周禮》校人"夏祭先牧，頒馬攻特"，賈疏云："攻其特，爲其蹄齧不可乘用者，亦謂騬其蹄齧者也。"鄭司農云："攻特謂騬之者。"《說文解字》第十（上）騬，"犗馬也"，《廣雅·釋獸》騬，"犗攻犗也"。孫詒讓在《周禮正義》中解釋攻特"謂割去馬勢，猶今之騸馬"。根據甲骨文中的材料，"攻特"在商代可能就出現了。

在甲骨文中，母馬和其它的動物母畜一樣，較爲常見。一般在畜體旁加一"匕"字（即牝）以表示之。如：

(40) 🐎。　　　　　　　　　　　　　　　　　　　　　　　　　（前 6·46·7）

(41) □卜□駤于□。　　　　　　　　　　　　　　　　　　　（前 6·46·6）

此二辭爲第一期物。第四十一辭馬字稍殘，但仍可辨出馬形，可隸定作駤。還有小牝馬：

(42) □少（即小）駤□子白□不白。　　　　　　　　　　　　（續 5·26·8）

此亦爲第一期卜辭。少即小。小駤即小的牝馬。值得注意的是，馬和其它畜類不同，甲骨文中不見用"丄"表示的牡馬（即特馬）。這並不是說商代沒有特馬，而祇能用商代爲了提高馬的經濟價值，大部分都經過去勢的處理，祇留下了較少的優良特馬——即種馬來解釋。動物的去勢處理，在甲骨文中有所反映。如豕去勢後，寫作豖形，據聞一多先生考證，"腹下一畫與腹連着者爲牡豕，則不連者殆即去勢之豕，因此，此字當釋爲'豖'字"，其本義"當求之於經傳之椓及剫斀等字"②。既然別的家畜已進行去勢的處理，那麼馬的去勢也不是不可能的。

---

① 郭沫若：《盠尊銘考釋》，《考古學報》，一九五七年，第二期。
② 聞一多：《釋豖》，《古典新義》，（《聞一多全集》選刊二）（下），第五四〇頁。

(43) □酉□☗。　　　　　　　　　　　　　　　　（歷史研究所拓本 5475）

此爲第一期武丁時卜辭，原骨現藏故宮。此辭之☗字，於馬腹下加一◊形。此◊形在甲骨文中不爲罕見，還有作◊形者。如：拾 11・11，後下 42・5，京 2458，金 556，乙 8909，京人 3245 等。∧即表示雙手所持。◊形與漢代遺址發現之鐵剪形近，但商代遺址迄今尚未發現此類銅質實物，因此很可能爲皮條（或繩索）。我們認爲此字可能是表示用繩（或皮條）爲套，將馬勢絞掉。

因此甲骨文中之☗字，可能爲表示馬匹去勢之專字。據研究生物學史的同志談，將風乾後的動物筋做成皮條（如農村彈棉花用的弓弦），其效果比用刀、剪給動物去勢還好，一直到近代我國農村還沿用此法。

馬匹經過去勢處理，既可免去牡馬對懷妊牝馬的傷害，保證了馬匹的順利繁殖；而且還可使經過去勢處理的馬體強壯，增強了任載力；同時，可把不純之劣種淘汰掉，保証優質馬種的繁衍。且不談傳說的黃帝時代就已經有了馬匹去勢的技術，就我國甲骨文中記載的商代馬匹去勢術的采用，在世界養馬史上也是名列前茅的。

養馬技術的改進，使商代馬群繁衍，馬種改良。而養馬業的發展，還必須不斷戰勝馬群的天敵——獸害和馬疾。商代爲患馬群最烈者當爲虎害：

(44) 貞我馬有虎，佳禍。　　貞我馬有虎，不佳〔禍〕。　　　　（丙 201 正）

這是商王武丁在貞問：我的馬群裏出現了老虎，造成了禍害吧？又從反面問：我的馬群裏竄來了老虎，沒有造成禍害吧？馬群不僅有時受到自然界動物的攻擊，而且可能還會因病致疾，引起死亡。

(45) 馬其死。　　　　　　　　　　　　　　　　　　　　　　（甲零 140）
(46) 貞馬不死。　　　　　　　　　　　　　　　　　　　　　（鄴初下 38・3）
(47) 馬〔不〕死。　　　　　　　　　　　　　　　　　　　　（簠文 13）
(48) ☐卜，宁，□馬其死。　　　　　　　　　　　　　　　　（珠 285）

以上四辭爲武丁時卜。使馬致死的原因固然多樣，但病疫當是一個很重要的因素。爲了使珍貴的馬匹不致死去，商王借助占卜，冀求神明的庇佑。除了通過這種"巫術"手段爲病馬治疾以外，可能還會對病馬施以某種治療。雖然甲骨文中還沒有發現這方面的材料，但"周因於殷禮"。《周禮・夏官》巫馬"掌養疾馬而乘治之，相醫而藥攻馬疾，受財於校人。馬死則使其賈粥之，入其布於校人"的記載，使我們有理由推測：可能商代也出現了相當於"巫馬"的馬醫。

（三）商代馬匹的使用

"國之大事，在祀與戎"。商奴隸主統治階級把馬匹主要用於祭祀和戰争這些國家最重大的事情中。

甲骨文裏有奴隸主階級用馬做祭祀時犧牲的記載。

(49) 癸未，貞叀今乙酉又父□歲于祖乙五馬（二），兹用。

（甲 696 + 甲 697）

此爲第四期卜辭，爲第二卜。此外還有佚 883 與此同文，爲第三卜。這是癸未日問：惟今乙酉這一天侑祭父某並歲祭祖乙用五匹馬麽？結果此卜施行了，將五匹馬做了祭牲。

(50) 其三馬，叀不勹馬，兄辛。　　　　　　　　　　（通别一·何8，佚203）

此爲第三期卜辭，兄辛即康丁稱其兄廪辛。勹字郭沫若同志隸定爲勹，謂即黧之初文，有一意爲黑色講①。這一辭是卜問祭祀兄辛時，用三匹馬麽？不用黑馬？還是用黑馬？這種"用馬爲牲，即春秋時宋人猶有此習。《左傳》襄九年'宋災，祝宗用馬于四墉，祀盤庚于西門之外'即其證"②。

(51) 貞攴馬。　　　　　　　　　　　　　　　　　　（京 257）

此爲第一期卜辭。攴字爲用牲之法，于省吾先生説："卜辭攴字，初義爲以朴擊蛇，引申爲割殺之意"③，此辭是問：割殺馬做祭牲麽？

有時還用馬駒（即子馬）爲祭牲。此即上引第三十八辭"甲辰卜，集子馬自大乙"（粹 135）。集字祭名，"字習見，上隹字例均倒書，或以曰以倒提之。羅振玉疑是'薦雞之祭'。然此言'集子馬'則所薦不必是雞"④。這是卜問用子馬祭自大乙以下的祖先否。

這種用馬做祭牲的遺迹，於安陽殷墟多有發現。殷墟第十一次發掘時，曾發

---

① 郭沫若：《釋勹勿》，《甲骨文字研究》。
② 郭沫若：《卜辭通纂考釋》别録，第一二頁，何八。
③ 于省吾：《釋攴》，《雙劍誃殷契駢枝》。
④ 郭沫若：《殷契粹編考釋》，第二五頁。

現幾座專門埋馬的馬坑。最小的馬坑內埋馬一匹，最大的馬坑埋馬卅七匹。其它還有一坑埋馬四匹，八坑各埋馬二匹的。坑中之馬，多帶籠頭，有銅飾①。《一九五〇年春殷墟發掘報告》(見《中國考古學報》第五冊，1951年)披露，在武官村大墓之北墓道"開馬坑三個，得馬骨十六架，轡飾多件"。在南墓道中"亦得馬坑二處，馬骨七架，轡飾多組，及正中跪葬人架一"。此跪葬人架，可能爲牧馬奴隸。此外，1973年小屯南地發現有埋一匹馬之祭祀坑，坑中埋有五具人架，其中三具成年，當爲牧馬奴隸②。近年在安陽小屯又有新的發現。

與祭祀同等重要的戎事，也大量使用馬匹。在商代的戰爭中，馬主要用於駕車，因此馬往往與車聯系在一起。在一次戰鬥中，商王朝曾俘獲馬、車等戰利品。

(52) □小臣牆从伐，率(擒)危美□人廿人四，而千五百七十，馨百，□丙，車二丙，◯百八十，函五十，矢□。又白㣇于大乙，用魋白印□于祖乙，用美于祖丁，堲甘京，卯□。 　　　　　　　　　　　　　　　　　(續存下915)

這是十分重要的虜獲戰利品的記錄。危爲方國名，美爲此方國之首領。而即馘。◯爲盾牌之類。堲字"爲城塞之塞"③。此爲第五期卜辭，追述了某次戰爭，有小臣名牆者被率出征，抓到危方首領名美者，俘虜二十四人，馘一千五百七十，馨百，馬若干匹，車二輛，盾牌之類一百八十，函五十付，矢若干。把一個首領白㣇用於祭祖先大乙，把另一個首領魋白用於祭祖乙，把美殺了祭祖丁。並築城塞於甘京……這說明，不僅商王朝使用車馬，而且周圍一些方國也使用車馬作戰了。可見當時車馬之普及。有人根據殷墟第十三次發掘時發現一人馬合葬小墓，推測騎射之制當自殷代始④。于省吾先生則更根據甲骨文材料，論證了殷代的單騎和騎射已經盛行了⑤。但正如恩格斯所說的"起初馬匹大概僅用於駕車，至少在軍事史上戰車比武裝騎手的出現早得多"⑥。在我國騎兵的出現也在這以後的事。

---

① 胡厚宣：《殷墟發掘》，第八二頁。
② 中國科學院考古研究所安陽工作隊：《一九七三年小屯南地發掘簡報》，《考古》，一九七五年，第一期。
③ 郭沫若：《卜辭通纂考釋》，別錄之一，第十頁。
④ 石璋如：《殷墟之重要發現附論小屯地層》，《田野考古報告》，第二冊。
⑤ 于省吾：《殷代的交通工具和馹傳制度》，《東北人民大學人文科學學報》，一九五五年，第二期。
⑥ 恩格斯：《騎兵》，《馬克思恩格斯全集》，一四卷，第二九八頁。

除了用馬拉車去打仗，狩獵時還要用馬拉車去逐獸。

(53) 癸巳卜，㱿，貞旬亡禍。王占曰：乃兹亦有祟。若偁，甲午王往逐兕，小臣叶車，馬硪，馭王車，子央亦墜。　　　　　　　　　　（菁1·1，通735）

"若偁謂如繇（筆者按：即占辭）所云也"，馭字"蓋傾覆字"①。此爲第一期卜辭。大意是癸巳日卜，貞人㱿問：這一旬沒有災禍吧？王看了兆以後說：這恐怕要有祟禍吧？以下是驗辭：果然如王所說的那樣，甲午那一天王駕着馬車去逐兕獸，小臣駕車，馬失前蹄，險些壓翻了王的車子，子央也從車上掉下來了。與此辭內容相同者還有掇一454（與外462、寧2·24、續存上972重）、前4·46·2等，雖然辭殘，但仍可據五十三辭補全辭義。

(54) □亥卜，㱿，貞旬亡禍。王占曰□丁卯王狩牧祓車馬□在車，皋馬亦□。　　　　　　　　　　（佚980，簠游122，續3·40·2，叕26）

(55) □亡禍，王固曰出（有）祟□牧祓車□車，皋馬□亦有□。　　　　　　　　　　（前7·5·3）

此二辭同文，可互補全其辭。這是說某日貞人㱿問：此旬亡禍否？王看了兆以後說有祟禍。果然出去狩獵時，車馬出了事。其它還有前5·6·4（鐵114·1）、軀1·7·11（珠1368）與上二辭同文，雖殘缺過甚，但亦可據上二辭補全辭意。

狩獵時，商王使用他豢養的好馬。如前引通730各辭，反復卜問用哪一匹名馬，最後選中了鴉及騽，終於使兕陷入窟穴。

商代的車和馬，用於戰爭和狩獵，也用於做祭祀時的貢獻。近年安陽發現了幾座完整的車馬坑②。值得注意的是：除去解放前在安陽殷墟小屯C區發現的M20爲一車四馬外，近年發現的殷代車馬坑多是一車二馬。這與上面我們所引述卜辭中馬是兩匹相並是一致的。"此足証殷末王者之事，所駕者僅二馬，即所謂駢。驂駟之制蓋後起者也"③。商代的車可能主要是駕二匹馬。而駕馬二匹以上，就需要掌握更複雜的駕馭技術和待車子的結構有了更進一步的改進以後。

綜上所述，我們可以看出：商代的養馬業受到商奴隸主統治階級的特別重視。商王朝設有專門養馬的馬廄和干預養馬事宜的"馬小臣"，養馬業的管理機

---

① 郭沫若：《卜辭通纂考釋》，第一五八頁。
② 殷代發現的車馬坑，楊泓同志在《殷周時代車子各部尺寸表》中有詳細統計。見《戰車與車戰》，《文物》，一九七七年，第五期。
③ 郭沫若：《卜辭通纂考釋》，第一五五頁。

构成为奴隶主专政国家机器的一个组成部分。我们研究养马业的上层建筑,即管理养马业的各种官吏和机构的"马政",当从商代的甲骨文记载起;由于马匹数量的增多和养马业的发展,从商代就开始有了相马、执驹、攻特等技术,繁殖出一批"名马"。商代养马业之所以受到奴隶主统治阶级的特别重视,是由于马匹在奴隶主阶级的国家大事——祀、戎的需要以及狩猎活动中的特殊作用所决定的。我国古代养马业的发展和在养马技术方面取得的突出成就,为世界科学文化的发展做出了宝贵的贡献。

原载《中国史研究》1980年第1期;收入宋镇豪、段志洪主编:《甲骨文献集成》第26册,四川大学出版社,2001年;又收入《中国甲骨学》,上海人民出版社,2009年。今据前者收入。

張亞初

甲骨金文零釋·釋祇(附 ▨、▨、▨、▨)

▨字孫詒讓釋求，陳邦懷釋東。郭沫若把杜國之姓▨根據文獻推定爲祁，召伯虎簋之▨推定爲祇，並從石鼓文中找到了這個字的對應關係（《金文叢考》二○五頁《釋嬸》）。這是很正確的。但對此字發生發展的脈絡還是不夠清楚的。

在甲骨文中，祇字第一二期作▨（《林》二六·十一—十一），第三期在其上部或者上下同時加甾作聲符，變爲▨（《戩》三七·十一），或簡化爲▨（《粹》九四五偏旁），由"重▨栥（《戩》三七·十一）等材料可證，此字係名詞，是商人祈祝求雨的對象。《粹》九四五此字从示旁，更說明它確爲神祇之祇。祇祇古本同字。三體石經《君奭》以甾爲祇，說明甾、祇、祇是同音字，故▨字加甾作聲符。這一條卜辭是貞問，是否向神祇祓求。早期文字由象形或會意演變爲形聲字，這是較爲普遍的現象。▨變爲▨、▨就是一例。祇字也是如此。▨字與金文之▨（杜伯鬲祁字偏旁）完全一致，差別只是金文之祇略爲簡化，中間的▨省爲▨，與甲骨文中的簡體寫法相同。召伯虎簋之祇進一步省▨而寫作▨。此字演變過程可圖示如下：

▨──▨ ▨──▨──▨

郭氏首釋之功不可磨滅。但是，由於對該字發生發展的全過程不清楚，在對造字本意的解說上，就不無可商之處。郭氏認爲此字象兩缶相抵，中間的▨則象兩缶間有物以墊之，原文當爲抵或氐之本字（此說亦見《文史論集》三○○頁《由壽縣蔡器論到蔡墓的年代·蔡侯鐘銘考釋》）。甲骨文之▨，根本沒有兩缶之形，又當如何解釋？可見認爲此字爲抵或氐之本字的說法是靠不住的。《說文》"祇，地祇，提出萬物者也"，許慎解此字，用的是聲訓，祇提音近，故云"提出萬物者"，亦非此字之本意。祇在石鼓文中的用法爲祁祁，文獻上祁祁訓盛、多、大和舒徐（參郭氏《釋嬸》一文）。

從甲骨文看，此字爲樹木枝葉茂盛、舒展狀。所以它應是祁字的本字，祈、祇則都是借字、後起字。

弄清了這個字之後，我們附帶要説明下面三字。

其一是甲骨文中的⌒字（《乙》二一一〇，《丙》一二、二〇等），爲祁的中間部分，應爲祁之省，讀如祁。祁之作⌒，猶如🌳加聲符作🌳，省作🌳（《前》四·二六·四），進一步省作🌳（《乙》六五三三），演變情況完全一致。⌒在甲骨文中爲國族名（《丙》一二、二〇）。此字張秉權釋飛，饒宗頤釋乙，謂从重乙（《殷代貞卜人物考》——二七頁）。从女从⌒的妞即⌒國族氏的女子。傳説黃帝之後裔有姓祁的（《史記·五帝本紀》）。《左傳》襄公二十一年傳"祁大夫"注云"祁奚也，食邑於祁，因以爲氏。祁縣今屬太原"。此祁有可能即甲骨文中的⌒。妞字劉心源釋妃，高田忠周釋姒，柯昌濟釋颮，都是没有根據的。

其二是🌳尊之🌳（《三代》十一·三三·二），吴大澂認爲从凸从刀，爲古文剔字，即梨（《字説》二八，《説文古籀補》二三）。丁佛言釋析或折，均不確。

我認爲，此字从木从⌒，即甲骨文中的祁字的析書，合起來即爲🌳字。斤旁爲後加的聲符。它應是祈字的異體字。祁姓的祁可以寫作祈。《晉語》"董叔將娶於范氏……他日，董祁愬於范獻子"，范氏爲杜國之後，女子稱姓，故董叔之妻稱爲董祁（或謂祁爲名，誤）。而《説苑·貴德篇》云："欒有叔祈之愬"，叔祈即董祁。又，僞古文《尚書·君牙》"冬祁寒"，《禮記·緇衣》或作"冬祈寒"，可證祁祈古字通。从木从⌒的祁字加上聲符斤，當即祈字，爲祈字的異體字。所以，該器我們可以稱之爲祈尊，過去或稱之爲析尊，誤。

其三，是作爲車馬器物的🌳、🌳、🌳，此字《金文編》亦置於附録之中（九七九頁—九八〇頁）。吴大澂釋之爲韣，徐同柏釋之爲幰，阮元釋之爲旆，孫詒讓釋之爲韎，陳夢家从之，柯昌濟釋之爲靳，郭沫若从之。説法很多，至今没有定論。

按，應以阮、柯二氏之説爲近是，尤以柯説爲長。但柯氏没有加以科學的論證，所以難以取信於人。

據上面的分析可知，甲骨文之祁可以析書爲🌳和省寫爲⌒，或者另加聲符斤，構成祈字。🌳、🌳、🌳諸字中，⌒斤爲聲符，亦可僅以⌒作聲符，十三年𤼈壺此字就作🌳，以⌒爲聲符。⌒斤和⌒都應該讀爲祁或祈。《金文編》所收五字，上面从朿者三字，从束者二字，省朿者一字（如包括新出土的十三年𤼈壺就有二字）。朿束二字，在獨體字中一般講是有區別的，但在偏旁中出現時，則往往通用無别，量字、鐘字、䚈字都是如此（參第八條）。所以，从朿从束不能看作是兩個

字。該字正體應該是从束,从東的是它的異構。《左傳》定公九年傳:"〔王〕猛笑曰:吾从子如驂之靳",注云:"靳,車中馬也",疏云:"靳是當胸之皮也。"《説文》:"靳,當膺也",膺即胸。可見注説非而疏説是。靳在文獻上又稱靰和纓,注釋者謂即"當胸",即束在馬胸前面的用來曳車的寬大的皮帶(參《從胸式繫駕法到鞍套式繫駕法》,孫機,《考古》一九八〇年第五期,四四八頁)。在金文中,此字从衣,當爲衣屬,上部从束,是表示用帶子束於馬。衣和束都是意符。前面已經講到,該字有祈或祁音,與从革斤聲的靳爲同音字。𩊷𩊸等字是靳字的初文,靳則是後起的形聲字。總之,𩊷之與靳,音義并通,當爲古今字無疑。阮氏釋斾從音講可從,義則不通。其他各種説法,都失諸穿鑿。

一九六五年初稿,一九八〇年修改稿

原載《古文字研究》第 6 輯,中華書局,1981 年;收入宋鎮豪、段志洪主編:《甲骨文獻集成》第 13 册,四川大學出版社,2001 年。今據前者收入。

沈建華

甲骨文釋文二則·釋雹

　　甲骨文"㊀"字或作"㊁、㊂"等形，王襄最早釋爲古"霽"字，謂此字"从雨从ooo，ooo古齊字，殷契作⋄⋄，齊乃化作⋏⋏，均可證"。陳夢家先生復引卜辭"生十月雨其隹㊀"（京津1）、"丁亥，昜日丙戌㊀"（續4·4·5）、"壬子夕㊀"（庫410）爲證，進一步説明㊀乃"霽"字，爲動詞，義乃雨止（《殷虚卜辭綜述》245頁）。李孝定指出甲骨文"齊"字作"⋏⋏"、"⋄⋄"，均"象禾麥吐穗形"，與"㊀"所从之"ooo"不類，㊀"非从齊也"（《甲骨文字集釋》十一卷"霝"字下按語）。這是對的。但他却把㊀和㊃、㊄混在一起釋爲"霝"字，殊誤。㊀从ooo，㊃从ㅂㅂ，形體遠隔，絶非同字，其字㊀乃"雹"字古文，从冖从ooo，像下雹子之形。甲骨文作oo或ooo，像星星點點的形狀。"雷"字或从oo，作⋄。"⋄"像閃電，"oo"像閃電時點點滴滴的物體狀態。又星字或作"⋆"，⋆爲聲，oo即像天上星星之形。"㊀"字从"ooo"，乃像所下冰雹之形。下冰雹總伴隨着雨，所以从冖。卜辭"雹"字用本義，最能説明問題的是《殷虚文字丙編》61兩條對貞的卜辭："癸未卜方貞，兹㊀（雹）隹降囚？癸未卜方貞，兹㊀（雹）不隹降囚？"與災咎聯繫的，當然絶不會是雨止的霽。

　　甲骨文"雹"字作"㊀"，从雨从ooo，乃會意字。《説文》雹字，古文作"䨔"，形體雖略有改易，但尚基本保留構形原意。上古會意字，增加聲符逐步演化爲形聲字，是古文字發展的一條通例，"㊀"字也不例外。到了後來，如長沙子彈庫帛書摹本"伏犧"之"伏"作"䨔"（《文物》1964年第9期），即演化中的過渡形態。"䨔"字所从之"䨔"，即由"㊀"到"䨔"進一步發展的變易形體。所加的"冫"形，即聲符"包"之所从。上古輕重唇不分，"包"與"伏"

聲同。由"▨"再進一步演變成了《説文》從雨包聲之"雹"。從"▨"至"雹"的發展綫索十分清楚，卜辭"▨"即《説文》之"雹"。

原載《古文字研究》第 6 輯，中華書局，1981 年；收入宋鎮豪、段志洪主編：《甲骨文獻集成》第 13 册，四川大學出版社，2001 年；又收入沈建華：《初學集：沈建華甲骨學論文選》，文物出版社，2008 年。今據《初學集》收入。

黄錫全

甲骨文"㞢"字試探

甲骨文中的"㞢"字，前人多有論及（詳見下），但迄今仍然是一個懸而未決的疑難問題。研者大都知道這個字在卜辭文例中的用法確與有無之"有"同義，而又可以假借爲"又"、"侑"、"佑"，但對其形體及其造字本義還没有見到一個比較合理而恰當的解釋。本文打算就這一問題提出一點新的看法，以就正於諸位專家和同志們。

關於對這個字的解釋，自來諸家亦不一致。最先對這個字加以解釋的是孫詒讓，他釋爲"之"，並認爲："凡云'之'者亦甚多，其義當爲'適'（《爾雅·釋詁》適、之往也）。……蓋竝謂卜適其廟而祭……"①羅振玉②、王國維與孫説並同③。胡光煒説"㞢"與《説文》屮形近，卜辭用"㞢"之例或以爲"又"，或以爲"有"，或以爲"告"之省。④葉玉森不同意是"告"字之省，但他仍從孫詒讓之説釋爲"之"，訓"適"，又用爲"獻"。⑤郭沫若先生説："㞢殆又字之異文，惟字形尚未得其解。"並可讀解爲有、右（佑）、侑。⑥吴其昌説："今綜合萬餘片甲骨，悉索其㞢字，駢臚而通觀之，始知'㞢'之一字其賦形有五，而其含義有六。"⑦胡厚宣先生認爲："惟㞢字究爲何字，終不可確知。但其字除有、又二義

---

① 孫詒讓：《契文舉例》上卷第十七頁。
② 羅振玉：《殷虚書契考釋》增訂本下卷第二十四頁。
③ 王國維：《戩壽堂所藏殷虚文字考釋》第十頁。
④ 胡光煒：《説文古文考》，據葉玉森：《殷虚書契前編集釋》一卷第三頁所引。
⑤ 葉玉森：《殷虚書契前編集釋》一卷第三頁。
⑥ 郭沫若：《卜辭通纂考釋》，參見十七、三五〇、三三一等片。《粹》：一八二、一八六、四二五等片。
⑦ 吴其昌：《殷虚書契解詁》第一片，載武大《文哲季刊》三卷二號。

之外，在早期卜辭中爲一極普遍之祭名則毫無可疑。然觀其既常用爲有、又之義，則用爲祭名者，或即假爲侑之一字也。"[①]

按以上諸家所釋，就形義而論，釋㞢爲之，形義俱乖。㞢與之卜辭書寫不同。之字作 ⿱ (《鐵》一六·一)、⿱ (《前》七·一四·三)、⿱ (《佚》一○三) 等形，與㞢字迥然有別。釋㞢爲之，形體不符，其義訓就無從論及了。卜辭"告"字雖有作 ⿱、⿱、⿱ 諸形，但亦有作 ⿱、⿱ 等形。胡氏未能明瞭"告"字的造字本義，就認爲"或以爲'告'之省"當屬猜測之詞。吳其昌說"㞢"字賦形有五是誤合㞢與 ⿱、⿱ 爲一字，因此就解釋出含義六種。其實只有三種，其餘三種實不可信。郭沫若、胡厚宣兩位先生認爲"㞢"字用爲"有"、"又"之義，又可假爲"侑"、"右（佑）"，這是對的。《甲骨文編》將"㞢"字列於"有"字之後，並解釋說"以文義覈之確與有無之有同義"，也是正確的。但"不知偏旁所從"及其造字本義。

作者認爲，"㞢"字的原始含義應當是來源於當時的社會生活實際，而又爲當時人們所熟知的很普通的概念。認真仔細的從文字的形體偏旁分析出發，並與有關聯的文字相互進行比較，再鈎稽古籍史實記載，參考或利用少數原始民族所保存的生產或生活上的某些風俗習慣來追溯這個字的造字本義，這個"㞢"字是應該能夠弄明白的。

我們知道，"㞢"字大都出現在武丁時期即第一期卜辭中[②]。這個字在武丁以後即已逐漸消失，而先後以其同音字"又"所代替[③]。至西周金文中才出現了從手持肉的"有"字[④]。綜觀全部甲骨卜辭，"㞢"字的形體大致可分下列幾種：

（一）㞢 甲2902　㞢 佚383　㞢 佚392　㞢 甲209　㞢 甲182

（二）㞢 乙1444　㞢 乙777　㞢 鐵189·3　㞢 乙6665反　㞢 菁5·1

（三）㞢 前4·4·2　㞢 前1·30·3　㞢 乙3290　㞢 乙4887　㞢 乙1916

（四）㞢 前7·40·2　㞢 甲3　㞢 鐵117·2　㞢 甲2809　㞢 甲140

作者認爲，上舉"㞢"字的基本形體就是人們熟知的牛頭象形字。商代的牛首鼎文，殷虛出土的牛頭形飾與現實生活中的牛頭一樣作

---

① 胡厚宣：《甲骨學商史論叢初集》第三冊《卜辭下乙說》一一二頁。
② 這裏所說的第一期卜辭包括自組、午組。
③ 第二期祖庚卜辭以後廢棄㞢。自組、午組卜辭中㞢、又并存。
④ 第五期卜辭中有一見，《後》上十一·五："癸未卜才⿱貞王旬亡⿱。""⿱"不是"有"字。島邦男《綜類》將此字錄作"⿱"，不確。

鼎文①　　玉牛首②　　鼎文　　牛頭形飾③

就是上舉二、三種形體的原始圖形。

上舉第一種形體的"𢍱"字，牛角呈弧形，日常生活中這種牛角形是很普遍的。因契刻只能作方筆很少作圓筆的關係，才刻呈"∪"形。"⊥"表示牛頭的上下端。牛頭上端作"一"形，卜辭中有"卯黃牛"、"幽牛"的"牛"字作"𢍱"形④，"𢍱"無疑是"牛"字，以"天"字有作"𠅃"（《甲》三六九〇）、"𠀑"（《前》二·二七·八）等形例之，所從的"口"、"一"均爲指示，表示人的頂部。《說文》："天，顛也。""顛，頂也。"那麼，"𢍱"字所從的"口"，"𢍱"字所從的"一"猶如"𠅃"字所從的"口"，"𠀑"字所從的"一"，應是指牛的頂部。下端略呈弧形"⌣"。"⊥"形表示除了牛角以外的頭部象形。這種形體只是出現在自組卜辭中，而自組卜辭中有些文字的構形是比較特別的。"𢍱"與"屮"無別。郭老早就指出："𢍱即常見之屮字。"⑤

第二種形體大都屬于賓組卜辭，表示主要特徵的牛角較之自組卜辭要直一些，由"∪"形趨于"⊔"形。牛頭頂部的"一"形逐漸省去，下端由"⌣"形逐漸變成"一"形了。斜劃與直劃互作卜辭習見，如"屯"字作"𠂆"也作"𠂉"，羊字作"𦍋"也作"𦍌"。在這種形體中尤其是賓組卜辭中的大字表示牛角的象徵性特別強。

第三種形體是因牛的頂部不太突出的緣故，加之正視牛頭的角度不同所造成。牛首鼎文及安陽出土的很多牛頭形飾都呈"𢍱"形，這種形體在卜辭中並不少見。

第四種形體已脫離象形文字的基本形態而變爲直綫條了，這種形體較之上例幾種形體爲晚，而且成爲比較通行的形體。

---

① 參見《金文編》附錄八四二頁。
② 天津藝術博物館藏，見《文物》一九五九年第七期，范汝森：《商周時代的幾件玉雕》。
③ 中國社會科學院考古研究所安陽工作隊：《一九六九——一九七七年殷墟西區墓葬發掘報告》，《考古學報》一九七九年第一期，圖版十六。
④ 牛字作𢍱形，如《續》二·一八·八，《明》二八〇。
⑤ 郭沫若：《卜辭通纂·別一》第九頁下。

根據以上的分析，我們認爲屮、ㄓ、ㄓ字象牛頭形。其演變序列應是：

$$\text{屮} \to \text{ㄓ} \to \text{ㄓ} \to \text{ㄓ}$$

這裏應該指出的是，文字產生的早期階段或圖形文字階段是以牛頭表示整頭牛的。如前所舉商代的牛頭形鼎文，後來演變作"ㄓ"形，以表示牛角、牛頭上下部的綫條勾劃出一幅牛頭形字。《說文》：牛"象角頭三封尾之形。"許慎實是以後來變化了的"牛"字作"ㄓ"形爲說解。早期的"牛"字下端作斜劃不出頭，後來才變成直劃，下端出頭。甲骨文中"牛"字的演變序列應該是：

$$\text{牛} \to \text{牛} \to \text{牛} \to \text{牛}$$

"屮"與"牛"字在形體上是略有區別，但透過區別的表面現象我們可以看出這兩個字實際存在的不可分割的聯繫，下列的兩種現象是夠說明一定問題的。

同形：

屮　ㄓ前4·4·2　ㄓ前1·30·3　ㄓ乙3290　ㄓ乙1916　ㄓ乙2487　ㄓ乙4887
　　ㄓ乙2236　ㄓ簠2·32

牛　ㄓ乙2103　ㄓ珠1106　ㄓ甲2486　ㄓ善2411　ㄓ存447　ㄓ甲365
　　ㄓ粹39　ㄓ簠3·14

省形：

屮　ㄩ乙766　ㄩ乙4057　ㄩ存632　ㄩ乙8684　ㄩ乙9085　ㄩ鐵97·2

牢　乙都2979　乙珠1106　乙佚212　乙甲2324　乙存1769　乙都3240

同形的一組表示主要特徵的牛角完全相同，牛頭上端不出頭。區別的地方僅僅在于"屮"字下端作直劃，"牛"字下端作斜劃，並稍出頭（如前所述，直劃與斜劃每每互作，如ㄓ亦作ㄓ，ㄓ字也作ㄓ。同一板上的"牛"字，一作ㄓ，一作ㄓ，是其例證）。①省形的一組，表示主要特徵的牛的角部相同，省略的只是下端的"一"和"∨"部分。"宰"字省形作（《甲》二七五九）、（《乙》八六八四反），與"牢"字省作是不同的，此爲"牢"字無疑，"屮"字省形作ㄩ亦屬事實，《乙》四○五七"甲午卜殼貞翌□未ㄩ于祖乙"。《乙》七六六"丙戌卜ㄩ于父丁叀巍"，以同例語"屮于祖乙"（《佚》一五四）、"屮歲于父丁"

---

① 例：《後》上二一·一三。《戬》一七·一八牛作ㄓ。

（《合》二五六）例之，"ㄩ"無疑是"㞢"字的省形。

還有一重要現象值得注意，即在一組卜辭中，每有當"㞢"字上部表示牛角的部分作彎筆"⌣"時，牛字變作直筆"凵"；而當"㞢"字上部作直筆"凵"時，牛字又作彎筆"⌣"。這種現象恰好說明了它們之間的同一關係。例：

自組大字		賓　　組	
㞢	牛	㞢	牛
(乙 9093)		(乙 2103)	
(乙 8660)		(乙 5227)	
(乙 412)		(乙 2171)	

自組小字		午　　組	
㞢	牛	㞢	牛
(甲 3045)		(乙 5328)	
(佚 599)		(乙 7261)	
(甲 248)①		(乙 4925)	

又如从"牛"的"告"字作㞢，也有从"㞢"作㞢（《甲》一五八一）、㞢（《甲》三三八二）的，這說明从牛从㞢無別。② 所以，我們說"㞢"與"牛"字既有區別，又有不可分割的聯繫，同屬牛頭象形的主要特徵是很明顯的。

那麼，為什麼同屬牛頭象形的字要在形體上有所區別呢？這是因為：隨著社會的不斷發展，文字的不斷演進和引申，本來同屬一個形體的字，為了表達幾種意思，往往在形體上稍加區別。如"人"與"尸"（夷）字，同為人之側視形，為了表明兩種意思，有時便在形體上稍加區別，即以"𠆢"表示"人"，以"⺈"表示"尸"（夷）。"白"與"百"字，為了表明兩種意思，"白"作 ⌂ ，而"百"便作 ⌂ 或 ⌂ ，形體上加以區別。又如"戌"與"王"字，同屬斧鉞象形字，只是為了

---

① 參見林澐：《甲骨文斷代中一個重要問題的再研究》表一。此文尚未正式發表。
② 所說的"告"字从牛，有另文專述。

表明兩種意思，在形體上加以區別，即以 ᶋ 表示"戌"，而以"戌"字上半部豎直之形的"ᐃ"表示"王"。① "牛"與"㞢"字也與上述人與尸、白與百、戌與王字一樣，爲了表明兩種意思，便在形體上稍加區別，即以 ᙱ 或 ᙳ、ᙲ 表示牲畜"牛"，而以 ᙸ 或 ᙹ、ᙺ 表示特定含義的"㞢"。

關于"㞢"字的音讀問題，我們既然認定"㞢"與"牛"字一樣同屬牛頭象形字，只是在形體上略有區別，那麼，"㞢"與"牛"字的讀音應該是相同或可通的。在某個獨體字上稍變其形賦予它以新的含義，但仍因原來的獨體字以爲音符而其讀音相同或略有轉變，這在古文字中是不乏其例的。② 如前所舉人與尸（夷）、戌與王、白與百等等。我們知道，"㞢"與"又"字在卜辭文例中是可以通用互作的。如：

  壬子卜，賓貞。㞯乞步伐呂方。受㞢又。十二月。   （《粹》一〇七二）
  壬戌卜，我弗入商。我又㞢。   （《粹》一二九八）
  ……辰卜，賓貞。受㞢年。   （《甲》三四三〇）
  ……籍 ᙴ 隹其受又年。   （《甲》一三六九）

"又㞢"即"㞢又"亦即"有佑"；"受㞢年"、"受又年"即"受有年"。"㞢"、"又"、"有"三字音同字通，與"牛"字音近可通。"又"、"有"屬喻母三等字，"牛"屬疑母字。疑母字與喻母三等字可以相通，如"僞"從"爲"得聲，"僞"是疑母字，"爲"屬喻母三等字。喻母三等字歸入匣母③，所以，疑母字又與匣母字相通。如"完"從"元"得聲，"元"爲疑母字，"完"爲匣母字；同是從"艮"得聲的"銀"、"齦"、"垠"爲疑母字，而"很"、"痕"、"恨"又屬匣母字。疑母字與喻母字往往混讀，如讀"顒"如"容"，讀"魚"如"余"，讀"銀"如"寅"，讀"堯"如"遥"，讀"牛"如"由"等等。④ "牛"與"又"、"有"古韻又同屬"之"部。所以，從聲韻上講，"牛"與"又"、"有"讀音可通，與"㞢"字讀音亦通應是沒有多大疑問的。

那麼，爲什麼以區別於牛的牛頭象形字來表示"㞢"即有無之"有"呢？

如前所述，由于表示有無之義的"㞢"字武丁以後已逐漸消失而先後以其同

---

① 吳其昌：《金文名象疏證》，載武大《文哲季刊》五卷三期第四九八—五〇九頁。林澐：《說王》，《考古》一九六五年第六期。
② 參見于省吾著：《甲骨文字釋林》第四四五—四六三頁。
③ 曾運乾：《喻母古讀考》，《東北大學季刊》一九二七年第二期。
④ 江永：《音學辨微》第十四—十八頁。

音字"又"、"有"所代替，因而"有"字的原始含義到後來就辨別不清了。《説文》"有"字下説："不宜有也。"段注："謂本是不當有而有之稱。"這説明許慎臆測無據，後來解釋《説文》者亦曲加附會，無可憑信。王國維曾經指出："有無之有，古本無正字，所用又、㕛、有三字皆假借也。"①有一定的獨到之處。但從文字的發展變化看，最初表示有無之"有"的正字應是牛頭象形的"㞢"字，"又"、"有"屬"㞢"字的同音假借字。

牛是一種大牲畜，以牛這類牲畜表示"有"或"富有"，這從古代典籍中可以窺見一斑。如《禮記·曲禮》："問庶人之富，數畜以對。"《漢書·五行志》中之上："牛，大畜。"《詩·無羊》："誰謂爾無牛，九十其犉。"《詩·魏風》："胡瞻爾庭有懸特兮。"

商的先公王亥僕牛，《世本·作篇》作"服牛"。《説文》：服"用也"。《易·繫辭》："服牛乘馬。"疏："服用其牛。"《管子·輕重戊篇》："殷人之王立帛牢服牛馬以爲民利。"②甲骨文中有不少"省牛"的記載③。由此可見殷民族是重視利用養牛來牟取利益的。

安陽殷墟出土的有些陶器上④以及有些銅器上就有以牛首形作爲裝飾的圖案⑤。在殷虛，考古發掘出有的房基遺址内的窖坑中專門儲有牛骨的現象⑥。墓葬中經常有以牛的大腿骨隨葬，甚至有的墓葬的填土中或二層臺上葬有牛頭。⑦從這些現象也可以看出殷人是重視牛的。

參照有些少數民族志的材料，發現有不少的民族都以牛這種牲畜表示富有。如雲南的拉祜族、景頗族、西盟瓦族、獨龍族、崩龍族⑧；貴州有海

---

① 王國維：《觀堂別集》二卷五頁上。
② 王念孫説"帛"當爲"阜"字之誤，阜以養馬，牢以養牛。見《管子集校》引。
③ 如：《乙》八四六一，《合》二二〇等。
④ 李濟：《殷周陶器初論》，《安陽發掘報告》第一期，一九二九年出版。
⑤ 甘肅省博物館文物隊：《甘肅靈臺白草坡西周墓》，《考古學報》一九七七年二期。參見容庚：《商周彝器通考》第二册（圖録）。
　補注：按：殷商銅器上的所謂"饕餮"紋，有些實際上就是牛首形紋。甘肅靈臺白草坡墓所出銅器上"銘文保持濃厚的殷商族徽遺風"，很多銅器上飾有牛首紋。
⑥ 《一九五五年秋安陽小屯殷墟的發掘》，《考古學報》一九五八年第三期六六頁。
⑦ 《一九六九——一九七七年殷墟西區墓葬發掘報告》，《考古學報》一九七九年第一期。全按：《禮記·祭統》："凡爲俎者，以骨爲主，骨有貴賤，殷人貴髀。"髀指大腿骨，這裏記載的雖然講的是俎祭，但反映了殷人貴髀的思想意識，聯繫到殷人墓葬中常常以牛的大腿骨隨葬，當可窺見殷人貴牛的意識。
⑧ 宋恩常著：《雲南少數民族社會調查研究》。滿都爾圖：《論父系家庭公社》，《民族研究》一九七九年第一期。

巴苗族①；西藏的僜人②等等民族。"牛成爲人們佔有和積累的主要財産。……牛的多少成爲區分貧富的標志，人們把宰殺的牛頭骨積累起來"或者"懸掛在房屋内外"。"牛頭骨越多越顯示富有"。這就意味着這些少數民族人們心目中的概念是有了象徵富有的"牛"就表示"有"。再從考古發掘的材料看，如雲南江川李家山③，晉寧石寨山④等古墓中有以銅牛角、銅牛、牛首銅杖頭等作爲隨葬品；不少的青銅器上都以牛的形象作爲裝飾的圖案。又如河北懷來⑤與内蒙古扎賚諾爾⑥一帶地區的古墓中大都有以牛頭或牛骨隨葬。這些現象從一定程度上再現了"牛"在當時當地人們心目中的地位。

有的民族還依托于"牛"來表示豐年的。如《廣東新語》："韶州十月朔日，農家大酺，爲米糍相餽，以大糍粘牛角上謂之'牛年'。""牛年"就是慶祝有年、豐年之意。這就猶如商代甲骨文中的"受㞢年"、周代《詩·有駜》中的"歲其有"，傳："歲其有，豐年也。"亦即富有之年。新疆出土的回鶻文文書中有可能是依托于牛來表示記年的。如"牛年十一月初九（日）"、"牛年十二月……"⑦。

再從甲骨文"㞢"字本身的材料看，它的基本含義的確等于有無之有的"有"字，而"㞢"字我們已認定爲表示"牛"的牛頭象形字，而"牛"與"有"又具有密切的關係。所以，我們説殷民族以區別于"牛"字的牛頭象形字來表示"㞢"即有無之"有"是不足爲怪的。

"㞢"字在卜辭文例中除了用作基本含義的"有"字之外，還用作祭名。祭祀用牛稱爲大牲，《易·萃》："用大牲。"鄭注："大牲，牛也。"也稱牢或大牢。殷代甲骨卜辭中以"牛"、"牢"或"大牢"作爲祭祀的犧牲是很多的。用數少則一頭、數頭，多者竟達三百牢、五百牛者。⑧由此可以看出殷王室祭祀的規模和擁

---

① 吳澤霖、陳國鈞著：《貴州苗夷社會研究》第二三二頁。又見《社會研究》第十六期，一九四〇年一月二十一日。
② 張江華：《略論原始社會瓦解時期的僜人社會》，《民族研究》一九八〇年第二期。吳從衆：《僜人父權制的家庭與婚姻》，《民族研究》一九八〇年第一期。
③ 《雲南江川李家山古墓群發掘報告》M二四、M一七、M二一、M二三等，《考古學報》一九七五年第二期。
④ 《雲南晉寧石寨山遺址及墓葬》，《考古學報》一九五六年第一期。
⑤ 《河北懷來北辛堡戰國墓》，《考古》一九六六年第五期。
⑥ 《内蒙古扎賚諾爾古墓群發掘簡報》，《考古》一九六一年第十二期六七五—六七六頁。
⑦ 耿世民：《幾件回鶻文文書譯釋》，《文物》一九八〇年第五期。
⑧ 胡厚宣：《釋牢》，載《史語所集刊》八本二分一五三頁，一九三九年本。

有的經濟實力。據《禮記·郊特牲》記載："殷人先求諸陽……用牲于庭，升首于室。……首也者直也……升首報陽也。"鄭注："制祭之後升牲首于北墉下，尊首尚氣也。""所以升首祭也，直或爲犆。"按"直"爲"犆"，亦即"特"。《韓詩》："實維我直。"《毛詩》："實維我特。""特"即"特牛"，《說文》特"朴特牛父也。"《禮記·王制》："用特。"注："特，特牛也。"由此看來，殷人祭祀用牛牲還需登其牛首。所以卜辭中以區別于牛的牛頭象形字"屮"假借爲祭名即後來之"侑"應該是可以理解的。《禮記·王制》記載周人"祭天地之牛角繭栗、宗廟之牛角握、賓客之牛角尺。"這一套用牛作爲犧牲的祭祀制度也應該是有一定的歷史淵源的。

綜括上述，我們以爲甲骨文中至今尚未明瞭形體結構的"屮"字應該是人們熟知的牛頭象形字。由于社會的不斷發展，文字的不斷演進和引申，到商代武丁時期的甲骨文中出現了本來是象徵牛頭的"牛"字，爲了表明兩種意思便在形體上稍加區別，即以 ψ、ψ、ψ、ψ 表示牲畜"牛"，而以 ψ、ψ、ψ、ψ 表示特定含義的"屮"；武丁以後這個"屮"字逐漸消失，而先後以其同音字"又"、"有"所代替。"牛"與"屮"、"又"、"有"不僅聲紐可通，而且古韻同屬之部。聯繫有關的文獻記載和考古發掘材料，可以窺視出牲畜"牛"與"有"字含義的一些關係，可以看出商人是重視和利用牛的。參考雲南、貴州、西藏等地少數民族以牛作爲財富的象徵，有牛就表明富有的材料，再從甲骨文"屮"字本身在卜辭文例中的用法的確又等于有無之"有"這一客觀事實，所以，我們說商民族以象徵牛而又區別于"牛"字的牛頭象形字來表示"屮"即有無之"有"這一特定含義，應該是符合造字原義的。商代祭祀大量用牲，用牛又爲大牲，因而又借"屮"字作爲祭名。

原載《古文字研究》第 6 輯，中華書局，1981 年；收入黃錫全：《古文字論叢》，藝文印書館，1999 年；又收入宋鎮豪、段志洪主編：《甲骨文獻集成》第 13 册，四川大學出版社，2001 年。今據前者收入。

陳煒湛

甲骨文異字同形例

甲骨文中有兩種正好相反的現象：一字異形和異字同形。兩者都反映了字形與字義的矛盾，説明甲骨文雖已形成體系，但字形還不十分固定。前者即所謂異體字，一個字有多種寫法，這是普遍現象，學者們已普遍地注意到了，除少數字外，意見也大都一致，毋庸贅言。後者亦可稱爲同形字，由於種種原因，一個字形代表兩個音義全然不同的字，爲數雖不多，却是特殊的現象，治甲骨者尚較少論及。識别異體字固然有助於文字的考訂，避免將一個字誤認作幾個字；而辨别同形字對於正確理解卜辭也頗關重要，可以免致釋讀上的錯誤。本文即擬選取若干有代表性的異字同形之例加以剖析，作些探討，希望讀者不吝指正。

下列兩種情况與異字同形相似而有别，不屬本文討論範圍。一種是古本一字，後世孳乳而分爲二字者，如隻與獲，帚與婦，晶與星，且匕與祖妣，宜與俎等等。另一種是假借字，如田與畋，又與有、侑、祐，帝與禘，卩與禦，兄與祝，巳與祀等等，或偏旁相同，或聲韵相通，與純粹的一形二字也不同。

一、下入∧

甲骨文入字多作∧，下通常作⌒，然亦可省作∧，遂與入字同形而易相混。《甲骨文編》將∧一律釋入（見該書卷五第18頁，合文卷第2—3頁）。

卜辭人名有下乙，或作了，或作彡。作彡者有的同志釋爲入乙，也有的釋爲内乙，均有未安。案《乙》4549片云"乙酉卜，虫歲于下乙"。另一辭同。兩辭對貞，下乙兩見，而一作了，一作彡，此爲下可作∧之有力佐證。《京津》701片

亦"又于𠂤"與"又𠂤"共見一版，足證∧爲下而𠂤非入乙。再如《乙》1783片"甲子卜羋羊于（案此字首畫適殘，不可誤認爲"七"）下乙又用"，3478片"乙卯卜又歲于下乙牢用"，7512片"癸酉卜□午下乙牢"，8670片"牢又羋于下乙"，諸辭之下乙亦均作𠂤。此下乙，胡厚宣先生謂即祖乙①，或以爲乃小乙②。案上述諸辭皆武丁時所卜，而武丁稱小乙爲父乙，安得呼爲下乙，當以胡氏之説爲是。又據《丙》39片，下乙的地位和大甲與咸一樣的崇高，也可"賓于帝"，可知下乙決非小乙。《丙》41片云："翌乙酉屮伐于五示：上甲、咸、大丁、大甲、祖乙。"而《乙》5303片則曰："奉上甲、咸、大丁、大甲、下乙。"二辭對比，亦可證明下乙即祖乙也。

卜辭又有下己之名，作𠂤，見《殷綴》149片："丙辰卜，歲牛于祖己𠂤？"

作爲下的∧與六亦相似而有別，不可混爲一談。《佚》76片（《粹》400片重出）云："癸未貞：𠂤又𢀛，不于妣囚？"𠂤，商承祚、郭沫若先生均釋六旬，無説，《甲骨文編》亦從之。案卜辭中六字多作介、∧、∧、∧諸形，如六示作𠂤，六祀作𠂤，六日作𠂤，六人作𠂤，六牛作介屮，六百作𠂤，六牢作𠂤，六字都不作∧，𠂤之∧釋六似有未安，實亦當釋下，與下乙之下作∧者同。下旬猶來旬也，與今旬相對。《乙》304片"今旬雨"，《粹》747片"自今旬雨"，《粹》751片"自今旬壬子雨"，《鐵》147·4片"癸酉卜自今旬不其〔雨〕"，其餘如《金》703，《續存》上340，《南北·坊間》4·42，《京都》209，《續》4·23·8，《乙》2629諸片亦均稱"今旬"。此稱"下旬又𢀛"與"旬亡囚"意同，乃於癸日即一旬之末日貞卜下旬是否有災禍，若釋六旬則了無意義矣。

∧作爲下字畢竟是少數，在大多數甲骨文中，∧則是入字，其辭例或稱入日，入商，王入，王勿入，義均爲出入之入，如《佚》407片即入日（∧日）與出日（𠂤日）共見一版；或稱某入若干，見於甲橋刻辭者不下數百例，義同入貢。而作爲入的∧，亦有誤認爲六字者。如《粹》757片（新版爲888之乙）有𠂤一語，郭沫若釋爲六百，謂"唯六百不合書，爲一異例"。案此實"入百"二字，"百"左下側之亘則爲史官簽名，"入"上一字剛好殘失，補足之，當讀爲"□入百。亘"。餘外"雨、易、日"三字則爲另一辭之殘，與本辭無涉。甲橋刻辭稱"入百"之例亦屢見。如《乙》776及1023片均稱"𠂤入百"。又如《佚》

---

① 胡厚宣：《卜辭下乙説》，載《甲骨學商史論叢》初集。
② 于省吾：《釋上乙下乙》（《雙劍誃殷契駢枝三編》）云："下乙即小乙，斷可識矣。"但1979年出版的《甲骨文字釋林》一書未收此文，殆作者已放棄此説。

370 片之背，商先生釋爲"□六百"，案此片第一字實妟，雖微蝕，尚可辨。二、三兩字作 [字形]，亦宜釋入百，連讀之則爲"妟入百"。妟入若干的記載亦見於《乙》5320 片，"妟入十"；6825 片，"妟入二"；7652 片，"妟入三十"（朱書）。

要之，甲骨文 ∧ 既是出入之入，又是上下之下，二者同形，但與六作 ∧ ∧ ∧ 者則仍有別。

二、女母 [字形]

甲骨文女均作 [字形] 或 [字形] 形，象一個女人跪跽在地雙手交叉於胸前之狀，又有少數作 [字形] 形，首部多一筆，象簪笄。甲骨文的母則多作 [字形]，即在女字中加上兩點，象胸前雙乳之形，金文亦多如此作，這在六書中可謂"指事"。小篆演變爲 [字形]，《說文》釋爲"牧也。从女，象懷子形。一曰象乳子也"，確是越說越糊塗。但甲骨文中的母字有時又不加兩點，而一去掉這標誌，便與女字相混了。這樣，[字形] 是母非女，很清楚，但 [字形] 却是女也是母，變成異字同形。不可不辨了。

[字形] 或 [字形] 作爲"女"字的辭例，卜辭屢見不鮮，如武丁時的卜辭說：

> 甲申〔卜〕，殷貞：帚（婦）好冥（娩）奼（嘉）？王固曰：其隹丁冥奼，其隹庚冥，弘吉。三旬出一日甲寅冥，不奼，隹女。　　　　《乙》7731（《續存》附圖八）

此辭謂婦好分娩，生了女孩，覺得掃興，認爲是"不奼"。甲骨文還有來女、取女、氐（致也）女的記載，如：

> 帚（婦）妌來 [字形]。　　　　《乙》7426
> 其氏角 [字形]。　　　　《乙》3507
> 貞[字形]〔氏〕角 [字形]。　　　　《乙》3005
> 乎取 [字形] 于林。　乎取 [字形]。　　　　《乙》3186
> 辛卯卜，爭：勿乎取奠 [字形] 子？
> 辛卯卜，爭：乎取奠 [字形] 子？　　　　《殷綴》276

這類"女"，姚孝遂同志認爲是作爲禮品或貢物進納給商王的女俘，是所謂"床上奴隸"[①]。此說能否成立，當然還可討論，但上引諸辭中的"女"不讀爲母，

---

① 姚孝遂：《商代的俘虜》，《古文字研究》第一輯。

則是肯定的。

在很多場合，根據文義可以判斷，⿱女𠂉 或 ⿱女𠂉 却是母字，不是女字，如《甲》2902 片，母庚、母壬、母癸並見，三母字一作 ⿱女𠂉、二作 ⿱女𠂉，中無兩點。《甲》2426 片母己作 ⿱女𠂉己，《乙》8661 片母壬亦作 ⿱女𠂉壬，再如《掇》1·195 片"母己"，母作 ⿱女𠂉，《粹》381 片"母戊"，母作 ⿱女𠂉，均與女同形。而在合文形式中，母甲、母乙、母丙、母丁、母戊、母己、母庚、母辛、母壬、母癸等等稱謂，母字均可作 ⿱女𠂉，與女同形（見《甲骨文編》合文卷，第 13—15 頁）。殷虛出土司母戊鼎母字亦作 ⿱女𠂉，結構與甲骨文同，可資參證。

三、正足 ⿱止一

正和足，小篆、金文都有明顯區別，不相混淆。但在甲骨文裏，正和足都可寫成 ⿱止一，二字完全同形，頗易弄錯。如《鐵》127·2 片云："戊寅卜，㱿貞：⿰宀⿱止一 ⿱止一？"末二字孫詒讓即釋爲定足，又說："未知爲正爲征，或別爲足字，皆無由決定。"案此二字當釋爲寔正，《甲骨文編》將此 ⿱止一 收在正字下是對的。此書卷二將正足分列兩字，並於足下注道："卜辭足與正字同形，從文義上可以別之。"其說是也。

從文義上看，甲骨文"正"大多用作征伐之征，例如：

丁酉卜，殻貞：今⿱止一王收人五千 ⿱止一 土方，受𡿧又？　　　　　　　《後》上 31·5

己酉卜，□貞：王⿱止一 舌方，下上若，受我又？二月。貞：勿 ⿱止一 舌方，下上弗若，不我其受又？　　　　　《鐵》244·2（《誠》354《粹》1084）

王來 ⿱止一 人方。　　　　　　　　　　　　　　　　　　　《甲》3355

……余其从多田于白 ⿱止一 盂方白。　　　　　　　　　　　　《甲》2416

或用爲正月之正，如《後》下 1·5 片稱"月一正"，《甲》2274，《粹》1350·1352·1570 諸片均稱"在正月"。正月二字合文之例亦甚多，見《甲骨文編》合文卷，第 26 頁。又有"又正"一語，多見於祭祀卜辭中，例如：

各日，又 ⿱止一。　　　　　　　　　　　　　　　　　　　　《甲》404

貞：叀乙酉酒，又 ⿱止一。　　　　　　　　　　　　　　　　《甲》1336

□眔大乙酒，又 ⿱止一。　　　　　　　　　　　　　　　　　《粹》143

王賓母戊歲，又𠂤。　　　　　　　　　　　　　　　　　　　《粹》383

叀小宰，又𠂤。叀牛，又𠂤。叀一牛，用。叀二牛，用。叀三牛，用。〔叀〕一宰用。
　　　　　　　　　　　　　　　　　　　　　　　　　　　　《粹》596

餘如《粹》233·234·455·542·559·659·1062·1274 諸片亦其例。此正，決也。《詩·大雅·文王有聲》："維龜正之。"注：正，決也。卜辭言又正，即有正，意謂有決，猶他辭言用，茲用。《粹》596 片"又正"與"用"並見，義當相近。

下列諸辭之𠂤或𠂤亦當釋正：

甲申卜，令喙宅𠂤？　　　　　　　　　　　　　　《乙》8893（8898同文）

庚寅卜，爭貞：旨𠂤妻？　　　　　　　　　　　　　　　《乙》1054

于𠂤京北。　　　　　　　　　　　　　　　　　　　　　《佚》374

令从永𠂤。　　　　　　　　　　　　　　　　　　　　《龜》1·26·18

而足，有用其本義者，如《甲》1640 片稱"疾足"，即文獻所謂"足疾"（《左傳》昭公二十七年"光偽足疾入掘室"，《史記·吳太伯世家》"公子光詳爲足疾入于窟室"）。不過，例不多見；有用其引申義者，常見的辭例有足雨或雨足：

帝其令雨𠂤？　　　　　　　　　　　　　　　　　　　　《乙》6951

己酉卜，黍年出𠂤雨？　　　　　　　　　　　　　　　《前》4·40·1

□□卜，黍年出𠂤雨？　　　　　　　　　　　　　　　　《金》373

貞：雨不𠂤，辰亡𠷚？　　　　　　　　　　　　　　　　《珠》454

庚辰卜，大貞：雨不𠂤辰不隹年？　　　　　　　　　　　《綴》252

或稱足年：

貞：帝令雨，弗其𠂤年？帝令雨，𠂤年？　　　　　　　《前》1·50·1

此數例之足，義均爲充足、豐足。足雨，即雨量充足，足年，意即豐足之年。若釋正，則諸辭均不可通。

值得注意的是，正除作𠂤與足同形外，也有寫成𤴓的，此字見於《甲》3940，即著名的鹿頭骨刻辭，辭稱"王來正□"，正下殘缺。也可以从屮或艸作𣥂𣥂，唯《甲骨文編》入之於附錄（附錄上，第 19 頁），故不見於正編。案𣥂實𠂤之繁，義亦同征，例如：

沚馘告曰：土方𣥂于我東啚（鄙），戈二邑。　　　　　　《菁》1

昔甲辰方𣥂于蚊，俘人十出五人。　　　　　　　　　　《菁》6

貞：弗其隻（獲）▢土方？　　　　　　　　　　　　　《甲》3346

　　貞：乎▢舌方？　　　　　　　　　　　　　　　　　《粹》1164

　　己酉卜貞：雀往▢犬，弗其半？十月。　　　　　　　《鐵》181·3

　　于辛巳王▢旨方？　　　　　　　　　　　　　　　　《佚》520

　　〔試比較："丁巳貞：王▢旨方？"《寧滬》1·424〕

文例與从▢之▢全同。以字形論，▢似多見於早期刻辭，▢通行於各期卜辭，▢則與金文相近，然僅一見，姑置不論。竊疑▢是正的本字，是早期寫法，所从之▢呈長方形，代表一個處所，雙止（趾）所至，是爲正，其意與韋之作▢或▢者相仿而有異。金文小篆从一實由▢演變而來（甲骨文从▢或▢而後世易爲一者尚有工作▢、天作▢），▢或▢字省變之則成▢或▢，與▢通用不悖，漸漸取而代之。故武丁以後，▢便很少見有使用了。

　　另一方面，足字所从的▢，也並不是口，它本是脛骨的俯視形，原當與▢相聯像小篆的▢字一樣的。《甲骨文編》附錄（上）第 17 頁錄有如下數文：

　　　　▢　　　　　　　　　　　　　　　　　　　　《甲》2878

　　　　▢　　　　　　　　　　　　　　　　　　　　《珠》542

　　　　▢ ▢　　　　　　　　　　　　　　　　　　《佚》392

恐怕就是足的初文，▢代表腳趾，亦即止，▢▢代表膝蓋以下的小腿骨。（金祥恆《續甲骨文編》即將此數文及《乙》1187 之▢，《甲》3067 之▢，《乙》647 之▢等均釋爲足，可供參考。）把這些字整齊規範化，也就是▢或▢字了。

　　如此說成立，則正與足本不同形，只是由於各自簡省而變得同形的。這兩個字的淵源關係略如下圖：

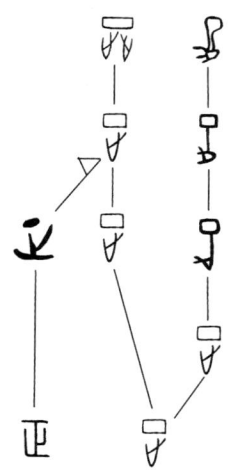

四、山火 ⛰

卜辭火字屢見，或作 ⛰ ⛰，象火焰上騰之形，或作 ⛰ ⛰，則與山字無別。蓋 ⛰ 既象山巒形，亦可象火焰之形。《甲骨文編》有"火"無"山"，僅收從山之嵒作 ⛰。其實，卜辭並非無山字，只因與火同形，《甲骨文編》把它歸入了火字而已。一般而論，下平者爲山，圓者爲火，但也往往互作，基本上兩字同形，只能根據句子的上下文來判斷究竟是山還是火。

下列諸辭之 ⛰ 或 ⛰ 不宜釋火，當釋山：

丁酉卜，扶：奠 ⛰ 羊□豕，雨？	《乙》9103
壬午卜，扶：奏 ⛰ 日□吉，雨？	《乙》9067
庚午卜，其寮雨于 ⛰ ？	《鄴三》下 38・4
□ ⛰ 奠。	《乙》2463

奠山，即奠于山，奏山，即奏于山。奠（奉）于山，義同奠（奉）于岳，與奠（奉）河相對。

□□卜，又于五 ⛰ ？在齊□□月卜。	《粹》72
丁丑卜，又于五 ⛰ ？在□隹，二月卜。	《鄴三》下 40・10
辛□貞□奠于十 ⛰ ？	《掇》1・376
甲申卜， 十 ⛰ ？（三辭同文）	《掇》2・159

郭沫若曰："'五山'，此例僅見，不知是否即五岳。"（《殷契粹編考釋》）案五岳之名屬後起，商代未必有之；且"五山"之外，又有"十山"一語，亦頗費解，或係泛指群山，"又于五山"，"奠于十山"意即祭（侑、奠）于群山。這五山、十山具體何指雖尚有疑問，但其不當讀爲五火（如《甲骨文編》然）、十火，却是十分明顯的。

庚午卜，王。在 ⛰ 卜。	《粹》1326
癸巳貞：其奠玉 ⛰ ，雨？	《甲》3642

⛰山，玉山，當是山名。

己酉貞： ⛰ 古王事？	《掇》1・431

己□貞：⛰古王事？　　　　　　　　　　　　　　　　　　　　《寧滬》1·496

　　貞：隹自⛰令？允隹自⛰令。　　　　　　　　　　　　　　　　《佚》67

此數辭之山似爲人名，某古王事爲武丁卜辭所習見；隹自山令即唯令自山，依文例，自山當是人名，是受"令"者。

　　當然，像下列各辭中的⛰或⛰就不是山字，而是火字了：

　　癸酉貞：旬亡⛰？　　　　　　　　　　　　　　　　　　　　　《粹》1428

旬亡囚（禍）爲卜辭恒語，此版有四條貞旬卜辭，三辭稱旬亡囚，囚分別作囚囚，獨此稱旬亡火，殆因火禍音近而通假，且"火"亦災禍之一也。

　　癸酉卜，扶：又山？　　　　　　　　　　　　　　　　　　　《殷掇》391

　　乙亥⛰。　　　　　　　　　　　　　　　　　　　　　　　　《前》4·19·7

　　⛰。一月。　　　　　　　　　　　　　　　　　　　　　　　《龜》2·21·3

　　貞：旬亡囚？⛰，婦妊子囚。　　　　　　　　　　　　　　　　《前》6·49·3

　　七日己巳夕㞢出新大星並⛰。　　　　　　　　　　　　　　　　《後》下9·1

此五例之火，殆焚火、起火之意。《後》下9·1謂"新大星並火"所言乃天象，其餘四例所言則爲人事，占卜是否有火災。《左傳》宣公十六年："人火曰火，天火曰災。"同書昭公十八年："陳不救火。"《公羊傳》襄公九年則謂"大者曰災，小者曰火"。凡此皆可爲卜辭"火"之佐證。特別是《前》6·49·3，貞一旬之內是否有禍，而驗辭則謂"火，婦妊子囚"，以此二者爲災異不吉（若釋囚〈冎〉爲死，則婦妊子因火災而致死，尤爲大災難）。由這幾條卜辭來看，"火"在商代是不吉利的象徵，確屬災害之一。

　　山、火異字同形還反映在以山、火爲偏旁的文字中，如栽作囧（《乙》959）囧（《誠》二），宀下从火，象室內起火，與《說文》栽之或體同，是爲災害。同樣，赤、焚、熹、炆、光等从火之字，其所从之火亦多有作⛰⛰⛰等形者（見《甲骨文編》卷十），與山無別。而孫詒讓所釋之岳（嶽），其下部所从除作⛰⛰⛰等形外，也有作⛰⛰⛰諸形的（此字《甲骨文編》從羅振玉說釋羔）。驗之辭例，从⛰之𡷗與从⛰之𡴚確係一字，並宜認作从山，釋岳，其例如：

　　貞：㞢年于𡷗？　　　　　　　　　　　　　　　《前》1·50·1《佚》375《契》33

　　戊午卜，亙貞：㞢年于𡷗？　　　　　　　　　　　　　　　　《續》2·28·1

丁未卜，又于🗆桒禾？
　　庚戌卜，又于🗆桒禾？　　　　　　　　　　　　　　　《寧滬》1·76
　　取🗆雨？　　　　　　　　　　　　　　　　　　　　　《京都》161
　　癸酉卜，其取🗆雨？　　　　　　　　　　　　　　　　《粹》28

其中《寧滬》1·76尤爲突出，🗆🗆共見一版，且辭例全同，亦可證明甲骨文中從山從火可相通。

　　既然甲骨文山火同形，且亦反映於偏旁中，那麽《甲骨文編》卷十自燀字以下二十八字所謂"《説文》所無"者，是否統統從火，也就不能無疑，而需作進一步的研究了。

五、臣目🗆🗆

　　甲骨文臣目兩字都象眼睛的形狀，總的來説寫法是有所區別的，即橫者爲目（🗆、🗆），竪者爲臣（🗆、🗆）。郭沫若謂臣"象一竪目之形，人俯首則目竪，所以'象屈服之形者'以此也"，其説甚是。目與臣有共見一辭而分別作🗆與🗆者，例如：

　　貞：子🗆亦毓，隹🗆？　　　　　　　　　　　　　　　《乙》7845
　　貞：子🗆亦毓，不其隹🗆？　　　　　　　　　　　　　《乙》7909

子目爲婦名，殷王嘗卜其娩妨之事：

　　庚午卜，賓貞：子🗆娩，妨？貞：子🗆娩，不其妨？王固曰：隹兹，勿妨。
　　　　　　　　　　　　　　　　　　　　　　　　　　　《乙》3069
　　子🗆妨。　　　　　　　　　　　　　　　　　　　　　《續存》上724

目均作橫目狀。但也有些目寫作🗆，則與臣同形。而臣有時又並不作竪目狀，却作橫目形，也寫成🗆🗆等形，遂與目字同形。故橫目者未必不是臣，竪目者也未必盡是臣，遇到🗆或🗆，同樣需要加以辨别，稍一不慎，仍有可能弄錯。

　　臣不作🗆而作🗆之例如：

　　□卯貞咒□令小🗆□　　　　　　　　　　　　　　　　《京都》2359
　　□方人其🗆商？　　　　　　　　　　　　　　　　　　《京津》1220

〔試比較："👁商？"《南北·無想》四〕

小臣爲卜辭習見之官名，多合文作🔣，今《京都》2359臣寫作🔣，若讀爲小目，於義不可通。臣商，臣服于商之謂也。臣，《說文》釋爲"牽也，事君也"，《廣韵》真部亦謂"伏也，仕于公曰臣，任于家曰僕"。是臣有事君、臣服義。若讀🔣商爲目商，義亦不通。

目不作🔣而作🔣者亦有其例：

　　☐京☐王田至🔣，隻豕五雉二，在四月。　　　　　　　　　　《明》99
　　正🔣其人又正。　　　　　　　　　　　　　　　　　　　《甲》3930

此目是人、地名，下列兩辭即作橫目狀：

　　王其田燬，至于🔣北，亡戋？　　　　　　　　　　　　　《京津》4468
　　叀🔣田，亡戋？　　　　　　　　　　　　　　　　　　　《戬》11·3
　　叀王令🔣歸？　　　　　　　　　　　　　　　　　　　　《摭續》185

臣、目異字同形的現象在偏旁結構中也同樣有所反映。一般來說，作爲偏旁的臣與目，也是一豎一橫，从臣者作🔣，从目者作🔣，分別相當明顯。如望从臣作🔣，見从目作🔣，前者舉目，後者平視，最易判別。但也有少數从目者作🔣的現象，例如相字，所从之目既可作🔣，又可作🔣。《前》5·25·5片相字兩見，作🔣🔣，實作豎目狀。《甲骨文編》卷六"柩"下列五文（🔣《乙》4211，🔣《天》39，🔣《京津》2670，🔣《束藏》109，🔣《佚》787）以爲"《說文》所無"。其實此五文以及《佚》999片之🔣（"甲辰婦🔣示二屯，岳。"）亦均相字，其从🔣與《前》5·25·5片之🔣亦同，正是小篆🔣之所本。又如面字，既可作🔣（《甲》415·416·2375），亦可作🔣（《續》1·9·8）。再如曼，雖多从🔣，然亦有从🔣作者，如《京都》3151片之🔣即是（《甲骨文編》卷四第1頁）。准此，《簠室·雜事》138片之🔣，《遺珠》564之🔣，565之🔣，實象左右視之形，可釋罡或眲，亦即瞗（小篆省冂）；《後》下24·6片之🔣，乃从目从寅，羅振玉釋瞋爲不誤，《甲骨文編》改釋矏，乃屬"《說文》所無"，反有未安。

六、姤多母🔣

🔣既是一個獨立的字，又是多母二字的合文形式，這是獨字與合文同形之

例。作爲一個獨立的字，𡚽，从女，多聲，《說文》謂"美女也"。卜辭有婦𡚽之名，乃武丁諸婦之一，其辭例如：

癸亥卜，婦𡚽亡囚？ 《乙》8877·8896

辛丑卜，乎𠂤婦𡚽孕？ 《乙》8896

婦𡚽亦可省稱婦多：

貞：婦多㚸？ 《乙》8711·8896

壬午貞：婦多亡囚？ 《乙》8882

貞：婦多亡囚？ 《乙》8884

癸丑卜，婦多在老。 《乙》8896

婦𡚽之𡚽省女而成婦多，猶婦𦍋（《乙》6758）之𦍋省女而作婦羊（《續》6·24·10），《乙》8896版婦𡚽與婦多並見，繁簡共存，尤爲明證。

但在下列各辭中，𡚽却是多母的合文形式：

貞：隹𠁟（多妣）？隹𡚽（多母）？ 《乙》5640

此版𡚽與𠁟（多妣）對文，可證此𡚽非𡚽字，亦非多女合文，而是多母合文（母女異字同形，說見前）。

貞𡚽亡囚？ 《乙》8717·8888

其所以知𡚽爲合文，是因爲甲骨文中同時也存在有多母析書之例，如：

庚戌□貞易多母㞢貝朋？ 《後》下8·5

貞：隹多母㞢？ 《庫》663

乙酉卜，韋貞：㞢于多母？ 《七集》丁·14

甲申卜，王：大衛于多母？ 《前》8·4·7

于多母禦？ 《鄴三》下37·8

既然𡚽與多母的合文異字同形，則《甲骨文編》卷十二許多从女的字，特别是"妣"字以下"《說文》所無"者五十餘字，是否全是獨體字而沒有合文在內；該書合文卷内母㚬以下至王母計二十條是否全屬合文，而無獨體字在內，也就有必要重新加以考慮，審慎地作出判斷了。

七、壬工示

卜辭十干之壬多作Ⅰ，工字早期多作ᙈ，象矩形，規矩爲工具，故其義引申爲工作，工巧，能事。但在祖庚祖甲以後，工字簡省爲Ⅰ，遂與壬字同形，唯於文義上可加以區別。

下列諸辭之Ⅰ均可釋工：

甲子酒妹，Ⅰ典。	《前》3·28·5
六月甲午Ⅰ典。	《前》3·28·5
在六月乙巳Ⅰ典。	《前》4·43·4
□于多Ⅰ。	《粹》1271
〔試比較："甲寅〔卜〕，叀貞：多ᙈ亡尤?"《粹》1284〕	
作學Ⅰ宮若。	《京都》60

工典即貢典，承奉典册。于省吾先生曰："其言貢典，是就祭祀時獻其典册，以致其祝告之詞也。"① 是工典爲獻典册於神前的儀式，Ⅰ若讀爲壬，"壬典"便難以理解。多工，殆即後世所謂百工。

作爲十干之名的壬，一般均與地支字相搭配以紀日，或用作人名，稱示壬、妣壬、母壬，極易分辨，不致誤認爲工，故其例從略。

示卜辭多作T或Ⅰ，其Ⅰ省上筆則成Ⅰ，乃與壬、工亦共一形，其例如下：

貞：不隹叔Ⅰ壱?	《京津》1918
㞢犬于叔Ⅰ。	《鐵》140·2
戊往Ⅰ沚。	《寧滬》2·52
三匚二Ⅰ卯，王祭于之若，又正。	《粹》542

三匚，即報乙、報丙、報丁；二Ⅰ，即指示壬、示癸。此類例不多見。示作Ⅰ者又見於合文中，如：

ꞩⅠ（示辛）	《甲》2764
∏（示壬）	《契》640

---

① 于省吾：《甲骨文字釋林·釋工》。

┃乂（示癸） 《甲》2381

〔試比較：乂┃《前》1·2·4〕

┃⺄（九示） 《乙》804

〔試比較：⺄┃《甲》267〕

其中《契》640較爲有趣。由於示省筆爲┃，與壬同形，示壬合文即成╂，就無法辨別其孰爲示孰爲壬了。

八、甲七十

甲骨文十干的甲與數目字的七都寫作十，完全同形。究其造字之初，作爲七，十代表從中切斷之意，實即切之初文。七爲指事，切爲七假作紀數專名後另造的後起形聲字。作爲甲，十又象甲坼之形，林義光《文源》曰：「甲者，皮開裂也，十象其裂文。」如是，同一個符號"十"實際上代表着兩個不同的概念，分屬兩個不同的字。或謂"七"之爲十，起源於以利器在器物上的刻劃，其音義與甲亦相近①，可備一説。

案卜辭之甲多與地支字搭配以紀日，或用作先公先王之名，如上甲、小甲、大甲、戔甲、羌甲、㽞甲，或見於稱謂，如父甲、祖甲、妣甲、母甲；七則或用爲序數，或用爲基數，作爲名詞的修飾語時，或置於名詞之前，或置於名詞之後。故甲、七二字雖異字同形，但使用範圍不同，用法各異，不致混淆，實際上研習甲骨文者，一般都不會弄錯。

九、妣刀人

甲骨文匕（妣）多作⺄或⺀，然亦可作⺄或⺀，遂與人形相近，又可作⺄（《佚》192），乃與刀同形。而人字，除一般作⺀外，亦可作⺄（《契》四）或⺀（《京津》4133），與匕同形，偶亦作⺀（《京津》2992），與刀形同。卜辭有⺀（⺀、⺀）者，或釋尸（夷）方（《殷契粹編》），或釋刀方（《甲骨文編》、《殷虛

---

① 劉宗漢：《釋七·甲》，《古文字研究》第四輯。

卜辭綜類》），均似有理，其實即釋爲人方亦無不可。可見，甲骨文人與匕基本同形（且从人之字亦多作𠆢）；匕與刀、人與刀也有少數同形之例，唯據文義均可判斷，不致相混，故其例亦可從畧。今復得从刀與从匕者同形之一例，即牝與剢共作 ⿰豕刂 形，需略爲一説。

《甲骨文編》卷二牝字條下注云 "匕形誤爲刀"，復列从豕之 ⿰豕刂 等十三文爲異體，謂 "或从豕"。案此十三文中實包含牝剢兩字。像《戩》43·5 片 "勿⿰豕刂 酋"，《後》下 25·12 片 "貞叀小⿰豕刂"，《甲》3022 "勿乎取 ⿰豕刂 芻"，《甲》3070 片 "庚申卜乎取 ⿰豕刂 芻"，《乙》5689 片 "屮于祖辛 ⿰豕刂 青"，諸例之 ⿰豕刂，釋牝（牝）誠可，其義爲牝豕，且在辭中均爲名詞。而其餘諸文，如《鐵》15·1 片 "壬戌卜王貞勿屮 ⿰豕刂"，《後》下 36·7 片 "王囧曰：其屮 ⿰豕刂。允弃，弗得夸"，《陳》17①片（《甲骨文編》誤爲 13）"丙辰卜，爭貞：自屮 ⿰豕刂" 均稱 "屮 ⿰豕刂"，辭例與 "屮 希"、"屮 囚"、"屮 來嬉" 等同，其義頗與災異不吉之事有關，與牝無涉，當是剢字，不應釋牝。剢，从豕从刀，其本義當爲殺豬，引申之則或有殺伐、凶殺義。此字古金文亦屢見，作一手操刀向豬的腹部（或背）砍去之形，容庚先生定爲圖形文字，《金文編》入之附錄（見附錄上第 27 頁）。甲骨文不如金文形象、填實，而是完全綫條化，抽象化，但其寫作 ⿰豕刂，从豕从刀，則與古金文一脈相承。

除《甲骨文編》所列十三文外，⿰豕刂 或 ⿰豕刂 之當釋牝（牝）者還有：

貞：⿰豕刂 青于父乙？	《乙》2833
貞：⿰豕刂 酋于祖乙？	《前》1·9·7
勿⿰豕刂 酋。	《戩》43·5

等數例，而當釋剢者爲例尚多，其辭較完整可讀者如：

戍亡其 ⿰豕刂。	《續》6·7·5《佚》142
射𢀝亡其 ⿰豕刂。	《南·明》251
貞：我在沚亡其 ⿰豕刂？	《寧滬》2·52
丙辰卜，爭貞：自屮 ⿰豕刂？	《前》1·24·3（《續存》下·182）
□征其屮 ⿰豕刂？六月。	《續》2·23·1
□酉卜，□貞：弜屮 ⿰豕刂，隻正方？	《拾遺》4·3
□未卜，貞：弜屮 ⿰豕刂？	《庫》696

---

① 編者按："17"，原文誤作 "16"，今據實際出處徑改。

均是其例。案 ↑ 實即 ↓ 之倒形，玼剢之共作 ⚬⚬ 形與此不無關係。

十、子巳 ⚬ ⚬

甲骨文子孫之子與十二支之巳同形，均作 ⚬ 或 ⚬。金文亦然。最初的研究者如劉鶚、孫詒讓囿於陳説，將 ⚬⚬ 皆釋爲子，反謂"唯巳字不見"。待到羅振玉作《殷商貞卜文字考》時，方根據殷虛出土獸骨刻辭中的干支表，考定 ⚬ 爲巳，進而證實古金文中所謂乙子、丁子、己子、辛子、癸子者即乙巳、丁巳、己巳、辛巳、癸巳，"有宋至今數百年間懷疑不能决者一旦涣然得確解"。另一方面，卜辭也有 ⚬ 字，其形與後世之巳同，但絶不見其用作十二支之巳，而多用爲祀。又如祀、汜、改諸字亦均從 ⚬ 作。爲何甲骨文不以 ⚬ 而以 ⚬ 爲辰巳之巳？誠如羅振玉所言，"此疑終不能明"。郭沫若則認爲"古十二辰中有二子"（《甲骨文字研究·釋支干》），故子巳同形。

卜辭子孫之子與十二支之巳雖然同形，但用法各異，後者又限於干支搭配的紀日，大都見於前辭（序辭）中，故尚易分辨，不致引起誤讀或誤解。卜辭中子某之名習見，如子商、子漁、子效、子羮、子目、子罒、子雗、子凡、子妻、子安（妟、窒、窂、宁）、子洋、子姼、子宫、子辟、子宋、子戠、子爵，等等，這些名稱究屬封號還是時王之子，目前意見尚未統一，還須進一步研究，方能論定。卜辭又有婦某屮子或婦某子之例，如《遺珠》620 片："辛丑卜，㱿貞：婦好屮子？三月。辛丑卜亘貞：王固曰：好其屮子？"《乙》2510 片："壬辰卜，㱿貞：婦良屮子？貞：婦良亡其子？"《通纂》別録Ⅵ12 片："貞：妣己耂婦好子？"此數例之子即今所謂兒子，自無疑問。卜辭又有以十干爲子名者，已發現者有子丁、子己、子庚、子癸四名，多爲祭祀對象。除子庚不致誤認爲"庚巳"，子己無合文形式外，子丁、子癸的合文 ⚬（《乙》8826）⚬（《乙》8748）⚬（《乙》9040）⚬（《京津》936）及 ⚬（《明》21、《乙》2961）⚬（《粹》340），如無上下文的關係及其它析書的辭例爲證，也難免認作丁巳、癸巳的合文，因爲甲骨文中干支合文之例亦屢見，如乙卯、乙巳、乙丑、乙未、乙亥、丙寅、丙午、戊申、庚子、庚辰、庚戌、庚寅、辛卯、辛亥、壬午、甲寅、庚午、癸亥等即均有合文形式（參見《甲骨文編》合文卷，第 29 至 30 頁）。而乙巳的合文 ⚬（《粹》629）如無上下文關係也未嘗不可讀爲子乙。但卜辭無子乙之名，故 ⚬ 只能是乙

巳合文。總之，子巳同形，也易判別，不像山火、牝牡之易混。

十一、从比 ⺈⺈ ⺉⺉

《說文》："从，相聽也。从二人。"又："比，密也。二人爲从，反从爲比。"段注："猶反人爲匕也。"驗之甲骨文，从比二字同形，均可作 ⺈⺈ 或 ⺉⺉，知許說爲不謬。蓋二人相隨爲从，从反書即成比；反从爲比，比反書又爲从。卜辭屢見王从某人伐某方之例，从字多作 ⺈⺈⺈ 或 ⺈⺈⺈⺈，亦作 ⺈⺈ 或 ⺉⺉，與比形無別。王从某人者，意即王以某人爲從。楊樹達曰："我从人爲从，平聲讀，使人从我爲从，去聲讀。《漢書·何並傳》云：'並自從吏兵追林卿'，猶今言並自帶吏兵追林卿也。從與从同。甲文王从洗（案即沚，下同）或，謂王以洗或自隨也。"①其說可信。卜辭中可確知爲比字者爲數不多，且假借爲妣，例如：

庚辰出于 ⺉⺉ 庚，宰？　　　　　　　　　　　　　　《京都》1822

⺉⺉ 己。　　　　　　　　　　　　　　　　　　　　《散》66②

比庚比己即妣庚妣己。

　　屈萬里氏嘗力辨从比二字，謂"以字形言，二字雖間有相似者，然大都固較然甚明；以字義言則尤爲風馬牛之不相及也"③。他把大量的王从某人征（伐）某方一類卜辭中的从釋爲比，只承認"㞢从雨"之从以及義同"自"、"于"者爲从。其實，即便根據他所引辭例分析，也只能得出从比同形的結論。因依屈說，从字从二人，比字从二匕，"从字作 ⺈⺈ ⺈⺈ ⺉⺉ 等形"，"比字作 ⺉⺉ ⺈⺈ 等形"，但屈氏所引諸辭之釋爲比者，亦有作 ⺈⺈ 或 ⺉⺉ 之例（如《契》85）。屈氏所未引的大量同類卜辭中，作 ⺈⺈ 或 ⺉⺉ 更是比比皆是，具見島邦男《殷虛卜辭綜類》（頁 19—23・65・110）。其次，屈氏所定爲从字者，固有作 ⺈⺈ 之例（如《粹》934・1017），而辭例之稱从東、从南、从西、从北者，从字亦有作 ⺈⺈ 或 ⺉⺉ 者（如《乙》7308・7826，《龜》1・28・3，《續存》上 753，《庫》247），依屈說，豈非並宜釋比？要之，甲骨文比从二字同形而間有變化，《甲骨文編》云"古从比同字"是也。

---

① 楊樹達：《積微居甲文說·甲文中之先置賓辭》。
② 《散》即《日本散見甲骨文字蒐彙》，松丸道雄著，刊《甲骨學》第七號，日本甲骨學會編。
③ 屈萬里：《甲骨文从、比二字辨》，《歷史語言研究所集刊》第十二本。

十二、月夕 ☽ ☾

　　總的說來，卜辭月夕二字都有兩種寫法：月作☽，亦可作☾；夕可作☾，亦可作☽，無論是☽還是☾，都是月夕二字同形。但在使用過程中，真正混淆不別，即月夕二字均作☽的時間並不長。而早期大多以☽為月，以☾為夕；以☾為月，以☽為夕者為例外。晚期則基本上以☾為月、以☽為夕；以☽為月、以☾為夕者為例外。這通例與例外的互易，是經歷了二百餘年的演變，"互用"而逐漸完成的，乃是長期積累的結果。①

十三、ナ又 ⺁

　　卜辭ナ（左）又（右）字分別作⺁和ㄟ，象人之左右手，引申之則為方位之左右，但甲骨文字大都可以反書，ㄟ反書即成⺁，遂與ナ同形。卜辭⺁，在相當多的場合下，乃是右的反書而不是ナ。其常見的辭例如牢⺁一牛、⺁豕、⺁羌、⺁雨、⺁大雨、⺁大風、⺁告、旬⺁禍、受⺁年、歲、⺁伐、王受⺁，等等，多假為有無之有、祭祀之侑或保祐之祐，這類辭例，大都屬於中期卜辭。卜辭中尚未見反ナ為又或以又為ナ的現象，故實際上ナ又二字只共⺁形而不共ㄟ形。②

　　上述諸例，都是一個形體符號而為兩個或兩個以上不同的字，反映着不同的概念，具有一定的代表性。此外，水與乙共作〜（水字多作〜，用為偏旁則為〜），內與丙共作冈，尹與聿均作冈（聿又可作冈），吉與南共作㕯或㕯，尸、弓、夷共作ʃ（弓一般作ʃ），毓（育）與後共作㐭，豊與豐共作豐，係與午共作㐅，以及婦妊之妊與母壬之合文共作壬等等，也都是異字同形之實例，不煩詳論。

　　既然甲骨文有異字同形的特殊現象，那麼，考釋單字，通讀卜辭，以及編纂工具書，也都應對這一特點充分予以考慮了。

---

① 說詳拙作《甲骨文字辨析·卜辭月夕辨》，《中山大學學報》（哲學社會科學版）一九八〇年第一期。
② 說詳拙作《甲骨文字辨析·卜辭ナ又說》，《中山大學學報》（哲學社會科學版）一九八〇年第一期。

從上述十餘例可知，甲骨文之所以存在異字同形現象，其原因是多方面的。第一，字形省簡，乃與另一字同形。如下本作 ⼆ 或 ⌒，契刻時為圖簡易，刻成 ∧ 而省去一點，遂與入字同形。正與足本不同形，也由於各自簡省而成同形。第二，異體字的存在，即一字異形現象，與異字同形有密切關係。如示與工均有異體字作 Ⲓ，遂與壬同形，若論其常見之形，則工作 ⲓ、示作 Ⲧ 或 Ⲓ，與 Ⲓ（壬）何嘗相同。第三，由於意義上的聯繫而致二字同形。臣字本義與眼睛有關，以豎目取義，乃與象形之目形同，不免相混。ナ與又本象人之左右手，从與比本象兩人之相隨，而甲骨文正反無別，一正一反，於是同形。第四，文字演變，由於歷史的因素而導致二字同形。第四期卜辭月夕同形作 ⟩，便是兩字演變過程中出現的現象，其它各期卜辭月夕兩字各有通例和變例，但若綜合觀之，便不能不承認兩字同形了。

　　應該指出的是，甲骨文這種異字同形現象，雖是漢字在甲骨文階段的特點之一，却是漢字發展過程中的支流，它與文字的性質是矛盾的。作為記錄語言的符號，文字應能準確地記錄和反映語言，一個符號與語言中某一個單位（詞或詞素）相對應；可是異字同形現象却允許一個符號同時與語言中兩個或兩個以上單位相對應，這便易造成歧義、混亂。隨着時間的遷移，文字日趨完備精密，這一現象亦逐漸減少消失。文字的使用者總是采取各種辦法，力圖使兩個不同的字在字形上有所區別，不相混淆。在兩周金文中，這種異字同形的現象便已大大減少，僅存極少數了（如七與甲、壬與工等）；而到小篆階段，"書同文"，文字定型化、規範化，這一現象便告絕迹。本文所論甲骨文中異字同形諸例，在《說文》中莫不判若涇渭，嚴然有別，其原因便在乎此。

1980 年 8 月初稿
1981 年元月修訂

　　原載《古文字研究》第 6 輯，中華書局，1981 年；收入中山大學中文系主編：《古文字學與語言學論集》，中山大學出版社，1986 年；又收入宋鎮豪、段志洪主編：《甲骨文獻集成》第 18 册，四川大學出版社，2001 年；又收入陳煒湛：《甲骨文論集》，上海古籍出版社，2003 年；又收入陳煒湛：《三鑒齋甲骨文論集》，上海古籍出版社，2013 年。今據《甲骨文論集》收入。

裘錫圭

論"歷組卜辭"的時代

李學勤同志在《論"婦好"墓的年代及有關問題》一文中,提出了"歷組卜辭"的名稱(《文物》1977年11期35頁)。這種卜辭絕大多數出於小屯村中和村南。基本上用骨不用龜。卜辭中通常不記卜人名,前辭作"干支卜"或"干支貞",偶爾也作"干支卜貞";只有少量卜辭記卜人㦰(以下寫作"歷")之名,這些卜辭的前辭多作"干支歷貞"。①歷組卜辭的字形一般比較大,書法比較恣肆,不像賓組卜辭的大字那樣秀麗整飭,字形結構有的與賓組相似,如"王"作

---

① 卜人歷見《後》下11·5【《合》32825】、《甲》544【《合》32826】、《京津》4387【《合》32815】、4709【《合》32823】、《存》上2202【《合》32822】、《懷》1621【《合補》10712】、1622【《合補》10719】、《金》396【《英》2483】、《庫》1678【《合》41663、《英》2484】、《寧》1·446【《合》32821】、《南》坊2·200【《合》32824】(《後》下11·6似即此片未拓全之本)等片。《京津》4709【《合》32823】作"癸亥貞歷……",《金》396作"癸卯貞歷……",《存》上2202【《合》32822】作"癸巳卜貞歷……",比較特殊。又《甲》556【《合》32816】"丙午貞"一辭之末有"歷口"殘字,屈萬里《殷虛文字甲編考釋》釋"歷貞",謂是置貞人之名於辭末的特例,恐不可信。卜辭"貞"字本皆作"鼎",是假借字。本文所引卜辭,釋文一般用寬式,借作"貞"的"鼎"都直接釋作"貞"。此外如"方"直接釋作"賓","帚"直接釋作"婦","弓"直接釋作"勿"等等,不一一加注。歷組卜辭前辭中的"歷",其實也有不是卜人名的可能。賓組卜辭的前辭裏,卜人名與"貞"字之間有時有"㕁"字,如"干支卜爭㕁貞"、"干支卜賓㕁貞",還有少數卜辭作"干支卜㕁貞"。一般以㕁爲貞人名,以"爭㕁貞"、"賓㕁貞"爲二人共貞之例。但唐蘭先生認爲㕁不是人名而應讀爲"再"(《天》第四片考釋)。劍橋大學藏片有"王㕁貞"語,饒宗頤讀㕁爲語辭之"載"(《人物》764頁。饒氏對其它賓組卜辭前辭中的㕁,仍認作人名)。這些意見是值得考慮的。歷組卜辭前辭中的"歷",似乎也有可能不是人名,而是說明"貞"的性質的。不過即使"歷"的確不是人名,也仍然可以保留"歷組卜辭"這個名稱,因爲治甲骨學的人很容易理解"歷組卜辭"指的是哪一類卜辭。基於同樣的理由,雖然陳夢家所謂"午組卜辭"實際上並沒有卜人午之名,但是我們在文章裏仍然沿用這個名稱。

大，"辛"作▽；有的則與晚期卜辭相似，如"未"作米，"酉"作▽。這種卜辭裏最常見的上一代稱謂是父丁，其次是父乙。

蕭楠同志《論武乙、文丁卜辭》一文①，認爲上述這種卜辭中有父丁稱謂的一類（以下簡稱"父丁類"）與有父乙稱謂的一類（以下簡稱"父乙類"），從字體上是可以分開的。前者"一般説來字體較大，筆劃較粗，筆風剛勁有力"，後者"字體較小，筆風圓潤而柔軟"。二者的字形結構也往往不同。如"庚"字，前者作 ，後者作 ；"酉"字，前者作 ，後者作 ，等等。蕭文的這些意見接近於事實。但是應該指出，如果全面地看，特別是跟其他各類卜辭對照起來看，這兩類卜辭的字體仍然是很接近的。在歷組父乙類卜辭裏，有些字的筆法的確顯得比較圓軟，但是多數字的筆法與父丁類卜辭並無多大不同，"剛勁的直筆與鋭利的轉折"②隨處可見。父乙類卜辭也有大字，只不過不如父丁類多而已。如果跟二、三、五諸期卜辭相比，父乙類卜辭的字形普遍顯得比較大。父乙類和父丁類卜辭的字形結構，大多數也完全相同或十分相似。此外，正如蕭楠同志所指出的，"具有武乙（按：即我們所謂父丁類）特點的字與具有文丁（按：即我們所謂父乙類）特點的字有時會出現交錯現象，即某些武乙卜辭中會出現具有文丁特點的字，一些文丁卜辭字體具有武乙字體的特點"。我們可以舉幾個實例來看看。《粹》1586【《合》32008】與《人文》2369【《合》32009】是歷組的同文卜辭，卜日庚午的"庚"字，前者作 ，屬蕭文的文丁字體，後者作 ，屬蕭文的武乙字體。《安明》2331【《合》34189】是歷組卜骨，"庚"字兩見，一作 ，一作 。《明後》2524是有父乙稱謂的歷組卜骨，"庚"字數見，大多數屬於蕭文的武乙字體。《寧》1·427與428【《合》33025】是一塊歷組卜骨的正反兩面。正面卜辭卜問"王正召方"之事，"召方"屢與"父丁"同辭或同版③，此辭應屬蕭文所謂武乙卜辭。但是此骨反面的卜夕之辭，"庚"作 ，"酉"作 ，"囚"作 ，却都屬於蕭文的文丁字體。可見僅僅根據字體很難把這兩類卜辭完全區分開來。

從其他方面來看，這兩類卜辭的關係甚至顯得更爲密切。它們的文例是基本一致的，如前辭都作"干支卜"或"干支貞"，都使用"兹用"、"不用"等占卜

---

① 蕭文據1979年古文字學年會上散發的打印本。以下引蕭楠同志意見未注出處者，皆出此文。（《論集》編按：此文已發表於《古文字研究》第三輯。）
② 引自陳夢家説歷組卜辭字體特點之語，見《綜述》142頁。
③ 同辭者見《甲》810【《合》33016】、《人文》2520【《合》33015】、《考古》1975年1期44頁圖18【《屯南》1116】，同版者見《明後》2630【《合》33017】、《明後》2537【《合》33033】（"召"作"刀"）。

術語。見於這兩類卜辭的重要人名也往往相同。例如："𢀧"與"父丁"同辭（《明後》2534【《合》32844】）或同版（《明後》2533【《合》32031】），又與"父乙"同版（《明後》2529【《合》34240】）。"犬祉"與"父丁"同版（《明後》2537【《合》33033】），又與"父乙"同版（《明後》2524）。"或"（即沚或）與"父乙"同版（《存》下764【《合》32879】），又與"召方"同辭（《掇一》450【《合》33020】），而"召方"屢與"父丁"同辭或同版。①"望乘"與"父丁"同辭（《綴》334【《合》32896】），又見於父乙類字體的卜辭（《鄴三》下38·1【《合》33112。編按：葛亮指出，從比較清晰的《合》33112看，此版上只有"望乘"而無"父丁"。此例不當引】，《懷》1637【《合補》10485】）。"歷貞"的卜辭從字體上看，也是既有父丁類，又有父乙類。②

總之，歷組父丁類和父乙類卜辭雖然在字體上各有一些特點，但是在很多方面都有共同點，字體上的區別也並非總是很明確的。事實上，有不少歷組卜辭，很難確定它們究竟屬於父丁類，還是屬於父乙類。所以"歷組卜辭"這個名稱的提出，還是很有必要的。

最早注意到歷組卜辭時代的甲骨學者，大概是加拿大人明義士。1928年，明義士將所藏一部分甲骨拓成墨本，名爲《殷虛卜辭後編》，其未完成的序言曾將1924年冬小屯村中一坑所出三百餘片加以分類，企圖以稱謂與字體決定甲骨時代。他認爲歷組卜辭中的父丁是武丁，父乙是小乙（《綜述》135—136頁）。按照明氏的說法，歷組卜辭的時代應屬董作賓甲骨分期系統中的一、二期。但是董作賓、郭沫若及其後的甲骨學者，幾乎全都把歷組卜辭中的父丁定爲康丁，父乙定爲武乙，認爲這種卜辭屬於武乙文丁時期。這種觀點統治甲骨學界達四五十年之久，直到1977年，李學勤同志才在《論"婦好"墓的年代及有關問題》一文中，重新提出了與明義士相似的說法，認爲歷組卜辭是"武丁晚年到祖庚時期的卜辭"（《文物》1977年11期37頁）。

明義士並沒有對自己的說法作有力的論證，因此他的意見長期沒有得到重視。李學勤同志是在深入考慮了與甲骨斷代有關的各方面的問題之後得出他的結論的，他的意見是不容忽視的。我們原來也相信歷組卜辭爲武乙文丁卜辭的傳統說法，讀

---

① 同辭者見《甲》810【《合》33016】、《人文》2520【《合》33015】、《考古》1975年1期44頁圖18【《屯南》1116】，同版者見《明後》2630【《合》33017】、《明後》2537【《合》33033】（"召"作"刀"）。

② 歷貞卜辭的字體多數屬父丁類。蕭文指出《甲》544【《合》32826】、《後》下11·6【《合》32824】爲父乙類，當據《甲》544的"酉"字"囚"字和《後》下11·6的"囚"字而定。

了李文以後，經過認真的考慮，覺得不能不放棄舊説而改從李説。①李文不是專門討論甲骨分期的，因此在有些方面談得不够充分。我們想順着李文的思路作一些補充的論證，錯誤之處希望李學勤同志及其他對這個問題感興趣的同志不吝指正。

我們先來看看主張歷組卜辭屬於武乙文丁時期的學者們的根據。有些學者的主要根據是卜辭的文例和字體。郭沫若在《殷契粹編考釋》裏的兩段話在這方面很有代表性。《粹》20【《合》32675】是有父丁稱謂的歷組卜辭，《考釋》説：

> 此蓋武乙時所卜，父丁者康丁也。知非祖庚祖甲之稱武丁，帝乙之稱文丁者以其辭例、字體均不類，祖庚祖甲時卜辭皆列卜人名，例爲"某日卜某貞"，帝乙時卜辭雖省去卜人名，但無省去卜字者，且字體秀麗，無此茁壯之作。

《粹》373【《合》32731】是有兄丁、父乙兩個稱謂的歷組卜辭，《考釋》説：

> 此兄丁、父乙同見於一片，以字跡而言，父乙蓋文丁之稱其父武乙。

公認屬於武丁時期的賓組卜辭屢見父乙、兄丁，而文丁時期有没有一個兄丁，本來是不清楚的。從親屬稱謂看，把《粹》373定爲武丁卜辭，顯然比定爲文丁合理。但是由於其"字跡"與賓組卜辭不類，就被定爲文丁卜辭了。

在甲骨文斷代研究初期，普遍存在把同一時期卜辭的文例、字體看得過於單純的傾向。董作賓把一些文例、字體比較特殊的卜辭，幾乎都定爲文丁卜辭，並以"文武丁復古"這一從來没有真正得到過證明的説法，來解釋這些卜辭裏與他心目中的常例不合的，文例、字體方面的一些現象。現在，絕大多數甲骨學者都認爲，自組、子組、午組等好幾種文例、字體比較特殊的卜辭，是屬於武丁時期的。也就是説，大家承認武丁時期卜辭有很多種文例和字體。其中如自組卜辭，本身的文例、字體就很不統一。此外，李學勤同志還指出，在村北所出的龜、骨並用的往往記卜人的第三期卜辭和主要出於村中的只用骨的不記卜人的第三期卜辭裏，有一些二者同卜一事的例子。②由此可知這兩種在文例、字體等方面都有

---

① 在1977年考古所召開的安陽殷墟五號墓座談會上，我們曾基於歷組卜辭可能是三、四期卜辭的想法，主張婦好墓的時代應在康丁或武乙時期（《考古》1977年5期343—344頁）。這個意見是錯誤的，應作廢。

② 看李著《評陳夢家〈殷虚卜辭綜述〉》（《考古學報》1957年3期124—125頁）及《殷代地理簡論》（以下簡稱"簡論"）73、77—80頁。《簡論》把前一種卜辭稱爲三期1類，後一種稱爲三期2類。我們還可以爲他補充一個三期1類與2類同卜一事的例子。《甲》1267【《合》27879】"叀小臣𢀖克又戠𢀖王"，屬三期1類。《明後》2322【《合》27878】"乙巳卜：叀小臣𢀖克又戠𢀖王"，屬三期2類。除前一辭無前辭外，二辭全同。又《簡論》77頁所引《甲》1707在《甲編考釋》中已與《甲編》未著録的碎片綴合【《合》26881】，全辭爲"癸丑卜狄貞：戍逐其雉王衆"。

相當明顯的不同的卜辭，至少有一部分是完全同時的。陳夢家把前者完全劃歸廩辛，後者完全劃歸康丁（《綜述》142—144頁），顯然是有問題的。有了上舉這些例子，主要根據文例、字體來確定歷組卜辭時代的作法，當然就不能再爲我們所接受了。

我們還可以具體地看一下，歷組卜辭文例、字體上的一些特點，是否真像董作賓等人所想象的那樣，只可能出現在晚期而決不可能出現在一、二期。

歷組卜辭的前辭一般作"干支卜"、"干支貞"。在已知的武丁卜辭裏，"干支卜"這種前辭也是很常見的。1973年考古所在小屯南地早期地層裏發現了七片屬於武丁時期的"𠂤組卜甲"，其前辭幾乎都作"干支卜"。① 屬於武丁時期的午組卜辭、子組卜辭和"婦女卜辭"等"非王卜辭"，其前辭也往往作"干支卜"。② 就是在賓組卜辭裏，也可以看到這種前辭。例如《乙》8669【《合》12974】、《人文》829【《合》13122】都是有賓組卜人爭之名的卜骨，前一骨上有一辭作"丁丑卜：翌戊寅不雨"，後一骨上有一辭作"戊午卜：翌己未不其啓"。在基本上不記卜人名的賓組早期卜辭裏，"干支卜"甚至是最常見的前辭形式。③ "干支貞"這種前辭在已知的武丁卜辭裏雖然不如"干支卜"常見，但也還不能算很稀少。𠂤組卜辭以及上面舉過的幾種非王卜辭，都有使用這種前辭的例子。④ 在賓組卜辭裏，同樣可以看到這種前辭。例如《合》11482是一塊典型賓組字體的卜旬骨版，正面的四條卜旬之辭，前辭皆作"干支貞"。《人文》848【《合》16846】是記賓組卜人𠂤之名的卜旬骨版，上端有一辭作"癸丑貞：旬亡囚"。《續》2·13·8【《合》16897】"癸丑貞：旬亡囚"一辭，也是典型的賓組字體。不少人以歷組卜辭基本上不記卜人，證明其時代不會早到習慣於記卜人的

---

① 蕭楠《安陽小屯南地發掘的"𠂤組卜甲"》，《考古》1976年4期238頁。這一批卜甲是否全都可以歸在"𠂤組卜辭"這個名稱之下，還是問題。但是從地層上看，它們都屬於武丁時期大概是没有問題的。
② 林澐《從武丁時代的幾種"子卜辭"試論商代的家族形態》，《古文字研究》第一輯315—316頁。午組卜辭相當於此文的乙種卜辭，子組卜辭相當於丙種，"婦女卜辭"是李學勤《帝乙時代的非王卜辭》（《考古學報》1958年1期）中所用的名稱，相當於林文的甲種卜辭。
③ 這部分卜辭從字體、內容看可以歸入賓組，但極少記卜人名而較多王親貞之辭，也許可以看作稍早於賓組的一種卜辭。
④ 𠂤組卜辭見《乙》413【《合》20351】、《甲》2337【《合》20583】、《乙》70【《合補》10207】、146【《合》19863】、156【《合》20922】、388【《合》20962】等。小屯南地"𠂤組卜甲"第五片也有一條前辭作"癸亥貞"（《考古》1976年4期235頁【《屯南》4514】）。關於非王卜辭，看林澐《從武丁時代的幾種"子卜辭"試論商代的家族形態》，《古文字研究》第一輯315—316頁。

一、二期。其實一、二期都有不少不記卜人的卜辭。武丁時代的午組卜辭、"婦女卜辭"，甚至完全不記卜人。①前面還說過，第三期的兩類卜辭，一類往往記卜人名，一類完全不記卜人名。可見決不存在同一時期的卜辭記不記卜人名必須一致的規律。

歷組卜辭裏屢見綴於辭末或單刻的"兹用"或"不用"。自組和午組卜辭有時也在辭末綴以"用"或"不用"之語②，"用"與"兹用"同義。"兹用"的說法也已經見於賓組卜辭和祖庚祖甲時期的出組卜辭。賓組卜辭綴於辭末的"兹用"見《前》1·51·1【《合》1824】，單刻的見《柏》44（《七》B·58）。出組卜辭綴於辭末的"兹用"見《京津》3454【《合》24502】、《文錄》555【《合》24402】、《明後》2153、《庫》1025【《合》23148】等，單刻的見《續》3·42·3【《合》24449】。歷組卜辭有時把"不用"說成"兹不用"（《粹》598【《合》33006】），出組卜辭也有這種說法（《前》5·5·7【《合》22758】、《文錄》555【《合》24402】）。

總之，認爲歷組卜辭的文例只能出現在晚期而不能出現在一、二期，是沒有道理的。相反，如李學勤同志所指出的，歷組卜骨上的署辭以及兆辭"二告"，倒顯然是接近於已知的武丁、祖庚時期卜辭的。③

字體可以分書法（即蕭文所謂字體風格）和字形結構兩方面來討論。

歷組卜辭的筆法的確與主要出於村中的字形較小的三、四期卜辭比較相似，但是另一方面，跟某些武丁時期的卜辭也相當接近。後面討論"歷、自間組"卜辭的時候，就可以看到這一點。賓組卜辭偶爾也有筆法很近於歷組的，如《粹》1053【《合》5058】殼貞卜辭便是一例。同樣，歷組卜辭也有筆法與賓組很接近的例子。如《人文》2477【《合》16801】"癸酉貞旬亡囧〔在〕 京"一辭，從

---

① 林澐《從武丁時代的幾種"子卜辭"試論商代的家族形態》，《古文字研究》第一輯 315—316 頁。午組卜辭相當於此文的乙種卜辭，子組卜辭相當於丙種，"婦女卜辭"是李學勤《帝乙時代的非王卜辭》（《考古學報》1958 年 1 期）中所用的名稱，相當於林文的甲種卜辭。
② 自組的"用"見《甲》182【《合》20015】、《乙》9092【《合》19813】、《佚》599【《合》19928】、《京津》2935【《合》19949】等，"不用"見《甲》460【《合》19806】、《京津》3110【《合》21267】等。午組的"用"見《乙》1783【《合》22060】、4064【《合》22069】、《前》8·8·4【《合》22116】等。"不用"見《乙綴》305【《合》22074】（不字倒書）。
③ 《文物》1977 年 11 期 36 頁。歷組卜辭的"二告"見《存》下 852【《合》35165】。李文提到《寧》1·349 的"弜台"，此片拓本見《掇一》448【《合》34158】，據拓本此二字似不能連讀。

文例和"囚"字寫法看，應屬歷組，所以《人文》列於第四期，但是"癸酉貞旬"四字完全是賓組作風，"酉"字作 𝌀，字形結構也同於賓組。這些都透露出歷組和賓組的時代可能很相近的消息。從書法的演變看，由字形較大的歷組卜辭到字形較小的三、四期卜辭，再到字形更小的五期卜辭，是一個很自然的過程。如果在三、四期卜辭與五期卜辭之間插入歷組卜辭，就有些奇怪了。總之，從書法上得不出歷組卜辭必屬晚期的結論。

討論歷組卜辭的字形結構，必須先破除董作賓關於卜辭字形演變的一種錯誤觀點。董作賓的第一期卜辭幾乎就等於賓組卜辭。他認爲卜辭字形以賓組爲最古，其他各種字形是從賓組的字形由簡到繁地演變出來的。例如他認爲"酉"字最古的字形是 𝌀（賓組作此形），然後演變爲 𝌀、𝌀、𝌀 等形。這裏舉的最後一種寫法，也就是歷組卜辭常見的寫法，在他的字形演變表裏要到第三期才開始出現。①董氏的這種觀點是與事實不符的，日本學者貝塚茂樹在《甲骨文斷代研究法的書體變遷觀批判》等文中，早就指出了這一點。②高去尋在《殷墟出土的牛距骨刻辭》一文中，也討論到這方面的問題。他認爲卜辭字體有其特殊性，某些常見的早期字形並不一定古於其他字形。他説："因爲在甲骨上刻字的不易，使字形或書體發生的變化，在今日可見到的約有兩種情形：一、將字的實體變成虛廓，圓筆變成方筆……二、有的字……省去了筆畫以便刻出。例如用爲地支之一的子字，金文作 𝌀 𝌀，與第五期卜辭中作 𝌀 𝌀 相近同，或本象小兒形，但早期卜辭則作 𝌀 𝌀 𝌀……如果我們認爲這些字形乃是由簡變繁的一種演進，何以在早期反不更爲象形，這在中國文字進化觀上便不容易解釋了。"（《中國考古學報》第 4 册 175 頁）他的意見是正確的。

屬於武丁時期的𠂤、午、子等組卜辭的字形，往往與賓組卜辭不同，而反與晚期卜辭相近。可見晚期卜辭中的有些字形，在早期並不是不存在，只不過賓組卜辭不用它們就是了。就拿上面舉過的"酉"字來説，𠂤組大字型多作 𝌀、𝌀、𝌀 等形，子組多作 𝌀，都跟歷組卜辭接近。賓組偶爾也作 𝌀，如《庫》1613。特別有意思的是《寧》2·56【《合》35257】的"酉"字。《寧》2·56 是 2·55【《合》4284】的反面。這一片卜骨的正面刻有賓組卜人穀的卜辭，反面有朱書的"癸酉"二字，"酉"字作 𝌀，寫法與歷組父丁類卜辭全同。這充分説明認爲這種寫法到第三期才出現是錯誤的。再拿"未"字來説，午組卜辭有時寫作 𝌀，𠂤

---

① 《甲骨文斷代研究例》"字形"節，《慶祝蔡元培先生六十五歲論文集》上册 409—411 頁。
② 此文收入貝塚茂樹所著《中國古代史學的發展》。

組卜辭有時寫作 ⚹ 或 ⚹（如《乙》69【《合》20822】），也與歷組卜辭相同或相近。所以我們決不能因爲歷組卜辭的某些字形與賓組常見的字形不符而與晚期卜辭接近，就斷定它們是晚期卜辭。

這裏附帶談一下用字習慣的問題。歷組卜辭的用字習慣跟賓組有一些顯著的不同。例如賓組既有"又"，又有"㞢"，二者用途有別，歷組只有"又"，凡賓組用"㞢"的場合歷組都用"又"。又如賓組"以"字作 ⚹，而歷組作 ⚹（目）；賓組用否定詞"弓"（勿），歷組不用"弓"而用"弜"。而且歷組的這些用字習慣又都是與較晚時期的卜辭相同的。這種現象也往往被用作歷組卜辭屬於晚期的證據。

其實，武丁時期各組卜辭的用字習慣是相當不一致的。就上舉各字而論，子組的用字習慣與歷組全同（"黃尹"子組作"伊尹"，也與歷組相同）。午組用"目"、"弜"，同於歷組；"又"、"㞢"兼用，同於賓組，但賓組用"㞢"的場合午組有時也用"又"（《綜述》162頁）。自組既用"以"（《掇一》256【《合》20639】），也用"目"（《乙》145【《合》20338】）；既用"弓"（《前》8‧8‧1【《合》19891】等），也用"弜"（《乙》474【《合》20805】等）；既用"又"，也用"㞢"，而且也像午組一樣，在賓組用"㞢"的場合自組有時也用"又"（《綜述》153頁）。屬於自組的《人文》3171【《合》20032】片有"又子宋"和"㞢司（姒）"二辭，用作祭名的"又"和"㞢"同見於一版。甚至在賓組卜辭裏偶爾也有"㞢"、"又"混用的現象。例如聯繫整數和零數的虛辭"又"，賓組一般作"㞢"，但是《後》下33‧10【《合》17525】的一條骨臼刻辭就寫作"又"："婦杞示七屯又一（，賓。"（《合》13447臼同文）出組卜辭裏也有"㞢"、"又"混用的現象（看《殷代貞卜人物通考》967、981等頁）。所以歷組卜辭的用字習慣在早期完全有可能存在。饒宗頤在《殷代貞卜人物通考》中曾根據自組大字型的《甲》2907【《合》19946】片上祭名"㞢"、"又"二字互用不別的現象，指出"據字體斷代之不易"（666頁。以下簡稱此書爲"人物"）。這話是有道理的。

總之，過去有些甲骨學者主要根據文例、字體，就斷定歷組卜辭裏的"父乙"、"父丁"不可能指小乙、武丁，而只能指武乙、文丁，顯然是沒有充分理由的。

董作賓還曾以坑位來證明有父丁稱謂的歷組卜辭屬於武乙時期。歷組卜辭多出村中。村中所出字形較小的一種卜辭，從親屬稱謂可以確定爲三、四期卜辭。

董氏據此認爲村中所出卜辭皆不早於第三期,從而斷定村中所出有父丁稱謂的歷組卜辭是武乙卜辭。他在《斷代例》中討論到有父丁、母辛稱謂的歷組卜辭時説:

> 本來,武丁之配有妣辛,康丁之配也名妣辛,稱父丁、母辛,固然可以是武乙時卜辭,但同時也可以説是祖庚、祖甲時的卜辭,至此,單以稱謂定時期的方法,便窮於應付了。在貞人、文法、字形方面,固然也可以幫着解決,而最有力的標準却是坑位。因爲這父丁、母辛的卜辭出土村中(第三區),我們就可以斷然説這是武乙時的卜辭。(1213 頁注①所引書 356 頁)

又説:

> 如果説父丁是武丁,便可在祖甲之世了,但村中無第三期以上的卜辭,而祖甲時又必有貞人,今此版出土村中,亦可見非祖甲時物。(同上 357 頁)

村中没有早於第三期的卜辭的説法,只有在證明了村中所出的歷組卜辭以及其他與已確定的三、四期卜辭不同類型的卜辭,都不早於第三期以後,才能成立。董氏以此作爲村中所出歷組卜辭屬於武乙時期的證據,顯然是不合邏輯的。就已發表坑位的殷墟第一次發掘所得甲骨來看,在村中出土的甲骨裏,除了三、四期卜辭和歷組卜辭之外,還有接近於𠂤組的卜辭以及後面將要討論到的"歷、𠂤間組"卜辭,它們都是屬於武丁時期的。村中没有早於第三期的卜辭的説法,純屬主觀臆斷。董氏以不記卜人證明歷組卜辭不可能屬祖甲時期(其實應説祖庚祖甲時期),也是不能成立的。這個問題在前面已經談過了。

近年來,主張歷組卜辭屬於武乙文丁時期的同志,又提出了考古學上的地層證據。1973 年考古所在小屯南地發掘到不少三期卜辭和歷組卜辭。上引蕭楠同志的文章分析了這批甲骨出土的情況,指出這批甲骨主要出土於中期地層。這一地層早於出"乙辛卜辭"的晚期地層,晚於出武丁卜辭的早期地層,並且與早期地層在時代上尚有一定間隔。中期地層本身又可以分爲時代較早的"一組"和較晚的"二組"。有父甲、父庚、父己、兄辛等稱謂的三期卜辭,以及父丁類歷組卜辭,"既出於中期一組地層與灰坑,也出於中期二組地層與灰坑",父乙類歷組卜辭"則只出於中期二組地層與灰坑,不出於中期一組地層與灰坑"。因此蕭文認爲從地層上看,父乙類卜辭要晚於父丁類卜辭,前者應爲文丁卜辭,父乙是文丁對武乙的稱呼,後者應爲武乙卜辭,父丁是武乙對康丁的稱呼。

殷墟第一次發掘中,35 坑出了三片歷組卜骨(《甲》412—414【《合》

35298、32689、32632】），其中一片有父丁稱謂（《甲》413）。50至60年代，鄒衡同志研究殷墟文化分期。他根據傳統說法以歷組父丁類卜辭爲武乙卜辭，認爲此坑卜辭的時代與陶器的時代相應。① 這也是有利於歷組卜辭屬於武乙文丁時期的説法的。

我們對於考古是外行，考古工作者的發掘、研究工作，本來是沒有我們置喙的餘地的。但是由於牽涉到歷組卜辭的時代問題，不得不在這裏談談我們很不成熟的一些看法。我們並不懷疑他們的發掘工作以及對地層、灰坑的時代先後的分析，但是仍然不認爲他們對於那些從有關地層和灰坑中出土的歷組卜辭的時代的判斷，是不可改變的最後結論。我們主要是從以下幾個方面考慮的。首先，較晚的地層和灰坑裏可以出較早的遺物，因此卜辭跟它們所從出的地層、灰坑以及同坑器物的時代，並不一定都是一致的。其次，僅僅依靠考古發掘和器物排隊，往往只能斷定不同地層、不同器物的時代先後，而不能把它們的時代跟歷史上記載的王世確切地聯繫起來。過去的殷墟文化分期工作，在一定程度上是依靠有關地層和灰坑中所出的甲骨文來定每個時期所對應的王世的。如果所根據的甲骨文的斷代有問題，由此得出的考古分期的時代也就多多少少會有些問題。婦好墓的發掘已經證明過去對一部分殷墟銅器的分期，存在把時代拉得過晚的傾向。會不會對歷組卜辭所從出的地層的時代也估計過晚了呢？第三，在全部歷組卜辭裏，出現父丁或父乙稱謂的卜辭只佔很小的比例，有父乙稱謂的尤其稀少。據蕭文，1973年小屯南地發掘所得的有父乙稱謂的歷組卜辭只有一片，大概蕭文主要是根據字體來區分這兩類卜辭的。前面已經說過，歷組父丁類和父乙類卜辭，從字體上並不全都是很容易區分的。蕭文還説這次出土的"武乙卜辭"有的"接近文丁字體"，"文丁卜辭"有的"近似武乙字體風格"。因此，蕭文對這兩類卜辭的區分能否做到完全合乎事實，也就是説"文丁卜辭""只出於中期二組地層與灰坑，不出於中期一組地層與灰坑"的結論是否完全合乎事實，恐怕不能説是完全沒有考慮餘地的。總之，我們覺得就目前的情況來説，考古學上的證據似乎還不足以確定歷組卜辭的時代。

通過以上的分析可以看到，主張歷組卜辭屬於武乙文丁時期的甲骨學者，並沒有爲自己的論點提出不容辯駁的確鑿證據。下面我們將在上引李文的基礎上，申述一下把歷組卜辭定爲武丁、祖庚卜辭的理由。

---

① 鄒衡《試論鄭州新發現的殷商文化遺址》，《考古學報》1956年3期97頁。又《試論殷墟文化分期》，《北京大學學報》（人文科學）1964年4、5期。

李文從字體的演變、卜辭的文例、卜辭出現的人名、占卜的事項和親屬稱謂這五個方面,來論證歷組卜辭是武丁、祖庚卜辭。我們準備在後三個方面爲李文作補充。

先談歷組卜辭的親屬稱謂。這個問題李文已經講得很清楚,由於問題比較重要,我們再重複一下,以引起注意。

不同時期甲骨卜辭中對祖、父、母、兄等人的帶日名的稱呼往往相同。因此孤立地以稱謂斷代是很危險的。但是,如果兩組卜辭的稱謂成套地相應,這兩組卜辭屬於同一時期的可能性就非常大了。

歷組卜辭中提到的父、母、兄,數量都很少。曾與父乙同見於一版的母,只有母庚(《論集》編按:"母"本作 ,似應釋"小母",參看徐中舒主編《甲骨文字典》序3頁):

　　庚申卜:叀("與"唯"略同)父乙☒用。茲用。
　　庚申卜:母庚示旬。不用。
　　壬戌卜:又伐甲子犬征吕(以)羌。　　　　　　　　　明後2524
　　丁未卜:牜母庚。　　　　　　　　　　　　　　　　明後2546

曾與父乙同見的兄,只有兄丁:

　　癸巳卜:叙兄丁凡父乙。
　　[甲午]卜:又于[子]戠[十]犬,[卯牛]一。　　　　甲611【《合》32730】
　　癸巳[卜]:叙兄丁凡父乙。
　　[甲]午卜:又于子戠十犬,卯牛一。懷1564【《合補》10470】(與上片同文)
　　甲午[卜]:叙[兄]丁于[父]乙。
　　甲午卜:又升于子戠十犬,卯牛一。
　　甲午卜☒又于子☒　　　　　　　　　　　　　　　佚194【《合》32775】
　　丙子貞:叙兄丁于父乙☒　　　　　　　　　　　　粹373【《合》32731】
　　(《論集》編按:應補引《後》上7·5【《合》32732】"丙子卜:叙兄丁于父乙凡"一辭)
　　辛酉卜:叙兄丁于父宗。　　　　　　　　　　　　摭續223【《合》32766】

我們知道,武丁之父小乙在周祭中的法定配偶是妣庚。在武丁時期的賓組和自組卜辭中,最常見最重要的父是父乙,母是母庚,兄是兄丁。情況與歷組父乙類卜辭正好完全相合。這很難說成偶然的巧合。並且,上引《明後》2524與父乙、母

庚同見一版的犬祉，在賓組卜辭裏也是常見的人名；上引《甲》611等片與父乙、兄丁見於同版的受"又"祭的子𢦏，在已知的武丁卜辭裏也有受"㞢"祭的記錄：

乙丑卜王：勿䒞㞢子𢦏。　　　　　　　　　　　　　存下462【《合》20037】
㞢☐子𢦏。　　　　　　　　　　　　　　　　　　　乙4817【《合》13517】

恐怕怎麼巧合也巧合不到這個程度吧（子𢦏又見《續》4·12·5【《合》20036】，也是武丁卜辭）。

根據商代晚期銅器肄簋（《三代》6·52·2【《集成》8·4144】），武乙的法定配偶是妣戊，而不是妣庚。顯然，從親屬稱謂上看，把歷組父乙類卜辭定爲武丁卜辭，要比定爲文丁卜辭合理得多。歷組卜辭裏還偶見"父庚"（《鄴三》下42·3【《合》27435】）、"父甲"（《明後》2223、2224【《合》27464】），可能是武丁稱盤庚、陽甲（《論集》編按：蕭楠《再論武乙、文丁卜辭》指出《明後》2223、2224不是歷組卜辭，是正確的，此文"父甲""陽甲"等字應刪去。蕭文見《古文字研究》第九輯157頁）。

歷組卜辭所祭之母，除母庚外還有母辛（《論集》編按："母"本作𢆶，似應釋"小母"，詳上）：

☐未卜：又母辛☐十犬十。茲用。　　　　　甲397【《合》32754】（《撫續》77同文）①
庚戌卜：㱃母辛宗。　　　　　　　　　　　　　　懷1566【《合補》10478】

母庚爲父乙之配，母辛應爲父丁之配。董作賓已經指出武丁之配有妣辛，康丁之配也有妣辛。但是，如果歷組卜辭裏的父乙和母庚是小乙及其配妣庚，父丁和母辛當然就只能是武丁及其配妣辛了。武丁配妣辛是見於周祭的法定配偶之一。在出組卜辭裏，母辛是諸母中最常見最重要的一位。歷組卜辭在武丁諸配中特別重視她是合理的。

李文還指出，歷組卜辭合祭重要先王時，往往把父丁排在小乙之後，"如把'父丁'理解爲康丁，那麼在祀典中竟略去了稱爲高宗的武丁及祖甲兩位名王，那就很難想象了"（57頁）。這也是歷組卜辭的父丁應爲武丁的有力證據。小乙在先王中並不是很重要的，但他是祖庚的祖父，祖庚祭先王的時候對他比較重視是

---

① 《撫續》77是歷組卜辭中極爲少見的用龜甲的例子。【編按：葛亮指出，此甲現藏上海博物館，已有學者指出實爲僞刻。】

合理的。如果是武乙祭祖，斷斷不會不祭地位既重要，跟自己的關係又比較密切的武丁、祖甲，而去祭地位既不那麼重要，跟自己的關係又比較疏遠的小乙。歷組卜辭所記的"日"祭次序，也是小乙後緊接父丁：

甲申貞：小乙日，亡尤。

丙戌貞：父丁日，亡尤。明後 2487【《合》32626】+人文 2288【《合》32696】

（許進雄《明後》序綴合【《合補》10460】）

甲申隔一天就是丙戌，其間也沒有容武丁、祖甲的餘地。

再談歷組卜辭裏的人名。歷組卜辭有大量與賓組卜辭和出組早期（大體相當於祖庚時期）卜辭相同的人名，李文已舉出不少例子，我們補充了一些，一併列表於下。凡卜辭有卜人名的，都在所列出處後用括號注明。大、出、兄、䝷、中是出組卜人，其餘都是賓組卜人。對於原來不記卜人或卜人名殘缺的卜辭，一般未注明屬於何組。這些卜辭有些顯然屬於賓組（排在注有賓組卜人名的卜辭之前的，一般都屬賓組），有些却難以確定究竟屬於賓組晚期，還是屬於出組早期，因爲二者的文例、字體很難區分。賓組晚期和出組早期卜辭不但有不少共同的人名，而且有時還同卜一事，可見二者有一段共存的時間。一部分賓組晚期卜辭已經晚至祖庚時期，詳後文及附錄一。下面是既見於賓組、出組卜辭又見於歷組卜辭的人名表。表中所舉卜辭，一般是舉例性質的。

	賓組出組	歷　　組
婦好	乙 2948【《合》6480】（争）、3383【《合》271】（殻）、6691【《合》10136】（殻）、佚 556【《合》13997】（賓）	鄴三下 43·8【《合》32762 甲】、掇一 444【《合》32762 乙】、寧 1·491【《合》32760】、甲 668【《合》32757】
婦妌	珠 371【《合》2726】（殻）、粹 879【《合》9968】（古）、續 3·26·2【《合》8991】（殻）、4·26·1【《合》9530】（殻）	南·坊 3·89【《合》39661】、佚 967【《合》32763】、京津 2004【《合》32764】、寧 3·238【《合》32765】（後三例妌作井）
子畫①	掇二 185【《合》6209】、京津 1461【《合》10426】、燕 16【《合》6053】、前 2·5·4【《合》8395】（賓）	京津 2175【《合》32774】、寧 1·494【《合》32773】、1·495【《合》32770】、安明 2717【《合》33059】

---

① 《安明》1303【《合》23529】有出組旅貞又祭子畫之辭，可能爲祖甲卜辭。

續表一

	賓組出組	歷　　組
畫	丙 81【《合》9525】（反面殼貞）、庫 1596【《合》40605、《英》634】（賓）、寧 2·52【《合》4284】（殼）、簠·雜 83【《合》3047】（㕚）	寧 1·347【《合》32856】、金 349【《合》41503、《英》2413】、續 6·15·4【《合》32772】
子㡇	鐵 151·1【《合》2955】（賓）、乙綴 178【《合》6572】（丙）、乙 6692（殼）【《合》6571】、前 2·37·7（竹、爭共貞）【《合》637】	安明 2692【《合》20027】、《考古》1975 年 1 期 54 頁圖 19（此例稱㡇。《論集》編按：後一例即《屯南》751）
子漁	鐵 184·1【《合》2978】（賓）、253·2【《合》6011】（同版賓貞）、佚 524【《合》13619】（殼）、續 3·48·3【《合》14782】（殼）	粹 1263【《合》32780】
子利	懷 965【《合補》3996】、合 3229、13726	粹 933【《合》33526】（此例稱利）
⿱囗侯	丙 298【《合》3291】、明後 1694【《合》6083】（同版賓貞）、甲 3510【《合》6】（賓）、珠 6【《合》3290】（古）	金 368【《合》41499】
⿻侯	存下 463【《合》3311】（賓）、後下 4·3【《合》5505】、前 4·5·1【《合》3314】、林 2·1·14【《合》8096】	粹 367【《合》32807】、甲 844【《合》32805】
⿱⿻侯	明後 1683【《合補》6202】（似賓組早期）	甲綴 19【《合》32810】、珠 897【《合》32046】
攸侯	金 597【《合》39701、《英》188】、林 2·3·18【《合》3330】	掇二 132【《合》32982】
犬侯	續 5·2·2【《合》6812】（㐺）、綴 157【《合》6813】（同版爭貞）	京津 4777【《合》32966】
射𦥑	前 7·18·1【《合》163】（殼）、續 3·43·3【《合》165】（㕚）、燕 235【《合》277】（賓）、鄴二下 38·7【《合》5749】	鄴三下 44·6【《合》32026】、後上 25·7【《合》32024】、安明 2674【《合》31996】、甲 868【《合》32886】
𦥑	鐵 258·3【《合》7629】（亘）、前 1·46·3【《合》2341】（賓）、4·50·6【《合》166】（殼）、珠 179【《合》6078】（賓）	掇一 550【《合》32028】、掇二 82【《合》32885】、鄴三下 39·9【《合》33056】、續 2·30·4【《合》4199】

續表二

	賓組出組	歷組
師般	後上 11・16【《合》8836】（賓）、金1【《合》39525、《英》609】（賓）、外107【《合》6185】（殼）、珠179【《合》6078】（同版賓貞）	後下 24・1【《合》32277】、安明 2336【《合》32273】、2684【《合》32900】、明 705【《合》32900】
般	乙 6988【《合》152】（丙）、存下 442【《合》4264】（古）、金 411【《合》39782、《英》374】（殼）、續 6・21・10【《合》23666】（大）	六・曾 24【《合》34193】
亞髟①	安明 658	鄴三下 44・1【《合》32987】、粹 1178【《合》31983】、安明 2336【《合》32273】、2679【《合》33114】
髟	林 2・12・12【《合》5834】（㲋）、甲 2121【《合》9560】（賓）、3338【《合》177】（殼）	甲 562【《合》34176】、896【《合》32035】、粹 915【《合》33237】、1224【《合》33218】
犬征	丙 442【《合》14755】（賓）、後下 37・3【《合》4632】（殼）、人文 281【《合》9479】（賓）、文錄 152【《合》23689】（出）	明後 2524、2537【《合》33033】、粹 934【《合》32903】、存上 1852【《合》33216】
望乘	丙 22【《合》32】（殼）、京津 1266【《合》6479】（爭）、佚 979（爭）、燕 596【《合》236】（賓）	鄴三下 38・1【《合》33112】、綴 334【《合》32896】、佚 875【《合》32021】、拾 3・4【《合》32895】
邑並②	粹 1213【《合》17171】（爭）、金 521【《合》39514、《英》608】（賓）、前 5・25・1【《合》14157】、文錄 362【《合》23675】（出）	文錄 257【《合》32891】
並	乙 4071【《合》376】（同版殼貞）、天 94【《合》9105】、後下 35・1【《合》52】（古）、庫 1542【《合》41023、《英》1948】（兄）	粹 915【《合》33237】、1535【《合》33042】、甲 727【《合》33065】
㠱	乙 2148【《合》671】（殼）、3338【《合》1173】（爭）、文錄 637【《合》24145】（出）、金 78【《合》41020、《英》1994】（出）	安明 2432【《合》32048】、摭續 143【《合》32275】、粹 1247【《合》32829】、人文 2283【《合》32700】

① 人名"髟"从"匕"从"㐫"。字或从"㞢"，實非"㓀"字，而爲"㐫"之異體，觀《摭續》87【《合》32044】、《乙》8670【《合》22062】、9047【《合》20737】等片"㞢"字自明。
② 邑並也可能指邑與並二人。

續表三

	賓組出組	歷　　組
雀	乙綴 302【《合》6946】（賓、爭）、乙 5303【《合》6947】（殼、爭）、5329【《合》10976】（丙）、鐵 194·4【《合》10352】（賓）	存下 733【《合》34011】
冓	丙 546【《合》1076】（背面殼貞）、前 5·27·1【《合》493】（賓）、甲 3539【《合》4888】（古）、人文 1630【《合》4073】	明後 2629【《合》32997】、安明 2711【《合》32994】
㠯①	出組常見的卜人，㠯貞之辭如存上 1507【《合》24132】、前 6·21·2【《合》23590】等，似皆屬出組早期。	人文 2322【《合》32909】、2540【《合》32908】、金 385【《合》40920、《英》2417】
黃	外 147【《合》15482】（爭）、存下 391【《合》13758】（殼）、燕 677【《合》4302】（爭）、庫 1209（中）	安明 2713【《合》32939】
𡖉	乙 2000【《合》6834】（爭）、存上 26【《合》5734】、人文 341【《合》5735】（賓）、前 3·33·6【《合》189】	後下 36·6【《合》32906】、前 6·5·3【《合》32907】
𠂤	丙 605【《合》7075】（同版殼貞、亘貞）、乙 2907【《合》5448】（爭）、林 2·19·16【《合》4567】（爭）、前 4·44·4【《合》4563】	《考古》1975 年 1 期 45 頁圖 19（《論集》編按：即《屯南》751）
㞢	丙 570【《合》274】（殼）、續 5·32·1【《合》13362】、甲 2415【《合》522】（正面㞢貞）、3524【《合》3726】（爭）	粹 722【《合》32875】、綴 184【《合》33035】、明後 2529【《合》34240】
扃	外 3【《合》14911】（賓）、燕 128【《合》9817】、金 616【《合》40106、《英》824】	摭續 106【《合》33225】、安明 2727【《合》32963】
受	前 2·28·7【《合》10923】（爭）、6·18·1【《合》5476】（爭）、7·25·3【《合》14436】（賓）、明 271【《合》23685】（大）	鄴三下 45·8【《合》32921】、後上 9·3【《合》33102】、寧 3·238【《合》32765】（後二例可能爲地名）
𠄣（正?）	乙 3331【《合》249】（同版賓貞）、甲 1098【《合》6044】（爭）、2121【《合》9560】（賓）、安明 103【《合》5854】（賓）	鄴三下 43·9【《合》32911】、京津 4782【《合》32910】

---

① 出組卜辭中，㠯之名除作爲卜人見於前辭外，尚見於《後》下 25·5【《合》24317】（旅貞）、《存》下 657【《合》23669】（王卜），似爲祖甲卜辭。㠯貞之辭亦有祖甲卜辭。

續表四

	賓組出組	歷　　組
旬	前4·28·3【《合》5560】、6·33·1【《合》4677】、後下34·5【《合》4090】（賓）、續5·19·5【《合》4679】	明後2505【《合》34132】
木	甲1167【《合》9575】（爭）、3512【《合》10067】（賓，稱戍木）、庫226【《合》39836、《英》530】、燕598【《合》7569】	甲600【《合》33193】
㞢	丙275【《合》13490】（爭）、乙4293【《合》136】（古）、前6·6·6【《合》552】、後下26·12【《合》10061】	安明2719【《合》33034】、存下804【《合》33037】
竹	京津1434【《合》1108】（㱿）、存上616【《合》1110】、乙7767【《合》6647】（賓）、文錄519【《合》23805】（矣，稱卜竹）	後下21·2【《合》32933】、《考古》1975年1期44頁圖18（《論集》編按：即《屯南》1116）
山	佚67【《合》7860】、寧2·46【《合》5562】	掇一431【《合》32967】
羽	金522【《合》39868、《英》564】（賓）、前7·23·1【《合》5452】（矣）、菁11·7（爭）、零拾116【《合》5717】（賓）	明後2452【《合補》10516】、2558【《合》32915】、安明2312【《合》32916】、掇一431【《合》32967】
章	前4·10·7【《合》13731】、乙5640【《合》1395】（㱿）、佚158【《合》8952】（㱿）、甲3510【《合》6】	後下27·14【《合》31981】、安明2536【《合》31970】、懷1650【《合補》10492】、存下846【《合》41500】
壴	乙綴307【《合》7996】（同版爭貞）、乙2027【《合》3816】（丙）、7205【《合》9811】（同版古貞）、簠·雜128（賓）	粹915【《合》33237】、1253【《合》32914】、後下38·6【《合》32881】、明後2629【《合》32997】
屮	乙591【《合》3536】（㱿）、1255【《合》947】（丙）、鐵108·4【《合》5503】、後下13·12【《合》23683】（大）	粹1545A【《合》32992】、庫119【《英》2418】
鑊	乙綴208【《合》5477】、乙8165【《合》946】（㱿）、後下14·13【《合》4834】、珠293【《合》4833】	粹1224【《合》33218】

續表五

	賓組出組	歷　　組
卯	丙 156【《合》667】（正面殻貞、爭貞）、甲 3429【《合》4960】（爭）、文錄 636【《合》8454】（王貞，似爲賓組）、人文 944【《合》4959】	佚 387【《合》32229】、913【《合》32897】、寧 1・247【《合》32871】、1・502【《合》32869】
剛	前 6・38・1【《合》13745】、存上 741【《合》10771】（爭）、甲 3510【《合》6】（賓）、粹 1306【《合》3236】	撥一 432【《合》32770】、粹 1221【《合》33210】、存下 846【《合》41500】
凸	粹 1306【《合》3236】	撥一 432【《合》32770】
𢆶	丙 185【《合》96】（賓）、前 4・10・3【《合》9477】（賓）、明後 1666【《合》4763】（賓）、懷 382【《合補》1989】（㘡）	甲 868【《合》32886】、明後 2471【《合》32033】、2629【《合》32997】、撥一 410【《合》31984】
癸	合 13886（殻）、珠 517【《合》13738】（古）、南・師 2・153【《合》3828】（古）、續 3・36・2【《合》22593】（同版出貞）	甲 808【《合》32001】、粹 232【《合》32536】、人文 2284【《合》32671】
陝	丙 98【《合》10613】（同版殻貞、賓貞）、乙 7393【《合》3291】、前 7・32・1【《合》6050】（同版賓貞）、後下 26・4【《合》4775】（爭）	粹 1225【《合》32926】
合	後下 14・1【《合》8731】（同版賓貞）、燕 290【《合》428】	安明 2718【《合》32835】、綴 46【《合》32834】
兔	明 2343【《合》234】（殻）、佚 323【《合》6528】（爭）、前 6・48・7【《合》4618】（爭）、珠 791【《合》14133】（亘）	佚 535【《合》34057】
困	丙 275【《合》13490】（同版爭貞）、442【《合》14755】（同版賓貞）、前 7・6・1【《合》7422】（殻）、文錄 519【《合》23805】（㘡）	佚 535【《合》34057】
蟲	乙 3290【《合》9503】（反面殻貞）、前 4・13・7【《合》5902】（賓）、6・22・6【《合》5900】（爭）、7・15・3【《合》9506】（葡）	鄴三下 40・6【《合》32056】
周	丙 442【《合》14755】（賓）、乙 5329【《合》10976】（丙）、7312【《合》1086】（古）、林 1・26・18【《合》5618】	撥二 82【《合》32885】

上表一共有五十個人名（子畫與畫，射𡥉與𡥉，師般與般，亞𠬞與𠬞，皆作一人計）。此外，賓組卜辭裏常見的"㞢𢦏"（《丙》22【《合》32】、24【《合》6476】、《粹》1317【《合》3952】、《綴》16【《合》25】等，亦稱𢦏）與歷組卜辭裏常見的"㞢𢦏"（《甲》695【《合》33104】、《京津》4395【《合》33058】、《後》下39·6【《合》32764】、《鄴三》下39·9【《合》33056】等，亦稱𢦏），實際上也應該是同一個人名。歷組"㞢𢦏"，《安明》2432【《合》32048】作"㞢戈"。"𢦏""𢦏"大概都从"戈"聲，所以可以通用。歷組《掇一》452【《合》33105】"㞢𢦏"的"𢦏"，仔細審視，似不从"口"而从"目"，字形與"𢦏"接近。賓組的"㾎"（《乙綴》213【《合》5447】、《乙》6373【《合》267】、7288【《合》10964】、《前》7·31·4【《合》6816】等）與歷組的"㾎"（《掇二》82【《合》32885】），賓組的"𠬝"（《後》下37·4【《合》6822】、《佚》746【《合》18745】）與歷組的"𠬝"（《掇二》82【《合》32885】），都很可能是同一個人名的異體字。①同見於賓組出組卜辭和歷組卜辭的人名，被我們遺漏的，一定還有不少。

　　主張歷組卜辭屬於武乙、文丁時代的甲骨學者，都用"異代同名"説來解釋上述現象。他們指出甲骨卜辭中的人名往往同時又是地名、國族名，這些人名實際上是族氏而不是私名，所以相隔很遠的兩個時期可以有不少同樣的人名。這種説法雖然就甲骨卜辭的一般情況來看，大體上符合事實，但是却不能用來解釋賓組出組卜辭和歷組卜辭之間的同名現象。

　　歷組卜辭中所見的與賓組出組卜辭相同的人名，數量遠遠超過其他各個時期或其他各組卜辭；而且歷組卜辭中所見的這些人的情況，也與賓組出組卜辭中的同名者非常相似。例如歷組卜辭中婦名很少見，除了個別文字不很清晰的例子以

---

① 歷組的㾎和𠬝曾與𡥉同見於一塊占卜"令周"之事的卜骨：

　　　　叀㾎令[周]。
　　　　叀𠬝令周。
　　　　叀𡥉令周。　　　　　　　　　　　　　　　　　　　　掇二82【《合》32885】

而在賓組卜辭裏，㾎、𠬝和𡥉正好也都在關於"璞周"的卜辭裏出現過（"璞"字暫從唐蘭先生釋，"璞周"的確切含義尚待研究）：

　　　　☐貞：令㾎比☐侯璞周☐　　　　　　　　前7·31·4【《合》6816】（同版矣貞）
　　　　☐[叀]𡥉令[比☐]侯璞周。五月。　　　　　　　　　　　　　　　合6821
　　　　貞：叀𠬝令比璞周。　　　　　後下37·4【《合》6822】（同版另一辭記"五月"）

這很可能是下文將要討論的歷組和賓組卜辭同卜一事的現象的一個實例。所以㾎和𠬝就是㾎和𠬝的可能是很大的。

外，只有"婦好"、"婦妌"各自出現了好幾次，可見她們是最重要的兩個婦。賓組卜辭中有大量婦名，但出現次數大大超過其他各婦的，地位最重要的，恰好就是"婦好"和"婦妌"。賓組卜辭提到的商王臣屬名中，出現次數最多、地位最重要的，是沚馘、望乘、□、共、師般、射□（有的也見於出組卜辭）。歷組卜辭中出現次數最多地位最重要的人名，同樣是這一些（沚馘作沚或）。歷組卜辭的□有時稱亞□，賓組晚期或出組早期卜辭中也有亞□（見上表）；歷組卜辭中沚或或稱伯或（《安明》2413【《合》32814】），賓組卜辭也有伯馘（《天》90【《合》5945】）。甚至賓組出組卜辭和歷組卜辭裏所見的、與這些同名者有關的事項，也往往是相類或相同的。下面談歷組卜辭占卜事項的時候，就會碰到不少這樣的例子。這裏先將與□有關的部分事項作一個簡單對比：

賓組出組	歷　　組
丁示蚩□　粹 1265【《合》14906】	上下蚩□　甲 562【《合》34176】
御□于丁，于婦御□　甲 2121【《合》9560】	□御于父丁　明後 2524【《合》32844】 御□　甲 562【《合》34176】
翌丁未酒□歲于丁尊屮□　前 5・4・6【《合》4059】	丁卯酒□尊饎又伐　安明 2350【《合》32235】
□以羌　後下 9・4【《合》261】	□曰羌　甲 896【《合》32035】
□以三百射　乙 7661【《合》5769】	□曰多射　庫 3【《合》41528、《英》2421】
□亡災　存下 371【《合》7946】、前 4・14・2【《合》4087】	□亡囚　甲 545【《合》32865】
□往　前 1・46・5【《合》4070】	□往　粹 1049【《合》32866】
令□田于京　燕 52【《合》10919】、前 4・45・5【《合》5715】	令□田　安明 2621、粹 1224【《合》33218】
令□堅田于京　燕 417【《合》9473】、明後 1699【《合》9474】	令□裛田于京　佚 250【《合》33220】
□以衆伐吾方　後上 16・10【《合》28】、粹 1082【《合》26】	□曰衆□伐召方　粹 1124【《合》31976】、人文 2523【《合》31977】
□其喪衆　佚 549【《合》58】、京津 2155【《合》56】	□唯其喪衆　懷 1639【《合補》10411】
□不喪衆　寧 3・43【《合》39481】	□不喪衆　安明 2691【《合》31999】
令□　金 569【《合》40075、《英》834】、粹 1137【《合》4041】、人文 951【《合》4036】	令□　戩 48・6【《合》32858】、京津 4779【《合》32853】、掇一 428【《合》32849】
令□ᚦ東土　粹 249【《合》7084】	令□ᚦ于東　安明 2723【《合》33068】
□勿立事　南・師 2・61【《合》4065】	弜立事叀□☐　掇一 428【《合》32849】

見於這兩種卜辭的與𢀛有關的事項，簡直相似得驚人。

上述這些情況，跟卜辭裏一般的異代同名現象有顯著的不同。我們不能相信相隔幾朝的武丁、祖庚時期和武乙、文丁時期，在人事上竟會存在這麼多如此相似的現象；不能相信商王朝各個重要的族在這樣長的時間裏，竟能全都始終保持他們的地位而沒有任何比較顯著的變化。

我們還可以從另一個角度來看這個問題。在以廩辛、康丁卜辭爲主體的三、四期卜辭裏（包括村北所出三期卜辭），沚馘、望乘、𢀛這幾個常見於賓組和歷組卜辭的重要人名，一次也沒有出現過。𢀛出現過一次：

辛亥卜：翌日壬王其比在成犬𢀛，弗每，亡戈，擒。　　撫續 1【《合》27925】

這個𢀛是駐在成地管理商王田獵事務的犬人，其地位與賓組出組和歷組卜辭裏的𢀛根本無法相比。第五期卜辭有"右牧𢀛"（《簠》征 38【《合》35345】），僅一見，顯然也遠不如早期的𢀛重要，情況與此相似。𤰈見於下引三、四期卜辭：

癸卯卜：戊王其比犬𤰈，亡□　　　　　　　　粹 1148【《合》27909】

叀𤰈比，擒。　　　　　　　　　　　　　　京津 4775【《合》33397】

叀𤰈比，湄日亡□　　　　　　　　　　　　掇二 167【《合》29297】

這個𤰈也是具體管理田獵事務的犬人，其地位也顯然不能與射𤰈比擬。三、四期卜辭中曾一見亞般：

□□卜：亞般歲玩𦉫□　　　　　　　　　　鄴三下 44・4【《合》27938】

看來也不像是很重要的。廩辛、康丁卜辭時常占卜戰事。在戰爭中起主要作用的人物是一些戍，如戍受、戍隹、戍辟、戍逐、戍䇂等等，跟賓組和歷組卜辭所反映的由沚馘、望乘、𢀛等人主持戰事的情況完全不同。

如果賓組出組卜辭和歷組卜辭裏的相同人名，真如主張歷組卜辭屬於武乙文丁時期的學者所想象的那樣，代表着異代的同族人的話，爲什麼武丁祖庚時期和武乙文丁時期起重要作用的族如此一致，而介於這兩個時期之間的廩辛、康丁時期的情況却截然不同呢？

還應該指出，沚馘、望乘這樣的人名顯然是由一個族氏和一個私名構成的。即使不承認沚馘、沚或是一名，望乘的例子總是無法否定的。這種人名爲什麼也重複出現於不同時期呢？立足於人名爲族氏這一基點上的異代同名說，對此也無法作出完滿的解釋。

我們把賓組出組卜辭和歷組卜辭看作同時代的卜辭，把見於這兩種卜辭裏的同名者看作同一個人，上述問題就都不存在了。①

最後談歷組卜辭的占卜事項。除了卜旬等類幾乎在各個時期的卜辭裏都可以看到的占卜事項以外，在歷組卜辭裏還可以找到很多與賓組或出組早期卜辭相同的占卜事項。有一些歷組卜辭與賓組或出組卜辭，甚至可以肯定是同時爲一件事而占卜的。這是歷組卜辭和賓組出組卜辭時代相同的最有力的證據。李文已經舉出了賓組出組卜辭與歷組卜辭所卜事項相同的幾個例子，我們在這裏再補充一批例子。引録卜辭時，採用左右對照的辦法，寫在左邊的是賓組或出組卜辭（有卜人名的都屬賓組，無卜人名的少數可能爲出組早期卜辭），寫在右邊的是歷組卜辭。

(1) 丙子卜賓貞：令央囗我于出自，囚告不茍。　續5·4·3【《合》17168】 ｜ 丙子貞：王叀（與"唯"略同）央令囗我。　粹1247【《合》32829】
（《人文》2537【《合》32831】同文）

上引兩辭卜日干支相同。歷組一辭内容較略，但所卜之事與賓組一辭顯然相同。二者當是在同一天爲同一事而占卜的。囗象人埋坑中而有"爿"薦之，囗象殘骨埋於坑中，應爲一字異體，或釋"葬"，似可從。

(2) □貞：叀乙亥用射𢎥[以羌自囗]。　京津2086【《合》5755】 ｜ [癸]酉[貞]：射𢎥呂（以）羌[用]自囗[叀]乙亥。　人文2265【《合》32023】
己卯卜賓貞：翌甲申用射𢎥以羌自囗。八月。　燕235【《合》277】 ｜ 癸酉貞：射𢎥呂羌用自囗于甲申。　京津3966【《合》32023】

上引兩組卜辭顯然是爲了射𢎥送來的同一批羌俘而占卜的，兩組卜辭提到的祭祀日期和祭祀對象完全相同，己卯是癸酉之後的第六天。在歷組卜辭裏還有於丁卯日卜問用"𢎥呂羌"於父丁的：

丁卯貞：𢎥呂羌其用自囗六至于父丁。
丁卯貞：𢎥呂羌于父丁。　　掇一550（《摭續》2）【《合》32028】

---

① 《人物》也認爲見於賓組卜辭、歷組卜辭的望乘等相同人名指同一個人，並把某些歷組卜辭的時代定爲武丁時期（517頁等）。但是《人物》似乎根本不承認異代同名現象，書中甚至把武丁卜辭和五期卜辭中的同名者也看作一個人，並且爲了使這些人的活動時間的上下限不致相距過遠，把有關的五期卜辭説成武乙卜辭。所以《人物》的出發點與我們是不同的。

丁卯是癸酉的前六天（上引《人文》2265 歷組卜骨上尚有於庚午日卜用"射𡧾以羌"之辭，丁卯與庚午只差三天），這兩條卜辭提到的"𡧾以羌"，與上引《人文》2265、《京津》3966 的"射𡧾呂羌"當是同一批羌俘。《人文》2265、《京津》3966 的字體也確是比較典型的父丁類字體。由此可知，與這些歷組卜辭同時的《京津》2086、《燕》235 等賓組卜辭的時代已經晚到祖庚時期。

（3）甲申［卜］爭貞：勿𡧾用望［乘來羌］。　　　　燕 618【《合》16061】
庚子卜賓貞：翌甲辰用望乘來羌。
　　　　燕 596【《合》236】

丁亥貞：用望乘呂羌自囧。
　　　　佚 875【《合》32021】

上引兩條賓組卜辭和一條歷組卜辭，應該是爲了望乘送來的同一批羌俘而占卜的。甲申是丁亥的前三天，庚子是丁亥之後的第十三天。上引《佚》875 歷組卜骨上尚有"丁亥貞用于父丁"一辭，可知上引《燕》596、618 等賓組卜辭的時代也已經晚到祖庚時期。

（4）壬午卜貞：翌甲申酒𠂤□牛自囧□□酒。　　甲 3651【《合》1198】
乙酉卜爭貞：酒𠂤方以牛自囧。一月。
甲 2029（《甲綴》340）【《合》10084】

癸亥貞：𠂤方呂牛其登于來甲申。
　　　　綴 334【《合》32896】
癸未貞：甲申□𠂤方呂［牛］自囧。
　　　　鄴三下 44·6【《合》32026】

上引賓組和歷組卜辭也應該是爲同一件事而占卜的（《甲》3651 無卜人名，據《甲》2029 暫定爲賓組卜辭）。第二條賓組卜辭的卜日是乙酉。大概當時先卜於甲申日用𠂤方送來的牛祭上甲以下的祖先，得兆不吉，或由於其他原因其事未實現，所以在甲申的次日乙酉再就此事進行占卜。【編按：葛亮指出，賓組第二條的"乙酉"他家皆釋"乙亥"，從圖版看，釋"亥"是對的。他的意見很正確。"乙亥"在"壬午"之前七天，"壬午"所卜較"乙亥"所卜更爲具體，二者所卜仍應爲一事。原文有關論述應删除。】第一條賓組卜辭"𠂤"作〵，未刻全。此辭於壬午日卜，上引第二條歷組卜辭於癸未日卜，二卜日緊接。上引《綴》334 歷組卜骨上尚有"丁未貞王其令望乘帚（歸）其告于祖乙一牛父丁一［牛］"等辭，《鄴三》下 44·6 歷組卜骨上尚有"癸卯貞射𡧾呂羌其用［于］父丁"一辭。由此可知上引《甲》2029 和 3651 兩條賓組卜辭也已經晚到祖庚時期。

(5) 辛丑卜貞：昷以羌，王于門尋。　　　辛酉貞：王尋昷呂羌南門。

　　　　後下9·4【《合》261】　　　　　　　懷1571【《合補》10646】

上引兩辭所卜之事相同，但卜日干支相距二十日。殷人常常在事先很多天就開始爲一件事占卜，所以上引兩辭卜問同一件事的可能性仍然存在。

(6) 癸卯［卜］賓貞：［令］昷堅田于京。　　□卯貞：王令昷㱿田于京。

　　　　燕417【《合》9473】　　　　　　　佚250【《合》33220】

很可能右方歷組卜辭"卯"上所缺一字爲"癸"，卜日與左方賓組卜辭相同。"堅"、"㱿"是一字異體。

(7) 貞：令昷✦東土，告于祖乙于丁。八月。　　丁巳卜貞：王令昷✦于東✦（生月？）□安明

　　　　粹249【《合》7084】　　　　　　　2723【《合》33068】

"令昷✦東土"與"令昷✦于東"應爲一事。

(8) 貞：令多馬衛于北。　　　　　　　　甲辰卜：呼多馬徬从北。　善齋舊藏

　　　甲3473【《合》5711】（同版爭貞）　　（《論集》編按：即《合》27943）

上引賓組卜辭在《甲》3473號卜甲上位於"癸卯卜"一辭上方。癸卯的第二天就是甲辰，上引兩辭所卜應爲一事。"衛"、"徬"是一字異體，有人釋作"衛"，也有人認爲是防衛之"防"的本字。

(9) □戌卜賓貞：令菁以多馬衛▨。　　　丙申卜：王令菁呂多馬。

　　　　合5712　　　　　　　　　　　　安明2711【《合》32994】

《合》8964的一條賓組或出組早期卜辭說："戊戌卜貞令菁以㞢友馬徬☐"，與上引之《合》5712當是一時所卜，可見後者"戌"上所缺一字應爲"戊"。戊戌與上引歷組卜辭的卜日干支丙申，中間只隔一個"丁酉"。二者所卜當是一事。

(10) ▨叀族馬令往。　　　　　　　　乙酉卜：于丁令馬。　　叀一族令。

　　　粹1291【《合》5728】（同版爭貞）　眾令三族。　　叀三族馬令。

　　　　　　　　　　　　　　　　　　　　　　　　　　　寧1·506

　　　　　　　　　　　　　　　　　　（《論集》編按：即《合》34136）

上引賓組卜辭在《粹》1291號卜甲上位於"甲申卜"殘辭上方。甲申的第二天就是乙酉。上引賓組與歷組卜辭可能爲同時所卜。

(11) 貞：叀木令衞。一月。　　　　　　壬午貞：癸未王令木歪。

　　　　燕 598【《合》7569】　　　　　　甲 600【《合》33193】

"歪"也是"衞"的異體，或析爲"方"、"止"二字，非是。

(12) 辛未卜貞：令戾以□射于斬，　　辛未貞：王令呂戋于魝。

布方我。　　　　　　　　　　　　辛未貞：冓呂新射于斬。

　　　續 3·46·6【《合》5766】　　　　明後 2629【《合》32997】

　　　　　　　　　　　　　　　　　乙亥貞：令戋于龜。

　　　　　　　　　　　　　　　　　乙亥貞：令辰呂新射于斬。

　　　　　　　　　　　　　　　　　　　安明 2710【《合》32996】

右方所引兩版歷組卜骨顯然是密切相關的。乙亥爲辛未之後的第四天。甲骨文常在地名字上加"山"、"水"等偏旁。上引賓組卜辭的"斬"與歷組卜辭所説的"斬"當指一地無疑。賓組卜辭所説的"令戾以□射于斬"，與歷組卜辭所説的"令辰呂新射于斬"應爲一事。"辰"和"戾"當是同一人名的不同寫法。

(13) 乙卯卜賓貞：䏦翌日。十三月。　　甲寅卜：叀翌日䏦。

　　　前 7·5·2【《合》10076】　　　　掇一 430【《合》34343】

（《金》355【《合》40761】同文）　　（《京津》4823 重，《撫續》201【《合》32787】同文，但"日"下多一"ㄓ"字）

上引兩辭當是爲同一事而占卜的。甲寅的第二天就是乙卯。見於這兩條卜辭的兩個怪字應爲一字異體。（校時案：《合》18567 歷組卜辭"甲寅卜，䏦翌日"，亦爲同時所卜。《論集》編按：以上爲原文按語。今按，《屯南》4080 亦同時卜。）

(14) 貞：于乙亥入黃尹祊(?)人。　　　□[今]日其取伊祊(?)人。

　　存下 229【《合》3099】（同版古貞）　□□貞：于乙亥[取]伊祊(?)人。

　　　　　　　　　　　　　　　　　　　　明後 2442

　　　　　　　　　　　　　　　　　　（參《寧》1·235【《合》32803】）

賓組的黃尹相當於歷組的伊尹。見於上引賓組卜辭的黃尹祊人也稱黃祊人：

癸卯卜貞：今日令昜取黃祊(?)人。七月。　　　前 7·3·2【《合》22】

與歷組卜辭的"伊祊人"當指同一種人。上引賓組卜辭的"入"字當"使進入"講，可讀爲"納"，與"取"義近。這條卜辭與上引歷組卜辭顯然是卜問同一件事的。

(15) 丁丑卜賓貞：㞢往。六月。　　　丁丑貞：往亡囚㞢。
　　　　　　前1·46·5【《合》4070】　　　　　粹1049【《合》32866】
（《甲》1492【《合》4071】同文，但貞
人爲爭）

這也是賓組、歷組同日卜同事的例子，上引《粹》1049的"㞢"字寫得較小較偏，顯然是寫漏後添補的，其本來位置也應在"往"字之前。

(16) 貞：翌乙亥令黃步。　　　　戊寅貞：王令黃翌己卯步。
　　　　　　　　　合7443　　　　　　安明2713【《合》32939】

己卯是乙亥之後的第四天，大概先卜於乙亥日命黃步，得兆不吉，或由於其他原因其事未實現，所以到戊寅日又卜於己卯日令黃步。上引《合》7443號卜骨未記卜人名，字體屬賓組，骨上尚有數辭，其中一辭僅記干支"己卯"二字，可能也與令黃步之事有關。

(17) 癸巳卜□貞：叀乙未令師般。　　癸巳貞：今日王令師般。
　　　　　　南·上68（《合》4216）　　王于乙未令。
　　癸巳卜古（?）貞：令師般涉于河東　　　　　　懷1651【《合補》10488】
　　北，尖于□奴王臣。　　　　　　□令師般眔央。
　　　　　甲釋圖版072（《合》5566）　　　　　　懷1649【《合補》6614】

上引《南》上68和《懷》1651，顯然是在同一天爲同一事而占卜的。其他兩條也有可能是跟它們同時占卜的。

(18) □翌乙酉呼子屵酒伐于父乙。　　壬午卜：屵又伐父乙。
　　　　　　續1·28·9【《合》969】　　　《考古》1975年1期45頁圖19
　　　　　　　　　　　　　　　　　　（《論集》編按：即《屯南》751）

乙酉是壬午後第三天，上引兩辭很可能是爲一事而卜的。

(19) 甲午卜賓貞：沚䵼啓王勿比，　　庚寅卜：叀𢀖[啓]我用若。
弗其受□　　乙綴192【《合》6471】　　叀沚䵼啓我用若。　　鄴三下39·9
　　　　　　　　　　　　　　　　　　（《綴》128）【《合》33056】
　　　　　　　　　　　　　　　　　　癸巳卜：王比沚䵼。
　　　　　　　　　　　　　　　　　　　　　　　甲695【《合》33104】

上引卜辭裏的"啓"指征伐時充當先行。① 庚寅是癸巳前第三天，甲午是癸巳後第一天，這幾條卜辭大概都是圍繞同一事件而占卜的。

(20) 辛酉卜争貞：王比望乘伐下危。
辛酉卜争貞：王勿唯望乘比。
貞：王叀沚馘比伐巴方。
貞：王勿唯沚馘比。
貞：王叀尸叨（方？）正。
貞：王勿唯尸正。
　　　　丙 24 + 京津 1266【《合》6476】
(《丙》插圖貳綴合。此版序數爲一)
貞：王比望乘伐。
王勿比望乘伐。
王叀止（沚）馘。
勿唯止馘。
王叀尸正。
勿唯尸正。　　乙 3797【《合》6583】
(與上版同文，此版序數爲五)

癸亥[卜]：王叀戉比。
[癸亥卜]：王叀望乘比。
癸亥卜：王叀尸（夷）正（征）。
乙丑卜：王叀戉比。
乙丑卜：王叀望比。
　　　　鄴三下 38・1【《合》33112】
甲[子卜]：王[叀戉]比。
甲子卜：王叀望乘比。
丁卯卜：王弜比戉。
丁卯卜：王弜比望乘。
　　　　懷 1637【《合補》10485】

在上引賓組卜甲和歷組卜骨上，王是否比望乘、是否比沚馘（歷組作戉）和是否征夷這三件事都同時並見（《懷》1637 征夷之辭殘去）。賓組卜日爲辛酉，歷組卜日爲癸亥、甲子、乙丑、丁卯。辛酉與癸亥中間只隔一個"壬戌"。這些賓組和歷組卜辭顯然是爲同一組事件而占卜的。

面對上引這些歷組卜辭與賓組或出組早期卜辭所卜事項相同的實例，除了承認歷組與賓組和出組早期時代相同以外，是没有其他辦法的。上面所引的卜辭裏，出組卜辭大概很少。不過一部分賓組卜辭已經晚到祖庚時期，正與出組早期的時代相當。

從前面討論過的各方面的情況來看，完全可以肯定歷組卜辭跟賓組和出組早期卜辭是同時代的。也就是説，歷組卜辭應該屬於武丁、祖庚時期。這種卜辭裏的父乙是武丁對小乙的稱呼，父丁是祖庚對武丁的稱呼。

---

① 胡厚宣：《殷卜辭中的上帝和王帝（上）》，《歷史研究》1959 年 9 期 39 頁。

在武丁卜辭裏，賓組卜辭的時代一般要晚於自組卜辭。①自組卜辭存在的時間可能比較長，文例、字體都比較複雜。其中一部分卜辭，行款整齊，字形不大不小，文字結體平正匀稱，與賓組卜辭頗爲相似。賓組卜辭中，在各方面與這類自組卜辭比較接近的，時代就早；反之，與出組早期卜辭比較接近的，時代就晚。與歷組卜辭有相同占卜事項的賓組卜辭，多數是偏晚的。前面對照賓組和歷組卜辭的占卜事項時已經指出，（2）（3）（4）諸例所引賓組卜辭已經晚到祖庚時期。這些賓組卜辭，除（2）例所引《京津》2086在形式上與較早的賓組卜辭難以區分外，其餘都明顯地屬於與出組早期相似的賓組晚期類型。上舉（1）至（12）諸例，在（2）（3）（4）三例之外，其餘各例所引賓組卜辭基本上也都屬於晚期類型。同時，與它們相應的歷組卜辭的字體，也大都可以歸入父丁型。所以賓組晚期卜辭很可能有相當大的一部分是屬於祖庚時期的。與歷組父乙類卜辭占卜相同事項的某些賓組卜辭，如上舉（18）（20）等例所引的賓組卜辭（18例歷組卜辭有"父乙"，20例歷組卜辭是比較典型的父乙類字體），時代顯然要早一些。如果把賓組分爲早中晚三期，它們大概可以歸入中期。但是就整個武丁時期來說，則仍應屬於後期。歷組父乙類卜辭中的重要人名，大都不見於自組卜辭而仍見於歷組父丁類卜辭，有的也見於出組早期卜辭。可見這些人在武丁時期的活動時間是偏晚的。這也說明歷組父乙類卜辭的時代不會很早。所以歷組卜辭時代的上限大概不會早於武丁後期。李學勤同志以歷組卜辭爲"武丁晚年到祖庚時期的卜辭"，是有道理的。

　　歷組卜辭與賓組、出組卜辭同時，並且也是"王卜辭"，爲什麼文例、字體却與賓組、出組有相當大的差異呢？貝塚茂樹認爲同屬武丁時期的賓組卜辭和自組卜辭，所以呈現不同的風格，是由於二者分屬於不同的占卜機關。他的看法很有啓發性。不過，自組卜辭，至少是其中相當大的一部分要早於賓組卜辭。二者風格的不同可能在很大程度上是由時代因素決定的。對於歷組卜辭和賓組、出組卜辭之間的風格差異來說，時代因素基本上無關，很可能占卜機關的不同是造成

---

① 林澐同志在《從武丁時代的幾種"子卜辭"試論商代的家族形態》一文中說："所謂'自組卜辭'，我在1965年已考定是武丁前期的王室卜辭。"（《古文字研究》第一輯317頁）李學勤同志也認爲自組卜人犾的卜辭在殷墟甲骨中時代最早（《盤龍城與商朝的南土》，《文物》1976年2期45頁）。自組卜辭的內容比較複雜，較晚的自組卜辭可能與較早的賓組卜辭同時。但總的來說，其時代無疑要早於賓組。陳夢家把自組卜辭的時代定在武丁晚期，是不正確的（《論集》編按：據黃天樹同志博士研究生畢業論文《殷墟王卜辭的分類與斷代》，自組卜辭的下限有延伸到武丁晚期的迹象。這一問題有待進一步研究）。

這種差異的主要原因。根據甲骨出土地點的資料來看，歷組卜辭主要出在村中村南，賓組、出組卜辭主要出在村北。這說明歷組卜人和賓組出組卜人分屬於不同占卜機關的可能性是非常大的。但是應該指出，這種不同決不會是貝塚茂樹處理賓組、自組關係時所設想的那種不同，即屬於王朝或屬於王族的不同。因爲從卜辭內容看，歷組卜辭顯然跟賓組出組卜辭一樣，也出自王朝正式卜官之手，只不過歷組卜人和賓組、出組的卜人大概分屬於不同的官署而已。其實，就是自組卜辭，也不可能出自與王朝卜官有別的王族私家卜官之手，"王族卜辭"這一名稱恐怕是不能成立的。

在討論了歷組卜辭的時代之後，還應該簡單討論一下與歷組卜辭有密切關係的另一組卜辭的時代問題。

李學勤同志過去在《殷代地理簡論》裏，曾經把歷組卜辭看作武乙至文丁初年的卜辭，把自組卜辭看作文丁卜辭。他分第四期甲骨爲四類。歷組卜辭稱爲四期 1 類，自組卜辭又分兩類，稱爲四期 3 類和四期 4 類。我們現在要討論的，是當時也被他看作文丁卜辭的所謂四期 2 類卜辭。①

這組卜辭龜、骨兼用，不記卜人名，前辭大多數作"干支卜"，少數作"干支卜貞"或"干支貞"。"貞"字兩鼎耳多作方形，干支字"子"多作 ☒ ☒，"丑"多作 ☒，"戌"多作 ☒，"未"、"酉"大部分似賓組，小部分似歷組，"王"字無頂上一橫，"雨"字橫畫幾乎都是傾斜的，"囚"字多作 ☒，"𡆥"字多作 ☒，"戎"字多作 ☒，"不"字大部分作 ☒，小部分作 ☒（以上參看《簡論》88 頁）。其筆法一般說來介於歷組父乙類卜辭與筆畫比較纖細流利的那種自組卜辭之間。不過，這一組卜辭的字體並不完全統一，一部分卜辭的字體特別近於歷組，還有些卜辭的字體比較怪。這組卜辭還有兩個顯著的特點。一是比較喜歡卜問"易（錫）日""不易日"。一是比較喜歡把先人稱謂中的日名放在前面，如稱"乙大"、"丁祖"、"己妣"等等。著錄這組卜辭最多的書，大概是《庫方》，其次是《人文》、《甲》、《粹》、《摭續》等書。爲了行文方便，我們姑且稱這組卜辭爲"歷、自間組"卜辭（《論集》編按：林澐同志在《小屯南地發掘與殷墟甲骨斷代》一文中指出，按時代先後的次序"歷自間組"應改稱"自歷間組"，見《古文字研究》第九輯 126—127 頁。這個意見是正確的。作者在後來寫的論文裏，已改稱"自歷間組"。又，本文在劃分歷組的兩類卜辭和劃定自歷間組的範圍時，沒

---

① 看《簡論》附錄"殷代王卜辭分類表"（101 頁）及書中有關各節。由於原書對甲骨分期問題談得比較簡單，我們的介紹可能有誤解原意之處。

有以字體爲唯一標準，這也是不妥當的。關於這個問題可參閱上引林文。至於自歷間組究竟應該包括哪些卜辭，還有待進一步研究）。

　　這組卜辭與歷組卜辭的關係是很密切的。《簡論》曾指出，《粹》1164【《合》33074】屬於此組而有歷組常見的人名沚或；《庫》972【《合》40866】屬於此組，而左下隅橫刻干支表一列，屬於歷組；《甲》2423（2422反面）【《合》21472】屬此組，《甲》884【《合》32182】屬歷組，二者皆有極爲罕見的"菱"字（89頁）。這兩組卜辭的文例、字體有時候非常相似，有些卜辭簡直難以斷定應該歸入它們之中的哪一組。例如《存》下731【《合》33076】很像是歷組卜骨（《存》列於三、四期），但是其上有"戊辰卜弗執獽"等辭，而屬於"歷、自間組"的《粹》1181【《合》33078】等片也有"癸酉卜王辜獽甲戌戠，"、"乙亥卜弗戠獽"等辭（詳後），戊辰、癸酉只相差五天，顯然爲一時所卜。這樣看來，此片似可歸入"歷、自間組"。又如《寧》1·12【《合》34012】片有"甲辰卜不易日"、"甲辰卜王步戊申易日"、"甲辰卜王步己酉易日"、"庚申不易日"等辭，"不"字有橫畫，"酉"字、"庚"字的寫法似歷組父乙類，就這一片孤立地看似乎可以歸入歷組。但是如與《人文》3222【《合》32941】片聯繫起來看，似乎還是歸入"歷、自間組"爲妥。後者有"甲辰卜王步丁未易日"、"甲辰卜王步戊申易日"、"不易日"、"乙卯卜王步丁巳易日"、"乙卯卜庚申易日"等辭，與前者顯然是同時所卜，而"不"字無橫畫，"庚"作甬，"未"作米，是標準的"歷、自間組"字體。有時一片卜骨上同時出現分別具有這兩個組的風格的卜辭。如《存》下733片【《合》34011】，上端卜旬一辭完全是歷組作風，其右下側一辭作"丙申卜王步丁酉易日"，與上舉《寧》1·12同類型，辭側記"二月"，更是不見於一般歷組卜辭而屢見於"歷、自間組"卜辭的作風。此片下端一殘辭有人名"雀"，也是屢見於"歷、自間組"卜辭而少見於歷組卜辭的。①

　　從以上所述的各種現象來看，"歷、自間組"與歷組的時代顯然是大致相同的。過去，李學勤同志把歷組卜辭看作武乙至文丁初年的卜辭，把"歷、自間組"卜辭看作文丁卜辭。現在歷組卜辭已經改定爲武丁後期到祖庚時期的卜辭，

---

① 提到"雀"的"歷、自間組"卜辭有《庫》1117+1151（《綴》141【《合》33089】）、《粹》1167【《合》20399】、1553【《合》20383】、《佚》604+《續》2·31·4（《綴》140）【《合》33071】、《甲》179【《合》20168】、183【《合》33072】、《鄴三》下40·3【《合》32839】、《存》上638【《合》20384】等。《存》上638的字體也比較接近歷組父乙類，但從卜辭內容可以確定爲"歷、自間組"卜辭，參看下文關於"歷、自間組"與賓組所卜事項相同一節。胡厚宣先生將《存》上638列入第一期，也不把它看作歷組卜辭。

"歷、自間組"卜辭當然也就應該改定爲武丁卜辭了。這種卜辭不會晚到祖庚時期，可以從以下兩方面得到證明。首先，從字體等方面看，歷組父乙類明顯地接近於"歷、自間組"，歷組父丁類跟"歷、自間組"的關係則比較疏遠。這既表現在筆法上，也表現在字形結構上。例如"貞"字，"歷、自間組"一般將兩耳寫作方形，這種寫法在歷組父乙類卜辭裏常常出現，但在歷組父丁類卜辭裏就相當少見了。其次，從親屬稱謂上看，這組卜辭也顯然屬於武丁時期。《掇二》170【《合》20530】"歷、自間組"卜骨有如下一辭：

　　癸未卜：祉覃父甲至父乙酒一牛。

郭若愚《自序》説："父甲至父乙當是象甲（按：當作兔甲，"兔"、"陽"二字陰陽對轉）、般庚、小辛、小乙，可知此片卜辭應爲武丁時物。"這是正確的。《粹》119【《合》31997】、《人文》3015【《合》2282】、3016【《合》22202】也是有"父乙"之稱的"歷、自間組"卜辭。①但"父丁"沒有在這種卜辭裏出現過。

歷組父乙類比歷組父丁類更接近於"歷、自間組"這一點，還透露出"歷、自間組"的時代可能略早於歷組父乙類的消息。也就是説，這些卜辭有可能是沿着"歷、自間組——歷組父乙類——歷組父丁類"這樣的途徑而逐漸演變的。

從"歷、自間組"卜辭中的占卜事項和人名，也可以看出這組卜辭確實屬於武丁時期，而且很可能要略早於歷組父乙類卜辭。

我們先來看占卜事項。武丁時期關於征伐方國的占卜，有一些既見於"歷、自間組"也見於賓組。例如"歷、自間組"有征伐獯②和翼（也作蠹）的卜辭：

　　戊辰卜：弗執獯。　　　　　　　　　　　　存下 731【《合》33076】
　　癸酉卜：雀覃（與伐義近）獯。　　　　　　甲 831【《合》32842】
　　癸酉卜：王覃獯，甲戌戕。

---

① 《人文》3016 字體較怪，而且有卜"屮囚"一辭，與一般"歷、自間組"卜辭用"又"不用"屮"的習慣不合。但是通過與其他"歷、自間組"卜辭的比較，可以肯定它也屬於"歷、自間組"。《人文》3113【《合》20779】有"乙酉卜丙戌步易日"等辭，從文例、字體看屬於"歷、自間組"無疑。這一版上還有"壬午卜屮戎才𠂤東北獲"一辭，也用"屮"字，而且與《人文》3016 的"壬午卜伐戎☐𠂤東北戕"一辭爲同時所卜。《人文》3016"戎"字的寫法，也是"歷、自間組"所特有的。

② 此方國名"歷、自間組"作"獯"。賓組少數作"獯"（《掇一》117【《合》6940】、《乙》6671【《合》7076】等），多數作"獯"，本文一律寫作"獯"。關於這個字，請參閱唐蘭《殷虛文字記》（唐先生認爲這個字从"豕"，我們改作从"犬"）。

乙亥卜：弗㞢𤉲。

乙亥卜：王章豐，㞢。旬一日乙酉王㞢。

　　粹1181【《合》33078】+懷1638(《懷》圖版117綴合【《合補》6622】)

乙亥卜貞：今日乙亥王章豐，㞢。

　　　　庫1094【《合》33080】(《懷》圖版117與上片綴合【《合補》6622】)

丙子卜：于丁丑㞢。

丙子卜：于戊寅㞢。

丁丑卜：㞢豐。

丁丑卜：今日㞢豐。　　庫104+1095(《北美》卡17綴合)【《合》33081】

賓組也有征伐𤉲和𦏧的卜辭，例如：

乙丑卜王貞：余伐𤉲。

　　　　　　前7·18·2【《合》6926】(《續》3·13·4【《合》6927】同文)

乙亥卜賓貞：勿伐𤉲。　　　　　　　庫1810【《合》39929、《英》604】

丁丑卜㱿貞：我伐𤉲。　　　　　　　七·W5【《合》6929】

庚寅卜㱿貞：呼雀伐𤉲。　　　　　　林2·15·11【《合》6931】

□雀伐𤉲。　　　　　　　　　　　　庫672【《合》39931、《英》603】

癸巳卜爭貞：亯㞢𤉲。　　　　　　　前7·12·1【《合》6939】

戊□卜□貞：亯㞢𤉲。

貞：[亯]弗其㞢𤉲。　　　　　　　　乙5303【《合》6947】

□亯𡩡𤉲。　　　　　　　　　　　　掇一117【《合》6940】

乙未卜㱿貞：勿唯王自正𤉲。

貞：我勿伐𤉲。　　　　　　　　　　通564(《通》別2·4·10)

□章㞢𤉲，不其㞢。　　　　　　　　乙6671【《合》7076】

辛巳卜㱿貞：呼雀伐𦏧。

辛巳卜㱿貞：勿呼雀伐𦏧。　　　　　乙綴249【《合》6959】

□□卜㱿貞：我㞢𦏧。　　　　　　　庫1750【《合》39937、《英》606】

"歷、自間組"卜問"雀辜𤉲"、"王辜𤉲"，賓組卜問"雀伐𤉲"、"王自征𤉲"，並有王親貞"余伐𤉲"之辭。"歷、自間組"於乙亥日卜"弗㞢𤉲"，賓組於乙亥日卜"勿伐𤉲"。"歷、自間組"於乙亥、丙子、丁丑等日卜辜𦏧、㞢𦏧，賓組於辛巳等日卜伐𦏧、㞢𦏧。丁丑與辛巳，中間只隔三個干支。賓組卜辭提到的伐

獿、伐𢀛之人，除王之外就是雀和㠱。雀不但見於上引"歷、自間組"辜獿卜辭，而且還屢見於其他"歷、自間組"卜辭，已見上述。㠱也見於下引"歷、自間組"卜辭：

己丑卜貞：㠱呂沚或伐猷，受又。　　　　　　　　　　粹1164【《合》33074】

甲午卜：王叀㠱配。　　　　　　　　　　　　　　　　懷1640【《合補》6625】

☐㠱☐亡正戎。　　　　　　　　　　　　　　　　　　庫1055【《合》20396】

從以上所説的來看，"歷、自間組"和賓組關於征伐獿和𢀛的卜辭顯然是同時的（請看文末追記）。

"歷、自間組"卜辭卜問"雀夆（執）亘"、"雀獲亘"：

辛亥貞：雀夆亘，受又。　　　　　　　　　　　　　　存上638【《合》20384】

癸亥卜：亘弗夕雀。

丁卯卜：雀獲亘。　　　　　　　　　　粹1553【《合》20383】（參《綴》141）

賓組也卜問"雀夆亘"、"雀獲亘"：

辛亥卜☐貞：自今至乙卯雀夆亘。　　京津1322（《存》上1097）【《合》6954】

貞：雀其夆亘。　　　　　　　　　　　　　　　　　　京津1324【《合》6953】

乙巳卜爭貞：雀獲亘。

乙巳卜爭貞：雀弗其獲亘。

辛亥卜㱿[貞]：雀獲亘。　　　　　　　　　　　　　　乙4693【《合》6952】

戊午卜㱿貞：雀追亘，㞢獲。　　　　　　　　　　　　乙5303【《合》6947】

"歷、自間組"卜"雀夆亘"的《存》上638一辭，與賓組卜"雀夆亘"的《京津》1322一辭，甚至連卜日干支也完全相同。上引這兩組卜辭無疑也是同時的。

"歷、自間組"卜問"辜缶"、"辜缶于㫚"：

辛巳卜：令☐☐☐辜缶。　　　　　　　　　　　　　　人文2153【《合》20526】

乙酉卜：王辜缶，受又。

　　　　粹1176【《合》20527】（《論集》編按：《甲》261【《合》20524】同文）

庚寅貞：辜缶于㫚，㞢又旅。才☐☐月。　　　　　　　懷1640【《合補》6625】

賓組也卜問"辜缶"、"辜缶于㫚"：

丁酉卜㱿貞：王叀乙辜缶，㞢。三月。　　　　　　　　人文364【《合》6867】

丁卯卜㱿貞：王叀岳于旬。二月。　　　　　　　　　　　後上9·7【《合》6863】

　　（《粹》1175【《合》6860】、《續》1·52·1【《合》6862】、《明》2330【《合》6861】等同文）

　　庚辰卜㱿貞：王叀岳于〔旬〕。　　　　　　　　　　　　　　續5·35·5

　　（《天》68重。《論集》編按：此片即《合》6864，《合》有反面拓，上有"☒旬。二月"殘辭。也有可能正反面當接讀，本無缺字）

"晌"和"旬"顯然指同一地點。上引這兩組卜辭應該是圍繞同一件事而占卜的。

"歷、自間組"卜問"辜畾"（《掇二》170【《合》20530】），賓組卜問"辜畾"（《乙綴》301【《合》1027】）"𢦏畾"（《丙》1【《合》6834】、《後》下25·1【《合》6832】）。"畾"和"畾"無疑是一字異體，這幾條卜辭大概也是圍繞同一件事而占卜的。

以上所引占卜事項與"歷、自間組"相合的賓組卜辭，沒有晚於賓組中期的，很可能比占卜事項與歷組父乙類相合的賓組卜辭要略早些，至少不會晚於後者。

如果跟卜辭中的人名結合起來看，"歷、自間組"應該略早於歷組這一點就比較清楚了。"歷、自間組"卜辭中所見的人名，最重要的就是上面提到的"雀"，但雀在歷組卜辭中則很少見。另一方面，除了上面提到過的記"亶曰沚戓"的《粹》1164之外，在"歷、自間組"卜辭中也幾乎從不見歷組卜辭中最常見的沚戓、望乘、𢀛、㠱等人名。雀這個人名沒有在賓組晚期和出組卜辭裏出現過，而他在前辭常作"干支卜"的賓組早期卜辭中則是屢見的[1]，在自組卜辭中也出現過。[2]他的活動時期顯然要略早於沚戓、望乘等人。[3]由此看來，"歷、自間組"卜辭的時代也應該略早於歷組卜辭。

除了相同的占卜事項和人名，"歷、自間組"和賓組的關係還表現在它們都有甲橋署辭上。《人文》3095【《合》21008】、3098【《合》21006】都是"歷、

---

[1] 《鐵》145·3【《合》4116】、176·2、226·1【《合》8006】、《天》80【《合》10201】、《粹》1293【《合》4146】、《前》7·5·4【《合》19191】、《乙》4718【《合》8984】等等。

[2] 見《甲》2902【《合》20576】。此版與《甲》2907【《合》19946】皆有"旧亡旧才南土"之辭，爲同時所卜。《甲》2907有自組卜人𠨘之名。

[3] 但晚期的雀與早期的沚戓（沚馘）、望乘等人可以同時，所以在賓組卜辭裏能看到"呼雀弜戓"（《乙》5303【《合》6947】）、"戓其啓雀"（《乙》7674【《合》10863】）等辭。

自間組"卜甲,前者背面甲橋部分刻有署辭"庚午☐",後者背面甲橋部分刻有署辭"庚寅☐示五",形式與賓組甲橋署辭相似。

前面説過,"歷、自間組"卜辭的筆法,一方面與歷組卜辭接近,一方面又與一部分自組卜辭接近。《簡論》還曾指出刻有自組卜辭的《甲》2904號【《合》20354】卜骨,其右下隅所刻干支表爲"歷、自間組"字體(89頁)。①此外,"歷、自間組"最重要的人名"雀"也曾見於自組卜辭。可見這兩組卜辭也有比較密切的關係。

1973年小屯南地出土的那批"自組卜甲"與"歷、自間組"卜辭的關係,尤其值得注意。這批卜甲中記自組卜人名的只有一片(《考古》1975年1期38頁圖13【《合》19838、《屯南》4517】),其筆法屬於纖細流利一類,字體跟有些"歷、自間組"卜辭相似,祭仲丁一辭稱"丁中",置日名於前,也與"歷、自間組"的作風一致。

這批"自組卜甲"的第五片卜問"子妥不妝(葬?)"、"其妝"(《考古》1976年4期235頁【《合》20578、《屯南》4514】)。"歷、自間組"卜辭也提到子妥:

辛丑卜:御子妥己妣。

庫974【《合》20038】(據《北美》卡6校正。參《庫》1146【《合》20039】)

此外,武丁卜辭裏提到子妥的,還有賓組卜辭,以及通常被研究非王卜辭的學者附於子組的一種書法草率的卜辭:

子妥囚凡。　　　　　　　　　　　　　　　　乙6273【《合》10936】

子妥囚凡☐　　　　　　　　　　　　　　乙4074【《合》3175】(以上爲賓組卜辭)

☐卯貞:子妥不死。　　　　　　　　　　　　　吉林4【《合》21890】

庚[子貞]:子妥不死。　　　　　　　乙綴418+乙1521【《合補》6912】

(參《乙》7718【《合》22459】。以上爲附屬子組的卜辭)

這些關於子妥的卜辭,占卜時間大概都相距不遠。賓組卜辭的"囚凡"當是卜辭常見的"囚凡有疾"一語的省文。卜問爲子妥舉行禦祭(一種被除災禍的祭祀),以及卜問子妥的"死"與"妝"(葬?),都應該與這場疾病有關。上引屬於

---

① 在《乙》474【《合》20805】自組卜辭,《乙》5388【《合》12314】賓組卜辭裏,以及在《人文》3074【《合》20323】可能屬於自組也可能屬於賓組早期的卜甲上,都有寫法很接近"歷、自間組"的干支字"子"。

"歷、自間組"的《庫》974號卜骨，與"自組卜甲"第五片的關係尤其密切。後者有"乙未卜王入☐三月"、"辛卯卜王入"、"弜入"等辭，《庫》974有"乙未卜王入今月"、"辛卯卜王弜入"等辭，二者顯然爲一時所卜。《考古》上發表的"自組卜甲"第五片的拓本，印得幾乎連一個字也看不清，估計其字體並非典型的自組類型。與其將這片卜甲附於自組，恐怕還不如附於"歷、自間組"來得妥當（《論集》編按：此片即《屯南》4514【《合》20578】，字體跟"歷、自間組"比較接近）。

"自組卜甲"第六片卜問"辜俑"、"伐歸"：

丁酉卜：今生十月王辜俑，受又。

弗受又。

己亥卜：王辜俑，今十月受[又]。

弗受又。

己亥卜：侯☐啓王伐歸，若。

庚子卜：伐歸，受又。八月。

弜伐歸。　　　　　　　　　　　　《考古》1976年4期236頁圖6上

（《論集》編按：即《屯南》4516【《合》33069】）

這兩件事也都見於"歷、自間組"卜辭：

丁酉卜：生十月王辜俑，[受]又。　　　粹1191（《京津》3135）【《合》20512】

己亥☐辜俑，受又。　　　　　　　　京津3136【《合》20513】

辛未卜：王一月辜俑，受又。

乙亥卜：生月王辜俑，受又。

丙子卜：王二月辜俑，受又。　　　　甲709【《合》20510】

壬戌卜貞：王生月辜俑，不蚩哉。

佚884（《續》1·2·4、《戩》1·9）【《合》34120】

壬寅卜：桒其伐歸，叀北巫用，卄示一牛，二示羊，以四戈彘。

粹221【《合》34122】

（《粹》222、《人文》2997【《合》34121】同文。同版有作凶的"子"及斜肩的"雨"）

☐伐歸伯，受又。　　　　　　　　　粹1180【《合》33070】

"自組卜甲"第六片與上引"歷、自間組"的《粹》1191、《京津》3136，都在丁酉日、己亥日卜伐俑，卜辭的文字也幾乎完全相同。"自組卜甲"第六片在己亥

日、庚子日卜伐歸，"歷、𠂤間組"的《粹》221等片在壬寅日卜問爲伐歸而舉行祭祀，庚子、壬寅之間只隔一個"辛丑"，二者提到的"伐歸"顯然也是一回事。上引《佚》884片在壬戌卜臺俑一辭上方尚有如下一辭：

> 癸卯卜貞：酒衆乙巳自囧廿示一牛，二示羊，四戈彘，四巫豕，土燎牢。

除未提"伐歸"外，内容與《粹》221等壬寅一辭基本相同，卜日癸卯又正好與壬寅緊接，可見所卜實爲一事。"𠂤組卜甲"第六片同時占卜"臺俑"和"伐歸"，"歷、𠂤間組"的"臺俑"和"伐歸"則通過關於祭祀"自囧廿示"的占卜而得到聯繫，這是很有意思的。在已著録的甲骨裏，還有不少卜問臺俑、替俑、征俑、執俑的卜辭①，從字體上看大都可以歸入"歷、𠂤間組"，至少可以附於此組。"𠂤組卜甲"第六片的字體既非典型的"歷、𠂤間組"，也非典型的𠂤組。從卜辭内容看，恐怕也與"𠂤組卜甲"第五片一樣，還是附於"歷、𠂤間組"爲宜。

小屯南地出土的七片"𠂤組卜甲"，雖然實際上並不都屬於𠂤組，但是從地層上看沒有問題都屬於武丁時期。"歷、𠂤間組"卜辭與這批卜甲的密切關係，又一次證明它確是武丁卜辭，同時還説明它的時代可能與"𠂤組卜甲"第一片所代表的那種筆畫纖細流利的𠂤組卜辭很接近。那種卜辭在𠂤組中大概是偏晚的（《論集》編按：是否如此尚待研究）。前面已經説過，𠂤組卜辭的文例、字體比較複雜，有一部分𠂤組卜辭與賓組卜辭很接近。很可能"歷、𠂤間組"卜辭和賓組卜辭都是由𠂤組卜辭發展出來的。不過，這樣説並不意味排斥下述那種可能性：在賓組卜辭和"歷、𠂤間組"卜辭出現以後，𠂤組卜辭還曾繼續存在一段時間。

過去，胡厚宣先生在他所編的幾種分期編排的甲骨著録書裏，把絶大多數"歷、𠂤間組"卜辭跟𠂤組卜辭等放在一起，附在第一期卜辭之後。貝塚茂樹、伊藤道治編的《人文》也把絶大多數"歷、𠂤間組"卜辭歸入以𠂤組卜辭爲主體的屬於第一期的"王族卜辭"。他們對這種卜辭的時代的判斷是正確的。不過，這種判斷與他們把歷組卜辭看作武乙文丁卜辭的觀點則是矛盾的。②

---

① 《粹》1192【《合》20522】、1193【《合》20516】、《摭續》146【《合》20511】、《佚》661【《合》20520】、《簠》文30【《合》31793】、《甲》3374【《合》19834】、《庫》1051【《合》20521】、《人文》3054【《合》20519】、3132【《合》20518】、《明後》2623【《合》20515】、《安明》2444【《合》20514】、《懷》1628【《合補》6664】。

② 他們都有偶爾把"歷、𠂤間組"卜辭誤認爲歷組卜辭而列入三、四期或四期的情況，如《存》上2115【《合》16802】、《人文》2400【《合》27801】。這也説明這兩種卜辭的確是比較相似的。

上面討論"歷、自間組"卜辭與"自組卜甲"的關係的時候，引用了兩條提到"自囲廿示"的"歷、自間組"卜辭（其中一條還有兩條同文卜辭）。過去大家一直認爲"廿示"指上甲到武乙這二十世的直系先王。因此這兩條卜辭幾乎被公認爲絶無懷疑餘地的文丁卜辭。現在看來，這種看法顯然是不正確的。僅僅根據辜佣、伐歸這兩件事，一方面與"自囲廿示"同見於一辭或一版，一方面又並見於已從地層上證明屬於武丁時代的"自組卜甲"第六片這個事實，就可以斷定這兩條提到"自囲廿示"的卜辭，也是武丁卜辭，"廿示"決不可能包括武丁以下諸王在内。有的同志既承認"自組卜甲"第六片屬於武丁時期，又承認提到"自囲廿示"的卜辭是文丁卜辭。這是自相矛盾的。關於卜辭裏的"示"，有很多問題還没有搞清楚。大示、小示究竟如何區分，就有很多不同説法。① 又如同樣是"五示"，賓組卜辭説："翌乙酉史伐于五示：囲、成、大丁、大甲、祖乙"（《丙》41【《合》248】），出組卜辭説："己丑卜大貞：于五示告，丁、祖乙、祖丁、羌甲、祖辛"（《佚》536【《合》22911】），所指先王就不一樣。有一條"歷、自間組"卜辭説："☐六示三、五示二、十示又☐"（《佚》882【《合》34119】）。"六示"應該指"囲六示"。② 與"六示"並提的"五示"，其内容顯然又與上引兩條卜辭的"五示"不同。如果我們對卜辭裏的"幾示"、"十又幾示"作帶有推測性的解釋，然後再據以定有關卜辭的時代，那是缺乏説服力的。

　　説到這裏也許有人要問，你們把歷組父乙類卜辭和"歷、自間組"卜辭都定爲武丁卜辭，殷墟甲骨裏究竟還有没有文丁卜辭呢？這的確是一個問題。但是我們不能因爲存在問題而否認事實。可能文丁卜辭的主要藴藏地不在殷墟已發掘的範圍之内，也可能已發現的甲骨文裏本來有不少文丁卜辭，但是被我們誤認爲其他時期的卜辭了。真相究竟如何，還有待探索。③

---

① 參看《丙》上（二）考釋 242 頁。
② 見《甲》712【《合》33313】、《明後》2470【《合》34111】、2533【《合》32031】、2586【《合》33296】、《存》上 1786【《合》32099】。
③ 1973 年小屯南地發掘中發現了兩片文例與三、四期"干支卜貞王其田亡戈"類型田獵卜辭相同，而字體則似五期卜辭的卜骨（《1973 年安陽小屯南地發掘簡報》，《考古》1975 年 1 期 43—45 頁。這種卜骨過去也發現過，如《人文》2507【《合》37793】），可見這種三、四期田獵卜辭的時代比較晚，有可能是文丁卜辭。《粹》341【《合》32658】的一條三、四期卜辭卜祭"三祖辛"，《粹編考釋》以三祖辛爲廩辛。《南》輔 61 殘存"康祖丁宗"四字，從字體上看也是三、四期卜辭（《論集》編按：此版即《合》38229，實非三、四期卜辭，《合》收入第五期是對的）。廩辛、康丁是文丁的祖父，這兩條卜辭也有可能是文丁卜辭。這些也許可以看作探索文丁卜辭的綫索。

還有一個問題，也應該在這裏提一下。歷組卜辭和主要出於村中村南的三、四期卜辭，在不少方面的確是很相似的。它們的文例、字體都比較接近，基本上都用骨而不用龜，並且都以村中村南爲主要儲藏地。它們的時代很可能是相接的。李學勤同志在没有把歷組卜辭定爲武丁祖庚卜辭之前，就認爲一般所謂三、四期卜辭的上限應延至祖甲時期。他認爲這種卜辭裏的兄己、兄庚、就是祖甲對孝己、祖庚的稱呼。①現在，歷組卜辭已經證明是武丁祖庚卜辭，"三、四期卜辭"包含祖甲卜辭的可能性，就顯得更大了。這個問題很值得進一步研究。此外，我們現在認爲歷組父丁類卜辭裏没有祖甲卜辭，主要根據是這種卜辭裏没有出現過"兄庚"。這是消極的證據。有没有可能歷組父丁類卜辭中也有祖甲卜辭呢？這也是可以研究的。

附錄一：一、二期的界綫應該劃在哪裏

按照董作賓在 30 年代建立起來的殷墟甲骨文斷代學説，第一期相當於武丁時期②，第二期相當於祖庚祖甲時期。這種分期方法長期爲甲骨學界所沿用。但是董氏自己，後來通過對卜辭祭典的研究，在一、二期的劃分問題上却有了新的看法。他在 1945 年出版的《殷曆譜》裏把祖庚劃入舊派，祖甲劃入新派，第二期實際上已經一分爲二。在 50 年代發表的《甲骨學五十年》裏，董氏比較明確地批評了自己過去劃分一、二期的辦法。他説：

> 所謂"五期"，是完全爲貞人關係而劃分的，如以祖庚祖甲爲第二期，以帝乙帝辛爲第五期，就是因爲這兩朝前後二王的貞人相同不易再爲區分。（《甲骨學六十年》71 頁）

> ……祖庚屬於舊派，一切制度仍武丁之舊而祖甲却改革了許多。因而祖庚卜辭又往往和武丁時不易分别，不似祖甲時顯然有異。所以我們寧可以説第一期應包括祖庚，不能只限於武丁。（同上 79 頁）

他把祖庚從第二期改劃入第一期，是可取的。

---

① 《評陳夢家〈殷虚卜辭綜述〉》，《考古學報》1957 年 3 期 125 頁，參看《簡論》101 頁"殷代王卜辭分類表"。
② 武丁之前的盤庚、小辛、小乙諸王的卜辭，直到現在還是没有從甲骨文裏找出來。董氏後來根據靠不住的殷代年曆定出來的早於武丁的卜辭是不可信的。

一般所謂武丁卜辭主要是指賓組卜辭，祖庚卜辭是指出組早期卜辭。賓組晚期和出組早期的卜辭，文例、字體以及所反映的制度都很相似。這是大家都承認的。此外，這兩種卜辭所占卜的事項和提到的人名，也有不少是相同的。《綜述》曾舉出出組卜人兄、出等人所卜的事項和所提到的人名，與賓組卜人相同的不少例子（190頁），我們在《論"歷組卜辭"的時代》（以下簡稱"時代"）裏討論歷組卜辭人名的時候，也舉出過不少既見於賓組卜辭又見於出組卜辭的人名，可以參閱。特別值得注意的，是出組卜人與賓組卜人有時在同一天占卜同一件事的現象，例如：

  （1）丙寅卜兄貞：令子齓亏（乂）。十月。   前5·4·2【《合》23536】

    丙寅卜賓貞：子齓奇（乂）畯四方。十月。 後下8·1【《合》3087】

  （2）癸亥卜兄貞：旬亡［囚。一日象甲子］夕燮大再☐

                    前5·33·4【《合》26631】

    癸亥卜事①貞：旬亡囚。一日象甲子夕燮大再至于☐ 【簠·雜116】

    （《論集》編按：即《合》18793，據《合》拓，"至于"下尚可辨出"相景"二字）

  （3）辛亥卜出貞：令𦰩伯［于］☐（"受"之誤摹？） 金413【《合》41011】

    （《論集》編按：即《英》1978，《英》拓"伯"下"于受"二字甚清晰）

    辛亥［卜］出貞：令𦰩伯于［受］。   拾6·7【《合》24155】

    辛亥卜爭貞：令𦰩伯于受。一月。   燕491【《合》10047】

上引第（1）、（2）兩例是饒宗頤在《人物》中舉出來的（見879頁）。李學勤同志在《簡論》中曾舉出如下一例（見66頁）：

  （4）［☐☐卜］大貞：令咸子奠子寧☐

                簠·人53（《論集》編按：即《合》23534）

    ［☐☐卜］賓貞：令咸子𦣞子寧。八月。   合6049

這兩條卜辭所缺的干支很可能也是相同的（《論集》編按：賓組、出組同日卜同事之辭尚可補《合》22594"丙戌卜大貞：告𡆥于河燎☐沜三牛☐"、《合》805"丙戌卜爭貞：其告𡆥于河☐"一例）。

  《簡論》還指出賓組甲骨記載進納甲骨等事項的署辭，在出組早期甲骨上有

---

① 卜人事，《綜述》作"吏"，未列入賓組。《人物》指出《存》下177【《合》1251】事、夂同版，《甲》3404【《合》8473】事（原作"史"，二字古通）、古、訁同版（575頁），可見事也是賓組卜人。

時也可以看到，例如（見 66 頁。例子略有增删）：

己酉，史戠☒　　　　　　　　　　燕 126 背【《合》24432】（骨，正面卜人出、大）
☒廿屯，小臣☒☒　　　　　　　　庫 1634 背【《合》41066】
（骨，正面卜人出、兄、矣。《論集》編按：即《英》2032，可與《英》2000 綴合，見本書所收《甲骨綴合拾遺》第 7 例。綴合後之署辭全文爲"辛丑，气自𠭯廿屯，小臣聓☒"。又據《英》2032 正，此骨正面"出貞""兄貞"二殘辭爲原刻，"矣貞"一辭則爲僞刻）

☒丑，小臣中示☒　　　　　　　　六・束 12（背甲背，正面卜人出）
☒☒气自☒　　　　　　　　　　　安明 1578（背甲，正面卜人出）

如果没有甲骨正面的卜人名，這些署辭很容易被誤認爲屬於賓組。《存》上 80【《合》15515】（《續》5・25・7 重）有下引骨背署辭：

己酉，戠示十屯。矣。

這與上引《燕》126 骨背署辭應爲同文之辭，但是其正面所記卜人却不屬於出組，而爲賓組的賓、爭、古等人（《存》上 79），署辭末的署名者矣也是賓組卜人。

上引《六》束 12 片署辭中的小臣中，與出組卜人中應爲一人（《綜述》182 頁）。他有時也署名於賓組卜甲反面的署辭。例如《存》上 24 號卜甲的卜人爲賓組的韋，背面甲橋署辭的署名者爲中（《存》上 25。《論集》編按：黃天樹同志指出，《存》上 25 即《合》4049 反，《存》上 24 非其正面，此例當删）。《零拾》21 號【《合》14859】卜甲的卜人爲賓組的爭，背面也有中的署名（請看文末追記）。

出組卜人矣的卜辭曾提到卜人竹：

丙寅卜矣貞：卜竹曰其出于丁宰，王曰弜圂，翌丁卯㚔若。八月。

文錄 519【《合》23805】

而賓組卜人爭曾與竹共貞：

丁巳卜，竹、爭貞：令䍙以子𡥆于盖。　　　前 2・37・7【《合》637】

上述這些現象説明賓組和出組的關係極爲密切。其中，賓組和出組卜人在同一天卜同一事的現象，以及他們使用的骨版上刻有同文署辭的現象，可以證明這兩組確實有過一段共存的時間。按照情理推測，這段時間可能在武丁晚期或祖庚早

期。我們在《時代》一文裏已經證明賓組晚期卜辭有相當大的一部分已經晚到祖庚時期。所以賓、出二組只是共存於武丁晚期的可能性可以排除。出組卜辭究竟有沒有早到武丁晚期的，目前還不能下斷語。

賓組晚期和出組早期卜辭在各方面都很接近，如果沒有卜人名或各組特有的親屬稱謂，往往難以區別。賓組晚期卜辭裏既有武丁卜辭，也有祖庚卜辭。因此那些有卜人名的賓組晚期卜辭，如果沒有可據以斷代的稱謂，通常仍然不能斷定究竟屬於武丁還是屬於祖庚。至於出組早期卜辭，一般把它們全都看作祖庚卜辭。由於出組上延到武丁晚期的可能性並不是完全不存在，這樣做也並不是絲毫沒有危險性。還有一件事更增加了劃分武丁晚期卜辭和祖庚卜辭的困難性。那就是在賓組晚期和出組早期卜辭裏，能據以斷代的親屬稱謂特別少。因爲在這些卜辭裏，"父某"一類稱呼很少見，最常見的親屬稱謂乃是"丁"。這既可以是武丁對祖丁的稱呼，也可以是祖庚對武丁的稱呼（參閱附錄二）。

在甲骨斷代上，爲了避免上述困難，只能把祖庚時期包括在第一期裏。歷組卜辭是武丁後期到祖庚時期的卜辭。從歷組卜辭的角度來看，也應該把祖庚時期包括在第一期裏。當然，對於肯定屬於祖庚時期的卜辭，完全可以明確地稱之爲祖庚卜辭，就跟肯定屬於武丁時期的卜辭可以稱爲武丁卜辭一樣。在把祖庚時期從第二期劃出去以後，"祖庚、祖甲卜辭"和"出組卜辭"，作爲與"第二期卜辭"含義不同的概念，仍然可以繼續使用。

有很多出組卜人兼事祖庚、祖甲兩朝。把祖庚劃歸第一期之後，就不能像過去那樣，一看到卜辭裏有出組卜人名，就把它們歸入第二期了。對於出組卜辭，需要根據文例、字體和內容，把它們分別劃入一期和二期。卜人供職的期限往往與王世不一致，並且也不一定與卜辭本身特點所構成的階段相應。"完全爲貞人關係"而分期本來就是不合理的，董作賓自己就已經指出了。過去把實際上包含着一部分祖庚卜辭的賓組卜辭，全都看作武丁卜辭，這與過分強調卜人在分期上的作用就是有關係的。

在這裏我們還要提出一個問題，是不是應該考慮把祖甲初期也劃在第一期裏。我們先來看下面兩條卜辭：

己丑卜大貞：于五示告，丁、祖乙、祖丁、羌甲、祖辛。

佚 536（《粹》250）【《合》22911】

貞：恵柰至于丁于兄庚。

掇二 137（《鄴初》下 38・4）【《合》2920】

這兩條卜辭的字體都像賓組，《掇二》137 背面（即《鄴初》下 38·5）並有賓組常見的甲橋署辭。前一條卜辭由於有出組卜人大之名，過去都定爲第二期。董作賓在《斷代例》裏、郭沫若在《卜辭通纂·後記》和《粹編考釋》裏，都認爲這一條的"丁、祖乙"指武丁、小乙。這樣解釋，"五示"先人之名由近到遠與商王世系密合，顯然是可信的。絕大多數甲骨學者都信從這一說法。"丁"這個稱謂在出組卜辭裏是常見的，解釋爲武丁，都沒有困難。

《掇二》137 片，從親屬稱謂上看顯然屬於祖甲時期，丁和兄庚應是祖甲對其父武丁和其兄祖庚的稱呼。日本學者島邦男就是這樣解釋的。① 但是由於這片卜甲的字體接近賓組，背面又有甲橋署辭，因此被不少甲骨學者定爲第一期。《綜述》以至最近出版的《甲骨文合集》（2920 片）都如此處理。本來，在武丁時期的賓組卜辭裏也常見"丁"的稱謂，島邦男認爲這種"丁"指祖丁，是可信的。他與祖庚祖甲卜辭裏的"丁"不是一個人（詳附錄二）。《綜述》則認爲武丁和祖庚祖甲卜辭裏的"丁"指同一個人，即武丁卜辭常見的兄丁，《掇二》137（《鄴初》下 38·4）的"丁"和"兄庚"都被解釋爲武丁之兄（437 頁）。但是《綜述》在另一處又說武丁卜辭裏的兄丁和丁，"是否一人，難以決定"（453 頁），可見對這個問題並無十分確定的見解。如果承認丁爲武丁之兄的說法，上引《佚》536 大貞卜辭就成爲不提時王之父武丁，而以未曾即位的伯父與祖父、曾祖等先王並列了。那是難以理解的。出組卜辭提到"丁"的次數很多，祖庚祖甲爲什麼特別重視一位沒有即過位的伯父呢？此外，在肯定屬於武丁時期的卜辭裏，從沒有出現過兄庚，《綜述》僅據《掇二》137 片就硬給武丁添一個兄庚，也是不合理的。總之，把這一片卜甲放在祖甲時期，把"丁"當作武丁，卜辭的內容可以得到十分合理的解釋；如果放在武丁時期就難以講通了。上文已經說過，出組早期卜辭，即祖庚卜辭，與賓組晚期卜辭是很接近的，而且這個時期的甲骨上也有賓組甲骨上常見的署辭。那麼，在與祖庚時期緊接的祖甲初期，爲什麼就不能有《掇二》137 片那樣的卜甲呢？認爲這片卜甲只能屬於第一期，是受甲骨斷代上的傳統觀點束縛的結果。

《珠》90 號【《合》23510】卜骨，文例、字體是出組早期的作風，骨上也有"兄庚"之稱。這片卜骨也應該屬於祖甲初期。

不少出組卜人的卜辭裏都有新舊作風混雜的現象，如有無之"有"等詞或寫

---

① 《殷墟卜辭研究》第一篇第二章"禘祀"。據《古文字研究》第一輯趙誠同志譯文（401—402 頁）。

作"屮"或寫作"又","王"字頂上一橫畫或加或不加等等（參看《人物》1209等頁）。可見第二期典型作風的形成有一個過程。從上舉的兩片祖甲甲骨來看，在祖甲初期的一段時間裏，這種作風顯然還沒有形成。不過，這段時間大概比較短，遺留下來的甲骨不多，所以其特點才會長期被人忽略。過去，有些甲骨學者認爲典型的第二期卜辭裏可能包含一部分祖庚卜辭。也就是說，他們認爲第二期典型作風在祖庚時期就已形成。這種看法似與事實不符。

甲骨斷代應以甲骨卜辭本身顯示出來的特點爲根據，既不能完全依靠卜人斷代，也不能要求一定把界綫劃在兩王交替的時候。過去爲什麽把兩個王甚至更多的王的甲骨劃爲一期呢？主要是由於他們的甲骨不好分。既然祖甲初期的甲骨與祖庚以及武丁晚期的甲骨不好分，爲什麽不能合爲一期呢？從上面所舉的兩片祖甲初期甲骨來看，在我們過去定爲祖庚時期甚至武丁時期的甲骨裏，肯定已經有祖甲初期甲骨混雜在裏面了。明確提出第一期包括祖甲初期，只不過是"正名"而已。在劃分二、三期和劃分四、五期方面，恐怕也都存在與劃分一、二期相類的問題。很難設想甲骨卜辭的作風會在某個新王即位之初立刻起很大的變化。至於三期和四期的劃分，根本是不合理的。因爲如果僅僅根據文例、字體，村中所出的康丁卜辭和武乙卜辭大部分無法區別。胡厚宣先生把三、四期合併爲一期，是有道理的。

按照我們的分期辦法，在實踐上也會碰到一些困難。有些介於一、二期之間的過渡性比較強的卜辭，究竟劃入哪一期很費斟酌。不過，這種問題在爲一個連續性的發展過程分期的時候總是會遇到的。

對於武丁、祖庚和祖甲初期的卜辭的分期，還可以有另一種設想。能不能把早於賓組晚期的武丁卜辭定爲第一期，把難以區分的武丁晚期、祖庚時期和祖甲初期的卜辭定爲第二期，把原來的第二期以下各期都推後一期呢？這樣做也有困難。首先，賓組中期、晚期的界綫具體怎樣劃，就很難講清楚。而且有時候從內容看應屬賓組晚期，甚至可以肯定是屬於祖庚時期的卜辭，在形式上却像較早的賓組卜辭，例如《時代》對照賓組和歷組卜辭中相同占卜事項時所舉的、第（2）例中的《京津》2086【《合》5755】。甚至有些出組卜辭，如不看卜人名，也會誤認爲早於賓組晚期的卜辭，如《京津》530【《合》24429】的大貞卜辭就比較典型。又如《庫》1551【《合》40914、《英》1977】殘甲存兩辭，上一辭記卜人出之名，作風是出組早期的；而下方"貞令屮伯于臺"一辭的作風，就有些像賓組中期（《論集》編按：此片即《英》1977，從《英》的拓本看，"屮伯"一辭

字形雖較大，字體作風仍與賓組中期有明顯不同。此例當刪）。這些複雜情況更增加了劃分賓組中、晚期的困難。其次，賓組中晚期的差別，應該說比自組與賓組的差別要小。自組和賓組早中期合爲一期，賓組中期和晚期反而分別劃入不同的期，從情理上似乎也說不過去。不過在有必要的時候，我們可以把賓組晚期和出組早期卜辭合稱爲一期晚期卜辭，以與較早的一期卜辭相區分，大部分歷組卜辭也可以歸入一期晚期。在我們對內容複雜的武丁卜辭有了深入的研究之後，也許可以定出一種更合理的分期辦法來。這就有待大家努力了。

附錄二：關於"丁"

在武丁、祖庚祖甲和廩辛康丁卜辭裏，都可以看到"丁"這個稱謂。丁究竟是誰，這是一個不大好解決的問題。研究這個問題成績最好的學者，大概要數島邦男。島氏在《殷墟卜辭研究》第一篇第二章"禘祀"中，對這個問題作了比較全面的考察。① 島氏認爲卜辭中有些"丁"指上帝，是不可信的；他對於他認爲是以"丁"指先人的那些卜辭的解釋，也並不完全正確。但是他的主要結論——武丁卜辭中的先人丁是祖丁，祖庚祖甲和廩辛康丁卜辭中的先人丁是武丁，則是可信的。關於出組卜辭和廩辛康丁卜辭中的丁的問題，島氏解決得不錯②，我們在附錄一裏對出組卜辭的丁也已經有所討論，所以這裏就不想再談了。下面談談賓組卜辭裏的丁（但我們討論到的有些沒有卜人名的卜辭，也有可能屬於出組早期）。

在賓組卜辭裏時常可以看到"丁"，在賓組晚期卜辭裏，"丁"的出現尤爲頻繁。③ 我們在《時代》和附錄一裏已經指出，賓組晚期卜辭實際上有相當大的一部分是祖庚卜辭。因此，賓組卜辭的"丁"指武丁的可能性，是不能排除的。在島氏心目中賓組卜辭和武丁卜辭是劃等號的，所以他論證賓組卜辭的丁是祖丁的方法很簡單。他的主要根據是下引這條卜辭：

貞：令宴㞢東土，告于祖乙于丁。八月。　　　　　粹249【《合》7084】

---

① 《殷墟卜辭研究》第一篇第二章"禘祀"。據《古文字研究》第一輯趙誠同志譯文（401—402頁）。
② 但是島氏對廩辛、康丁時代的《甲》2647片【《合》27875】的解釋恐怕有問題。
③ 出現"丁"的賓組卜辭見《合》1905—1997（可能有少數出組早期卜辭在內），但所收不全。

他説："這一版的'□'列於祖乙之後。因爲在第一期，祖乙以後的先王只有祖丁，而把命令殷將㠱征伐（島氏釋✢爲伐）東土這件事報告給'□'的這個'□'，只能是祖丁。"①這條卜辭，我們在《時代》中對照賓組和歷組卜辭的相同占卜事項的時候曾經引用過（見第7例）。從卜辭作風看，似屬賓組晚期（其實也不能完全排除屬於出組早期的可能性）。與它相應的歷組卜辭，很像是屬於父丁類的。因此，這條卜辭很可能是祖庚卜辭，辭中提到的"丁"很可能與出組卜辭中的"丁"一樣，是祖庚對武丁的稱呼，而不是武丁對祖丁的稱呼。歷組祖庚卜辭屢次説"告于祖乙、父丁"：

　　叀夕㝬酒告于祖乙、父丁。　　　　　　　　明後2535【《合》32578】
　　□□貞：有來告［方出］从北土，其燎告［于祖］乙、父丁。
　　　　　　　　　　　　　　　　　　　　　　　粹366【《合》33050】
　　丁未貞：王其令望乘帚（歸），其告于祖乙一牛，父丁一［牛］。
　　　　　　　　　　　　綴334（《粹》506＋《南》明499）【《合》32896】

把"告于祖乙、父丁"與上引《粹》249的"告于祖乙于丁"對比一下，就可以知道後者的"丁"是祖庚稱呼其父武丁的可能性是非常大的。從附錄一所引《粹》250【《合》22911】大貞卜辭稱武丁、小乙爲"丁、祖乙"來看，上舉各辭的祖乙也有可能是指小乙而言的。

　　大概屬於賓組晚期的《後》下12·13【《合》281】説："庚子卜貞：牧以羌征于丁㽞用。"屬於歷組的《明後》2533【《合》32031】説："□□卜：用逊（牧）㠯羌于父丁。"這兩條卜辭所卜問的很像是一件事，所以前者的"丁"很可能也指武丁。

　　在賓組晚期卜辭裏，父乙是很少見的，而丁則常見。如果説賓組晚期卜辭絕大多數屬於武丁時期，丁是武丁對祖丁之稱的話，爲什麽武丁如此輕其父而重其祖呢？而且何以在賓組較早的卜辭裏父乙出現得相當頻繁，與晚期卜辭大不一樣呢？這種現象使我們懷疑賓組晚期卜辭大部分是祖庚卜辭，這種卜辭裏的丁大部分是祖庚對武丁的稱呼。

　　不過，稱祖丁爲丁的確鑿例子，在賓組晚期卜辭裏還是找得出來的。我們可以看下面這條卜辭：

---

① 《殷墟卜辭研究》第一篇第二章"禘祀"。據《古文字研究》第一輯趙誠同志譯文（401—402頁）。

丁丑卜賓貞:子雍其御王于丁妻二妣己，㞢羊三，卯羌十。

　　　　　　　　　　　　　　　　　　　　　　佚 181（《續》1·39·3）【《合》331】

這條卜辭的作風似屬賓組晚期，但是它所提到的丁不可能是武丁。因爲這條卜辭的時代再晚也不可能晚於祖庚祖甲，祖庚祖甲稱武丁之配，是只能稱母不能稱妣的。這個丁顯然是指以妣己爲法定配偶之一的祖丁。祖丁之配稱二妣己，也許是相對於也稱妣己的祖乙之配而言的。在祖庚時期不會把祖丁、武丁兩個先王都稱爲"丁"。所以上引這條卜辭應該屬於武丁時期。在下引兩片賓組晚期作風的卜甲上，"丁"與"母庚"同見：

　　　丙寅卜貞:來丁亥子𥎦見以歲于示于丁于母庚于婦。

　　　　　　　　　　　　　　　　　　　　　　　　　前 1·2·9【《合》3101】

　　　甲辰卜貞:告于丁一牛。五月。
　　　甲辰卜貞:翌乙巳忧出于母庚宰。　　　　　安明 157【《合》2543】

上引卜辭裏的母庚似應指武丁父小乙之配妣庚，所以這兩片卜甲大概屬於武丁時期，"丁"自然也以解釋作祖丁爲宜。

　　有些"丁"見於肯定屬於武丁時期的賓組中期卜辭。這些"丁"當然也應該解釋爲祖丁，如《乙》3797【《合》6583】"自成告至于丁"的"丁"。在賓組早期卜辭中，"丁"似乎很少見。

　　有些賓組卜辭裏的"丁"，從某一個角度看很像是武丁，從另一個角度看又很像是祖丁，使人感到迷惑。例如《甲》2124【《合》339】、2121【《合》9560】的"丁"就是這樣。這兩版都屬於殷墟第三次發掘所得的"大龜四版"，卜辭作風屬於賓組晚期。董作賓早就懷疑《甲》2124 的丁是武丁。他在《安陽侯家莊出土之甲骨文字》一文中說:

　　　殷人常有對最切近之人，僅舉忌日，不加稱謂者。如大龜四版之一（按：即《甲》2124）載祭丁之辭十三，皆但稱丁，不加祖或父之稱謂。同版有祖乙之祀，若祖乙爲小乙，則此丁即父丁，武丁了。此版皆武丁時舊史，或係祖庚時之卜辭。（《田野考古報告》一册 125 頁）

從我們對賓組晚期卜辭的觀點來看，董氏的説法顯然是很有道理的。《甲》2121 也有關於"丁"的卜辭：

　　　壬午卜賓貞:御𥁕于丁。

　　　　貞：于婦御㝬。

歷組祖庚卜辭曾提到"㝬御于父丁"（《明後》2524），對照起來看，《甲》2121 的"丁"似乎也應該是武丁，正可與董氏之説互證。但是《甲》2121 以"御㝬于丁"與"于婦御㝬"對貞，上引《前》1·29·2 説："子𪒠見以歲于示壬丁于母庚于婦"以丁與婦並提，二者的"丁"似乎應該指一個人。如果真是這樣，《前》1·29·2 的丁既不是武丁，《甲》2121 以至同出的《甲》2124 的丁，就也都不可能是武丁了。當然，也可能我們對《前》1·29·2 的解釋是錯誤的，也許這條卜辭裏的丁就指武丁，而母庚則指武丁的一個配偶而不是指小乙的配偶。

　　總之，賓組卜辭中所見的"丁"的問題很複雜，還有待進一步深入細緻地加以研究。只有在把這個問題真正搞清楚以後，我們對祖庚卜辭在賓組卜辭中所佔的分量，才能有比較明確的認識。

　　歷組卜辭中也有"丁"，例如：

　　　（1）丙辰卜：柔（𧛣）壴（鼓）鞀于丁。
　　　（2）于八月酒升歲于丁。　　　　　　　　　　安明 2337【《合》32014】
　　　（3）丙寅貞：其征昜于丁。　　　　　　　　　粹 1271【《合》32981】
　　　（4）癸酉卜：其告于丁牛一。　　　　　　　　粹 529【《合》32649】
　　　（5）癸未貞：其告于丁牛☐。　　　　　　　　明後 2440【《合》32648】
　　　（6）☐告方于丁。　　　　　　　　　　　　　鄴三下 39·9【《合》33056】
　　　（7）甲寅卜：又燎于丁。
　　　（8）乙卯卜：又燎于丁。　　　　　　　　　　明後 2457【《合》32647】
　　　（9）乙酉卜貞：㝢于丁。　　　　　　　　　　存上 1785【《合》34115】
　　　（10）丁丑貞：昇丁羌八☐牛一。　　　　　　　摭續 86【《合》32084】
　　　（11）丁丑貞：㝢其即丁。　　　　　　　　　　明後 2482【《合》32440】

　　　　（《鄴三》下 40·2【《合》34102】同文。此"丁"或當釋"祊"）

前五條似屬父乙類字體，後三條似屬父丁類字體，中間三條較難下斷語。看來，歷組卜辭裏的"丁"似乎也分兩類，有的是武丁對祖丁的稱呼，有的是祖庚對武丁的稱呼。

　　　　　　　　　　　　　　　　　　　　　　　　　1980 年 7 月 26 日夜寫完

追記：

《合》6937 賓組卜辭"乙酉卜囗貞：呼亶比沚伐獿"，與前引《粹》1164【《合》33074】歷、𠂤間組卜辭"己丑卜貞：亶眔沚或伐狃受又"，應該是爲同一件事而占卜的。乙酉與己丑只差四天。"獿""狃"當是一字異體。賓組卜辭的"獿""獿"也許不應釋爲"獿"。

關於出組署辭還應該補充一條資料。《合》列入第一期的17582號卜甲，背面有署辭"戊寅出示囗"，這裏的出當即祖庚祖甲時主要卜人出。

《論集》編校追記：

李學勤同志在發表於《古文字研究》第三輯的《關於𠂤組卜辭的一些問題》一文中，已把他在《簡論》中定爲"四期2類"的卜辭歸入𠂤組（37—39頁）。

原載《古文字研究》第6輯，中華書局，1981年；收入裘錫圭：《古文字論集》（文中簡稱"《論集》"），中華書局，1992年；又收入《裘錫圭學術文集·甲骨文卷》，復旦大學出版社，2012年。今據後者收入。

林 澐

甲骨文中的商代方國聯盟

在世界史上，目前確知的最早的國家形式，都是小型的奴隸制城邦國家。列寧在《論國家》一文中早已指出："……國家是在比現在狹小得多的地理範圍內形成起來的。技術薄弱的國家機構只能爲一個版圖較小、活動範圍較小的國家服務。"但是，對中國史上最早國家形式的探討，長期受着黃帝以來就是"大一統"的傳統觀念的影響，50 年代以後又加了一個所謂"東方專制大國"的模式的束縛，至今缺乏實事求是的具體分析。雖然"茫茫禹迹，畫爲九州"之類的説法，幾乎已没有人再據以爲信史，但商代有龐大的專制集權國家，在古代史著作中仍是一種流行的觀點。

其實，古代典籍中有不少提到周代以前存在衆多的小國。《呂氏春秋·用民》："當禹之時，天下萬國，至於湯而三千餘國。"《逸周書·世俘解》記載：武王克商，"遂征四方，凡憝國九十有九國，凡服國六百五十有二"。但東周時人們的觀念中，總想象着自古就有"天子"、"諸侯"的名位區别和隸屬關係，故《墨子·非攻》説："古者天子之始封諸侯也，萬有餘。"《逸周書·殷祝解》把湯時的三千餘國也説成是"天子"湯和三千"諸侯"的關係。

由甲骨文可確知，商代確實存在着衆多的"方"，或稱"丰（邦）方"（合 36243、36530、36528 反），即典籍中所見之"方"或"邦"。關於這種"方"，田野考古已提供了初步的具體概念。如湖北黄陂縣灄口公社葉店大隊的盤龍城已查明是一座商代古城。城内有宫殿，城外有居址和墓地，總面積約 1 平方公里，城垣面積約 7 萬餘平方米[①]。有趣的是，這種以一座城爲中心而城外廣布居民的布局，和河

[①] 湖北省博物館、北京大學考古專業盤龍城發掘隊：《盤龍城一九七四年度田野考古紀要》，《文物》1976 年 2 期。

南鄭州商城是一致的。只是鄭州商城的面積和城外居民活動區的面積都比盤龍城遺址大了 25 倍而已①。北京大學歷史系考古教研室商周組編著的《商周考古》明確認爲盤龍城這樣的遺存就是一個"方國"，而且説："這樣的方國在早商時代應該是不少的。"（見該書 62 頁）根據這種觀點，自然可以把鄭州商城内外的遺存也推定爲一個大了 25 倍的"方國"。但是，鄭州商城遺存總面積也不過 25 平方公里，和傳統中商之"邦畿千里"相差也太遠了，而《商周考古》的作者又是相信有"龐大的商王國"的。於是，問題又只好回到"天子"和"諸侯"的傳統觀念去了。

早在 50 年代，于省吾先生根據甲骨文資料，大膽地突破了傳統觀念，認爲商代諸"方"的關係，可能有相當於古墨西哥阿兹忒克軍事聯盟的一面，試圖把商王從專制君主的傳統形象改變爲軍事聯盟首腦的新形象②。可惜，這一見解在史學界中一直未被重視。當前，由於整個世界史研究的深入，古代東方最早的國家一開始就是專制集權大國的説法已引起越來越多的懷疑。例如，傳統認爲，古埃及第一王朝的第一個王美尼斯就建立了統一的中央集權的專制國家，後來的研究却表明，早王朝初年，不論是上埃及還是下埃及，仍然是分立的許多"斯帕特"（後來希臘語稱爲"諾姆"，即"州"之意）。屬於美尼斯時代的"利比亞人民貢賦調色板"，描寫了聯盟的七個"州"分別攻擊大概是另一個聯盟的七座城。聯盟的首領和其他各州的首領處於平等地位，他領導聯盟的各州對共同敵人進行戰鬥，却不是後來具有無限權力的專制君主③。這種"斯帕特"在前王朝時代已經形成。一個"斯帕特"是小型的奴隸制城邦國家。從希拉康坡里的發掘來看，它正像鄭州商城或盤龍城一樣，也是以城市爲中心而四周有居民活動區的遺址。較小的城邦國家經過城邦聯盟階段而發展成較大的國家，在世界各地歷史中已成爲普遍值得研究的課題了。因此，我想就甲骨文資料所反映的商代諸方國的關係，再作一次研究，爲探討我國古代國家形式的發展提供一些新的綫索。

一、"比"字的考定

本文試圖討論商代的方國之間的軍事聯盟問題。其基本出發點，是卜辭中商

---

① 河南省博物館、鄭州市博物館：《鄭州商代城址發掘簡報》，《文物》1977 年 1 期。
② 于省吾：《從甲骨文看商代社會性質》，《東北人民大學人文科學學報》1957 年 2～3 期。
③ 見《劍橋古代史》，1 卷 2 分册，1971 年英文版，10～11 頁。

王親自"比"某征伐某方，或商王令其下屬"比"某征伐某方的記載，舉例如下：

  王叀侯告比正（征）尸。   （合 6460 正）

  貞：王令帚（婦）好比侯告伐尸。   （合 6480）

這類卜辭中的"比"字，早期甲骨文考釋著作中均釋"从"，後來雖有人改讀爲"比"，但未有定論。小篆从作𠓜，比作𠤎𠤎，《説文》以爲"二人爲从，反从爲比"，從前的文字學家多信從之。後來發現古文字中"从"、"比"二字均正反無別，故《甲骨文編》、《金文編》均以爲"从"與"比"爲一字。島邦男《殷墟卜辭綜類》也仍然以"从"、"比"爲一字。

實際上，甲骨文中"从"、"比"兩字是判然有別的。屈萬里早在 1948 年發表的《甲骨文从、比二字辨》（載《史語所集刊》第 13 本）中指出，"从"字確係从二人，而"比"字則本來並非从人，是从二匕。這一正確的見解，一直沒有得到公認。後來，李孝定在《甲骨文字集釋》中又提過"比字疑當从二匕"（《甲骨文字集釋》2693 頁），張日昇却駁斥説："其説非是。"（《金文詁林》5152 頁）可見這個問題有進一步論證之必要。

"比"字本从二匕，先舉武丁賓組卜辭爲例來證明。

  乙卯卜，㱿，貞：王𠂤望乘伐下𢆉，受屮又。

  貞：王𠂤望乘。   （合 32 正）

  庚辰卜，賓，貞：今𡆥王𠂤望乘伐下𢆉，受…… （合 6491）

凡是武丁賓組卜辭中"比"某征伐某方的"比"字，只有以上三種寫法，即（1）从二𠂤（最常見），（2）从二𠂤（較少見），（3）从二𠂤（最少見）。武丁賓組卜辭中用作先妣之妣的寫法，恰恰也有這樣三類：

  癸未卜，㱿，貞：告于匕己眔匕庚。

  貞：勿告于匕己眔匕庚。   （合 1248 正）

  辛卯卜，賓，貞：隹（唯）匕庚虫（害）……   （《通》別二 10.1）

而且略作統計，也同樣是匕最常見，匕次之，匕最少見。還可以用从匕的𦣞字作旁證，在武丁賓組卜辭中𦣞字所从之匕也是這三種寫法：

  勿令𦣞三百射。   （合 5769 正）

  貞：勿令𦣞田于京。   （合 10919）

  □丑卜，□，貞：叀令𦣞……   （合 4043）

所以，"比"字原从二匕，是不容置疑的。而且，在武丁賓組卜辭中還偶見有以"比"爲先妣之匕的：

　　　　庚申，出于𠂤庚。　　　　　　　　　　　　　　　　　　（合 2450）

可證从二匕的"比"字，確實讀若匕，是根本不能讀爲"从"的。

　　武丁賓組卜辭中的人字，絕大部分作𠂉，間或作𠂊。如伐字作𠇍，疾字作𤶀，所从之人，和匕之作𠤎、𠥌、𠥋也是不相混的。所以，武丁賓組卜辭中的𠤏、𠦫、𠦬等字，分明是从二人，不論正反，都是"从"字，不能讀爲"比"。

　　在字形上分清了武丁賓組卜辭中的"比"、"从"二字後，就可以看出兩者的用法是有嚴格區別的。在"比某伐某方"這類卜辭中，"比"字均从匕，不从人。相反，"从雨"一詞中的"从"字，均从人，不从匕；"从東"、"从西"、"从南"、"从北"等詞中的"从"，也均从人，不从匕。（在《殷墟卜辭綜類》中，由於作者不明武丁賓組卜辭中人、匕之別，摹錯了不少，可核對原著錄。）這些例證就足以說明"比"、"从"二字是可以而且應該區分清楚的。

　　既然"比"、"从"二字在字形和用法上分明是有別的，那爲什麽許多古文字學者至今仍把這兩字混爲一談呢？主要的原因是：在不同時代、不同類別的甲骨文中，人、匕的寫法是有變化的。不少甲骨學者對甲骨分期和分類在文字研究上的重要性認識還不夠，一方面未能就同期、同類卜辭的人、匕寫法細加區別，如武丁賓組卜辭的人和匕本來比較容易區別，但《殷墟卜辭綜類》仍把《存》下 308（即合 6799）、《乙》8132（即合 3521 正）等片上分明是从人、从壬的"任"字，誤歸爲匕壬合文；另一方面又把不同期不同類的卜辭中寫法相近的人和匕混淆起來。例如，《殷墟卜辭綜類》把《存》下 320（即合 5944）這片武丁自組卜辭从人从壬的𠂆字，既歸入"任"字條，又收入"匕壬"條。所以，像《殷墟卜辭綜類》是認爲人、匕兩字在字形上分不開的，哪裏還能區別"从"和"比"呢？

　　上文我們已分析了武丁賓組卜辭中人作𠂉、𠂊，匕作𠤎、𠥌、𠥋，是可以區別的。然而在武丁自組卜辭中人、匕的寫法就不同了：人字寫成𠂉、𠂊（伐字相應作𠇍、𠇘，疾字相應作𤶀、𤶀），匕字則僅見作𠤎者。人和匕的區別，主要只在下部，人字垂直向下，匕字彎曲向旁。所以在武丁自組卜辭中，"从"字作𠤏、𠦫，如：

　　　　己丑卜：舞，庚𠤏雨。允雨。　　　　　　　　　　　　　　（合 20975）
　　　　戊申卜：今日奏舞，出𠦫雨。　　　　　　　　　　　　　　（合 12828）

而"比"字作 𠤎𠤎，如：

□申卜，徣，令🧍𠤎𠤎□侯。　　　　　　　　　　（合20164）

由此可見，自組卜辭人、匕的寫法雖然和賓組卜辭不同，但只要會區別自組卜辭的人和匕，自組卜辭的"从"字和"比"字也是可以區分的。

但是，自組卜辭人、匕的差別既然只在下部，所以刻寫時對匕字的下部往往很強調地向旁彎曲。而賓組卜辭人、匕二字上部的區別就已經很明顯，寫刻時對匕字下部的旁彎就不很強調了。所以賓組作𠂉形的匕字和自組作𠂉形的人字是最容易相混的。如果研究者不懂得區分自組卜辭和賓組卜辭，或區分不精審，就會把自組卜辭中从二人的𠆧和賓組卜辭中从二匕的𠤎𠤎混爲一談，這正是"从"、"比"兩字至今仍被許多研究者視爲一字的癥結所在。

下面我們把王室卜辭各期的人、匕兩字的區別，以及"从"、"比"兩字的區別列成一表。由此表可以看出，只要會區別各期卜辭中人、匕的不同，那麼"从"、"比"兩字的區分是很容易的。

	武丁自組	武丁賓組	祖　庚	祖甲(尹群)	廩辛康丁	武乙文丁	帝乙帝辛
人	𠂉 𠂉	𠂉 𠂉	𠂉	𠂉	𠂉	𠂉 𠂉	𠂉
匕	𠤎	𠤎 𠤎 𠤎	𠤎 𠤎	𠤎	𠤎	𠤎 𠤎	𠤎
从	𠂉𠂉 𠂉𠂉	𠂉𠂉 𠂉𠂉	𠂉𠂉		𠂉𠂉	𠂉𠂉	𠂉𠂉
比	𠤎𠤎	𠤎𠤎 𠤎𠤎 𠤎𠤎	𠤎𠤎		𠤎𠤎	𠤎𠤎	𠤎𠤎

根據以上區別"从"、"比"兩字的原則，在十二種甲骨著録中一共查檢了二百八十八條有"比"的卜辭、八十四條有"从"的卜辭，結果發現，應該寫作"比"字的，有一例寫錯了半個字（合6477正，𠤎𠤎㞢乘），有兩例寫得不夠正確（合811正，𠤎𠤎奚伐𠤎；合6813，多子族𠂉𠂉犬）；應該寫作"从"字的，有一例誤寫爲"比"（合14206反，𠤎𠤎西）。這種只占總數百分之一的例外，顯然只能視爲當時契刻者的疏誤，無法據之以否定"从"、"比"有別的結論。

可見，《說文》"反从爲比"之説固不符實際，認爲古文字中"从"、"比"是一字的長期誤會也應該結束了！

既然"王叀侯告比征尸"這類卜辭中的"比"字是確定無疑的了，這類卜辭的意義應該如何理解呢？《論語》"君子周而不比"，鄭注"阿黨爲比"，則比有結黨之義。但按鄭注所説，似有貶義。其實，《晉語》有"事君者比而不黨"的説

法，可見"比"本身並無貶義。《周禮·形方氏》"大國比小國"注："比猶親也。"《左傳》昭公三年"燕大夫比以殺公之外嬖"杜注："比，相親比。"《楚語》"比爾兄弟親戚"注："比，親也。"以上"比"字均作動詞用，是親密聯合之義。《晉語》："褒姒有寵，生伯服，於是與虢石甫比，逐太子宜臼，而立伯服。"和"王叀侯告比征尸"語法相同。所以，像"王叀侯告比征尸"這樣的句子，字面的意義只是王和侯告聯合征伐尸方，在文辭中王和侯告的地位是相對等的，看不出有什麼主從之別。因此，這類卜辭是證明商王在軍事行動中和其他方國有聯盟關係的基本依據。

二、確定聯盟方國的標準

有"比"的卜辭，不一定都是同別的方國聯合作戰。例如，"丙寅卜，貞：令逆比畫于☉"（《珠》610），其中的畫是人名，是族名還是方國名？就很難確定。所以，要討論方國聯盟問題，首先必須討論一下確定聯盟方國的標準。

第一類：被"比"者明確稱為某方者，當然是聯盟的方國。如：

貞：王比興方伐下☉。　　　　　　　　　　　　　（合 6530 正，據兩條殘辭互相補足）

第二類：被"比"者在原辭中雖未稱為"方"，但根據它辭可知為某方，則可定為聯盟的方國。如：

王勿比鬼。　　　　　　　　　　　　　　　　　　　　　　　　　　（合 6474）

根據它辭有"鬼方易亡囗"（合 8591、8592），可知鬼為方國名。《易·既濟》爻辭："高宗伐鬼方，三年克之。"《殷本紀》記載，紂以西伯、鄂侯、九侯為三公。九侯，《集解》："徐廣曰：一作鬼侯。"則在武丁伐鬼方以後，鬼方就和商結為盟國，一直保持到商末。

第三類：被"比"者稱為某伯，根據卜辭中"盂方伯"、"人方伯"、"羌方伯"等辭例，可知"伯"是方國的首領。故可據之以推定聯盟的方國。如：

貞：王叀𠂤（戠）伯龜比，伐□方……　　　　　　　　　　　　　（合 6480）
乎比井伯——勿乎比井伯。　　　　　　　　　　　　　　　　　　（合 716 正）

井之為方國，卜辭中有"井方"（合 1339、6796），可直接證明。

屬於此類的還有：

辛巳卜，殼，貞：王比易伯兟。　　　　　　　　　　　　　　　　　　（合 3380）

乙酉，貞：王其令⺁以……比魝伯○鷹，屮王事。　　　　　　　　　（補 10516）

己亥卜，在彳（彭），貞：王……亞其比凵伯伐……方；不⻀戕（翦）

在十月又……　　　　　　　　　　　　　　　　　　　　　　　　（合 36346）

第四類：被"比"者在原辭中雖未稱"伯"，但根據它辭可知爲某伯，亦可據之以推定聯盟的方國。如：

貞：呼比彳（彭）告取事。　　　　　　　　　　　　　　　　　　　（合 4555）

根據它辭有"貞：乎取彳（彭）伯——貞：勿乎取彳（彭）伯"（合 6987 正），可知爲方國名。

第五類：被"比"者稱爲某侯，根據前引鬼方之首領稱鬼侯之例，可知"侯"也是方國首領之一種。故可據之以推定聯盟的方國。如：

貞：今……比▢侯虎伐芇方，受屮又。　　　　　　　　　　　　　　（合 6553）

己酉卜，夋，貞：令多子族比犬侯撲周，屮王事，五月。　　　　　　（合 6812 正）

己未貞：王其告，其比▢（崇）侯。　　　　　　　　　　　　　　　（合 32807）

貞：呼比虢（暴）侯。　　　　　　　　　　　　　　　　　　　　　（合 697 正）

第六類：被"比"者在原辭中只稱"侯某"，但根據它辭可確知爲"某侯"，亦可據之推定聯盟的方國。如：

……余步比侯喜征人方……　　　　　　　　　　　　　　　　　　（合 36483）

根據其他同期卜辭中有"攸侯喜"（合 36484），可知侯喜爲攸侯，則可推定攸方是聯盟的方國。

卜辭中還有許多"比侯某"的記載，除前舉之"侯告"外，還有"癸亥卜，王，貞：余比侯專"（合 3346），"呼比侯豖"（合 3353），"王比侯中伐……"（合 32813）等等。根據"▢侯虎"省稱爲"侯虎"（合 10080、3297 正等），"攸侯喜"省稱爲"侯喜"，可知侯後面的一個字是私名，而不是方國名。卜辭中既有"攸侯喜"，又有"攸侯屮"（合 32982），可見不同的私名不一定就是不同方國的侯。因此，只有私名的"侯某"是不能和有方國名的"某侯"並列統計的。

第七類：被"比"者可根據卜辭而定爲"任"，亦可據之以推定聯盟的方

國。如：

> 貞：王□🩻比——勿隹🩻比。　　　　　　　　　　　　（合 13490）

根據"呼羍取🩻任"（合 7859 正）、"呼羍取🩻任伐，⺁（以）"（合 7854 正）可知🩻（肩）爲"任"。任、男古代音同字通，《酒誥》"侯甸男衛邦伯"，《白虎通·爵篇》作"侯甸任衛作國伯"；《夏本紀》"二百里任國"，《漢書·地理志》作"二百里男國"。可見任即男，亦古代方國首領之一種。在卜辭中，"𠕋（䛐）伯"又稱"𠕋（䛐）任"（合 10989 正），也可證"任"是方國首領之稱。則可推定🩻方也是聯盟的方國之一。

第八類：被"比"者在卜辭中未見明確的稱謂，但可用間接方法推定爲聯盟方國。

武丁卜辭中最常見的"比望乘"和"比沚𢦔"即屬此類。在大量的有關望乘和沚𢦔的卜辭中都沒有對他們身份的稱謂。當然根據"貞：伯𢦔執，四月"（合 5945 正）、"甲子卜，其往望，叀伯令"（合 26993）都可以推測他們是"伯"，或者把合 8408 讀成"丁卯，貞：望、🔶多方……"則可定望爲"方"，但這種解讀法都可以引起爭議。然而，有一點是可以肯定的：武丁卜辭中㚔、雀、婦好、子𠭯（商）等人地位頗高，也都參加征伐，但從未見到過"王比㚔"、"王比雀"、"王比婦好"、"王比子𠭯（商）"這類記載。而對望乘和沚𢦔，則經常稱"王比望乘"、"王比沚𢦔"，並有明確稱"王自比望乘"（合 7528）的例子。可見在征伐活動中，他們和商王是處於對等地位的。所以，把他們理解爲商王屬下的將領是不妥的，望、沚應該和前舉各類例子一樣，是和商王聯盟的方國名。又如：

> 癸丑卜，亙，貞：王比奚伐🔶方。　　　　　　　　　　（合 811 正）

卜辭中雖未見"奚方"，但于省吾先生已考定奚爲辮髮民族，非商之同族，故亦可推定其爲和商曾有聯盟行動的方國。

綜上所述，卜辭確實反映出商代有許多方國和商王發生聯盟關係。可考知者已有興、鬼、𠕋（䛐）、井、易、鈇、⺁、𢆉（彭）、🔶、犬、🔶（崇）、暴、攸、🩻（肩）、望、沚、奚等"方"。絕大多數這類卜辭都明確地涉及征伐，所以説，商代是存在着方國間的軍事聯盟的。

商王既然和不少方國有聯盟關係，當然可以推想在和商王敵對的諸方國之間，也是存在着同樣的聯盟的。卜辭在這方面也提供了某些線索。如武丁卜辭有"丙辰卜，殼，貞：🩻方⺁（以）䳂方羍吕、允……"（合 8610 正），如以"㚔以眾

伐𢀛方"等辭例對比，上辭當是𢀛方領着䝞方辜伐呂地之意，可推測在這一行動中𢀛方和䝞方是聯盟者。又如乙辛卜辭有："……晉叡方、羌方、羞方、䜌方，余其比侯、田甾𢦔四邦方"（合36528反），可推測被伐的四個方國也是一個聯盟。

用這種觀點去看典籍記載，如《殷本紀》叙成湯率諸侯伐桀，應當就是成湯組織一個軍事聯盟去攻打桀。而《詩·長發》所謂"韋、顧既伐，昆吾、夏桀"，則反映夏桀方面也有一個包括顧、韋、昆吾等方國的聯盟。[武丁卜辭中有"貞：呼取雇伯"（合13925正），可證顧方在商代猶存。]又如《牧誓》之叙武王伐紂，有"友邦冢君"庸、蜀、羌、髳、微、盧、彭、濮等參加，也是一個方國軍事聯盟。而後來周公東征所遇到的敵人，則是商的殘餘力量在東方重新組織起來的軍事聯盟。可見有商一代的歷史自始至終貫穿着方國聯盟的問題，是值得認真研究的。

三、聯盟的形成和聯盟諸方國的關係

摩爾根在論阿兹忒克軍事聯盟時指出："這一聯合可説是他們從前互相争鬥的結果。"[1]商代方國聯盟的形成也大體如此。前面在談到鬼方時，已經參照典籍記載指出鬼方和商的結盟，可能是武丁和鬼方三年作戰的結果。這類情形，在卜辭本身也有所反映。例如，武丁時卜辭有：

癸巳卜，殼，貞：呼雀伐望……　　　　　　　　　　　　　　　　（合6983）

令𢀛沚。　　　　　　　　　　　　　　　　　　　　　　　　　（合21035）

最後一辭中的𢀛即伐，由合6834正"庚申卜，王，貞：余伐不"伐字同一版上或作𢀛、或作𢀛，可證。可見武丁時期的"比望乘"、"比沚𢦔"也是互相鬥争的結果。當然，也可以設想相反的情況，即本來互相聯盟的方國又轉爲互相争鬥，例如前舉武王伐紂時的同盟方國——微，很可能就是武丁時和商王聯盟的"𢀛伯"。可見，方國聯盟不僅是前一時期方國間互相鬥争的結果，又隨着鬥争形勢的發展而變化。所以，方國聯盟只是一種在某段時間内保持相對穩定的共同體。

從片斷的卜辭可以作一個大膽的推測，武丁之所以成爲商代的中興名王，通

---

[1] 莫（摩）爾根：《古代社會》，生活·讀書·新知三聯書店，1957年，214頁。

過軍事勝利而擴大方國聯盟應是其主要功業之一。在屬於比武丁賓組卜辭時代更早的自組卜辭中，我們見到如下記載：

　　　壬午卜，自，貞：乎禦方于商。　　　　　　　　　　　　　　　（合 20450）

　　　□巳卜，王，貞：于中商呼禦方。　　　　　　　　　　　　　　（合 20453）

　　　癸亥卜，王：方其章大邑。　　　　　　　　　　　　　　　　　（合 6783）

按"禦方"一詞卜辭習見。郭沫若、陳夢家均以禦方爲方國名，是不對的。所引以爲證的"太公望令禦方來"（《逸周書·世俘》），實際也是命令太公望抵禦"方來"之意（可參看顧頡剛《逸周書世俘篇集訓校釋》）。"禦方于某地"和"禦羌于某地"辭例相同，是抵禦"方"的意思。"方"是武丁時代的一個重要敵國，其言商、中商或大邑，當即後來卜辭中所謂"大邑商"。可見當時商之邊防能力頗弱，故"方"能長驅直入而至商的腹地。在賓組卜辭中，仍有"方"的記載，如"乙巳卜，爭，貞：告方出于祖乙于大……"（合 651）但只有"□辰卜，賓，貞：方圣井方"（合 6796）、"貞：方允其來于沚"（合 6728）等爲禍於聯盟方國的記載，而未見有深入商本土的例子。這可能就是因爲武丁後期軍事聯盟的發展，商本土的周圍均有聯盟方國爲其屏障。這些聯盟方國可考知大體方位者，如"丁酉，允有來媿（艱）自西，沚聝告曰：土方征于我東鄙，（戔）二邑；𠂤方亦牧（侵）我西鄙田"（合 6057 正）。則沚方在商本土之西。又如侯告，王常比其伐尸（合 6457 正、6460 正、6480、33039），則其方國當在商本土之東。鬼方，據後世隗姓分布區推測，當在商本土之西北。𠂤方，據卜辭中常比其撲周（合 6816、6817）、伐兒（合 6553），當在商本土之西南（按于省吾先生認爲兒方即《牧誓》中之髳，詳見《甲骨文字釋林·釋兒》）。環繞着商本土的聯盟方國，顯然有利於商本土的和平繁榮。《左傳》昭公二十三年記載："楚囊瓦爲令尹，城郢。沈尹戌曰：子常必亡郢。苟不能衛，城之無益也。古者，天子守在四夷，天子卑，守在諸侯。諸侯守在四鄰；諸侯卑，守在四竟。慎其四竟，結其四援，民狎其野，三務成功，民無內憂，而又無外懼，國焉用城。"沈尹戌的這段話，不能說是完全沒有歷史根據的。

所謂天子"守在諸侯"的歷史真實背景，就是方國聯盟的盟主以盟國爲軍事屏障。商代甲骨文中未見"天子"一稱，商的最高統治者的名號是"王"。我在《說王》一文中提出過，王字本象斧鉞形，是表示軍事統率權的。古代以斧鉞爲軍事統帥的權杖，近來河北平山戰國中山王墓出土的一件銅鉞上鑄有"作兹軍鈇

（斧），以敬（警）厥衆"之銘，是新添的一個有力實證。而王字本象斧鉞形，合32444"成求王"一辭中王字作🔣，是一個直接證明。在金文中，豎立的鉞作🔣，橫置的鉞作🔣、🔣者習見，不煩一一舉證。如集成5465尊銘中的🔣字，上部所從之🔣和🔣字無異。由此可知王字初形即爲橫置之鉞，武丁卜辭中通行的🔣字是已經簡化了的。① 總之"王"的本義應該就是軍事總指揮，和"天子"的概念是根本不同的。結合商代實際存在的方國軍事聯盟來看，與商王結盟的其他方國首領都只稱"伯"、"侯"、"任"而不稱"王"，那末可以斷言，商代的"王"的實際意義顯然並不是指某一方國的軍事首領，而是方國聯盟的最高軍事統帥。摩爾根在叙述阿兹忒克聯盟時寫道："關於任何地方自治事件各部落②都是獨立的，但是在對外關係上，不拘是攻或守，三個部落則是一個整體。雖然各部落各有其酋長會議及領袖軍務酋長，但阿兹忒克的軍務酋長則是聯盟軍的總指揮官。"看來，商王也正是這樣的"聯盟軍的總指揮官"。

　　上文已經説過，商王和聯盟方國共同征伐中一般均用"比"的説法，反映了一種地位上的對等性。但這是和商王對㠱、雀、婦好、子𡚬（商）等人從來不稱"比"這一點相對而言的。在有關征伐的卜辭中，偶爾也可以見到商王對聯盟方國的首領使用"令"這個詞，如：

　　　　癸卯卜，賓，貞：叀甶（甫）呼，令沚蚩（害）𠦪方七月。　　　　（合6623）

　　　　庚辰，貞：令望乘伐🔣方。　　　　　　　　　　　　　　　（合32899）

　　　　癸亥，貞：王令🔣侯伐……　　　　　　　　　　　　　　　（合41499）

在不涉及征伐的卜辭中，商王對諸方國首領用"呼"、"令"這個詞還有不少例子，就不一一列舉了。這正反映了商王是聯盟的盟主。

　　從卜辭看來，商王作爲聯盟的盟主，有以下權力是值得注意的。

（1）徵取貢物

　　關於興方有：

　　　　亡取專、興。　　　　　　　　　　　　　　　　　　　　　（合21746）

---

① 附帶説一下，胡厚宣先生説該字爲"我王"合文。我們知道，在武丁王室卜辭中，"我"字一律作🔣，在從我旁的字如🔣、🔣、🔣、🔣中也均作🔣形。只有子卜辭中才有作🔣形的。"成求🔣"一辭是武丁王室卜辭，顯然不是子卜辭。如果是"我王"合文，應作🔣才對，既然作🔣，是無法釋爲"我王"合文的。

② 本文作者按：摩爾根把古墨西哥的城邦國家説成是"部落"，是不妥的，詳後文。

壬寅卜，殻，貞：興方⚑（以）羌，用自上甲至于下乙。　　　　（合 270 正）

關於⚑（臶）方有：

　　戊午卜，⚑（臶）弗其⚑（以）我史女不。　　　　　　　　　　（合 673）

關於⚑（彭）方有：

　　貞：呼取⚑（彭）伯。　　　　　　　　　　　　　　　　　　　（合 6987 正）

關於⚑方有：

　　己酉卜，殻，貞：勿呼⚑取⚑任，伐弗其⚑（以）。　　　　　　（合 7854 正）

關於夒方有：

　　甲辰卜，殻□：夒來白馬？王固曰：吉，其來。　　　　　　　　（合 9177 正）
　　貞：今⚑夒不其來牛。　　　　　　　　　　　　　　　　　　　（合 9178 乙）

關於望方有：

　　丁亥貞：用望乘以羌自上甲。　　　　　　　　　　　　　　　　（合 32021）

從有明確記載的"貢物"來看，是牲口、女子和用作人牲的"羌"、"伐"。後代所謂天子班貢、諸侯助祭，當與此有聯繫。像阿茲忒克聯盟那樣按一定比例分配戰利品，在卜辭中尚無直接證據。因爲在卜辭中只見到聯盟國家單方面向商王貢納，而王對於聯盟方國則稱"賞"〔如"王弜商望"（合 32968）〕，可能聯盟諸方按比例分配戰利品已演變爲聯盟方國將戰利品之部分獻給"王"。周代各諸侯國戰勝之後，向周天子或霸主獻俘告捷，也可能是這種習慣的遺迹。

（2）入境狩獵

　　戊子卜，賓，貞：王逐麋于汕，亡災。之日王往逐麋于汕，允亡災，隻（獲）麋八。
　　　　　　　　　　　　　　　　　　　　　　　　　　　　　　　（合 9572）
　　己未卜，雀隻（獲）虎。弗隻。一月，在⚑（臶）。　　　　　　（合 10201）
　　貞：在攸田戈其來告。　　　　　　　　　　　　　　　　　　　（合 10989 正）

後代典籍如《孟子·梁惠王下》說："天子適諸侯曰巡狩。"看來，巡狩就是起源於方國聯盟之盟主到聯盟各國去打獵。孟子以爲"巡狩者，巡所守也"，殆非本義。

最後，想結合文獻記載，討論一下軍事聯盟盟主的另一種權力——仲裁和懲罰的權力。

作爲軍事聯盟的總指揮官，在軍事行動時對全軍操有生殺大權，這在《牧誓》中看得很清楚，就不多說了。在日常事務中，方國聯盟的盟主對諸方國之間的糾紛也有仲裁權。像周在西土逐漸建立與商對立的聯盟這一過程中，"虞、芮質厥成"就是一件重大的事情，故在《詩·綿》中加以歌頌。孟子說，啓之所以能代益爲"天子"，是因爲"朝覲訟獄者不之益而之啓"，也反映了同類的情況。于省吾在《從甲骨文看商代社會性質》一文中提出，卜辭中習見的"王聑（聽）"是聽訟，是很值得重視的看法。在較晚的文獻中仍可看到春秋時代的盟主對各盟國之間的糾紛有仲裁權，甚至可以對一些國君加以處罰。如《左傳》襄公十六年記載晉平公在溴梁會諸侯，"命歸侵田，以我（按指魯）故，執邾宣公、莒犁比公"就是一例。春秋時代的這種盟主處罰國君的做法仍然同干涉別國內政是有別的。卜辭中如"己巳卜，王、貞：其執屵任？六月，允執"（合 5944），亦應是拘執聯盟方國的首領。所以，《殷本紀》所述紂之幽西伯、醢九（鬼）侯、脯鄂侯，固然是對盟主權力的濫用，但若據此而以紂爲專制帝王，顯然是一種誤會。

四、方國聯盟和"諸侯"的由來

相信商代有龐大的專制國家，往往和傳統的天子分封諸侯的說法有關。孟子說古代有公侯伯子男五等爵制，至今史學界也仍然有人是信以爲真的。

從甲骨文來看，孟子所說的五等爵制在商代是根本不存在的。胡厚宣先生早年在《殷代封建制度考》中實際上只是列舉了甲骨文中所見的稱謂和五等爵的爵號有相合的表面現象。

甲骨文中"公"這個稱謂雖然頗常見，但只有用作先公之公，沒有一條是可以確定爲生者之爵稱的。甲骨文中的"伯"和"子"，確是對生者使用的稱號，但都是通用的尊號，而非等級性的封爵。因爲，直到周代金文中，伯和子仍是通用性尊號，而不是封爵之專號，楊樹達先生早已詳細列舉證據，在此就不再贅述了。

根據金文來看，"諸侯"是周代確實存在的一種概念，但周初的諸侯只有三

種。令方彝銘：“明公告至于成周，徣令舍三事令、眾鄉事寮、眾諸尹、眾里君、眾百工、眾諸侯：侯、田、男。”大盂鼎銘則只舉了兩種：“唯殷邊侯、田、雩殷正百辟，率肄于酒。”

在甲骨文中，"侯"這一稱謂很常見。前文已經舉出許多王比某侯和王比侯某的例子，可見侯是聯盟方國首領的一種專用稱號。

"男"在甲骨文中作"任"（甲骨文中另有男字，但均無法確定爲爵稱），前文已舉過王比肩任的例子；而且，王所比的 ⌇（鹹）伯，也稱"⌇（鹹）任"（合10989 正）。此外，還見有：

  貞：呼取⌇任。   （合 13934 正）
  貞：呼取⌇任于⌇。   （合 1248 正）
  丁卯卜，曰蔷任出咸歸？允咸。   （合 7049 正）
  己巳卜，王，貞：史其執岢任？六月，允執。 （合 5944）
  ……多任……   （合 19034）

足見"任"也是對聯盟方國首領的一種專用稱號。

"田"這一稱謂在甲骨文第一至三期未見，第四期卜辭有"以多田、亞、任"（合 32992 正，按：《合集》將之誤爲反），是和亞、任這兩種身份性稱謂相並舉的。第 5 期卜辭中"田"這一稱謂較多見。如：

  余其比多田于多伯征盂方白蚩。   （合 36511）
  ……比多田于多伯征盂……   （合 36513）
  ……比多田……盂方伯……   （合 36521）
  余其比侯田甾戋四邦方。   （合 36528 反）
  余其[比]……田甾征盂方……   （合 36514）

因爲在武乙以前的卜辭中迄今未見"田"這一稱謂，推想"田"是一個較晚發生的稱號。

總之，周初金文中所見的三種諸侯稱號，在卜辭中都存在，而且又恰恰都是王在征伐中所比的對象。這不能不使人想到，實際存在過的諸侯制度正是源自方國軍事聯盟制度。

這種實際存在過的制度，在較晚的典籍中是以"服"的名義來描述的。《周語》記載：“夫先王之制，邦內甸服，邦外侯服，侯衛賓服，夷蠻要服，戎狄荒服。”《禹貢》説得更詳細：“五百里甸服：百里賦納總，二百里納銍，三百里納秸服，

四百里粟，五百里米。五百里侯服：百里采，二百里任服①，三百里諸侯。……"當然，那時天子"邦畿千里"的説法已經流行，而且把天下五百里、五百里地整齊劃一起來，顯然是理想化的説法，但畢竟還是保存了"諸侯：侯、田（甸）、男（任）"的真實内核。按《禹貢》的説法，還可以看出任（男）是包括在侯服之中的，故大盂鼎只稱"殷邊侯田"，想來是把任（男）包括在侯之内而言的。

按照《周語》和《禹貢》的説法，甸（田）服是在邦内的，而且似乎不在"諸侯"之列。這種説法，同令方彝把侯、田、男並列爲諸侯是不合的，也和大盂鼎稱"殷邊侯田"不符。《左傳》桓公二年稱"今晉，甸侯也"，是甸（田）亦諸侯之證。不過據此推斷"田"在地域上應更接近"王"（即後世稱爲"天子"者）的本土，是合乎情理的。

在《左傳》和《國語》中，也有一些證據可證明周初諸侯本來只有侯、田、男三種。除上引"今晉，甸侯也"一語可推知晉之始封本爲"田"之外，《左傳》定公四年云："曹，文之昭也；晉，武之穆也，曹爲伯甸，非尚年也。"可推知曹之始封亦爲"田"。又《左傳》昭公十三年："子産爭承，曰：昔天子班貢，輕重以列，列尊貢重，周之制也，卑而貢重者，甸服也。鄭伯，男也，而使從公侯之貢，懼弗給也。"《周語》亦云："鄭伯南也，王而卑之，是不尊貴也。"南、男是同音假借字，可推知鄭之始封爲男（任）。後代注疏家惑於五等爵之成説，面對這種反映古代實際諸侯制度的記載反而迷惑不解，所以鬧了不少笑話，却仍然難以自圓其説。

從《左傳》和《國語》的上述記載作邏輯推理，周初的侯、田、男是有等級差別的。男的地位不是最低，故曰："王而卑之，是不尊貴也。"又據"卑而貢重者，甸服也"，可知甸（田）的地位比男低。但男的地位也不是最高的，因此子產可據"列尊貢重"爲理由而要求不從"公侯之貢"，可見侯比男的地位高。所以周初實際存在的是三等爵制：侯、男、田。由此而上推商代，在方國聯盟首領的地位上也可能已形成了這種差別。

爲什麽"田"等級最低而貢反而重呢？從《禹貢》本文來看，甸是要向天子交納農作物，侯和任（男）則没有這種義務。後代注家如《職方氏》孔晁注："甸，田也，治田入穀。"《王制》鄭玄注："服治田，出穀税。"均無異説。在甲骨文中有許多貢納的記載，武丁時代卜辭中有關貢納的尤多，却尚未發現過一條聯盟方國向商王貢納穀物的記載。只有商王呼令本土内的臣屬治田的記載，如：

---

① 按《職方氏》作"男服"、《夏本紀》作"任國"、《漢書·地理志》作"男國"。

丁酉卜，㱿，貞：呼畾（甫）秬于姛，受㞢年。

畾（甫）秬于姛，受年。　　　　　　　　　　　　　　　　（合13505正）

庚戌卜，□，貞：王呼黍在姛，受㞢年。　　　　　　　　　（合9517）

貞：呼雷秬于名。　　　　　　　　　　　　　　　　　　　（合14正）

辛丑卜，殷，貞：婦姘呼黍［于］商。　　　　　　　　　　（合9530正）

乙卯……貞：呼……田于𡿨，受年。　　　　　　　　　　　（合9556）

壬戌卜，王，貞：令雀田于……　　　　　　　　　　　　　（合10567）

……雀步于𡿨。　　　　　　　　　　　　　　　　　　　　（合13514正甲）

這種被呼令參加服田事的人物，往往同時又有呼令其參加征伐的記載。在這種人物中，如雀是有作"亞雀"的（參《殷墟卜辭綜類》237頁"亞雀"條），可知其身份當爲"亞"。推測第四期卜辭中始見第五期卜辭中常見的"田"，可能就是從這類原在商本土內自有邑落和領地的人物中發展起來的。第四期卜辭中"多田、亞、任"並舉，西周金文中"諸侯、大亞"並舉（見䚄簋），爲"田"這種諸侯是從有勢力的"亞"所發展而成的推測提供了初步綫索。至於他們怎樣從直接爲王服田而發展成"入穀"，尚有待今後進一步探究。不過，從第五期卜辭中多田和多亞並舉，或田、侯並舉，而且在征伐中取得了與王相比的地位，顯然已有了更大的獨立性。當然，這種從商本土分化出去的新的"諸侯"，不應只限於"田"。因爲，根據金文中"族徽"的研究，商代的異侯，就是從本來是"亞"的亞吴族獨立出去的（詳拙作《關於早期銅器銘文的幾個問題》）。

　　根據以上分析，可以看出，周初肯定已經存在的"諸侯"一詞，在起源上實際是由兩條途徑形成的。一方面，是由本來分立的諸方國，在互相鬥爭的過程中結成有相對穩定性的主要是軍事性的聯盟。在這種聯盟的發展過程中，加盟各國從平等成員的地位逐漸變爲盟主——"王"的諸侯。另一方面，是由母方國逐漸分化出取得相對獨立地位的子方國，它們作爲母方國的天然同盟者，也成爲母方國的"王"的諸侯。只有在後一種情況下，才可能有真正意義的"裂土分封"。當然，不能排除像希臘的殖民城邦或周初大封建那樣的遠離母方國本土而去建立新的子方國的可能性。

　　在西周金文中已經有實際證據說明當時的"王"認爲自己是天的兒子，即"天子"，所以"天子"和"諸侯"都是古代實際存在過的概念。但如果認爲自古以來就有至高無上的"天子"，把先秦時代的國家組織形式按"天子分封諸侯"的傳統觀念描繪成龐大的專制國家，離歷史真相實在是相差太遠了。

五、方國聯盟的實質

　　商代甲骨文中所見的"方"，究竟是部落還是進入階級社會的國家，是不能一概而論的。考慮到北方和西方廣大地區的各游牧集團也可能被商人稱爲"方"，則"方"不一定都是進入階級社會的國家。但在中原地區，如河南鄭州商城遺存、湖北黄陂盤龍城遺存、山西夏縣東下馮商城遺存等二里崗期考古遺存表明，在早於殷墟甲骨文的時代，無疑已存在着衆多的以頗大的城市爲中心的城邦國家了。從甲骨文來看，商本身顯然已進入了階級社會，並有官吏、監獄、常備軍等國家機器。所以甲骨文所反映的以商本土爲核心的方國聯盟，其實質應是城邦國家聯盟，不應視爲部落聯盟。

　　于省吾當年把商代的方國聯盟同阿兹忒克聯盟對照的做法，是否錯了呢？我認爲，這種對照本身是没有錯誤的。阿兹忒克聯盟的原始資料是西班牙作家報道的，摩爾根批判他們"曾採用了一種謬誤的見解，以爲阿兹忒克的政治在本質上是和歐洲現存的諸君主國全然相同的一種君主制"，所以現存的阿兹忒克聯盟的文獻報道是一種歪曲的報道，正像我國封建時代的人去描寫商代的歷史是歪曲了的一樣。但是，摩爾根又過分誇大了阿兹忒克人報道中有關氏族制度和原始民主的一面，把阿兹忒克聯盟描述爲部落聯盟，這實際上是矯枉過正了。根據西班牙作家的報道，當時在所謂氏族成員即普通平民之下，已經出現了奴隸和無產者，甚至提到了債務奴隸的存在。在氏族成員之上已出現了貴族武士階級，有了專門的僧侶，有了終身甚至變成世襲的官職。全民動員時的軍隊雖和血緣組織仍有密切關係，但也有了特殊的常備軍。這些情況都是和甲骨文反映的商代社會很接近的。所以，所謂"墨西哥王國"和"墨西哥帝國"，正像我們現在歷史著作上所説的"商王國"一樣，既不應該按封建時代君主國的模式去理解，也不應該認作部落聯盟，而是在城邦國家基礎上結成的城邦國家聯盟。

　　商代的方國究竟有多大，這個問題目前還難有十分明確的結論。當然，不能刻板地把"城邦國家"理解爲只有一個城市而周圍均爲農村。商代的一個方國可能在發展中建造起相當數量的"邑"，而且各方國領土的大小也允許有相當大的差别。考古學成果表明，以小屯式陶器爲代表的晚期商文化的主要分布區，僅佔有河南北部和河北南部，這和吴起所説的"殷紂之國，左孟門，右太行，常山在

其北，大河經其南"（《史記·吳起傳》）是基本一致的。如果考慮到在這一地區內還可能有商所分建的侯、田之"方"，則商作爲方國來說，本土是不會太大的。這和周早期本土僅在周原，而後直接統治的地區也不過擴大到豐鎬一帶，是相似的。

商在中國歷史上被作爲一個王朝，實際上不過是一個方國的王朝，至多是一個較强大的方國聯盟的王朝。商王朝覆滅的主要原因，除商方國的内部矛盾之外，是因爲它和它的重要聯盟方國：周、鬼、鄂關係破裂而被孤立。周却在西方組織了一個新的强大的聯盟。所以，在那個時代，能否保持王權的根本之點，就是能否維持一個穩定而强有力的方國聯盟。武王伐紂之所以速戰速决，是因爲打擊的只是一個本土有限的商方，而伐紂之後商的本土也没有併入遠在西方的周，只是盟主的地位轉入了周的手中而已。直到春秋時代的所謂"爭霸"，實質上仍然是在方國林立的原有基礎上不斷試圖結成新的方國聯盟，涌現出一個個新的盟主。只是在事情發展到兼併其他方國的領土和建立郡縣制度的時候，方國聯盟這種國家組織形式才逐漸被更大的統一國家所取代，結束了我國中原歷史上的城邦國家時代。

當然，用片斷而殘缺的甲骨文資料去恢復商代歷史，往往會"失之毫釐，謬以千里"。因此對本文所描述的商代方國聯盟的圖景，我也並不敢十分自信。但這一研究至少説明，要抛開東方專制大國的模式而從新的角度來考慮商代的國家組織形式，不但和甲骨文資料不相抵觸，倒可能是更相符的。那麽，爲什麽不可以希望有更多的同志打破傳統的框子來作新的嘗試呢？

1980 年 7 月 3 日

按語：

文中在討論確定聯盟方國的標準時，所舉第三類中除井伯外還有丹伯，實際甲骨文中井字和丹字同形轉注，故删去丹伯條（在總結聯盟方國一小節中也删去"丹"這個方國名）。又，所舉第七類實例有誤，是把點 ⿳ 和 ⿱ 都釋爲囧造成的。"⿱方"才是聯盟方國之一。

寫此文時，我還不知道甲骨文中的 ⼺ 和 ⼻（彡）是不同的兩個字，因爲甲骨文中實際存在的"⼺伯"，便造出一個甲骨文中並不存在的"⼻伯"，推論武王伐紂時周的同盟方國——微，在武丁時是和商王聯盟的。這當然是錯的。

文中第三部分在論證商王的聯盟方國是互相鬥爭的結果時，引用了鐵181·3（即合6979）"雀往征犬"，證商王"比犬侯"也是鬥爭的結果。其實"雀往征犬"是"征豕"之誤讀，與"犬方"無涉，今删去。

寫此文時，我還没認識到歷組卜辭的時代應該提早到武丁到祖甲時代，出現"多田、亞、任"的合32992是歷組二類卜辭，應該不晚於祖庚、祖甲時代。而且師賓間組卜辭合6963、補2240都有"侯、任"並舉現象，賓組卜辭合19034有"多任"，則任在武丁時已經存在。並非文中所言要武乙時才出現。而且，關於"甸"的產生，並非商王派去墾田的人都會發展爲"甸"，應以裘錫圭《甲骨卜辭中所見"田""牧""衛"等職官的研究》所論爲是。

該文把方國説成是"城邦國家"，是不够確切的。在我後來寫的《關於中國早期國家形式的幾個問題》一文中，才較詳細地討論了與希臘城邦不同的"都鄙制"國家的產生、發展和聯合體的形成。

原載《古文字研究》第6輯，中華書局，1981年；收入《林澐學術文集》，中國大百科全書出版社，1998年；又收入《林澐文集·古史卷》，上海古籍出版社，2019年。今據後者收入。

常正光

"辰爲商星"解
——釋"辰、辳、農"

"辰爲商星"是一段神話故事裏的一項結語,記載在《左傳·昭公元年》裏。這是鄭子產出使於晉探望晉侯病症時,回答晉叔向問及爲崇晉侯的實沈、臺駘究屬何神而講的神話。神話本身雖然並不一定具有什麼意義,但是透過神話所反映的歷史實際與天文學史上的成就却值得注意。本文就這一問題試加探討。

作爲十二支之一的"辰",自殷代用於干支紀日以來,便成爲最常見的一個字。就是這樣一個普通字,曾在中國古代天文學史的研究中佔有重要的地位。宋代沈括曾試圖對"辰"字進行探討①,以便弄清天文學史上的一些問題;近世以及當代的中外天文史學者也對這項研究頗爲重視,認爲"……倘若能够瞭解字(指辰字)的意義和來歷,就可以明白上古天文學的大概"②。因此,探明"辰"字的源與流,辨析其本義與引申義的發展變化,無論從古文字學或天文學史的研究來說都是有意義的。

"辰"字早在東漢時期許慎作《說文解字》時,就已經對於其所象者究爲何事何物弄不清了。許慎根據小篆字形認爲這是會意兼聲的字③,把它肢解爲四個部份反復說解還是沒有解釋通。近世以及當代研究甲骨文、金文的中外學者,多數仍然墨守《說文》,有的認爲是"象雷電振動",有的認爲是"象龍之首足鱗甲形"。④這

---

① 沈括:《夢溪筆談》卷七。
② 陳遵嬀:《中國古代天文學簡史》頁82。新城新藏《東洋天文學史》頁4也有類似說法。
③ 許慎:《說文解字》卷十四下:"辰,震也。三月陽氣動,雷電振,民農時也,物皆生。从乙,匕。匕,象芒達;厂聲;辰,房星,天時也,从二。二,古文上字。"
④ 周法高:《金文詁林》頁8278。

些説法都是不可靠的。郭沫若根據甲骨文認爲是農具，"其作貝壳形者蓋蜃器也。其作磬折形者則爲石器"①是接觸到了實際。但是爲什麽一個"辰"字却有二象呢？也是語焉不詳。

甲骨文裏的"辰"字早期作"丙"形，其中所從的"厂"，確與出土的殷代玉磬作"⌒"形者很相近②，難免要使人誤認爲是象磬折形的，但是早期的磬並不是折形而是具有半圓弧作"⌒"形③，而且原始樂器多是在利用生産工具的基礎上發展起來的。磬又是從何種工具發展而來呢？所以如果説"辰"字象磬折形，既不是早期磬形的實際，而且也没有反映出所象的最原始工具究竟是什麽。另一方面對於"辰"字作"厂"形的折角，也要考慮到甲骨文爲求刀筆契刻之便，經常把圓弧形的字刻成折角。如"日"字本爲圓形，却有很多是刻成四角的方形或多角形，特别是"月"字本來是具有圓弧形的一鉤彎月，有的在後期竟然刻成近似磬折形而作"〉"。因此我們就應當透過"辰"字所從的折角形看出它本來具有的圓弧。徐中舒老師就是這樣不爲演變後的字形所限，在研究出土文物的基礎上，指出"辰"字的原始形象。

徐中舒老師指出："辰"字所從的"厂"，本是收割禾穗的蚌鐮或石鐮作"⌒"形，書寫時爲求行款整齊而改作"⊲"形，而其圓弧形的刃部也在長期契刻過程中演變爲磬折形而作"厂"。鐮，本是套在拇指上用來掐斷禾穗的，穿過其背部的雙孔附有繩索以便緊套住手指，於是使用"戶"形來表現，這樣再與手連結起來就構成完整的"丙"字了。因此應該説"辰"字是象套在手指上的鐮。

"辰"是鐮，更確切地説，原始的"辰"應該是蚌鐮。因爲"辰"的得名是由"蜃"而來的，二字古音相同，郭沫若指出："辰與蜃在古當係一字"。④蜃是大蛤，"辰"既是蛤蚌，又是代表用蚌殼做的農具。原始的蚌製農具也是構成商族文化的一種特點。

商族是在龍山文化地區發展起來的。龍山文化的中心區是"圍繞着泰山的許多小河河谷丘陵高地"⑤。它與峙立於西方黄土高原上發展起來的仰韶文化東西遥遥相對，各自形成獨立的文化體系。從泰山脚下直到太行山麓，古時曾是一片

---

① 郭沫若：《甲骨文字研究》，《釋干支》頁 25。
② 于省吾：《雙劍誃古器物圖録》玉磬。
③ 參見武官村大墓出土的虎紋大石磬形，據：《中國考古學報》第五册。又據：常任俠：《古磬》，《文物》1978 年第 7 期。
④ 郭沫若：《甲骨文字研究》，《釋干支》頁 25。
⑤ 徐中舒：《試論周代田制及其社會性質》，《中國的奴隸制與封建制分期問題論文選集》頁 445。

廣大的沮洳藪澤地區。商族生活在這片沼澤地區的東部邊緣一帶，不僅是氣候溫暖，灌莽叢生，草木繁茂，鳥獸集聚；而且由於這裏在地質史上是一條沉降地帶，它與新華夏構造體系第二條巨大隆起帶緊密相鄰，距離海浸綫較近，因而水生生物也極爲豐富，魚鱉螺蛤的游息孳生更是得天獨厚的。

這樣的自然條件，使商族的祖先能夠比較容易地獲得生活資料，在漁獵的同時，還可以采集螺蛤以資補充。《韓非子·五蠹》所說的"太古之初……近水則食魚鱉螺蛤"，也只有商族所居住的這類鄰近沼澤的地區才更有可能。進入母系氏族公社出現原始農業生產之後，這裏還能夠比較容易地得到生產工具。因爲采集蛤蚌頗爲方便，只要把食後棄置的蚌壳稍爲加工便是適用的農具。《淮南子·氾論訓》所說的"摩蜃而耨"也應該說是對古代商族製作農具情況的追憶和描述。

隨着以辰（蜃）爲原始農具的農業生產逐步發展，也推動了農具的改進與發展。可以看出，後世所用的銚、鎒、銍、鐮等幾種農具，就是在辰的基礎上發展起來的。

銚是周秦時期的常用農具。關於銚和辰的關係，在《爾雅·釋魚》裏是說"蜃小者珧"，認爲蜃與珧在古代是同物異名，有時還連稱爲"蜃珧"，如《山海經·東山經》就說"激女之水多蜃珧"。在《說文》裏還認爲珧是專指蚌壳，釋爲"珧，蜃甲也"。蚌壳因其晶瑩如玉，所以古時"珧"字的偏旁也從"玉"；當磨製蚌壳用爲工具並演進爲石製乃至金屬製的以後，便把由珧而得名的農具改從"金"字偏旁而寫成"銚"。銚就是《詩·臣工》"庤乃錢鎛"的"錢"，在《爾雅·釋器》裏又叫做"斛"，郭璞注"即古鍬、臿字"。《釋名》說："錊（臿），插也，插地起土也。或曰銷。銷，削也，能有所穿刺也。"可見銚在古代是由辰演進的掘地起土的農具。

鎒就是鋤。"摩蜃而耨"的"耨"作動詞用，指除草。古代漢語中多有動詞與名詞不分，因此除草的工具也叫做"耨"，後世爲了區別才加偏旁寫作"槈"或"鎒"，用以表示農具的專名。鎒就是"庤乃錢鎛"的鎛。《釋名》"鎛，迫也，迫地去草也。"這種除草工具也是由辰演進而來的。

銍和鐮都是收割工具。蚌製的銍和鐮在龍山文化和殷代文化遺址中曾有大量出土。《小爾雅·廣物》說："禾穗謂之穎，截穎謂之銍。"銍也是鐮，同爲收割工具，後世才區別銍是套在手指上掐斷禾穗的工具，使用時是操刃向外裁割，而鐮是裝有木柄操刃向內鈎刈的工具。蚌銍和蚌鐮的大量出土，說明直到殷商晚期這種農具還在生產上發揮作用。

銚、鎒、銍、鐮都是由辰演進而來的重要農具，是從翻土、除草到收割等項作業環節中必備的農具。"庤乃錢鎛，奄觀銍艾"，是說準備好錢鎛（即銚、

鎒）進行耕耘，接着就要看到用銍來收割，也反映了這幾種農具在生產中的地位。《莊子·外物篇》也説"春雨日時，草木怒發"的季節來臨，應該是"銚鎒於是乎始修"。反映戰國時期社會情況的《管子·輕重篇》甚至强調説，"一農之事，必有一耜、一銚、一鐮、一鎒、一錐、一銍"，更明確指出這幾種農具是必備的基本工具，同時他們反映的這種情況又都是屬於古代商族活動的地區。

根據上述農具的發展情況，可知辰在原始農業發展中確實起過重要作用；農業生產離不開辰以及由辰演進創製的農具，有了辰也標誌有了農業。郭沫若指出"農事之字每多从辰，如農如辱如蓐皆是"①，其中的"辱"與"蓐"應當是一個字，都表示手持辰進行農業勞動，因此説"辱者蓐與農之初字也"。儘管後世蓐與農字代替了辱字的功用，使辰字的含義發生轉化，但是從這幾個字都是以辰爲字根而構成來説，也反映了以辰爲農具曾是商族農業發展的一項因素。

進行農業生產不僅需要農具，判知季節也是必須掌握的大事。

商族的先祖每當嚴冬已過，氣候轉暖，春草萌發，燕子飛來而進行農業生產時，就會發現恰好"天蝎座 α"星（大辰星，亦名大火或心宿二）也於黄昏後出現於南天。"天蝎座 α"及其前後相鄰的兩顆星所聯成的弧綫，與地上使用的農具辰所具有的圓弧形刃部是相似的，人們對此也引起格外的注意。《史記·天官書》以及一些天文志裏都以爲位於中心的這顆星是"明堂"、"天王"，其"前後星，子屬，不欲直，直則天王失計"。這雖是占星家的胡説，但也反映了自古以來人們對於這三顆星已形成習慣看法，如果看到它竟然弧而不弧，類是直綫，也當然認爲是反常現象的。因此商族人民便把地上的農具比擬於天上的星象，而稱之爲"大辰"。"大辰"的含義就是天上的辰。殷商時期的"大"與"天"是混稱的，如"大邑商"也叫做"天邑商"；卜辭中的"大乙"在《世本》中爲"湯名天乙"，《史記·殷本紀》也説"主癸卒，子天乙立，是爲成湯"。可見"大辰"就是"天辰"。每年在天上新出現的辰形星與地面上開始用辰進行農業生產活動，上下交映，步驟一致，從而使人們在長期農業生產實踐中，把"大辰"星用爲標定季節進入春天的天象，使其在安排農業生產中具有指導作用。這正如古代埃及人通過觀察天狼星在日出前的出現，用來判定尼羅河即將泛濫一樣，商族人民則是以大辰星在黄昏的出現來判知農耕季節的開始。從此，大辰星進入商族人民的認識領域中。

隨着農業生產的發展，比較準確地判知季節以定農時顯得更加重要，於是大

---

① 郭沫若：《甲骨文字研究》，《釋干支》頁 25。

辰星便在人們對星象的觀察中被突出起來，而爲辨識星象的基點。事實上人們對於滿佈夜空的繁星，不可能在短期的漫無邊際的觀察中識別些什麼的。必然是在辨識個別或少數某些星座的基礎上，逐漸擴大範圍，才能獲得更多的比較全面的認識。後世有關"辰"的概念內涵逐漸擴大，其原因也在於此。辨識出大辰，掌握其規律，以大辰爲基點擴大對其他星象的辨識，可以說這是中國古代天文學發展的軌跡（有關這方面問題，在《殷曆考辨》一文中有詳細論述）。由於大辰星在觀察天象中受到人們的特殊注意，逐漸發展到把它擺在同整個星象並立的地位，由"星辰"的連稱，而有如《左傳・昭公三年》的"日、月、星、辰之神"的尊重待遇。關於這一點，在甲骨文裏也是有所反映的，"䢅、䢈"二字就是如此。

在《說文》的"農"字條下，收錄農字的古文，其中有一個作"䢅"，在小徐本裏改作"䢈"，因此直到今天研究甲骨文字的人都遵循之而釋爲"農"字。其實"農"字應如上文所指的"辱、蓐"等字，是由從手，從辰或再加上從艸、木會意而成，不從手的"䢅、䢈"並不具有"農"的含義。試讀下面列舉的卜辭：

1. 丙□□貞：翌丁卯且辛歲，叀䢅？　　　　　　　　（《粹》二五一）
2. □□旅□：後且乙歲，今䢅酒？　　　　　　　　　（《鄴》二・四〇・一）
3. 癸亥卜□貞乙歲，叀今䢅酒，　　　　　　　　　　（《前》五・四七・六）
4. 壬申卜即貞：兄壬歲，叀䢅？　　　　　　　　　　（《後》上七・十一）
5. 貞：中丁歲，叀䢅？　　　　　　　　　　　　　　（《明》六七八）
6. 丙午卜即貞：翌丁未丁䢅歲？其又伐？　　　　　　（《佚》九二四）
7. 己酉卜即貞：告于母辛叀䢅？　　　　　　　　　　（《前》五・四八・一）

這七條卜辭無論是據《說文》釋爲"農"，或依通假釋爲"醲"都是講不通的。如果再與下列卜辭對照一番：

1. 其又父己叀莔（暮）酒，王受有又？　　　　　　　（《粹》三一七）
2. 其又父己叀莔酒，王受□？　　　　　　　　　　　（《鄴》一・四〇・九）
3. 巳歲叀莔酒？　　　　　　　　　　　　　　　　　（《後》上五・十二）
4. □□卜且丁莔歲三牢，王受□？　　　　　　　　　（《粹》二六三）
5. 貞：叀莔酒？　　　　　　　　　　　　　　　　　（《佚》二七九）
6. 其又莔歲？　　　　　　　　　　　　　　　　　　（《遺》六二七）
7. 貞：莔（暮）酒？　　　　　　　　　　　　　　　（《庫》一〇二五）
8. 癸丑卜行貞：翌甲寅後且乙歲？朝酒？玆用。　　　（《庫》一〇二五）

可以清楚地看出這裏的"暮酢"、"暮歲"、"朝酢"是與前舉的"褻酢"、"褻歲"、"今褻酢"等屬於同一類型。"朝、暮"都是殷代紀時所用的字，只有釋"褻"爲"晨"，才能符合殷代在朝暮舉行祭祀的實際情況。此外，還可以從字形結構來分析這三個字，發掘它們之間的共同聯繫。

甲骨文的"暮"字作①🀄（《粹》一九五）、②🀄（《粹》三七〇）、③🀄（《南坊》①五・六〇）、④🀄（《人》二七八）、⑤🀄（《鄴》一・四〇・九）、⑥🀄（《粹》三七一）、⑦🀄（《甲》二五九八）、⑧🀄（《庫》一〇二五）。"朝"字作①🀄（《後下》三・八）、②🀄（《庫》一〇二五）、③🀄（《佚》二九三）。《說文》對"暮"字的解釋是"日且冥也，從日在茻（莽）中"，甲骨文從"林"或從"茻"是相通的，其偏旁的繁簡增省也是互通的，因此前八個字都應釋爲"暮"。後三個字有人釋爲"萌"，不確。唐蘭和董作賓都釋爲"朝"②。董作賓認爲"朝暮字均以草木叢中爲日出、日落時之背景……朝字又當取象於下弦以後之早晨，其時一輪紅日已騰輝於林木之中，而明月如弓猶復高懸碧落"。既然朝暮二字是通過草木的背景與日月等天象的會意而成，那末褻莀二字用大辰星在草木叢中，以表示天色將曉的天象也就可以理解了。因此把褻莀釋爲"晨"，從字形結構的分析來說也是有根據的。

同時這樣分析也是符合殷代的天象實際。大辰星自春分昏見以後，經夏而秋逐漸西移，到了秋分便伏而不見了。迨冬至以後的清晨又可以看到大辰星於南天逐漸上升，當人們在漫長的冬夜裏，看到大辰星在草木叢中緩緩上升時，就可以判定黑夜即將過去，清晨已經到來。清晨和辰星是相伴而來的，以辰來表示晨古音既同，事實也是有據的。《國語・周語》說"農祥晨正"，東漢韋昭注解："農祥，房星也；晨正，謂立春之日晨中於午也。農事之候，故曰農祥。"農祥可以理解爲農業活動的先兆；晨正，是指大辰星於清晨位於中天。韋昭認爲當房星（靠近大辰星）在立春以後的清晨位於中天時，是向人間啟示農祥。東漢時期的天象實際雖然是這樣，但在殷商時期却要較早一些，是提前在冬至後就出現的天象。

甲骨文中褻莀二字的出現，一方面說明商族人民是把大辰星與日月同等看待，用同一方法會意成字，滿足紀時的需要，從而反映了大辰星在觀察天象中的特別地位；另一方面也說明商族很早以來就熟知大辰星運行的全年規律。他們根據大辰星的昏見而開始春耕，並且伴隨大辰星橫過南天乃至西流伏没而進行夏耘

---

① 編者按："坊"，原文誤作"塲"，今徑改。
② 唐蘭：《殷虛文字記》。董作賓：《殷曆譜》上編卷一《殷曆鳥瞰》頁6下。

與秋收。特別是在冬至以後，他們還注意到大辰星的中天與清晨的關係，進而預知農祥的來臨。於是在後世爲做好生產準備的"三之日于耜"的詩章也出現了。

以辰爲原始農具而發展起來的商族農業生產，也促進商族社會結構的發展，於是在商族進入父系氏族公社，出現父系始祖契以後，一些神話傳說也結合這類特點而流傳下來。《詩·商頌》所說的"天命玄鳥，降而生商"，"有娀方將，帝立子生商"都是傳述商族始祖契的事跡。契母爲有娀氏之女，名簡狄，因吞食上帝遣使送來的玄鳥卵而生契。玄鳥就是燕子。根據對殷商時期物候的研究，那時的燕子每當春分時節就飛臨於商族居住區。《左傳·昭公十七年》："使玄鳥氏司春"，孔疏是"以春分來秋分去，故以名官，使主二分"，也反映了當時的物候情況。由於作爲報春使者的燕子曾向人間啟示春耕的到來，對商族的農業發展有過貢獻，所以商族的後世子孫在追念其先祖的功業時，便把燕子加以神化，尊爲商族的圖騰。重視農業發展的商族，既然把地上的報春使者燕子尊之爲"降而生商"，那末天上標誌春耕開始的大辰星，當然也會被尊爲商族的代表，因而"辰爲商星"的神話也創作流傳下來了。

有關"辰爲商星"的故事是比較簡略的，只談到高辛氏之子閼伯因與其弟實沈日相征討被帝譴罰遷於商丘，主祀辰星，後代商族因襲下來，所以說"辰爲商星"。爲什麼要這樣說呢？神話中的材料固然是不足信，但並不是完全不可信，也是有其歷史實際的依據。總結上文，我們可以說，商族的原始農業是辰農業，其中包括辰爲農具，辰爲農時。辰本是蜃即蛤蚌是商族居住區的一項特產。早在原始農業生產中，商族就已經使用蚌製農具，其中的蚌鎌又是甲骨文中所據以象形的"辰"字。後世幾種主要農具如銚、鎒、銍、鎌等的發展是同蚌製農具有聯繫的。再從甲骨文的農字是以辰爲字根來說，也反映了辰農具是構成商族農業的一項特點。在判知農時方面，商族是以大辰星爲依據的，大辰星的得名由來是地上辰農具在天上的比擬。根據甲骨文中"農"字的考釋，可知商族已經掌握了大辰星周年昏見晨中的規律。由此可見，"辰爲商星"說也是包含豐富内容的。特別是涉及天文、曆法方面，更有待進一步詳細闡明，爲了避免與《殷曆考辨》相重複，本文也就不再多說了。

原載《古文字研究論文集》（《四川大學學報叢刊》第 10 輯），1982 年 5 月；收入宋鎮豪、段志洪主編：《甲骨文獻集成》第 32 册，四川大學出版社，2001 年。今據前者收入。

曹錦炎

釋甲骨文北方名

甲骨文的四方和四方風名，既見於一版大龜的奉年之卜，又見於一版大骨的記事刻辭。胡厚宣先生首先以此與《山海經》、《尚書·堯典》等典籍相印證，頗有創獲。經過各家的考證，甲骨文的四方和四方風名基本上得到了解決。但是，對於北方名的解釋，仍然存在着一些問題。

甲骨文稱："北方曰勹，風曰伇。"勹，胡厚宣先生隸定作勹，並謂："甲骨文勹爲匀省，即宛字重文，與《山海經》作鵷者，爲同字。"（見《釋殷代求年於四方和四方風的祭祀》，《復旦學報》1956 年 1 期）陳邦懷先生釋爲夗，云："爲宛之初文。"（見《殷代社會史料徵存》）楊樹達先生也釋爲宛（見《積微居甲文説》）。

按甲骨文北方名的勹字（善齋藏大胛骨作入，見《京津》520），殷墟發掘所得的龜腹甲作凡（見《合》261。島邦男的《殷墟卜辭綜類》把前者摹作凡，後者摹作弓，與泐痕連在一起，並誤），而甲骨文智（從于省吾先生釋，見《甲骨文字釋林》）字所從的"夗"字偏旁作？、弓、凡等形，與此字構形截然不同，因此決非夗（或宛）字甚明。甲骨文的禁、鼻、飼、梵等字所從的勹字偏旁作勹、凡、勺等形，與此字構形正同。于省吾先生指出："勹、凡、勺象人側面俯伏之形，即伏字初文。"（見《甲骨文字釋林》）所論甚確。所以，甲骨文的北方名實爲"伏"。

"北方曰伏"，除了見於甲骨文外，尚見於典籍，《史記·五帝本紀》司馬貞《索隱》引《尸子》曰："北方者，伏方也。"北方何以名爲"伏"？《漢書·律曆志》："太陰者，北方。北，伏也，陽氣伏於下，于時爲冬。"《史記·天官書》："北方木，太陰之精，主冬，曰壬癸。"《管子·四時》："北方曰月，其時爲冬。"

《尚書·堯典》："申命和叔，宅朔方，曰幽都，平在朔易，日短星昴，以正仲冬。厥民隩，鳥獸氄毛。"《爾雅·釋詁》："朔，北方也。"《尚書》的這段話，《史記·五帝本紀》作："申命和叔，居北方，曰幽都，便在伏物。"《索隱》注："使和叔察北方藏伏之物，謂人畜積聚等，冬皆藏伏。"這里都把北方與冬季聯系在一起。《吕氏春秋·有始覽》："北方曰寒風"，而甲骨文的北方"風曰伇"正讀作"風曰洌"（詳于省吾先生《甲骨文字釋林》），寒、洌同義。甲骨文雖然沒有四時之分，但殷人對自然現象應該是覺察得到的，冬季寒風凛洌，萬物皆藏伏，故稱北方為"伏"。

《山海經·大荒東經》："有人名曰鵷，北方曰鵷，來風曰狹，是處東北隅以止日月，使無相間出没，司其短長。"可知北方也稱"鵷"，鵷即鵷，雷浚《說文解字外編》謂："《說文》無鵷字，《文選》司馬長卿《子虚賦》，鵷鶵孔鸞，《漢書·司馬相如傳》作宛。"知鵷可讀為宛。《說文》："宛，屈草自覆也"，宛從夗得聲，《說文》："夗，轉卧也"，是宛也有屈伏之義。宛與鬱音義俱可通，《詩·秦風·晨風》"鬱彼北林"，《周禮·考工記·函人》鄭注引作"宛彼北林"；《史記·扁鵲倉公列傳》："寒濕氣宛"，宛字《集解》云："音鬱"，《索隱》注："又如字"，均是其證。鬱字初文甲骨文作 ，金文作 （叔卣），其造字本義正與八（伏）字有關。所以，《山海經》稱北方名為"鵷"，與甲骨文稱北方名為"伏"，其來源都是一樣的。

總之，甲骨文北方名為"伏"，不僅從文字上而且從典籍記載上都得到了證明。

附記：本文曾以補白形式刊載於《中華文史論叢》1982年第3輯，删削過半，幾不成文，今一仍其舊。

《釋甲骨文北方名》，原載《中華文史論叢》第3輯，上海古籍出版社，1982年；收入宋鎮豪、段志洪主編：《甲骨文獻集成》第13册，四川大學出版社，2001年。《讀甲骨文劄記（二則）》"釋北方名"，原載《上海博物館集刊》第4期，上海古籍出版社，1987年。今據後者收入。

裘錫圭

釋"蚩"

甲骨文裏有一個寫作 ? ? 等形的字（以下隸定爲"蚩"）①，用法跟"希"（祟）、"囚"（憂）②等字相類，例如：

父庚弗蚩王。

父庚蚩王。　　　　　　　　　　　　　　　　　　　　乙綴 177【《合》2146＋2148】

貞：南庚不蚩。

貞：南庚蚩。　　　　　　　　　　　　　　　　　　　前 1·13·8【《合》1481】

貞：疒（疾）齒，隹（唯）父乙蚩。　　　　　　　　　　乙 4600【《合》13649】

隹且（祖）辛蚩王目。　　　　　　　　　　　　　　　　乙 6727【《合》1748】

貞：不隹帝蚩我年。

貞：隹帝蚩我年。二月。　　　　　　　　　　　　　　乙 7456【《合》10124 正】

丙午卜：隹岳蚩雨。　　　　　　　　　　　　　　　　屯南 2438

（《金》201【《合》41655】同文。《論集》編按：拓本見《英》2444）

甲寅卜㱿貞：王隹出（有）蚩。六月。　　　　　　　　甲 2032

（《論集》編按：《綴新》37【《合》16994】已將此片與《甲》1654 綴合，對貞之辭爲"甲寅[卜]㱿貞：王亡蚩。六月"，應補入）

壬戌卜亘貞：出疒齒，隹出蚩。　　　　　　　　　　　續 5·5·4【《合》13644】

---

① 看《甲骨文編》511—512 頁"它"字條（此條所收 ? ? 等文實爲另一字，應剔出）。? 不當釋"它"，詳後文。丁山將此字隸定爲"蚩"（如《商周史料考證》55 頁所引《前》1·52·1【《合》4368】二辭釋文），今從之。

② 關於"囚"字，詳拙作《説"囚"》。（《論集》編按："希"字實當釋爲"求"，疑當讀爲"咎"，參看《釋"求"》。）

貞：王亡㞢。　　　　　　　　　　　　　　　　　　　　乙 2378【《合》17035】
　　丙午卜行貞：翼（翌）丁未祭于中丁，亡㞢。　　　　　後上 2·10【《合》22863】

羅振玉釋此字爲"它"，他說：

> 《說文解字》：它，虫也。上古艸居患它，故相問無它乎。或从虫作蛇。卜辭中从止（即足也）下它，或增从彳。其文皆曰亡㞢，或曰不㞢，殆即它字。上古相問以無它，故卜辭中凡貞祭於先祖，尚用不它、亡它之遺言，殆相沿以爲無事故之通稱矣（卜辭中亦有單稱它，則當是有故不可以祭矣）。又案：它與虫殆爲一字，後人誤析爲二，又并二字而爲蛇，尤重複無理。許書於虫部外別立它部，不免沿其誤矣。（《增訂殷虛書契考釋》中 34）

羅說頗爲世人所信，但是實際上並無可靠的根據。

金文"虫"字作 ꙮꙮ 等形①，"它"字作 ꙮꙮꙮ 等形②，二字毫不相混。甲骨文裏有一個寫作 ꙮꙮ 等形的字③，舊或釋作"蠶"，張政烺先生改釋爲"它"，十分正確④。甲骨文和金文的"它"字有一個共同特點，就是象身體的部分比較粗。金文"它"字中間的一豎是甲骨文"它"字蛇身花紋的簡化，省去中間一豎的是較晚的寫法。甲骨文的 ꙮꙮ 變爲金文的"虫"，ꙮꙮ 則變爲金文的"它"，系統分明。羅氏說"它與虫殆爲一字，後人誤析爲二"，是不可信的。⑤

我們認爲"㞢"字與"它"無關，應該是傷害之"害"的本字。要證明這一點必須從"𡴎"字談起。

大徐本《說文·舛部》：

---

① 看《金文編》681 頁"虫"字及 682—683 頁从"虫"諸字。（《自選集》編按：見 1985 年版 873—876 頁。）
② 看《金文編》683—685 頁"它"字、571—572 頁"沱"字。（《自選集》編按：見 1985 年版 876—878、727—728 頁。）
③ 《甲骨文編》附錄 876 頁。
④ 《釋它示——論卜辭中沒有蠶神》，《古文字研究》第一輯。
⑤ 上注所引張政烺先生文仍從羅氏釋 ꙮꙮ 爲"它"，這是我們所不同意的。張先生釋《人文》2979【《合》22159】ꙮ 字爲"柁"（64 頁），似尚有待研究。《說文·䖵部》"蠹"字或體作 𧌎，"象蟲在木中形"，疑 ꙮ 即"蠹"字。甲骨文"蚩"（蚑）字从"虫"（《甲骨文編》139 頁），這似乎是"它"、"虫"本爲一字的一個證據。但是从"虫"的"蚩"字可以看作象以攴擊虫之形的表意初文，不必把它所从的"虫"看作聲旁，所以仍然不是"它"、"虫"一字的確證。而且這個字究竟是不是"蚑"字，其實也還是可以討論的。有人釋甲骨文 ꙮ 字爲"扡"（《甲骨文編》468 頁），此說從卜辭文義絲毫也得不到支持，不足辨。

𨍋，車軸耑鍵也。兩穿相背。从舛，萬省聲。

在《四部叢刊》影印的《說文解字繫傳》的影宋抄本裏，這個字的篆文寫作𨍋（蒙張政烺先生指示，馮桂芬翻刻的宋本《說文解字均譜》篆形與此同），可以隸定爲"𨍋"。《說文》玉、㝊、蚰三部都有从"𨍋"聲的字。在上引影宋鈔本《繫傳》裏，"瓁"、"蠹"二字所从的"𨍋"也都寫作𨍋（馮刻《均譜》同）。

雲夢睡虎地 11 號秦墓所出竹簡有"萬"字：

> 稷辰　正月二月：子，秀。丑、戌，正陽。寅、酉，危陽。卯，敫。辰、申，萬。巳、未，陰。午，徹。亥，結。

（《雲夢睡虎地秦墓》圖版一一八·755。"萬"字還見於 756 至 760 及 769 等簡）

字亦作"𢝊"：

> 正月二月：子，采。丑、戌，[正]陽（"正"字據 943 等簡推補）。寅、酉，危陽。卯，敫。[辰]（此字原簡漏寫，據 943 等簡推補）、申，𢝊。巳、未，陰。午，徹。丑（"亥"字之誤），結。

（同上書圖版一四七·942。"𢝊"字還見於 943 至 947 及 954 等簡）

所謂"秀（或作"采"，即"褎"字聲旁）、正陽、危陽、敫、萬、陰、徹、結"，是早期建除家所用的術語。① 雲夢簡 730 至 742 號還記有如下一套早期建除術語（同上書圖版一一六至一一七。簡上尚有其他文字，已略去。"絶紀日"三字據 918 號簡補）：

濡	嬴	建	陷	彼（破）	平	寧	空	坐	蓋	成	甬
結日	陽日	交日	害日	陰日	達日	外陽日	外害日	外陰日	[絶紀日]	夬光日	秀日

見於前引二簡的"敫、萬（𢝊）、陰、徹"，顯然相當於這一套簡的"交、害、陰、達"（"交"、"敫"音近。"徹"、"達"音義皆近）。這說明秦簡"萬"（𢝊）字應讀爲"害"。

---

① 秦簡所記關於"建除"的術語，跟漢代建除家所用的有出入，我們姑且稱之爲早期建除家所用的術語。

"鍵"（銉）、"轄"二字古通。《說文》以"車軸耑鍵"爲"鍵"字本義（此義實非"鍵"字本義，讀後文自明），古書則多用"轄"或"鎋"字。《毛詩》有《車舝》篇，《左傳·昭公二十五年》引《詩》作"《車轄》"。"轄"从"害"聲。从"鍵"聲的"達"字，《說文》也讀作"害"。由此看來，"蠆"（憂）跟"鍵"（銉）應該是一字的異體。江陵天星觀 1 號楚墓所出竹簡有从"車"从"蠆"的 字①，可見"蠆"是較古的寫法。"憂"當是"蠆"的變體，"銉"似是揉合這兩種寫法而成的，"鍵"是最後出的訛體。楚簡"轄"字疑即"轄"字異體。上引秦簡上的"外害日"，同出另一簡作"外達日"。②"達"跟《說文》的"達"可能是一個字。（《論集》編按：李家浩同志指出，長沙楚帛書乙篇，即篇幅較長的一篇的第一段末一句"于其王"上一字作 ，即"蠆"字，當讀爲傷害之"害"。此字前人皆誤釋。）

馬王堆三號墓出土的西漢前期帛書本《周易》，把《損》卦"曷之用二簋可用享"的"曷"、《大有》卦"无交害"的"害"都寫作 。③這也是"蠆"的變體。"曷"、"害"二字古音極近。《說文》"達"讀若害"，而"瑋"則"讀若曷"，就是一個例證。

甲骨文"禺"字應該就是"蠆"的初文。容庚先生指出："甲骨文 ，金文作 ，後漸變爲 ，爲 。"④" "演變爲"萬"，跟" "演變爲"萬"同例。甲骨文的 ⑤後來演變爲"禽"字所從的"离"，情況也是類似的。甲骨文有 字，聞一多釋"齲"。⑥其說可信。這個字所從的" "後來也演變爲"禹"，跟" "字的演變如出一轍。"齲"字由从"虫"變爲从"禹"，大概還跟"齲"、"禹"二字讀音相近有關（《說文》"齲"字从"牙""禹"聲，或體作"齲"）。"蠆"音"害"，"害"與"禹"古音也相近。"害"爲匣母字，"禹"爲于母（喻母三等）字。于母古歸匣母。"禹"屬魚部，"害"屬祭部，韻似相隔。但是從古文字資料看，"害"的古音跟魚部實有密切的關係。⑦所以"蠆"字由从"虫"變爲

---

① 此墓發掘報告見《考古學報》1982 年 1 期。所據竹簡的照片承湖北省荆州地區博物館提供，謹致謝忱。
② 《雲夢睡虎地秦墓》圖版一四五·916。
③ 見即將出版的《馬王堆漢墓帛書》第 2 輯。（《論集》編按：馬王堆《周易》釋文，已發表於《文物》1984 年 3 期。《損》卦見 2 頁，《大有》卦見 6 頁。）
④ 自《金文詁林》7368 頁轉引。
⑤ 看《甲骨文編》542 頁"禽"字及 542—543 頁从"禸"諸字。
⑥ 見《釋齲》，收入《古典新義》。《甲骨文編》誤以釋"龕"爲聞氏之說（86 頁）。
⑦ 看裘錫圭、李家浩《曾侯乙墓鐘磬銘文釋文說明》，《音樂研究》1981 年 1 期 18 頁。

从"禹",可能也有兼取"禹"字以爲音符的用意。

《説文》以"傷"爲"害"字本義。周法高指出"害"字本象下器上蓋之形,跟"會"、"蓋"等字音義皆近。①其説可信。《説文》顯然是把"害"字的假借義誤認爲本義了。"虫"(萬)字有"害"音,其字形象人的足趾爲蟲虺之類所咬嚙,也與傷害之義相合,應該就是傷害之"害"的本字。後世習慣於以假借字"害"表示傷害之義,"萬"字就被廢棄了。

卜辭"虫"字有動詞、名詞兩種用法,意義跟"布"(祟)字相近(《論集》編按:關於"布"字參看1284頁注②),讀爲"害"顯然十分合適。羅振玉指出"無它"是古代成語,但是用"它"爲動詞之例從未見於古籍。僅僅從這一點看,把"虫"讀作"害"也要比釋作"它"合理。"有害"、"亡害"也是古代成語。《詩·邶風》中《泉水》和《二子乘舟》兩篇都有"不瑕有害"之語。《書·金縢》記周公卜得吉兆後"啓籥見書,乃並是吉。公曰:'體,王其罔害。'""罔害"顯然就是卜辭的"亡虫(害)"。

《屯南》著録下引對貞卜辭:

丙寅鼎(貞):岳㞢雨。

弗㞢雨。　　　　　　　　　　　　　　　　　　　　　屯南644

第二辭以"虫"爲"虫"。《前》1·16·6【《合》23110】有下引殘辭:

□□卜王[貞]:□乙酉□□小乙□□亡㞢。

也以"虫"爲"虫"。這類"虫"字疑是刻漏"止"形的"虫"字,但是也有可能並非誤刻,而是以音近借用爲"虫"的。"虫"與"虺"同音,是曉母微部字。曉、匣二母,微、祭二部,關係都很密切,可知"虫"、"虫"(害)二字古音相近。上古時代,蛇虺之類爲害極烈。"虫"(害)大概就是由"虫"孳生的一個詞。所以卜辭有時以"虫"爲"虫"並不奇怪。

在甲骨卜辭裏,"亡虫"有時也寫作"亡徣"。②商代金文也有"徣"字。③西周中期的衛鼎(乙)銘文所記的車上器物,有"棻㡩、虎冟、布𢾿、畫

---

① 《金文詁林》6184頁。
② 看《甲骨文編》512頁、《綜類》84—85頁。用"徣"字者多爲五期卜辭。《文編》所收 𢾿 字,用法與"虫"字不同,與"徣"是否一字尚待研究。
③ 《金文編》91頁。(《自選集》編按:見1985年版117頁。)

轊"等物①，"布"下一字作"徫"，應是"徫"字較晚的寫法。人爲蟲虺所傷多在行路之時，"徫"字有可能如前人所説是"䖝"的繁體。不過這個字也有可能是小篆"逢"字的初文，卜辭以其音與"䖝"同而借作"䖝"字。衛鼎（乙）"徫"字究竟借爲何字，尚待研究。②

1975 年岐山縣董家村西周窖穴所出的䚄匜的銘文，有"義（宜）便（鞭）女（汝）千，黙䵣女"之語。③"䵣"上一字的右旁與"䖝"形近，但其實並無關係。唐蘭先生把"䵣"上一字隸定作"䵣"，認爲"䖝"與甲骨文 𐤇 是一字，《説文》"䖝"字即其訛體。④李學勤同志把這個字隸定作"䵣"，讀爲《説文》訓"刺"的"鼓"。⑤李説似可信。

　　原載《古文字學論集初編》，香港中文大學中國文化研究所吳多泰中國語文研究中心，1983 年；收入《古文字論集》（文中簡稱"《論集》"），中華書局，1992 年；又收入《裘錫圭自選集》（文中簡稱"《自選集》"），河南教育出版社，1994 年；又收入《裘錫圭學術文集·甲骨文卷》，復旦大學出版社，2012 年。今據後者收入。

---

① 《文物》1976 年 5 期 39 頁圖 16【《集成》5·2831】。
② "害"、"蓋"古音相近，衛鼎"徫"字也許應讀爲"蓋"，指車蓋。過去釋此字爲"韋"，讀爲"幃"（《文物》1976 年 5 期 28 頁、57 頁注④）。釋作"韋"是錯誤的，但是"韋"、"害"二字古音頗爲相近（"韋"是于母微部字），"徫"讀爲"幃"的可能性似不能完全排除。如果把"徫"讀爲車轄之"轄"，當然是很直捷的，可是從上下文看這裏似乎不應該説到轄。
③ 《文物》1976 年 5 期 42 頁圖 24【《集成》16·10285】。
④ 《陝西省岐山縣董家村新出西周重要銅器銘辭的釋文和注釋》，《文物》1976 年 5 期 59 頁注⑮。
⑤ 《岐山董家村訓匜考釋》，《古文字研究》第一輯 153 頁。

姚孝遂

牢宰考辨

甲骨刻辭"牢"字作⟨字⟩、⟨字⟩；或從羊作⟨字⟩、⟨字⟩，二者區分極爲嚴格。《三代吉金文存》一五·一二《宰爵》猶從羊作⟨字⟩，當爲商器。西周以後，"牢"、"宰"即合併作"牢"，從羊之"宰"已廢而不用。這也如同商代"牝"與"羟"，"牡"與"羝"，從牛與從羊區分極嚴，西周以後即趨於統一是一致的。

自羅振玉、王國維以來，諸家釋"牢"無異辭，且均承認"牢"與"宰"在卜辭有别。問題在於："牢"與"宰"的具體内容究竟是什麽，則有不同的認識。

葉玉森《前編集釋》一·四六據《晉語》韋昭注："凡牲一爲特，二爲牢"，以爲"稱牢當非一牲。殷世或即以二牲爲牢"。並據《大戴禮》"牛曰大牢，羊曰少牢"，以爲"宰"專指羊，"宰"即"小宰"之省。卜辭或從牛作"小牢"，或從羊作"大宰"，乃"契刻偶誤"。

吴其昌《殷虚書契解詁》一八八——一九〇基本是沿襲葉氏之説，而特别强調"大宰"與"小牢"爲誤文。

胡厚宣先生曾有專篇論文《釋牢》（載於《集刊》八本二分册），博徵歷代舊説，並蒐羅了大量的有關原始資料，作了非常詳細的論證。

胡先生除了申述"牢"必爲二牛；"大牢"必爲"牢"，"小宰"必爲"宰"之外，尚提出了一個新穎的見解，即"疑牢者當專指一牡牛與一牝牛而言"。

李孝定先生《集釋》三一三"牢"字下則力主"牢爲牛、羊、豕三牲具"，"三牲具爲大牢"，"羊豕曰少牢"。其根據是"羊與小宰并言，足證宰非特羊"，"牛、牢對舉，足證牢非特牛"。

所有以上的説解，驗之於甲骨刻辭，皆有所不合，因此有重新加以檢討的必要。

一、牲二爲牢

韋昭注《國語》保存了很多古訓，值得我們加以重視。但是韋昭的説解是否合乎商代卜辭的實際情況，則有待於通過卜辭辭例的檢驗，看看是否講得通。

  甲午卜，又于父丁，犬百、羊百、卯十牛？
  叀犬百，卯十牢？　　　　　　　　　　　　　　　《京津》四〇六六

"十牛"與"十牢"顯然是相對的。"十牛"既不能等於"五牢"，"十牢"也不能等於"廿牛"。這片卜辭《綜類》四六八引錄時，"十牢"作"七牢"。我們的意見是：其中間一橫畫乃是泐痕，不當釋"七"。

  甲戌卜，王其又河、叀牛，王受又？
  叀牢用，王受又？　　　　　　　　　　　　　　　《小南》二六九九

"牛"與"牢"對貞，相同的例子還有：

  王又伐于且乙牢、牛？　　　　　　　　　　　　　《南明》四四〇
  壬戌卜，求于河，三牢沈，三牛囧？　　　　　　　《小南》七三二
  丙子卜，于丁，卯牢？
  其一牛卯？　　　　　　　　　　　　　　　　　　《小南》三五六五
  丙午卜，濰伐二牢？
  叀牛？　　　　　　　　　　　　　　　　　　　　《小南》一〇六〇

"牛"和"牢"是不同的祭牲名稱，不可能是數量的差别。下面的辭例能進一步證明這一點：

  王其又于囧三牛，王受又？
  五牛？
  其牢？　　　　　　　　　　　　　　　　　　　　《小南》二六一七

很顯然，"其牢"不可能是"二牛"。

  貞，求于土三小牢，卯二牛，沈十牛？　　　　　　《前》一·二四·三

在同一段卜辭中，既稱"三小牢"，爲什麽不稱"卯牢"、"沈五牢"，而要稱

"卯二牛"、"沈十牛"？相同的例子還有：

其燎禾于河,耒三宰,沈牛二？

河耒三宰,沈牛二？　　　　　　　　　　　　　　　　　　　　《小南》九四三

爲什麼既稱"宰"和"牢"，而不稱"沈牢"，却稱"沈牛二"？

"牛"與"牢"對稱之例，在卜辭中多得不可勝數，二牲爲牢之説，無法解釋此種大量的、不稱牢而稱牛的現象。

《小南》三三八八尚有"牢又三牛"①，這再一次有力地證明"牢"與"牛"是不同的祭牲，"牢又三牛"不可能是"五牛"，從而也就證明"牢又一牛"不可能是"三牛"。"牢又一牛"祇能是與"羊𠂤豚"（《天》三四）、"犬𠂤羊"（《佚》一四）、"牢𠂤𡰥"（《乙》四五二一）、"其酚十牢又羌；廿牢又羌、卅牢又羌"（《佚》二二五）屬於同一性質，都是卜問用不同的祭牲。

"匕庚召牢又一牛……"（《佚》二五一），商承祚先生《考釋》作"牢又二牛"，《綜類》一二八—四、五四二—三亦作"牢又二牛"。諦審原拓片，上爲泐痕，當釋"牢又一牛"爲是。

二、太牢、少牢

牛羊豕三牲具爲"太牢"，羊豕爲"少牢"，這種説法是否合乎兩周秦漢的實際，在此暫且不論，至於其不符合於殷商的實際，則是肯定無疑的。

庚子卜,豕羊匕乙？　　　　　　　　　　　　　　　　　　　《乙》七二六一

癸未卜,钔余于且庚羊豕𡰥？　　　　　　　　　　　　　　　《乙》四五二一

出匕己二羊二豕不？　　　　　　　　　　　　　　　　　　　《人》三〇二四

燎生于……庚匕丙……羌豕？　　　　　　　　　　　　　　　《粹》三九六

辛未卜,卯于且乙牝牡？　　　　　　　　　　　　　　　　　《乙》二八五四

耒于河一羊一豕？　　　　　　　　　　　　　　　　　　　　《京津》五九五

以上這一些，爲什麼不稱"牢"或"小牢"，而要稱之爲"羊豕"？

甲午卜貞,翌乙未出于且乙羌十出五,卯宰一出一牛？

---

① 此爲殘片，且卜辭從未見此句例，當釋讀爲"……牢,卯三牛"。

甲午卜貞，翌乙未出于且乙羌十出五，卯窜出一牛？五月。　《佚》一五四

既然"窜"是羊豕，"牢"是牛羊豕，爲什麽在此既不稱"牛羊豕"，又不稱"牢"，而要稱之爲"窜出一牛"？此足以證明"牢"不是"牛羊豕"，"窜"不是"羊豕"。

與此相同的例證尚有：

……母辛……窜一牛用？　　　　　　　　　　《明》一六三四
乙巳出于母辛窜出一牛？十月。　　　　　　　《金》六九四
翌乙巳出且乙窜出牝？　　　　　　　　　　　《乙》四五九〇

卜辭也有同時用牛羊豕，但不稱"牢"或"大牢"，而是指明其牝、牡。

辛巳貞，其奠生于匕庚牡、牝、白豭？　　　　《粹》三九六
貞，來庚戌出于示壬妾匕……牝、牝、牝？　　《續》一·六·一

自葉玉森、吳其昌以來，均以爲大牢之牢必從牛，小窜之窜必從羊，而以卜辭中從羊之"大窜"與從牛之"小牢"爲誤刻。這不過是在不能自圓其說的情況下的一種遁詞，或者是囿於漢代經師的說解而習非成是。

卜辭在某些情況下確有誤刻，但必須有大量的有關辭例予以證明。卜辭所見的"大牢"與"小牢"，不僅僅是葉玉森所列舉的那幾條，更不是吳其昌所説的"厪有一處偶誤而已"。

僅據《綜類》二一二、四九七蒐集之資料，作"大窜"者有：

《金》四六六、《鐵》一七六·四、《掇》二·一二五、《甲》二六九八

作"小牢"者有：

《京津》五二四、《粹》八二八、《甲》三八九、《乙》四六〇三（二）、四五〇七（二）、《摭續》七八、《人》一八九四、《存》一·一九〇八、《南明》五一一、《乙》八八八六、《庫》七三六

從比例上來説（按《綜類》所引錄計算）：

"大牢"　七　　　"大窜"　五
"小窜"　一四　　"小牢"　一三（《乙》四六〇三有二"小牢"，《綜類》漏引其一。）

此外，《小南》有"小牢"見於下列諸片：一〇六〇、二八〇三、三七三〇。像上述這樣非常接近的比例，怎麼也不能説成是"懸殊"，不能根據漢代經

師的說法就判定"大宰"與"小牢"是"筆誤"。

尤其是下列諸片：

  庚子卜，叀小宰卯龍母；

  庚子卜，叀小宰匕司；

  辛丑子卜，貞，用小牢龍母；

  辛丑子卜，貞，用小牢匕司？   《乙》四五〇七

  貞，父戊戌叀羊；

  貞叀小宰；

  貞叀大宰？   《掇》二・一二五

  庚寅卜，彭貞，其大宰；

  庚寅卜，彭貞，其小宰？   《甲》二六九八

像這樣嚴格的對貞形式，其辭例本身不僅充分說明這些都不可能是"筆誤"，而且也充分說明"小宰"、"大宰"、"小牢"、"大牢"都是具體有所指的。這些名稱都是確實存在的，而不是由於什麼"筆誤"所造成的。"小牢"之不同於"小宰"，"大牢"之不同於"大宰"，猶之乎"宰"之不同於"牢"一樣，它們都是指不同的祭牲而言。

三、牝牡爲牢

胡厚宣先生僅僅祇是偶爾懷疑牢當專指一牡、一牝而言，並未提出任何例證來足成這一說法，也未堅持這一說法。

我們的意見則認爲，這種可能性是不存在的。

  甲申卜，卯帚鼠匕己二牝？   《前》一・三三・七

葉玉森《集釋》以爲牝乃牝牡合文。如果"牢"是一牝一牡的專用字，何以不稱"牢"而稱"牝"？

  ……生于高匕……牡牝？

  其十牢？   《戩》二三・一〇、《續》二・一五・二

何以不稱"牢"而稱"牡牝"？且"牢"與"牡牝"對貞，祇能證明它們是屬於不

同的祭牲。

殷人祭祀，對於犧牲的品類、毛色、牝牡，以至於殺牲的方法，均選擇極爲嚴格。卜辭所見同時用牝牡的絶少。據《綜類》所收録，除了上引《前》一·三三·七、《戬》二三·一〇以外，僅有《後上》二五·一〇之"……牝…三牡……"。

卜辭經常的情況是牝牡不同用：

其衆生于匕庚、匕丙、牡、羝、白豭？
衆生于（匕）庚、匕丙（牝）、羖、死？　　　　　　　　　《粹》三九六
业且乙宰业牝？
貞，弓业牝，叀牡？　　　　　　　　　　　　　　　　　《乙》四五九〇

如果假定"牢"爲一牝一牡，那麽《南明》四四〇之"王又伐于且乙牢、牛"，以及其它常見之"牢又一牛"，是否可以解釋爲："用一公牛、一母牛，再加上一頭不論是公或母之牛？"這顯然是説不通的。

四、牢爲享牛

以上諸説既已證明其均不能成立，而可以肯定者僅有一點，即："牢"專指牛，"宰"專指羊，但又有别於一般的牛或羊。然則，它究竟應如何正確地加以理解？

陳夢家先生在《卜辭綜述》中曾提到："甲骨文中有牢、宰、寫，前兩者是牲品，乃指一種豢養的牛羊。"（五五六頁）儘管説得不夠明確，也缺乏任何例證，但是已接近於正確的理解。鄭玄早就曾經指出："繫養者曰牢。"（見《詩·瓠葉序箋》）

《説文》："牢、閑，養牛馬圈也。从牛、冬省，取其四周帀也。"（據大徐本）

許慎的説解，得"牢"字之本義，但釋其形謂從冬省，則非是。徐鍇《繫傳》謂從冬省聲，不可據。王筠《釋例》以爲"從冬省者，牛冬乃入牢，若夏日有汗入牢，則毛盡禿矣"。其所以從牛者，"牛于六畜中最畏冷"。王筠的這種説法，可以説是極牽强比傅之能事。段玉裁謂"冬取完固之意"，亦想當然之詞。唯朱駿聲《通訓定聲》謂"外象匊帀堅固形，一以閑之……，非冬省也"，實得"牢"字之本形。林義光《文源》據《貉子卣》"𥁕"字以爲"象牛在牢中形"是對的。

卜辭所有"牢"或"宰"字，不是用"牢閑"之本義，而是用其引申義，指繫於牢閑之牛羊而言。

《周禮·牧人》："凡祭祀，共其犧牲，以授充人繫之。"鄭《注》："授充人者，當殊養之。"賈《疏》："牧人養牲，臨祭前三月，授與充人繫養之。"

又《牛人》："凡祭祀共其享牛、求牛，以授職人而芻之。"鄭玄謂"享，獻也，獻神之牛，謂所以祭者也。求，終也，終事之牛，謂所以繹者也"。鄭衆則謂"求牛，禱於鬼神祈求福之牛也"。

又《充人》："掌繫祭祀之牲牷，祀五帝，則繫於牢，芻之三月，享先王亦如之，凡散祭祀之牲，繫於國門，使養之。"

《公羊傳》宣公三年："帝牲在於滌，三月。"何休《注》："滌，宮名，養帝牲三牢之處。"

基於上述，可見凡是用於祭祀之犧牲，必繫之於牢，經過特殊之飼養，所謂"衣以文繡，食以芻菽"。一般是十天到三個月。《國語·楚語》楚昭王問於觀射父："芻豢幾何？"對曰："遠不過三月，近不過浹日。"

古代祭祀，對於圈養之牛與非圈養之牛區分甚嚴：

> 《春秋》宣公三年："春王正月，郊牛之口傷，改卜牛，牛死，乃不郊。"《左傳》以爲"不郊而望，皆非禮也"。孔《疏》："牛死在正月，郊當用三月，其間足得養牛，牛雖一傷一死，當更改卜，取其吉者。郊天之禮不可廢也。牛死而遂不郊，非禮也。"

郊祭之牛，必須用經過特殊圈養之牛，而且還得通過"卜吉"的儀式。這種專供祭祀之用的牛，如果或死或傷，甚至可以作爲停止祭祀的藉口。所以《春秋》僖卅一年有"四卜郊，不從，乃免牲"；成七年有"鼷鼠食郊牛角，改卜牛，鼷鼠又食其角，乃免牛"。這在我們今天是不可思議的事情，而在古人則是鄭重其事的。

根據卜辭所反映的情況，殷人稱普通的牛爲"牛"：

其見牛？	《京津》三一三三
追弗其氐牛？	《後下》四〇·七
乎共牛？	《乙》七九五五

羊的情況也相同，不贅述。牛經過特殊飼養之後，則稱爲"牢"。作爲祭牲，用"牢"要比用"牛"隆重：

> 王其又于囧三牛,王受㞢?
> 五牛?
> 其牢?　　　　　　　　　　　　　　　　　　　　《小南》二六一七

此可以説明,一牢是較五牛爲隆重。

> 己酉貞,㝩以牛其用自囧,汎大示叀牛?
> 己酉貞,㝩以牛其用自囧,三牢汎?
> 己酉貞,……以牛其(用)自囧五牢?汎大示五牢?　　　《小南》九

牛是由"㝩"貢獻來的,其經過特殊飼養的就稱之爲"牢",未經過特殊飼養的仍稱之爲"牛"。此亦可以證明牢衹能是牛,而不能是牛羊豕。

這種經過特殊飼養的牛羊,其大者謂之"大牢"、"大宰";其小者謂之"小牢"、"小宰"。

殷人在祭祀的時候,並不是每一次都對於其毛色、大小、牝牡均有所限制,因此也就不一定要每次都冠以大小、幽黄、牝牡。這正如同用人爲牲時,在有的情況下限於專用某方之俘,有的情況下則泛稱"人"而已。

殷人用牲時,經常也要"卜吉"。如:

> 甲戌卜,王其又河,叀牛,王受又?吉;
> 叀牢用,王受又?弘吉。　　　　　　　　　　　　《小南》二六九九

除了"牢"、"宰"以外,卜辭尚有"䮺"字:

> 叀小䮺用?　　　　　　　　　　　　　　　　　　《福》二九
> 叀騳眔大䮺比伐?　　　　　　　　　　　　　　　《佚》九七〇

商承祚先生《福》二九《考釋》謂"大䮺、小䮺則大馬、小馬也。用以祭祀,故加牢以别之",其説近是。更爲確切的解釋則是:"䮺"爲經過特殊飼養而用於祭祀之馬。

後　記

《牢宰考辨》一文是一九七六年的舊作。由於從目錄上知道孔德成先生一九六六年八月在《文史哲學報》第十五期有《釋牢宰》一文,未見原文,不知道孔

先生是怎樣論證這一問題的，所以不敢貿然予以發表。祇是在與一些同志互相切磋時，請他們看過。直至一九八〇年，承許禮平先生的盛情，以《釋牢宰》一文見寄，始得見原文。孔先生認爲牢、宰爲繫養之牛羊，這一點拙見是與之相同的。不過孔先生未見到陳夢家先生已早有此說。至於孔先生同意"大宰"、"小牢"爲"大牢"、"小宰"之誤字的舊說，這一點則是拙見與之完全不同的。拙作主要是從甲骨刻辭本身以論證商代"牢"、"宰"之含義，並以之與典籍相印證。近讀新出版的《小屯南地甲骨》（簡稱《小南》），略事補充有關卜辭，謹以之獻於中國古文字學會第四屆年會，以就正於方家。

原載《古文字研究》第9輯，中華書局，1984年；收入宋鎮豪、段志洪主編：《甲骨文獻集成》第13册，四川大學出版社，2001年；又收入《姚孝遂古文字論集》，中華書局，2010年。今據後者收入。原文引述甲骨刻辭例句一般單起並加引號，因此次重排已在格式上加以區別，故將此種引號略去。

林 澐

小屯南地發掘與殷墟甲骨斷代

甲骨斷代研究實質上包括兩個方面：甲骨分類以及確定每類甲骨的存在年代。董作賓在 30 年代初創立甲骨斷代學時，是把殷墟甲骨分爲五大類，而將其分別定在武丁、祖庚祖甲、廩辛康丁、武乙文丁、帝乙帝辛五個時期。

董氏在《殷虛文字乙編序》中所説的"文武丁卜辭"是他在殷墟甲骨中分出的第六大類。50 年代以來，對該類卜辭的進一步分類和確定年代，提出了極爲分歧的見解。因此，1973 年中國科學院考古研究所在小屯南地對富含甲骨的多層堆積進行新的發掘，是引人矚目的。

我在 1965 年寫的《甲骨文斷代中一個重要問題的再研究》一文中，把陳夢家從"文武丁卜辭"中分出的自組卜辭，考定爲武丁時代而且早於賓組卜辭。另一方面，則認爲董氏"四期卜辭"中有父乙稱謂的，有一部分可據字體劃爲獨立的一類；郭沫若根據"自上甲廿示"而定爲文丁時代的粹 221（即合 34122）、粹 222（即合 34121）及戩 1·9＝佚 884＝續 1·2·4（即合 34120）等片，據字體也可劃出獨立的一類。以上兩類卜辭，我都認爲是"真正的文丁卜辭"。前一類是我首先分出的，後一類則比李學勤在《殷代地理簡論》中所分出的"四期 3 類"範圍更窄。關於這些觀點，我曾同發掘小屯南地甲骨而正在整理這批資料的肖楠同志交換過意見。

1976 年，肖楠正式報道了小屯南地早期堆積（相當於大司空村一期）中發現的𠂤卜之卜甲，自組卜辭之屬於武丁時代已成爲定論。但肖楠仍同陳夢家一樣，把自組卜辭當作晚於賓組卜辭的武丁晚期之物。①

---

① 肖楠：《小屯南地發現的"自組卜甲"》，《考古》1976 年 4 期。

1976年李學勤在以筆名發表的文章中，也提出了卜人𠂤的卜辭在殷墟甲骨中時代最早的看法。①接着又提出了"歷組卜辭"（即董氏舊定的"四期卜辭"）應改定爲武丁至祖庚時期。②這在甲骨斷代研究中引起了一場新的尖銳爭論。肖楠從小屯南地的地層現象對李說進行駁辯③，裘錫圭則從卜辭內容的分析支持李說④。肖楠根據地層分析而考定的"文丁卜辭"，雖有分類標準不夠精密的缺陷，但大體上同我過去所認爲的"真正的文丁卜辭"是相同的。因此，我在這場爭論中起初是堅決支持肖楠同志的。但在同裘錫圭同志幾次交換意見，並讀了他的《論"歷組卜辭"的時代》（以下簡稱《論歷組》）之後，同他一樣覺得"不能不放棄舊說而改從李說"。但在小屯南地所獲全部甲骨尚未發表的情況下，對肖楠所堅持的地層根據，殊難作出確切的解釋。

　　最近，在仔細研究了新出版的《小屯南地甲骨》中發表的全部甲骨和坑位記錄之後，我對肖楠同志在該書《前言》中就甲骨分類和諸類年代而重申的意見，再一次作了認真考慮。現就以下幾個問題，談一些個人的看法。

一、𠂤組和賓組的時代孰早？

　　同屬於武丁時期的𠂤組卜辭和賓組卜辭，在年代上的相互關係究竟如何？目前仍然意見不一。裘錫圭同志在《論歷組》中基本同意我的看法，認爲"賓組卜辭的時代一般要晚於𠂤組卜辭"⑤，肖楠曾一度贊成陳夢家的意見⑥，認爲𠂤組晚於賓組。謝濟則認爲兩者時代基本一致，"一點也不能看出晚期和前期的痕迹"⑦。李學勤在最近的文章中，只是駁斥了陳夢家把𠂤組插在賓組和出組之間是行不通的，並不再談𠂤組早於賓組，而認爲"𠂤組卜辭體例特異，數量不多，與賓組有同時的證據，它不能作爲卜辭發展中一個獨立的階段"⑧。

---

① 江鴻：《盤龍城與商朝的南土》，《文物》1976年2期。
② 李學勤：《論"婦好"墓年代及有關問題》，《文物》1977年11期。
③ 肖楠：《論武乙·文丁卜辭》，《古文字研究》第3輯，中華書局，1980年。
④ 裘錫圭：《論"歷組卜辭"的時代》，《古文字研究》第6輯，中華書局，1981年。
⑤ 裘錫圭：《論"歷組卜辭"的時代》，30頁。
⑥ 肖楠：《小屯南地發現的"𠂤組卜甲"》，240頁。
⑦ 謝濟：《武丁時另種類型卜辭分期研究》，《古文字研究》第6輯，中華書局，1981年。
⑧ 李學勤《關於𠂤組卜辭的一些問題》，《古文字研究》第3輯，中華書局，1980年，32頁。

在《小屯南地甲骨》前言中，肖楠對這個問題的提法變得更加審慎，認爲"目前解決這一問題的條件還不成熟。因爲，雖然從某一點上看，如字體方面，自組卜辭的部分字體帶有某些早期階段的特點，但僅靠此點就斷言自組早於賓組卜辭，還爲時過早。第一，截止目前爲止，只發現過賓組、自組同出的地層，而尚未發現它們之間的叠壓打破關係；第二，此組出自組卜甲的 T53（4A）不是最早的地層……"

在考古學上，要確定出土遺物的相對早晚關係，層位學的研究的確非常重要，但並不能視爲唯一的手段。型式學（typology）的研究方法同樣有很大的意義。不同時代的遺物往往出於同一地層，故同一層位出土遺物的年代早晚，往往有賴於型式學的研究而得以確定。在我國考古界，型式學多應用於器物形狀的排比，實際上，它可以應用於遺物的各個方面。因此，研究自組卜辭與賓組卜辭的相對早晚關係，並不是沒有層位差別就無法作進一步討論。

當然，像提出"自組卜辭的部分字體帶有某些早期階段的特點"，是根本無法據之以考定自組早於賓組的，甚至這種提法本身就難以成立。因爲，如果我們先不能肯定自組早於賓組，賓組卜辭就是目前所知最早的甲骨文；顯然，我們不能憑空推測比賓組卜辭更早的字體該是什麼樣，那麼，又有什麼根據來談論自組卜辭的字體帶有"早期階段"的特點呢？

我之論證自組早於賓組，首先是以發現自組和賓組之間的無法否定的"過渡"現象爲出發基點的。

衆所周知，區別自組卜辭和賓組卜辭的基本標準之一是卜人，而其核心是有同版關係的卜人，在自組卜辭是自、𠂤、𠂤三人；在賓組卜辭是賓、㱿、𠂤、古、永、亘、箙等人。有自、𠂤、𠂤所卜之辭的字體特徵（包括書體、字形結構和用字習慣三個主要方面），則是劃定自組卜辭的另一基本標準，不見卜人名之卜辭可根據字體特徵而歸於自組，與自、𠂤、𠂤三人沒有同版關係的卜人之所以被確定爲自組卜人，也是由字體特徵相同而建立聯繫的。賓組卜辭的劃定也是一樣。

過去主張自組和賓組同屬武丁時代的研究者，往往以自組卜人和賓組卜人有同版關係作爲證據之一。實際上，到目前爲止還沒有人能找到確切可靠的實例。謝濟在去年年會上提出的《武丁時另種類型卜辭分期研究》一文中指出：過去所舉出的所謂自組卜人和賓組卜人同版的例子，往往在辭中無法確定是否卜人，所以並不可靠。這是很對的。因爲嚴格地說，只有確切是在前辭中出現的人名，以及在繇辭部分的"㫃曰"或"曰"之前出現的人名，纔可確知爲卜人。所以，像

貝塚茂樹所舉的燕141（即合20149），實際上只有𑿁可肯定爲卜人，亙、箙則無法肯定爲卜人。但是，謝濟又認爲：甲2361、合集21029卜人𠂤和卜人賓同版，甲234卜人内和卜人𠂤同版，"這些是可信的"。這却是不對的。甲234和254、196、248、235可綴合（即合集19817），甲234上的所謂卜人内，實際是"㞢卜丙乎？"的殘辭。①甲2361和合集21029均爲殘辭，也無法確定是否爲卜人。因此　根據卜人和字體把賓組和自組區分爲兩組，目前仍認爲是可行的。

但是，根據以上兩項基本標準來區分自組和賓組卜辭時，我們會遇到以下幾種現象：

1. 自組小字字體（即肖楠在《小屯南地甲骨》前言中所說的"第三類"自組字體）的成段刻辭和賓組字體的成段刻辭，見於同一版上。

例一，合20149正面的㞢卜之辭，令字作𠂤，是自組小字字體特點，但背面"辛酉卜：不其雨？"一辭，字體與賓組無別。

例二，合19890中央部分爲自、𠂤所卜之辭，字小，㞢作㞢，母作𠂤，爲典型自組小字字體；但上部兩側之"辛酉卜，王：兄于匕已迺取且丁。——辛酉卜，王：勿兄于匕已"二辭，字大，字體與賓組無別。

例三，合20007有卜人𠂤所卜之辭，爲自組小字字體，另有兩條刻辭亦同。但左上角又有賓組字體刻辭"……莑……用"。

例四，合20066有卜人𠂤所卜之辭，爲自組小字字體，其上方和下方又有較大的賓組字體刻辭。

貝塚茂樹已經指出，燕141（即合20149）背面的賓組字體，乃屬於前辭多作"干支卜"，"干支卜，貞"形式的一類②，和一般賓組有一定差別性，也就是注意到賓組卜辭字體還可以進一步細分爲不同亞組。

2. 有些卜人所卜之辭，既有作自組小字字體，又有作賓組字體，或介於兩者之間。

例一，𠂤卜之辭，合3929爲自組小字字體，故陳夢家將此卜人附屬於自組。但合3931、合3932、合3930、合12800各片𠂤之辭字體屬賓組。

例二，𡈼卜之辭，不少作自組小字字體，以合20921、合20163、合20160、合20472、合21287等片最爲典型，故陳夢家將此卜人附屬於自組。但如合集20165𡈼卜之辭，字頗大，除令作𠂤猶存自組特點外，與賓組頗難區別。該卜人

---

① 嚴一萍：《略論饒著"貞卜人物通考"的基礎問題》，《大陸雜誌》23卷9—10期。
② 貝塚茂樹、伊藤道治：《甲骨文字研究》正文篇，同朋舍，1980年，78頁。

名又寫作衙，見於合 20276、20158。有趣的是，陳夢家一面説 F36 坑所出"全是自組卜辭"，"此坑不出賓組卜辭"（《綜述》148 頁），一面又把該坑出土的合 20276 之卜人衙"約略就字體暫定其附屬組別"而附屬於賓組（《綜述》166 頁）。説明他對合 20276 的字體究竟歸爲自組或賓組把握不定。

例三，㭝卜之片，合 3357 在字體上與賓組無别，合 10514 字雖較一般自組小字爲大，近賓組，但隻字所从之隹，足部作曲筆的㠯，辰字作末筆彎曲的㠯，猶存自組小字之特點（而且該片有自組小字龜甲習見的右尾甲刻辭）。

例四，㱿卜之片，大量屬賓組典型字體，故被歸爲賓組主要卜人。但合 6885 㱿卜之片，辛字上部加短劃作㠯；合 5758 叀字作㠯，令字作㠯；合 10977 在字作㠯。均有自組小字的字體特點，而且這幾片上的㱿字均作㠯，和賓組字體常見的㠯形不同。

例五，如按大多數研究者目前的意見而承認爲㠯卜人名，則㠯卜之辭除多數爲賓組字體外（如合 3912、3755），也有貞字作㠯的典型自組小字字體，如合 16670。

由以上現象的啓發，在舊稱"第一期卜辭"的賓組卜辭中，可發現其中有一部分實際上也是處於自組字體和賓組字體的過渡狀態的。總結這部分甲骨的字體特點，初步歸納如下：

1. 從書體上看，比較嚴正，字較大，故一般被認爲屬賓組。但因字較窄長，比一般賓組字體清秀。

2. 貞字作㠯，和自組作㠯不同，兩耳較一般賓組尖狹些。干支字的寫法相當劃一，基本同於賓組。惟辛字偶有作㠯（賓組絶大多數作㠯），辰字有作㠯、㠯（賓組絶大多數作㠯），同於自組。

3. 字形結構尚有自組小字特點的主要表現是人作㠯（从人傍之字也如此）、令作㠯。隹作曲足的㠯、㠯，乍作㠯，因作㠯，冥作㠯，和一般賓組之作㠯、㠯、㠯、㠯、㠯、㠯多異。其他如用作㠯、㞢作中豎較短的㠯、㠯，在作㠯，女作㠯，耳作㠯，和一般賓組的㠯、㠯、㠯、㠯、㠯互作。

這類卜辭，我過去稱爲"自組過渡組"，現因考慮到和裘錫圭的"歷自間組"的提法統一起見，建議命名爲"自賓間組"。而且，由於其賓組的特點較多，我贊成把它作爲賓組範圍内的一個特殊亞組。（裘錫圭在《論歷組》一文中，已提到賓組中可以分出"與出組早期相似的賓組晚期類型"，故賓組實際上可分成"自賓間組"、"典型賓組"、"晚期賓組"三個亞組。）貝塚茂樹所謂前辭多作"干支卜"、"干支卜貞"的那類賓組卜辭，和"自賓間組"大體相當。前舉與自

組小字卜辭同版的賓組卜辭，多可歸入此組，合集 20165 徣卜辭、合 10514 ⿰卜之辭、合 6885 及 10977 殻卜之辭均可明確肯定爲此組。（參看圖一）

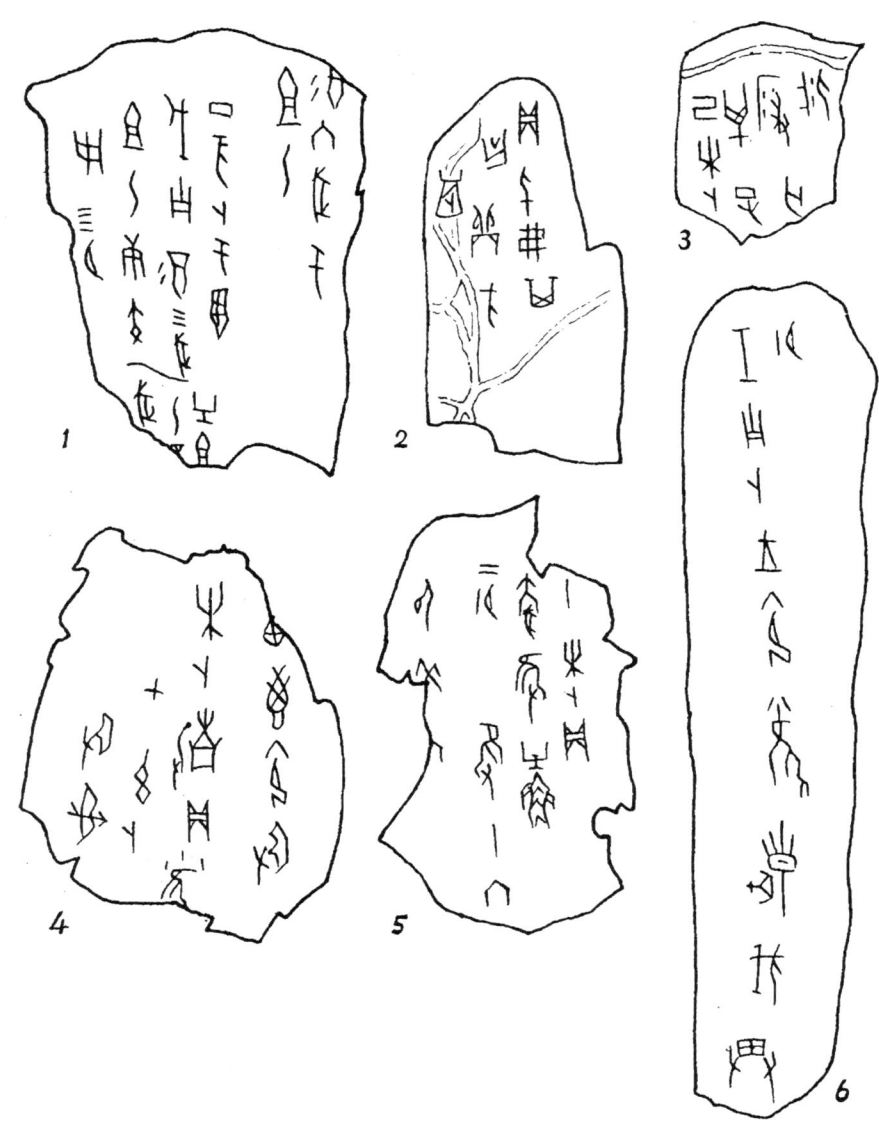

圖一　自賓間組字體舉例

1. 續 1·13·3　2. 甲 3115　3. 下 29·4　4. 前 7·10·3　5. 前 7·8·4　6. 下 19·3

肖楠認爲小屯南地 T53（4A）層中八片疊壓在一起的卜甲均爲"自組卜甲"。實際上，其中的屯南 4511，正應歸爲"自賓間組"。

肖楠認爲自組卜辭有三種字體，其中"第一類"字體爲自組、賓組所共有。這是認識到了自組和賓組在字體上有一部分是互相接近的，但缺乏深入分析。這種籠統的提法，勢必在劃分自組和賓組兩類卜辭上造成混亂。像肖楠所舉自組

"第一類"的例子中，合 1029 並無卜人，既然這一類字體爲𠂤組與賓組所共有，爲什麼劃爲𠂤組而不劃爲賓組呢？單就肖楠所舉的三個例子來看，所謂𠂤組第一類是難以成立的。合 20731 祜卜之片，翌作 ，咒作 ；合 20608（上半）𠂤卜之片，貞作 ，子作 。均與一般賓組顯然有別，且字較小，應歸入𠂤組小字無疑。合 1029 字較大，但人作 ，以作 ，保持𠂤組寫法特點，應歸爲"𠂤賓間組"。

"𠂤賓間組"，從型式學的觀點來看，也就是在賓組和𠂤組這兩個字體類型之間的中間類型。我們可以擴大範圍來考察一下，全部𠂤組字體和賓組字體之間，究竟是否存在逐步"過渡"的現象呢？在表一中，把𠂤組字體分爲"大字"和"小字"兩個亞組和"典型賓組"就部分常見字的寫法逐字對照，而把"𠂤賓間組"不同於"典型賓組"的寫法用括號標出，附於賓組一欄内。從表中可以看出，𠂤組小字的字體，正介於𠂤組大字和賓組之間。𠂤組大字的字形，它幾乎都有；賓組的字形，它也幾乎都有；此外還有介於兩者之間的其他異體。從𠂤組大字到賓組字體的總的演變趨勢是：由多體而趨向劃一，由多曲筆而趨向便於刻寫的折筆，由圖形性強而趨向較簡單的符號化。"𠂤賓間組"正是這一總的演化趨勢中的一個環節。而且，𠂤組大字卜辭和𠂤組小字卜辭有同版現象（如合集 19921、20088、20046），𠂤組小字卜辭又有和賓組卜辭（𠂤賓間組）同版之例（詳上文）。目前尚未發現𠂤組大字卜辭和賓組卜辭有同版之例，這顯然有利於說明𠂤組大字——𠂤組小字——賓組在字體上的逐步過渡關係。

表一 𠂤組→賓組之字形演變

組別	出	用	人	令	在	大	隹	王	其	不	于	叀	止
𠂤組大字													
𠂤組小字													
賓組													

續表

組別	來	尞	豕	牛	羊	貞	丙	丁	戊	庚	辛
自組大字											
自組小字											
賓組											

組別	子	丑	寅	卯	辰	巳	午	未	申	酉	戌
自組大字											
自組小字											
賓組											

把考察範圍再擴大到字體以外的特徵，還有很多方面可以發現自組大字——自組小字——自賓間組——典型賓組的逐步過渡性。

1. 鑽鑿形式

自組大字甲骨采用單獨的小圓鑿（所謂"圓鑿"可能一部分爲鑽成，舊稱"鑽"，下同），即許進雄所謂異常型第二式[①]，如合 20975 右列上方的兩個拓痕。也采用單獨的小長鑿，例如合 20975 右列下方的兩個拓痕，這種小長鑿爲弧肩而肥短，有短於 1.5 釐米者。至於從拓本上看似乎有小長鑿旁附有小圓鑿者，據許進雄分析，認爲都是燒灼而形成的剥裂面，我未有機會考察過這類實物，不能斷其確否。

自組小字甲骨，仍采用單獨的小圓鑿，如合 21433 林卜之骨版（參閱許書圖 56）。也采用較短的小長鑿，如許書圖 210 林卜之骨版，但一部分長鑿變窄而兩肩之弧度變小，趨向直肩。我在吉林大學藏骨中也找到一些例子，如吉大藏骨 528 即是，而且鑿的內壁也比自組大字的規整。

自賓間組甲骨，盛行淺大圓鑿包攝長鑿的形式，即許進雄所謂異常型第一式，觀察其中的長鑿，多爲接近自組小字的那種狹而規整的小長鑿，且有一部分作直肩而頭尾尖伸者，如合 7731、20172（參見《甲骨文字研究》本文篇圖 19），外廓已和賓組甲骨之長鑿相仿。

典型賓組甲骨，單獨的小圓鑿或圓鑿包攝長鑿的形式已很少見，可舉庫 1937（許書圖 22）、庫 1029（許書圖 49）、人文 707（《甲骨文字研究》本文篇圖 19）爲例。單獨的長鑿，多作內壁規整、直肩、頭尾尖伸的形狀，長度多在 1.5—2 釐米之間。長鑿旁附有燒灼以前先修治成的淺圓穴者頗常見，許進雄以爲這種"異常型第三式"是"第一期（按指賓組卜辭）所特有"，但他所舉的例子中，如許書圖 82（ROM 編號 77・19）的疾𣦵，應定爲自賓間組，可知此種形式至少在自賓間組已經有之。

由此可見，就鑽鑿形式而言，從自組大字到典型賓組也有連續過渡的性質。特別是長鑿由短到長，由肥到窄，由弧肩到直肩，由頭尾不尖出到尖出，內壁由不規整到規整的漸變現象，尤爲明顯。

2. 卜辭行款

自組大字卜辭行款最不規則。有旁行者，如合 19921 "乙巳卜，林：囯子

---

① 許進雄：《卜骨上的鑿鑽形態》，藝文印書館，1973 年。

宋?"；有下行而又折向上者，如合 20463 反"乙亥卜：令虎追方"；有旁行而折向上者，如合 21120"戊戌卜，𠂤：㞢季牛"；有下行而第二行之末字錯向第一行之下者，如合 21373"囗亥卜，𠂤：帚不婡"。自組小字卜辭行款趨於規整。賓組卜辭最整齊。

3. 前辭形式

自組卜辭"干支卜"式比例很大，"干支卜貞"式少見。自賓間組"干支卜"式比例仍較大，賓組卜辭則以"干支卜某貞"式爲常例。

4. 兆側刻辭

自組大字甲骨上未見。自組小字甲骨偶有之，如合 20185、合 20715、甲考 164 均有"二告"，合 20611 有"二告"、"不若"、"見"，合 20228 有"不⿰丨丨㞢"。自賓間組較常見，如合 9758 之二告、不㞢，合 16870 之二告，合 5945 之不㞢。典型賓組甲骨則爲普遍現象。

5. "某入"之記事刻辭

自組大字已見者僅一例，刻於胛骨之下方，作"丁丑，敊入七"（合 20850）。自組小字作"右尾甲刻辭"而頗常見。自賓間組仍有"右尾甲刻辭"（綴合 354 = 甲考 178，合 6852）。賓組改爲甲橋刻辭，常見。

6. 王親卜

自組卜辭中王親卜比例甚大，自賓間組仍有之，賓組罕見。

在以上排比分析中，我特意排除了稱謂、人名、事項等可作多方面解釋的現象，僅取與占卜內容無關的方面作爲型式學的研究對象。可以看出，從多方面的平行演變現象存在，把自組大字——自組小字——自賓間組——典型賓組排成依次相銜的一個序列，是合理的。

當然，兩種類型之間存在中間過渡類型的現象，既可以解釋爲因時代推移而逐漸演進，也可能是兩種類型同時並存而互相影響所致。但因爲上述序列是多項特徵互相平行的漸變，殊難以用並存的兩種類型互相影響來解釋。而且，自組卜辭和賓組卜辭的區別，主要僅在於字體和卜人，至於卜人的身份和所卜內容的性質，看不出有什麼不同。因此，貝塚茂樹假設賓組爲王室卜辭而自組爲"王族"卜辭是缺乏積極證據的。

承認自組——賓組的這一漸變序列是時代早晚的演進序列，還要解決這一序列的何端爲早。過去主張自組、賓組同屬武丁時代的研究者，也或多或少地看出自組和賓組的過渡現象，但多以爲這種演進是由賓組向自組進行的。分析其原

因，主要是誤信董氏五期分類法中對字形演變的一些過時的假設，而認爲𠂤組字體有所謂"晚期"的特點。例如陳夢家說："𠂤組的干支字有和賓組相同的，有接近晚期的。"所謂接近晚期的，舉了子作 🔲、🔲、🔲，午作 🔲 等（《綜述》150頁）。貝塚茂樹誤將合20921的卜人㕣當作卜人 🔲，而説此片子作 🔲 是晚期寫法，作爲賓組向𠂤組過渡的重要資料（《甲骨文字研究》本文篇114—115頁）。其實，造成字體多樣性的因素是很複雜的，哪些寫法是書寫者的個人習慣，哪些寫法反映早晚之別的時代特徵，尚有待我們根據不斷發現的新資料，作深入分析，如果只根據𠂤組卜辭中某些字的寫法和帝乙帝辛時的黄組卜辭（即舊稱"第五期卜辭"）相近，就認爲它時代上晚於賓組，這和因爲商末周初的金文中有的字比甲骨文的寫法還要富於圖形性，就認爲它比甲骨文時代還早，同樣是可笑的。

陳夢家對於𠂤組之晚於賓組還舉出另一些理由：①𠂤組卜辭在月份前有加"在"之例，不見於賓組而見於祖甲卜辭。②𠂤組卜辭前辭有作"干支卜曰貞"之例，和祖甲卜辭常見的"干支卜王曰貞"相類。③𠂤組卜辭稱成湯爲大乙，和祖甲卜辭同。④𠂤組卜辭祭祀之"侑"，屮、又並用，作又者和祖甲卜辭同。我們且不説①、②兩條根據的只是罕見的特例，最難理解的是，𠂤組卜辭既然没有稱謂足以證明它可以延續到祖庚時代，而即使比賓組晚也只能晚到武丁晚期，却又跳過了祖庚時代，先有了祖甲時代的特徵，在干支字上又和祖甲時代也不一樣，有了更"晚期"的特徵。實際上，這種個別舉例式的方法，與型式學所要求的全面排比，是風馬牛不相及的。如果抛開這種個別舉例的不科學方法，而從全面來看，則賓組卜辭在向晚期發展的方向上，已經有"賓組晚期"這一亞組與出組卜辭緊密銜接，實在不容再有𠂤組介於其中。因此，唯一合理的結論是把𠂤組置於賓組之前，在總體上構成𠂤組→賓組→出組這樣一個連續漸變的序列。

總之，我就是根據這樣的分析推理方法，得出𠂤組應早於賓組的結論的。𠂤組之早於賓組，還有一個積極的證據。大家知道，在早於小屯商文化的二里崗期商文化中，卜用甲骨是盛行單獨的小圓鑽（鑿）的[①]。最近我在厦門大學人類學博物館有機會目驗鄭州出土的二里崗期卜骨標本，上面也有刀挖的短肥的弧背小長鑿。因此，𠂤組卜辭，是目前殷墟有字甲骨中鑽鑿形式最接近二里崗期甲骨的。

利用型式學的方法推定𠂤組比賓組早，目前是否就完全没有層位學上的根據呢？我不這麽認爲。

---

① 河南省文物工作隊：《鄭州二里崗》，科學出版社，1959年，圖版拾陸。

肖楠同志説，賓組和𠂤組同出於小屯南地早期地層，是把在 T55（6A）中所出的屯南 4575 定爲賓組卜辭（《小屯南地甲骨》前言 17 頁），但此片僅存四字，其中貞作𤔲。衆所周知，賓組卜辭中的貞字幾乎全都作𤔲，並未見過作𤔲之例。很難理解肖楠爲什麽把屯南 4575 定爲賓組卜辭。此外，這次發掘中出於早期地層中的有字甲骨，只有 H102 的屯 2698（午組），H104 的屯 2765—2766（均𠂤組小字），H107 的屯 2767—2769（𠂤組小字），2770—2771（午組），H115 的屯 2777（字迹模糊，不能分類），T53（4A）的屯 4511（肖楠原定𠂤組，應爲𠂤賓間組）、4512—4518（𠂤組），即在相當於大司空村一期的地層中，未見典型賓組及賓組晚期卜辭。

　　解放前殷墟發掘中出土過大量賓組卜辭，但當時限於田野工作的水平，缺乏層位學分析。解放後考古研究所在安陽地區的發掘中，把殷墟堆積劃分爲大司空村一至四期，也不曾報道過在大司空村一期堆積中有賓組卜辭出土。鄒衡把"大司空村一期"（實際是 1953 年發掘的大司空村 H117 和 H126）歸入他所劃分的"殷墟文化第二期第二組"①，同時把解放前發掘的出有典型賓組卜辭的 YH006、YE16 也歸爲此組。但是，這種歸屬是可以討論的。因爲大司空村一期以鬲、簋爲主要標準器，而鄒衡僅根據盤、罐、鉢、器蓋等在分期上僅起次要作用的器物形態而將 YH006、YE16 排定在該組的位置，證據尚欠堅實。所以，典型賓組及賓組晚期卜辭是否出於大司空村一期的地層，目前尚屬疑問。

　　在賓組卜辭中，婦好是常見人名之一。近年在小屯發掘的婦好墓，由於是殷墟發掘史上第一座未經盗掘的高級貴族墓，人們炫目於大量青銅器和玉雕之工藝高超，而產生了它時代偏晚的錯覺。實際上，從該墓出土的陶爵來看，無疑以定爲大司空村二期爲是②。去年我到安陽工作站，鄭振香同志進一步告知該墓出土的骨簪、骨鏃也應定爲大司空村二期。而且在該墓近旁發掘的 M17、M18 中的成組陶器也都是大司空村二期的。M18 的銅器上有子漁之銘，他和婦好一樣是賓組卜辭的常見人名。M18 出土玉戈上的朱書文書和典型賓組字體一致。這些都表明賓組卜辭的存在年代應與大司空村二期器物有重合關係。婦好之名，在𠂤組卜辭中僅一見，即合集 19998，屬𠂤組小字字體，爲占卜生育之事。在賓組卜辭中則大量出現，有占卜她是否死亡之事。子漁一名則不見於𠂤組而僅見於賓組。因

---

① 鄒衡：《試論殷墟文化分期》，《夏商周考古論文集》，文物出版社，1980 年，60 頁表四。
② 考古所安陽隊：《安陽殷墟五號墓的發掘》，《考古學報》1977 年 2 期，圖版 36∶1。參看：《1969—1977 年殷墟西區墓葬發掘報告》，《考古學報》1979 年 1 期，表四。

此，鄭振香同志認為，既然婦好墓和子漁墓屬大司空村二期，只要有自組卜辭出於大司空村一期地層，就可以間接確定自組卜辭在時代上早於賓組，我認為這個看法是很正確的。

自組卜辭雖早於賓組，但在其全部稱謂中找不出它早於武丁的證據，而我們又沒有理由推測它在武丁即位時就開始存在，所以只能稱之為"武丁卜辭"，倒是賓組卜辭應稱為"武丁晚期卜辭"。

我過去有一個看法，認為王室的卜用甲骨上刻寫卜辭，恐怕就是以自組大字為起點。這是因為自組大字的書體很像毛筆字，應該是在甲骨上刻字的最原始形態。但肖楠同志根據這次發掘指出："此次出現自組卜甲的 T53（4A）不是最早的地層"，它壓在 H111、H112 上，H112 之下又發現 H115，"在 H115 中出了一片卜甲 2777，但其上僅有兩字，其中一字還不清楚，所出幾塊陶片，又小又碎，難以分期"。實際上是提出了有比自組卜辭更早的卜辭的問題。提出這個問題是很有意義的。但我堅信：即使有比自組卜辭更早的卜辭，那也決不是賓組卜辭。將來的發掘一定會證明這一點的。

二、真正的文丁卜辭為何？

肖楠同志認為文丁卜辭共有四種字體類型[①]，並以它們只出於小屯南地中期二組以上地層作為論證它們是文丁卜辭的主要根據。然而，在分析卜辭的層位時，首先應對卜辭分類有統一的見解。例如上文提到的屯南 4575，肖楠在分類上認為它屬於賓組，就說小屯南地早期地層出賓組卜辭，我認為它不屬賓組，故云小屯南地早期地層"未見典型賓組及賓組晚期卜辭"。又如裘錫圭在分類上把肖楠的文丁卜辭第一、二類字體合稱"歷自間組"，並認為 T53（4A）所出的屯南 4514—4515、4516 兩片也可以附入此組，則肖楠所定的文丁卜辭，就可以說是也見於小屯南地早期地層了。所以，我先討論分類，再談對層位現象的看法。

肖楠所分的文丁卜辭第一類，在《論武乙、文丁卜辭》中，只說"以粹 221（即合 34122）為例"，《小屯南地甲骨》前言中雖加了"這種字體筆劃較纖細瘦長"，我們仍無法知道，肖楠認為除粹 221 究竟外還有哪些卜辭屬此類。肖楠

---

① 肖楠：《論武乙、文丁卜辭》，《古文字研究》第 3 輯。又，中國社會科學院考古研究所編：《小屯南地甲骨》，中華書局，1980 年，前言。

所分的文丁卜辭第二類，只舉了佚 884（即合 34120）為例，而指出這類卜辭"貞字皆作冂"即"斜方頭形"，也語焉不詳。裘錫圭在《論歷組》中把粹 221 及佚 884 均劃歸"歷自間組"，並認為就是李學勤在《殷代地理簡論》中所分的"四期 3 類卜辭"，對該類卜辭字體特徵作了較詳細說明。

我認為，把合 34122 和合 34121 在字體上歸為一類，是正確的。現以合 34121 的貞作"斜方形耳"（確切說是"梯形耳"）出發，作簡要說明。在眾多的卜旬辭中，確實有一批貞作冂的卜旬辭，如合 20584、22404、33180、34862、34866、34991、34995、35116、35123、16802，歷史所藏善齋拓本 1873，字體相當一致。合 21472 亦屬此，但書法拙劣，似習刻。這批卜旬辭，前辭一律作"干支卜貞"，與冂同版的貞也有一些作方形耳或三角形耳的，或兩耳形狀不一。因字以囗最常見，也有作囚之例，干支之子（巳）作子，於偏旁中偶作子，丑強調指尖之折部，以作又為典型，卯作尖耳之卯，未均作未，酉卣、卣互見。書體風格亦可自成一類。據此，收集除佚 884 之外有冂而書體風格相似的卜辭，可進一步推定該類卜辭的其他特徵性字體，並根據已知特徵性字體的組合關係，把聯繫範圍可擴大到無冂的卜辭，這種歸納方法，擇要以表二示之。

表二　自歷間組的特徵性字形及其同版關係

著錄號	丑	未	酉	囚	貞	人	戌	辰	雨	不	庚	又	隹	用	其	午	壬	癸	戈	兌	辛
甲考209	△	△		△	△			△			△										
合34991	△	△		△	△																
合34866			△	△																	
善1873				△	△								△								
合35116					△			△		△											
合34120				△	△			△							△						
合32198			△	△	△			△			△				△						
合33080				△	△																
合32843			△	△					△		△		△								
合21032			△		△	△															
合20786				△	△	△					△										
合33074	△																				
合40866		△		△	△		△		△		△				△				△		
合20038	△		△																△		△
合33838	△		△		△														△		
庫1016					△				△	△											

由以上方法歸納出來的字體特徵，可以相當容易地把這類卜辭同其他類別的卜辭區分開來。例如這次小屯南地發掘所獲的屯南 940、1080、2173、2250、2628、2841、3911、4242、4573 等，均可劃歸此類。

合 34122 及同辭的合 34121 均無❒字，但這兩片卜甲上的 ❒、❒、❒、❒、❒ 的寫法均同於此類卜辭，雖人旁之作❒與本類常見之❒形不同，不過本類卜辭本有❒、❒混用之現象，如合 61 眔字下部三個人形，兩個作❒，一個作❒。只有以字作❒，近於自組，與本類卜辭合 33074 之作❒不同，而且，在書體風格上，合 34122 及合 34121 比合 34120 更近於自組。但是，我們無法在全部已發現的卜辭中，根據合 34122 和合 34121 的這方面特殊性，劃分出相當數量的卜辭而另立一類，所以還是劃歸本類而承認本類字體有一些不大的差別爲好。

過去，不少研究者對這種卜辭之自成一類缺乏應有的認識。所以，貝塚茂樹一方面把屬於這類的卜甲人文 2982（即合 33309）、卜骨人文 3222（即合 32941）等劃歸"王族卜辭"，另一方面又把同類的卜甲人文 2400（即合 27801）①、卜骨人文 3295（即合 32392）劃歸"三、四期卜辭"。許進雄則把這類卜辭中有❒的定爲"王族卜辭"，無❒的則籠統的歸入"文武丁時期"。近出《甲骨文合集》第七册，把這類卜辭有的歸入附於第一期的"甲類"（按：即自組），有的歸入"丙二類"。這是因爲這類卜辭的字體，有些方面和自組相似，有些方面和歷組相似。所以，裘錫圭稱這類卜辭爲"歷自間組"，是有道理的。不過裘錫圭是從討論歷組的角度出發，在命名時把"歷"放在前；我則認爲按時代先後的次序稱爲"自歷間組"更妥當。

但是，我所稱爲"自歷間組"的這類卜辭，範圍比裘錫圭所謂"歷自間組"範圍要窄一些。這是因爲對於不記卜人的卜辭進行分類，除書體之外，主要只能根據特徵性字體的組合關係。由於每一片卜辭上的字數有限，特殊字形和用字習慣的組合關係是根據許多同版關係轉輾聯繫而推定的。比如 A、B、C、D 共見一版，A、B、C、E 共見一版，則可認爲 A、B、C、D、E 都是共組的特徵字體，如果 A、C、E、F、G 又共見一版，就可能把 F、G 也歸入該組的特徵字體。這樣連續推演下去，勢必有一個把界限劃定在何處的問題。我在推定"自歷間組"的特徵字體時，是以梯形耳的貞字爲核心，對於同❒沒有直接同版關係的特殊字形是否歸屬本組，采取相當審慎的態度，力求在擴大聯繫時，能保持書體風格的較大

---

① 編者按：本片實爲卜骨（參看《人文》拓片，特別是 240 頁照片）。

的一致性。因此，裘錫圭（包括李學勤）所舉出字形的不作 ⩝、子作 ⩗，能否歸於本組，我是表示懷疑的。以裘錫圭同志在《論歷組》中劃歸"歷自間組"的甲709（即合 20510）爲例，該片子作 ⩗、⩗，不作 ⩝、未作 ⩘、寅作 ⩙，用作 ⩚、⩚，受作舟形橫置的 ⩛。這和我所劃的"自歷間組"的子作 ⩗，未作 ⩘、不作 ⩜、用作 ⩚、寅作 ⩙（如合 40866、32198），受作 ⩛（如合 33074），都不合。而合 20510 上這些字的寫法，大都在有自組卜人名的卜辭中可以找到。在書體上，合 20510 多曲筆，和"自歷間組"多折筆也呈不同風格。所以，我認爲合 20510 應劃歸自組，而不應歸入本組。又如裘錫圭認爲人文 3016（合 22202）也歸"歷自間組"，當然，該版如 ⩝、⩘、⩙，及 ⩞（疾字所从）、⩟（伐、北、千所从），都符合"自歷間組"的特徵，但除了 ⩞、⩟ 互作在自組尚未見它例之外，都是自組可以有的特徵。而在作 ⩠，有因之有作 ⩡，則是自組特有的特徵。如果我們把該片劃歸自組，只不過在自組字體特徵中附加"人有作 ⩟ 之特例"。如果劃歸本組，則要在本組用字習慣上增加 ⩡、又互作，字形上增加在作 ⩠，就像如因合 20510 子作 ⩗ 和本組子作 ⩗ 近似而把合 20510 劃歸本組，就要承認 ⩘、⩝、⩙ 等也是本組應有的特徵字形。但這樣一來，我們就不清楚裘錫圭同志究竟把自組和"歷自間組"的界限劃在哪里，最後推演的結果，恐怕只好承認"歷自間組"和自組卜辭之無卜人之片是不可分割的一體，而像貝塚茂樹和《甲骨文合集》那樣，把許多"歷自間組"都附於自組了。

當然，在"自歷間組"可以獨立劃爲一類，以及自歷間組和自組卜辭有密切關係，字體有過渡現象這些主要看法方面，我和裘錫圭同志是完全一致的。但正因爲如此，如將"自歷間組"的界限定得太寬，將和自組難以區劃。這個問題希望和裘錫圭同志作進一步討論，以取得一致意見。就我個人看法，T53（4A）所出的屯 4514—4515、4516 並非"自歷間組"，而應依肖楠定作自組爲是。

下面我們再來討論肖楠的文丁卜辭的後兩種類型。

第三種類型，肖楠在《論武乙、文丁卜辭》中舉合 32723 爲例，說是"字體剛勁有力，近似武乙字體風格"。在《小屯南地甲骨》前言中，另行提出屯 582、3874、4103 作爲此類型的代表，仍說是"字體風格略近於武乙卜辭"。對合 32723 的所屬則改變了看法，認爲它和合 34240、明後 2524、合 32571 等片"上有父乙稱謂，但字體完全與武乙卜辭一樣"。

第四種類型，《論武乙、文丁卜辭》中舉屯 751、2100、2126、2601 爲例，在地層分析時又稱之爲"中期第三類卜辭"。認爲"此類卜辭與第二類（此處指

'中期第二類'，即'武乙卜辭'）相比字體較小，筆風圓潤而柔軟，主要稱謂有父乙等"。在字形上舉出庚多數作中、少數作中，子作凸，辰作冈，子（巳）作卩、夬，午作丨，未作朱、少數作朱，酉作酉、酉，戌作钅，有、侑作孓，羌作肖、肖，伐作戈，叀作吏、吏，灾作宀，啓作启、启，用作用，弜作弜，囚作囚，允作夂等。在《小屯南地甲骨》前言中，談到"中期第三類卜辭"時，在代表片中取消了 2100 而增加了屯 2628；在叙述文丁卜辭第四種類型時又補充了屯 739。字形上取消了庚作中，灾作宀；增加了戌作钅，酉作酉，召作邑，受作孓、孓。

　　肖楠所説的第三、四兩種類型，均屬李學勤所稱之"歷組卜辭"之列。肖楠把"歷組卜辭"分成了"武乙卜辭"、"文丁第三種類型"、"文丁第四種類型"三類，但界綫是模糊不清的。

　　所謂文丁卜辭第三種類型，如依肖楠最初用合 32723 爲代表，則該類字體和肖楠所謂"武乙卜辭"的字體是完全一致而無法作區別的。肖楠把合 32723 定爲文丁卜辭，無非是因爲其上有"父乙"稱謂，但這種字體之有"父乙"稱謂者，除《小屯南地甲骨》前言中所舉的合 34240、明後 2524、合 32571 之外，還可以舉出合 32732 + 32767 + 32768 + 34317、合 32731、明後 2523 等片。同類字體的卜辭中又常見有"父丁"稱謂（但與"父乙"無同版關係），則爲人所共知。至於肖楠後來把合 32723 取消而另舉屯 582、3847、4103 作爲文丁卜辭第三類型的代表，則這三片的字體，實在看不出和肖楠所列舉的第四種類型代表片的字體有什麽不同。特别是後來補充的第四種類型特徵性字形中，受作孓、召作邑，顯然就是根據屯 4103 而言的，但却又把屯 4103 作爲第三種類型的代表片，這實在令人費解。因此，肖楠所分的文丁卜辭第三種類型，在字體上並不能成爲一個獨立的類型。

　　"第四種類型"的分類標準，肖楠説得比較詳細，但也並不十分確切。特別是肖楠在《前言》中所補充的該類型字體代表片屯 2628，不作凸、其作凵、卯作卯、未作朱，這樣的字形組合關係，顯然屬於"自歷間組"這説明肖楠在掌握字體分類標準上，尚欠成熟的考慮。

　　裘錫圭在《論歷組》中，把肖楠對"歷組卜辭"所作的進一步分割工作，不很確切地歸納爲"歷組卜辭父丁類"和"歷組卜辭父乙類"。裘錫圭説："歷組父丁類和父乙類雖然在字體上各有一些特點，但是在很多方面都有其共同點。"所以，"僅僅根據字體很難把這兩類卜辭區分開來"。這個意見我認爲是不對的。我認爲歷組卜辭完全可以"僅僅根據字體"而分爲兩個亞組，但不應從稱謂考慮而

分成什麼"父丁類"、"父乙類"。

我認爲，根據以下字形的組合關係，即貞作方形耳，而且多數下方兩斜劃不相觸而成❰，乙多作曲筆之✓，丁作扁方形之▢與扁圓形之◯互見，戊作✝，庚多作✦，子作較扁的𠙵、𠙻，寅多作偏尾之𝄋，卯有相當比例作圓耳之❊，辰作❋或❋，子（巳）✦、✦互見，未作首部方折或曲弧的❊、❊（有少量的❊）而不見❊，申作鉤曲頗甚的❋，酉作❊、❊、❊、❊而有頸無頸者往往共見於一版，戌一般作弧刃的❋而有相當比例的❋，王字有相當比例底部作弧形的❋，因一律作寬首的❋或❋，吏作❊、❊，自作❊、❊而不見❊、❊。弜字作❊之外有一定比例❊；以及字較小，筆劃較細，有圓潤感。完全可以在歷組卜辭中分出一個亞組，我建議名之爲"歷組卜辭第一類"，簡稱"歷組一類"。它大體上相當於肖楠的"文丁卜辭第四種類型"。其餘的歷組卜辭則可稱爲"歷組卜辭第二類"，簡稱"歷組二類"。大體上相當於肖楠的"武乙卜辭"。這次小屯南地發掘的甲骨中，可定爲歷組一類者，見表三。

表三　歷組一類卜辭在小屯南地出土情況

單　位	期　別	著　錄　號
H2	晚	87　100　313·　325·　339　405?　406　422　436
H17	晚	580·　582　616　663—664
H23	中二	717·　739　751　756·　759·　771—772·　774·　783—784·　792
H24	中二	911—912　944·　961　976?　983?　1049　1051·　1552　1759?　2022　2024
H39	中二	2100·　2104·
H47	中二	2126
H50	中二	2161　2201　2243
H57	晚	2272　2282—2283·　2305·　2287—2288　2308—2309　2347—2348　2351—2352　2439
H58	晚	2482
H65	?	2525
H75	中二	2534　2541·
H83	晚	2564
H85	中二	2601　2604　2605
H103	中二	2761—2762

續表

單 位	期 別	著 錄 號
F1	中	2782 2783
M13	隋	3171 3174 3279 3300 2916˙ 3006˙ 3092 3113 3391 3407 3534
M16	隋	3537? 3580 3593
M20	?	3612
T1③	?	3646˙
T2③	?	3682 3770
T12③_A	?	3834?
T21②_A	?	3847
T22②	?	3966
T23②_A	?	4053 4072
T31③	?	4100˙ 4103 4188 4232 4246
T44③	晚	4318
T44④_C	中	4350
T52②_C	?	4399
T53②	?	4414
T53②_B	?	4477˙ 4507?
T55③	晚	4577?

　　根據字體而分出的歷組一類中，稱謂只見父乙而未見父丁；歷組二類則兼有父乙和父丁，但不同版。裘錫圭之所以感到"父乙類"和"父丁類"僅僅用字體很難區別，是因爲同時要把字體和稱謂均作分類標準是行不通的。肖楠把歷組卜辭分爲"武乙卜辭"和"文丁卜辭"，却又說兩者在字體上有相混現象，也是因爲把稱謂當成分類標準而造成的混亂。

　　應該指出，歷組一類和歷組二類在字體上雖然有可區分的一面，但又有相聯繫的一面。在歷組二類卜辭中之有父乙稱謂者，有一部分在個別字的寫法上同歷組一類相同。如合 32724 酉作 而不作 、 ，合 32730 之貞作 而不作 ，合 32879 之庚作 而不作 ，但它們的書體却和歷組一類不同，字較長大，刀法粗獷有力，多折筆。類似的卜辭，在這次小屯南地發掘的甲骨中，可舉出屯 19、81—

82、93、112、194、340、484、503、562、603、844、994、1051、1074、1918、2123、2124、2198、2426、2836、2845、2914、3006、3798、4185 等。它們只是有個別的 ⟨字⟩、⟨字⟩、⟨字⟩、⟨字⟩、⟨字⟩ 同歷組二類習見的 ⟨字⟩、⟨字⟩、⟨字⟩、⟨字⟩、⟨字⟩、⟨字⟩ 相異，書體風格則完全是歷組二類的。所以仍應劃歸歷組二類。這類卜辭中也見"父丁"稱謂，如屯 503、合 33025 即是。

另外，從表三中可以看出，在我劃歸歷組一類而加有·號的各片，就特徵性字形的組合關係而言，它們是歷組一類的，但書體風格已接近歷組二類。

所以，歷組一類和歷組二類雖可區分為各自獨立的亞組，但在字體上顯然存在相承演進的關係。

綜上所述，肖楠所認為的"文丁卜辭"，包括了我所劃分的"自賓間組"、"歷組一類"和"歷組二類"中有父乙稱謂者。據此而檢查這次發掘中所得全部甲骨的坑位記錄，除了《前言》中未能說明期別的灰坑和地層外，凡出有"自歷間組"和"歷組一類"卜辭的灰坑和探方地層，確實都是屬於小屯南地中期二組堆積及更晚的堆積。至於"歷組二類"雖在中期一組堆積中也存在，可是"歷組二類"字體而有父乙稱謂的卜辭，這次一片也未遇到，故無從檢查。所以，肖楠把"自歷間組"、"歷組一類"和有父乙稱謂的"歷組二類"定為文丁之物，就這次發掘的層位現象來說，並無明顯破綻。

但是，我覺得肖楠同志所堅持的地層根據，並非不容置疑。第一，單就這次發掘來說，出土的有字甲骨號稱五千，但是在比中期二組要早的堆積中，共計才出了 71 片。其中早期堆積的四個灰坑和兩個探方地層中出 17 片，中期一組堆積的 7 個灰坑和一個探方地層中出 54 片。這個數字和中期二組堆積以後的各單位中所出的甲骨實在不成比例。因此，根據這次發掘的層位現象來判定各類甲骨的年代，只能說某類甲骨出於早期堆積一定是早的，如說某類甲骨不出於早期堆積就一定是晚的，就很不保險。在這次發掘中，連典型賓組卜辭都不出於早期和中期一組堆積，却出於中期二組（H47 的屯 2113）及晚期（H57 的屯 2390）堆積中，如果根據這種現象來論證典型賓組卜辭中的父乙也是指武乙而將其定為文丁卜辭，難道是可信的嗎？第二，這次小屯南地發掘區中，沒有遇到相當於大司空村二期的地層和單位。是這一地區原無此期堆積，還是有過此期堆積而被後期破壞無遺，發掘報告中並沒說得很清楚。自從解放以後把殷墟地層劃分為大司空村一至四期以來，在大司空村一期堆積層中明確出土的甲骨也就只有這次發掘的 17 片。至於《1958—1959 年殷墟發掘簡報》

所報導的大司空村出的那片卜骨①，原報告定爲大司空村一期，據鄭振杳同志告知，乃出於 H114，而該坑陶器據現行四期分法，應定爲大司空村二期。在大司空村三期地層中，河南文物工作隊一隊 1955 年在小屯 H1 中得到過一片卜骨②，而該坑出土的陶器群顯然和這次小屯南地中期二組的陶器相同，即屬大司空村三期的後半，而大司空村三期前半期堆積中出土的甲骨，也就只有這次小屯南地所得的 54 片。總之，解放以來在大司空村三期前半及更早的堆積中一共只出 72 片有字甲骨，而大司空村二期堆積中究竟能出什麼樣的甲骨，尚待解決。在這種情況下，由於這次小屯南地發掘所獲的 "自歷間組" 和 "歷組一類" 卜辭，都是和其他類別的卜辭混出於中期二組及更晚的堆積之中，就很難說它們一定不是從更早的地層中被翻移到晚期地層和灰坑中的再生堆積。所以單就這次發掘中 "自歷間組" 和 "歷組一類" 只見於中期二組以上的堆積就認爲其 "父乙" 稱謂不可能是武丁之稱小乙而一定是文丁之稱武乙，是缺乏說服力的。

我們還是從型式學來考察一下吧。

從字體上說，歷組一類和歷組二類字體之間有過渡的關係，已如上述。而董氏所分的 "第三期卜辭" 中不記卜人的那種卜辭，即李學勤名爲 "無名組"③者，在字體上顯然接近於 "歷組二類"，這是人所共知的。不過按肖楠的觀點，這種字體連續演變的方向，是由無名組→歷組二類→歷組一類，而不是相反。這是因爲從董作賓以來，無名組主要屬於康丁時代而歷組二類主要屬於武乙時代的看法，在甲骨斷代研究中一直占統治地位。實際上，我們如果試圖將這一字體連續演變的序列再向兩頭伸展，就可以看出：歷組一類是通過自歷間組而跟地層上已確證爲武丁時代的自組相聯繫的，無名組則是和公認屬於乙辛時代的黃組卜辭相聯繫的。

前文已述，自歷間組在字體上介於自組和歷組之間。單從裘錫圭所劃的 "歷自間組" 中包含有我認爲是自組的卜辭，就足以說明 "自組" 和 "自歷間組" 在字體上的密切關係了。對歷組來說，歷組一類字體在很多方面比歷組二類更接近自歷間組，屯南 4566 就是說明自歷間組和歷組一類在字體上過渡關係的最好例子。

---

① 考古所安陽發掘隊：《1958—1959 年殷墟發掘簡報》，《考古》1961 年 2 期，圖 16。
② 河南文物工作一隊：《一九五五年安陽小屯殷墟的發掘》，《考古學報》1958 年 3 期，圖 6。
③ 李學勤：《小屯南地甲骨與甲骨分期》，《文物》1981 年 5 期。

無名組和黃組在字體上有直接聯繫，這在從前的甲骨著錄中只透露了一點綫索，這次小屯南地發掘則提供了較多的能說明問題的新資料，已經引起不少研究者的注意。

《小屯南地甲骨》前言在叙述小屯南地晚期地層出土的甲骨時說："值得注意的是在 H17、H57、H48、H58 等灰坑中出土了字體屬於帝乙或接近帝乙時代的卜辭，如屯南 648、2157、2405、2263、2489 等。這些卜辭盡管數量不多，但已說明這些坑的堆積年代已進入帝乙時代。"可見，肖楠同志認爲這些卜辭應附入董氏"第五期卜辭"，亦即黃組卜辭。

這里我們又遇到一個分類上的問題了。第一，這類卜辭的共同特徵是什麼？第二，還有哪些卜辭可歸入此類？第三，這類卜辭究竟能否說是"字體屬於帝乙"，即是否可與"第五期卜辭"並爲一類？

從肖楠所舉五例總結，這類卜辭字小而棱角顯明，貞字作兩脚微外撇之 ⿱，有少數上下斜劃相通（屯 2405 之 ⿱），其幾乎全作 ⿱，災均作 ⿱，辛作 ⿱，庚作 ⿱，戊作 ⿱，子作 ⿱，寅作 ⿱，辰作 ⿱，子作 ⿱，未作 ⿱，申作 ⿱，酉作 ⿱，戌作 ⿱，亥作 ⿱。據此，這次發掘的甲骨中可歸此類的還有屯 2617、2917、3564、4343、4363、4474 諸片。其中 2617、3564、4343 不是田獵卜辭，但其均作 ⿱，2617 酉作 ⿱，4343 庚作 ⿱，4343 和 3564 的武字從戈作 ⿱，和上舉 ⿱、⿱ 一致，故可定爲同類。2917 的災全部作 ⿱，但全部干支字的寫法和上舉各字均一致，故可歸入此類。由這些補充之片，可增加午作 ⿱（2917），辰作 ⿱（4474，比 2263 清晰），"于"作 ⿱（2617、3564），受又之又作 ⿱（3564、2617），吉作 ⿱，翌作 ⿱。在以前著錄中，合 37993 干支字寫法全同，而 ⿱、⿱ 互見，貝塚茂樹歸入"第四期卜辭"；合 33521、合 33523 顯屬本類，許進雄歸爲"第三期卜辭"。

這類卜辭的字體，確有接近黃組卜辭的一面，除書體較相近外，其、子、未、庚、受又之又的寫法和黃組一致，王、寅、災、吉、午的寫法也很接近。但和黃組卜辭又有相異的一面，在書體上，字較黃組爲大，且筆劃間較疏朗；字形和黃組也有許多不同：

本類卜辭							
黃組卜辭							

此外如黃組卜辭癸絕大多數作 ⿱，而屯 2263—2264 反面之記事刻辭癸作 ⿱；

黄組卜辭亥多作 [字], 而本類止作 [字]; 黄組之貞多作 [字], 而本類僅一見, 都說明它與黄組字體仍有一定差別。所以, 說這類卜辭的字體"接近"黄組是對的, 說它"屬於"黄組就是分類上的混淆了。

許進雄把這類卜辭歸入"第三期卜辭", 即認爲和無名組是一類, 我認爲是有道理的。這類卜辭和無名組的關係, 可以從屯660、2172、2178、2182、2219、2230、2279、2286、2301、2306、2323、2440、2630、2640、3550等片得到證明。這里所舉的卜辭, 災字 [字]、[字] 互見, 受又之又多作 [字], 叀均作 [字], 接近於黄組, 但其字仍均作 [字], 貞字兩腳不外撇, 庚仍作 [字] 或 [字](屯2630), 子作 [字], 辰作 [字], 災仍有作 [字] 者, 和以屯648爲代表的字體也有一定差別, 但它們可以令人信服地說明典型的無名組卜辭字體是怎樣逐步過渡到以屯648爲代表的字體。從書體上說, 以屯660爲代表的這批卜辭, 顯屬無名組的性質而與黄組有相當顯然的區別, 以屯648爲代表的卜辭的書體與以屯660爲代表的書體之接近性, 要大於它與黄組卜辭的接近性。而且它們和整個無名組一樣有單記干支的記事刻辭, 如屯660、2301、2306、2263, 這是黄組所沒有的。所以我建議把屯660、648這樣的卜辭稱爲"無名組晚期卜辭", 如果將來有更多的發現, 可以割爲"無名黄間組"這樣一個亞組, 而仍歸爲無名組。

從字體上看, 自組→自歷間組→歷組一類→歷組二類→無名組→無名組晚期→黄組是一個逐步過渡的連續序列, 從字體以外的其他方面可找出不少證據, 證明排成這樣一個序列是完全合理的。

1. 鑽鑿形式

許進雄在《卜骨上的鑿鑽形態》中舉了許多實例來論證"王族卜辭"(即自組卜辭和部分自歷間組)和"四期卜辭"(即歷組卜辭和部分自歷間組)在鑽鑿形式上是一致的, 因此斷言: "王族卜辭之與第四期卜辭同時是不能不承認的事實。"但他先已相信"第四期卜辭"是武乙文丁卜辭, 故認爲"王族卜辭與第四期卜辭有相同鑿鑽習慣的事實, 使王族卜辭與第一期同時的說法, 難以令人信服。"現在既已由地層上證明自組卜辭是武丁之物, 則許進雄的說法應改爲"歷組卜辭與自組卜辭有相同鑿鑽習慣之事實, 便歷組卜辭屬武乙文丁時期的方法, 難以令人信服"了。

細緻些分析, 自組和自歷間組的鑽鑿形式是基本一致的。按許進雄的說法, 其長鑿"大部分是特別短或是比武乙時(按指歷組, 主要是歷組二類)短些, 頭尾都是尖的, 或是兩弧綫相交如水滴形, 或是窄長而彎曲不定形"。歷組一類的

情況不夠清楚。歷組二類，即許進雄所謂"第四期武乙時的勁峭字大的卜辭"，其長鑿"經常是比較長，肩也比較寬，頭尾都尖的很少，多半是平的或平圓頭尾的，肩部的綫條較文武丁時（按指自組和自歷間組）顯得挺直多了"。無名組，即許進雄所謂"第三期卜辭之不署貞人名的"，"大部分則是平圓頭尾的長而寬"的長鑿。由此可見，根據長鑿的長度不斷增加，肩部由彎曲度大變直，頭尾由尖變平圓，可將自組→歷組→無名組構成一連續演變的序列。許進雄同時還特別指出，字體屬我稱爲"無名組晚期"的 ROMB2625、ROMB2627（即合 33523、33521，見許書圖 203、照片 16 以及圖 204），有的長鑿"長而寬，顯然是兩肩再挖寬的"、"内壁都是相當緩"，"和第四期（即歷組）兩弧相交的橄欖狀長鑿的挖法是非常不同的"。而和"第五期（即黃組）卜骨 ROM 之 B3169（即合 39080，見許書圖 126、照片 34）的長鑿很相似"。許進雄實際上已經認識到無名組和黃組在字體和鑽鑿形式上是直接過渡的，把合 33523、33521 列爲"到第五期的過渡期"。可惜他當時還未能完全抛開文丁復古的説法，所以仍將自組和歷組安插在有直接過渡關係的無名組與黃組之間。

2. 卜骨骨臼之整治

自組卜辭就已發表的拓本而言，我還沒有找到有截去臼角的例子。自歷間組也有不截除臼角便用於占卜的（如合 32941、合 20038、庫 1125），又有截除臼角的（如合 32198）。字體上介於自歷間組和歷組一類之間的屯 4566 仍是截除臼角的，歷組一類卜骨不截臼角者已很罕見（如屯 2161），歷組二類卜骨則未見不截臼角之例。無名組和黃組卜骨也是都截去臼角的。（無名組晚期截臼角之例如屯 2306—2307。）

因此，從全不截臼角→部分截臼角→全截臼角的觀點來看，自組→歷組→無名組→黃組這樣的連續序列也是合理的。

3. 記事刻辭

倒刻的"干支￥……"這種記事刻辭盛行於歷組一類字體向歷組二類過渡之際，在有這種刻辭的卜骨中，書體風格最有歷組一類特點的是屯 2308—2309，最接近歷組二類的是屯 2282—2283。許多歷組一類卜骨上則肯定沒有這種刻辭（如屯 2351—2352、2601），自歷間組和自組也沒有。在歷組二類卜骨上，辭中之￥改爲￥，由倒刻變成正刻，很常見。無名組卜骨上，這種刻辭省略爲只記干支，或倒或正。有正刻干支者，書體風格更接近於歷組卜辭（如屯 2718—2719 最明顯）；無名組晚期卜骨則只見倒刻的（屯 660、2301、2306、2263）。黃組卜骨就

没有了。

肖楠排定的時代系列是𠂤組→無名組→歷組二類→歷組一類及𠂤歷間組→無名組晚期→黃組，如按這種序列，上述記事刻辭就是出現於康丁，發達於武乙，衰落於文丁，到帝乙之初忽然又出現而恢復康丁的形式，這是難以理解的。

既然根據與卜辭占卜内容無關的多項特徵，用純型式學的方法可以肯定𠂤組→𠂤歷間組→歷組一類→歷組二類→無名組→黃組的發展序列的合理性，那麽，𠂤歷間組、歷組一類和少量歷組二類卜辭中的父乙稱謂，顯然應理解爲武丁之稱小乙，而不可能是文丁之稱武乙了。

我們知道，𠂤歷間組和歷組一類卜辭中只有父乙稱謂而不見父丁稱謂，所以它們應該和賓組卜辭在時代上有重合關係。歷組二類卜辭則既有父乙稱謂，又有父丁稱謂，且父丁稱謂常見，應該上限始於武丁而延於祖庚（但因未見兄庚稱謂，未敢斷言其必延至祖甲），且主要存在於祖庚時代，所以和出組卜辭在時代上有重合關係。這次小屯南地發掘所獲的屯 910—911，正面爲歷組一類卜辭，反面有賓組字體的"壬子，㱿〔示〕……"記事刻辭。屯 2384 上端爲出組字體的"庚辰卜，王"共九辭，下部爲歷組二類卜辭。證明上述推斷是完全正確的。肖楠同志企圖用"同版不同期卜辭"這種新概念來解釋這兩片甲骨，却似乎没有考慮全部甲骨斷代研究都是基於"没有一版甲骨刻着兩個世代的卜辭"這條公設的（《殷虛卜辭綜述》137 頁）。

在確定了以上各組的發展序列之後，我們再討論一下地層問題。根據小屯南地發掘，已知𠂤組出於大司空村一期地層，在相當於大司空村三期前半的小屯南地中期一組地層中，除歷組二類之外，已出無名組卜辭。因此，在發展序列中處於歷組二類跟𠂤組之間的歷組一類卜辭，其原生層位可以推定爲大司空村二期。上文提到的大司空村 H114 所出卜骨，是很值得注意的。這片卜骨只發表了摹本，據摹本來看，貞字作方耳而字較窄長，正是歷組一類的特點；不切臼角，也是歷組一類可以有的特徵。"在衣"之衣與歷組一類字體的屯 2564"在衣"之衣一樣，中央有數點。當然，由於該片出於大司空村，辭例又較特殊，在未見原骨的情況下，不能肯定它就是歷組一類，甚至不敢說它一定是王室卜辭，但在目前，它仍是討論歷組一類卜辭能否出於大司空村二期地層的唯一綫索，如果考古所的同志能檢出原骨，以拓本和照片形式連同該坑陶器正式發表，相信對解決歷組卜辭的年代問題是有好處的。

那麼，究竟什麼是真正的文丁卜辭呢？我認爲，前面所討論過的"無名組晚期卜辭"才是文丁卜辭，李學勤已經指出，屬於這類字體的屯3564上有"武乙宗"，這是文丁時代纔可能出現的稱謂①。裘錫圭在《論歷組》中則先已提出合38229字體不屬黃組，而有"康祖丁宗"，也是文丁時代才能有的稱謂②。應該注意，合38229的康字摹作 ，所从的 ，適和前舉屯2182之庚字寫法相同。因此，當無名組字體發展到屯南2182的時期，已經進入了文丁在位之世，故"無名組晚期"字體應是文丁時代的。

過去我在對李學勤把歷組卜辭提早到武丁時代的想法還很不理解的時候，曾以爲歷組卜辭提前，必將在甲骨斷代上造成空白期。這是因爲我過去對無名組卜辭所歷王世之多，缺乏應有的認識。肖楠把無名組卜辭仍稱爲"康丁卜辭"，這是很不妥當的。陳夢家已經指出，無名組有父丁稱謂，故時代可以下延到武乙③。李學勤又根據無名組有兄庚兄己稱謂而把它的時代上推到祖甲④。但是，既然把上限推到祖甲，則父丁就也有可能是祖甲之稱武丁，不能同時又作爲證明其下限一定到武乙的堅强證據了。但這次小屯南地發掘所獲的屯3564之出現"武乙宗"以及前舉合38229之出現"康祖丁"，都顯然是文丁之世才能出現的稱謂，則無名組卜辭之於武乙之世存在，不待父丁稱謂即可證明。另外，肖楠舉出屯2281的"中宗祖丁，祖甲……父辛"爲武乙稱武丁、祖甲、廩辛，該片正是無名組字體。無名組卜辭中還有兄辛、子癸見於同版之例（如粹340），可知康丁有子名癸，故無名組卜辭之祭兄癸者，如合41495、27634、27571，當亦是武乙時所卜。所以，整個無名組存在的年代，歷祖甲、廩辛、康丁、武乙、文丁五王，其中所見父丁，當既有祖甲之稱武丁，又有武乙之稱康丁。據周初之《無逸》記載，商代祖甲以下諸王在位年數都較短，無名組卜辭共歷五王是不足爲怪的。尤其是無名組字體本身是有差異的，除了無名組晚期之外，還可以分出其他亞組，將另文作專門討論。

最後，還要談一談地層問題。

肖楠認爲，在這次發掘中，以屯648爲代表的那部分無名組晚期卜辭只出於小屯南地晚期地層。而且只注意了它們和黃組卜辭相似的一面，就判定它們

---

① 李學勤：《小屯南地甲骨與甲骨分期》，《文物》1981年5期。
② 裘錫圭：《論"歷組卜辭"的時代》，注㊵。
③ 陳夢家：《殷虛卜辭綜述》，科學出版社，1956年12月，142頁。
④ 李學勤：《評陳夢家〈殷虛卜辭綜述〉》，《考古學報》1957年3期，125頁。

"屬於帝乙"。所以斷言小屯南地晚期堆積"已進入帝乙時代"。但是，出有這種卜辭的 H57，在原發掘簡報中是定爲"中期"堆積的①，在《小屯南地甲骨》前言中才改定爲"晚期"。然而由於分類上的疏忽，似乎没有注意到有個被 H57 所打破的 H85 中，而 H85 中出土的屯 2617 也是這種卜辭，在《前言》中仍把 H85 定爲中期二組堆積。肖楠對 H57 由中期改定爲晚期未作具體説明，從《前言》注③的總説明來看，像 H57、H99、H102 開口都在同一擾亂層下，它們之所以被分別定爲早、中、晚三期，"主要根據平面的打破關係和坑内出土的遺物（甲骨、陶器）來斷定"。當然，按照室内整理的常規，對於開口於同一層的各單位，根據出土遺物來區別時代早晚，這是無可非議的。但是，把本身正在作爲斷代研究的對象而有待地層研究來確定其時代早晚的甲骨，也用來作爲判定各單位所屬期別的依據，這不能不説是方法上的不夠嚴密了。按照這種方法，如果發現 H85 中的屯 2617 在字體上也是"屬於帝乙或接近帝乙時代的卜辭"，又將如何處理這個灰坑的期別判定問題呢？既然甲骨和陶器都可以作爲判定期別的根據，就可以有多種選擇了。比如，可以單根據陶器把 H85 定爲中期二組，而因爲共存的甲骨中已經有字體屬於武乙的，得出中期二組堆積的時代下限也已經"進入帝乙時代"；也可以單根據屯 2617 應屬晚期而把 H85 定爲晚期堆積；甚至可以因爲 H85 既然有晚期甲骨而説它出的陶器也應劃歸晚期陶器。這還是假定每個單位都出有可確定期別的陶器資料，如果某一單位陶片很少或很碎，不能分期，則該單位期別的判定，就只能由整理者對甲骨時代的認識來決定了。可是，用這種方法而判定的各單位的期別，在討論甲骨斷代時又要用來作爲論證甲骨年代早晚的根據，就不能没有"乞貸證明"之嫌。人們可以懷疑：中期一組堆積之所以不含有自歷間組和歷組一類卜辭，是否也是對甲骨時代先有定見而整理的結果呢？否則爲什麽中期一組堆積所出甲骨是那麽少呢？

三、甲骨斷代研究的方法問題

根據以上討論，殷墟全部王室卜辭的分類和時代可以歸納爲：

---

① 考古所安陽工作隊：《一九七三年安陽小屯南地發掘簡報》，《考古》1975 年 1 期。

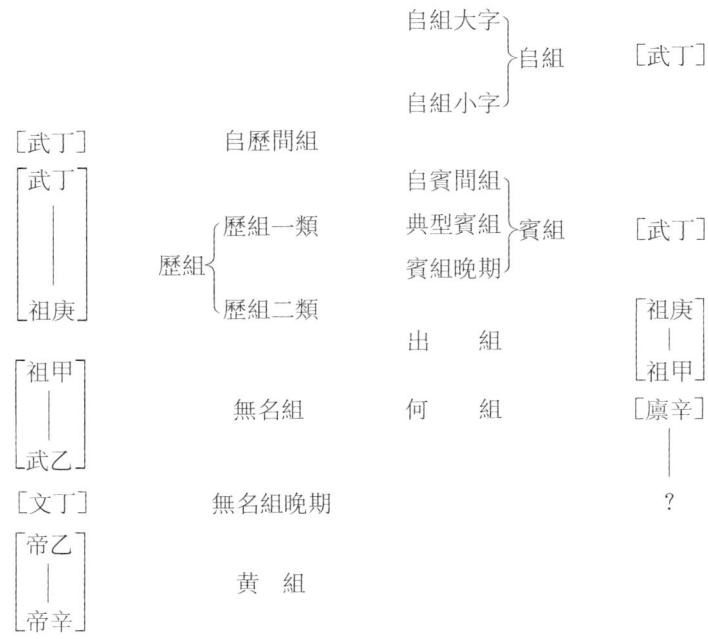

　　殷墟王室卜辭在演進上可以分爲兩系的思想，是李學勤先生在第一屆古文字討論會上首次公開提出的。在甲骨斷代研究史上開創了一個新的時期。我認爲，王室卜辭是由自組卜辭而分化爲兩個各有特點的演進序列的，這和李先生認爲自組不能成爲卜辭發展中的一個獨立階段的看法稍有差異。黃組卜辭則反映兩系後來又合流的迹象。王室卜辭之分化爲兩系，如說是出現了兩個獨立的占卜機構，在卜辭內容中還找不出積極的證據，我覺得目前還是解釋爲王室占卜集團中因師承關係而形成的不同流派爲妥。

　　用李學勤的"兩系說"斷代體系取代董作賓"復古說"的斷代體系，想必在甲骨學界還會有一段時間的熱烈爭論。爲了早日取得統一的看法，首先有必要在斷代研究方法上取得一致。

　　自從董作賓提出甲骨斷代的十項標準後，他自己在《乙編序》中又進而指出，甲骨斷代實際上只有稱謂和卜人這"兩大法寶"。陳夢家則把世系、稱謂、占卜者定爲甲骨斷代的第一標準。他們所說的"斷代標準"，都是把甲骨分類和確定某類甲骨的年代範圍這兩件事情混爲一談的。

　　甲骨斷代研究的最終目的，是把每一片甲骨的年代縮到盡可能小範圍。對於確定年代來說，王室卜辭定年代的根本依據，是將稱謂同商王世系進行對照。但是，如果某片甲骨上只有一個稱謂，比如只有父丁，則在遷殷後的諸王中，可以是盤庚、小辛、小乙之稱祖丁，也可以是祖庚、祖甲之稱武丁，或可以是武乙之

稱康丁，又可以是帝乙之稱文丁。必然出現"公說公有理，婆說婆有理"的現象。王國維、羅振玉僅根據稱謂而把後上 25·9（即合 2131）定爲武丁時代之所以正確無誤，是因爲其上同時有父甲、父庚、父辛，而遷殷之後諸王的父輩兼有甲、辛、庚三名者，只有武丁。然而，多數甲骨卜辭是不含有稱謂的，加以後來的研究又表明，各代商王的祭祀男性亡靈，並不限於即位的先王，有許多是商王世系中找不到的，使問題更複雜化了。所以，只有把零散的甲骨先進行分類，對每類甲骨中所見的全部稱謂加以總結，並統計各種稱謂的數量比例以明確其主次，由這種"稱謂系統"與商王世系進行對比，才能較可靠地確定每類甲骨的存在年代。董作賓發現的"貞人"（卜人），是對署卜人名卜辭的一個最有效的分類標準。但它本身並不具有確定年代的直接意義。

雖然有了分類和"稱謂系統"，某一類甲骨的年代仍可以有多樣的解釋。以自組卜辭爲例，它的"稱謂系統"和賓組很接近，故有人據此定其亦屬武丁時期。但有人則認爲雖然兩者祭祀對象均以父乙爲主，父甲、父辛也相同，但賓組有父庚，爲自組所未見（實際上是因爲自組逕稱"盤庚"，不稱"父庚"），故仍堅持把自組之父乙解釋爲文丁稱武乙，而自組的父甲、父辛則可說成是王系以外的諸父。只有這次小屯南地發掘中有幾片自組卜辭出於殷墟早期地層後，才能使自組屬武丁之說成爲定論。可見，每類甲骨的出土層位，是稱謂系統之外的另一個確定年代的原始根據。

除了稱謂系統和世系對照，以及地層學的方法，再沒有其他方法可以作爲確定年代的原始根據。但要正確使用這兩種方法，都必須首先解決甲骨分類問題。上文已經指出，稱謂系統是從同類甲骨中總結出來的。每類甲骨的範圍如不能確定，不同研究者各自總結的稱謂系統就不一樣。比如，貝塚茂樹在對京都大學人文科學研究所的甲骨進行分類時，是把一部分自賓間組的卜辭劃歸王族（即自組）卜辭的。自賓間組是有父庚稱謂的，故按貝塚的分類法，自組的稱謂系統中就可以有父庚了。又如屯 3564 之有"武乙宗"，我根據翌作🀄，武从戈作🀄，"弘吉"不合書，認爲在分類上不屬黃組卜辭而屬無名組晚期，才作爲無名組卜辭下限進入文丁之世的證據，如按肖楠分類認爲它屬於帝乙卜辭，則帝乙之世當然可以有武乙稱謂，就根本不會去考慮它可不可能是文丁卜辭了。使用地層學的方法，同樣也有一個先要確定甲骨類別的問題，前文已說過不少，就不再贅述了。從這個意義上說，甲骨分類學實爲甲骨斷代研究之基礎。

目前在甲骨分類上，使用的標準很不統一，把稱謂當作分類標準的做法，仍

頗流行，肖楠所分的"康丁卜辭"、"武乙卜辭"、"文丁卜辭"，就是基於主要稱謂的一種分類。"歷組卜辭"本來是和稱謂無關的分類概念，再分成"歷組父丁類"和"歷組父乙類"，也是受到了以稱謂作分類標準的影響。從理論上說，既然賴以確定年代的稱謂系統是在分類的基礎上才總結出來的，先就把稱謂也作爲分類標準，顯然是不科學的。

董作賓原先所舉的十個斷代標準中，坑位、方國、人物都根本不應當作分類標準，"事類"和"文法"也多半不能作爲分類標準。董氏所謂"坑位"的本義是指發現甲骨的探坑、探溝所在的位置，這種按地點來對甲骨進行分類的想法已證明是行不通的。後來的研究者們使用的"坑位"一詞，是指甲骨所出的灰坑或其他單位。由於發掘經驗表明，同一灰坑或其他單位所出的甲骨，即使是在早期地層中，時代雖較單一，類別也很複雜；在較晚的地層中，則往往混出各個時代各種類別的甲骨。所以這種意義的"坑位"，在甲骨分類上也是沒有用處的。至於根據卜辭內容來分類，只是徒然造成種種混亂而已。從歷史經驗來看，在對署卜人名的卜辭進行分類時，卜人及其同版關係，是正確分類的基本依據。但同一卜人集團所卜諸片要進一步分成細類、卜人組之間互相交錯過渡現象的區劃界限，以及不見卜人諸片的歸類，字體（即書體風格，字形特徵和用字習慣三個方面）是起很重要的作用的。至於對習慣上不署卜人名的一大批卜辭。堪稱分類第一標準的，只是字體而已。

對賓組、出組、何組的研究表明，字體是隨着時代而演變的，它既有連續過渡的性質，又呈現一定的階段性。據我推想，當時卜人雖很多，但在甲骨上刻字這一種專門技術工作，恐怕不是很多卜人同時進行的，否則就不能解釋同一時期多人所卜的諸辭，在書法和刀法上何以如此一致而看不出各自的特點。所以，甲骨刻辭之字體的連續過渡性的演變，很可能只是同一刻手早晚期書法和刀法的變化；演變又呈現的階段性，則多半是因爲一位新手在刻意摹仿其業師的字迹時，又不能不表現出自己的風格和特點。由於字體演變比較快，而且呈現一定的階段性，所以從型式學觀點來看無疑是分類的最好標準。其他如獨立於卜辭內容之外的鑽鑿形式、甲骨整治形式、記事刻辭形式等等，當然在型式學上也有分類的意義，但都不如字體所能分的類細緻。而且，在多數人只能據拓本來分類的情況下，字體最便於使用。

由於在署卜人名的卜辭中得到了字體可作甲骨分類標準的經驗，對於不署卜人名的卜辭進行分類，實際上主要是依靠字體而進行的。但過去在分類上有兩種

缺點：第一，有的人過分相信書體風格上的印象，而不重視對字形和用字習慣的具體分析。似乎培養甲骨分類的能力，首先在於多看。看的甲骨多了，自然能達到看它像哪一類就是哪一類的地步，把甲骨分類法變成只可意會不可言傳的東西。第二，不少研究者雖注意了字形和用字習慣的分析，但偏執於個別字的寫法，而不是着眼於它們的組合關係。由於不同類的卜辭個別字寫法相同，就把它們互相混淆起來。舉一個簡單的例子來説，《甲骨文合集》把 ROMB2692 定爲第一期附甲類（即自組卜辭），見合 20027，謝濟同志説自組卜辭中有子商，即指該片。該片上除兆序外只存五字，《甲骨文合集》顯然是因爲貞作 ꩜ 與自組習見寫法相同而歸入此類。當然，同片上 ꩜꩜ 兩字寫法，也是自組所有的，但子作折足的 ꩜，却是自組未見的，這種折足的子是歷組一類的特點，如合 32762 好作 ꩜。而且歷組一類的屯 751 商作 ꩜，也和本片之 ꩜ 的簡化方式相似。所以單據 ꩜ 而定爲自組是片面的做法，因爲除自組外，自歷間組、歷組一類和歷組二類貞均有作 ꩜ 的。應該根據 ꩜、꩜、꩜ 這種特殊組合定爲歷組一類才對。因此，根據字體來分類，應該在重視書體一致的前提下，着重於總結每類卜辭在特徵性字形和用字習慣上的特有組合關係，才能使以字體分類的方法成爲科學而易於把握的方法。

　　怎樣才能確定某類卜辭的特徵性字形和用字習慣的特有組合關係呢？在署卜人名的卜辭中可用有同版關係的卜人名作爲歸納這種特有組合關係的依據，對於習慣上不署名的卜辭來説，這種特有組合關係是通過同版關係轉遞式地推定的，上文在討論自歷間組和無名組晚期字體時已經舉例説明過了。由於轉遞式的推定無限進行下去必然會使各類之間漫無界限，必須以保持書體的一致性作爲一種限制。而且，每類甲骨中字的寫法都會有例外現象，因而保持書體的基本一致在分類上是有重要意義的。據我個人的經驗，這種轉遞式的推定法，有一個選擇起點的問題。比如我在劃出自歷①間組時，是以梯形耳的 ꩜ 和有 ꩜ 的卜旬辭爲起點的。因爲它在開始時較有效地保持書體的一致性。李學勤先生則似乎是先把 ꩜、꩜ 當作同類寫法而作爲起點的，所以他推定的該類範圍就比我的大了。

　　過去有些研究者未能把分類和確定年代這兩件事情分開，不知道字體只能作爲分類的標準，而把字的寫法逕直當作確定年代的標準。比如因爲自組干支字的寫法和黄組有一些相近之處，就説自組卜辭應定在殷墟晚期，這種把分類標準和

---

① 編者按："歷"，原文誤作"賓"，今徑改。

確定年代的標準混爲一談的做法，是今後甲骨斷代研究中應該堅決擯棄的。

利用字體對現有的各類卜辭作更細緻的分類，是有廣闊前景的工作，希望有更多的研究者能仔細從事這方面的研究，才能使整個甲骨斷代研究從粗疏的估計而變成更精確的科學工作。

要想確定每類甲骨的具體年代，原始根據只有稱謂和地層二者。但二者又均有其局限性。考古發掘中的層位，只能用以判斷遺物的相對早晚關係，對遺物的具體年代則只能提供大致的估計。比如可以推想殷墟的最下面的商文化層時代應接近盤庚，最上的商文化層應屬帝辛前後，但要確定哪層是哪個商王在世的年代，靠地層本身是無法做到的。而且某一次有限的發掘中所提供的各類甲骨的層位，並不一定都是它們各自的最早原生層位。對稱謂的解釋，更有多樣的選擇性。比如，我是在無名組卜辭上接歷組二類而下接黃組卜辭的考慮下，才認爲該組卜辭中已發現的全部稱謂，可以從三輩五王的角度加以解釋。如果一定要堅持它只是康丁卜辭，則父庚、父甲以外的諸父也可以解釋成都是祖庚祖甲的兄弟，兄辛以外的諸兄也可以解釋成都是廩辛康丁的兄弟，不見得就一定說不通。即使把層位和稱謂結合考慮，也不能保證對稱謂的解釋都只有唯一的選擇。

因此，從分類到確定年代之間，還要注意一個非常重要的中間環節，就是盡可能弄清各類卜辭之間的互相關係。裘錫圭同志在《論歷組》一文中詳細討論的同日占卜同事的現象，是確定不同類卜辭在橫向上同代關係的可靠原則，不同類卜辭見於同版也是判定它們基本同代的另一種根據。我在本文中所強調的型式學上的演變序列，則是確定諸類卜辭在縱向上接續關係的有效方法。如果我們能用上述方法把各類卜辭的關係構成一個大體的框架，那麼，只要能由稱謂和層位結合而對其中某幾類卜辭的年代有了定論，其他各類卜辭的年代問題就不難解決，不至於因爲個別稱謂的錯誤理解或某種偶然的層位現象而走入歧途。

我相信，如果肖楠同志能基本上同意我對斷代研究方法的這些意見，肯定是會對這次小屯南地發掘的地層現象，作出跟我現在一樣的重新理解的。

1981 年 6 月 12 日定稿

《林澐文集・文字卷》按語：

本文第一部分末尾提到在𠂤組卜辭中有"婦好"之名，是把合 19998 "尋姓女㞢子"中的"姓"字右旁和右面的"子"字誤爲一字，實際在𠂤組卜辭中並未

出現"婦好"之名。

　　本文在討論無名黃間組卜辭字體時，尚未注意到該組卜辭有相當數量的"酉"字作🙾，所以把字形仍誤摹作🙾。而且在列舉和屯 660 相同字體（即無名黃間一類）的各版時，屯 3793 實際應是無名黃間二類。屯 4326、4327、4447 均非此組，故一併删去。

　　原載《古文字研究》第 9 輯，中華書局，1984 年；收入《林澐學術文集》，中國大百科全書出版社，1998 年；又收入《林澐文集・文字卷》，上海古籍出版社，2019 年。今據後者收入。

胡厚宣

八十五年來甲骨文材料之再統計

在四十七年以前，我曾寫過一篇《甲骨文材料之統計》，登在1937年4月2日天津《益世報·人文周刊》第13期，轉載在開明書店出版胡愈之先生主編的《月報》第1卷第5期。在當時曾經引起一般學人的注意。

抗日戰爭期間，1942年在成都編印《甲骨文商史論叢》，我又寫過一篇《甲骨文發現之歷史及其材料之統計》。《論叢》1944年由齊魯大學國學研究所出版，印數不多，但後來臺灣大通書局和香港文友堂書店都有翻印。

解放初，我根據新的情況，把它改寫成一本名叫《五十年甲骨文發現的總結》的小書，1951年3月商務印書館出版。幾年之間，一連印了三次。1954年1月，商務編審部同我商量，要印第4版，我建議等我補充修改後再印，人事旁午，不覺已是三十年。這本小書，在國外，聽說也有幾處加以翻印，有的論文集，還收錄了小書裏有關的篇章。直到最近，還有人引用這本小書裏的一些材料，這就使我感到非常惶恐，不能不趕快再寫這一篇補充修訂的文章了。

當我寫《統計》一文的時候，那是在解放以前，大學畢業剛進研究院不久。到我寫《總結》那本小書的時候，我們國家才剛剛解放。今年已是我們偉大祖國建國三十五周年；就甲骨學這一門學科來說，從1899年開始認識到現在，也已經八十五周年了。今天改寫這本小書，對八十五年以來甲骨文發現的材料，重新作一統計，條件已經比較成熟。

過去作甲骨文材料的統計，以流散到國外的材料最難瞭解，根據傳聞，或間接引用別人的說法，常常會造成許多錯誤。這個問題，在今天就比較容易解決。

譬如說，流散到國外的甲骨，以日本為最多，過去瞭解，比較困難。這些年

來，除了京都大學人文科學研究所①、東京大學東洋文化研究所②、東洋文庫③和書道博物館④等幾大宗甲骨都陸續發表之外，東京大學松丸道雄教授還在《甲骨學》雜誌上，陸續發表了《日本散見甲骨文字蒐彙》1至6期⑤，神户大學的伊藤道治教授除與京都大學貝塚茂樹合著《京都大學人文科學研究所藏甲骨文字》之外，也陸續發表了《故小川睦之輔氏藏甲骨文字》⑥，《大原美術館所藏甲骨文字》⑦，《藤井有鄰館所藏甲骨文字》⑧，《檜垣元吉氏藏甲骨文字》⑨，《關西大學考古學資料室藏甲骨文字》⑩，《國立京都博物館藏甲骨文字》⑪和《黑川古文化研究所藏甲骨文字》⑫等論文。1981年我去日本開會並訪問，在東京大學東洋文化研究所的一次懇談會上⑬，我同松丸道雄教授談起日本收藏甲骨的問題⑭，他不久就寫了《日本搜儲的殷墟出土甲骨》一文⑮。日本收藏甲骨較多迄今還未曾發表的單位，有一個天理大學參考館。據香港中文大學饒宗頤教授說數量有3500片之多⑯。這次我在日本，承伊藤道治教授和天理大學金關恕教授的美意，用了一整天的時間，陪同我仔細觀察了天理的全部甲骨，一大木箱，内裝38盒，係羅振玉、王國維兩氏舊藏，總計不到1000片。

其次藏甲骨較多的是加拿大安大略博物館。這幾年來，許進雄博士先後發表了安大略博物館所藏《明義士收藏甲骨》⑰及《懷特氏等收藏甲骨文集》⑱，並作

---

① 貝塚茂樹、伊藤道治：《京都大學人文科學研究所藏甲骨文字》，圖版册1959年，本文篇1960年，索引1968年。增補版改名《甲骨文字研究》，1980年。
② 松丸道雄：《東京大學東洋文化研究所藏甲骨文字》，1983年。
③ 東洋文庫中國史研究委員會：《東洋文庫所藏甲骨文字》，1979年。
④ 青木木菟哉：《書道博物館藏甲骨文字》，刊《甲骨學》6—10期，1958—1964年。
⑤ 松丸道雄：《日本散見甲骨文字蒐彙》（一）至（六），刊《甲骨學》7—12期，1959—1980年。
⑥ 伊藤道治：《故小川睦之輔氏藏甲骨文字》，刊《東方學報》京都第37册，1966年。
⑦ 伊藤道治：《大原美術館所藏甲骨文字》，刊《倉敷考古館研究集報》第4號，1968年。
⑧ 伊藤道治：《藤井有鄰館所藏甲骨文字》，刊《東方學報》京都第42册，1971年。
⑨ 伊藤道治：《檜垣元吉氏藏甲骨文字》，刊《神户大學文學部紀要》1，1972年。
⑩ 《關西大學考古學資料室藏甲骨文字》，刊《史泉》51號，1977年。以上⑥—⑩注論文5篇。又統名《日本所見甲骨録》，附在重印本《卜辭通纂》後，日本朋友書店出版，1977年。
⑪ 伊藤道治：《國立京都博物館藏甲骨文字》，刊神户大學《文化學年報》第3號，1984年。
⑫ 伊藤道治：《黑川古文化研究所藏甲骨文字》，刊同上。
⑬ 浦野俊則：《圍繞胡厚宣先生的座談會》，刊《不於非止》第四號，1981年。又東京大學東洋文化研究所：《圍繞胡厚宣先生的懇談會》，1981年。
⑭ 松丸道雄：《日本現存的殷墟出土甲骨》，1981年8月21日《朝日新聞》。
⑮ 松丸道雄：《關於日本蒐儲的殷墟出土甲骨》，刊《東洋文化研究所紀要》第86册，1981年。
⑯ 饒宗頤：《日本所見甲骨録》（一），刊香港大學《東方文化》3卷1期，1956年。
⑰ 許進雄：《明義士收藏甲骨》圖版1972年，釋文1977年。
⑱ 許進雄：《懷特氏等收藏甲骨文集》，1979年。

了《皇家安大略博物館所藏甲骨文字索引》①，就連明義士舊藏的甲骨拓本，也編輯出版了《殷虛卜辭後編》②一書。流散到加拿大的7 000多片甲骨，可以說基本上發表凈盡了。

關於美國所藏的甲骨，近年先有李棪教授的《北美所見甲骨選粹》③和饒宗頤教授的《歐美亞所見甲骨錄存》④，後有周鴻翔教授發表的《美國所藏甲骨錄》⑤，更作了全面的搜集。1982年和1983年，我兩次前往美國，在周書的基礎上，也作了一點補充的調查。

關於歐陸所藏的甲骨，在法國的，饒宗頤教授發表了《巴黎所見甲骨錄》⑥，在瑞士的，饒宗頤教授發表了《海外甲骨錄遺》⑦。西德的甲骨，我們從王俊銘先生處，借到了全部照片，1958年我去蘇聯，也搜集了收藏在愛米塔什博物館的甲骨⑧。

關於英國所藏的甲骨，除了饒宗頤教授的《歐美亞所見甲骨錄存》⑨發表了一小部分拓本和照片之外，我們從吳子臧（世昌）教授借到大英博物院舊藏全部甲骨的照片⑩，我們還經羅惟一教授的協助，借到劍橋大學圖書館所藏全部甲骨的照片。1982年和1983年，李學勤同志和齊文心同志先後到英國，對英國全國收藏的甲骨作了全面的調查，齊文心同志並以半年多的時間，將所有甲骨予以墨拓。這些拓本和照片，現都要編輯成專書，出版公佈。

這樣，在早期方法斂所摹《庫方二氏藏甲骨卜辭》⑪、《甲骨卜辭七集》⑫和《金璋所藏甲骨卜辭》⑬等三書之外，不但將摹本換成了照片和拓本，而且所瞭

---

① 許進雄：《皇家安大略博物館所藏甲骨文字索引》（一）至（五），《中國文字》新4—8期，1981—1983年。
② 許進雄：《殷虛卜辭後編》，1972年。
③ 李棪：《北美所見甲骨選粹考釋》，刊香港中文大學《中國文化研究所學報》3卷2期，1970年。
④ 饒宗頤：《歐美亞所見甲骨錄存》，1970年。
⑤ 周鴻翔：《美國所藏甲骨錄》，1976年。
⑥ 饒宗頤：《巴黎所見甲骨錄》，1956年。
⑦ 饒宗頤：《海外甲骨錄遺》，香港大學《東方文化》4卷1—2期，1957—1958年。
⑧ 胡厚宣：《蘇聯國立愛米塔什博物館所藏甲骨文字》，刊《甲骨文與殷商史》第3期。
⑨ 饒宗頤：《歐美亞所見甲骨錄存》，1970年。
⑩ 英國大英博物院舊藏甲骨現歸倫敦圖書館收藏。
⑪ 方法斂：《庫方二氏藏甲骨卜辭》，1935年。
⑫ 方法斂：《甲骨卜辭七集》，1938年。
⑬ 方法斂：《金璋所藏甲骨卜辭》，1939年。以上三書又曾合編爲《方法斂摹甲骨卜辭三種》一書，1966年。

解的材料，也增加許多了。

至於我國臺灣省所藏的甲骨，本來遷自大陸，我們早有瞭解。而且重要的都已先後發表爲《殷虛文字甲編》①、《殷虛文字甲編考釋》②、《殷虛文字乙編》③、《殷虛文字丙編》④、《甲骨文錄》⑤和《殷虛文字存真》⑥等書。

香港地區所藏的甲骨，除了饒宗頤教授在《歐美亞所見甲骨錄存》⑦已發表一部分之外，李棪教授又出版了《聯合書院圖書館新獲東莞鄧氏甲骨簡介》⑧一文。1983 年我去香港中文大學，順便也核對了香港所有的甲骨實物材料。

關於國内收藏的甲骨，由於近些年來，編輯《甲骨文合集》一書，我們也作了近乎普查的工作。計全國收藏甲骨的，有 25 個省市自治區，40 個城市，98 個機關單位和 47 個收藏家，共藏甲骨將近 10 萬片。這一數字，雖然不見得就十分完全或絶對正確，這也是不可能的。但比起過去的統計，往往根據傳聞，那就比較接近確切的多了。

現在試就我們最近瞭解所得，先國内後國外，再作一次重新的統計：

國内各單位收藏甲骨，總數超過 2 萬片以上者，有：

北京圖書館　　　34 512⑨
故宫博物院　　　22 463⑩

收藏甲骨在萬片以下，5 千片以上者，有：

　山東省博物館　　5 468
　上海博物館　　　5 275⑪
　中國社會科學院考古研究所　　5 064⑫

收藏甲骨在 5 千片以下千片以上者，有：

---

① 董作賓：《殷虛文字甲編》，1948 年。
② 屈萬里：《殷虛文字甲編考釋》，1961 年。
③ 董作賓：《殷虛文字乙編》，上、中輯，1948 年；下輯，1953 年，1956 年重印。
④ 張秉權：《殷虛文字丙編》，上、中、下輯，1957—1972 年。
⑤ 孫海波：《甲骨文錄》，1938 年。
⑥ 關百益：《殷虛文字存真》，1931 年。
⑦ 饒宗頤：《歐美亞所見甲骨錄存》，1970 年。
⑧ 李棪：《聯合書院圖書館新獲東莞鄧氏甲骨簡介》刊香港中文大學《聯合書院學報》7 期，1969 年。
⑨ 已除去僞片及無字甲骨。
⑩ 内有碎片 500 片左右。
⑪ 1979 年 5 月 7 日濮茅左同志告以數字是 5 276 片。
⑫ 綴合後數字是 4 534，《小屯南地甲骨》拓片號是 4 589。

北京大學歷史系　　　3 001
　　旅順博物館　　　2 925①
　　南京博物院　　　2 921
　　中國社會科學院歷史研究所　　　1 987
　　天津市歷史博物館　　　1 847②
　　清華大學圖書館　　　1 694
收藏甲骨在千片以下 5 百片以上者，有：
　　中國歷史博物館　　　862③
　　河南省博物館　　　839
　　南京大學圖書館　　　575
收藏甲骨在 5 百片以下百片以上者，有：
　　吉林大學歷史系　　　493
　　北京市文物工作隊　　　484④
　　新鄉市博物館　　　480
　　北京師範大學歷史系　　　430
　　遼寧省博物館　　　394
　　浙江省博物館　　　339
　　復旦大學歷史系　　　335
　　吉林省博物館　　　293
　　河北大學歷史系　　　209
　　廈門大學人類學博物館　　　199⑤
　　安陽市博物館　　　195
　　重慶市博物館　　　192
　　山西省文物工作委員會　　　185⑥
　　安徽省博物館　　　145
　　廣東省博物館　　　128
　　武漢市文物商店　　　127

---

① 　包括未編號的一些有字甲骨，待核實。
② 　已除去僞片及無字甲骨。
③ 　包括少量借陳甲骨。
④ 　舊存 274 片，又市財政局實物庫 210 片，共 484 片。
⑤ 　舊藏 10 片，又 89 片，又新購 100 片，合共 199 片。
⑥ 　舊藏 175 片，新獲送北京展覽 10 片，共 185 片。

湖北省博物館　　　115
　　華東師範大學歷史系　　101①
　　武漢師範學院　　　100

收藏甲骨百片以下 10 片以上者，有：

　　雲南省文物商店　　　96②
　　旅大市文物商店　　　85
　　中國社會科學院考古研究所殷墟陳列室　　79
　　東北師範大學歷史系　　77
　　雲南省博物館　　　73
　　陝西師範大學歷史系　　72
　　開封市博物館　　　65
　　中山大學歷史系　　63
　　遼寧大學歷史系　　48③
　　四川省博物館　　　47④
　　青島市博物館　　　44⑤
　　北京市文管處　　　40
　　華南師範學院　　　39
　　江西省博物館　　　37
　　蘇州市博物館　　　33⑥
　　河北省博物館　　　31
　　河南省歷史研究所　　31
　　河南大學歷史系　　31
　　天津市藝術博物館　　25
　　廣東師範學院　　　25
　　哈爾濱師範大學歷史系　　24
　　天津師範學院圖書館　　23
　　內蒙古大學歷史系　　21

---

① 已除去偽片。
② 私人藏主收回，今不知原甲骨何在。
③ 舊藏 37，新獲 11，共 48 片。
④ 舊藏 39，新獲 8 片，已除去偽片。
⑤ 舊藏 37，新獲 6，又 1 片，共 44 片。
⑥ 舊藏 25，新獲 2，倉庫舊存 6，共 33 片。

廣州市博物館　　　21
　　北京師範學院歷史系　　20
　　鄭州市博物館　　　20
　　台州文管會　　　20
　　鄭州大學歷史系　　18
　　甘肅省博物館　　　18①
　　中山大學中文系　　17
　　貴陽師範學院　　　17
　　南京市文管會　　　16
　　天津市文物商店　　16
　　南京師範學院　　　13
　　鎮江市博物館　　　13
　　浙江省圖書館　　　13
　　甘肅師範大學歷史系　13
　　四川大學博物館　　13
　　河北師範學院歷史系　12
　　南開大學　　　　　10
　　內蒙古師範學院　　10
　　西南師範學院　　　10

收藏甲骨不到10片者，有：
　　河北師範大學歷史系　9
　　湖南省博物館　　　9
　　山東大學歷史系　　8
　　西北大學歷史系　　8
　　武漢大學　　　　　8
　　徐州市博物館　　　7
　　杭州大學歷史系　　6②
　　上海師範學院歷史系　5
　　福建省博物館　　　5
　　北京市文物商店　　4

---

① 已除去偽片。
② 已除去多量偽片。

揚州市博物館　　　4
　　陝西省博物館　　　4
　　貴州省博物館　　　4
　　山丹縣文化館　　　4①
　　廣州市文物商店　　3
　　福建師範大學歷史系　　3
　　武漢市二十八中　　3
　　濟寧一中　　3
　　山東師範學院歷史系　　2
　　河南文物工作隊　　2
　　黑龍江省博物館　　1
　　避暑山莊博物館　　1
　　晉祠保管所　　1

以上國内 38 個城市 98 個單位，共藏甲骨 95 880 片。

　　至於私人收藏，因爲流動量大，不易瞭解，瞭解後不久，可能又有變化。姑舉解放以來，我們先後瞭解情況，略備參考。

在北京的有 10 家 354 片。
　　董希文舊藏　　111
　　張瑋舊藏　　65
　　康生舊藏　　59
　　高君謨舊藏　　38
　　王壽之舊藏　　30
　　何春畬舊藏　　19
　　鄧拓舊藏　　16
　　臧勝遠　　10
　　梁思永舊藏　　4
　　耿鑒庭　　2

在上海的有 18 家 926 片。
　　曹仁裕舊藏　　600
　　潘景鄭舊藏　　100
　　孫鼎舊藏　　76

---

① 參看 1981 年 9 月 30 日《人民日報》。

羅伯昭舊藏	40
杜亞詒舊藏	22
陳漢第舊藏	15
沈曾植舊藏	14
張鳳舊藏	14
張丹斧舊藏	11
邊政平舊藏	10
李旭舊藏	6
朱鎮生舊藏	4
陳器成舊藏	4
孫叔仁舊藏	3
龔心釗舊藏	3
童大年舊藏	2
吳思進舊藏	1
郭士祺舊藏	1

在天津的有 3 家 17 片。

謝宗陶	8
徐寶祠舊藏	8
胡敬之	1

在哈爾濱的有 2 家 18 片。

游壽	14
周瑛	4

在濟南的有 1 家 8 片。

欒調甫舊藏	8

在開封的有 3 家 18 片。

孫作雲舊藏	10
郭人民	7
趙寶俊	1

在南京的有 2 家 196 片。

陳中凡舊藏	186
孫望	10

在徐州的有 1 家 25 片。

黄龍　　　25

在杭州的有 2 家 6 片。

　　黄賓虹舊藏　　5
　　姜亮夫　　　　1

在紹興的有 1 家 10 片。

　　王永元　　　10

在廣州的有 1 家 100 片。

　　商承祚　　　100

在桂林的有 1 家 8 片。

　　温雄飛舊藏　　8

在西安的有 1 家 15 片。

　　党晴梵　　　15

在成都的有 1 家 30 片。

　　易忠籙　　　30

以上 14 個城市 47 個藏家，共收藏甲骨 1 731 片。這些甲骨，有的可能早已易主①。有待進一步向各方面調赴瞭解，加以核實。

　　臺灣省收藏甲骨的有 5 個單位，30 191 片。

　　"中央研究院"歷史語言研究所　　25 700②
　　歷史博物館　　　　　　　　　　3 656③
　　"中央圖書館"　　　　　　　　　744④
　　"中央博物院"　　　　　　　　　79
　　臺灣大學考古人類學系　　　　　12

3 個私人收藏家，13 片。

　　莊尚嚴舊藏　　7
　　金東溪舊藏　　4
　　方豪舊藏　　　2

---

① 以上這些甲骨收藏的數字，是在編輯《甲骨文合集》一書的過程中，前前後後隨時瞭解的，中間經過了"文化大革命"的查抄，又經過了粉碎"四人幫"後的落實政策，賠退、認領、贈與、捐獻或價讓，甲骨收藏的變動，是很有可能的。
② 12 次發掘所得 24 918 片，購自王伯沆舊藏 662 片，購自南京 45 片，1928 年調查所得 16 片，歷年同人檢購 59 片，共計 25 700 片，整理綴合後數字未詳。
③ 河南博物館兩次發掘所得。
④ 金祥恒:《"國立中央圖書館"藏甲骨文字》著錄 648 片。

公私收藏，合共 30 204 片。

香港地區收藏甲骨的有 4 個單位：

中文大學聯合書院圖書館　　56
中文大學中國文化研究所　　26
香港大學馮平山博物館　　　6
香港大會堂美術博物館　　　1

共藏甲骨 89 片。

總上大陸機關收藏 95 880 片，私人收藏 1 731 片，臺灣省收藏 30 204 片，香港地區收藏 89 片，合共 127 904 片。

國外收藏的甲骨，以日本爲最多。計有 31 個單位，7 667 片。

京都大學人文科學研究所　　3 256
東京大學東洋文化研究所　　1 641
天理大學天理參考館　　　　809
書道博物館　　　　　　　　600
東洋文庫　　　　　　　　　591
東京國立博物館　　　　　　223
東京大學文學部考古學研究室　　113
亞非圖書館　　　　　　　　81
京都大學文學部考古學研究室　　56
大原美術館　　39
富氏短期大學　　35
東京理科大學人類學室　　30
慶應義塾大學文學部考古學研究室　　22
關西大學考古學資料室　　22
早稻田大學東洋美術陳列室　　21
藤井有鄰館　　16
大阪市立美術館　　14
九州大學教養學部資料室　　13
明治大學文學部考古學研究室　　12
不言堂美術店　　12
國學院大學文學部考古學資料室　　11
國立京都博物館　　10

黑川古文化研究所　　9
　　東京教育大學東洋史研究室　　7
　　築波大學歷史人類學系　　7
　　早稻田大學高等學院　　6
　　武藏大學歷史學研究室　　5
　　出光美術館　　3
　　東京大學教養學部美術博物館　　1
　　慶應義塾大學圖書館　　1
　　桃山中學舊藏　　1
31個私人收藏家，4 776片。
　　三井源右衛門舊藏　　3 000
　　富岡謙藏舊藏　　800
　　田中慶太郎舊藏　　400
　　中島玉振舊藏　　200
　　今井凌雪　　76
　　小倉武之助　　53
　　秋山公道　　42
　　加藤某氏　　40
　　小林斗庵　　33
　　內藤虎次郎舊藏　　25
　　藤田豐八舊藏　　20
　　谷邊橘南　　18
　　白川一郎　　10
　　宕間德也舊藏　　10
　　工藤愚盦　　9
　　小川睦之輔　　7
　　川合尚雅堂　　7
　　宕井大慧　　5
　　狩野直禎　　3
　　園田湖城　　3
　　江口寬　　3
　　三浦清吾　　2
　　松谷石韵　　2

　　　　佐藤武敏　　　1

　　　　松丸道雄　　　1

　　　　菅原保　　　1

　　　　植村清二　　　1

　　　　西川靖庵　　　1

　　　　長島健　　　1

　　　　富岡昌池　　　1

　　　　曾我部静雄　　　1

公私共藏 12 443 片①。

　　加拿大安大略博物館藏明義士舊藏懷履光舊藏及其他零散收藏及最近所得碎片，總數不少，僅次於日本所藏。

　　　　安大略博物館　　　7 802

　　　　英國收藏甲骨的，有 7 個單位，3 329 片。

　　　　蘇格蘭博物館　　　1 777②

　　　　劍橋大學圖書館　　　850

　　　　英國倫敦圖書館　　　490

　　　　英國倫敦博物館　　　150

　　　　亞士摹蘭博物館舊藏　　　35

　　　　倫敦維多利亞與阿爾伯特博物館　　　20

　　　　倫敦大學　　　7

2 個私人收藏家 26 片。

　　　　雷德哈斯特（LYNOHURST）　　　22

　　　　倫敦某氏　　　4

公私合共 3 355 片③。

　　　　美國收藏甲骨的，有 21 個單位，1 779 片。

　　　　哈佛大學皮巴地博物館　　　960

　　　　卡内基博物館　　　440

　　　　普林斯頓大學圖書館　　　115

---

① 日本甲骨，基本上據松丸道雄《日本散見甲骨文字蒐彙》（一）至（六）（《甲骨學》7—12 期，1959—1980 年）及《關於日本蒐儲的殷墟出土甲骨》（《東洋文化研究所紀要》第 86 册，1981 年）兩文，並參考其他文獻。又筆者實地調查。

② 加拿大安大略博物館原藏 7 786 片，新獲碎片 16，合共 7 802 片。

③ 英國甲骨，根據吳世昌教授、艾蘭教授、李學勤同志及齊文心同志提示。

又補遺　　24
哥倫比亞大學東亞圖書館　　73
又補遺　　36
大都會美術博物館　　25
自然歷史博物館　　24
哈佛大學福格美術博物館　　14
納爾遜美術陳列館　　12
佛利亞美術陳列館　　11
聖路易斯美術博物館　　7
夏威夷東西中心圖書館　　7
舊金山亞洲藝術博物館　　5
歷史與工藝博物館　　5
國會圖書館　　4
加州大學人類學博物館　　4
普林斯頓大學藝術博物館　　3
丹佛藝術博物館　　3
耶魯大學美術陳列館　　2
洛杉磯美術博物館　　2
西雅圖藝術博物館　　2
加州大學東亞圖書館　　1

9個私人收藏家，103片。

顧立雅（Prof. H. G. Creel）　　50
星格（Dr. P. Singer）　　25
發納（Mrs. J. M. Farnior）　　15
福斯特（Dr. C. F. Forester）　　5
沙克來（Sackler）　　3
本奈（Dr. D. W. Bennett）　　1
吉德煒（Prof. D. N. Keigbtley）　　1
劉先（羅吉眉夫人）　　1
某婦女　　2

公私合共1 882片[①]。

---

①　美國甲骨，根據吉德煒教授、周鴻翔教授、夏含夷博士及筆者實地調查。

西德收藏甲骨的，有 2 個單位，712 片。
　　西伯林民俗博物院　　　711
　　法蘭克福中國學院　　　1
私人收藏家 1 個，3 片。
　　某氏　　3①
公私合共 715 片。
　　蘇聯收藏甲骨的，1 個單位，199 片②。
　　國立愛米塔什博物館　　199
　　瑞典收藏甲骨的，1 個單位，100 片③。
　　遠東古物博物館　　　100
　　瑞士收藏甲骨的，1 個單位，70 片。
　　巴賽爾人種志博物館　　　70
私人收藏家 1 個，29 片④。
　　某氏　　29
公私合共 99 片。
　　法國收藏甲骨的，有 4 個單位，54 片。
　　法京國家圖書館　　　28
　　歸默博物院　　　13
　　策努斯奇博物院　　　9
　　巴黎大學中國學院　　　4
私人收藏家 1 個，10 片。
　　甘茂德　　10
公私合共 64 片。
　　新加坡收藏甲骨的，1 個單位，28 片⑤。
　　南洋大學李光前文物館　　28
　　比利時收藏甲骨的，1 個單位，7 片。
　　比利時皇家藝術博物院　　7
　　南朝鮮收藏甲骨的，1 個單位，6 片。

---

① 據張光裕博士搜集。見徐錫臺：《西德瑞士藏我國殷墟出土的甲骨文》，刊《人文雜志》1980 年 5 期。
② 蘇聯莫斯科國立東方文化博物館藏有 17 版完整的龜甲文字，全偽。
③④　據張光裕博士提示。
⑤　看李孝定：《李光前文物館所藏甲骨文字簡釋》，1976 年。

漢城大學博物館　　6

總上國外收藏的甲骨，日本 12 443 片，加拿大 7 802 片，英國 3 355 片，美國 1 882 片，西德 715 片，蘇聯 199 片，瑞典 100 片，瑞士 99 片，法國 64 片，新加坡 28 片，比利時 7 片，韓國 6 片，十二國合共收藏甲骨 26 700 片。

中國大陸及港臺地區收藏甲骨 127 904 片，加上國外十二個國家收藏甲骨 26 700 片，國内外總共收藏甲骨 154 604 片。舉成數而言，我們就可以説，85 年來殷墟出土的甲骨文材料，總共約有 15 萬片左右。

至於有關甲骨文材料的著録書刊，不下 100 多種，著録甲骨達 10 萬片。又國内各單位還收藏有甲骨拓本，計 200 餘種，20 餘萬片。其中很有一些甲骨，其原來的實物，不知道現在收藏在什麽地方①。又有一些私人收藏家，我們只聽説他們藏有甲骨或曾經藏有甲骨，但不知具體數字②。再就是我們所没有瞭解到的公私藏家，一定還有。對於這些，我們就無法統計在内。

然而就以上所列，15 萬片，其數量之豐富，已經大有可觀。這對於中國古代史特別是商代史，中國古文字學，特別是甲骨學的研究，確實具有極爲重大的意義。

最後我們還要聲明，這一統計雖然比幾十年前的統計較爲接近確切，但要説絶對正確，那還是不可能的。因爲甲骨的數字，隨時都在變化，今天發掘出一坑，數字馬上增加，明天拼合一些，數字馬上又要減少。私人收藏，由於饋贈、捐獻、出讓、轉手，不斷易主，更是難以究詢。特別是在"文化大革命"期間，對於文物的查抄，以及粉碎"四人幫"後對於文物的退還，其間變化更多。兹將這一統計列出，有什麽錯誤，敬請中外各單位專家予以糾正③。

1984 年 7 月 25 日

原載《史學月刊》1984 年第 5 期；又《古籍整理出版情況簡報》第 129 期，1984 年 10 月；收入宋鎮豪、段志洪主編：《甲骨文獻集成》第 34 册，四川大學出版社，2001 年。今據前者收入。

---

① 如羅振玉舊藏甲骨，現藏故宮博物院、北京圖書館、吉林博物館、吉林大學、遼寧博物館、旅順博物館和山東博物館等處。但羅氏所編《殷虚書契前編》及《後編》等書，其自藏甲骨，現在找不到原物的有許多片。聽旅順博物館的同志説，東北解放時，旅順羅家的文物有損失，甲骨尤甚。
② 如我過去有關甲骨文材料之統計的論文中所舉。
③ 關於各單位專家所藏甲骨的内容、來源與著録情況，筆者另有論述，不詳於此。

張政烺

065 殷墟甲骨文中所見的一種筮卦

一、近幾年來對古筮資料之探索

1978年11月末,在長春開中國古文字學術討論會,頭一天下午徐錫臺同志作周原出土甲骨文的報告,內中最後一節是"奇字"問題。會後散場有幾位同志問我那些"奇字"是什麼字,晚間又不斷有人問,第二天會上我講了《古代筮法與文王演周易》。這是臨時增加的題目,事先毫無準備,客中又無必要的材料可以詳細引證,未免大膽,幸好得到學識淵博的張頷同志(山西省考古研究所)、洪家義同志(南京大學)發言支持,大家熱烈鼓掌,算是全場通過了。回到北京後,把歷代著錄金文的書籍徹底檢查一過。1979年春,參觀周原發掘品,又見湖北江陵天星觀楚墓竹簡照片,其中有八個變卦,由某卦之某卦,兩卦並列,共十六個單卦,資料遂多起來了。這時,紐約大都會博物館籌備開"偉大的中國青銅器時代"展覽會,並舉行學術討論會,我應邀參加,報了一個題目是《試釋周初青銅器銘文中的易卦》(後收入《考古學報》1980年第4期,以下簡稱《試釋》),遂着手寫論文。後來,因爲天星觀竹簡遲遲未發表,我不好搶先發旁人發掘的材料,把論文中牽涉到天星觀的材料全部摘除了。1980年春,見到巴納、張光裕合編的《中日歐美澳紐所見所拓所摹金文匯編》(1978年,臺北),中有日本寧樂美術館藏的父乙🖻盉蓋銘(第八册,730頁,1125號),又加入論文中。這兩次修改很累人,篇中的數目字許多處都要改動,不勝其煩,所以後來得到的材料便未再增加。其中重要的有,考古研究所張長壽同志把《安陽苗圃北地發掘報告》的稿本給我看,內有兩張陶器銘文拓本,共三個卦。翻閱《考古》1961年第2期中關於苗圃北地的發掘簡報,在同書中又看到《山東平陰縣朱家橋殷代遺址》的陶器上的一個卦。這時陸續見到周原溝東

（扶風縣召陳公社）發現的陶片、獸骨上刻的易卦。到紐約後，見到薩克萊爾先生所藏一個鼎①，上有"八五一"銘文。同時聽林巳奈夫教授說，日本大倉古物館藏有一個鳥尊，足部有陽識六個數目字的銘文。我在大都會博物館的青銅器討論會上宣布的論文共舉了三十二個卦例，事實上當時所知道的已經超出一倍了。近三年來，安陽殷墟、扶風周原不斷發現重要的資料，不僅數量增多，內容更是"匪夷所思"。有一個龜腹甲在四條腿的位置上各刻一行六個數目字，皆由內向外寫，突出四維的地位，類似漢唐式占所用的地盤（參考嚴敦傑《跋六壬式盤》，見《文物參考資料》1958 年第 7 期）。筮人既用龜，自然不免有龜甲的形象縈迴於腦際，流露在書上。宋本《周易本義》卷首有《易圖》（朱熹集錄），其《洛書圖》云"洛書蓋取龜象"，又有《伏羲八卦方位》、《文王八卦方位》兩圖，皆四方四維並舉，而後者尤重在四維，類似這龜甲的布局。可見先天之學、後天之學皆有來歷，不是陳摶、邵雍輩妄作。看來，古代筮法的清算還得在殷墟、周原下工夫。

截至今日，考古資料上出現的三個數目字一組、六個數目字一組的易卦，有百十來個，"其經卦皆八，其別皆六十有四"，和《周易》是一個體系，將別爲文述之，今天講的則是另外一種。

二、四個數目字的卦

殷墟卜辭中找到兩個只有四個數目字的卦。先把材料擺出來。

壹、《甲骨文合集》第九册，29074 片（圖一）。

圖 一

---

① 《張政烺論易叢稿》《張政烺文集·論易叢稿》整理者案：薩克萊爾先生，即 Arthur M. Sackler，今多譯爲賽克勒。

這片卜骨《甲骨續存》(1980片)曾著錄過,是第三期田獵卜辭;有"〔于〕桑亡戈"、"吉"等字。關於筮法的有"六七七六"四個數目字,是倒寫的,所以未被學者們注意。第三期卜辭,過去董作賓、陳夢家都認爲是廩辛、康丁時的,今估計其年代約在公元前1200年前後,無論如何,可斷言其在"太王去邠遷岐"之前。

貳、《小屯南地甲骨》上册第二分册,4352片(圖二)。

T44(4C):43 反
4352

圖 二

這是考古研究所1973年的發掘品,片上卜辭殘缺不完,關於筮法的是"八七六五"這四個數目字,也是倒刻的。這片應當定在哪一期不清楚,無論如何是第四、五期以前的。我因爲它倒刻着四個數目字,和上面所舉的一片情況相同,所以看作一類。

在卜骨上突然出現一行四個數目字，無其它文字連接，如果是近代的，很容易被認爲是博物館或圖書館的登錄號碼，但中國古代卻決無此事。從《尚書》、《周禮》、《左傳》、《史記》等書知道古人龜（卜）策（筮）同時進行，因此我推測這是殷代一種筮法的記錄。

再説一件事情。1979 年，我寫《試釋》時，從《續殷文存》（卷上，7 頁）找到一件鼎銘，上有"八八六八"四個數目字。當時我只注意三個數目字或六個數目字的銘文，想不到會有四個數目字的，所以我認爲它原本是六個數目字，遭到毁壞，剩下了這四個字。這有幾種可能，一是後天的，器已殘破經過修復，或字被銹掩未曾剔出。這個鼎現在上海博物館，我寫信去問，沈之瑜館長親筆答覆，説：

> 根據你提出的幾點，我細緻觀察了八八六八鼎。此鼎非常完整，没有修補的痕迹。銘文上下均無銹斑。經目驗是鑄的，不是刻的。

並惠寄拓片一紙，今揭出如次（圖三）。

圖 三

我的解釋落空，又有一個想法，即先天不足。古代鑄造銅器銘文，陶範内芯磨得很平，再用細泥寫上文字，鑄成便是陰文。銅的比重大，幾十斤、上百斤的高温銅汁傾入範内，會把細泥作的筆畫冲壞。我曾摩挲過扶風出土的周厲王胡

簋，銘文中缺幾個字，底部平滑，毫無痕迹，就是這樣造成的。有一個師酉簋（《陶齋吉金錄》卷二，第 14 頁，《兩周金文辭大系圖錄考釋》《錄編》78 頁），銘文第一行末一字是"各"字，分成"夂"和"口"，離開很遠，也是這種情況。數目字的筆畫簡單，被銅汁沖走不見是完全可能的。總而言之，我當時只承認有三個數目字一組、六個數目字一組的，不相信曾經有過四個數目字一組的。直到發現上舉兩片卜骨，才知道它們是一類。這樣就有了三組數目字，六七七六、八七六五、八八六八，可以一併討論。

三、試對四爻作解釋

筮法中列舉四爻的有揚雄的《太玄》，但是組成卦爻所使用的數目字是一、二、三，故其蓍策是三十六而虛其三，實用三十三策而揲之以三。這和上舉兩片卜骨、一個鼎銘毫無相同之處，可以不必比敷。《太玄》中"方、州、部、家"各專一爻的名稱，在此也用不上。要想解決問題，仍當於《周易》求之。

朱熹《易學啓蒙》之原卦畫第二，用圖象解釋"易有太極，是生兩儀，兩儀生四象，四象生八卦"之後，接着畫出了 ☰、☱、☲、☳、☴、☵、☶、☷、☰、☱、☲、☳、☴、☵、☶、☷ 十六個僅有四爻的形象，並作說明：

> 八卦之上各生一奇一偶而爲四畫者十六，於經無見，邵子所謂"八分爲十六"者是也。又爲兩儀之上各加八卦，又爲八卦之上各加兩儀也。

邵雍説"八分爲十六"是推理之辭，朱熹作了分析：一、八卦之上各加兩儀。二、兩儀之上各加八卦。由於"於經無見"，也説不明白。古人稱三爻爲單卦，六爻爲重卦，即兩個單卦重叠之意。這大概是分析的結果，而不一定是發生的歷程。從考古資料看，六爻和三爻同時出現，甚至於六爻比三爻早，或許是六爻簡化爲三爻。《繫辭下》：

> 《易》之爲書也，廣大悉備，有天道焉，有人道焉，有地道焉。兼三才而兩之，故六。六者非它也，三才之道也。

《説卦》也有"兼三才而兩之，故《易》六畫而成卦"。向來的解釋都説初二爻象地，三四爻象人，五上爻象天，則六爻不是三加三，而是二加二、加二。周原甲骨 177 號：

父乙𐅁盉蓋：

𐅁

似乎也看出一些苗頭，此事非片言可決，暫時不談。無論如何，按《易學啟蒙》來看，前舉的那三個四爻卦當是未完成的卦，但是鼎銘卻以爲氏（族）名，故可斷言其決非如此。

漢代學者解釋易卦，喜歡講互體，最有名的是鄭玄。鄭玄《周易注》曾一度風行，列於學官。王弼尚名理，譏互體，其作《周易注》所廓清的主要是互體。後來王注顯，鄭注微。北宋亡後，鄭玄注本竟失傳。南宋末，王應麟輯《周易鄭康成注》，並作序文，主要談互體問題，引如下：

> 鄭康成學《費氏易》，爲注九卷，多論互體。以互體求易，左氏以來有之。凡卦爻二至四、三至五，兩體交互各成一卦，是謂一卦含四卦，《繫辭》謂之中爻，所謂"八卦相盪"、"六爻相雜，唯其時物"、"雜物撰德"是也。唯乾、坤無互體，蓋純乎陽、純乎陰也。餘六子之卦皆有互體。坎之六畫其互體含艮、震，而艮、震之互體亦含坎。離之六畫其互體含兌、巽，而兌、巽之互體亦含離。三陽卦之體互自相含，三陰卦之體亦互自相含也。

王應麟又從《左傳正義》、《禮記正義》、《周禮疏》中鈔出以互體說易卦的八條，附於卷末。自來講互體的學者多以《繫辭》"二與四同功而異位"、"三與五同功而異位"爲根源，但《繫辭》中的這幾句是什麼時期的作品，卻不易斷定，所以大家公認較早的證據是《左傳》莊公二十二年：

> 周史有以《周易》見陳侯者，陳侯使筮之，遇觀䷓之否䷋，曰：……坤，土也。巽，風也。乾，天也。風爲天，於土上，山也。有山之材而照之以天光，於是乎居土上，故曰："觀國之光，利用賓於王。"

這裏觀卦的第四爻動，六四變爲九四，所以"之卦"是否。巽變爲乾，所以說"風爲天"。自二爻至四爻是艮，艮爲山，所以說"有山之材"。此事《史記·十二諸侯年表》記載在陳厲公三年（前704年）。《左傳》成書年代在戰國前期，也肯定比《繫辭》寫定的時間早。總而言之，互體說是有來歷的，所以歷代《周易》學家常言之。宋代流傳的麻衣道者《正易心法》第十九章：

> 一卦之中，凡具八卦，有正有伏，有互有參。（正，謂上下二體也。伏，謂二體

從變也。互,謂一卦有二互體也。参,謂二互體参合也。與本卦凡八,是謂一卦具八卦也。……)

全祖望《經史答問》評之曰:

> 至宋所傳《麻衣易》,則又有参互之法,謂除本卦之二體,但以所互之上下二卦重而参之,又得六畫之卦一,是又一法也。然此皆但於二互中離合以求之,不参以他說,其於古法不悖。

互體説重視"中四爻",初爻、上爻置之不論,專從二、三、四、五爻下工夫,把四個爻當作一個卦。試師其意,將前舉甲骨金文中的三組四個數目字畫出來:

六七七六　䷹兌䷸巽　大過
八七六五　䷜坎䷝離　既濟
八八六八　䷁坤䷁坤　坤

易學是中國古老的文化遺産,典籍記載伏羲始作八卦,考古資料或許可以早到新石器時代,其源之遠,流之長,有時我們會估計不足。《左傳》所記"變卦"或"之卦",殷周考古資料中常見。互體説可溯源於《左傳》,我們用以解釋甲骨金文之四爻,也就不爲離奇了。

四、筮法不容易解決

這三個四爻卦所使用的數目字是五、六、七、八,没有一、二、三、四。在《試釋》中三十二例皆不見二、三、四,但有"一"字。這決不是偶然現象,而是筮人有意如此。我們看敦煌卷子《周公卜法》採用"上斜、中豎、下斜"的辦法,知道筮人所苦在二、三、三(四)這幾個字皆積畫爲之,容易混淆,在算籌(或蘇州碼子)盛行之後,故採用此法。古代没有算籌(或蘇州碼子),不能避免混淆,索性把二、三、四都省掉了。我寫《試釋》時根據所見到的資料六最多,一次之,推測三變一,二、四變六,有的同志不相信,現在各地考古發現的易卦資料有百十來個,全無二、三、四字,足以補證前説。從這一點看,四字一組的和三字一組的、六字一組的有共同點,可能出於一個來源,終是一家眷屬。至於爲什麽這三個四爻卦中不出現"一",由於材料太少,不便妄測。

我寫《試釋》時,曾作"筮法擬測"(見第三節)。我曾説明這只是虚構,並

非復原，不是古筮真正如此，但是有的專家還不諒解。我並不固執，不妨大家各擬一套筮法，最後比較一番，看哪一種有接近真實的可能性。《試釋》限於字數，不能扯得太遠，事實上民間處理疑難問題常有類似的辦法。其見於記載的，楊恩壽《坦園日記》卷三，同治乙丑（1865 年）四月十九日記入潯陽府城（今廣西壯族自治區桂平縣）所見：

> 河市頗盛，而賭館充斥焉。粵人垂布簾於外，懸大燈如桶，內設大席，主人隨手掬錢約百餘，覆碗下，任人猜單雙爲勝負，竟有以千金爲孤注者，土人稱爲"番攤館"。

這種賭的方法很簡單，只問數之單雙便決勝負。主人掬錢約百餘，數目很大是爲了使人無從估計其內容，而辨別單雙，事實上就是揲之以二。主人隨手掬錢後，餘錢必多（少則會被人看出單雙），籌碼數大，可不作什麼限制。這是把人的命運寄托在一個單雙（奇偶）數上，其用意和筮占是相同的，可以看作一爻卦。有用兩個爻的，見陶宗儀《輟耕錄》卷二十"九天玄女課"：

> 其法，折草一把不計草數多寡，苟用算籌亦可，兩手隨意分之，左手在上豎放，右手在下橫放，以三除之，不及者爲卦。一豎一橫曰太陽，二豎一橫曰靈通，二豎二橫曰老君，二豎三橫曰太吳，三豎一橫曰洪石，三豎三橫曰祥雲，皆吉兆也。一豎二橫曰太陰，一豎三橫曰懸崖，三豎二橫曰陰中，皆凶兆也。……《離騷經》云："索藑茅以筳篿兮，命靈氛爲余卜。"《注》曰："藑茅，靈草也。筳，小破竹也。楚人名結草折竹以卜曰篿。"據此則亦有所本矣。

《水滸傳》（第六十八、八十一、八十二等回）說宋江曾受"九天玄女課"，可見這種筮法元明時期在江湖上流行很廣。其法只有二爻，而使用的籌碼是一、二、三，故揲之以三。折草不計數之多少，籌碼是無限的，所以九個卦都有出現的機會。卦用三爻的有敦煌卷子《周公卜法》，其設三爻是模仿《周易》，數目字用一、二、三、四，是爲了奇偶數相等，故揲之以四。蓍策三十四是偶數，則三爻相加一定是偶數，有局限性（三爻相加是奇數的卦出不來），只能成十六個卦。術士們有十六個卦已足夠用，可以走江湖騙飯吃，遂不計其它。我推測《周公卜法》所用的筮法是有來頭的，是從一種古筮法簡化來的，故據以擬測易卦的筮法。

易卦比較麻煩，爻要反映奇偶，卦是以奇數偶數相配而成。單卦是三爻，有八個，重卦六爻有六十四個，卦的數目和爻的奇偶都是死的，不能增減改動。蓍

策不能是無限的，要有個固定數目，而爲奇爲偶不能兩全。所以我推測有"上牌"的辦法，這樣可以使蓍策的實用數奇偶無定，每一個卦都有機會可以出得來。《周易·繫辭》"大衍之數五十，其用四十有九"，是立一虛策。《太玄》的蓍策是三十六而虛其三，《潛虛》的蓍策是七十五而虛其五，這一、三、五個虛策就是"上牌"，但是它們都把不用的策固定下來，只減少幾根策，起不到調劑奇偶的作用。比較起來，"上牌"的辦法原始一些，也會收實際效果。

前一章說過，這兩骨一鼎上的卦雖是四爻卻不同於《太玄》，那麼卦是怎麼成的呢？我想這有兩種可能，一是仍用我在《試釋》中擬測的辦法求得上下兩卦，然後把初上兩爻省略不寫（參考王弼《周易略例·辯位》），故只有四爻。但是何必如此，卻想不通。另一個辦法是一次得出四爻。蓍策是六十四，"上牌"後隨手分爲四部分，皆揲之以八，餘數小的一、二、三、四依次變爲五、六、七、八。試筮如下：

上牌	六	取出不用		
初爻	十四	去八得六		六
二爻	十九	去十六得三	變七	七
三爻	十五	去八得七		七
上爻	十	去八得二	變六	六

六七七六 ☱ 分成兩單卦是 ☱兑、☴巽，合成一重卦是爲大過。現在從甲骨金文中只見到這樣三個卦，資料太少，不敢保不再發現其它情況，例如"一"不是不可能出現的，又如這三個卦的數目字自加皆是偶數（二十六、二十六、三十），本來可以不"上牌"，但是一卦四字相加是奇數的也不是不可能出現，要爲它留有餘地，這就不能免去"上牌"。希望此後能發現更多的資料，暫時只申論前法。

最後，應當聲明一下，我不是說這二骨一鼎的銘刻必須這樣講，既然發現了三個四爻卦，順便說出自己對它的解釋，這只是個人一時的意見，並不排斥其它的說法，還請方家多多指教。

補 記

《文史》20輯饒宗頤教授《殷代易卦及有關占卜諸問題》後記中說到巴黎歸

默博物館藏的一片卜甲，正反皆有文字。正面即《巴黎所見甲骨録》第 24 片，其文爲：

乙丑〔卜，□〕貞：多……〔王占〕曰：父乙……

這是武丁時期標準字體，父乙即武丁之父小乙。背面摹本也印出來了（見《文史》20 輯 12 頁），有"弋"及"六一一六"等字。這樣，四爻卦便多出一卦，並且是最早一卦。我在前文説，因爲材料少，不敢保"一"不出現，現在果然有了兩個"一"，由此斷定四爻卦所用數目字是一、五、六、七、八，和三爻卦、六爻卦是一樣的。六一一六畫成卦爻和六七七六相同，這也可注意，終因材料太少不便作過多的推測。我對於這片材料非常高興，但是心中還不滿足，幾時安陽、江陵的材料發表，才可以把古代筮法問題徹底研討一番。

原載《文史》第 24 輯，中華書局，1985 年；收入《張政烺文史論集》，中華書局，2004 年；又收入《張政烺論易叢稿》，中華書局，2010 年；又收入《張政烺文集·論易叢稿》，中華書局，2012 年。今據後者收入。

姚孝遂　趙　誠

小屯南地甲骨考釋·今來翌

2106（1）己亥貞，今來翌受禾
　　（2）不受禾
　　（3）甲子卜，隹䖈壱禾

第（1）辭與第（2）辭爲對貞。"今來翌"很費解，前此所未見。

卜辭於時間概念的區分很是細微。"今"指"現在"，"來"指"未來"。"今"之前爲"昔"；"今"之後爲"來"。但"翌"亦是表示未來之時間概念。"翌"與"來"的區分在於："翌"是表示距"今"較短的，一般是一、二日；"來"則是更遠一些的未來。

《粹》692："自今辛至于來辛又大雨"，"今辛"與"來辛"相距十一日。

《存》1·1467："乙亥卜，大貞，來丁亥易日"，"乙亥"與"丁亥"相距十三日。

在大多數的情況下，"翌"是表示第二日，不得超出旬日之內：

　《河》178：癸未卜，行貞，今日至于翌甲申不雨。
　《乙》6385：甲寅卜，殼貞，翌乙卯易日。

至於《前》7·4·1："乙亥卜，㱿貞，翌乙亥酒䙴易日？乙亥酒，允易日"，相距六十日，則是比較特殊的例子。

卜辭"翌"有兩種概念：一爲祭名，一爲將來時間。

作爲將來的時間概念，"今翌"或"今來翌"連言，都是非常特殊的。

《粹》878："今翌受黍（年）"，"今翌"顯然是表示時間概念。然則，是否可以認爲"今翌"是同時表示"現在"和"將來"這兩個時間概念？

卜辭"今來"經常連言：

《乙》979：今來戈我受年
《合》109：今來戈我不其受年

陳夢家先生以爲"今來云云近乎'最近的將來'……'今來戈''今翌'當指最近的下季"(《綜述》119)。這種理解是值得商討的。

據《粹》447："丁亥卜，叀今庚寅酚用戋。"又《佚》883："癸未貞，叀今乙酉又伐于且乙五豕，兹用"。

丁亥與庚寅相距四日；癸未與乙酉相距三日，均可稱之爲今。

《丙》一關於時日的記載最爲完整，也最爲明確，能給我們以啓示：

癸丑卜，爭貞，自今至于丁巳，我找囚？王固曰：丁巳我毋其找，于來甲子找。旬又一日癸亥，車弗找，之夕望。甲子允找。

可以肯定，以"癸丑"（今）爲基點，"丁巳"不能稱"來丁巳"，無疑也包括"甲寅"不能稱爲"來甲寅"。

質言之，以"今"爲起點，第一輪的天干之內，不得稱作"來"，而可以稱作"翌"。

然則，我們於《粹》447及《佚》883就可以解釋。

《粹》447的"丁亥卜"而稱"今庚寅"，"丁亥"後的第一個"庚"日是"庚寅"，故可稱之爲"今庚寅"；《佚》883的"癸未貞"而稱"今乙酉"，"癸未"後的第一個"乙"日是"乙酉"，故可稱之爲"今乙酉"。

《合》282的"辛亥卜，爭貞，今來乙卯出于成十牛"，以及《續》1·48·3的"丁丑卜，今來乙酉出于成五宰，七月"，都可以進一步證明當如此解釋。

"今來乙卯"應是兩個"乙卯"。一是距"辛亥"五日的最近一個"乙卯"；一是距"辛亥"六十五日的較遠一次的"乙卯"。"今來乙酉"同樣也是如此。

當然，我們應該注意到，相對地說來，像這樣的紀時方法，終究是少數。在大多數的情況下，就"干支"日來說，當日稱今，次日以後的十日之內稱"翌"，十日以外的"干支"日稱"來"。

卜辭經常見有"今戈受年"，"來戈受年"。"今"和"來"是相對的。

"今戈"只能理解爲本收穫年度，"來戈"只能理解爲下一個收穫年度。"年度"實際上也就是收穫"季節"。這一點大家的意見是一致的。

那麼，"今來戈"就不可能解釋爲"最近將來"的一個收穫年度，否則的話，

就與"來戋"無法區分。"今來戋"只能是指"今戋"和"來戋"。

　　卜辭只有"日"稱"翌","戋"和"月"都不稱"翌"。而收穫是不以"月"、"日"為單位，而是以"戋"為單位的。此片之"今來翌受禾"，難以理解。

　　節選自《小屯南地甲骨考釋》，中華書局，1985年。

詹鄞鑫

甲骨文字考釋二則·釋㫃

㫃字甲骨文象人張口坐地,舉手拭臉形(見古文字表1—3)①。這個字舊或釋爲"次"②,修訂本《甲骨文編》收於附錄,表示待考。于省吾先生則釋爲"次"③。今按甲骨文次字象人口流涎(古文字表4),其特點是手臂下垂,或支在膝腿上,與㫃字迥然有别。從用例看,兩者決不相混,凡川河衍溢,"衍"字只用"次"(字或加舟旁),其非一字明矣。

《金文編·附録》收有幾個以㫃爲聲符的字(古文字表5—6),高田忠周釋爲"旂",李孝定釋爲"旃",皆謬。孫詒讓早已釋之爲"旛",以爲即肵字異文④。其説至確。其所從的聲符字(古文字表7—8)即昏之古文㫃字,而與甲骨文寫法基本相同。查周器《大盂鼎》、《克盨》的"䎽"(古"聞",辭中借爲"婚")字及《三年師兑簋》、《番生簋》的"䡅"字(《説文》讀如閔),它們的聲符字均與甲骨文㫃字構形相同或相近(古文字表9—12)。其形於頭上或加三點,乃是口旁三點上移所致,後來訛變爲"尔"形。又在人之足下或加"夂",與不加者無别,如《説文》稷古文作䄺,稷籀文作䄻,金文孔旁或加夂作㲻,甲骨文㚅字或作㚂(《屯南》2123)等,皆其例。甲骨文從耳㫃聲的䎽字(古文字表13),唐蘭先生釋爲"聞"(聞字從耳門聲,㫃與門古音同),這已是公論。這是我們釋 🖼 爲㫃的確證。

《説文》以爲㫃是古文昏字,又以爲是籀文婚字,又"讀若閔"。據此可知甲

---

① 1—2,《屯》751;3,《明》733。
② 見《甲骨文字集釋》第八,2829頁。
③ 于省吾:《甲骨文字釋林》,382頁。
④ 諸説俱見《金文詁林附録》,1879頁。

骨文㪅字讀與昏或㪅同，古音在文部明母。

㪅字構形，象人張口噴沫（或者是汗水涕淚類），以手揩抹，參以音讀，當即《説文》"捪"字初文。此字異體頗多，或寫作揹、抿、扻、抻等。由於語音變化，唐宋以來或借搵字爲之。《説文》捪的釋義爲"撫也，一曰摹（同摸）也"。此爲廣義，狹義應爲扻拭（揩抹涕淚涎沫之類）。《廣雅·釋詁二》："扻，拭也。"《呂氏春秋·長見》"吴起抿泣而應之"，《文選·洞簫賦》"搵涕扻淚"，《楚辭·九章·悲回風》"孤子吟而扻淚"，《稼軒詞（二）·水龍吟》"搵英雄淚"等，其義皆爲揩抹扻拭。許氏以爲它是昏之古文，又以爲是婚之籀文，其實都是通用關係。

卜辭㪅字有兩類用法。卜辭云："叀（與"唯"的用法相近）翌日㪅"（庫1093），"叀七牛㪅用王受［佑］"（摭續88）等，㪅字都是紀時詞，應讀爲昏暮之"昏"。他辭有云"翌日暮"（戩13·9），與前一辭同例，又云"二牛今日用"（前1·11·4），與後一辭同例。卜辭紀時固已有昏字，然則㪅昏二字之通用不自金文始，早在卜辭中已然。

又《屯》中出現新的用法，頗爲罕見，只在751版云"又伐自上甲㪅示"凡三見。于省吾讀爲"延示"，自然不可信。"㪅示"我們曾懷疑表示"衆示"①，但文獻中未見同類語，暫且存疑待考。

一九八二年七月初稿

附古文字表：

1	2	3	4	5
6	7	8	9	10
11	12	13		

原爲《甲骨文字考釋二則》之一，《語言研究》1986年第2期；後改爲《釋甲骨文"捪"和"舡"》第一則，收入《華夏考——詹鄞鑫文字訓詁論集》，中華書局，2006年。今據後者收入。

---

① 典籍中與"昏"字通用的"民"、"緜"等，都有衆義。例見《韓詩·載芟》和《小雅·緜蠻》等。

常玉芝

晚期龜腹甲卜旬卜辭的契刻規律及意義

　　殷墟甲骨卜辭中的卜旬卜辭，據筆者檢視，大都是數條集中刻在一版牛胛骨或龜腹甲上，基本不刻於龜背甲上（只見《甲》3177一版背甲刻辭）。早期（除黃組外的其他組卜辭①）絕大多數刻在牛胛骨上，少數刻在龜腹甲上，一版刻於龜背甲上；晚期（黃組卜辭）刻在牛胛骨上的仍然很多，但刻在龜腹甲上的已爲數不少②。刻於牛胛骨上的卜旬卜辭，早期雖然多數是自下而上一句接一句契刻的，但尚有不少例外（以賓組居多③），規律性還不強；而晚期的全部刻辭（約678版左右）中，凡是契刻在兩句以上的，皆是自下而上一句接一句契刻的，規律性已很强。刻於龜腹甲上的卜旬卜辭，早期有78版左右，但其中只有一版是比較完整的（屬賓組），董作賓先生已指出它的契刻特點是："先右後左……先外後内，先下後上，先中部後四隅，先疏後密，有時爲填滿空隙而上下内外錯落"④；而晚期龜腹甲卜旬卜辭的契刻特點至今尚未見到總結，故本文擬在前人研究早期龜腹甲卜旬卜辭契刻特點的基礎上，再對晚期龜腹甲卜旬卜辭的契刻特點進行分析，并兼及其意義。

---

① 卜辭的分組情况見李學勤先生的《小屯南地甲骨與甲骨分期》，《文物》1981年5期。筆者贊同歷組卜辭的時代應提前的觀點，故只將黄組卜辭劃爲晚期。
② 據筆者統計，早期刻於牛胛骨上的約有1 405版左右，刻於龜腹甲上的約有78版左右；晚期刻于牛胛骨上的約有678版左右，刻于龜腹甲上的約有167版左右。
③ 其他的契刻情况有自上而下的（如《粹》1439、《珠》202、《粹》1435），先右後左的（如《前》7·12·2、《鐵》250·2+《鐵》260·3），先右後左再中間的（如《寧》2·24+《寧》2·26），先左後右再中間的（如《菁》3·1），上下旬不是連續兩旬的（如《珠》198、《續》4·45·8），還有的契刻雜亂無章（如《粹》1429、《續》4·44·3）。
④ 董作賓：《大龜四版考釋》，《安陽發掘報告》第3期，1931年。

一

探討晚期龜腹甲卜旬卜辭的契刻特點，可根據下面兩版卜辭：
（1）《合集》39018（圖一）

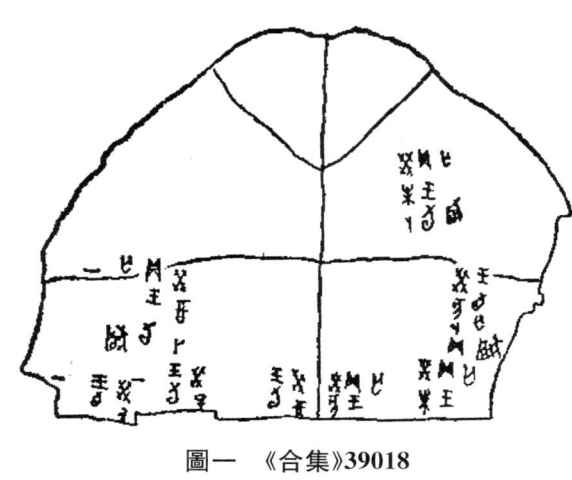

圖一　《合集》39018

此龜腹甲殘片上殘留八條卜旬卜辭，以腹甲中縫爲界，左右兩半部分各殘留四條。左半部各辭的行文皆左行，右半部各辭的行文皆右行。如果按照干支日次序排列各旬卜辭，其契刻部位分別是：

癸亥［卜］，貞：王［旬］亡［禍］？（右半部）

癸酉［卜］，［貞］：王旬［亡禍］？（左半部）

癸未［卜］，貞：王［旬］亡［禍］？（右半部）

癸巳［卜］，［貞］：王旬［亡禍］？（左半部）

［癸卯卜］，［貞］：［王旬亡禍］①？（右半部）

癸丑［卜］，［貞］：王旬［亡禍］？（左半部）

癸亥卜，貞：王旬亡禍？（右半部）

癸酉卜，貞：王旬亡禍？（左半部）

癸未卜，貞：王旬亡禍？（右半部）

很明顯，在中縫右半部刻一旬卜辭之後，下一旬卜辭即刻於中縫的左半部，再下

---

① 此辭殘掉了，這裏是根據干支日次序補上的。

一旬又回刻到中縫的右半部，如此循環往復。這樣對每半部分來說，各相鄰的兩句都不是連續的兩句，而是都間隔了一句；其次，每半部分都是先從內部的中縫處刻起的，以後依次外移；再者，每半部分都是先從下部刻起的，以後依次上移。綜合以上契刻特點就是：先右後左，先內後外，先下後上。

（2）《珠》214＋《安明》3069（圖二）

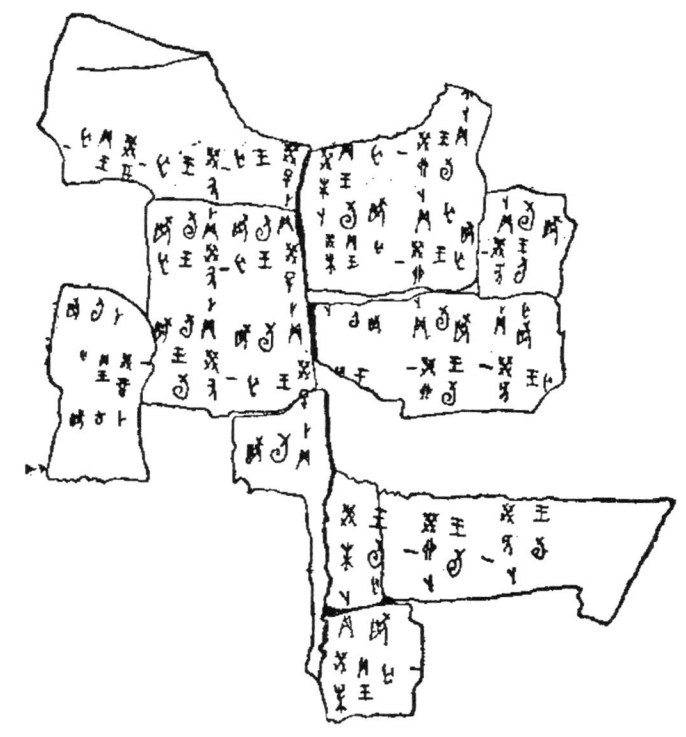

圖二　《珠》214＋《安明》3069

這是筆者新拼合的一版龜腹甲，是由《珠》214（即《合集》39171）和《安明》3069（即《合集》39175）拼合而成的。上面殘留二十三條卜旬卜辭，以腹甲中縫爲界，左半部分殘留九條，右半部分殘留十四條。左半部各辭的行文皆左行，右半部各辭的行文皆右行。每半部分的卜辭都刻成三豎排，每豎排卜辭的干支日都相同，因此，每一橫排卜辭的干支日就分別一致。這樣，只要弄清楚兩橫排卜辭的契刻特點，就可以明瞭全版卜辭的契刻特點了。下面按照干支日次序，將保留比較完整的兩橫排，即倒四排和倒五排卜辭排列起來，其契刻部位的安排分別是：

癸未卜，貞：王旬亡禍？（右半部）

癸巳卜，貞：王旬亡禍？（左半部）

癸卯卜,貞:王旬亡禍?(右半部)
癸丑卜,貞:王旬亡禍?(左半部)
癸亥卜,貞:王旬亡禍?(右半部)
[癸酉]卜,[貞]:[王]旬[亡]禍?(左半部)
癸未卜,貞:王旬亡禍?(右半部)
癸巳卜,貞:王旬亡禍?(左半部)
癸卯卜,貞:王旬亡禍?(右半部)
癸丑卜,貞:王旬亡禍?(左半部)
[癸亥]卜,貞:[王]旬[亡]禍?(右半部)
癸酉[卜],貞:王[旬]亡[禍]?(左半部)

顯然，與上版一樣，其契刻特點也是先右後左，先内後外，先下後上的。

以上契刻特點并不僅見於此兩版龜腹甲，檢查迄今所能認定的約165版左右的晚期龜腹甲卜旬卜辭，其契刻均符合上述特點。因此可以説：先右後左，先内後外，先下後上是晚期龜腹甲卜旬卜辭的契刻規律。這個規律與董作賓先生指出的那版早期龜腹甲卜旬卜辭的契刻特點相同之處有：都是先右後左，先下後上的。不同之處是：早期是先外後内，而晚期是先内後外；早期"先中部後四隅，先疏後密，有時爲填滿空隙而上下内外錯落"的特點，晚期是没有的，而是契刻的比較整齊。

二

掌握龜腹甲卜旬卜辭的契刻規律對甲骨學和商代歷史文化的研究是很有意義的。經筆者初步探究，發現它至少可在以下幾個方面幫助我們取得更大的成績：

1. 準確地拼合龜版

殷墟甲骨在地下埋藏已數千年，極易毀壞，今天我們所見到的甲骨大多是殘缺不全的，一塊甲骨的碎片天各一方，給研究工作帶來一定的困難和損失，因此拼合甲骨就成了甲骨學中一項重要的内容。拼合甲骨需要多方面的知識，下面是筆者根據龜腹甲卜旬卜辭的契刻規律拼合的一塊龜版①：

---

① 前面圖二的拼合版主要是根據殘字互足和殘辭互補以及骨碴兒的銜接拼合的。

（3）《安明》3072＋《珠》215（圖三）

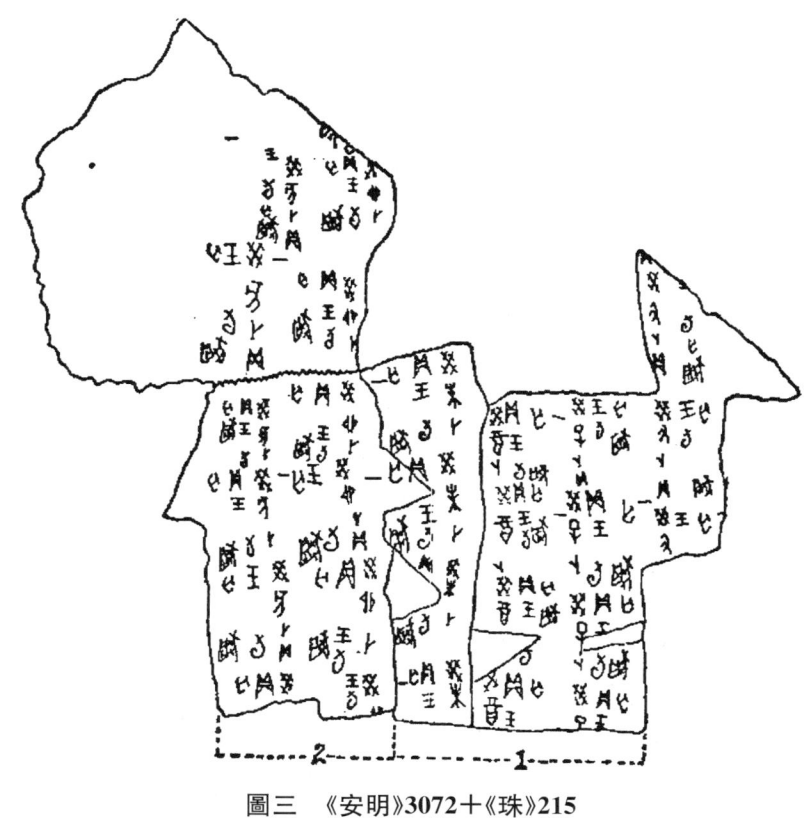

圖三　《安明》3072＋《珠》215

這塊龜版是由《安明》3072（即《合集》39035）和《珠》215（即《合集》39174）拼合而成的。它們都是龜腹甲殘片，上面刻的都是晚期卜旬卜辭，卜辭的字體也一致，因此有可能是一塊龜甲的殘片，也就是説有拼合的基礎。首先看《安明》3072（圖三，1），上面有腹甲中縫，中縫的右半部刻着三竪排卜旬卜辭，各辭的行文皆右行，每竪排卜辭的干支日各自相同，其由内向外依次是癸酉、癸巳、癸丑，相鄰的兩旬都間隔一旬，所缺的各旬依次應是癸未、癸卯、癸亥，按照前面所揭示的契刻規律，它們當是刻在腹甲中縫的左半部的。今該版中縫左半部緊靠中縫處已刻有一竪排癸未旬的卜辭，那麼還缺一竪排癸卯旬，一竪排癸亥旬的卜辭。而《珠》215（圖三，2）正有這樣兩竪排卜辭，並且各辭的行文皆左行，也正是腹甲左半部的殘片，試將其接到《安明》3072（圖三，1）的左半部，結果兩版的破損處正好相互銜接，殘辭部分也正好能互足，故拼合是準確無誤的。

2. 正確地釋讀卜辭

有不少卜旬卜辭並不是只單純地卜問每旬有無災禍，而是在卜問有無災禍之後附記着祭祀、戰爭等方面的内容①，它們無疑是研究商代歷史文化的重要資料。但在以往的研究中，由於没有掌握龜腹甲卜旬卜辭的契刻規律，故在釋讀此類卜辭時，往往將干支日讀錯，影響了研究效果。如對下面兩版卜辭的釋讀就有此種情況：

（4）《前》3・28・4+《續》6・1・8+《續》6・5・2（圖四，2）

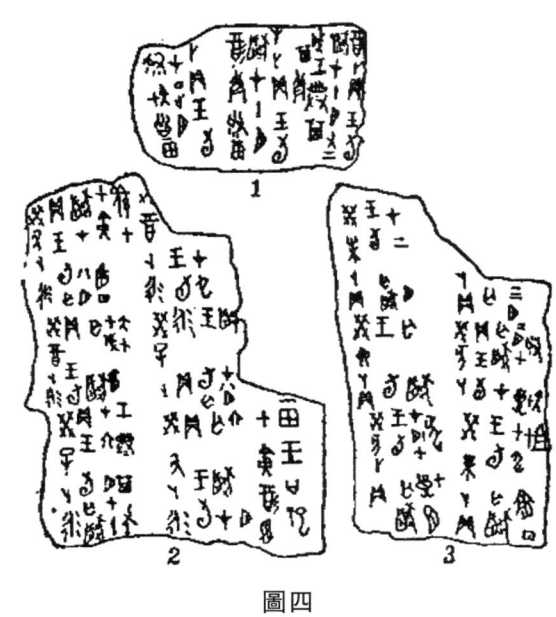

圖四

1.《後・上》21・3　2.《前》3・28・4+《續》6・1・8+《續》6・5・2　3.《綜述》21・8

此版龜腹甲上有六條晚期卜旬卜辭，各辭的行文皆是右行，故是龜腹甲右半部的殘片。根據龜腹甲卜旬卜辭先内後外、先下後上的契刻規律，各辭的卜問次序應是：

癸巳卜，泳，貞：王旬亡禍？在六月，甲午工典其㱃。

癸丑卜，泳，貞：王旬亡禍？在六月，甲寅酒翌上甲。王二十祀。

癸酉卜，泳，貞：王旬亡禍？甲戌翌大甲。

癸巳卜，泳，貞：王旬亡禍？在八月。

癸丑卜，泳，貞：王旬亡禍？在八月，甲寅翌日羌甲。

---

① 有時根據研究的角度不同，研究者又或稱這種卜辭爲祭祀卜辭、戰爭卜辭等。

癸酉卜，泳，[貞]：王旬[亡禍]？在九[月]。

每相鄰的兩旬都間隔一旬，所缺的各旬按照契刻規律當是刻在腹甲左半部的。各辭在卜問本旬有無災禍之後都有附記，内容有月份、翌祀的祭祀和年祀，翌祀是周祭中的祀典，故研究周祭者往往根據需要又稱其爲周祭卜辭①。辭中的"工典其㓝"即是翌祀的工典祭②，"工典"，于省吾先生謂即貢典，是祭祀時獻其典册③，典册的内容大約記載的是以某祀典在某日祭祀某先王或某先妣的④，因此翌祀的工典祭就是獻翌祀的典册于神前的祭祀。辭中的"王二十祀"即是王二十年，祀即年，《爾雅·釋天》説："夏曰歲，商曰祀，周曰年，唐虞曰載"；又周祭中對先公先王先妣輪番祭祀一周需要三十六旬或三十七旬的時間，與一年的日數相當，因此是可以借"祀"以名"年"的⑤。前人研究周祭時因不知龜腹甲卜旬卜辭的契刻規律，又囿於周祭的三十六旬型周期中，翌祀的工典祭與翌祭上甲是在連續的兩旬舉行的觀念，而認爲該版的翌祀工典祭與翌祭上甲間隔一旬舉行是不對的，因此他們都將翌祀工典祭即"工典其㓝"的卜日看作癸卯日，祭日看作甲辰日，即比原刻後移了一旬，使翌祀的工典祭與翌祭上甲在連續的兩旬内舉行。今用卜旬卜辭在龜腹甲上的契刻規律來檢查，知原刻是正確的，因爲就龜腹甲的每半部分來説，相鄰的兩旬都不是連續的兩旬，而是都間隔一旬，故該版中翌祀的工典祭與翌祭上甲間隔一旬舉行是正常的，是契刻者的本意，翌祀工典祭的卜日、祭日並没刻錯。但爲什麽與三十六旬型周期不同，翌祀的工典祭要與翌祭上甲間隔一旬舉行呢？這是因爲周祭中除了三十六旬型周期外，還有三十七旬型周期，這多出的一旬正是三十七旬型周期的證據。前人研究周祭，雖然存在着各種分歧，但在有三十七旬型周期，並且都是由三十六旬型周期增加一旬構成的這一點，意見却是一致的，分歧只在於這增加的一旬應是在何處，由於没有人從卜辭中找到證據，故各家擬出多種方案⑥，互相不能説服，使問題久而不决。現

---

① 晚期卜旬卜辭附記周祭祀典時，只附記甲名先王的祭祀，祭日均選在卜日癸日的第二天甲日，即祭日與先王的日干名（廟號）一致。
② "㓝"字從陳夢家先生釋，見《殷虚卜辭綜述》394頁。
③ 于省吾：《甲骨文字釋林》71頁。
④ 董作賓：《殷曆譜》下編卷二，2—3頁。
⑤ 董作賓：《殷曆譜》上編卷三，2頁；又見常玉芝的《商代周祭制度》一書（待出）。
⑥ 見董作賓：《殷曆譜》下編卷二；陳夢家：《殷虚卜辭綜述》395頁；島邦男：《殷墟卜辭研究》中譯本113頁；許進雄：《殷卜辭中五種祭祀的研究》，1968年；許進雄：《殷卜辭中五種祭祀研究的新觀念》，《中國文字》第35册，1970年。

在根據卜旬卜辭在龜腹甲上的契刻規律，得知在翌祀工典祭與翌祭上甲間（也包括"祭"祀的工典祭與"祭"上甲間和彡祀的工典祭與彡祭上甲間。見下文）多出的一旬正是大家尋而不得的三十七旬型周期中增加的那一旬。

（5）《後·上》21·3（圖四，1）

此版龜復甲上殘留三條晚期卜旬卜辭，各辭的行文皆左行，故是龜腹甲左半部的殘片。根據龜腹甲卜旬卜辭先內後外的契刻規律，各辭的卜問次序應是：

[癸]酉卜，貞：王旬[亡]禍？在十月又二，[甲]戌工典其[妹]其冒①。
[癸]巳卜，貞：王旬[亡]禍？在十月[又二]，[甲午]酒冒祭上甲。
[癸丑]卜，貞：王旬[亡禍]？在正月，[甲寅]祭大申酓上甲②。

各辭在卜問本旬有無災禍之後都有附記，內容有月份、"祭"祀和酓祀的祭祀，"祭"祀和酓祀都是周祭中的祀典。辭中的"工典其妹其冒"的"冒"祭，于省吾先生謂即毛炰之祭，也即炙肉之義③；而"祭"祀是用肉之祭④。故二者意義相近，因此"工典其妹其冒"即是"祭"祀的工典祭。第一條辭于癸酉日卜問舉行"祭"祀的工典祭，第二條辭于癸巳日卜問舉行"酒冒祭上甲"即"祭"上甲，兩旬之間相隔一旬（按照契刻規律這一旬應是刻在腹甲的右半部的），與上版一樣，也是在工典祭與祭上甲旬之間多出了一旬。由于與前面所說的相同的原因，即不知龜腹甲卜旬卜辭的契刻規律和囿于三十六旬型周期中，"祭"祀的工典祭與"祭"上甲是在連續的兩旬舉行的觀念，前人研究周祭時，無一例外地都將"祭"上甲的卜日癸巳日寫成癸未日，也即使"祭"祀的工典祭與"祭"上甲在連續的兩旬內舉行。這樣釋讀以龜腹甲卜旬卜辭的契刻規律檢查是錯誤的，因為就龜腹甲每半部分來說，相鄰的兩旬都不是連續的兩旬，而是都間隔一旬；不僅如此，就是從卜辭的實際記錄看也是錯誤的，辭中"祭"上甲的卜日癸巳日的巳字尚保留着下半部的丫形，在殷墟甲骨卜辭中，地支字"巳"晚期都寫成𠂤，其下半部都作丫⑤形；而"未"字，早晚期的寫法雖然不盡相同，早期多寫作𣎵，晚期多寫作𣎴，但其下部都是作木形。巳與未兩個字下半部的區別是很明顯的。因此將巳字釋成未字，一字之差又丟掉了三十七旬型周期的證據。

---

① "冒"字從陳夢家先生釋，見《殷虛卜辭綜述》394頁。
② 此辭的卜日和祭日均殘掉，這裏是根據周祭的祭祀次序和龜腹甲卜旬卜辭的契刻規律補上的。
③ 見于省吾：《雙劍誃殷契駢枝·續編》，1941年。
④ 見董作賓：《殷曆譜》上編卷一，1945年。
⑤ 編者按："丫"，原文誤作"木"，今徑改。

3. 糾正卜辭的誤刻

殷墟甲骨卜辭雖是商朝人所刻，但古人也會發生這樣那樣的誤刻，今天我們利用這些寶貴資料時，應有一個辨誤工作，否則會使研究的問題得不出正確的結論。下面舉一版卜辭說明掌握龜腹甲卜旬卜辭的契刻規律可以幫助辨誤。

（6）《綜述》21·8（圖四，3）

此版龜腹甲上有六條晚期卜旬卜辭，各辭的行文皆是右行，故是龜腹甲右半部的殘片。根據龜腹甲卜旬卜辭先內後外、先下後上的契刻規律，各辭的卜問次序應是：

癸亥卜，貞：王旬亡禍？在十[二]月，甲子翌陽甲。
癸未卜，貞：王旬亡禍？甲申翌日祖甲。
癸卯卜，貞：王旬亡禍？
癸亥卜，貞：王旬亡禍？在二月，甲子祭大甲。
癸未卜，貞：王旬亡禍？在二月。
[癸卯]卜，貞：[王旬]亡[禍]？[在]三月。

上面有的辭在卜問本旬有無災禍之後附記着翌祀或"祭"祀的祭祀。前已說過，翌祀和"祭"祀都是周祭中的祀典，因此，這是一版研究翌祀與"祭"祀接續關係的重要材料，歷來爲研究者所重視。但因前人不知龜腹甲卜旬卜辭的契刻規律，看不出該版的月份有誤刻，故有的對其祀序和月份的不合感到棘手；有的則採取錯誤的由上往下讀的方法，說該版證明了翌祭祖甲（翌祀的終止旬）與"祭"祀的工典祭（"祭"祀的起始旬）是相隔一旬舉行的，即認爲三十七旬型周期是在翌祭祖甲之後，"祭"祀的工典祭之前增加一旬構成的①。情況究竟如何？用龜腹甲卜旬卜辭的契刻規律按照月份、旬、翌祀和"祭"祀的祭祀次序排列此右腹甲刻辭和殘掉的左腹甲刻辭即可明白。因右腹甲（即該版）上的一條卜辭記錄卜問"祭"大甲的癸亥旬是在二月，其後兩旬的癸未旬也是在二月，那麽

---

① 見陳夢家：《殷虛卜辭綜述》395頁。陳先生從二月"祭"大甲開始數，到"祭壹啓"祀組祭祀週期結束，再經過整個彡祭祀祀週期，到翌祀祀組的翌祭陽甲，共是三十一旬，說這個祀序證明了翌祭祖甲與"祭"祀的工典祭是相隔一旬舉行的。但研究過周祭問題的人都知道，翌祭陽甲的後兩旬才是翌祭祖甲的一旬，"祭"大甲的前三旬才是"祭"祀工典祭的一旬，陳先生從"祭"大甲數到翌祭陽甲，恰恰是沒有經過翌祭祖甲和"祭"祀的工典祭這兩旬，怎麽能證明它們之間有增加的一旬呢？

"祭"大甲的癸亥旬就是二月的第一旬（其第二旬癸酉旬刻於腹甲的左半部），故我們用二月作定點進行排列：

月份	旬	祀序	契刻部位
十[二]月	癸亥	翌陽甲	右半部
十二月	癸酉	○①	左半部
[十二月]②	癸未	翌祖甲	右半部
一月	癸巳	祭工典	左半部
[一月]③	癸卯	[祭上甲]④	右半部
一月	癸丑	○	左半部
二月	癸亥	祭大甲	右半部
二月	癸酉	祭小甲	左半部
二月	癸未	○	右半部
三月	癸巳	祭戔甲	左半部
三月	[癸卯]⑤	[祭羌甲]⑥	右半部
三月	癸丑	祭陽甲	左半部

表中"祭"大甲是在癸亥旬，由此旬上推到前一個癸亥旬即翌祭陽甲的一旬共有六旬，一個月有三旬，六旬就正好是兩個月的時間。因爲"祭"大甲的癸亥旬是二月的第一旬，所以其前的六旬就分別是一月份的三個旬和上一年十二月份的三個旬，這樣翌祭陽甲的癸亥旬就是十二月份的第一旬。但原辭中此旬的月份刻的是十月，漏刻了個"二"字。由於將本是十二月的月份刻成了十月，就使周祭的祀序和月份不合了，故前人感到棘手；今糾正了翌祭陽甲月份的誤刻，知其是十二月的第一旬，那麼其後兩旬的翌祭祖甲就是在十二月的第三旬，而"祭"祀的工典祭就是在一月的第一旬，這樣翌祭祖甲與"祭"祀的工典祭就分別是在前後連續的兩旬內舉行的，中間並不間隔一旬，因此諸學者的三十七旬型周期是在翌祭祖甲之後，"祭"祀的工典祭之前增加一旬構成的説法就不能成立了⑦。如前所

---

① 這裏的"○"是表示該旬沒有甲名先王被祭祀。
②③ 月份省略未記。
④ "祭"上甲省略未記。
⑤ "癸卯"二字殘掉了。
⑥ "祭羌甲"幾字殘掉了。
⑦ 與陳夢家先生持相同意見的還有日本學者島邦男（見《殷墟卜辭研究》中譯本113頁）和加拿大籍華裔學者許進雄；許先生還認爲增加的一旬也可在祭祖甲與彡祭祀工典祭或彡祭祖甲與翌祀工典祭之間，即翌祀、祭（壹翌）祀、彡祀三個祀組都有增加一旬的機會（見《殷卜辭中五種祭祀的研究》，1968年）。但都無證據。

述，周祭中的三十七旬型周期都是在各個祀組的工典祭與祭上甲旬之間增加一旬構成的。目前雖然尚未見到在彡祀的工典祭與彡祭上甲旬之間增加一旬的材料，但據研究，商人設置三十六旬和三十七旬兩種周期類型的目的是爲了迎合天時，即使兩個祭祀周期約相當於兩個太陽年的時間，從而保持周祭周期與太陽年的日數基本平衡。如果確實如此，則三十七旬型周期中增加的一旬有時也可能是在彡祀的，即在彡祀的工典祭與彡祭上甲旬之間的。

三

本文分析了晚期龜腹甲上卜旬卜辭的契刻規律及掌握此規律對甲骨學商史研究的重要意義。應該指出，其意義肯定不只上述三種，隨着研究工作的日益深入，它必定會在其他方面顯示着自己的作用。

原載《考古》1987 年第 10 期；收入宋鎮豪、段志洪主編：《甲骨文獻集成》第 17 册，四川大學出版社，2001 年。今據前者收入。

黄德寬

卜辭所見"中"字本義試説

"中"字甲骨文、金文異體甚多，大致可分三種基本類型：

Ⅰ. 🚩（作妣己觶） 🚩（中婦鼎） 🚩（㞢卣） 🚩（合集 13357）

Ⅱ. 🚩（合集 39883） 🚩（合集 41059 正） 🚩（孟鼎）

Ⅲ. 中（通 735） 中（令鼎）

"中"的構形本義，曾有不少古文學家予以探討，但衆説紛紜，未有定論。由於三種類型的差别，有人將Ⅰ型釋"游"（柯昌泗）、釋"旗"（高田中周）或"旂"的初文（馬叙倫）、釋"於"（高鴻縉）。Ⅱ型都一致釋"中"，然於其構形本義，也各呈異辭：高田中周謂"中"字"从㫃从中，中亦聲"，爲"中廷專義字"；林義光説"本義爲射中之中'○象正鵠'，🚩象矢有繳形"；郭沫若謂"中字竪畫上下有同數之旅，或二或三，乃指事字，與本末同意，謂中央之圓適當正口也"；商承祚："竪㫃宜正，故从丨在○中間以見義"；馬叙倫："🚩爲什伍集中之義。"Ⅲ型，郭沫若認爲是"箭射中的之中，一圈示的，一竪示矢，乃會意字"；高田中周也説"象射侯形"，"其本訓當爲矢箸正也"。①上引諸説，可歸納爲"旂屬"和"中的"二説，而於三類字型關係的認識殊不明確。唐蘭先生分析"中"字字形演化最爲詳審，他指出三種類型代表同一字發展變化的不同階段。對於"中"的構形本義，唐先生却也未能擺脱"旂旗"之屬的解釋，并申論"中""最初爲氏族社會中之徽幟"，"上下爲游，中間之方框乃由直畫飾點，以雙

---

① 上引諸家之説的出處，周法高主編的《金文詁林》"中"字條下均有徵引，該書易檢，爲求省便，本文不再一一注明。

鈎寫出而成"。①

根據殷墟卜辭提供的材料，我們認爲"中"可能不是"旂旗之類"，而是我國古代測風工具的象形字，試述如次：

卜辭有以"中"測風的記載。卜辭"立中"一語多次出現，在有些卜辭中，我們看到一個有趣的現象，卜問"立中"時，"亡（無）風"、"允亡（無）風"常常同時出現，如：②

(1) ☐亡風，易日。/丙子其立中，亡風。八月。　　　　　　　　(7369)

(2) ☐酉卜，亘貞：翌丙子其☐立中，允亡風。　　　　　　　　(7370)

(3) ☐其立中，亡風。/☐亡風，易日。　　　　　　　　　　　　(7371)

(4) 癸卯卜，爭貞：翌☐中，亡風。丙子☐允亡〔風〕。　　　　　(13357)

(5) ☐中，丁酉☐風☐。　　　　　　　　　　　　　　　　　　(13343)

(6) ☐爭貞：翌丙子其立☐風，丙子立中，〔允〕亡風，易日。　　(40345)

從這些卜辭可以看出，"立中"可以確定風之有無，因此，可以肯定占卜"立中"與測風活動有關係。（1）（2）（3）（4）（6）等例都無疑表明這一事實，（5）例雖殘，也存"中""風"二字，其缺可補。

當然也有出現"立中"而不出現"亡風""允亡風"記錄的卜辭：

(7) ☐卜，爭貞：王立中？　　　　　　　　　　　　　　　　　(7365)

(8) 己亥卜，爭貞：王勿立中？　　　　　　　　　　　　　　　(7367)

(9) 辛亥貞：生月乙亥酚系，立中。　　　　　　　　　　　　　(32227)

這一類"立中"是否與上舉各例相同？我們認爲答案應該是肯定的。只是"立中"所測結果未曾記錄而已。有些殘辭，保留了"立中"如7376、7372反等。也可能殘損的正是"亡風"、"允亡風"之類的驗詞。例（9）"立中"出現於"酚系"等祭祀之辭之後，殘片33096作："☐亥☐乡系，立中"，34563作"☐乡酚☐中"，都與此例相近，這三片卜辭均見於四期。爲什麼貞卜祭祀之辭要附記"立中"，還值得進一步研究。但是祭祀卜辭後附記有關氣象情況的却甚爲常見，如《粹》13、16、26、70、217、456等片，及《續》6·11·3、《庫》29等，都可參證。《合集》32214片，同版有"伐"祭，也有貞卜"立中"的。

---

① 唐蘭：《殷虚文字記·釋"中"》，48—54頁，中華書局，1981年。
② 本文材料取自郭沫若主編的《甲骨文合集》（簡稱《合集》），爲方便起見，只標明著録號；也間或引用其他著録，文中簡稱一如島邦男《殷墟卜辭綜類》。

7369、7371、40354 等片，同辭還出現"易日"一語，32226 片云："甲寅卜：㱃立中，乙卯不易日。""易日"郭沫若讀爲"晹日"，指的是一種天象，即《説文》所謂"日覆雲，暫見也"，"猶言陰日"。① "立中"不僅與"亡風"而且與"易日"同辭或同版出現，可進一步證明"立中"與氣象觀測活動的密切關係，因爲風向與天氣陰晴相關，測風也就可以預知天氣的變化。

卜辭中保存了大量占卜"風"的記録，就有關卜辭看，當時已形成了初步的分級概念，有"小風"、"大風"、"大掫（驟）風"之别。14294 片卜骨云："東方曰析，風曰劦；南方曰𠀇，風曰屴；西方曰丯（介），風曰彝；［北方曰夗］，風曰役"，14295 版也有四方風的記載，風名和方名與此骨稍有差異②。據此可知當時四方與四方風已有專門的命名，殷代對風的觀測已經達到相當高的水平。"風"之所以引起殷人的高度重視，一方面是由於風的大小直接影響人們的生産和生活，另一方面，通過對風的觀測，可以幫助預測天氣的陰晴冷暖變化。我國農村至今仍十分重視利用這方面的經驗，這種經驗凝結在大量的農諺中。卜辭有關"風"的大量記録，也説明殷代完全可能已運用某種工具對風進行觀測。

唐蘭先生以"中"爲"旂旗"之屬，建旗以致衆人的説法影響甚大③。但是從卜辭内容看，"立中"以致衆人，尚未發現十分有力的證據。《合集》中有以下幾例，看起來好象與戰争之事相關，如：

（10）a. 貞：今㲋勿正土方
　　　b. 貞：立中
　　　c. 貞：☒立☒　　　　　　　　　　　　　　　　　　　　　（39883）

（11）a. ☒今㲋勿收☒人
　　　b. 貞：勿立中　　　　　　　　　　　　　　　　　　　　　（7374）

（12）a. ☒爭貞：戉戈，出☒
　　　b. 戉弗其☒
　　　c. ☒來甲辰立中☒　　　　　　　　　　　　　　　　　　　（39981）

（13）癸酉貞：方大出，立中于北土　　　　　　　　　　　　　　（33049）

以上各例，都不能直接證明"立中"與"立旗致衆"有關。考察圖版可知：

---

① 郭沫若：《古代銘刻彙考四種·"易日"解》，日本文求堂書店，1933 年影印。
② 本條刻辭釋文和增補參見以下二文：胡厚宣：《釋殷代求年於四方和四方風的祭祀》，《復旦學報》1956 年第 1 期；于省吾：《釋四方和四方風的兩個問題》，《甲骨文字釋林》，123—129 頁。
③ 唐蘭：《殷虚文字記·釋"中"》，48—54 頁。

39883 片 a 與 b、c 兩條卜辭之間，7374a 條與 b 條之間，都刻有分界綫，表明"正土方""奴☐人"與"立中"是兩條内容不同的卜辭。39981 片，a、b 兩辭明顯爲對貞句關係，b 條可補爲"戍弗其戋，出☐"，因而同版 c 條雖有"立中"，却可能是另一條卜辭。這種同版之中，不同内容卜辭交錯的現象，在甲骨刻辭中是大量存在的，如 39701 片云："貞：不其受年/貞：王勿奴人"，前者是關於年成的，後者一般則認爲屬於征伐一類。僅以《卜辭通纂·征伐》一類卜辭爲例，與"征伐類"内容同版出現的就有占卜"生死"、"祭祀"、"生育"、"寧風"等内容的卜辭，如 492、493、496、504、525、554、565 等片。因此，上舉三條卜辭，不能因爲同版有"戰爭征伐"等内容的卜辭出現，就認爲它們可以證明"立中"是"立旗致衆"。例（13）"中"寫作"屮"，與卜辭"立中"的"中"通常寫法有很大的差別，"立中"的"中"，竪畫上下都有曲畫，中間是比較方正的矩形，這個"中"，則與"立事"的"事（叓）"上部相同，我們懷疑它可能是"立叓"的"事"省刻了"又"，不管如何，應注意到其形體的特殊性。根據卜辭"立中"等材料出現的情況，我們難於遵從唐蘭先生的説法。

從辭例和卜辭有關"風"的記録入手，我們認爲"中"是測風的工具，考之於字形，"中"作爲測風器具的象形字，也甚契合。舊釋"中"字構形本義，多以爲是旌旗之屬，乃是根據"中"字有類似"斿"的附着物立論的，因有九斿、六斿、四斿旗之説，進而在典籍中尋找證據。這可能是一種誤會。與卜辭其他旗類字相比，"中"字所從，與"㫃"是有明顯的差別的，"中"有斿無旗，這一點唐蘭先生也已指出①。我們認爲，"中"所附之物，不是旗之斿，而是用於測定風之有無和方向的"綌"。"綌"用帛條或羽毛編織成帶狀，只是與斿類似而已。就"中"字 I 型而言，直畫乃象長標竿，上下對稱地系以"綌"用來測風。"綌"之所以取上下對稱，則是爲了確定風向的準確性。唐蘭先生認爲 I 型是"中"字原型②，而這種原型正是早期原始而又簡單的測風器具的形狀。II 型"中"字在中部加上了方框，我們覺得它不是標明中間位置的指事符號，也非"飾點"以雙鈎寫成，而是代表四方。四方坐標的確定，就可以準確無誤地測定八面來風了。這類字形代表了測風器具的發展。方框甲骨文有時寫得亦方亦圓，不甚規整，金文則大多變爲橢圓形，這是文字書寫和風格流變所致，也正是文字之所以爲文字而不等同於實物的特點的反映。而 III 型"中"字，則完全是后來字形的省簡，一般

---

① ② 唐蘭：《殷虛文字記·釋"中"》，48—54 頁。

不用於本義。根據"中"字字形提供的材料，我們大致可以瞭解殷代測風器的形制及其發展。

考察古籍中關於我國古代測風器的記載，也還能看到"中"字所象與后來測風器原理的一致性。古代測風器，典籍中叫"相風"、"相風鳥"或"五兩"。這方面零星記載現存最早的材料是漢代的。西漢劉安等撰《淮南子·齊俗訓》云："故終身隸于人，辟若綄之見風也，無須臾之間定矣。"許慎注云："綄，候風也，楚人謂之五兩。"據《北堂書鈔》卷一百三十八"舟部""伍兩"條所引，許注原爲"綄者，候風之羽也"。① 唐李淳風《乙巳占》云："凡候風者，必於高迥平原，立五尺長竿，以雞羽八兩爲葆，屬竿上以候風，風吹羽葆平直則占……羽葆之法，先取雞羽中破之，取其多毛處，以細繩逐緊夾之，長短三四尺許，屬于竿上，其扶搖、獨鹿、四轉、五復之風各以形狀占之。"② 這段記載可以幫助我們理解《淮南子》所記及許慎的注文。劉安等所見和唐代李淳風所描述的測風器，與"中"的形製未必就完全一致，但顯然與 I 型"中"字所象類似。"綄"本從"糸"，顯係絲帛之屬，編爲羽繩的"羽葆"，當爲後來的改進。《後漢書·張衡列傳》記載，"陽嘉元年（公元 132 年），復造候風、地動儀"，但未見關於"候風"的詳細記述。佚名氏《三輔黃圖》引晉郭延生《述征記》曰："長安宮南有靈台，高十五仞，上有渾儀，張衡所制，又有相風銅鳥，遇風乃動。"③ 此相風銅鳥是否即爲張衡所造的"候風"儀，不得確知。《藝文類聚》引晉傅玄《相風賦》云："乃構相風，因象設形。蜿盤獸以爲趾，建修竿之亭亭。體正直而無橈（撓），度經高而不傾。栖神鳥于竿首，俟祥風之來征。"這篇賦文《太平御覽》也節引了，只是文字上稍有出入，題爲鄭玄所作④。據傅玄賦文的描述，可以得知另一種形製稍不相同的測風器——"相風鳥"，其所異於"中"字所象和《淮南子》所記者，應是測風器由簡樸向復雜、美觀的一種發展，其基本原理並無大的差別。魏晉之後，關於相風的記載更多，無須備列。

西漢以後典籍所載之"相風"有簡單實用的，也有高級、復雜、講究美觀

---

① 劉文典：《淮南鴻烈集解》卷十一《齊俗訓》。
② 李淳風：《乙巳占》卷十"候風法"條，叢書集成初編本。
③ 《三輔黃圖》，作者佚名，其成書不晚於南北朝，據四部叢刊廣編本，臺灣商務印書館印行。
④ 《太平御覽》卷九"天部"九所引，題"鄭玄相風賦"，全部引文比《藝文類聚》卷六十八所引多出 39 字，僅此段文字有出入者，如"獸"作"虎"，"橈"作"撓"，"經"作"徑"，"高"作"挺"，"俟"作"候"。史書不言鄭玄有賦作，傅玄所作賦多有傳世，風格與此接近，且《藝文類聚》出於《御覽》之前，引證也較嚴謹，故從之。

的，那麼，其原始形製到底怎樣？又起源於何時？這是研究科技史所要提出的問題。晉崔豹云："伺風鳥，夏禹所作也。"①這未必有據，只極言來源之古。《宋書·禮志五》載："《周禮》辨載法物，莫不詳究，然無相風、罼網、旄頭之屬，此非古制明矣。何承天謂戰國並爭，師旅數出，懸烏之設，務察風祲，宜是秦制矣。"何是劉宋著名科學家，曾參與《宋書》編纂，其中《天文志》、《律曆志》即出自他之手，這裏記録的只是他對"相風"起源的推測。根據卜辭提供的資料，今天我們可以推定，"相風"之原始形製類似"中"字所象，至遲殷代已經有了這種測風器具。沿經周秦，到東漢經科學家張衡的改造，它變得更加精密、複雜而美觀。但從傅玄對"相風鳥"的描述來看，其基本結構和原理與"中"字還是一致的，只不過將"綖"改爲"神鳥"而置於"竿首"而已。王仁裕《開元天寶遺事》"相風旌"條載，唐代"五王宮中，各于庭中豎長竿，掛五色旌于竿頭，旌之四垂綴以小金鈴，有聲即使從者視旌之所向，可以知四方之風候"，可見到唐代類似Ⅰ型"中"的構形簡單的測風器還在使用。

　　古籍中關於"相風"的各種文字，可佐證我們關於"中"字所象乃爲測風器之説，因此，"中"不是會意字，也不是指事字，乃是一個象形字，中豎象長竿，上下等數曲畫象"綖"，中方框代表四方的坐標。問題是"中"在典籍中没有作爲"相風"之名的材料保存。我們認爲這一問題，可作如是答："相風"乃是根據"中"的作用——"觀測風"作的一個新的命名。由於"中"的引申義增多，詞義系統日趨複雜，"相風"遂取代了"中"表示測風器具這一義項，"中"字則只用於各種引申義項。時代更移，典籍湮没，"中"之本形本義遂致不可考。今有甲骨卜辭之文，才爲我們解決這一問題提供了新的綫索。類似這種情形的，在漢語詞彙發展中並非絶無僅有。有典籍可考的，如"領"本指"頸"，到後代只用於引申義，而本義由"頸"表示，發展到現代漢語，"脖子"又取代了"頸"。如果"領"變爲"脖子"的中間環節缺乏材料，或古籍中不保存"領"作爲"脖子"的材料，那麼二者的關係也同樣茫然難解了。"書"本有"信"一義，"信"古指"信使"，後以"信"取代"書"這一義項，"書"只保留了"書寫"和"書寫後訂成册的作品"之類的義項，也屬相同的現象②，這只是隨手取來的例子。在漢語詞彙發展史中，類似以"相風"取代"中"，以"相風鳥"取代"相風"，又以"伍兩"取代"相風鳥"之類的更名換姓而不易其主的現象不是個別的，這牽涉

---

① 崔豹：《古今注》卷上，四部備要本。
② 王力：《漢語史稿》（修訂本），497、547頁，中華書局，1980年。

到詞語命名及其發展問題，不便深論。

確定了"中"的構形來源，關於"中"的各項引申義就比較容易理解了。對"中"爲何有"中央"、"正"等引申義項，舊説多所牽强。唐蘭先生説"中本徽幟，而其所立之地，恒爲中央，遂引申爲中央之義，因更引申爲一切之中"①。此説雖比較圓通，也還難令人信服。就我們所釋字形而言，"中"作爲測風器，其標竿立於四方坐標（囗）之中心，故"中"有"中央"之義，同時觀測風向，總是以測點爲中心，因此"中"引申出"中心"、"中點"、"中間"諸義項是順理成章的。卜辭"王作三㠯，左中右"②（《粹》597），"中"即對左右師而言，位屬於"中"，還有大小上下之"中"，如卜辭"中宗者承大宗而言。中丁者承大乙、大丁、大戊而言"，"中子者乃對大子、小子而言"③；伯仲之仲作"中"，則是就其位居"伯"之下、"叔"之上而言，"仲"乃後起分別字。"中"有"正"一義，也是由構形本義引申。中所立之長竿不僅位居於中，而"體正直而無橈（撓）"，"既修且貞（正）"④，自然就引申出"正"這一義項。"中"的引申義進一步抽象，"正"可以引申出"中的"之"中"，"中央"即不偏倚，又可引申出"中和"一義。盡管引申義可以越來越抽象，而溯本求源，又都與"中"字構形本旨相關聯。

綜上所述，謂"中"爲測風器的象形字，就卜辭辭例、字形、典籍材料和詞義的引申系統諸方面看均無抵牾。這一結論如能成立，不僅對解決"立中"等卜辭的釋讀問題提供新的綫索，而且爲古代科技史的研究提供了較可靠的古文字資料。我們撰寫此文時，查閱了有關科技史論著⑤，發現一些著者根據甲骨文有"䧹"字，而確定殷代有測風器。這是由上引《淮南子·齊俗訓》"辟若綂之見風"之"綂"字，傳世版本作"䧹"所致。"䧹"爲"綂"之訛，莊逵吉、王念孫等考證甚精，已正其誤⑥。引者忽略了這一點，根據"䧹"卜辭中有對應字，就草率肯定卜辭"䧹"就是殷代測風器的證據，這顯然是不妥當的。實際上甲骨文

---

①③ 唐蘭：《殷虛文字記·釋"中"》，48—54頁。
② 編者按："左中右"，原辭作"右中左"（《合》33006）。
④ （晉）傅玄《相風賦》云："翟翟竹竿，在武之庭，厥用自然，既修且貞，插羽其首，丹漆弗營，經之營之，不日而成。"見《太平御覽》卷九"天部"。
⑤ 王鵬飛：《中國古代對天氣現象的觀測和理論》，見自然科學史研究所主編：《中國古代科技成就》，中國青年出版社，1978年；杜石然等編著：《中國科學技術史稿》，193頁，科學出版社，1982年。
⑥ 劉文典：《淮南鴻烈集解》卷十一《齊俗訓》。

的"倪"與側風器毫無關係，這一點應該予以糾正，而應以"中"字及相關卜辭提供的材料來替換這一錯誤的引證。

原載《文物研究》總第3期，黄山書社，1988年；收入黄德寬：《開啟中華文明的管籥——漢字的釋讀與探索》，北京師範大學出版社，2011年。今據前者收入，並吸收了後書的一些編校處理意見。

裘錫圭

關於殷墟卜辭的命辭是否問句的考察

命辭指卜筮時提出所卜或所筮之事的話。在殷墟出土的商代後期甲骨卜辭裏，命辭往往用"鼎"（貞）字引出。古人說"卜以決疑"（《左傳·桓公十一年》），《說文》把"貞"字訓爲"卜問"，所以長期以來，研究殷墟卜辭的學者都把命辭一律看作問句。但是絕大多數命辭所用的句子，在語法形式上跟占辭、驗辭所用的陳述句並無區別，至少在字面上看不出區別。因此從 70 年代開始，有些研究殷墟卜辭的外國學者，對命辭是問句的傳統看法提出了疑問。

漢語裏雖然有專門表示疑問的句末語氣詞，但並不是非用不可，有時是非問句和陳述句除了語調不同外，形式上可以毫無區別。由於這個原因，並由於殷墟卜辭裏句末語氣詞很少見，研究卜辭的中國學者一直沒有把命辭跟占辭、驗辭形式上沒有區別這一點，看作把它們理解爲問句的障礙。外國學者在很長一段時間裏也是接受這種看法的。最先提出懷疑的是美國加州大學伯克利分校的吉德煒（David N. Keightley）和華盛頓大學的司禮義（Paul L-M. Serruys）兩位教授。

1972 年，吉德煒在提交給太平洋沿岸亞洲研究學會在加州蒙特利舉行的會議的論文《釋貞——商代貞卜本質的新假設》裏，提出了命辭不是問句的主張。我們沒有讀到這篇論文，下面引的是法國學者雷煥章（Jean A. Lefeuvre）神父在《法國所藏甲骨錄》釋文部分裏對此文內容所作的概括：

> Keightley 在一篇題作《釋貞》之論文中，提出一就當時而言非常新的意見：甲骨文中之"命辭"，不是疑問句，而是一有關未來之陳述命題；這些"命辭"之文法，亦皆無任何問句之形式；若將其視爲某種"意圖"或"預見"之宣示，則有關甲骨文命辭解釋上的許多困難，便可迎刃而解。……《說文》釋"貞"爲"卜問"，乃屬後起之解釋；……最後，他將"貞""正"連結，而釋序辭中之"某（貞

人）貞"爲"由某（貞人）正之"。（123 頁）

司禮義在刊登於 1974 年《通報》的《商代卜辭語言研究》中，也主張命辭不是問句，並以"正""定"一類意義來解釋貞卜之"貞"。他認爲"貞"的意義近於檢驗、校正，命辭所說的就是需要檢驗、校正的行動方針等等。此外，他還批評了有些學者認爲卜辭裏常見的"其"和"唯"以及出現在句末的某些"乎"和"不"是表疑問的語詞的看法（《通報》卷 60・I -3，21 頁以下）。

此後，美國斯坦福大學的倪德衛（David S. Nivison）教授在提交給 1982 年在檀香山舉行的商代文明國際討論會的論文《問句的問題》（以下簡稱"倪文"）裏，對命辭是否問句的問題進行了更爲深入的探討。他接受了我國學者李學勤教授關於𠂤組卜辭語末助詞的研究成果，在承認𠂤組卜辭的命辭裏確有一些具有語法標誌的問句的前提下，從多方面論證一般的命辭並非問句。這篇論文裏的不少意見在後面的討論中將會引到，這裏就不多作介紹了。

倪德衛的學生，現在執教於芝加哥大學的夏含夷（Edward L. Shaughnessy）教授，在他的博士論文《周易的構成》裏也對殷墟卜辭的命辭進行了研究。在命辭是否問句的問題上，他的意見大致與倪德衛相同。此外，他還論述了殷墟卜辭在形式和內容上從早期到晚期的變化，以及與之相應的占卜作用的變化（1983 年縮微膠卷複印本 52—57、66—67 等頁）。這篇論文還指出，周原卜辭往往以"囟……"一類話結尾（如"……囟有正"），"囟"應該讀爲"思"，訓爲"願"；典籍等所載的東周時代卜筮的命辭，幾乎都使用"尚"字（如"余尚得天下"），也是表示願望的，所以它們也都不可能是問句（同上 58—59、76—81 等頁。參看夏含夷《試釋周原卜辭囟字——兼論周代貞卜之性質》，1983 年 8 月手寫中文稿複印本）。

在上述幾位之外，還有一些研究卜辭的外國學者也是主張命辭非問句的，如前面提到過的雷煥章和加拿大英屬哥倫比亞大學的高嶋謙一教授（參閱《法國所藏甲骨錄》123—126 頁）。

近年來，國內學者中也有人對命辭是問句的傳統看法產生了懷疑。李學勤在提交給 1983 年在香港中文大學舉行的國際古文字學研討會的論文《續論西周甲骨》裏，根據他對周原卜辭"囟"字的研究，也認爲周原卜辭的命辭都不是問句，並提出了殷墟卜辭的命辭有些也不是問句的意見。這篇論文已在《中國語文研究》第 7 期和《人文雜志》1986 年 1 期上公開發表。李學勤的意見是有一個發展過程的。他很早就把周原卜辭的"囟"字讀爲"斯"，但起初仍把用"囟"字的

卜辭看作問句（李學勤、王宇信《周原卜辭選釋》,《古文字研究》第四輯250等頁）。在發表於《文物》1981年9期的《西周甲骨的幾點研究》裏，他指出周原卜辭有些不是問句，"與殷墟卜辭大多爲問句不同"（8頁），但仍然把周原卜辭裏用"囟"的句子看作問句（8、9、10等頁）。到《續論西周甲骨》裏，他提出了周原卜辭裏的"斯……"和《左傳》《國語》所載卜筮之辭裏的"尚……""這樣以命令副詞開首的句子，絶不是問句"的看法，並認爲"既然西周卜辭的'斯正'、'斯有正'之類不是問句，殷墟卜辭的'正'、'有正'也肯定不是問句"（《人文雜志》1986年1期71頁）。看來，他已經改變了"殷墟卜辭大多爲問句"的觀點。不過，絶大部分國内學者目前仍持命辭都是問句的傳統看法。

命辭是否問句的問題"涉及對所有卜辭的理解"（同上71頁）。對這樣重要的問題有必要繼續進行研究和討論，以求取得比較一致的認識。我們準備就這個問題提供一些資料和看法，希望能有助於研究和討論的深入。主張命辭不是問句的學者，大都撇開《説文》的定義，對"貞"字另作解釋。但是正如倪文已經指出的那樣，"貞"字的意義實際上並不能決定跟在它後面的命辭的語氣（倪文1、10等頁）。所以我們不想涉及"貞"字的解釋問題，只準備具體討論一下在殷墟卜辭的命辭裏，究竟有哪些可以確定是問句，有哪些可以確定不是問句。下文引用卜辭時，釋文一般用寬式，如讀爲"貞"的"鼎"直接寫作"貞"，讀爲"在"的"才"直接寫作"在"。有些有争論的字暫用一説，如"㞢"字暫釋作"正"（此種"正"字右上角加＊號作標誌）。釋文中句末一律標句號，即使已經確定是問句的也標句號不標問號。卜辭附記的月名等，釋文中一般略去。

一、卜辭句末疑問語氣詞和置於辭末的否定詞"不"

在殷墟卜辭裏，曾被認爲是句末疑問語氣詞的字，有"乎""才"（哉）和"抑""執"。此外，出現在卜辭末尾的否定詞"不"，很多人也認爲是古漢語反復問句所用的"否"的前身。這些意見是否可信，需要分別加以討論。

（一）關於"抑"和"執"

見於殷墟卜辭的最確鑿無疑的句末疑問語氣詞，是李學勤在《關於自組卜辭的一些問題》一文（以下簡稱"李文"）的"語末助詞"節裏指出來的"🦅"（亦

作 ⿰) 和 "執"（《古文字研究》第三輯 39—43 頁）。但是李文把前者釋爲"屷"，則是有問題的。

羅振玉把⿰字釋作"屷"，⿰字釋作《說文》認爲"从反'印'"的"抑"字古體，並指出"印""抑"古本一字（增訂本《殷虛書契考釋》中 54—55 頁）。這些都是正確的。古文字表意偏旁中"爪"形和"又"形往往可以通用，所以⿰也可作⿰。但是由於羅振玉考釋"屷""抑"二字時強調从"又"从"爪"之別，後來《甲骨文編》《甲骨文字集釋》等書都誤把⿰歸入"屷"字。島邦男《殷墟卜辭綜類》才加以糾正（參看張桂光《古文字中的形體訛變》，《古文字研究》第十五輯 177 頁）。在卜辭裏，"屷"多指祭祀人牲，"抑"則用爲句末語氣詞，有時也用爲國族名或人名（如《合》21708、21710 等。《合》22590、25020 兩條出組同文卜辭裏的"抑"疑亦人名）。兩個字的用法截然有別。

李文所以把"抑"釋作"屷"，是有原因的。李文討論自組語末助詞時，舉了下引兩組卜辭加以對比（標點依原文，出處改用《甲骨文合集》片號）：

(1) 丙辰卜，丁巳其陰（本作"雀"，從于省吾釋）不？允陰。　　合 19781
(2) 丙辰卜，丁巳其陰屷？允陰。　　合 19780
(3) 丁丑卜，方其正*今八月不？　　合 20473
(4) 辛亥，方正*今十一月屷？　　合 20818

（1）（2）爲一組，（3）（4）爲一組。李文認爲這兩組卜辭可以證明"屷"和"不"在句中的作用相同，並說"兩字均屬古之部，音近可通"（《古文字研究》第三輯 40 頁）。如果採釋"抑"之說，跟"不"就音遠不可通了。但是上引（3）辭末尾的"不"其實並非"語末助詞"，詳後文（本節第四小節）。（1）（2）兩辭原來是完全同文的，只是前一條"抑"字的下部已殘去，乍看起來有些像"不"。既然與"不"相通的證據有問題，這個字當然仍以釋"抑"爲宜。倪文雖然採用了李文的研究成果，却仍然把這個字釋作"抑"，可謂有識。

下面就來看看自組卜辭使用句末疑問語氣詞"抑"和"執"的例子。凡李文已舉之例都在辭前加*號，但釋文有時略有出入。

李文指出自組卜辭有時"把正反兩問併於一辭之中，正問用助詞'屷'，反問用助詞'執'（有時相反）"（41 頁）。李文所說的這種命辭，可以認爲是由兩個正反相對的分句組成的選擇問句（其實也未嘗不可以就稱爲反復問句），兩個分句分別綴以句末語氣詞"抑"或"執"。其例如下：

*(5) 癸酉卜貞：方其正*今二月抑，不執。余曰：不其正*。允不。　合 20411

*(6) 癸酉卜，王貞：自今癸酉至于乙酉，邑人其見方抑，不其見方執。
合 799

*(7) 乙酉卜，王貞：余辥朕老工延我莫，貞：允唯余受馬方祐抑，弗其受方祐執。　合 20613

(8) □辰卜，王□于(？)大方□敦抑，不執。　合 20468

(9) □獲正*方抑，弗獲執。　合 20427

*(10) 丙寅卜，□貞：衣今月虎其凶抑，不凶執。旬六日壬午凶。
合 40819 + 21390

（李文未拼。《論集》編按："月"下一字，虎頭上有"m"形，或非"虎"字，李文隸定爲"麂"）

*(11) 丙寅□今月虎不其凶[抑]，凶執。　英 1779【《合》40820】

*(12) 丙寅□衣今月[虎]不其凶[抑]，凶執。　合 21394

(13) 辛丑卜，白貞：子辟霽疾臣不其囚曾抑，囚曾[執]。　合 21036

*(14) 壬□貞：□牛在□弗克以抑，其克以執。　合 19779

(15) □□卜，冄：不其延雨□（李文釋爲"至丙"合文）抑，延雨執。
合 19778

(16) □貞：□有囚抑，亡囚執。　合 19784

*(17) □疾抑，亡執。　合 21047

以上爲前一分句用"抑"後一分句用"執"之例。前一分句有的是正面問有的是反面問。以下爲前一分句用"執"後一分句用"抑"之例：

*(18) 癸卯卜，王：缶蔑正*戎執，弗其蔑抑。三日丙午邁方，不獲。
合 20449

(19) 庚戌卜，白貞：方其正*今日執，不[抑]。　京津 2984

*(20) □唯□咎執，不抑。　合 19785

*(21) 辛酉卜，貞：有至今日執，亡抑。亡。　合 20377（參看《庫》1194摹本）

《合》20224（即《甲》2271）有如下一辭：

(22) 辛丑卜，曰：缶亡以□，有以抑。

據文例，"亡以"下一字應爲"執"，但原拓此字不清，難以確定。如果不把上引諸例的"抑"和"執"理解爲句末疑問語氣詞，辭義絕大多數根本講不通，看作

句末疑問語氣詞就文從字順了。可見李說是不可移易的。

從上引諸例看，前一分句用"抑"的比較常見。較晚的古漢語裏置於選擇問句的兩個分句之間的連詞"抑"，也許就是由這種"抑"演變而成的。"執"相當於古書中的哪個詞，或者跟哪個詞有關，尚待研究。

在"把正反兩問併於一辭之中"的選擇問句式的命辭之外，自組卜辭中也有他組卜辭中常見的那種正反對貞的命辭。這種命辭之末有時也加"抑"字：

(23A) 戊申卜：方𤰔自南，其正*抑。
(23B) 戊申卜：方𤰔自南，不其正*抑。　　　　　　　　合 20415
(24A) 涉三羌，既獲抑。
(24B) 毋獲抑。　　　　　　　　　　　　　　　　　合 19755
(25A) 甲午卜，彶：亡𩫖抑。
(25B) 甲午卜，彶：由(?)𩫖抑。　　　　　　　　　屯南 4310
(26A) 甲戌卜，☐麀☐獲抑。
(26B) 甲戌卜☐象麀☐抑。　　　　　　　　　　　合 21768

這些"抑"字無疑也是用作句末疑問語氣詞的。《合》20196 是一塊殘卜骨，右下方有如下一辭：

(27A) 甲戌卜，玦：𢀛其出抑。

其上方尚有一條殘辭：

(27B) ☐不其出。

這兩條卜辭大概也是正反對貞的關係，但反面命辭未加"抑"字，似可說明不加句末疑問語氣詞的命辭也有可能是問句。

此外，在自組卜辭裏還可以看到一些句末加"抑"的命辭：

*(28) 辛亥卜：方正*今十一月抑。　　　　合 20818（即前引第 4 辭）
(29) 癸亥卜：小方不正*今秋抑。　　　　　　　　　合 20476
*(30) 戊戌卜：王貞：余並立員宁史眔見莫抑。　　　　英 1784
*(31) 戊午卜，曰：今日啓抑。允啓。　　　　　　　合 20898
*(32) 戊戌卜：其陰翌己抑。啓不見雲。

合 20988（《合》19786 有同文殘辭）

*(33) 丙辰卜：丁巳其陰抑。允陰。

合 19780（《合》19781 同文。即前引 1、2 兩辭）

*（34）己酉卜：晕陰其雨抑。不雨，曲（曾）啓。　　　　　　　合 21022

（35）己未卜：不𫝀（義近"遘"）雨抑。狩取。　　　　　　　合 20757

*（36）甲辰卜：乙其焚又□中（?）風抑。小風，延陰。　　　　合 20769

（37）□麐抑。明陰，不其□　　　　　　　　　　　　　　　合 20717

（38）庚戌卜：今日狩，不其擒抑。　　　　　　　　　　　　合 20757

（39）戊辰卜，王□豕允獲抑。　　　　　　　　　　　　　　合 19782

（40）己巳□岳豕遘豕抑。　　　　　　　　　　　　　　　　合 19787

（41）辛亥卜，貞：犬囚凡疾抑。　　　　　　合 21053（倪文已引此條）

（42）辛卯[卜]：𫝀其疾抑。　　　　　　　　　　懷 1518【《合補》6740】

*（43）壬申卜，玖：弜（勿）又，其若（?）抑。　　　　　　合 20805

（44）戊戌卜：弜追□抑。　　　　　　　　　　　　　　　　合 19783

（45）□王貞：馬方□亟陟曰喪抑。□　　　　　　　　　　　合 20407

（46A）丙寅卜：又涉三羌，其得□抑。

（46B）丙寅卜：又涉三羌，其畜至白抑。　　　　　　　　　合 19756

*（47）丙寅卜：□羌，其畜涉河抑。不畜。　　　　　　　　　合 19757

李文認爲這些命辭末尾的"抑"也是疑問語氣詞，其説可信（《論集》編按：《懷》1507【《合補》6666】"壬子卜，𠂤：其至五日抑"，也是這一類的例子，應補入）。這些命辭有的可能原來也是屬於對貞卜辭的，只是跟它有對貞關係的辭没有發現而已。

在殷墟卜辭裏，句末用疑問語氣詞"抑"和"執"的，實際上並非只限於自組。下引兩條賓組卜辭的命辭，也用"抑"和"執"組成正反相對的選擇問句：

（48）壬午[卜]，爭貞：□其來抑，不其來執。　　　　　　　合 800

（49）貞：禦婦抑，勿執。　　　　　　　　　　　　　　　　合 802

《合》797 和 798 兩條用"抑"和"執"的殘辭，從字體看大概也屬於賓組。

另有兩條午組卜辭，句末也加"抑"：

（50）壬戌卜：𠂤侯□余𫝀乎見尹以𫝀侯抑。　　　　　　　　合 22065

（51）□申卜：𠂤禦子自祖庚至于父戊抑。　　　　　　　　　合 22101

這兩條也應是問句（《論集》編按：子組卜辭也有加"抑"之例，如《合》21586"甲子卜，我貞：呼象，獲抑""不獲抑"這一對正反對貞之辭）。

（二）關於"乎"

《粹》425 是一片自組殘甲（《合》20098 即此片加《甲》264），上部有如下二辭：

(52A) 丁未卜，玖：虫咸戊、學戊乎。

(52B) 丁未，玖：虫咸戊牛。不。

郭沫若解釋説："案此二辭，一綴以'乎'，一綴以'不'，蓋均表示疑問之語詞，不者否也。凡卜辭本均是疑問語。"（《殷契粹編考釋》66 頁下）"不"的問題後面再談，這裏先討論"乎"。

司禮義不同意郭沫若那種意見。他質問説，如果命辭是問句，"乎"是句末疑問語氣詞，"爲什麽在大量所謂問句裏只有一個用'乎'的例子呢？"（《通報》卷 60·Ⅰ-3，23 頁）但是在自組卜辭中，跟上引（52A）同類型的以"乎"結尾的命辭，實際上是屢見的，如：

(53A) 乙巳卜，玖：虫卜丙乎。
(53B) ☐玖：☐兄☐乎。　　　　　　　　　　　　　合 19817
(54) 丙午卜，王：牢卜丙乎。　　　　　　　　　　合 19891
(55) 丁酉卜，王：虫祖丁乎。　　　　　　　　　　合 1843
(56) 甲午卜☐又升歲大乙乎。　　　　　　　　　　合 19815
(57) ☐☐卜：☐大庚乎。　　　　　　　　　　　　合 22168
(58) ☐巳卜，王：虫兄戊乎。　　　　　　　　　　合 2403
(59A) [庚]辰卜，☐：𠂤兄戊乎。
(59B) [庚]辰卜，王：𠂤☐丁乎。辛巳。　　　　　英 1803
(60) 戊寅卜：又子族乎。不。　　　　　　　　　　合 21288
(61) 戊子卜，𠂤：☐母乎。　　　　　　　　　　　合 19890
(62) ☐未卜，☐：虫母庚乎。　　　　　　　　　　合 19963
(63) 己未☐又妣☐乎。　　　　　　　　　　　　　合 15868
(64) 壬午卜：燎土，延巫帝乎。　　　　　　　　　合 21075

既然自組卜辭中"乎"字句屢見，郭説是不是就可以成立呢？那倒不一定。上引各辭都是卜祭之辭，而且句式相當一致，"乎"字一般緊接在被祭者之名後面，前邊不出現牲名等詞。如果"乎"確是疑問語氣詞，爲什麽只在這種句子裏

出現呢？它會不會指跟祭祀有關的某件事呢？所以用"乎"字結尾的這種命辭究竟是不是問句，還有待研究。

（三）關於"哉"

下引三辭的末一字都是"才"：

（65A）貞：呼伐舌人才。
（65B）貞：勿人才。 合6252
（66）☐五牡二☐用才。 合34406

《合》6252即《粹》1089，屬賓組。《合》34406即《粹》552，屬歷組。《殷契粹編釋文》把這三條卜辭的"才"都讀爲"哉"。在古漢語裏，表疑問語氣的"哉"通常用於反詰句，"而且要靠疑問代詞或反詰副詞的幫助，才能表示反詰"（王力《漢語史稿》中冊449頁，中華書局，1980）。從這種情況看，把卜辭的"才"讀爲"哉"顯然是不合適的。

上引（65）的兩條卜辭是相間刻辭，其間尚有如下一辭：

（65C）辛亥卜，古貞：于。

命辭只有一個"于"字，無義可說，其後當有未刻出的字。兩條同版卜辭的"才"字之後，是否也有未刻出的字呢？（66）說不定也屬於這種情況。

（四）關於"不"

自組卜辭裏常見末尾有否定詞"不"的卜辭（參看李文39—40頁）。賓組早期卜辭（如《合》12910、11787、11790、11953等）、歷組卜辭（如《合》33829、33943、《屯南》325、4350、《英》2429等）以及午組等字體較特殊的一些卜辭（如《合》22067、22045、22187、22289、22290等，參看李文42頁）裏，也都有一些這樣的例子。前面已經說過，郭沫若認爲出現在卜辭末尾的否定詞"不"是"表示疑問之語詞，不者否也"。這種意見得到了相當廣泛的贊同。

陳夢家在《殷虛卜辭綜述》裏，曾提到以"不"結尾的問句的來源。殷墟卜辭裏有一些"V不V"格式的卜辭，如"雨不雨"（這是最簡單的例子，這種格式裏的謂詞是可以有主語、賓語或修飾語的）。很多人把它們看作與現代漢語的反復問句相當的句式。陳氏在《綜述》的"文法"章中，曾以跟"雨"有關的卜辭爲例，對卜辭語法進行過分析。他認爲卜辭的"'雨不雨'省而爲'雨不'，就是

後來的'雨否'"（87 頁）。

應該承認，"V 不 V"和"V 不"這兩種格式的反復問句，在殷代語言裏都有可能存在。

本文開頭已經提到過，漢語問句句尾不一定都帶疑問語氣詞。無論現代漢語或古代漢語都是如此。呂叔湘《中國文法要略》說："是非問句在口語裏可以單用語調來表示……古代口語裏想來也應該有這樣的句法，但文言中實例甚少。"（商務印書館，1956，287 頁）楊樹達《高等國文法》從典籍中舉出了一些例子，如："我生不有命在天？"（《書·西伯戡黎》）"功成而不居，其不欲見賢？"（《老子》）"虞帝之明，在茲壹舉，可不致詳？"（《漢書·薛宣傳》）等（商務印書館，1955，533 頁），但也大都是反詰句。古代書面語中少見這種句例，大概是怕人誤認爲非問句，這種現象恐怕不反映當時口語的實際情況。

在現代口語裏，選擇問句，尤其是其中的反復問句，不用句末疑問語氣詞的情況更爲常見。像"你去不去"這類反復問句，甚至是以不用爲常的。在古代典籍中，一般的選擇問句幾乎都用句末疑問語氣詞；反復問句常見的是"V 否"式，"V 不 V"式幾乎看不到。這種現象恐怕也不能反映古代口語的實際情況。70 年代發現的雲夢秦簡的"法律答問"等部分有很多選擇問句，絕大多數都不用句末語氣詞（兩個分句間一般有連詞"且"）。此外還有不少"V 不 V"式反復問句及其變式（如"……論不論""……當論不當"），這些問句全都不用句末語氣詞（參看馮春田《秦墓竹簡選擇問句分析》，《語文研究》1987 年 1 期）。

我們在"關於'抑'和'執'"那一小節中，舉過（10）"……其禽抑，不禽執"和（20）"……咎執，不抑"等例句。如果去掉句尾的語氣詞，就變成"V 不 V"和"V 不"式反復問句了（這裏只是作平面的比較，並不認爲用句末語氣詞的形式一定先產生）。此外，如陳夢家所設想的，由"雨不雨"省略成"雨不"的可能性，也是存在的。所以在殷代語言裏，這兩種問句有可能都已經出現了。70 年代岐山董家村出土了西周中期的五祀衛鼎，銘文中有"正乃訊厲曰：汝賈田不"之語（《文物》1976 年 5 期 38 頁【《集成》5·2832】）。這裏的訊辭顯然是"V 不"式問句。這對殷代已有這種問句的想法是一個有力支持。

但是承認殷代語言裏可能有"V 不 V"式和"V 不"式的問句，並不一定導致承認"V 不 V"和"V 不"這兩種格式的卜辭是問句。如果撇開"××卜"之類序辭不說，除了單獨由命辭構成的卜辭之外，還存在很多包含命辭、占辭、驗辭三部分的卜辭，以及很多包含命辭和占辭或驗辭兩部分的卜辭。而且各部分之

間的界綫,尤其是命辭跟驗辭的界綫,並非總是很清楚的。所以"V 不 V"或"V 不"格式的卜辭究竟能不能看作反復問句式的命辭,是需要仔細推敲的。下面先討論"V 不","V 不 V"在下一節討論。

如果把末尾爲否定詞"不"的卜辭跟有關的卜辭聯繫起來進行考察,就能發現這種卜辭末尾的"不"字實際上並不屬於命辭,而是簡化的驗辭或用辭(用辭指記於命辭、占辭之後,或記於兆旁的"兹用""不用"一類詞語)。

屬於𠂤組的《合》21052 有如下一對正反對貞的卜辭:

(67A) 癸酉卜:自今至丁丑其雨不。

(67B) 自今至丁丑不其雨。允不。

仔細對比一下這兩條卜辭就可以看出,A 辭末尾的"不"跟 B 辭末尾的"允不"一樣,也是驗辭。所以釋文中"不"字前邊應該加句號,把它跟命辭隔開(下文引用卜辭時,就直接按我們的理解加標點)。這一對卜辭貞卜從癸酉日到丁丑日這段時間裏會不會下雨。結果沒有下雨,所以在反面命辭後面記上"允不",等於説"允不雨",意即果然没下雨。由於結果是否定的,在正面卜辭後面當然不能用"允"字,所以只記一個"不"字,等於説"不雨",意即没有下雨。在小屯南地發現的𠂤組卜甲上也有這類對貞卜辭:

(68A) 乙未卜:其雨丁。不。

(68B) 乙未卜:翌丁不其雨。允不。　　合 20398(《屯南》4513 + 4518)

正反對貞的卜辭在兩條命辭後都加驗辭的現象屢見不鮮。例如《合》32171 有一對己亥日貞卜的卜辭:

(69A) 己亥卜:不雨。庚子夕雨。

(69B) 己亥卜:其雨。庚子允雨。

兩辭正反對貞,"庚子夕雨""庚子允雨"説的是同一件事,其爲驗辭確鑿無疑。

屬於𠂤組的《合》21387 有三對正反對貞的卜辭:

(70A) 辛卯卜,𠂤:自今辛卯至于乙未虎㚔。不。

(70B) [辛卯卜,𠂤:自今辛卯]至[于]乙未虎不其㚔。允不。

(70C) 丁酉卜,𠂤:自丁酉至于辛丑虎[㚔]。不。

(70D) 丁酉卜,𠂤:自丁酉至于辛丑虎不其㚔。允不。

(70E) 丁巳卜,𠂤:自丁至于辛酉虎不其㚔。允。

(70F) 丁巳卜，㱿：自丁至于辛酉虎㝈。不。

這些卜辭也都是在正面命辭後加驗辭"不"，在反面命辭後加驗辭"允不"，或簡化爲"允"。（《論集》編按：上引諸辭中的"虎"原來也是在虎頭上加"ㅁ"形的。）

也是屬於自組的《合》20961有兩條相鄰的同日貞卜的卜辭：

(71A) 丙戌卜：雨今夕。不。

(71B) 丙戌卜：三日雨。丁亥唯大食雨。

A辭貞卜丙戌當天晚上是否下雨，B辭貞卜三天内是否下雨。結果丙戌晚上没下雨，到丁亥大食之時下了雨。所以B的命辭後記"丁亥唯大食雨"，A的命辭後記"不"。"不"爲驗辭也是很明顯的。

屬於賓組早期的《合》12909正有兩組卜辭。一組在乙卯日卜，共三辭，分別貞卜丙辰、丁巳、戊午這三天是否會下雨。一組在庚申日卜，也有三辭，分別貞卜辛酉、壬戌、癸亥這三天是否會下雨。原文如下：

(72A) 乙卯卜：丙辰雨。不。

(72B) 丁巳雨。允雨。

(72C) 戊午雨。不。

(72D) 庚申卜：辛酉雨。允雨。

(72E) 壬戌雨。不。

(72F) 癸亥雨。允雨，小。

A、C、E三辭末尾的"不"，顯然跟其餘三辭末尾的"允雨"和"允雨小"一樣，也是驗辭。

屬於歷組的《合》33874有五條卜雨之辭：

(73A) [甲戌卜]：丙子[雨]。不。

(73B) 甲戌卜：丁丑雨。允雨。

(73C) 己卯卜：庚辰雨。允雨。

(73D) 庚辰卜：今日雨。允雨。

(73E) 庚辰卜：辛巳雨。不。

A、E兩辭末尾的"不"顯然也是驗辭，情況跟上例相同。自組、賓組早期和歷組的卜雨之辭末尾的"不"，大概都是驗辭。

從字體看似屬賓組晚期或出組早期的兩片甲骨上,也有末尾爲否定詞"不"的卜雨之辭:

(74) 貞:今夕雨不。　　　　　　　　　　　　　　　　合 12221

(75) 貞:今夕雨不。　　　　　　　　　　　　　珠 1164【《合》12037】

這兩個"不"也以是驗辭的可能性爲大。

下引兩條自組卜辭雖然不同版,卜日也差一天,但顯然是從正反兩方面貞卜同一件事的:

(76) 丙子卜:小方不其正*今八月。允不。　　　　　　　　合 20475

(77) 丁丑卜:小方其正*今八月。不。　合 20473(即第 1 小節所引第 3 辭)

(77)的"不"顯然是驗辭,意即"不正*"。自組卜辭中屢見末尾爲"不"的卜"方正*""方至"之辭,如:

(78) 壬申卜,曰:今五月方其正*。不。　　　　　　　　　合 20412

(79) 癸酉卜,方至今。不。　　　　　　　　　　　　　　合 20409

(80) 乙巳卜:今日方其至。不。　　　　　　　　　　　　合 20410

(81) 丁未卜:今日方正*。不。　乙 106(《合》將此片拼入 20412,似非)

這些卜辭裏的"不"都應該是驗辭。

這類驗辭偶爾也有可以不説"允不"而只説"不"的,如:

(82) 壬寅卜:自今三日方不正*。不。　　　　　　　　　合 20412

這並不奇怪,因爲在其他類型的驗辭裏也有這種省説"允"的情況,如:"貞:今夕不雨。之夕不雨。"(《合》12433)

有一條自組卜辭説:

(83) 戊寅卜:方至。不。之日有日方在崔鄙。　　　　　　合 20485

這條卜辭的"不"也應是驗辭,意即"不至"。"至"當指至於商之近畿。後面説有人報告方在某地之鄙,這跟方不至並不矛盾。

有些卜辭末尾的"不"是用辭。在殷墟卜辭裏,最常見的表肯定的用辭是"茲用"和"用",最常見的表否定的用辭是"不用"和"不"。在刻於兆旁的用辭裏,否定的用辭往往是"不"。例如《合》32041 和《屯南》783 都是歷組卜骨,前者在三個卜兆旁刻有用辭,一個刻"用"兩個刻"不",後者在六個卜兆

旁刻有用辭，兩個刻"茲用"四個刻"不"。這種用辭"不"的性質明確，不會引起誤解。但是當用辭"不"刻於卜辭之末時，就很容易被誤解爲是命辭的一部分了。

下面所引的是分別見於三片甲骨的三組卜辭：

（84A）又刀妣庚升。不。
（84B）弜又刀妣[庚]□。用。　　　　　　　　　　合 22374
（85A）又六妣一豕。不。
（85B）六妣即日。用。　　　　　　　　　　　　合 19906
（86A）乙巳卜，㱿：㞢大乙母妣丙一牝。不。
（86B）丙午卜，㱿：㞢大丁牡。用。　　　　　　合 19817

（86）屬𠂤組，（84）（85）字體較特殊，甲骨學者一般也都把它們歸入第一期。（84）A、B 是一對正反對貞的卜辭。（85）（86）的 A 和 B 也都有密切關係。各組 A 辭末尾的"不"，顯然跟 B 辭末尾的"用"一樣，也是用辭，意即"不用"。在𠂤組卜辭刻在辭尾的用辭裏，"不用"出現的次數比"用"少得多，這是因爲大部分"不用"都簡化爲"不"了。

總之，卜辭末尾的否定詞"不"，有些是驗辭，有些是用辭，我們還沒有發現任何確與後世的"否"相當的用例。

卜辭末尾的否定詞"不"，有時寫得特別小，跟前面的字極不相稱，如《合》11787、20961 的"不"。有時"不"跟命辭之間有月名隔開，如：

（87）己酉卜，王：司娥冥（?）允其于壬。一月。不。　合 21068
（88）乙亥卜：今日雨。三月。不。　　　　　　　　合 20903
（89）癸卯[卜]，王曰：㞢其艱，余呼延。九月。不。　合 21386

這些正是它們不屬於命辭的證據（卜辭中偶有月名隔斷命辭末一字與其前文字的反常現象，但與上舉諸例似不能混爲一談）。

二、殷墟卜辭中是否有"V 不 V"式問句和
其他不用句末疑問語氣詞的選擇問句

我們認爲"V 不 V"式卜辭，包括用否定詞"弗"的同型卜辭"V 弗 V"，也

跟上面剛討論過的很多"V不"式卜辭一樣，是由命辭和驗辭構成的，並非反復問句式的命辭（當然也不可能是由兩個正反相對的獨立問句構成的命辭，下文對這種情況不一一指出）。

　　屬於自組的《合》21022有如下一對正反對貞的卜辭：

　　　　（90A）☐雲其雨。不雨。
　　　　（90B）格雲不其雨。允不，啓。

A辭"其雨"後的"不雨"，顯然跟B辭"不其雨"後的"允不，啓"一樣，也是驗辭而不是命辭的一部分。

　　屬於歷組的《英》2429有癸未日卜的一組卜辭，共三條，分別貞卜甲申、乙酉、丙戌這三天會不會下雨：

　　　　（91A）癸未卜：甲申雨。允甲（原缺刻橫畫）雨。
　　　　（91B）癸未卜：乙雨。不。
　　　　（91C）癸未卜：丙戌雨。不雨。

C辭的"不雨"、B辭的"不"，無疑跟A辭的"允甲雨"一樣，也都是驗辭。B的命辭把"乙酉"省說成"乙"，驗辭也把"不雨"省說成"不"。

　　下引兩組歷組卜辭都有一條"雨不雨"式卜辭，通過跟同組卜辭對比，也都可以看出是應該分成命辭和驗辭兩部分的：

　　　　（92A）戊戌卜：今日雨。允。
　　　　（92B）癸卯卜：雨。不雨。　　　　　　　　　　　　　　　　屯南2288
　　　　（93A）癸巳卜：乙未雨。不雨。
　　　　（93B）己酉卜：庚戌雨。允雨。　　　　　　　　　　　　　　屯南4399

《屯南》釋文把（93）的A、B兩辭標點爲："乙未雨？不雨。""庚戌雨？允雨。"這是正確的（命辭應不應加問號不是這裏所要討論的問題）。但是（92B）却標點爲："雨？不雨？"跟（93）的標點相矛盾（《論集》編按：姚孝遂、肖丁《小屯南地甲骨考釋》已指出《屯南》2288的"不雨"是驗辭，見125—126頁）。

　　屬於歷組的《屯南》744有如下一對正反對貞的卜辭：

　　　　（94A）癸卯卜：甲啓。不啓，終夕雨。
　　　　（94B）不啓。允不啓，夕雨。

A辭的"不啓,終夕雨"跟B辭的"允不啓,夕雨",説的是一件事,都是驗辭。"甲啓不啓"不能連讀。《屯南》釋文的標點把"不啓終夕雨"全都包括在命辭裏,更無道理。

在自組、歷組的"V不V"式卜辭裏,跟氣象有關的佔了很大一部分,下面再舉些例子:

(95) 壬午卜:來乙酉雨。不雨。　　　　　　　　　　　　　　合 21065

(96) ☐今夕雨。不雨。　　　　　　　　　　　　　　　　　合 20916

(97) 己丑卜,☐:自今五日至癸巳雨。不雨,癸☐　　　　　　　合 20921

(98) 丙戌卜:舞❂舞❂,雨。不雨。　　　　　　　　　　　　合 20974

(99) ☐鹿,啓。不啓,☐往。　　　　　　　　　　　　　　　合 20718

(100) 乙酉卜:今日雨。不雨。　　　　　　　　　　　　　　合 33875

(101) 壬子卜:今日雨。不雨。　　　　　　　　　　　　　　合 33889

(102) 癸丑卜:甲雨。不雨。　　　　　　　　　　　　　　　合 34490

(103) 甲戌卜:今日雨。不雨。　　　　　　　　　　　　　　屯南 87

(104) 戊申卜:啓。不啓。　　　　　　　　　　　　　　　　合 33974

(105) 甲辰卜:乙巳錫日。不錫日,雨。　　　　　　　　　　　合 34015

跟上面討論過的那些例子比較,可以看出這些卜辭裏的"不雨""不啓""不錫日"也都是驗辭。

下邊兩條歷組卜辭裏的"己不雨"和"丁未不雨"之爲驗辭,極爲明顯:

(106) 己未卜:今日雨。己不雨。　　　　　　　　　　　　　合 33895

(107) 丁雨。丁未不雨。　　　　　　　　　　　　　　　　　屯南 254

但是如果省去了"己"和"丁未",我們就有可能會把"雨不雨"連起來讀。這個例子對於我們分析"雨不雨"式卜辭,是很有啓發的。

上文指出,自組的"方其至不""方其正*不"一類卜辭裏的"不"是驗辭,意思就是"不至""不正*"。由此可見下引自組卜辭裏的"方至不至""方其正*不正*"等辭中的"不至""不正*"也都是驗辭:

(108) 丁卯卜:今日方至。不至。　　　　　　　　　　　　　合 20470

(109) 辛亥卜:方至。不至。　　　　　　　　　　　　　　　合 20486

(110) ☐☐卜:今日方其正*。不正*。延雨自西北,小。　　　　合 21021

見於賓組早期和歷組卜辭裏的"獲不獲""擒不擒"等,也應該屬於同類情況。下面舉兩個例子。爲了便於比較,同版有關的卜辭也一併抄出:

(111A) 丁酉卜,王:逐壴告豕,獲。不獲。
(111B) 己亥卜,王:[逐]雙告豕,[獲]。允獲。　　　　　合40153
(112A) 壬午[卜]:癸未王齒,擒(原作"隼",下同)。不擒。
(112B) 弗擒。
(112C) 乙酉卜:今日王[逐]兕,擒。允擒。
(112D) 弗擒。　　　　　　　　　　　　　　　　　　屯南664

(111)屬賓組早期,(112)屬歷組。只要跟同版的有關卜辭對照一下,就可看出"不獲"和"不擒"都是驗辭。

下引兩辭裏的"弗擒""弗獲"也都應該是驗辭(113屬歷組,114屬賓組早期):

(113) 戊戌卜:王其逐兕,擒。弗擒。　　　　　　　　屯南2095
(114) 己未卜:雀獲虎。弗獲。　　　　　　　　　　　合10201

(《合》10202有同文之辭,同版尚有"辛酉卜:王獲。不獲"一辭)

不過前引(112)的A、B和C、D都以"擒"與"弗擒"對貞,A的驗辭則不用"弗"而用"不"。也許會有人根據這一點,懷疑(113)的"弗擒"和(114)的"弗獲"應該屬於命辭。按照這種看法,這兩條命辭都可以理解爲反復問句(把"雀獲虎弗獲"看作問句,其結構與秦簡"今郡守爲廷不爲"相同,參看上引馮文28頁)。我們知道,殷墟卜辭的驗辭雖然以用"不"爲常,但是也有用"弗"的例子,如:

(115) 丁巳卜,王:巫弗其獲正*方。九日癸告弗及方。　合40833
(116) 庚午貞:辛未敦召方,錫日。允錫日,弗及召方。　合33028

所以上引(113)(114)的"弗擒""弗獲"恐怕還是以看作驗辭爲妥。

賓組早期卜辭裏有如下兩辭:

(117) 小馷子白。不白。　　　　　　　　　　　　　合3411
(118) 丙申卜:巫𠂤。不𠂤。　　　　　　　　　　　合5651

根據上文的討論,"不白""不𠂤"也應是驗辭。(117)貞卜小牝馬將生的崽是不是白色的。賓組早期卜辭裏還有一條殘辭說:"☐ 騎子白。不。"(《合》3412)

"不"也應是驗辭，意即"不白"。

下面討論一下使用動詞"有"和"亡"的一些卜辭。

在現代漢語裏，反復問句"有没有×"也可以説成"有×没有×"。殷墟卜辭所用的跟"没有"相當的詞是"亡"（應讀爲"無"或"罔"）。有些卜辭在説了"有×"之後緊接着就説"亡×"，從形式上看跟"有×没有×"這類問句很相像。例如：

（119）于己丑有來。亡來。　　　　　　　　　　　合 33063（《合》35328 同文）
（120）☐其有遘。亡遘。　　　　　　　　　　　　懷 642
（121）己亥卜，争貞：旱有夢（?），勿求有匃。亡匃。　　合 17452

我們在討論"抑"和"執"的問題的時候，舉過（16）"☐有囚抑，亡囚執"那樣的正反相對的選擇問句。如果不用句末語氣詞，跟上引那些卜辭就很像屬於同一類句型了。那末上引那些卜辭是不是就可以看作正反相對的選擇問句呢？我們的回答是傾向於否定的。

上引（119）（120）是歷組卜辭。與（119）同版的，有"弗及方。允及"一辭。"允及"顯然是驗辭。依通例，"弗及方"的驗辭應爲"允不及"或"及"。此辭"允"字下可能漏刻一"不"字，也可能"允"字是衍文。《京津》350【《合》24771】一辭說："貞：今夕雨。之夕允不雨。"依例，驗辭中的"允"和"不"必有一字爲衍文，情況與此相似。從"弗及方。允及"這條辭的情況來看，同版"于己丑有來亡來"一辭中的"亡來"大概也是驗辭。同屬歷組的（120）的"亡遘"，似乎也應以看作驗辭爲妥。上引的（121）屬賓組。我們在《釋"求"》一文中曾指出，卜辭中"求有匃""求雨匃"等語屢見，並把（121）的"勿求有匃"四字連起來讀（《古文字研究》第十五輯 202—203 頁）。如果這種讀法符合實際的話，後面的"亡匃"即使屬於命辭，也不可能跟"有匃"構成選擇問句。

有一條歷組卜辭在説了"亡囚"後，緊接着又説"有囚"：

（122）[癸]未[貞]：旬亡囚。有囚。　　　　　　　合 34989

同版還有兩條卜旬之辭，"亡囚"後都没有"有囚"二字。（122）的"亡囚"之"囚"和"有囚"之"囚"的寫法很不一樣，"有囚"二字顯然是後刻的，大概也是驗辭。

還有些卜辭説了"弗×"緊接着又説"有×"，或是説了"有×"緊接着又説"不其×"（下引 123 屬自組，124、125 屬出組，126 屬賓組早期）：

（123）癸未卜，㱿貞：㱈弗疾。有疾囚【編按：此字字形中間無"卜"，其釋讀參看《說"㞢凡有疾"》】凡。　　　　　　　　　　　　　　合21050

（124）癸亥卜，出貞：子㝬弗疾。有疾。　　合23532（《合》23533同文）

（125）丁酉卜，貞：子弗疾。有疾。　　　　　　　　　　　　　　英1948

（126）壬申卜，貞：弜（此字在此用爲人名）其有囚。不其囚。　合4331

【編按：此辭"貞"字及二"囚"字下原來都還可能有字，"有囚"後恐不能加句號，且"不其囚"的"囚"，字形中間無"卜"，前一"囚"字殘去下半，是否有"卜"不詳。故此例應删去。】

這些卜辭有沒有可能是正反相對的選擇問句或兩個獨立的問句呢？既然"有×""亡×"疊用的卜辭都不大可能是這種問句，這些卜辭是這種問句的可能性當然就更小了。前三辭裏的"有疾""有疾囚凡"多半是驗辭。（126）的"不其囚"要說成驗辭似有困難，因爲在卜辭裏"其"似乎通常是不出現在述說已經實現的事情的句子裏的。我們懷疑這條卜辭的"不其囚"是占辭。上文中被我們看作驗辭的那些字句，有的說不定實際上也是占辭。【編按：自"（126）"以下之文應删去。上文"前三辭"應改爲"這三辭"，"多半是驗辭"應改爲"可能是占辭或驗辭"。】

下引出組卜甲上一辭疊用"有""亡"二字：

（127）癸酉卜，出貞：旬有亡囚在入（内）。　　　　　　　　　合41228

此辭"有"字寫作"㞢"，同於賓組卜辭，當屬出組早期。卜甲在"入"字下缺損，原來可能記有月名。"囚"字一般讀爲"禍"，竊疑當讀爲"憂"，另詳他文【編按：參看《裘錫圭學術文集》所收《說"囚"》《從殷墟卜辭的"王占曰"說到上古漢語的宵談對轉》】。"入"字古通"内"。殷墟卜辭所見先祖名"入乙"，陳夢家釋爲"内乙"（《綜述》417頁）。《合》34189有下引兩條對貞卜辭：

（128A）庚辰卜：于卜勺（？）土。

（128B）庚辰卜：于入勺（？）土。

卜辭中"外丙"作"卜丙"，上引兩辭中的"于卜""于入"顯然應該讀爲"于外""于内"【編按：《合》34189即《安明》2331，許進雄《明義士收藏甲骨釋文篇》早已指出，寫此文時因未加注意而失引，是嚴重失誤】。卜辭或言"其自卜有來囚"（《合》32914）、"在（或應釋"于"）卜有囚"（《屯南》550。參看《小屯南地甲骨綴合篇》6號，《考古學報》1986年3期270頁）、"于卜□彷（防）□"（《合》34530），"卜"皆應讀爲"外"；或言"王曰彷，亡囚在入"（《屯南》

756)、"彷在入，亡至囚"（《屯綴》14號，《考古學報》1986年3期277頁）、"在入戍（此字形近"旬"，疑即"旬"之誤刻）有囚"（《屯南》附12。《論集》編按：此辭全文爲"辛酉卜：在入戍有囚"，其下方尚有"辛☐入束☐王☐"一殘辭。《合》32962與《屯南》附12同文，有"辛酉〔卜〕：在入束有〔囚〕，王曰彷""〔辛〕酉卜：〔在入〕戍〔有〕囚"二辭。可知原以"在入束有囚"與"在入戍有囚"對貞，"戍"不會是"旬"的誤字。上引《屯南》756"王曰彷，亡囚在入"一辭的序辭作"辛酉貞"，亦當爲同時所卜。此版尚有"甲午☐王☐入束☐"殘辭，內容亦與上引諸辭有關），"入"皆應讀爲"內"（《論集》編按：卜辭中當讀爲"內"之"入"與當讀爲"外"之"卜"還有一些，因與卜囚無關，不具引）。"有亡"相當於現代漢語的"有沒有"，"旬有亡囚在內"的意思，就是一旬之中有沒有內憂，這肯定是一個問句。但是（127）所據的是摹本，而且這種疊用"有""亡"的句式在已著錄的卜辭中是一個孤例，所以此辭可能有誤刻或誤摹之處。【編按：《合》41228的拓本見《合》23620、《上海博物館藏甲骨文字》17647·403、《雲間朱孔陽藏戩壽堂殷虛文字舊拓·殷虛文字拾補》15·5，後者並附摹本。《合》41228所摹"囚"字乃"其"之誤摹，"其"上一字不清，但斷非"亡"字。參看《雲間朱孔陽藏戩壽堂殷虛文字舊拓》（綫裝書局，2009年12月）所附孫亞冰《〈甲骨文集錦〉校勘記》636頁。故卜辭確無"有亡×"的文例。】

總之，在殷墟卜辭大量不帶句末疑問語氣詞的命辭裏，撇開上面提到的"旬有亡囚"一條不論，我們還沒有找到一條確鑿無疑是選擇問句或反復問句的命辭。

有的研究者不但把"V不V""V不"等格式的卜辭看作問句，甚至認爲下邊這類卜辭也是問句（標點依《屯南》釋文）：

(129) 庚子卜：辛雨，至壬雨？　　　　　　　　　　　　　　　屯南197

(130) ☐丑（同版有丁酉卜一辭，"丑"上缺文可補爲"辛"）卜：今日雨？至壬雨？　　　　　　　　　　　　　　　屯南154

從標點可以看出來，《屯南》釋文把（129）理解爲一個選擇問句，把（130）理解爲兩個獨立的問句。不過這種差別並不重要，重要的是《屯南》釋文認爲這兩條卜辭都是要求在並非正反相對的兩件事（129的"辛雨"和"至壬雨"，130的"今日雨"和"至壬雨"）之間進行選擇。這種看法顯然不妥。由於占卜本身性質的限制，卜辭裏不但不可能出現特指問句（參看倪文4頁），也不可能把兩項

並非正反相對的陳述組成問句（不論是組成單一的選擇問句，還是用兩個獨立的問句組成一條命辭）。舉例説，殷代人貞卜用牲數時，供選擇的不同數字總是一個個分開貞卜的，決不會在一條命辭裏提出兩個數字。因爲在一次占卜中，占卜者只能從卜兆看出用某個數是否合適，無法看出在兩個數裏哪一個數比較合適。上引（129）（130）兩辭是在緊挨着的前後兩天裏進行的兩次占卜的記録。庚子那天貞卜第二天辛丑是否下雨，辛丑那天貞卜當天是否下雨，其實卜的是一件事。結果辛丑那天没下雨，第二天壬寅才下雨，所以兩條卜辭的命辭後面都記上了驗辭"至壬雨"。《屯南》釋文把"至壬雨"當作命辭的一部分是不對的。《屯南》釋文中還有一些類似的錯誤，這裏不能詳細討論了。

三、殷墟卜辭命辭裏的非問句

根據上兩節的討論，在殷墟卜辭的命辭裏，目前能够確定爲問句的，只有自、賓、午等組中帶句末疑問語氣詞"抑""執"的那一部分（最多再加上出組早期的"旬有亡囚在内"那條命辭）。倪文認爲既然卜辭中確有句末疑問語氣詞，因此不帶句末疑問語氣詞，同時也無法從其他方面證明是問句的命辭，就都應該看作非問句（4—5等頁）。這個意見我們不能同意。前面已經説過，漢語裏問句不用句末疑問詞的情况相當普遍，是非問句跟陳述句除了語調之外可以毫無區別。第一節講帶"抑"的對貞卜辭時舉過的（27B）"☐不其屮"一辭，就很可能是不用句末疑問語氣詞的是非問句。所以我們不能肯定字面上無問句特徵的命辭一定不是問句。要證明這一點，必須拿出正面的證據來。倪文提出了命辭不是問句的一些具體論證，但是這些論證恐怕都有問題。

倪文引用了下面這條卜辭：

(131) 丁酉卜王貞勿死玖[曰]不其[死]　　　　　　　外240（即《合》21370）

認爲命辭"勿死"是一個祈禱，不可能是問句（4頁）。但是"勿"在這裏應爲人名，其下尚有缺文。李文34頁引這條卜辭，釋爲："丁酉卜王貞，勿[不]死。"是正確的。"勿不死"當然不一定是問句，但也無法斷定它一定不是問句。

倪文又引《尚書》和卜辭裏以"余其"開頭的一些句子，認爲這些句子都有決斷語氣，不可能是問句（7頁）。其實在他所引的卜辭的例子裏，只有下引一辭

裏的"余其"句可以這樣解釋：

（132）戊戌卜殻貞王曰侯虎往余不爾其合以乃使歸

菁7（即《合》3297正）

可是此辭貞卜王應否跟侯虎說"往（？）余不爾其合以乃使歸"，"余其"句的語氣並不能決定整條命辭的語氣。所引其他諸例如"余其作邑""余其從"等，都無法證明一定表示決斷語氣。《尚書·多士》有問句"我其敢求位"。《左傳》有"吾其廢乎"（閔公二年）、"吾其濟乎"（僖公五年）、"吾其何得"（襄公二十八年）、"吾其入乎"（哀公二十六年）等問句。因此說"余其"句一定不是問句是缺乏理由的。

倪文還認為用幾個句子構成的命辭也不宜看作問句。他說，由 A、B、C 三句構成的命辭，如果當作問句看待，不可理解為"A？B？C？"，而只能理解為"A，B，C——這是確實的嗎？"因為占卜者不可能從一個卜兆得到對三個問題的回答。可是作後一種理解時，"這是確實的嗎"這層意思是解釋者加上去的，命辭本身並沒有說（8—9頁）。這種說法也不是很有力的，因為 A 和 B 可能是 C 的條件。拿倪文所舉的實例，"王叀乙往于田，丙迺啓，亡災"（《合》28605）這條命辭來說，就可以譯為："如果王在乙那天'往于田'，而天到丙那天才開朗，不會有災禍嗎？"我並不是說這條命辭非這樣理解不可，只是說目前還難以斷定它一定不是問句。

倪文指出理解命辭時不應憑空補上它本身沒有說過的話，這當然不錯。但是應該承認命辭往往有省略。這裏只舉一個簡單的例子。《合》29654 有如下兩條命辭：

（133A）叀小宰。

（133B）叀牛，王受祐。

如果我們說，A 辭的意思實際上是"叀小宰，王受祐"，大概不會有很多人反對。（《論集》編按：這跟理解卜辭時憑空加上"這是確實的嗎"的意思不同，此段應刪。）

倪文還提出一個論證：人們通常在對是否會下雨沒有主觀看法，或者認為不能下雨時，才問"會下雨嗎"。在預料天會下雨時，才問"不會下雨嗎"。因此，卜雨的命辭如果是問句的話，在記應驗之辭時，應該在正面命辭，即"雨"這類命辭之後記"允不雨"；在反面命辭，即"不雨"這類命辭之後記"允雨"。可是

實際上却是正面命辭後記"允雨",反面命辭後記"允不雨"。這也可以證明命辭不應看作問句(9—10頁)。這種分析對反詰句也許是合適的,但是命辭大概不會是反詰句。如果殷人卜雨時從正面問會下雨嗎,得兆有雨,結果真的下了雨,驗辭當然記"允雨"。即使貞卜者提問時覺得下雨的可能性極小,或者主觀上不希望有雨,那也不會影響驗辭。要知道驗辭"允"字後所記的事,並不一定是貞卜者所希望出現的,賓組卜辭中屢見的"允有來艱"就是例子。所以驗辭的記法並不能用來判斷命辭是不是問句。

上文曾經提到李學勤在《續論西周甲骨》裏,指出殷墟卜辭的"正""有正"肯定不是問句。他的論證也是可以商榷的。周原卜辭的"囟"究竟應該讀爲"斯"還是讀爲"思",或者應該讀爲別的什麽字,現在還難以斷定。即使確實應該讀爲"斯",從《論語》《孟子》有"斯謂之仁已乎"(《顏淵》)、"斯不亦惠而不費乎"(《堯曰》)、"斯可受禦與"(《萬章下》)等問句的情況來看,也不能說"斯正""斯有正"等語一定不是問句。至於不用"斯"字的"正""有正"等語表示何種語氣,就更無從説起了。附帶説一下,就是以"尚"開頭的卜筮辭,恐怕也很難從語義上證明它們絕對不可能是問句。《禮記·檀弓上》就有"尚行夫子之志乎哉"這樣的問句(《檀弓上》鄭玄注:"尚,庶幾也。"古書中以"庶"或"庶幾"開頭的問句屢見)。

那麽,殷墟卜辭裏究竟有沒有可以確證爲非問句的命辭呢?我們認爲下舉這種卜辭裏的命辭可以肯定不是問句:

（134）辛酉卜,殼貞:今𠂤王勿比望乘伐下𠱾,弗其受有祐。　　合6482

這種命辭可以分成兩部分。前一部分説的是不做某件事或不以某種方式做某件事,後一部分説的是不能受保祐、出外將碰上雨等等不吉利的情況。它們通常屬於正反對貞卜辭裏的反面卜辭。例如上引（134）就有一條同版的正面卜辭:"辛酉卜,殼貞:今𠂤王比望乘伐下𠱾,受有祐。"如果把（134）的命辭當作問句理解,只能翻譯爲:"今𠂤"(時間詞)王不跟望乘一起去伐"下𠱾",不能受到保祐嗎?這跟正面命辭的意思——王跟望乘一起去伐"下𠱾"能受到保祐,實際上不是正反相對的,而是一致的。而且殷人正是爲了想知道王跟望乘一起去伐"下𠱾"能不能受到鬼神保祐而進行這次占卜的。如果先提出不準備跟望乘一起去伐"下𠱾",還問什麽受不受保祐呢?所以這種命辭只能理解爲陳述句。

作爲陳述句,（134）的命辭應該譯爲:"今𠂤"王不要跟望乘一起去伐"下

户",（如果跟望乘一起去伐"下户",）將不能得到保佑。這種在否定形式的陳述句之後，隱含一個意義相反的假設句的例子，在金文和典籍中都可以看到，例如：

　　其唯我諸侯百姓，厥賈毋不即市，毋敢或入絲（關？）变（完？）賈，（如不即市，或敢入絲变賈，）則亦刑。　　　　　　兮甲盤【《集成》16·10174】

　　無敢寇攘，踰垣牆，竊馬牛，誘臣妾，（如敢寇攘，踰垣牆，竊馬牛，誘臣妾，）汝則有常刑。　　　　　　　　　　　　　　　　　　　《尚書·費誓》

　　古者聖王唯毋得賢人而使之，（如得賢人而使之，）般爵以貴之，裂地以封之，終身不厭。　　　　　　　　　　　　　　　　《墨子·尚賢中》

　　人君唯毋聽寢兵，（如聽寢兵，）則群臣賓客莫敢言兵。

　　　　　　　　　　　　　　　　　　　　　　　　《管子·立政九敗解》

　　吾獨不得廉頗、李牧時爲吾將，（如得廉頗、李牧時爲吾將，）吾豈憂匈奴哉！

　　　　　　　　　　　　　　　　　　　　　　　　　　《史記·馮唐傳》

　　毋妄言，（如妄言，）族矣！　　　　　　　　　《史記·項羽本紀》

這種句法其實直到現在還在使用。例如說："别碰它，會觸電的！"意思是說，如果碰了它，就可能觸電。在這種句子裏，末一個分句有時可以用反詰式的感嘆句，但決不會用真正的問句。楊樹達在《古書疑義舉例續補》的"省句例"中，周法高在《上古語法札記·（二）"唯毋"解》（《史語所集刊》二十二本）中，都對這種句子作過討論，可以參閱。

　　我們所討論的這類命辭在殷墟卜辭裏相當常見，下面再舉些例子：

　　（135）☐㚔舞今日，不其雨。允不。　　　　　　　　合20972

上條屬自組，舞是求雨的一種方法。

　　（136）貞：翌辛巳王勿往逐兕，弗其獲。　　　　　　合40126
　　（137）翌丁卯勿（從正面卜辭可以知道是指"勿奏舞"），亡其雨。

　　　　　　　　　　　　　　　　　　　　　　　　　　合14755正

（《論集》編按：本文發表後，承吉德煒教授寄示《釋貞》複印本。此文23—24頁已指出"翌丁卯勿，亡其雨"一辭如作爲問句理解，與其對貞卜辭"貞：翌丁卯奏舞，有雨"不能構成正反對立；如作爲陳述句理解，就不存在這個問題。這一意見是很正確的）

以上屬賓組。

(138) 弜逆執,亡若。　　　　　　　　　　　　　　　　　合 32185

上條屬歷組。

　　(139) 貞:馬弜先,其遘雨。　　　　　　　　　　　　　　合 27950

上條屬何組。

　　(140) 弜呼射,弗擒。　　　　　　　　　　　　　　　　　合 28815
　　(141) 弜用黑羊,亡雨。　　　　　　　　　　　　合 30552(《屯南》2623 同文)

以上屬無名組。(141)的對貞之辭是:"叀白羊用于之,有大雨。"跟(141)不構成嚴格意義的正反關係,情況稍有些特殊。

　　跟上舉這種命辭有對貞關係的正面命辭,如果孤立的看,一般是既可理解爲問句,也可理解爲陳述句的。但是既然它們的對貞之辭肯定是陳述句,把它們看作陳述句顯然要比看作問句合理。

　　何組和無名組卜辭裏常見的"貞:壬弜田,其雨"(《合》28716)、"辛王弜田,其雨"(《合》33533)、"弜省噩田,其雨"(《合》28993)一類反面命辭,也只能看作陳述句。拿"壬弜田,其雨"這條來説,我們只能把它譯成"壬日不要去田獵,天將下雨",如果當作問句譯成"壬日不要去田獵,天將下雨嗎",就不知所云了。這類命辭一般也有對應的正面命辭,如《合》28993 的"叀噩田省,不雨"。這些正面命辭當然也以看作陳述句爲妥。這類命辭跟前面講過的那一些,情況略有不同。例如前面所舉的(135)"☐弜舞今日,不其雨",從表面上看似乎跟"壬弜田,其雨"完全同類型,而且也未嘗不可以按照翻譯後者的辦法,翻譯爲"……今日不要舉行舞祭,天將不會下雨",但是實際上兩者是有區别的。因爲舉行舞祭正是爲了求雨,提出不要舉行舞祭,是怕舉行後老天無動於衷仍然不下雨;至於是否舉行田獵,對於天是否下雨則根本没有影響。所以我們認爲"☐弜舞今日,不其雨"這類命辭的第一個分句之後隱含一個意義相反的假設句(就此例來説,就是"如果在今日舉行舞祭"),"壬弜田,其雨"這類命辭的第一個分句之後則並不隱含這種假設句。但是如果把"壬弜田,其雨"這條命辭裏的"其雨"改爲"其遘雨",就應該把它歸到"☐弜舞今日,不其雨"那種類型裏去了。因爲如果不去田獵而呆在家裏,根本談不到遘不遘雨的問題,我們只能認爲"其遘雨"是指如果去田獵將會遇到雨。

　　在下引的一對正反對貞的歷組卜辭裏,反面的命辭大概也是跟"壬弜田,其雨"同類型的:

（142A）辛亥卜：北方其出。

　　（142B）弜稱眾，不出。　　　　　　　　　　　　　　合 32030

"稱眾"之意當近於"舉眾"。殷人不"稱眾"，不可能使敵方不出犯。但是敵方如不出犯，就不必"稱眾"來對付它了。所以（142B）的意思不可能是："不稱眾，北方不出犯嗎？"而只能是："不要稱眾，北方不會出犯。"屬於無名組的《合》28012 有"弜注涂人，方不出于之"等辭，顯然也是同類型的。

　　在自組卜辭裏，卜旬之辭的命辭幾乎全都只有一個"旬"字（《合》19863、20966、21314、21316 等等），卜夕之辭的命辭也大都只有一個"夕"字（《合》20103、20918、21350 等等）。"旬"這種命辭偶爾也見於賓組早期卜辭（《合》13361、13376 正）以及自歷間組和歷組卜辭（《合》32821、34995、《美》13、19【《合》33142】、130【《合》33141】）。在一片大概屬於出組晚期的卜骨上，也有"癸巳，王：旬"等卜旬之辭（《合》26709）。"夕"這種命辭偶爾也見於賓組早期卜辭（《合》13363）。

　　自組卜辭在已知各組殷墟卜辭中時代上限最早。既然自組卜辭裏的卜旬、卜夕之辭基本上都用上述這種簡單的命辭，我們就沒有理由把它們看作"旬亡囚""夕亡囚"之類命辭的省略。"旬""夕"這種命辭當然也無法看作問句。如果把卜辭序辭中的"貞"或"卜"跟"旬"或"夕"連讀，字句的結構就跟古書裏的"卜日"（《周禮·春官·大宗伯》）、"卜立君""卜大封"（同上《大卜》）以至倪文引用過的"問政"屬於一類了。

　　有一條字體跟自組接近的卜辭説：

　　（143）癸酉卜，貞：旬在入（內）。　　　　　　　　合 20609

"貞旬在內"可以理解為貞卜一旬中有無內憂，雖與第二節舉過的"貞旬有亡囚在內"同意，但也不必看作後者的省略形式。"旬在內"這樣的命辭也難以看作問句。

　　如果再仔細找一下，大概還可以在殷墟卜辭裏找出一些不能看作問句的命辭來。

四、結　語

　　在殷墟卜辭的全部命辭裏，我們現在能夠確定是問句或非問句的命辭只佔一

小部分。在承認問句可以不帶句末疑問語氣詞的前提下，大部分命辭可以看作陳述句，也可以看作是非問句。説不定有些命辭在當時就有不同的讀法，既有人讀成陳述句，也有人依靠語調讀成問句。鑒於確實存在非問句的命辭，同時大部分命辭又無法斷定是不是問句，我們建議今後引用殷墟卜辭時，句末一律標句號，不標問號。因爲給非問句加問號，錯誤要比給問句加句號嚴重得多。

倪德衛和夏含夷都認爲命辭用問句限於武丁卜辭中時代最早的自組卜辭（倪文4—5、13等頁，《周易的構成》52—53頁）。我們已經指出賓組和午組卜辭也有問句。不過這類例子比起自組卜辭裏的問句來要少得多，而且其時代也都不晚於武丁時期。就是"旬有亡囚在內"那條出組早期卜辭，大概也不會晚於跟武丁緊接的祖庚時期。另一方面，在時代較晚的卜辭裏，可以肯定是問句的命辭還没有找到，而肯定不是問句的命辭却已經發現了一些。這樣看來，雖然晚於自組的卜辭不再用問句的説法不能成立，可是武丁或祖庚之後的卜辭不再用問句的可能性目前還無法排除。在自組之後的武丁時期，問句的使用已經大大減少的可能性，當然也是存在的。

最後，還有一個跟命辭是否問句有關的問題需要在這裏討論一下。

夏含夷認爲殷墟卜辭的命辭由問句變爲非問句以及卜辭形式和內容上的其他變化，反映了從武丁到帝乙帝辛這段時間裏，占卜的作用曾經發生過重大變化。下面先簡單撮述一下他的意見。夏含夷認爲在各組卜辭中時代最早的自組卜辭有三個特點：一、通常針對特定的具體事件進行占卜，公式化的卜辭很少。二、往往把正面和反面的問題放在一條卜辭裏提出，一般不用對貞形式。三、命辭時常用問句。繼之而來的賓組卜辭普遍使用對貞形式，命辭也不再用問句。但是占卜的形式及目的，一般説來在當時似乎還没有發生變化。賓組卜辭在各組卜辭中數量最大，占卜主題的範圍也極廣。占卜作用的巨大變化發生在祖甲時期，一直延續到商王朝之末。這時，占卜主題的範圍縮小了，占卜次數也大大減少。除了數量上的變化之外，占卜的性質也發生了重大變化。自組、賓組卜辭所具有的那種針對特定事件進行貞卜的現象，在帝乙帝辛卜辭裏已難以見到。占卜基本上已經公式化，似乎已經喪失了原來的神秘性，而且看來發生了一種不尋常的神學上的轉變。在武丁卜辭裏，不但命辭比較有特性，占辭也是這樣，而且占辭是有吉也有凶的。到了帝乙帝辛時代，占辭永遠是公式化的"吉""大吉"或"引吉"；命辭也總是正面的，如"旬亡囚""往來亡災"，"旬有囚""往來有災"是從不出現的。"這反映出在商代末期，占卜已經不僅僅是解決關於即將來到之事的疑問的

一種嘗試，而已經變成控制它們的一種手段了。"(《周易的構成》52—56 頁）或者說，"占卜已經不再僅僅是知道未來的一種手段，而是控制未來的一種嘗試了"（同上 67 頁）。這些意見裏有不少合理的成分，但是總的來説是不能被我們接受的。

夏含夷似乎認爲除了問句形式的卜辭，只有正反對貞的卜辭才能充分反映出占卜的決疑的性質。這是不全面的。在正反對貞卜辭之外，提出供選擇的事物或對象的對貞或系列卜辭（以下簡稱"選擇性卜辭"），同樣能夠充分反映出占卜的決疑的性質。正反對貞的和選擇性的卜辭在各時期的卜辭裏都是常見的，並非武丁時期的賓組卜辭所特有。

在自組卜辭裏就可以看到上述兩類卜辭的不少例子。在第一節裏已經引了自組卜辭中用句末語氣詞"抑"的正反對貞卜辭（如 23 至 26 諸辭），此外在第一、二節裏還陸續引過一些不用"抑"的例子（如 67、68、70、90 諸辭），下面再補充兩個例子：

(144A) 辛丑卜，𠂤：自今至于乙巳日雨。乙陰（此字據施謝捷釋），不雨。
(144B) 自今至于乙巳不雨。　　　　　　　　　　　　　　　　合 20923
(145A) 辛酉卜，王：祝于妣己，迺取祖丁。
(145B) 辛酉卜，王：勿祝于妣己。　　　　　　　　　　　　　合 19890

選擇性卜辭在自組卜辭裏好像不如正反對貞卜辭常見，下邊引的是兩個較典型的例子：

(146A) 辛酉卜：又祖乙卅宰。
(146B) 辛酉卜：又祖乙廿宰。　　　　　　　　　　　　　　合 19838
(147A) 甲申卜：禦婦鼠妣己二牝（此字爲"牝""牡"合文）。
(147B) 一牛一羊禦婦鼠妣己。
(147C) 一牛禦婦鼠妣己。　　　　　　　　　　　　　　　　合 19987

在歷組、出組以及其後的各組卜辭裏，正反對貞的和選擇性的卜辭都是常見的。爲了節省篇幅，這裏只引跟我們現在的討論關係最密切的黃組卜辭裏的一些例子：

(148A) 乙亥卜，貞：今日不雨。
(148B) 其雨。　　　　　　　　　　　　　　　　　　　　　合 38122
(149A) 戊辰卜，貞：今日王田敦，不遘雨。

(149B) 其遘雨。　　　　　　　　　　　　　　　　合 37647

(150A) 其戠日。

(150B) 弜巳戠日。　　　　　　　　　　　　　　　合 38115

以上是正反對貞之例。

(151A) 乙巳卜，在兮：叀丁未蠚眔。

(151B) 叀丙午蠚眔。　　　　　　　　　　　　　　合 35343

(152A) 癸巳卜，貞：祖甲丁（?），其宰。

(152B) 其宰又一牛。

(152C) 叀騂。

(152D) 叀物。　　　　　　　　　　　　　　　　　合 35931

以上是選擇性卜辭之例。可見占卜的決疑的性質一直到商末仍然沒有改變。在這方面，命辭是否問句並沒有多大關係。

倪文認爲《尚書·金縢》所敍述的占卜，是爲了祈求鬼神同意占卜者的請求，不是爲了決疑而進行的，並指出在《金縢》的全部敍述中連一個問句也看不到（4頁）。這是一個誤解。《金縢》原文説：

> 既克商二年，王（武王）有疾，弗豫。二公曰："我其爲王穆卜。"周公曰："未可以戚我先王。"公乃自以爲功……植璧秉珪，乃告太王、王季、文王。史乃册祝曰："惟爾元孫某，遘厲虐疾。若爾三王，是有丕子之責于天。以旦代某之身……今我即命于元龜。爾之許我，我其以璧與珪，歸俟爾命。爾不許我，我乃屏璧與珪。"乃卜三龜，一習吉。啓籥見書，乃并是吉。

仔細讀一下這段文字就可以知道，周公正是由於不同意爲武王之疾進行占卜，而採用"册祝"的方式向先王提出讓武王病愈的要求的。册祝跟占卜是兩回事。册祝後所以還要占卜，"即命于元龜"，是爲了判斷先王是否答應周公的要求。這正好説明占卜僅僅是決疑的手段（《論集》編按：《論衡·知實》："武王不豫，周公請命，壇墠既設，策祝已畢，不知天之許己與不，乃卜三龜，三龜皆吉。"把這一點説得很清楚）。

在殷墟卜辭裏可以看到的，占卜逐漸變得公式化的現象，占辭從有吉有凶變到有吉無凶的現象，只能説明人們對占卜的信仰在逐漸減弱，占卜者越來越傾向於只作出符合自己願望的判斷。這些現象並不能證明占卜從決疑的手段轉變成了控制將來的手段。

附記：

本文蒙朱德熙先生仔細審閱修改，作者十分感謝。

　　本文是提交給 1987 年在安陽召開的中國殷商文化國際討論會的論文，修改後發表於《中國語文》1988 年 1 期。收入《古文字論集》時，所引卜辭的釋文的寫法一般改從初稿。今據《古文字論集》收入。此文後由 Edward L. Shaughnessy（夏含夷）譯成英文，發表於 *Early China* 第 14 期（1989）。

對《關於殷墟卜辭的命辭是否問句的考察》一文的評論的答覆①

　　我非常感謝把拙文譯成英文的夏含夷教授和各位對拙文發表批評意見的學者。希望我們的討論能對殷墟卜辭、古漢語語法和中國古代占卜的研究起一些促進作用。

　　我想先説一下拙文中的幾處錯誤和疏失：

　　1. 拙文所引卜辭（69）一例的釋文有誤。（69A）一條應刪去，"（69B）" "（69C）" 應改爲 "（69A）" "（69B）"。【編按：編集《古文字論集》時已據此刪改。】

　　2. 倪德衛教授認爲用幾個句子構成的命辭不可能是問句。拙文第三部分曾就此提出疑問。我在指出由 A、B、C 三句構成的命辭中的 A 和 B 有可能是 C 的條件之後，還根據有些命辭確實略去了某些話的現象，指責倪德衛認爲理解命辭時不應該憑空添上它本身沒有説過的話的意見有片面性。這種指責是錯誤的。倪德衛指出，如果 "A，B，C" 本身不是問句，我們不能通過把它理解爲 "A，B，C——這是確實的嗎？" 的辦法，把它看成問句。這是完全正確的。"這是確實的嗎" 這層意思是外加到命辭上去的。這跟我所説的根據同類命辭爲某些命辭補出所省略的話的情況，完全是兩回事。我接受倪德衛教授在這次所寫的意見中就這個問題對我所作的批評。

　　3. 拙文發表後，承吉德煒教授寄贈《釋貞》複印本。讀後才發現有些我自以

---

① 拙文《關於殷墟卜辭的命辭是否問句的考察》（原載《中國語文》1988 年 1 期）由夏含夷教授譯爲英文發表在 *Early China* 14 期（1989）上。此期同時刊登了一些學者對此文的評論和我的這篇答覆的英譯文（亦由夏含夷教授翻譯）。

爲是創見的意見，《釋貞》中早已提出來了。如此文 23—24 頁指出，"翌丁卯勿，亡其雨"一辭（即拙文第 137 例，譯文略去未譯），如作爲問句理解，跟它的對貞卜辭"貞：翌丁卯奏舞，有雨"不構成正反對立；如作爲陳述句理解，就不存在這個問題。我的意見跟他完全相同。我在寫拙文時，沒有先想辦法把《釋貞》找來讀一下，是不應有的疏失。

4. 饒宗頤教授的《殷代貞卜人物通考》，我在多年前曾經借來讀過。但是當時對書中"舊說於貞字下每施問號，多不可通"的意見以及全書引卜辭都不標問號"但作斷句"的做法沒有給予應有的注意，以致寫拙文時根本沒有提到。這也是一個不應有的疏失。直到這次讀饒教授所寫的意見時，才發現這個問題。

下面，依次就下列四個問題發表一些意見：1.占卜具有決疑的作用是否能決定命辭必爲問句。2.關於"抑"和"執"。3.關於"旬有亡囚"。4.在商代後期，占卜的性質是否起過根本性的變化。

1. 在這次討論中，王宇信、范毓周兩位教授主張命辭都是問句。他們主要是根據占卜具有決疑作用這一點立論的。在語言方面，他們強調指出漢語中存在陳述句式的是非問句，但是並沒有爲命辭都是問句的論點提出積極的證據。范毓周以命辭常用"其"來證明它們是問句，這是沒有說服力的。我們翻一下楊樹達的《詞詮》（中華書局，1965，160—161 頁），就可以看到，"副詞"性質的"其"字既可以用於疑問句，也可以用於陳述句（如"予其大賚女""日月其除"等），而且還可以當"庶幾"講（如"帝其念哉""其雨其雨，杲杲出日"）。認爲命辭裏的"其"都表示疑問語氣，是由於先已有了命辭必爲問句的成見。這一點司禮義教授等學者早就指出來了。

主張命辭不是問句的學者，並沒有否定占卜的決疑作用。倪德衛在《問句的問題》和這次所寫的意見裏都強調指出，研究者應該把占卜者說什麼和做什麼這兩件事區分開來，不能因爲占卜的作用是決疑就斷定命辭是問句。這是很正確的。在拙文中已經舉出了一些從辭義看無法當作問句理解的命辭。例如"辛王弜田，其雨"（《合》33533）這條命辭，如果當作問句，無論是理解爲"辛日王不要去田獵，將會下雨嗎？"還是理解爲"是不是辛日王不要去田獵，將會下雨？"辭義都講不通。既認爲命辭都是問句，就應該令人信服地駁倒我們關於這類命辭的意見。可是王、范二位對此都連一句話也沒有說。王宇信爲了證明他的論點的正確，引用了幾個見於《左傳》的占卜實例。然而他在翻譯文公十八年、昭公五年、十三年和十七年的《傳》文中的命辭的時候，却並沒有把它們譯成問句。例

如"余尚得天下"譯成了"我希望能得到治理楚國的權力"。這豈不是正好證明儘管占卜的作用是決疑，命辭却可以不是問句嗎？

2. 范毓周教授説，甲骨文中的🖐和🖐本爲一字，應該釋爲"皮"而不應該釋爲"抑"。其實🖐和🖐是一個字，手形在後的🖐則是另一個字。這兩個字的用法截然有別，前者爲"抑"字，後者爲"皮"字。對這個問題拙文已經作過説明（見《中國語文》1988 年 1 期 3 頁，譯文略去未譯），這裏就不重複了。附帶説一下，吉德煒教授在他所寫的意見的注 2 裏，説我在拙文中文本 3 頁上承認🖐（或作🖐）既可釋"皮"，也可釋"抑"。這是一個誤解。在那裏我只討論了李學勤教授爲什麽會把"抑"釋爲"皮"，並没有承認這個字也可以釋爲"皮"。不過對於我們現在的討論來説，這個字究竟應該怎樣釋只是一個次要問題。我們需要弄清楚的，是自組卜辭中使用在句末的"🖐"和"執"究竟能不能看作句末疑問語氣詞。即使在没有確定🖐究竟是什麽字的情況下，這個問題也還是有辦法加以討論的。

范毓周説："在李、裘所列舉的自組卜辭在句末使用'皮'和'執'的諸例中，除了極少數可能爲方國部族或人名外，絕大多數是用爲人牲的名稱的。"我認爲即使承認"🖐"可釋"皮"，范説也是不能成立的。把"🖐"和"執"理解爲句末疑問語氣詞究竟是否正確，當然可以討論。但是我們至少應該承認，按照這種理解，全部有關的卜辭都可以講通。然而按照范説，不少有關的卜辭却講不通。下面所舉的就是一些明顯的例子（辭前加拙文編號，"抑"字改作"皮"）：

(15) □□卜，叉*：不其延雨□皮，延雨執。

(16) □貞：□有囚皮，亡囚執。

(33) 丙辰卜：丁巳其陰皮。允陰。

(34) 己酉卜：□陰其雨皮。不雨，曾啓。

(41) 辛亥卜，貞：犬囚凡疾皮。

何况釋"🖐"爲"皮"還有問題呢？附帶説一下，在范毓周所引的《合》21708 諸辭裏，"乙未余卜：皮敔"一辭中的"皮"是"夲"（執）的誤釋。這些卜辭裏的"皮"（其實是"抑"）和"敔"應該是國族名，"執"是動詞，都與祭祀無關。

吉德煒認爲"抑"和"執"可能都應該當"或"（or）講，並根據"或"並不一定含有疑問語氣這一點，主張不必把用"抑"和"執"的命辭看作問句。對這一意見我也不能同意。拙文曾指出"較晚的古漢語裏置於選擇問句的兩個分句之

間的連詞'抑'"，也許就是由殷墟卜辭的句末疑問語氣詞"抑"演變而成的，但是並没有把這兩種"抑"等同起來的意思。我並不認爲卜辭裏的"抑"可以當"或"講，更不用説"執"了。"抑"或"執"往往是命辭的最後一字，但是按照語言通例，當"或"講的詞的後面是不可能什麼話也没有的。爲了解決這個矛盾，吉德煒提出了一種解釋，然而説服力並不强。還應該指出，雖然古漢語裏的"或"並不一定含有疑問語氣，可是當"或"講的連詞"抑"却總是用來連接選擇問句的兩個分句的，連接非問句的"抑"是當"然而"（but）講的（參看《詞詮》368—369頁）。如果承認自組命辭裏的"抑"是後來當"或"講的"抑"的前身，把有關命辭看作問句顯然要比把它們看作非問句合理。

吉德煒還對"抑"和"執"提出了另一種説法。他認爲它們也有可能起着類似標點符號的作用，是用來區分命辭，指示占卜過程中的停頓的。這種假設在古今文獻裏找不到任何依據，而且對"抑"和"執"屢屢使用在没有區分命辭的需要的場合的現象無法作出妥善解釋，所以也不能被接受。

但是正如吉德煒所指出的，把"抑"和"執"看作句末疑問語氣詞，也會碰到一些不好解釋的問題（這些問題對於吉德煒的兩種假設來說也是存在的）。我們不但没有在自古流傳的古漢語文獻裏找到在語音和用法上都跟它們相合的詞，而且還無法解釋以下問題：殷代人爲什麼要使用它們的作用看起來似乎没有區別的"抑"和"執"兩個詞？如果二者有别，區别究竟在哪裏？爲什麼"執"只能跟"抑"配合起來使用，"抑"則可以單獨使用，但是在一條命辭的兩個分句後面又不能全都用"抑"呢？所以關於"抑"和"執"的問題的確還需要進一步研究。但是就目前情况來看，李學勤的句末疑問助詞説仍然是各種説法中最爲合理的一種。

3. 倪德衛認爲拙文所舉的（127）"旬有亡囚在内"一辭並不是問句。他把這條命辭跟《南》所收的"《明》215"（即《明後》1838【《合》16348】）"☐亡不若在内"一辭相比較，認爲既然"《明》215"的"不若"是動詞"亡"的賓語，（127）的"亡囚"也應該是動詞"有"的賓語。所以他把"旬有亡囚在内"譯爲"In the next ten days there will be absence of misfortune in the interior"。我認爲他的意見是有問題的。"亡"跟"不"的詞性不同，"有亡囚"和"亡不若"的語法結構不能相提並論。現代的中國人還在説"心有不安"這種帶有點文言味道的話，"不安"是"有"的賓語，就跟上引卜辭裏的"不若"是"亡"的賓語一樣。可是像"心中有無内疚"或"心中有没有内疚"這種格式的話，則只能理解爲問

句,而不能理解爲以"無……"或"沒有……"爲"有"的賓語的陳述句。人們決不會把用"心中無內疚"就可以表達清楚的意思說成"心中有'無內疚'"。我想殷代人也決不會把用"旬亡囚"就可以表達清楚的意思說成"旬有亡囚"。所以這條命辭只能理解爲一個問句。不過拙文已經指出,"有亡"連用的問句在卜辭裏只有這一個孤例,而且根據的還是摹本,其可靠性的確是有懷疑餘地的。【編按:關於此辭,參看《關於殷墟卜辭的命辭是否問句的考察》"二"節尾所加編按。】

4. 我還是認爲在從武丁到帝乙、帝辛這段時間裏,占卜的性質並沒有發生過根本性的變化。直到帝乙、帝辛時代,占卜的作用仍然是決疑,它並沒有變成主要用來謀求鬼神祐助或既用來謀求鬼神祐助也用來決疑的一種手段。關於這個問題,我有兩點要說。

首先,從中國上古文獻來看,謀求鬼神祐助一般用祭祀、祝告等方法,占卜則是人們瞭解鬼神意志的一種手段。

其次,把占卜者說什麼和做什麼這兩件事區別開來,不但對於命辭是否問句的討論是必要的,就是對於占卜性質的討論也是必要的。占卜者往往有自己所希望得到的占卜結果。例如爲出行占卜的人,一般都希望出行時能平平安安,沒有意外。這種情緒當然有可能在命辭裏反映出來。我們不能只根據反映出這種情緒的命辭,就斷定占卜具有謀求鬼神祐助的作用。

夏含夷指出,商代晚期只有"旬亡囚""往來亡災"這樣的命辭,而沒有"旬有囚""往來有災"這樣的命辭。依我看,這種現象並不能說明占卜的性質已經有了巨大變化。在武丁時代的卜旬之辭裏,"旬有囚"這種命辭也是極其罕見的。在絕大多數場合,武丁時代的卜人跟帝乙、帝辛時代的一樣,也是只貞"旬亡囚"而不貞"旬有囚"的,儘管他們的真正用意是想知道在新的一旬裏會不會有可憂之事。我想商代卜人在對占卜結果沒有明顯傾向性的情況下,一般大概是採用正反對貞一類占卜方式的;在對占卜結果有明顯傾向性的情況下,則既可採用對貞的占卜方式,也可採用只從對自己有利的一方面提出命辭的占卜方式。看來,時代越晚,占卜者就越傾向於採用單方面的占卜方式。周代的占卜者甚至習慣於用表示願望的口氣來提出命辭。這是一種值得注意的變化,但是對占卜的本質並不會產生多大影響。我並不否認,在從武丁到帝乙、帝辛這段時間裏,殷人對占卜的態度有了不小的變化,占卜的方法和卜辭的形式也都有了一些變化。但是我看不出占卜的性質有什麼根本性的變化。

最後，對《金縢》的問題再說幾句。倪德衛指出，在《金縢》關於占卜的敘述中連一個問句也看不到。這的確是事實。但是他認爲《金縢》所說的册祝和占卜的儀式是結合在一起而不可分的，並且認爲占卜儀式還起着使册祝生效的作用。這些意見我都不能同意。迷信鬼神的古人顯然相信，他們對鬼神的祝告，鬼神全都能知道；不可能有通過占卜儀式來使祝告生效的想法。但是鬼神對他們的祝告採取什麽態度，他們却無法直接知道，只能通過占卜來判斷。《金縢》所記的册祝之辭在最後提到，將要進行占卜來判斷先王是否答應周公的要求，以決定是否把圭璧獻給他們。說這些話，顯然只是爲了敦促先王同意周公的請求。不能由此得出册祝和占卜的儀式不可分以及占卜儀式具有使册祝生效的作用的結論。《論衡·知實》説："武王不豫，周公請命，壇墠既設，策祝已畢，不知天之許己與不，乃卜三龜，三龜皆吉。"我們同意王充對《金縢》所說的册祝與占卜的關係的理解。

1989 年 5 月 7 日寫完

《關於殷墟卜辭的命辭是否問句的考察》，原載《中國語文》1988 年第 1 期；又由 Edward L. Shaughnessy（夏含夷）譯出提要，載《古代中國》第 14 卷（*Early China*，14），1989 年；收入裘錫圭：《古文字論集》（文中簡稱"《論集》"），中華書局，1992 年；又收入《裘錫圭學術文集·甲骨文卷》，復旦大學出版社，2012 年；又收入《中西學術名篇精讀·裘錫圭卷》，中西書局，2015 年。

《答覆》英譯文由 Edward L. Shaughnessy（夏含夷）譯，載《古代中國》第 14 卷（*Early China*，14），1989 年；收入《裘錫圭學術文集·甲骨文卷》，復旦大學出版社，2012 年。

今皆據《裘錫圭學術文集·甲骨文卷》收入。

蔡哲茂

釋"🔥""🔥"

殷卜辭中有"🔥"字，見於：

(1) ☐殼貞：乎雀☐
　　☐殼貞：雀其牽☐
　　☐王往🔥伐獲？　　　　　　　　　合集 39930（英藏 602、金 685）
(2) 貞：☐🔥☐　　　　　　　　　　　合集 18532（前 6、42、1）
(3) 貞：勿🔥屮于河？　　　　　　　　乙 8077
(4) ☐🔥☐王☐　　　　　　　　　　　京 3085

而🔥字有時也可把🔥中的兩點或三點代表水的部分省去作"🔥"，見於：

(5) 王固☐亦🔥☐　　　　　　　　　　乙 7064
(6) ☐🔥☐雨　　　　　　　　　　　　乙 6901
(7) ☐🔥☐十二月　　　　　　　　　　後下 41、10
(8) 辛亥卜，王車壬田🔥不雨？　　　　明續 1910
(9) 弜田🔥雨？　　　　　　　　　　　屯南 217
(10) 丙申卜：王尸🔥🔥　　　　　　　　屯南 4429
(11) ☐🔥☐　　　　　　　　　　　　　合集 18533（前 6、61、8）

金文中也有一個字和此相同作🔥（三代吉金文存 15 卷 35 頁）及🔥（三代吉金文存 15 卷 36 頁）、🔥 🔥（三代吉金文存 2 卷 14 頁）、🔥（商周金文錄遺 402）（附圖一）。由於卜辭中从🔥的字，有時也可以省去下面的圈足从∪，如🔥又可作🔥，🔥又可作🔥，🔥又可作🔥，🔥又可作🔥，🔥又可作🔥①，因此🔥字也應可省

---

① 詳見裘錫圭《釋祕》，《古文字研究》第三輯。

作 [字], 見於:

（12）貞:乎望于[字]？二月　　　　　　　　　續 2、26、1

（13）□[字]　　　　　　　　　　　　　　合集 18524（拾 13、14）

（14）貞:令从[字]　　　　　　　　　　　明續 S0665

羅振玉氏在《增訂殷虛書契考釋》卷中 68 頁，引（2）（7）（11）三片的字體，把它釋爲"盥"字，其説云：

《説文解字》："盥，澡手也，从臼水臨皿。"此象仰掌就皿以受沃，是盥也。

此後學者們皆從羅説，無異辭。

卜辭又有"[字]"字，字形是"[字]"字的顛倒，見於：

（15）辛未卜，爭貞:帚好其从沚盛伐巴方，王自東[字]伐重虛于帚好立？

帚好其从沚盛伐巴方，王自東[字]伐重虛于帚好立？

合集 6480（乙 2948＋乙 2950）

（16）己卯卜□貞:叀□[字]伐獲？　　　　　合集 6934

（17）貞:[字]其出疾？　　　　　　　　　合集 13747（文 841）

（18）□丑卜貞:□[字]□　　　　　　　　合集 420

（19）乙酉卜貞:叀[字]令戈羌？十月　　　　陳引

（20）癸亥卜，㞢貞:旬亡囚？之夕[字]，甲子[字]歧王□

合集 16158（南南 2、131）

（21）庚戌卜:[字]隻嘼隻八？　　　　　　甲釋 178（甲 3113）

（22）貞:[字]弗其入見？五月　　　　　　合集 4542（存下 473）

（23）□叀[字]□界□中□帚□　　　　　　人 417

（24）貞:叀臣告令戈[字]？　　　　　　　合集 19092（前 6、9、2）

（25）□子[字]□王漁？十月　　　　　　　掇 2、20（京 1516）

（26）□乙□徙[字]□　　　　　　　　　南坊 4、230

（27）貞:□今夕□　　　　　　　　　　合集 4543（存上 1335）

（28）□乎[字]□　　　　　　　　　　合集 4540（甲 3188）

（29）貞:□[字]　　　　　　　　　　　合集 4541（佚 947）

（30）□[字]□豕□出□　　　　　　　　合集 15069

李陸琦先生在《甲骨文字集釋》第三 946 頁舉（17）（21）（29）三片，以爲"[字]"字是：

从又从覆皿，《説文》所無，字當與盟字同義，从覆皿者，奉匜沃盟之意也，《甲編》3113辭云"庚戌卜隻(獲)一网雒隻八"❍疑爲人名。屈翼鵬云"❍未識，疑亦狩獵之法"見《甲釋》402葉，恐未然也。

❍有當作人名的例子，《京都大學人文科學研究所藏甲骨文字考釋》417片下，也曾提出相同的看法。其云：

> 人名或是國族名。"貞：❍其业疾。"(録841)"貞：叀臣❍命戈❍"(前6、9、2)的❍和本片的❍或是同一個人。

前舉卜辭中除了殘泐之外（3）（14）（17）（19）（20）（21）（22）（23）（24）等辭大概都是人名，但是如果把❍當作盟的意義去解釋（15）（16）兩條，則難以通讀。最近寒峰氏"甲骨文所見的商代軍制數則"[①]一文中，把❍釋成"騷"字，其云：

> 騷字上从倒皿，下从又即手，亦有作爪形，騷伐連詞見前6、30、2，前6、30、1，金525，契80等；可隸定爲蚤，亦即古書裏的騷字，《詩經·常武》"徐方繹騷"《國語·鄭語》"王室方騷"，"王室始騷"均注爲擾，爲亂虐。

因此寒氏解釋（15）條卜辭爲：

> 婦好將隨从沚䛐征伐巴方，商王也將親自領兵另从東邊作騷擾性的進攻。

按《説文》蚤下云："齧人跳蟲也，从䖵叉聲，叉古爪字，蚤或从虫。"段注"叉古爪字"下說："按此四字，妄人所沾，不言古文而言古某字，許無此例，且叉手足甲也，爪丮也，未嘗謂叉爲爪之古文，直由俗謂爪爲手足甲，乃謂叉爲其古字，徑注之於此，不可不删去。"因此，如果只因爲❍字从又，又可寫作爪（ ），就把❍字釋成騷，顯然是有問題的，而且寒氏對❍字所从的倒皿（ ）和蚤字的關係，也沒有任何說解，即使❍字可讀成騷，（15）（16）的"騷伐"一辭，古來文獻未見，也是很可疑的，卜辭另有作爲地名的❍（前2、19、3，前2、19、5，金544）與《説文》訓爲手足甲也的 字相同，而❍字， 旁的兩點或三點是表示皿中之水，與 的 中兩點所指的不同，這就是寒說無法成立的理由，但是寒氏把"❍"和"❍"看成是同一個字，這是正確的，❍字見於卜辭者如下：

(31) ☐❍伐西土？ 　　　　　　　　　　　　　　　　　　合集7082（燕80）

[①] 《甲骨探史録》四一一頁。

(32) □貞□王䍐伐土方受□　　　　　　　　　合集 6425（前 6、30、1）

(33) 己丑卜，殻貞：令𠂤來？曰𠂤䍐伐𢀛方？七月。　合集 39873（金 525）

(34) □丑卜，殻貞：令𠂤來□𠂤䍐伐𢀛方？七月。

　　　　　　　　　　　　　　　　　　　合集 6379 正（前 6、30、2）

(35) □卜貞：□䍐□于□　　　　　　　　　　合集 18620

(36) □䍐□　　　　　　　　　　　　　前 6、10、1（林 2、2、8）

與卜辭䍐字相同的金文見於䍐甗（三代 5、4、6），其銘云：

　　　䍐乍寶彝（按此器現藏日本東京出光美術館，附圖二）

吳大澂在《說文古籀補》釋此字爲"罙"，按《說文》罙字作"𤴙"云"深也"段注：

　　　此以今字釋古字也，罙深古今字，篆作𤴙深，隸變作罙深，水部深下但云水名，不言淺之反，是知古深淺字作罙，深行而罙廢矣。有穴而後有淺深，故字從穴，《毛詩》"罙入其阻"，傳曰"罙，深也"。此罙字見六經者，毛公以今字釋古字，而許襲之，此罙之音義原流也。

段注釋罙之義甚確，《詩·殷武》所言"撻彼殷武，奮伐荊楚，罙入其阻，裒荊之旅，有截其所，湯孫之緒"。所謂"奮伐荊楚，罙入其阻"，即卜辭"罙伐"之意。古書中以"深"爲"深入"之意，尚見於：

《國語·晉語》：

　　　六年，秦歲定，帥師侵晉，至於韓，公謂慶鄭曰："秦寇深矣，奈何？"

韋昭注：

　　　深，入境深也。一曰深猶重也。

《左傳·僖公十五年》記此事云：

　　　三敗及韓，晉侯謂慶鄭曰："寇深矣，若之何？"

秦兵至韓原即深入晉境，故當以"入境深也"釋"深"爲是。

《戰國策·秦策四》：

　　　三國攻秦，入函谷，秦王謂樓緩曰："三國之兵深矣，寡人欲割河東而講。"

高誘注：

深猶盛也。

三國之兵入函谷則深入秦地，故秦不得不割河東以講和，深即深入之意，高注未得。因此把（31）（32）（33）（34）的"㴱伐"釋爲"深伐"印證古籍，可謂信而有徵矣。前舉李先生文以爲卜辭的 ㆝、㆟ 是同一個字，這也是正確的，比較（1）和（15）（16）的辭例即可知"㴱伐"和"㴱伐"是相同的，卜辭上不管獨體或合體的字，倒書但意義仍然相同，如且字倒書作"㆟"（合集 1777，甲 1174），"㆝"（合集 1824 正，7772 正）又可倒書作"㆞"（福 2，金 675，金 402），㆟（人 2138）又可倒書作 ㆟（粹 1590），殷武丁時曾大規模的征伐獲，且並帶著多子一同去，也就是王族和多子族一齊伐獲，卜辭稱"深伐獲"即深入獲境之意。①

近年出土的中山王䛐壺有辭云"䛐愛深則賢人親"，深字作"㴱"，諸家考釋以爲"深"字，無異辭。與卜辭比較，已變㆟㆟爲㆟，而且多出"㆟"來。石鼓文戊鼓（霝鼓）亦有辭云"隹舟以衎，或陰或陽，極深以□，于水一方"，其深字作"㴱"，與中山王䛐壺銘同，唯移㆟於㆞旁，而成後來小篆深字。由於深字由甲文的从倒皿，演變成从㆟，所以段注解釋說"有穴而後有淺深，故字从穴"。最近李裕民氏在《侯馬盟書疑難字考》一文②也和段注提出類似的看法，其云：

> ㆟、㆟、㆟爲穴之象形，㆟象洞穴之外形，…象水滴，或作㆟。穴内潮溼，不免有水滲入。正因爲是滲入的水滴，只作…等形，而與河水之水作㆟者不同。㆟、穴本意相同，故二者通用。……㆟爲手形，㴱字象以手伸入穴中摸取，深淺難測，故又引伸爲深。《爾雅·釋詁》"深，測也"，《老子》"深矣遠矣"注"深不可測也"。

按由卜辭的㴱字作㆟或倒書作㆟，可以了解㴱字的取義是用手在水中探其深淺，而水是裝在器皿之中，後來所从的倒皿訛變成㆟，就和家室等字的从㆟無別，最後㆟又訛成㆟，使得後人以爲㴱是从穴，也就是由 ㆟→㆟→㆟。由 ㆟變成 ㆟ 金文中亦有他例，如造字作 ㆟（頌鼎）、㆟（頌殷），又可作 ㆟（公孫造壺）。㆟（邵鐘），又可作 ㆟（秦公殷）。卜辭中㴱字的…是表示皿中有水，後代深字加水旁，正是由此重複而來，也就是增加意符，這在其它的字也有同樣的例子，如金文从阜的字後來又增加意符土。當然深和探在語源上應該是有關係的，探而後

---

① 詳林小安《殷武丁臣屬征伐與行祭考》，《甲骨文與殷商史》第二輯。
② 《古文字研究》第五輯。

知深淺，但卜辭的罙字在前舉（1）（15）（16）（31）（32）（33）（34）等所表示的應該是深淺字的本義，而非引伸則可斷言，其它的地方是當作人名或地名。罙字的演變如下所示：

追記：

馬王堆竹簡《十問》："息必探而久，新氣易守。"影本探讀爲深，謂呼吸必深而長久。《史記·信陵君列傳》："臣之客有能深得趙王陰事者。"《索隱》："譙周作探得趙王陰事。"《正義》："探一作深。"按《論語》有"見不善如探湯"，則卜辭 似爲探湯之形。又合 6357 有"貞：方弗西土？""□其西土？"，當讀作探，深探同源，但字形解釋當以探爲本義。

附圖一　作 見於三代 15 卷 35 頁、36 頁，作 見於三代 2 卷 14 頁，作 見於録遺 402。

録遺

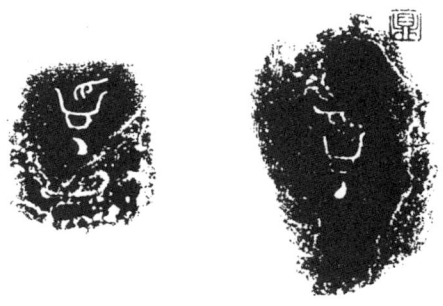

三代 2 卷 14 頁

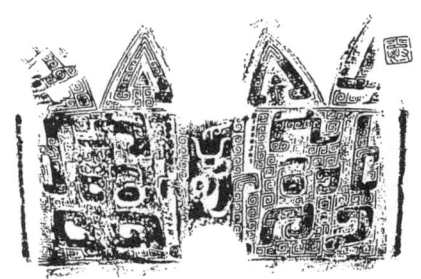

三代 15 卷 35 頁

三代 15 卷 36 頁

附圖二　（出光美術館"中國古代の美術"）

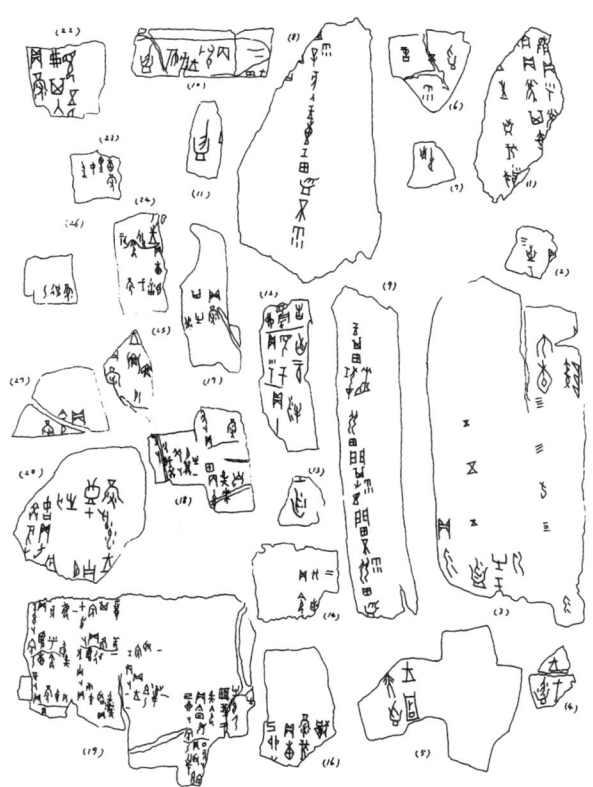

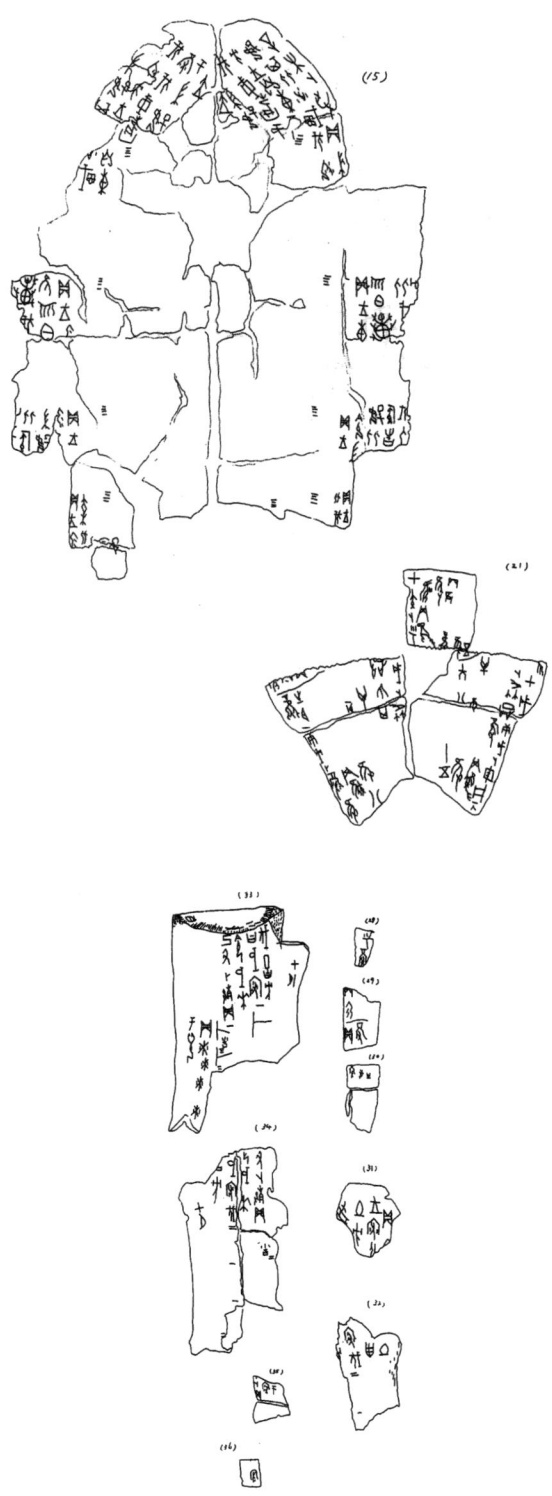

原載《故宮學術季刊》第 5 卷第 3 期,1988 年;收入宋鎮豪、段志洪主編:《甲骨文獻集成》第 13 冊,四川大學出版社,2001 年。今據前者收入。

張玉金

卜辭中表示兩事時間關係的詞的意義和用法

本文主要是以甲骨卜辭中表示兩件（或兩件以上）事情之間的時間關係的詞作爲研究對象，旨在弄清這些詞的意義和用法。

我們知道，兩件事情説在一起，當中可以有種種關係，如並列關係、選擇關係、因果關係、轉折關係及假設關係等等。有時候，兩件事情之間只有時間關係或主要是時間關係。例如：

（1）于入自日延敗。　　　　　　　　　　　　　　　　　　　（合集 29713）

（2）辛酉卜，王：兄(祝)于妣己，延取祖丁。　　　　　　　　（合集 19890）

在例（1）中，"入自日"這件事和"敗"這件事之間是時間關係。在例（2）中，"兄于妣己"一事和"取祖丁"一事之間也是時間關係。

表示兩件事情之間的時間關係，可以只憑語序這種語法手段。例如：

（3A）甲寅貞：伊歲，遘報丁日。

（3B）甲寅貞：伊歲，遘大丁日。　　　　　　　　　　　　　（屯南 1110）

這個例子在討論遘字句的結構時曾引用過。在（3A）中，"報丁日"這件事是"遘"這件事的時間背景；在（3B）中，"大丁日"這件事爲"遘"這件事的時間背景。"報丁日"、"大丁日"兩事與"遘"之間的時間關係的表達手段僅是語序。

語序這種語法手段在表達兩件事情之間的時間關係上有局限性，因爲有些時間關係並不是語序所能表達出來的。在多數情況下，表示時間關係要用一定的詞（主要是虛詞）。依據我們的考察，甲骨卜辭中的"惠"、"邲"（必）、"于"、"即"、"由"、"並"、"戠"、"先"、"既"、"咸"、"延"（乃）、"後"、"延"、"眔"

等等詞常用來表示事情之間的時間關係。

　　呂叔湘先生在《中國文法要略》一書中認爲，在現代漢語和古代文獻中，有很多句子是只有時間關係或是以時間關係爲主的。他把這些句子分成兩類，一是以一事爲另一事的時間背景的，一是兩事不分賓主的。他還論述了在這兩類句子中常用的表示兩事時間關係的詞。① 從呂先生的論述中，我們可以看到，在前一類句子中使用的詞，一般不在後一類句子中出現；反之亦然。這説明，有一類詞可用來表示一事爲另一事時間背景這樣的關係，而另一類詞則不用來表示這樣的時間關係。既然如此，現代漢語和古代文獻中表示兩事時間關係的詞就可分成兩類了。甲骨卜辭中的這種詞也可以分爲兩大類，每大類又可分爲一些小類。詳見下表（表中的"VP"，代表謂詞或謂詞語，"NP"代表名詞或名詞語，"VT"代表通過記叙一件事來記時間的詞語）：

表一

A 類詞——用來表示或事實上表示一事爲另一事的時間背景（同時也可以表示出兩件事情有先後或共時關係）這樣的關係	Aa 類詞——出現在"□＋VT＋VP"或"VP＋□＋VT"中"□"的位置上，用來表示一事爲另一事時間背景這樣的關係	Aa1 類詞——用來表示一事在（或當、正當）某一時間進行這樣的關係：惠、即
		Aa2 類詞——用來表示一事到（等到、臨近）或趕在某一時間進行這樣的關係：于、邲（必）、戠₁
		Aa3 類詞——用來表示一事從某一時間起進行這樣的關係：由
	Ab 類詞——出現在"NP1＋□＋NP2＋VP"中"□"的位置上，事實上用來表示一事爲另一事時間背景這樣的關係：眔、暨、戠₂、先₁、後₁	
B 類詞——不用來表示一事爲另一事時間背景這樣的關係，只用來表示兩事有先後或共時這樣的關係	Ba 類詞——用來表示兩事時間的先後關係：先₂、既、咸、後₂、廼（乃）、延	
	Bb 類詞——用來表示兩事同時進行這樣的關係：並	

　　A 類詞和 B 類詞明顯不同。首先，在使用 A 類詞的句子中説出的兩件事都是分賓主的，而在使用 B 類詞的句子中説出的兩件事情則多數是不分賓主的，有少

---

① 呂叔湘：《中國文法要略》，370—385 頁，1982。

數雖然分賓主，但卻不是 B 類詞的作用（卜辭或言"丙寅卜：王己巳步，往迺易日"《合集》21079，這個例子中的"往"這件事應是"易日"一事的時間背景，它們之間的這種時間關係並不是用"迺"表示出來的——它只是用來表示"往"和"易日"有先後關係的，而是用語序這種語法手段表示出來的，語序這種語法手段可以用來表示一事為另一事時間背景，如前引第 3 例）。既然如此，我們就可以說，A 類詞是用來表示一事為另一事時間背景的，B 類詞則不是用來表示這樣的時間關係的。其次，A 類詞大都能帶上賓語出現在"VP"之前或其後，作"VP"的修飾成分；B 類詞則沒有這種功能。Aa 類詞和 Ab 類詞也有差異：Aa 類詞出現在"□ + VT + VP"或"VP + □ + VT"中"□"的位置上，表示"VT"這件事是"VP"這件事的時間背景。Ab 類詞一般出現在"NP1 + □ + NP2 + VP"中的"□"的位置上，表面上看它是表示"NP2"這一物件和"VP"這一行為的關係的，但事實上表示出了"NP2 + VP"這件事為"NP1 + VP"一事的時間背景的。

下面，我們將按照"表一"中諸詞排列的次序，對它們的意義和用法逐個進行探討。

（一）A 類詞

上面講過，這類詞可分為 Aa、Ab 兩類，Aa 類詞出現在"□ + VT + VP"或"VP + □ + VT"中"□"的位置上，表示一事為另一事的時間背景這樣的關係，Ab 類詞一般出現在"NP1 + □ + NP2 + VP"中"□"的位置上，事實上可以表示出一事為另一事時間背景這樣的關係。

1. Aa 類詞

這類詞又可分為 Aa1、Aa2、Aa3 三類詞，Aa1 類詞是用來表示一事在（或當、正當）某一時間進行這樣的關係的，Aa2 類詞是用來表示一事到（或等到、臨近）、趁著某一時間進行這樣的關係的，Aa3 類詞則是用來表示一事從某一時間起進行這樣的關係的。

（1）Aa1 類詞

屬於這類詞的有"惠"和"即"。

a. 惠

先看下例：

（4A）貞：惠翌癸未酒。

（4B）貞：于來乙酉酒。　　　　　　　　　　　　　　　　　　（合集 3290）

在（4A）的"□+時間詞語+VP"中"□"的位置上用的是"惠"，在（4B）的同樣位置上用的則是"于"。這種例子，在甲骨卜辭中常見。例如：

（5）癸酉卜，㱿貞：雀惠今日戎。

　　癸酉卜，㱿貞：雀于翌甲戌戎。　　　　　　　　　　　　（丙 263）

（6）癸未貞：惠乙酉延伐。

　　癸未貞：于來月延伐。　　　　　　　　　　　　　　　　（合集 32243）

（7）惠夕酒。

　　于來日酒。　　　　　　　　　　　　　　　　　　　　　（合集 27396）

上引諸例中的"惠"字，應是語氣副詞。但是它經常在一對選貞卜辭中出現在與"于"相對的位置上，如上引例（4）、例（5）、例（6）、例（7）；在"□+VT+VP"中"□"的位置上（這種"惠"與"□+時間詞語+VP"中"□"的位置上的"惠"是一個詞），"惠"和"于"有時換用，例如：

（8）丁未貞：升歲，惠祭遘。

　　升歲，于劦遘。　　　　　　　　　　　　　　　　　　　（合集 34613）

（9）丁未貞：升歲，于祭遘。

　　丁未貞：升歲，于劦遘。　　　　　　　　　　　　　　　（合集 34615）

這說明，這種"惠"客觀上應具有把時間修飾語介紹給"VP"的作用。

上舉這類卜辭中，"惠"後所記之時一定比"于"後所記之時較近於占卜之時，而且往往即爲卜月、卜日或卜日中的一個時段。如上引例（5）、例（7）。又如：

（10）惠今日辛圍，禽。　　　　　　　　　　　　　　　　　　（甲 638）

（11）惠今夕用，其言。　　　　　　　　　　　　　　　　　　（甲 499）

（12）惠今昏酒。　　　　　　　　　　　　　　　　　　　　　（甲 558）

（13）惠今六月出。　　　　　　　　　　　　　　　　　　　　（甲 931）

上引諸例中的"惠"都可譯爲"在"。有些"惠"字，其後記載的時間遠於卜

日，如上引例（4）、例（6）。這種"惠"似也可譯爲"在"，因爲同樣用法的"惠"，似不必做兩種解釋。

當然，"惠"字本身沒有什麽實在意義，它之所以可譯爲"在"，只是因爲它處在特定的位置上，有特定的作用。

"惠"不但可以把"時間詞語"介紹給"VP"（如前引第 4 至 7 例），還可以把"VT"介紹給"VP"（如前引第 8 例），這類"惠"就是我們所說的 Aa1 類詞了。

前引例（8）在討論遘字句的結構的時候曾引用過，可以參看。下引三個例子也曾引用過：

（14）惠又㕣日遘又升，王受又。　　　　　　　　　　（合集 26992）

（15）［惠］又㕣日遘，王受又。　　　　　　　　　　（合集 30852）

（16）惠上甲史遘酒。　　　　　　　　　　　　　　　（合集 27051）

上引三個例子中的"惠"都是作 Aa1 類詞用的。下引諸例中的"惠"亦然：

（17A）惠日敳。

（17B）于入自日迺敳。　　　　　　　　　　　　　　（合集 29713）

上引（17B）中的"日"明顯是祭名，他辭或言"惠今入自祼告"（合集 23403），可以爲證。"入自日"的"入"似是指進入宗廟，"日"祭似是在宗廟外舉行。"入自日"一語，大概是離開"日"祭這種儀式進入（宗廟）的意思。從（17B）來看，（17A）中的"日"也應是祭名。這對卜辭卜問，是在"日祭"的時候舉行"敳"祭好，還是等到從"日"祭場所進入（宗廟）的時候舉行"敳"祭好。

（18）惠各（格）于藝祼敳，王受又。　　　　　　　　（合集 30925）

在"王其田，藝入，不雨。夕入，不雨。"（合集 28572）一例中，"藝"和"夕"相對，"藝"明顯是個時間詞。在"祼"字之前，"藝"有時也和"夕"相對，例如："其又妣庚，惠入自己夕祼酒。惠入自藝祼酒。"（合集 27522）這種"藝"也應是時間詞。"藝祼"當是在"藝"時（有人認爲掌燈之時）舉行的祼祭，"夕祼"則是在太陽落的時候舉行的祼祭。"各"讀爲"格"，是來到的意思。"各于藝祼"從字面上講是來到"夕祼"祭這種儀式上，可以理解爲參加"藝祼"祭。例（18）卜問，在參加"藝祼"時舉行"敳"祭好不好。

(19) □酉卜，旅貞：妣庚歲，叀出敁。　　　　　　　　　　　　　　（明2360）

此例中的"出"和前引（17）、（18）中的"入"、"各"一樣，都是指王在祭祀時的行動。① 前面講過，"入"可能是指進入宗廟，然則"出"可能是指從宗廟出去。例（19）卜問，將要"歲"祭妣庚了，是否在（王）出去的時候舉行"敁"祭。此例中的"敁"祭是在"歲"祭中舉行的。

(20A) 其又（侑）父己，叀莫（暮）酒，王受又[又]。
(20B) 叀入自父庚夕酒，王受又又。　　　　　　　　　　　　　　（合集27396）

上引（20B）中的"夕"是祭名，"入自父庚夕"同（20A）中的"莫"一樣，表示"酒"祭舉行的時間。（20）這對卜辭卜問，將要侑祭父己了，是在傍晚舉行酒祭好，還是在從"夕"祭父庚的場所進入（宗廟）時舉行酒祭好。此例中的"酒"作爲一種輔助祭祀在父己的侑祭中舉行。

(21A) 其又（侑）妣庚，叀入自己夕祼酒。
(21B) 叀入自藝祼酒。　　　　　　　　　　　　　　　　　　　　（合集27522）

這對卜辭卜問，將要侑祭妣庚了，是在從"夕祼"祭妣己的場所進入（宗廟）時酒祭好，還是在從"藝祼"祭的場所進入（宗廟）時酒祭好。

(22A) 弜祝于妣辛。
(22B) 其祝妣辛，叀翌日辛酒。
(22C) 弜翌日辛酒。
(22D) 叀今入自夕祼酒，又正。　　　　　　　　　　　　　　　　（屯南261）

此例當是庚日占卜的記錄。（22B）、（22C）中的時間詞語都是"翌日辛"，"辛"前的日子是"庚"。在（22D）中，有"夕祼"一語，當是指對妣辛的祭祀。依例，妣辛的"夕祼"祭舉行的時間應在"辛"日的前一天——庚日之夕。"入自夕祼"當是在庚日時的事兒，這一詞語前用個"今"字，這也能說明占卜的日子。上引（22）先問要不要祝祭妣辛，占卜的結果當是吉利的。於是再問，是在從"夕祼"祭場所進入（宗廟）時酒祭，還是在第二天辛日酒祭。此例中的"酒"當是爲妣辛的祝祭而舉行的。

(23A) 叀今日己酒。

---

① 裘錫圭：《釋祕》，《古文字研究》第3輯，7—13頁，北京：中華書局，1980。

(23B) 于來日己酒。

(23C) 叀入自夕祼酒。

(23D) 王夕酒。　　　　　　　　　　　　　　　　　　　　（屯南 4242）

從（23A）來看，此例是己日的占卜記錄。（23C）中的"夕祼"祭應也是在己日舉行的，"夕祼"祭的對象可能是廟號爲"庚"的先王或先妣。（23）這四條卜辭仍是在卜問酒祭的時間。

(24) 王其☐，叀入自日酒，王受☐。　　　　　　　　　　（屯南 2483）

(25) 乙未[卜]，[旅]貞：其又(侑)于妣，叀今入自祼告。　　（合集 23403）

此例中的"告"爲祭名。卜辭常言"入自祼"、"入自藝祼"、"入自夕祼"，前面說過，"入"可能指進入宗廟，然則"祼"祭可能通常是在宗廟外舉行的。

(26) 貞：其用竹黽羌，叀酒彡用。　　　　　　　　　　　（合集 451）

（26）中的"竹"，當是人名。"竹"後那個難以隸定的字，其意義當爲"獻"或"送"。"酒彡"當是爲"彡"祭舉行酒祭的意思，這裏表示"用"的時間。此例卜問，將要用竹獻來的羌俘了，在"酒彡"祭的時候使用好不好。

(27) 叀入自延用，王受又。　　　　　　（合集 30699）(《合集》31211 同文)

"延"在這裏當指一種祭祀，"用"當是指用牲。

(28) 癸亥卜，☐貞：其兄(祝)于妣，叀祼用。　　　　　　（合集 26899）

此例卜問，將要祝祭某妣了，是否在"祼"祭時爲之用牲。

(29) 丁卯卜，行貞：叀又(侑)用。　　　　　　　　　　　（文 557）

總之，在甲骨卜辭中，有些"叀"字出現在"☐＋VT＋VP"中"☐"的位置上，表示一事在某一時間進行這樣的關係。

b. 即

在古代文獻中，有些"即"字出現在"☐＋時間詞語＋VP"中"☐"的位置上。例如：

(a) 於是高帝即日駕，西都關中。　　　　　　　　　　　（史記·留侯世家）

(b) 項伯許諾，即夜復去。　　　　　　　　　　　　　　（漢書·高帝紀）

(c) 即日夕，入未央宮。　　　　　　　　　　　　　　　（漢書·文帝紀）

這種"即"是"就在"、"當"的意思，可看成介詞或動詞。

在甲骨卜辭中，這種"即"已可見到。例如：

(30) 即日甲酒，王受又。　　　　　　　　　　　　　　　　　　(合集 29705)

此例中的"即日甲酒"是說當甲日那天酒祭，"即"是把時間詞語"日甲"介紹給"酒"的詞（看《說卜辭中的"至日""即日""戠日"》）。

在上引（30）中，"即"出現在"□＋時間詞語＋VP"中"□"的位置上。在卜辭中，有些"即"字出現在"□＋VT＋VP"中"□"的位置上，這種"即"字就是作 Aa1 類詞用的了。例如：

(31A) 歲一牛。

(31B) 歲牢。

(31C) 歲其即杏。

(31D) 歲其莫（暮）。　　　　　　　　　　　　　　　　　　(合集 41662)

上引（31C）中的"杏"，寫作"𣐺"，它不是杏樹的"杏"，而是"祭名"，他辭或言"丁丑卜，文甲杏牢"（存 2·763），可以為證。上引（31A）和（31B）卜問，是用一頭牛進行"歲"祭好，還是用"牢"進行"歲"祭好。（31C）和（31D）卜問，"歲"祭是就在"杏"祭時進行，還是傍晚再進行。（31C）和（31D）以"即杏"和"莫"構成對貞，"即杏"中的"即"明顯地是把表示時間的"杏"介紹給"歲"的。這種"即"與前面講過的"惠"作用相近。

(32A) 父甲□歲，即祖丁歲祊。

(32B) 弜即祖丁歲祊。　　　　　(屯南 2294)(《屯南》173 與(32B)同文)

此例中的"祊"當是祭名，他辭或言"☐祊十又五牢，其即☐"（拾 315）、"☐祖丁祊五牢"（甲 814），可證。此例卜問，父甲將要受……"歲"祭了，就在"歲"祭祖丁時"祊"祭好，還是不要在這時"祊"祭好。

(33) 即大乙升歲，王[受][又]。　　　　　　　　　　　　　　(粹 152)

此例卜問，就在"升"祭大乙時舉行"歲"祭好不好。

總之，作 Aa1 類詞用的"即"，是用來表示一事就在或當某一時間進行這樣的關係的。

(2) Aa2 類詞

屬於這類詞的有"于"、"邲"（必）、"戠$_1$"。

a. 于

前面講過，在卜辭中，"惠"常出現在"□＋時間詞語＋VP"中"□"的位置上，"于"也常在這種位置上出現。關於這種"惠"和"于"用法上的區別，陳夢家曾有這樣的説法："卜辭近稱的紀時之前加虛字'惠'，遠稱者加虛字'于'。"① 陳氏此説，大致可信。"于"後所記之時確實都遠於卜日。例如：

(34) 癸丑卜，争貞：自今至于丁巳，我戋𦎫。王占曰：丁巳我母（毋）其戋，
于來甲子其戋。　　　　　　　　　　　　　　　　　　　　　　　　（丙 1）

(35) 丙辰卜，古貞：其敗羌。
貞：于庚申伐羌。　　　　　　　　　　　　　　　　　　　　　　　（丙 7）

(36) 乙未余卜：于九月又（有）事。
于九月又事。……
丁酉余卜：今八月又事。
唯今八月又事。　　　　　　　　　　　　　　　　　　　　　　　（丙 611）

(37) 于翌庚禦王。　　　　　　　　　　　　　　　　　　　　　　　（丙 166）

(38) 于來乙卯侑祖乙。　　　　　　　　　　　　　　　　　　　　　（丙 198）

(39) 貞：于生一月步。　　　　　　　　　　　　　　　　　　　　　（丙 485）

上引（34）的卜日是"癸丑"，在"于"後記載的時間是"甲子"，"甲子"是癸丑後的第十一天。例（35）的卜日是"丙辰"後的第四天。例（36）占卜的月份是八月，而在"于"後記載的月份是九月。（37）、（38）、（39）三例的"于"後的時間詞語中有"翌"、"來"、"生"三個詞，這三個詞都是表示"未來時"的。② 可見，"于"後所記載的時間大都是在卜日（或卜月）後的日子（或月份），陳夢家之説近是。

既然"于"後所記之時大都是在卜日（或卜月）後的日子（或月份），那麼，出現在"□＋時間詞語＋VP"中"□"的位置上的"于"就應譯爲"到"，"于＋時間詞語"是到（未來的）某一時間的意思。

"于"不但出現在"□＋時間詞語＋VP"中"□"的位置上，也可在"VP＋□＋時間詞語"中"□"的位置上出現（這種位置上的"于"也是"到"的意思，看下引第 40 例）：

---

① 陳夢家：《殷虛卜辭綜述》，227 頁，北京：科學出版社，1956。
② 陳夢家：《殷虛卜辭綜述》，119 頁，北京：科學出版社，1956。

(40) 癸酉貞:射徣以羌用自報甲于甲申。　　　　　　　　　（京 3966）

這説明,"于"應是個介詞。

當這種"于"字出現在"□+VT+VP"或"VP+□+VT"中"□"的位置上時,它就是作 Aa2 類詞用的了。例如:

(41) 丁巳卜,貞:旡于王循入。　　　　　　　　　　　　（合集 7235）

上例中的"旡"為人名,"循"是動詞。這條卜辭卜問,"旡"到王"循"的時候再進入好不好。此例中的"于"表示"王循"一事為"旡入"一事的時間背景。

(42A) 貞:王勿卒(猝)入。
(42B) 辛亥卜,㱿貞:王入。
(42C) 貞:王于舂酒于報甲入。　　　　　　　　　　　　（合集 1210）

(42C)中的"舂酒"可能是指在"舂"祭中舉行"酒"祭,"于"是把"舂酒于報甲"介紹給"入"的。這條卜辭卜問,王是否到"舂酒"祭上甲的時候進入。

(43A) 貞:沈十牛。
(43B) 王勿于舂酒入。　　　　　　　　　　　　　　　（合集 16113）

上引(43A)卜問,是否以"沈"的方式用十頭牛。"沈"祭應是在宗廟外舉行的。(43B)可能是在卜問,王是否要到"舂酒"祭時(從"沈"祭的場所)進入(宗廟)。

(44A) 舂酒王入。
(44B) 貞:勿入。
(44C) 己亥卜,㱿貞:王入。
(44D) 己亥卜,㱿貞:王勿于舂[酒][入]。　　　　　　　（合集 39781）

上引(44A)中的"舂酒"是"王入"的時間背景,它們之間這種時間關係的表達手段是語序。(44A)卜問,到"舂酒"祭時王進入好不好。

(45A) 王其又父己,惠卯各(格)[于]日酒,王受又。
(45B) 于入自日酒,王受又。
(45C) 于入自夕祼酒,王受。　　　　　　　　　　　　（屯南 2483）

（45A）中的"卯"，與古文獻中的"比"音義俱近（説詳見下文）。（45）卜問，王將侑祭父己了，是趁著參加"日"祭時舉行酒祭好，還是等到從"日"祭或"夕祼"祭場所進入（宗廟）時舉行酒祭好。此例中的"酒"祭是爲父己的侑祭而舉行的。

（46）☐妣癸，于今入自夕祼酒。　　　　　　　　　　　　（屯南 1442）

此例中的"夕祼"若是祭祀"妣癸"的，那麽，這一祭祀當是在"癸"日的前一天——壬日之夕舉行，"入自夕祼"也應是壬日的事兒，這一詞語前加"今"，這説明占卜的日子當是在壬日。

（47）癸亥卜，殼貞：于出酒。　　　　　　　　　　　　　（合集 9990）
（48A）虢惠卯各于祼用，王受又。
（48B）于入自祼用，王受又。　　　　　　　　　　　　　（合集 27281）

上引（48A）中的"虢"指俘虜。（48）這對卜辭卜問，是趁著參加祼祭時用人牲，還是到從祼祭的場所進入（宗廟）時用人牲。

（49）丁酉卜，賓貞：有來告方圍，于尋祼告于丁。　　　　（合集 6672）

（49）卜問，有人來報告説，敵方來犯了，到"尋祼"時把此事報告給丁好不好。"尋祼"中的"尋"，可能是重複的意思。

（50）貞：王于出尋。　　　　　　　　　　　　　　　　　（合集 16064）

此例中的"尋"，可能是祭名。"尋"前的"出"應是指王在祭祀時的行動。

（51）丁未貞：升歲，惠祭邁。
　　　升歲，于祭邁。　　　　　　　　　　　　　　　　（合集 34613）
（52）丁未貞：升歲，于祭邁。
　　　丁未貞：升歲，于祭邁。　　　　　　　　　　　　（合集 34615）

上引兩例在討論邁字句的結構及表示時間關係的"惠"時都曾引用過，可參看。

（53）乙巳貞：升歲，惠彡邁。
　　　丁未貞：升歲，于祭邁。
　　　［丁］［未］貞：［升］歲，于祭邁。　　　　　　　（合集 34614）

（53）的後兩條卜辭與（52）兩條卜辭同文。

以上諸例中的作 Aa2 類詞用的"于",都出現在"□＋VT＋VP"中"□"的位置上。下引兩例中的"于",則出現在"VP＋□＋VT"中"□"的位置上。例如：

(54) 戊申卜,貞：其品司于王出。　　　　　　　　　　　　(合集 23712)

上例中的"品"當是"祭名",他辭或言"乙卯卜：來丁卯酒品,不雨"(掇 1·426)、"辛卯卜,貞：王賓品,亡尤"(前 5·35·4),可以爲證。"司",或釋爲"后",有人認爲是"祭名",有人認爲是"神名"。從"于司禦子辟"(庫 429)、"乙丑卜：其又歲于二司一牝"(甲 875)兩例來看,"司"當是"神名"。(54)卜問,到王出去的時候"品"祭"司"好不好。

(55) 乙酉卜,何貞：祖丁礿,遘于日。　　　　　　　　　　(合集 27282)

這條卜辭在討論遘字句的結構時曾引用過,可參看。

總之,上述兩種位置上的"于"都是用來表示一事到某一時間進行這樣的時間關係的。

在現代漢語中,出現在"□＋VT＋VP"中"□"的位置上的"到"和出現在"VP＋□＋VT"中"□"的位置上的"到"表示的時間關係不同,前者表示一事到某一時間進行這樣的關係(例如"到吃飯時又哭起來了"),後者表示一事一直到某時仍如此這樣的關係(例如"一直哭到吃飯時")。甲骨卜辭中的"于"卻不然,它出現在"VP＋□＋VT"中"□"的位置上時,也表示一事到某一時間進行這樣的關係。理由如下：

首先,"VP＋□＋時間詞語"中"□"的位置上的"于"不是用來表示一事一直到某一時間仍然如此的。例如：

(56A) 癸酉貞：射徝以羌自上甲乙亥。

(56B) 癸酉貞：射徝以羌用自上甲于甲申。　　　　　　　　(人 2265)

上引 A、B 兩條卜辭以"乙亥"和"于甲申"構成對貞,卜問在乙亥那天從上甲開始對先王使用射徝帶來的羌俘好,還是到甲申那天用好。"于"在這裏表示的是一事到某一時間進行這樣的關係,依此類推,"VP＋□＋VT"中"□"的位置上的"于"也應表示這種時間關係。

其次,"VP＋□＋VT"中"□"的位置上的"于"可用,也可以不用。例如：

(57) 乙酉卜,何貞:祖丁磔,其遘于日。　　　　　　　　　　（合集 27282）

(58A) 甲寅貞:伊歲,遘報丁日。

(58B) 甲寅貞:伊歲,遘大丁日。　　　　　　　　　　　　　（屯南 1110）

上引（57）中的"遘"與"日"之間用了"于",但在（58）中的"遘"與"報丁日"、"大丁日"之間就沒有用"于"。這種"于"使用與否,並不影響句子的基本意思。可見,"VP＋囗＋VT"中"囗"的位置上的"于"並不是用來表示一事一直到某一時間仍如此的,因爲,它若表示這種關係,就是非用不可的了；若不用它,會影響句子的基本意思。

再次,在甲骨卜辭中,常用"至"、"至于"來表示一事一直到某時仍如此這樣的關係。這種用法的"至"、"至于"常與"自"相照應。例如：

(59) 自乙至丁又（有）大雨。　　　　　　　　　　　　　（合集 30050）

(60) 貞:自今庚申至于甲子雨。　　　　　　　　　　　　（合集 14470）

在甲骨卜辭中,未見到表示時間關係的"于"和"自"相照應的用例（當"自"和"于"的賓語都是處所詞時,"自"常和"于"相照應,如"癸丑卜,行貞:王其步自𦫺于𦫺,亡災。"《佚》271）,表示一事一直到某時仍如此這樣的關係不用"于"。

由上述三點看來,"VP＋于＋VT"中的"于"同"于＋VT＋VP"中的"于"一樣,也是用來表示一事到某一時間進行這樣的關係的。

"于"字既可單獨使用,以表示兩事間的時間關係,也可以和"既"、"廼"等詞聯合使用,以表示時間關係。先看看"于"和"既"聯合使用的例子：

(61) ☐祖丁莫（暮）歲,于既祭酒。　　　　　　　　　　（合集 27273）

上引（61）中的"祭"是祭名。這條卜辭卜問,祖丁傍晚將受"歲"祭,是否到"祭"祭結束後進行酒祭。此例中的"酒"祭當是爲祖丁的"歲"祭而舉行的。

(62) 貞:于既父丁升歲酒。　　　　　　　　　　　　　　（合集 23224）

上引（62）卜問,到了父丁的"升歲"祭結束後再舉行酒祭好不好。

(63A) 其置庸（鏞）鼓于既卯。

(63B) 惠卯卯。　　　　　　　　　　　　　　　　　　　（合集 30693）

這對卜辭卜問,是等到"卯"祭以後設置鐘鼓好,還是趁著"卯"祭舉行之時(設置鐘鼓)好。①

(64A) 貞:中丁歲,惠晨。
(64B) 于既日。　　　　　　　　　　　　　　　　　　　　(合集 22859)

(64A)和(64B)以"惠晨"和"于既日"構成對貞,卜問中丁的"歲"祭是在晨時舉行好,還是到"日"祭結束時舉行好。

(65) 于日既。　　　　　　　　　　　　　　　　　　　　(粹 485)

在這條卜辭中,"VT"出現了,但"VP"沒有出現。這是在卜問,對某神的某種祭祀是否到"日"祭結束後舉行。

上引例(61)到例(65)是"于"和"既"聯合使用的例子,"于"和"既"共同表示了這樣的時間關係:到了某一件事情結束後再進行另一件事情。

下面我們再看看"于"和"廼"相照應的用例:

(66) 王出,于彡酒廼入。　　　　　　　　　　　　　　　(乙 4166)

前面講過,祭祀卜辭中的"出"和"入"都指王在祭祀時的行動,所出入的場所可能是宗廟。"彡酒"是說在"彡"祭中舉行酒祭。這條卜辭卜問,王將出去,是否到"彡酒"祭時才進入。

(67) 于月出廼往,亡災。　　　　　　　　　　　　　(安明 1918+2096)

這條卜辭卜問,到月亮出來的時候才前往吉利不吉利。

(68) 于來自牢廼逐辰麋,亡災。　　　　　　　　　　　　(屯南 3599)

上例中的"牢"、"辰"皆爲地名。這條卜辭卜問,是否到從牢地回來時才追逐辰地的麋鹿。

(69) 于彡衣廼又△,王受又。　　　　　　　　　　　　　(合集 41410)

(69)中的"△",或以爲是祭品名。這條卜辭卜問,到"彡衣"祭時才用"△"舉行侑祭好不好。

(70) 惠日妝。
　　 于入自日廼妝。　　　　　　　　　　　　　　　　(合集 29713)

---

① 裘錫圭:《釋䄆》,《古文字研究》第 3 輯,7—13 頁,北京:中華書局,1980。

這個例子在討論作 Aa1 類詞用的"叀"字時已引用過,可參看。

(71A)［于］［入］自□廼敃小丁,又正。

(71B) 于入自☒。　　　　　　　　　　　　　　　　　　(合集 27332)

上引這兩條卜辭都有殘缺,依據(71B),可以在(71A)中的"自"前補出"于"和"入"兩字。(71A)卜問,是否到從某種祭祀的場所進入(宗廟)時才"敃"祭小丁。

上引例(66)至例(71)是"于"和"廼"相照應的用例,"于……廼……"表示了這樣的時間關係:到了一事發生時才進行另一件事。

在卜辭中,還可見到"于"、"既"、"廼"聯合使用的例子:

(72A) 戍興伐,卯方食☒。

(72B) 于方既食戍廼伐,戋。　　　　　　　　　　　　　(合集 28000)

(72)中的"戍"是武官名。這對卜辭卜問,戍是趁著敵人吃飯時進行攻擊會勝利,還是等到敵人吃完飯時才進攻會勝利。①

(73) 于既酒父丁翌日祭日彡日,王廼賓。　　　　　　　(合集 32714)

這個例子在討論賓字句的結構時已引用過,可參看。這是卜問,到了爲父丁的"翌日"、"祭日"、"彡日"舉行完酒祭時,王才去迎導神靈好不好。

(74) 于父己父庚既祤廼酒。　　　　　　　　　　　　　(合集 27416)

(74)卜問,到了"祤"祭完父己父庚時才舉行酒祭好不好。

上引例(72)至例(74)是"于"、"既"、"廼"聯合使用的例子,它們共同表示了這樣的時間關係:到了一件事結束後才進行另一件事情。

在上面,我們討論了單獨使用的"于"以及和"既"、"廼"聯合使用的"于",這兩種"于"都屬於 Aa2 類詞。

b. 卯(必)

甲骨卜辭中有"卯"和"丨"字,裘錫圭先生釋爲"卯"和"必",這是可信的。②

卜辭中的"卯"(必)和古文獻中的"比"聲音極近,而且有些"卯"(必)和

---

① 裘錫圭:《釋秘》,《古文字研究》第 3 輯,7—13 頁,北京:中華書局,1980。
② 裘錫圭:《釋秘》,《古文字研究》第 3 輯,7—13 頁,北京:中華書局,1980。下文所引的關於"卯"(必)的說法皆見於此文,不再贅注。

有些"比"在用法上也相同（比如，兩者都可出現在"□＋VT＋VP"或"VP＋□＋VT"中"□"的位置上，把"VT"介紹給"VP"）。這種"卯"（必）跟"比"的意義當是相近的（裘錫圭先生疑此種"卯"（必）即當讀爲"比"），應是到或趁著的意思。

裘先生認爲，第三、四期卜辭裏的"卯"和一、二期裏的一些"必"字，好像是用作表示時間關係的介詞的，此說甚是。先請看裘先生舉過的三個例子：

(75A) 戌興伐卯方食☐。
(75B) 于方既食戌廼伐，戈。　　　　　　　　　　　（合集 28000）
(76) 辛卯卜：卯彡酒，其又于四方。　　　　　　　　（合集 30394）
(77A) 虢叀卯各于祼用，王受又。
(77B) 于入自祼用，王受又。　　　　　　　　　　　（合集 27281）

上引（75）、（77）兩例，在討論"于"字的時候都曾引用並解釋過，可參看。在（75）中，A、B以"卯方食"和"于方既食"構成對貞，"方食"和"方既食"都是表示"戌"舉行"伐"的時間的，"方既食"前的"于"是表示兩事時間關係的，"方食"前的"卯"也應是表示兩事時間關係的。又從上引（75A）來看，"卯"可以出現在"VP＋□＋VT"中"□"的位置上；從上引（76）來看，"卯"又可以出現在"□＋VT＋VP"中"□"的位置上。這種"卯"與表示兩事時間關係的"于"有著相同的分佈，"卯"應跟"于"一樣屬於介詞（裘先生疑這種"卯"當讀爲"比"，若此說可信，則"卯"無疑當看成介詞，因爲古文獻中的把"VT"介紹給"VP"的"比"即是介詞）。上引（77A）中的"卯"前用了"叀"，表示時間關係的"于"前也可以用"叀"，他辭或言"丙午卜，叀于甲子酒甗"（合集 32053，合集 32485 同文），可以爲證。由上述看來，把"卯"看成是跟"于"有同樣性質、同樣作用的詞應是沒有問題的。

除了上引三個例子之外，裘先生在《釋秘》一文中還舉了下面一些"卯"（必）用作表示兩事時間關係的詞的例子（因裘先生對這些例子已作了較具體的解釋，故這裏不再解釋）：

(78) 乙丑卜，出貞：大史必酒，先酒，其侑匚于丁卅牛。七月。

　　　　　　　　　　　　　　　　　　　　　　　　（合集 23064）

(79) 己丑卜，彭貞：其爲祖丁賓門于魯卒卯彡。　　　（甲 2769）
(80) 兄辛歲，叀卯各于日皮。　　　　　　　　　　　（合集 27625）

(81) 禱父己父庚,惠㘱往△。 （合集 27415）

(82) 丙辰卜,即貞:惠必出于夕禦馬。 （合集 23602）

(83) 癸亥卜,即貞:翌甲子其又于兄庚,惠必賓祊。 （合集 23481）

下面三個例子,在《釋柲》一文中未曾引到:

(84A) 惠癸登黍,王受又。

(84B) 王其登二勺,惠㘱各藝祼酒。

(84C) 其登黍祖乙,惠翌日乙酉酒。 （屯南 618）

上引（84）中的"登"可訓爲"升",是奉獻的意思。"勺",陳夢家釋爲"升",以爲同"宗"一樣是藏王之所（看《殷虛卜辭綜述》470 頁）。上引（84A）卜問,是否在癸那天奉獻黍子。（84B）卜問,王將要對"二勺"奉獻黍子,到參加"藝祼"時舉行酒祭好不好。（84C）卜問,將奉獻黍子給祖乙,在乙酉那天舉行酒祭好不好。引例中的"酒"祭是爲"登"祭舉行的。

(85) 惠㘱各日酒。 （懷特 1386）

這條卜辭卜問,是否趁著參加"日"祭時舉行酒祭。

(86A) 其磔父己,惠入自▢。

(86B) 惠㘱各祼。

(86C) 于入自祼。 （屯南 2140）

上引（86A）中的"磔"是祭名。（86A）的"自"後有殘缺。（86B）、（86C）後都省說了一個祭名,這個祭名所表示的祭祀當是爲父己的"磔"祭舉行的。（86B）、（86C）卜問,是趁著參加祼祭時舉行某種祭祀好,還是等到從祼祭的場所進入（宗廟）時舉行某種祭祀好。

由上述可見,甲骨卜辭中的"㘱"（必）有些是作 Aa2 類詞用的。

作爲 Aa2 類詞,"于"和"㘱"（必）很相近,但是,兩者是有區別的。在甲骨卜辭中,有的"㘱"可當趁著講,比如前引例（75）"戍興伐,㘱方食"中的"㘱"即是此義;"于"字則無此義。又從前引例（75）、例（77）、例（86）來看,"㘱"後所記之時比"于"後所記之時距卜時近。此外,"㘱（必）+ VT + VP"前常用語氣副詞"惠",但是,在"于 + VT + VP"前則少用"惠"（由於其所處的位置與作 Aa2 類詞的"惠"的不同,這種"惠"不必看成是表示兩事時間關係的詞,它的作用當是對其後的成分的強調）。"于"可在一對對貞卜辭中出現

在與"惠"相對的位置上,而"卯"(必)則不在這種位置上出現。

c. 戠₁

在甲骨卜辭中有"戠"字。裘錫圭先生發現,有些"戠"字跟好多動詞(如"占"、"步"、"出"、"入"、"歸"、"比"、"酒"、"用"、"退"、"使"等等)正反相對。他認為,這些"戠"應讀為"待",因為從語音上看,"戠"和"待"很相近;從語義上看,把各辭裏的"戠"讀為"待"都很合適。①

在先秦時代的文獻中,"待"字也跟好多動詞正反相對。例如:

(a) 不待而歸。　　　　　　　　　　　　　　　　　　　　(左傳·定公五年)
(b) 弗待而出。　　　　　　　　　　　　　　　　　　　(左傳·襄公二十四年)
(c) 子産不待而對客。　　　　　　　　　　　　　　　　(左傳·昭公十九年)
(d) 如不待其招而往。　　　　　　　　　　　　　　　　　(孟子·滕文公下)
(e) 是不待教而誅也。　　　　　　　　　　　　　　　　　　(孟子·萬章下)
(f) 以治伐亂,不待戰而後知克。　　　　　　　　　　　　　　(荀子·大略)

上引諸例中的"待"與"歸"、"出"、"對"、"往"、"誅"、"知"等動詞正反相對,正與卜辭中有些"戠"相類。又試把上引例(a)、例(b)和下兩類相比較,可知"待"與"戠"正相當:

(87) 弜戠,歸。　　　　　　　　　　　　　　　　　　　　　(合集 33980)

試與前引例(a)"不待而歸"相比較。

(88) ☒王勿出,戠。　　　　　　　　　　　　　　　　　　　(合集 5067)

當要表達與例(88)相反的意思時,就要說"王勿戠,出"。試與前引例(b)"弗待而出"相比較。

可見,卜辭中有些"戠"確實應讀為"待",裘先生之說不可易。

卜辭中有些讀為"待"的"戠",是表示時間關係的。例如:

(89A) 于丁卯酒。
(89B) 戠辛酒。　　　　　　　　　　　　　　　　　　　　　(合集 30173)
(90) 戠日甲申酒,王受又。　　　　　　　　　　　　　　　　(合集 29699)

---

① 裘錫圭:《說甲骨卜辭中"戠"字的一種用法》,見《古文字論集》,111—116 頁,北京:中華書局,1992。

上引（89A）和（89B）以"于丁卯"和"哉辛"構成對貞，"于丁卯"中的"丁卯"是時間詞，"于"是表示時間關係的介詞；"哉辛"中的"辛"也是時間詞，"哉"應同"于"一樣具有把時間詞介紹給"VP"的作用。上引（90）中的"哉"與（89）中的"哉"作用相同（參看《説卜辭中的"至日""即日""哉日"》）。這種"哉"應看成動詞或介詞。

卜辭中讀爲"待"的"哉"有時出現在"□＋VT＋VP"中"□"的位置上，把"VT"介紹給"VP"，這種"哉"就是表示兩事之間時間關係的詞了。例如：

（91）己丑[卜]，古貞：哉侑酒。（合集 15761）

這條卜辭卜問，等到侑祭的時候舉行酒祭好不好。

（92）哉陟酒。（合集 41636）

上例中"哉"後的那個字，島邦男疑是"陟"字①。若此説可信，則此例中的"哉"也是作 Aa2 類詞用的了。

總之，卜辭中有些"哉"字是用來表示一事等到某一時間進行這樣的時間關係的。

在卜辭中，還見到下面兩個用"哉"的例子：

（93A）己丑貞：弜哉，辛步。
（93B）哉禱，于乙步。（合集 33707）
（94）□亥卜，貞：弜哉禱，辛步。（合集 33706）

從（94）來看，（93A）中的"哉"後省説了"禱"。（93）這對卜辭卜問，不要等待（舉行禱祭），在辛那天就"步"好，還是要等待舉行禱祭，到乙那天再"步"好。（94）這條卜辭與（93A）意思相同。上引兩例中的"哉"，並不是用來表示等到禱祭時再"步"這樣的關係的。這種"哉"還不能算是表示兩事時間關係的詞。

"哉"和"于"、"卯"（必）雖然都可作 Aa2 類詞用，但是，它們有分別："哉"基本意思是等待，而"于"、"卯"（必）則不是。

(3) Aa3 類詞：由

屬於 Aa3 類詞的，只有"由"字。

---

① 島邦男：《殷墟卜辭綜類》，355 頁，日本：汲古書院，1977。

在古代文獻中,"由"字和它的賓語可以表示時間的起點。例如:

(a) 由周而來,七百有餘歲矣。　　　　　　　　　　　　(孟子・公孫丑下)
(b) 由孔子而來至於今,百有餘歲矣。　　　　　　　　　(孟子・盡心下)

在甲骨卜辭中,有"凷"字,唐蘭釋爲"由",可信。

有些"由"字,出現在"□+時間詞語+VP"中"□"的位置上,把時間詞語介紹給"VP"。這種"由"字,可看成是介詞或動詞,是"從"的意思。例如:

(95) 壬寅卜,貞:由郭往,有□。　　　　　　　　　　　(合集 3417)

上引(95)中的"郭",應是個時間詞,他辭或言"今日乙郭啟,不雨"(合集 30203)、"戾至郭不雨"(掇 1・394)、"□至郭啟"(粹 652),可以爲證。這條卜辭卜問,是否從"郭"時起出去。

(96) □□[卜],賓貞:巤告曰:方由今春凡,受有又。　　　(合集 4596)
(97) 乙酉卜,爭貞:巤告曰:方由今春凡,受有又。　　　(合集 4597)

上引兩例中的"凡",于省吾先生讀爲侵犯之"犯",可信。其中的"由"字,于先生以"從"字釋之,亦有據①。上兩例中的"由",或讀爲"酋",認爲"方由"即是"方酋",此說不可從。從"壬戌卜:方其凡"(鐵 237・1)一辭來看,"方由今春凡"中"凡"的施事是"方";又把"方由今春凡"和"由郭往"相比較,可知這兩小句中的"由"都是表示時間關係的詞,都當譯爲"從"。可見,于說爲是。"方由今春凡"是說敵人從今年春天起進犯。

上引(95)至(97)中的"由",出現在"□+時間詞語+VP"中"□"的位置上,把時間詞語介紹給"VP"。有些"由"字,出現在"□+VT+VP"或"VP+□+VT"中"□"的位置上,把"VT"介紹給"VP"。這種"由"字,就是表示兩事時間關係的詞了。例如:

(98) 戊子卜,殷貞:王勿由昝往出。　　　　　　　　　　(合集 16108)
(99) 貞:王勿往出由昝。　　　　　　　　　　　　　　　(合集 16108)

試把上引(98)中的"由昝往出"和前引(95)中的"由郭往"相比較,當知(98)中的"由"同(95)中的"由"一樣是用來表示時間關係的,當知

―――――――――
① 于省吾:《甲骨文字釋林》,426—427 頁,北京:中華書局,1979。

（98）中的"叠"同（95）中的"郭"一樣是表示時間的（"叠"本是"祭名"，但常用來表示時間，他辭或言"升歲，于劦叠"《合集》34615，可以爲證。"叠"和"劦"記錄的是同一個詞）。王的"往出"這種活動是要經歷一段時間的（試對有"王往出"的卜辭進行考察，可以知道，"王往出"後的動詞有"狩"、"省"、"田"等等，如："王勿往出狩"《七》T14、"王往出省"《佚》381、"王往出田"《合》220；"王往出"後的處所詞有"甘"、"庙"、"敦"、"宿"等等，如："王往出于甘"《後》上12·4、"王往出于庙"《存》1·616、"王往出于敦"《簠·游》13、"〔王〕往出于宿"《佚》538。由上述兩點看來，王"往出"這種活動是需時較久的），"由叠"即表示"往出"這種活動的時間起點。上引（98）卜問，王不要從"叠"祭時起出去好不好。（98）中的"由叠"出現在"往出"前，（99）中的"由叠"出現在"往出"之後。儘管如此，（98）、（99）中命辭的基本意思是相同的。

　　總之，卜辭中有些"由"字作 Aa3 類詞用，表示一事自某一時間起進行這樣的關係。

　　上面，我們討論了卜辭中 Aa 類詞的意義和用法。前面講過，Aa 類詞是指把"VT"介紹給"VP"的詞。把時間詞語、代詞（指代時間）及專有名詞（用來表示時間）介紹給"VP"的詞，我們則稱之爲 Aa' 類詞。這兩類詞的關係非常密切（Aa 類詞多數同時作 Aa' 類詞用），因此，我們在這裏附帶講講卜辭中的 Aa' 類詞。

　　由前面的敘述中，我們可以看到，"惠"、"即"、"于"、"戠"、"由"諸詞既可把"VT"介紹給"VP"，也可以把時間詞語介紹給"VP"。那麼，這幾個詞既屬於 Aa 類詞，也屬於 Aa' 類詞。

　　"孖"（必）的情況比較特殊，它一般是出現在"□＋VT＋VP"中"□"的位置上。只有在後面帶上"至"，才可出現在"時間詞語＋VP"前。例如：

（100）翌日庚其柬乃雩，孖至來庚亡大雨。
　　　翌日庚其柬乃雩，孖至來庚又大雨。　　　　　　　　　　（合集 31199）

　　在卜辭中，還有一些詞，我們只見到其作 Aa' 類詞用的例子，未見到其作 Aa 類詞用的例子，如"唯"、"在"、"及"、"至"（至于）、"自"、"終"、"湄"等。

　　作爲 Aa' 類詞，"唯"和"在"是用來表示一事在基本一時間進行這樣的關係的。例如：

(101) 帝唯今二月令雷。　　　　　　　　　　　　　　　（合集 14129 反）

(102) 唯今夕癸見丁。　　　　　　　　　　　　　　　　（合集 667 反）

(103) 己巳卜，彭貞：禦于河羌三十人。

　　　在十月又二卜。　　　　　　　　　　　　　　　　（甲 2491）

　　卜辭中的作 Aa' 類詞用的"惠"、"唯"和"在"、"即"雖然都是用來表示一事在（或當）某一時間進行的，但它們有所不同。"惠"、"唯"都是語氣副詞，它們只是客觀上具有把時間詞語介紹給"VP"的作用，"在"、"即"則應看成是介詞或動詞；"惠"、"唯"義虛而"在"、"即"義實。

　　"唯"可作 Aa' 類詞用，"惠"也可以這樣用，這兩個詞有相同處，也有相異處。

　　"在"與"即"有別，"即"是當或就在的意思，"在"就是在的意思。

　　卜辭中的"及"有時用來表示一事趕在某一時間之內進行這樣的關係。例如：

(104) 戊子卜，殻貞：帝及四月令雨。　　　　　　　　　（合集 14138）

(105) 乙酉卜，大貞：及兹二月有大雨。　　　　　　　　（合集 24868）

　　在卜辭中，有一部分"至"是用來表示一事到某一時間進行這樣的關係的。例如：

(106) 惠今夕酒。

　　　于翌日甲酒。

　　　其至日戊酒。

　　　磔其至父甲。

　　　弜。　　　　　　　　　　　　　　　　　　　　　（合集 27454）

(107) 夔祭，[弜]至日酒。

　　　其至日。　　　　　　　　　　　　　　　　　　　（屯南 4582）

　　上引兩例中標有著重號的"至"，是把時間詞語（"日戊"、"日"）介紹給"酒"的，用來表示"酒"祭到某一時間舉行（看《説卜辭中的"至日""即日""哉日"》）。

　　卜辭中另一部分"至"（至于）是用來表示一事一直到基本一時間仍如此的。例如：

(108) 自今庚子至于甲辰帝令雨。
　　　至甲辰帝不其令雨。　　　　　　　　　　　　　　　（合集 900）

(109) 丁至庚不遘小雨。
　　　丁至庚其遘小雨。　　　　　　　　　　　　　　　　（合集 28546）

(110) 昃至郭兮不雨。　　　　　　　　　　　　　　　　　（合集 29793）

(111) 己巳帝允令雨至于庚。　　　　　　　　　　　　　　（合集 14153 反）

(112) 今日至于丁亥易日。　　　　　　　　　　　　　　　（合集 22915）

　　這種用法的"至"（以下稱爲"至$_1$"）跟前面講過的表示一事到某一時間進行這樣的關係的"至"（以下稱爲"至$_2$"）應當區別開來：當"至"與前面的"自"配合使用時，它一定是"至$_1$"；當"至＋時間詞語＋VP"前又有一個時間詞語時（如前引第 109 例、第 110 例），它也應是"至$_1$"；當"至"出現在"□＋時間詞語＋VP"中"□"的位置上時，它就可能是"至$_1$"，也可能是"至$_2$"，須根據上下文仔細判別。在卜辭中，"至于"一般只用來表示某事一直到某時仍然如此這樣的關係。

　　卜辭中作 Aa' 類詞用的"哉"、"于"、"至"、"及"很相近，但它們之間有差異。前面講過，"哉"的基本意義是等待，這有別於"及"、"至"、"于"諸詞。"及"的意思是趁著，這和"至"、"于"不一樣。"至"和"于"的意思雖然大致相同，但兩者仍有區別："于"還常作 Aa 類詞用，"至"則一般不這樣用；"至"有時用來表示某事一直到某時仍然如此，"于"則不能表示這樣的關係；"于"常在一對選貞卜辭中出現在與"叀"相對的位置上，"至"則不在這種位置上出現。

　　在甲骨卜辭中，有些"大"字出現在："□＋時間詞語＋VP"中"□"的位置上。例如：

(113) 貞：大今三月雨。　　　　　　　　　　　　　　　　（合集 12528）

(114) 大今月不其雨。　　　　　　　　　　　　　　　　　（合集 12529）

　　對於這種"大"，郭沫若解釋說："大假爲達，達从羍聲，羍从大聲。又達或作达，正从大聲。"①若郭氏此說爲是，則這種"大"就是用來表示一事到某一時間進行這樣的關係的詞了。但是，這種用法的"大"字僅此兩見，顯然可有幾種解釋；在古代文獻中，"達"並沒有作 Aa' 類詞用的，把上兩例中的"大"讀爲

---

① 郭沫若：《殷契粹編考釋》，555 頁，日本東京：文求堂石印本，1937。

"達"，缺乏文獻上證據；若把這種"大"讀爲"達"，"達今"相連，語意不貫。這種"大"的意義待考。

卜辭中有些"气"字，或以爲當讀爲迄至之"迄"，是表示時間關係的詞，其說也有問題。

卜辭中的"自"常用來表示某事從某一時間起進行這樣的關係：

(115) 辛亥卜，師：自今五日雨。　　　　　　　　　　　　（合集 20902）

(116) 自今旬雨。　　　　　　　　　　　　　　　　　　　（合集 12480）

作 Aa' 類詞用的"自"常與"至"、"至于"相照應，"自……至……"、"自……至于……"用來表示一事在某一段時間内進行這樣的關係。例如：

(117) 自今五六日至壬辰有至。　　　　　　　　　　　　　（合集 11661）

(118) 癸酉卜：自今至丁丑其雨。不。
　　　自今至丁丑不其雨。允不。　　　　　　　　　　　（合集 21052）

(119) 自今至己卯雨。　　　　　　　　　　　　　　　　　（合集 10516）

(120) 丁巳卜，㫃貞：自今至于庚申不雨。　　　　　　　　（合集 12324 正）

作 Aa' 類詞用的"自"和"由"很相近，但它們有差異："自"常與"至"、"至于"相照應，而"由"字在卜辭中不與"至"、"至于"相照應；"自"字常見而"由"字不常見。

卜辭中"从"字常見，但未見其作 Aa' 類詞用的例子。

卜辭中的"終"和"湄"是表示某事在某一段時間内一直都在進行這樣的關係的。例如：

(121) 癸卯卜：甲啟。不啟，終夕雨。　　　　　　　　　　（屯南 744）

(122) 辛未卜，内：翌壬申啟。壬終日陰。　　　　　　　　（合集 13140）

(123) 辛酉卜：今日辛王其田，湄日亡災。　　　　　　　　（屯南 659）

(124) 翌日乙王其省田，湄日不遘雨。　　　　　　　　　　（屯南 272）

上引（123）、（124）中的"湄"，楊樹達以爲應當讀爲"彌"，訓爲"終"①，此說現在已爲大多數甲骨學者所接受。卜辭中"湄"和"終"的意義可能是相近的，但是，兩者用法有所不同："湄"字出現在田獵卜辭中，而"終"字則不然；"湄"字大都出現在否定句中，而"終"字則在肯定句、否定句中都可出

---

① 楊樹達：《楊樹達文集》之五，73頁，上海古籍出版社，1986。

現；"湄"帶上它的賓語出現在句子中的否定詞前（例如："湄日不遘雨"《屯南》272），"終"帶上它的賓語出現在否定詞後（例如："貞：不其終夕雨"《福》32）；"終"的賓語除"日"外，還有"夕"，而"湄"的賓語只有"日"。

在甲骨卜辭中，還有"衣"和"屯"字，有時也出現在"□＋時間詞語＋VP"中"□"的位置上，有人認爲它們的意義和用法與"終"、"湄"相近，是否可信待考。

總之，在甲骨卜辭中，"唯"、"在"、"及"、"至"（至于）、"自"、"終"、"湄"等詞有時是作 Aa' 類詞用的，它們一般不作 Aa 類詞用。

在周秦時代的文獻中，"唯"、"至"、"及"、"自"等詞有作 Aa 類詞用的例子：

(a) 唯四月，白懋父北征，唯還，呂行黃，孚貝。

(呂行壺)(《雙劍誃吉金文選》下 2・5)

(b) 王南征，伐角僪，唯還自征，在砠，噩侯馭方內豐于王。

(噩侯馭方鼎)(三代 4・32・1)

(c) 子列子笑謂之曰：君非自我知也。以人之言而遺我粟。至其罪我也，又且以人之言。此吾所以不受也。 (莊子・讓王)

(d) 及反，市罷，遂不得履。 (韓非子・外儲說左上)

(e) 及其飲酒也，先伐諸。 (左傳・昭公十年)

(f) 自有生民以來，未有孔子也。 (孟子・公孫丑上)

(g) 楚自克庸以來，其君無日不討國人而訓之于民生之不易、禍至之無日、戒懼之不可以怠。 (左傳・宣公十二年)

2. Ab 類詞

屬於這一類詞的有"眔"、"摯"、"戠₂"、"先₁"、"後₁"等。

a. 眔

"眔"，本是個動詞，表示一種動作，多是"跟……一塊兒"的意思。例如：

(125) 貞：惠師乎眔甾。 (合集 6857)

(126) 惠△令眔多子族。 (合集 14921)

(127) 壬子卜，爭貞：惠戊乎眔甾。

貞：惠師令旋眔長。 (合集 6855 正)

(128) 壬子卜，爭貞：惠戊乎眔。　　　　　　　　　　　　　　（合集 6856）

(129) 勿乎宁鼓眔。　　　　　　　　　　　　　　　　　　　（合集 3508）

從上引（127）來看，（128）中的"眔"後應是省說了一個名詞，（129）中的"眔"後亦然。上引（125）是說，讓"師"跟"㠯"在一塊兒，此例中的"眔"是表示（師）跟（㠯）在一塊兒這樣的行為的。其餘幾個例子中的"眔"類此。

下例中的"眔"也是動詞。例如：

(130A) 甲寅卜：其登鬯于祖乙，小乙眔。

(130B) 弜眔。

(130C) 祖乙卯牢。

(130D) 牢又二牛。

(130E) 二牢。

(130F) 小乙其眔，一牛。　　　　　　　　　　　　　　　　（屯南 657）

上引（130A）"其登鬯于祖乙"後有"小乙眔"一小句，這個小句是在說小乙跟（祖乙）一起（受"登鬯"），其實就是在奉獻鬯酒給祖乙的同時奉獻鬯酒給小乙這樣的意思，這小句中的"眔"字事實上是用來表示兩事時間關係的。（130B）中的"眔"亦然。上引（130C）、（130D）、（130E）是在卜問，用"牢"、"卯"祭祖乙好，還是用一"牢"加二頭牛或二"牢"（"卯"祭祖乙）好。（130F）中的"小乙其眔"這一小句是說小乙跟（祖乙）一起（受"卯"祭），其實就是在"卯"祭祖乙的同時"卯"祭小乙這樣的意思，這小句中的"眔"事實上也是用來表示兩事時間關係的。

下引兩例中的"眔"似是使動用法的動詞。例如：

(131A) 辛亥貞：又升于二示。

(131B) 弜又。

(131C) 眔奭。

(131D) 弜眔奭。　　　　　　　　　　　　　　　　　　　　（合集 34106）

(132A) 眔羌甲。

(132B) 弜眔。　　　　　　　　　　　　　　　　　　　　　（合集 27260）

（131A）中的"二示"是指示壬、示癸。（131A）、（131B）卜問，是"又升"祭示壬示癸好，還是不"又"祭好。（131C）中的"眔奭"似乎不能解釋為（"二示"）跟他們的配偶一塊兒（受"又升"祭），即不是在"又升"祭其配偶的同時

"又升""二示"這樣的意思,因爲在殷代先妣一般隨所配之王受祀,而不是相反。"眾奭"中的"眾",似乎是使動用法的動詞(這種用法的動詞在卜辭中常見,如"貞:不其來象"中的"來"。《後》下 5·11),"眾奭"似是説讓"二示"的配偶跟("二示")一塊兒(受"又升"祭),實際上可能是讓"二示"的配偶在"二示"受"又升"祭的同時受"又升"祭這樣的意思,其中的"眾"事實上也是用來表示兩事之間的時間關係的。(131D)、(132A)、(132B)中的"眾"字同此。

下例中的"眾"當看成介詞,事實上也是用來表示兩事時間關係的:

(133A) 辛丑卜:公禱,惠今日酒,王受又。

(133B) 于癸酒,王受又。

(133C) 于父己父庚既祭廼酒。

(133D) 夕酒,王受又。

(133E) 公眾二父酒。　　　　　　　　　　　　　　　　　　　(合集 27416)

上引(133A)至(133D)都是在卜問在什麼時候爲公的禱祭舉行酒祭好,(133E)也應是卜問爲公的禱祭舉行酒祭的時間的。(133E)中的"眾"出現在"NP1(公)+□+NP2(二父)+VP(酒)"中的"□"的位置上,把"NP2"介紹給"VP"。(133E)一句,從字面上講,是公跟父己父庚一起受酒祭的意思,其實就是在酒祭父己父庚的同時酒祭公的意思,其中的"眾",事實上表示出了"酒父己父庚"一事爲"酒公"一事的時間背景這樣的關係。這種用法的"眾"在甲骨卜辭中很常見。例如:

(134A) 甲辰卜:大乙眾上甲酒,王受又。

(134B) 弜眾。

(134C) ☐先上甲酒。

(134D) 三匚二示眾上甲酒,王受又。

(134E) 弜眾。　　　　　　　　　　　　　　　　　　　　　(屯南 2265)

上例中的"三匚",是指報乙、報丙、報丁,"二示"是指示壬、示癸。(134A)、(134B)卜問,大乙是否跟上甲一起受酒祭。(134D)、(134E)卜問,"三匚二示"是跟上甲一起受酒祭好,還是不一起受酒祭好。(134C)中的"先"字前面當殘去"神名",這條卜辭可能是在卜問,某神或某幾位神在上甲之先受酒祭好不好。

(135A) 其禱年,河眔岳酒,又大雨。

(135B) 弜眔酒。　　　　　　　　　　　　　　　　（人1943）

上引（135）中的"酒",顯然是爲"禱"祭舉行的,或者説是在"禱"祭這種儀式中舉行的。這對卜辭卜問,將要爲年成舉行"禱"祭,河神是跟岳神一起受酒祭會有大雨,還是不一起受酒祭（會有大雨）。

(136A) 于辛酉酒。

(136B) 岳眔河酒,王受又。　　　　　　　　　　　（合集30412）

這兩條卜辭是卜問岳神受酒祭的時間的。辭主不知是在辛酉那天酒祭岳神好,還是在酒祭河神的同時酒祭岳神好,故有此卜。

(137A) 父己眔父庚酒。

(137B) 于來日己。　　　　　　　　　　　　　　　（合集27419）

上例中的"父庚",其受酒祭的日子當是庚日。這兩條卜辭卜問,父己是在受酒祭好,還是到下一個己日受酒祭好。

(138) 丙午卜,貞:三祖丁眔祖丁酒,王受又又。　　（合集27181）

(139A) 己巳貞:示先入于商。

(139B) ［己］［巳］貞:示眔［羌］入。　　　　　　（合集28099）

從"示其先羌入。示其配羌。"（合集32029）一例來看,（139A）中的"先入",也當是指先羌而入,（139B）中的"眔"後殘掉了"羌"。（139）中的"示",是指廟主,"羌"指羌俘。這對卜辭卜問,廟主是在羌俘之先進入商好,還是跟羌俘一起進入（商）好。

(140A) 弜尊。

(140B) 庸鼓其眔熹鼓尊。　　　　　　　　　　　　（合集31017）

上引（140）中的"尊"應是置的意思（卜辭中的"尊"是個動詞,上引第一條卜辭中的"尊",受否定副詞"弜"修飾,這表明了它的性質。"尊"所涉及的對象有時是"鼓",他辭或言"癸丑卜,史貞:其尊鼓,告于唐牛。"《佚》870、"尊新鼓示"《前》5·4·4,可以爲證。"尊"在古代文獻中多用作名詞,但也有用作動詞的,例如:"側尊一甒醴"《儀禮·士冠禮》、"側尊甒醴於房中"《儀禮·士冠昏禮》。這種"尊"字,鄭玄以"置"訓之。甲骨卜辭中動詞用法的"尊",

也應當訓爲"置","尊鼓",應是設置鼓的意思,"尊新鼓",是說設置新的鼓,上引兩條卜辭中的"尊"與"尊鼓"之"尊"同義)。"庸",當讀爲"鏞",指大鐘,"熹"也是一種樂器的名稱①。(140B)卜問:與鏞配合的鼓是否跟與"熹"配合的鼓一起設置。

　　(141A) 己巳貞:其禘祖乙,眔父丁。
　　(141B) 弜眔父丁劀。　　　　　　　　　　　　　　　　(屯南 1128)

從(141B)來看,(141A)中的"眔父丁"當是"眔父丁劀"之省。"禘"和"劀"都是祭名,"劀"當是爲"禘"祭而舉行的。卜辭或言"其劀祖乙禘"(這是說將爲祖乙的"禘"祭舉行"劀"祭,參看第一篇文章②)(寧 1·178),可以爲證。上引這對卜辭卜問,將要"禘"祭祖乙了,(祖乙)是跟父丁一起(受"劀"祭)好,還是不跟父丁一起受"劀"祭好。

　　(142A) 祖乙奭眔酒。
　　(142B) 弜眔酒。　　　　　　　　　　　　　　　　　(合集 27519)

上引(142)中的"眔"後省說了一個神名,這個神名可能是祖乙。這對卜辭卜問,祖乙的配偶是跟(祖乙)一起受酒祭好,還是不一起受酒祭好。

　　(143A) 庚子卜:多母弟眔△。
　　(143B) 弜眔△。　　　　　　　　　　　　　　　　　(合集 41331)

上引(143)的"眔"後,也是省說了一個神名,"多母弟"應是祭祀的對象,"眔"後那個怪字應是祭名。這對卜辭卜問,"多母弟"是跟某神一起受某種祭祀好,還是不一起受某種祭祀好。

在上面,我們講了一些事實上用來表示兩事時間關係的"眔",這種"眔"字,多出現在"NP1 + □ + NP2 + VP"中"□"的位置上。這種位置上的"眔"字和一些連詞用法的"眔"字需加區別。

較易和表示時間關係的"NP1 + □ + NP2 + VP"中"□"的位置上的"眔"字相混的是表示兩個物件的聯合關係的"眔"字。讓我們先看看有這種連詞"眔"的例子:

　　(144A) 貞:邁眔永獲鹿,允獲。

---

① 裘錫圭:《甲骨文中的幾種樂器名稱》,《中華文史論叢》1980 年第 2 輯。
② 編者按:指作者《賓字句和邁字句的句法分析》一文。下同。

(144B) 貞：遘眾永不其獲鹿。　　　　　　　　　　　　　　　　（合集 1076）

上例中的"NP1＋眔＋NP2"作句子的施事主語。

(145A) 惠[囗]眔[囗]用，亡災。
(145B) 惠[囗]眔大騂，亡災。　　　　　　　　　　　　　　　（合集 36985）

上例中的"NP1＋眔＋NP2"作句子的受事主語。在（145B）的"騂"後省說了動詞"用"。

(146A) 惠母己眔子癸酒。
(146B) 惠兄辛眔子癸先。　　　　　　　　　　　　　　　　（合集 27633）

（146B）中的"先"後，應是省說了"酒"。此例中的"神名＋眔＋神名"是祭祀動詞"酒"涉及的對象，這個聯合結構因其前加"惠"而前置於"VP"，作句子的主語。

(147A) 王往于田，弗以祖丁眔父乙，唯之。
(147B) 王弗以祖丁眔父乙，不唯之。
(147C) 王弗以祖丁眔父乙，唯之。　　　　　　　　　　　　（合集 10515）

上例中的"NP1＋眔＋NP2"作句子的受事賓語。

(148) 翌日□王令右旅眔左旅甾見方，戉，不雉眾。　　　　（屯南 2328）

上例中的"NP1＋眔＋NP2"作句子的兼語。

(149) 其又兄丙眔子癸。　　　　　　　　　　　　　　　　（合集 27501）

上例中的"NP1＋眔＋NP2"爲動詞涉及的對象，作句子的賓語。

(150A) 癸未卜，殻貞：告于妣己眔妣庚。
(150B) 貞：勿告于妣己眔妣庚。　　　　　　　　　　　　　（合集 1248）

上例中的"NP1＋眔＋NP2"作介詞的賓語。

(151) 辛眔壬王弜往于田，其毎。　　　　　　　　　　　　（合集 28605）
(152) □□卜：丁眔戊王□。　　　　　　　　　　　　　　（合集 31729）

上兩例中的"NP1＋眔＋NP2"出現在主謂結構前作時間修飾語。

(153) 戊子卜，疑貞：王曰：余其曰多尹，其令二侯：上絲眔倉侯，其□周。
　　　　　　　　　　　　　　　　　　　　　　　　　　　（合集 23560）

（154）戊寅卜，貞：令甫从二侯：及眔元，王循于□，若。　　（合集 7242）

　　上兩例中的"NP1＋眔＋NP2"爲本位語。（144）至（154）中的"眔"，都是連接兩個名詞語的。從這些例子中，我們可以看到，作主語、賓語的"NP1＋眔＋NP2"中的連詞"眔"跟表示兩事時間關係的"眔"雖然很相近，但仍有明顯區別：

　　首先，表示時間關係的"眔"前可以出現副詞性的修飾成分。例如：

　　庸鼓其眔熹鼓尊。　　（合集 31017）

　　其禱年，河眔岳酒，又大雨。

　　弜眔酒。　　（人 1943）

　　己巳貞：其禘祖乙，眔父丁。

　　弜眔父丁卯。　　（屯南 1128）

上引第一例的"眔"前出現了"其"，第二例、第三例的第二條卜辭中的"眔"前都用了"弜"。"其"、"弜"都是副詞。上引第二、第三例第一條卜辭中的"眔"前，若從其否定語意的那條卜辭來看，也可以出現副詞性的修飾成分。但是表示兩個物件聯合關係的"眔"前從不出現也不可能出現副詞性修飾成分。當"NP1＋眔＋NP2"作句子的主語時，副詞性的修飾成分或出現在"NP1＋眔＋NP2"的前出現（如前引第 145 例、第 146 例），或出現在其後：

　　豚眔羊皆用。　　（合集 31182）

　　雪眔門皆用，又雨。　　（合集 41411）

當"NP1＋眔＋NP2"作動詞賓語或介詞賓語時，副詞性的修飾成分就只能出現在句子中的動詞前（看前引第 149 例、第 150 例）。

　　其次，連詞"眔"前的"NP1"、其後的"NP2"都是不可省說的（看前引第 144 例至第 154 例），但是，表示時間關係的"眔"前的"NP1"有時省去，"眔"後的"NP2"有時也省去，有時甚至把"眔"前的"NP1"、其後的"NP2"一齊省掉，這種例子在前面都已經舉過了。

　　再次，表示時間關係的"眔"和"先"有時在一對選貞卜辭的相對位置上出現。例如：

　　示先入于商。

　　示眔［羌］入。　　（合集 28099）

但是，連詞的"眔"不會如此。

表示時間關係的"眔"和連詞"眔"之所以有上述的差異，是因爲兩者的性質及作用不同。表示時間關係的"眔"不是連詞，有的可看成動詞，有的可看成介詞。表示時間關係的"眔"的實際作用是表示一事爲另一事時間背景，而連詞"眔"的作用則是表示兩個物件的聯合關係。

在甲骨卜辭中，連詞的"眔"不但用來表示兩個物件的聯合關係，而且用來表示兩件事情的聯合關係。例如：

(155) 丙午卜，賓貞：血八羊眔酒卅牛。　　　　　　　　　（合集 16223）

(156) 庚寅卜：父乙歲眔妣。　　　　　　　　　　　　　（合集 32879）

(157A) 庚戌卜：其禱禾于河，沈三牢。

(157B) 庚戌卜：河卯三牢。

(158) 庚戌卜：高敔沈眔卯，兢。　　　　　　　　　　　（屯南 2667）

上引三例中的"VP1 + 眔 + VP2"或自成一句（如上引第 155 例、156 例），或自成一小句（如第 158 例）。

(159) 壬申卜，行貞：王賓兄己奏眔兄庚奏叔，亡尤。　　（合集 22624）

此例在討論賓字句的結構時曾引用過。此例中的"兄己奏眔兄庚奏"是"叔"的定語。"VP1 + 眔 + VP2"還可作賓語，這種例子在討論賓字句的結構時已引用過，可參看。我們之所以把這種"眔"字看成是連詞，是因爲這種"眔"字前面從不出現副詞性的修飾成分，而且這種"眔"字前後的"VP"從不省去（有時"VP"中的主要動詞可承前省去）。

這種連詞"眔"不是用來表示兩事的時間關係的，而是用來表示兩件事情的聯合關係的。其理由如下：

首先，在古代文獻中，連詞"及"出現在兩個"NP"之間，表示的是兩個物件的聯合關係；出現在兩個"VP"之間，則表示的是兩件事情的聯合關係。例如：

(a) 每吳中有大繇役及喪，項梁皆爲主辦，陰以兵法部勒賓客及子弟。

（史記・項羽本紀）

(b) 匈奴右賢王怨漢奪之河南地而築朔方，數爲寇盜邊，及入河南，侵擾朔方，殺略吏民甚衆。　　　　　　　　　　　　　　　　（史記・匈奴傳）

(c) 滇王與漢使者言曰：漢孰與我大。及夜郎侯亦然。（史記・西南夷傳）

卜辭中的意義爲"及"的"眔"字當跟文獻中的"及"字一樣，當字出現在兩個"NP"之間時，表示的是兩個物件的聯合關係；當它出現在兩個"VP"之間時，表示的則是兩件事情的聯合關係。

其次，若把"VP1＋眔＋VP2"中的"眔"解釋爲表示兩件事情間的聯合關係的詞，則可講通有這種"眔"出現的卜辭。例如，（156）"父乙歲眔妣"是說父乙受"歲"祭並受"妣"祭，（159）的"王賓兄己奏眔兄庚奏叔"是說王爲"兄己奏眔兄庚奏"的"叔"祭舉行迎神儀式，"兄己奏眔兄庚奏"是說兄己的"奏"祭和兄庚的"奏"祭。在討論賓字句的結構時，我們曾引用過下面兩個例子：

庚午卜，即貞：王賓兄庚登眔歲，亡尤。　　　　　　（合集 23485）
乙酉卜，囗貞：王其賓祖乙登眔□□登。　　　　　　（合集 27211）

上面第一例的"王賓兄庚登眔歲"是說王爲兄庚的"登"祭和"歲"祭舉行迎神儀式，上面第二例的"王其賓祖乙登眔□□登"是說王爲祖乙的"登"祭和某神的"登"祭舉行迎神儀式。總之，"VP1＋眔＋VP2"中的"眔"都應看成是用來表示兩件事情的聯合關係的。

再次，我們看到，不管是"王賓＋VP"這樣結構的卜辭，還是"王賓＋VP1＋眔＋VP2"這樣結構的卜辭，緊繼其後的另一條卜辭都是"王賓叔"。例如：

丁酉卜，行貞：王賓父丁歲，亡尤。
丁酉卜，行貞：王賓叔，亡尤。　　　　　　　　　　（合集 23184）
丁卯卜，行貞：王賓祖丁歲眔父丁歲一宰，亡尤。
丁卯卜，行貞：王賓叔，亡尤。　　　　　　　　　　（合集 24305）

這種現象可能反映出"王賓＋VP"和"王賓＋VP1＋眔＋VP2"中的"VP"和"VP1＋眔＋VP2"功能相同。既然如此，"VP1＋眔＋VP2"中的"VP1"和"VP2"之間應是聯合關係，"眔"應是表示這種關係的詞。"王賓＋VP1＋眔＋VP2"中的"眔"既然是表示兩事的聯合關係的，單獨成句的"VP1＋眔＋VP2"中的"眔"也應是如此。

總之，出現在兩個"VP"之間的"眔"是用來表示兩事之間的聯合關係的，不是用來表示兩事的時間關係的。

b. 攣

在甲骨卜辭中的"攣"，爲丁山所釋（《金文詁林》2531 至 2532 頁），較可

信。卜辭中有的"䜌"字的用法似是與有些"眔"字相近。例如：

(160A) 甲申卜：令以示先步。
(160B) 弜先、䜌王步。　　　　　　　　　　　　　　　　　　　　　（屯南 29）

（160A）中的"以示"，是説帶著廟主。從（160B）來看，（160A）中的"先步"，顯然是指先王而步。（160A）中的"先"事實上是用來表示兩件事情時間關係的詞（其説詳見下文），那麽，處在與這個"先"相對位置上的"䜌"也應看成是這種詞。這條卜辭中的"䜌"，或以爲"其音義同'聯'、'連'相近，有'從屬'、'相隨'之義"①。若此説可信，上引（160B）中的"䜌王步"就可解爲某人隨王一起"步"，也就是在王"步"的同時某人"步"的意思，其中的"䜌"字跟上面所述的"眔"一樣實際上表示出了一事爲另一事時間背景這樣的關係。

c. 戠₂

在甲骨卜辭中，還可見到下面這種用法的"戠"字。例如：

(161A) 毓□□先□□酒。
(161B) 毓祖丁戠大乙酒。　　　　　　　　　　　　　　　　　　　（合集 27145）

在上引（161A）中的"毓"後殘缺的兩字應是"祖丁"，"先"後殘缺的兩字應是"大乙"。在（161B）中，"戠"字出現在"NP1 + □ + NP2 + VP"中"□"的位置上，具有把"NP2"介紹給"VP"的作用。（161B）一句，從字面上講，是毓祖丁等待大乙一起受酒祭的意思，其實就是等到酒祭大乙時酒祭毓祖丁的意思，其中的"戠"實際上表示出了一事等到某一時間進行這樣的關係。

d. 先₁

在甲骨卜辭中，可見到下面這種用法的"先"字：

(162A) 癸亥示先羌入。
(162B) 示弜先、配羌。　　　　　　　　　　　（懷特 1644）（《合集》41465 同文）

上引（162A）中的"先"，出現在"NP1 + □ + NP2 + VP"中"□"的位置上（"NP1"前還出現了時間詞），具有把"NP2"介紹給"VP"的作用。（162A）中的"示先羌入"，從字面上講，是廟主在羌俘之先進入的意思，其實是在羌俘進入之先廟主進入的意思，其中的"先"事實上表示出了一事在另一事之先進行這樣的關係。這種"先"字，在甲骨卜辭中較常見。例如：

---

① 高智群等編：《西周金文選讀教學大綱》，復旦大學歷史系内部材料。

(163A) 示其先羌入。

(163B) 示其配羌。　　　　　　　　　　　　　　　　　（合集 32029）

上引（163）與前引（162）當是爲同一件事情而占卜的。

(164A) 己巳貞：示先入于商。

(164B) ［己］［巳］貞：示眔［羌］入。　　　　　　　　（合集 28099）

(165A) 甲申卜：令以示先步。

(165B) 弜先、擘王步。　　　　　　　　　　　　　　　　（屯南 29）

（164）在討論"眔"字的時候已引用過，（165）在討論"擘"字的時候也曾引用過，可參看。

(166) 大乙先上甲酒，王受又。　　　　　　　　　　　　（合集 27055）

這條卜辭卜問，大乙在上甲之先受酒祭好不好。

(167A) 毓［祖］［丁］先［大］［乙］酒。

(167B) 毓祖丁戠大乙酒。　　　　　　　　　　　　　　（合集 27145）

(168A) 甲辰卜：大乙眔上甲酒，王受又。

(168B) 弜眔。

(168C) ☐先上甲酒。　　　　　　　　　　　　　　　　（屯南 2265）

（167）在討論"戠"字的時候已引用過，（168）在討論"眔"字的時候也曾引用過，可參看。

　　總之，上引諸例中的"先"字，實際上是用來表示一事在另一事之先進行這樣的時間關係的詞。

　　e. 後$_1$

　　卜辭中有的"後"字可能也是作 Ab 類詞用的。例如：

(169A) 後王射兕，其叙。

(169B) 弜叙。　　　　　　　　　　　　　　　　　　　（屯南 2358）

上引（169）中的"叙"受"其"、"弜"修飾，應是個動詞。（169A）中的"後"前，應是省說了一個"NP"。"後王射兕"可能是某人在王後射殺"兕"的意思，其中的"後"，可能事實上表示出了一事在另一事之後進行這樣的時間關係。

(二) B 類詞

這類詞不用來表示一事爲另一事時間背景這樣的關係，只用來表示兩事有先後或共時關係。這類詞可分爲 Ba、Bb 兩類，Ba 類詞是用來表示兩事有先後關係的，Bb 類詞是用來表示兩事同時進行這樣的關係的。

1. Ba 類詞

屬於這一類詞的有 "先₂"、"既"、"咸"、"後₂"、"迺"（乃）、"延" 等。

a. 先₂

"先"，本是個動詞，表示一種動作。例如：

(1) 丁酉卜：馬其先，其每。　　　　　　　　　　（合集 27946）
(2) 其乎馬先，弗每。　　　　　　　　　　　　　（合集 27954）
(3) 丁卯卜，貞：禽往先。
　　貞：勿先。　　　　　　　　　　　　　　　　（合集 4068）
(4) 貞：勿乎帚井先。　　　　　　　　　　　　　（合集 2732）

(1)、(2) 中的 "馬"，乃是職官之名。(3) 中的 "禽"、(4) 中的 "帚井" 都是人名。(1) 至 (4) 中的 "先"，表示一種動作行爲，是走在前頭、先行的意思。在先秦典籍中，有些 "先" 字即是此義。例如：

(a) 壽子載其旌以先。　　　　　　　　　　　　（左傳・桓公十六年）
(b) 寧子先。　　　　　　　　　　　　　　　　（左傳・僖公二十八年）
(c) 子姑先乎。　　　　　　　　　　　　　　　（左傳・襄公十八年）

在甲骨卜辭中，上述這種意義的 "先" 字有用如使動的。例如：

(5) 弜先馬，其雨。　　　　　　　　　　　　　　（合集 27955）

(5) 中的 "先馬"，即是説讓 "馬" 先行。這種用法的 "先" 字，也見於先秦典籍中。例如：

(a) 狄人囚史華龍滑與禮孔，以逐衛人。二人曰："我，大史也，實掌其祭，不先，國不可得也。" 乃先之。　　　　　　　　　（左傳・閔公二年）

下例中的"先"與前引（1）至（4）中的"先"字同義：

  （6）戊申卜：馬其先，王兌（銳）从。   （合集 27945）

（6）中"馬其先"一小句後，又出現了"王兌从"一小句，這兩個小句是說，"馬"先行，王急速跟從。此例中的"先"雖主要是表示一種行爲動作的，但兼有表示兩事（"王行"和"王兌从"）時間關係的作用。

在先秦典籍中，有些動詞用法的"先"是居先、在先之義。例如：

  （a）故紀子以伯先也。   （穀梁傳·隱公二年）
  （b）先者見獲必務進。   （左傳·隱公九年）

這種意義的"先"應源於前一種意義的"先"，因爲走在前頭的必定是處在前面的。

前面講過，作 Ab 類詞用的"先₁"可看成介詞，是在……之先的意思，"先₁"應是由意義居先、在先的動詞用法的"先"虛化而成。

意義爲走在前頭、先行的動詞用法的"先"可用如使動（如上引第五例），意義爲居先、在先的動詞用法的"先"也可用如使動，例如：

  （a）先親而後祖也。   （穀梁傳·文公二年）
  （b）先大而後小，順也。   （左傳·文公二年）

甲骨卜辭中，這種用法的"先"字比較常見，而且大都是用來表示事情之間的先後關係的。例如：

  （7A）丙申卜，即貞：翌丁酉惠中丁歲先。
  （7B）貞：惠父丁。   （合集 22860）

上引（7A）中的"中丁歲"是"先"的受事，因其前出現"惠"而前置於"先"。（7B）的"父丁"後，明顯是承前省說了"歲先"。（7）中的"先"，是把……放在先的意思。這對卜辭卜問，丁酉那天是把中丁的"歲"祭放在先好，還是把父丁的"歲"祭放在先好。（7A）中的"先"實際上表示出了"歲中丁"一事在"歲父丁"一事之先，這種"先"事實上是表示兩件事的時間關係的詞。下引幾例中的"先"與上引（7A）中的"先"相同。

  （8A）先庚歲酒。
  （8B）先祖乙歲酒。   （合集 32532）

（8A）中的"庚歲酒"應解釋爲"庚歲"之"酒"，（8B）中的"祖乙歲酒"應解釋爲"祖乙歲"之"酒"（參看第一篇文章）。這對卜辭卜問，是把爲"庚"的"歲"祭舉行的酒祭放在先好，還是把爲祖乙的"歲"祭舉行的酒祭放在先好。

  （9A）辛亥卜，[行]貞：先□□歲妝。
  （9B）貞：先祖辛歲妝。　　　　　　　　　　　　　　（合集 22992）

（9A）中的"先"後殘掉了神名。這對卜辭卜問，是把爲某神的"歲"祭舉行的"妝"祭放在先好，還是把爲祖辛的"歲"祭舉行的"妝"祭放在先好。

  （10A）先高祖尞酒。
  （10B）惠河尞先酒。　　　　　　　　　　　　　　　（合集 32308）

（10A）中的"先"是動詞，（10B）中的"先"則應看成是副詞。（10）這對卜辭卜問，是把爲高祖的尞祭舉行的酒祭放在先好，還是先爲河神的尞祭舉行酒祭好。

  （11A）壬申貞：王又禦于祖乙，惠先。
  （11B）壬申貞：王又禦祖丁，惠先。　　　　　　　　　（屯南 4583）

前引（7A）"惠中丁歲先"中"先"的受事即是"中丁歲"，"中丁歲"用了"惠"，故前置於"先"。上引（11A）中的"先"的受事應是"又禦于祖乙"，但是"又禦于祖乙"卻出現在"惠先"前的小句中，在"惠先"中沒有出現。（11B）與（11A）情形相同。這對卜辭實際上是在卜問，王是把"又禦"祭祖乙一事放在先好，還是把"又禦"祭祖丁一事放在先好。

  上面列舉的都是成對選貞卜辭的例子。有時，由於某些原因（或因辭殘，或因未刻等），只出現了一對選貞卜辭中的一條卜辭。這條卜辭中的"先"也是用來表示兩事時間關係的，只是時間在後的事不可知而已。例如：

  （12）貞：惠父丁歲先。　　　　　　　　　　　　　　（合集 23230）
  （13）惠示壬歲先。　　　　　　　　　　　　　　　　（合集 32398）
  （14）惠示癸歲先。　　　　　　　　　　　　　　　　（合集 32401）

可把上引三例與前引例（7）相比較。

  （15）壬申貞：王又禦于祖丁，惠先。　　　　　　　　　（合集 32597）

（15）與前引（11A）係爲同一件事而占卜的。

在卜辭中，副詞用法的"先"已很常見。這種"先"，當是由意義爲走在前頭、先行的動詞用法的"先"虛化而成的（動詞虛化成副詞，這在漢語中很常見。比如古籍中作範圍副詞用的"畢"、"咸"就是由動詞"畢"、"咸"虛化而成的）。副詞用法的"先"常與"廼"相照應，表示兩事的先後關係。例如：

  （16）乙亥卜：先㲅，廼又祖辛。   （合集 32712）

  （17）□□卜：先又，廼祖辛㲅。   （合集 1733）

上引兩例中的"㲅"是祭名。（16）卜問，先舉行"㲅"祭，然後侑祭祖辛好不好。（17）則是卜問，先舉行侑祭，然後"㲅"祭祖辛好不好。辭主不知對祖辛的"又"祭和"㲅"祭哪一個先舉行好，故有此兩卜。

  （18）叀岳先酒，廼酒五云，又（有）雨。   （屯南 651）

（18）中的"岳"，"五云"都是神名。這條卜辭卜問，先酒祭"岳"，然後酒祭"五云"是否有雨。

  （19）乙亥卜：王先敗卜丙歲，廼申。   （合集 27164）

此例在討論賓字句的結構時曾引用過，可參看。這是卜問，先爲卜丙的"歲"舉行"敗"祭，然後再"申"好不好。"申"，應是個動詞，其義未詳。

  （20）先置，廼□。   （合集 27590）

上例中的"廼"後殘掉了"VP"。這條卜辭卜問，是否先設置（某種樂器），然後再進行某種活動。

  （21）其又大丁大甲，先酒，廼□。   （合集 27106）

此例中的"廼"後也殘掉了一個"VP"。這條卜辭卜問，將要侑祭大丁和大甲了，先舉行酒祭，然後再舉行某種活動好不好。此例中的"酒"，是爲大丁大甲的侑祭而舉行的。

  （22）其先尞，廼省鼓。   （屯南 658）

（22）中的"鼓"當是地名。這是卜問，是否先舉行尞祭，然後省視鼓地。

  （23A）戊午卜：今日戊王叀喪田□。

  （23B）叀盂田先省，廼从宮入，湄日亡災。 （合集 28975①）

---

① 編者按："28975"，原文誤作"28976"，今據實際出處徑改。

上引（23）中的"喪"、"盂"、"宮"都是地名。（23B）卜問，先省視盂田，然後從宮地回來好不好。

(24) 王先狩，廼鄉，禽又鹿，△。　　　　　　　　　　（合集 28333①）

此例中的"鄉"字當指與田獵有關的活動。（24）卜問，王若先"狩"，然後"鄉"，那麼會不會擒到鹿。

上面舉了副詞用法的"先"和"廼"相照應、共同表示兩事時間關係的例子。副詞用法的"先"不和"廼"相照應，也能表示兩事（或幾事）的時間關係。例如：

(25) 乙丑卜，出貞：大史必酒，先酒，其侑匚于丁卅牛。　（合集 23064）

上例中的"先酒，其侑匚于丁卅牛"，應是先舉行酒祭，（然後）用三十頭牛"侑報"祭丁的意思。

(26A) 叀上甲先酒。
(26B) 叀示壬先酒。　　　　　　　　　　　　　　　　（合集 28272）

上引（26）是一對選貞卜辭，在這對選貞卜辭的第一條卜辭中用了"先"，第二條卜辭中也用了"先"。第一條卜辭中的"先"實際上表示出了"酒上甲"一事在"酒示壬"一事之先，第二條卜辭中的"先"實際上表現出了"酒示壬"一事在"酒上甲"一事之先。以下十二個例子中的"先"字同此：

(27A) 叀母先酒。
(27B) 叀兄先酒。
(27C) 叀父先酒。　　　　　　　　　　　　　　　　　（合集 27489）
(28A) 壬戌卜：叀岳先又(侑)。
(28B) 叀河先又。
(28C) 叀王亥先又。　　　　　　　　　　　　　　　　（屯南 342）
(29A) 壬戌卜：叀岳先［又］。
(29B) 叀王亥先又。　　　　　　　　　　　　　　　　（合集 34291）
(30A) 叀中彔（麓）先鼎。
(30B) 叀東彔（麓）先鼎。　　　　　　　　　　　　　（合集 28124）

---

① 編者按："28333"，原文誤作"28338"，今據實際出處徑改。

此例中的"鼎"是個動詞,意義未詳。這對卜辭卜問,是先"鼎"中麓好,還是先"鼎"東麓好。

　　(31A) 王叀襄兕先［射］,［亡］［災］。
　　(31B) 弜襄兕先射,其若。
　　(31C) 王叀⿰兕先射,亡災。
　　(31D) 弜⿰兕先射,其若。　　　　　　　　　　　　　　(合集 28407)

上列中的兩個怪字都是地名。這是卜問,王是先射襄地的"兕"好,還是先射⿰地的"兕"好。

　　(32A) 戊辰卜:其示于妣己,先妝妣己示。
　　(32B) 叀父己示先妝。　　　　　　　　　　　　　　　　(合集 27412)

這個例子在討論賓字句的結構時曾引用過,可以參看。這對卜辭卜問,將要"示"祭妣己了,是先爲妣己的"示"祭舉行"妝"祭好,還是先爲父己的"示"祭舉行"妝"祭好。

　　(33A) 先酒宜。
　　(33B) 叀升先酒。　　　　　　　　　　　　　　　　　　(合集 15291)

上引(33A)中的"酒宜"是個動賓結構,"宜"是賓語,"酒"是爲動用法的動詞,"酒宜"是爲"宜"祭而舉行酒祭的意思(參看第一篇文章)。這對卜辭卜問,是先爲"宜"祭舉行"酒"祭好,還是先爲"升"祭舉行"酒"祭好。

　　(34A) 癸未貞:叀翌甲子酒。
　　(34B) 于來甲午酒。
　　(34C) 叀歲先酒。
　　(34D) 叀尞先酒。　　　　　　　　　　　　　　　　　　(屯南 639)

上引前兩條卜辭卜問,是在甲子那天舉行酒祭好,還是到甲午那天舉行酒祭好。後兩條卜辭卜問,是先爲"歲"祭舉行酒祭好,還是先爲"尞"祭舉行酒祭好。

　　(35A) 己［亥］［卜］:先［又］祖□十［牢］。
　　(35B) 己亥卜:先又大甲大牢。　　　　　　　　　　　　(屯南 751)

例(35)卜問,是先用十"牢"侑祭祖某好,還是先用十"牢"侑祭大甲好。

　　(36A) 史(使)人,先曰屰。

　　　　　(36B) 先曰何。　　　　　　　　　　　　　　　　（合集 22246）

此例中的"屰"、"何"都是人名。這對卜辭卜問，將要派遣人了，是先命令"屰"好，還是先命令"何"好。

　　　　　(37A) 辛酉卜，㱿貞：于矢先冒。
　　　　　(37B) 貞：于𩫖先冒。　　　　　　　　　　　　（合集 11016）

上例中的"矢"、"𩫖"都是地名。"冒"是動詞，陳夢家認爲是設網以獵的意思①。這對卜辭卜問，是先到"矢"地設網以獵好，還是先到"𩫖"地設網以獵好。

　　上面列舉的都是成對或成組的選貞卜辭的例子。有時，由於某些原因，只出現了一對（或一組）選貞卜辭中的一條卜辭。這條卜辭中的"先"也是表示兩事時間關係的，只是時間在後的事情不可知而已。例如：

　　　　　(38) 戊午卜，㱿貞：叀成先酒。　　　　　　　　（合集 1351）

試把（38）與前引（26）"叀上甲先酒。叀示壬先酒"一例相比較，可知此例中的"先"，表示"酒成"一事在先，但此事先於何事，則不得而知。

　　　　　(39) 貞：叀母先酒。　　　　　　　　　　　　　（合集 30642）

此例可與前引（27）例相比較。

　　　　　(40) 叀犧先田，亡災。　　　　　　　　　　　　（合集 29360）

此例可與前引（37）例相比較。

　　　　　(41) 叀升伐先酒。　　　　　　　　　　　　　　（合集 32252）

此例可與前引（33）例相比較。

　　　　　(42) 先侑于唐。　　　　　　　　　　　　　　　（合集 1276）

此例可與前引（35）例相比較。

　　　　　(43) 侑匚于報甲，先酒。　　　　　　　　　　　（合集 1162）

上例中的"先"表示"酒"一事在時間上居先，但先於何事，在卜辭中並沒有説出來。

---

① 陳夢家：《殷虛卜辭綜述》，514 頁，北京：科學出版社，1956。

總之，卜辭中意義爲把……放在先的動詞用法的"先"及意義爲先的副詞用法的"先"，大都是用來表示兩事的先後關係的。

b. 既

"既"，本是動詞，例如：

(44) 辛巳貞：雨不既，其祭于稷。不用。

弜祭，啟。

辛巳貞：雨不既，其祭于亳土。　　　　　　　　　　　　（屯南1105）

(45) 癸巳卜王：旬二月四日丙申昃雨自東，小采既，丁酉雨至東。

（合集20966）

(46) 庚寅雨，中日既。　　　　　　　　　　　　　　　　　（合集21302）

(47) 不其既。　　　　　　　　　　　　　　　　　　　　　（合集16055）

(48) 至于庚寅妝祃既。　　　　　　　　　　　　　　　　　（丙76）

(49) 丁亥卜，貞：既雨。

貞：毋其既雨。　　　　　　　　　　　　　　　　　　（合集1784）

上引（44）中的"既"字當訓爲"盡"，"雨不既"就是雨不止的意思。例（45）至例（47）中的"既"同此。（48）中的"既"也當訓爲"盡"，"至于庚寅妝祃既"是說一直到庚寅那一天"妝"祭才結束。（49）中的"既"用如使動，"既雨"是說使雨停止，可能當時陰雨連綿，殷人欲舉行活動以使雨停止，但不知能否達到目的，故有此卜。

下例中的"既"也應訓爲"盡"：

(50) 貞：告侑既一羊。　　　　　　　　　　　　　　　　　（合集7248）

試把例（50）與"……告亞其入于丁一牛"（合集5685正）一例相比較，可知（50）中的"一羊"同上例中的"一牛"一樣是爲"告"祭而"用"的、（50）中的"侑既"同上例中的"亞其入"一樣是"告"的內容。（50）其實是說，侑祭已畢，用一頭羊把此事報告給某神，（50）中的"既"事實上表示出了兩件事（"侑"和"告一羊"）的先後關係。

意義爲"盡"的動詞用法的"既"有的就是用來表示兩事的先後關係的。例如：

(51) 貞：于既父丁升歲酒。　　　　　　　　　　　　　　　（合集23224）

(52) 于日既。　　　　　　　　　　　　　　　　　　　　　（粹485）

這兩個例子在討論"于"字的時候已引用過,可參看。

在卜辭中,有些"既"是已經的意思,作副詞用。這種"既"字當是由動詞用法的"既"字虛化而成的。例如:

(53) 庚寅卜,殼貞:沚化各戋戈舁隹。

　　　貞:沚化各弗其戋。

　　　王占曰:叀既。三日戊子允既戋戈方。　　　　　　　　　(合集 6648)

(54) 貞:戊既戋。　　　　　　　　　　　　　　　　　　　(合集 7686)

(55) 辛巳卜貞:告既尞于河。　　　　　　　　　　　　　　(合集 14534)

上引(53)前辭中的"庚寅",是占卜的日子,驗辭中的"戊子",是戰勝戈方的日子。"戊子"是"庚寅"前的第三天,那麼占卜一事在後,戰勝戈方一事在先。因此,驗辭中"戋戈方"前用"既"。這個"既"事實上表示了兩事(占卜和戰勝戈方)的先後關係。(53)中的"既尞"是"告"的內容,"告既尞于河"其實是說,舉行完"尞"祭後,把此事報告給河神。(55)中的"既"事實上也表示出了兩事("尞"與"告于河")時間的先後關係。

在卜辭中,多數副詞用法的"既"字即是用來表示事情間的時間關係的。這種"既"有時與"于"聯合使用,有時與"于"、"廼"聯合使用,這種例子,在討論"于"字的時候已引用過了。

這種"既"字有時是和"廼"相照應的。例如:

(56A) 丁丑卜:☐小丁史,又正。

(56B) 既妝祖丁歲,廼止妝。　　　　　　　　　　　　　(合集 32642)

上引(56B)中的"止"應是停止的意思。(56B)卜問,爲祖丁的"歲"祭舉行完"妝"祭,就停止進行"妝"祭好不好。

"既"和"廼"相照應的例子,在周代金文中也可以見到。例如:

> 武王既戋殷,微史烈祖廼來見武王,武王則令(命)周公舍宇。①

"既……廼…"和"先……廼……"都用來表示兩件事情的先後關係,但是,卻有區別:前者是用來表示甲事結束後再進行乙事這樣的時間關係的,後者是用來表示先進行甲事然後進行乙事這樣的時間關係的,乙事進行時甲事不一定結束。

---

① 唐蘭:《西周青銅器銘文分代史徵》,448—450 頁,北京:中華書局,1986。以下簡稱"史徵"。

這種"既"字除了與別的表示時間關係的詞聯合使用外,也單獨使用。例如:

(57) 既禱,王其田咏。　　　　　　　　　　　　　　（合集 29382）

這條卜辭卜問,舉行完禱祭,王就到咏地田獵好不好。

(58) 貞:王勿狩乂,既陷麋,歸。　　　　　　　　　（合集 40133 正）

這條卜辭卜問,王是否不要在"乂"地"狩",用陷阱捕到麋鹿後,就回去。

(59) 壬戌卜,爭貞:既出狋,尞于土宰。　　　　　　（合集 14396）

上例中的"狋"義未詳。這例卜問,是否在"出狋"後,用"宰"尞祭"土"。

(60) 既侑于王亥,告囗。　　　　　　　　　　　　　（合集 14753）

例（60）卜問,是否侑祭完王亥,就對某種神舉行告祭。

(61) 己亥卜,永貞:翌庚子酒囗。王占曰:茲唯庚雨卜。之夕囗雨。庚子酒三酋云△其囗,既祝,啟。　　　　　　　　　　　（合集 13399 正）

上例中的"啟"當讀為"啓"。"既祝,啟"為驗辭,是說舉行完祝祭,天就晴了。

總之,甲骨卜辭中的副詞用法的"既"字單獨使用也可以表示出兩件事情的先後關係。

在古代文獻中,有些"既"字自成一小句,用在兩個句子中間,以表示兩件事情的先後關係。例如:

(62) 新築人仲叔于奚救孫桓子,桓子是以免,既,衛人賞之以邑,辭。

（左傳・成公二年）

在甲骨卜辭中,有的"既"字的用法似與上例中的"既"的用法相同。例如:

(63) 丁未卜:象來涉,其乎麋射,吉。
　　　己未卜:象麝,既,其乎囗。　　　　　　　　　（屯南 2539）

c. 咸

在《詩經》中,有"敦商之旅,克咸厥功"（魯頌・閟宫）一句,對於其中的"咸"字,楊樹達《積微居小學述林》卷六解釋說:"咸者,終也,竟也。"西周金文中的"咸",多是此義。這種"咸"常用來表示兩件事情的時間關係。

西周金文中表示時間關係的"咸"字有兩種用法,一是"咸"字自與一小

句,用在兩個句子中間,表示事情間的先後相繼的關係。例如:

(a) 王在周,各(格)大室,咸,井叔入右(佑)趞。

(趞觶)(史徵367至368頁)

(b) 唯八月既死霸戊寅,王在鎬京濕宮,親令(命)史懋路算,咸,王乎(呼)伊白(伯)易(錫)懋貝。

(史懋壺)(史徵367至368頁)

(c) 甲戌,王令毛白庿虢城公服,粵王立(位),乍(作)四方極,秉繁、蜀、巢令。易鈴勒,咸,王令毛公以邦冢君、徒御、戭人伐東國偃戎,咸,王令吳白曰:"以乃師左比毛父。"

(班簋)(史徵346至347頁)

(d) 唯三月,王在成周,延武王祼,自郊,咸,王易德廿朋。

(德方鼎)(史徵70頁)

第二種用法是,"咸"字出現在一個小句之中,在這個小句後尚有另一個與之相關聯的句子,"咸……,……"表示事情間的先後相繼的關係。例如:

(a) 十又一月癸未,史獸獻功于尹。咸獻功,尹賞史獸曼,易方鼎一、爵一。

(史獸鼎)(史徵140頁)

(b) 二月既望乙亥,公太史咸見服于辟王,辨于多正。

(作冊䰜卣)(史徵326頁)

(c) 王咸誥,何易貝卅朋。　　　　　　　　(何尊)(史徵73至74頁)

(d) 王休宴,乃射,馭方合王射,馭方休闌。王宴,咸酒,王親易馭[方][玉]五瑴、馬四匹、矢五[束]。

(噩侯馭方鼎)(史徵404頁)

上面講了西周金文中表示時間關係的"咸"的兩種用法。"咸"的前一種用法不見於甲骨卜辭,而後一種用法則可以見到。例如:

(64) 咸奏于曾,又伐☐。　　　　　　　　　　　　(合集32164)

(64)中的"曾",可能是地名。這條卜辭卜問,到曾地舉行"奏"祭後,就用"伐"侑祭某神好不好。

(65) 貞:王咸酒登,勿賓翌日。　　　　　　　　　(合集9520)

上引這條卜辭卜問,王爲"登"祭舉行完"酒"祭,是否不要爲"翌日"祭舉行迎神儀式。

(66) 咸伐,亦雨。　　　　　　　　　　　　　　(合集11497)

例（66）爲驗辭，是說"伐"祭之後，又下了雨。

總之，卜辭中有些"咸"字是用來表示兩件事情的先後關係。

表示兩事先後關係的"咸"和"既"的意義很相近，但兩者用法有別，比如"既"字常和別的表示時間關係的詞（如"于"、"廼"）聯合使用。

d. 後₂

在古代文獻中，有些"後"應看成爲副詞，即是後的意思。例如：

先事後得，非崇德與。　　　　　　　　　　　　　　　　（論語·顔淵）

這個例子中的"後"，與前面的"先"相照應，"先……後……"是用來表示兩事先後關係的。

在卜辭中，有些"後"字似乎也可看成爲副詞，也是後的意思。例如：

（67A）河［尞］五。

（67B）河尞十。

（67C）河尞十又五。

（67D）岳尞，後酒。　　　　　　　　　　　　　　　　　　（屯南 4397）

上引（67）的前三條卜辭是在卜問，用多少犧牲"尞"祭河神好。（67D）可能是在卜問，岳神先受尞祭，後受酒祭好不好。（67D）中的"後"大概是表示"岳尞"和"酒"兩事之間的先後關係的詞。下引三例中的"後"字可能也是用來表示兩事之間先後關係的，但是時間在先的那件事没有説出來：

（68）貞：後酒。　　　　　　　　　　　　　　　　　　　（合集 25948）

試把（68）與（67D）"岳尞，後酒"一句相比較，可知（68）的"後"前應是有省略。這可能是在卜問，後舉行酒祭好不好。

（69）貞：其後升歲。　　　　　　　　　　　　　　　　　（合集 25986）

上例中的"升"是祭名，"歲"可能是祭名，也可能是祭牲。這條卜辭可能是在卜問，後舉行"升歲"祭好不好。

（70）後束求。　　　　　　　　　　　　（合集 22287）（合集 22288 同文）

此例中的"束"，爲"刺"之古文，是刺殺的意思①。"束"後的那個字，當釋爲

---

① 于省吾：《甲骨文字釋林》，174—176 頁，北京：中華書局，1979。

"求",是祭名①。"束求"是说爲求祭而刺殺犧牲。(70)可能是在卜問,後進行"束求"好不好。下引一例的"後"前還用了"先",比較特殊:

    (71)先後束。   (合集 22283)

這條卜辭可能是説,先刺殺(犧牲)或後刺殺(犧牲)而不在做某事的同時刺殺(犧牲)。

  總之,卜辭中有些"後"可能是作 Ba 類詞用的。

  e. 廼(乃)

  甲骨卜辭中表示兩事時間關係的"廼"(乃)可譯爲"才"或"然後"。這種"廼"字,有時和"于"、"既"等詞聯合使用,有時和"先"聯合使用,這種例子在前面均已舉過,這裏不再重複。

  "廼"字除了與別的表示兩事時間關係的詞聯合使用外,還單獨使用。單獨使用的"廼"亦用來表示兩事先後相繼的時間關係。例如:

    (72)丁卯貞:升盧豕于妣己,廼酉。   (合集 22231)

上例中的"酉"是祭名。這條卜辭卜問,用黑色的豬"升"祭妣己,然後舉行"酉"祭好不好。

    (73)辛酉卜,王:祝于妣己,廼取祖丁。   (合集 19890)

(73)中的"取"是祭名。這例卜問,祝祭妣己,然後"取"祭祖丁好不好。

    (74)庚辰卜,王:祝父辛羊豕,廼酒父乙。   (合集 19921)

此例是在卜問,用豬和羊祝祭父辛,然後酒祭父乙好不好。

    (75)癸酉卜貞:取岳,廼尞。   (合集 14457)

例(75)卜問,"取"祭岳神,然後舉行尞祭好不好。

    (76)貞:方禘,廼酒岳。   (合集 14470)

這是卜問,禘祭方神,然後酒祭岳神好不好。

    (77)旦其敃鼎,廼各日,又正。   (合集 31116)

上例中的"鼎"是祭名,他辭或言"其鼎兕祖丁。其鼎兕父丁"(寧 1·193),可

---

① 裘錫圭:《釋求》,《古文字研究》第 15 輯,195—206 頁,北京:中華書局,1986。

以爲證。"敁鼎"可能是爲"鼎"祭而舉行"敁"祭的意思。這條卜辭卜問，早晨舉行"敁鼎"祭，然後參加"日"祭好不好。

　　　　（78）己卯卜：奏酒，廼叟。　　　　　　　　　　　　　　（合集 34565）

此例中的"奏酒"，當是在"奏"祭這種儀式中舉行"酒"祭的意思，卜辭或言"壬子卜，即貞：祭，其酒奏，其在父丁。"（佚 172），《佚》172 中的"酒奏"，應是爲"奏"祭舉行"酒"祭的意思。"奏酒"、"酒奏"基本意思可能是相同的。"叟"，也是祭名。這條卜辭卜問，舉行"奏酒"祭，然後舉行"叟"祭好不好。

　　　　（79）癸卯礿，廼燎。　　　　　　　　　　　　　　　　　（合集 21885）

上例中的"礿"是祭名。這是卜問，癸卯那天先舉行"礿"祭，然後舉行燎祭好不好。

　　　　（80）王入，廼格于祭。　　　　　　　　　　　　　　　　（合集 27165）

這是卜問，王進入（宗廟），然後參加"祭"祭好不好。

　　　　（81）☑其燎，廼奏又。　　　　　　　　　　　　　　　　（屯南 4411）

（81）卜問，舉行燎祭，然後"奏又"好不好。

　　　　（82）□□卜，殻貞：王次于曾，廼乎𢦔屮☑。　　　　　　（合集 6536）

上例中的"次"，與古文獻中有些"次"同義，是停留的意思。"曾"爲地名。"𢦔"的意思可能是擒。"屮"爲方名。這條卜辭卜問，王停留在曾地，然後派人去擒屮人好不好。

　　　　（83）辛巳卜：今日告父丁一牛，廼令。　　　　　　　　　（屯南 965）
　　　　（84）以多田伐又封，廼☑。　　　　　　　　　　　　　　（合集 27893）

例（84）中的"田"當讀爲"甸"，是官職名。"又封"即右境。"廼"後殘去了一個"VP"。這例卜問，帶領諸甸去征伐右境之國，然後再做某事好不好。

　　上面舉的是"廼"字單獨使用以表示兩事先後關係的例子。

　　"乃"字在卜辭中未見與別的表示兩事時間關係的詞聯合使用的例子。它一般是單獨使用，以表示兩事先後相續的時間關係。例如：

　　　　（85）丁巳卜，賓貞：令鬲易（錫）止食，乃令西史。　　　（合集 9560）

這條卜辭卜問，命令"鬲"賜給"止"食物，然後命令"西史"好不好。

(86) □亥貞：王令吴以子方，乃奠于幷。　　　　　　　　（合集 32833）

卜辭或言"于京其奠剢竕"（人 2512），貝塚茂樹等認爲這一句是説把剢地的竕人安置到京地，貝氏以安置解釋"奠"①。（86）中的"奠"也是此義。（86）卜問，王命令帶領子方，然後（把他）安置在幷地好不好。

(87) 辛巳貞：𢍰以畫于蜀，乃奠。　　　　　　　　（英國所藏甲骨集 2413）

此例卜問，𢍰把畫帶到蜀地，然後安置（在那兒）好不好。

(88A) 翌日庚其秉，乃雩，卯至來庚亡大雨。
(88B) 翌日庚其秉，乃雩，卯至來庚又大雨。
(88C) 來庚剢秉，乃雩，亡大雨。　　　　　　　　（合集 31199②）

上例中的"秉"爲動詞，他辭或言"□戌秉于盂，遘大雨"（粹 780），可證。"雩"，祭名。"剢"字音義未詳。上引（88A）、（88B）卜問，若在最近這個庚日"秉"，然後舉行"雩"祭，那麼，等到下一個庚日會有大雨呢，還是没有大雨。（88C）卜問，若在下一個庚日"剢秉"，然後舉行雩祭，會不會有大雨。

(89) 其將，乃鼓，其□，又正。　　　　　　　　　　　　（人 1886）

這條卜辭卜問，將舉行"將"祭，然後舉行"鼓"祭好不好。

總之，卜辭中的"乃"有時用來表示兩事先後關係。

卜辭中這種用法的"廼"和"乃"雖然有些細微的差別（比如"乃"字不與別的表示兩事時間關係的詞聯合使用），但是，兩者不見得是兩個不同的詞，而可能與周秦時代的典籍中的"廼"和"乃"一樣是一個詞的兩個不同書寫形式。

"廼"（乃）是甲骨卜辭中常見的表示事情間先後關係的詞。在周代金文中，這種"廼"（乃）也很常見。例如：

(a) 乙亥，王誥畢公，廼易史話貝十朋。　　　　（史話簋）（史徵 165 頁）
(b) 丁酉武公在獻宮，廼命向父詔多友，廼從于獻宫。
　　　　　　　　　　　　　　　　　　　　　　（多友鼎）（人文雜志 1981 年第 4 期）
(c) 昔饉歲，匡衆厥臣廿夫寇舀禾十秭。以匡季告東宫，東宫廼曰："求乃人，乃弗得，女匡罰大"，匡廼稽首于舀。　　　　　　　　　　（舀鼎）（三代 4·45）

---

① 貝塚茂樹：《京都大學人文科學研究所藏甲骨文字釋文》，607 頁，日本：京都同朋舍，1980。
② 編者按："31199"，原文誤作"31189"，今據實際出處逕改。

（d）王南征，伐角僑，唯還自征，在砥。鄂侯馭方内豊（？）于王，乃鄂之，馭方䞆王。王休宴，乃射，馭方合王射，馭方休闌。　　（鄂侯馭方鼎）（史徵404頁）

在周代金文中，"廼"和"乃"也是一個詞的兩個不同書寫形式。

f. 延

甲骨文、周代金文中常見的"延"，當即是"延"字。

卜辭、金文中有些"延"字是作Ba類詞用的。請看下引兩對例子：

（a）王其省盂田，延从宫。　　（屯南2357）
　　　惠盂田先省，廼从宫入。　　（合集28796）
（b）既㲋祖丁歲，廼止㲋。　　（合集32642）
　　　既聰于心，延中厥德。（蔡侯鐘）（《壽縣蔡侯墓出土遺物》圖版貳壹：2）

上引（a）例兩條卜辭的基本意思相同，第一條卜辭的"从宫"前用了"延"字，第二條卜辭的"从宫"前則用了"廼"字。上引（b）例第一個句子中的"既"與"廼"相照應，第二個句子中的"既"與"延"照應。由上述可見，甲骨文、周代金文中有些"延"字與表示時間關係的"廼"字用法相同。

從"延"的一般字義推測，這種"延"字應是繼續、接著的意思，它表示出兩事的先後相繼的關係。這種用法的"延"字在甲骨文、周代金文中都常見。下面先舉甲骨卜辭的例子：

（90）丙子卜貞：翌日丁丑王其振旅，延祕，不遘大雨。　　（安明3139）

上例中的"延"，許進雄以然後釋之，近是①。"祕"字，裘錫圭先生讀爲"毖"，認爲是敕戒鎮撫的意思②。此例卜問，丁丑那天王將整頓軍旅，接著去鎮撫是否不會遇上大雨。

（91）丁丑王卜貞：其振旅，延祕于盂，往來亡災。　　（合集36426）

（91）所卜之事與（90）同類。

（92）丁丑卜：翌日戊王其田△，延田☐。　　（安明1998）

此例卜問，戊那天王將在"△"地田獵，接著到某地田好不好。

（93）王其田瀼，延射叔兕，亡災。　　（屯南1098）

---

① 許進雄：《明義士收藏甲骨釋文篇》，241頁，加拿大：皇家安大略博物館，1973。
② 裘錫圭：《釋祕》，《古文字研究》第3輯，7—31頁，北京：中華書局，1980。

(93) 卜問，王將在"瀼"地田獵，接著去射殺"叔"地的兕好不好。

(94) 王叀南田省，延往于率，弗每。　　　　　　　　（人 2070）

這是卜問，王省視南方的田，接著到率地去好不好。

(95) 叀亞戠田省，延□于向，亡災。　　　　　　　　（合集 30122）

"延"後殘缺的字，從其所剩的殘畫來看，應當是"往"字（又參看前引第 94 例）。這是卜問省視亞戠的田，接著到向地去好不好。

(96) 叀喪田省，延至于彶，亡災。　　　　　　　　　（合集 28991）

這條卜辭卜問，省視喪田，接著到彶地去是否吉利。

(97) 叀□省，延至于夢。　　　　　　　　　　　　　（屯南 2578）

上例中的"叀"後殘掉了"地名＋田"。

(98) □王□□田，延至笄，亡災。　　　　　　　　　（懷特 1438）

此例蓋卜問，王將省視某田災，接著到笄地去好不好。

(99A) 戊寅卜：王㳄于向。

(99B) □其省向，翌日延射鹿，禽。　　　　　　　　（屯南 598）

(99B) 卜問……將省視向地，第二天接著射鹿，是否有所擒獲。

(100) 己亥卜，貞：王往觀耤，延往□。　　　　　　　（合集 9501）

上例中的"耤"，是指用耒耜耕種。此例卜問，王去視察耕種情況，接著去……好不好。

(101) 丁丑卜，㱿貞：王往立刈，延从沚戛。　　　　　（合集 9557）

這條卜辭卜問，王親往立臨收刈穀物之事，接著跟從沚戛這個人好不好。

(102A) 辛卯卜，㱿貞：王往，延漁，若。

(102B) 辛卯卜，㱿貞：王勿延漁，不若。　　　　　　（合集 12921）

這兩條卜辭卜問，王前往某地，是否接著捕魚。

(103) □貞：王□㳄，延□于夫，延至盂，[往]來亡災。（合集 36557）

(103) 卜問，王將去鎮撫，接著到夫地去，然後到盂地去好不好。

(104) ☐步,延取。　　　　　　　　　　　　　　　　　　（合集 20757）

(105) 癸卯卜,王貞:旬亡禍。甲辰△,延祭于上甲。　　　　（合集 40928）

此例中的"甲辰△,延祭于上甲"是説甲辰那天舉行"△"祭,然後"祭"祭上甲。

(106) 辛丑卜,大貞:中子歲,其延酒。　　　　　　　　　（合集 23545）

(107) 壬午卜,燎于土,延巫帝乎。　　　　　　　　　　　（合集 21075）

這條卜辭卜問,燎祭"土"神、接著禘祭"巫"神好不好。

(108) 己酉卜,旅貞:伐,其延伐于兄己。　　　　　　　　（合集 22609）

（108）卜問,"伐"祭某神,接著"伐"祭兄己好不好。

(109) 辛亥卜,貞:其衣翌日,其延尊于室。　　　　　　　（合集 30370）

前面講過,卜辭中動詞用法的"尊"多是置的意思,（109）中的"尊"亦當是此義。這條卜辭卜問,將"衣翌日",接著到室裏舉行"尊"這種活動好不好。

(110) 丙辰卜:禱,延立人三百。　　　　　　　　　　　　（合集 5515）

上例中的"立人三百",其義未詳。這條卜辭卜問,舉行禱祭,接著"立人三百"好不好。

在上引諸例中,都出現了表示兩事時間關係的"延"字,而且用"延"字表示出的有先後關係的兩件事情都説出來。在有些用"延"字的卜辭裏,只説出了兩件事情當中的一件。例如:

(111) 王其延至于薝,亡災。　　　　　　　　　　　　　（合集 28342）

試把上引（111）例和前引（97）"惠☐省,延至于薝"一例相比較,即可知兩例中的"延"的意義和用法是相同的,只是例（111）没有象例（97）那樣説出在"至于薝"前的那件事。下引八個例子都與例（111）相類:

(112) 戊戌卜:其延示于妣己。　　　　　　　　　　　　（合集 27518）

(113) 貞:翌丁酉延示于大丁。　　　　　　　　　　　　（合集 672）

(114) 貞:勿延歲于南庚。　　　　　　　　　　　　　　（合集 23081）

(115) 貞:勿延侑于有。　　　　　　　　　　　　　　　（合集 15050）

(116) 貞:翌癸未延酒卅牛。　　　　　　　　　　　　　（合集 15514）

(117) 延升丁麑。　　　　　　　　　　　　　　　　　　（合集 22258）

(118) 癸丑卜:王其延史于父甲。　　　　　　　　　　　（合集 27475）

(119A) 己亥卜：其延禱于兄己。

(119B) 弜延禱。　　　　　　　　　　　　　　　　　（合集 27613）

上引諸例都是未說出時間在先的那件事，而下引兩例，則是未說出時間在後的那件事。例如：

(120) 癸巳卜，□貞：父丁歲，其延。　　　　　　　（合集 23231）

試把上引例（120）與前引（106）"中子歲，其延酒"一例相比較，可知兩例中的"延"的意義、用法都是相同的，只是例（120）沒有說出在"父丁歲"之後的那件事。

(121) 癸巳卜：燎于束，延。　　　　　　　　　　　（合集 22074）

此例中的"束"是地名。這條卜辭卜問，到束地燎祭，接著做某事好不好。在甲骨卜辭中，像（120）、（121）這樣的例子罕見。

上面列舉的是甲骨卜辭中的"延"字作表示兩事時間關係的詞用的例子。下面，再舉一些周代金文中的例子：

(a) 唯王大禴于宗周，延饗鎬京年。　　　（臣辰文癸尊）（史徵 257 頁）

上引（a）例中的"延"，唐蘭先生譯為"接著"，甚是（看《西周青銅器銘文分代史徵》257 頁）。下引六個例子中的"延"字與上引（a）例中的"延"意義和用法相同：

(b) 王來伐商邑，延令康侯啚于衛。　　（康侯簋）（《商周金文錄遺》157）

(c) 唯王伐迷魚，延伐朝黑。　　　　　　（郭伯馭簋）（史徵 342 頁）

(d) 唯十月又一月丁亥，我乍禦，祉祖乙妣乙祖乙妣癸，延祐叔二母。

（我方鼎）（三代 4·21）

(e) 乙卯，王令保及殷東國五侯，延兄六品。（保卣）（《商周金文錄遺》276）

(f) 王在周，客新宮，王延正師氏。　　　　　（師遽簋）（三代 8·53）

(g) 唯戎大出□□，井侯博戎，延令臣諫□□亞旅處于□。

（臣諫簋）（《考古》79·1）

在古代文獻中，我們沒有見到這種用法的"延"字，但是，可以見到這種用法的"誕"字。例如：

(a) 天乃大命文王，殪戎殷，誕受厥命。　　　　　　　　（尚書·康誥）

(b) 乃話民之弗率，誕告用亶。　　　　　　　　　　　（尚書·盤庚）

(c) 皇天改大邦殷之命，惟周文武誕受羑若，克恤西土。

（尚書·康王之誥）

(d) 上帝不寧，不康禋祀，居然生子。誕寘之隘巷，牛羊腓字之。誕寘之平林，會伐平林。誕寘之寒冰，鳥覆翼之。　　　　　　（詩經·大雅·生民）

上引（a）例中的"殪戎殷"和"受厥命"顯然是前後相繼的兩件事，"誕"用於"受厥命"前，以表示這兩件事情之間的時間關係。餘例中的"誕"同此。我們知道，"誕"字从"言"，"延"聲，"誕""延"聲音相近。古籍中這種用法的"誕"的前身顯然就是甲骨文中表示兩事時間關係的"延"字。表示時間關係的"延"，當是由動詞用法的"延"字虛化而成的。在甲骨文、周代金文中，這兩種"延"都寫作"延"，但是，在古代文獻中，兩者的寫法就不同了，動詞的"延"寫作"延"，而表示時間關係的"延"則寫作"誕"。"誕"和"延"的這種關係，有些學者似已看到了。比如，郭沫若在解釋"王令保及殷東國五侯，延兄六品"（保卣）中的"延"時説："延即語詞誕，猶遂也。"①周永珍在解釋"王來伐商邑，延令康侯啚于衛"（康侯簋）中的"延"時説："延，與誕通用"，並以"乃"解釋"延"②。但是，他們都沒有具體討論到古籍中虛詞用法的"誕"的意義。古籍中的這種"誕"字，古人多以"大"訓之（比如"誕受厥命"中的"誕"，《僞孔傳》就解釋爲"大"），這是不正確的。古籍中還有一些"誕"字，雖然也可以譯爲"乃"，但它難以看成是表示兩事時間關係的詞。例如：

(a) 帝謂文王，無然畔援，無然歆羨，誕先登于岸。　（詩經·大雅·皇矣）
(b) 矧今卜並吉，肆朕誕以爾東征。　　　　　　　　　（尚書·大誥）
(c) 殷小腆誕敢紀其敘。　　　　　　　　　　　　　　（尚書·大誥）

（a）中的"誕"應訓爲"乃"，主要是用來表示"無然畔援、無然歆羨"爲"先登于岸"的條件這樣的關係的。在古籍中，"則"既可以表示時間關係，又可以表示條件關係，"誕"與"則"情形相同。表示條件關係的"誕"和表示時間關係的"誕"應是同源的。（b）、（c）中的"誕"也可以譯爲"乃"，跟表示時間關係的"誕"也是同源的。在古籍中，還有一些"誕"字，用於句子之首或句子之中，沒有什麽實在意義。例如：

---

① 郭沫若：《〈保卣〉銘釋文》，《文史論集》，320—322 頁，北京：科學出版社，1957。
② 周永珍：《釋康侯簋》，《古文字研究》第 9 輯，296 頁，北京：中華書局，1984。

(a) 誕惟厥縱淫泆于非彜，用燕喪威儀。　　　　　　　　　　　（尚書・酒誥）

(b) 誕后稷之穡，有相之道。　　　　　　　　　　　　　（詩經・大雅・生民）

(c) 王命周公後，作冊逸誥，在十有二月，惟周公誕保文武受命，惟七年。
　　　　　　　　　　　　　　　　　　　　　　　　　　　　（尚書・洛誥）

(d) 後暨武王誕將天威，咸劉厥敵。　　　　　　　　　　　（尚書・君奭）

這種用法的"誕"，應看成爲語氣副詞，應是由表示兩事時間關係的"誕"進一步虛化而成的。楊樹達把古籍中的虛詞用法的"誕"字都看成是沒有意義的"助詞"，這當然是不正確的，但有些"誕"字確實是沒有實在意義的所謂"助詞"。在西周金文中，有些"延"字似也應看成是語氣副詞。例如：

(a) 唯八月既望，辰在甲申，昧爽，三左三右多君入服酒。王格周廟，□□□賓。延邦賓尊其旅服，東嚮。　　　　　　（小盂鼎）（三代4・44至45）

(b) 雩若翌日乙酉，□三事□□[入][服]酒。王各廟，獻王邦賓。延王命賞盂□□□□[弓]一……　　　　　　　　　　　　　　　　　　　（小盂鼎）

在甲骨卜辭中，還有下面這種用法的"延"字。例如：

(122) 戊戌卜：祖丁史，其延妣辛妣癸。　　　　　　　　　（合集27367）

上例中的"延"字，出現在"S1，其+□+NP"中"□"的位置上（在有些例子裏，這種"延"字後用"于"字）。(122)"祖丁史，其延妣辛妣癸"從字面上講，是祖丁（當是武丁）的"史"祭將延及到妣辛妣癸（此兩妣爲武丁之配偶）的意思，實際上是說，"史"祭祖丁，接著"史"祭妣辛妣癸，(122)中的"延"字事實上表示出了兩事（"史祖丁"與"史妣辛妣癸"）的先後相繼的關係。這種"延"字在甲骨卜辭中較常見。例如：

(123) 魯甲史，其延般庚小辛，王受又。
　　　弜延。　　　　　　　　　　　　　　　　　　　　　　（屯南738）

這對卜辭卜問，魯甲的"史"祭是否延及到般庚和小辛。

(124) 壬辰卜：妣辛史，其延妣癸，惠小宰。
　　　惠牛。　　　　　　　　　　　　　　　　　　　　　　（屯南323）

(125) 己未卜：祖丁大升，王其[延]父甲。
　　　弜延。　　　　　　　　　　　　　　　　　　　　　　（屯南2276）

(126) 壬申卜，逐貞：示壬歲，其延于[示]癸。　　　　　　（合集22714）

在上例中的"延"後出現了"于"字。這是卜問，示壬的"歲"祭是否延及到示癸。

  （127）庚午卜，王：燎河，延于油。 （佚 9）

此例中的"油"，可能是神名。

  （128）甲戌卜，行貞：歲，其延于祖甲。 （合集 23097）

這是卜問，某神的"歲"祭是否要延及到祖甲。下引（129）至（132）諸例類推。

  （129）己亥卜，何貞：翌庚子升歲，其延于父甲。 （合集 27424）
  （130）癸丑卜，貞：歲，延于羌甲。 （安明 12＋2995）
  （131）己巳卜，行貞：翌庚午歲，其延于羌甲爽妣庚。 （合集 23326）
  （132）庚子卜：史，其延于☐。 （合集 30771）
  （133）登鬯，延父己父庚，王受又。
    弜延于之，若。 （屯南 210）

上例中的"之"爲代詞，這裏指代父己父庚。這對卜辭卜問，奉獻鬯酒這一活動是延及到父己父庚好，還是不延及到他們好。

  （134）其延卜丙。 （合集 1419）

此例"其延卜丙"前，未出現另一小句。這例也應是在卜問，某神的某種祭祀是否延及到卜丙。

  總之，出現在"名詞語"或"于＋名詞語"前的"延"字，事實上也表示出了兩事的先後關係。

  卜辭中作 Ba 類詞的"延"和"廼"很相近，但是兩者有別："延"是繼續、接著或延及的意思，而"廼"（乃）則是才、然後的意思，"延"字義實而"廼"（乃）字義虛；"廼"字常與"于"或"既"或"先"等表示兩事時間關係的詞聯合使用，而"延"字在卜辭中一般不與它們聯用；用"廼"（乃）表示出的有先後關係的兩件事一般都要說出來，而用"延"字表示出的有先後關係的兩件事可以都說出來，也可以只說出其中的一件事。總之，無論從意義上看，還是從用法上看，兩者都有區別。

  2. Bb 類詞：並

  Bb 類詞表示兩事之間同時進行這樣的時間關係。屬於這類詞的只有一個

"並"字。

甲骨卜辭中有"𝇗"字，學者們都認爲它是"並"字。卜辭中又有"𝇘"字，唐蘭先生把它也釋爲"並"①，可從。

作 Bb 類詞用的"並"都用在謂語中動詞的前面，可譯爲同時，用來表示兩件事情同時進行這樣的時間關係。例如：

（135A）貞：妣庚歲，並酒。

（135B）貞：弜並酒。　　　　　　　　　　　　　　　（合集 23326）

上引這對卜辭卜問，妣庚要受"歲"祭了，是同時受酒祭好，還是不同時受酒祭好。此例中的"並"表示出了"妣庚歲"和"酒"兩事的共時關係。

（136）丙午卜：中丁歲，並酒。　　　　　　　　　　（合集 32498）

（137A）丙午卜，旅貞：翌丁未其又于祖丁。

（137B）丙午[卜]，[旅]貞：翌[丁][未]其並又[于]小丁。（合集 23029）

（137A）卜問，丁未那天侑祭祖丁好不好。（137B）卜問，丁未那天同時侑祭小丁好不好。（137B）中的"並"是用來表示"又于祖丁"和"又于小丁"這兩件事同時進行這樣的關係的。

（138）弜並酒。　　　　　　　　　　　　　　　　　（合集 23360）

這是卜問，不要同時舉行酒祭好不好。與"酒"同時進行的那件事沒有說出來。

總之，卜辭中的有些"並"字是作 Bb 類詞用的。

上面較詳細地探討了卜辭中表示兩件事情之間時間關係的詞的意義和用法。在這裏，我們想附帶談談下面這樣的問題，即卜辭中表示兩事時間關係的詞有哪些在春秋戰國時代的文獻中仍可見到，有哪些見不到了；春秋戰國時代的文獻中有哪些不見於卜辭的表示兩事時間關係的詞。

作 Aa1 類詞、Aa' 類詞用的"惠"，在甲骨卜辭中常用，但在春秋戰國時代的文獻中就不再使用了。"即"字在漢代的文獻中有作 Aa' 類詞用的例子，但在春秋戰國時代的文獻中，我們還沒有找到其作 Aa1 類詞、Aa' 類詞用的例子。

"于"（"于"出現的時代早，後來逐漸被"於"替代）在甲骨卜辭中是作 Aa2 類詞用的。在春秋戰國時代的文獻中，有些"於"（于）似仍是作 Aa2 類詞用

---

① 唐蘭：《古文字學導論》下編 53 頁，山東：齊魯書社，1981。

的。例如：

(1) 於其出焉，使公子彭生送之；於其乘焉，搚幹而殺之。

（公羊傳·莊公元年）

(2) 於其歸焉，用事乎河。　　　　　　　　（公羊傳·定公四年）

另一些"於"（于）字，由於進一步虛化，意義發生了轉變。意義轉變了的"於"（于）常作 Aa1 類詞用。例如：

(3) 於天子之崩也爲魯主。　　　　　　　　（穀梁傳·隱公三年）

(4) 於鄭子國之來聘也，四月，晏弱城東陽而遂圍萊。（左傳·襄公六年）

在春秋戰國時代的文獻中，"於"（于）作 Aa' 類詞用的例子仍常見。例如：

(5) 鄭僖公之爲大子也，於成之十六年，與子罕適晉，不禮焉。

（左傳·襄公七年）

在春秋戰國時代的文獻中，除了"於"（于）常作 Aa1 類詞用外，"方"和"當"也常作這類詞用。例如：

(6) 楚子使工尹襄問之以弓，曰："方事之殷也，有韎韋之跗注，君子也。識見不穀而趨，無乃傷乎？"　　　　　　　　（左傳·成公十六年）

(7) 夢飲酒者，旦而哭泣；夢哭泣者，旦而田獵。方其夢也，不知其夢也。

（莊子·齊物論）

(8) 當齊無君，制在公矣。當可納而不納，故惡內也。（穀梁傳·莊公九年）

(9) 當武王邑姜方震大叔，夢帝謂己曰："余命而子曰虞，將與之唐，而屬諸參，而蕃育其子孫。"　　　　　　　　（左傳·昭公元年）

"先"字在卜辭中常見，但我們沒有找到其作 Aa1 類詞用的例子。在春秋戰國時代的文獻中，可以見到這種例子：

(10) 先戰，夢河神謂己曰："畀余：余賜汝孟諸之麋。"

（左傳·僖公二十八年）

前面講過，卜辭中作 Aa2 類詞用的"必"，裘錫圭先生讀爲"比"。在春秋戰國時代的文獻中，"比"仍常作 Aa2 類詞用。例如：

(11) 王之臣有托其妻子於其友而之楚遊者。比其反也，則凍餒其妻子。

（孟子·梁惠王下）

(12) 比君之駕也，寡人請攝。　　　　　　　　　　　　（左傳·定公十三年）

在春秋戰國時代的文獻中，"比"作 Aa' 類詞用的例子罕見。

作 Aa2 類詞用的"待"（在甲骨文中寫作"敔"）在殷虛卜辭中就不常見，在春秋戰國時代的文獻中，我們沒有找到其作 Aa2 類詞用的典型例證。

除了"於"（于）、"比"之外，在春秋戰國時代的文獻中常作 Aa2 類詞用的還有"至"、"及"、"迨"、"逮"諸詞。"至"、"及"作 Aa2 類詞用的例子在前面已舉過。"迨"、"逮"作這類詞用的例子如下：

(13) 迨天之未陰雨，徹彼桑土，綢繆牖戶。　　　　　（詩經·豳風·鴟鴞）
(14) 請迨其未畢濟而擊之。　　　　　　　　　　　（公羊傳·僖公二十二年）
(15) 逮吳未定，君其取分焉。　　　　　　　　　　　（左傳·定公四年）

在殷墟卜辭裏，"由"可作 Aa3 類詞用，也可以作 Aa' 類詞用。在春秋戰國時代的文獻中，我們沒有找到其作 Aa3 類詞用的例子，但可以找到其作 Aa' 類詞用的例子：

(16) 由周而來七百有餘歲矣。　　　　　　　　　　　（孟子·公孫丑下）
(17) 由湯至於文王五百有餘歲矣。　　　　　　　　　（孟子·盡心下）
(18) 由孔子而來至於今百有餘歲。　　　　　　　　　（孟子·盡心下）

在卜辭中，"由"不與"至于"相照應，在春秋戰國時代的文獻中，"由"這樣使用了。

在春秋戰國時代的文獻中，常作 Aa3 類詞用的是"自"，這種例子在前面已舉過了。

在卜辭中，作 Ab 類詞用的"眔"常見，"敔"（待）、"孿"不常見。在春秋戰國時代的文獻中，沒有見到這三個詞作 Ab 類詞用的例子。

作 Ab 類詞用的"先$_1$"、"後$_1$"在春秋戰國時代的文獻中仍可見到。例如：

(19) 鄭先衛亡，逼而無法。　　　　　　　　　　　　（左傳·昭公四年）
(20) 告子先我不動心。　　　　　　　　　　　　　　（孟子·公孫丑上）
(21) 齊王聞之，恐後天下得魏，以事屬犀牛首。　　　（戰國策·魏策一）
(22) 故迂其途，而誘之以得，後人發，先至，此知迂直之計者也。

　　　　　　　　　　　　　　　　　　　　　　　　（孫子兵法·軍事）

除"先$_1$"、"後$_1$"外，在春秋戰國時代的文獻中常作 Ab 類詞用的，還有

"與"、"及"、"以"等詞。例如：

(23) 虎以爲然，故遂與之行。　　　　　　　　　　　　（戰國策・楚策）

(24)（楚王）與之馳騁乎雲夢之中。　　　　　　　　　（戰國策・楚策）

(25) 德音莫違，及爾同死。　　　　　　　　　　　　（詩經・邶風・谷風）

(26) 滔滔者，天下皆是也，而誰以易之。

　　　　　　　　　　　　　（論語・微子）（"而誰以易之"是說你跟誰一起改變它）

在春秋戰國時代的文獻中，沒有見到意義爲"把……放在先"的"先$_2$"作 Ba 類詞用的例子，作 Ba 類詞用的副詞用法的"先$_2$"仍較常見。春秋戰國時代的文獻中的副詞用法的"先$_2$"一樣，既可以單獨使用，也可以和"迺"聯合使用。在卜辭中，已有"後"字，但未見其與副詞用法的"先$_2$"相照應的。在春秋戰國時代的文獻中，可以見到這種"先$_2$"和"後"、"而後"相照應的例子：

(27) 先事後得，非崇德與？　　　　　　　　　　　　　（論語・顏淵）

(28) 先行其言而後從之。　　　　　　　　　　　　　　（論語・爲政）

(29) 曷爲先言王而後言正月。　　　　　　　　　　　（公羊傳・隱公元年）

在卜辭中，作 Ba 類詞用的"既"可以和表示時間關係的"于"聯合使用；在春秋戰國時代的文獻中，未見到這樣使用的"既"字。在卜辭中，"既"還可單獨使用，與"迺"聯合使用，春秋戰國時代文獻中的"既"也可以這樣使用。此時文獻中的"既"還和"而後"、"則"相照應，這種例子卜辭中未見：

(30) 既食而後食之。　　　　　　　　　　　　　　（左傳・襄公二十四年）

(31) 既戰而後圖之。　　　　　　　　　　　　　　（左傳・僖公二十八年）

(32) 既見君子，我心則降。　　　　　　　　　　　　（詩經・召南・草蟲）

作 Ba 類詞用的"咸"字，在殷墟卜辭及西周銅器銘文中都較常見，但在春秋戰國時代的文獻中就見不到了。

在甲骨卜辭中，作 Ba 類詞用的"後$_2$"單獨使用。在春秋戰國時代的文獻中，"後$_2$"單獨使用的例子罕見，可以見到"後$_2$"和"先"相照應的用例（這在前面已經舉過了）。在此時的文獻中，"後"還和"而"、"然"組成"而後"、"然後"，這兩個詞語不但能表示出兩事的先後關係，還能表示出無甲事則無乙事這層意思。例如：

(33) 歲寒然後知松柏之後雕也。　　　　　　　　　　　（論語・子罕）

(34) 宋人既成列，楚人未既濟。司馬曰："彼眾我寡，及其未既濟也，請擊之。"公曰："不可。"既濟而未成列，又以告。公曰："未可。"既陳而後擊之，宋師敗績。
（左傳・僖公二十二年）

在卜辭中，作 Ba 類詞用的"廼"常與"于"聯合使用，這種用例，基本不見於春秋戰國時代的文獻中。在此時的文獻裏，有些"乃"字不但可以表示出兩事一先一後這樣的關係，還可以表示出無甲事則無乙事這層意思。例如：

(35) 知己知彼，勝乃不殆。　　　　　　　　　　　　（孫子兵法・地形）
(36) 雨霽日出，視之晏陰之間，而棘刺之母猴乃可見也。
（韓非子・外儲說左）

這種"乃"字未見於甲骨卜辭。此外，卜辭中的"廼"和春秋戰國時代的文獻中的"乃"的用法大體相同：或單獨使用，或與"先"、"既"等詞聯合使用。

作 Ba 類詞用的"延"，在殷墟卜辭西周時的銅器銘文及西周時的典籍中（在典籍中這種用法的"延"寫作"誕"）較常見，但在春秋戰國時的文獻中，這種"延"字就很少見到了。

除了"先₂"、"既"、"乃"之外，在春秋戰國時的文獻中用來表示事情間的一般的先後關係的，還有"已"、"則"、"而"、"斯"、"遂"、"焉"等詞。例如：

(37) 晉已取虢，還。　　　　　　　　　　　　　　　（韓非子・喻老）
(38) 吾已見孔子，則視子猶蚤蝨也。　　　　　　　　（韓非子・說林上）
(39) 既見君子，我心則降。　　　　　　　　　　　　（詩經・召南・草蟲）
(40) 入竟而問禁，入國而問俗，入門而問諱。　　　　（禮記・曲禮上）
(41) 鄉人飲酒，杖者出，斯出矣。　　　　　　　　　（論語・鄉黨）
(42) 楚人和氏得玉璞楚山中……王乃使玉人理其璞而得寶焉，遂命曰："和氏之璧。"
（韓非子・和氏）
(43) 盡逐群公子，乃奔齊，焉始為令，國無親族焉。　（國語・晉語二）

作 Bb 類詞用的"並"，不見於春秋戰國時的文獻中，代之而起的是"且"字。例如：

(44) 狄應且憎，是用告我。　　　　　　　　　　　　（左傳・成公十三年）
(45) 及滑，鄭商人弦高將市於周，遇之，以乘韋先牛十二犒師，曰："……"，且使遽告于鄭。
（左傳・僖公三十三年）

總而言之，表示兩事時間關係的"惠"、"即"、"哉₁"、"由"、"眾"、"擎"、"哉₂"、"咸"、"延"、"並"等詞在甲骨卜辭中可以見到，但在春秋戰國時的文獻中則不見或罕見；表示兩事時間關係的"于"、"卯"（比）、"先₁"、"後₁"、"先₂"、"既"、"後₂"、"乃"等詞，在甲骨卜辭中可以見到，在春秋戰國時的文獻中亦可見到；表示兩事時間關係的"方"、"當"、"至"、"及"、"迨"、"逮"、"自"、"與"、"及"、"以"、"已"、"則"、"而"、"斯"、"遂"、"焉"、"且"諸詞只見於春秋戰國時的文獻中，而不見於甲骨卜辭中。

《甲骨卜辭語法研究兩篇》之一，北京大學中文系古典文獻博士學位論文，1988年；正式發表於《文物研究》第7、8、9輯，黃山書社，1992—1994年；收入張玉金：《甲骨卜辭語法研究》，廣東高等教育出版社，2002年；又收入張玉金：《20世紀甲骨語言學》，學林出版社，2003年。今據作者提供的定稿收入，並做了校訂。

高嶋謙一

殷代貞卜言語の本質（殷代貞卜語言的本質）

概　要

　　中國最初の歷史王朝であった殷代後期、凡そ紀元前一二五〇年から一〇五〇年程の約二〇〇年間繼續的に契刻された甲骨文とは、一體、何であったのだろうか。通常、それは神々に問いをなげかけた「うらない」の言葉、所謂、「卜辭」である、と思われている。それは正しい理解と言えるであろうか。

　　卜辭の本質を考えるに、問題はかなり廣岐に亙るが、例えば、「卜」、「貞」、「正」、「命・令」といった語の適釋、「疑問・質問」、「選擇」、「祈禱」、「呪文」、「豫言」といったもので性格づけられる卜辭例の分類、卜辭の「命辭」の言語型式の解釋、傳世の古典にある「うらない」に關する記載と卜辭の內容との關連性、最近提唱された「抑・執句末疑問詞說」の妥當性、等が擧げられる。

　　このような問題を十二名程の研究者の所論にそって、研究發展史をも念頭に入れつつ、考察してみると、次の六つほどの說が檢出できる。即ち、（i）卜辭疑問・質問說、（ii）卜辭命龜說、（iii）卜辭修祓・祝禱說、（iv）卜辭豫言・宣言說、（v）卜辭マジック說、（vi）卜辭二元論的マジック說、と命名したものである。これらの諸說を言語學的觀點から分析し、解釋を加えてみると、卜辭の本質は、以上の六說の中、（i）を除いた五つの說により性格づけられる、という結論に至った。

目　次

はじめに
一、羅振玉及び早期研究者の見解
二、董作賓說
三、白川靜說
　　1　卜辭命龜說斥棄の評價
　　2　卜辭修祓・祝禱說の分析
四、饒宗頤、張秉權及び李學勤說
五、キートリー說
　　1　「貞」の字形
　　2　『說文』の「貞卜問也」の由來
　　3　古典に於ける「貞」、「卜」、「命」の意味
　　4　卜辭の言語型式
　　5　キ氏の「貞」字對象說とその評價
　　6　マジックとしての卜辭說
六、「貞」字解釋をめぐって
　　1　セロイス說とその擴充論
　　2　ニビソン說とその評價
　　3　ラフーブレ說とその評價
七、ショナシー說
八、裘錫圭說
　　1　「抑」・「執」句末助詞說の問題點と「印」・「摯」名詞試釋說
　　2　試釋說の再檢討
おわりに

はじめに

　中國の有史時代は、ほぼ紀元前十三世紀中頃から前十一世紀中頃まで繼續的に契刻されたとみなされている殷代後期の甲骨文を以って始まる、とされている。「有史」とは言え、それは、『尙書』、『春秋』三傳、或いは、正史の『史記』、『漢書』等のように作者が意識的に「史實」として諸行諸事を記述したものが、甲骨文にも窺われるということではない。そのため、甲骨文を史料として研究する際、それが上記のような傳世書とは異なり、殷代後期の同時資料の主流として貴重な價値を有する一方、その性質はどのようなものであるかを認識しておかなくてはならないと思われる。契刻された甲骨文とは、殷人にとって一體何を意味するものであったのかということは、史學の分野でも語言學の分野でも基本的な問題である。今迄、それは神の託宣を得るための占いの言葉である、とかなり安直に解答されがちであった。かかる性格づけは全く誤りであるとは言えないのであるが、追究してみると、諸般に亙る問題が續出し、我々には未だ充分に究明できていないように感じられる。甲骨文自身の檢討を通して貞卜の意義を追究するいうことは、とりもなおさず貞卜言語の性質について考えるということである。このことは斯學の多産性にもかかわらず、そうあるものでもなかった。例えば、貝塚茂樹氏は、「龜卜と筮」[①]にて

　　「……甲骨文字はまた殷墟卜辭とも呼びならはされてゐるやうに、本來はトひの言葉であったのであるのにトひの言葉としての本質的な研究が割合に閑却されてゐる」

とし、期待がいだける。ところが、それに續く文は、

　　「殷人はどんな方法によって龜卜を行ったのであらうかといふことは、一度甲骨を手にした一般の人が知りたがるところであるに係はらず、甲骨學者は割合に冷淡で立ち入って考へやうともしなかった」

とあり、期待が別の方向にそらされてしまうように思えてならない。龜卜の方

[①] 『東方學報』京都、第一五册、第四分、一九四七年、頁二五。

法と龜卜の際に用いられた言葉とを區別して、後者の本質を考えようとする本稿とは、問題意識にズレがある、ということに注意しておきたい。尤も、貝塚氏は、特に繇辭の性質について、それを占筮と關連づけ、巫が神籤によって判斷し、それを王がト兆の判定として宣告したものであると性格づけており、その意味合いで「卜ひの言葉」と表現したと思われる②。しかしながら、言葉を言葉として言及したところは、あまり窺われなかった。本稿では、うらないの言葉の性格について、樣々な問題を取り上げ、整理分析を試みてみたい。

　最近、中國の北京大學の裘錫圭氏が一九八八年に「關于殷墟卜辭是否問句的考察」③（以下、裘論文とも略稱することあり）という長論を出版した。また、歐米の專門家も、近々、裘論文をめぐり、*Early China*（『古代中國』）誌にシンポジウムのフォラムで論叢を出版するということである④。米國では、一九七二年にカリフォルニア大學バークレー校のD. N. キートリー（Keightley）氏が "Shih Cheng 釋貞: A New Hypothesis about the Nature of Shang Divination"⑤（以下、キ氏論文とも略稱することあり）という長論を發表した。この論文は、北米では多くの研究者に影響を與えたが、中國の社會科

---

② 近年、龜卜と占筮の關係が問題にされ、例えば、周原甲骨によく見られる數字が占筮の結果の記錄であろうとする張政烺氏の「試釋周初青銅器銘文中的易卦」『考古學報』（一九八〇年、第四期）や李學勤「西周甲骨的幾點研究」（頁一一～一二參照）、周立強氏の第二十回國際漢藏語言和語言學會發表論文「周原甲骨筮辭考證和商殷甲骨筮辭初探」（一九八七年、カナダ・ブリティッシュ・コロンビア大學）等、數篇あるが、何れも貝塚氏の假說をとりあげるまでには至っていない。氏の假說について、未だ深く考慮してはいないが、それをテストし得る資料が容易に得られない。後世、例えば、漢代あたりからの記述からは、むしろ、占卜と占筮を關連づけるには、否定的なものが思い浮かぶ。例えば、『禮記』曲禮の「卜筮不相襲」や『周禮』筮人の鄭注の「當用卜者、先筮之、于筮之凶、則止不卜」などである。
③ 『中國語文』一九八八年、第一期、總二〇二期、頁一～三五。
④ 『古代中國』誌の新編集長に一九八八年春就任したシカゴ大學のエドワード・L・ショナシー（Edward L. Shaughnessy）氏が、その年の夏、歐米の專門家に呼びかけ、論考を募った。氏は、先ず裘論文を英譯し、そのコピーをシンポジウム參加希望者に配付し、裘氏所揭の例文等の劃一的理解を計らんと試みた。ショ氏の英譯は、裘氏の閱讀・校正を受けており、『中國語文』の原文より判然とするところがある。原文では、甲骨文の例文を引用するのみで、裘氏の細緻に亙る解釋が不明の部分も出てくることもあるからである。筆者は、事情があり、該シンポジウムへの參加を斷念したが、ショ氏の英譯を氏の御好意で一部わけていただいた。茲に記して謝意を表したい。本稿では、ショ氏の英譯—これは『古代中國』誌に出版されるとのことである—と裘論文とを對照しつつ利用することにする。
⑤ 「太平洋岸に於ける東洋學會々議」（Asian Studies on the Pacific Coast Conference, Monterey, California, June, 1972）發表論文。

學院歷史研究所の李學勤氏[6]や裘錫圭氏にも、最近になってではあるが、刺激を與えたのである[7]。日本では、早くも一九四八年に京都の立命館大學の白川靜氏が「卜辭の本質」という題の好論を出版しているが、その後、進展を見ていないようである。本稿では、甲骨文とは、龜の腹甲や牛の肩胛骨等を用いた占卜行爲、卽ち、「占い」の言語であるという在來の性格づけから一步前進し、「甲骨文」が殷王朝關係の人々により發話され、更に契刻された根本的インパルス——起動的理由とでも言えようか——は何であったのか、という問題を主に言語學的觀點から考察してみたい。

現在に至る迄、實際の甲骨文にそくしその本質に關して注意すべき見解を示した研究者は、管見によれば、既述の四名も含めて、次の十二名である。年代順に記すと、次記の通りである。

　　（一）　羅振玉（一九一〇年）[8]（早期研究者代表）
　　（二）　董作賓（一九三一年）[9]
　　（三）　白川靜（一九四八年）（注７參照）
　　（四）　饒宗頤（一九五九年）[10]
　　（五）　張秉權（一九六五年）[11]
　　（六）　Ｄ・Ｎ・キートリー（一九七二年）（注５參照）
　　（七）　Ｐ・L-M・セロイス（Serruys）（一九七四年）[12]
　　（八）　李學勤（一九八〇年及び一九八五年）（注６參照）
　　（九）　Ｄ・Ｓ・ニビソン（Nivison）（一九八二年）[13]

---

[6] 李氏の所論は次の二つの論文に見られる。「關于自組卜辭的一些問題」『古文字研究』第三輯（一九八〇年）、頁三二～四二。これを李論文一と稱する。「續論西周甲骨」『中國語文研究』第七期（一九八五年）、頁四～六。これを李論文二と稱する。この論文は『人文雜誌』第一期（一九八六年）にも再揭載された、と裘論文（頁三）にある。

[7] 『立命館文學』第六二號（一九四八年）、頁一九～四一。以下、「白川論文」とも略稱。

[8] 『殷商貞卜文字攷』（玉簡齋石印本、一九一〇年）、卜法第三、頁二二ォ―二五ォ。

[9] 「大龜四版考釋」『安陽發掘報告』第三期（中央研究院歷史語言研究所、專刊之一、一九三一年）、頁四二六～四三四。

[10] 『殷代貞卜人物通考』（香港大學出版社、一九五九年）上册、頁七〇―七一。

[11] 『殷虛文字丙編・考釋』（"中央研究院"歷史語言研究所、一九六五年）、中輯（二）、頁四四四～四四七。

[12] "Studies in the Language of the Shang Oracle Inscriptions," *T'oung Pao*, Vol. LX, 1-3 (1974), pp.21-27.

[13] "The 'Question' Question." Paper presented at the International Conference on Shang Civilization, Honolulu, Hawaii, September, 1982.

（十）　E・L・ショナシー（Shaughnessy）（一九八三年）⑭

（十一）　J・A・ラフーブレ（Lefeuvre）（一九八五年）⑮

（十二）　裘錫圭（一九八八年）（注3参照）

　本稿では、主に以上の十二名の研究者の所論を紹介し、問題意識の歴史的展開をも考慮に入れつつ論考してみたい。上記の（一）から（三）迄、（六）のキートリー氏、（十）のショナシー氏、及び（十二）の裘錫圭氏の論文は項をそれぞれ設けて論じ、その他は数説まとめて検討することにした。そのため、内容は（一）から（十二）の順序にならず、最初に目次を掲げた如く、一から八までの各項に配分したようになっている。

一、羅振玉及び早期研究者の見解

　一九一〇年の羅振玉の著以前にも殷墟出土の甲骨片を殷代の遺物と考え、『周易』に傳えられる占筮と同じように、人閒が未知に對してその含むところを感知せんとする、所謂、うらない（divination）に用いたものとした著論があることは確かである。それらには、未定・不定を豫期し得る方法として、「問う」という言語行爲が極めて自然なことと思われていたようである。例えば、一九〇三年の劉鶚（字、鐵雲）著『鐵雲藏龜』序（頁三ォ）には、今では、例えば「乙酉卜、大貞翌丁亥易日」（『鐵雲』二二・三）、また、「庚子卜、殻貞帚好有子」（『鐵雲』一二七・一）と釋文されるべき卜辭中の「貞」（鼎）字を「問」などとして解釋しているところからも分かるのである。また、一九〇四年には、古典・金石學で著名な清朝末の碩學、孫詒讓が『契文擧例』二卷を著し、劉鐵雲の「問」と釋した甲骨の原字は、金文の「貝」という字に近似しており、「問」ではなく、「貞」字であり、それは『說文』（三下）の「貞卜問也」という意味において解釋するべきだ、としている（上掲書、上、頁六）。この「貞」字說は、楷書化の限りでは、今でも正しいとされるが、その意味解

---

⑭　The Composition of the *Zhouyi*. Ph.D. dissertation, Stanford University, 1983. Cf. pp.52-57, 66-67.

⑮　*Collections of Oracular Inscriptions in France*. Taipei, Paris, Hong Kong: Ricci Institute, 1985, pp.123-126（Chinese）/pp.195-200（French）/pp.294-298（English）.

釋に關しては、未だ定説がないということが言えよう。しかしながら、權威ある『說文』の定義を引用したことは、孫詒讓以來、甲骨文研究者に絶大な影響を及ぼしつづけているのである。

　『說文』は權威的ではあったが、劉鐵雲や孫詒讓が「うらない」とは所詮問うことだ（to divine is to question）という理解を更に深め浸透せしめたのは、やはり、清朝末の考證學者羅振玉の名を舉げるべきかと思う。彼は、其の一九一〇年の著『殷商貞卜文字攷』にも見られるよう「貞卜」という表現——これは『左傳』哀公十七年の「衞侯貞卜」が初出か——を用い、それが「文字」を修飾している結構を書名とし、『說文』の定義に「肉付け」をしたのである。先ず、「貞」に關し、『周禮』春官、大卜の「凡國、大貞卜立君、卜大封則眂高作龜」を引き（頁二三オ）、許愼が依據したと思われる鄭司農の注「貞問也」に注意を向ける。これは、『說文』の定義と校勘してみると、より直接的に「貞」字を定義している。さらに、「卜」字に關しても、羅振玉は『說文』（三下）の「卜、灼剝龜也」というテクニカルな定義に從っていないか、或るいは、それを意識していない。どちらかと言えば、彼の引用した『周禮』の「卜ㇾ立ㇾ君」や「卜二大封一」で卜が他動詞に用いられているため、「一を卜う」とう意味にとらえているようでさえある。甲骨文を讀解せんとしたその當時の學者は、古典に造詣が深く、「卜」を他動詞にとってしまうのに抵抗を感じなかったのではなかろうか。甲骨文では「卜」というコトバは、目的語をとらないため、自動詞である。このことについては、その名詞としての用法とともに後でも觸れよう。「卜」の原義は、「火で灼いて龜裂を生じさせる」、また、殷代では骨も用いたから、骨のヒビ割れも含むが、前掲の『說文』の解は、古義を傳えていると思われる。羅振玉の考えでは、「貞卜」とは、要するに、「問いて卜う」（to divine/foretell by enquiring）ということであったのであり、かかる意味の卜辭として、有貞字、或るいは、有卜字の文例を十頁以上にわたり羅列している（頁二五オ—三〇オ）。本稿ではこれを稱して「卜辭疑問・質問説」と呼ぶことにする。

　孫詒讓や羅振玉などの早期研究者は、以上述べたように、貞卜とは問うことであると理解していたのだが、實際の甲骨文において、貞字が自動詞としての卜字の前に用いられることがない事實やその意義については、考えてもいなかったようである。そのような事實を踏まえ、所謂、「卜下貞上」の文字が殷

王室に仕えた、或るいは、殷王室と何らか關係のあった、「貞人」（diviner）であると提唱し、更に、本稿で對象としている卜辭の本質をもはじめて究明せんとしたのが、次項で取り上げる董作賓である。

二、董作賓說

　　一九三一年の董作賓の論文は、その二年前の十二月十三日に殷墟の大連坑と呼ばれた坑から出土した四枚の刻字大龜版を資料にして書かれ、それ迄出土した零細な有字甲骨片に基づかざるを得なかった先人の研究よりも一段と優れた結果をもたらした。既に觸れた「卜下貞上」の字が貞人名を表わすという說も大龜四版の卜辭が基礎となり、殷代の甲骨文を歷史的にふり分ける斷代研究を可能ならしめたのである。貞人說は、董作賓の劃期的な論文「甲骨文斷代研究例」（一九三二年）⑯以來、斯學の定說となったのは周知のことである。卜辭の性質についても、董作賓（注9所揭論文、頁四二六）は、次のように述べている。

　　「在四版中、關於書契卜辭一項、…貞卜法中最大的發現、就是左右對貞、一事兩決之例…今由此大龜版所啟示、可知吾人所稱爲卜辭者、實即卜時命龜之辭、亦卽貞辭。貞訓"卜問"、卜以決疑、因有疑而問之於龜、所以貞辭也就是問事命龜之辭。『周禮』春官"以邦事作龜之八命"、『史記』龜策列傳也載有漢時太卜"命龜"之法、分反正兩項、如所舉占病者之辭：

　　　　"今某病困、死。──首上開、內外交
　　　　駭、身折節。不死、──首仰足胎。"

這知9、10兩辭〔見下〕甚相似。凶、象人在棺中、丁山先生疑是死字。今並列比較之。

　　　　今某病困、死。不死。
　　　　貞、其死(10)。壬子卜、賓貞、𡩋洮不死(9)。」

ここでのキー・ワードは、「對貞」、「命龜之辭」、「卜問」、「卜以決疑」の

---

⑯　『中央研究院歷史語言研究所集刊外編、蔡元培先生六十五歲慶祝論文集』上冊、頁三二三〜四二四。

四つであると思う。この中、「卜問」は既に引用した『説文』の貞字の定義であり、更に「卜以決疑」は、『左傳』桓公、十一年の「卜以決疑、不疑何卜」からの出典である。これらは董作賓自身の理解と巧みに織成している感がある。「卜問」と「卜以決疑」の二つのキー・ワードで表現される考えは、前項で述べた孫詒讓や羅振玉の影響が董作賓にも及んでいたと思われる。「卜うとは問うことだ」という認識は、一九三〇年前半頃もごく自然な解釋であり、また、別に反對意見も出されていなかったこともあって、當時の研究者にすんなり受容されていたと思われる。⑰そのような折に、董作賓は、新出の見事な大龜四版中、卜旬の一版（『甲編』二一二二）を除き、殘りの三版（『甲編』二一二四、二一二一、二一二三）の卜辭に注目し、それら腹甲にはしる「千里路」と呼ばれる中央の縫線を左右對稱に、右は肯定文、左は否定文、とかなり規則的に契刻されている事實を發見し、左右對貞、一事兩決による「卜辭命龜説」を打ち出したのであった。

　「卜辭命龜説」とは、實は、董作賓自身の命名ではなく、次項（第三項）で取り上げる白川靜氏のものである。しかし、白川氏は命龜説と呼びながら、それが、究極的には、何であるのか充分説明し得ていないと思う。また、董氏自身の考えもいま一つ明瞭さを缺くようである。董氏は、上記の文中に『史記』龜策列傳の「命龜」という表現を徴引しているのだが、實は、『史記』より古い『尚書』にも「龜に命ずる」というような記載がある。我々は、「命龜説」を如何に性格づけるかによって、或るいは、殷代の貞卜言語の性質を理解する面での一つの手がかりが得られるかも知れない。まず『史記』より古い記載に『尚書』金縢篇の「今我卽命于元龜」があり、この文中の「卽」の解釋に、「既」の意味にとるべしとか、また、「就」、あるいは、「受」の義にとるべしとかいう異説があって、原義を客觀的に確定し難いが、ここでは、「命」（charge, command）と「龜」が密接に關係しているということは認め

---

⑰　例えば、一九三三年に出版された郭沫若著『卜辭通纂』（東京、文求堂）の序（頁五ゥ）に次のような言辭がある。
　　「…"某日卜某貞某事"之例所在皆是、曩於卜貞之間一字未明其意、近時董氏彥堂解爲貞人之名、遂頓若鑿破鴻濛。今據其説以詮之、乃謂於某日卜、卜者某、貞問某事之吉凶、貞下辭語當付以問符。」この引用文最後のところの疑問符をつけるべしということは、言語學的に、また、甲骨文の性質を考える上、問題である。このことについては、後に詳考することにする。

られよう。思うに、元龜が人間名詞（human noun）である「我」（＝ここでは周公を指す）に命ずるとは考え難く、その逆であろう。この判斷は、とりあえず一つの作業假定（working hypothsis）としておくことにしたい。しからば、重要なのは「何を」龜に命ずるかということを解決し、しかる後に、殷代でも卜辭命龜說が畢竟妥當であるか吟味する、ということであろう。後者の問題は、次項（第三項）の白川靜氏の論考對象になっているので、そこに初步的考察を讓ることにする。前者の問題であるが、龜に命ずるとは、『左傳』の「卜以決疑、不疑何卜」からすると、「疑問」を命ずると考えられなくもないかも知れない。しかし、疑問を命じても、解決の道がどのように龜から得られるか必ずしも明瞭ではない。董氏は具體的に答を示してくれていないのだが、私は、ここで、言語學的觀點から考えて、それは「選擇」（alternative choice, selection）であるということが言えると思う。「選擇」を命ずるということは、卽ち、肯定文と否定文とを龜に告訴し、そのどちらかに對して可決か否決か、或るいは、その「程度の差」（吉、大吉、弘吉、不牾黽といった表現）で現われる卜兆を求めることである。これは、究極のところ、ある事項の可否、正反の選擇、卽ち、二者擇一に等しい。二者擇一のみではなく、所謂、多項式選擇（multiple choice）の場合もあるが、對貞の場合は、二者擇一と言ってよい。ここで言う「選擇」であるが、その基底にあるものは、疑問の念であった、としてよいと思われるが、かかる解釋には、意味論的に考えると、一つの條件を付けなければならない。それは、選擇すべき項目、卽ち、肯定文と否定文が意味的に完全に同質と考えられる場合に於いてのみ適應する、ということなのだが、このことについては、追って考えることにしたい。

　董作賓自身は、「選擇」という表現こそ用いていないのだが、實は、氏の卜辭命龜說の內容をみると、かかる表現がふさわしいことがわかると思う。董氏は、大龜四版中の卜辭に（１）から（８９）の番號を施し、例えば、（９）「壬子卜賓貞辜沘不死」と（１０）の「貞其死」の對貞を「決死不死」という言葉で表わし、「純粹卜旬」の辭は「反」がないため、例外とし、他の二十八對貞を全て「決一」としている。肯定と否定との組み合わせは、現代中國語で「去不去」、「行不行」、「有没有」のように疑問文となる。しかし、これらの表現はそれぞれ、統辭論（syntax）により一つの文中に動詞句として收められなければならない。ところが、甲骨文では、「貞」というコトバが肯定の前

にも否定の前にも用いられ、更に、同一主語が各對貞文に用いられることが頻見することから、正反の對貞文を一つの文章である、と認めることが不可能である。してみると、（９）の「…辜洇不﹂死」と（１０）の「…其死」をそれぞれ一つの獨立文としてとらえなければならない。この際、もしそれらが二つとも疑問文であるとしたら、可能な解答は二通りずつ出ることが起こり得るし、或るいは、その「解答」がコンフリクトにならないとも限らない。従って、（９）と（１０）の獨立文は疑問文であるとは解釋し難く、非疑問文であると思われる。この點は、後述するニビソン氏の論文（頁二、九――一〇）から得るところ大であるが、今の段階では、作業假定の類として受けとどめておいても構わない。先の現代中國語の例でも、たとえば、「去」が肯定、「不去」が否定で、各々、非疑問文がベースになっている。このことから言えることは、物事を解決する答が必要な時、潜在的・心理的には、疑問の念があったであろうことは認めてもよかろうが、言語表現としては疑問文ではない、と言えるであろう。

　董作賓氏の「卜辭命龜說」は、以上述べたように、正反の選擇、或るいは、多項式選擇を龜に告詫し、そのいずれかを選ぶことを目的としたと理解されるべきだと考える。このことは、殷代の、特に、對貞形式の卜辭の本質をある程度迄正確に把握できていると思う。「ある程度」とは、殷人にとって、正反の命辭のどちらもが、情報として「有益」であったと思われる場合のみを指すのであるが、このようなことをも含めた命龜說補正案を本稿では提出したく思う。（第三の１項参照。）しかしながら、白川靜氏は、卜辭命龜說を否定しているので、次に、氏の所說を紹介し、その根據をも分析してみよう。

三、白川靜說

　一九四八年の白川論文には一つの大前提がある。それは、そもそも龜版獸骨に刻文するということは、中國古代の占卜の歷史上、殷王朝にのみ特有であることなどからして、かかる占卜行爲は殷王の神聖な王者としてまたシャーマンとしての性格を表象するものであった、とする前提である。

　しかしながら、この大前提は、四十年程經った現在、額面どおり受けとれないように思える。少なくとも、それを再考してみる要素がでできたことを指

摘しなくてはならない。今、立ち入った議論は避けて、三つの點を舉げておくことにする。先ず、自組、子組、午組、歷組という卜辭グループが、殷王朝「直轄」と思しき賓組、出組、何組、無名組、黃組と實質的な面（例えば、自組では繇辭を述べた占者が殷王でないという事實が認め得るなど）に於いて區別可能という點。第二の點として、一九七〇年代後半に陝西省岐山縣鳳雛村の西周建築遺址から出土した有字周原甲骨二九三片の發見にともなって、新たに提出された諸問題が考えられよう。たとえば、これら周原甲骨を殷王朝との關係面で如何に解釋するかの大問題を浮上せしめた、ということが舉げられるべきであろう。この問題は、或るいは、白川論文の大前提を支持するような議論の發展を見る可能性も內在している。しかし、かかる可能性だけでは不充分であるし、我々はそのような大前提から離れて考察を進めるべきであろう。また、第三の點として、「王」というコトバの意味の問題もある。それが果たして殷王のみに許された稱號であったのか、それとも齊文心が論ずるように、「某王」、「王某」等と殷墟卜辭上に現われるように殷王以外にも用いられたのか[13]、等の問題があるのである。要するに、白川論文の大前提は、現在では、その比重が薄らいだと言わなくてはならない。

　　次に、白川氏は、龜卜の詳細を傳える唯一の古文獻『史記』龜策列傳には龜版上に文を契刻するなどということが一切書かれていないため、殷代の卜法には異なるところがあったのであろう、としている。そして、龜策列傳に三十二條ほどある「命曰」で始まる一連の文章——これを白川氏は「命龜の辭」と稱する——が董作賓をして卜辭を命龜の辭とする先入觀的な解釋を導かしめたとしているのである。

　　殷代の卜法が龜策列傳所見のものと異なっていたであろうと推測するのは

---

[13] 齊文心「關于商代稱王的封國君長的探討」『歷史研究』二（一九八五年）、頁六三～七八。齊氏の說を檢討した結果、私は「某王」と稱されるもの—例えば、「𠘧王」、「㦰王」、「羋王」等（齊氏は前者二王を「應王」、「麋王」と釋字している。後者の一王の名は引用していない）—は、殷王と區別する上で、「某地の王」と呼ばれた可能性があると思うに到った。しかし、「王某」は、にわかに贊成しかねる。「某」の字は、何らかの職能を任った名前—例えば、「㞢」、「臥」、「侑」、「𠦪」、「𣢉」、「貯」等—と解釋することが可能で、「王の某」、即ち「殷王に屬する、或るいは、殷王と何らかの關係ある某」と捉えた方が言語構造的には自然であるからである。更に、『乙編』九〇八一片の「辛巳貞卜王而…」の「卜王」は「外王」と訓む可能性が生じるわけであるが、該刻は恐らく習刻であるようでもあって、資料として信を置くには不安が殘る。

自由であり、恐らくそうであったろうと思われる。しかし、先程の「命曰」で始まる三十二條の『史記』の文に關しては、人間が龜に「命じて曰く」ではなく、龜から人間に對する「命」であり、「命に曰ふ」と訓むべき内容がかかる表現の後に續くのである[19]。かかる「命」とは、人間が各兆を、恐らく經驗的知識に基づいて解釋し、それらに判斷の辭を結びつかせたものと捉えるべきものであると思われる。ところが、董作賓氏の言う「命龜之辭」というのは、「命曰」で始まる三十二條の文ではなく、その前の「卜…（曰）」で始まる二十三條の文章なのである[20]。このことは、龜策列傳を見れば分かるはずであって、董氏は始めにくる「卜占病者祝曰」を省略したまでのことにすぎない。してみると、白川氏が董作賓の「卜辭命龜説」を退けてしまったのは、一つには、氏の誤解に基づいていることにもなるわけである。

　白川氏は、次に、「卜辭命龜説」が成立しない理由として卜法上の問題を提起する。これには四つある。（イ）大龜第一版には合計二十八辭の命辭（貞辭とも言われる）が刻されているが、實際に觀察し得る卜兆は六十兆ほど數えられる。刻辭のない卜兆は三十二も殘ることになるわけだが、それは何故かが命龜説では説明できていない。更に、大龜四版の卜辭中に於いても、左右對貞、一事兩決の原則が保持できない文例がある。即ち、肯定・否定の兩貞法は、董氏が思った程、絶對的ではない。（ロ）多數の卜辭――例えば田遊、卜旬、卜夕刻辭など――が一事一貞の形式をとり、董作賓が考えたような兩貞法は、卜法の全體に通ずるものではない。むしろ、兩貞（または、對貞）法の方が、祖祭或るいは天象に關するものとして、特殊なのではないか（ハ）「癸亥卜王」など『文録』一七四以下に累見する一事多貞の卜法は、十卜を重ねる如き例が多く、これらは命龜説では解決の道がない。（ニ）命辭の後に繇辭（占辭とも言う）と驗辭と呼ばれる附記が見受けられる例があるが、命龜説では、それらの

---

[19] 例えば、第一條に「命曰横吉安。以占病、病甚者一日不死、不甚者卜日瘳、不死…云々」とあり、また、第二條には、「命曰呈兆。病者不死。繋者出。行者行。來者來。市買得。追亡人得、過一日不得。問行者不到。」とある。これから考えても、「命曰」は、龜に「命じて曰く」とは訓めないことが分かるであろう。

[20] 例えば、第一條には、「今某病困。死、首上開、内外交駮、身節折。不死、首仰足胎」（ここでの句點の施し方は、董作賓氏のと少しく異なる）とあり、第二條には、「今病有祟、無呈。無祟、有呈…云々」とある。第三條以下には、「卜…曰…」の「曰」の字が用いられていないが、これは省略されたものであろうことは、容易に推測し得る。

例を説明することができない。以上の四つの理由により、白川氏は卜辭命龜說を斥棄し、卜辭は修祓・祝禱（purification and prayer）的意義を有したものとする議論を展開することになる。本稿では、これを「卜辭修祓・祝禱說」と呼ぶことにするが、次にこれら四つの指摘に簡評を加えておこう。

1　卜辭命龜說斥棄の評價

（イ）の兩貞法が殷代の卜法の全體に卽せず絕對的ではないとするのは正しい觀察である。例えば、大龜四版の第一版の第六辭「丁未卜賓貞今日㞢于丁、六月」等は、その否定形も、また、コントラスティブな對貞もない。しかしながら、刻辭なき卜兆の意味を命龜說が說明しなくてはかかる說が成り立たない、とすることまでは言えないのではあるまいか。少なくとも、命龜說の致命傷にはならないと思われる。白川氏の卜辭修祓・祝禱說は、刻辭にのみ注意することによって、刻辭なき卜兆の意味を探索しなくてもよいように論を進めた。しかしながら、修祓・祝禱說にせよ、命龜說にせよ、刻辭なき卜兆に對して何らかの說明が欲しいところであるのは認めてよいだろう。これは私の假說なのだが、命龜說の補正案の一つとして、次のことを提起したい。刻辭なき卜兆の意味は、董作賓が假設しては毀棄した四つの事項[21]の外に、ただ單に、無意味、ニュートラル（meaningless, neutral）であったか、或るいは、かかる卜兆に魔術的な効力（potency）がないと繇の擔當者に判斷され、何らの命辭をもその卜兆の側に刻することがなかった、ということである。この假說については、實際の甲骨文の用例の解釋に基づいて推論していくのが良いと思われるの

---

[21]　これらは次記のとおりである。（「大龜四版考釋」『安陽發掘報告』第三期（中央研究院歷史語言研究所、專刊之一、一九三一年）、頁四三四參照。）

一、所問之事、已經一卜再卜、然後刻辭記之者。
二、因小事而不刻辭記之者。
三、刻辭者先卜、以後再卜因無隙不容刻辭者。
四、卜于此版而刻辭記事于彼版者。

以上の中、一は必ずしも間違いであると簡單に片付けられないかも知れぬ。たとえば、意味ありとよまれた卜兆に刻辭されたかも知れないのである。二は、「小事」なら、そもそもなぜ貞卜したか疑問を殘すし、董氏が考えた如く、成立し難いと思える。三は、「犯兆」という現象—即ち、大部分の刻辭が卜兆を避けて現れ、このことは先卜後刻の事實を示す—から正しいが、空閒があっても無刻辭のものがある。四は、完全になかったとは言えないが、そのような假說は卜辭研究にケイオスをもたらしてしまう。

て、ここで少々試みてみよう。

(1) 王占卜、曰我其田、〔受〕甫耤在妰年。　　　　『丙編』三八二・(3)
(2) 壬寅卜、大貞卜有祟、在茲內有不諾。　　　　　『京津』三四八八
(3) 丁丑卜、大貞卜祟其于王。　　　　　　　　　　『人文』一四六九
(4) 己未卜、王貞㞢有求于祖乙、王吉茲卜。　　　　『佚存』八九四
(5) 貞宙茲卜用。一月。　　　　　　　　　　　　　『方法』七、X1
(6) 庚申卜、旅貞宙元卜用。在二月。　　　　　　　『續編』一・三九・九
(7) 二月貞卜子亡諾。二月卜有諾。三月卜有諾。茲三卜亡諾。
　　　　　　　　　　　　　　　　　　　　　　　　『粹編』一二五五
(8) 丁卯卜、賓貞勮、卜不興、亡勾。五月。　　　　『甲編』二一二四

　先ず、例文（1）を見ると、動詞「占」の對象は「卜」、即ち、卜兆であることがわかる。（1）は繇辭であり、それは王が卜兆を解釋して、「我々が田するに、甫なる人物が妰地にて耕した作物の年を受けん」といった意味の文を口宣したものと解釋できる。（1）で重要なのは、動詞「占」の目的語が明瞭に「卜」であることである。通常、「王占曰」と表現されるものの深層構造が「王占卜曰」であることを證佐する例は、（1）以外に見當たらないようであるが、『丙編』からの用例は、YH一二七坑出土の信賴すべき龜版で疑いの餘地がない。『英國』一一七五（正）に「…王占卜曰…」なる表現があるが、殘念なことに、該片は僞刻の可能性があると思われる。姚孝遂主編の『殷墟甲骨刻辭摹釋總集』（北京、中華書局、一九八八年、頁一〇七三）に於いても、編者はこれを僞刻としている。しかし、僞刻たる所以は「王占卜曰」なる表現があるからではなく、別の理由によるとすべきである。例えば、「王占卜曰」のすぐ上に「壬戌卜賓貞」という表現が見られ、かかる表現自體は何ら問題ないが、拓本を見ると、明らかに異ったスタイルで契刻されており、文意からも「王占卜曰」は「貞」字の對象にならない。（「貞」字の解釋については後論する。特に、第六の1項を參照されたし。）この外、繇辭の內容をみても、重要な語（例えば干日など）を缺いていることから僞刻と判斷できる。
　例文（2）では、名詞「卜」が動詞句である「有祟」の主語に用いられている。文意は、「卜に祟あり、茲の內には不諾（スムーズに事がはかどらない、帝の意にかなわない狀態）がある」という豫言めいたことを「貞」してい

ると思われる。

　例文（３）は（２）と似ているが、倒置法をとっているとみられる。正置法では、「卜其祟于王」と表現し得ると思われる。「祟」が他動詞に用いられることについては、例えば、『丙編』一〇四・（９）（１０）に「貞黃尹祟王」、「貞黃尹弗祟王」とあり、そのコトバが「外向性」（extrovertive）の動詞に用いられたり、「內向性」（introvertive）の名詞的用法（例えば（２）にて）に用いられたりする。例文の意味は、「（ある特定の）卜兆が祟するは、（他人にではなく）王（の上）にならん」というように解釈できると思われる。ここで特に注意したいのは、「卜」の効力（potency）が具體的に王の身に及ぼすことの可能性が考えられていたことである。意味的に望ましくないことである。

　例文（４）の前半は詳らかにし得ないが、恐らく祖乙に對し何かを祈求しているものであろう、ということは言えよう。しかし、後半の「王吉茲卜」は重要で、その意味は「王が茲の卜を吉とせん」と訓むべきものだと思える。「吉とせん」ということは、卜兆に何かしらのパワーがあったと信じられていたに相違ない。

　例文（５）も（４）と同じようなことが言えるが、繫辭「甶」（第六の３項参照）により目的語の名詞句「茲卜」が前置され、動詞「用」の對象になっている。例文（５）の對貞は「其用茲卜」であり、これは該卜兆を用いるかどうかの疑念の意を「其」字にて表現していることが分かる。（「其」字の解釋については後述する。）

　例文（６）も（５）と同じ構造であるが、ここでは、「卜」に「元」という形容詞が用いられている。この形容詞の意味は、はっきり理解できないが「元の」とか「オリジナル」な卜兆ととれるかも知れない。卜には、外に、「二卜」、「三卜」、「四卜」等というように序數が冠せられることがよくある。また、「一卜」もあることから、「元卜」とは意味上何か區別があったかとも思える。更に、「用五卜」（『甲編』二六八）や「用六卜」（『乙編』五三九九）もあることから、一事に對して數卜されていたことがあったということが分かる。そして、例文（４）、（５）、（６）等から選擇の自由があったこともうかがえよう。もし、例えば、「六卜」が用いられたとしたら、それまでの五卜には効力なしとか、或るいは、無意味、卽ち、「兆不呈」というように判斷さ

れた可能性を含んでいたかも知れないのである。しかし、どのようにして判斷されたかは不明である。

　例文（7）の「二月貞卜子亡諾」は、郭沫若の解釋によると、「卜子」を人名としてとらえ、その證として『粹編』一二五三の「其自卜有來擇」を引き、「卜」を地名、從って、人名にも用いられるとする。更に、例文（7）の語順が不自然とし、「…如"卜子"不連文、例當云"二月卜貞"、不得云"貞卜"也」としている（『粹考』頁一六三ォ―一六三ゥ）。例文（7）の「二月貞卜…」を「二月卜貞…」の誤りとするのは、下辭に「二月卜」、「三月卜」、「兹三卜」とあり、一應根據があると認められるであろう。しかし、そのように解釋するなら、「卜子」を人名としてとらえることができないはずである。「卜子」は、周知の「卜竹」や「卜賓」（卜者たる竹、卜者たる賓の意）なる表現と構造が同じになり、ことによったら、正しい解釋とみなせないことはないが、郭沫若は「卜」を個有名詞にとっており、その意味は「卜地の子」でなければならない。また、その構造は、「限定句」であろう。ところが、「卜竹」や「卜賓」の「卜」は普通名詞であって、その構造は「限定」ではなく、「同格竝置」である。この際、「卜賓」の構造を限定にとり、「卜を行う賓」というふうに解釋できなくはないが、かかる限定は「卜地の子」というのと意味論的に異なっている。また郭氏は『粹編』一二五三の例を引くも、これは「其自外有來禍」と理解すべきかと思われる。「卜」字を「外」字に解釋する可能性をここで打ち出したのであるが、これは上例の（1）及至（8）にはあてはまらないことに注意されたい。例文（2）は、或るいは、「外」にとれるかも知れないが、（3）は無理である。

　例文（7）の初辭は、正確には、恐らく「二月卜貞子亡諾」であったと思われる。そして、第二辭以後、「二月の卜は、（子）に諾あらん」、「三月の卜は、（子）に諾有らん」、「兹の三卜は（子に）諾亡からん」と解釋し、ここでも「卜」にある種のパワーがあった、と信じられていたのではないかと推測し得るのである。

　最後に、例文（8）であるが、この辭の解釋には異說が出されると豫想できる。我々の今迄の論點からすれば、「…卜興、亡凶」の部分の意味は「卜兆が興らなかったが、害亡かれ」と解釋でき、ここでは、しかるべき卜兆が期待されていたのであろうが、それが得られなかった。從って、その「凶（＝害）」

は亡かれと祝禱的な言辭を宣告したと思われる。どうやら、卜兆がないというのも良いことではなかったらしいということがてくる。

　以上の例文（1）から（8）まで「卜」字に關し我々の解釋を施したのであるが、刻辭なき卜兆の意味は、その卜兆に效力がないとか、無意味だとか、或るいは、ニュートラルだとかいうように判斷されていたのではあるまいか、そして、そのような場合には、刻辭することをしなかったのではないか、と推測するわけである。

　我々が卜辭命龜說の補正案を出すにあたり、もう一つ重要と思われることがある。それは次のようなことである。

　正反の對貞、または、多項式選擇から構成される命辭は、ある特定の卜兆と關係が成立し、その卜兆がパワーのあるものとして取り扱われたのであろう。そして、それが正と對應するものであるにせよ、反と對應するものであるにせよ、どちらも殷人にとって無益な内容ではなかったのであろう。多項式選擇の場合もしかりである。そして、その場合、次に舉げる例のように、正反が言語の型式的な面からも意味的な面からも「均等」な價値があると認められる對貞が命龜說の對象になると思われる。

　　（1）王隹有不諾。　　　　　　　　　　『丙編』九六・(6)
　　（2）王不隹有不諾。　　　　　　　　　『丙編』九六・(7)
　　（3）丙戌卜韋貞令役往于虘。　　　　　『丙編』一一〇・(3)
　　（4）丙戌卜韋貞勿令役〔往〕于虘。　　『丙編』一一〇・(4)
　　（5）貞夒其取。　　　　　　　　　　　『丙編』三〇六・(12)
　　（6）貞夒弗其取。　　　　　　　　　　『丙編』三〇六・(13)

例文（1）と（2）では、「王が不諾」を有するということが、「隹・不隹」というバランスのとれた正反の對應により構成されている。例文（3）と（4）も「役」〔人名〕が虘に往くことを命ずるか否かを「令・勿令」で均等に命龜している。例文（5）と（6）も夒が（何かを）取れるかどうかを、（5）では肯定、（6）では否定の「弗」を用いて表現している。そして、この場合、「其」字が正反兩方に用いられ、第五の6項にて詳述する「其」字のモダリティーが共通して表現されている。そのことから考えても、正反のいずれかが卜兆により啓示され、その「情報」價値は等しいものであったと思われる。次に白川氏が

「卜辭命龜說」が成立しないとして擧げた四點の中の第二、(ロ)の卜辭の言語型式についてであるが、氏の言う貞卜對象によって一事一貞法とか兩貞法とかが大體に於いて區別しうるという觀察は正しいと思われる。「旬亡禍」とか「今夕亡禍」とか「往來亡禍」という各辭には、その「肯定形」、即ち、意味的に反に相當する辭が貞字の後に用いられることがない。これはきまり文句であったようだ。かかる表現は、特に後期の卜辭に顯著であり、その事實をふまえ、「卜辭修祓・祝禱說」を形成した白川氏の貢獻を本稿では高く評價し、容認できるところは採用したく思う。それは、後述するように、主に一事一貞法に認められよう。

　(ハ)で述べられた、例えば、『文錄』一七四の「癸亥卜王」を白川氏は「癸亥の日に王を卜す」と理解しているが（白川論文、頁三五）、これは誤解である。「卜」を他動詞に解釋するのは、孫詒讓や羅振玉もそうであったが（一項參照）、古典での用法であり、殷代の甲骨文にそぐわない。『文錄』一七四以下に累見する「干支卜王」は、例えば、一八〇にある「甲戌卜、王在自渲卜」や一八二の「甲辰卜、王在自寮卜」のように、「卜」字が二度現われ、その略式記述である。後者の例で言えば、「甲辰の日の卜、王、師の寮に在りて卜す」と訓むべきであると思う。このことは饒宗頤氏も指摘しているとおりである㉒。文末の「卜」は自動詞である。さらに、その意味は、甲骨を焦灼し、「プック」という輕い音とともに龜裂を生ぜしめることである。これは『說文』の定義でもある。また、白川氏は、一事多貞の卜法は十卜を以ってする例が多いと指摘した。これは正しいが、一事兩貞の場合でも十卜は數多くあり㉓、一事多貞のみに特別の意味を持たせんとしたのは妥當ではない。

　(ニ)の繇辭と驗辭は命龜說では解釋できないとするのは當然であって、董氏は命辭・貞辭に限って論じたのである。本稿では、甲骨文を記事刻辭と非記

㉒　『殷代貞卜人物通考』、頁六四～六五。饒氏は同著（頁六〇～六三）で、「干支卜王」を「干支卜王貞」の省略型でもあり得るとしている。屈萬里氏も同樣な意見である。『殷虛甲編考釋』（頁一八/一〇四片）參照。

㉓　『丙編』に例が多く、例えば、四九・(1)(2)、六七・(7)(8)、一〇八・(5)(6)等。しかし、常に十卜とは限らず、三卜から十卜まで色々ある。これらの例は次の論考を參考されたし。張秉權「卜龜腹甲的序數」『慶祝胡適先生六十五歲論文集』史語所集刊、第二十八本、下冊（一九五六年）、頁二二九～二七二。饒宗頤「由卜兆記數推究殷人對于數的觀念」『慶祝董作賓先生六十五歲論文集』・下冊、史語所集刊外編、第四種（一九六一年）、頁九四九～九八二、特に、頁九五八～九六一を參照されたし。

事刻辭に大分し、前者には署名、前辭、驗辭、兆辭等を、後者には命辭と繇辭を含める、という慣習に基づいて考察を進めることにする。

以上、白川氏の卜辭命龜說斥棄[24]の理由について檢討を試みてみたが、氏の大前提の不確實性、「命曰」の「命」字についての誤解等もあり、命龜說を抹殺してしまうには至らないと思われる。更に、四つの理由の中、（ハ）と（ニ）は見當違い、（イ）の刻辭なき卜兆の意味を考慮外にしてしまったことは、重大な缺陷と思う。要するに、（ロ）で述べられた一事一貞法とか兩貞法に分類可能という型式學的見地から建立した卜辭修祓・祝禱說が最も重要な、また、受容できる出發點（point of departure）になっている。では、次に、氏の說の內容を見て、些少細かく檢討を加えてみよう。

2 卜辭修祓・祝禱說の分析

先ず、「修祓」とは、「みそぎはらえ」することだと思われるが、誰が如何なる目的で何をそうするのか。白川氏の答えは、明白であって、貞人か或いは殷王自身が王者を聖化（sanctify）するために、その支配する時間と空間を清めるのだという（頁三四—三五）。そして、「祝禱」とは、殷王が巫祝者（shaman）として神龜を通じて宇宙の統一者に向かって、その卜意の實現を要求する祈りであるとする（頁三七—三八）。ここには、卜辭を質問（question）と捉える餘地はない。命辭とは、疑問文ではなく、選擇や祝禱などを目的とする非疑問文と解釋する本稿の考えとも一致する。問題は、殷代後期の貞卜の意義を白川氏の考えたような修祓・祝禱說がどの程度まで實際の卜辭の言語の分析・理解により支持することができるか、ということである。そこで、先

---

[24] 白川氏は、命龜說以外にも別說を二つほど擧げ、批判を加えている。「卜辭繇辭說」と「卜辭記錄說」と名付けられたものである。前者は、瞿潤緡「大龜四版考釋商榷」『燕京學報』第十四期（一九三三年）、頁一六一～一八三。後者は、平岡武夫「王者の記錄としての龜甲文と銅器銘」『東方學報』京都、第十二冊第一分（一九三一年）、頁三九～七〇、竝びに松田壽男「殷の卜辭と古代支那人の生活」『加藤博士還曆記念東洋史集說』（東京、冨山房、一九三一年）、頁七四五～七六七。以上の兩說には、卜辭の性質を考える上で、心得ておくべき指摘もある。例えば、瞿氏の「契刻は占卜の後に行われた」ということなど、また、平岡氏の「純然たる記錄體の"帚杞示七屯一、賓"」—即ち、我々の「記事刻辭」—という刻辭グループが存在した事實などが擧げられよう。しかし、現在では、繇辭說も記錄說も甲骨文のある一部にのみ、それもかなり修正を經てから、採るべきものであると思え、全般的には、白川氏の批判が認められよう。故に、本稿では、項を設けて議論することは避けることにした。

ず、白川論文で引用している卜辭の主な例を中心に檢討してみることにする。
　貞卜形式には、簡單なものから述べて、二つのタイプがあるとする。一つは、旬末の癸の日に來旬の吉凶を「貞ふ」卜旬と呼ばれているもので（ここで「貞」字を「とふ」と訓んでいるのは白川氏）、この外に「卜夕」と呼ばれる毎晩の「吉凶」を「貞ふ」卜辭も含むとする。例えば、「癸巳卜、賓貞旬亡禍」（大連坑出土大龜第四版、『甲編』二一二二）という定型的刻辭を十日（＝一旬）毎に九ヶ月間に亙ってくりかえしているもの。更に「己卯卜、貞王今夕寧」（『前編』三・二五・四）、もしくは、「甲申卜、旅貞今夕亡禍。在十一月。」（『文錄』四二）という型式のもの。もう一つのタイプは、先程も引用したが、「卜王」とするもので、例えば、「癸未卜王」（『文錄』一七八）などの型式のもの。前者のタイプは、ひとしく一事一貞、後者のタイプは、一事多貞の型式であるとしている。我々は、後者に關しては、旣に白川氏の理解を受容しがたいと論じたが、前者の卜旬、卜夕、及び卜寧に關しては、それらを言語活動としてとらえる時、氏の修祓・祝禱説はかなりの説得力を持っていると思う。卜旬と卜夕は、恐らく殷王武丁期から帝辛期まで繼續的に行なわれたのではないかと推測され、それらに見える「亡禍」という表現に肯定形がないことが多いという事實は、正反や、或るいは、犧牲動物の數とか種類などを決定する「選擇」を神龜に命ずる、と理解した命龜説では、うまく説明できない。「亡禍」を純疑問文にとり、「禍亡からんか」と訓むものも神龜からの具體的な答えが永遠に得られないため、不自然のように思える。ちなみに記しておくと龜ほど靜かな生き物はいないと言われるし、龜が「質問」に對して答を與えるということは、尋常ではない。
　これとは對照的に、卜寧の「王今夕寧」とか「乙酉卜、貞今夕師亡禍、寧」（『粹編』一二〇六）の「寧」には、意味的に正のみで反がない。これも、從って、祝禱的に、或るいは、修祓的（？）に解釋するのが自然のようである。つまり、これらの卜辭は、卜者の將來に對する「答」そのものであり、白川氏の力説するところの儀禮的・慣習的言・語行爲として受けとめられよう。ここには、本來の意味であるべき未來を豫知せんとするうらない行爲の意義が喪失し、むしろ、未來に對し働きかけているように解釋できそうである。この點は、第五項で取り上げるキートリー氏の論文に詳説されているので、そこで追考したく思う。卜旬、卜夕、卜寧の外に、「卜田遊」と言われる一事一貞の

定型的刻辭があり、これも董作賓の二者擇一、及び我々が補充した公平選擇の命龜說ではうまく說明できない。實例は無數にあるが、「戊午卜、貞王其田、往來亡災」（『甲編』三九一八）等は典型的なものである。これらを命龜說で解釋しようとすれば、正反の選擇ではなく、意味的に正なるもののみを貞卜手段を通して命龜するということになる。それは、少なくとも、「祝禱的」と捉え得るのではあるまいか。

　以上に述べた卜旬、卜夕、卜寧は時間という觀念で、また、卜田遊（卜往來）の方は場所の觀念で、殷人に理解されていたとする白川說には、我々は積極的に反對できないかも知れない。しかし、氏が次の卜辭例を根據として時間を具體的な存在者であったとするのは、如何であろうか。

　　癸酉卜有燎于六旬、六豕劉羊六。　　　　　　　　　　『後編』上・二二・三

この文（白川氏は拓本でみられる「六」及び「劉」の二字を、それぞれ「于」字の後と「豕」の後に見落としている）で問題なのは、白川氏が「旬」と釋字したものであるが、これは甲骨文では「𠣥」と刻され、「𠣥」の別體であることは、例えば、『乙編』五三一七の

　　己丑卜、爭貞亦乎雀燎于𠣥犬

を見れば分かる。この字は「旬」ではなく、「雲」に釋字するのが通例である。燎祭は祖先神をはじめ方向性のある雲や河等の自然神に對して行われたと思える。從って、時間を具體的な存在者と考える根據は消滅してしまうのである。一方、白川氏が「卜田遊」を場所的修祓とするのも、「往來亡災」の卜辭以外に適例を舉げていない。この方は、未開社會や原始社會によくみられるとされている土地の禍患性と人間との關係という文化人類學的議論に賴っているのみで、卜辭からの實例は引用していない。また積極的に思いあたる用例も考え及ばない。これらを要するに、王の支配する時間と空間を淸めるというのは、かなり抽象的な言い方で、言語學的に實證、ないしは、支持するレベル迄には達していないと言わざるを得ない。

　以上を小結してみると、我々は白川氏の卜辭修祓・祝禱說を卜辭言語型式の簡單な卜旬、卜夕等から評價し、實證こそ難しい面もあるとしながらも、董作賓の命龜選擇說よりは優れているところがあるとした。殘された問題の一つとして、修祓・祝禱說が卜辭の言語型式の複雜な肯定的命題と否定的命題を具

えた兩貞法にも適應するか否か、ということがあり、次にそのことについて考えてみたい。

　白川論文では兩貞法に於いても修祓・祝禱說を維持するのであるが、正反二命題の反の意義をどう說明するかが意味論的に最大の問題になろうと豫想される。何故ならば、正反の對偶により「選擇」ということが必然的に生じてくるからである。ところが、白川氏のその問題に對する解釋は「選擇」というより「質問」の觀念（question, rather than selection）でとらえているようであり、その點では孫詒讓や羅振玉の考えから脫し切れていない。氏は次のように言っている（白川論文、頁三六）。

　　「…祭祀・天象における卜問の對象が、上天の帝處にあって自由に下土に降臨來格する神々であるために、一義的に修祓のための行爲といふよりは貞ふといふことの意識がなほ強くはたらいてゐたことを示すのであるが、しかしなほ肯定的命題が卜意に適ふべきものとして期待されてゐたらしいことは、いはゆる繇辭的な刻辭の大體からもこれを察することができる」と。

そして、繇辭的な刻辭例として、「吉・大吉・弘吉・亡尤・亡𡆥・若・受屮・用・茲用・御・茲御」を肯定的なもの、「凶・𡆥・不若」を否定的なものとして舉げている。本稿では繇辭とは、王などが卜兆を實際に觀察してその意味するところを記した刻辭のみを指すという一般的に認められている定義に基づいて考えを進めるため、これらの表現中に不適當なものもある。例えば、「大吉・用・茲用・茲御」等は驗辭であり繇辭ではない。また、「凶」字については甲骨文字にその原形が檢出されていない。從って、白川氏の繇辭的表現諸例は、氏の重要なインサイトと思われる「肯定的命題が卜意に適ふべきものとして期待されてゐたらしい」という可能性を如何に支持しているか明らかではない。本稿では、かかる可能性を追述する三つの點から補正してみたい。また、「其」という語氣助詞の意味論的分析、及びディスプレー・インスクリプション（展示銘刻）と呼ばれる卜辭の內容分析（contextual analysis）による結果を導入することによってその可能性を具體的に支持してみたい。前者の「其」字に關する解釋は、主にポール・L-M・セロイス氏の硏究成果[25]、後者のディス

---

[25] Paul L-M. Serruys, "Studies in the Language of the Shang Oracle Inscriptions," *T'oung Pao*, Vol. LX, 1-3 (1974), pp. 12-120; particularly see pp. 25-34.

プレー・インスクリプションは、デイヴィッド・N・キートリー氏の貢獻[26]である。今、その主旨のみをここに記すと、先ずセ氏は次の如く述べている。

> "... we find that the presence or absence of *ch'i* is a sign of very clear contrast between two different kinds of oracular propositions: presence of *ch'i* marks the proposition of the alternative among possible courses of action, which is considered less desirable, less preferred, often positively feared and resorted to only if really unavoidable. This rule applies to regardless of whether the proposition is expressed in negative of affirmative sentences."(p.25)

ここで述べられていることは、「其」字が命辭の肯定文か否定文のどちらかに用いられている場合にあてはまる。「そのどちらの場合にでも意味的に（貞卜者側にとって）望ましくない」というのであるから、かなり強力なインプリケーションがある。それは、兩貞法に關し白川氏の考えた「貞ふことの意識が強くはたらいてゐた」ということを否定さえするものである。これが、補正しなくてはならない第一の點である。

次に、白川氏の「肯定的命題が卜意に適ふべきものとして期待されてゐたらしい」というのを、セ氏の説明に從うと、必ずしも肯定的命題に限らず、文法的に否定的命題の場合でも考え得るわけである。例えば、次の兩貞（對貞）の卜辭を見てみよう。

(1) 丙辰卜、㱿貞帝隹其終玆邑。貞帝弗終玆邑。　『丙編』七一・(1)(2)
(2) 戊申卜、爭貞帝其降我艱。戊申卜、〔爭〕貞帝不我艱。
　　　　　　　　　　　　　　　　　　　　　　　　　『丙編』六七・(7)(8)
(3) 貞祖乙其壱王。貞祖乙弗壱王。　『丙編』三三二・(13)(14)

以上の三組の外にも例はかなりあるが、これらに共通して言えることは、動詞の意味するところが貞卜者側にとって好ましくないということである。例文(1)の對貞の肯定の方に「其」字が用いられ、「帝が玆の邑を終らしむ」ということは確かに望ましいことであったとは言えない。同樣に、(2)では「帝が我々に艱を降らしむ」ということは望ましくないため、婉曲の意味をも含んだ「其」

---

[26] David N. Keightley, *Sources of Shang History*. Berkeley: University of California Press, 1978, p.46, n.90.

字が用いられていると解釋できる。（3）では「祖乙が王に壱す」というネガティブなことが「其」字によって弱められているが如くである。從って、これらの例からも分かるように、「肯定的命題」というのは、文法的範疇が肯定というのではなく、意味論的範疇で考えねばならない。これが白川氏の指摘に對しての補正すべき第二の點である。本稿では、今までも既に用いたが、「正・反」の「正」という術語をこの意味論的な範疇に用い、「肯定」という術語を文法的範疇でとらえることにしたい。「反」は正に對する反對語、「否定」は肯定に對する反對語である。前者は意味論的、後者は文法的範疇を指すことは言うまでもない。

さて、かかる補正を加えた上で、兩貞法に於いての正反の辭は、そのいずれか一方に「其」字が用いられている場合に限り、かなりバイアスのかかったものであると理解されねばならないであろう。正反の對偶による「選擇」とは、必ずしも完全にバランスのとれた、公平なものではなかったのである。その意味で、白川氏の「肯定的（＝正の）命題が卜意に適ふべきものとして期待されてゐた」という可能性が支持され得ると思うのである。これは豫測されることだが、「其」字が正反兩辭に用いられたり、或るいは、全く用いられたりしない場合は、そのような期待はニュートラルであり、公平な選擇として受けとめるべきであろう。

以上述べた「其」字の意味論的分析に加え、更にマクロな觀點から正の命題が貞意に適うべきものとして期待されていた可能性を支持できるものにキートリー氏の提唱するディスプレー・インスクリプションというものがある。今、その定義の部分を記すと次のとおりである。（注 26 参照。）

> "… certain 'display inscriptions' appear to have been written all at one time. As I define them, the essential characteristics of these display inscriptions are: (1) bold, large calligraphy; (2) the prognostication and verification written as a single, continuous, and usually placed immediately next to the charge; the verification, frequently detailed, confirms the accuracy of the prognostication."

この定義を具現するものとして、キ氏は、『丙編』一・（3）、五七・（1）、二四七、『菁華』二〔これは一或るいは三の誤〕、『庫方』一五九五、『鐵雲』五・三等を擧げている。これらは全て第一期の賓組卜辭である。それらには、命辭、繇辭、驗辭と齊整しているため、零細な斷片上の不完全な刻辭が甲骨文の大部分という事實からして、ややマクロな觀點からの内容分析が可能であ

る。ここでは、二つほどの刻辭例を見てみよう。

　　（1）癸未卜、爭貞旬亡禍。王占曰有祟。三日乙酉夕斷丙戌允有來入齒。十三月。　　　　　　　　　　　　　　　　　　　　『庫方』一五九五＝『英國』八八六

　　（2）甲申卜、殻貞婦好冥嘉。王占曰其隹丁冥嘉、其隹庚冥引吉。三旬又一日甲寅冥、不嘉。隹女。　　　　　　　　　　　　　　　　『丙編』二四七・（1）

例文（1）では、命辭にて「旬に禍亡からん」という、白川氏の説く修祓・祝禱的な言辭（utterance）を謳いながらも、王が「祟有らん」とト兆を占み、更にト日である癸日から三日經った乙酉の夕が翌日の丙戌を「斷る」頃（＝過ぎた頃か）、まことに闌入してきた齟齬が來らされたこと有り、と驗している。ここで「齒」を「齟齬」の意としておいたが、これは定かではない。但し、命辭中の「禍」は繇辭中の「祟」に呼應していることは確かであろうから、好ましくない意味にとるのが自然だと思われる。例文（2）では、命辭にて「婦好が分娩（冥）するに、嘉ならん」と解釋できる祝禱的な言辭を神龜に告詫しているようである。それに對する繇辭は單純ではなく、先ず「丁の日に分娩するようになれば、嘉となるであろう」とし、更に、「庚の日に分娩するようになれば、引吉（恐らく、單なる吉よりも良い意味）となるであろう」としている。驗辭では、甲申の日から「三十一日經った甲寅の日に分娩があり、それは嘉ではなかった。というのは、女だったからだ」としている。甲寅の日は、王の豫言した丁の日でもなく庚の日でもない。故に（とまで言えるか自信はないが）、嘉ではなかった、ということにでもなるのであろうか。「嘉」の意味は、男子の出世であるということは分かるが、「引吉」が表現として「嘉」とどう違うのかは不明である。もしかしたら、「吉」とか「引吉」というのは、ト兆及び筮の組み合わせに對應する專門用語であったかも知れない。ともあれ、キ氏の指摘で重要だと思われるのは、貞人の命辭ではなく、王の繇辭が、第一、二例でも、また、外のディスプレー・インスクリプションでも、驗辭にて立證されていることである。驗辭が繇辭と全く反對の意味を表わすということは、キートリー氏も指摘する如く㉗、ないようである。この點でも、意味論的範疇での「肯定的命題がト意に適ふべきものとして期待されてゐた」ということが汲みとれるであろう。但し、ディスプレー・インスクリプション（及びそれに

㉗　キ氏論文（頁五五）參照。Cf. also Keightley, *Sources of Shang History*, p.44, n.83.

準ずる例）の場合、「卜意」とは、實は、命辭そのものではなく、繇辭に表現されているものである。そして、既に指摘したように、繇辭は卜兆に潛むと信じられていたパワーを人間の言辭で「翻譯」したものである、と捉え得ると思う。これが、補正しなくてはならない第三の點である。しかしながら、ディスプレー・インスクリプションは、多數の卜辭中、實例が少ない。そのため、白川氏が引用した例の如く、繇辭がなく、命辭から驗辭に直行している場合（何故直行するようになったかという問題は、卜辭の性質の歷史的變遷とも關係があると思われる）、命辭が卜意を表現していると解釋することが許されるのではないだろうか。ここでは、かかる例を二つのみ擧げておくことにする。

(1) 〔己亥〕卜、賓貞翌庚子有告麥。允有告麥。　　『前編』四・四〇・六
(2) …申卜、貞蠱禍、有疾。旬又二日…未蠱允禍、百日又七旬又…蠱亦有疾。　　　　　　　　　　　　　　　　　　　　　　　　『鐵雲』五・三

例（1）は賓組後期の刻辭と思われるが、卜日の己亥の翌日、庚子の日、に「告麥」という農耕儀禮的な祝典をなさんとする意向を神龜に告げたところ、恐らく兆に「吉」が出たのであろう、實行に移したことを驗辭に記している。この場合、命辭は白川氏の修祓的というよりは、貞人も含めた王室側の意志・意向を述べたもの、卽ち「宣言」とする方が自然のようだが、このことは、キートリー氏の說を檢討する際に、更に考えてみたい。例（2）では、地名としても現われる蠱が自然神等により禍わされ、疾病することあらんと祝禱的というよりむしろ呪文的な言辭を神龜に告詫している。その結果、先ず十二日目に命辭の言うところが實現され、また、百七十何日目にも蠱に疾することありとしている。ここで、白川氏は、郭沫若の「是則永無不應之卜矣」[28]を引用し、「卜者は實にその命意の飽くなき實現を求めてやまなかったことが知られる」としている。これは、白川氏の修祓・祝禱說の最も强力な論點であり、命辭を呪術的なマジックの一種であると判斷した一つの理由である（白川論文、頁三八）。しかし、その反面、全ての卜兆が命辭に對して反應したということにはならない。むしろ、ある特定の卜兆が百七十數日という長期間保存され、結果が契刻された、と考える方が自然ではないだろうか。(2)のような例は珍しいし、また、前述した刻辭なき卜兆のこともあるからである。

---

[28]　郭沫若『卜辭通纂攷釋』頁一六九／第九八八片。

以上、白川說をかなり詳細に分析し、批判を加えてきたが、次のようにまとめられると思う。言語形式が簡單で意味論的範疇で考えて正か反しかない命辭は、卜意が貞卜者側の期待するところのものであり、修祓・祝禱的な性格がある。これには祝文的な內容も含められよう。但し、それが王の支配する時間と空間を清めるとするのは、きわめて抽象的且つ形而上學的であり、論證不足の憾みがある。白川說では、兩貞法は、基本的には「質問」という發想法に根ざしていると考え、從來の解釋からぬけ切れていない。これは、「貞」字を「とふ」などと訓じているところからも伺える。但し、氏の「肯定的命題が卜意に適ふべきものとして期待されてゐた」という考えは、それを（一）意味論的に捉え、（二）「其」字の含意するところをも吸收し、（三）ディスプレー・インスクリプションの場合は、命辭そのものではなく繇辭に卜意が表現される、という三點の修正を經た上で、受容できると論じた。今、かかる修正以前の白川說を卜辭の言語的性質問題に關し、歷史的に位置づけるとすれば、羅振玉や董作賓等の先學に見られなかった新しい面が打ち出されたと言うことができよう。また、本稿で修正した後の修祓・祝禱・呪文的內容の命辭及び繇辭の性質は、「とう」という言語行動とはかなり距離があることを示すと思われる。それらの具體的な檢討をこれからも心がけてみるが、今まで論考してきたことを豫備知識として活用したい。

四、饒宗頤、張秉權及び李學勤說

　一九四八年の白川論文からほぽ十年後、饒宗頤氏は古典の經・傳に基づき、卜辭の本質を解明する一つの手がかりともなる「貞」字の釋義に次の四つがあるとした。（i）卜問する、（ii）（一の役に）當たる、（iii）正す（或るいは、正しい）、（iv）定める（注10參照）。（i）の「卜問」するという義は、例えば、「乙巳卜賓貞翌丁未酚彡歲于丁尊出珏」（『續存』下、七二）に伺えるとし、この卜辭例の最後にある「出珏」は「侑珏」にして、『周禮』春官天府の「季冬陳玉、以貞來歲之媺惡」の「陳玉」に等しいとする。しかるに、鄭司農の注に「貞問也」とあり、當該卜辭例の「貞」は鄭注に依るべしとしている。このような見解は、他の無數の「干支卜某貞」の例が「玉」と關係なく、どのように扱うか不明にもなるため、全く議論にならない。（ii）の「當」の義は

『尙書』洛誥の「我二人共貞」に對する馬融の「貞當也」に基づいている。そして、饒氏は、「卜官某、當值其事、卽所謂涖卜也」と解說し、この義は（ⅰ）の義と倂せて理解できようとしている。この馬融の注は、「共貞」すというのを機能的に說明したものである可能性が强く、必ずしも「貞」の原義を說明したものとは考え難い。語源的にも關係ないことは、それらの屬する上古韻部が全く異なるということからも分かる。このような注にのみ依據した解釋は、出來る限り避けたいものである。（ⅲ）の「貞」を「正」とする解釋は、『周禮』の鄭注や『周易』の彖傳や『廣雅』釋詁にある「貞正也」を引いてその證とする。更に、『詩經』文王有聲の「維龜正之」も引用し、これは「問事得其正」の意味であるとしている。「正」については、例えば、「戊子卜賓…正。王占曰吉正」（『續存』上、六五五）などに見られるように、「良貞」を「吉、正」とし、「不良貞」を「凶」とする「判斷之詞」としている。「貞」字に「正」の義があるという說は、語源學的にも傍證を得られるものであり[29]、正しいと思われる。問題は、しかし、かかる「正」が命辭の性格とどうかかわるか、また「正」が「判斷の詞」としたら、「貞」と「正」はその用法からして有機的にどう考えられるかということになると思うのだが、その方面の追及はない。（ⅳ）の「貞」を「定」とする解釋も、漢の『釋名』の「貞定也」を引いて、その證としているのみである。饒氏は、更に「定」は「鼎」と同音とし―これは誤りで、「定」は去聲、「鼎」は上聲である―、『說文』の鼎字下

---

[29] このことは、語源的に貞と正が同根であるということを古人が感知した結果、それが注に「貞正也」などと現われたりした、というべきであろう。甲骨文での資料から、殷代でも貞と正が深く關係していたことは、次のような對貞からも讀みとれる。

　　　戊戌其貞雨。　　　　　　　　　　　　　　　　　『丙編』五二七・（5）
　　　其雨。　　　　　　　　　　　　　　　　　　　　『丙編』五二七・（6）

「正雨」という「形容詞＋名詞」の表現があり（『綜類』七一・三參照）、それは「ほどよい雨」とか「適量の雨」という意味だと思われる。しかるに、ここでは、「正雨」のかわりに「貞雨」が用いられている。出典の『丙編』五二七の拓本を見ると、この腹甲には熟練契刻者と未熟な契刻者と思える者が「貞雨」なる表現を不注意にも用いたと推察するわけであるが、「正」というコトバ（字形ではない）と「貞」というコトバが密切に關係あることを如實に示した好例と言えよう。尙、この件に關しては、次の二著をも參照されたし。
　　一、Bernhard Karlgren, *Grammata Serica Recensa*. Reprinted in offset from the *Bulletin of the Museum of Far Eastern Antiquities*, No.29 (1957), pp.220-221/833j, 834g.
　　二、藤堂明保『漢字語源辭典』（東京、學燈社、一九六五年）、頁四六四～四六八。

にある「籀文以鼎爲貞字」を引き、その源流は甲骨文に遡るとして、『乙編』八八八八片の「己巳鼎帚婡老亡禍」と「貞妙亡禍」の同版例を擧げている。ここにいう「源流は甲骨文に遡る」には同意できるが、「鼎」と「貝」の字形のあいまいさの指摘はない。（これに關しては後述。）『乙編』の例文は「鼎」字と「貞」字が假借に用いられているのがわかるだけであって、それが「定」の義であるという證據にはならない。「定」字は、甲骨文にて地名のみに用いられており、甲骨文からは『釋名』の定義を支持する證據は求められない。

以上簡評してきたように、饒宗頤氏の見解は、學問的價値が薄いといわざるを得ないのだが、一つだけ我々の問題意識に觸れることとして、次の如き言及がある。

「總上而論、貞字有取疑問語氣者、爲『貞問』之義；有取肯定語氣者、則爲『當値』之義；或卜事得『正』之義。舊說於貞字下、每施問號、多不可通。今參諸經典、得條析其異訓如上、言卜辭者所宜詳辨也。」（注10所揭書、頁七一。）

饒氏は上文にて「貞」字の下に來る文每に疑問符を施すことは、多分に義不通になると言っている。そして、千三百頁にも及ぶ饒書の引用卜辭例に疑問符をつけ加えなかったのである。このことは、因襲的中國人研究者に「占い」とは「問うことだ」と信じられていた「常識」の束縛から抜け出した感じを與える。饒氏のこの考えは、その當時、衝動的效果はあったと思われるが、說得力のあるものと見做されることがなかったとみえ、臺灣の張秉權氏により強い反駁を受けることになる。

一九六五年刊行の『殷虛文字丙編・考釋』（中輯㈡、頁四四五）で、張氏は、先ず、卜辭中の「貞」字の釋義を饒氏の擧げた四つの中から選ぶ必要があるとする。これは、勿論、そのとおりなのであるが、重要なのは、何を基準にしたら選べるかということである。基準になる手がかりが求められないのである。次に、張氏は「二人共貞」の卜辭例の一つとして饒氏の引用した「癸未卜爭◯貞旬亡禍」（『粹編』一四二四）を問題にとりあげる。二人共貞の場合は、饒氏に依れば、馬融の注に從い「貞當也」ということになる。（これが「基準」らしきもののある僅か一例。）故に、上例中の「貞」は「肯定語氣的"當値"之義」という風に饒氏は解釋していると思われる。ところが、張秉權氏は、貞字の下の「旬亡禍」に疑問符を施すべきなのかどうか結局のところ饒氏の考えが分からないとし、次のように決めつける。

「假如可以〔加個疑問符〕、當然無所謂"不可通"了、假如不可、則命辭非疑問、占卜所爲何來？除非根本否定"貞"下"旬亡禍"三字是命辭、否則那一條還是應當屬於疑問語氣的卜辭、它下面還是應該施以問號的。」

前項、第三、で白川氏の所説をレヴューしてきた我々にとって、饒宗頤、張秉權兩氏の爭論は觀念的で啓發されるところに乏しいと言わざるを得ない。上引した張氏の所論も占卜とは問うことだと思い込み、命辭なら命辭の性格を吟味し、探究しようとする所がない。我々は、少し前に、「貞」字と「正」字の分佈用法などから有機的にどう考えられるかが問題だとした（これに關しての我々の分析・解釋は第六の1項を參照）が、張氏の見解は次のような指摘にとどまるのみである。

「…那一類卜辭〔卽、前所揭的『續存』上、六五五〕中的"正"字、是否經傳中的"正龜"之事有關、實在還是問題、其不能用以解釋卜辭的序辭中的貞字、則可斷言。」

この張氏の饒説に對に對する反駁自體は、饒説がもとより實證性に乏しいため正當だと認められるのであるが、そこから發展していこうとする所がみられない。これでは、第一項でレヴューした羅振玉及び早期研究者による見解と大差ない。

饒、張兩氏の所説とは對照的に、時代が下るが、一九八〇年に出版された李學勤氏の論文（李論文一、注6參照）は、第八項で檢討する裘錫圭氏の説の一つのインピタスにもなっていて興味深い。李論文一は、自組卜辭などでは、「由占曰…」のように貞人「由」が王のかわりに用いられること、貞人「衍」の卜辭の特異性、「自上甲廿示」が必ずしも直系の先王を指さないこと等を論じたあと、特に、命辭の言語性格の究明に深く關連してくる「語末助詞」について、注目すべき提言をしている。（李氏の言う「語末助詞」を裘錫圭氏は「句末助詞」としており、その方が用語としては「正しい」ので、以下「句末助詞」に統一することにする。）今迄の解釋は、主に『説文』の「貞、卜問也」という定義に基づき、觀念的に命辭は疑問文にとるのがよかろうと思われてきた。しかし、李氏は、一つの文である命辭そのものに次の四つの句末助詞が用いられていると指摘し、用例も若干擧げている。（ⅰ）「不」（否）、（ⅱ）「乎」、（ⅲ）「㞢」、（ⅳ）「執」。つまり、もしこれらが句末助詞として用いられるのだとしたら、命辭は明らかに疑問文として解釋すべきである、ということになる。李氏のこの説は、後考するニビソン、ショナシー、裘錫圭氏の説

に深遠な影響を與えたのである。もっとも、ニビソン氏は、李氏説を容認した上で、これらの句末助詞が殷の貞人によって用いられていない大多數の命辭は、論理的に考えると、疑問文ではないとすべきだ、という逆手論法をとっている。（注13所揭論文、頁四—五參照。）つまり、もしこのような句末助詞により疑問文が明白にマークされるなら、マークのないものは肯定文と見做すべきであろうというのである。この四つの「句末助詞」に關しては、本稿第八項の裘錫圭氏によりかなり重要な修正案が出されているために、そこで詳しく論ずることにしたい。ここでは、ただ私の分析の結果として、李氏説はことごとく成立しないということのみをつけ加えておくにとどめておく。

次に、一九八五年の李論文二では、上述の李論文一の内容には觸れることなくして、次の如く論じている。

「…殷墟黃組卜辭辭末也常有『正』或『有正』、古代『貞』、『正』二字相通假、所以洪洞坊堆卜骨辭尾的"貞"也就是"正"、恰與『周易』文例相合。…『左傳』、『國語』所載卜筮命辭、辭的末句常冠以"尚"字、"尚"當依『爾雅』訓爲"庶幾"楊樹達先生認爲是命令副詞。西周卜辭的"囟"（斯）字應訓爲"其"、也是義爲"庶幾"的命令副詞。…必須注意的是、"斯…"或"尚…"這樣以命令副詞開首的句子、絕不是問句。這表明、西周卜辭都不是問句。我們在「幾點研究」文中㉚、認爲有些問句、有些不是、這個看法是錯誤的、現在應該更正。」（注6所揭李論文二、頁五—六）。

李學勤氏は、周原甲骨の「囟」字を「囟」（斯）に釋字し、それが「其」（＝庶幾）を意味するという判斷に基づいて、周原卜辭は疑問文ではなく、命令文か祈求文であると解釋していることが分かる。李氏は更に安陽卜辭にもあてはまるとして、次のように述べている。

「既然西周卜辭的"斯正"、"斯有正"之類不是問句、殷墟卜辭的"正"、"有正"也肯定不是問句。卜辭是否問句、近年在學術界一個爭論問題、涉及對所有卜辭的理解。上面的分析可能對解決這一問題有所裨益。」（頁六）

安陽甲骨には、周原甲骨の「囟」に似た字として、「囟」があり、これを「囟」（小篆⊗）字としたのは、陳夢家の說に遡れる㉛。陳氏は、「囟」を

㉚ 李學勤「西周甲骨的幾點研究」『文物』一九八一年、第九期、頁七～一二。李學勤「關于自組卜辭的一些問題」に言及がないことを考えると、李氏は、命辭が疑問文であると判斷できるものは自組卜辭のみに限定しているようでもある。

㉛ 陳夢家『殷虛卜辭綜述』（北京、科學出版社、一九五六年）、頁三二七。

「脺」卽ち脳蓋を象どったものとし、「首脳」または「脳殻」の意味があったとする。例えば、「⊕」は「羌方」（『甲編』五〇七）とか「觸（或釋として危）方」（『南明』六六九）等の直後に出現し、それぞれ「羌方の首領、或いは、その頭顱」、「觸方の首領、或いは、その頭顱」という義であろうとしている㉜。注32で考慮した義も含め、周原卜辭の用例にそくして考えると、文脈上不自然ではないと思える解釋は、李氏の「斯」という語詞的解釋の外に、名詞にとることだと思われる。如何なものであろうか㉝。安陽卜辭では、

㉜　この説は、于省吾氏や李棪氏等により部分的に受容され、「⊕」字が羌方や觸方の首領の頭顱を意味し、それが『甲編』五〇七（羌方⊕其用、王受祐）と『南明』六六九（…用觸方⊕于妣庚、王賓）では犠牲になっているとする。（于省吾氏の解釋は『東北人大學報』（第二、三期、一九五七年）にあるとのことだが未見。）李棪氏の解釋は「殷墟斫頭坑髑髏與人頭骨刻辭」『中國語文研究』（第八期、一九八六年）、頁三四、三七）を参照。李氏は、人間の頭蓋骨を後から見ると⊕のようになると言っているのだが、これはどうであろうか。むしろ、△のように見え、「頗似⊕形」とまでは言えないようである。上の『甲編』と『南明』の用例は、もしかしたら、△（白＝伯）の誤増畫にて、それぞれ、「羌方の伯」（伯は地方のリーダー一格の人間）と解釋すべきかも知れない。『京津』四〇三四に次のような例がある。「…亥左羌二方△、其用于祖丁父甲」。「左」はここでは恐らく「切る」というような意味の祭祀動詞であろう。この文では「羌二方伯」が「左」の目的語になっているようだ。すると、ここでは、△が頭蓋骨を表わしたとは解釋できない。最も自然な解釋は、例えば、『甲編』二四一六などにある「盂方伯炎」などと同じく名詞句にとることだと思われる。このように考えてくると、△が頭蓋骨であることは斷定できない。また小篆文字に⊗（凶）ではなく、⊕があり、この方が甲骨の形に近い。この小篆文字は、「由（フツ）」と楷書化され、『説文』によると「鬼頭也、象形」とされている。もし△（白）がどんぐりの象形としたら、凶も由も白も、字形の面のみからは、「人間の頭」（白＝「ドングリ頭」か）で共通性が見い出せなくもない。しかし、字形の共通點は、音と意味との結合した實際の言語とは、本來、關係ない。

㉝　今、李氏の釋文に從つて、周原卜辭の用例を示すと、次の十三例を數える。

　　　囟亡咎。　　　　　　　　　　　　　　　　H11:28、35、77、96、H31:3
　　　囟亡眚　　　　　　　　　　　　　　　　　H11:20
　　　囟正。　　　　　　　　　　　　　　　　　H11:82、84、114、130
　　　囟尚（當）。　　　　　　　　　　　　　　H11:2
　　　囟克事。　　　　　　　　　　　　　　　　H11:21
　　　囟克往密。　　　　　　　　　　　　　　　H11:136
　　　囟城（成）。　　　　　　　　　　　　　　H31:5
　　　囟又（有）罵。　　　　　　　　　　　　　齊家村采112
　　　囟不妥王。　　　　　　　　　　　　　　　H11:174
　　　囟不大追。　　　　　　　　　　　　　　　H11:47
　　　囟御于永冬（終）。　　　　　　　　　　　齊家村H31:1
　　　囟御于永令（命）。　　　　　　　　　　　齊家村H31:1

⊕の用例が稀少なため（『綜類』二四八・一參照）、比較しがたいが、周原卜辭のとは、用法が異なる。注33で引用した周原卜辭からの文例、もしくは、それらに似た例は、皆無であるからである。從って、周原卜辭の「囟（斯）正」と「囟（斯）有正」——ここで△の釋文を認め得たと假定して——から、安陽卜辭の「正」と「有正」も疑問句ではないという論理は成立しない。我々は、李學勤氏の「正」と「有正」が疑問句ではないという判斷には贊成なのだが、氏の論理推進過程に疑いを抱いているのである。安陽卜辭の⊕と周原卜辭の△が全く違ったコトバを表わしていると言ってしまえば、勿論、それで終りなのだが、問題はそこにある。周原卜辭の字形・字釋が安陽卜辭のそれから推して理解できるものがあるのに、どうしてこの場合はできないのか。また、何故に周原卜辭の方では「囟」（斯）なるコトバが「正」と「有正」の前に必要とされ、安陽卜辭では、かかるコトバが不必要であったか、等の問題を考えることによって、兩者の相違が研究されてしかるべきである。李學勤氏の提起したような周原卜辭と安陽卜辭の短絡的な因果關係は、要注意の態度で受けとめておきたい。

五、キートリー說

一九七二年六月、米國カリフォルニア州モントレー市開催の「太平洋岸に於ける東洋學會々議」で發表されたキートリー氏の論文は九十一頁にもなる長論で、その會議に參加した筆者をはじめ、次項以降で紹介・檢討するセロイス、ニビソン、ラフーブレ、ショナシー等の研究者に絕大な影響を及ぼしたのである。その當時から現在にかけて、西ドイツには張聰東（Tsung-tung Chang）、北米には許進雄（James Chin-hsiung Hsü）、周鴻翔（Hung-hsiang Chou）、張光直（Kwang-chih Chang）、スタンレー・ミケル（Stanley Mickel）等の研究者もいるが、彼らにはキ氏の論旨は受容されなかったことも事實である。（その理由は、公けにされていないため、不明である。）このことだけからみれば、一般的に言って、キ氏の說は歐米人には支持され、中國人にはされないということが言えそうであるが、學問とはそのようなものであるはずがない。以下、しばらくキ氏の論旨を追ってみたく思う。

キ氏の論文名は、「はじめに」でも觸れたが、「釋貞—商代占卜の性質に關しての新假説」とでも譯されよう。論文の主旨は、一口で言うならば、「商代の卜辭とは、質問ではなく豫言であり、神祇の諾不諾を得るために宣言した人間の意向聲明である」ということである。

　　"It is the thesis of this essay that ... the oracle-bone inscriptions of Shang were not questions but predictions. What they recorded were not queries, but tentative statements of intent proclaimed to the spirits for their spproval or disapproval."(p.1)

本稿では、これを稱して、「卜辭豫言・宣言説」と呼ぶことにする。この説は、それ迄の研究者が卜辭（命辭）を全て疑問文であると理解していた、所謂、「卜辭疑問・質問説」に正面から反對し、1「貞」の字形の吟味、2『説文』の「貞卜問也」の由來解明、3古典に於ける「貞」、「卜」、「命」の意味解釋、4卜辭の言語型式の分析、5「貞」の意味、6マジックとしての卜辭説から成る六つの節、その下に合計三十五以上の細目での論證から構成されている。論文全體からみると、4の卜辭の言語型式の分析から導こうとする貞字以下の命辭の性質究明に本文の約四分の一（二十二頁）を割き、この點では、我々が既にレヴューした白川論文で用いられた問題アプローチの方法と似ていると言えよう。また、特に、6の卜辭をマジックとして解釋する點などでも、兩者の論文には似かよった見解がみられる。結果的にはそう言えるのであるが、前述した如く、白川氏は卜辭とは殷王が王者として、またシャーマンとしての神聖な性格を表象するものであるといった前提から始まり、卜辭修祓・祝禱説といった、いくらかは豫期できる結論につながっていく論法を取っている。これに對して、キ氏の論文は、時には關係薄いかと思われるようなエヴィデンスを引き出したり、不可思議な議論（追述）を展開してはいるものの、大局的に見て、理論構成が緻密にできているように思える。今、以上の1から6までの各節の内容を紹介し、檢討してみたい。

1　「貞」の字形について

先ず、字形の問題であるが、貞字は「卜」＋「貝」から作られている。ところが、甲骨文では「𠾗」に書かれ、それは鼎（𠾗、𠾗）字の簡略化した形とする。𠾗イコール貞というのは、孫詒讓以來、ただそう言われいるだけなので、

キ氏はそれに對し二つの例を提出する。一つは、饒宗頤氏も引用した『乙編』八八八八の「己巳㊉婦嬕老亡禍」と島氏『綜類』三九六・一で竝列して出ている『乙編』八六九五の「己巳㊉婦嬕老亡禍」である。この二例は同文刻辭であり、㊉と㊉が互換可能ということが分かる。このような例はほかにも見い出せるし（『綜類』三九六・一、二）、更に貞と丁は、『綜類』五七七・一（例えば、『前編』八・六・三、八・十二・四）にもあるように假借として用いられている。しかるに、これらの字音は、カールグレンの上古再構音㉞によると、鼎が、＊tieng、貞が＊tiĕng、丁が＊tiĕngで音韻的に假借が支持されるから、㊉を貞字と考え得る。もう一つの例としては、『說文』（七上）の鼎字項に「…籒文以鼎爲貞字」とあり、鼎と貝が則＝劓、員＝鼎、賔＝霸のように關係づけられることを擧げている。そして、貝は＊pwadのように發音されていたから、貞や鼎と音韻的に關係ない。故に㊉を貞と見做してよい、と判斷している。キートリー氏のこの結論は正しいと思われる。しかし、甲骨文の㊉が字形的に㊉や㊉の「簡略形」（"simplified picture"）とするのは、郭沫若（『通纂』一三/頁六ｫ）なども同じ見解であるが、私は、百パーセント同調することができない。㊉の形については、瞿潤緡氏が「卜」と龜版の形を組み合わせたものとする意見もある㉟。しかし、そのような複雜に微析統合の創造は、或るいは、可能かも知れないが、他の例が想い當たらず、いささか疑問である。やはり、孫詒讓（既述）や羅振玉（『書契考』中、頁一八オ）が「…㊉與㊉字相似而不同」とした如く、貝（㊉―『甲編』七七七）とは別字なるも、それが樣式化された形とするのも捨てがたい。また、ラフーブレ氏の分類（『法國』、頁一三四）に從うと、鼎（㊉―『乙編』一六〇七）の樣式化された形とも考えられる。要するに、貝と鼎の字形上のあいまいさは、甲骨文にまで遡れるのである。（この問題に關しては、更に第六の項で追究してみたい。）但し、キートリー氏の指摘にある如く、字音から言えば、鼎や丁と關係づけられ、貝とは關係ない。コトバとしても、貝と關係ない。

2 『說文』の「貞卜問也」の由來

許愼の『說文』にある「貞卜問也」は、鄭司農（活躍期八九年頃、沒一一

㉞ Bernhard Karlgren, *Grammata Serica Recensa*. Reprinted in offset from the *Bulletin of the Museum of Far Eastern Antiquities*, No.29（1957），pp.221/834.a 參照。

㉟ 瞿潤緡「大龜四版考釋商榷」『燕京學報』第十四期（一九三三年）、頁一七〇～一七二參照。

四年)の『周禮』春官、天府での注「貞問也」に從っているのではないかとする段玉裁や陳邦懷の說㊱をキ氏は正しいとしている。また、鄭司農の注は、王弼(二二六—二四九年)の『易注』や賈逵(三〇—一〇一年)の『國語解詁』、鄭玄(一二七—二〇〇年)の『周禮』の注等の「貞正也」とする傳統を汲んでいないと指摘する。このことは、一九一四年刊の羅振玉の『書契考』(中、頁一八ォ)に「古經注貞皆訓正、惟許書有卜問之訓…」とある如く、我々の知る所であるが、『易』、『國語』、『周禮』、『禮記』等の貞字に對する諸注は、確かに「正也」とする方が「問也」とするより適義であると思われる㊲。上文の羅振玉の『書契考』からの引用文の直後に「古誼古說、賴許書而僅存者、此其一也」と續くが、これは、その當時の卜辭の性質の理解を反映している一方、キ氏の見解とは對照的である。羅振玉はここで『說文』の定義の「稀少價値」を生かそうとし、キ氏はミニマイズしようとしているからである。我々は、かかる「稀少價値」をミニマイズせんとする迄には至らないが、甲骨文に於いてのそれは、要注意として受けとめておくべきであろう。

3 古典に於ける「貞」、「卜」、「命」の意味

漢代以前の古典に於けるこれら三つの語の意味解釋に關しては、『易』、『書』、『左傳』、『論語』、『老子』、『淮南子』等のテキストの中で、これらの語がどのように用いられているかを調査した、とキ氏は言う。先ず、「貞」であるが、「問う」という意味では本義を失するのではないかとして、『左傳』哀公十七年の「衛侯貞卜」を引用する。これをイギリスのジェームズ・レッグが

"The marquis again consulted the tortoise shell"

と英譯し㊳、一見、『說文』の定義に合い、しかも文脈上正しいかと思えるも、これは、實は違うのではないかとし、次の如く論ずる。「衛侯貞卜」の前文は、哀公十七年に衛公が筮で自分のみた夢について占い(「公親筮之」)、

㊱ 段玉裁は、『段注』(『說文解字詁林』三下/頁一三八三)でキ氏の言うようには明記していないようである。一方、陳邦懷は、一九一七年のその著『殷虛書契考釋小箋』(頁一〇ゥ)でそのように明記していることを確め得た。

㊲ キ氏論文(頁四~八)、注29、及び本稿第六の1項を參照されたし。

㊳ James Legge. *The Chinese Classics*, Vol.V: *The Ch'un Ts'ew with the Tso Chuen*. Hong Kong and London, 1872; reprinted in Taipei: Wen-hsing Shu-tien (1966), p.850.

それに對しての占辭が胥彌赦によって「害あらず」とよまれた。しかし、胥彌赦は結局宋に遁走してしまったため、衛侯が今度は自分で「貞卜」したのである。そこで、キ氏は、『說文』の「貞卜問也」に基づき、「衛侯卜問卜」いうようにパラフレーズしてみると、

"The marquis of Wei questioned the cracks by crack-making"

となり、意味的にリダンダントになる。故に、キ氏は『說文』の意味では不自然であるとする。氏は、更に、『左傳』に於いて、「うらなう」という意味の動詞は「貞」よりはむしろ「卜」であるという事實に基づいて、この場合、「貞」は「正」の意味に用いられていると解釋したわけである。從って、「衛侯貞卜」の「貞卜」は「正ﾚ卜」と理解し、「卜」は胥彌赦が係わった筮占を指した、という判斷を下したのである。杜預（二二二—二八四年）が『左傳』の「衛侯貞卜」に注して、「正卜夢之吉凶也」と言ったのは、衛公が行った筮占を不滿とし、それを「正」した、と理解すべきであるとしている。

以上、キ氏の解釋を紹介したが、私は、曲解であると思う。「卜」とは、『左傳』にても龜卜を意味し、蓍筮は含まないからである。「うらなう」という意味の動詞は、その方法によって「卜」か「筮」になり、二つが共存していたと考えられる。確かに龜卜の方が蓍筮よりも權威あるものとして尊重されていたということはある。しばしば引用される「筮短龜長」（『左傳』僖公四年）や「龜重威儀多、筮輕威儀少」（『儀禮』士喪禮・注）や「凡國之大事、先筮而後卜」（『周禮』筮人）などが佐證として擧げられる。しかしながら、「卜」を蓍筮とし、それを「正ﾚ卜」とするのは如何であろうか。「衛侯貞卜」の「貞卜」なる表現は『左傳』にのみ、それもただの一例しかないため、確實なことは言えないが、動詞的（verbal）に用いられていることは確かである。『國語』吳語に「貞於陽卜」とあり、この場合は、「貞」が動詞であるから、『左傳』の「衛侯貞卜」の「貞」も動詞であり、「卜」が名詞であると言えないことはない。ともあれ、「貞」は、その道德的な意味に用いられる場合は別として、古典にて蓍龜の占いに共通したテクニカルなコトバと意識されていたであろうということは推測できるのではあるまいか。『易』などにはよく用いられるコトバである。『尙書』洛誥の「我二人共貞」の「貞」も動詞であるが、この場合は、龜卜を指す。但し、ここで重要なのは、その意味なのである

が、キ氏の論ずるように、「問也」でなければ通じない、という例はない。むしろ、「正也」の說明の方がどちらかと言えば優っている。卜辭の用例から言えば、「…卜貞」は頻見するが、「…貞卜」なるパターンは皆無と言ってよい。

次に、「卜」の意味であるが、キートリー氏は、その古典に於ける用法を調べた結果、「卜」字が文法的に疑問句を支配している例は絶無であるとし、「問う」ではなく、「豫言する」（to predict）という意味に用いられているとする。例えば、『詩經』天保と楚茨から引用し、カールグレンとレッグの譯を施しつつ論じている。

「君曰卜爾萬壽無疆」 "… the (dead) lords say: 'We predict for you a myriad years of life, without limit.'" (Karlgren)

「神嗜飲食、卜爾百福」 "… the spirits enjoy the wine and food; they predict for you a hundred blessings …" (Karlgren)[39]

レッグは、カールグレンと異なり、「卜」を「與える」（to give, confer）と譯し、これは『爾雅』釋詁や『毛詩訓詁傳』の解釋であるが、いずれにせよ疑問のニュアンスはない。キ氏はカールグレンの「豫言する」（"predict"）という譯語が卜占の性質を良く捉えているとして、『左傳』中の數例にも言及する。例えば、文公十八年から、

「…公聞之、卜曰"尙無及期"、惠伯令龜、卜楚丘占之曰"齊侯不及期"」

を擧げ、特に「尙」字に注目する。このコトバは、疑いもなく豫言的、切望的、祈願的（predictive, wishful, optative）なものであって、「問う」というコンセプトとは適合しないと主張する。私は、キ氏のこの主張は受け入れられると思う。しかし、強いて言えば、豫言的な言辭は楚丘の占辭「齊侯不及期」であって、「尙無及期」は祈願文である。

最後に「命」字についてであるが、キ氏はこのコトバの意味を「命龜」とか「令龜」という表現の解釋中に求め、『尙書』金縢篇の「今我卽命于元龜」を問題にする。この文は、本稿でも既に第二項にて引用し、注釋家によって「卽」の意味は「既」、「就」、あるいは「受」の義であるべしというように

---

[39] Bernhard Karlgren, *The Book of Odes*. Stockholm: Museum of Far Eastern Antiquities, 1950, p.110 and p.163, respectively. Also, James Legge, *The Chinese Classics*, Vol.IV: *The She King or the Book of Poetry* (cf. n.38 for bibliographical information), p.257 and p.371, respectively.

異說があるとしたが、我々は「元龜が人間名詞の我（＝周公）に命ずるとは考え難く、その逆であろう」とし、それを作業假定とする、としておいた。キ氏の解釋もこれと同じなのであるが、氏は、そもそも注釋家やレッグなどの翻譯者が異說を唱えたのは、うらないとは「問う」ことではなく「命令を下す」という考えになじめず、抵抗感をいだいたからではないかとしている。

　キ氏が注釋家や翻譯者等にかかる抵抗感があったと推測するのは、もしかしたら、正しい見解かも知れない。しかし、これは、レッグや、特に、この金縢の文に「就受三王之命于龜、卜知吉凶」という注を施した漢の孔安國の占卜に對する考えを究明し得てから言えることであろう。そのような研究ルートを探るのも一案だが、私は、「命」が所謂「反訓」の兩義を備えていたコトバであるが故に「受三王之命」という注を生じせしめたのではないかと思う。かかるコトバは動詞で、文法的には能動・受動の關係に表現される場合がある。これは一種のアスペクトの問題であり、どこに基點を据えて見るかによって、「受・授」、「買・賣」、「之・止」、「有・侑」、または「賜ふ・賜はる」等のように主體・客體の關係が逆になる。本稿の第三項では、『史記』龜策列傳の「命曰」で始まる三十二條の辭に關して、それらは「神龜から人間に對する命」であるということを言ったが、それもこの「反訓」性の表われであると思われる。

　しからば、この金縢の一文はどのように解釋すべきなのであろうか。「今我卽命于元龜」の虛辭「于」も、實は反訓的であり、この方はちょうど日本語の助詞「に」のように方向性が從格になったり向格になったりして—例えば、從格として「某々にもらう」、向格として「某々にあげる」—始末に困るコトバである。從って、この金縢の文の場合は、コンテクストに賴らざるを得ないのだが、そのコンテクストも今一つ明白ではない。赤塚忠氏は、「今、わたしくは、大きな龜に命じ御意を卜い問う」と邦譯し、「史乃册祝曰」以下の文を全て命辭であるという解釋を採用している[40]。一方、池田末利氏は、「今、私は（あなたがた三王の）命を大龜に受ける」と邦譯し、これは孔安國の注に從っている[41]。どちらでも意味は通じないことはないが、私は赤塚氏の說—これは結局キ氏の說とも合致—が正しいと思う。赤塚氏は、「史乃册祝曰」以下を

---

[40]　赤塚忠譯注『書經・易經』中國古典文學大系1（東京、平凡社、一九七二年）、頁二〇四、二〇七。

[41]　池田末利譯注『尙書』全釋漢文大系11（東京、集英社、一九七六年）、頁二六六、二六七。

命辭としたが、周公と史の命辭は、「今我卽命于元龜」の直後に、

「爾之許我、我其以璧與珪歸俟爾命。爾不許我、我乃屏璧與珪」

とある。私は、これが命辭でなければならないと思う。何故なら、これは正反からなる二者擇一（第一項参照）であるからである。この解釋が正しいとすれば、金縢の該文は「元龜に命ずる」という意味にとらねばならない。結論として言えることは、龜卜を行うときに用いた言辭は龜に「命じた」ものであり「命ぜられた」ものではなかった。また、「三王が命じた」ものでもなかった。更に言えば、「問いかけた」ものでもなかったのである。今日の甲骨文研究者は、董作賓以來、「命辭」とか「貞辭」という表現を用いているが、「命辭」とは、その意味するまま（卽ち、能動）にとるべきであるとするキートリー氏の解釋に、私は、以上で論じた古典の分析に基づいた範圍で贊意を表すことができる。また、實際の甲骨文に則しても、稀例ではあるが、「貞隹龜令」（『卜辭』一九二）の例—圖一参照—がある。これは、「邑を作する」ことに關連した龜卜であると思え、『尚書』洛誥篇の周公の洛邑建設を彷彿させるものである。「貞隹龜令」の上に境界線をはさみ「其作玆邑、三月」という刻辭に注意されたい。また、「貞隹龜令」の意味は、「龜に（こそ）令する」である。

圖1

4　卜辭の言語型式

　卜辭の言語型式の分析に關しては、白川論文の出發點になっているように、キートリー氏の論文でも重要な部分である。白川論文では、氏の解釋が卜辭修祓・祝禱說をもたらしたのであるが、キ氏のここでの解釋は、「貞」字以下の命辭を疑問文ではなく、豫言・宣言文と見做す議論を展開するに結びつ

く。氏の論旨は、卜辭の性質をそのように解釋すれば、「貞卜工程の解釋の平易化」が得られるであろうというということである。このことは、更に、「オッカムのかみそり」の命題にも則しているとし、次のように述べている。

"It [this section] relies foe part of its persuasiveness upon the use of 'Ockham's razor'(entities should not be multiplied needlessly), for it can be shown that treating the oracle-bone inscriptions as statements simplifies the interpreting of the divination process."(p.18)

キ氏はこの節で約三十の甲骨文の例を引用しつつ、以上に掲げた内容について論じている。その論旨を簡潔に表現してしまえば、前述した命名のごとき「卜辭豫言・宣言説」とでも言えるであろう。本稿では、このキ氏の卜辭豫言・宣言説と從來の「卜辭疑問・質問説」とを比較しながら、前者が如何なる點で「貞卜工程解釋の平易化」をしているか分析してみることにしたい。「平易化」とは、究極的に言って、事の正否と關係があることなのかということにも、折に觸れて、考えてみたく思う。以下の引用卜辭はキ氏論文からのを軸として探用し（これは○印を施して表示）、原著録集と照合した上、引用することにする。字釋や文の解釋は、キ氏のと較べて變動があることを附記しておくが、重要なディスクレパンシーにば言及する。

（1）○戊辰卜、壹貞又來辥自戠、今日其祉于祖丁。　　　『甲編』二七七二

この文は、「干支卜某貞」の序文型式を除けば、句讀點迄が事實の供述である。その部分を "since disasters have come from hunting" という[42]意味の原因・理由の從屬節に、また「今日」以下の質問を表わす "should we continue yesterday's sacrifice to Tsu Ting?" という主節に解釋することが不可能であるとは斷定こそできないが、その場合、文法的なインディケーターがないため、複文ではなく重文と捉える方が平易であるとする。從って、キ氏はこの文を "there have come disasters from hunting and (thus) today we continue (yesterday's) sacrifice to Tsu Ting" と解釋したのである。

---

[42] この解釋は、屈萬里氏の『甲編』二七七二の考釋に從う、としている。「辥」と「戠」の意味は、それぞれ「災害」、「狩獵」であるとしているが、同意しがたい。未だ研究の餘地を殘すと言えども、「辥」は人身犧牲の一種、「戠」は地名と解釋すべき可能性が大であることを記しておく。

思うに、主節・從屬節を明示する文法的なインディケーター、もしくはマーカー（通常虛詞と呼ばれるもの）を甲骨文や金文や早期古典語に求めることは、かかるマーカーがもともと極少のため、無理である。してみると、そもそもこの文を重文と解釋すること自體正しいのであろうか、という疑問があらたに擡頭してくる。結論から言ってしまえば、私は、實際、この文は主節と從節から成る複文でもなければ重文でもない單文であると思うのだが、先ず次の例文を見て、キ氏の解釋の檢討に供したい。（以下の例文は私が選出し、それらには●印を施しておく。）

(2) ●丙午卜、卽貞又氐羌、翌丁未其用。　　　『續存』一・一六〇五
(3) ●乙未卜、旅貞又氐牛、其用于妣、㞢今日。　『庫方』一一七二
(4) ●丙寅卜、賓貞有來羌、來甲戌鬯用。　　　『前編』六・六七・四

　これらの文は、貞字以下の句讀點を施した部分がキ氏の言うように事實の供述ではあるようだが、如何なる面で「貞卜工程解釋の平易化」をしているのだろうか。キ氏の考えだと、結局のところ、文構造が合成からなる重文なら平易、主節・從節の複合からなる複文なら平易ではないということになってしまう。これは、理論的につめていけば、氏の英譯からも議論からも抽出し得ることであり、誰が分析しても同じ結果が得られると思う。

　しかしながら、そのような解釋は、キ氏自身の卜辭の英譯中に複文解釋が窺えられるために、おのずから破綻してしまうことになるのである。例えば、次の如き解釋である[43]。

(5) △辛酉卜、㱿貞今載王從望乘伐下危〔艅〕、受有祐。

『丙編』一二・(1)

"This season, the king should follow Wang Ch'eng to attack the Hsia Wei [= Hsi], (for if he does, we) will receive assistance in this case."

(6) △辛酉卜、㱿貞今載王勿從望乘伐下危〔艅〕、弗其受有祐。

『丙編』一二・(2)

"This season, the king should not follow Wang Ch'eng to attack the Hsia Wei [= Hsi], (for if he does, we) will not perhaps receive assistance in this case."

---

[43] David N. Keightley, *Sources of Shang History*. Berkeley: University of California Press, 1978, p.78. 例文の頭に△印を施したが、それはキ氏論文以外の著からの引用である。

この對貞が正反兩文とも複文であることは、第七項の裘錫圭氏の解釋でもあり、現在異議を唱える研究者はいないと思われる。裘氏をはじめ他の研究者もそのように解釋する理由を明記したのを知らないが、言語學的に見れば、次のようなことが言えるのではないだろうか。この（5）・（6）の對貞には、それぞれ主な動詞が「從」と「受」の二つがある。「從」の支配する節は「王從望乘伐下𦎫」であり、今これをS1とする。「受」の支配する節は「（王）受有祐」であり、これをS2とする。否定形の方の文は、「勿」と「弗」が主動詞に附加されたただけで、文の構造に變化がないから、この方もS1＋S2である。問題は、S1＋S2の「＋」の解釋である。この「＋」をS1とS2の論理關係に求めて解釋を得る、というのが意味論的にも統辭論的にも問題になることである。この論理關係には、順接、逆接、假定・條件、原因・理由、竝列、選擇、時間、場所等といろいろあるが、どれを適當と認めるかによって解釋が大いに異なる。この（5）・（6）の對貞の場合には、どうやらS1を主節にS2を從節に、そして「＋」を「理由」に解釋するのが良かろうということで意見が定說化してきたと言えるのではないだろうか。これに對する私個人の解釋には未だ釋然としないところがないわけではない⑭。しかし、一應、かかる解釋を一つの有力なる分析・解讀法であることは認めておく。

　さて、以上で試みた分析をふまえて、キートリー氏の〇印を施した文（1）と我々が●印を施した三文（2）〜（4）とを比較してみると、句讀點までの「又來艱自㠱」、「又氐羌」、「又氐牛」、「有來羌」は事實の供述ではあるようだが、それらをS1と見做し、その後に續く「今日其祉于祖丁」、「翌丁未其用」、「其用于妣、宙今日」、「來甲戌盤用」をS2と解釋することが、果たして、妥當なのだろうか。そしてS1とS2の論理關係如何を求めるべきなのだろうかという疑問が生じてくるわけである。キ氏の解釋は「重文」であるから、「＋」の論理關係は「竝列」である。

　私は、この場合、S1を單なる名詞句と解釋する方が平易で、しかも正しいのではないかと思う。卽ち、例文（1）の「S2」中の動詞「祉」―ここでは「坼（さ）」くという意か―と例文（2）、（3）、（4）の三文共通の「用」の目的語とみなすのである。これを古典漢語調で言い表わすと、（1）は「有來艱自㠱者」、

---

⑭ Cf. K. Takashima, "Subordinate Structure in Oracle-Bone Inscriptions with Particular Reference to the Particle *Ch'i*," *Monumenta Serica*, Vol. 33 (1977-1978), pp. 36-61.; particularly, pp. 51-55.

（2）は「有所氐（＝致）羌者」、（3）は「有所致牛者」、（4）は「有所來羌者」の如くなり、これは、全て、名詞句で、その文法的機能は、主題目的格である。従って、○印の文も●印の文もことごとく單文である。例文（2）〜（3）に關し、「羌」や「牛」が動詞「用」の目的語に使われるのは周知のことだが、例文（1）の「辟」としておいた字も、例えば、「…王其用辟、叀…」（『甲編』七五七）のように「用」の目的語として用いられることがあるのである。（注42参照。）

以上を小結してみると、キ氏の説くところの「貞卜工程解釋の平易化」として提起した重文解釋は、その根據としている基準が我々の取るべきものであるとは限らないと言えるであろう。ましては、キ氏の言う「平易」であることが正しいかどうかということになると、却って我々の單文解釋の方が平易であるようであって、「正不正」の問題の核心に觸れていないようでもある。「オッカムのかみそり」の命題に限って言えば、複文の方が重文よりも、更に、重文よりも單文の方が平易になるわけだが、そのような議論は成立しないのである。甲骨文には、單文もあり、複文もある。そして、それらは、全て文法的インディケーターなしで（少なくとも字面からはなしで）、摘出できるのである。

單文についても、また複文についても、以上考慮したので、次に重文の問題について考えてみよう。

　　（1）○庚申貞今來甲子彫王、大禦于大甲燎十六小宰劉九牛、不遘雨。

　　　　　　　　　　　　　　　　　　　　　　　　『南明』四三二

この文は張聰東氏によりドイツ語に譯され[45]、それを参考にしてキ氏が英譯を施している（頁二一）。今、これを漢文訓讀調に和譯すると、次の如くなる。

　　「庚申に貞す、今（ど）來（たる）甲子、王を大禦するに大甲に酒〻せんか、六〻小宰を燎せんか、九牛を劉せんか、雨に遘あわざらんか、と」[46]。

---

[45] I.e., "Am Tage Keng-shen wurde das Orakel befragt: 'Soll am kommenden Tage Chia-tzu Wein vergossen werden und der König sich einer Großreinigung vor Ta-chia unterziehen?　Sollen hierbei sechzig Lämmerpaare durch kultische Verbrennung und neun Rinder aufgeschnitten dargebracht werden?　Werden wir nicht vom Regen überrascht werden?'" Tsung-tung Chang, *Der Kult der Shang-Dynastie im Spiegel der Orakelinschriften: Eine paläographische Studie zur Religion im archaischen China* (Wiesbaden: Otto Harrassowitz, 1970), p.91/5.26 b.

[46] この解釋は、そもそも重要な點において、間違っていると思うのだが（後述、頁五三参照）、最後の部分の譯は、貝塚茂樹・伊藤道治氏の著『京都大學人文科學研究所藏甲骨文字・本文編』（京都大學人文科學研究所、一九六〇年）、頁四〇五／S－四六〇に既に正しい解釋が提出されているので、それにしたがっておくことにする。

このような張聰東氏の理解は、卜辭疑問・質問說の一つのヴァリエーションである。キートリー氏はこれに反論し、もしこれらが一つ一つ疑問文なら、それらに對する「答」はどのようにして得られたのであろうか、と問う。このような命辭に對して、卜兆が複數あるならまだしも、一つしかないのが規則である。從って、この文は、「王を大禦するに」を除き、それ以下を重文にとり、「酒」、「燎」、「劉」、「不遘雨」の「パッケージ・ディール」、つまり、それらを一括した全體に對して兆を求めたと解釋した方が、「貞卜工程解釋の平易化」につながるのではないかとする。思うに、卜兆が一貞辭につき一つということは重要であり、その點から貞卜工程解釋の平易化を唱えたキ氏の論點は支持されよう。しかし、これにもまだ二つほど大きな問題を殘していると思われ、以下、それについて分析してみたい。

　上述した張聰東氏の理解は卜辭疑問・質問說の一ヴァリエーションと言ったが、まだいくつか考えられる。その一つは、この文の五つの動詞句を竝列式に解釋することである。つまり、

　　　「庚申に貞す、今(ど)來(たる)甲子、王を大禦するに大甲に酒し、六小宰を燎し、九牛を劉せんか。雨に遘わず、と」

ということになる。この譯文は「重文のパッケージ・ディール」として捉えてはあるものの、疑問文型式を含むことで、キ氏の理解—それは重文にとり、非疑問文の竝列にとるもの—と異なる。そこで、この疑問文型式とキ氏の說く宣言型式とを比較してみると、いかなる點で、後者の方が貞卜工程解釋の平易化に關連しているかという問題も生じてくるわけである。疑問文型式では、答が「イエス」か「ノー」であろうが、かかる答は見當らない。豫言・宣言型式なら、それに對し柔軟に反應する「吉」の意味で對應できたであろう、とキ氏は說く（キ氏論文、頁二二、二六）。

　ここでの疑問文か非疑問文かという問題に、そのリスポンスである結果を記した兆語から答を見出そうとするのは、妥當であると思える。そして、キ氏の說くように上文の解釋は究極的には非疑問文に捉えるべきだと思う。理由は、後でも言及するが、「玆用」とある表現からして、「玆」は命辭を指すと思われる。そして、それは「疑問・質問文である命辭を用いる」とは考え難いことからも察せられよう。「玆用」なる表現は、兆語である場合とそうでない場合（つまり驗辭）の兩方あるが、第一期卜辭から第五期卜辭迄を通して、兆

語でない場合の方が多く、命辭の後に直結するものである。例はかなりあるが、好例としては、『南明』七〇五、六二〇、『續存』二・七五八等が擧げられる。兆語として用いられた例は、第三・四期の數片に限られ、例えば、『戩壽』一五・一、『粹編』一〇〇四、『南明』五九八等ある。これらの場合、「玆用」なる表現は、「玆卜用」、或るいは、「用玆卜」の意味であったと思われる。キ氏が論文を書いた時點では、第一期の賓組卜辭などに頻見の兆語「㞢」、「二㞢」、「小㞢」をそれぞれ「吉」、「上吉」、「小吉」と解釋しており、現在では、それらを「告」、「二告」、「小告」と釋字すべきであるという風に考えを訂正しているため㊼、その點は割引して評價しなくてはならない。

前揭の『南明』四三二の例文（1）について、五つの動詞並列句になる「重文のパッケージ・ディール」とキ氏は解釋したが、この問題について我々はどう考えるべきであろうか。注46でも觸れたが、張聰東氏もキートリー氏も、文意を正しく理解していないと思われ、基礎的なことなので、まず、それを正しておきたい。

「今來甲子酒王大禦于大甲」までを「…王を大禦せんに大甲に酒し」と訓むのは誤りである。これは「今（ど）來（たる）甲子に酒し、王が大禦するに」と訓むべきである。その理由は、（一）酒祭は酒祭とは違い、天候と密切に關係し、それは屋外にて他の祭祀に先立って執行された準備祭祀である㊽。從

㊼ Cf. David N. Keightley, "Reports from the Shang: A Corroboration and Some Speculation," *Early China*, 9-10 (1983-1985), pp.20-39. (The title should be amended to "... A Correction and Some Speculations" according to the errata in the subsequent issue.)

㊽ 甲骨文の「𢨋」は、字形から判斷して「酒」とするのに無理がある。それは酒と釋字でき、字素の「彡」は、「彤」、「彩」、「彫」、「彥」、「彰」等の字に用いられ、「鮮かできれいな文樣」という義符であると思う。酒を大地や犧牲物に注ぐ、所謂、ライベーションの祭祀は、「𤲞」（灌＝祼）というコトバによって表わされたと思える。さらに、「酒」の典型的な文型は「（勿）＋酒＋（于）＋間接目的語＋直接目的語」であり、否定詞「勿」によって否定されていることから、統御可能の意味をもつ動詞に用いられていることが分かる。もし「酉」が聲符なら、＊rəgwxのように發音され、語源的に關連ある「彫」＊tjəgw（傷也）といったコトバで解釋できるのではあるまいか。「乙巳卜、爭貞今日酒伐、啓」（『乙編』三四七一）の如き例にもあるよう、天候と密切に關連していることから晴天の時に實行されたらしいということが言える。そのことは、「酒」の處理する犧牲がきれいに、また鮮かに仕上がることをも可能ならしめたのではないだろうか。また、酒祭が「燎」、「侑」、「歳」等の動詞とは別の祭祀動詞として、それらの準備的な祭祀行爲であったらしいことについては、周國正氏の博士論文に詳說されている。Chow Kwok-ching, Aspects of Subordinative Composite Sentences in Period I Oracle-Bone Inscriptions (Vancouver: University of British Columlsia, 1982), pp.341-346.

って、「酻」で文を區切るべきである。(二) 禦祭の執行者は、この場合、「王」であり、王は被祭者ではない。かかる訂正を施した後、『南明』四三二の例文 (1) は、次の如く讀み下せよう。

　　「庚申に貞するは、今ど來たる甲子に酻し、王の大甲 (の示前にて) 大禦せんに十六小宰を燎し、九牛を劉さん、と。雨に遘わざり。」

もしこの解釋が正しいなら、キートリー氏の提起した「重文のパッケージ・ディール」のうち、「重文」は「酻し」と「燎し」の二個所のみであり、五つの動詞から成るという「パッケージ・ディール」は成立不可能になる。この文には、主從關係が看取され、主要なフォーカル・ポイントは「十六小宰を燎し、九牛を劉さん」であるからである。このフォーカル・ポイントに兆が求められていたことは、『南明』四三二の刻辭全體を見れば推測可能と思われるので、少々煩雜になるが、ここに引用しておく。(尙、「主從關係」の「從」は準備祭祀の「酻」と思われる。)

(2) ●癸丑貞甲寅酻、大禦自上甲、燎十六小宰。茲用。
(3) ●上甲不遘雨。大乙不遘雨。大丁遘雨。
(4) ●庚申貞今來甲子酻、王大禦于大甲、燎十六小宰、劉九牛。不遘雨。
(5) ●貞甲子酻、王大禦于大甲、燎十六小宰、劉九牛…。

今、簡單に說明を加えると、(2) は (王が) 大禦をするにあたり、その受祭者を上甲から始め、十六小宰を燎祭にすることを貞し、その命辭が採用されたことを意味する。このことは「茲用」から判斷できる[49]。(3) は (2) の驗辭と考えられ、上甲と大乙を受祭者とした時には、雨に降られなかったが、大丁の時には雨に降られた、ということが讀みとれる。(4) は、大丁の次王である大甲を受祭者として王が大禦する際、十六小宰の燎祭に加え九牛を劉祭することを貞し、その時も雨に降られなかったことが分かる。(この「不遘雨」をキ氏は命辭の一部としてとらえているが (頁二二)、これは (3) と同樣、驗辭である。氏も頁二七ではそのように理解しており、自己矛盾している。) 最後に、(5) は (4) と同じであったようだが、完文ではないため、些少疑問が殘される。

このように見てくると、キ氏の「貞卜工程解釋の平易化」として引用さ

---

[49] 「茲用」なる表現が宣言文には適應するが、疑問文には適應しないとするキートリー氏の指摘 (キ氏論文、頁二七) は、正しいと思われる。

れた例文は、その文構造を極端な重文としてとらえられたために、フォーカル・ポイントが消滅してしまうことになる。このことは、貞辭としてのスラスト、パワー、貞意といつたものが失われるということでもある。「パッケージ・ディール」説は成立しないのである。また、この説が複文解釋の例として舉げた『丙編』一二・（1）の「辛酉卜、殻貞今載王從望乘伐下𦥑、受有祐」及びその否定形の「辛酉卜、殻貞今載王勿從望乘伐下𦥑、弗其受有祐」にそくしても成立しないのは、容易に理解できるであろう。この場合、S1の主動詞は「從」、S2の主動詞は「受」であり、パッケージ・ディール說に從えば、その兩方の意味するところが貞されてしまうことになるからである。フォーカル・ポイントもディフューズされてしまう。

　しからば、複文解釋が妥當と判斷できる場合、貞意はどのようにして得られるのであろうか。この問題に關しては、次のようなことが考えられることを指摘しておきたい。言語學、特に、イギリスの言語哲學の分野において、「イロキューショナリー・フォース」（illocutionary force）と言われる歸納法がある。それは一つの文をそのトータルのメッセージとして解釋する方法である。「イロキューショナリー・フォース」は「從辭言」とも譯せるであろう。從辭言は、イロキューション、つまり「直辭言」と對照的に用いられる。この從辭言を該複文解釋例に適應させてみると、肯定形の場合は、「王が、今載[50]、望乘という名の軍の指揮官に從うべきである」という意味になり、それがまたフォーカル・ポイントにもなるわけである。否定形の場合は、「王が、今載、望乘という名の軍指揮官に從うべきではない」というのがイロキューショナリー・フォース、且つフォーカル・ポイントとなる。卜兆は、まさしくそのフォーカル・ポイントに對應するものとして理解されていたのではあるまいか。フォーカル・ポイントというものは、もともと人間の言語行爲に見い出せるものであっても、卜兆はそうではない。そこで、相互關係についていろいろな解釋が生じる可能性があると思う。キ氏の「貞卜工程解釋の平易化」もその一つであろう。しかし、以上分析してきて明らかになったと思われるが、キ氏の言う貞卜工程解釋の平易化にはかなりの修正が必要である。ましてやそれが「卜辭宣

---

[50] この表現の意味は定かではないが、ある時間帶を表わすことは確認し得る。もしかしたら、六十日（干支）の一サイクルを指す語かとも思われるが、詳しくは、拙著『殷虛文字丙編注釋』（臺北、"中央研究院"出版豫定）、頁一〇八～一一三を參照されたし。

言・豫言說」を支持し、「疑問・質問說」をしりぞけるという充分な根據を與えてくれる、とは斷定し難い。私は前者の方にその說明力—例えば、兆語や「兹用」の表現から判斷して—が些少たりともあると思うのだが、必ずしもそれが證明されるというレベル迄には達していない。もっと別の觀點から考えてみる必要があるようだ。

5　キ氏の「貞」字對象說とその評價

キ氏論文の第五節は、第一節の「貞」の字形の考察に基づき、甲骨文での意味について論じている。

キ氏は先ず「鼎」、「貞」、「正」、「定」字等を含む單語群に「正」（"correct, regulate, proper"）及び「定」（"settle, establish, fix"）という意味の兩義があるとし、とりわけカールグレン氏の『尙書』洛誥中の一文「我二人共貞」の「貞」字の解釋が優れているとする。力氏の解釋は、次のとおりである[51]。

「…貞というコトバが"問い占い"の意味に用いられる時、その眞義は"確かめる"とか"正しいことを決める"ということだ。」

力氏自身の言葉がここでは問題になるため、原文を引用する。

"The word cheng is common in the sense of 'straight, correct, proper' (it is etym. closely cognate to 正), and when it has its sense of 'divination enquiry' it really means 'to verify, to determine what is correct'."

キートリー氏は、このカ氏の解釋に從って、例えば、「庚子卜、爭貞翌辛丑啓」（『菁華』七）を英譯すると、

"Crack-making on the day keng-tzu, Cheng determining/verifying what was correct: 'On the next hsin-ch'ou day it will be clear'…"

となり、「貞卜工程の如何なる局面が"正されたり""正しさを確かめられたり"、する必要があったのであろうか」という疑問を投げかける。キ氏は、解答として、四つほどの局面が考えられるとして、次のように言う。

（ⅰ）貞卜工程というものを考えるに、まず第一に鑽鑿がうがてられ、次に

---

[51] Bernhard Karlgren, "Glosses on the Book of Documents," *Bulletin of the Museum of Far Eastern Autiquities* (*BMFEA*), No.21 (1949), p.76/＃1752.

燃えさしか何かで火がそこに加えられる。その時に甲骨に向かって「宣言」をする、といった順序で行われたであろうとする。卜兆が現われると、その順序を記す序數が卜兆の傍に刻され、それから宣告の内容を記す卜辭が契刻される、という手續きを踏む。その際、どの宣言文句がどの卜兆とコレスポンドしていたかを分別するのは紛らわしかったであろうから、貞人がそのような技術的な、官僚が從事するような手續きに携わっていたであろうとし、それを「確かめたり」したのであろう。このような技術的な局面の外に、

（ⅱ）儀禮的な局面もあったであろうし、『丙編』等に見られる鑿の焦灼使用狀況を問題にする。これには、張秉權氏の『丙編』の考釋での記述（例えば頁九四所見のもの）等から察せられるような嚴格な規律があったはずであり、もしそうならば、貞人がそれらを「貞」、即ち、「定」していたのではなかろうか。さらに、

（ⅲ）命辭の實際の言いまわし（"wording"）を按排するのも「正したり」「確かめたり」する對象であったろう。

最後に、

（ⅳ）貞字が鼎の字で表わされたことは、かなえが實際に貞卜工程に用いられたのではあるまいかとし、それは「ちょうどかなえをしっかりと据えるが如く、龜を正しい位置に"貞"する」ということも意味したのであろう。

ここでは、『周禮』春官、大卜の「國大遷、大師則貞龜」の「貞龜」という表現に對する鄭玄の注「正龜於卜位也」も傍證として引用している。以上の四つの局面は、それぞれ排他的な性質ではなかろうとした上、「貞」の甲骨文での意味は、"regulate"（規定する）という譯が最も包括的で妥當な解釋であると結論づけている。

キ氏論文の第五節を以上のごとくまとめてみたが、我々は如何に批評できるであろうか。先ず、一般的な反應として、このようなことがあり得たであろうかという素朴な疑問が腦裡をかすめる。ニビソン氏も氏の論文（注13所掲、頁一〇～一一）にてそのように感じたようであるが、深く分析していない。效果的に反駁し得るエヴィデンスに不足するようだが、少々論じてみることにしたい。

先ず第一に、キ氏の出發點が不可解である。氏はカールグレンの洞察力に富んだ解釋 "... [*cheng*] means 'to verify, to determine what *is* correct'" を "... determining/verifying what *was* correct" とカ氏の現在形 is を過去形の was

に置き換えている。その理由は施されていない。そして、キ氏は「貞卜工程の如何なる局面が"正される"必要があったのであろうか」（"... what aspects of the divination process would require verifying, rectifying or determining ..." — p.41）という自問自答をしているのである。しかし、カ氏が解釋を施した『尚書』洛誥の「我二人共貞」の前後文を讀んでも分かる如く、「貞」の對象は「貞卜工程」ではなく、洛邑に於ける新都建設の適所選擇である。貞卜工程とは全く關係がない。言うまでもなく、キ氏は貞字の甲骨文での意味をカ氏の解釋に基づいて推察したのだが、それならそれを用法は限られているとは言え、甲骨文の中で考えてみるより仕方があるまい。私は「貞」字の支配するもの（對象となるもの）は、命辭の内容以外には考え難いと思うのだが、これについては、第六の2項で考察することにしたい。

　　（ii）の儀禮的な問題の鑿の使用狀況であるが、「嚴格な規律」の詳細が判明していないこともあって、これも貞字の意味的スコープに入るとは考え難い。キ氏は、『丙編』五八の場合に二つの鑿が焦灼され、卜兆も現われはしているが、序數が刻されていない事實に注意する。張秉權氏は、『丙考』（頁九四）にて次のように述べている。

　　　　「也許那兩個已灼之穴、在灼卜的時候、發現有什麼不合規距的地方、所以作廢了…。」

キ氏はこれに同意しているのだが、「規則に合わない」という解釋が成立するのは、その規則が何であったかを明らかにし得てから可能であると思われる。我々の論理から考え、第三の1項にて既述したところに従って、ただ單にその卜兆に効力がないとか、或るいは、無意味・ニュートラルであると殷王に判斷されたために採用されなかった、ということに結びつけるのが自然な解釋と思われる。このことは、逆に、卜兆に序數があるのは、その卜兆が採用された、または、少し弱めて、採用される可能性があった、ということになるわけである。卜兆に序數があるのは頻見するが、序數に貞字が施されている例は、ごくわずかのようである。このことは、貞字の「貞」する對象が人間の言葉であったことを意味するものであると思われる。

　　（iii）の命辭の言いまわし、つまりワーディングの問題について、キ氏は命辭と繇辭との對應關係を追究する。次の例文は『丙編』二四七・（1）からの卜

辭であるが、ごく簡單な命辭に對して、繇辭が比較的に詳細である。

　　○甲申卜、殻貞婦好冥嘉。王占曰其隹丁冥嘉、其隹庚冥引吉。三旬又一日甲寅冥、不嘉。隹女。（第三の２項、ディスプレー・インスクリプションに關して既引。）

　張秉權氏によると、このような現象が見られるのは、命辭の原型がここにあるよりもっと複雜であったはずで、それが契刻された時に省略されたのではないか、という（『丙考』頁四五八）。キ氏は、この張氏の推測を正しいであろうとし、貞人こそそのような命辭の省略の按排を擔當していたのではないかと論ずる（キ氏論文、頁四五）。

　ここには二つの大きな問題がある。一つは張秉權氏の考え自體が正しいかどうかということである。これについて、我々が確認できるものはない。もう一つは、省略の按排というのは、どちらかというと、フォーム（形式）の問題であり、コンテント（內容）の問題は二の次になる。張氏やキ氏の想像した「命辭省略說」は複雜な問題であり、本稿では詳說できないが、命辭のフォーカル・ポイントは前例の卜辭でも明瞭であるし、繇辭が詳細な事實には、いろいろな理由が考えられるであろう。（例えば、ある卜兆が「甲」のもの、「乙」のものというように十干の數位で順序が決まっていたのかも知れない。序數が十迄あるということも無關係ではないようで、肯定文・否定文で千里路を中心に左右に分かれたり、奇數干・偶數干といったことも關連してくるかも知れないのである。このことは待考。）

　（ⅳ）の「龜を正しい位置に規定する〔配置する〕」というのは、想像的である。しかし、これはテストの困難な假定である。キ氏は、『周禮』の「貞龜」という表現を引くが、鄭玄が注を施す位であるから、かかる表現の意味が後漢末では分かりにくくなっていたことであろうし、また、鄭玄の注「正龜於卜位也」以外にも別の說明が不可能ではない。例えば、カールグレンの解釋に從って「龜に貞たす」とも理解できようし、またこの場合は、『周禮』の大凡の成立時代から考えて、『說文』の定義に從って「龜に貞とう」とも說明できるかもしれない。

　以上、キ氏論文の第五節を檢討してきたが、貞字のカバーする意味範圍があまりにも包括的に過ぎ、複雜である。それは、貞卜工程及び命辭に見られるとする「省略形」のフォームを中心に考え、コンテントを深く考えなかったか

らだと思われる。より簡単な説明を求める方が、キ氏自身第四節でアピールした「オッカムのかみそり」の命題にもそくしていてよいのではあるまいか。我々は、この問題に對して、具體的な提案を第六の1項にて出してみたい。

6 マジックとしての卜辭說

　キ氏の論文の最終節、第六節は、白川靜氏の卜辭を一種の呪術的なマジックであるとする說に近似している。兩氏とも甲骨文が單に毛筆で書かれたものでなく、契刻された、という事實に注目する。特に、キ氏は、その事實がマジシャンによる呪術的性格を暗示しているのではないかとしている。契刻されたということは、史官による記錄を殘そうとする意向があったに違いないのではあるが、そのことよりも未來に對しての積極的な働きかけをキ氏は契刻という行爲に讀みとらんとしたわけである。我々は、第三の1項（イ）にて、卜兆には魔術的效力があるものとないもの（もしくはニュートラル）というふうに、殷人により判斷されていた可能性があると論じた。このことはキ氏の說と矛盾するものではないことに注意しておきたい。イギリスのアーサー・ウェイリーなども易の研究に關して、「前兆」というものは、それ自身つかの間のものでしかなく、それを印象的且つ效果的なものにするには"フィックス"（固定化、法典化）する必要がある」[52]と言っている。また、ジョセフ・ニーダムも易の八卦をただの數のシンボルではなくして「自然現象の背後に潛むところの引起的な要素である」[53]としている。キ氏はこれらの先學の考えを利用しつつ（頁五〇）、もし、假說として受容できるものであるなら、契刻された（つまり、固定化、法典化された）卜辭にもあてはまるであろうとし、次のように論じる。

　　「命辭は未來に對する呪文である。卜兆は未來のシンボリックな表示であり、それは（人間によって）解釋されなくてはならなかったのであるが、未來そのものでもあった。そして、卜兆がそのような意味をになっていると

---

[52] Arthur Waley, "The Book of Changes," BMFEA, No.5 (1933), p.136. To quote as provided by Keightley (p.50): "... an omen is regarded as in itself a momentary, evanescent thing. Like silver-prints, it requires 'fixing.' Otherwise it will refer only to the moment at which it was secured."

[53] Joseph Needham, *Science and Civilization in China*, Vol.2 (Cambridge: Cambridge University Press, 1954), p.336, n. (b). To quote as given by Keightley again: "... causative factors behind natural phenomena."

したら、命辭にもあてはまることだろう」と。

"... the charges represent spells applied to future events ... The crack was a symbolic representation of the future, which had to be read. But it was, at the same time, the future itself. And if this were true of the crack, it would also have been true of the charge. "(p.50)

キ氏はさらにこの說を卜辭疑問・質問說と比較して、「命辭を疑問文としてとらえたら、呪文ではなくなってしまい、また、疑問文を甲骨に刻みつけても、未來には何の影響も及ぼすことはないであろう」と說く。命辭は、かくして、氏の言う「アナロジカル・マジック」（模倣魔術）としてとらえ得るのである。

このような提唱は、議論としては、アピーリングのようだが、證據はと問われると、何を擧げたらよいのであろうか。キ氏も筆書よりは勞力及び巧妙さを要求されたはずの契刻という所爲以外に何も建言しておらず、かかる所爲そのものに深い意味を求めたのではないかと思われる(54)。私は、このアナロジカル・マジックというものが、殷王朝後期の甲骨文の（ひいては文化的）性格をデリニエイトするのに格好なものの一つだと思い、それを、既述した卜兆の解釋に加えて、さらに甲骨文中適例と思えるものの解釋を通じて、支持してみたく思う。（本稿「おわりに」を參照されたし。）本稿で支持するということは、言語行爲と貞卜行爲との關係を有機的に、つまり、發話から行爲に至るまでのプロセスを主に從辭言的に、解釋するということになる。しかし、アナロジカル・マジックがそう簡單に支持できない例もある。故に、その問題から考えてみたく思う。

キートリー氏は、以上で概觀したような「卜辭マジック說」とも呼べるものを力說したのであるが、それには大きな障碍があるとして、「反」の意味の命辭

---

(54) 契刻は書と比較して、高度な、というよりは、別の技術を用すると思われ、この點キ氏（頁四九）も白川靜氏（頁二〇）も意見が一致している、しかしながら、契刻という所爲を格別なものとして解釋するのは、多分に主觀的な觀察に基づいているとも思われる。例えば、松丸道雄氏は、ある熟練した篆刻家が篆書の「田中」印をわずか十秒で、篆書「伊藤」印を三十五秒で刻し、朱押しの結果、そのまま使用できるものであった、という實際の觀察報告をしている。そして、「慣れてくれば、一刀刻りの場合、書くのと刻るので、それほどスピードは異ならないようである」としている。このことは刻るスピードについていっているものであるが、甲骨に刻字する場合にも參考になる情報であるに違いない。そして、書くモノの相違も我々現代人の考えている程技術的に考えて特別な意味があったか不明である。松丸道雄「甲骨文における書體とは何か」『書道研究』十二號（一九八八年）、頁四〇參照。

を問題にとりあげる。これは當然である。もし命辭がアナロジカル・マジックとして魔術的なパワーがあるとするならば、殷人は、何故、命辭にその約半數をも占めよう「否定形」を用いたのであろうか、として、次の例文を擧げる。ここでは、以前（第三の2項）でも觸れたことだが、意味論的範疇での否定である。

  （1）戌午卜、㱿貞般往來亡禍。　　　　　　　　　　　　『丙編』一三〇・（1）
  （2）貞般往來其有禍。　　　　　　　　　　　　　　　　　『丙編』一三〇・（2）

 例文（1）は、白川氏の卜辭修祓・祝禱說を以って解釋すれば、「般〔人名〕の往來するに禍亡からん」となり、卜辭マジック說を以って解釋すれば、「…禍亡かれ」とでも訓めるであろう。ところが、例文（2）の方は、訓讀式にのっとって訓むと修祓・祝禱說では「般の往來するに、其れ禍有らん」、マジック說では「…其れ禍有れ」とでもなるであろう。ところが、「般」なる人物は殷王朝の重要な味方であったらしく、王室に入貢したり、外敵征伐に從事したりしている。（『綜類』四六四・一〜四、『丙編通檢』、頁三六三參照。）從って、般に禍あることは避けたかった筈であり、マジック說にとってはなはだ都合が惡く、大きな問題である。これに對する氏の說明は、現在では氏自身も撤回するのが明らかなため（注47所掲の論文から判斷）、ここで議論するには及ばない。我々の觀點からすれば、この問題は、一見、さしたる障礙ではないかとも思われる。それは、語氣助詞「其」の意味的役割により「說明」できるからである。以前（第三の2項）、我々は、セロイス氏の貢獻を引き「其」字には、「貞卜者側にとって望ましくない」という意味があることを指摘した。また、正反の對偶による選擇は、そのどちらか一方に其字が用いられている場合、バランスのとれた公平なものではないということも指摘しておいた。上例（2）の場合も、マジック說では、「般往來亡禍」が貞人を含めた王室側の期待するところであるが、「般往來其有禍」はその逆である。ところが、「其」字の使用によって、あたかも「有禍」の可能性が意味的に薄められているようにとらえ得る。してみると、漢文訓讀調にのっとって、「其れ禍有らん」とか「其れ禍有れ」と訓んだところで、本義は全く傳わってこないわけである。どのように訓んだらいいのか適案に苦しむが、英譯だと、

  "Pan, in his coming and going, might have misfortunes"

とでもなるであろう。これはただの叙述文である。私はかかる解釋が正しいと思

うのであるが、それを和譯してみると、「般の往來するに禍が有るかも知れぬ」とでもなる。これは語調が漢文訓讀式にそぐわないため、スムーズとは言えない。しかし、本義としては、かかる和譯が正しいと思われ、それをさらにパラフレーズしてみると、「…禍は可能性としてはあり得ようが、不確實であり、また望ましくない」と解釋できると思う。しかし、問題は、やはり、何故そのような、貞人を含んだ王室側に望ましくない、言わば、無益な命辭を用いたのかということになってしまう。卜辭マジック説では説明が極めて困難になる所以である。

説明困難という點では、實は、マジック説にのみ限られていることはではない。我々は既に白川氏の卜辭修祓・祝禱説を論評してみたが、マジック説で説明困難なことは、そのまま、修祓・祝禱説にもあてはまり、問題解決に至らない。董作賓氏の二者擇一の卜辭命龜説は、それが卜辭を一々どのような意圖の下に發話されたかを究めんとする內容分析の領域にまで入っていないので、問題自體浮上してこない。「其」字のもつ特別な意味に對する配慮なども研究對象に含められるレベル迄進歩していなかったということなどもあるが、問題自體浮かんでこないというのも問題である。卜辭疑問・質問説によると、反の意味の命辭は、「般の往來するに、其れ禍有らんか」と解釋でき、一見、最も良く意味を捉えているかのようである。しかし、これは熟考してみると、ディセプティブであり、ミスリーディングでもある。何故か。「有らんか」の「ん」は、推量の助動詞「む」の連體形にして、その意味するところは、「まだ實現していないことについて豫想し、婉曲に推量する」（三省堂『大辭林』頁二三四六・①⑤）であって、これは、我々が其字の意味を汲み取って正しいとした解釋「…可能性としてはあり得ようが、不確實であり、また望ましくない（だから婉曲に推量する）」ということに近似している。その上、「其れ禍有らんか」は語調が整っている感じを與えるため、ディセプティブであると言えよう。それだけではない。「有らんか」の「か」は、通常、疑問の終助詞に解釋するようであって(55)、そうだとすると、卜辭疑問・質問説をこの解釋のみで支持することにも

(55)　「有らんか」の「か」を反語の終助詞に解釋すると、ん（＝む、現代語の「う」）と相俟って、「般の往來するに其れ禍あろうか—いやない」というように自然に、また、從辭言的（イロキューショナリ・フォース的）に答が出て來るようであって、あたかも善處したかのようでもある。しかし、この反語解釋を「般往來亡禍」にそくして考えると、論理的に不思議なことになってしまう。というのは、「般の往來するに禍亡からんか—いやある」となってしまい、これは從辭言的に全く逆の意味になってしまうからである。

なりかねない。これはミスリーディングである。この外にも考慮に入れなければならないことがあり、我々は既に疑問文としてとらえた時に生じる二通りの解答のコンフリクト性（第二項）、兆語、「玆用」なる表現等から考えて、疑問・質問説が成立し難いことなどを述べた。卜辭豫言・宣言說では、「般往來其有禍」は殷王室側にとっても望ましくないことでこそあれ、豫言と解釋することで一應納得できる。しかし、「般往來亡禍」をマジック說、或るいは、修祓・祝禱說で解釋し、その對貞である「其有禍」を豫言說で解釋するというのも、奇異に感じられる。正反兩方とも豫言說で解釋するのが最適なのであろうか。

以上、「戊午卜、㞢貞般往來亡禍」と「貞般往來其有禍」の對貞、特に後者の反の一見無益と思える命辭の解釋を今迄考え得た卜辭何々說によって試みたが、何れも滿意を得られないようである。強いて言えば、卜辭豫言說が無難のようでもあるが、このような無益な反の意味の文が發話され、更に契刻された根本的な理由は、結局、何であったのか、もう少し追求してみよう。

キートリー氏のこの疑問への解答は、今迄、どの研究者にも見られなかった新しい提言がある。一言で表現すれば、それは「卜辭二元論的マジック說」とでも言えるであろう。キ氏は、肯定・否定の命題—この場合、意味論的に考えた正・反の命題—を「形而上學的均衡性」（"the metaphysical balance"）としてとらえたのである（頁五七）。中國人の世界觀というものがバランスのとれた二元論的なものであるとよく言われるが、かかるコンセプトを殷代にまで遡らせ、次のように說く。

　「幸と不幸、善と惡は矛盾したものではなく、分離不可能な程密着したものである。肯定と否定があるのは、世界がそのように構成されていると意識されていたからだ。それらは原理的な、また、有機的な緊張關係にあり、人間の前にそのどちらかが實現する可能性として現われる。そのような二つの可能性に接し、いずれかが未來に對し徵効が現われるように公平なチャンスを與えてこそ、貞卜そのものが公平な、現實的な、また正當なものになるのである」と。

原文は次の通りである。

　"Lucky and unlucky, good and bad, were seen as inextricably entwined, not as contradictory. Both alternatives were presented for choice because that was the way the world was viewed. There was a fundamental, organic tension, between the possible choices facing man. Only by facing both possibilities, by giving each possibility, a fair chance to make its mark on the future, could the divination itself be fair, in accord with reality, and thus valid."(p.57)

キ氏はこれに引き續き二元論的マジック說（この表現はキ氏自身のものではなく、私が命名したもの）について論じているが、論旨をまとめると、次の如くである。

　正反の選擇に於いて、たとえ反が期待に沿ぐわなかったことが判明した後でも契刻したということは、そこに記錄・歷史として保存しておこうとするインパルスがあったに違いない。それは、貞卜というものが公平で現實的なものとして意識され、殷王の執政上の決定や行爲を正當化させていたのではあるまいか。貞卜行爲は單なるマジック的なものではなく、反を契刻することによって、現實の世界と一體化を計らんとしたことが考えられないだろうか。そして、もし以上のようなことが正しいとしたら、殷王は貞卜することにより、未來の方向を轉換せんとするというよりは、吉と不吉、人間と神などとのあるべき關係を正しく規定せんとする儀禮的機能をも果たしていたのではないか。それが、「貞」の意味でもある。（ここでは、我々が既に紹介したキ氏の「規制する」"to regulate"という解釋に關連してくる。）從って、ここで言うマジックとは、何かを引起せしむというよりは、協和的に正反を調整する手段であった、とキ氏は結論づけている。

　以上、キ氏の命辭の本質、特に反の解釋について、氏の論旨を紹介してみたのであるが、兩貞法・對貞法における反の處理方法によって、白川靜氏の「勝義に於て貞とふといふことにその儀禮的意義が存した」（頁三二）という解釋が生じたり、キートリー氏のように「二元論的マジック說」が生じたりすると言えるであろう。また、儀禮的意義を白川氏のように人間の疑問を解決するということに求めたり、キ氏のように協和的に正反を調整するといった形而上學的・抽象的な關係に求めたりして意見の分かれるところである。この點について、もう少し考えてみよう。

　前項第5迄のキ氏の說を本稿では「卜辭豫言・宣言說」として批評し、修正すべきことは多いとしながらも、結論としては、容認できると論じた。本項第6では、卜辭豫言・宣言說が二元論的マジック說に發展したわけである。そこで、その發展段階なのであるが、これは、我々の納得のいくものであろうかとい

う問題が生じるわけである。私は、結論から言ってしまえば、理論的に考えて、特に障碍はなかろうと思う。豫言・宣言が正反の對貞、もしくは多項式選擇で表現された場合、いずれかが當事者にとって、特に望ましかったであろうことは充分考えられる。それに對して、言辭的、從辭的に積極的に働きかけた一方、望ましくなかったことも契刻した事實は、キートリー氏の言うように公平な、均衡のとれた觀念が働いたからだ、とするより外いい說明がなさそうである。たとえ、その望ましくなかったことが、「其」字の使用により、弱められたとしても、從辭言的に考えると、そこに殘るのは、依然として、「反」の意味である。ここでは、アナロジカル・マジック的な性質が抑えられているというように解釋できると思われる。このことは、未來の「反」を含めた可能性を包容することにもなる。このような「卜辭二元論的マジック說」は、我々が均等な正反の選擇を目的とすると解釋した「卜辭命龜說」とコントラスティブである。後者の方は、白川氏の言う「疑問の解決」の場としてとらえても、深層レベルに於いては大きな支障にないと思われる。しかし、「其」字を伴なった反の命辭には、やはりマジカルな性格が殘ると言えるであろう。私は、前者の二元論的マジック說が卜辭の本質を適切に具現できる實例搜索をしてみた結果、この說はただの理論に終わらず、卜辭の性格づけが可能である例もあるという見解を得た。それについては「おわりに」の第（vi）項にて論じてみたい。特に「其」字の解釋をめぐって、キートリー氏の所說との相異點等も指摘しつつ、考察することにする。

六、「貞」字解釋をめぐって

　本項では、前項第五にて詳察したキートリー氏の說に影響を受けつつ、貞字の解釋、及び貞卜の意義などについて論じたセロイス、ニビソン、ラフーブレの三氏の見解を紹介し檢討を加えてみたい。

　　1　セロイス說とその擴充論

　セロイス氏の論文（注12所掲）は、キ氏論文の二年後の一九七四年に出版されたが、脫稿はキ氏論文より四ヵ月程先んずる一九七二年二月であった。（筆者はセ氏の未定稿を受けとった。）セ氏は、命辭が疑問文ではないと論じ（頁

二一～二五）、英譯を全て叙述文にしているのである。この解釋は、結論としては、キ氏の命辭非疑問說と同じであるが、「貞」の字義等に關して交流があったことは、キ氏論文（頁四八）からもうかがえる。一九七〇年前半、ちょうど甲骨文が發見されてから約七〇年間、外國では注意されなかった白川氏のト辭修祓・祝禱說（一九四九年）のような變化をはさみつつも、ト辭疑問・質問說が一般的であった。それが米國に於いて本格的に疑問視されだしたわけである。

セ氏論文は、そもそも、張聰東氏の著書（注45所揭）に對するレヴュー・アーティクルとして書かれたものである。特に、張氏が「卜、貞、乎、不、隹、叀、其」の七つの語詞に疑問・質問を表示する機能があるとしたのをセ氏は問題にとりあげ、それらにことごとく反駁を加えたのである。その際、セ氏の判斷の基準となったのは文法であった。ここでは、「卜」と「貞」、主に後者について檢討してみることにする。

張氏は「卜」にも「貞」にも"fragen"（問う）という獨語譯を施している。「卜」に關しては、張氏は『說文』の定義である「卜、灼剝龜也」を引きながらも、それをまともに受けとめていないことがわかる。これは、第一項にて羅振玉がかかる定義にアグノスティックであったことに相通じるものがある。セ氏は張氏の"fragen"を「龜甲や骨を焦灼し、ヒビ割れを生じせむ」（"to apply a firing process to cause cracks in the shell or bone"）と正している。かかる手續きは人間が神の「諾不諾」を得るために行なったのではあるが、それだからと言って、「卜」が文法的に疑問文を導引するとは言えないとしている。セ氏は、ここで「諾不諾」がどのようにしたら得られるか明記していないが、「卜」が文法的に疑問文を導誘しないという判斷は、キートリー氏も論じた如く、正しいと思える。我々が第一項にて注意したように、「卜」を他動詞にとり、「うらなう」とは、所詮「問う」ことだと信じていた初期研究者の考えが張氏によって無批判に受け入れられていることが分かる。

次に、「貞」の意味であるが、「貞」字の用例として「形容詞＋名詞」があり、貞は形容詞の機能で、「正也、定也、善也、信也」といった意味に用いられているとする。そして、甲骨文では、前辭・序辭において動詞として用いられていることからして、その意味は"to test, to try out; to *make* true, correct"であり、「人間が進むべき正しい行路を探るために測驗する」というのが適解だ、としている。「干支卜某貞」という前辭は、從って、

> “In the bone divination of day XX, diviner Y *tested* the proposition, or *proposed* for test(i.e., rectification) the following course of action or alternative courses of action...”(p.23)

という意味であるとする。私自身、この「命辭を正さん」という解釋に永い間從ってきたが、それに、は實、はもう一つの言語學的理由がある。そのことについて、セ氏の說の擴充論とでもいえるものを展開したく思う。

以前、注29でも觸れたことだが、「正」と「貞」は語源的に同根であるということである。そして、ただ單に同根というだけではなく、形態論的(morphological)にも密切な關係があったと思われる。今、李方桂氏の上古漢語再構音系統(56)に基づいて音價を與えると、正は耕部で＊tjing(h)—ここで語尾の(h)は去聲、括弧は去聲または平聲で讀まれたこともあるという符號—となる。貞は同じく耕部であるが介音の＊-r-が入って、＊trjingである。ここで重要なことは、介音＊-r-には「使役的機能」が認められると言われることがあることである。正は、つまり「正しい」という意味であり、その使役的機能を適用すると、貞は「正しくす、正さむ」という意味になるわけである。以下、貞は「貞しくす、貞さむ」と訓ずることにする。セ氏の“to *make* true, correct”は、まさにこのことを表わしたものと解釋するわけである。「正」と「貞」以外にも、ミニマル・ペア(最小的對比)として次のような例が考えられよう。

至 ＊tjidh “いたる” 致 ＊trjidh “いたらしむ”
合 ＊gəp “あう” 袷 ＊grəp “あわしむ”(通常“うるおす”の義だが,「洽比」などの熟語に“あわせる、仲よくす”などの意が潛在していることに注意)
敗 ＊padh “やぶれる” 敗 ＊pradh “やぶる”(並母もあり)
暴 ＊pagwh“あばれる” 爆 ＊pragwh“(火などを)はず”
弘 ＊gwəng“ひろい” 宏 ＊gwrəng“ひろくす”(ひろいの意もある)
梜 ＊kiap “はさみいた” 夾 ＊kriap “はさむ”
索 ＊sak “なわ” 索 ＊srak “たぐる、もとむる”

---

(56) 李方桂「上古音研究」『清華學報』新九卷、第一・二期合刊(一九七一年)、頁一～六一。同「幾個上古聲母問題」『蔣公逝世周年紀念論文集』(臺北南港、“中央研究院”、一九七六年)、頁一一四三～一一五〇。

結　＊kit　"むすび"　　袺　＊krit　"(きものの裾を)つまどる"
穫　＊gwak　"かりいれ"　獲　＊gwrak　"える"
卜　＊puk　"ひびわれ"　剝　＊pruk　"はぐ"（諧聲音として「錄、祿」＊lukを參照）

　以上擧げた例の中、「至」から「弘」までは使役的要素を含む意味の語が下段にくるよう配列してみた。「梜」から「卜」のペアーまでは、名詞對動詞であって、「至」から「弘」までのペアーと些少異なるが、形態論的に關連ありそうなことは認められると思う。ここでは、「使役的機能」と假稱しておいたが、「強輔的」とでも言った方が適當であるかも知れない。

　しかしながら、かかる介音＊-r-は、古典漢語の段階で能產的(productive)なものであったとは、必ずしも言えない。何故なら、例えば、「甲」＊krap、「百」＊prak、「皆」＊krid等、介音＊-r-を含みながらも、「使役的・強輔的」な意味は存在していそうにないし、また、「繫」＊kigh/＊gigh對「解」＊krigx/＊grigxなどのように、聲調こそ異にするも、意味は"つなぐ"と"ほどく"で使役・強輔關係が逆になっている印象を與える。（「崩」＊pəng"くずれる"對「繃」＊prəng"つかねる、くるる"はよかろうか。）しかしながら、これらの例は、必ずしも、介音＊-r-の使役・強輔說の反證にはならないことに注意しておきたい。このような形態論的構詞法は、往々にして歷史的に安定したものでは決してないからである。太古漢語から上古漢語の發展に於いて、ある機能が變化したり、あるいは、失效してしまったりすることはよくあることである。現代英語の-sなど、動詞の三人稱單數を表わしたり、名詞の複數形を表わしたり、もしくは、所有格を表わしたりするのに用いられ、歷史的發展の結果、かかる異なった機能が收束した、ということが言えるであろう。中國語の歷史にもそのようなプロセスがあったことは想像に難くない。

　さて、元にもどり、「正」と「貞」の形態論的關係であるが、前者は「正しい」という意味にして、後者はその使役・強輔的な意味の「貞しくす、貞さむ」であると言えるであろう。私は、以前（第五の5項）、カールグレンの"[cheng] means 'to verify, to determine what is correct'"を「洞察力に富んだ解釋」であると言っておいたが、それは、このような使役・強輔的機能を念頭に置いていたからであった。

　我々は、第四項にて、饒宗頤、張秉權、及び李學勤の三氏の說を紹介、檢

討を試みた。その際、特に饒氏と李氏が「貞」と「正」或るいは「有正」なる表現を問題にしたが、兩氏の分析が不充分だと指摘した。更に、かかる表現の分佈用法から有機的にどう考えられるのかが問題だ、ともつけ加えておいた。今、以上で述べた形態論的假設により、その問題を追求するにある程度の準備ができたと思われるので、少し例文を見て、實際に應用してみたい。

(1) 貞勿詳酌妣癸舞、正。　　　　　　　　　　『乙編』四一一九
(2) 甲午卜、賓貞侑于妣甲一牛、正。　　　　　『乙編』三四二四
(3) 辛亥卜、殻貞王其乎供爰伯出牛、允正。　　『丙編』四七一・(1)
(4) 貞勿乎供爰伯出牛、不其正。　　　　　　　『丙編』四七一・(2)
(5) 壬子卜、賓〔貞〕…正。王占曰吉、正。　　『續存』上・六五五
(6) 貞燎五牛、正。貞正。　　　　　　　　　　『前編』一・四八・六
(7) 乙丑卜、貞王其侑升于文武帝(祕)、其以羌五人、正、王受有祐。
　　　　　　　　　　　　　　　　　　　　　　『續編』二・七・一
(8) 貞叀乙未酌、有正。　　　　　　　　　　　『甲編』一六四五
(9) 貞叀羊、有正。　　　　　　　　　　　　　『甲編』一六六四
(10) 貞叀十宰、有正。　　　　　　　　　　　　『撫續』九四

以上、とりあえず十例ほど選んでみたが、(1)から順次に說明を加えてみる。(1)の文意は、「先妣の妣癸に舞〔犠牲〕をとりわけ(詳)酌祭として施さなくても、(本祭が)正しく運行せん」というようなことだと思われる。(ここで、「勿かれども」と「逆接」の解釋をしたが、これについては第八の項で詳說する。)尚、酌祭に關しては、注48でも觸れることがあったが、それは一種の準備祭であったと思われる。しかるに、かかる準備祭を行わなくても、本祭の推移に支障なく、「正しく」本祭が進まんことを「貞」* trjing、つまり、「正さむ」とした、と理解できるであろう。「貞」と「正」* tjingとは呼應し、そこには、有機的な關係があったのである。

例(2)では、(1)の「酌」と同種の統御可能動詞の「侑」が用いられているが、否定詞「勿」がないため、「妣甲に一牛を侑めんば、正ならん」と訓め、かかる命辭は、前辭の「貞」字に呼應していると解釋できると思われる。

例(3)の場合は、王が爰伯なる人物の派出した牛を供御せしめば、それは「允(まこと)に正ならん」を「貞さむ」とした貞卜言語であると解釋するわけである。

例(4)は、(3)の否定形であるが、(1)とは對照的に、統御可能動

詞の「供」には「勿」が、統御不可能動詞の「正」には「不」が用いられている(57)。そのような「勿＋V_1」＋「不＋V_2」といったパターンの場合は、V_1で構成するS_1とV_2で構成するS_2と二文節になり、複文になると思われる。そして、「不＋V_2」、つまり、S_2の方が原因・理由を表わす節になる。(この點は重要であるが、我々は第五の項の例文(5)・(6)(頁四九)のところで、原因・理由解釋説が一つの有力な見解であることを指摘しておいたので、そのところの分析を參考されたい。)してみると、「勿乎供爰伯出牛、不其正」は「爰伯の出せし牛を供せ乎ㇾむこと勿かれ、正なら不れば(なり)」と訓むのが正しいと思う。(このことについては、後でさらに追求する。)

例文(5)は、冒頭の部分が缺落しているが、命辭はやはり、「正」で終結している。そして、繇辭がすぐ後に續き、「王占いて曰く、吉なりと。正ならん」と結ばれており、ここでは「正」と「吉」が呼應していることが分かる。

例文(6)は、「貞燎ㇾサバ五牛ヲ、正ナラン」の貞卜の後、その「速記的」な省略形と思われる「貞正」のみが刻辭されている。これは、我々の提起した＊-r-使役・強輔説によると、決して「正貞」とはならない筈であり、また、かかる例も現實にないのである。

例(7)は第五期卜辭であって、上述したような「貞」と「正」の有機的關係が殷代後期迄保たれていたと推察できるものである。ここでは、「正」が「王ハ受ニケン有ゆう祐ゆきヲ」と呼應していること、そして、「正、王受有祐」が一つのユニットとして前辭中の「貞」と有機的に關係があったであろうことを示していると思われる。

例文(8)から(10)までは、「正」が動詞「有」の目的に用いられている。その場合、ただ「正ならん」という意味ではなくて、「正なる狀態を獲有(獲得)できん」といったニュアンスを含むものだと思われる(58)。(8)は「叀ㇾテニ

---

(57) 否定詞の研究には、筆者は永い間携ってきたが、ここで述べたことはその一斑である。詳しくは、次の二點を參照されたし。

1. K. Takashima, Negatives in the King Wu Ting Bone Inscriptions. Ph.D. dissertation. Seattle: University of Washington, 1973.

2. K. Takashima, "Morphology of the Negatives in Oracle-Bone Inscriptions," *Computational Analyses of Asian and African Languages*, No.30 (1988), pp.113-133.

(58) この點に關しては、注48所掲の周國正氏の博士論文(頁一三六～一四一)に詳說があり、參照されたし。周氏は、特に條件節の後に用いられる「有」字には「獲有・獲得」するという意味が讀み取れると論じており、私は同意である。

乙未ニノヒニ酢サバ、有ラン正」のように、(9)は「更ニセシメバ羊ニ、有ラン正」のように訓むべきものであろう。

　以上のように考えてくると、命辭には、使役・強輔的意味を擔った貞字が冠されるのが通例であることから、貞字以下をその目的格の文、或るいは、文節であると見做すことができる。しばしば引用される『周禮』の鄭注に「問事之正曰貞」とあり、「問」をむしろ同根の「聞」で解釋し、必ずしも疑問文を導びかない、ということを念頭に入れれば、鄭玄も「貞」と「正」とを有機的にとらえていたということが言えるかも知れない。言うまでもないが、鄭玄の場合は、甲骨文の理解ではなく、古典でのそれであった。

　以上、例文（1）から（10）に於ける「貞」を「正」の分佈用法から、その關係如何について、一つの試釋を提起してみたのであるが、自己批判の餘地があるかも知れない。それは、甲骨文に於いて「貞」字は萬をも數えるのに對し、それと呼應しているとした「正」字の用例は百程度であり、その差があまりにもありすぎるようである。何故なのか。ここで、一つの可能性として、全ての命辭が終わりに「正」とか「不其正」とか、或るいは、「有正」とかいう表現が省略されていたとみることが考えられよう。この説明ルートを採用し、考察していくこともできるであろうが、私は、それよりも、殷人の「貞」字に對する「無頓着さ」に注目したい。この無頓着さとは、例えば、「己卯卜、余羍于蔑三牛、允正」（『前編』六・七・六）の卜辭に於いて「貞」字が用いられなくても「正」字で結ばれていることから、「貞」字がなくても「正」字との關係はあったことを指すと思われる。換言して言えば、「貞」字は前辭の一部として實に頻繁に現われ、紋切り型のフォーミュラに過ぎないようでもある。その場合、「貞」というコトバに本來流れているはずの意味を殷人はかなり無頓着に認識していた可能性があるのではあるまいか、ということである。このことは、我々が提起した「貞と正の有機的解釋」説を弱めるものではあるが、必ずしもそれを無効にするものでもないと思われる。更に、かかる「正」字の實例というものは、「潛在意識の表面化」と言われる、言語學ではおなじみの現象としてとらえられるのではないだろうか。この現象については、ラフーブレ氏の「貞」字の字形分析のところでも考えることにするが、要するに、無意識にたまたま眞相が出現することもある、ということである。かかる原理は、「オッカムのかみそり」と同様、注意して取り扱わねばならない。そのこ

とを念頭におきつつ、推測すると、「貞」と「正」との關係の場合、例文（1）から（10）迄のように、有機的な呼應があったであろうということになる。眞相がたまたま表面化されたのではないだろうか。音韻的に、また、形態論的に關係があったのは、歪められないことであろうし、我々の分析は、かかるエヴィデンスに基づいたものだからである。

2 ニビソン說とその評價

貞字の後に續く命辭の法（ムード）に關しては、ニビソン氏も、第八項で檢討する裘錫圭氏も意見が合い、貞字の意味を考えることにより法の解釋が可能になることはない、と言っている[59]。ニビソン氏は、貞イコール正という、嚴密に言えば誤った解釋で法の問題を考えたために、そのような見解を持つに至ったのではないかと思われる。しかし、貞と正は同根ではあるものの形態論的に密切な關係があり、その相違は、貞が使役・強輔的で、正は狀態・情態を表わすということであった。さらに、貞は統御可能動詞であるのに對し、正は統御不可能動詞（即ち、非使役・非強輔的）であることも、前項の例（1）から（10）迄から推察できることである。してみると、このことは法の問題にも一つの解決の道を與えてくれるであろう。

先ず、貞字以下を「疑問文」であると假定し、それを「貞しくす、貞さむ」とは、不思議なことである。ニ氏論文（頁一二）でも、貞＝正と解釋し、疑問文を「正」することは不可解であるとしている。言語學の分野に於いては、通常、「疑問」というのは、何らかの新情報を得るための言語活動であって、「正」とか「不其正」といった評語は與えられない場合が非常に多いのである。かかる評語が適應するのは、言語理論的に考えて、叙述文に限る。祈願文については、「正しいかどうか」という評語が適應するかどうか簡單に判斷下せないが、私はやや否定的に考える。命令文の場合は、言語でのリスポンスよりも行動や狀態でのリスポンスが要求されるのが普通である。このような見識に基づいて、前項の（1）から（10）までの例文をもう一度考えてみると、どのようなことになるであろうか。

「正」、「允正」、「不其正」、「有正」の前にくる部分は、（1）から

---

[59] ニ氏論文（"The 'Question' Question."）、頁一、一〇、及び裘論文（「はじめに」及び「關于殷墟卜辭是否問句的考察」）、頁二を參照。

（3）、及び（6）から（10）では、從屬節である。この分析で重要なのは、「從屬節」ということは、疑問文ではあり得ないということである。例文（4）の場合は、「不其正」の前の文がもし從屬節とすると、「爰伯の出せし牛を供せ乎むこと勿かれば、正なら不らん」となってしまい、これでは何のために貞卜しているのか分からなくなってしまうのである。このことは、かって、私が指摘しておいたことである[60]。故に、この文を「爰伯の出せし牛を供せ乎むこと勿かれ、正なら不れば（なり）」と訓み、「不其正」は「勿乎供爰伯出牛」という主節に對して、理由をつけ加えた從節であると判斷したわけである。その際、それを文としては、叙述文に解釋し、そのトータルなメッセージ、つまり從辭言としては、命令調・勸告調（advisory）にとるべきであろう。卜辭疑問・質問說にのっとって主節を「爰伯の出せし牛を供せ乎むこと勿からんか」と疑問文にとり、從節の方も「正なら不らんか」と疑問文にとることは、一つの卜兆から二つの「答え」を得るようになってしまい不自然のようである。このことは、ニビソン氏も注意していることである（頁八）。では、次に、本題の貞字の意味の探究に入ろう。

　　ニビソン氏の「貞」字の解釋は、カールグレン氏の『グラマタ・セリカ・リセンサ』（頁二二一／八四三 g—i、注 29 所揭）での語譯「確かめる、神託を讀みとる」（"verify, read off an oracle"）に基づいている。この語譯は、我々も既に囑目した力氏の "Glosses on the Book of Documents"（注 51 所揭）の要約であり、詳しくは後者の方を參考にするべきであった。力氏のここでの語句注解は、『尙書』洛誥の「我二人共貞」の「貞」字についてである。ニビソン氏は、洛誥篇のコンテクストから判斷して、「貞」の對象を洛邑に於ける新都建設の適所選擇結果であると正しく認識し、それを「あたかも公證人が正式に "正しい" と認定する」という意味であると解釋したのである。そして、甲骨

---

[60] 注 57 所揭の拙著學位論文（頁二九五）にて、次のように論じてある。

"But in (457)〔辛酉卜㱿貞今載王勿從望乘伐下危，弗其受祐〕, where the 'wu ... fu...' construction is observed, to translate the sentence as 'If the king does not follow Wang Ch'eng to attack Hsia Wei [Hsi] this spring [60-day cycle], he (the king) will not perhaps receive abundant assistance' ...seems rather strange. That is, if the king does not follow Wang Ch'eng to attack the Hsia Wei [Hsi], why does he need assistance from ti-God anyway? Here it may be considered that 'receive abundant assistance' referred to the proposed act of 'following Wang Ch'eng to attack Hsia Wei [Hsi]', rather than to some other act of the king."

文での貞の意味も、「貞卜の結果の正しさを正式に認定する」ということであるとしている。氏の原文は次の如くである。

"officially certify the correctness of the result of divination about... the following sentence."(p.12)

ニ氏は、洛誥の一文に基づき、命辭の内容を結果としてとらえ、それを公式に認定すると解釋したわけである。洛誥のコンテクストに卽せば、確かにそのようにもとれる。しかし、前にも注意しておいたように、『尙書』にかかる用例はただ一つあるのみであって、それを更に甲骨文にまで適應させようとするのは、かなり勇敢である。このことは、命辭の内容が過去のものとしてとらえられ、時制の解釋の問題にも發展すると思われる。私には、卜辭に於ける貞卜内容の時制が過去であった、とは考え難い。命辭が繇辭、驗辭とともに契刻されていることからして、それらは全て言辭活動の後になされたことであるとは認められようが、そのことが「結果の正しさを公式に認定する」ということには結びつかないと思う。また、洛誥では、西周の成王が「我二人共貞」と言ったとされていることから、「公式」にという解釋が生じたわけであろう。しかし、「公式」か如何ということを殷代にもそのまま適用することは、貞人の社會的地位にも涉及し、問題が多岐に亙る。このことは、以前檢討したキートリー氏の貞の對象を廣範圍に求め過ぎたこと（つまり複雜化）という點とは反對に單純化の憾みがある。

ともあれ、ニビソン氏は、以上述べたような貞字の解釋に基づいて、『庫方』一五〇六（＝『英國』二六七四）と『庫方』一九八九の有名な「家譜刻辭」に關して論じ、その二つとも眞刻であるとしている。（前者は牛の肩胛骨に刻字されており、以下、「牛骨」と略稱することにし、後者は雕花鹿角に刻字されており、以下、「鹿角」と略稱することにする。）これら「牛骨」と「鹿角」上の所謂家譜刻辭は眞僞問題にかかわり、胡厚宣氏や于省吾氏等數名の研究者の所論がある[61]。しかしながら、未だ問題の決着を見るには至っておら

---

[61] 胡厚宣「甲骨文"家譜刻辭"眞僞問題再商榷」『古文字研究』第四輯（一九八〇年、頁一一五～一三八）は、この問題の研究史などをも紹介しつつ氏の見解について論じている。胡氏の結論は、これら「牛骨」・「鹿角」刻字を僞と判斷している。また、于省吾「甲骨文"家譜刻辭"眞僞辨」同書（頁一三九～一四六）は、「牛骨」の方の「貞」字を僞刻とし、殘辭は眞の記事刻辭としている。

ず、ニビソン氏の所論は、貞字の語釋のみから推論したものである。以下、氏の主な論點を簡單に紹介し、檢討を加えてみたい。

圖2(縮小率約70%)

　ニ氏は、「牛骨」と「鹿骨」家譜刻辭の背景に次のようなことがあったのではないかとしている。殷代のある貴族が殷王の所へ自分の家の家系譜を牛骨上に契刻し、それを公式に認證してもらいに來る。(圖二參照。)王は同意し、鑽鑿を「工人」に作らしめ、その後、焦灼する。〔とニ氏は言うが、刻字した後に焦灼はしない。これは「犯兆」という現象から推察できることである。つまり、卜兆はその大部分が刻字の際避けられていることからして契刻の前に生じさしめられたことが分かる。「犯兆」というのは、かかる事實にそぐわない、ごく限られた現象を指すのである。〕王は卜兆を見て、その家系譜が「有効且つ正しい」と宣言する。牛骨刻辭が公式な認定を經たものであるという記錄として、王はおかかえの契刻者に命じて「貞」字を家系譜の右上に契せしむ。家系譜本文の契刻者と「貞」字の契刻者が異なっているのはそのためである、とする。〔このことは後述するが、讀者をしてかなり強烈な印象を與えしむ。〕家系譜本文以外に別の刻辭が何もないのに、その上に境界線が一本引かれているのは、「貞」の對象がそこに記されている家系譜全體に及ぶことを示す、とする。〔そのような例は、類例がない。〕該貴族は、その牛骨を家寶として保存することになる、とニビソン氏は想像するのである。

　次に、鹿角刻辭に移るが、該貴族の子孫が牛骨上の家系譜を彫花鹿角に轉寫刻する。〔外に類例なし。〕この鹿角家系譜は展示用のためだとする。牛骨

上の刻字とは異なり、鹿角上には、「王曰貞」と刻す。かかる表現は他例を見出せないが〔と二氏は言い、ここでは注意深い態度だが、實は、『佚存』三九一に一例を擧げ得る〕、この意味は、「王曰く、朕が認定するに…」と解釋でき、これは、この貴族の子孫が自分の身分を展示するために王に言ってもらいたいことである、とする。ところが、牛骨の方が實際に王の認定を受けた、言わば、「公式文書」であるから、それは貴重であり、コピーである鹿角は、二氏が再構したような貞字の意味—つまり、事後承諾ということ—を熟知した者、すなわち、殷人以外にはなし得なかった筈である、と結論づけたのである。牛骨・鹿角刻字も正眞正銘殷人の手によるとするわけである。二氏がつけ加えて言うには、この牛骨と鹿角が市場に出廻り出したのは、一九〇五年あたりであり、その頃の學者は全て貞字を『說文』の「貞卜問也」で解釋していたから、貞字以下の家系譜本文は疑問文であると見做されていたに違いない。しかるに、金祥恆氏のように、家系譜本文が疑問文であるとは考え難いと氣付き、牛骨刻辭を僞刻と判斷したのである[62]。金祥恆氏は、貞字以下の命辭を疑問文であると信じて疑わず、それに基づいて、さらに誤斷をした、と二氏は批判する。〔以上のように二氏は言うが、我々が第一項で見たように、孫詒讓が『契文擧例』を著し、『說文』の定義を引用したのは一九〇四年であった。一九〇五年あたりでは、僞刻者が頻見する「貞」字を分別なくして契刻したということは充分考えられる。〕

　以上、ニビソン氏の貞の語釋が家系譜刻辭の眞僞問題にどのようなインプリケーションをもつか紹介した。我々は二氏の想像力の逞しさを評價することにためらいを感じない。しかし、既に角括弧を施し、寸評を加えたことからも察せられるように、果敢に過ぎるようである。また、かかる歷史的背景の再構は、說明不可能なものを全てないがしろにする威力をもっている。例えば、牛骨に於いて、家系譜本文の契刻者と貞字の契刻者が異なるということは、于省吾氏も言うように（注61所掲于氏論文、頁一四二）、少なくとも貞字は後世の僞刻とすべきものであろう。一つの甲骨文を契刻する際、それが二人以上の契刻者によってなされた、と判斷できる例は、ごく少數の「習刻」と言われるもの以外、ないと思われる。鹿角刻字の方は、胡厚宣氏の論じたように、全て僞

---

[62] 金祥恆「庫方二氏甲骨卜辭第一五〇六片辨僞兼論陳氏兒家譜說」『大陸雜誌』第二期（一九六二年、頁一三七～一九二）、及び松丸道雄「甲骨文僞作問題新探」『池田末利博士古稀記念東洋學論集』（同刊行會編、一九八〇年）、頁二一、二五、三〇を參照。

刻であると思う。彫花鹿角に家系譜や普通の卜辭を殷代に於いて轉寫刻するといった例は、未だ發見されていない。

　甲骨文に於ける貞字の解釋について、我々は、前項第五の1、2、5にてキートリー氏の說、本項の1にてセロイス氏說及びそれを形態論的に發展させた拙說、そして本項の2にてニビソン氏の說を紹介し檢討をしてきた。この外に、もう一つ、ラフーブレ氏の說がある。それについても考察を加えたいが、ここで小結をしておきたい。

　孫詒讓の『契文舉例』での指摘以來、約七十年間、『說文』の「貞卜問也」が決定的な影響力をもちつづけている。それに疑問をいただき、『說文』の解は「貞、正也」という傳統的な解釋になじまず、恐らく鄭司農の『周禮』での注「貞、問也」に從っているのではないかと指摘し、「貞、不問也」と結論づけたキートリー氏の貢獻は評價するべきである。しかし、貞の意味を"to regulate"（規定する）とし、その對象を命辭の內容に求めず、貞卜工程及び命辭の省略形、つまりコンテクストではなくフォームに求めたのは、贊成しかねる。次に、セロイス氏の"to test, to try out; to *make* true, correct"（試す、正す、「貞測」す）は、我々の從うことのできる解釋であるとした。その理由について、我々は貞と正の形態論的分析を展開したわけであるが、それは、卜辭の「干支卜某貞……正、允正、不其正、有正」といったパターンを有機的に解釋することが重要だ、と考えたからである。ニビソン氏の『尚書』洛誥に基づいた、貞とは「貞卜の結果の正しさを公式に認定する」という意味である、という解釋は、『庫方』採錄の二片の家譜刻辭、特に鹿角刻辭まで巧妙に理解してしまう威力がある。本稿では、かかる解釋は愼重さに缺けるのではないかとし、資料批判をもっと嚴密に行う必要性があろうとしたのである。

3　ラフーブレ說とその評價

　「貞」字解釋論も、一九八五年のラフーブレ氏の說をみて最後になる。ラ氏の考釋（注15所揭書）を讀むと、まず明らかになるのは、氏が言語學的アプローチに對して、かなり強い疑念をいだいていることである。そして、その代わりの方法論として、ラ氏は「古代は、古代人の眼でみよ」という方法論的モットーを打ち出している。このことは、個別の議論をする以前に、結論が左右されるおそれがあるのではないかと思い、少しく氏の考えを廣い角度から檢討

し、然る後に詳細な檢討に移りたい。先ず、ラ氏自身の言葉を引用する。

「原始泛靈論與人類初面對宇宙不可控制的力量時的驚訝、是同時發生的。所以、語言學者在探求的原始意義時、應該捐棄現代人的觀念、盡可能以古代人的眼光來看宇宙。」(頁一二〇)

ここに述べられていることは、言語學としての分野と文化人類・宗教學的（？）分野が對立的にとらえられ、後者の視野から前者をみるべきだ、ということのようである。このことがもう少し明瞭に理解できるかと思われることとして、數文章後にラ氏は次のように言う。

「下文中我們將討論的那些字、有些是與生命和存有起源之某些基本觀念有關、有些則與占卜儀式有關。」

人間の生命と存在の起源に關する言葉として、ラ氏は繫辭（例えば英語の"be"動詞）の「隹」と「叀」とを擧げる。「隹」は「鳥」であり、殷人が鳥を神聖な祖先、つまり自分達の生命・存在の根源であると信じていたことを示すものであるとしている。氏の言葉では、「隹 "to be" 則表示分受鳥之生命」である。また、「叀」に關しても、ラ氏はそれが「～であるべし」（"should be"）という意味であることは認めるが、やはり殷人はその言葉に神聖な意味合いを感じていた、として次のように述べている。

「…"使其是"之主格當指說話者、而如果誠如前文所述商末人相信自己與神明閒能有一密切之接觸―尤其是與氏族始祖和居地守護神閒―那麼、"使其是"的主格應指神明。這麼一來、"叀"當意爲…"因神明使其如此、故該是…"」

ラ氏に依ると、「非情態繫辭（non-modal copula）である「隹」も「情態繫辭」（modal copula）である「叀」も[63]、殷人の宗教的觀念を暗示し、それが世俗化

---

[63] 二つの繫辭「隹」と「叀」に對する簡稱として、それぞれ「非情態繫辭」と「情態繫辭」という術語を用いたが、その内容詳細に關しては、拙論 "Two Copulas or One Copula in Proto-Sino-Tibetan? : *Wei*（隹）and *Hui*（叀）in Oracle-Bone Inscriptions," to appear in *Monumenta Serica*, Vol.38を參照されたし。尚、「叀」については、上記拙論の外に、伊藤道治「語詞"叀"の用法に關して」『立命館文學』第四三〇、四三一、四三二號（一九八一年）『白川靜博士古稀記念中國文史論叢』頁二六五～二七四をも參照されたし。
【付記】
注63所掲の拙論は、更に手を加え、タイトルも "A Study of the Copulas in Shang Chinese" と改題し、本紀要第百十二册に掲載することになりました。この件に關し、MS誌からは撤回許可を得ました。

（secularize）されるに従って、神明との關係が薄らいでいった、ということである。そして、この世俗化が進んだ現代、中國人の研究者が「隹」と「叀」とは同義であると「感じている」ことをも説明し得るとしている。

このような解釋は、言語そのものが文化的要素を表わす具體例のように思われ、一見、魅惑的な印象さえ與えるかも知れない。例えば、「隹」は「弗」以外の否定詞により否定されるが、「叀」はそれ自體否定されることがないという事實がある。このことは、ラ氏の解釋では、「叀」は「因神明使其如此、故該是…」、卽ち「神の命により～であるべし」であるから、それが否定されないということは、「神の命であるから、それに逆えない」とでもなり、氏の說に都合が良さそうでもある。氏が果たしてそのように言うか不明であるが、かかる否定詞の分佈狀態は、格好のリサーチ・トピックになる。何故か。それは、ラ氏の主張するところの「應該捐棄現代人的觀念、盡可能以古代人的眼光看宇宙」が、「叀字不被否定」という言語學的現象を文化・宗教的に一見スムーズに說明し得ている一方、しからば、言語學的には、如何に說明できるであろうか、という一課題が提出されるからである。

私は、この課題に關しては注63で引用した拙論（頁五〇一五七）にて既に考察を試みたことがある。今、ここで立ち入った議論するのを避けて、要點のみを記すことにする。

先ず、當然なことであるが、「叀」字に神聖な意味を與えたのは、ラフーブレ氏であり、殷人ではない。語源學の觀點からすれば、「叀」＊gwidh（中古漢語ではγiwei）は、ジェームス・マティソフ氏の言うシナ・チベット祖語の「神」という言葉＊wayと同根であるかも知れない(64)。私はこのマティソフ氏の論文のコピーをラ氏にお送りしたところ、これを傍證として引用された（頁一三）。それも當然のことである。殷人の觀點からものを見るべきだ、と主張するラ氏にとって、氏の考えがシナ・チベット語系統の言語によって支持されていたようだからである。そうなのではあるが、我々は、語源と實際の言語の用法・意味は明瞭に區別しなくてはならないことがあることも忘れてはならない。そして、この言語學の分野では周知のことが「隹」と「叀」字にも適應す

(64) Cf. James A. Matisoff, "God and the Sino-Tibetan Copula with Some Good News Concerning Selected Tibeto-Burman Rhymes," *Journal of Asian and African Languages*, No.29 (1985), pp.1-81.

ると思われるのである。「叀」字の用法を研究して判明したことであるが、

（ⅰ）叀字の用いられている對貞の否定文には、統御可能動詞を否定する「勿」（典型的には「勿隹」）が用いられる。ここで、統御可能動詞の「統御」とは、人間（殷人）を指していることである。

（ⅱ）同じく對貞の正反いずれか一方に於ける「其」字—これは前述したように「將來が不確實で、殷人にとって望ましくない」意味を擔っているコトバ（第三の2項、第五の6項參照）—が用いられることがある。

（ⅲ）同じく對貞の正反いずれか一方に於いて、場所・時間を表わす虛辭の「于」が用いられる時、その後にくる時間帶は、例外なく「叀」が先行した時間帶よりも後、つまり、貞卜時より遠く離れた將來ということがある。時間帶が後ということは、その對貞に於いて、異った、コンピーティングな選擇を命龜しているわけである。

以上述べた三つのポイント[65]の意味するところは何か。それは次のようなことだと思われる我々がラ氏に從って「叀」字に神聖な意味を認めるとしたら、その神聖なる叀字と對貞中に表現された人間（殷人）の意志・意向・願望とが正面から衝突することになりはしまいか。殷代の貞卜、特に兩貞法というものは、そのように人間と神が對立する場を供給していた、とは到底考え難いことである。では、何故叀字は否定されることがないのであろうか。それは、叀字の意味するところが「神の命であるからそれに逆えない」ということではなくして、叀というコトバの情態性・樣態性（modality）が非常に強く、外向性（extrovertive）の語氣が顯著であったからだと思われる。このことも注63所揭の拙論（頁二八—三一、四五—四七）で論じたことだがごく簡單に次の對貞例をみておこう。

　　（1）貞王叀沚馘夏從伐〔巴方〕。　　　　　　　　　　『丙編』二二・（11）

---

[65] この三つのポイントのベースになっている例文を一組ずつ記しておく。

　　（ⅰ）叀霊田省、不雨。勿省霊田、其雨。　　　　　　　　　　　『明義』一九〇〇
　　（ⅱ）癸卯卜、㱿、其牢。叀小牢。　　　　　　　　　　　　　『明義』二四〇八
　　（ⅲ）丙寅貞叀丁卯酚于堯。丙寅貞于庚午酚于堯。　　　　　　『通纂』二五九

　尚、この（ⅲ）の對貞で貞卜日の「丙寅」は干支の第三日、「丁卯」は四日、「庚午」は七日であり、「于」で表わす時間帶が「叀」で表わす時間帶より（貞卜日を基準として）離れていることが分かる。

（2）貞王勿從沚戛伐巴〔方〕。　　　　　　　　　『丙編』二二・（12）

（1）の意味は、「王が巴方を伐たんとするに從う〔者、つまり、將軍、斥候軍の指揮者の類か〕は、沚戛なるべし」ということであり、（2）の意味は、「王は巴方を伐たんとするに沚戛に從うことなかるべし」であろうと思う。（2）での否定詞「勿」は、注57所揭の拙論にて論じたごとく、統御可能動詞を否定し、そのモダリティーは非常に強く、外向的な語氣があるということである。この「勿」は、後の古典漢語でも禁止の否定詞「～なかれ」として用いられ、強いモダリティーと外向性を保存している。然るに、（1）と（2）は對貞であり、「宙」字のモダリティーに限って言えば、「勿」のそれと同じ價値を與えるのが至當と思われる。このような分析により、繫辭の「宙」は、「勿」が否定する動詞と同じように、統御可能動詞の一種であるという言語學的な結論に到達したわけである。ここには神聖な意味は讀みとれない。かかる言語學的な解釋は、ラ氏の主張する「現代人の觀念から脱却し、古代人の觀念からものを見よ」というモットーと比較すると、如何なる相違があると言えるであろうか。前者は、我々の解釋（假說）が或いは誤っている、という可能性が內潛している說を打ち出している、ということになると思われる。後者は、モットーそれ自體は望ましいことであると思われるのではあるが、結局のところ、不可能なプロポジションであり、その方法論、從って、實證性に問題がある、ということが言えるのではないだろうか。學問の發展があるとすれば、上述したような言語學的解釋のどこが誤っているかを追求するべきであろう。

　　以上、ラフーブレ氏の考えについて、「隹」と「宙・叀」の例をとり、論じてみたが、本項で直接關係あるのは、氏の「貞」字の解釋である。それは次の如くまとめられよう。

　　先ず、氏は貞字の研究史の如きものを簡單に紹介した後、甲骨文に於ける「𠂤」、「𠁥」、「𠁧」（及びこれら三字の異體）が「鼎」字に該當するとし、序辭や命辭に用いられたりすることに注意する。音韻方面からとして、李方桂氏の上古・中古再構音（注56所揭文獻參照）の「鼎」字の音 *tingx＞tieng 及び「貞」字の音 *trjing＞tjäng を引き、前者が名詞、或いは、自動詞に、そして後者が恐らく他動詞にコレスポンドしたのであろう、としている。（これは正しい判斷であると思われる。）甲骨文に於いて最もよく用いられる「𠁥」も「鼎」*tingx であり、「貞」*trjing にはコレスポンドないとし、次の如く述べる。

　　　　　　「就字形、字音言、"鼑"當爲"鼎"…、當名詞或不及物動詞用、而非
　　　　　"貞"…。說文之前、"貞"竝無"卜龜"之意…。」（ラ氏論文、頁一二四）

ラフーブレ氏は、この「鼑＝鼎」という解釋に基づき、更に次のように論じている。

　　　　　　「命辭中、"鼎"經常表祭儀、卽"用鼎以祭"；序辭中之"鼑"（卽"鼎"）、應有相
　　　　　近的意義。和祖先或神明接觸、只有藉奉獻祭品的隆重儀式才能進行。…"卜"卽
　　　　　表示以火占卜時連續的形式動作；"鼎"則代表在祖先或神明之前所舉行的整個
　　　　　祭儀。…商末時、君王或其代表貞人、應先立於祖先或神明之前、以莊嚴之祭儀禮
　　　　　敬之後、再宣示"命辭"。這便是爲甚麼有時在序辭中"鼑"字前常有王禮者之名
　　　　　之原因。果其如此、則"某鼑"、或可釋爲"某主禮占儀"。」（頁一二五—一二六）

これを要するに、ラ氏は「干支卜某貞」とすべきところを「干支卜某鼎」としてとらえ、「鼎」は嚴かな「鼎祭」の儀禮を行うことにほかならないとしたわけである。

　ラ氏の解釋は、我々が「貞」を形態論に基づいて、使役・強輔的な「貞す」＊trjingという意味のコトバと解釋したのとはかなり異なる。ラ氏の「某主禮占儀」にコレスポンドする英文テキストの方は、"X celebrated the divination"（某が占卜の儀式を擧行する）であり、それは「鼎」字の解釋であるわけである。これは、前にも觸れた「古代人の觀念からものを見よ」という氏のモットーを實踐したものと思える。現代人の我々の觀點からみるとどうなるかは、勿論、分析者によって異なるであろうことは豫想されるが、一つの見解を示しておきたい。

　先ず、字形の問題である。ラ氏は「鼑」及びその異體字をことごとく「鼎」字とし、「貞」字ではないと斷定しているのである。その「根據」として、「說文之前、貞竝無卜龜之意」（頁一二四）とし、これはキートリー氏が強調した通りであると言う。我々は旣にキ氏の所說を檢討してみたが、キ氏の強調したのは、貞字には「問う」という意味はなかったということで、「貞竝無卜龜之意」とは言っていない。（第五の3項參照。）實際、『尚書』洛誥の「我二人共貞」、『左傳』哀公十七年の「衞侯貞卜」、『國語』吳語の「貞於陽卜」等、數は多いとは言えないが、これらは全て『說文』以前のテキストであり、また「卜龜」に關連する時に用いられたことは明らかである。また、『周

禮』も参考とするならば、春宮、天府に「…以貞來歳之媺惡」とか、小宗伯に「右國大貞」等あり、これらの中、「貞」字は全て龜卜を指すと解釋されている。從って、ラ氏の「根據」は我々が受容できる根據たり得ない。

字形の問題は、やはり字形の分析により解決されるべきである。これに關して、ラ氏はパラグラフを改め（頁一二五）、金文の「」（『金文詁林』九二九/頁四四二四－四四二五）を引用し、この字の上部にある「卜」は卜兆の卜ではなく、鼎の蓋を表わしたものであるとする。故に、この金文の字形は、「貞」の字の前形ではない、と判斷している。金文の字形の「卜」が鼎蓋を表わしたとは、未だ信じ難しと感じるが、該金文の字が「貞」の意味に用いられていないことは確かである(66)。この場合、金文の字形よりも甲骨文の字形分析が問題にされるべきである。しかし、ラ氏はそれには言及していない。我々は、第五の1項に於いて、「貝と鼎の字形上のあいまいさは甲骨文にまで遡れる」とした。(貝）と（鼎）は、それらが様式化（stylize）された時、兩者ともになると思われ、混同される可能性を含んでいたのである。しかし、「貞」は占卜のテクニカルなコトバであったため、かかる混同は字形上のみに限られ、コトバとしては、明白に區別されていたと思われる。スタイライズされた「」字は、命辭中にはほとんど皆無に近いということもある。「貝」の上に義符と思われる「卜」をつけたのは、刻字者のイディオシンクラシーが「⺊がつくべきであるという潛在意識」の表面化としてとらえられるのではなかろうか。その理由であるが、先ず、周原卜辭では、「」（H11・1）、「」（H11・174、H11・84）、「」（H11・13、H11・10）等と契刻され、それらは「」、（H11・1）や「」（H11・14）等と區別されている。前者は、

(66) リチャード・クンスト（Richard A. Kunst）氏は、氏のカリフォルニア大學（バークレー校）での博士論文 "The Original *Yijing*: A Text, Phonetic Transcription, Translation, and Indexes, with Sample Glosses"（1985）, p.237, n.85; pp.210-211にて、散氏盤での「」と利簋の「」が、それぞれ、動詞の「貞」の意味（氏は「問いただす」と解釋している）に用いられている可能性があるとしている。思うに、散氏盤での刻字の用法は、動詞であるとは認め難い。これは、文脈から言って、人名にとるべきであろう。（一連の人名が列擧されているところに用いられている。）利簋に於いての刻字は、明らかに「鼎」であり、それを「貞卜」の動詞「貞」であるとする說は成立しないと思う。詳しくは、拙論 "Some Problematic Aspects of the *Li kuei* Inscription," *Ancient Chinese and Southeast Asian Bronze Age Culture*（tentative title; ed. by Noel Barnard; in press), pp. 34-36（original mss）を參照されたし。

「貞」であり、後者はそれぞれ「鼎」と「「劓」（＝則）の字に相當すると思われる。從って、この場合、「卜」を「貝」・「鼎」の上につけたのは、周原卜辭の刻字者グループのイディオシンクラシーとしてとらえうる。（但し、これは殷墟卜辭の刻字者グループと比較してのことである。）殷墟卜辭では、著録された例として、僅かに一例を『鐵雲』四五・二に「閌」とあるのを發見しえたが、何萬とある貞字中一例あるのみということは不思議である。この『鐵雲』四五・二は僞刻でもなさそうで、陳夢家氏も松丸道雄氏もリスト・アップしていない[67]。ところが、最近明かるみに出たことだが、肖楠氏が意外の收穫として一つの腹甲を紹介した[68]。それは殷墟小屯南地の陶片と混って發見されたものであり、腹甲の五つの部位に文字と易卦の數字が刻されていることが後になって（つまり、泥落としした後）判明した。文字は數字と同樣に極めて小さいが、はっきりと「閌吉」（貞吉）と契刻されていたことが見てとれる。肖楠氏は、この腹甲の

　　（ⅰ）攻治方法と形制
　　（ⅱ）鑽鑿
　　（ⅲ）字形の特徵

の三點から、大體に於いて周原卜辭と近似しているが、鑿がやや丸味を帶び、中央の千里路を境にした鑽鑿の對應關係の體系が違ったりしている點などから周原卜辭とは異物のものであるとしている。肖氏は、結論として、この「易卦腹甲」を殷末周初、恐らくは、周初のものであろうとしている。このようなモノが、どうして殷墟の小屯南地から出土したか、その真相はつかみ難い。しかし、もしこれが外地からもたされたものでないとしたら、貞字の原形として、時代こそ隔たるが、殷墟に「閌」字と「閌」（後者は第一期の賓組卜辭と思える）の二つあったことになる。そして、この場合は、特異ではあるが、「卜」が本來は意符としてつくべきものであるという刻字者の潛在意識が表面化されたのではないだろうか。私はそのように問題の整理を試みたのであるが、これらの「貞」字の原形が金文の「貞」字とは意味的にも時代的にも連接しないのは確かである。これは、金文の該字の音價が＊trjingとは全く違ったものであったからであろう。

---

[67] 陳夢家『殷虛卜辭綜述』（北京、科學出版社、一九五六年）、頁六四九、及び松丸道雄「甲骨文僞作問題新探」『池田末利博士古稀記念東洋學論集』（同刊行會編、一九八〇年）、頁二三の注（1）參照。

[68] 肖楠「安陽殷墟發現"易卦"卜甲」『考古』一九八九・一、頁六六〜七〇。

最後に、ラフーブレ氏の「鼎」を「用鼎以祭」とする解釋であるが、それが合辭中に於いて一つの動詞であることは確認可能である。次の如き文は好例である。

(1) 貞鼎宰。　『人文』九九
(2) 王其鼎、又大雨。　『京津』三八七五
(3) 其鼎、又正。　『京津』四三三〇

（1）では、「貞」（）と「鼎」（）が明瞭に區別されていることが分かる。「鼎」をコトバとしてとらえる時、ラ氏の言う「〔與貞〕應有相近的意義」は受容し得ると思われるが(69)、それを直ちに「祖先や神明の前での莊嚴なる占卜儀式」と解釋することは如何なものであろうか。それは、古代人の眼から見るべきだとするラ氏のモットーが氏をして想像の域に行かしめたということにもなるかも知れない。資料の制限を卓越した見解とも言える性質のものであるなら、これは要注意の態度で受けとめざるを得ないと思う。いずれにせよ、ラ氏の解釋は「貞」ではなく「鼎」という語に對してなされたのであって、我々のここでの關心からはずれるのである。そして、字形の分析から言えることは、「」字が「貞」ではなくして「鼎」字のみにコレスポンドするというラ氏の說は成立しないのである。

七、ショナシー說

最初に斷わっておかねばならないことであるが、私は本稿を執筆する時、ショナシー氏の一九八三年の博士論文（注14所掲）に直接目を通せる境遇にいあわせなかった。從って、氏の說は裘錫圭氏の論文（「はじめに」にて引用）で紹介されているところに依ることにする(70)。裘論文は、注4にても記した

(69) この點に關しては、次の二つの拙論にて考えたことがあるので、參照されたし。K.Takashima,"Some Philological Notes to Sources of Shang History," *Early China*, 5 (1979-1980), p.53. Idem,"Settling the Cauldron in the Right Place: A Study of *Ting*  in the Bone Inscriptions," *Wang Li Memorial Volume* (Hong Kong: Joint Publishing Co.,1987), pp.405-421.

(70) 裘論文でショ氏の所說が述べられているところは、頁二、一七、一八の三個所ある。ショ氏の裘論文英譯原稿では、頁四、五三、五四～五六にそれぞれ分佈している。

が、ショ氏により英譯されている。そのため、裘論文中ショ氏說に關連するところは、氏の博士論文と同文のところもあるであろう。しかも、氏の檢閱を經ていると推測される。また、裘論文でショ氏の見解が分かるところは、ニビソン氏の論文（注 13 所掲、頁一三）で記述されているところと一致している。

ショナシー氏の見解で新しいところは、殷墟卜辭の性格について、共時的に劃一的な解釋を下すのに滿足せず、歷史的發展が窺えるとすることにある、と言ってよい。ショ氏は、李學勤氏の李論文一（注 6 所掲）の說—卽ち、𠂤組卜辭中の「不（否）、乎、㞢、執」という「語末助詞」（＝「句末助詞」）が用いられている卜辭は疑問文と見做すべきだという說—をまず認める。更に、ショ氏は、李論文二の說—卽ち、「斯正」、「斯有正」などの表現がある文は疑問文ではないとする說—を認めた上で、次の如く論ずる(71)。𠂤組卜辭が現存する最古の卜辭であるという說に基づき、そのグループには、三つの特徵があるとする。一つには、何らか特定なイベントがあった時に應じて貞卜し、その言語は一定の句型型式にのっとっていないということ。次に、𠂤組卜辭では、正反の問題を一つの文に收め、對貞型式は、通常、用いていないということ。ここでは、李學勤氏の意見「…把正反兩問併于一辭之中」（李論文一、頁四一）にそのまま從っていることが分かる。最後に、命辭はしばしば疑問文として提起されていること。これら三つの特徵を𠂤組に續く賓組卜辭と比較してみると、次のようなことが言えるとしている。卽ち、賓組卜辭では對貞型式がよく用いられ、疑問文は用いられなかったとする。この段階では、一般的に言って、「占卜の形式も目的も特に變化の萌芽はないようだ」としている。ここのところの原文は次の如くである。

> "…the general form and purpose of divination at that time[i.e., during the Pin-tsu Group inscriptions] seems not to have undergone any change."(p.55)

賓組卜辭は數も多く、貞卜のトピックも廣範圍に亙る。しかし、祖甲の代になると、貞卜の性質にも大きな變化が見られ、それは殷王朝滅亡時まで繼續的に進んでいったとする。祖甲以降、貞卜のトピックも貞卜する頻度も少なくなっていき、帝乙・帝辛時代の卜辭には𠂤・賓兩組に見られた臨時的な、また應變

(71)　以下、ショ氏の說は、裘論文の頁一八、ショ氏の裘論文英譯原稿の頁五四～五六に基づいて紹介する。

的なものがなくなる。その時代には、貞卜行爲に本來具わっていたであろう神秘性が消滅してしまい、卜辭も形式化されたものになっていった。武丁時代の賓組卜辭では、比較的に言って、命辭のみが臨時應變的なものではなく、繇辭もそうであった。これは、繇辭に「吉」や「不吉」などといった表現を記すこともあったことからも推察できる、とショ氏は言う。しかし、帝乙・帝辛の時代になると、繇辭は「吉」、「大吉」、及び「引吉」と全て良い意味にて形式的なスタイルで記されるようになる。命辭の方も「旬亡禍」とか「往來亡災」のように「正」の概念を表わし、決して「旬有禍」とか「往來有災」などといった「反」の概念を表わすことがない。このように考えてくると、殷代末期では、「貞卜という儀式は、單に緊迫した事態に對處すべきことを量らんとする手段ではなくなり、それらをコントロールするための手段になっていたのである」とショ氏は結論づけている。ここの部分の氏の原文は次の通りであるが、氏の説は「卜辭マジック説」を彷彿させるに足る、と言ってよいと思う。

　　　"This[referring to the summary just presented] suggests that for the last Shang kings, the ritual of divination was no longer simply an attempt to resolve doubts about impending events but rather had become a means of controlling them."(p.56)

ショナシー氏のこのような説は、殷王朝の貞卜の意義を歷史的な流れの中に求めたものとして、評價出來るところもある。例えば、卜辭の內容から考えて、殷人が貞卜により對處せんとしたことが臨時應變的なものかどうかを考えてみることは、祭祀、戰法、農耕生活等に對する思想を知る上で、重要なことと思われる。また、本稿で紹介できたところは、ショ氏の説の骨格に過ぎないであろうから、更に充實もしくは修正可能なところも出て來るであろう。ともあれ、今迄、我々が羅振玉の説を始めとし、前項のラフーブレ氏迄の諸説を紹介・檢討してきた過程で言えることが三つほどあると思うので、次に簡單に述べてみよう。

　先ず第一に、ショ氏が甲骨文の初期には疑問文があると認めたことである。これは、羅振玉や張秉權氏などの因襲的甲骨文研究者の考えと同じであり、「卜辭疑問・質問説」である。しかし、ショ氏の理由は、「うらなうということは問うことだ」という、いわば、先入觀的なものではなく、李學勤氏の提起になる句末疑問助詞によって明白にマークされる、ということである。我

々は、既にこの句末助詞そのものが成立しないということを述べ、それを次項の第八の1で詳考するとしておいた。もし、私が信ずるように、甲骨文の初期にも疑問文がないとしたら、ショ氏の歴史観には大きな影響をもたらすであろう。

第二に言えることは、ショ氏の判斷である「賓組卜辭でよく對貞型式が用いられ、疑問文は用いられない。この段階では、一般的に言って、占卜の形式も目的も特に變化の萌芽はない」ということに關してである。賓組卜辭によく見られる對貞型式に疑問文が用いられないとするのは、ショ氏の論據こそ不明であるが、正しい。これは、我々が第二項で董作賓氏の卜辭命龜説を正反の選擇を神龜に命ずると解釋することにより、疑問文ではなく非疑問文、叙述文であると判斷したことと一致する。「對貞型式による占卜の目的に特に變化の萌芽が見られない」(72)ということは、ショ氏が武丁時代の貞卜の目的を神祕的な手段によって疑問や問題を解決するものとしてとらえていることを意味する。但し、この解決方法として、言語の「質問形式」を用いてはいないのだが、「質問の意識」がはたらいていた、と理解しているようである。これは、白川靜氏の兩貞法の解釋（第三の2項）を「貞ふことの意識がなほ強くはたらいてゐた」とすることと同じである。しかし、白川氏の「肯定的な命題が卜意に適ふべきものとして期待されてゐたらしい」というインサイトは、ショ氏説には窺われない。我々は白川氏のインサイトを「其」という語氣助詞の意味論的分析とディスプレー・インスクリプションの內容分析によって支持してみた。もしかかるインサイトが受容できるものであるたら、これもまたショ氏の卜辭の性格の理解に大きな影響を與えるであろう。

最後に言えることは、「貞卜という儀式は、單に緊迫した事態に對處すべきことを量らんとする手段ではなくなり、それらをコントロールするための手

(72) ショ氏がここで實際に言っていることは、前にも引用したことではあるが、「…占卜の形式も目的も特に變化の萌芽はないようだ」である。私は、この「占卜の形式」（…the general form…of divination）ということが具體的に何を指しているのかよく分からない。裘論文の中國文でも「占卜的形式」であるが、これは貞卜の言語形式のことなのか、それとも、龜骨卜の際のいろいろ想像し得る儀式的なことなのか、或いは、その兩方をまとめて一般的に言ったことなのか、決定できないのである。當初は、「貞卜の際の命辭の言語形式」ではないかと思ったが、それなら、ショ氏の自組の命辭形式の記述と一致しない。ここで引いたショ氏の言葉は、武丁時代の卜辭に對して「變化の萌芽はない」であるからである。そのような理由により、ショ氏の「占卜の形式も…特に變化の萌芽はない」の部分を除外して、以下、考えを進めることにする。

段になっていた」についてである。これは第五期の卜辭についての性格づけであるが、白川靜氏の「卜辭は一種の呪術的なマジックである」という考え、さらにキートリー氏の「アナロジカル・マジック」(模倣魔術)、即ち、「卜辭マジック說」に非常に近似している。むしろ、それらをより一層強調した如くである。しかし、かかる判斷の根據となっている二つの點―即ち、第五期卜辭には繇辭として「吉、大吉、引吉」があり、また、「旬有禍」とか「往來有災」などといった命辭がないということ―は、實は、何らの效果もないものである。何故なら第一期にも繇辭として「吉、引吉」があるし(例えば『丙編』九七・(12)、二四七・(1))、また、「旬有禍」とか「往來有災」などといった命辭は、甲骨文全期を通じて、皆無であるからである。從って、第五期の貞卜言語の目的を第一期のそれと比較して變化したとする說は、薄弱な根據にのみ立脚していて、サブスタンスがない。確かに第五期の繇辭には「不吉」などはなく、第一期のそれにはある。しかし、それからだけでは滿足のいく歷史的說明は得られない。第一期の卜辭には、キートリー氏が指摘したごとく、時として、卜兆が深く切り込まれている。その意義についての解釋は一樣なものになるとは言えないであろう。キ氏の解釋によると、かかる事實は未來に對してはたらきかけるシンボルということである。我々も甲骨文に於いて卜兆が實際にどのように用いられているかを考慮した結果(第三の1項(イ))、キ氏の解釋は穩當なものであるとしたわけである。また、「旬有禍」というような表現はないが、「某往來其有禍」はあり、問題は「其」字の解釋になる。(第三の2項參照。)このように、多角的な、また細分析を伴った硏究をすることにより、「卜辭マジック說」は檢討されるべきと思う。

　以上をまとめると、ショナシー氏が武丁期迄の貞卜言語の性質が祖甲以後に大きく變化し、殷王朝滅亡まで繼續的に進化していったとする說は、我々としては、受容できるものではない。

八、裘錫圭說

　一九八八年の裘論文とショナシー氏による英譯(以下、「ショ譯」と略稱、注4參照)との最も重要な相違は、例文の數がショ譯ではかなり減ってい

ることである。裘氏はショ譯を入念にチェックしたとあるから（ショ譯、頁一、注一）、例文は裘氏の精選を經たものと受けとめてよいと思う。本稿では、念の爲に、ショ譯では引用されていない裘論文の全ての例文を拓本と對照しつつ考えてみた。斷片的な資料か解釋が不確實の場合は擧例を憚んだということであるなら理解できるが、ショ譯に採用された卜辭例には、裘氏の説に却って不利になるというようなものもあるようである。少なくとも別の解釋を導くようでもある。また、その逆に裘氏の説に有利なものも極めて少數ながらあるようでもある。從って、本稿では、ショ譯で除外された例文も全て考慮の對象に入れて論じてみることもあるし、また、裘論文に引用されていないものも考えに入れることもある。

　裘論文の主旨は、大體、次の如くである。甲骨文に於ける命辭は、過去約七〇年の間、大多數の專門家により一律に疑問文としてとらえられてきたのであるが、これを分析してみると、疑問文であると認められるものと認められないものとに分類可能である。前者に屬する例は賓組卜辭にもあることはあるが、特に、第一期早期の自組卜辭に多くある。それらには句末助詞の「抑」と「執」が用いられ、明白に識別できる。郭沫若（『粹考』頁六六ウ／四二五片）や李學勤氏（李論文一、頁四〇、注6）が句末疑問助詞として「不」（＝否）と「乎」をも擧げているが、それは間違いである。さらに、郭沫若（同書、頁八〇オ／五五二片、頁一四〇ウ／一〇八九片）が「才＝哉」としているが、それも間違いである。現代語に見える「動詞＋不＋動詞」（以下、Ｖ不／弗Ｖと表記する）の構造をもった選擇タイプの質問型式は、甲骨文には存在しない。それらは、ことごとく「Ｖ、不／弗Ｖ」と表わされるょうにＶの後で文を切るべきであって、「不／弗Ｖ」は驗辭と解釋すべきである。最後に、裘氏は疑問文ではないと斷定できる文例を若干擧げて説明を加えているが、それらは全て複文型式である[73]。以上の論旨の中、我々が本稿でとりあげたい問題は、裘氏が句末疑問助詞とする「抑」と「執」の解釋である。裘氏のそれ以外の説は、細部に至っては疑問點もないわけではないが、大局的には受容できる印象を得た。何故受容できるかを再檢討するのも有益ではあろうが、紙幅にも制約を課したく思うため、本稿では直接關連あるところのみ述べることにしたい。

---

[73] 我々は第五の4項にて單文、重文、複文の問題について考察してみたので、そこの部分も參照されたい。本項での議論も理解しやすくなると思われる。

1 「抑」・「執」句末助詞說の問題點と「印」・「摯」名詞試釋說

前述した如く、李學勤氏は、自組卜辭には疑問を表わす句末助詞の「𠬝」と「執」が用いられる、という說を發表した（注6所揭の李論文一）。この說はニビソン、ショナシー、そして裘錫圭三氏の考えに絕大な影響を及ぼしたのである。裘氏はまず第一に「🖋」もしくは「🖋」と刻される文字を「𠬝」ではなくして、「抑」に訂正する。李氏がそもそも「𠬝」としたのは、實は、音韻的な理由が字釋の決定に先だった、ということがある。つまり、「不」（＝否）は之部陰聲の＊pjəg（X）であり、「𠬝」は之部入聲の＊bjəkであることから、李氏はその二語とも句末助詞ととらえ、音韻的に近いと考えたわけである（李論文一、頁四〇）。しかるに、「抑」は＊・jitであり、音韻的に比較しえないと判斷した、と推測できる。ところが、裘氏は字形上「🖋」と「🖋」は、既に羅振玉が『殷虛書契考釋』（中、頁五四ウー五五オ）にて「印・抑」と釋字すべしとしていることを指摘する。かかる字は明らかに「🖋」と異なる。後者は人牲としてしばしば用いられ、これが「𠬝」であるのは間違いない、としたわけである（裘論文、頁三、及び羅振玉の『書考』中、頁五九ウ）。裘氏のこの字釋訂正は正當である。次に、甲骨文にて「🖋」と刻される字は「執」とされ、この方は字形の面からは問題はない。

問題は、しかし、「抑」字と「執」字が、結局のところ、裘氏が提唱したょうに、疑問の句末助詞の機能を果している、と認め得るかどうかということである。結論から述べるとすれば、私の解釋は否定的であり、かかる二語は疑問助詞にも句末助詞にも認定できない。例外としては、ほんの一例もしくは二例を數える程度であり、それを根據にして句末助詞說を支持することは難しい。

先ず、裘氏が「抑」と「執」を疑問の句末助詞と解釋しなければ意味が通じないとする例から考察してみよう。裘論文中の例文（3）（以下、數字番號は全て裘論文からのを用いることにする）は「不」のため、それを除き、（1）から（22）までの合計二十一例を對象にする。この中、さらに（7）、（13）、（17）に對する裘氏の釋文にクルーシャルな部分で疑問が殘るようであり、本稿ではひとまず「抑」と「執」の考慮から除外したい。拓本のコピーを圖三として揭げておくが、（7）などは別の議論をするときに用いることもある。（注

82参照。)

21047　　　　21036　　　20613（＝『前編』4.46.1）
圖3

　（7）を裘氏は「乙酉卜、王貞余辥朕老工延我莫、貞允唯余受馬方祐抑、弗其受祐執」としている。拓本を見ると、「二月」の下の「方」の字を裘氏は見落としているのが分かる。李學勤氏（李論文一、頁四一）は、最後の部分を「…弗其受方又執、二月」とし、「方」字を見落としてはいないが、裘氏の釋文と異なる。「乙酉卜」から「…余受馬方祐」までは、兩氏が釋文した如くに何とか讀めても、最後の部分は語順に疑問が殘る。兩氏の釋文とは別に、「…余受馬方祐、印弗執、其受方祐、二月」とすることも考えられるかも知れないが、このような不明瞭な例は、資料から除外しておいた方が無難である。

　例（13）を裘氏は「辛丑卜、自貞子辥□疾臣不其禍□（此字从"目"从"舟"）抑、禍□執」としているが、クルーシャルな「抑」は明瞭さに缺き、「執」などは句末に認めることができない。もし右から三行目の第一字が「執」字であるとしたら、裘氏は（13）を不可解な語順で訓んでいる。□字は『柏根』一三では地名に用いられていることから、ここでは人名にとることも考えられる。しかし、（13）は前後文を缺き、資料價值が問われるべきであろう。

　　（17）は更に絶望的である。

　以上見てきたように、（7）、（13）、（17）は資料的に我々の考察の對象外とした方が安全であると思う。

　資料不信は、容易に強調できようが、注意を轉じて、殘りの二十一例を考えることにする。私は「抑」と「執」が疑問の句末助詞と解釋しなければ意味不通とする說に疑問を持ち、別の假說を立ててみた。それは「抑」と「執」は二つとも名詞に解釋すべき統辭論的ビヘィヴィアーが窺われる、ということで

ある。そしてこのように解釋することにより、かかる語の前に用いられるコトバは動詞であるべしということが導かれるわけてある。そこで、(3)(これは「不」を使用)、(7)、(13)、(17)の四例を除いた(1)から(22)までの例文中、次の八個の一見動詞と見做される字が問題として擡頭してくる。今、それらを列記し、簡單なフィロロジカルなコメントを施し、「抑」、「執」名詞説に一歩接近してみたい。

（ⅰ）〔甲骨文〕　この甲骨文の形は一種のモンタージュ字であり、『合集』一九七八〇、二〇九八八、一九七八一がそれぞれ由來している原著錄集の『乙編』三〇七、四四五、『京津』二九二二に見える五つの異體字をベースにして構成したものである。(『合集』よりは原著錄集の方が一般的に言って質がよい。)この字は、賓組卜辭にでる「〔字〕」(『續編』五・一〇・三)、即ち「隺」、裘氏の「陰」とする字とは區別すべきである。今、「雀」と隷書化しておくが、その意吠は「擒」、即ち「いけどる、とらえる」であると思う。

（ⅱ）〔甲骨文〕　この字を「正」とも「征」とも解釋することは、大いに疑問である。「〔字〕」が別に存在し、それが「正」あるいは「征」の意味を表わすと思われる。しかし、上記の甲骨文字が「征伐」とか「軍役」に關連のあるコトバを表わしたであろうことは、そのコンテクストから察せられることである。本稿では、周永珍氏の説でもある「圍」字と解釋しておく。意味は「かこむ」であると思われる。詳細は、氏の論文「殷代"韋"字銘文銅器」『出土文獻研究』(北京、文物出版社、一九八五年)、頁四一～六〇、及び該論文所掲の參考文獻などを參照されたし。

（ⅲ）〔甲骨文〕　これは「見」で格別に問題はなかろうと思われる。目で實際に「見る」とか「見わける」という意味で、「見牛」、「見豕」、さらに「見壹在之」等の表現に用いられる。頻見の「見王」は「謁見する」の意であろう。

（ⅳ）〔甲骨文〕　隷書化すれば、「𩰎」となり、小篆では「攴」が右旁につき、楷書では「敦」と變化した。意味は「うつ、うちくずす」であると思われ、卜辭では「敦缶」とか「敦大邑」などがある。

（ⅴ）〔甲骨文〕　これは、自組卜辭（のみ？）に用いられ、その外（後）は別の字によって契刻された可能性がある。楷書化は不明だが、「〔字〕」や「〔字〕」(『簠殷』雜五六)というコトバと深い關係があると思われる。後世の「屈せしむ」とか「折る」という意味をもつ「拐」字で理解すると分かり易いようである。

（vi）𖡄　通常、「氐」とか「以」などと釋字され、その意味は「もたらす、ひきいる」であると思われる。コトバ及び字形からは、「氐」（至＝致）の方が「以」よりもディフェンシブルであると思う。「氐」は＊tjidであり、それは後の「致」＊trjidhの假借であると思われる。字形上も甲骨文、金文（令鼎）、小篆と綿々と引き繼がれていくようである。甲骨文での用例は、「氐衆」、「氐羌」、「氐易」、「氐═羌㽞═」、「氐═䙷㽞═」など豐富にあり、「氐」の後にくるこれらの字は人間名詞を表わす。

（vii）𖡇　この文字は「咼」（＝禍）と釋字するのには問題ないと思われるが、通常、名詞として用いられ、動詞には用いられない。從って、裘氏の擧げた一例（氏の（16））は名詞、それもここでは個有名詞の可能性が大である。人名・族名としての用例はいくつかあるが『丙編』二七五・（7）（8）などは好例である。（vi）に擧げた「氐䙷㽞」も「䙷の㽞（兵士）をひきいる」の意味であると思われる。

（viii）𖡉　字の構成からは、「䘮」であるが「蔑」字が當てられる。この字は、普通、黄伊などと並んで犧牲をうける神格、即ち個有名詞として用いられる。動詞として用いられる場合は、後世の「ないがしろにする、さげすむ」という意味にとるより、同根である筈の「滅」、すなわち、「ほろぼす」という意味に解釋した方がよいであろう。

　以上、簡單に「抑」と「執」の前に用いられている語に注釋を加えてみたが、（i）から（vi）まで、及び（viii）は他動詞としてとらえられる公算が強い。（自動詞、というよりは、受身の用法も含んだ狀態動詞（stative verb）としてとらえられることもあるが、それはコンテクストや否定詞「不」の出現によって決定できるであろう。）上の（i）、（ii）、（iv）、（v）、（viii）、そして恐らくは（vi）も、大部分「戰争」とか「追及」といった行動に關連あるコトバである。してみると、「抑」と「執」は、しばしば「ペアー」として現われる一種の特別な「人間」（或るいは「動物」）であったのではあるまいか。その點、「執」の方は、動詞としては「手かせをはめる、とりおさえる」という意味であることには問題ない。（『綜類』三七六・二、三、例えば、『乙編』三三八一、四六九三等參照。）その派生名詞（derived noun）としての用法は充分考えられることである。例えば、裘論文未收の『合集』七九八（圖四）の刻辭は好例であると思う。意味は「とらわれもの（囚人）、囚人たるべきもの」であろう。（ここ

で、「囚人たるべきもの」としたが、他にも、例えば、「伐」も「首を伐られてしかるべきもの」という意がある。例えば、「伐十羌」とか「數＋伐」が目的語として用いられている場合などである。）圖4の例では「執」のみではなく、「抑」も動詞「用」の目的語として使われていることが分かる。ここて、「抑」も「執」も疑問の句末助詞と解釋するのは、極めて不自然である。

　不自然と言えば、裘論文（頁四）で、「以上爲前一分句用"抑"后一分句用"執"之例。〔（5）〜（17）を指して〕前一分句有的是正面問有的是反面問。以下爲前一分句用"執"后一分句用"抑"之例、〔（18）〜（22）〕」という觀察は、言語學的に考えて、非常に不自然である。疑問文や選擇を表わすコトバは、例えば、日本語の「か」（「行くか、行かないか」等の例）のように、一つのコトバで經濟的に言い表わせる。それとも、英語に於ける間接疑問の "whether…or…" の如き二つのコトバが考えられるのであろうか。しかし、英語の "whether"（OE hwæþer）は、"which of the two" という意味であって、"or"（OE oððe, oðða）のような語源的に不透明な助詞的（particle like）なコトバとは違う。日本語の「か」も現代中國の「嗎」と同樣に語源的にも不透明な、また虛辭的な助詞であるが、「抑」も「執」も虛辭的（particle like）ではなく、實辭的なコトバである。どうしても虛辭的、助詞的にとらえる必要があるときのみ、そのように解釋した方が良いように思える。また、裘氏のいう「較晚的古漢語裏置于選擇問句的兩個分句之間的連詞"抑"、也許就是由這種"抑"演變而成的。"執"相當于古書中的哪個詞、或者跟哪個詞有關、尚待研究」（頁四）などは、中國語を歷史言語學の觀點から記述する際、愼重さを要求されることである。（これに關してはさらに追述する。）「抑」は古代漢語に於いて二つの文節に用いられる接續詞だと裘氏は言うが、もっと正確に言えば、次の例の如く、「S1 + S2」のS2の初頭に用いられるのである。

圖4

○皇父卿士、…豔妻煽方處、抑此皇父、豈曰不時、胡爲我作、不卽我謀…

『詩經』十月之交

（注、この句の「抑」は「噫」という感嘆詞にとられるとされているが、コンテクストから考えると、「それとも」の方が良いと思われる。冒頭の「皇父」に對應し、「此皇父」と續いており、「それとも」の意が自然であると思われるからである。）

○善哉、民之主也、抑武也不足以當之。　　　『左傳』襄公二十七年
○若不從三臣、抑社稷實不血食、而君焉取餘。　『左傳』莊公六年
○求之與、抑與之與。　　　　　　　　　　　　　　『論語』學而
○仲子所居之室、伯夷之所築與、抑亦盜跖之所築與…

『孟子』滕文公、下

　以上の例からも分かる如く、「抑」はS2の文頭にくる選擇の接續詞である。裘氏は、甲骨文では、それを疑問の句末助詞にとらえるのだが、これは統辭論的に説明困難である。文頭にくる語が文末であったとするのは、にわかに信じがたいからである[74]。そして、「執」に至っては、古典のどのコトバに相當するか、或るいは、どのコトバに關連あるか「尚待研究」としているが、これは不毛な想像であると思われる[75]。もとより、そのようなコトバはないからである。甲骨文において、「執」は動詞に用いられたり、「執」、卽ち「とらわれもの」という名詞に用いられたりしており、そこには、＊tjəp

---

[74] 甲骨文、金文、早期古典（『易』、『詩』、『書』、『左傳』等の言語）での繋辭「隹・維」は、文頭的であり、それが文末的な「也」に機能的に變化した例はある。（理由は、恐らく音韻とも關連してくるであろうが、未詳。）しかし、裘氏が「演變而成的」とする「抑」は、かかる繋辭の發展と逆方向である。氏の言う變化發展は不可能ではないかも知れないが、それには綿密な論證が必要である。

[75] 實は、私も裘論文を初讀したとき、「執」＊tjəpは、もしかしたら、「之＋不」＊tjəg＋＊pjəg（x）の約音（phonetic contraction）か、などと想像したりもした。「之」にアクセントがあったと假定すれば、ちょうど日本語の「〜だ、（そう）じゃない」、獨語の"…, nicht war?"、佛語の"…, n'est-ce pas?"、英語の"…, isn't it?"のような反問句（tag question）かとも解釋できはしまいか、と想像したのである。しかし、その場合、「之」の指示するところのも心は、事物とか狀態のはずであろうと思われる。しかるに、裘論文の例を通覽したところ、指示するものと假定した「之」のレファレントは、ことごとく「行動」であるようだ。更に、「執」は、裘氏に依れば、氏の例文（7）（圖3參照）のように「弗」が先行したり、或るいは、肯定文（例文（18）など）が先行したりして、一定していない。このような理由により、私は「之＋不」の音約説は成立しないと判斷するに至ったのである。

（執）對＊tjiəbh（摯）といった入・去聲間にある形態論的名詞派生關係があったのである(76)。以後、名詞の場合は「摯」と釋字し、動詞の場合は「執」と書き表わすことにする。

「抑」が古典にて名詞に用いられている例を、私は、認知していない。しかし、甲骨文の「・」が「抑」＊・jitとも「印」＊・jinhとも關係あることは明白であって、そこにも形態論的な名詞派生關係があったに違いない。「印」は去聲でもあるし、語尾が＊－nである。ピーター・プードバーグ氏に依れば、かかる語尾は、しばしば、「内向的な側面」（introvertive aspect）があるように認められる、と言っている(77)。「抑」の動詞としての意味は、「禹抑洪水」（『孟子』滕文公）でも知られている「おさえる」、「印」はそれから派生した名詞の「おさえつけられたしるし」である。これから推論すると、「・」は「印」と釋字し、その甲骨文での意味は、「（烙）印を押されたもの、押されるべきもの」、つまり、人間（或るいは、動物）とするのが妥當なのではあるまいか。圖 4の「用摯用印」とは、そのパラレリズムを生かすと、「摯」と「印」の二つの種類の犠牲者（或るいは、犠牲動物）として用いられたのではないか、という假說をここに提起したい所以である。

以上のようにして得られた「摯」と「印」の名詞解釋說を、裘氏の舉げた例文（1）から（22）まで（（7）、（13）、（17）は前述した理由により除外）に應用してみると、氏が、「疑問の句末助詞と解釋しなければ意味不通」としたのが、かなりスムーズに說明可能になる。ここでは、その中から代表的なものと思える例に說明を加え、しかる後に、裘論文に引用されている（23）から（51）までの例文にも目を通し、假說の檢證に供したい（第八の2項）。以下の

(76)　「執」が「とらわれもの、手かせをはめられたもの」という意味に解釋できることは、裘氏自身も認めているようである。氏の例文（138）（頁一六）に「勿逆執、亡若」とあり、ショ譯（頁四八）にも次のように殆んど正しく解釋されている。"Do not go to meet the shackled one（s），（for if you do） there will not be approval." かつて、私はこの「執」名詞說に關し、研究したことがあるので、詳しくは、次の拙論を參照されたい。
K Takashima，"Nominalization and Nominal Derivation with Particular Reference to the Language of Oracle-Bone Inscriptions，" *Papers in East Asian Languages*，Vol.2（1984），pp.25-73.この論文では、「執」對「摯」の外、「獲」（とらえる）＊gwrak 對「擭」（えもの）＊＊gwraks 等、約二〇例ほど舉げて論じている。

(77)　Boodberg，Peter A. *Selected Works of Peter A. Boodberg*（Comp. by Alvin P.Cohen. Berkeley: University of California Press，1979），p.433.

例文は、番號とも裘論文によるが、釋字には多少異動がある。（＊印は李論文一に引用されている例、裘氏の表記をそのまま踏襲する。）

（1）丙辰卜、丁巳其雀印。允雀。
『合集』一九七八一（＝『鄴中』二・三六・四、『京津』二九二二重出、又一片綴合）

（4）辛亥卜、方圍今十一月印。　　　　　　　　　　　『合集』二〇八一八

（5）＊癸酉卜、貞方其圍今二月印、不執。余曰不其圍。允不。
『合集』二〇四一一（＝『乙編』一三五）

（6）＊癸酉卜、王貞自今癸酉至于乙酉、邑人其見方印、不其見方摯。一月。
『合集』（＝『外編』三四）

（8）…辰卜、王…于大方…敦印、不執。　　　『合集』二〇四六八

（10）丙寅卜…貞衣今月虎其捐印、不捐摯。旬六日壬午捐。
『合集』二一三九〇＋四〇八一九（＝『南北』師二・一〇八）

（14）壬…貞…牛在…弗克氐印、其克氐摯。三月。
『合集』一九七七九（＝『拾掇二』四六八）

（16）…貞…有禍印、亡禍摯。九月。　　　　　　『合集』一九七八四

（18）癸卯卜、王…缶蔑圍戎摯、弗其蔑印。三日丙午…方不獲。
『合集』二〇四四九（＝上、『前編』五・三九・二、下、八・一二・五）

以上の九つの例に注釋を施すことにする。

　例（1）の命辭の意味は、「丁巳の日に印を擒えん」であると思われ、驗辭で實際に「印」を擒捉したことを記している。別版に同辭の刻辭があり（裘論文例文（2））、その「事件」は、武丁時代の前期と思われる自組卜辭に關連する人人に何らか特別な意味があったのであろうと推察できる。

　（4）は、（5）でもそうだが、日付である「今十一月」（（5）では「今二月」）が「印」を修飾していると解釋できるのではあるまいか。名詞句であり、その構造は「限定」であろう。如何なる限定かは不明だが、想像できることの一つとして、異なった日付に烙印のごときものを押されたもの、或いは、何かしらその日にマークされるものだったのであろうか。また、（4）では如何なる事情があったか言えないが、「今十一月の印」を方が圍むことを卜している。

　（5）は命辭、繇辭、驗辭の三つがそろっているため、得られる情報が（4）より大である。命辭では「其」字が用いられており、「圍」の語氣をやわ

らげている。意味は、「方が今二月の印を圍まん（とすれども）、「不埶」、すなわち「埶らえられん」というような受身であろうか。（上文での「〜とすれども」の「逆接」については後述する。）「不埶」は、別解として、「埶るようにはならない」（"will not be catching" [not so much in its progressive aspect as in its stative/eventive aspect]）というような、當事者の意志では統御不可能なイベントの意味に解釋するのがよいであろうか。いずれにせよ、「埶」は「不」により否定されているため、不可控制（統御不可能）動詞にとるべきであろう。（注57所掲の拙論の解釋による。）繇辭には、「余が曰うには、（方は）包圍するようにはならないであろう」とある。そして、驗辭にて「實際に包圍するようにはならなかった、（故に、「今二月の印」は埶らえられなかった、或るいは、埶るようにはならなかった）、という内容で完結している。ここで言外の意味を汲みとらんとすれば、繇辭と驗辭の間に「方が二月の印を包圍しないほうが望ましい」ということが言えるかも知れない。「允」の語氣は、しばしば、その前にくる潛在的な意味と呼應し、それを總體的に肯定し、追認すると認められるからである[78]。

　例文（6）は、一つの文の中で（と假定して）、肯定形と否定形が包容された「選擇、二者擇一」（裘氏の「選擇疑問」でも可）の構造を擁しているとみなして考えてみよう。この假定に從うと、（6）の意味は、「今日、癸酉の日より乙酉の日までの間に邑人は方の印を見るようになるであろうか、或るいは、方の埶を見るようにならないであろうか」ということになろう。しかし、この解釋は理論的に考えて「選擇、二者擇一」になっていない。それは、肯定の對象である「方印」が否定の對象である「方埶」と一致していない、つまり「公分母的」、または「同指謂的」ではないからである。もし、例文（6）を二者擇一に解釋しようとすれば、裘錫圭氏の句末助詞説の「…邑人其見方抑、不其見方埶」とする説が考え得る。しかし、この句末助詞説は、なぜ、肯定に「抑」、否定に「埶」が用いられるのか説明されていないばかりでなく、例文

---

[78] かかる「允」の意味的性質を、私は "total confirmation" と性格づけ、「有／亡＋動詞」の構造で表現される一種の強調表現と比較し、後者を "partial confirmation" と解釋した。詳しくは、次の拙論を参照されたい。
K. Takashima, "An Emphatic Verb Phrase in the Oracle-Bone Inscriptions," *Memorial Volume Dedicated to Li Fang-kuei* (Taipei: Institute of History and Philology, Academia Sinica; in press).

（5）や（8）に於いて「執」が、なぜ、何の動詞もなしに直ちに否定詞「不」に續くかも說明されていない。また、既述したように古典漢語への歷史的發展がどのようになっていったかも解明されていない。ここで、一步讓って、「…邑人其見方、抑不其見方摯」とするのも、裘氏の說よりは、古典漢語の「抑」とも比較できる點で、優れていそうである。今、この「…邑人其見方、抑不其見方摯」を表層構造としてとらえてみるとする。しかし、問題は、その深層構造であるはずの「…邑人其見方摯[1]、抑不其見方摯[2]」から變形文法の削除法（deletion rule）により「摯[1]」が削除されねば、表層構造は得られないことになる。文法理論からすれば、可能な解釋だとは思われるのであるが、私はかかる削除法が他の例にも適應する實例を知らない。從って、（6）に限って「…邑人其見方、抑不其見方摯」とする解釋は、急場凌ぎの處置であり、愼まねばならないであろう。しからば、（6）は、畢竟、どのような意味であったのであろうか。私は、次のように解釋することを提案したく思う。即ち、「…邑人は方を見るようにはなるであろうが、方の摯を見るようにはならないであろう」とするのである。これは、S1とS2とを「逆接關係」にとることである。この解釋は、甲骨文讀解に關して深遠なインプリケーション、また、アプリケーションがでてくるため、以下、少し詳しく考えてみたい。

甲骨文に於いて、逆接や順接は、S1の意味とS2の意味の「緊張關係」・「論理關係」から生成されると思われる。一般的に言って、甲骨文や金文や早期古典語では文法的マーカー、即ち、虛辭が非常に少ない。その一つの理由は、その當時の言語が形態論的なプロセスがかなり發達していたということが考えられる。上古漢語の音韻再構がドラスティカルに進步しない限り、形態論學、構詞法は低迷せざるを得ない、と言わざるをえないのではあるが、統辭論の面から言えることとして、逆接と順接は、例文（6）のみではなく、他例が見い出せるのである。例えば、逆接として、次のような例がある。

　　　〇有保、死。
『丙編』三〇五・（2）（これには對貞があり、それは順接になっている。後述。）
　　　〇貞勿侑牝、宙牡。
『丙編』三一七・（8）（これにも對貞があり、それも順接になっている。後述。）
　　　〇王占曰魚彫、隹有祟、亡禍。　　　　　　　　　　　　『丙編』四八・（1）（2）
　　　〇丁丑貞卜有祟、非禍。　　　　　　　　　　　　　　　『粹編』一二六二

第一文の「有保」は「神の保（庇護、保護）が有る」であり、そのS1はポジティブなことである。しかし、S2の「死」はネガティブなことである。從って、その「緊張關係」は相反撥し合う逆接という論理關係が成立すると解釋できよう。第二文の「勿有牝」は「牝を侑することなかれ」でネガティブであるが、「叀牡」は「牡であるべし」であるからポジティブである。しかも、犧牲動物の牛が雌から雄に變わっている。これも從って逆接である。第三文は繇辭であり、そこにも逆接が檢出されよう。「𩵋」は天候狀態を表わす語と思われ、そのような時に酌祭（注48参照）を行うことは、「祟あるであろうが、禍は亡からん」と王が占っていることが分かる。最後の例文も「卜に祟あるとも、それは禍にあらず」ということを貞している。このように、逆接はS1とS2との緊張關係をロジカルな意味分析で解釋することから得られるのである。

順接の場合も、同じような方法で導き出せるのである。例えば、

〇亡保、其死。　『丙編』三〇五・(3)

〇翌乙巳侑祖乙宰、又牝。　『丙編』三一七・(7)

〇王占曰吉、勿隹禍。

『丙編』四九五・(6)（同文刻辭として、五〇五・(5)、五一四・(10)等ある。）

〇貞王𡚸多屯、不左、若于下上。　『丙編』五二三・(2)

ここで、全文に共通して言えることは、S1とS2（或るいは、N1とN2）の緊張關係が論理的に順當に連なっているということである。一つ一つの解說は不必要と思われるので、ここでは省略するが、第二文と第四文のみに對し、簡單な說明を加えることにする。前者では、「又」は「それに加えて」という意味の接續詞であり、それは(79)順接である。この場合は、從って、N1（宰）とN2（牝）との論理關係が順接ということである。後者の第四文での「左」は「左（たが）う、さからう」と理解するのが正しいと思われ(80)、「不左」、つまり「左（たが）わず」は「若于下上」と順接關係を形成しているのである。

裘論文の例文（6）の解釋とそこから派生した逆接と順接の問題處理に紙

(79) これに關しては、次の拙論で論じたことがあるので、參照されたい。
K. Takashima, "Noun Phrases in the Oracle-Bone Inscriptions," *Monumenta Serica*, Vol. 36 (1984-1985), pp.229-302. Cf. particularly pp.283-284, pp.235-244.

(80) 注76所揭の拙著、頁六〇、及び注48所揭の周國正氏の博士論文、頁四六～五〇、二七一～二七三を參照されたし。

面をかなり費してしまったが、先に擧げた殘りの例文（8）、（10）、（14）、（16）、（18）に簡單な解說を加え、本項、第八の1に一應の結末をみたい。

　例文（8）の主要部分「…敦印、不執」は、「印」を族名か人名にとるのが最も無理のない解釋であると思われる。それは、動詞「敦」が「擊つ、襲う」というように理解されているからである。裘錫圭氏自身も、實は、『合集』二一七〇八、二一七一〇、二二五九〇、二五〇二の四例（圖5參照）を擧げ、「有時也用爲國族或人名…」（頁三）としているのである。

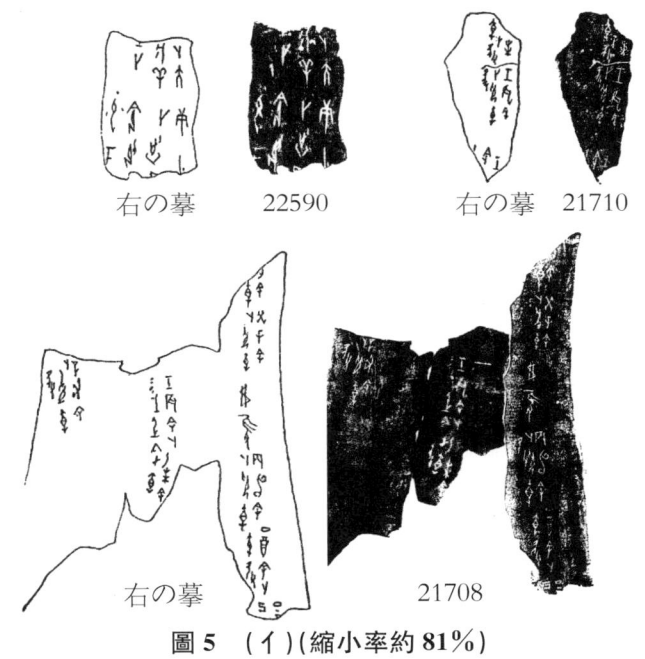

圖 5　（イ）(縮小率約 81%)

　裘氏は例文（8）を氏の言う「國族或人名」に含めていないが、含めてはならない理由はない。圖5中の二一七〇八と二一七一〇で用いられている動詞は、「𢁉」（＝執）で、例えば、「癸巳余卜、印𢁉。弗獲」（二一七〇八）は、「印は（…を）𢁉（とら）えん。〔驗辭として〕獲えられず」、または、「印は𢁉えられん。獲えられず」の如く解釋できる。私は後者の解釋の方が正しいと思う。二二五九〇と二五〇二〇は出組卜辭で、そこでは、印は動詞「令」の對象になっているようだが、後者の拓は明瞭ではない。自組卜辭では、印はまだ殷王朝の支配下にいなかったと思われ、前にもみたように、「印執」や「敦印」の如き內容の表現が可能であったと思える。このように考えてくると、印は羌と同じように考えられる族名に用いられていた可能性を拂拭することができない。先程は、印を抑と同根とみなし、圖4の「用摯用印」のパラレリズムから考えて普通名詞とし

てとらえておいたが、ことによると、印は全て個有名詞であったかも知れない。それが羌のように屬名詞（generic noun）として用いられたり、族名として用いられたりした、と考えても何の支障もない。むしろ、その方が自然のように思えはしないわけではない。例文（4）（…方圍今十一月印）と（5）（…方其圍今二月印…）では、各々、「今十一月」と「今二月」が印を限定修飾しているとしておいた。この解釋は、一方では古代漢語の文法にのっとっていると考えられるか、他方では意味的に「某時の印」、つまり某時に烙印のごときものを押されたもの、とするのに一抹の危懼がないわけではない。そこで、かかる日付を時間副詞にとり、動詞「圍」を「逆方向修飾」していると解釋し、さらに印は族名・屬名とみなすのも不可能ではないかも知れない。文法的に考えると、「逆方向修飾」は認め難いが、印を族名・屬名詞とする解釋は、普通名詞にとるより魅力的であるようだ。先程、敢えて普通名詞解釋說を提起しておいたのは、形態論的名詞派生關係（抑＊・jit ⌒ 印＊・jinh）が、自組卜辭の時代まで、文化的、社會的にも何かしらのミッシング・リンク、或るいは、「橋渡し的役割」を果たすことも可能かと考えたからであった。本稿では、從って、以下、印の普通名詞說を一歩前進させた（羌のような）族名・屬名詞說に焦點を絞り、推論していくことにするが、必ずしも普通名詞說を抹殺してしまうまでには至らない。少なくとも、その根據が見い出せない。しかしながら、私には上記の時間語の「逆方向修飾」は容認しがたく、何らかの意味で屬名詞である印を限定修飾していると解釋したいのである。（「今來羌」なる表現は名詞句であることは確實で〔例えば、『丙編』四一・（6）～（9）〕、その意味は「今來らされた羌」であり、「今」はタイム・ワードであり、「逆方向修飾」にはなっていない。参考附記まで。）

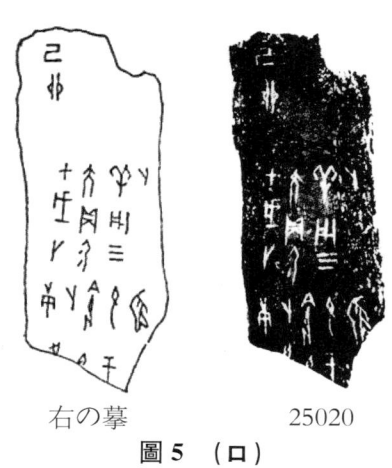

右の摹　　　25020

圖5 （ロ）

例文（10）（…今月虎其拐印、不拐摯。旬六日壬午拐）は、タイム・ワードの「今月」が時間副詞として、文法的に位置すべきところに用いられ、その點では問題はない。もし、我々の語釋である「折る、屈せしむ」という意味の「拐」が正しければ、S1の「今月虎其拐印」は、「今月、虎が印族を屈伏せん」という解釋につながる。S2の「不拐摯」は、S1がポジティブであって對立的であるため、先程論じた意味論的論理に從って、「逆接關係」が成立すると思われる。故に、（10）は、「…今月、虎は印族を屈伏せんようにはなろうが、摯（または、摯たるべきもの）は屈伏するようにはなるまい」という豫言的な言辭であると解釋できる。

　例文（14）の主要部分は、「…弗克氏印、其克氏摯」であり、ここでもS1が否定、S2が肯定の逆接關係が成立する。故に、意味は「…印族を致らしむること克はずとも、摯（たるべきもの）を致らしむることになるであろう」とすべきであろう。

　例文（16）の主要部分は、「…有禍印、亡禍摯」であり、これも（10）と同じく、S1が肯定、S2が否定で對立的である。「禍」がS1とS2との兩方に用いられ、それは"co-referential"「（公分母的、同指謂的）であるとすべきである。「禍」は、前述したように（（viii）の字釋の項）、人名である證據が『丙編』二七五・（7）（8）（「貞钾、甴禍從」、「勿隹禍從」）に見られる。（16）でも禍は人名であると思われる。そのように理解すると、今度は「禍印」、「禍摯」の構造をどのように解釋するかという問題を解決する必要がある。これを「禍の印族」、「禍の摯（もしくは、摯たるべきもの）」としたら良いのか、「禍と印族」、「禍と摯（もしくは、摯たるべきもの）」としたら良いのか。また、もし印がここでは動物を表わしたというように解釋できるならば、それは屬名詞であり、「禍の印（もしくは、印たるべきもの）」と「禍の摯（もしくは、摯たるべきもの）というように、對照的に意識されていたものであろうか。この最後の解釋が論理的には滿足感を與えるようにもとれるが、必ずしも、正しいものであるとは言えない。それは、殷の社會構成に係わる問題に發展してしまい、我々は簡單に判斷を下せない。いずれにせよ、理想論の程度を少し下げて、「禍印」と「禍摯」を名詞句に解釋することは許されるであろう。

　ここで角度を全面的に變えて、「…有禍、抑、亡禍、執」とし、「…禍有らば、抑し、禍亡からば、執せん」とする解釋は如何であろうか。「抑」を動詞にみなすことに新鮮味はあるが、管見の及ぶ限り、「抑」の甲骨文での動詞

的用例がない。意味的にも、「有」と「亡」が對立的、「抑」と「執」が對照的で、複雜に過ぎるようである。しからば、（16）は、やはり、「…禍印は有ろう（或るいは、有った）が、禍摯は亡からん」（或るいは、亡かった）と訓むべきだと思う。括弧内に驗辭としての解釋も可能であることを示しておいたが、コンテクストが不足しているため、いずれが適釋か判斷できない。括弧外の解釋は命辭にでも驗辭にでもあてはまるようにしてある。

最後に、例文（18）を考えてみよう。ここで、クルーシャルな部分は「…缶蔑圍戎摯、弗其蔑印。…不獲」である。この文も、S1が肯定、S2が否定の意味的緊張關係が見られる。その關係は逆接であると思われ、意味は「缶は、…摯（たるべきもの）を滅ぼしえょうが、印族（或るいは、印たるべきもの）は滅ぼせまい」とするべきと思う。S1中の「圍戎摯」の意味は不明であるが、構造的に考えると、「圍まれた戎と摯」、「圍まれた戎の摯（たるべきもの）」、または、「圍まれるであろう…云云」というような内容の名詞句であるに違いない。

以上、裘論文の例文（1）から（22）までの代表的な文について分析し、我々の解釋を試みてきた。裘錫圭氏に依ると、これらは全て「抑」と「執」という疑問の句末助詞としなければ義不通ということなのであるが、我々の檢討したところ、それらは全て名詞に解釋すべき（少なくとも、解釋できる）という結果になったわけである。このことは、裘氏の「抑」・「執」使用の「命辭疑問文說」に對し、根本的な見直しを促すことに外ならない。

「𢎥・𢎥」と「𢻬」が如何なる名詞であるかについても、我々は「印」と「摯」であろうとし、前者は羌の如く、時には族名として、時には屬名詞として用いられたのではないか、と提起した。また、「印」が動物扱いを受けていたこともあろうかという推測もしてみた。ここに於いて、裘氏の「抑・執句末助詞說」に對して、我々の「印・摯名詞說」の解釋が一つの假說に足る根據、及び議論が成立しうる基盤ができたものと信じる。では、次項にて再檢討を行い、假說の域から一歩前進を圖りたい。

2　試釋說の再檢討

前項、第八の1にて、S1とS2との緊張關係をロジカルな意味論的分析にアッピールして、逆接關係と順接關係を抽出した。それにしたがって、裘論文の例文若干に異なった解釋を施してみたのであるが、そのような新しい解釋は、

對貞形式そのもの、または、對貞形式の歴史的發展と何らかの關係があったのであろうか。一瞥してみると、無關係のような印象を與える。結論から述べるとすれば、實はその通りなのであるが、順接はまだしも逆接は、既にみたように一種の「正反」の組み合わせでもある。李學勤氏が「這種卜辭〔これは、前項で我々が新解釋を施した例文を指すとみなしてよい〕把正反兩問併于一辭之中」（李論文一、頁四一、強調のための横點は筆者）と言っており、この意見が裘錫圭氏やショナシー氏等に絶大なインパクトを與えたことは、我々も既に觸れたことである。李氏の言う「正反兩問」が、たまたま、「抑」と「執」とも釋字される甲骨文字と一緒に用いられることもあるために、裘氏やショ氏がこれらを二つの「句末助詞」として「發見」（李學勤氏を最初とすれば、「再發見」）してしまったのである。我々の見地からすれば、「發見」ではなく、「發明」なのであるが、それは、そもそも、質問の言語型式（疑問文）及び選擇文というものの認識不足がその根底にあると言えるであろう。「正反兩問」の「問」も先入觀的判断が先走っている。我々は、既に第二項で董作賓氏の「卜辭命龜說」を検討した際、對貞形式について次のように論じた。すなわち、肯定文と否定文が意味的にバイアスなしに(81)組み合わせられた場合、そこに潛在的な疑問の念があったことは認めてもよいが、かかる組み合わせは直ちに質問の言語型式にはつながらない。更に、それは「選擇」型式であり、選擇を形成する個々の文は非疑問文にとるべきである、と。「選擇」があれば、それは質問だという考えが、裘氏にもショ氏にもうかがえるが、實はそうではないのである。例えば、次の基本的な用例について考えてみよう。

〇丁亥…貞自今五六日至。壬辰有至。　『福氏』三七

〇癸酉卜、亘貞臣得。王占曰其得、隹甲乙。甲戌臣涉舟祉㞢、弗告、旬有五日丁亥執。十二月。　『丙編』二四三・(3)

〇王占曰吉。亩有乎己。其伐其弗伐不吉。　『丙編』二七七・(4)

第一の例について、『福氏』の編者である商承祚は、「董彦堂先生云此段

(81)　バイアスのかかったものとしては、第三の2項にて白川靜氏の「卜辭修祓・祝禱說」を分析した際、次の二つの「不公平な」選擇が命龜の對象になっていた、ということを指摘した。（一）肯定文と否定文を意味論的範疇の正反で解釋した上で、そのいずれか一方に「其」字が用いられている場合。（二）キートリー氏の「ディスプレー・インスクリプション」に於ける繇辭と驗辭との呼應關係から正反のどちらかが期待されていたと思われる場合。

以文繹之五六日一行殆是後人所刻」（頁一一ォ）と言っているが、拓本を見ると、後人にょる僞刻の疑いがあるのは、むしろ、問題の表現の後に續く「至壬辰有至」であろうかとも思われる。私見によれば、『福氏』三七は全て眞刻と認められるものであって、「至壬辰有至」の頭の「至」は、「自今五六日」の直後に續けて「今日より五日か六日して（某）が（どこそこに）至らん」と訓み、「壬辰有至」は驗辭で「壬辰の日に至れる有り」と訓むべきと思う。一應、拓のコピーを圖6に掲げておく。第二例は繇辭にて「（臣）が（何かを）獲得することになるのは、甲か乙の日であろう」とあって、ここにも「選擇」がみられるのである。第三例は、『丙編』二七六・（3）（4）の裏側に刻され、「庚寅卜、賓貞今𡆥王其伐夷」と「庚寅卜、賓貞今𡆥王勿步伐夷」の對貞にコレスポ

圖6

ンドする繇辭である。重要なのは、「伐の行爲をしようがしまいが不吉なり」とあって、ここでも「選擇」がうかがえる。古典漢語の語法からすれば、「其伐、抑其弗伐、不吉」とでもなろうが、甲骨文では「抑」なる虛辭は用いずとも知るべしであったと思われる。いや、古典漢語でさえも、S1とS2が對照的である場合は、「抑」は不要であったと思われる。前項で引用した『詩經』や『左傳』からの文例を再度吟味すると、「抑」の後に續くのは、通常、「新情報」（a piece of new information）を供給する一方、特にコントラスティブなことを浮きぼりにしている。ここには廣い意味での「選擇」が讀みとれるであろう。

　以上のように考えてくると、「選擇」という言語學的性質がかなり明確に想

起し得るのではないかと感ずるのであるが、「逆接」にしろ「順接」にしろ全てロジカルな意味論的分析から得られるのである。甲骨文に於いては、これら「選擇、逆接、順接」を表わすのにマーカーは基本的には必要としなかった、ということが判斷できるのである。對貞形式は、根本的には「正反」の組み合わせであり、それはまさしく選擇文である。疑問文ではない。從って、「句末疑問詞」も「句中選擇詞」も必要としない。典型賓組卜辭等見られる對貞形式への發展は、一つの文が分解して、然る後に成立したとする考えは誤りだと思う[82]。

　我々に殘された課題としては、裘論文中に引用された（24）から（51）までの例文は如何に説明できるか、ということで盡きると思われる。前項で例文（1）から（22）までを檢討した際、資料として信を置き難いものは除外した。（23）から（51）までにもそのような例が含まれているだろう。入念に調査した結果、私は次の四つの例をブラック・リストにのせた。卽ち、（26）A・（26）B、（35）、（40）、（41）である。（（40）に關しては、董作賓の「殷虛文字乙編摹本」『中國文字』2、獨立頁一二、及び同3、頁一九を參照。）拓本のコピーを掲げることは割愛した。以前と同樣、例文の番號は裘論文のものであるが、釋字、釋文には異動がある。

　裘氏は、先ず賓組卜辭などによく見られる對貞が自組卜辭にも現われ、そこにも句末疑問詞の「抑」が加えられることもあるとして、次の例を引用する。

(23) A　戊申卜、方啓自南、其圍印。
　　　　　　　　　　　　　　　　『合集』二〇四一五（＝『乙編』一五一）
(23) B　戊申卜、方啓自南、不其圍印。
　　　　　　　　　　　　　　　　『合集』二〇四一五（＝『乙編』一五一）
(24) A　涉三羌既獲印。　　『合集』一九七五五（＝『乙編』一八四＋α）
(24) B　允獲印。　　　　　『合集』一九七五五（＝『乙編』一八四＋α）
(25) A　甲午卜、徣亡囏印。　　　　　　　　　　　　『屯南』四三一〇
(25) B　甲午卜、徣古囏印。十月。　　　　　　　　　『屯南』四三一〇

---

[82] 圖3中の例文（7）は、我々が刻字に不明瞭なところがあるため、語順を確定できないとしたものである。しかし、興味深いこととして、「貞」字があたかも文の中間に用いられていることである。これには、いくつか解釋が考えられようが、もし前半と後半に內容的に關連があるとしたら、「貞」はそれらを二つに分解する役割があった、とも考えられよう。裘錫圭氏の理論からすれば、「貞」字ではなく、「抑」字がその位置に用いられてしかるべきである。しかし、それはもとより不必要だった、ということが言えるのではあるまいか。

(27) ┌ A 甲戌卜、扶往其古印。　　　　　　　　『合集』二〇一九六
(27) └ B …不其古。　　　　　　　　　　　　　　『合集』二〇一九六
(46) ┌ A 丙寅卜、有涉三羌其得…印。
　　　　　　　　　　　　　　　　　　　　　　『合集』一九七五六（＝『乙編』一〇四＋四五二）
(46) └ B 丙寅卜、有涉三羌其得至自印。
　　　　　　　　　　　　　　　　　　　　　　『合集』一九七五六（＝『乙編』一〇四＋四五二）

　上記五つのペアーについて説明を加えてみたい。
　（23）Aが肯定、（23）Bが否定であるから、選擇は必然的に浮かんでくる。その兩方に「選擇詞」ともとれる「抑」が出現するとは却って裘氏の説にとって不利であると思われる。些少讓歩し、「抑」を選擇詞とよばずに、裘氏の言う「疑問詞」として解釋することは如何であろうか。裘氏のいままでの議論は、「抑」と「執」が肯定文と否定文に用いられるということであり、その際、大體の趨向として、「抑」を最初の文（肯定文が多い）がとり、第二の文（否定文が多い）が「執」を句末疑問助詞として指定する、ということであった。しかし、ここでの場合、「執」は用いられずして「抑」が再度用いられている。このことは、上記の全例に對してもあてはまることである。もし裘氏の議論が説得力のあるものとしたら、このような對貞には何故「執」が全く用いられないかを説明されてしかるべきである。我々の説からすれば、「執」も「抑」も句末疑問助詞ではない、ということであり、更にこの場合「抑」と解釋しないで「印」という名詞にとることになるわけである。「印」は前出した動詞「圍」（第八の1項、例文（5）及び動詞（4））の直接目的語として族名、或るいは、屬名詞（または、動物扱いの名詞）である、と解釋した方が滿足出來る。「方啓自南」は、「方が南より啓くに」というふうに方の戰場（もしくは、狩獵）での攻撃體勢を描寫しているのではあるまいか。「啓」字は、天候狀態を表わすコトバ以外に、戰爭に關連あるコトバだからである。そのように理解できる「方啓自南」に續いて、肯定では「印を圍まん」とし、否定では「印を圍むようにはなるまい」としている。
　（24）Aは恐らく驗辭ではないかと思われる。「涉三羌」は名詞句の構造を持ち、「（河）を涉った三羌」の意味であるに違いない。（ここで、「河を涉った」というように、河を括弧内に入れた理由は、後出の例文（47）を參照されたい。）「既獲印」は「既に印を獲えたり」と解釋するのが最も自然である。

（24）Bは典型的な驗辭スタイルであり、意味は「允に印を獲えたり」である。このように解釋すると（24）Aと（24）Bは對貞ではない。そして對貞でもない文に句末疑問詞は必要ない。

　（25）Aと（25）Bは、刻辭の配置具合からしても對貞であることが拓本にて確認できる。しかし、主動詞がそれぞれ「亾」と「古」で異なっている。その理由は理解できないが、そのまま受けとめれば、（25）Aは「嚚印亾からん」となり、「嚚」は前述の「禍」（例文（16））と同様に人名・族名にとるのがよいと思われる。但し、その際、「嚚の印（もしくは、印たるべきもの）」とするか、「嚚族と印族」とするべきか、如何なる意味關係にあったかは、殘念ながら、依然として決め手になるものがない。（25）Bは「嚚印を古めん」[83]と解釋するのが妥當だと思われる。

　（27）Aも印が同じ動詞「古」の直接目的語になっており、印をおさめる、統御するということは、その當時重要な關心事であったことが想起できる。（27）Bに對し、裘氏は、「這兩條卜辭大概也是正反對貞的關係、但反面命辭未加"抑"字、似可說明不加句末疑問語氣詞的命辭也有可能是問句」と言っている。しかし、このようならば、對貞は殆んど疑問文にとっても差し支えないということになってしまう。「抑」があってもよし、なくてもよし、という理論は、裘氏の說を非常に弱體化することになりかねない。我々の解釋では、もし（27）Bが（27）Aと對貞をなし、完結文だとしたら（そのように判斷するエヴ

---

[83] 「山」は後の「古」にあたり、それは郭沫若も指摘した如く、「盬」の初文とするのが良いであろう。（『甲骨文研究』上册、「釋寇」、頁二ゥ参照。）「盬」は『詩經』鴇羽に次のように用いられている。

　　　　「肅肅鴇羽、集于苞栩、王事靡盬、不能蓺黍稷、父母何怙、悠悠蒼天、易其有所、云々」

舊說では、「盬」の意味は「もろい、堅固でない」とされている。これにしたがうと、「王事はもろからず」となり、次に續く「不能蓺黍稷」と「父母何怙」と意味の流れにスムーズさが缺けるようである。コトバとしても「盬」は「古、故」（ふるい、かたい）と同根であるから、元來、動詞としては「かたくす、かたくなる」であったと思われる。それからの轉義の一つとして「堅固にする、よくする、よく〜をなす」は十分考えられる。その意味をこの鴇羽の句にあてはめると、どうなるであろうか。「靡」は言うまでもなく否定詞であり（「非」と同じ）、「王事靡盬」を條件節としてとれば、後文にもスムーズに連接する。つまり、「もし王事〔祭祀・戰役〕がよくなされねば、（誰も）植うる營みあたはず、父や母は何に賴れるか」と首尾一貫した意味にとれるわけである。甲骨文に於いても、「古王事」や「古我事」が出てくるし、その外に「古車馬」などのように「古＋動物」、また「古＋人名」もある。その場合も、「〜をよくする」、「〜をよくあつかう、統御する、おさめる」といった意味が考えられるのである。

ィデンスはない)、動詞「古」の目的語である印が省略された、とすることになろう。しかし、資料が定かでないため、詮索は避ける。

最後に、(46) Aと (46) Bの對貞では主語が「有涉三羗」であり、これは (2-) Aの主語「涉三羗」と比較できる。「有」は、ここでは「經驗」を意味するコトバであると思われ、「(河) を涉ること有りし三羗」と訓むべきであろう。古典漢語調でかかる名詞を表現すると、「有渡河之三羗者」の如きものであろう。そのように理解される「三羗」の實體が何であったか不明なるも、彼等が「至自印」、卽ち、「師に至れりし印」を「其得」、つまり「獲得せん」、と解釋するわけである。

次に、裘錫圭氏は、句末疑問詞の「抑」が對貞法を形成していない命辭に用いられているとして、(28) から (51) までの例文を列擧している。既に指摘しておいた如く、この中 (35)、(40)、(41) は資料として充分活用できるか疑問である。(46) Aと (46) Bは既に考察した。(28) と (33) はそれぞれ (4) と (2) と同文のため除外する。その他の全文について、以下簡單に注釋を施していくことにしたい。

(29) 癸亥卜、方不圍今秋印。　　　　　　　　　　『合集』二〇四七六

ここでは、動詞が例文 (5) や (23) と同一の「圍」であり、その目的語と見做される表現が「タイム・ワード＋印」の「今秋印」である。タイム・ワードとして、我々は既に「今十一月」(例 (4))、「今二月」(例 (5)) 等に注意しておいた。その外、例 (32) の「翌日己亥」もある。

(30) 戊戌卜、王貞余併立員宁史眔見鄭印。六月。　　『英國』一七八四

この例の始めの部分はよく理解できないが、「余が員の宁 (＝貯?) と史とを竝立させん」というような意味であろうか。後半の「〜と共に、及び」の意を表わした「眔」字 (注 79 所揭の拙論參照) 以下は、動詞が (6) と同じ「見」、その目的語とみたてられるのが名詞句の「鄭印」である。「鄭」は人名・地名である。この外にも「方」(例 (6))、「禍」(例 (16))、「舞侯」(例 (50)) などがある。

(31) 戊午卜、曰今日啓印。允啓(?)。　　　　　　　『合集』二〇八九八

この文の否定形があったとしたら、「勿曰今日啓印」とでも表現されたのであろう。動詞「曰」は、ただ單に「曰う」ではなく、曰うことに何らか特別な儀

禮的・宗教的な意味合いが含まれていたかと想像できる。動詞の「啓」に關しては、例文（23）の個所を參照されたい。

　　　　（32）戊戌卜、其雀翌日己亥印。　　　『合集』二〇九八八（『乙編』四四五）

例文（1）、（4）、（5）、及び（29）の注釋を參照されたい。「翌日己亥」はタイム・ワードではあるが、それは貞卜日の戊戌からみて未來のことである。從って、以前「印」を「ある日付に烙印のごときものを押されたもの」と述べたこともあるが、その可能性は減少するであろう。もしこの例のように未來の日付が印を修飾しているのだとしたら、やはり、その時間帶に何かしらの方法でマークされ得るもの、と考えるべきであろう。今、具體的な修飾關係は詳らかにし得ないが、「翌日己亥の印」と訓んでおくことにする。

　　　　（34）己酉卜、…牵雀（?）…其雨、抑不雨。西啓。
　　　　　　　　　　　　　　『合集』二一〇二二（＝『乙編』三八＋一〇八）

裘氏の引用した例文中、この例（34）のみが我々の解釋にとって説明不可能のものである。故に後にこれをとりあげて考えてみたい。

　　　　（36）壬辰卜、乙其焚又羌（?）十、風印小風…
　　　　　　　　　　　　　　『合集』二〇七六九（＝『乙編』一九四）

これも後でとりあげる。

　　　　（37）…陷印。明雀、不其…
　　　　　　　　　　　　　『合集』二〇七七（『乙編』二〇三及び三〇八を參照）

動詞は「陷」であり、次の例（38）の動詞が「禽」であることからすると、「印」はもしかしたら、人間ではなくて動物かも知れない。例（37）の「雀」も（38）の「禽」もコトバとしては同じであったかも知れず、そうだとすると「雀」と釋字した甲骨文の原形と「禽」と釋字したものとは、單なる異形（graphic variants）であった可能性もある。

　　　　（38）庚戌卜、今日狩不其禽印。
『合集』二〇七五七（＝『乙編』一四三＋二一三＋一五三＋四四＋三九二＋三六九）

ここでは「今日狩をせば（或るいは、……狩をしても）、印を禽えることにはならないかも知れぬ」とあるから、「印」は例文（37）と同じく、人間ではな

く動物であったのかとも思える。

  （39）戊辰卜、王…豕。允獲(?)印。　　　　　　　『合集』一九七八二

この刻辭は小破片の上にあるので、「豕」と「印」が果たして對照的（或るいは、同種の動物と對比的）に用いられていたかどうか判斷できず、殘念である。

  （42）辛卯…〔禦〕昌(?)其葬印。十二月。　　　　　　　『懷特』S一五一八

許進雄氏は、王國維や李孝定氏の釋字に從って動詞と思える「其」の後の字を「葬」としてあり（『集釋』一、頁二四三―二四四參照）、私もそのようにしておいた。しかし、確信は持てない。そのこともあって、印が動物か人間か決定することができない。もし「葬」であるとしたら、印は人間の可能性の方が強いようである。

  （43）壬申卜、扶勿侑、其若(?)印。　　　　　　　『合集』二〇八〇五

ここでの動詞を「若」としておいたが、契文は明らかに通常用いられる「若」（𦥑）と異なっている。尚、ここでの「勿」は否定詞ではなく、人名である。「扶」は貞人名で、その後に「貞」字を補って理解すべきであろう。

  （44）戊戌卜、勿追…印。　　　　　　　『合集』（＝『佚存』六三七）

「印」が動詞「追」のスコープに入るのであるならば、それは族名の可能性もある。動物を追跡するのは、通常「遂」が用いられるからである。

  （45）…王貞馬方…巫陋曰喪印…

            『合集』二〇四〇七（『前編』四・四六・三）

ここでは動詞が「喪（うしなう）」であり、「喪衆」、「喪人」などの常用句からすると、「印」は人間である可能性がある。

  （47）丙寅卜…、羌其得涉河印。不得。

            『合集』一九七五七（＝『乙編』三六三）

ここでは動詞が「得」であり、その目的語が「河を渉った印」である。別に「得羌」なる表現もあることからすると、「印」は人間なのであろうか。

  （48）壬午〔卜〕、爭貞…其來印、不其來摯。　　　　　　　『合集』八〇〇

この例文は裘氏が賓組卜辭にも「疑問の語氣詞」として「抑」と「執」が用いられているとするものである。しかし、これは例文（6）の「…邑人其見方印、

不其見方摯」(既見)の文章構造と同じである。從って、文意は「…印を來(もたら)すようにはなろうが、摯を來すようにはならないであろう」というように解釈するべきだと思う。動詞が(6)では「見」、ここでは「來」の相違のみである。頻見する「來羌」なる表現も參考になる。

(49) 貞禦帚印、勿摯。　　　　　　　　　　　　『合集』八〇二

この例は、拓を見ると、「勿」が欠畫であることが分かる。よって資料としていささかの不信感を殘す。「勿摯」とし、「勿執」の如く解釈しなかった理由は、次の通りである。「執」は「とらえる」という意味にして、人間が實際にその行爲を遂行できるかどうかは事前には分からない、故に「統御不可能動詞」である。かかる動詞は「勿」によって否定されることがない、という解釋によっている。(注57所揭論文參照)。してみると、「勿摯」は、恐らく、「勿禦帚摯」といった表現の省略であるかと思われる。「勿禦帚摯」の意味は、「帚(某)を禦祭するに摯を以ってするなかれ」ということではなかろうか。つまり、摯は禦祭のときに祭られた犠牲動物か人身犠牲であると解釈するわけである[84]。例

---

[84] 注48所揭の周國正氏の博士論文(頁一九一以下)で、氏は卜辭の祭祀動詞の詳細な分析を行っている。氏によると、祭祀動詞には「タイプA動詞」と「タイプB動詞」の二種類に分類され、それぞれの統辭論的性格を分析することによって、「禦」、「告」、「求」などの動詞には「工具賓語」(object-instrument)とも言われる犠牲動物が用いられる。これらの動詞を稱して、「タイプA」と氏は言っており、それは認められる解釈だと思う。「工具賓語」は「被祭賓語」(object-patient)と明確に文の構造から區別できるものである。例えば、

「…戌卜、…禦子央于母己二小宰」　　　　　　　　　『南北』無一三四

を見ると、「子央」は被祭賓語であり、「二小宰」が工具賓語である。勿論、「二小宰」は犠牲として用いられたものである。「于母己」は間接目的語で、意味論的には「受祭賓語」とでも云えよう。このように、タイプA動詞である「禦」は、工具賓語を伴って用いられる。それは、言わば付随語である。古典漢語の感覺からすると、「以~」で表現できよう。(例えば、『左傳』閔公二年の「以賂求共仲于莒」など參考になろう。)甲骨文では、「以」のかわりに、タイプB動詞の「酌」、「劉」、「侑」、「翌」等が用いられる例もかなりあるが、上揭の『南北』からの例文のように、タイプB動詞を用いないで、間接目的語「母己」——これを周氏は"object-beneficiary"と言っている——の直後に統辭論により配置される場合もある。例文(49)の場合は、間接目的語が用いられず、被祭賓語であるはずの「帚」の後に印が用いられており、これは工具賓語と解釋すべきものであろう。「印」は、例えば圖4の「用摯用印」のようにペアーとして用いられている。

周國正の博士論文は入手に時間を要するので、手短かには次の論文を參照されるのが便利かと思われる。「卜辭兩種祭祀動詞的語法特徵及有關句子的語法分析」『古文字學論集』初編(香港中文大學中國文化研究所、一九八三年)、頁二三〇～三〇七。

文（49）の前半は、「禦帚印」なので、そこに現われる印も同様に犠牲動物か人身犠牲とするべきである。してみると、（49）の深層構造の文は、「禦帚印、勿禦摯」となり、S1とS2とは逆接関係になり、意味は次の通りにとるべきであろう。即ち、「帚を禦祭するに印を以ってなすとも、摯を以って帚を禦祭するなかれ」となり、一つの完結した文として解釋するわけである。

(50) 壬戌卜、侯□余□乎見君以舞侯印。

『合集』二二〇六五（＝『乙編』五三九四）

この例の一貫した文意は汲みとれないが、「舞侯印」は限定の名詞句であると思われる。しかし、如何なる限定か詳らかにできない。「舞侯」と「印」が両者とも「人間」であると假定した場合、それらはどうもイコール・フッティングにあったとは思い難い。前者は犠牲として祭られることはないのに対し、後者の「印」はあるからである。（注84参照。）もしそうだとすれば、「竝列」の名詞句、即ち「舞侯と印」とは解釋しがたい、と言えるのではあるまいか。先程、前項の例文（16）について、「禍印」なる表現の意味を考慮した際、「禍族と印族」という意味も考えられないことはない、としておいた。しかし、例文（50）にて「舞侯印」が「舞侯と印」というように解釋しがたいということならば、「禍印」が「禍と印」とは解釋しがたい。従って、例文（25）の「嚣印」なる表現にもあてはまるということになり、これも「嚣族と印族」とはしがたい。このように考えてくると、これらに共通した「某印」とは「某の印」と解釋すべきであろう。現に「印＋某」という表現はないことからも「印」は何かしらの制約を受けていたに違いない。このことは、言語學的に言うと、「限定」ではあるが、「所有」を意味したのか、「某が印たるべきもの」として何らかの「制裁」を加えたもの（動物も除外できない）であったのか、また別の意味関係があったか判断できない。待考としておくことにする。尚、例文（50）は、裘氏も指摘しているごとく、次の（51）と同樣、午組卜辭である。しかし、ここでより重要と思われることは、（50）には實は對貞文がある。即ち、

壬戌卜、子夢見邑幸父戊

の如く釋文できる。この文の最後の「父戊」は文法的に解釋し難いが、「見邑幸」は「邑の幸（＝執＝摯）を見る」と理解できそうである。これは例文

（6）の「見方摯」と比較できる。してみると、「見方摯」は（50）の「…見君以舞侯印」と對句になっている可能性があり、その意味は「君が以いた舞侯の印」ということではないだろうか。そのように解釋することによって、（6）の「邑人其見方印」とも比較できるし、また（30）の「見鄭印」とも比較できるわけである。つまり、これらは一種のパラレリズムを構成している、と判斷できよう。

　　　　…申卜、柵〔人名〕禦子辟〔于〕祖庚至于父戊印。　　　『合集』二二一〇一

この例も（49）と同じように禦祭があらわれ、文末の「印」は犧牲動物か人身犧牲であると思われる。（注84參照。）文の構造に關しては、（49）では禦祭の被祭賓語のみが記され、間接目的語（受祭賓語）の祖先神は用いられていないが、（51）では「祖庚至于父戊」と祖先神が用いられている。尚、（51）では禦祭の被祭賓語も「子辟」として、また施禦者名も「柵」として、用いられている。

　以上、裘論文の例文（23）Aから（51）まで、資料として不確實な數例を考察外としたものを除き、大多數の例が「名詞說」で解釋可能であるとしてきた。具體的にも「印」と「摯」がどのように性格づけられるか推論してみた。しかし、人間か動物かは未だ確定し得ない。私には人間說の方が可能性大のように思える。

　裘錫圭氏の「抑・執句末疑問詞」說に不利なことに關しては、結局、次の四點ほど擧げることができよう。

　（i）一つの文中に意味論的な對照が見い出されるということは、廣い意味での「選擇」になり得ようが、それは必ずしも「疑問文」を形成するわけではない。

　（ii）甲骨文に於いては、「選擇」も「順接」も「逆接」も基本的には表面化されたマーカーを必要としなかった。これはある條件の下では古典漢語にも言えることである。

　（iii）對貞形式に於いて、裘氏の「抑」が句末疑問助詞として正反兩貞に用いられるという說は奇怪である。かかる正反兩貞文に「執」などは一例も用いられていないことから判斷すると、「執」のみではなく、「抑」までもが句末疑問助詞ではないだろう、ということになる。

（ⅳ）裘氏が對貞に於いて（例えば（27）B）、「抑」がなくても疑問文になり得るとするのは、氏の說の弱體化を意味する。

　最後に殘しておいたが、裘氏の所揭例文中の（34）と（36）について考えなくてはならない。私見によると（34）のみが我々の名詞說では說明不可能と思える。これは重要なので、先ず、圖7として拓本のコピーを揭げ參考に供したい。ちなみにつけ加えておくと、これら二例ともショ譯に採られていない。

(34)　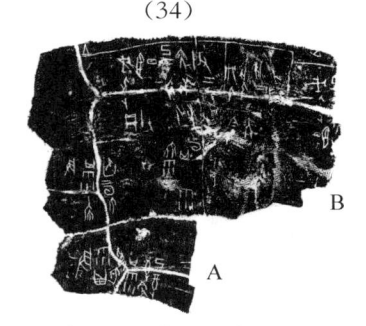　(36)　

21022（＝A＝『乙編』38，B＝108）　　20769（＝『乙編』194）

圖7

　例文（34）の裘氏の釋文は、次の通りである。

「己酉卜：□陰其雨抑。不雨、曾啓。」

裘氏はここで「不雨、曾啓」を驗辭としている。「曾」と釋字してある原字は、通常、「🅑」の如く刻され、「🅑」のような例はない。また、「曾啓」（意味は「ますます啓（は）れた」か）なる表現も他例に見ない。どの字に釋したらよいのか不明だが「西」の字の可能性もなくはない。しかし、「西啓」（「西啓れたり」の意か）なる表現も他例に見ない。命辭に關しては、裘氏は一字「卒」を見落としている。「卒」字に續く「陰」（裘氏は「くもる、くもり日」という意味に解釋している）を我々は「雀」（＝禽）としてきたが、ここでは、その字の上部分のみが見え、下半分がよく分からない。島邦男氏は「令」とし、もう一つの例を『坎』TO—〇—一—[85]に引くが、明白でない。してみると、この字は「陰」でもなく、「雀」でもなく、「令」でもない、全く別の字であるかも知れない。もし「雀」であるなら、その前の字が「卒」なの

---

[85] William C. White, *Bone Culture of Ancient China*（Toronto：The University of Toronto Press, 1945），p.94/Plate XIV. 島氏『綜類』頁三七五・三參照。

で、二つの「とらえ方」が並列しているとも考えられなくはない。しかし、その後に「印」が直結せず、少くとも「其雨」なる表現が「浸入」している。これは、どう見ても、不可解である。従って、ここでは名詞の「印」には解釋できそうもない。この例のみが、我々の名詞説で説明不可能であり、裘氏の句末疑問詞説に有利である。しかし、我々は古典漢語の「抑」の用法を前項でみたように、句末疑問詞説に抵抗を感じるのを禁じ得ない。従って、少し讓歩し、「抑」を接續詞にとり、「…其雨、抑不雨」とするべきなのだろうか。それ以外に解釋の方法がないようである。意味は「雨が降るようになるか、それともならないか」になり、これは「選擇」ではあるが、「逆説」でもなく「順接」でもない疑問である、と判斷せざるを得ない。驗辭は「西啓」、「曾啓」、あるいは、「～啓」で、メッセージは「晴れたり」と解釋できる。

例文（36）も（34）と同様に名詞説は保持困難であろうことが豫想されるので、少しく檢討してみよう。先ず、裘氏の釋文は次の通りである。

「甲辰卜：乙其焚又□中（？）風抑。小風、延陰。」

拓本を見ると、裘氏の「延陰」とする刻辭は、必ずしも「甲辰卜…云々」の一部であるとは言えない。別の辭に屬する可能性を殘している。その意味も、裘氏の理解している「引きつづき曇った」が唯一の正確の解釋ではないかも知れない。「延雀」とも考えられる。「延」には、例えば、「延夷」なる表現（『京津』二三五〇）、すなわち、「夷を征（さ）く（＝戔坼の初文か）」という意味があると思われるから、「延雀」は「雀えられたものを征く」という解釋も不可能ではないのである。ともあれ、（36）で肝要な部分は、「乙其焚又羌（？）十、風￤小風」である。（釋文は裘氏のと異なる。）ここでも「￤」は「印」では文意不通で、接續詞の「抑」とせざるを得ないのであろうか。もしそうならば、この命辭の意味は、「乙の日に焚さんに、羌人十人を侑めん。風が吹くか、抑（そ）れとも小風が吹くか」ということになる。裘錫圭氏は、我々が「十」とした字を「中」にし、「中風抑、小風…」、即ち「中風が吹かんか。小風であった」と理解している。もしこれが正しいなら、「抑」は句末疑問助詞である。しかし、「小風」なる驗辭も他例にないので、命辭の一部とみなし、「中風、抑小風」とするべきなのだろうか。もしそうならば、「抑」は選擇接續詞になり、例文（34）でみた「其雨、抑不雨」と比較できることになる。

しかしながら、そのように解釋するにも問題があるのである。それは、「焚」の字にまつわることなのだが、『綜類』（頁四八八・一）の用例を見ると、殆んどが狩獵關係であり、祭祀とは關係がない。してみると、羌人の侑祭と天候（特に風）との關係がどうであったかという問題が出てくる。そして、「小風」以下に「摯」字か「印」字があった可能性がある。すると、風は族名にとれないこともなく、字體こそ少しく異にするが、例えば、『甲編』三一一二にて「丙辰風獲五」と明らかに人名・族名に用いられている。このように見てくると、例文（36）の釋文は次のように解釋すべきかも知れない。

「丙辰卜、乙其焚…。…又羌十（或、中）風印、小風〔印、或、摯〕。」

ここでクルーシャルになるのは、「又羌」の前に來るコトバが何であったか、という問題だが、例えば、「隹」であったかも知れない。してみると、上の釋文の意味は、「乙の日に焚さん。又（ユウ）羌十、風族の印、小風族の印（或、摯）を〔隹〕（とら）えたり」とでもなり、この辭は狩獵に關連したもの、という推測も可能であるかも知れない。勿論、このような解釋を我々はアドヴォケートするわけでもない。意圖するところは、このような推測を許す資料の信憑性不足である。つまり、(36)は選擇疑問詞としての「抑」の資料には充分に援用しうるとは言えないということである。

第八項を1と2に分け、裘錫圭氏の説を批判しつつ、我々の解釋を試みてきた。ここで第八項を大局的に回顧してみると、如何なることが言えるのであろうか。一つには、たとえ裘論文所掲の五十程の例文全てに「句末疑問助詞」が用いられていると認め得たとしても、その數は誠に少ないと言わざるを得ない。「執」などはわずか十數例である。むしろ、ショナシー氏が勇敢にも殷虛卜辭の性質を歷史的發展の上にとらえ、自組卜辭にはしばしば選擇質問形式が用いられた、というのを更に發展させ、自組卜辭の命辭は全て疑問文である、とした方が理論的には清楚である。「オッカムのかみそり」のこともある。勿論、そのように議論することは無謀であって、表層構造に現われた「句末疑問助詞」を重視した結果の一つとして、裘論文は評價されねばならない。本項でも同じ資料を別の角度から表層構造としてとらえ、言語學的に檢討した結果が「印・摯名詞説」になったわけである。例文（34）の「𩚨」のみがどうしても裘氏の説に近い（同じではない）選擇疑問を表わす接續詞にとらざるを得なかっ

たわけであるが、このことから自組卜辭の性質一般について云々することは妥當ではない。

おわりに

本稿では、第一項から第八項までの各項をトピック別ではなく、研究者別に設け、そこにて彼等の說を紹介し、さらに我々の評價と解釋を織り込むという方式を採用した。またト辭でも壓倒的に多い命辭の性質について、專ら共時的に考えてきた。そのようなフォーマットをとったことから、それなりの制約を必然的に受けた、ということもある。一方、「共時的に考える」ということは、制約をむしろ意圖的に加えた、と言ったほうが正しい。それは、通時的、即ち歷史的にものを考える場合、資料の斷代問題もさることながら、資料を與えられたものとして理解することが先決問題だと考えたからである。その資料も歷史的資料としてではなく、言語學的資料として扱ってきたことは言うまでもない。しかし、卜辭の言語を理解した上で、それを歷史的に位置づける試みは有意義なことである。これは本稿ではなし得なかった。

卜辭の言語を性格づける意味で、本稿では「卜辭〜說」と命名してきたが、考察の對象になり得たのは全部で次の六說であった。

　　（i）卜辭疑問・質問說（孫詒讓、羅振玉等の早期研究者、その他張秉權などの現代の因襲的研究者、及び李學勤、ニビソン、ショナシー、裘錫圭等の條件付でこの說を容認する研究者）
　　（ii）卜辭命龜說（董作賓）
　　（iii）卜辭修祓・祝禱說（白川靜）
　　（iv）卜辭豫言・宣言說（キートリー、セロイス、ニビソン？）
　　（v）卜辭マジック說（白川靜、キートリー、ショナシー）
　　（vi）卜辭二元論的マジック說（キートリー）

括弧內にこれら各說を提唱した研究者名を記してみたが、本稿で檢討の對象になりながら、登場してこない名前がある。饒宗頤とラフーブレの二名の研究者である。この二名の見解は、命辭を全て非疑問文とすることには變わりない。

ただ、その非疑問文說を（ⅱ）の命龜說に含めたら良いのか、（ⅳ）の豫言・宣言說に含めたら良いのか、明白ではないようである。したがって、ここでは、その歸屬を控えておくことにする。

我々に殘された課題は、本稿で議論してきた内容を踏まえて、貞卜の言語の性格づけを行うことである。そこで、上記の（ⅰ）から（ⅵ）までを表題として掲げ、その下に結語と實例を施すことにしたい。

（ⅰ）卜辭疑問・質問說

「今日雨降らんか」、「今日雨降らざらんか」、または、「某々に禍有らんか」、「某々に禍亡からんか」といった對貞の解釋が疑問・質問說を代言すると思われるが、かかる解釋は「占うことは問うことだ」という先入觀的な前提に基づいている。『說文』の「貞、卜問也」という定義は、殷代の甲骨文の「貞」字の意味を傳えているとは信じがたい。命辭への反應である卜兆に見られる兆語から判斷すると、命辭は正反ともに非疑問文にとることが論理的である。非言語的（non-linguistic）な卜兆は、疑問文に對しては無言で應ずるより外ないと思われる。マジック的效果も認められないであろう。從って、この說に該當する卜辭の實例はない。貞卜する際、發話するということは、早期研究者及び因襲的現代の研究者の考えたように、質問するということではなかった。

李學勤氏が自組卜辭には句末疑問詞が用いられているという說を提起して以來、裘錫圭氏はその說に修正を加え、一擴充論を展開した。それに依ると、「抑」と「執」という助詞的マーカーの使用により、疑問の念がうかがえるとされ、ここに一種の疑問・質問說の復活化が提唱されるに至った。一九八八年のことである。しかし、この說に適う實例として我々が認めざるを得なかったのは、次の一例のみであることを論じた。

　　　己酉卜、…卒雀（？）…其雨、抑不雨。西（或、曾）啓。（裘論文の例文（34））

この例は、選擇疑問文であるようだが、何故このような疑問文が可能であったか、私は、不可解である。あるいは、「其」字が肯定文の方に用いられているので、意味的に弱め、雨が降るのは望ましくないという語氣を含ませ、「不雨」を卜兆に求めたのであろうか。いずれにせよ、「抑」を句末疑問詞とするのには問題があり、もし選擇疑問接續詞ならば「句末」ではなく「句頭」にす

べきであると論じた。

(ii) 卜辭命龜說

　　この説の本質を我々は龜や骨に「選擇を命ずる」と性格づけた。董作賓はそれを例えば「決死不死」という言葉で表現している。「決死不死」ということは、その根底には疑問の念があったであろうことは否定できないが、命辭としては、正反とも非疑問文であり、それらに對して、卜兆が可決か否決かをイエス・ノーではなく、「吉」の程度の差でリスポンドした、というように解釋した。更に、卜兆にはあるパワーが内在していたと殷人に信じられ、時には、そのパワーが無意味であったり、ニュートラルであったりした可能性があった、という卜辭命龜補正說を提起した。

　　卜辭命龜說として、我々は次のような例が考えられると思うのであるが、一般的に言って、對貞の正反が意味的に「均等價値」を有しているものである。例えば、「隹」と「不隹」などのように、正反のモダリティーが等しいと判斷されるものである。以下、説明の必要があると思うもののみに簡單な注を加える。

　　　⎰丙午卜、賓貞翌丁卯侑于丁。　　　　　（大龜一版＝『甲編』二一二四）
　　　⎱勿侑于丁。五月。　　　　　　　　　　（大龜一版＝『甲編』二一二四）
　　　⎰癸丑卜、貞小示侑羌。　　　　　　　　（大龜三版＝『甲編』二一二二）
　　　⎱勿侑羌。二月。　　　　　　　　　　　（大龜三版＝『甲編』二一二二）
　　　⎰隹父甲　　　　　　　　　　　　　　　　　　　　　『丙編』一五・（1）
　　　⎱不隹父甲　　　　　　　　　　　　　　　　　　　　『丙編』一五・（2）

このペアーは、張秉權氏も『丙考』で指摘した如く、『丙編』一二・（8）、（9）、（10）で問題になった王武丁の疾齒の原因追及の辭であると思われる。「隹父甲」とは、つまり、「（武王の疾齒は）父甲（のたたりのため）なり」と解釋できる。「不隹父甲」はその單純否定である。本片には、父庚、父辛、父乙の三近祖名が見られる。

　　　⎰王宙出值。　　　　　　　　　　　　　　　　　　　『丙編』二二・（7）
　　　⎱王勿隹出值。　　　　　　　　　　　　　　　　　　『丙編』二二・（8）

このペアーの意味は、肯定文の方が「王の（なすことは）出動して（外族）を

値（ただ）すことであるべし」、否定文の方が「王の（なすことは）出動して（外族）を値すことでなかるべし」と思われる。「叀」のモダリティーと「勿」のそれとは（正反の相違をとびこえて）同價値のものであると思う[86]。「叀」と「勿隹」の文法的性格の一つに、それらの後にくる一見動詞的表現（この場合は「出値」）を名詞句化し、それをハイライトする、ということがある（見注86）。

$$\begin{cases}戊寅卜、殻貞沚戛其來。 & \text{『丙編』二八・（1）}\\ 貞戛不其來。 & \text{『丙編』二八・（2）}\end{cases}$$

このペアーには、正反ともに「其」字が用いられ、そのモダリティーは相い等しい。

　以上の對貞例からも分かるように、正反のどちらかが、貞卜の結果、選擇されても、その「情報價値」は當事者にとって無益ではなかったらしい、ということが推測できるのではないだろうか。つまり、これらの對貞は、意味的にバランスのとれたものであり、當事者のディシジョン・メーキングに役立たせたと思える。

　最後に、「無益ではなかった」という角度から考えて、正反の對貞ではなく、多項式選擇を構成する卜辭も命龜說がふさわしいと思える。例えば、次の如き例が典型的なものであろう。

(1) ｜己酉… 　　　　　　　　　　　　　　　　　　　　　　『合集』二八六〇五
(2) ｜辛䍃壬王勿往于田、其悔。　　　　　　　　　　　　　『合集』二八六〇五
(3) ｜王叀乙往于田、丙廼啓、亡災。　　　　　　　　　　　『合集』二八六〇五
(4) ｜乙王勿往于田、其悔。　　　　　　　　　　　　　　　『合集』二八六〇五

右の（1）から（4）までは、一骨片の上に刻され、「己酉」（46）を始めに、（2）では「辛䍃壬」の日、恐らく「辛亥（48）と壬子（49）の日に、王は田に往くべきではない、（何故なら）後悔するようになりかねないからだ」とトしたものと思える。引き續き（3）にて「王が田に往くのは乙の日（＝乙卯〔52〕）にすべきである。そうすれば、丙の日（＝丙辰〔53〕）も啓れ、災は亡からん」とトし、（4）には（3）の否定形である「乙の日に王は田に住くべき

---

[86] この點に關しての詳細は、注63所掲の拙論を參照されたい。

ではない、（何故なら）後悔するようになりかねないからだ」とトしている。ここで分かることは、二日が一つのユニットになっていることであって、それは、（3）の從辭言（イロキューショナリー・フォース）的メッセージの「乙の日に往けば、丙の日も啓れ、災も亡からん」から明白に讀みとれよう。この一連の多項式選擇も、二日をユニットとして決定せんとしたものであり、卜辭命龜說がふさわしいと思う。

(iii) 卜辭修祓・祝禱說

この說は、白川靜氏が殷代の貞卜を宗敎學的觀點からみて解釋した結果、得られたものであり、優れて卜旬、卜夕、卜田遊などの一事一貞の場合、擧例に値するものがある。數は多いが、パターンは少なく、大體、次のような例である。「旬亡禍」、「王今夕寧」、「今夕亡禍」、「往來亡災」等で、ここでは著錄書の出典明記は省略する。このような言辭は白川氏の言う「儀禮的慣習的言語行爲」であり、かかる言辭が實現化されんことを祝禱しているとする說は正しいと思える。意味的には、ことごとく「正」の觀念を傳えている。かかる說を認めた上で、我々は、白川論文の「殷王を絕對的存在」と位置づける前提からは距離を置いたのである。それは、一つには、「卜王」という表現が白川氏の考えた如く、「王が王を聖化する」という意味には解釋不可能である、ということにもよる。

白川氏の卜辭修祓・祝禱說は、一事一貞法の卜辭のみではなく、兩貞法・對貞法の卜辭にも適應するとしているのである。しかし、氏は正反の辭を「選擇」ではなく「質問」の概念でとらえている。その點では、（i）の卜辭疑問・質問說の影響から脫け出ていない、ということが言えよう。但し、白川說には「肯定的命題が卜意に適ふべきものとして期待されてゐたらしい」というインサイトがある。本稿では、それを「其」という語氣助詞の意味論的分析及びディスプレー・インスクリプションの内容分析の兩側面から支持してみた。その結果、正反の對偶による選擇は、必ずしもバランスのとれた、公平な選擇を神龜に詑したことではないことが判明した。例えば、次のような對貞がそれに適應すると思われる。

｛辛亥卜、爭貞翌乙卯雨。乙卯允雨。　　　『丙編』三〇四・(1)
　貞翌乙卯不其雨。　　　　　　　　　　『丙編』三〇四・(2)

このペアーでは、驗辭「乙卯允雨」が用いられ、肯定命題の「翌乙卯雨」、卽ち、貞卜日の辛亥から五日目(その當時の計算法による「乙卯の日に雨降らん」が望まれていたことが分かる。しかるに、否定命題の方では「其」字が用いられ、それが望ましくないことを示している。「不其雨」、つまり「雨が降らざらん」ということは、「其」、卽ち望ましくない、と婉曲に述べられている、と理解できよう。次のペアーも同樣である。

  ⎰庚戌卜、𤉲貞王其疾骨。   『丙編』三三四・(2)
  ⎱庚戌卜、𤉲貞王弗疾骨。王占曰勿疾。 『丙編』三三四・(3)

ここでは、文法的には肯定の命題に「其」字が用いられ、「王が骨を疾む」ことは望ましくないことであったに違いないから、かかるコトバを挿入し、王の疾骨の可能性を弱めている、と解釋できる。文法的には肯定形であるが、意味的には反である。否定命題の後には、繇辭である「勿疾」が刻辭され、それは白川氏の修祓・祝禱的な義で解釋できると思われる。しかし、この繇辭自體は、(v)のマジック說でも性格づけが可能である。兩者の差は、マジック說の方が「勿疾」の意味をさらに强調して理解するということであり、祝禱とマジックとは一線上に存在するものであろう。

 以上の二つの對貞以外にも實例はかなりある。本文の第三の2項に擧げた例をも參考にされたい。

(iv) 卜辭豫言・宣言說

 この說は、從來の疑問・質問說のよりどころとなっていた『說文』の貞字の定義や卜辭の言語型式など五つのトピックについて分析し、命辭を疑問文と見做すのは妥當ではなく、非疑問文の豫言か宣言をするものだ、と性格づけられる。しかし、どちらかと言えば、卜辭マジック說へ導誘していく過渡的なものであったということが言えよう。

 我々は、キートリー氏のトピックにそってその論旨の評價を試みたのであるが、例えば貞字の對象を命辭ではなく貞卜工程とするなど、不思議な解釋もみられるようだと論じてみた。また、キ氏は「オッカムのかみそり」の命題などにアッピールした論證を多角的にしてはいるが、我々は單文、重文、複文等の分析を實際の命辭例に卽して統辭論的分析を加えた結果、氏の「パッケー

ジ・ディール説」（第五の項）などは成立し難いのではないかとした。このようにキ氏の論證にこそ難點はあるものの、究極的には、命辭を豫言・宣言とする説そのものは、取るに足るものであると判斷したのである。例えば、次の如き單文は卜辭豫言・宣言説を支持することができると思われる。

　　○戊辰卜、壴貞有來辥自𢦏、今日其征于祖丁。　　　　『甲編』二七七二
　　○丙午卜、卽貞又氏羌、翌丁未其用。　　　　　　　　『續存』一・一六〇五
　　○丙寅卜、賓貞有來羌、來甲戌鬯用。　　　　　　　　『前編』六・六七・四
　　○〔乙亥〕卜、賓貞翌庚子有告麥。允有告麥。　　　　『前編』四・四〇・六
　　○貞隹龜令。　　　　　　　　　　　　　　　　　　　『卜辭』一九二

以上の例は全て本文中で引用したものである。また、卜辭豫言・宣言説は單文によってのみ支持されるわけではない。次の如き重文も充分考えられるであろう。

　　○癸丑貞甲寅彡、大禦自上甲燎十六小宰。兹用。　　　　『南明』四三二
　　○庚申貞今來甲子彡、王大禦于大甲燎十六小宰、劉九牛。不遘雨。
　　　　　　　　　　　　　　　　　　　　　　　　　　　　『南明』四三二

以上の二つの卜辭を獨立したものととれば、宣言説である。但し、ここで注意しなくてはならないことがある。それは、右の命辭を一つのユニットとしてとらえた場合、命辭の内容が異なり、さらに「其」字などもないため、「選擇」の可能性が生じてくる。故に、宣言説よりも命龜説で解釋した方が理にかなっていると言えよう。

　今、上文で卜辭豫言・宣言説の一つだけとり、「宣言説」という表現を用いたが、實は、「豫言説」のみで解釋できる例がある。それらは「王占曰」で緒言する繇辭である。例えば、次の如き本文中でも考えたものを擧げておく。

　　○癸未卜、爭貞旬亡禍。王占曰有祟。三日乙酉夕斷丙戌允有來入齒。十二月。
　　　　　　　　　　　　　　　　　　　　　　　　　　『庫方』一五九五
　　○甲申卜、𣪊貞婦好冥嘉。王占曰其隹丁冥嘉、其隹庚冥引吉。三旬有一日甲寅冥、不嘉。隹女。
　　　　　　　　　　　　　　　　　　　　　　　　　　『丙編』二四七・（1）

（v）卜辭マジック説

ここでいうマジックとは、キートリー氏の説く「アナロジカル・マジック」、即ち「模倣魔術」と言われているものである。前項（ⅳ）で我々は、豫

言・宣言說はマジック說に發展していく過渡的な說として想定された、と述べた。それと同樣のことが、(v) から次項 (vi) の「卜辭二元論的マジック說」に發展していく際にも認められる。キ氏はそのように過渡的なものとして想定したようなのではあるが、マジック說が適應する例があると思う。貞卜行爲から得られる卜兆には或る種のパワーが潛在するとした我々の觀點からすると、かかる卜辭例が存在するのは豫期できよう。特に繇辭に適例がある。例えば次の通りである。

(1) 庚戌卜、亘貞王弗疾骨。王占曰勿疾。　　　　　『丙編』三三四・(3)
(2) 王占曰吉、勿泇。　　　　　　　　　　　　　　『丙編』四六・(1)
(3) 王占曰勿余壱。　　　　　　　　　　　　　　　『丙編』一七六・(3)
(4) 己巳卜、㱿貞允不死。王占曰吉、勿死。　　　　『丙編』四三八・(1)
(5) 貞不隹禍。王占曰吉、勿隹禍。　　　　　　　　『丙編』五一四・(20)
(6) 王占曰吉、黽勿余壱。　　　　　　　　　　　　『丙編』五二三・(7)
(7) …卜。貞蠱禍、有疾。旬又二日…未蠱允禍、百日又七旬又…蠱亦有疾。
　　　　　　　　　　　　　　　　　　　　　　　　『鐵雲』五・三

例文 (1) は (iii) の修祓・祝禱說にも適用したが、特に命辭の部分はその說で說明できるであろう。但し、もう少し掘り下げてみると、「疾骨」は統御不可能なことである。またその事實が否定詞「弗」をも誘導している。繇辭の「勿疾」の部分はあたかもある特定の卜兆が得られるように王が命令しているが如きである。例文 (2) も「泇」なる語の意味が不明なるも (案ずるに「とどこおる、さわりあり」という意か)、「吉」を受けていると思われる。そのため、「勿泇」は殷人にとって好ましい意味であったに違いない。ここでも、王は「泇すること勿かれ」と命令している語氣がうかがえるのであろう。(3) は明らかに「余に壱すること勿かれ」の意である。(4) も命辭では「允は死なず」という豫言・宣言的な言辭であるが、繇辭では、またもや「吉」に呼應した「勿死」である。(5) も何かのトピックに對し、「(それは) 禍にはあらず」と豫言・宣言的な言辭に對して王が登場し、「吉、勿隹禍」と統御可能的言辭で結んでいる。(6) は (3) と比較できるが、「壱」という他動詞の主語が具體的に「黽」と表面化している。この「黽」なるコトバこそ、人が後世「神黽」と呼ぶところの神格 (numen) を表わした精靈ではあるまいか。第一期卜辭にのみ頻見の「不悟黽」という兆語の「黽」と同一無二のものである。かかる兆語

の意味は、「黽に悟せず」、つまり、龜・骨の精靈である黽の意向に反しない、というような、いわば、ニュートラルなト兆だ、ということであると思う[87]。例文（7）は、本文でもとりあげたが、「黽禍、有疾」にて黽があたかも呪いをかけられているようであり、マジック的色彩が濃厚である。これらのマジック的言辭は未來に對してただの豫言や宣言をするというのではなく、積極的に働きかけている、と解釋できよう。

　最後に、これは論爭必至になると豫想される一例を引用し、卜辭マジック說で解釋する假說を提起しておきたい。

───

[87]　この兆語の解釋には、諸說あるが、一つの言語學的解釋をここに提出しておきたい。「黽」と釋字した原型は「📷」であり、金文での「📷」（邾伯鬲）、「📷」（邾公華鐘）、「📷」（邾公牼鐘）などと字形の面からは比較できる。これら金文の形には「朱」という聲符らしきものを内包していることに注意されたい。これを聲符としたエヴィデンスに賴ると、甲骨文の形は金文の「📷」（＝黿＝黽）の前身と見做されてよかろうから、「黽」に「朱」の聲符がついたものと考えられる。上古漢語では恐らく、＊tjugであろうと思われ、これは「殊・誅」＊djug（「死ぬ、殺す」の意）と同根である。『懷持』B〇九五九には、次のような刻字がある。

　　📷

金祥恆氏「加拿大多倫多大學安大利澳博物館藏一篇牛胛骨刻辭考釋」『中國文字』三八、頁一〇ォ～一〇ゥ）に依ると、該甲骨文字は「殊」とすべしとあり、これは正しいと思える。（文意も失われない。）但し、本文の例文（6）での「黽」は明らかに名詞であるから、「殊、誅」、卽ち＊tjug～＊djugと解釋しうるとしても、意味的に如何なる關係があったかは不明である。或るいは、全く關係のない假借的用法ということもありうる。

　次に、「悟」（📷）であるが、これは例えば、『丙編』九〇・（1）～（6）に

　　　「丁巳卜、王〔貞〕余勿悟肜」

とあり、意味は「余は肜祭に悟（さから）うこと勿かれ」ということだと思われる。「悟」は『說文』に「逆也、从午吾聲」とあることから、音は＊ngagであろう。實は、「午」自體＊ngagxであるから、『說文』の「吾聲」はリダンダントであると言える。ともあれ、「午」の基本義は「ぶつかる」とか「かみあう、あざなう」であると思われ、「杵」＊skjagx、「牙」＊ngrag、「禦」＊ngjagx、「五」＊ngagx等の語と單語家族を形成する。これらの語は、それぞれ、「きね」（上下運動をしながら"ぶつける"もの）、「きば」（上下にかみあう齒）、「禦」（おはらい、邪氣とコンフロントし、それをはらう）、「五」（藤堂明保氏によると、ゆびおりで數える時、五でリターンして〔つまり、交叉して〕十まで數える）の意味が檢出できる。「不悟黽」なる表現は、よって、「黽に悟（さから）わず」と理解できよう。この際、否定詞が狀態否定の「不」であることにも注意すべきである。すなわち、狀態否定である上に、統御不可能な狀態（「不悟黽」の主語が卜兆であることから判斷して）でもある。「余勿悟肜」では、「勿」が用いられており、この方は非狀態否定であり、また「さからう」という統御可能なふるまいを意志的に否定している。從って、「余は肜祭に悟うこと勿かれ」と理解できるわけである。

(8) 乙巳卜、帝日叀乙又日、叀辛又日。　　　　　　　　　　『美國』USB11

このト辭の解釋は定かではないが、一つの可能性として、次の如く考えられはしまいか。

「帝の日〔卽ち、或る王―武乙のことか？―が死去し、その廟號の十干を選擇する必要性から"帝日"としたとする見解に從って〕は、乙〔偶數干〕を又日〔吉日の意〕とすべし、(また)辛〔"8"の偶數干〕を又日とすべし。」[88]

もし、ここで「叀乙又日」と「叀辛又日」を「順接」にとらず、「選擇」で解釋すると、それは裘錫圭氏の言う「選擇疑問」となる。これを準古典語調にパラフレーズすると、「叀乙又日、抑叀辛又日」とでもなろうか。しかし、このように解釋すると、それに對する答として如何なる卜兆が必要とされたかが分からなくなってしまう。我々は、既に第八項で裘論文を別の角度から檢討した際、このように何とも不可解な「選擇疑問」は僅か一文の例外を除き認め難いとした。してみると、「叀乙又日、叀辛又日」は、「順接」に解釋し、しかも、S_2の「叀辛又日」は「追加」、つまり、ファースト・チョイスは乙が又日だが、辛も又日であるべし、と加えたということが言えるのではないだろうか。そうだとすると、例文(8)は「帝日は乙でも又日、また、辛でも又日なるべし」となり、これはマジック說が適應するように考えられると思う。以上の(1)から(8)までの例文は全て命令文の語氣があるようであり、それらは言語活動から貞卜行爲を通して未來に働きかけているように解釋できる。

(vi) ト辭二元論的マジック說

キートリー氏は(iv)のト辭豫言・宣言說も(v)のマジック說もこの二

---

[88] キートリー氏は例文(8)を次のように英譯している。

"It should be *xin* for which there is a sun/day." (David N. Keightley, "Lucky Days, Temple Names and Social Aspiration in Ancient China," p. 26. Paper presented at the International Conference on Yin-Shang Civilization in China, Anyang, Septembe 10-17, 1987.)

この英譯は「乙に太陽・日があるべし」、「辛に太陽・日があるべし」とでも和譯され、「又」を「ある」の意味に解釋していることが分かる。不可能な解釋であるとは決して言えないが、「又日」なる表現がそのように解釋できる傍證に乏しい。私は「又日」を名詞句にとり、「又」は「又示」、「又年」、「又工」、「又土」、「有祖」、「有母」、「有弟」、「有兄」等に用いられている「美稱」の「又・有」にもとれるのではないかと思う。しかし、「又日」の「日」はこれらの名詞と性質を異にするようでもあり、問題がないわけでもない。故に、これは一つの假說として待考としておくことにする。

元論的マジック説に結着するための過渡的なものとして設定したょうだ、ということは我々も既に述べた。しかし、本稿ではそれらを單なる過渡的なものとしてはとらえず、實例を舉げて、採用したのである。最後に、この二元論的マジック説に到達した理由であるが、これにも適應する實例を見出せることができると思う。ここで、またもや問題になるのは、貞卜者側にとって望ましくなかった「反」の解釋、處理方法である。次の對貞例を資料にして考えてみよう。

(1) 戊午卜、㱿貞殷往來亡禍。　　　　　　　　　　　『丙編』一三〇・(1)
(2) 貞殷往來其有禍。　　　　　　　　　　　　　　　『丙編』一三〇・(2)
(3) 丙辰卜、㱿貞我受黍年。　　　　　　　　　　　　『丙編』八・(1)
(4) 丙辰卜、㱿貞我弗其受黍年。　　　　　　　　　　『丙編』八・(2)
(5) 乙卯卜、㱿貞王從望乘伐下危（危）、受有祐。　　『丙編』二二・(1)
(6) 乙卯卜、㱿貞王勿從望乘伐下危（危），弗其受有祐。『丙編』二二・(2)

例文（1）と（2）は本文（第五の6項）で既に檢討してあるので、そこを參照されたい。例文（4）の反の「我、黍の年を受けざらん」は、「其」字によりその語氣が抑えられている。とは言え、收穫がないといったことは、現實に起こり得ることである。かかる反の刻辭をも敢えて施したのは、單なるマジック説では説明できない。例文（5）と（6）のペアーの構文は複文である。（5）の主節は「王從望乘伐下危」であり、從屬節は「理由」を表わす「受有祐」である。（6）も同じく「王勿從…」が主節で、「弗其受…」が理由の從屬節である。そこにも「其」字が用いられ、「有祐を（帝から）受けられない」ということを婉曲に表現していると解釋できる。しかしながら、實際問題として、帝からの祐がないことも考えられたはずであり、そこでも單なるマジック説は成立しない。次の二つのペアーにも同じことが言えよう。

(7) 戊申卜、爭貞帝其降我艱。一月。　　　　　　　　『丙編』六七・(7)
(8) 戊申卜、爭貞帝不我降艱。　　　　　　　　　　　『丙編』六七・(8)
(9) 貞方其戈我史。　　　　　　　　　　　　　　　　『丙編』七六・(3)
(10) 貞方弗戈我史。　　　　　　　　　　　　　　　　『丙編』七六・(4)

例7の反の命題にも「其」字用いられ、「帝が我々に艱を降（くだ）す」可能性が、いわば「アナロジカル・マジック的コトバの其」により弱められている。

とは言え、ここにもかかる可能性があったはずである。(9)の反にも同様なことが言えよう。「方が我が史を戈する」ことは、王朝側にとって望ましいことではない。故に、「其」字により意味的に「修祓」をしかけている、とも言えよう。しかし、可能性としてはあったであろう。一方、次の例(11)のように、望ましくない意味の「左」に「其」字が冠されていないのもある。

　　　(11)　示左王。　　　　　　　　　　　『丙編』九八・(18)
　　　(12)　示弗左。　　　　　　　　　　　『丙編』九八・(19)

例文(11)は「示が王に左う」という意味だと思われ、「示其左王」というように表現されてしかるべきである。従って、このペアーの場合、卜辭二元論的マジック説ではうまく説明ができない。勿論、單なるマジック説もふさわしくない。豫言・宣言説も不適應のようである。ただ一つの可能性として、命龜説が殘されるようである。それは、正反の意味が「均等價値」を有しているものと考えられ、(11)か(12)の選擇が殷人にとって無益なインフォメーションではなかったからではないだろうか。マジカルな要素は窺われず、それこそバランスのとれた、純粋な二元論的なものであり、命龜することにより(11)か(12)の神的反應を引きださんとしているが如くである。次のペアーもそのように考えられる。

　　　(13)　貞黃尹祟王。　　　　　　　　　『丙編』一〇四・(9)
　　　(14)　貞黃尹弗祟王。　　　　　　　　『丙編』一〇四・(10)

　以上のようにみてくると、二元論的マジック説がふさわしい例文とそうでない例文の區別がかなり明確にできるようになったと思われる。「其」字が用いられ、それがあたかもアナロジカル・マジック的にある動詞の語氣を抑えている。かかる解釋は、「二元論的マジック説」の「マジック」的要素を反に附加している、と見ることが許されるのではなかろうか。「其」字を除去した場合、正反の組み合わせは、從辭言的にみると、バランスのとれた、公平な貞意がそこにあった、と思われる。これは二元論的なことである。「有禍」、「弗受年」、「弗受有祐」、「帝降我艱」、「方戈我史」といったことは、全て、現實化する可能性が十分にあったはずである。また、これらが全て當事者の意のままにならぬ統御不可能な意味があることは、注意を促すことである。このことは、單に儀禮的・形式的な必要性から對貞の對象に採用されたということを

否定するようである。これら反の意味は、究極のところ、現實の世界と一體化を圖らんとした精神の表われであったと解釋できるのではあるまいか。そうだとすると、ここでいうマジックとは、神祕的に何かをおこらしめるというようなものではなく、正反に對し、そのいずれかが實現する可能性を與えるという、二元論的な、調和的な手段であったということが言えるであろう。「其」字の使用は、その二元論的な解釋にマジック的で、實に人間的な側面を備えている、ということであった。

「おわりに」を終結させるにあたり、我々の言えることは、（ii）のト辭命龜說から（vi）のト辭二元論的マジック說までの五つの說が殷代貞ト言語の本質を性格づけるということである。

初稿脫稿一九八九年五月九日
補一九八九年七月六日

［追記］　本稿執筆中、東アジア第一部門・考古の松丸道雄教授から何かと御教示・御便宜を賜った。記して謝意を表したい。

The Nature of the Shang Divination Texts
by Ken-ichi Takashima

What did the Shang think they were writing, on the turtle plastrons and the bovine scapula, during the latter part-for a period of about 200 years, ca. 1250—1050 B.C.-of China's first historical dynasty?

This basic question has led us to examine various issues associated with it. To mention just a few of them, they have to do with the precise understanding of such frequently used words as *pu* 卜, *chen(g)* 貞, *cheng* 正, and *ming/ling*, 命・令, with the nature of questions, selections, prayers, spells, commands, and predictions, with the linguistic formula of oracle-bone "queries" (charges), with the relationship between the scattered accounts seen in traditional classical texts and our own formulation of the oracle-bone texts, and with the true nature of the recently proposed "particle-like" function words: *yi* 抑 and *chih* 執. Issues such as these are treated not thematically, but more or less chronologically, in the context of the researches of a dozen scholars, Chinese, Japanese, and Western. These scholars, who appear in the Table of Contents, are primary contributors to our understanding of the Shang oracular texts.

The paper has identified six major theories which have been offered up to now to characterize the nature of the charges of Shang oracle-bone inscriptions. They are referred to hereinafter as follows:

(i) the theory that the charges are questions(卜辭疑問・質問說).

(ii) the theory that the charges are alternative selections put to the plastromantic and scapulimantic numina(卜辭命龜說).

(iii) the theory that the charges are purificatory mantra and prayers(卜辭修祓・祝禱說).

(iv) the theory that the charges are predictions(prophecy) and proclamations(卜辭豫言・宣言說).

(v) the theory that the charges are analogical magic, an attempt to influence and control the future(卜辭マジック說).

(vi) the theory that charges are dualistic magic, an attempt to balance the positive and negative forces of the universe(卜辭二元論的マジック說).

These theories are analyzed and evaluated with a view toward enabling us to throw light on the nature of the charges. The frame of reference in which our analyses and evaluations are conducted is almost strictly linguistic and philological, and thus our crossreferences to, and interpretations of, the actual inscriptions are of paramount importance. We suggest, in short, that any single one of the above six theories is insufficient to account for the nature of the Shang oracular texts and that all but the first theory, (i) above, are required for a proper characterization of the different "types" of inscriptions that are distinguished in the body of the paper.

原載《東京大學東洋文化研究所紀要》第 110 冊,1989 年;收入宋鎮豪、段志洪主編:《甲骨文獻集成》第 18 冊,四川大學出版社,2001 年。今據前者收入。

夏含夷

試論周原卜辭㕣字
——兼論周代貞卜之性質

周原卜辭裏"㕣"字最爲常見,幾乎每條完整的卜辭都含有:

H11:1:癸子(巳)彝文武帝乙宗,貞:王其邵祭成唐,鼎禦及二女,其彝血牲三豕三;㕣又正。

H11:2:自三月至于三月=唯五月;㕣尚。

H11:6:咎曰:並㕣克事。

H11:11:子(巳)王其乎更乒父陟;㕣亡……。

H11:20:祠自蒿于壹;㕣亡咎。

H11:21:曰:吝㕣克事。

H11:28:戠;㕣亡咎。

H11:32:囦㕣克事。

H11:35:八屮㐅;㕣亡咎。

H11:47:大禳;㕣不大追。

H11:77:……㕣亡咎。

H11:82:……于文武……王其㝵帝天……晉周方白□;㕣正亡ナ……王受又又。

H11:84:貞:王其㸚又大甲,晉周方白盍;㕣正,不ナ于受又又。

H11:96:……告于天;㕣亡咎。

H11:114:弜巳(祀),其若及;㕣正。

H11:130:㕣正……受又又。

H11:136:今秋王㕣克往竅。

H11:174：貞：王其□用胄東丁胄乎水受；◊不奻王。

H11:248：……◊不……

H31:3：隻其五十人羊；◊亡咎。

H31:4：㕢曰：戍既弗克𢦏𢦏徒；◊亡咎。

……迺荆東……。

H31:5：寇◊城。

周原卜辭出土僅有幾年，對"◊"字仍未有詳細考證。陝西周原考古隊或釋爲"東"，或釋爲"迺"。"東"契文作 、 、 諸形，"迺"契文作 、 諸形；不但字形與"◊"迥然不同，並且標準"東"字、"迺"字均出現於含有◊字的周原卜辭裏：

H11:174：貞：王其□用胄東丁胄乎水受；◊不奻王。

H31:4：……◊亡咎……迺荆東。

由此可斷言，◊絕非"東"，也非"迺"。

李學勤和王宇信以◊隸定爲"囟"，釋作"思"（見《周原卜辭選釋》，《古文字研究》第四輯，頁250—251），得之。《說文》："恖……从心从囟"，可見於戰國時代陶文""（見高明，《古文字類編》，頁150）。从"心"之字，多至春秋戰國時代纔加心旁。因此，◊和諒必即古今字。於後時之字書也可求其旁證。《集韻》謂："囟古作顖。"《正字通》謂："顖俗顋字。"《玉篇》亦云："顖同顋。"顋和顖若是同字，則囟和恖同樣地也爲一個字。

然而，李、王二氏以此"思"釋爲虛辭，與"唯"同意，恐怕仍有可商之處。在周原卜辭裏，◊字的用法很規律，或謂"◊又正"（H11:1、H11:12、H11:84、H11:114、H11:130），或謂"◊亡咎"（H11:11、H11:28、H11:35、H11:77、H11:96、H31:13、H31:4），或謂"◊克事"（H11:6、H11:21、H11:32、H11:136），均爲卜辭的尾語，而且最重要的是，均表示積極的意思。"又正"、"亡咎"、"克事"似是卜人向鬼神之祈求，"◊"（思）乃應該爲動辭，即"願"之意思。《詩·大雅·文王》"思皇多士"，《鄭箋》謂："思，願也"。《爾雅·釋詁》："願，思也。"《方言·一》："願，欲思也。"皆說明"思"有"願"之意。《說文》："顖，大頭也，从頁原聲。""◊"即大頭之形象，在字形上"思"與"願"也不矛盾。在《詩經》裏可以找到類似周原卜辭"思"的這種用法。《魯頌·駉》謂：

駉駉牡馬,……思無疆,思馬斯臧。
駉駉牡馬,……思無期,思馬斯才。
駉駉牡馬,……思無斁,思馬斯作。
駉駉牡馬,……思無邪,思馬斯徂。

清陳奐《毛詩說》謂"皆祝辭也",很有見地。如此,無論是"⛎又正"、"⛎亡咎"或者"⛎克事",以"⛎"釋作"願"皆可通,即"願意是正確的"、"願意沒有災難"、"願意能夠做得到",是祝辭一類的用語。

如果完整的周原卜辭一律都含有祝辭式的尾語,周代貞卜之意義恐怕就不完全像傳統說法所謂"貞卜問也"、"卜以決疑"的那種目的,而也是爲了祈求鬼神的贊同和幫助。除了在周原卜辭裏以外,周代貞卜之性質也可尋求於東周時代的文獻記載。譬如,《左傳》裏的三十六條卜筮實例之中,有五條相當完整,具有貞卜之"命辭",於下一一引用:

文公十八年:春,齊侯戒師期而有疾,醫曰:"不及秋將死。"公聞之,卜曰:"尚無及期。"惠伯令龜,卜楚丘占之曰:"齊侯不及期,非疾也,君亦不聞,令龜有咎。"

昭公五年:吳子使其弟蹶由犒師,楚人執之,將以釁鼓。王使問焉,曰:"女卜來吉乎?"對曰:"吉。寡君將治兵於敝邑,卜之以守龜曰:'余亟使人犒使,請行以觀王怒之疾徐,而爲之備;尚克知之。'龜兆告吉,曰:'克知也。'"

昭公十三年:靈王卜曰:"余尚得天下。"不吉,投龜詬天而呼曰:"是區區者而不余畀,余必自取之。"

昭公十七年:吳伐楚;陽匄爲令尹,卜戰,不吉。司馬子魚曰:"我得上流,何故不吉。且楚故司馬令龜,我請改卜。"令曰:"魴也以其屬死之,楚師繼之,尚大克之。"吉。

昭公七年:衛襄公夫人姜氏無子,嬖人婤姶①生孟縶。孔成子夢康叔謂已立元。……婤姶生子,名之曰元。孟縶之足不良,弱行。孔成子以《周易》筮之,曰:"元尚享衛國,主其社稷。"遇屯䷂。又曰:"余尚立縶,尚克嘉之。"遇屯䷂之比䷇。以示史朝,史朝曰:"'元亨',又何疑焉。"

僅以"命辭"提出予以相比:

---

① 編者按:"姶",原文誤作"姤",今徑改。下同。

> 文公十八年：尚無及期。
>
> 昭公五年：尚克知之。
>
> 昭公十三年：余尚得天下。
>
> 昭公十七年：尚大克之。
>
> 昭公七年：元尚享衛國，主其社稷。
>
> 余尚立縶，尚克嘉之。

一瞥可見，《左傳》裏貞卜的命辭也有其一律的形質，即以"尚"爲樞紐。並且，這種性質不限於《左傳》一書，也見於戰國時代各種各樣貞卜記載。譬如，《國語·晉語》謂：

> 公子親筮之曰："尚得晉國。"得貞屯䷂悔豫䷏，皆八也。筮史占之，皆曰："不吉；閉而不通，爻無爲也。"司空季子曰："吉；是《周易》皆'利建侯'。不有晉國以輔王室，安能建侯？我命筮曰：'尚得晉國。'筮告我曰：'利建侯。'"

《儀禮·少牢饋食禮》曰：

> 筮於廟門之外；主人服西面于東門。史朝服，左執筮，右抽上韇，兼與筮執之。東面受命于主人。主人曰："孝孫某，來日丁亥，用薦事于皇祖伯某以其妃配某氏；尚饗。"①

《儀禮·特牲饋食禮》同樣曰：

> 宰自主人之左贊命，命曰："孝孫某筮來日某諏此某事，適其皇祖某子；尚饗。"

《儀禮》的這些例子像一個表格一樣，可以證明"尚某某"一律爲貞卜命辭的尾語。除了上述文獻記載以外，這種貞卜的性質猶可以見於戰國時代的出土品；譬如，湖北天星觀楚簡謂：

> 鄦遝呂邡答爲君貞："既㞢雁疾以心䣄；尚毋以其古（故）又（有）大咎。"占之吉。

饒宗頤先生解釋這個貞卜命辭爲，"先生已經有了大雁疾及心悸，希望沒有因爲這個原因有大問題"（《殷代易卦及有關占卜諸問題》，美國夏威夷商代文化國際討論會論文，頁17），甚是。

---

① 編者按：本段引文與古書原文頗有出入，"東門""薦""其"，《儀禮》作"門東""薦歲""某"。

過去學者們沒有注意東周貞卜記載的這種形質，拘於"貞卜問也"之訓詁，沒有考慮而自動地理解這些貞卜命辭爲問話。譬如，毛奇齡《春秋占筮書》注《左傳》昭公七年之"元尚享衛國"曰："問辭。"如此，"尚克知之"就翻成白話文的"我們能夠知道嗎？"，"余尚得天下"同樣地翻成"我會不會得到天下？"。但是，古代"尚"字決無問話之用法，於這種文句中，如《左傳杜氏解》已經説得很明白，尚即"庶幾也"（見文公十八年、昭公十三年）。鄭玄注《儀禮》亦同。《儀禮正義》就更清楚："云尚庶幾也者，《説文》同，蓋願望之辭。"不但《説文》亦同，《爾雅》也曰："庶幾尚也。"《爾雅疏》就謂："尚爲心所希望也。"《爾雅》另外訓"庶幾"爲"僥倖"；"僥"（與徼、憿可假借通用）即"要也"、"求也"，與今所常用"憿福"同意。因此，這些貞卜命辭（於此應該注意，"命辭"的意思就是"用以發命令的辭"，而不是"用以問問題的辭"）應該翻成白話文的"希望我們能夠知道"、"我希望可以得到天下"等。由此可斷言，東周貞卜之性能是卜人向鬼神表示祈求，而不僅僅是問將來之事如何。

　　再歸到周原卜辭，卜辭尾語一律謂"🜨又正"、"🜨亡咎"、"🜨克事"，可知"🜨"（即思）與"尚"有同樣的用法和意義，也可知周原卜辭的性質就像東周貞卜之性質一般，是卜人向鬼神表示"心所希望"。

一九八三年五月十八日

　　原載《古文字研究》第 17 輯，中華書局，1989 年；收入夏含夷：《古史異觀》，上海古籍出版社，2005 年。今據前者收入，並吸收了後者的一些修訂整理意見。

075 釋戉

劉桓

　　甲骨文 ✦（粹一六），或作以下諸形，✦（明藏四四二）、✦（粹一四）、✦（甲七八一）。

　　對於該字的解釋一向衆説紛紜①。諸家中唯郭沫若注意到此字象形，指出："字象一人倒執斧鉞之形，舊釋伐，不確。此蓋人名，乃殷之先公。"②郭説中其它問題，將留待後面討論；他指出象形這點，確是考釋此字的關鍵。

　　我認爲該字象形，活畫出一個側身西立、眉髮豎起、相貌奇異的人，右手倒提着一把長柄大斧，顯出威風凛凛的樣子。字應隸定爲戉。因爲，✦即戌字之倒；字的左旁，似當作夏，夏本象人有兩手側身而立③，與卜辭字形恰相吻合④。

　　根據該字在甲骨卜辭中用作人名，聯想到古文獻記載，戉分明是蓐收的形像。《國語·晉語二》載：

　　　　虢公夢在廟有神，人面白毛，虎爪執鉞，立于西阿（按，"阿"指深曲處。段玉裁注《説文》阿字謂"引申之，凡曲處皆得稱阿"）。公……覺，召史嚚占之。對曰："如君之言，則蓐收也，天之刑神也，天事官成。"

　　　　韋昭注："蓐收，西方白虎金正之官也。傳曰：少皞氏有子該爲蓐收。"

---

① 參閱陳夢家：《殷虛卜辭綜述》三三四、三三五頁。
② 《殷契粹編·考釋》一四片，三五三頁。
③ 《説文》五篇下夂部："夏，中國之人也。从夊、从頁、从臼，臼，兩手，夊，兩足也。"
④ 甲骨文另有一✦字，易與戉相混。字象一人側立以右手揮鉞形，卜辭一般用爲征伐義，如"乎✦兕（髦）……"（前六·一八·六）。但有極個別的兩字混用者，如京都一、乙二四九八均以此字代戉，疑刻寫之誤。舊釋戉爲伐，也是由於未能將此二字區分開的緣故。

白毛者，指其眉髮之白；虎爪者，指其手如虎爪（甲骨文虎字帶爪者，爪有 ⚡ 形。見《甲骨文編》），《説文》云："覆手曰爪"，是言手的形狀異於常人。這皆與魃的威武形像相吻合，魃正是少皞該。

又《山海經・海外西經》載：

> 西方蓐收，左耳有蛇，乘兩龍。
>
> 郭注："金神也。人面、虎爪、白毛、執鉞，見《外傳》。"桓按：《外傳》即《國語》。説見韋昭《國語解叙》。

同書《西山經》云：

> 又西二百九十里曰泑山，神蓐收居之。
>
> 郝懿行《山海經箋疏》："懿行案《北堂書鈔》一百四十九卷引泑作岰，李善注《思玄賦》引此經作濛山，蓋即《淮南子》云日至於蒙谷是也……"

所謂"左耳有蛇，乘兩龍"，應是在神話傳說過程中添接的枝葉，證據是同書記四方之神，于東方勾芒，南方祝融皆言"乘兩龍"（《海外東經》、《海外南經》），北方禺彊則"珥兩青蛇"（《海外北經》）；夏后開（啓）也是"珥兩青蛇，乘兩龍"（《大荒西經》）。這説明給蓐收添上珥蛇乘龍之類的説法，意在增加其神秘色彩，使"神蓐收"更有神味，本無足爲怪。由此反而可知，《國語・晉語》比《山海經》的記述爲原始。

《左傳・昭公二十九年》記魏獻子與蔡墨一問一答的一段文字，其中有：

> 對曰："夫物物有其官，官脩其方……故有五行之官，是謂五官。實列受氏姓，封爲上公，祀爲貴神，社稷五祀，是尊是奉。木正曰句芒，火正曰祝融，金正曰蓐收，水正曰玄冥，土正曰后土……"獻子曰："社稷五祀，誰氏之五官也？"對曰："少皞氏有四叔，曰重、曰該、曰脩、曰熙，實能金木及水，使重爲句芒，該爲蓐收，脩及熙爲玄冥，世不失職，遂濟窮桑，此其三祀也。顓頊氏有子曰犂，爲祝融，共工氏有子曰句龍，爲后土，此其二祀也。……"

所謂少皞四叔，都是少皞族的著名人物，未必同時。少皞該之作爲五行之官（五官）的"金正"，無疑是因爲他對金（銅）有所擅長。

下面，且看在甲骨卜辭中是如何記述對魃舉行祭祀的。卜辭説：

1. □□貞：〔其告〕龝（秋）□□〔于〕魃□牛。　　　　　（粹一四）〔四〕
2. 其桒雨于魃，尞九宰。　　　　　　　　　　　　　（粹一五）〔四〕

3. 其桒年于戠,叀☐酌,又(有)大雨。　　　　　　　　　　　（粹一六）〔三〕
4. ☐☐卜,其桒禾于戠,尞二牛。戠,尞一牛。　　　　　　（後上二四·九）〔四〕
5. 壬辰卜,其桒年于戠,又羌。兹用。
　　戠,尞二牛。　　　　　　　　　　　　　　　　　　　（續一·五一·五）〔四〕
6. 于戠宗酌,又雨。
　　于芇宗酌,又雨。
　　于帝臣,又雨。　　　　　　　　　　　　　　　　　　（甲七七九）〔三〕
7. 戊申卜,尞于戠,雨。
　　辛未卜,尞于河,☐于禾。　　　　　　　　　　　　　（明藏四二三）〔三〕
8. ☐申卜,其淑戠。　　　　　　　　　　　　　　　　　　（粹一五三八）〔三〕
9. 貞:乎刚目、光、河氐戠、洹。　　　　　　　　　　　　（寧滬三·四〇）〔一〕
10. 辛酉卜,宂,貞:尞于戠白牛,二月。　　　　　　　　　（京都1）〔一〕
11. 貞:屮戠尞、卯。　　　　　　　　　　　　　　　　　　（後下一四·九）
12. 壬寅卜,王其淑戠,于盂田又雨,受年。
　　淑,又雨。　　　　　　　　　　　　　　　　　　　　　（屯南二二五四）
13. 于來甲辰酌戠。　　　　　　　　　　　　　　　　　　　（綴合一六）

由上所引,可知戠有宗廟,是商代統治者桒雨（祈雨）、桒年（又作"桒禾",祈求好年成）和告秋（報告禾穀成熟）的對像,他或與芇（有人釋爲岳）、帝臣（上帝的臣）同祭,或與目、光、河及洹河同祭,或與河對貞行祭,祭法如尞（燒柴祭天,但此爲用牲之法）、酌、淑、刚、又（即屮祭,"又羌"是殺羌人行祭。又、屮當讀爲侑）等等,也多種多樣。我們知道,芇有宗廟,是介於殷先公高祖與自然神祇之間的人物。帝臣亦稱"帝五臣"、"帝五丯臣"或"帝五臣正",他們組成了上帝的朝廷,應屬於自然神祇之類。至於目、光,皆爲傳説時代人名,性質尚不能肯定。河在卜辭中用法有二:一爲先公高祖一類人物,一爲大河之河,但二者可能是二而一的。續補五六三二片:"尞于河、王亥、上甲十牛,卯十宰。五月。"此是合祭先公先王的,河、王亥被排在先公高祖之列。《國語·周語上》:"河竭而商亡",這説明殷人是把河視爲發祥地的,河即河神。至於洹,即殷墟附近洹河,此指洹水之神,屬於自然神祇。戠既與上述早商傳説人物和自然神祇同祭,説明其性質必相接近。由戠有宗廟,可見他是受享祭的人鬼,而非自然神祇。又由對戠致祭之講究（如用白牛,擇日而祭等）,可窺知他在殷人心目中的地位。

卜辭又有"右宗戠"的説法，與此密切相關。如：

王其又酚于又宗戠，又（有）大雨。　　　　　　　　　　（甲一二五九）〔三〕
即又宗夒，又雨。　　　　　　　　　　　　　　　　　　（續存一一七五九）〔三〕
貞：即于又宗，又雨。　　　　　　　　　　　　　　　　（粹一六）〔三〕
貞：即于又宗，又大雨。　　　　　　　　　　　　　　　（粹六八五）〔三〕
若于屮宗。　　　　　　　　　　　　　　　　　　　　　（零八九）〔一〕

郭沫若謂："即于又宗，又殆左右之右，古人以西爲右，右宗蓋謂宗祭于西方也，它辭言：其于西宗。"①郭説以又爲右，爲西，均是。屮宗亦是右宗。但古人以右爲尊②，右宗之右，當取此義。在卜辭中，在上甲微之前只有兩個人被明確稱爲高祖，一爲高祖夒，一爲高祖王亥。在此處戠、夒同稱"右宗"，爲殷王祈雨的對像，則右宗必只此一家，只能是一個集合的宗廟。戠與商的遠祖夒皆屬於傳説時代的人物，大概他們都對商族產生過大的影響，才被如此尊奉。

值得提出的是，卜辭戠所在的"右宗"爲西宗，依豨與蓐收立於（廟之）西阿的方位闇合，可知傳説是有所本的。據考證，帝乙征人方，要在西宗舉行宗教儀式，才決定出師③。則西宗即右宗，又與征伐有關。古時兵刑不分，少皞該被奉爲刑神，即相當於戰神，故主征伐。卜辭與傳説史料是一致的。

釋戠爲少皞該的根據，還不僅在於甲骨文中這個象形字本身，以及卜辭與古文獻之間的聯繫，而且在於對此可以從民族、地域和考古年代幾個方面作出相應的解釋。

首先，少皞該之見於甲骨卜辭，可以與少皞族的歷史聯繫起來，可證我國古史傳説時代確有少皞存在過。馬克思認爲，人是名副其實的社會動物，不僅是一種合羣動物，而且是只有在社會中才能獨立的動物。在我國古代一定的時間，一定的地域，所出現的某一著名人物，都不是獨立於社會之外的，而必然是當時某一族的代表。我們知道，少皞族在歷史上據説一度有過"少皞之國"（《山海經·大荒東經》），並曾設立官職，以鳥名官（《左傳·昭公十七年》），擁有若干著名人物，在金、木、水幾方面都有擅長，對我國古代社會的發展起過相當的作用。今得卜辭此證，參以《國語·楚語》的説法："及少皞之衰也，九黎亂德"，

---

① 《殷契粹編·考釋》一六片，三五四頁。
② 屌敖簋銘的"屌敖……用訟告其右，子歆史孟"，指"訟告"他的上司"子歆史孟"。銘見郭沫若：《屌敖簋考釋》，《考古》，一九七三年二期。
③ 李學勤：《殷代地理簡論》四一頁。

可知確有少皞時代。

在當時，由於生產的發展，因而各族的活動範圍擴大，相互往來增多。"他們相互間經常有冲突，也經常有經濟上文化上的相互影響以至於融合或部份融合。"① 如古代太皞亡而少皞興，從其名稱、地域上看，似乎有太皞之裔融合於少皞。而夏代夷族有窮氏的羿，恃其武力"革孽夏民"（《楚辭·天問》），"因夏民而代夏政"（《左傳·襄公四年》），通過戰爭，夷夏是否也會發生一部份融合呢？值得思索。我國古代華夏民族的形成，就是各個民族融合的結果，然則少皞的一支，與早期商族融合，因而傳說其本族酋長之事，神乎其神地讓他與商高祖同宗並列受祭，不也是合乎情理的嗎？

其次，在地域上考察。據《左傳》等古書記載，前人早已論定山東是少皞的大本營。但少皞有西移的一支，《左傳·昭公元年》記鄭國的子產說："昔金天氏有裔子曰昧，爲玄冥師，生允格、臺駘，臺駘能業其官，宣汾洮，障大澤，以處大原，帝用嘉之，封諸汾川，沈、姒、蓐、黄，實守其祀，今晉主汾而滅之矣。"據杜預注和《尸子》說，金天氏即少皞。這樣說來，在上古就有少皞的一支活動於山西一帶了。而《左傳·文公十八年》舜"流四兇族"、"投諸四裔"，其中包括少皞氏不才子窮奇，不知是否與此是同一支。《左傳》郯子所述的少皞歷史與鄭子產所講的却是截然兩回事。蓐收之名，似與"沈、姒、蓐、黄"的"蓐"有關，卜辭用"蓐"爲地名，可證"蓐"地甚古；而《山海經》又說蓐收居於西方之泑山（見《西山經》），由此看來，少皞該似乎出於西遷的一支，故《國語·晉語》載其傳說形像。但古史茫昧，難以肯定，姑且不管他在東在西，要之都未出於商族活動範圍之外。可證融合之說有據。

再其次，就考古年代上說，唐蘭先生從古文獻上考察，提出大汶口文化即少皞文化②，這個新見解富有啓發性。夏鼐先生根據利用 C-14 測定年代法獲得的數據研究，以爲"大汶口文化至少跨着公元前四五〇〇—二三〇〇年"③。據此，可以認爲少皞文化的下限約在公元前二三〇〇年左右。其西移的一支雖無直接的年代證據，其年代也不會差很多。這與夏朝的建立上下只隔二百年，與先商年代上限的間隔幾乎一般長。關於商的上限可以推得，《國語·周語上》："玄王勤

---

① 范文瀾：《中國通史簡編（修訂本）》，第一編，九九頁。
② 《從大汶口文化的陶器文字看我國最早文化的年代》，見《光明日報》一九七七年七月十四日"史學"六九期。
③ 《碳-14 測定年代和中國史前考古學》，《考古》，一九七七年四期。

商，十有四世而興"，即在公元前十六世紀加上十四世約三百年，再加上未載世系而商族實已存在的一段時間，大致不會比公元前二十一世紀夏啓建國晚。故在年代上，夏初或先商，距少皞末期都晚不了二三百年以上。我國古代氏族組織維持二三百年不變的，並非罕見。那末，少皞的一支，隨着少皞的衰落而融合於商族，於情理可通。

《左傳·僖公三十一年》説："冬，狄圍衛，衛遷于帝邱。卜曰：三百年。衛成公夢康叔曰：相奪予享。公命祀相，寗武子不可，曰：鬼神非其族類，不歆其祀。杞鄫何事？相之不享於此久矣，非衛之罪也，不可以間成王、周公之命祀，請改祀命。"衛祭其祖康叔，而不祭曾居帝邱的夏后相，此事有助於我們對商代祭祀的理解，從"鬼神非其族類，不歆其祀"的舊傳統看，戜要是與商族無關，就不會受祭。《世本》説"少皞名契"，這正暗示着少皞與商的融合情況，但卜辭從不稱戜（少皞該）爲高祖，看來他是被視爲與商族祖先有着親緣關係和直接影響的傳説人物。

總之，少皞該之見於甲骨卜辭，給我國古史的傳説時代增添了新資料，對於先商史的研究也具有一定的意義。

原收入劉桓：《殷契新釋》，河北教育出版社，1989年。

馮　時

殷曆歲首研究

目　次

序文
一、從武丁時期五次月食的推定證殷曆歲首
二、殷曆歲首的天文學依據
三、卜辭與殷曆歲首的對證
四、主要結論

序　文

《史記·曆書》云："夏正以正月，殷正以十二月，周正以十一月。"若配以月建，則夏曆歲首當建寅之月，殷曆歲首當建丑之月，周曆歲首當建子之月，這三朝曆法的歲首便構成了中國古曆中傳統的三正①。千百年來，三正論雖已爲人們所普遍接受，但也確曾有人在懷疑。唐司馬貞著《史記索隱》時就明確提出："唯黄帝及殷、周、魯并建子爲正。"清人顧觀光更備論其義，刊陳補苴，發揚此説②。這種獨標新意的見識卓爾不群，開風氣且省人思，我們自不該視之爲古人偶發的懸斷或奇想。

中國的先秦古曆一直未能詳知，以丑月爲歲首的殷曆乃是漢傳古六曆的一部

---

① "三正"在文獻中首見於《尚書·甘誓》，云："威侮五行，怠棄三正。"陸德明《經典釋文》卷三引東漢馬融《注》云："建子、建丑、建寅，三正也。"
② 顧觀光：《六曆通考》，《武陵山人遺書》，重印光緒九年刊本。

分,依此研究甲骨文所反映的殷商歷史,會在很多問題上難以深入。我們無權指摘甲骨文是錯誤的,它是出於時人之手、未經僞造的真實史料,那麼,唯可懷疑的自然只有殷曆本身。漢傳的丑正殷曆非時王之術,自晉杜預以來時有議論。《宋書·律曆志中》云:"考其遠近,率皆六國及秦漢時人所造。"祖冲之亦云:"古之六術,并同《四分》,《四分》之法,久則後天。以食驗之,經三百年,輒差一日。古曆課今,其甚疏者,朔後天過二日有餘。以此推之,古術之作,皆在漢初周末,理不得遠。且却校《春秋》,朔并先天,此則非三代以前之明證矣。"[①]僅據古六曆之一的殷曆而言,其合天年代約在公元前五世紀,相當於中國的戰國時期,本非時王之曆自可肯定。然而,真正的時王殷曆又是怎樣的一種面貌?

曆法是年代學的重要內容,而年代學則是古史研究的框架和基礎,曆法不明,一切史實便無從附著,因此,正確地瞭解殷曆對正確地研究商史無疑有着重要的意義。目前研究殷正,可尋的方法有兩種:第一,利用卜辭記錄的殷代氣象和農事材料,同後世的氣象及農事情況衡量比較,以求得二者相互符合的理想時段;第二,根據卜辭記錄的殷代天文現象做天文學分析。結論的客觀首先需要材料和方法的客觀,本文擬依甲骨文提供的月食材料,運用天文學方法爲復原殷正進行一次新嘗試。

一、從武丁時期五次月食的推定證殷曆歲首

目前所見殷卜辭中的月食刻辭共八條,從卜辭斷代的角度講,都屬於殷王武丁時的"賓組"刻辭,它們分別記述了武丁時期發生的五次月食,習慣上稱爲"乙酉月食"、"庚申月食"、"甲午月食"、"壬申月食"和"癸未月食"。五次月食中有一次月食明係殷曆月份,有兩次月食的殷曆月份可以推得。

乙酉月食

　　癸未卜,爭貞:旬亡禍?三日乙酉夕,月有食,聞(昏)。八月。　　(《甲釋》55)

此次月食發生於殷曆武丁某年八月望日。

庚申月食

(一)癸丑卜,貞:旬亡禍?七日己未夕斷,庚申月有食。

---

① 《宋書·律曆志下》,中華書局標點本,1974年10月。

癸亥卜，貞：旬亡禍？

癸酉卜，貞：旬亡禍？

癸未卜，爭貞：旬亡禍？王占曰："有咎。"三日乙酉夕鬥，丙戌允有來入齒。
十三月。　　　　　　　　　　　　　　　　　　　　　　（《庫方》1595 正、反）

董作賓先生主張依（一）讀，則庚申月食發生於殷曆十二月望日①。陳夢家先生參考《金璋所藏甲骨卜辭》（*Hopkins Collection of the Inscribed Oracle Bone*）594（正、反）所記庚申月食卜辭，主張（二）讀：

（二）癸亥。

癸未。十三月。

癸巳卜，貞：旬亡禍？

癸卯卜，貞：旬亡禍？

[癸丑卜，貞：旬亡禍？七日]己未夕鬥，庚申月有食。

依（二）讀，則庚申月食發生於殷曆一月望日②。

最近，李學勤先生等編錄的《英國所藏甲骨集》選收了兩辭的拓本③。經過反覆比較，我們更傾向於陳夢家先生的讀法。兩版卜辭同記"庚申月有食"，并同於癸未日係記"十三月"，所卜為一事當無疑問，其貞卜次序可整理如下：

《英國所藏甲骨集》885 正、反	《英國所藏甲骨集》886 正、反
	癸[卯]
	癸丑（十二月）
癸亥	癸亥
（癸酉）	（癸酉）
癸未　十三月	癸未　十三月
癸巳	[癸巳]
癸卯	[癸卯]
[癸丑]庚申月有食（一月）	[癸丑]庚申月有食（一月）
	[癸亥]
	癸酉

---

① 董作賓：《殷曆譜》下編卷三《交食譜》，中央研究院歷史語言研究所，1945 年。
② 陳夢家：《殷虛卜辭綜述》，238—239 頁，科學出版社，1956 年 7 月。
③ 李學勤、齊文心、艾蘭：《英國所藏甲骨集》，中華書局，1985 年。

圓括號內是原辭所無、按順序擬補的干支或月份，方括號內是原辭殘掉的干支。據此可知，庚申月食發生於殷曆武丁某年一月望日。

甲午月食

　　　[己]丑卜，賓貞：翌乙[未酚]，黍烝于祖乙？王占曰："有咎，不其雨。"六日[甲]午，月有食。乙未酚，多工率條遣。　　　　　　　　　　（《綴合》230）

此辭干支殘缺，董作賓先生擬補爲"甲午月食"是可信的①。卜辭命辭記"黍烝于祖乙"，"烝"當古之烝祭。《左傳·桓公五年》："閉蟄而烝。"杜預《集解》："建亥之月，昆蟲閉戶，萬物皆成，可薦者衆，故烝祭宗廟。"《爾雅·釋天》："冬祭曰烝。"郭璞《注》："進品物也。"《周禮·春官·大宗伯》："以烝冬享先王。"古代烝祭有兩個特點：一、烝祭多行於夏曆孟冬十月；二、烝祭的對象是先王先祖。卜辭所記烝祭用物有黍、稷、秫、米、鬯等，且皆祀先王，與文獻契合。依殷禮，烝祭多行於殷曆一月或十二月，卜辭云：

　　　辛丑卜，于一月辛酉酚，稷烝？十二月。
　　　辛丑卜，衍，稷烝，辛亥？十二月。　　　　　　　　　　（《綴合》62）
　　　□□卜，王，弜今日烝？一月。　　　　　　　　　　　　（《合集》4321）

一辭卜在十二月辛丑日。古之卜祀，如郊之用辛②乃"以十二月下辛卜正月上辛，如不從，則以正月下辛卜二月上辛"③，如此者數。殷制未必這樣嚴格，但辛酉歸屬一月，從占卜時間看，應是首先考慮的日期。二辭卜在一月。以此比較"甲午月食"卜辭，其在一月的可能性要大些。因此可以初步確定，甲午月食發生於殷曆武丁某年一月望日。

對這五次月食發生年代的推考，繼董作賓先生之後又有很多學者有所涉及④。近年來，不少天文學者注意到古代月食的推算，并編制出一些精度較高的古代月食表。這裏，我們以劉寶琳先生所制《公元前1500年至公元前1000年月

---

① 張秉權：《殷虛文字丙編》上輯（一），90—95頁，"中央研究院"歷史語言研究所，1957年8月。
② 《禮記·郊特牲》："郊之用辛。"
③ 《穀梁傳·哀公元年》。
④ 主要的論文有張培瑜：《甲骨文日月食紀事的整理研究》，《天文學報》16卷2期，1978年；范毓周：《甲骨文月食紀事刻辭考辨》，《甲骨文與殷商史》第二輯，上海古籍出版社，1986年6月。

食表》（以下簡稱《劉表》）①爲基礎推定這五次月食。

需要說明的是，《劉表》採用的記日法是現代通行的子夜零時制，這與殷人以一日之旦至次日之旦計算一日的記日法略有不同。記有月食的卜辭有些詳記"夕"字，"夕"在殷代是整個夜晚的通稱②。所以，我們在實際考慮上述五次月食發生時間的時候，必須含括自同一干支的子夜零時至下一個干支日出之前的一段時間。

《劉表》所列公元前1500年至公元前1000年間安陽可見的庚申月食共十一次（表一）。

表一　庚申月食表（表中所列爲安陽時）

編號	儒略曆	儒略周日	干支	初虧		食甚		復圓		食分
1	－1480.7.18	1180687	庚申	02^h	48^m	04^h	31^m	06^h	14^m	1.308
2	－1433.1.13	1197667	庚申	00	02	01	42	03	22	1.220
3	－1428.4.16	1199587	庚申	02	02	03	06	04	09	0.335
4	－1263.5.20	1259887	庚申	15	57	17	41	19	26	1.316
5	－1217.11.15—16	1276867—8	庚申、辛酉	22	36	23	49	01	02	0.395
6	－1191.12.27—28	1286406—7	己未、庚申	20	31	22	27	00	23	1.663
7	－1165.8.14	1295767	庚申	03	18	05	11	07	05	1.620
8	－1144.6.23—24	1303386—7	己未、庚申	21	06	22	37	00	09	0.841
9	－1113.5.12—13	1314666—7	己未、庚申	23	28	00	02	00	36	0.091
10	－1067.11.7	1331647	庚申	05	04	06	43	08	22	0.833
11	－1020.5.4—5	1348627—8	庚申、辛酉	22	17	00	07	01	56	1.307

這十一次月食的時間若按殷人記日法加以調整的話，則第1—3、6—10次均應排除，原因是這八次月食一般都發生在晚21時至次日凌晨6時之間，這在殷代基本上屬於前一干支—己未的範圍，而不能視爲庚申月食。其餘的三次月食，第11次年代太晚，也應排除。至此，表一中可供選擇的就只有第4、5兩次月食了。

由於殷代記日法與今天不同，所以，發生在庚申次日，亦即辛酉凌晨的月食事

---

① 文見《天文集刊》第一號，1978年。
② 董作賓：《殷代的記日法》，《文史哲學報》5卷，1953年12月。

實上也屬於庚申月食。安陽可見的這類月食在《劉表》中共列有五次（表二）。

表二 辛酉晨月食表（表中所列爲安陽時）

編號	儒略曆	儒略周日	干支	初虧		食甚		復圓		食分
1	-1310.11.24	1242908	辛酉	01^h	15^m	03^h	00^m	04^h	44^m	1.646
2	-1118.2.9	1312748	辛酉	03	32	05	29	07	27	1.792
3	-1072.8.6	1329728	辛酉	03	28	04	32	05	37	0.355
4	-1041.6.25	1341008	辛酉	03	28	04	52	06	16	0.672
5	-1025.2.1	1346708	辛酉	03	03	04	11	05	18	0.428

這五次月食只有第 1 次可與表一的第 4、5 兩次月食相適應，其餘四次在年代上都嫌過晚，可以舍棄。經過這樣的刊選，我們便得到了庚申月食可能發生的三個時間：

A 組：
（1）-1310.11.24
（2）-1263.5.20
（3）-1217.11.15

依照這種方法，我們再去檢查乙酉月食。《劉表》所錄安陽可見的乙酉月食（含丙戌晨月食）共十三次，經殷人記日法加以調整後尚餘七次（表三）。

表三 乙酉（含丙戌晨）月食表（表中所列爲安陽時）

編號	儒略曆	儒略周日	干支	初虧		食甚		復圓		食分
1	-1495.10.30	1175312	乙酉	17^h	02^m	18^h	43^m	20^h	25^m	1.175
2	-1417.3.16	1203573	丙戌	05	40	06	11	06	43	0.067
3	-1278.9.2	1254513	丙戌	00	16	01	36	02	57	0.629
4	-1226.5.31—6.1	1273412—3	乙酉、丙戌	22	29	00	10	01	52	1.339
5	-1180.11.25	1290392	乙酉	18	02	19	54	21	45	1.728
6	-1081.2.19	1326272	乙酉	18	30	20	02	21	34	0.698
7	-1035.8.17	1343253	丙戌	00	55	02	49	04	42	1.463

由於武丁王的在位時間目前比較一致地認爲是五十九年，因此，如果我們以前面推得的庚申月食可能發生的三個時間作爲年代基點，并將 A 組（1）與 A 組（3）分別加減五十九年的話，便可得到一個年代範圍，即公元前 1369 年至公元前 1158 年，這是否可以被認爲是武丁王在位的最大年限。用這個假設的年限去

衡量表三中的月食，能夠適應的只有第 3、4、5 三次。於是我們又推得了乙酉月食可能發生的三個時間：

$$
B 組：\begin{cases} (1) & -1278.9.2 \\ (2) & -1226.5.31 \\ (3) & -1180.11.25 \end{cases}
$$

現在，我們將 A、B 兩組年代做一一對應的組合，共成九組。九組之中有七組年代與我們考慮的某些基本原則不符，需要排除。具體說明如次：

1. 其中的三組年代彼此相距八十年以上，已遠遠超出武丁王的在位年數五十九年，故舍。

2. 另有一組年代彼此相距六十一年，鑒於記有庚申、乙酉月食的卜辭均由貞人"爭"所行占，而"爭"供職的時間能夠跨越六十一年的可能性又極小[①]，故亦舍。

3. 我們在嘗試推步所餘五組年代的殷曆歲首後發現，有三組年代的歲首誤差在四個月以上。因此，如果我們承認殷人使用的是一種陰陽合曆的話，那麼這三組結果就必須舍棄。換言之，一旦我們允許殷曆的歲首可以擺動在四個月之間，那就意味着這種曆法實際已經失去了以閏月調節的陰陽曆的性質了。

在排除了以上七組年代後，最終餘下的年代有兩組：

$$
C 組：\begin{cases} -1310.11.24 & 庚申月食 \\ -1278.9.2 & 乙酉月食 \end{cases}
$$

$$
D 組：\begin{cases} -1217.11.15 & 庚申月食 \\ -1226.5.31 & 乙酉月食 \end{cases}
$$

推步歲首的結果是，C 組年代歲首誤差兩個月，D 組年代歲首誤差在一個月內。這是僅存的可供選擇的月食年代。

我們繼續檢查甲午月食。甲午月食卜辭所記貞人爲"賓"，"賓"與庚申、乙酉月食卜辭的貞人"爭"同屬武丁時期的"賓組"貞人，而且兩人在卜辭中又有同版互見的例子[②]，故其時間相隔不會太遠。在《劉表》中，安陽可見的甲午月食（含乙未晨月食）共列有十二次，經殷人記日法調整後尚餘六次（表四）。

---

① 張培瑜、盧央、徐振韜：《試論殷代曆法的月與月相的關係》，《南京大學學報》1984 年 1 期。
② 陳夢家：《殷虛卜辭綜述》，174—175 頁，科學出版社，1956 年 7 月。

表四　甲午（含乙未晨）月食表（表中所列爲安陽時）

編號	儒略曆	儒略周日	干支	初虧		食甚		復圓		食分
1	-1465.4.5—6	1186061—2	甲午、乙未	20^h	35^m	22^h	21^m	00^h	06^m	1.548
2	-1228.12.17	1272882	乙未	00	00	01	30	03	00	0.755
3	-1197.11.4	1284161	甲午	20	31	21	56	23	21	0.724
4	-1150.5.2	1301142	乙未	00	51	02	38	04	26	1.126
5	-1129.3.12	1308761	甲午	14	43	16	31	18	18	1.738
6	-1052.7.25	1337021	甲午	19	08	20	42	22	16	0.718

上列 C 組年代彼此相去三十二年，將其早晚年代分別擴大二十七年，即是武丁王在位的最大年限。以此衡量表四，沒有一次甲午月食能夠適應。上列 D 組年代彼此相去九年，將其早晚年代分別擴大五十年，亦即武丁王在位的最大年限。以此衡量表四，則有第 2、3 兩次甲午月食可得安排。至此可以確定，D 組年代是庚申月食和乙酉月食發生時間的唯一答案①。

D 組年代的正確與否，取決於壬申月食和癸未月食能否在此年代範圍內得到合理的安排。

壬申月食

　　□旬。壬申夕，月有食。　　　　　　　　　　　　　　　　　（《簠·天象》2）

癸未月食

　　［癸］未卜，爭貞：翌甲申易日？之夕月有食。甲，蒙，不雨。　（《丙編》59）

《劉表》所列安陽可見的壬申月食（含癸酉晨月食）共十次，經殷人記日法調整後、并符合上述年代範圍的只有二次（表五）。

表五　壬申（含癸酉晨）月食表（表中所列爲安陽時）

編號	儒略曆	儒略周日	干支	初虧		食甚		復圓		食分
1	-1188.10.25	1287439	壬申	19^h	27^m	20^h	40^m	21^h	53^m	0.507
2	-1182.1.28	1289360	癸酉	04	04	05	13	06	23	0.413

《劉表》所列安陽可見的癸未月食（含甲申晨月食）共十三次，經殷人記日

---

① 張培瑜先生等也傾向於這種選擇。見張培瑜、盧央、徐振韜：《試論殷代曆法的月與月相的關係》，《南京大學學報》1984 年 1 期。

法調整後、并符合上述年代範圍的只有四次（表六）。

表六　癸未（含甲申晨）月食表（表中所列爲安陽時）

編號	儒略曆	儒略周日	干支	初虧		食甚		復圓		食分
1	－1231.8.23—24	1271670—1	癸未、甲申	22^h	53^m	00^h	14^m	01^h	35^m	0.612
2	－1200.7.11—12	1282950—1	癸未、甲申	22	24	23	39	00	54	0.508
3	－1184.2.18—19	1288650—1	癸未、甲申	22	31	23	53	01	15	0.692
4	－1179.5.22	1290570	癸未	17	22	19	08	20	54	1.172

范毓周同志通過對甲午、壬申、癸未三次月食及其刻辭的研究，主張選擇表四第3、表五第1和表六第2次①，我們同意這種選擇。

在今見的全部八條月食卜辭中有這樣一種有趣的現象，即僅有乙酉月食的卜辭附記"聞"字，而其他四次月食的卜辭不記此字。我們且看另一版由貞人"㱿"所行占的卜辭：

[癸未卜]，㱿[貞：旬亡]禍？三日[乙]酉夕，[月有]食，聞。[八月]。

(《燕》632)

與由貞人"爭"所行占的乙酉月食卜辭一樣，貞人"㱿"的卜辭也同樣附記"聞"字。"聞"字的真正含義究竟是什麼？澄清這個問題將有助於檢驗我們推定的五次月食的正確性。

董作賓先生曾經指出，"聞"意即方國報聞，因此乙酉月食安陽不可見②。這種意見已遭到一些學者的反駁。屈萬里先生認爲，"聞"於此當讀爲"昏"，言月食發生時月色昏暗③，乃真知灼見。我們認爲，乙酉月食的卜辭獨記"昏"字，證明乙酉月食是月全食。發生全食，月球被地影完全遮蔽，月面變暗，呈紅銅色，所以記"昏"。相反，其餘四次月食的卜辭不記"昏"字，則反證了它們爲月偏食。驗之我們所推定的五次月食，恰恰只有乙酉月食爲全食，另外四次月食皆爲偏食，而且除甲午月食外，其他三次偏食的食分都很小，即在發生月食時，月面的大部分仍很明亮。這應該不是偶然的巧合！

這一步說，假如我們把表四、表五和表六中所録的全部八次月食都作爲武丁

---

① 范毓周：《甲骨文月食紀事刻辭考辨》，《甲骨文與殷商史》第二輯，上海古籍出版社，1986年6月。
② 董作賓：《殷曆譜》下編卷三《交食譜》，中央研究院歷史語言研究所，1945年。
③ 屈萬里：《殷虛文字甲編考釋》上冊，"中央研究院"歷史語言研究所，1961年6月。

時期可能發生的月食來加以考查，結果只有表六第 4 次爲月全食，其餘七次皆爲偏食，而這僅有的一次全食又正是年代最晚，被選擇的可能性最小的一次。因此，即使這樣也不能動搖我們上面的推論。或者我們也可以這樣理解，因爲無論做怎樣的處理，除癸未月食以外的其他四次月食的類別都只能有一種選擇，而這唯一的一種選擇又與卜辭的記録完全吻合，那麼，反過來也可以證明癸未月食必爲一次月偏食。這種互證的方法應該是被允許的。

現在，我們把最後推定的發生在殷王武丁時期的五次月食制成表七。

表七　殷武丁時期月食表

儒略曆	儒略周日	殷曆曆日干支	殷曆月	貞　人	食甚時刻（安陽時）	食　分
－1226.5.31	1273412	乙酉	八月	争、㱿	00^h　10^m	1.339
－1217.11.15	1276867	庚申	一月	争	23　49	0.395
－1200.7.11	1282950	癸未		争	23　39	0.508
－1197.11.4	1284161	甲午	一月	賓	21　56	0.724
－1188.10.25	1287439	壬申			20　40	0.507

表七中，乙酉、庚申、甲午三次月食所在的殷曆曆月，卜辭或已明記，或可推知。現在我們根據張培瑜先生編制的《冬至合朔時日表（公元前 1500 年至前 105 年）》①推步這三次月食所反映的殷曆歲首。可以相信，該表是目前國内外精度最高的合朔表。

首先我們考慮庚申月食，此年閏十三月，置閏的目的在於正四時，顯然次年的歲首已經過調整。

一月庚申月食

表八

前	冬至	冬至月	二月	三月	四月	五月	六月	七月	八月	九月	十月	十一月	十二月	十三月
1218	辛丑	12 11 辛巳 11 12	1 9 庚戌 22 58	2 8 庚辰 11 15	3 10 庚戌 00 12	4 8 己卯 14 09	5 8 己酉 05 06	6 6 戊寅 20 38	7 6 戊申 11 55	8 5 戊寅 02 15	9 3 丁未 15 30	10 3 丁丑 03 51	11 1 丙午 15 38	12 1 丙子 02 58

---

① 張培瑜：《中國先秦史曆表》，齊魯書社，1987 年 6 月。本表採用世界時，《劉表》採用曆書時，兩種計時系統因起算之年的不同而有一年之差。

續表

前	冬至	冬至月	二月	三月	四月	五月	六月	七月	八月	九月	十月	十一月	十二月	十三月
1217	丁未	12 30	1 28	2 27	3 27	4 26	5 25	6 24	7 24	8 22	9 21	10 21	11 19	
		乙巳	甲戌	甲辰	癸酉	癸卯	壬申	壬寅	壬申	辛丑	辛未	辛丑	庚午	
		13 37	23 45	09 41	20 15	08 06	21 38	12 37	04 29	20 38	12 30	03 37	17 24	

表八左起第二列是冬至日干支，上起第一行是周曆，"冬至月"即冬至所在之月，"二月"即冬至月後一月，餘類推。第二行是儒略曆，第三行是朔日干支，第四行是合朔時間。

查表八得：公元前 1218 年 11 月 1 日是丙午日，後推至 11 月 15 日正逢庚申日。由於月食只能發生在太陽和月球的地心黃經等於 180°的時候，這實際就是朔望月的望日。所以，我們設此庚申日爲殷曆某年的一月十五日，則是年殷曆一月朔即爲丙午。此去冬至六十二日，若按中國農曆的節氣換算，則殷曆某年一月朔丙午在霜降前二日。

一月甲午月食

表九

前	冬至	冬至月	二月	三月	四月	五月	六月	七月	八月	九月	十月	十一月	十二月
1198	丙戌	12 30	1 29	2 27	3 28	4 27	5 26	6 24	7 24	8 23	9 21	10 21	11 20
		乙酉	乙卯	甲申	癸丑	癸未	壬子	辛巳	辛亥	辛巳	庚戌	庚辰	庚戌
		14 09	00 14	08 51	16 59	01 27	1105	22 24	11 57	03 57	21 53	16 39	10 30
1197	壬辰	12 20	1 18	2 17	3 17	4 15	5 15	6 13	7 12	8 11	9 9	10 9	11 8
		庚辰	己酉	己卯	戊申	丁丑	丁未	丙子	乙巳	乙亥	甲辰	甲戌	甲辰
		02 11	15 01	01 17	09 48	17 24	00 48	08 47	18 15	06 25	21 50	16 09	11 49

查表九得：公元前 1198 年 10 月 21 日是庚辰日，後推至 11 月 4 日得甲午日。我們設此甲午日爲殷曆某年的一月十五日，則是年殷曆一月朔即爲庚辰。此去冬至七十二日，若按節氣換算，則殷曆某年一月朔庚辰在霜降前十二日。

八月乙酉月食

表一〇

前	冬至	冬至月	二月	三月	四月	五月	六月	七月	八月	九月	十月	十一月	十二月
1228	己酉	12 31	1 29	2 28	3 30	4 28	5 28	6 26	7 26	8 24	9 23	10 22	11 21
		己酉	戊寅	戊申	戊寅	丁未	丁丑	丙午	丙子	乙巳	乙亥	甲辰	甲戌
		02 02	17 47	10 04	02 13	17 39	07 56	20 45	08 06	18 20	04 09	14 15	01 04

续表

前	冬至	冬至月	二月	三月	四月	五月	六月	七月	八月	九月	十月	十一月	十二月
1227	甲寅	12 20	1 19	2 17	3 19	4 17	5 17	6 16	7 15	8 14	9 12	10 12	11 10
		癸卯	癸酉	壬寅	壬申	辛丑	辛未	辛丑	庚午	庚子	己巳	己亥	戊辰
		12 41	00 56	13 49	03 33	18 12	09 38	01 04	15 44	05 12	17 39	05 29	16 53

查表一〇得：公元前 1227 年 5 月 17 日是辛未日，後推至 5 月 31 日得乙酉日。我們設此乙酉日爲殷曆某年的八月十五日，前推七個半月，則是年殷曆一月朔爲甲辰，相當於公元前 1228 年 10 月 22 日。此去冬至七十一日，若按節氣換算，則殷曆某年一月朔甲辰在霜降前十一日。

我們將依此三次月食推定的殷曆歲首時間列表如下（表一一）：

表一一

月　食	殷曆一月朔日干支	儒略曆（B.C.）	儒略周日	農曆節氣
一月庚申月食	丙午	1218.11.1	1276853	霜降前 2 日
八月乙酉月食	甲辰	1228.10.22	1273191	霜降前 11 日
一月甲午月食	庚辰	1198.10.21	1234147	霜降前 12 日

甲午和庚申兩次月食所反映的殷曆歲首時間，可以認爲是表一一中三個時間的上、下限。據此我們初步認爲，殷曆的一月朔日擺動在儒略曆的 10 月下旬至 11 月上旬，當中國農曆節氣的寒露至霜降間。殷人測定合朔不很精確，所以，真實的殷曆正月月首可以允許較真朔出現±1 日的誤差。

二、殷曆歲首的天文學依據

曆法的發展大致經歷了自原始物候曆、觀象授時到推步曆法三大時期。殷曆無疑已擺脱了物候曆的原始内容，但又遠未達到推步的水平，所以它應該處在觀象制曆的階段。

觀象授時在中國古代關涉到兩個重要方面，即測日晷和觀候星象。這些對於長期從事户外生産活動的古代先民是十分容易掌握的事情，現存民族志材料也清楚地反映了這一點[①]。因此，殷曆歲首的天文學依據也不可能超越這兩項内容。

---

① 盧央、邵望平：《雲南四個少數民族天文曆法情況調查報告》，《中國天文學史文集》第二輯，科學出版社，1981 年。

《周禮·地官·大司徒》："以土圭之法測土深，正日景，以求地中。日南則景短，多暑；日北則景長，多寒；日東則景夕，多風；日西則景朝，多陰。"很多學者認爲，殷人已知測定二至，因爲度量日晷不僅可以確定季節，同時也可以確定時間和方向，而這些內容在卜辭和考古發掘中都有所反映。在此基礎上，經過一段時間的觀測以求得二至，恐怕并不是件困難的事。但是，問題在於我們已限定了殷曆歲首的時間範圍，其正月朔日擺動於儒略曆的 10 月下旬至 11 月上旬，相當於農曆節氣的寒露至霜降間，這無論從哪一個角度看都與冬、夏至日存在着一定距離。因此，殷人觀測晷影的活動對於確定歲首并沒有直接意義。

事實上，在否定了測度日影對殷人確定歲首的作用之後，我們就只有在觀候星象方面尋找答案了，而中國古文獻恰恰在這方面有明確的記載。

《左傳·昭公元年》：

> 昔高辛氏有二子，伯曰閼伯，季曰實沈，居於曠林，不相能也，日尋干戈，以相征伐。后帝不臧，遷閼伯於商丘，主辰。商人是因，故辰爲商星。

《左傳·襄公九年》：

> 陶唐氏之火正閼伯居商丘，祀大火，而火紀時焉。相土因之，故商主大火。商人閱其禍敗之釁，必始於火，是以日知其有天道也。

《國語·晉語四》：

> 吾聞晉之始封也，歲在大火，閼伯之星也，實紀商人。

大火也叫大辰，即中國二十八宿東宮蒼龍七宿的心宿二，西名天蝎座 α 星（Antares α Scorpius）。上引文獻說明了兩個問題：（一）殷人主祀大火星；（二）殷人以觀測大火星的周天視運動作爲紀時的標志。

大火之謂大辰，前人有過很好的解釋。《左傳·昭公十七年》孔穎達《正義》："大火謂之大辰。李巡云：'大辰，蒼龍宿之心，以候四時，故曰辰。'孫炎曰：'龍星明者以爲時候，故曰大辰。大火，心也，在中最明，故時候主焉。"《公羊傳·昭公十七年》："大辰者何？大火也。大火爲大辰，伐爲大辰，北辰亦爲大辰。"何休《注》："大火謂心，伐謂參伐也。大火與伐，天所以示民時早晚，天下所取正，故謂之大辰。辰，時也。"[①]何休的解釋尤其透徹！所謂"天下所取

[①] 《爾雅·釋天》云："大火謂之大辰。"郭璞《注》："大火，心也。在中最明，故時候主焉。"均以大火爲授時的標準星。

正",大概指的就是標準時間。辰以紀時,確實充當着"天上的標記點"①。

古人以大火爲授時的標準星,對其周天變化自然有着詳密的觀測。現在,我們根據先秦文獻提供的材料,將大火星的周天變化情況揭示如次:

《國語·周語中》:

> 火朝覿矣,道茀不可行。……駟見而隕霜,火見而清風戒寒。……火之初見,期於司里。

韋昭《注》:"火,心星也。覿,見也。……朝見,謂夏正十月,晨見於辰也。……霜降以後,清風先至,所以戒人爲寒備也。"

《左傳·莊公二十九年》:

> 火見而致用。

杜預《集解》:"大火,心星,次角、亢見者。"孔穎達《正義》:"十月之初,心星次角、亢之後而晨見東方也。"這是記大火的偕日出,此周之天象。

《禮記·月令》:

> 季冬之月,日在婺女,昏婁中,旦氐中。

孔穎達《正義》引《三統曆》:"大寒,日在危初度,昏昴二度中,去日八十度,旦心五度中。"這是記大火的旦中天。此戰國之天象。

《左傳·昭公四年》:

> 火出而畢賦。

杜預《集解》:"火星昏見東方,謂三月、四月中。"楊伯峻《注》:"則夏正三月,天蠍座 α 星於黃昏時出現,於是食肉者皆可以得冰。"

《左傳·昭公六年》:

> 火見,鄭其火乎!

《左傳·昭公十七年》:

> 火出,於夏爲三月,於商爲四月,於周爲五月。

《左傳·昭公十八年》:

---

① J. Needham, *Science and Civilisation in China*, Vol. Ⅲ, The Sciences of the Heavens, Cambridge University Press, 1959.

> 夏五月，火始昏見。

這是記大火的昏見，時值夏曆三月。校之歲差，殷代大火星昏見於清明、穀雨間，比統言三月，若以較殷商晚十日計算，則相差約七百餘年。此戰國以前之天象。

《尚書·堯典》：

> 日永星火，以正仲夏。

《夏小正》：

> 五月，……初昏大火中。

這是記大火的昏中天。竺可楨先生定《堯典》之"日永"爲夏至日，此則殷末周初之天象①。《夏小正》所記當亦如之②。

《左傳·昭公三年》：

> 火中，寒暑乃退。

杜預《集解》："心以季夏昏中而暑退，季冬旦中而寒退。"孔穎達《詩經正義》引服虔云："火，大火，心也。季冬十二月平旦正中在南方，大寒退；季夏六月黃昏火星中，大暑退。"這是記大火的昏、旦中天，古人視此可知寒來暑往。服虔、杜預不知歲差，他們所測大火昏、旦中天的時間，比《左傳》的記載要晚得多，《左傳》反映的天象應屬戰國。

《詩·豳風·七月》：

> 七月流火。

鄭玄《箋》："大火者，寒暑之候也。火星中而寒暑退，故將言寒，先著火所在。"王先謙《集疏》："流火，火下也。火向西下，暑退將寒之候也。"這是記大火的西流。此周之天象。

《夏小正》：

> 八月，……辰則伏。

---

① 竺可楨：《論以歲差定〈尚書·堯典〉四仲中星之年代》，《竺可楨文集》，科學出版社，1979年。
② 趙莊愚：《從星位歲差論證幾部古典著作的星象年代及成書年代》，《科技史文集》第10輯，上海科學技術出版社，1983年4月。

盧辯《傳》："辰也者，心也。伏也者，入而不見也。"這是記大火的昏伏。

《夏小正》：

> 九月，內火。……辰繫於日。

王聘珍《解詁》："九月日躔心、尾，故大火入而不見也。"這是記大火的伏没。此皆殷末周初之天象。

  古文獻所提供的材料應該說是充實的，幾乎對大火的每一次記録，都涉及了它的授時作用。同時我們也看到，古人所測大火所在的天球視位置俱十分完美，這使我們領略了先民對大火星周天變化規律的精審認識。龐樸先生曾經指出，中國古代確曾存在過一部以火紀時的曆法，它的濫觴約當大火處於秋分點的公元前二千八百年左右，即傳說的所謂堯舜時代①。當然，這個時間或可能更早。古人通過長期的辛勤觀測，對大火星運行規律的認識在逐漸深化，儘管隨着時代的發展和人類文明的進步，人類具備的有關各種天象的知識在日益豐富，但是，這種以火紀時的古老方法却長時間地爲人們所沿用。"商主大火"并"火紀時焉"這兩條文獻明確地向我們表示，殷人仍以大火星的周天變化作爲其授時的標志，這同樣在我們推定的殷曆歲首期間有着充分的反映。

  在表一一中，我們據卜辭所記的殷王武丁時期三次月食發生的時間，得到了三個殷曆歲首時間，它們的正月朔日擺動於儒略曆的 10 月下旬至 11 月上旬，所以，此三年的正月均擺動於儒略曆的 10 月下旬至 11 月，約當中國農曆節氣的霜降前至立冬後。這樣，我們便可以檢驗大火星在此時間範圍内的變化特點。

  由於歲差的緣故，春分點在黄道上約每 71.6 年西移 1°。我們以公元 1950.0 年爲今之曆元，則今日春分點在室 7°13′。表七中，我們推定的武丁王時期最早的一次月食發生在公元前 1227 年，據此推算，則今之春分點已較殷商西移 44°。我們將依此推得的公元前 1200 年前後的日躔和昏、旦中星情況列成表一二。

  查表一二"殷"欄得，寒露、霜降間日躔房、心兩宿，此時天空中大火星伏而不見。經過二十天左右的時間，當太陽走到心宿以東 15° 以外的地方時，火始晨見，即太陽將出之前，大火星朝覿於東方，時間約當霜降後九日。如果我們將這一現象同前節推定的殷曆歲首時間聯繫起來考慮，則大火星的偕日出都發生

---

① 龐樸：《"火曆"初探》，《社會科學戰綫》1978 年 4 期；《"火曆"續探》，《中國文化研究集刊》第一輯，復旦大學出版社，1984 年 3 月。

表一二

節氣	今(A.D.1950.0 年) 日躔 黃經	今(A.D.1950.0 年) 日躔 約古宿度	殷(B.C.1200 年) 日躔 約古宿度	殷(B.C.1200 年) 昏中星 約古宿度	殷(B.C.1200 年) 旦中星 約古宿度
立春	315°	女宿 4°00′	室宿 6°	參宿 2°	箕宿 6°
雨水	330	虛 7°18′	壁 5.1	井 12	斗 4
驚蟄	345	危 12°20′	奎 7.8	井 32	斗 16
春分	0	室 7°13′	婁 10.4	柳 14	牛 3
清明	15	壁 6°32′.5	胃 12.35	張 12	女 3
穀雨	30	奎 9°43′	畢 5.95	翼 13	虛 2
立夏	45	婁 11°44′	參 4.7	軫 15	危 2
小滿	60	昴 1°17′	井 9.03	亢 6	危 12
芒種	75	畢 7°14′	井 24.03	氐 15	室 9
夏至	90	參 6°01′	柳 3.9	尾 4	壁 9
小暑	105	井 10°24′	星 1.9	箕 1	奎 15
大暑	120	井 25°24′	張 8.5	斗 2	胃 5
立秋	135	柳 5°24′	翼 5.05	斗 13	昴 10
處暑	150	星 3°25′	軫 3.4	斗 25	參 2
白露	165	張 10°00′	角 5.5	女 2	井 11
秋分	180	翼 7°00′	亢 9.8	虛 1	鬼 1
寒露	195	軫 4°58′	氐 14.4	危 1	星 6
霜降	210	角 6°51′	心 6.5	危 11	張 17
立冬	225	氐 0°37′	尾 13	室 7	翼 16
小雪	240	房 2°16′	斗 4.2	壁 1	角 2
大雪	255	尾 0°00′	斗 19.2	奎 7	亢 1
冬至	270	箕 0°00′	女 2.6	婁 5	氐 7
小寒	285	斗 5°31′	虛 5.9	胃 11	心 1
大寒	300	斗 20°31′	危 10.9	畢 1	尾 11

在殷曆一月，準確時間約相當：

　　一月十一至十二日（依庚申月食推算）

　　一月二十至二十一日（依乙酉月食推算）

　　一月二十一至二十二日（依甲午月食推算）

我們再檢查與大火星相關的參星的變化情況。查表一二"殷"欄得，處暑日躔軫 $3°.4$，旦參 $2°$ 中。時過約兩個半月，即至霜降與立冬間，參伏。

據此我們認爲，殷人以大火星的偕日出作爲確定歲首的標志，即將大火星朝覿，同時參星伏没之月定爲殷曆的一月。《國語・晉語四》："大火，閼伯之星也，是謂大辰。……且以辰出而以參入，……而天之大紀也。"韋昭《注》："所以大紀天時。"上面的分析與《晉語》的記載正相吻合。

李約瑟先生指出，以一顆恒星的偕日出或偕日没確定季節，相差不會超過很少幾天[①]。我們推得的結果符合這一看法。毫無疑問，這種曆法較之推步是疏闊的。殷人通過對大火星兩次晨見的觀測得到的是恒星年，但它與真實的恒星年必然存在着一定誤差。當然，恒星年與回歸年之間存在的微小差別，古人就更無法感受了。

古人以恒星定季節，礙於太陽過於明亮，因此只有偕日法和冲日法兩種方法可行[②]。傳統的觀點認爲，中國素以冲日法觀測恒星而自成體系，因爲，諸如《吕覽》十二月紀、《禮記・月令》、《淮南子・時則訓》一類的古籍，每月都非常系統地列出了日躔和昏、旦中星的情況。但是，這些書籍的年代最早不能超過公元前四世紀。那麽，更早些時候的人們是否也習慣於冲日法呢？這確實是我們感興趣的問題。

對於古人，運用偕日法觀測恒星實際上比之冲日法更爲簡單易行。"進行這種觀測并不需要天極、子午綫或赤道等的知識，也不需要任何計時制度"[③]。冲日法則不同，它起碼需要有比較精確的記時制度和子午綫的概念。從《吕覽》上推一千年的殷人是否已很好地掌握了這兩點，我們還不敢下此斷語。

德莎素（de Saussure）認爲，以偕日法觀測恒星會受到地平綫上的霧和其他大氣現象的影響，所以時間很難準確確定[④]。客觀地講，在文明時代的初期，人類的活動非常有限，這一方面表現爲當時大氣的透明度遠勝於今日，另一方面則可以完全不必考慮光源的干擾。基於這些因素而形成的優越的觀測條件，使得古人對恒星的觀測遠較今人爲易。因此對於古人，相對簡易的偕日法似更爲實用。同時我們也注意到，以偕日法觀測恒星在世界其他文明古國中均得到了廣泛採用，古埃及人以天狼星（Sirius α Canis Major）的偕日升爲一年之始，這一天約

---

①②③ J. Needham, *Science and Civilisation in China*, Vol. Ⅲ, The Sciences of the Heavens, Cambridge University Press, 1959.

④ de Saussure, L., *Le Zodiaque Lunaire Asiatique*, ASPN, 1919.

當公曆的 7 月 19 日；古巴比倫以五車二（Capella α Auriga）之晨見爲歲首；古印度人則以觀測阿耆尼（Agni，即昴星團，西名 Pleiades）的朝覿確定歲首；古希臘人、古羅馬人以及古墨西哥的阿芝特克人也都以恒星的偕日升作爲確定歲首的標志①。世界上幾乎所有文明古國的這種以觀測恒星的偕日出或偕日没確定歲首的方法，不僅反映了人類早期文明史的發展規律，同時也爲殷人以觀測大火星的偕日升確定歲首的分析提供了有力的佐證。

不容否認，古代中國人對於某些恒星的偕日出和偕日没的觀測同樣給予了高度重視，古文獻的詳確記載清楚地反映了這一點，這除我們前面徵引的有關大火朝覿的文獻外，還有大量的這方面的例證。

《夏小正》：

> 正月，……鞠則見。

王聘珍《解詁》："《小正》凡星言'則見'者，皆謂旦見東方。"

《夏小正》：

> 四月，昴則見。初昏，南門正。

盧辯《傳》："南門者，星也。歲再見，壹正。"王聘珍《解詁》："《傳》云：'歲再見壹正'者，亢宿四月正於中，九月旦見東方，六月昏見西方也。"

《夏小正》：

> 五月，參則見。

這是以危、昴、參星的偕日出定季節②。

《左傳·昭公四年》：

> 西陸朝覿而出之。

孔穎達《正義》引鄭玄《答其弟子孫皓問》云："西陸朝覿，謂四月立夏之時。《周禮》'夏頒冰'是也。"這是以昴星的偕日出定季節③。

---

① 古墨西哥阿芝特克人的授時星象爲休脱庫特里（Xiuhtecutli），它同古印度的阿耆尼一樣，都是代表火神的星，這與中國古人以大火星授時有着相同的意義。
② 《夏小正》正月"鞠則見"之"鞠"，舊注或以爲柳，或以爲匏瓜，或以爲司禄，不能一定。我們根據歲差推算，認爲應是危宿。"危"與"居"古文字相近，傳寫之中極易訛舛，"居"與"鞠"古音雙聲可通。
③ 杜預《集解》以爲夏曆三月，《詩疏》引服虔以爲夏曆二月，皆據奎星朝見而言。《爾雅·釋天》："西陸，昴也。"此鄭意所本。

《國語·周語中》：

> 夫辰角見而雨畢，天根見而水涸，本見而草木節解，駟見而隕霜，火見而清風戒寒。

這是以角、亢、氐、房、心星的偕日出定季節①。

《楚辭·天問》：

> 角宿未旦，曜靈安藏？

王逸《章句》："角、亢，東方星。曜靈，日也。言東方未明旦之時，日安所藏其精光乎？"這是觀測角宿的偕日出。

所有這些記載表明，觀測恆星的偕日出以確定季節與觀測昏、旦中星一樣，也是古代中國人所常用的方法，甚至在早期人類社會中，這還應該是更爲主要的方法。

值得注意的是，《夏小正》一書在全部有關星象的記錄中，僅一條記錄了日躔。

《夏小正》：

> 九月，內火。……辰繫於日。

不能説這個記錄毫無意義，也不能認爲它的意義僅與《月令》所記的日躔一樣，旨在指明一個月的天象。我們認爲，這一記錄的實際作用在於定歲首，對一部曆法而言，歲首的確定有着第一位的重要性。

測度日躔有兩種方法，一是觀測恆星的偕日没和偕日出，一是以可見天體的位置來推斷不可見天體的位置。從《夏小正》原文分析，當以偕日法的可能性爲大。查表一二"殷"欄知，秋分後日躔氐宿，此時當太陽西落之後，大火星昏見西方，不久便伏没不見了。這個時間會一天短於一天，終於當有一天大火星完全看不到的時候，人們便領悟到這是大火與太陽俱出俱入的時刻。

可以設想，殷人一旦看到了這種天象，於是知道再過二十幾天，大火星將於凌晨重新朝覿於東方。所以，人們可根據大火星偕日没的日期，確定此年是平年還是閏年。換言之，由於殷人以大火星晨見之月爲歲首，因此，如果在前一年的

---

① 韋昭《注》："天根，亢、氐之間也。……本，氐也。"王引之據《爾雅·釋天》以天根爲氐，又疑本、亢二字形近而訛，以本爲亢，且上下互易。依星見之前後次第，當云"亢見而水涸，天根見而草木節解"。説見《經義述聞》卷二十。

十二月，大火星沒有走到它應該走到的位置，那麼無疑就需要置閏以調整年歲的誤差。《左傳·哀公十二年》："冬十二月，螽。季孫問諸仲尼，仲尼曰：'丘聞之，火伏而後蟄者閉。今火猶西流，司曆過矣。'"孔子的觀測同殷人確定歲首的方法該有多麼相似！

　　《夏小正》的這一記載，反映了早期曆法的特點。出於確定歲首的需要，人們通過長期觀測得到了九月的日躔，而他月無記，原因不言而喻。更爲有趣的是，表一二表明，殷代日躔心宿時值寒露至霜降，正合夏曆九月。《夏小正》的這一內容恐怕是抄錄了更古老的曆書。

三、卜辭與殷曆歲首的對證

　　以卜辭對殷曆歲首的檢討可以在兩方面審慎展開，即在理論上，卜辭的記錄是否存在我們論證的殷曆歲首的天文學依據；同時在時間上，卜辭的記事又是否符合我們所排定的殷曆。由於第二點涉及的問題相當廣泛，所以，這裏僅就第一點試做探索。

　　我們既已論定，殷人主祀大火星，并以此作爲其授時的標志，殷曆歲首確定在大火星偕日而升的一月。這些推論於卜辭可在如下三方面得到證實。

　　（一）祭火

　　應該說明，卜辭"火"、"山"二字字形酷肖，常混淆不能辨識。兩字都作平底或圓底三凸形，其中"火"或加點以飾火焰，但大多并無點飾，而"山"却絕不應有點飾。這種字形如與卜辭中已釋定的燎、焚、熹、赤、炆諸字所從的"火"符比較，都能找到相同的字例。陳夢家先生曾主張將無點之字統釋爲"山"①，但那樣又勢必會誤釋很多無點的火字。孫海波先生《甲骨文編》和高明先生《古文字類編》均將此類字歸釋於"火"②，而將"山"字條空置，應該有其一定的道理。當然，這是在目前尚不易區分"火"、"山"二字的前提下所採取的一種權宜之計。

---

① 陳夢家：《殷虛卜辭綜述》，342頁，科學出版社，1956年7月。
② "火"字入《甲骨文編》卷十·七，哈佛燕京學社石印本，1934年10月，中國科學院考古研究所改訂本，中華書局，1965年9月；入《古文字類編》504頁，中華書局，1980年11月。

一些主要的火祭卜辭見如下録：

(1) 七日己巳夕斲，㞢(有)新大星並火。 (《後編·卷下》9·1)

董作賓先生認爲，“火”即大火星，“並”訓近，“新大星”即新星之大星。辭意是：有大星傍近大火星[①]。董先生賦予“火”字的含義確鑿無誤，但對全辭我們則更傾向於另一種讀法。胡厚宣先生認爲，“㞢”、“新”、“並”俱爲祭名[②]，可謂的解。准此，應將上辭釋寫爲：

七日己巳夕斲、侑、新，大星，並火。

這是一條卜辭的驗辭。“斲”亦祭名[③]。“大星”即大晴[④]，卜辭以晝晴爲“啟”，以夜晴爲“星”[⑤]。辭意是：(癸亥)後第七天己巳晚上行“斲”、“侑”、“新”三祭，於是天大晴，大火星見於夜空，卜官賡行“並”祭祀大火。這是殷人主祀大火星的珍貴史料。

(2) 癸酉卜，扶，侑火？ (《綴合》391)

“火”字從石璋如先生釋[⑥]。“侑”，原辭作“又”，祭名。辭記侑祭大火星。

(3) 丙寅卜，㱿貞：其侑火？

丁卯卜，㱿貞：今日夕侑于兄丁，小牢？ (《甲編》3083)

此爲武丁卜辭。“侑”，原辭作“㞢”，祭名。“火”，屈萬里先生所釋，其謂：“卜辭祭山，皆舉山之專名，無泛言祭山者。則此當是火字無疑。疑此乃《詩》‘七月流火’之火，星名。”[⑦]説甚諦。“兄丁”蓋即武丁，此以武丁配祭大火星。

(4) 乙亥卜，賓貞：勿首用火，羌？ (《後編·卷下》37·8)

“火”字從《甲骨文編》所釋。“用”，祭名。“勿首”，繼續之意[⑧]。“羌”，人牲。

---

① 董作賓：《殷曆譜》下編卷三《交食譜》，中央研究院歷史語言研究所，1945年。

② 胡厚宣：《殷代之天神崇拜》，《甲骨學商史論叢》初集，第二册，成都齊魯大學國學研究所石印本，1944年。

③ 龍宇純：《釋甲骨文⾖字兼解犧尊》，《沈剛伯先生八秩榮慶論文集》，1976年12月。

④ 李學勤：《論殷墟卜辭的“星”》，《鄭州大學學報》1981年4期。

⑤ 陳夢家：《殷虚卜辭綜述》，244、246頁，科學出版社，1956年7月。

⑥ 石璋如：《“扶片”的考古學分析》，《“中央研究院”歷史語言研究所集刊》第五十六本第三分，1985年9月。

⑦ 屈萬里：《殷虚文字甲編考釋》下册，“中央研究院”歷史語言研究所，1961年6月。

⑧ 張政烺：《殷契首字說》，《古文字研究》第十輯，中華書局，1983年7月。

辭記繼續用羌奴致祭大火星。

  （5）☐［于］火燎？   （《乙編》2463）

"火"字從《甲骨文編》所釋。"燎"，本作"尞"，祭名。《説文》："尞，柴祭天也。"段玉裁《注》："示部祡下曰：'燒柴尞祭天也。'"《周禮·春官·大宗伯》："以實柴祀日月星辰。"辭記燎祭大火星。

  （6）丙，燎岳、夒、火、兕？   （《戩》21·8）

"火"，李孝定先生所釋①，兹從之。"燎"，祭名。"岳"、"夒"、"兕"爲神帝，學者多有異説，今暫存疑。"火"與上三神并舉，亦當爲神帝。李孝定先生謂即星名②，是。辭記燎祭諸自然神。

  （7）壬申卜，王，陟火，黄，癸酉易日？   （《珠》922）

"陟"，祭名③。《説文》："陟，登也。"《爾雅·釋詁》："陟，升也。"《尚書·君奭》："殷禮陟配天。"孔穎達《正義》："故殷有安上治民之禮升配於天。""黄"即尪，用爲人牲④。"易日"即"錫日"⑤，意即上天賜以日照⑥。辭言賜日曝尪，祭獻於大火。《左傳·僖公二十一年》："夏大旱，公欲焚巫尪。"《禮記·檀弓下》："歲旱，穆公召縣子而問然，曰：'天久不雨，吾欲暴尪而奚若？'"知古代祈雨用尪有焚、曝兩法。今觀卜辭，兩法當殷皆有之，但目的却并不限於求雨。

  （8）辛，戠于火？   （《京津》2522）

"戠"，祭名⑦。辭記戠祭大火星。

  （9）其鬱火？   （《戩》39·8）

"火"王國維所釋⑧，兹從之。"鬱"，原辭作从"曰"从"鬯"，"曰"爲聲，今暫

---

①② 李孝定：《甲骨文字集釋》卷十，"中央研究院"歷史語言研究所，1965年。
③ 陳夢家：《殷虚卜辭綜述》，580頁，科學出版社，1956年7月。
④ 裘錫圭：《説卜辭的焚巫尪與作土龍》，《甲骨文與殷商史》，上海古籍出版社，1983年3月。
⑤ 羅振玉：《增訂殷虚書契考釋》卷中，東方學社，1914年。
⑥ 卜辭云："乙未卜，王，翌丁酉彫、伐，易日？丁明蒙，大食易日。"（《續編》6·11·3）又云："丙申卜，翌丁酉彫、伐，啓？丁明蒙，大食日啓。"一月。（《庫方》209）兩辭所卜爲一事，"易日"與"啓"互稱，是二者同意之證。
⑦ 陳夢家：《殷虚卜辭綜述》，587頁，科學出版社，1956年7月。
⑧ 王國維：《戩壽堂所藏殷虚文字考釋》。

釋鬱。字於《說文》本从"臼"而不从"林",云:"一曰鬱邑,百草之花,遠方鬱人所貢芳草,合釀之以降神。"《周禮·春官·鬱人》:"凡祭祀,賓客之祼事,和鬱鬯,以實彝而陳之。"故字於卜辭當爲祭名。李旦丘先生云:"其字从邑,必有以邑降神之意,而下一字必其所降之神號。"① 辭記鬱祭大火星。

除此之外,卜辭中還有一些祭祀大火星禱雨的內容。

(10) 丁酉卜,扶,燎火,羊子、豭,雨? (《乙編》9103)

"燎",祭名。"羊子"即羔羊。"豭",唐蘭先生所釋②,茲從之。《說文》:"豭,牡豕也。"辭記用羔羊和牡豬爲犧牲燎祭大火以祈雨。

(11) 壬午卜,扶,奏火,日南雨? (《乙編》9067)

"奏",祭名。卜辭屢見"日雨"、"夕雨"二辭,與此相類。"日"指白晝③,則"南"應指殷都之南。此於夜間卜問白天殷都南是否降雨,爲奏祭大火祈雨之辭。

(12) 甲子卜,其祓雨于東方?
庚午卜,其祓雨于火? (《鄴三》38·4)

"祓",除惡求福之祭④。"東方",殷之方神,與"火"并舉,知"火"當爲星名。辭記祈雨於大火、東方。此以大火配屬東方,與後世二十八宿之大火配屬東宮相同,這種觀念的形成可能很早,而殷人確定歲首也正是觀測朝覿東方的大火星。

(13) 癸巳貞:其燎丰火,雨? (《甲編》3642)

"燎",祭名。"丰",舊釋玉,誤。卜辭別有玉字,形與此異⑤。字於此當爲祭品。卜辭云:

其貞:用三丰、犬、羊? (《佚》783)

---

① 李旦丘:《鐵雲藏龜零拾考釋》,40 頁,孔德圖書館叢書第二種,上海中法文化出版委員會,1939 年 5 月。
② 唐蘭:《天壤閣甲骨文存考釋》,35 頁,北平輔仁大學,1939 年 4 月。
③ 屈萬里:《殷虛文字甲編考釋》上冊,"中央研究院"歷史語言研究所,1961 年 6 月。
④ 胡厚宣:《殷代婚姻家族宗法生育制度考》,《甲骨學商史論叢》初集,第一冊,成都齊魯大學國學研究所印本,1944 年;龍宇純:《甲骨文金文𢆶字及其相關問題》,《"中央研究院"歷史語言研究所集刊》第三十四本,下冊,1963 年 12 月。
⑤ 連劭名:《甲骨文"玉"及相關問題》,《出土文獻研究》,文物出版社,1985 年 6 月。

可證。《説文》："丰，草蔡也，象草生之散亂也。讀如介。"字用於祭品當假爲韭，韭、丰古音同屬見紐，雙聲可通。或可逕釋爲韭。《詩·豳風·七月》："獻羔祭韭。"《禮記·王制》："庶人春薦韭。"是古以韭爲祭品之證。辭記薦韭燎祭大火以祈雨。

(14) 取火，迺有［大雨］？　　　　　　　　　　　　　　　　　（《後編·卷下》23·10）

"取"通"橾"，祭名①。《説文》："橾，積木燎之也。"《詩·大雅·棫樸》："薪之橾之。"孔穎達《正義》："豫斫以爲薪，至祭皇天上帝及三辰。"此橾祭大火祈雨之辭。

以上諸條禱雨卜辭中的"火"字或可釋"山"，在此不做定論。

殷人主祀大火星，遍行侑、燎、陟、并、用、鬱、祓、奏、戠、橾等多種祭祀，用牲有羔羊、牡豬乃至人牲，足見祭禮之隆重。既然殷人對大火星如此重視，也就必然設有專以司掌大火爲職的"火正"。

(二) 火正

(15) 貞：隹阜火令？
　　　貞：允隹阜火令？　　　　　　　　　　　　　　　　　　　　（《佚》67）

"隹"，虛詞，意在强調賓語，"隹阜火令"即令阜火。"火"，商承祚先生謂爲火正②，暫從。"阜"於卜辭中用作人名或地名，在此應以人名解之。卜辭中人名冠於官職之前的辭例并不鮮見，卜辭云：

　　丙寅卜，子效臣田，獲羌？　　　　　　　　　　　　　　　　（《鐵》175·1）
　　乎雀臣正？　　　　　　　　　　　　　　　　　　　　　　　　（《盧》）
　　己亥卜，貞：令先小藉臣？　　　　　　　　　　　　　　　　（《前編》6·17·6）

諸辭之"臣"、"臣正"、"小藉臣"皆爲官職名，此前之"子效"、"雀"、"先"皆爲人名。胡厚宣先生認爲，卜辭中"子某"之人與殷王有着親族關係③，則"子效"應是貴族子弟，這是殷代小臣的來源之一④。"雀"、"先"同樣是武丁時期顯

---

① 陳夢家：《殷虛卜辭綜述》，355頁，科學出版社，1956年7月。
② 商承祚：《殷契佚存考釋》，金陵大學中國文化研究所影印本，1933年10月。
③ 胡厚宣：《殷代婚姻家族宗法生育制度考》，《甲骨學商史論叢》初集，第一册，成都齊魯大學國學研究所石印本，1944年。
④ 張永山：《殷契小臣辨正》，《甲骨文與殷商史》，上海古籍出版社，1983年3月。

赫一時的重要人物，他們都曾充任過小臣之職。"阜火"辭例與此相同，所以"阜"當是火正的私名。

依卜辭通例，殷代官職的名稱很多採自該官所司之職項，如司犬之官名"犬"、司馬之官名"馬"、司卜之官名"卜"①、司牧畜之官名"牧"、司郊甸之官名"奠"等②。卜辭中還有一些火字用作人名，能否將其理解爲官職名，尚不能確定。

(三) 以火紀時

這類卜辭多係月份，因此對驗證我們所推定的殷曆歲首更顯得重要。

(16) 丁未卜，今者火來母？　　　　　　　　　　　　　　　　　(《綴合》27)

"者"字從郭沫若先生釋③，"今者"即今時④。"來"訓還歸、反歸。《易·雜卦》："而升不來也。"孔穎達《正義》："來，還也。"《詩·小雅·采薇》："我行不來。"鄭玄《箋》："來，猶反也。"《左傳·文公七年》："其誰來之。"杜預《集解》："來，猶歸也。""母"，假爲悔，意訓賜予⑤，故"來悔"意即星迴於天。《夏小正》云："八月辰則伏。"夏曆八月，約合殷曆十一至十二月。查表一二"殷"欄知，夏曆八月節曰躔角$5°.5$，去大火約$38°$。設日沒地平綫$15°$時火始見，則時過約一小時半大火始沒。八月中，日躔亢$9°.8$，此時日落約半小時後大火伏沒。所以，殷曆年終正是大火星伏而不見之時。當太陽再次運行到心宿以東$15°$以外的地方時，大火星才在凌晨日出之前重新升現於東方。此辭貞問：現在大火星會重新出現嗎？顯然，這是在注意觀測大火的偕日出。卜辭雖未系月，但據"今者"的範圍在一旬之內可推知，此辭卜在年末或年初。

(17) 辛酉卜，火，氐？一[月]。　　　　　　　　　　　　　　　(《甲編》1074)

"火"字從《甲骨文編》所釋。"氐"，讀如眡，同視⑥。時系"一月"。這是記觀

---

① 陳夢家：《殷虛卜辭綜述》，514、519頁，科學出版社，1956年7月。
② 張亞初：《商代職官研究》，《古文字研究》第十三輯，中華書局，1986年6月。
③ 郭沫若：《卜辭通纂考釋》三十六片眉批，《郭沫若全集·考古編》卷二，科學出版社，1982年。
④ 陳夢家：《殷虛卜辭綜述》，228頁，科學出版社，1956年7月。
⑤ 郭沫若：《殷契粹編考釋》一五四三片，科學出版社，1965年5月。
⑥ 高明：《中國古文字學通論》，311頁，文物出版社，1987年4月。

測大火的偕日出。

  (18) 壬寅卜,賓貞:氐?

    己巳卜,爭[貞]:火,今一月其雨?

    火,今一月其雨?

    火,今一[月]不其雨?   (《綴合》209)

"火"字從嚴一萍先生釋①。此辭亦記"氐",即觀測大火,日在壬寅,已巳再卜,時大火已見。兩次行占相隔二十八天,知殷人觀測大火星之偕日出應有固定日期,大約從前一年的十二月下旬即已開始。辭問一月雨否,意在降雨則影響觀測。此卜於一月。

  (19) 火?一月。   (《林》2·21·3)

"火"字從《甲骨文編》所釋。此辭系貞問大火星的偕日出。卜在一月。

  (20) 王于□御火?一月。   (《京津》2537)

"御",祭名。辭記王於某地御祭大火星。時記"一月",正當大火朝覯之際。

  卜辭中有關大火星的材料,凡係記曆月者多集中在年末和年初,時間齊整,并無參差,這反映了大火星對於確定殷曆歲首的意義。

  (21) 貞:隹火?五月。   (《後編·卷下》37·4)

"火"字從李亞農先生釋②。卜辭僅此一條時記"五月"。殷曆之五月約當夏曆二月,二月的中氣是春分。殷人以五月觀測大火星,想必與確定春分有關。然而,殷人是否能夠認識分至?這使我們不禁想起殷人祭祀出入日的情況。據宋鎮豪同志研究,祭日的時間當殷曆二、三月之交③,正合夏曆十一月,中氣冬至,這表明祭日與確定冬至密切相關。可以堅信,殷人對分至的認識已經具備,那麼,我們承認殷人於春分之時觀測大火,甚至祭祀出日、入日,便能獲得一種和諧而統一的授時關係。

  值得注意的是,在"祭火"和"以火紀時"兩項内容的全部二十條卜辭中,有八條是記有貞人的卜辭,其中由殷王親自行占的有二條,另外六條則分別屬於貞人扶、㱿、賓、爭的卜辭。王是商族的領袖,扶、㱿、賓、爭同爲武丁時期的

---

① 嚴一萍:《殷商天文志》,《中國文字》新二期,藝文印書館,1980年9月。
② 李亞農:《李亞農史論集》上冊,528頁,上海人民出版社,1978年11月。
③ 宋鎮豪:《甲骨文"出日"、"入日"考》,《出土文獻研究》,文物出版社,1985年6月。

重要貞人，而且扶的地位在某種意義上甚至比殷王更爲重要①。這清楚地顯示了祭祀和觀測大火星的活動在殷代是一項"國之大事"。

最後指出，我們所推定的殷曆歲首約當夏曆十月，用後世的月建法去安排，約合所謂的"建亥"説。戰國時期的楚曆和秦朝漢初的曆法都以此月爲歲首②。當然，月建的産生是晚起的事情，因而我們自然不能同意"殷正建亥"的説法。

通過以上討論，我們論定的殷主大火并以大火的偕日出確定歲首這兩方面内容，都獲得了卜辭的印證。討論卜辭的記事内容，即有關殷代氣象和農事活動的卜辭，對查驗我們所推定的殷曆同樣十分重要。限於篇幅，容另文論之。

四、主要結論

綜觀全文的論述，我們可得到若干重要認識，現鳌定其要點如次：

（一）我們考定了殷王武丁卜辭中記録的五次月食，準確時間分别當儒略曆：公元前 1227 年 5 月 31 日，乙酉月食；公元前 1218 年 11 月 15 日，庚申月食；公元前 1201 年 7 月 11 日，癸未月食；公元前 1198 年 11 月 4 日，甲午月食；公元前 1189 年 10 月 25 日，壬申月食。

（二）根據已考定的武丁時期五次月食的時間推步了殷曆歲首，結論是：殷曆正月朔日擺動於儒略曆的 10 月下旬至 11 月上旬，大致相當於中國農曆節氣的寒露至霜降間，則殷曆正月當在儒略曆的 10 月下旬至 11 月，也即中國農曆節氣的霜降至立冬前後，相當於夏曆的九至十月。這個結論否定了漢傳的丑正殷曆爲殷代時王曆的傳統觀點。

（三）中國古文獻中明確記載，殷人主祀大火星，即中國二十八宿東宫七宿的心宿二。據歲差校正的計算結果表明，大火星於殷正期間正呈偕日升，授時標志十分理想，從而論定，殷人以大火星的朝覿作爲確定歲首的標志。

（四）觀測恒星的可行方法有兩種，即偕日法和沖日法。傳統的觀點認爲，中國素以沖日法觀測恒星而自成體系。我們通過沖日、偕日兩法的比較，古代埃

---

① 丁驌先生云："余讀各貞占辭後，似卜貞人物皆不贊一辭，而以王判兆之吉凶解釋其意義，由王作最後之决斷於占辭。卜貞人中惟扶一人有在王占之後而仍發言者，曰'扶曰'。"見《殷貞卜之格式與貞辭允驗辭之解釋》，《中國文字》新二期，藝文印書館，1980 年 9 月。
② 因古曆法疏闊，《春秋》紀年亦時有建亥。見王應麟《困學紀聞》卷九。

及等文明古國所採用的觀測恒星的方法及中國古文獻中大量的有關以偕日法觀測恒星的記述，證明對於古人，運用偕日法事實上比冲日法更爲簡易，同時説明，偕日法應該是殷人觀測恒星的主要方法。

（五）通過研究殷人祭祀、司掌大火星和以大火星紀時的卜辭，印證了以上各項挂論。

附記：本文完成後，曾承胡厚宣、王世民、張培瑜和劉家蔭諸位先生審閲，并得到他們的很多幫助，兹謹志銘感。

一九八七年十二月

原載《考古學報》1990 年第 1 期；收入馮時：《古文字與古史新論》，臺灣書房出版有限公司，2007 年；又收入馮時：《尚樸堂文存》，中國社會科學出版社，2021 年。今據前者收入，並吸收了後者的一些校訂意見。